PROPERTY AND LAWYERING

Second Edition

By

R. Wilson Freyermuth
Professor of Law
University of Missouri-Columbia

Jerome M. Organ
Professor of Law
University of St. Thomas

Alice M. Noble-Allgire
Associate Professor of Law
Southern Illinois University

James L. Winokur
Professor of Law, Emeritus
University of Denver

AMERICAN CASEBOOK SERIES®

Mat #40453379

© West, a Thomson business, 2001
© 2006 Thomson/West
      610 Opperman Drive
      P.O. Box 64526
      St. Paul, MN 55164–0526
      1–800–328–9352
Printed in the United States of America

ISBN–13: 978–0–314–16782–8
ISBN–10: 0–314–16782–X

TEXT IS PRINTED ON 10% POST CONSUMER RECYCLED PAPER

To my mother Margaret, and in loving memory of my father,
the Rev. Robert W. Freyermuth

To my parents, Ray and Ruth Organ, and my wife Debbie,
in gratitude for their constant support, inspiration and love

To my husband, Rich, and in loving memory of my parents,
John and Catherine Noble

To my mother, dearest friend and source of the very best in my
spirit,
Rosalie Frankel Winokur Silverman (1912-2001),
of blessed memory

*

Preface to the Second Edition

In many ways, this book is much like other property casebooks. It covers the basics of the law of property, in much the same order as some other casebooks, and uses some of the same leading cases. Like many other casebooks, it provides ample historical and policy perspective throughout. So what distinguishes this book from any other property casebook? While all property casebooks are designed to give you a thorough grounding in the law of property, the goal of this casebook is broader. We assembled, edited, and wrote this casebook with the goal of helping you to see the law of property from the perspective of law practice and to identify (and to begin to develop) a broad range of fundamental lawyering skills.

In recent years, there has been a continuing national debate about whether law schools are doing an adequate job preparing their students for the practice of law. The conventional wisdom has been that legal education—especially in the first year—is designed to teach you the elusive skill of "thinking like a lawyer" through learning and refining basic skills of case analysis. Increasingly, many outside of legal academia have complained that a substantial gap exists between legal education and the actual practice of law. Consider, for example, the view of Judge Harry T. Edwards of the United States Court of Appeals for the District of Columbia Circuit:

> I fear that our law schools and law firms are moving in opposite directions. The schools should be training ethical practitioners and producing scholarship that judges, legislators, and practitioners can use. The firms should be ensuring that associates and partners practice law in an ethical manner. But many law schools—especially the so-called "elite" ones—have abandoned their proper place, by emphasizing abstract theory at the expense of practical scholarship and pedagogy. Many law firms have also abandoned their place, by pursuing profit above all else. While the schools are moving toward pure theory, the firms are moving toward pure commerce, and the middle ground—ethical practice—has been deserted by both. This disjunction calls into question our status as an honorable profession. [Harry T. Edwards, *The Growing Disjunction Between Legal Education and the Legal Profession*, 91 Mich. L. Rev. 34, 34 (1992).]

Nor have the voices of criticism come only from outside law schools. One such voice is Professor Alex Johnson, who has written about how some of his former students, now in law practice, have reflected upon their law school experience:

> I am struck by the returning graduates' frustration and disillusionment with their careers. When they drop by my office to say hello or

elicit information about current students, they complain about the practice of law and especially about their lack of preparation for what the practice of law truly entails....

At first I believed that their complaints simply reflected these new lawyers' adjustments to the long hours and tedious work required of young associates. However, I realized that my own and my peers' transition from law school to law practice did not create the same deep dissatisfaction. The nature and the number of my students' complaints seemed unusual and revealed to me the seriousness of the problem that currently plagues American law school graduates.

Why the difference?... [T]he problem really lies in the process by which we educate law students and prepare them (or fail to prepare them) for legal practice. [Alex M. Johnson, Jr., *Think Like a Lawyer, Work Like a Machine: The Dissonance Between Law School and Law Practice*, 64 S. Cal. L. Rev. 1231, 1231-32 (1991).]

Partly in response to this type of criticism and debate, the American Bar Association in 1989 formed a task force on "Law Schools and the Profession: Narrowing the Gap." This task force, which represented all segments of the legal profession, undertook an extensive study of the processes by which students are prepared for the practice of law. In 1992, the task force issued its report, "Legal Education and Professional Development—An Educational Continuum." Most persons refer to the report as the "MacCrate Report" (after the chairperson of the task force, Robert MacCrate).

The MacCrate Report identified what it considered to be ten fundamental lawyering skills "essential for competent representation." These include:

- problem solving
- legal analysis and reasoning
- legal research
- factual investigation
- communication
- counseling
- negotiation
- litigation and alternative dispute resolution procedures
- organization and management of legal work
- recognizing and resolving ethical dilemmas

MacCrate Report, page 135. The MacCrate Report took note of the finger-pointing in which academics and practitioners had engaged over who was "responsible" for the shortcomings in legal education. It concluded, however, that one honestly could not allocate blame for lawyer unpreparedness in any precise fashion:

The Task Force's collective effort has resulted in the recognition that the task of educating students to assume the full responsibilities of a lawyer is a continuing process that neither begins nor ends with three years of law school study. Having reached this conclusion, the Task Force ... has identified the roles of law schools and the practicing bar in assisting prospective lawyers as they move along the continuum from applicant to student to qualified lawyer.

Thus, we have concluded that there is no "gap." There is only an arduous road of professional development along which all prospective lawyers should travel. It is the responsibility of law schools and the practicing bar to assist students and lawyers to develop the skills and values required to complete the journey. [*Id.* at 8.]

The spirit of the MacCrate Report also suggests that there are lawyerly perspectives on law and law practice, and that an appreciation of these perspectives is a necessary part of the foundation of lawyering skills and values. Lawyers see relationships evolve over time—through periods of friendly "courting" (both in the personal and commercial senses); through the period in which parties to a transaction establish their relationship; through periods of doubt or confusion about how parties to a previously negotiated transaction should act in light of new and unanticipated circumstances; and through periods of outright legal combat, whether through litigation (often overemphasized in law schools) or through some alternative form of dispute resolution. To function effectively across this time continuum, the practicing lawyer must have both a capacity for detached objective analysis and a capacity for a zealous connection with and advocacy for her client. More importantly, the practicing lawyer must develop and possess the essential lawyering quality of foresight—the ability to "see around corners" to recognize potential problems (such as an unanticipated transaction pitfall, a potential change in the law, or how a client's objectives could be influenced or compromised by future circumstances unanticipated by the client) and to use this recognition in effective representation of her client.

To the surprise of no one, the MacCrate Report generated substantial disagreement within the legal academy. Some academics criticized (to some extent, fairly) the MacCrate Report's recommendations as unrealistic and too expensive to implement. *See* John J. Costonis, *The MacCrate Report: Of Loaves, Fishes, and the Future of American Legal Education*, 43 J. Legal Educ. 157 (1993). Others decried the MacCrate Report as an attempt by the bar to regulate the law school curriculum at the expense of academic freedom. Yet others hailed the MacCrate Report as the blueprint for legal education in the 21st Century.

We wonder if the debate perhaps missed the point. Even those on opposite sides of the debate never really disagreed that (a) the MacCrate Report does identify a core group of fundamental lawyering skills, and (b) effective legal education (wherever that occurs, in law school or in practice) requires the acquisition and refinement of that core group of skills. And everyone engaged in this debate—even the most vocal of the pro-reformers—knows and understands that even in a perfect world, law schools cannot fully teach all of these fundamental lawyering skills to completion in a three-year period. The best that any law school can hope to do is to expose students to the skills they will need to function as effective lawyers and to equip students with the basic tools they will need to continue learning these skills throughout their legal careers. We are confident, however, that law teachers can do an effective job—even operating within current resource constraints—of (a) helping students to become aware of these fundamental lawyering skills during law school, and (b) helping students begin to acquire these basic skills, along with a solid foundation for lifelong continuing education and professional development.

We have written this book, then, with the purpose of presenting the substantive doctrine of property law—including the history and policy considerations familiar to other property casebooks—but in a way that pervasively identifies and reinforces the early development of the fundamental lawyering skills identified in the MacCrate Report. So, to the students who will use this book: Throughout, these materials will consistently challenge you to take the practitioner's perspective in considering a legal relationship or transaction. These materials will challenge you to consider, recognize, and understand the concerns and interests of the people who comprise legal relationships or engage in property transactions. These materials will challenge you to learn from the mistakes of prior lawyers and clients—and your own in-class mistakes—as a means of helping to develop the skill of foresight that will serve your future clients. Our goal is modest. As we have already stated, we cannot hope to make you expert negotiators, expert writers, expert counselors, expert transaction-builders, expert mediators, expert investigators, or expert problem-solvers. [If you are, for example, an expert negotiator at the end of this course, so much the better—but then you were probably close to being an expert negotiator when you started, and no teacher or author can take credit for that!] Our goal is to help you realize this: that learning to "think like a lawyer" about a problem involving property is not merely to learn the rules of law that courts apply in property disputes. To borrow an analogy that you will soon encounter, "thinking like a lawyer" about a property transaction or dispute requires you to remember that the knowledge of the rule of law is but one "stick" in the "bundle of sticks" that all competent lawyers must possess. We hope that our materials help you to begin the lifelong process of learning these skills.

Edited Changes to the Second Edition

In preparing this book, we have heavily edited many of the principal cases. Where we have omitted text from a court's opinion, we have indicated the omission by an ellipsis; however, we chose not to indicate the deletion of footnotes or string citations that we felt would add little to student understanding. Furthermore, we have taken editing license to correct misspellings in opinions, rather than to provide annoying "[sic]" references. In using the book, if you conclude that our editing of a particular case has omitted a valuable or necessary portion of the opinion, we would appreciate your calling it to our attention for future consideration.

Where footnotes appear in the principal cases, they typically come directly from the reported opinion, although they have been renumbered for ease of presentation here. [In a few cases, we have added footnotes that are not part of the opinion to highlight a particular point or raise a question; these footnotes are prefaced by "Editors' Note."] Because we have numbered all footnotes seriatim within each chapter, footnote numbers in the principal cases do not match the numbers used in the published decisions.

In Gratitude

Professor Jimmy Winokur retired in 2004, and understandably decided to enjoy his retirement rather than participate actively in the preparation of the second edition of this book. Professors Freyermuth, Organ, and Noble-Allgire envy his retirement. We are profoundly grateful to him for his many contributions to the first edition, and we are pleased that he wishes to remain associated with us as a co-author of the book.

Each of us is grateful for the many people whose prior work and inspiration is reflected in this book. The credit is theirs, and the errors are ours.

Professor Freyermuth: I wish to thank my students at the University of Missouri-Columbia School of Law, whose enthusiasm has inspired me throughout the preparation and revision of this book and continues to do so. I am especially grateful for the research assistance of former and current students Rich Hill, Myia McKenna, and Ryan Paulus; for the able and cheerful administrative assistance of Cheryl Poelling; and for the patient encouragement of my wife Shari Freyermuth. I am also thankful for the encouragement and insights of the following colleagues, both generally and in numerous discussions over various portions of this book: Grant Nelson, Dale Whitman, Len Riskin, the late Tim Heinsz, Bob Lawless, Chris Wells, David English, Jim Devine, Steve Easton, Jim Levin, Jen Robbennolt, Bill Henning, Royce Barondes, Jerry Organ, and Alice Noble-Allgire. Finally, a special word of thanks to Jimmy Winokur for his many insights and contributions to this book.

Professor Organ: There are a number of people who deserve my appreciation with respect to this casebook: Len Riskin, whose efforts to develop Missouri's program of integrating dispute resolution into the first-year curriculum inspired our decision to integrate lawyering skills and values into a first-year casebook; Bill Henning, who helped catalyze our interest in writing a casebook; my colleagues at Missouri, who provided encouragement and helpful advice on the first edition—particularly Bob Bailey, Melody Daily, Jim Devine, Steve Easton, Bill Fisch, Chris Guthrie, Tim Heinsz, Jim Levin, Grant Nelson, Jim Westbrook and Dale Whitman; my students at the University of Missouri-Columbia School of Law, who helped us work through (and improve upon) earlier drafts, and my students here at the University of St. Thomas School of Law, who provided great feedback on the first edition; and my research assistants and administrative assistants over the years, at Missouri and here at St. Thomas. My co-authors deserve special thanks—Jimmy Winokur, for his unique insights, Wilson Freyermuth, for his patience and perseverance; Alice Noble-Allgire, for her judgment and attention to detail. Finally, I am particularly indebted to my wife, Debbie Organ, for her constant love and support throughout the writing, editing and proofing of both editions of this casebook.

Professor Noble-Allgire: I wish to thank my co-authors, Wilson Freyermuth, Jerry Organ, and Jimmy Winokur, for inviting me to participate in the refinement of this innovative teaching resource. Our discussions during the past year have deepened my appreciation for the finer points of property theory and practice. I also am grateful to Jennifer Claire Sprague for research and editorial assistance that always went above and beyond my expectations; to Sara Ingram, Joseph Reed, and Rebecca Van Court for assisting Claire in the painstaking effort of updating the index; to Susan Williams for her administrative assistance; to my past property classes for helpful comments about the prior edition; and to my husband, Rich Allgire, for his patience and support. Finally, I wish to thank the following colleagues and mentors for inspiring and supporting the methodology and ideas embodied in this book: Wenona Whitfield, Taylor Mattis, the late Brian Mattis, Suzanne Schmitz, Cheryl Anderson, R.J. Robertson, Jill Adams, Gene Basanta, Robert Beck, Dean Peter Alexander, and former deans Thomas Guernsey and Harry Haynsworth.

R. WILSON FREYERMUTH
JEROME M. ORGAN
ALICE M. NOBLE-ALLGIRE

March 2006

Acknowledgements

The authors gratefully acknowledge permission to reprint from the following material.

ABA Model Code of Professional Responsibility (1980). Copyright © 1980 by the American Bar Association. Reprinted with permission.

ABA Model Rules of Professional Conduct (2004 Edition). Copyright © 2003 by the American Bar Association. Reprinted with permission.

ABA Special Committee on Residential Real Estate Transactions, The Proper Role of the Lawyer in Residential Real Estate Transactions (1974). Copyright © 1974 by the American Bar Association. Reprinted with permission.

American Law of Property, Vol. 4, § 17.18. Copyright © 1952. Reprinted with permission from American Law of Property.

Robert M. Bastress and Joseph D. Harbaugh, Interviewing, Counseling, and Negotiating (1990). Reprinted with permission of Aspen Publishers, Inc.

David A. Binder, Paul Bergman, and Susan C. Price, Lawyers as Counselors (1991). Reprinted with permission of the West Group.

Ira Mark Bloom, *How Federal Transfer Taxes Affect the Development of Property Law*, 48 Cleveland State Law Review 661, 676 (2000). Reprinted with permission of Cleveland State Law Review.

Board of Student Advisers, Harvard Law School, Introduction to Advocacy: Research, Writing, and Argument (6th ed. 1996). Reprinted with permission of Foundation Press.

Michael Braunstein, *Remedy, Reason, and the Statute of Frauds: A Critical Economic Analysis*, 1989 Utah Law Review 383. Reprinted with permission of the Utah Law Review.

Louis M. Brown and Edward A. Dauer, *Preventive Law—A Synopsis of Practice and Theory*, published in The Lawyer's Handbook (1975). Copyright © 1975 by the American Bar Association. Reprinted with permission.

Guido Calabresi and A. Douglas Melamed, *Property Rules, Liability Rules and Inalienability: One View of the Cathedral*. Reprinted with the permission of the authors and the Harvard Law Review Association and William S. Hein Company from *The Harvard Law Review*, Vol. 85, pages 1089–1128.

Felix Cohen, *Dialogue on Private Property*, 9 Rutgers Law Review 357 (1954). Reprinted with permission of the Rutgers Law Review.

Rance L. Craft, Comment, *Of Reservoir Hogs and Pelt Fiction: Defending the* Ferae Naturae *Analogy Between Petroleum and Wildlife*, 44 Emory Law Journal 697 (1995). Reprinted with permission of the Emory Law Journal.

Charles Donahue, Jr., *The Future of the Concept of Property Predicted from Its Past*, Nomos XXII: Property (1980). Reprinted with permission of New York University Press and Charles Donahue, Jr.

Jesse Dukeminier & James E. Krier, *The Rise of the Perpetual Trust*, originally published in 50 UCLA Law Review 1303 (2003). Reprinted with the permission of James E. Krier and the Estate of Jesse Dukeminier.

Harry T. Edwards, *The Growing Disjunction Between Legal Education and the Law Profession*, 91 Michigan Law Review 34 (1992). Reprinted with the permission of The Michigan Law Review Association and the Honorable Harry T. Edwards.

Melvin A. Eisenberg, *Private Ordering Through Negotiation: Dispute-Settlement and Rulemaking*, 89 Harvard Law Review 637 (1976). Reprinted by permission of the Harvard Law Review Association and William S. Hein Company from *The Harvard Law Review*, Vol. 89, pages 627–681.

First American Title Insurance Company, Standard Owners' Policy of Title Insurance. Reprinted with permission of First American Title Insurance Company.

Jonathan Hoffman, *Estoppel Certificate Pitfalls of Which Tenants Should Be Aware*, Commercial Leasing Law & Strategy (Nov. 1998). Reprinted with permission from the November 8, 1998 edition of Law Journal Newsletter © 1998 ALM Properties, Inc. All rights reserved. Further duplication without permission is prohibited.

Alex M. Johnson, *Think Like a Lawyer, Work Like a Machine: The Dissonance Between Law School and Law Practice*, 64 Southern California Law Review 1231 (1991). Reprinted with the permission of the Southern California Law Review.

Stefan H. Krieger & Richard K. Neumann, Jr., Essential Lawyering Skills: Interviewing, Counseling, Negotiation, and Persuasive Fact Analysis (2d ed. 2003). Reprinted with permission of Aspen Publishers, Inc.

Jeff Lewin, Boomer *and the American Law of Nuisance: Past, Present, and Future*, 54 Albany Law Review 189 (1990). Reprinted with permission of the Albany Law Review.

Legal Education and Professional Development—An Educational Continuum ("MacCrate Report"). Copyright © 1992 by the American Bar Association. Reprinted with permission.

Carrie Menkel-Meadow, *Toward Another View of Legal Negotiation: The Structure of Problem Solving*, originally published in 31 UCLA Law Review 754 (1984). Reprinted with permission of Carrie Menkel-Meadow.

Thomas W. Merrill, *Property Rules, Liability Rules and Adverse Possession*, 79 Northwestern University Law Review 1122 (1984). Reprinted by special permission of the Northwestern University School of Law, *Northwestern University Law Review*.

Missouri Association of Realtors, Contract for Sale of Residential Real Estate. Copyright © 1970, Revised August 2001. Reprinted with permission of the Missouri Association of Realtors.

Grant S. Nelson, *The Contract for Deed as a Mortgage: The Case for the Restatement Approach*, 1998 BYU Law Review 1111. Reprinted with permission of the Brigham Young Law Review.

Grant S. Nelson and Dale A. Whitman, Real Estate Transfer, Finance and Development (6th ed. 2003). Reprinted with permission of the West Group.

Grant S. Nelson and Dale A. Whitman, Real Estate Finance Law (4th ed. 2001). Reprinted with permission of the West Group.

Richard K. Neumann, Jr., Legal Reasoning and Legal Writing: Structure, Strategy, and Style (4th edition 1991). Reprinted with permission of Richard K. Neumann, Jr.

Note, *Administrative Discretion in Zoning*, 82 Harvard Law Review 668 (1969). Reprinted by permission of the Harvard Law Review Association and William S. Hein Company from *The Harvard Law* Review, Vol. 82, page 668-685.

Steven L. Pepper, *Counseling at the Limits of the Law: An Exercise in the Jurisprudence and Ethics of Lawyering*, 104 Yale Law Journal 1545 (1995). Reprinted by permission of The Yale Law Journal Company and William S. Hein Company from *The Yale Law Journal*, Vol. 104, pages 1545–1610.

Richard A. Posner, Economic Analysis of Law (4th ed. 1992). Reprinted with permission of the Honorable Richard A. Posner.

William L. Prosser, Handbook of the Law of Torts (1st ed. 1941). Reprinted with permission of the West Group.

Margaret Jane Radin, *Property and Personhood*, 34 Stanford Law Review 957 (1982). Reprinted with permission the Copyright Clearance Center.

Charles A. Reich, *The New Property*. Reprinted by permission of The Yale Law Journal Company and William S. Hein Company from The Yale Law Journal, Vol. 73, pages 733–787.

Restatement (Third) of Property—Servitudes. Reprinted with permission of the American Law Institute.

Restatement (Second) of Torts. Reprinted with permission of the American Law Institute.

Restatement (Second) of Contracts. Reprinted with permission of the American Law Institute.

Leonard L. Riskin and James E. Westbrook, Dispute Resolution and Lawyers (2d ed. 1997). Reprinted with permission of the West Group.

Leonard L. Riskin, James E. Westbrook, and James H. Levin, Instructor's Manual to Accompany Dispute Resolution and Lawyers (2d ed. 1998). Reprinted with permission of the West Group.

Leonard L. Riskin, James E. Westbrook, Chris Guthrie, Timothy J. Heinsz, Richard C. Reuben & Jennifer K. Robbennolt, Dispute Resolution and Lawyers (3d ed. 2005). Reprinted with permission of the West Group.

Florence Wagman Roisman, *Teaching About Inequality, Race, and Property*, 46 St. Louis University Law Journal 665 (2002). Reprinted with permission of the Saint Louis University Law Journal © 2002 St. Louis University School of Law, St. Louis, Missouri.

Carol M. Rose, *Possession as the Origin of Property*, 52 University of Chicago Law Review 73 (1985). Reprinted with permission of the Copyright Clearance Center.

Rick Rush, "The Masters of Augusta," reprinted with permission of Jireh Publishing, Inc.

Elizabeth J. Samuels, *Stories Out of School: Teaching the Case of* Brown v. Voss, 16 Cardozo Law Review 1445 (1995). Copyright © Cardozo Law Review; originally published in 16 Cardozo Law Review 1445 (1995).

Richard Sander, Comment, *Individual Rights and Demographic Realities: The Problem of Fair Housing*, 82 Northwestern University Law Review 874 (1988). Reprinted by special permission of Northwestern University School of Law, *Northwestern University Law Review*.

Frank E.A. Sander and Stephen B. Goldberg, *Fitting the Forum to the Fuss: A User-Friendly Guide to Selecting an ADR Procedure*, Negotiation Journal 54–59 (Jan. 1994). Reprinted with permission of Blackwell Publishing.

Robert G. Schwemm, Housing Discrimination: Law and Litigation (1990). Reprinted with permission of the West Group.

Helene S. Shapo, Marilyn R. Walter, and Elizabeth Fajans, Writing and Analysis in the Law (3d ed. 1995). Reprinted with permission of Foundation Press.

Joseph W. Singer, *The Reliance Interest in Property*, 40 Stanford Law Review 614 (1988). Reprinted with permission of the Copyright Clearance Center.

Joseph William Singer, *Legal Theory: Sovereignty and Property*, 86 Northwestern University Law Review 1 (1991). Reprinted by special permission Northwestern University School of Law, *Northwestern University Law Review*.

William B. Stoebuck and Dale A. Whitman, The Law of Property (3d ed. 2000). Reprinted with permission of West Group.

Uniform Commercial Code. Reprinted with permission of the American Law Institute and the National Conference of Commissioners on Uniform State Laws.

Uniform Statutory Rule Against Perpetuities. Reprinted with permission of the National Conference of Commissioners on Uniform State Laws.

Uniform Vendor and Purchaser Risk Act. Reprinted with permission of the National Conference of Commissioners on Uniform State Laws.

Peter T. Wendel, A Possessory Estates and Future Interests Primer (2d ed. 2005). Reprinted with permission of the West Group.

Dale A. Whitman, Internet Title Search Exercise. Reprinted with permission of Dale A. Whitman.

James L. Winokur, *Critical Assessment: The Financial Role of Community Associations*, 38 Santa Clara Law Review 1135 (1998). Reprinted with permission of the Santa Clara Law Review.

James L. Winokur, *The Mixed Blessings of Promissory Servitudes: Toward Optimizing Economic Utility, Individual Liberty, and Personal Identity*, 1989 Wisconsin Law Review 1. Copyright © 1989 by The Board of Regents of the University of Wisconsin System. Reprinted with permission of the Wisconsin Law Review.

*

Summary of Contents

Table of Contents

*

Table of Cases

The principal cases are in bold type. Cases cited or discussed in the text are roman type. References are to pages. Cases cited in principal cases and within other quoted materials are not included.

purposes and policies evolve in public debate and in the reasoning of legal decisionmakers, this evolution effectively modifies a legal rule—or, at the least, clarifies its application to circumstances that the original decisionmaker may not have foreseen or failed to address sufficiently.

As you begin, you should appreciate that a variety of policy perspectives have shaped (to varying degrees over many centuries) how the law has defined property, and how notions of property may change in the future. To assist your identification and analysis of these policy perspectives, we very briefly preview a few of them here.

Property as Socio–Political Structure. Centuries ago, "property" law existed primarily to define socio-political structure. Our property law first developed within the feudal manor of the Middle Ages. There, a man's property in land defined the man's position within a complex social hierarchy. Each man's tenure included mutual obligations and expectations with another man (his "lord"). His "property" tied him, from birth to death, into a web of social relations between a host of "lords" and "tenants" that accounted for his home, livelihood, physical security—and potentially his mate, religious experience, and political niche. Thus, a man's property defined the nature and pattern of his life.

The emergence of capitalism and the development of the "market" unraveled this carefully integrated socio-political structure. Significantly, the marketplace began to transform some elements of the feudal relationship—most notably, one's labor—into marketable commodities. Common ownership of manor lands yielded to enclosure and exclusive private ownership, a movement that forced hordes of peasants off the land and into emerging cities. These changes in the conception of property contributed to the emergence of urban life and property-based markets as dominant in western culture, and they profoundly changed existing social structures and relationships.

Throughout American history, property has served as the backbone of important social and political structures. Under the leadership of Justice John Marshall, the United States Supreme Court ratified and legitimated the violent manner (conquest) by which European powers acquired property rights to North American land from Native Americans. See *Johnson v. M'Intosh,* 21 U.S. (8 Wheat.) 543, 5 L.Ed. 681 (1823), which appears on page 92. Initially, the fundamental political right of voting in this country was an incident of property ownership. Further, our initial Constitution appallingly recognized and expressly sanctioned slavery—the ownership of human beings as legal objects of property. Applying property concepts in these settings, thereby broadening the parameters of property as defined and enforced by our legal system, profoundly shaped our American social structure.

Even today, the concept of property heavily influences social and political structures, though perhaps less consciously so. As we will see in Chapter 7, the rules governing the landlord-tenant relationship first developed in the context of feudal relationships. More recently, however, contract law has begun to inform the analysis of the landlord-tenant relationship—and this trend has produced results that have tended to provide tenants with greater economic and political power than tenants possessed historically. Evolution of property concepts has enabled the development of condominiums and modern suburban subdivisions, governed either by zoning schemes or by private restrictive covenants administered by community associations (which serve as private "mini-governments" within the relevant community). This evolution has provided neighbors with an exclusionary legal mechanism that allows them to avoid the harm that undesired land uses can present. Unfortunately, this evolution also creates the possibility that neighbors might exercise this exclusionary power based upon race, ethnicity, political beliefs, creed, or wealth characteristics—with the significant social and political consequences occasioned by such exclusion. Thus, in evaluating and advocating for evolution of property law, lawyering alters and refines our social and political relationships and structures.

Property as Efficient Resource Allocator. For the past several centuries, many theorists have argued that law should seek to maximize society's wealth by facilitating commerce and the operation of a free market economy. This perspective—first articulated in the mercantile era by such classical market economic theorists as Adam Smith (*The Wealth of Nations*) and recently rearticulated in great depth by a significant group of "law and economics" scholars such as Judge Richard Posner—sees a free market as an "invisible hand" that can operate to allocate each of society's scarce resources to the members of society that value those respective resources most highly. More importantly, many economic theorists suggest that the market accomplishes this allocation in a fashion that is presumptively superior to governmental regulation. The effectiveness of the market as resource allocator assumes that each person is a rational maximizer of her self-interest who will respond to incentives by altering her behavior when the market creates an opportunity to improve her circumstances. If the parties to a transaction have full information and there are no barriers to the transaction, parties will voluntarily exchange resources when each party perceives that the exchange will increase that party's respective well-being. In turn, such exchanges should increase the aggregate value that society can derive from those resources, unless the exchange has effects on third parties (economists refer to these third-party effects as *externalities*) that are negative and outweigh the benefits to the transacting parties.

This theory has profoundly influenced the development of property law, because the idea of markets as efficient resource allocators rests on the legal recognition of private property rights to resources, and upon the premise that these rights are both *exclusive* (identifiable to one person or group of persons) and *transferable* (capable of being reallocated), making use of the resource obtainable by one who values it more highly than its current owner. The policy goal of aggregate value maximization is further served by a system that is also *universal*—i.e., one that potentially subjects all valuable resources to private ownership. Lawyering influenced by this policy perspective advocates for establish-

markets as efficient allocation of resources

*

PROPERTY AND LAWYERING

Second Edition

*

Chapter 1

THE CONCEPT OF PROPERTY
AND ITS PARAMETERS

A. INTRODUCTION

What does it mean to say that something is "property"? As Professor Charles Donahue has explained, "property" derives from the French *prepriété* (peculiar nature or quality) and the Latin *proprietas* (ownership). *Proprietas* is in turn a derivation of *proprius* (one's own, or peculiar), as contrasted with *communis* (common) or *alienus* (another's). In this regard, we could think of "property" abstractly as a "separator"—something that "distinguishes an individual or a thing from a group or from another." Charles Donahue, Jr., The Future of the Concept of Property Predicted from Its Past, Nomos XXII: Property 28 (1980).

Not surprisingly, however, we often tend to use the term "property" in a more tangible way. Several years ago, one of the authors of this book invited his new first-year students to provide some brief biographical data about themselves. One of the students wrote proudly of his two-year-old daughter, who "had already learned everything that she needed to know about Property law—the terms 'NO' and 'MINE.'" Even at two, that student's daughter had already conceptualized property in a sense familiar to all of us—as something tangible and under one's special control—pointing to an object and saying "this is mine." As Professor Donahue explains, this conception

> seems to characterize the legal concept of property in the definitional sense in the West: a tendency to agglomerate in a single legal person, preferably the one currently possessed of the thing that is the object of inquiry, the exclusive right to possess, privilege to use, and power to convey the thing. . . . [Donahue, *supra*, at 31–32.][1]

1. Our experience also tells us, however, that we cannot take too literally this tendency toward agglomeration of rights relating to an object in a single person. In fact, we experience the separation of rights among different persons in a variety of contexts. Landlords rent land to tenants for a limited period of time; siblings inherit an object from a parent as co-owners; one person may have an easement for access across the adjacent land of another. Our legal system has developed to view ownership of

1

Our purpose in Chapter 1 is to help you explore, as lawyers-in-training, the richness and complexity of the process that ultimately leads the law to conclude that something is my "property"—that "this is mine." From the outset, we attempt to place this exploration in the broader context of *lawyering*. We hope to focus your attention on the practice of law regarding real and personal property—not only how advocacy and legal decisions unfold in courtrooms, legislatures, and government offices, but how planning, drafting, counseling and negotiation take place in law offices. Before we begin, however, a little more background is in order.

__Rules, History, Policies and Change.__ Rules about "property" have changed over time as changes in social and economic life have changed the way that people interact with one another. And because changes in social and economic life continue, we can expect the rules about "property" will continue to change in the future. Changes in life that precipitate changes in the law are among the most inevitable realities of law study and law practice.[2] Thus, to understand the development of legal rules and the definitions inherent in them, you must appreciate the context of the *history* of our current rules (which can often help predict future changes in those rules) and the *purposes* or *policies* that we expect these evolving rules will serve in governing interpersonal relationships.

An appreciation of history allows us to make sense of rules and transactions that are otherwise nonsensical to the current mind. In law, as in life more generally, it is often the case that "a page of history is worth a volume of logic."[3] When we study a rule's history, we can focus upon the context in which a legal decisionmaker (*e.g.*, court, legislature, executive officer, administrator, or drafter of a contract) first established that rule. In doing so, we can gain an appreciation for the thoughts, opinions, and debates that shaped the purposes or policies the decisionmaker hoped to serve by that rule. This understanding provides a framework for us to appreciate how later decisionmakers culled, interpreted, enriched, shaded, or adapted those purposes and policies when facing subsequent disputes. As we will see throughout this book, as these

"property" as the aggregate of many component property rights (sometimes referred to colloquially as a "bundle of sticks"), and to view many of these component rights as separable and transferable to others in the marketplace.

2. Changes in law often follow (and hopefully address) societal changes, or changes in society's perspective on some recurrent problem. These changes occur more frequently than many new law students expect. Moreover, the inevitability of change in the smaller scale of an individual client's life—her situation or motivations (or those of other parties related to her transaction or conflict)—is a more frequent inevitability in law practice. To a significant degree, a good lawyer must be a specialist

in the "time travel" of foresight—anticipating remote and collateral consequences of rules and anticipating changes that will affect her clients and the rules that govern them. The good lawyer thus anticipates, for example, the potential for buyer's or seller's remorse after completing a transaction; the potential for a change in a client's current fortunes, goals and abilities; or the potential for a change in public attitudes or market valuation of competing interests.

3. This famous legal quotation comes from Justice Oliver Wendell Holmes in the United States Supreme Court's decision in *New York Trust Co. v. Eisner*, 256 U.S. 345, 41 S.Ct. 506, 65 L.Ed. 963 (1921).

ing legal rules that strengthen the market system and thus maximize efficiency.

Property as Guardian of Individual Liberty. We often say that "One's home is one's castle." Land ownership does not make one a king, of course—yet the rhetoric behind this statement does influence the way the law has viewed interpersonal disputes. As Professor Charles Reich explains:

> Property . . . draw[s] a boundary between public and private power. Property draws a circle around the activities of each private individual or organization. Within that circle, the owner has a greater degree of freedom than without. Outside, he must justify or explain his actions, and show his authority. Within he is master, and the state must justify and explain any interference. . . .
>
> Thus property performs the function of maintaining independence, dignity and pluralism in society by creating zones within which the majority has to yield to the owner. [Charles A. Reich, *The New Property*, 73 Yale L.J. 733, 771 (1964).]

As we shall see in this chapter and throughout this book, the law not only protects the individual owner against governmental intrusion into her "property," but also enlists the government in protecting against intrusion by other private actors. These protections implement fundamental policies (such as recognition of and respect for boundaries) that the law can serve by recognizing and protecting something as property.

Nevertheless, the designation "property" does not suggest that an owner of property may act with impunity. The law recognizes a number of limitations upon an owner's freedom to act with respect to her own property (*e.g.*, laws governing taxation of land, nuisances, zoning, and eminent domain). These limitations reflect the outcomes of collisions between the policy of property as guardian of individual liberty and other potentially conflicting goals of property law (including the other policies briefly previewed here). Defining and altering the boundaries of each owner's freedoms, based upon a careful and sophisticated analysis of the respective interests of the client and other parties, is a central task of property lawyering.

Property and the Reward of Labor. The view that one's labor should have a vital place in the allocation of property rights has long had significant appeal and for many years formed a classic liberal theory of property. As John Locke argued in his *Two Treatises on Civil Government*:

> Though the earth and all inferior creatures be common to all men, yet every man has a "property" in his own "person." This nobody has any right to but himself. The "labour" of his body and the "work" of his hands, we may say, are properly his. Whatsoever, then, he removes out of the state that Nature hath provided and left it in, he hath mixed his labour with it, and joined to it something that is his own, and thereby makes it his property. It being by him

removed from the common state Nature placed it in, it hath by this labour something annexed to it that excludes the common right of other men. For this "labour" being the unquestionable property of the labourer, no man but he can have a right to what that is once joined to, at least where there is enough, and as good left in common for others. [Book II, § 27 (G. Routledge 2d ed. 1887).]

In some cases, the law's recognition of property rights may well operate as a reward to a person's investment of labor (*e.g.*, the rule allocating ownership of a wild animal to its capturer, as discussed in Chapter 2). In other cases, the law refuses to allocate (or re-allocate) property rights notwithstanding a person's substantial investment of labor (*e.g.*, the law's general refusal to recognize "property" rights in a job). Identifying the extent to which a person's labor influences her legal rights—and the extent to which those rights can or should rise to the level of property rights—is often a fundamental part of the lawyering process.

Property, Personal Identity and Community. Capitalism and the development of markets has had the effect of splitting once-integrated life components (such as one's labor) into marketable commodities. This modern process of *commodification* has the potential to convert *anything* people are willing to sell and buy—from tangible land and appliances to more abstract rights like rights to control another's uses of her own land ("servitudes"), rights to ideas or a person's likeness, and even human reproductive components like eggs, sperm and/or space in the womb during gestation—into market commodities, and potentially "property."

This transformation has profound consequences for both the way that we view objects of property and the way that we view ourselves as persons. Parties engaged in modern commerce produce and market increasingly standardized products, businesses, and even entire communities. This standardization, however, means that as individuals, our experience of various places and times can become increasingly undifferentiated. Products and the companies that market them become progressively more difficult to distinguish from each other. Even the cities and towns in which we live have become increasingly similar in many respects. Further, as society has become more mobile, bonds between the individual and her social context—bonds that provided personal identity in earlier times—have become increasingly attenuated. Many of us no longer have a sense of having deep roots in a particular place, with a unique identity that derives from our relationship to that place and a particular community. In reaction to this dilemma of personal identity a communitarian movement has arisen in recent years; persons sharing this perspective have decried our society's "overemphasis" on individualism and individual rights at the expense of meaningful community and interpersonal connections.

At the same time, this standardization has tended (ironically) to abstract the concept of personal identity. Increasingly, the market views persons as fungible—each of us is a social security number, a credit card number, or a member of some generic classification (*e.g.*, retiree, "Gen–X," "18 to 35," white, female, or Hispanic). While such classification plays a significant role in the operation of markets that have brought relative affluence, it also ignores or de-emphasizes qualitative differences that would otherwise highlight personal identity. As a result, many people feel alienated and personally powerless in the face of the powerful and impersonal marketplace that surrounds and molds us—an alienation that French sociologist Emile Durkheim identified as *anomie.* Emile Durkheim, The Division of Labor in Society 1–3 (trans. G. Simpson, 1964). Against this backdrop, some have argued that society and law must operate to preserve personal identity—to allow the individual to connect to the outside world in a way that allows her to shape her life by her own unique values, rather than by being pressured to conform to the standardized values of others. In this respect, property law might play a central role—perhaps (as Professor Margaret Jane Radin has argued in her influential article *Property and Personhood*, 34 Stan. L. Rev. 957 (1982)) providing greater protection for those "property" rights that are most closely bound up with a person's identity (such as her home). In the lawyering process, consideration of the personhood and communitarian perspectives invite consideration of how the law can and should influence our ability as individuals to preserve our own personal identity while also functioning as integral, connected members of meaningful social communities.

B. THE RIGHT TO EXCLUDE

Regardless of the philosophical perspective through which one views the concept of property, the concept of property does have one unifying or necessary characteristic—the right to exclude. As Professor Thomas Merrill has explained, "[The right to exclude] is the *sine qua non.* Give someone the right to exclude others from a valued resource, *i.e.*, a resource that is scarce relative to the human demand for it, and you give them property. Deny someone the exclusion right and they do not have property." Thomas W. Merrill, *Property and the Right to Exclude*, 77 Neb. L. Rev. 730, 730 (1998). As you read the following materials, consider what role the right to exclude plays in the meaning and importance of property.

FELIX COHEN, DIALOGUE ON PRIVATE PROPERTY
9 Rutgers L. Rev. 357, 365–369 (1954).

C. Mr. F., there's a big cottonwood tree at the southeast corner of Wright Hagerty's ranch, about 30 miles north of Browning, Montana, and under that tree this morning a mule was born. Who owns the mule?

F. I don't know.

C. Do you own the mule?

F. No.

C. How do you know you don't own the mule? You just said you didn't know who owns the mule. Might it not be you?

F. Well, I suppose that it is possible that I might own a mule I never saw, but I don't think I do.

C. You don't plan to declare this mule on your personal property tax returns?

F. No.

C. Why not, if you really don't know whether you own it? Or do you know?

F. Well, I never had any relation to any mules in Montana.

C. Suppose you did have a relation to this mule. Suppose it turns out that the mule's father was your jackass. Would that make you the owner of the mule?

F. I don't think it would.

C. Suppose you owned the land on which the mule was born. Would that make you the owner of the mule?

F. No.

C. Suppose you owned a piece of unfenced prairie in Montana and the mule's mother during her pregnancy ate some of your grass. Would that make you the owner of the mule?

F. No, I don't think it would.

C. Well, then you seem to know more about the ownership of this Montana mule than you admitted a few moments ago. Now tell us who really owns the mule.

F. I suppose the owner of the mare owns the mule.

C. Exactly. But tell us how you come to that conclusion.

F. Well, I think that is the law of Montana.

C. Yes, and of all other states and countries, as far as I know. For example, the Laws of Manu, which are supposed to be the oldest legal code in the world, declare: "50. Should a bull beget a hundred calves on cows not owned by his master, those calves belong solely to the proprietors of the cows; and the strength of the bull was wasted." Now how does it happen, do you suppose, that the law of Montana in the twentieth century A.D. corresponds to the law of India of 4000 years or so ago? Is this an example of what Aristotle calls natural justice, which is everywhere the same, as distinguished from conventional justice which varies from place to place and from time to time?

F. Well, it does seem to be in accordance with the laws of nature that the progeny of the mother belong to the owner of the mother.

C. Wouldn't it be just as much in accordance with the laws of nature to say that the progeny of the father belong to the owner of the father?

F. I suppose that might be so, as a matter of simple biology, but as a practical matter it might be pretty hard to determine just which jackass was the mule's father.

C. Then, as a practical matter we are dealing with something more than biology. We are dealing with the human need for certainty in property distribution. If you plant seed in your neighbor's field the biological connection between your seed and the resulting plants is perfectly natural, but under the laws of Montana and all other states the crop belongs to the landowner. And the Laws of Manu say the same thing: "49. They, who have no property in the field, but having grain in their possession, sow it in soil owned by another, can receive no advantage whatever from the corn, which may be produced." Would you say here that as a matter of certainty it is generally easier to say who owns a field than to say who owned the seeds that were planted in it?

F. Yes, as a general rule I think that would be the case.

C. Then whether we call our rule of property in livestock an example of natural law or not, its naturalness has some relation to the social need for certainty, which seems to exist in 48 different states and 48 different centuries. Do you think that property law reflects some such human demand for certainty?

F. I think it does in the cases we have been discussing.

C. Couldn't we have some other equally certain and definite rule, say that the mule belongs to the owner of the land where it was born?

F. It might be a hard thing to do to locate the mule's birth-place, but the young mule will show us its own mother when it's hungry.

C. Suppose we decided that the mule should belong to the first roper. Wouldn't that be a simple and definite rule?

F. Yes, but it wouldn't be fair to the owner of the mare who was responsible for its care during pregnancy if a perfect stranger could come along and pick up the offspring.

C. Now, you are assuming that something more than certainty is involved in rules of property law, and that somehow such rules have something to do with ideas of fairness, and you could make out a good case for that proposition in this case. But suppose you are trying to explain this to a cowboy who has just roped this mule and doesn't see the fairness of this rule that makes it the property of the mare owner. Are there any more objective standards that you could point to in support of this rule? What would be the economic consequences of a rule that made the mule the property of the first roper instead of the mare-owner?

F. I think that livestock owners wouldn't be so likely to breed their mares or cows if anybody else could come along and take title to the offspring.

C. You think then that the rule that the owner of the mare owns the mule contributes to economic productivity?

F. Yes.

C. But tell me, is there any reason to suppose that the owner of the mare will be able to raise the mule more economically than, say, the first roper or the owner of the ground on which the mule was born?

F. Well, so long as the mule depends upon its mother's milk, it will be less expensive to raise it if the owner of the mother owns the offspring. And presumably the owner of the mother has physical control over his animals, and no extra effort is involved in his controlling the offspring as long as they are dependent upon their mother.

C. So, in effect, the rule we are talking about takes advantage of the natural dependency of the offspring on the mother animal. By enlisting the force of habit or inertia, this rule economizes on the human efforts that might otherwise be expended in establishing control over the new animal. The owner of the mare has achieved the object of all military strategy—he has gotten there "fustest with the mostest." We don't need to pay a troop of Texas Rangers to seize the mule and deliver it to the owner of the jackass father who may be many miles away. But why should we have a simple definite rule in all these cases? Wouldn't it be better to have a more flexible standard so that we might consider in each case what the owner of the mare contributed, what the owner of the jackass contributed, what was contributed by the grass owner who paid for the mare's dinners, then on the basis of all the facts we might reach a result that would do justice to all the circumstances of each individual case?

F. The trouble with that is that the expense of holding such investigations might exceed the value of the mule.

C. And would it be easier or harder to borrow from the bank to run a livestock business if the owner of a mare or a cow didn't know in advance that it would own the offspring?

F. If I were a banker I'd certainly hesitate to make a livestock loan to a herd owner without such a simple definite rule.

C. Could we sum up this situation, then, by saying that this particular rule of property law that the owner of the mare owns the offspring has appealed to many different societies across hundred of generations because this rule contributes to the economy by attaching a reward to planned production; is simple, certain, and economical to administer; fits in with existing human and animal habits and forces; and appeals to the sense of fairness of human beings in many places and generations?

F. I think that summarizes the relevant factors.

C. And would you expect that similar social considerations might lead to the development of other rules of property law, and that where these various considerations of productivity, certainty, enforceability, and fairness point in divergent directions instead of converging on a single solution, we might find more controversial problems of private ownership?

GUIDO CALABRESI & A. DOUGLAS MELAMED, PROPERTY RULES, LIABILITY RULES AND INALIENABILITY: ONE VIEW OF THE CATHEDRAL

85 Harv. L. Rev. 1089, 1090–1092 (1972).

The first issue which must be faced by any legal system is one we call the problem of "entitlement." Whenever a state is presented with the conflicting interests of two or more people, or two or more groups of people, it must decide which side to favor. Absent such a decision, access to goods, services, and life itself will be decided on the basis of "might makes right"—whoever is stronger or shrewder will win. Hence the fundamental thing that law does is to decide which of the conflicting parties will be entitled to prevail. The entitlement to make noise versus the entitlement to have silence, the entitlement to pollute versus the entitlement to breathe clean air, the entitlement to have children versus the entitlement to forbid them—these are the first order of legal decisions.

Having made its initial choice, society must enforce that choice. Simply setting the entitlement does not avoid the problem of "might makes right"; a minimum of state intervention is always necessary. Our conventional notions make this easy to comprehend with respect to private property. If Taney owns a cabbage patch and Marshall, who is bigger, wants a cabbage, he will get it unless the state intervenes. But it is not so obvious that the state must also intervene if it chooses the opposite entitlement, communal property. If large Marshall has grown some communal cabbages and chooses to deny them to small Taney, it will take state action to enforce Taney's entitlement to the communal cabbages. . . .

The state not only has to decide whom to entitle, but it must also simultaneously make a series of equally difficult second order decisions. These decisions go to the manner in which entitlements are protected and to whether an individual is allowed to sell or trade the entitlement. In any given dispute . . . the state must decide not only which side wins but also the kind of protection to grant. . . .

An entitlement is protected by a property rule to the extent that someone who wishes to remove the entitlement from its holder must buy it from him in a voluntary transaction in which the value of the entitlement is agreed upon by the seller. It is the form of entitlement which gives rise to the least amount of state intervention: once the original entitlement is decided upon, the state does not try to decide its value. It lets each of the parties say how much the entitlement is worth to him, and gives the seller a veto if the buyer does not offer enough. Property rules involve a collective decision as to who is to be given an initial entitlement but not as to the value of the entitlement.

Whenever someone may [acquire] the initial entitlement if he is willing to pay an objectively determined value for it, an entitlement is protected by a liability rule. This value may be what it is thought the original holder of the entitlement would have sold it for. But the holder's complaint that he would have demanded more will not avail him once the objectively determined value is set. Obviously, liability rules involve an additional stage of state intervention: not only are entitlements protected, but their transfer or destruction is allowed on the basis of a value determined by some organ of the state rather than by the parties themselves.

JACQUE v. STEENBERG HOMES, INC.

Supreme Court of Wisconsin.
209 Wis.2d 605, 563 N.W.2d 154 (1997).

WILLIAM A. BABLITCH, JUSTICE. Steenberg Homes had a mobile home to deliver. Unfortunately for Harvey and Lois Jacque (the Jacques), the easiest route of delivery was across their land. Despite adamant protests by the Jacques, Steenberg plowed a path through the Jacques' snow-covered field and via that path, delivered the mobile home. Consequently, the Jacques sued Steenberg Homes for intentional trespass. At trial, Steenberg Homes conceded the intentional trespass, but argued that no compensatory damages had been proved, and that punitive damages could not be awarded without compensatory damages. Although the jury awarded the Jacques $1 in nominal damages and $100,000 in punitive damages, the circuit court set aside the jury's award of $100,000.... We conclude that when nominal damages are awarded for an intentional trespass to land, punitive damages may, in the discretion of the jury, be awarded.... Accordingly, we reverse and remand for reinstatement of the punitive damage award....

The relevant facts follow. Plaintiffs, Lois and Harvey Jacque, are an elderly couple, now retired from farming, who own roughly 170 acres near Wilke's Lake in the town of Schleswig. The defendant, Steenberg Homes, Inc. (Steenberg), is in the business of selling mobile homes. In the fall of 1993, a neighbor of the Jacques purchased a mobile home from Steenberg. Delivery of the mobile home was included in the sales price.

Steenberg determined that the easiest route to deliver the mobile home was across the Jacques' land. Steenberg preferred transporting the home across the Jacques' land because the only alternative was a private road which was covered in up to seven feet of snow and contained a sharp curve which would require sets of "rollers" to be used when maneuvering the home around the curve. Steenberg asked the Jacques on several separate occasions whether it could move the home across the Jacques' farm field. The Jacques refused. The Jacques were sensitive about allowing others on their land because they had lost property valued at over $10,000 to other neighbors in an adverse possession action in the mid–1980's. Despite repeated refusals from the Jacques, Steenberg decided to sell the mobile home, which was to be used as a summer cottage, and delivered it on February 15, 1994.

On the morning of delivery, Mr. Jacque observed the mobile home parked on the corner of the town road adjacent to his property. He decided to find out where the movers planned to take the home. The movers, who were Steenberg employees, showed Mr. Jacque the path they planned to take with the mobile home to reach the neighbor's lot. The path cut across the Jacques' land. Mr. Jacque informed the movers that it was the Jacques' land they were planning to cross and that Steenberg did not have permission to cross their land. He told them that Steenberg had been refused permission to cross the Jacques' land.

One of Steenberg's employees called the assistant manager, who then came out to the Jacques' home. In the meantime, the Jacques called and asked some of their neighbors and the town chairman to come over immediately. Once everyone was present, the Jacques showed the assistant manager an aerial map and plat book of the township to prove their ownership of the land, and reiterated their demand that the home not be moved across their land.

At that point, the assistant manager asked Mr. Jacque how much money it would take to get permission. Mr. Jacque responded that it was not a question of money; the Jacques just did not want Steenberg to cross their land. Mr. Jacque testified that he told Steenberg to "[F]ollow the road, that is what the road is for." Steenberg employees left the meeting without permission to cross the land.

At trial, one of Steenberg's employees testified that, upon coming out of the Jacques' home, the assistant manager stated: "I don't give a * * * * what [Mr. Jacque] said, just get the home in there any way you can." The other Steenberg employee confirmed this testimony and further testified that the assistant manager told him to park the company truck in such a way that no one could get down the town road to see the route the employees were taking with the home. The assistant manager denied giving these instructions, and Steenberg argued that the road was blocked for safety reasons.

The employees, after beginning down the private road, ultimately used a "bobcat" to cut a path through the Jacques' snow-covered field and hauled the home across the Jacques' land to the neighbor's lot. One employee testified that upon returning to the office and informing the assistant manager that they had gone across the field, the assistant manager reacted by giggling and laughing. The other employee confirmed this testimony. The assistant manager disputed this testimony.

When a neighbor informed the Jacques that Steenberg had, in fact, moved the mobile home across the Jacques' land, Mr. Jacque called the Manitowoc County Sheriff's Department. After interviewing the parties and observing the scene, an officer from the sheriff's department issued a $30 citation to Steenberg's assistant manager.

The Jacques commenced an intentional tort action ... seeking compensatory and punitive damages from Steenberg.... At the completion of the Jacques' case, Steenberg moved for a directed verdict under Wis. Stat. § 805.14(3) (1993–94). For purposes of the motion, Steenberg admitted to an intentional trespass to land, but asked the circuit court to find that the Jacques were not entitled to compensatory damages or punitive damages based on insufficiency of the evidence. The circuit court denied Steenberg's motion and the questions of punitive and compensatory damages were submitted to the jury. The jury awarded the Jacques $1 nominal damages and $100,000 punitive damages. Steenberg filed post-verdict motions claiming that the punitive damage award must be set aside because Wisconsin law did not allow a punitive damage award unless the jury also awarded compensatory damages.... The circuit court granted Steenberg's motion to set aside the award....

This case presents three issues: (1) whether an award of nominal damages for intentional trespass to land may support a punitive damage award and, if so; (2) whether the law should apply to Steenberg or should only be applied prospectively and, if we apply the law to Steenberg; (3) whether the $100,000 in punitive damages awarded by the jury is excessive....

Steenberg argues that, as a matter of law, punitive damages could not be awarded by the jury because punitive damages must be supported by an award of compensatory damages and here the jury awarded only nominal and punitive damages. The Jacques contend that the rationale supporting the compensatory damage award requirement is inapposite when the wrongful act is an intentional trespass to land. We agree with the Jacques....

... [W]hether nominal damages can support a punitive damage award in the case of an intentional trespass to land has never been squarely addressed by this court. Nonetheless, Wisconsin law is not without reference to this situation. In 1854 the court established punitive damages, allowing the assessment of "damages as a punishment to the defendant for the purpose of making an example." *McWilliams v. Bragg*, 3 Wis. 424, 425 (1854). The *McWilliams* court related the facts and an illustrative tale from the English case of *Merest v. Harvey*, 128 Eng.Rep. 761 (C.P.1814), to explain the rationale underlying punitive damages. ^

In *Merest*, a landowner was shooting birds in his field when he was approached by the local magistrate who wanted to hunt with him. Although the landowner refused, the magistrate proceeded to hunt. When the landowner continued to object, the magistrate threatened to have him jailed and dared him to file suit. Although little actual harm had been caused, the English court upheld damages of 500 pounds, explaining "in a case where a man disregards every principle which actuates the conduct of gentlemen, what is to restrain him except large damages?" *McWilliams*, 3 Wis. 424 at 428.

To explain the need for punitive damages, even where actual harm is slight, *McWilliams* related the hypothetical tale from *Merest* of an intentional trespasser:

> Suppose a gentleman has a paved walk in his paddock, before his window, and that a man intrudes and walks up and down before the

[handwritten margin note: difference between punitive nominal damages]

window of his house, and looks in while the owner is at dinner, is the trespasser permitted to say "here is a halfpenny for you which is the full extent of the mischief I have done." Would that be a compensation? I cannot say that it would be.... [*McWilliams*, 3 Wis. at 428.]

[handwritten marginalia: punitive damages from right to exclude from property]

Thus, in the case establishing punitive damages in this state, this court recognized that in certain situations of trespass, the actual harm is not in the damage done to the land, which may be minimal, but in the loss of the individual's right to exclude others from his or her property and the court implied that this right may be punished by a large damage award despite the lack of measurable harm.

Steenberg contends that the rule established in *Barnard* [*v. Cohen*, 165 Wis. 417, 162 N.W. 480 (1917)] prohibits a punitive damage award, as a matter of law, unless the plaintiff also receives compensatory damages. Because the Jacques did not receive a compensatory damage award, Steenberg contends that the punitive damage award must be set aside. The Jacques argue that the rationale for not allowing nominal damages to support a punitive damage award is inapposite when the wrongful act involved is an intentional trespass to land. The Jacques argue that both the individual and society have significant interests in deterring intentional trespass to land, regardless of the lack of measurable harm that results. We agree with the Jacques. An examination of the individual interests invaded by an intentional trespass to land, and society's interests in preventing intentional trespass to land, leads us to the conclusion that the *Barnard* rule should not apply when the tort supporting the award is intentional trespass to land.

We turn first to the individual landowner's interest in protecting his or her land from trespass. The United States Supreme Court has recognized that the private landowner's right to exclude others from his or her land is "one of the most essential sticks in the bundle of rights that are commonly characterized as property." *Dolan v. City of Tigard*, 512 U.S. 374, 384, 114 S.Ct. 2309, 2316, 129 L.Ed.2d 304 (1994). This court has long recognized "[e]very person['s] constitutional right to the exclusive enjoyment of his own property for any purpose which does not invade the rights of another person." *Diana Shooting Club v. Lamoreux*, 114 Wis. 44, 59, 89 N.W. 880 (1902) (holding that the victim of an intentional trespass should have been allowed to take judgment for nominal damages and costs). Thus, both this court and the Supreme Court recognize the individual's legal right to exclude others from private property.

Yet a right is hollow if the legal system provides insufficient means to protect it. Felix Cohen offers the following analysis summarizing the relationship between the individual and the state regarding property rights:

[T]hat is property to which the following label can be attached:

> To the world:
>
> Keep off X unless you have my permission, which I may grant or withhold.
>
> Signed: Private Citizen
>
> Endorsed: The state

Felix S. Cohen, Dialogue on Private Property, IX Rutgers Law Review 357, 374 (1954). Harvey and Lois Jacque have the right to tell Steenberg Homes and any other trespasser, "No, you cannot cross our land." But that right has no practical meaning unless protected by the State. And, as this court recognized as early as 1854, a "halfpenny" award does not constitute state protection.

The nature of the nominal damage award in an intentional trespass to land case further supports an exception to *Barnard*. Because a legal right is involved, the law recognizes that actual harm occurs in every trespass. The action for intentional trespass to land is directed at vindication of the legal right. W. Page Keeton, Prosser and Keeton on Torts, § 13 (5th ed.1984). The law infers some damage from every direct entry upon the land of another. *Id.* The law recognizes actual harm in every trespass to land whether or not compensatory damages are awarded. *Id.* Thus, in the case of intentional trespass to land, the nominal damage award represents the recognition that, although immeasurable in mere dollars, actual harm has occurred.

The potential for harm resulting from intentional trespass also supports an exception to *Barnard*. A series of intentional trespasses, as the Jacques had the misfortune to discover in an unrelated action, can threaten the individual's very ownership of the land. The conduct of an intentional trespasser, if repeated, might ripen into prescription or adverse possession and, as a consequence, the individual landowner can lose his or her property rights to the trespasser.

In sum, the individual has a strong interest in excluding trespassers from his or her land. Although only nominal damages were awarded to the Jacques, Steenberg's intentional trespass caused actual harm. We turn next to society's interest in protecting private property from the intentional trespasser.

Society has an interest in punishing and deterring intentional trespassers beyond that of protecting the interests of the individual landowner. Society has an interest in preserving the integrity of the legal system. Private landowners should feel confident that wrongdoers who trespass upon their land will be appropriately punished. When landowners have confidence in the legal system, they are less likely to resort to "self-help" remedies. In *McWilliams*, the court recognized the importance of " 'prevent[ing] the practice of dueling, [by permitting] juries [] to punish insult by exemplary damages.' " *McWilliams*, 3 Wis. at 428. Although dueling is rarely a modern form of self-help, one can easily imagine a frustrated landowner taking the law into his or her own hands when faced with a brazen trespasser, like Steenberg, who refuses to heed no trespass warnings.

People expect wrongdoers to be appropriately punished. Punitive damages have the effect of bringing to punishment types of conduct that, though oppressive and hurtful to the individual, almost invariably go unpunished by the public prosecutor. The $30 forfeiture was certainly not an appropriate punishment for Steenberg's egregious trespass in the eyes of the Jacques. It was more akin to *Merest*'s "halfpenny." If punitive damages are not allowed in a situation like this, what punishment will prohibit the intentional trespass to land? Moreover, what is to stop Steenberg Homes from concluding, in the future, that delivering its mobile homes via an intentional trespass and paying the resulting Class B forfeiture, is not more profitable than obeying the law? Steenberg Homes plowed a path across the Jacques' land and dragged the mobile home across that path, in the face of the Jacques' adamant refusal. A $30 forfeiture and a $1 nominal damage award are unlikely to restrain Steenberg Homes from similar conduct in the future. An appropriate punitive damage award probably will.

In sum, as the court of appeals noted, the *Barnard* rule sends the wrong message to Steenberg Homes and any others who contemplate trespassing on the land of another. It implicitly tells them that they are free to go where they please, regardless of the landowner's wishes. As long as they cause no compensable harm, the only deterrent intentional trespassers face is the nominal damage award of $1, the modern equivalent of *Merest*'s halfpenny, and the possibility of a Class B forfeiture under Wis. Stat. § 943.13. We conclude that both the private landowner and society have much more than a nominal interest in excluding others from private land. Intentional trespass to land causes actual harm to the individual, regardless of whether that harm can be measured in mere dollars. Consequently, the *Barnard* rationale will not support a refusal to allow punitive damages when the tort involved is an intentional trespass to land. Accordingly, assuming that the other requirements for punitive damages have been met, we hold that nominal damages may support a punitive damage award in an action for intentional trespass to land....

Next we consider the effect of our holding on the parties before us. Steenberg argues that its reliance at trial on the well-established *Barnard* rule compels this court to either apply our holding prospectively, or grant a new trial.

Steenberg argues if we should hold, as we do, that punitive damages can be awarded with only a nominal damage award, our holding should not apply to them. Steenberg cites *Colby [v. Columbia County]*, 202 Wis.2d 342, 550 N.W.2d 124 [(1996)], for the proposition that a holding that departs from past precedent should only be applied prospectively. Steenberg argues that because it relied on the well-established *Barnard* rule at trial, and our holding today recognizes an exception to the *Barnard* rule, today's holding should not apply to this case. Steenberg misunderstands *Colby* and the doctrine of sunbursting.

Sunbursting[4] is an exception to the general rule referred to as the "Blackstonian Doctrine." *Fitzgerald v. Meissner & Hicks, Inc.*, 38 Wis.2d 571, 575, 157 N.W.2d 595 (1968). This classic doctrine provides that a decision which overrules precedent is accorded retroactive effect.

At times, inequities will occur when a court departs from precedent and announces a new rule of law. In an effort to avoid inequity on these rare occasions, the court has recognized exceptions to the Blackstonian Doctrine and used the device of prospective overruling, known as "sunbursting," to limit the effect of a newly announced rule when retroactive application would be inequitable.

Prospective application of a judicial holding is a question of policy to be determined by this court. The court allows sunbursting for the purpose of mitigating hardships that may occur with the retroactive application of a new rule. This court will not sunburst absent a compelling judicial reason for doing so. No simple rule helps us determine the existence of a judicial reason for sunbursting. Instead, the equities peculiar to a given rule or case determine the rule adopted by the court in each case.

Steenberg contends that its reliance on *Barnard* at trial creates a compelling judicial reason to sunburst. Steenberg explains that its trial strategy was dependent on the *Barnard* rule. Therefore, it contends that a holding in this case, recognizing an exception to the *Barnard* rule should only apply prospectively, *i.e.*, not to Steenberg Homes. We disagree. We find Steenberg's contention that it relied on the *Barnard* rule misleading. Steenberg did not concede the intentional trespass until after the Jacques rested at trial. At this point, when overwhelming evidence clearly established Steenberg's intentional trespass on the Jacques' land, then and only then, did Steenberg rely on *Barnard* and concede intentional trespass. This type of "reliance" does not give rise to the inequity that sunbursting is designed to prevent.

Steenberg's reliance on the *Barnard* rule is not the type of reliance that normally forms the basis for sunbursting. The court does not prospectively apply a holding merely because of reliance on an old rule. *Rolo v. Goers*, 174 Wis.2d 709, 723, 497 N.W.2d 724 (1993). Prospective application of a holding based on reliance on an old rule has occurred when there has been reliance on an overruled decision by a substantial number of persons and considerable harm or detriment could result to them. *Id.* When tort law is changed, the court is concerned about exposing many individuals and institutions to liability who would have obtained liability insurance had they known they would no longer enjoy

---

4. Judge Thomas Fairchild has suggested that "[i]f one thinks of a judicially pronounced new rule of law as the rosy dawn of a new day, 'sunbursting' has an appropriate connotation." Thomas E. Fairchild, Limitation of New Judge-Made Law to Prospective Effect Only: "Prospective Overruling" or "Sunbursting," 51 Marq.L.Rev. 254, 255 (1967–68). However, the illustrative nature of the term is purely coincidental. Prospective overruling earned the nickname "sunbursting" from the name of a party to litigation involving prospective application. *Great Northern Railway Company v. Sunburst Oil & Refining Co.*, 287 U.S. 358, 53 S.Ct. 145, 77 L.Ed. 360 (1932).

immunity. *Harmann* [*v. Hadley*, 128 Wis.2d 371, 381, 382 N.W.2d 673 (1986)]. Steenberg does not claim that others will be adversely affected by our recognition of an exception to the *Barnard* rule. Steenberg only refers to its own reliance, and to its own punishment.

The Jacques' interests also prevent us from sunbursting in this case. In determining whether hardship or injustice will occur, the court must also consider the effect of prospective application on the party who sought to change the law. Retroactivity is usually justified as a reward for the litigant who has persevered in attacking an unsound rule. To refuse to apply the new rule here would deprive the Jacques of any benefit from their effort and expense in challenging the old rule which we now declare erroneous. That, we conclude, would be the greater injustice. Accordingly, we hold that the exception to *Barnard* that we recognize today shall be applied to Steenberg. . . .

In conclusion, we hold that when nominal damages are awarded for an intentional trespass to land, punitive damages may, in the discretion of the jury, be awarded. Our decision today shall apply to Steenberg Homes. . . . Accordingly, we reverse and remand to the circuit court for reinstatement of the punitive damage award. . . .

Notes

1. *Property and the Power of Exclusion.* The *Jacque* case reflects our popular conception of "property" as those objects over which one has legally sanctioned dominion and control. This conception has a long pedigree. Sir William Blackstone—namesake of the "Blackstonian" doctrine mentioned prominently in *Jacque* and an 18th Century scholar whose *Commentaries on the Laws of England* had significant impact upon the development of both English and American law—spoke of the concept of property in near absolute terms: "There is nothing which so generally strikes the imagination, and engages the affections of mankind, as the right of property; or that sole and despotic dominion which one man claims and exercises over the external things of the world, in total exclusion of the right of any other individual in the universe." II Blackstone, Commentaries on the Laws of England at 2 (9th ed. 1783).

Why should the law accord this exclusive dominion to the Jacques? As Calabresi and Melamed suggest, there are other alternatives.

- The law could say that the Jacques had no "entitlement" at all—*i.e.*, it could treat the land as a communal asset and let Steenberg cross the land as it wished, without interference from the Jacques.

- Alternatively, the law could say that the Jacques had a general "entitlement," but that Steenberg could "take" this entitlement (*i.e.*, it could cross the land over the objection of the Jacques) as long as it paid the Jacques the objectively determined "fair market value" of this right. [In the terminology of Calabresi and Melamed, this would protect the Jacques using a "liability rule."]

So why does the law instead choose to protect the Jacques by a "property" rule, *i.e.*, by giving them a state-sanctioned power to exclude Steenberg?

Does Professor Cohen's dialogue with his hypothetical student give you any insight as to the reasons why this remedy is socially useful?

2. *The Court's Remedy in* Jacque. The jury in *Jacque* awarded the Jacques $1 in nominal damages, $0 in compensatory damages, and $100,000 in punitive damages. Was the jury correct not to award compensatory damages to the Jacques? If not, how should the jury have measured their compensatory damages?

3. *"Sunbursting" Versus Retroactive Application of the Law.* Prior to the dispute in *Jacque*, state courts in Wisconsin (*e.g., Barnard v. Cohen*) had refused to impose punitive damages in cases in which the plaintiff suffered no actual harm to person or property. The court in *Jacque* decided to change the law and permit punitive damages even in the absence of actual damages. Steenberg argued that the court should have applied its rule only prospectively—*i.e.,* the law should assess punitive damages against future intentional trespassers, but not Steenberg. The court clearly did not agree. Do you agree? Why should a court ever apply a rule only prospectively, against future parties? Might a court decide to apply a rule prospectively (*i.e.,* only as to causes of action that arise after the date of the court's judgment), and yet still apply the new rule in the lawsuit in which the court announces the change? If so, why? *See, e.g., Theama v. City of Kenosha*, 117 Wis.2d 508, 344 N.W.2d 513 (1984).

LAWYERING EXERCISE
(Counseling: Evaluating Precedent and Legal Risk)

BACKGROUND: When a client is faced with a decision—*e.g.,* whether to take certain actions or forgo them—one of the lawyer's most important functions is to give the client the data she needs to make an informed decision. Typically, this may require the lawyer to evaluate existing legal authority, such as a statute or a prior judicial decision, and to provide the client with the lawyer's best predictive judgment about whether that authority would permit the client's intended conduct without legal consequences. This requires the lawyer to develop the skills of analogizing and distinguishing:

> An analogy is a demonstration that two situations are so parallel that the reasoning that justified the decision in one should do the same in the other. When a court is persuaded by an analogy to precedent, the court is said to "follow" the precedent. Distinguishing is the opposite of analogy: a demonstration that two situations are so fundamentally dissimilar that the same result should not occur in both. Analogizing and distinguishing have been two of the most important intellectual tools in the slow and gradual construction and evolution of the common law. Both help find and state the rule for which a precedent stands, together with something about how that rule is to be applied. (Distinguishing does so by showing what the rule is not and how it is not to be applied). There are three steps in analogizing or distinguishing. First, make sure that the issue in the precedent is the same one you are trying to resolve. Second, identify the precedent's determinative facts. Do not look for

mere coincidences between the precedent and the current case; look instead for facts that the precedential court treated as crucial and on which it really relied. Finally, compare the precedent's determinative facts to the facts you are trying to resolve. . . . Your conclusion should . . . be the most logical and plausible one that is consistent with the heart of the precedential court's reasoning and with public policy. [Richard K. Neumann, Jr., Legal Reasoning and Legal Writing: Structure, Strategy and Style 138 (4th ed. 2001).]

SITUATION: Assume that your law firm generally represents Steenberg Homes (Steenberg) in its activities. Steenberg wants to deliver the home across the land of the Jacques, because it will cost them an additional $1,000 in transportation expenses to deliver the home via public roads. Steenberg informs you that the Jacques have refused to give permission to cross their land. Steenberg's president tells you: "Delivering the home across their land would take about 20 minutes and would cause no physical damage. They're being unreasonable. If we just went across their land anyway, and we did no physical damage, would we face a risk of serious liability?"

TASK: Read the opinion in *Barnard v. Cohen*, 165 Wis. 417, 162 N.W. 480 (1917) (you can find it in your library or on WESTLAW). Using Professor Neumann's steps in analogizing and distinguishing, explain to your client whether delivering the home without permission poses an unacceptable risk of a punitive damage award, or whether the rule in *Barnard v. Cohen* would insulate Steenberg from punitive damages as long as it did no physical harm to the land.

As Professor Cohen suggested, we find more controversial problems of private ownership when various social considerations may justify different and potentially conflicting views regarding what legal rule is ideal. Compare the *Jacque* court's view of the right to exclude with the view expressed in *State v. Shack*, a legendary New Jersey decision dealing with the scope of a farmer's ability to exclude unwanted persons from his farm.

STATE v. SHACK

Supreme Court of New Jersey.
58 N.J. 297, 277 A.2d 369 (1971).

WEINTRAUB, C.J. Defendants entered upon private property to aid migrant farmworkers employed and housed there. Having refused to depart upon the demand of the owner, defendants were charged with violating N.J.S.A. 2A:170–31 which provides that "[a]ny person who trespasses on any lands . . . after being forbidden so to trespass by the owner . . . is a disorderly person and shall be punished by a fine of not more than $50." Defendants were convicted . . . .

Before us, no one seeks to sustain these convictions. The complaints were prosecuted in the Municipal Court and in the County Court by counsel engaged by the complaining landowner, Tedesco. However Tedesco did not respond to this appeal, and the county prosecutor, while defending abstractly the constitutionality of the trespass statute, expressly disclaimed any position as to whether the statute reached the activity of these defendants.

Complainant, Tedesco, a farmer, employs migrant workers for his seasonal needs. As part of their compensation, these workers are housed at a camp on his property.

Defendant Tejeras is a field worker for the Farm Workers Division of the Southwest Citizens Organization for Poverty Elimination, known by the acronym SCOPE, a nonprofit corporation funded by the Office of Economic Opportunity pursuant to an act of Congress, 42 U.S.C.A. §§ 2861–2864. The role of SCOPE includes providing for the "health services of the migrant farm worker."

Defendant Shack is a staff attorney with the Farm Workers Division of Camden Regional Legal Services, Inc., known as "CRLS," also a nonprofit corporation funded by the Office of Economic Opportunity pursuant to an act of Congress, 42 U.S.C.A. § 2809(a)(3). The mission of CRLS includes legal advice and representation for these workers.

Differences had developed between Tedesco and these defendants prior to the events which led to the trespass charges now before us. Hence when defendant Tejeras wanted to go upon Tedesco's farm to find a migrant worker who needed medical aid for the removal of 28 sutures, he called upon defendant Shack for his help with respect to the legalities involved. Shack, too, had a mission to perform on Tedesco's farm; he wanted to discuss a legal problem with another migrant worker there employed and housed. Defendants arranged to go to the farm together. Shack carried literature to inform the migrant farmworkers of the assistance available to them under federal statutes, but no mention seems to have been made of that literature when Shack was later confronted by Tedesco.

Defendants entered upon Tedesco's property and as they neared the camp site where the farmworkers were housed, they were confronted by Tedesco who inquired of their purpose. Tejeras and Shack stated their missions. In response, Tedesco offered to find the injured worker, and as to the worker who needed legal advice, Tedesco also offered to locate the man but insisted that the consultation would have to take place in Tedesco's office and in his presence. Defendants declined, saying they had the right to see the men in the privacy of their living quarters and without Tedesco's supervision. Tedesco thereupon summoned a State Trooper who, however, refused to remove defendants except upon Tedesco's written complaint. Tedesco then executed the formal complaints charging violations of the trespass statute. . . .

The constitutionality of the trespass statute, as applied here, is challenged on several scores. . . . [Editors' Note: Tejeras and Shack raised two federal constitutional arguments: (1) that their actions were protected speech under the First Amendment; and (2) that applying the

New Jersey trespass statute would defeat the purpose of federal statutes that fund organizations (such as SCOPE and CRLS) that aid migrant farmworkers, in violation of the Supremacy Clause. The New Jersey State Office of Legal Services also filed an amicus brief, in which it argued that by denying the migrants access to legal services, application of New Jersey's trespass statute deprived the migrants of their right to counsel in civil matters under various provisions of the Constitution.]

These constitutional claims are not established by any definitive holding. We think it unnecessary to explore their validity. The reason is that we are satisfied that under our State law the ownership of real property does not include the right to bar access to governmental services available to migrant workers and hence there was no trespass within the meaning of the penal statute. The policy considerations which underlie that conclusion may be much the same as those which would be weighed with respect to one or more of the constitutional challenges, but a decision in nonconstitutional terms is more satisfactory, because the interests of migrant workers are more expansively served in that way than they would be if they had no more freedom than these constitutional concepts could be found to mandate if indeed they apply at all. . . .

Property rights serve human values. They are recognized to that end, and are limited by it. Title to real property cannot include dominion over the destiny of persons the owner permits to come upon the premises. Their well-being must remain the paramount concern of a system of law. Indeed the needs of the occupants may be so imperative and their strength so weak, that the law will deny the occupants the power to contract away what is deemed essential to their health, welfare, or dignity.

Here we are concerned with a highly disadvantaged segment of our society. We are told that every year farmworkers and their families numbering more than one million leave their home areas to fill the seasonal demand for farm labor in the United States. The Migratory Farm Labor Problem in the United States (1969 Report of Subcommittee on Migratory Labor of the United States Senate Committee on Labor and Public Welfare), p. 1. The migrant farmworkers come to New Jersey in substantial numbers. The report just cited places at 55,700 the number of man-months of such employment in our State in 1968 (p. 7). The numbers of workers so employed here in that year are estimated at 1,300 in April; 6,500 in May; 9,800 in June; 10,600 in July; 12,100 in August; 9,600 in September; and 5,500 in October (p. 9).

The migrant farmworkers are a community within but apart from the local scene. They are rootless and isolated. Although the need for their labors is evident, they are unorganized and without economic or political power. It is their plight alone that summoned government to their aid. In response, Congress provided under Title III-B of the Economic Opportunity Act of 1964 (42 U.S.C.A. § 2701 *et seq.*) for "assistance for migrant and other seasonally employed farmworkers and their families." Section 2861 states "the purpose of this part is to assist migrant and seasonal farmworkers and their families to improve their living conditions and develop skills necessary for a productive and self-sufficient life in an increasingly complex and technological society." Section 2862(b)(1) provides for funding of programs "to meet the immediate needs of migrant and seasonal farmworkers and their families, such as day care for children, education, health services, improved housing and sanitation (including the provision and maintenance of emergency and temporary housing and sanitation facilities), legal advice and representation, and consumer training and counseling." As we have said, SCOPE is engaged in a program funded under this section, and CRLS also pursues the objectives of this section although, we gather, it is funded under § 2809(a)(3), which is not limited in its concern to the migrant and other seasonally employed farmworkers and seeks "to further the cause of justice among persons living in poverty by mobilizing the assistance of lawyers and legal institutions and by providing legal advice, legal representation, counseling, education, and other appropriate services."

These ends would not be gained if the intended beneficiaries could be insulated from efforts to reach them. It is in this framework that we must decide whether the camp operator's rights in his lands may stand between the migrant workers and those who would aid them. The key to that aid is communication. Since the migrant workers are outside the mainstream of the communities in which they are housed and are unaware of their rights and opportunities and of the services available to them, they can be reached only by positive efforts tailored to that end. The Report of the Governor's Task Force on Migrant Farm Labor (1968) noted that "One of the major problems related to seasonal farm labor is the lack of adequate direct information with regard to the availability of public services," and that "there is a dire need to provide the workers with basic educational and informational material in a language and style that can be readily understood by the migrant" (pp. 101–102). The report stressed the problem of access and deplored the notion that property rights may stand as a barrier, saying "In our judgment, 'no trespass' signs represent the last dying remnants of paternalistic behavior" (p. 63).

A man's right in his real property of course is not absolute. It was a maxim of the common law that one should so use his property as not to injure the rights of others. Although hardly a precise solvent of actual controversies, the maxim does express the inevitable proposition that rights are relative and there must be an accommodation when they meet. Hence it has long been true that necessity, private or public, may justify entry upon the lands of another....

The subject is not static. As pointed out in 5 Powell, Real Property (Rohan 1970) § 745, pp. 493–494, while society will protect the owner in his permissible interests in land, yet

... [S]uch an owner must expect to find the absoluteness of his property rights curtailed by the organs of society, for the promotion of the best interests of others for whom these organs also operate as protective agencies. The necessity for such curtailments is greater in a modern industrialized and urbanized society than it was in the relatively simple American society of fifty, 100, or 200 years ago. The current balance between individualism and dominance of the social interest depends not only upon political and social ideologies, but also upon the physical and social facts of the time and place under discussion.

Professor Powell added in § 746, pp. 494–496:

> As one looks back along the historic road traversed by the law of land in England and in America, one sees a change from the viewpoint that he who owns may do as he pleases with what he owns, to a position which hesitatingly embodies an ingredient of stewardship; which grudgingly, but steadily, broadens the recognized scope of social interests in the utilization of things. . . .

> To one seeing history through the glasses of religion, these changes may seem to evidence increasing embodiments of the golden rule. To one thinking in terms of political and economic ideologies, they are likely to be labeled evidences of "social enlightenment," or of "creeping socialism" or even of "communistic infiltration," according to the individual's assumed definitions and retained or acquired prejudices. With slight attention to words or labels, time marches on toward new adjustments between individualism and the social interests.

The process involves not only the accommodation between the right of the owner and the interests of the general public in his use of this property, but involves also an accommodation between the right of the owner and the right of individuals who are parties with him in consensual transactions relating to the use of the property. Accordingly substantial alterations have been made as between a landlord and his tenant. *See Reste Realty Corp. v. Cooper*, 53 N.J. 444, 451–453, 251 A.2d 268 (1969); *Marini v. Ireland*, 56 N.J. 130, 141–143, 265 A.2d 526 (1970).

The argument in this case understandably included the question whether the migrant worker should be deemed to be a tenant and thus entitled to the tenant's right to receive visitors, *Williams v. Lubbering*, 73 N.J.L. 317, 319–320, 63 A. 90 (Sup.Ct.1906), or whether his residence on the employer's property should be deemed to be merely incidental and in aid of his employment, and hence to involve no possessory interest in the realty. *See Scottish Rite Co. v. Salkowitz*, 119 N.J.L. 558, 197 A. 43 (E. & A. 1938). These cases did not reach employment situations at all comparable with the one before us. Nor did they involve the question whether an employee who is not a tenant may have visitors notwithstanding the employer's prohibition. Rather they were concerned with whether notice must be given to end the employee's right to remain upon the premises, with whether the employer may remove the discharged employee without court order, and with the availability of a particular judicial remedy to achieve his removal by process. We of course are not concerned here with the right of a migrant worker to remain on the employer's property after the employment is ended.

We see no profit in trying to decide upon a conventional category and then forcing the present subject into it. That approach would be artificial and distorting. The quest is for a fair adjustment of the competing needs of the parties, in the light of the realities of the relationship between the migrant worker and the operator of the housing facility.

Thus approaching the case, we find it unthinkable that the farmer-employer can assert a right to isolate the migrant worker in any respect significant for the worker's well-being. The farmer, of course, is entitled to pursue his farming activities without interference, and this defendants readily concede. But we see no legitimate need for a right in the farmer to deny the worker the opportunity for aid available from federal, State, or local services, or from recognized charitable groups seeking to assist him. Hence representatives of these agencies and organizations may enter upon the premises to seek out the worker at his living quarters. So, too, the migrant worker must be allowed to receive visitors there of his own choice, so long as there is no behavior hurtful to others, and members of the press may not be denied reasonable access to workers who do not object to seeing them.

It is not our purpose to open the employer's premises to the general public if in fact the employer himself has not done so. We do not say, for example, that solicitors or peddlers of all kinds may enter on their own; we may assume for the present that the employer may regulate their entry or bar them, at least if the employer's purpose is not to gain a commercial advantage for himself or if the regulation does not deprive the migrant worker of practical access to things he needs.

 And we are mindful of the employer's interest in his own and in his employees' security. Hence he may reasonably require a visitor to identify himself, and also to state his general purpose if the migrant worker has not already informed him that the visitor is expected. But the employer may not deny the worker his privacy or interfere with his opportunity to live with dignity and to enjoy associations customary among our citizens. These rights are too fundamental to be denied on the basis of an interest in real property and too fragile to be left to the unequal bargaining strength of the parties. *See Henningsen v. Bloomfield Motors, Inc.*, 32 N.J. 358, 403–404, 161 A.2d 69 (1960); *Ellsworth Dobbs, Inc. v. Johnson*, 50 N.J. 528, 555, 236 A.2d 843 (1967).

It follows that defendants here invaded no possessory right of the farmer-employer. Their conduct was therefore beyond the reach of the trespass statute. The judgments are accordingly reversed and the matters remanded to the County Court with directions to enter judgments of acquittal.

Notes

1. *The Source of the Rule of Decision in* State v. Shack. For any particular dispute, there may be a variety of potential sources of law that are relevant to that dispute:

- Constitutional (*i.e.*, the constitution, the written document establishing the character and structure of a government)

- Statutory (*i.e.*, an act of the legislature acting within its authority)

- Administrative (*i.e.*, a regulation issued by a governmental agency acting within the scope of its authority)

- Common law (*i.e.*, legal principles as established by previous judicial decisions)

- Private law (*e.g.*, an agreement between parties that governs certain aspects of their subsequent relationship)

What source of law does the court rely upon to reverse the convictions of Tejeras and Shack? On what specific language in the opinion do you base your conclusion?

2. *Articulating the Rationale in* Shack. What "rule" does Tedesco want the court to establish? What justifications can you articulate for that rule? In contrast, what "rule" might Tejeras and Shack want the court to establish? What justifications can you articulate for that rule?

3. *The Precedential Impact of* Shack—*Predicting the Effect of a Decision on Future Court Decisions.* Two of the lawyer's core functions in counseling are to analyze correctly the legal "holding" of a case and to predict for the client how the court's opinion may influence future legal decisionmakers. Notably, the mere fact that a court makes a statement in an opinion does not make that statement a "holding" or give the statement the force of law. Some statements in judicial opinions are "dictum"—statements that are not necessary to the court's resolution of the particular dispute. In contrast, the court's "holding" is the court's answer to the precise legal issue presented by the dispute, in the context of the specific facts of a given case. The court usually justifies its "holding" by elaborating the "rationale" of its decision—the reasons why the court's conclusion is preferable to some other conclusion. Sometimes that rationale is expressed overtly, as in *State v. Shack*; sometimes it is expressed implicitly, frequently by reference to prior judicial decisions that addressed similar legal issues. What is the holding in *State v. Shack*?

Suppose that you represented Tedesco. Tedesco wants to exclude someone from the Salvation Army from entering his farm to deliver donated clothes to the farmworkers. How would you analogize or distinguish *State v. Shack* in advising him? How would you advise him if he wished to exclude someone from entering his farm to solicit farmworkers to join a farmworkers' union? How would you advise him if he wished to exclude a door-to-door solicitor who wanted to sell clothing and personal supplies to the farmworkers?

4. *"Externalities" and Efficiency.* From time to time, you will encounter the term "externality." An externality is a consequence of a person's actions that the person need not take into account in her decisionmaking. The term is more easily understood by an example. Suppose Pushaw paints his house orange and burns old tires on his land. This conduct will have a negative effect upon his neighbor Henning in several respects. First, if Henning dislikes orange, he will be quite annoyed by the sight of Pushaw's house. Second, the smoke from the burning tires may irritate Henning's eyes and cause him breathing difficulties. Third, if would-be buyers share Henning's distaste for orange homes and the odor of burning tires, it is unlikely that anyone else will want to live next door to Pushaw. Thus, the value of Henning's land will likely decrease; no one will be willing to buy it from him at the price he could obtain without Pushaw's obnoxious conduct.

If Pushaw can paint his house orange and burn old tires—and Henning legally can do nothing to stop him—then the cost to Henning from Pushaw's conduct is an externality. In other words, it is a cost that is *external* to Pushaw, because Pushaw does not have to take that cost into account in deciding whether to paint his house orange and burn old tires. The primary problem with externalities is they often encourage inefficient conduct. If Pushaw saves himself $10,000 burning the tires (the amount it would cost him to dispose of them properly), but Henning and his surrounding neighbors are suffering losses valued at $10,000 or more (due to illnesses caused by the smoke and the reduced value of their land), Pushaw's conduct is not "efficient" under either of the traditional economic concepts of efficiency:

- First, Pushaw's conduct is not *Pareto-superior.* A Pareto-superior transaction (so named for the economist Vilfredo Pareto) is one that makes one person better off and no one else worse off. Here, allowing Pushaw to burn tires is not Pareto-superior; although it makes Pushaw better off (the $10,000 profit he makes), it reduces the value of neighboring land parcels (such as Henning's). Pareto-superiority is a very austere concept of efficiency; none of us live in a vacuum, and most everything we do can or does have potentially negative effects on third parties.

- Second, Pushaw's conduct is not *Kaldor-Hicks efficient* or *wealth-maximizing.* A Kaldor–Hicks efficient transaction is one in which one person is made better off by an amount that exceeds the losses thereby imposed on others. Because the losses of Henning and the other neighbors exceed $10,000 (the benefit to Pushaw), Pushaw's conduct is not wealth-maximizing. When economists state that some conduct is efficient, they typically mean it is efficient in the Kaldor–Hicks sense of wealth-maximization.

The law often attempts to deal with the problem of external costs by forcing the actor to *internalize those costs*—in other words, to take account of those costs in her decisionmaking. Consider the case of Pushaw burning old tires. In how many different ways could the law force Pushaw to internalize the costs of his conduct? *See* David W. Barnes and Lynn A. Stout, The Economics of Property Rights and Nuisance Law 21–32 (1992).

To what extent does the problem of externalities manifest itself in the dispute in *Shack*? Suppose that Tedesco makes the following argument:

"Farming is expensive and my profit margin is already small. The conduct of Tejeras and Shack (entering onto my farm) creates administrative complications, such as the costs of extra security, that threatens my ability to farm profitably. It would be efficient to allow me the right to exclude Tejeras and Shack in order to force them to bear the cost of their conduct (such as by paying me for the additional costs, like security costs, that I would incur by allowing them access to the farm)." How would you respond to Tedesco?

5. *The Process of Dispute Resolution—Trial and Its Alternatives.* The parties in *State v. Shack* resolved their dispute by judicial trial, where (generally speaking) one party "wins" and one party "loses." Because of the long history of decisionmaking by judicial trial, the pervasive use of court opinions as legal tools for subsequent decisionmaking and legal education, and the organized bar's emphasis upon its role as client advocate in adversarial disputes, many Americans have come to expect that judicial trial is the standard way to settle disputes. Over the past few decades, however, growing disenchantment with the delay and expense of litigation has spurred a boom in the study, development, and use of alternative dispute resolution techniques. This growth in alternative forms of dispute resolution has resulted in a corresponding decline in the number of civil cases resolved by a jury trial. In a study of state court decisions in 1992, only 2% of the civil cases were decided by juries. Brian Ostrom, *A Step Above Anecdote: A Profile of the Civil Jury in the 1990s*, 79 Judicature 233 (1996). Some of the alternatives with which you should familiarize yourself, as a lawyer-in-training, include the following:

Arbitration. In arbitration, the parties agree to submit their dispute to a neutral party whom they have, at least theoretically, selected to make a decision. Arbitration is used extensively in industrial labor relations and in commercial and consumer disputes. The parties have an opportunity to select an arbitrator with background and experience suitable for dealing with the particular issues in dispute. Because the parties can customize the proceedings to suit their needs, arbitration has the potential to be less formal, faster, and less expensive than the judicial process. . . .

Negotiation. In negotiation, persons seek to resolve a disagreement or plan a transaction through discussions, which may include reasoned argument. The discussions may be conducted between the parties themselves or through representatives. Negotiation is used in all manner of disputes and transactions and is common in everyday life. It is a constant activity of lawyers. . . .

Much negotiation in law practice, particularly that involved in resolving disputes, is based on adversarial assumptions—i.e., that the purpose of the negotiation is to divide a limited resource. In recent years, however, scholars have argued that problem-solving approaches to negotiation, long-used in putting together business deals and other transactions, can and should be applied to dispute resolution. . . .

Mediation. Mediation is an informal process in which an impartial third party helps others resolve a dispute or plan a transaction but does not impose a solution. In other words, mediation is facilitated negotiation. The parties often enter into mediation voluntarily, but many courts have programs that require parties to mediate before proceeding to trial. The desired result is an agreement uniquely suited to the needs and interests of the parties. Normally the agreement is expressed in a contract or release and is enforceable according to the rules of contract law. . . .

Mediation-Arbitration. "Med-Arb" begins as a mediation. If the parties do not reach an agreement, they proceed to arbitration, which may be performed either by the person who mediated or by another neutral. . . .

Mini-trial. "Mini-trials" or "structured settlement negotiations" refer to specifically designed processes, usually employed to resolve complex disputes that would otherwise be the subject of protracted litigation. . . .

Mini-trials are tailored to the needs of the participants and may embody a number of dispute resolution processes. In one model, lawyers for both sides present their cases in abbreviated form to a panel composed of a neutral advisor, who usually is a lawyer with expertise in relevant areas of law, and decision-making executives of the two organizations. The neutral advisor then gives his opinion of what would happen if the matter were litigated. Next, the executives retire to negotiate a settlement, with or without the neutral advisor. . . .

Summary jury trial. Summary jury trial is an adaptation of some mini-trial concepts to cases that would be tried before a jury. It consists of lawyers giving brief presentations of their cases to a jury that has no authority, but whose members are drawn from the same population as real jurors. The jury's non-binding verdict on liability and damages helps the parties better understand their cases, and, thus, it encourages settlement. [Leonard L. Riskin, James E. Westbrook, Chris Guthrie, Timothy J. Heinsz, Richard C. Reuben & Jennifer K. Robbennolt, Dispute Resolution and Lawyers 14–17 (3d ed. 2005).]

Is saving time and money the only "goal" to be sought in considering alternative means of dispute resolution? If not, what other goals or motives might the parties to a dispute have? Does society have an interest in having a public record of how certain types of disputes are resolved? *See* Kent D. Syverud, *ADR and the Decline of the American Civil Jury*, 44 UCLA L. Rev. 1935, 1943–44 (1997). Why do you think that the parties in *State v. Shack* did not resolve this dispute through one of these non-judicial methods of dispute resolution?

LAWYERING EXERCISE
(Counseling and Evaluating Precedent)

BACKGROUND: Reread the excerpt from Professor Neumann in the Lawyering Exercise on page 20.

SITUATION: Donald Trump's Taj Mahal Casino (located in Atlantic City, New Jersey) has barred Raymond from playing blackjack in its casino. Raymond is an accomplished "card-counter." Card-counting is a process that permits a gambler to effectively shift the odds away from the casino's advantage to the card-counter's advantage (*i.e.*, it would permit the successful card counter to win more often than not).

TASK: Raymond wants to retain you to file a lawsuit seeking an injunction that would force the casino to allow him to play blackjack. Raymond thinks that the *State v. Shack* decision may be helpful because it purports to limit a landowner's right to exclude. Is that decision relevant to the dispute between Trump and Raymond, and would it provide support for the relief Raymond is seeking? How would you explain to Raymond whether he should litigate this case? What additional information (if any) might you like to know before advising Raymond?

————————

gov's eminent Domain

Recently, we have experienced a resurgence of academic and public debate about the right to exclude and the proper limits of that right—particularly in the context of the ability of the government to use the power of eminent domain to "take" property for a public purpose. In the vocabulary of Calabresi and Melamed, an owner whose land is taken by eminent domain is no longer protected by a "property" rule (*i.e.*, the owner cannot exclude the government if it is properly exercising its eminent domain power). Instead, the former owner of the land is protected by a "liability" rule—payment of an amount equal to the fair market value of the land taken. Indeed, under our federal Constitution's "Takings Clause," a governmental entity can take land only upon payment of "just compensation," and even then only for "public use."

The classic explanation for the eminent domain power is a utilitarian one. Suppose that a city council decides to construct a new public highway to accommodate growth and traffic within the community. To do that, the council must obtain title to the land on which it plans to locate the highway. Although the democratic process led the city to conclude that the public interest is best served by building the highway, an individual landowner in the path of the highway could subvert that democratic process if it could exercise a "property" right of exclusion and refuse to sell to the city. By preventing individual landowners from exercising this unilateral veto power, the Takings Clause reflects our collective social contract as governed people. If a private person wants to purchase my land, I can agree to sell only at my own price, or refuse to sell at any price. But if the government proposes to take my land for a public use, the Takings Clause reflects my presumed consent to accept "just compensation" (in the form of a payment equal to the fair market value of the land).

Takings clause

The government's power to take land for public use—for the construction of highways, parks, buildings (such as schools) and other public facilities—is well-established. But in the last few decades, governments have begun using eminent domain power in ways that involve the re-allocation of land from one private owner to another (albeit for an alleged public purpose). Recently, the U.S. Supreme Court had the opportunity to revisit the issue of whether the "public use" requirement of the Takings Clause can be satisfied if a government takes land from one private owner and reallocates it to another private owner.

KELO v. CITY OF NEW LONDON

Supreme Court of the United States.
125 S.Ct. 2655, 162 L.Ed.2d 439 (2005).

JUSTICE STEVENS delivered the opinion of the Court. In 2000, the city of New London approved a development plan that, in the words of the Supreme Court of Connecticut, was "projected to create in excess of 1,000 jobs, to increase tax and other revenues, and to revitalize an economically distressed city, including its downtown and waterfront areas." In assembling the land needed for this project, the city's development agent has purchased property from willing sellers and proposes to use the power of eminent domain to acquire the remainder of the property from unwilling owners in exchange for just compensation. The question presented is whether the city's proposed disposition of this property qualifies as a "public use" within the meaning of the Takings Clause of the Fifth Amendment to the Constitution.

I

The city of New London (hereinafter City) sits at the junction of the Thames River and the Long Island Sound in southeastern Connecticut. Decades of economic decline led a state agency in 1990 to designate the City a "distressed municipality." In 1996, the Federal Government closed the Naval Undersea Warfare Center, which had been located in the Fort Trumbull area of the City and had employed over 1,500 people. In 1998, the City's unemployment rate was nearly double that of the State, and its population of just under 24,000 residents was at its lowest since 1920.

These conditions prompted state and local officials to target New London, and particularly its Fort Trumbull area, for economic revitalization. To this end, respondent New London Development Corporation (NLDC), a private nonprofit entity established some years earlier to assist the City in planning economic development, was reactivated. In January 1998, the State authorized a $5.35 million bond issue to support the NLDC's planning activities and a $10 million bond issue toward the creation of a Fort Trumbull State Park. In February, the pharmaceutical company Pfizer Inc. announced that it would build a $300 million research facility on a site immediately adjacent to Fort Trumbull; local planners hoped that Pfizer would draw new business to the area, thereby serving as a catalyst to the area's rejuvenation. After receiving initial approval from the city council, the NLDC continued its planning activities and held a series of neighborhood meetings to educate the public about the process. In May, the city council authorized the NLDC to formally submit its plans to the relevant state agencies for review. Upon obtaining state-level approval, the NLDC finalized an integrated development plan focused on 90 acres of the Fort Trumbull area.

The Fort Trumbull area is situated on a peninsula that juts into the Thames River. The area comprises approximately 115 privately owned properties, as well as the 32 acres of land formerly occupied by the naval facility (Trumbull State Park now occupies 18 of those 32 acres). The development plan encompasses seven parcels. Parcel 1 is designated for a waterfront conference hotel at the center of a "small urban village" that will include restaurants and shopping. This parcel will also have marinas for both recreational and commercial uses. A pedestrian "riverwalk" will originate here and continue down the coast, connecting the waterfront areas of the development. Parcel 2 will be the site of approximately 80 new residences organized into an urban neighborhood and linked by public walkway to the remainder of the development, including the state park. This parcel also includes space reserved for a new U.S. Coast Guard Museum. Parcel 3, which is located immediately north of the Pfizer facility, will contain at least 90,000 square feet of research and development office space. Parcel 4A is a 2.4–acre site that will be used either to support the adjacent state park, by providing parking or retail services for visitors, or to support the nearby marina. Parcel 4B will include a renovated marina, as well as the final stretch of the riverwalk. Parcels 5, 6, and 7 will provide land for office and retail space, parking, and water-dependent commercial uses.

The NLDC intended the development plan to capitalize on the arrival of the Pfizer facility and the new commerce it was expected to attract. In addition to creating jobs, generating tax revenue, and helping to "build momentum for the revitalization of downtown New London," the plan was also designed to make the City more attractive and to create leisure and recreational opportunities on the waterfront and in the park.

The city council approved the plan in January 2000, and designated the NLDC as its development agent in charge of implementation. The city council also authorized the NLDC to purchase property or to acquire property by exercising eminent domain in the City's name. The NLDC successfully negotiated the purchase of most of the real estate in the 90–acre area, but its negotiations with petitioners failed. As a consequence, in November 2000, the NLDC initiated the condemnation proceedings that gave rise to this case.

II

Petitioner Susette Kelo has lived in the Fort Trumbull area since 1997. She has made extensive improvements to her house, which she prizes for its water view. Petitioner Wilhelmina Dery was born in her Fort Trumbull house in 1918 and has lived there her entire life. Her husband Charles (also a petitioner) has lived in the house since they married some 60 years ago. In all, the nine petitioners own 15 properties in Fort Trumbull—4 in parcel 3 of the development plan and 11 in parcel

4A. Ten of the parcels are occupied by the owner or a family member; the other five are held as investment properties. There is no allegation that any of these properties is blighted or otherwise in poor condition; rather, they were condemned only because they happen to be located in the development area.

In December 2000, petitioners brought this action in the New London Superior Court. They claimed, among other things, that the taking of their properties would violate the "public use" restriction in the Fifth Amendment. After a 7–day bench trial, the Superior Court granted a permanent restraining order prohibiting the taking of the properties located in parcel 4A (park or marina support). It, however, denied petitioners relief as to the properties located in parcel 3 (office space).

After the Superior Court ruled, both sides took appeals to the Supreme Court of Connecticut. That court held, over a dissent, that all of the City's proposed takings were valid. It began by upholding the lower court's determination that the takings were authorized by chapter 132, the State's municipal development statute. That statute expresses a legislative determination that the taking of land, even developed land, as part of an economic development project is a "public use" and in the "public interest." Next, relying on cases such as *Hawaii Housing Authority* v. *Midkiff*, 467 U.S. 229 (1984), and *Berman* v. *Parker*, 348 U.S. 26 (1954), the court held that such economic development qualified as a valid public use under both the Federal and State Constitutions.

Finally, adhering to its precedents, the court went on to determine, first, whether the takings of the particular properties at issue were "reasonably necessary" to achieving the City's intended public use, and, second, whether the takings were for "reasonably foreseeable needs." The court upheld the trial court's factual findings as to parcel 3, but reversed the trial court as to parcel 4A, agreeing with the City that the intended use of this land was sufficiently definite and had been given "reasonable attention" during the planning process. . . .

III

Two polar propositions are perfectly clear. On the one hand, it has long been accepted that the sovereign may not take the property of *A* for the sole purpose of transferring it to another private party *B*, even though *A* is paid just compensation. On the other hand, it is equally clear that a State may transfer property from one private party to another if future "use by the public" is the purpose of the taking; the condemnation of land for a railroad with common-carrier duties is a familiar example. Neither of these propositions, however, determines the disposition of this case.

As for the first proposition, the City would no doubt be forbidden from taking petitioners' land for the purpose of conferring a private benefit on a particular private party. Nor would the City be allowed to take property under the mere pretext of a public purpose, when its actual purpose was to bestow a private benefit. The takings before us, however, would be executed pursuant to a "carefully considered" development plan. The trial judge and all the members of the Supreme Court of Connecticut agreed that there was no evidence of an illegitimate purpose in this case. Therefore, as was true of the statute challenged in *Midkiff,* 467 U.S., at 245, the City's development plan was not adopted "to benefit a particular class of identifiable individuals."

On the other hand, this is not a case in which the City is planning to open the condemned land—at least not in its entirety—to use by the general public. Nor will the private lessees of the land in any sense be required to operate like common carriers, making their services available to all comers. But although such a projected use would be sufficient to satisfy the public use requirement, this "Court long ago rejected any literal requirement that condemned property be put into use for the general public." *Id.,* at 244. Indeed, while many state courts in the mid–19th century endorsed "use by the public" as the proper definition of public use, that narrow view steadily eroded over time. Not only was the "use by the public" test difficult to administer (*e.g.,* what proportion of the public need have access to the property? at what price?), but it proved to be impractical given the diverse and always evolving needs of society. Accordingly, when this Court began applying the Fifth Amendment to the States at the close of the 19th century, it embraced the broader and more natural interpretation of public use as "public purpose." . . .

The disposition of this case therefore turns on the question whether the City's development plan serves a "public purpose." Without exception, our cases have defined that concept broadly, reflecting our longstanding policy of deference to legislative judgments in this field.

In *Berman* v. *Parker,* 348 U.S. 26 (1954), this Court upheld a redevelopment plan targeting a blighted area of Washington, D. C., in which most of the housing for the area's 5,000 inhabitants was beyond repair. Under the plan, the area would be condemned and part of it utilized for the construction of streets, schools, and other public facilities. The remainder of the land would be leased or sold to private parties for the purpose of redevelopment, including the construction of low-cost housing.

The owner of a department store located in the area challenged the condemnation, pointing out that his store was not itself blighted and arguing that the creation of a "better balanced, more attractive community" was not a valid public use. Writing for a unanimous Court, Justice Douglas refused to evaluate this claim in isolation, deferring instead to the legislative and agency judgment that the area "must be planned as a whole" for the plan to be successful. The Court explained that "community redevelopment programs need not, by force of the Constitution, be on a piecemeal basis—lot by lot, building by building." The public use underlying the taking was unequivocally affirmed:

use by public

We do not sit to determine whether a particular housing project is or is not desirable. The concept of the public welfare is broad and inclusive.... The values it represents are spiritual as well as physical, aesthetic as well as monetary. It is within the power of the legislature to determine that the community should be beautiful as well as healthy, spacious as well as clean, well-balanced as well as carefully patrolled. In the present case, the Congress and its authorized agencies have made determinations that take into account a wide variety of values. It is not for us to reappraise them. If those who govern the District of Columbia decide that the Nation's Capital should be beautiful as well as sanitary, there is nothing in the Fifth Amendment that stands in the way." [*Id.*, at 33]

In *Hawaii Housing Authority* v. *Midkiff*, 467 U.S. 229 (1984), the Court considered a Hawaii statute whereby fee title was taken from lessors and transferred to lessees (for just compensation) in order to reduce the concentration of land ownership. We unanimously upheld the statute and rejected the Ninth Circuit's view that it was "a naked attempt on the part of the state of Hawaii to take the property of *A* and transfer it to *B* solely for *B*'s private use and benefit." (internal quotation marks omitted). Reaffirming *Berman*'s deferential approach to legislative judgments in this field, we concluded that the State's purpose of eliminating the "social and economic evils of a land oligopoly" qualified as a valid public use. Our opinion also rejected the contention that the mere fact that the State immediately transferred the properties to private individuals upon condemnation somehow diminished the public character of the taking. "[I]t is only the taking's purpose, and not its mechanics," we explained, that matters in determining public use. ...

Viewed as a whole, our jurisprudence has recognized that the needs of society have varied between different parts of the Nation, just as they have evolved over time in response to changed circumstances. Our earliest cases in particular embodied a strong theme of federalism, emphasizing the "great respect" that we owe to state legislatures and state courts in discerning local public needs. For more than a century, our public use jurisprudence has wisely eschewed rigid formulas and intrusive scrutiny in favor of affording legislatures broad latitude in determining what public needs justify the use of the takings power.

IV

Those who govern the City were not confronted with the need to remove blight in the Fort Trumbull area, but their determination that the area was sufficiently distressed to justify a program of economic rejuvenation is entitled to our deference. The City has carefully formulated an economic development plan that it believes will provide appreciable benefits to the community, including—but by no means limited to—new jobs and increased tax revenue. As with other exercises in urban planning and development, the City is endeavoring to coordinate a variety of commercial, residential, and recreational uses of land, with the hope that they will form a whole greater than the sum of its parts. To effectuate this plan, the City has invoked a state statute that specifically authorizes the use of eminent domain to promote economic development. Given the comprehensive character of the plan, the thorough deliberation that preceded its adoption, and the limited scope of our review, it is appropriate for us, as it was in *Berman*, to resolve the challenges of the individual owners, not on a piecemeal basis, but rather in light of the entire plan. Because that plan unquestionably serves a public purpose, the takings challenged here satisfy the public use requirement of the Fifth Amendment.

To avoid this result, petitioners urge us to adopt a new bright-line rule that economic development does not qualify as a public use. Putting aside the unpersuasive suggestion that the City's plan will provide only purely economic benefits, neither precedent nor logic supports petitioners' proposal. Promoting economic development is a traditional and long accepted function of government. There is, moreover, no principled way of distinguishing economic development from the other public purposes that we have recognized. . . .

Petitioners contend that using eminent domain for economic development impermissibly blurs the boundary between public and private takings. Again, our cases foreclose this objection. Quite simply, the government's pursuit of a public purpose will often benefit individual private parties. For example, in *Midkiff*, the forced transfer of property conferred a direct and significant benefit on those lessees who were previously unable to purchase their homes. . . . The owner of the department store in *Berman* objected to "taking from one businessman for the benefit of another businessman," 348 U.S., at 33, referring to the fact that under the redevelopment plan land would be leased or sold to private developers for redevelopment. Our rejection of that contention has particular relevance to the instant case: "The public end may be as well or better served through an agency of private enterprise than through a department of government—or so the Congress might conclude. We cannot say that public ownership is the sole method of promoting the public purposes of community redevelopment projects." *Id.*, at 34.

It is further argued that without a bright-line rule nothing would stop a city from transferring citizen *A*'s property to citizen *B* for the sole reason that citizen *B* will put the property to a more productive use and thus pay more taxes. Such a one-to-one transfer of property, executed outside the confines of an integrated development plan, is not presented in this case. While such an unusual exercise of government power would certainly raise a suspicion that a private purpose was afoot, the hypothetical cases posited by petitioners can be confronted if and when they arise. They do not warrant the crafting of an artificial restriction on the concept of public use.

Alternatively, petitioners maintain that for takings of this kind we should require a "reasonable certainty" that the expected public benefits will actually accrue. Such a rule, however, would represent an even greater departure from our precedent. "When the legislature's purpose is legitimate and its means are not irrational, our cases make clear that empirical debates over the wisdom of takings—no less than debates over the wisdom of other kinds of socioeconomic legislation—are not to be carried out in the federal courts." *Midkiff*, 467 U.S., at 242.... The disadvantages of a heightened form of review are especially pronounced in this type of case. Orderly implementation of a comprehensive redevelopment plan obviously requires that the legal rights of all interested parties be established before new construction can be commenced. A constitutional rule that required postponement of the judicial approval of every condemnation until the likelihood of success of the plan had been assured would unquestionably impose a significant impediment to the successful consummation of many such plans.

Just as we decline to second-guess the City's considered judgments about the efficacy of its development plan, we also decline to second-guess the City's determinations as to what lands it needs to acquire in order to effectuate the project. "It is not for the courts to oversee the choice of the boundary line nor to sit in review on the size of a particular project area. Once the question of the public purpose has been decided, the amount and character of land to be taken for the project and the need for a particular tract to complete the integrated plan rests in the discretion of the legislative branch." *Berman*, 348 U.S., at 35–36.

In affirming the City's authority to take petitioners' properties, we do not minimize the hardship that condemnations may entail, notwithstanding the payment of just compensation. We emphasize that nothing in our opinion precludes any State from placing further restrictions on its exercise of the takings power. Indeed, many States already impose "public use" requirements that are stricter than the federal baseline. Some of these requirements have been established as a matter of state constitutional law, while others are expressed in state eminent domain statutes that carefully limit the grounds upon which takings may be exercised. As the submissions of the parties and their *amici* make clear, the necessity and wisdom of using eminent domain to promote economic development are certainly matters of legitimate public debate. This Court's authority, however, extends only to determining whether the City's proposed condemnations are for a "public use" within the meaning of the Fifth Amendment to the Federal Constitution. Because over a century of our case law interpreting that provision dictates an affirmative answer to that question, we may not grant petitioners the relief that they seek.

The judgment of the Supreme Court of Connecticut is affirmed.

JUSTICE KENNEDY, concurring.... My agreement with the Court that a presumption of invalidity is not warranted for economic development takings in general, or for the particular takings at issue in this case, does not foreclose the possibility that a more stringent standard of review than that announced in *Berman* and *Midkiff* might be appropriate for a more narrowly drawn category of takings. There may be private transfers in which the risk of undetected impermissible favoritism of private parties is so acute that a presumption (rebuttable or otherwise) of invalidity is warranted under the Public Use Clause. This demanding level of scrutiny, however, is not required simply because the purpose of the taking is economic development.

This is not the occasion for conjecture as to what sort of cases might justify a more demanding standard, but it is appropriate to underscore aspects of the instant case that convince me no departure from *Berman* and *Midkiff* is appropriate here. This taking occurred in the context of a comprehensive development plan meant to address a serious city-wide depression, and the projected economic benefits of the project cannot be characterized as *de minimus*. The identity of most of the private beneficiaries were unknown at the time the city formulated its plans. The city complied with elaborate procedural requirements that facilitate review of the record and inquiry into the city's purposes. In sum, while there may be categories of cases in which the transfers are so suspicious, or the procedures employed so prone to abuse, or the purported benefits are so trivial or implausible, that courts should presume an impermissible private purpose, no such circumstances are present in this case....

JUSTICE O'CONNOR, with whom THE CHIEF JUSTICE, JUSTICE SCALIA, and JUSTICE THOMAS join, dissenting.... [The "public use" and "just compensation" requirements] serve to protect "the security of Property," which Alexander Hamilton described to the Philadelphia Convention as one of the "great obj[ects] of Gov[ernment]." 1 Records of the Federal Convention of 1787, p. 302 (M. Farrand ed.1934). Together they ensure stable property ownership by providing safeguards against excessive, unpredictable, or unfair use of the government's eminent domain power—particularly against those owners who, for whatever reasons, may be unable to protect themselves in the political process against the majority's will....

This case returns us for the first time in over 20 years to the hard question of when a purportedly "public purpose" taking meets the public use requirement. It presents an issue of first impression: Are economic development takings constitutional? I would hold that they are not....

[The *Berman* and *Midkiff* cases] hewed to a bedrock principle without which our public use jurisprudence would collapse: "A purely private taking could not withstand the scrutiny of the public use requirement; it would serve no legitimate purpose of government and would thus be void." *Midkiff,* 467 U.S., at 245, 104 S.Ct. 2321. To protect that principle, those decisions reserved "a role for courts to play in reviewing a legislature's judgment of what constitutes a public use ... [though] the Court in *Berman* made clear that it is 'an extremely narrow' one." *Midkiff, supra,* at 240, 104 S.Ct. 2321 (quoting *Berman, supra,* at 32, 75 S.Ct. 98).

The Court's holdings in *Berman* and *Midkiff* were true to the principle underlying the Public Use Clause. In both those cases, the extraordinary, precondemnation use of the targeted property inflicted affirmative harm on society—in *Berman* through blight resulting from extreme poverty and in *Midkiff* through oligopoly resulting from extreme wealth. And in both cases, the relevant legislative body had found that eliminating the existing property use was necessary to remedy the harm. Thus a public purpose was realized when the harmful use was eliminated. Because each taking *directly* achieved a public benefit, it did not matter that the property was turned over to private use. Here, in contrast, New London does not claim that Susette Kelo's and Wilhelmina Dery's well-maintained homes are the source of any social harm. Indeed, it could not so claim without adopting the absurd argument that any single-family home that might be razed to make way for an apartment building, or any church that might be replaced with a retail store, or any small business that might be more lucrative if it were instead part of a national franchise, is inherently harmful to society and thus within the government's power to condemn.

In moving away from our decisions sanctioning the condemnation of harmful property use, the Court today significantly expands the meaning of public use. It holds that the sovereign may take private property currently put to ordinary private use, and give it over for new, ordinary private use, so long as the new use is predicted to generate some secondary benefit for the public—such as increased tax revenue, more jobs, maybe even aesthetic pleasure. But nearly any lawful use of real private property can be said to generate some incidental benefit to the public. Thus, if predicted (or even guaranteed) positive side-effects are enough to render transfer from one private party to another constitutional, then the words "for public use" do not realistically exclude *any* takings, and thus do not exert any constraint on the eminent domain power.

There is a sense in which this troubling result follows from errant language in *Berman* and *Midkiff*. In discussing whether takings within a blighted neighborhood were for a public use, *Berman* began by observing: "We deal, in other words, with what traditionally has been known as the police power." From there it declared that "[o]nce the object is within the authority of Congress, the right to realize it through the exercise of eminent domain is clear." Following up, we said in *Midkiff* that "[t]he 'public use' requirement is coterminous with the scope of a sovereign's police powers." This language was unnecessary to the specific holdings of those decisions. *Berman* and *Midkiff* simply did not put such language to the constitutional test, because the takings in those cases were within the police power but also for "public use" for the reasons I have described. The case before us now demonstrates why, when deciding if a taking's purpose is constitutional, the police power and "public use" cannot always be equated.

The Court protests that it does not sanction the bare transfer from A to B for B's benefit. It suggests two limitations on what can be taken after today's decision. First, it maintains a role for courts in ferreting out takings whose sole purpose is to bestow a benefit on the private transferee—without detailing how courts are to conduct that complicated inquiry. For his part, Justice Kennedy suggests that courts may divine illicit purpose by a careful review of the record and the process by which a legislature arrived at the decision to take—without specifying what courts should look for in a case with different facts, how they will know if they have found it, and what to do if they do not. Whatever the details of Justice Kennedy's as-yet-undisclosed test, it is difficult to envision anyone but the "stupid staff[er]" failing it. The trouble with economic development takings is that private benefit and incidental public benefit are, by definition, merged and mutually reinforcing. In this case, for example, any boon for Pfizer or the plan's developer is difficult to disaggregate from the promised public gains in taxes and jobs.

Even if there were a practical way to isolate the motives behind a given taking, the gesture toward a purpose test is theoretically flawed. If it is true that incidental public benefits from new private use are enough to ensure the "public purpose" in a taking, why should it matter, as far as the Fifth Amendment is concerned, what inspired the taking in the first place? How much the government does or does not desire to benefit a favored private party has no bearing on whether an economic development taking will or will not generate secondary benefit for the public. And whatever the reason for a given condemnation, the effect is the same from the constitutional perspective—private property is forcibly relinquished to new private ownership.

A second proposed limitation is implicit in the Court's opinion. The logic of today's decision is that eminent domain may only be used to upgrade—not downgrade—property. At best this makes the Public Use Clause redundant with the Due Process Clause, which already prohibits irrational government action. The Court rightfully admits, however, that the judiciary cannot get bogged down in predictive judgments about whether the public will actually be better off after a property transfer. In any event, this constraint has no realistic import. For who among us can say she already makes the most productive or attractive possible use of her property? The specter of condemnation hangs over all property. Nothing is to prevent the State from replacing any Motel 6 with a Ritz–Carlton, any home with a shopping mall, or any farm with a factory.

The Court also puts special emphasis on facts peculiar to this case: The NLDC's plan is the product of a relatively careful deliberative process; it proposes to use eminent domain for a multipart, integrated plan rather than for isolated property transfer; it promises an array of incidental benefits (even aesthetic ones), not just increased tax revenue; it comes on the heels of a legislative determination that New London is a depressed municipality. . . . But none has legal significance to blunt the force of today's holding. If legislative prognostications about the secondary public benefits of a new use can legitimate a taking, there is nothing in the Court's rule or in Justice Kennedy's gloss on that rule to prohibit property transfers generated with less care, that are less comprehensive, that happen to result from less elaborate process, whose only projected advantage is the incidence of higher taxes, or that hope to transform an already prosperous city into an even more prosperous one.

Finally, in a coda, the Court suggests that property owners should turn to the States, who may or may not choose to impose appropriate limits on economic development takings. This is an abdication of our responsibility. States play many important functions in our system of dual sovereignty, but compensating for our refusal to enforce properly the Federal Constitution (and a provision meant to curtail state action, no less) is not among them.

It was possible after *Berman* and *Midkiff* to imagine unconstitutional transfers from A to B. Those decisions endorsed government intervention when private property use had veered to such an extreme that the public was suffering as a consequence. Today nearly all real property is susceptible to condemnation on the Court's theory. In the prescient words of a dissenter from the infamous decision in *Poletown* [*Neighborhood Council v. Detroit*, 410 Mich. 616, 304 N.W.2d 455 (1981)] "[n]ow that we have authorized local legislative bodies to decide that a different commercial or industrial use of property will produce greater public benefits than its present use, no homeowner's, merchant's or manufacturer's property, however productive or valuable to its owner, is immune from condemnation for the benefit of other private interests that will put it to a 'higher' use." 410 Mich., at 644–645, 304 N.W.2d, at 464 (opinion of Fitzgerald, J.). This is why economic development takings "seriously jeopardiz[e] the security of all private property ownership." *Id.*, at 645, 304 N.W.2d, at 465 (Ryan, J., dissenting).

[handwritten margin note: dissent by Justice O'connor]

Any property may now be taken for the benefit of another private party, but the fallout from this decision will not be random. The beneficiaries are likely to be those citizens with disproportionate influence and power in the political process, including large corporations and development firms. As for the victims, the government now has license to transfer property from those with fewer resources to those with more. The Founders cannot have intended this perverse result. "[T]hat alone is a *just* government," wrote James Madison, "which *impartially* secures to every man, whatever is his *own*." . . .

Notes

1. *Takings and the "Public Use" Requirement.* The *Kelo* majority concludes that a taking for economic development is analytically comparable to a taking to address blight (previously approved in *Berman*) and to address excessive concentration of land ownership within a relevant market (previously approved in *Midkiff*). By contrast, the dissenting justices viewed *Kelo* as analytically distinct. Why so? Should the United States Supreme Court be the final arbiter of whether a redevelopment plan serves a "public purpose," or should that judgment be left to the people living in New London, Connecticut, and their democratic processes?

As the opinions in *Kelo* suggest, many state statutes or state constitutions impose a greater restriction upon takings for economic development purposes. For example, one of the most notable early "economic redevelopment" takings involved the City of Detroit's condemnation of large sections of the Poletown neighborhood. The City proposed to transfer the condemned land to General Motors as part of a plan in which GM would commit to retaining manufacturing facilities in Detroit. The Michigan Supreme Court upheld the condemnation against a challenge that it violated the "public purpose" requirement of Michigan's constitution. *Poletown Neighborhood Council v. Detroit*, 410 Mich. 616, 304 N.W.2d 455 (1981). Recently, however, the Michigan Supreme Court overruled *Poletown*—concluding that Wayne County lacked the power to condemn land for a privately owned business and technology park adjacent to the local airport, because the condemnation did not advance a "public use." *County of Wayne v. Hathcock*, 471 Mich. 445, 684 N.W.2d 765 (2004). As a policy matter, is it problematic that cities in some states can engage in "economic redevelopment" condemnations while cities in other states cannot? Why or why not? *See generally* Charles Tiebout, *A Pure Theory of Local Expenditures*, 64 J. Pol. Econ. 416 (1956).

Berman, *Midkiff*, and *Kelo* seem to establish the clear proposition that if a city has decided to pursue a legitimate end (a public purpose within its police power authority), it is for that city to determine the appropriate means for accomplishing that end—so long as that means is within the city's power under state law and the city's decision is made in accordance with proper procedures. Professor Thomas Merrill has suggested, however, that courts should instead direct the "public use" inquiry more to the question of "means" than "ends." Merrill argues that the "means" (*e.g.*, condemnation) is more appropriate to accomplish the city's "ends" (*e.g.*, economic redevelopment) when the city would face high transaction costs and the possibility of holdouts—such as when the city has to assemble numerous discrete parcels into one large parcel, or when only one specific parcel will satisfy the intended use. By contrast, if the city did not face high transaction costs or holdout risks (such as when numerous parcels might satisfy the intended use), condemnation is less appropriate. Thomas Merrill, *The Economics of Public Use*, 72 Cornell L. Rev. 61, 109–14 (1986). Is Professor Merrill's approach a workable one? Why or why not?

2. *Takings and the "Just Compensation" Requirement.* If the government and the landowner cannot agree on the price for land taken by eminent domain, a judicial procedure is used to establish the price, which is based upon the objectively determined fair market value for the land. In this process, any "idiosyncratic" value that the owner may place on the land—*i.e.*, value not shared by objective buyers and sellers in the marketplace—goes uncompensated.

Is this measure of compensation appropriate? Consider the "property as personhood" perspective offered by Professor Margaret Jane Radin:

> Most people possess certain objects they feel are almost part of themselves. These objects are closely bound up with personhood because they are part of the way we constitute ourselves as continuing personal entities in the world. They may be as different as people are different, but some common examples might be a wedding ring, a portrait, an heirloom, or a house.
>
> One may gauge the strength or significance of someone's relationship with an object by the kind of pain that would be occasioned by its loss. On this view, an object is closely related to one's personhood if its loss causes pain that cannot be relieved by the object's replacement. If

so, that particular object is bound up with the holder. For instance, if a wedding ring is stolen from a jeweler, insurance proceeds can reimburse the jeweler, but if a wedding ring is stolen from a loving wearer, the price of a replacement will not restore the status quo—perhaps no amount of money can do so.

The opposite of holding an object that has become a part of oneself is holding an object that is perfectly replaceable with other goods of equal market value. One holds such an object for purely instrumental reasons. The archetype of such a good is, of course, money, which is almost always held only to buy other things. A dollar is worth no more than what one chooses to buy with it, and one dollar bill is as good as another. Other examples are the wedding ring in the hands of a jeweler, the automobile in the hands of the dealer, the land in the hands of the developer, or the apartment in the hands of the commercial landlord. I shall call these theoretical opposites—property that is bound up with a person and property that is held purely instrumentally—personal property and fungible property respectively. . . .

The personhood dichotomy comes about in the following way: A general justification of property entitlements in terms of their relationship to personhood could hold that the rights that come within the general justification form a continuum from fungible to personal. It then might hold that those rights near one end of the continuum—fungible property rights—can be overridden in some cases in which those near the other—personal property rights—cannot be. This is to argue not that fungible property rights are unrelated to personhood, but simply that distinctions are sometimes warranted depending upon the character or strength of the connection. Thus, the personhood perspective generates a hierarchy of entitlements: The more closely connected with personhood, the stronger the entitlement. [Margaret Jane Radin, *Property and Personhood*, 34 Stan. L. Rev. 957, 959–60, 986 (1982).]

Consider also Judge Richard Posner, who has articulated the same basic concern using more purely economic analysis:

The familiar argument that the eminent domain power is necessary to overcome the stubbornness of people who refuse to sell at a "reasonable" (that is, the market) price is bad economics. If I refuse to sell for less than $250,000 a house that no one else would pay more than $100,000 for, it does not follow that I am irrational, even if no "objective" factors such as moving expenses justify my insisting on such a premium. It follows only that I value the house more than other people. This extra value has the same status in economic analysis as any other value. [Richard A. Posner, Economic Analysis of Law 56–57 (4th ed. 1992).]

Can the law reasonably compensate private landowners for idiosyncratic value not shared by actors in the marketplace? Should Wilhelmina Dery (one of the plaintiffs in *Kelo*) be entitled to greater compensation because she was born in the home and lived there since 1918? What about the people of Poletown (as referenced in note 1)? Should they receive greater compensation because they also lost their "community"? *See also* Merrill, *supra* note 1, at 109–14 (courts should exercise heightened judicial scrutiny if condemnation will result in significant loss of subjective value for affected landowner and also presents significant potential for profit for those who benefit from condemnation).

Another influential scholarly view regarding the right of exclusion is reflected in the work of Professor Joseph W. Singer. His article *The Reliance Interest in Property* focuses on how a rigid conception of property is inconsistent with the expectations that result from our complex interpersonal interactions over time:

> [A] wide variety of current legal rules can be justified in terms of an underlying moral principle that I call "the reliance interest in property.". . . These currently enforceable doctrines encompass the full range of social relationships, from relations among strangers, between neighbors, among long-term contractual partners in the marketplace, among family members and others in intimate relationships, and finally, between citizens and the government. At crucial points in the development of these relationships—often, but not always, when they break up—the legal system requires a sharing or shifting of property interests from the "owner" to the "non-owner" to protect the more vulnerable party to the relationship. The legal system requires this shift, not because of reliance on specific promises, but because the parties have relied on each other generally and on the continuation of their relationship. Moreover, the more vulnerable party may need access to resources controlled by the more powerful party, and the relationship is such that we consider it fair to place this burden on the more powerful party by redistributing entitlements. . . . [L]egal rules reflect a choice between the freedom of the stronger party to do whatever she wants with "her" property and the security of the weaker party who has relied on access to the other's property in the past or who has relied on the continuation of the relationship. . . . [Joseph W. Singer, *The Reliance Interest in Property*, 40 Stan. L. Rev. 614, 622–23 (1988).]

Perhaps the best example of Professor Singer's "reliance interest" is reflected in the law of equitable distribution of property upon divorce (a topic we explore briefly in Chapter 6). Equitable distribution statutes authorize a court to characterize assets acquired during the marriage as "marital property"—even if one of the spouses took title to the assets individually—and to distribute that marital property between the spouses upon divorce in an equitable (presumptively equal) fashion.

Professor Singer's reliance interest could also come into play in the context of plant closings. Can General Motors close its Flint, Michigan, assembly plant without regard to the effect that this decision might have on its employees and the community? Those who have seen Michael Moore's film *Roger and Me* will say that the answer is "yes." Even if the ultimate legal conclusion is "yes," what does property law have to say (if anything) about how the law reaches that conclusion?

LOCAL 1330, UNITED STEEL WORKERS
v. UNITED STATES STEEL CORP.

United States Court of Appeals, Sixth Circuit.
631 F.2d 1264 (1980).

EDWARDS, CHIEF JUDGE. This appeal represents a cry for help from steelworkers and townspeople in the City of Youngstown, Ohio who are distressed by the prospective impact upon their lives and their city of the closing of two large steel mills. These two mills were built and have been operated by the United States Steel Corporation since the turn of the century. The Ohio Works began producing in 1901; the McDonald Works in 1918. The District Court which heard this cause of action found that as of the notice of closing, the two plants employed 3,500 employees.

The leading plaintiffs are two labor organizations, Locals 1330 and 1307 of the United Steel Workers of America. This union has had a collective bargaining contract with the United States Steel Corporation for many years. These local unions represent production and maintenance employees at the Ohio and McDonald Works, respectively.

In the background of this litigation is the obsolescence of the two plants concerned, occasioned both by the age of the facilities and machinery involved and by the changes in technology and marketing in steelmaking in the years intervening since the early nineteen hundreds.

For all of the years United States Steel has been operating in Youngstown, it has been a dominant factor in the lives of its thousands of employees and their families, and in the life of the city itself. The contemplated abrupt departure of United States Steel from Youngstown will, of course, have direct impact on 3,500 workers and their families. It will doubtless mean a devastating blow to them, to the business community and to the City of Youngstown itself. While we cannot read the future of Youngstown from this record, what the record does indicate clearly is that we deal with an economic tragedy of major proportion to Youngstown and Ohio's Mahoning Valley. . . .

In the face of this tragedy, the steel worker local unions, the Congressman from this district, and the Attorney General of Ohio have sued United States Steel Corporation, asking the federal courts to order the United States Steel Corporation to keep the two plants at issue in operation. Alternatively, if they could not legally prevail on that issue, they have sought intervention of the courts by injunction to require the United States Steel Corporation to sell the two plants to the plaintiffs under an as yet tentative plan of purchase and operation by a community corporation and to restrain the piecemeal sale or dismantling of the plants until such a proposal could be brought to fruition.

Defendant United States Steel Corporation answered plaintiffs' complaints, claiming that the plants were unprofitable and could not be made otherwise due to obsolescence and change in technology, markets, and transportation. The company also asserts an absolute right to make a business decision to discharge its former employees and abandon Youngstown. It states that there is no law in either the State of Ohio or the United States of America which provides either legal or equitable remedy for plaintiffs. . . .

[Editors' Note: The court first analyzed the terms of the collective bargaining agreement between the steel workers and United States Steel, concluding that the decision to close the plants did not violate the terms of that agreement. The court then turned its attention to the steel workers' other arguments: (1) that United States Steel should be prevented from closing the plants on the grounds of promissory estoppel; and (2) that the steel workers possessed a "property" interest in the plants.]

The primary issue in this case is a claim on the part of the steel worker plaintiffs that United States Steel made proposals to the plaintiffs and/or the membership of the plaintiffs to the general effect that if the workers at the two steel plants concerned put forth their best efforts in terms of productivity and thereby rendered the two plants "profitable," the plants would then not be closed. . . .

II. *Promissory Estoppel.* The doctrine of promissory estoppel recognizes the possibility of the formation of a contract by action or forbearance on the part of a second party, based upon a promise made by the first party under circumstances where the actions or forbearance of the second party should reasonably have been expected to produce the detrimental results to the second party which they did produce. Restatement (Second) of Contracts § 90 (1932) states:

> A promise which the promisor should reasonably expect to induce action or forbearance of a definite and substantial character on the part of the promisee and which does induce such action or forbearance is binding if injustice can be avoided only by enforcement of the promise.

Thus, appellants' contract claim depends essentially upon oral statements and newspaper releases concerning the efforts of the company to secure increased productivity by enlisting the help of the workers of the plant and upon the employee responses thereto. The representations as set forth in the steelworkers' complaint include many oral statements made over the "hotline" employed by management in the plants to advise U.S. Steel employees of company policy. They began in the Fall of 1977 in the midst of much public speculation that the Ohio and McDonald works at Youngstown were to be closed. . . .

[Editors' Note: The steelworkers' complaint provided an extensive litany of facts to support the request that U.S. Steel be estopped from closing the plants. For sake of conciseness, we have omitted most of those facts in favor of the following summary that should provide sufficient insight into the nature of the company's alleged "representations" and the steelworkers' alleged "reliance."

As the court mentions, the company communicated many of its "representations" by means of a company "hotline" used to communicate with employees. In September 1977, after rumors began circulating that U.S. Steel would close the plants, William Ashton (U.S. Steel's then-superintendent for its Youngstown District) made the following announcement on the hotline:

> In response to many rumors, I want to tell you that there are no immediate plans to permanently shut down either the Ohio Works or McDonald Mills. However, steps will have to be taken to improve these plants' profitability....

A few months later, in January 1978, Bill Kirwan (the new superintendent of the Youngstown District) announced on the hotline that the company's position had not changed since the previous September:

> At that time United States Steel said that continued operation in Youngstown would depend on the plant's ability to become profitable. Since that time some progress *has* been made in reducing our losses. With your help, this effort will continue and if and when there will be a phase-out depends on the plant's profitability, but no time table has been set. I intend to give this my best effort and I am confident you will too.

Three months later, in April 1978, Kirwan stated on the "hot line" that "[i]n the month of March, for the first [time] in a long long time, the Youngstown Works earned a profit for the United States Steel Corporation. We didn't make a bundle, and we are still in the hole for the year, but this is the first indication that the changes in our operations, and our attitudes are turning the place around." A few days later, Kirwan stated to the press: "We'll be doing business here for some time to come," and Randall Walthius, another spokesman for U.S. Steel, stated to the press: "Company management has repeatedly said that the works will stay open if they become profitable. Well, now they are profitable."

The Company continued issuing comparable statements to the employees and the press during the ensuing year. In April 1979, Kirwan wrote a letter to the editor published in the Wall Street Journal, taking the Journal to task for reporting that the Youngstown plant was inefficient and should be closed. Kirwan's letter stated: "You imply by this statement that Youngstown is eroding U.S. Steel Corporation's profit. Factually, this is nonsense and reflects the opinions of someone who doesn't know the facts and never bothered to get them.... A complete turn-around has been achieved at Youngstown in the past year due to an aggressive management effort, streamlining of operations, and hard work on the part of all employees." A few weeks later, on May 2, 1979, Kirwan stated to the press that "[w]e currently have an operation here that's been going profitably since the early part of 1978...." On June 18, 1979, David Roderick, U.S. Steel's Chairman of the Board of Directors, announced on ABC television: "Simply stated, we have no plans for shutting down our Youngstown operation. Only two things would result in a Youngstown shutdown: [massive expenditures to meet environmental requirements or an unproductive plant operation.] The Youngstown plant is profitable. We're operating in the black there."

The steelworkers argued that their members had taken specific actions reflecting their reasonable and detrimental reliance upon the assurance that U.S. Steel would not close the plants if they remained profitable. For example, the steelworkers alleged that the unions had agreed to workshift changes, changes in layoff policies, and job-combining that cut labor and energy costs, without resorting to grievance procedures that the unions could have pursued had the company imposed the changes unilaterally. Finally, the workers argued that numerous individual workers made employment and financial decisions based upon the company's statements, such as forgoing other employment opportunities, purchasing cars and homes, or sending their children to more expensive schools.

Notwithstanding these statements, later in 1979, U.S. Steel announced plans to close both plants. The steelworkers requested that U.S. Steel instead sell the plants, either to the workers or to a competitor who would operate the plants, but U.S. Steel refused to do so, prompting the unions to file this lawsuit.]

The District Judge ... rejected the promissory estoppel contract theory on three grounds. The first ground was that none of the statements made by officers and employees of the company constituted a definite promise to continue operation of the plants if they did become profitable. The second ground was that the statements relied upon by plaintiffs were made by employees and public relations officers of the company and not by company officers. The third ground was a finding of fact that "The condition precedent of the alleged contract and promised profitability of the Youngstown facilities was never fulfilled, and the actions in contract and for detrimental reliance cannot be found for plaintiffs."...

Our examination of this record offers no ground for our holding that this finding of fact is "clearly erroneous." See Fed.R.Civ.P. 52(a).

[Editors' Note: At this point, the court reviewed the evidence in the record concerning the profitability of the plant. The plaintiffs had argued that the plants were operating with a positive "gross profit margin," meaning that revenues exceeded the variable costs of production. Plaintiffs' exhibits demonstrated that the gross profit margin for the Youngstown facilities were as follows: for 1977, $24,899,000; for 1978, $41,770,000; for 1979, $32,571,000; for 1980 (projected), $32,396,000. Based on these figures, the plaintiffs argued that the plants were indeed profitable. The defendants had argued, however, that the appropriate measure of profit should include fixed costs (including depreciation), and that the company actually projected a loss of $9,387,000 for 1980 with fixed costs taken into account.]

... This Court is loath to exchange its own view of the parameters of profitability for that of the corporation. It is clear that there is little argument as to the production figures for the Youngstown mills—the controversy surrounds the interpretation of those figures. Plaintiffs read the figures in light of a gross profit margin analysis of minimum profitability. Defendant sees capital expenditure, fixed costs and technical obsolescence as essential ingredients of the notion of profitability. Perhaps if this Court were being asked to interpret the word "profit" in a written contract between plaintiffs and defendant, some choice would have to be made. Given the oral nature of the alleged promises in the case at bar and the obvious ambiguity of the statements made, this Court finds that there is a very reasonable basis on which it can be said that Youngstown facilities were not profitable. Further, plaintiffs have made no showing of bad faith on the part of the Board of Directors in the Board's determination of profitability, nor have they given any grounds to suggest that defendant's definition of profitability is an unrealistic or unreasonable one. The condition precedent of the alleged contract and promise—profitability of the Youngstown facilities—was never fulfilled, and the actions in contract and for detrimental reliance cannot be found for plaintiffs. . . .

We believe that this record demonstrates without significant dispute that the profitability issue in the case depends in large part upon definition. The plaintiffs wish to employ the direct costs of operating the two plants, compared to the total selling price of their products. The difference, they contend, is "profit." This formula would eliminate such charges as corporate purchasing and sales expense allocable to the Youngstown plants, and allocable corporate management expenses including, but not limited to marketing, engineering, auditing, accounting, advertising. Obviously, any multiplant corporation could quickly go bankrupt if such a definition of profit was employed generally and over any period of time.

Plaintiffs-appellants point out, however, that this version of Youngstown profitability was employed by the Youngstown management in setting a goal for its employees and in statements which described achieving that goal. The standard of Restatement (Second) of Contracts § 90, upon which plaintiffs-appellants rely, however, is one of reasonable expectability of the "promise" detrimentally relied upon. The District Judge did not find, nor can we, that reliance upon a promise to keep these plants open on the basis of coverage of plant fixed costs was within reasonable expectability. We cannot hold that the District Judge erred legally or was "clearly erroneous" in his fact finding when he held that the "promise" to keep the plants open had to be read in the context of normal corporate profit accounting and that profitability had not been achieved. . . .

III. *The Community Property Claim.* At a pretrial hearing of this case on February 28, 1980, the District Judge made a statement at some length about the relationship between the parties to this case and the public interest involved therein. He said:

> Everything that has happened in the Mahoning Valley has been happening for many years because of steel. Schools have been built,

roads have been built. Expansion that has taken place is because of steel. And to accommodate that industry, lives and destinies of the inhabitants of that community were based and planned on the basis of that institution: Steel. . . .

We are talking about an institution, a large corporate institution that is virtually the reason for the existence of that segment of this nation [Youngstown]. Without it, that segment of this nation perhaps suffers, instantly and severely. Whether it becomes a ghost town or not, I don't know. I am not aware of its capability for adapting. . . .

But what has happened over the years between U.S. Steel, Youngstown and the inhabitants? Hasn't something come out of that relationship, something that out of which not reaching for a case on property law or a series of cases but looking at the law as a whole, the Constitution, the whole body of law, not only contract law, but tort, corporations, agency, negotiable instruments—taking a look at the whole body of American law and then sitting back and reflecting on what it seeks to do, and that is to adjust human relationships in keeping with the whole spirit and foundation of the American system of law, to preserve property rights. . . .

It would seem to me that when we take a look at the whole body of American law and the principles we attempt to come out with and although a legislature has not pronounced any laws with respect to such a property right, that is not to suggest that there will not be a need for such a law in the future dealing with similar situations—*it seems to me that a property right has arisen from this lengthy, long-established relationship between United States Steel, the steel industry as an institution, the community in Youngstown, the people in Mahoning County and the Mahoning Valley in having given and devoted their lives to this industry*. Perhaps not a property right to the extent that can be remedied by compelling U.S. Steel to remain in Youngstown. But *I think the law can recognize the property right to the extent that U.S. Steel cannot leave that Mahoning Valley and the Youngstown area in a state of waste, that it cannot completely abandon its obligation to that community, because certain vested rights have arisen out of this long relationship and institution.*

Subsequently thereto, steelworkers' complaint was amended . . . as follows:

2nd theory of workers ←

52. A property right has arisen from the long-established relation between the community of the 19th Congressional District and Plaintiffs, on the one hand, and Defendant on the other hand, which this Court can enforce.

53. This right, in the nature of an easement, requires that Defendant:

a. Assist in the preservation of the institution of steel in that community;

b. Figure into its cost of withdrawing and closing the Ohio and McDonald Works the cost of rehabilitating the community and the workers;

c. Be restrained from leaving the Mahoning Valley in a state of waste and from abandoning its obligation to that community.

This court has examined these allegations with care and with great sympathy for the community interest reflected therein. Our problem in dealing with plaintiffs' fourth cause of action is one of authority. Neither in brief nor oral argument have plaintiffs pointed to any constitutional provision contained in either the Constitution of the United States or the Constitution of the State of Ohio, nor any law enacted by the United States Congress or the Legislature of Ohio, nor any case decided by the courts of either of these jurisdictions which would convey authority to this court to require the United States Steel Corporation to continue operations in Youngstown which its officers and Board of Directors had decided to discontinue on the basis of unprofitability.

This court has in fact dealt with this specific issue in *Charland v. Norge Division, Borg–Warner Corp.*, 407 F.2d 1062 (6th Cir. 1969). . . . [Editors' Note: Charland was a thirty-year employee of Norge at its Muskegon Heights plant. When the plant was relocated to Fort Smith, Arkansas, Charland and other employees were given the option of two alternatives negotiated by their union—limited severance pay of $1,500 or the right to keep the job by relocating to Fort Smith. Liking neither alternative, Charland sued Norge claiming that their actions constituted a deprivation of his property rights in his job in violation of Article V of the United States Constitution.]

This court's response to Charland's claims bears repetition here:

Article V of the Constitution, of course, makes no mention of employment. But it (and the Fourteenth Amendment) does prohibit deprivation of property without due process of law. Thus [Charland's] assumption submits the fundamental question of whether or not there is a legally recognizable property right in a job which has been held for something approaching a lifetime. . . .

Whatever the future may bring, neither by statute nor by court decision has [Charland's] claimed property right been recognized to date in this country. . . . [*Id.* at 1065.]

[The unions], however, cite and rely upon a decision of the Supreme Court of the United States, *Munn v. Illinois*, 94 U.S. 113 (1977), claiming "that a corporation affected by the public interest, which seeks to take action injurious to that interest, may be restrained from doing so by the equitable powers of a court of law.". . . [Editors' Note: In *Munn*, the Supreme Court decided that an Illinois statute fixing the maximum legal charge for the warehouse storage of grain did not violate the Commerce Clause or the Due Process Clause of the U.S. Constitution.]

The case is undoubtedly important precedent establishing power on the part of state legislatures to regulate private property (particularly public utilities) in the public interest. It cannot, however, properly be cited for holding that federal courts have such legislative power in their own hands....

The problem of plant closing and plant removal from one section of the country to another is by no means new in American history. The former mill towns of New England, with their empty textile factory buildings, are monuments to the migration of textile manufacturers to the South, without hindrance from the Congress of the United States, from the legislatures of the states concerned, or, for that matter, from the courts of the land.

In the view of this court, formulation of public policy on the great issues involved in plant closings and removals is clearly the responsibility of the legislatures of the states or of the Congress of the United States.

We find no legal basis for judicial relief as to [the union's claimed property interest.]...

Notes

1. *Whose Plant Is It, Anyway?* Consider Prof. Singer's criticism of the *United States Steel* decision:

> [A]t a community meeting in Youngstown, Ohio, concerning a threatened plant closing, a steelworker cried out, "Those are our jobs!" Another worker answered him, "But it's their mill." I want to argue that people who think this way are wrong. In part, I mean to emphasize that "Who owns the mill?" is a hard, not an easy, question to answer; I also mean to call attention to the fact that even if it is "their mill," they do not necessarily have the legal power to use it in a way that destroys the community. But I mean something more fundamental than either of these things. I want to argue that phrasing the problem as "identifying the owner" is fundamentally wrong. It is simply not the right question. To assume that we can know who property owners are, and to assume that once we have identified them their rights follow as a matter of course, is to assume what needs to be decided....
>
> When several parties share legal rights in property, any identification of a single person as the "owner" is likely to be both arbitrary and misleading. It is arbitrary because we could just as easily identify someone else as the owner. It is misleading because it denies the existence of joint interests and the need to determine the legal relations among all the persons with legally protected interests in the property. The "owner's" rights are limited by the rights of others with entitlements in the property. Identifying the owner does not tell us who these other people are or what their rights are.
>
> We ask who the owner is because we need to resolve a specific question of how to allocate control of resources among all the parties with legally protected interests in access to those resources. Can the company blow up the plant when the workers want to buy it? To answer this question by looking for the owner is like asking how many angels

can dance on the head of a pin. It is a species of conceptualism; to say the company can blow up the plant *because* it owns it states a conclusion rather than a premise. It does not give us a *reason* to allocate rights between the workers and the company in this way. [Joseph W. Singer, *The Reliance Interest in Property*, 40 Stan. L. Rev. 614, 637–38 (1988).]

So how *should* the law solve this dilemma and why? Singer argued that the court should have used the "reliance" principle to reallocate partial ownership of the plant to the workers, in the same sense that the law has reallocated property rights between spouses upon divorce. Why do you think that the court refused to do so, and instead chose to say that the workers had no entitlement? In what ways is the situation in *U.S. Steel* different from (or similar to) the divorce context?

2. *The Concept of Estoppel.* In *U.S. Steel*, the workers also raised an estoppel argument. To understand the estoppel principle, a little historical background is in order. In English law, there were two parallel systems of justice. One was "Law," in which one set of courts resolved disputes by reference to rigid rules established by legislation or prior judicial decision. The other system was "Equity," in which a designate of the King (called the Chancellor) could exert the royal prerogative to resolve disputes without rigid adherence to the rules of "Law." Equity was grounded upon the recognition of divine moral obligations, rather than technical legal obligations. Further, Equity recognized rights unrecognized at Law through the imposition of remedies—notably, the injunction—that were unavailable at Law. Today, American law has merged Law and Equity so that the same judicial system (our public courts) exercises both the traditional jurisdiction of Law and Equity.

Estoppel is an example of the exercise of equitable jurisdiction. Essentially, the workers in *U.S. Steel* argued that even though U.S. Steel did not make a binding promise to keep the plants open according to the rules of contract law (the "Law"), the court should nevertheless exercise its equitable jurisdiction ("Equity") to "estop" U.S. Steel—*i.e.*, to issue an injunction requiring U.S. Steel to keep open the plants, based upon its representations to the workers and their reliance on those expectations. Suppose that the court in *U.S. Steel* had ruled in favor of the workers on their estoppel claim, and had entered an injunction to prevent the company from closing the plants. At that point, would the workers have a property interest in the plants? Why or why not? Once the court enters the injunction, what do you think would happen in the future?

3. *The Court's Fact–Finding in* U.S. Steel. The *U.S. Steel* case provides a good example of the practical difficulty that a losing party faces in challenging a trial court's findings of fact. The court of appeals upheld the district court's findings of fact, concluding that they were not "clearly erroneous." Do you agree? Would it have been as easy for the court of appeals to rule in favor of U.S. Steel if the district court's findings of fact had favored the steelworkers (*i.e.*, that U.S. Steel, through its officers, did make a promise to keep the plants open and that the plants were still profitable)? Why or why not?

4. *The Role of the Law (and the Courts) in Reviewing Business Decisions.* Notice that the court in *U.S. Steel* eventually resolves the dispute by

accepting the company's definition of "profitability" regarding the two plants in question. But suppose that United States Steel, *as a whole*, was profitable even taking into account the continued operation of the Youngstown plants. If you had been the judge in *U.S. Steel*, would that have mattered?

In thinking about this question, consider the following (nonhypothetical) situation: In January 1991, the Green Giant division of the British conglomerate, Grand Metropolitan PLC, closed its processing plant in Watsonville, California, and relocated the plant to Mexico—laying off 375 workers who earned $7.50/hour. At the time, Grand Met was the eighth largest food products producer in the world—its prior year's net income was $1.8 billion ($1.85 per share of outstanding stock). Upon opening in Mexico, Grand Met paid its Mexican employees $4 *per day*. According to James W. Donovan, if Grand Met had remained in Watsonville rather than moving its processing facilities to Mexico, Grand Met's per share earnings would have been reduced by only one cent per share. James W. Donovan, *A Case Study: Laying Off American Workers, Gouging Mexican Workers*, New Oxford Rev., Jan.-Feb. 1992, at 10–13. Should the shareholders of Grand Met be able to insist upon earning the extra penny per share regardless of the consequences to the workers and to the community?

One might argue that the Mexican workers were entitled to these jobs (at the expense of the Watsonville workers) by virtue of their willingness to do them for less money. By contrast, Donovan argued that even in Mexico, a subsistence wage was $26 per day—such that by paying only $4 per day, Grand Met was exploiting the relatively less powerful Mexican workers and earning a socially unacceptable windfall. Donovan's criticisms echo the earlier social criticism of Martin Luther King, Jr., who argued that society could not achieve true justice as long as it was a "thing"-oriented society that considered profit-making and property rights to be more important than people. Martin Luther King, Jr., "Beyond Vietnam: A Time to Break Silence." Do the criticisms of King and Donovan carry any legal force (*i.e.*, do they carry any weight as authority in the resolution of legal disputes such as the plant closing cases)? Can one simply dismiss them as legally irrelevant because they are theologically based? Why or why not?

LAWYERING EXERCISE
(Counseling: Statutory Interpretation and Analysis)

BACKGROUND: The effective lawyer must understand the relationship of statutory law and the common law, and this requires the lawyer to develop an understanding of the tools of statutory interpretation:

> Interpretation is the art of finding out ... what [the drafter] intended to convey.—*Francis Lieber*

> I don't care what their intention was. I only want to know what the words mean.—*Oliver Wendell Holmes*

> [These] two quotations ... might seem to express contradictory approaches to interpreting any source of law. The first focuses on

what the lawmaker intended to do, and the second on what the lawmaker did. The first approach might use any reliable evidence of intent, but the second concentrates on the words actually used. This is a classic tension in statutory interpretation, and it grows partly out of a history of struggle—now mostly halted—between legislatures and courts. As you know, in English common law, courts were the original lawmakers, and legislatures arose afterward, acquiring the power to make new law and to change law already made by courts. Courts, of course, retained the ultimate power to enforce all law. And, because interpretation is essential to enforcement, courts used their power to limit the effect of intrusive statutes, which judges treated with suspicion and even condescension until well into the twentieth century. [There are many reasons why this kind of struggle is mostly behind us, but perhaps the most important is this: modern life is so complex and so difficult as to humble anyone who undertakes to make law, and judges today are grateful for a partnership with legislatures, who are better equipped to gather masses of detailed information and to work out compromises between competing interest groups.] [Richard K. Neumann, Jr., Legal Reasoning and Legal Writing: Structure, Strategy, and Style 157–58 (4th ed. 2001).]

To ascertain the meaning of a statute (and its potential application to a dispute), courts may use a variety of sources, including the words of the statute, statutory or historical context that might indicate the legislature's intent, interpretation by other courts, governmental officials or scholars, and certain "maxims" or "canons" of statutory construction that you will often see cited in judicial opinions. [Keep your eye out for these "maxims" as you read cases dealing with statutory interpretation.]

SITUATION: The U.S. Congress (acting in response to the political pressures that arose due to notorious plant closings) enacted the Worker Adjustment and Retraining Notification Act (known as the "WARN Act"). Subject to several exceptions explained in the statute, the WARN Act generally requires persons who employ 100 or more full-time employees to give at least 60 days of advance notice prior to closing a plant or instituting a mass layoff, if the shutdown or layoff results in 50 or more employees (excluding part-time employees) losing their jobs at a single site of employment for more than 30 days. 29 U.S.C. §§ 2101–2102. For the sake of this exercise, assume that the WARN Act had been in effect at the time of the dispute in *U.S. Steel*.

TASK: Look at the WARN Act. Is it at all relevant to the resolution of the legal issues presented by the steelworkers' complaint? If so, how? How would you argue that the WARN Act provides support for the workers' property argument? For the company's position that the workers have no valid property claim?

The use of property rules makes possible the efficient reallocation of entitlements through voluntary transfer. This might tempt one to conclude that *transferability* is a necessary characteristic of property rights, and indeed, most property rights are transferable. In fact, however, transferability is not a *necessary* characteristic of property; as Calabresi and Melamed have noted, in some cases society chooses to protect an entitlement by virtue of a rule of "inalienability"—one that prevents the voluntary transfer of that entitlement. If one cannot transfer an entitlement, should we consider it "property" at all? And why does it make a difference? Consider the following celebrated case.

MOORE v. REGENTS OF THE UNIVERSITY OF CALIFORNIA

Supreme Court of California.
51 Cal.3d 120, 271 Cal.Rptr. 146, 793 P.2d 479 (1990).

[Editors' Note: The following factual background is derived from the facts of John Moore's complaint—taken as true by the court given the procedural posture of the case—and from the work of Professor Henry Greely, who has studied, written, and spoken about the "true facts" of the *Moore* case.

In October 1976, John Moore—suffering from hairy-cell leukemia—went to Dr. David Golde of the UCLA Medical Center for treatment. Moore consented to and underwent a splenectomy based upon Golde's recommendation that the disease threatened Moore's life—Moore's spleen weighed 16 pounds (32 times the weight of a normal spleen).

Moore's T-lymphocytes (certain white blood cells) overproduced certain lymphokines (proteins that regulate the immune system). Following Moore's surgery and three years of research, Golde and Shirley Quan (another UCLA researcher) used Moore's T-lymphocytes to establish a cell line, which in turn could produce large quantities of lymphokines using recombinant DNA techniques. In 1981, the Board of Regents of the University of California (the "Regents") applied for a patent on the cell line (now called the "Mo" cell line), listing Golde and Quan as the inventors. Golde later negotiated an agreement with a private company, Genetics Institute, under which Genetics received exclusive rights to the research materials associated with the Mo cell line and any products derived from it. In exchange, Golde received options to acquire 75,000 shares of Genetics common stock and Genetics agreed to pay Golde and the Regents $110,000 per year (including a portion of Golde's salary and benefits) for a period of three years.

Upon discovering the nature and extent of Golde's research and the resulting Mo cell line, Moore filed suit against, among others, Golde, Quan, Genetics and the Regents. Moore's complaint alleged that the defendants had converted his T-lymphocytes by using them in their research, without his consent, to produce the Mo cell line. The complaint also alleged that by failing to inform Moore of the planned use of

Moore's cells, Golde had not obtained Moore's informed consent to the splenectomy and thus breached his fiduciary duty as Moore's physician.

Golde argued that he did explain his research to Moore prior to the surgery—at the time, he was trying to create cell lines from all of his hairy cell leukemia patients as part of his continuing medical research—and that he had obtained Moore's oral consent. Golde argued (and Moore admitted) that Moore knew Golde conducted research specializing in hairy cell leukemia.

The defendants filed a general demurrer to the complaint (the procedural equivalent of a motion to dismiss the case for failure to state a cause of action), and the superior court—taking the allegations of the complaint as true—sustained that demurrer. The court of appeal reversed, concluding that Moore's complaint stated a cause of action for conversion. On appeal, the California Supreme Court concluded that Moore's complaint had stated a cause of action for lack of informed consent and breach of fiduciary duty. The portion of the opinions reprinted below focuses upon Moore's conversion claim.]

PANELLI, JUSTICE. . . . Moore also attempts to characterize the invasion of his rights as a conversion—a tort that protects against interference with possessory and ownership interests in personal property. He theorizes that he continued to own his cells following their removal from his body, at least for the purpose of directing their use, and that he never consented to their use in potentially lucrative medical research. Thus, to complete Moore's argument, defendants' unauthorized use of his cells constitutes a conversion. As a result of the alleged conversion, Moore claims a proprietary interest in each of the products that any of the defendants might ever create from his cells or the patented cell line.

No court, however, has ever in a reported decision imposed conversion liability for the use of human cells in medical research. While that fact does not end our inquiry, it raises a flag of caution. In effect, what Moore is asking us to do is to impose a tort duty on scientists to investigate the consensual pedigree of each human cell sample used in research. To impose such a duty, which would affect medical research of importance to all of society, implicates policy concerns far removed from the traditional, two-party ownership disputes in which the law of conversion arose. Invoking a tort theory originally used to determine whether the loser or the finder of a horse had the better title, Moore claims ownership of the results of socially important medical research, including the genetic code for chemicals that regulate the functions of every human being's immune system. . . .

Accordingly, we first consider whether the tort of conversion clearly gives Moore a cause of action under existing law. We do not believe it does. Because of the novelty of Moore's claim to own the biological materials at issue, to apply the theory of conversion in this context would frankly have to be recognized as an extension of the theory. Therefore, we consider next whether it is advisable to extend the tort to this context.

torts =
conversion

LD must have
expected to
retain
ownership
after
surgery

1. *Moore's Claim Under Existing Law.* "To establish a conversion, plaintiff must establish an actual interference with his *ownership* or *right of possession* . . . . Where plaintiff neither has title to the property alleged to have been converted, nor possession thereof, he cannot maintain an action for conversion." *Del E. Webb Corp. v. Structural Materials Co.* (1981) 123 Cal.App.3d 593, 610–611, 176 Cal. Rptr. 824 (emphasis added).

Since Moore clearly did not expect to retain possession of his cells following their removal, to sue for their conversion he must have retained an ownership interest in them. But there are several reasons to doubt that he did retain any such interest. First, no reported judicial decision supports Moore's claim, either directly or by close analogy. Second, California statutory law drastically limits any continuing interest of a patient in excised cells. Third, the subject matters of the Regents' patent—the patented cell line and the products derived from it—cannot be Moore's property.

Neither the Court of Appeal's opinion, the parties' briefs, nor our research discloses a case holding that a person retains a sufficient interest in excised cells to support a cause of action for conversion. We do not find this surprising, since the laws governing such things as human tissues, transplantable organs,[5] blood,[6] fetuses, pituitary glands, corneal tissue, and dead bodies[7] deal with human biological materials as objects sui generis, regulating their disposition to achieve policy goals rather than abandoning them to the general law of personal property. It is these specialized statutes, not the law of conversion, to which courts ordinarily should and do look for guidance on the disposition of human biological materials.

Lacking direct authority for importing the law of conversion into this context, Moore relies, as did the Court of Appeal, primarily on decisions addressing privacy rights. One line of cases involves unwanted publicity. *Lugosi v. Universal Pictures* (1979) 25 Cal.3d 813, 160 Cal. Rptr. 323, 603 P.2d 425; *Motschenbacher v. R.J. Reynolds Tobacco Company* (9th Cir.1974) 498 F.2d 821. These opinions hold that every

---

5. See the Uniform Anatomical Gift Act, Health and Safety Code section 7150 *et seq.* The act permits a competent adult to "give all or part of [his] body" for certain designated purposes, including "transplantation, therapy, medical or dental education, research, or advancement of medical or dental science." Health & Saf. Code, §§ 7151, 7153. The act does not, however, permit the donor to receive "valuable consideration" for the transfer. Health & Saf. Code, § 7155.

6. See Health & Safety Code section 1601 *et seq.*, which regulates the procurement, processing, and distribution of human blood. Health and Safety Code section 1606 declares that "[t]he procurement, processing, distribution, or use of whole blood,

plasma, blood products, and blood derivatives for the purpose of injecting or transfusing the same . . . is declared to be, for all purposes whatsoever, the rendition of a service . . . and shall not be construed to be, and is declared not to be, a sale . . . for any purpose or purposes whatsoever."

7. *See* Health and Safety Code section 7000 *et seq.* While the code does not purport to grant property rights in dead bodies, it does give the surviving spouse, or other relatives, "[t]he right to control the disposition of the remains of a deceased person, unless other directions have been given by the decedent. . . ." Health & Saf. Code, § 7100.

person has a proprietary interest in his own likeness and that unauthorized, business use of a likeness is redressible as a tort. But in neither opinion did the authoring court expressly base its holding on property law. Each court stated, following Prosser, that it was "pointless" to debate the proper characterization of the proprietary interest in a likeness. For purposes of determining whether the tort of conversion lies, however, the characterization of the right in question is far from pointless. Only property can be converted.

Not only are the wrongful-publicity cases irrelevant to the issue of conversion, but the analogy to them seriously misconceives the nature of the genetic materials and research involved in this case. Moore, adopting the analogy originally advanced by the Court of Appeal, argues that "[i]f the courts have found a sufficient proprietary interest in one's persona, how could one not have a right in one's own genetic material, something far more profoundly the essence of one's human uniqueness than a name or a face?" However, as the defendants' patent makes clear—and the complaint, too, if read with an understanding of the scientific terms which it has borrowed from the patent—the goal and result of defendants' efforts has been to manufacture lymphokines. Lymphokines, unlike a name or a face, have the same molecular structure in every human being and the same, important functions in every human being's immune system. Moreover, the particular genetic material which is responsible for the natural production of lymphokines, and which defendants use to manufacture lymphokines in the laboratory, is also the same in every person; it is no more unique to Moore than the number of vertebrae in the spine or the chemical formula of hemoglobin.

Another privacy case offered by analogy to support Moore's claim establishes only that patients have a right to refuse medical treatment. *Bouvia v. Superior Court* (1986) 179 Cal.App.3d 1127, 225 Cal.Rptr. 297. In this context the court in *Bouvia* wrote that " '[e]very human being of adult years and sound mind has a right to determine what shall be done with his own body....' " *Id.*, at p. 1139, 225 Cal.Rptr. 297. Relying on this language to support the proposition that a patient has a continuing right to control the use of excised cells, the Court of Appeal in this case concluded that "[a] patient must have the ultimate power to control what becomes of his or her tissues. To hold otherwise would open the door to a massive invasion of human privacy and dignity in the name of medical progress." Yet one may earnestly wish to protect privacy and dignity without accepting the extremely problematic conclusion that interference with those interests amounts to a conversion of personal property. Nor is it necessary to force the round pegs of "privacy" and "dignity" into the square hole of "property" in order to protect the patient, since the fiduciary-duty and informed-consent theories protect these interests directly by requiring full disclosure.

The next consideration that makes Moore's claim of ownership problematic is California statutory law, which drastically limits a patient's control over excised cells. Pursuant to Health and Safety Code section 7054.4, "[n]otwithstanding any other provision of law, recognizable anatomical parts, human tissues, anatomical human remains, or infectious waste following conclusion of scientific use shall be disposed of by interment, incineration, or any other method determined by the state department [of health services] to protect the public health and safety." Clearly the Legislature did not specifically intend this statute to resolve the question of whether a patient is entitled to compensation for the nonconsensual use of excised cells. A primary object of the statute is to ensure the safe handling of potentially hazardous biological waste materials. Yet one cannot escape the conclusion that the statute's practical effect is to limit, drastically, a patient's control over excised cells. By restricting how excised cells may be used and requiring their eventual destruction, the statute eliminates so many of the rights ordinarily attached to property that one cannot simply assume that what is left amounts to "property" or "ownership" for purposes of conversion law.

It may be that some limited right to control the use of excised cells does survive the operation of this statute. There is, for example, no need to read the statute to permit "scientific use" contrary to the patient's expressed wish. A fully informed patient may always withhold consent to treatment by a physician whose research plans the patient does not approve. That right, however, as already discussed, is protected by the fiduciary-duty and informed-consent theories.

Finally, the subject matter of the Regents' patent—the patented cell line and the products derived from it—cannot be Moore's property. This is because the patented cell line is both factually and legally distinct from the cells taken from Moore's body. Federal law permits the patenting of organisms that represent the product of "human ingenuity," but not naturally occurring organisms. *Diamond v. Chakrabarty* (1980) 447 U.S. 303, 309–310, 100 S.Ct. 2204, 2208, 65 L.Ed.2d 144. Human cell lines are patentable because "[l]ong-term adaptation and growth of human tissues and cells in culture is difficult—often considered an art ...," and the probability of success is low. It is this inventive effort that patent law rewards, not the discovery of naturally occurring raw materials. Thus, Moore's allegations that he owns the cell line and the products derived from it are inconsistent with the patent, which constitutes an authoritative determination that the cell line is the product of invention....

2. *Should Conversion Liability Be Extended?* ... There are three reasons why it is inappropriate to impose liability for conversion based upon the allegations of Moore's complaint. First, a fair balancing of the relevant policy considerations counsels against extending the tort. Second, problems in this area are better suited to legislative resolution. Third, the tort of conversion is not necessary to protect patients' rights. For these reasons, we conclude that the use of excised human cells in medical research does not amount to a conversion.

Of the relevant policy considerations, two are of overriding importance. The first is protection of a competent patient's right to make autonomous medical decisions. That right, as already discussed, is grounded in well-recognized and long-standing principles of fiduciary duty and informed consent. This policy weighs in favor of providing a remedy to patients when physicians act with undisclosed motives that may affect their professional judgment. The second important policy consideration is that we not threaten with disabling civil liability innocent parties who are engaged in socially useful activities, such as researchers who have no reason to believe that their use of a particular cell sample is, or may be, against a donor's wishes . . . .

The extension of conversion law into this area will hinder research by restricting access to the necessary raw materials. Thousands of human cell lines already exist in tissue repositories, such as the American Type Culture Collection and those operated by the National Institutes of Health and the American Cancer Society. These repositories respond to tens of thousands of requests for samples annually. . . . At present, human cell lines are routinely copied and distributed to other researchers for experimental purposes, usually free of charge. This exchange of scientific materials, which still is relatively free and efficient, will surely be compromised if each cell sample becomes the potential subject matter of a lawsuit . . . .

[T]he theory of liability that Moore urges us to endorse threatens to destroy the economic incentive to conduct important medical research. If the use of cells in research is a conversion, then with every cell sample a researcher purchases a ticket in a litigation lottery. Because liability for conversion is predicated on a continuing ownership interest, "companies are unlikely to invest heavily in developing, manufacturing, or marketing a product when uncertainty about clear title exists." [U.S. Congress, Office of Technology Assessment, New Developments in Biotechnology: Ownership of Human Tissues and Cells, at 27 (1987).] . . . .

If the scientific users of human cells are to be held liable for failing to investigate the consensual pedigree of their raw materials, we believe the Legislature should make that decision. Complex policy choices affecting all society are involved, and "[l]egislatures, in making such policy decisions, have the ability to gather empirical evidence, solicit the advice of experts, and hold hearings at which all interested parties present evidence and express their views. . . ." *Foley v. Interactive Data Corp.*, [47 Cal.3d 654, 694, fn. 31, 254 Cal.Rptr. 211, 765 P.2d 373 (1988)]. Legislative competence to act in this area is demonstrated by the existing statutes governing the use and disposition of human biological materials . . . .

ARABIAN, JUSTICE, concurring. . . . Plaintiff has asked us to recognize and enforce a right to sell one's own body tissue for profit. He entreats us to regard the human vessel—the single most venerated and protected subject in any civilized society—as equal with the basest commercial commodity. He urges us to commingle the sacred with the profane. He asks much . . . .

It is true, that this court has not often been deterred from deciding difficult legal issues simply because they require a choice between competing social or economic policies. The difference here, however, lies in the nature of the conflicting moral, philosophical and even religious values at stake, and in the profound implications of the position urged. The ramifications of recognizing and enforcing a property interest in body tissues are not known, but are greatly feared—the effect on human dignity of a marketplace in human body parts, the impact on research and development of competitive bidding for such materials, and the exposure of researchers to potentially limitless and uncharted tort liability.

Whether, as plaintiff urges, his cells should be treated as property susceptible to conversion is not, in my view, ours to decide. The question implicates choices which not only reflect, but which ultimately define our essence. A mark of wisdom for us as expositors of the law is the recognition that we cannot cure every ill, mediate every dispute, resolve every conundrum. Sometimes, as Justice Brandeis said, "the most important thing we do, is not doing."

Where then shall a complete resolution be found? Clearly the Legislature, as the majority opinion suggests, is the proper deliberative forum. Indeed, a legislative response creating a licensing scheme, which establishes a fixed rate of profit sharing between researcher and subject, has already been suggested. Such an arrangement would not only avoid the moral and philosophical objections to a free market operation in body tissue, but would also address stated concerns by eliminating the inherently coercive effect of a waiver system and by compensating donors regardless of temporal circumstances....

BROUSSARD, JUSTICE, concurring and dissenting.... If this were a typical case in which a patient consented to the use of his removed organ for general research purposes and the patient's doctor had no prior knowledge of the scientific or commercial value of the patient's organ or cells, I would agree that the patient could not maintain a conversion action. In that common scenario, the patient has abandoned any interest in the removed organ and is not entitled to demand compensation if it should later be discovered that the organ or cells have some unanticipated value. I cannot agree, however, with the majority that a patient may never maintain a conversion action for the unauthorized use of his excised organ or cells, even against a party who knew of the value of the organ or cells before they were removed and breached a duty to disclose that value to the patient. Because plaintiff alleges that defendants wrongfully interfered with his right to determine, prior to the removal of his body parts, how those parts would be used after removal, I conclude that the complaint states a cause of action under traditional, common law conversion principles....

... [T]he pertinent inquiry is not whether a patient generally retains an ownership interest in a body part after its removal from his body, but rather whether a patient has a right to determine, before a body part is removed, the use to which the part will be put after removal. Although the majority opinion suggests that there are "reasons to doubt" that a patient retains "any" ownership interest in his organs or cells after removal, the opinion fails to identify any statutory provision or common law authority that indicates that a patient does not generally have the right, before a body part is removed, to choose among the permissible uses to which the part may be put after removal. On the contrary, the most closely related statutory scheme—the Uniform Anatomical Gift Act—makes it quite clear that a patient does have this right.

The Uniform Anatomical Gift Act is a comprehensive statutory scheme that was initially adopted in California in 1970 and most recently revised in 1988. Although that legislation, by its terms, applies only to a donation of all or part of a human body which is "to take effect upon or after [the] death [of the donor]"—and thus is not directly applicable to the present case which involves a living donor—the act is nonetheless instructive with regard to this state's general policy concerning an individual's authority to control the use of a donated body part. The act, which authorizes an anatomical gift to be made, inter alia, to "[a] hospital [or a] physician[,] . . . for transplantation, therapy, medical or dental education, research or advancement of medical or dental science", expressly provides that such a gift "may be made to a designated donee or without designating a donee" and also that the donor may make such a gift "for any of the purposes [specified in the statute or may] limit an anatomical gift to one or more of those purposes. . . ." Thus, the act clearly recognizes that it is the donor of the body part, rather than the hospital or physician who receives the part, who has the authority to designate, within the parameters of the statutorily authorized uses, the particular use to which the part may be put.

Although, as noted, the Uniform Anatomical Gift Act applies only to anatomical gifts that take effect on or after the death of the donor, the general principle of "donor control" which the act embodies is clearly not limited to that setting. In the transplantation context, for example, it is common for a living donor to designate the specific donee—often a relative—who is to receive a donated organ. If a hospital . . . decided on its own to give the organ to a different donee, no one would deny that the hospital had violated the legal right of the donor by its unauthorized use of the donated organ. Accordingly, it is clear under California law that a patient has the right, prior to the removal of an organ, to control the use to which the organ will be put after removal.

It is also clear, under traditional common law principles, that this right of a patient to control the future use of his organ is protected by the law of conversion. As a general matter, the tort of conversion protects an individual not only against improper interference with the right of possession of his property but also against unauthorized use of his property or improper interference with his right to control the use of his property. Sections 227 and 228 of the Restatement Second of Torts specifically provide in this regard that "[o]ne who uses a chattel in a manner which is a serious violation of the right of another to control its use is subject to liability to the other for conversion" and that "[o]ne who is authorized to make a particular use of a chattel, and uses it in a manner exceeding the authorization, is subject to liability for conversion to another whose right to control the use of the chattel is thereby seriously violated.'' . . .

The application of these principles to the present case is evident. . . . If these allegations are true, defendants clearly improperly interfered with plaintiff's right in his body part at a time when he had the authority to determine the future use of such part, thereby misappropriating plaintiff's right of control for their own advantage. Under these circumstances, the complaint fully satisfies the established requirements of a conversion cause of action. . . .

One of the majority's principal policy concerns is that "[t]he extension of conversion law into this area will hinder research by restricting access to the necessary raw materials''—the thousands of cell lines and tissues already in cell and tissue repositories. The majority suggests that the "exchange of scientific materials, which still is relatively free and efficient, will surely be compromised if each cell sample becomes the potential subject matter of a lawsuit.''

majority policy concerns

This policy argument is flawed in a number of respects. First, the majority's stated concern does not provide any justification for barring plaintiff from bringing a conversion action against a party who does not obtain organs or cells from a cell bank but who directly interferes with or misappropriates a patient's right to control the use of his organs or cells. Although the majority opinion suggests that the availability of a breach-of-fiduciary-duty cause of action obviates any need for a conversion action against this category of defendants, the existence of a breach-of-fiduciary-duty cause of action does not provide a complete answer. Even if in this case plaintiff may obtain the same remedy against such defendants under a breach-of-fiduciary-duty theory as he could under a conversion cause of action, in other factual settings an unlawful interference with a patient's right to control the use of his body part may occur in the absence of a breach of fiduciary duty. . . .

Second, even with respect to those persons who are not involved in the initial conversion, the majority's policy arguments are less than compelling. To begin with, the majority's fear that the availability of a conversion remedy will restrict access to existing cell lines is unrealistic. In the vast majority of instances the tissues and cells in existing repositories will not represent a potential source of liability because they will have come from patients who consented to their organ's use for scientific purposes under circumstances in which such consent was not tainted by a failure to disclose the known valuable nature of the cells. Because potential liability under a conversion theory will exist in only the exceedingly rare instance in which a doctor knowingly concealed from the patient the value of his body part or the patient's specific directive with regard to the use of the body part was disregarded, there is no reason to think that application of settled conversion law will have any negative effect on the primary conduct of medical researchers who use tissue and cell banks.

Furthermore, even in the rare instance—like the present case—in which a conversion action might be successfully pursued, the potential liability is not likely "to destroy the economic incentive to conduct important medical research," as the majority asserts. If, as the majority suggests, the great bulk of the value of a cell line patent and derivative products is attributable to the efforts of medical researchers and drug companies, rather than to the "raw materials" taken from a patient, the patient's damages will be correspondingly limited, and innocent medical researchers and drug manufacturers will retain the considerable economic benefits resulting from their own work. Under established conversion law, a "subsequent innocent converter" does not forfeit the proceeds of his own creative efforts, but rather "is entitled to the benefit of any work or labor that he has expended on the [property]. . . ."

Finally, the majority's analysis of the relevant policy considerations tellingly omits a most pertinent consideration. In identifying the interests of the patient that are implicated by the decision whether to recognize a conversion cause of action, the opinion speaks only of the "patient's right to make autonomous medical decisions" and fails even to mention the patient's interest in obtaining the economic value, if any, that may adhere in the subsequent use of his own body parts. Although such economic value may constitute a fortuitous "windfall" to the patient, the fortuitous nature of the economic value does not justify the creation of a novel exception from conversion liability which sanctions the intentional misappropriation of that value from the patient.

This last point reveals perhaps the most serious flaw in the majority's public policy analysis in this case. It is certainly arguable that, as a matter of policy or morality, it would be wiser to prohibit any private individual or entity from profiting from the fortuitous value that adheres in a part of a human body, and instead to require all valuable excised body parts to be deposited in a public repository which would make such materials freely available to all scientists for the betterment of society as a whole. The Legislature, if it wished, could create such a system, as it has done with respect to organs that are donated for transplantation. To date, however, the Legislature has not adopted such a system for organs that are to be used for research or commercial purposes, and the majority opinion, despite some oblique suggestions to the contrary, emphatically does not do so by its holding in this case. Justice Arabian's concurring opinion suggests that the majority's conclusion is informed by the precept that it is immoral to sell human body parts for profit. But the majority's rejection of plaintiff's conversion cause of action does not mean that body parts may not be bought or sold for research or commercial purposes or that no private individual or entity may benefit economically from the fortuitous value of plaintiff's diseased cells. Far from elevating these biological materials above the marketplace, the majority's holding simply bars plaintiff, the source of the cells, from obtaining the benefit of the cells' value, but permits defendants, who allegedly obtained the cells from plaintiff by improper means, to retain and exploit the full economic value of their ill-gotten gains free of their ordinary common law liability for conversion. . . .

MOSK, JUSTICE, dissenting. . . . Being broad, the concept of property is also abstract: rather than referring directly to a material object such as a parcel of land or the tractor that cultivates it, the concept of property is often said to refer to a "bundle of rights" that may be exercised with respect to that object—principally the rights to possess the property, to use the property, to exclude others from the property, and to dispose of the property by sale or by gift. "Ownership is not a single concrete entity but a bundle of rights and privileges as well as of obligations." *Union Oil Co. v. State Bd. of Equal.* (1963) 60 Cal.2d 441, 447, 34 Cal.Rptr. 872, 386 P.2d 496. But the same bundle of rights does not attach to all forms of property. For a variety of policy reasons, the law limits or even forbids the exercise of certain rights over certain forms of property. For example, both law and contract may limit the right of an owner of real property to use his parcel as he sees fit. Owners of various forms of personal property may likewise be subject to restrictions on the time, place, and manner of their use. Limitations on the disposition of real property, while less common, may also be imposed. Finally, some types of personal property may be sold but not given away,[8] while others may be given away but not sold,[9] and still others may neither be given away nor sold.[10]

In each of the foregoing instances, the limitation or prohibition diminishes the bundle of rights that would otherwise attach to the property, yet what remains is still deemed in law to be a protectible property interest. . . . The same rule applies to Moore's interest in his own body tissue: even if we assume that section 7054.4 limited the use and disposition of his excised tissue in the manner claimed by the majority, Moore nevertheless retained valuable rights in that tissue. Above all, at the time of its excision he at least had *the right to do with his own tissue whatever the defendants did with it: i.e.*, he could have contracted with researchers and pharmaceutical companies to develop and exploit the vast commercial potential of his tissue and its products. Defendants certainly believe that their right to do the foregoing is not barred by section 7054.4 and is a significant property right, as they have demonstrated by their deliberate concealment from Moore of the true value of his tissue, their efforts to obtain a patent on the Mo cell line, their contractual agreements to exploit this material, their exclusion of Moore from any participation in the profits, and their vigorous defense of this lawsuit. The Court of Appeal summed up the point by observing that "Defendants' position that plaintiff cannot own his tissue, but that they can, is fraught with irony." It is also legally untenable. As noted

8. A person contemplating bankruptcy may sell his property at its "reasonably equivalent value," but he may not make a gift of the same property. *See* 11 U.S.C. § 548(a).

9. A sportsman may give away wild fish or game that he has caught or killed pursu-ant to his license, but he may not sell it. Fish & Game Code, §§ 3039, 7121. . . .

10. *E.g.*, a license to practice a profession, or a prescription drug in the hands of the person for whom it is prescribed.

above, the majority cite no case holding that an individual's right to develop and exploit the commercial potential of his own tissue is not a right of sufficient worth or dignity to be deemed a protectible property interest. In the absence of such authority—or of legislation to the same effect—the right falls within the traditionally broad concept of property in our law. . . .

The majority begin their analysis by stressing the obvious facts that research on human cells plays an increasingly important role in the progress of medicine, and that the manipulation of those cells by the methods of biotechnology has resulted in numerous beneficial products and treatments. Yet it does not necessarily follow that, as the majority claim, application of the law of conversion to this area "will hinder research by restricting access to the necessary raw materials," *i.e.,* to cells, cell cultures, and cell lines. The majority observe that many researchers obtain their tissue samples, routinely and at little or no cost, from cell-culture repositories. . . .

. . . [T]o the extent that cell cultures and cell lines may still be "freely exchanged," *e.g.,* for purely research purposes, it does not follow that the researcher who obtains such material must necessarily remain ignorant of any limitations on its use: by means of appropriate record-keeping, the researcher can be assured that the source of the material has consented to his proposed use of it, and hence that such use is not a conversion. . . . "Record keeping would not be overly burdensome be-cause researchers generally keep accurate records of tissue sources for other reasons: to trace anomalies to the medical history of the patient, to maintain title for other researchers and for themselves, and to insure reproducibility of the experiment." As the Court of Appeal correctly observed, any claim to the contrary "is dubious in light of the meticulous care and planning necessary in serious modern medical research." . . .

The inference I draw from the current statutory regulation of human biological materials, moreover, is the opposite of that drawn by the majority. By selective quotation of the statutes the majority seem to suggest that human organs and blood cannot legally be sold on the open market—thereby implying that if the Legislature were to act here it would impose a similar ban on monetary compensation for the use of human tissue in biotechnological research and development. But if that is the argument, the premise is unsound: contrary to popular misconcep-tion, it is not true that human organs and blood cannot legally be sold.

As to organs, the majority rely on the Uniform Anatomical Gift Act for the proposition that a competent adult may make a post mortem gift of any part of his body but may not receive "valuable consideration" for the transfer. But the prohibition of the UAGA against the sale of a body part is much more limited than the majority recognize: by its terms the prohibition applies only to sales for "transplantation" or "therapy." Yet a different section of the UAGA authorizes the transfer and receipt of body parts for such additional purposes as "medical or dental education, research, or advancement of medical or dental science." No section of the

UAGA prohibits anyone from selling body parts for any of those additional purposes; by clear implication, therefore, such sales are legal. Indeed, the fact that the UAGA prohibits no sales of organs other than sales for "transportation" or "therapy" raises a further implication that it is also legal for anyone to sell human tissue to a biotechnology company for research and development purposes. . . .

With respect to the sale of human blood the matter is much simpler: there is in fact no prohibition against such sales. The majority rely on Health and Safety Code section 1606, which provides in relevant part that the procurement and use of blood for transfusion "shall be construed to be, and is declared to be . . . the rendition of a service . . . and shall not be construed to be, and is declared not to be, a sale. . . ." There is less here, however, than meets the eye: the statute does not mean that a person cannot sell his blood or, by implication, that his blood is not his property. . . . [D]espite the statute relied on by the majority, it is perfectly legal in this state for a person to sell his blood for transfusion or for any other purpose indeed, such sales are commonplace, particularly in the market for plasma.[11]

It follows that the statutes regulating the transfers of human organs and blood do not support the majority's refusal to recognize a conversion cause of action for commercial exploitation of human blood cells without consent. On the contrary, because such statutes treat both organs and blood as property that can legally be sold in a variety of circumstances, they impliedly support Moore's contention that his blood cells are likewise property for which he can and should receive compensation. . . .

The majority's final reason for refusing to recognize a conversion cause of action on these facts is that "there is no pressing need" to do so because the complaint also states another cause of action [for breach of fiduciary duty or lack of informed consent] . . . .

The [informed consent/fiduciary duty] remedy is largely illusory. "[A]n action based on the physician's failure to disclose material information sounds in negligence. As a practical matter, however, it may be difficult to recover on this kind of negligence theory because the patient must prove a *causal connection* between his or her injury and the physician's failure to inform." There are two barriers to recovery. First, "the patient must show that if he or she had been informed of all pertinent information, he or she would have declined to consent to the procedure in question." As we explained in the seminal case of *Cobbs v. Grant* (1972) 8 Cal.3d 229, 245, 104 Cal.Rptr. 505, 502 P.2d 1, "There must be a causal relationship between the physician's failure to inform and the injury to the plaintiff. Such a causal connection arises only if it is established that had revelation been made consent to treatment would not have been given."

The second barrier to recovery is still higher, and is erected on the first: it is not even enough for the plaintiff to prove that he personally would have refused consent to the proposed treatment if he had been

11. Editors' Note: Justice Mosk is correct on this point. What, then, is the purpose of Section 1606? *See, e.g., Hyland* *Therapeutics v. Superior Court*, 175 Cal. App.3d 509, 220 Cal. Rptr. 590 (1985).

fully informed; he must also prove that in the same circumstances *no reasonably prudent person* would have given such consent. . . .

. . . [I]n the case at bar no trier of fact is likely to believe that if defendants had disclosed their plans for using Moore's cells, no reasonably prudent person in Moore's position—*i.e.*, a leukemia patient suffering from a grossly enlarged spleen—would have consented to the routine operation that saved or at least prolonged his life. . . . In this context, accordingly, the threat of suit on a nondisclosure cause of action is largely a paper tiger.

The second reason why the nondisclosure cause of action is inadequate for the task that the majority assign to it is that it fails to solve half the problem before us: it gives the patient only the right to refuse consent, *i.e.*, the right to prohibit the commercialization of his tissue; it does not give him the right to grant consent to that commercialization on the condition that he share in its proceeds. . . .

Third, the nondisclosure cause of action fails to reach a major class of potential defendants: all those who are outside the strict physician-patient relationship with the plaintiff. Thus the majority concede that here only defendant Golde, the treating physician, can be directly liable to Moore on a nondisclosure cause of action. . . .

In sum, the nondisclosure cause of action (1) is unlikely to be successful in most cases, (2) fails to protect patients' rights to share in the proceeds of the commercial exploitation of their tissue, and (3) may allow the true exploiters to escape liability. It is thus not an adequate substitute, in my view, for the conversion cause of action. . . .

Notes

1. *To the Victor Go the Spoils.* So who won this case, exactly?

2. *Another Exercise in Statutory Interpretation.* Which of the Justices do you believe most satisfactorily interpreted the relevance of the UAGA and the other statutes discussed in the *Moore* opinions? Why?

3. *"Entitlements."* Does Moore have any "entitlement," as Calabresi and Melamed use that term? If so, what is his entitlement, and how does the law protect it? In answering this question, consider the following problems:

   (a) Assume Golde did inform Moore about his intention to use Moore's cells in research, and that Moore had agreed to consent to the surgery only if Moore received 5% of all profits that Golde derived from the future use of Moore's cells. After making such an agreement, and then using the cells to produce the Mo cell line, Golde refuses to perform the agreement. Moore sues Golde for damages. Based on the reasoning in the court's decision in *Moore v. Board of Regents,* would the court enforce the agreement? Why or why not? Do you believe such an agreement should be enforced?

   (b) After having a kidney stone removed in January 2006, the actor William Shatner—famous as Captain Kirk of Star Trek™ fame, and more recently as Denny Crane of the TV show *Boston Legal*—asked his doctor to return the kidney stone so that Shatner could sell it. The doctor returned the stone as requested and Shatner sold it in an online auction for $25,000 (which he donated to Habitat for Humanity). *See* David Goldberg, "You Want a Piece of Me?," *Newark Star–Ledger*, January 29, 2006. Suppose, however, that Shatner's doctor had refused to return the stone as requested. In that case, would Shatner have been able to recover the stone under the reasoning of *Moore*? Should Shatner's charitable intent matter?

(c) A fertility clinic takes an embryo from a donor and transplants it into another patient without the consent of the donor. After discovering this conduct, the donor sues the clinic for conversion of the embryo. Given the decision in *Moore*, how would you advise your client about the likely success of the conversion claim? Does a patient have a continuing property right in her eggs and embryos? Are a fertility clinic's patient's interests adequately protected through other possible claims, such as breach of fiduciary duty and/or failure to obtain consent, as the court concludes in *Moore*?

4. *Markets in Body Parts and Bodies—Justice Arabian's Nightmare, or a Logical Solution?* Assume that currently, the following conditions exist in the state of West Dakota: (a) there are more persons waiting for kidney transplants than there are available kidneys for transplantation; (b) there are more persons wanting to adopt healthy babies than there are such babies available for adoption. West Dakota state law prohibits both the sale of organs for transplantation and the sale of babies for adoption. [Assume that there are no relevant federal laws governing the sale of organs or babies.] Representative Pushaw, who thinks these conditions are unacceptable, proposes legislation that would permit the sale of kidneys for transplantation and the sale of babies for adoption in West Dakota. Why would this be a good idea? Why would this be a bad idea?

In pondering these questions, consider Calabresi and Melamed's explanation for why the law sometimes regulates or prohibits the sale of certain things. First, they observe that "inalienability" rules may be justified in the case of "moralisms," which occur when a transaction would create externalities that "do not lend themselves to collective measurement which is acceptably objective and nonarbitrary." Guido Calabresi and A. Douglas Melamed, *Property Rules, Liability Rules, and Inalienability: One View of the Cathedral*, 85 Harv. L. Rev. 1089, 1111–12 (1972).

> If Taney is allowed to sell himself into slavery, or to take undue risks of becoming penniless, or to sell a kidney, Marshall may be harmed, simply because Marshall is a sensitive man who is made unhappy by seeing slaves, paupers, or persons who die because they have sold a kidney. Again, Marshall could pay Taney not to sell his freedom to Chase the slaveowner; but again, because Marshall is not one but many individuals, freeloader and information costs make such transactions practically impossible. Again, it might seem that the state could intervene by objectively valuing the external cost to Marshall and requiring Chase to pay the cost. But since the external cost to Marshall does not lend itself to an acceptable objective measurement, such liability rules are not appropriate. [*Id.* at 1112.]

Calabresi and Melamed offer two additional efficiency reasons for forbidding the sale of certain entitlements—"self-paternalism" and "true paternalism":

Examples of [self-paternalism] are Ulysses tying himself to the mast or individuals passing a bill of rights so that they will be prevented from yielding to momentary temptations which they deem harmful to themselves. . . . Self-paternalism may cause us to require certain conditions to exist before we allow a sale of an entitlement; and it may help explain many situations of inalienability, like the invalidity of contracts entered into when drunk, or under undue influence or coercion. But it probably does not fully explain even these.

True paternalism brings us a step further toward explaining such prohibitions and those of broader kinds—for example the prohibitions on a whole range of activities by minors. Paternalism is based on the notion that at least in some situations the Marshalls know better than Taney what will make Taney better off. Here we are not talking about the offense to Marshall from Taney's choosing to read pornography, or selling himself into slavery, but rather the judgment that Taney was not in the position to choose best for himself when he made the choice for erotica or servitude. [*Id.* at 1113.]

Finally, Calabresi and Melamed note that inalienability rules may advance "distributional goals":

Whether an entitlement may be sold or not often affects directly who is richer and who is poorer. Prohibiting the sale of babies makes poorer those who can cheaply produce babies and richer those who through some nonmarket device get a free "unwanted" baby. Prohibiting exculpatory clauses in product sales makes richer those who were injured by a product defect and poorer those who were not injured and who paid more for the product because the exculpatory clause was forbidden. [*Id.* at 1114.]

To what extent are these observations relevant to Representative Pushaw's legislative proposal?

Chapter 2

POSSESSION, FIRST–IN–TIME, AND ACQUIRING PROPERTY INTERESTS

possession + 1st possession

How is it that something comes to be "property"? A pen (or a book, or a home, or any other object) may become my property because I purchased it, but only if my seller had a "property" interest in it or the power to convey a "property" interest. But how does an object become "property" *in the first instance*? How, and why, did the law first allocate a "property" interest in a certain object? Chapter 2 focuses upon the way in which the common law uses the concepts of *possession* and *first possession* to allocate property rights and resolve disputes between persons who claim competing rights.

A. "FIRST-IN-TIME" AND DISCOVERY/CAPTURE

PIERSON v. POST

Supreme Court of New York.
3 Caines 175 (1805).

This was an action of trespass on the case commenced in a justice's court, by the present defendant against the now plaintiff.

The declaration stated that Post, being in possession of certain dogs and hounds under his command, did, "upon a certain wild and uninhabited, unpossessed and waste land, called the beach, find and start one of those noxious beasts called a fox," and whilst there hunting, chasing and pursuing the same with his dogs and hounds, and when in view thereof, Pierson, well knowing the fox was so hunted and pursued, did, in the sight of Post, to prevent his catching the same, kill and carry it off. A verdict having been rendered for the plaintiff below, the defendant there sued out a *certiorari*, and now assigned for error, that the declaration and the matters therein contained were not sufficient in law to maintain an action. . . .

TOMPKINS, J., delivered the opinion of the court. This cause comes before us on a return to a *certiorari* directed to one of the justices of Queens county.

Issue of case
⌐↳

The question submitted by the counsel in this cause for our determination is, whether Lodowick Post, by the pursuit with his hounds in the manner alleged in his declaration, acquired such a right to, or property in the fox, as will sustain an action against Pierson for killing and taking him away?

The cause was argued with much ability by the counsel on both sides, and presents for our decision a novel and nice question. It is admitted that a fox is an animal *ferae naturae*, and that property in such animals is acquired by occupancy only. These admissions narrow the discussion to the simple question of what acts amount to occupancy, applied to acquiring right to wild animals?

If we have recourse to the ancient writers upon general principles of law, the judgment below is obviously erroneous. Justinian's Institutes, lib. 2, tit. 1, s.13, and Fleta, lib. 3, c.2, p.175, adopt the principle, that pursuit alone vests no property or right in the huntsman; and that even pursuit, accompanied with wounding, is equally ineffectual for that purpose, unless the animal be actually taken. The same principle is recognised by Bracton, lib. 2, c.1, p.8.

Puffendorf, lib. 4, s.2, and 10, defines occupancy of beasts *ferae naturae*, to be the actual corporal possession of them, and Bynkershoek is cited as coinciding in this definition. It is indeed with hesitation that Puffendorf affirms that a wild beast mortally wounded, or greatly maimed, cannot be fairly intercepted by another, whilst the pursuit of the person inflicting the wound continues. The foregoing authorities are decisive to show that mere pursuit gave Post no legal right to the fox, but that he became the property of Pierson, who intercepted and killed him.

It therefore only remains to inquire whether there are any contrary principles, or authorities, to be found in other books, which ought to induce a different decision. Most of the cases which have occurred in England, relating to property in wild animals, have either been discussed and decided upon the principles of their positive statute regulations, or have arisen between the huntsman and the owner of the land upon which beasts *ferae naturae* have been apprehended; the former claiming them by title of occupancy, and the latter *ratione soli*. Little satisfactory aid can, therefore, be derived from the English reporters.

uses this for theory for possession↓

Barbeyrac, in his notes on Puffendorf, does not accede to the definition of occupancy by the latter, but, on the contrary, affirms, that actual bodily seizure is not, in all cases, necessary to constitute possession of wild animals. He does not, however, *describe* the acts which, according to his ideas, will amount to an appropriation of such animals to private use, so as to exclude the claims of all other persons, by title of occupancy, to the same animals; and he is far from averring that pursuit alone is sufficient for that purpose. To a certain extent, and as far as Barbeyrac appears to me to go, his objections to Puffendorf's definition of occupancy are reasonable and correct. That is to say, that actual bodily seizure is not indispensable to acquire right to, or possession of, wild beasts; but that, on the contrary, the mortal wounding of such beasts, by one not abandoning his pursuit may, with the utmost propriety, be deemed possession of him; since, thereby, the pursuer manifests an unequivocal intention of appropriating the animal to his individual use, has deprived him of his natural liberty, and brought him within his certain control. So also, encompassing and securing such animals with nets and toils, or otherwise intercepting them in such a manner as to deprive them of their natural liberty, and render escape impossible, may justly be deemed to give possession of them to those persons who, by their industry and labour, have used such means of apprehending them. . . . The case now under consideration is one of mere pursuit, and presents no circumstances or acts which can bring it within the definition of occupancy by Puffendorf . . . or the ideas of Barbeyrac upon that subject. . . .

We are the more readily inclined to confine possession or occupancy of beasts *ferae naturae*, within the limits prescribed by the learned authors above cited, for the sake of certainty, and preserving peace and order in society. If the first seeing, starting, or pursuing such animals, without having so wounded, circumvented or ensnared them, so as to deprive them of their natural liberty, and subject them to the control of their pursuer, should afford the basis of actions against others for intercepting and killing them, it would prove a fertile source of quarrels and litigation.

However uncourteous or unkind the conduct of Pierson towards Post, in this instance, may have been, yet his act was productive of no injury or damage for which a legal remedy can be applied. We are of opinion the judgment below was erroneous, and ought to be reversed.

LIVINGSTON, J. My opinion differs from that of the court. Of six exceptions, taken to the proceedings below, all are abandoned except the third, which reduces the controversy to a single question.

Whether a person who, with his own hounds, starts and hunts a fox on waste and uninhabited ground, and is on the point of seizing his prey, acquires such an interest in the animal, as to have a right of action against another, who in view of the huntsman and his dogs in full pursuit, and with knowledge of the case, shall kill and carry him away?

This is a knotty point, and should have been submitted to the arbitration of sportsmen, without poring over Justinian, Fleta, Bracton, Puffendorf, Locke, Barbeyrac, or Blackstone, all of whom have been cited; they would have had no difficulty in coming to a prompt and correct conclusion. In a court thus constituted, the skin and carcass of poor *reynard* would have been properly disposed of, and a precedent set, interfering with no usage or custom which the experience of ages has sanctioned, and which must be so well known to every votary Diana. But the parties have referred the question to our judgment, and we must dispose of it as well as we can, from the partial lights we possess, leaving to a higher tribunal, the correction of any mistake which we may be so unfortunate as to make. By the pleadings it is admitted that a fox is a "wild and noxious beast." Both parties have regarded him, as the law of nations does a pirate, *hostem humani generis,* and although *"de mortuis nil nisi bonum,"* be a maxim of our profession, the memory of the deceased has not been spared. His depredations on farmers and on barn yards have not been forgotten; and to put him to death wherever found, is allowed to be meritorious, and of public benefit. Hence it follows, that our decision should have in view the greatest possible encouragement to the destruction of an animal, so cunning and ruthless in his career. But who would keep a pack of hounds; or what gentleman, at the sound of the horn, and at peep of day, would mount his steed, and for hours together, *"sub jove frigido,"* or a vertical sun, pursue the windings of this wily quadruped, if, just as night came on, and his stratagems and strength were nearly exhausted, a saucy intruder, who had not shared in the honours or labours of the chase, were permitted to come in at the death, and bear away in triumph the object of pursuit? Whatever Justinian may have thought of the matter, it must be recollected that his code was compiled many hundred years ago, and it would be very hard indeed, at the distance of so many centuries, not to have a right to establish a rule for ourselves. In his day, we read of no order of men who made it a business, in the language of the declaration in this cause, "with hounds and dogs to find, start, pursue, hunt, and chase," these animals, and that, too, without any other motive than the preservation of Roman poultry; if this diversion had been then in fashion, the lawyers who composed his institutes would have taken care not to pass it by, without suitable encouragement. If any thing, therefore, in the digests or pandects shall appear to militate against the defendant in error, who, on this occasion, was the foxhunter, we have only to say *tempora mutantur:* and if men themselves change with the times, why should not laws also undergo an alteration?

It may be expected, however, by the learned counsel, that more particular notice be taken of their authorities. I have examined them all, and feel great difficulty in determining, whether to acquire dominion over a thing, before in common, it be sufficient that we barely see it, or know where it is, or wish for it, or make a declaration of our will respecting it; or whether, in the case of wild beast, setting a trap, or lying in wait, or starting, or pursuing, be enough; or if an actual wounding, or killing, or bodily tact and occupation be necessary. Writers on general law, who have favoured us with their speculations on these point, differ on them all; but, great as is the diversity of sentiment among them, some conclusion must be adopted on the question immediately before us. After mature deliberation, I embrace that of Barbeyrac, as the most rational, and least liable to objection. If at liberty, we might imitate the courtesy of a certain emperor, who, to avoid giving offence to the advocates of any of these different doctrines, adopted a middle course, and by ingenious distinctions, rendered it difficult to say (as often happens after a fierce and angry contest) to whom the palm of victory belonged. He ordained, that if a beast be followed with *large dogs and hounds,* he shall belong to the hunter, not to the chance occupant;

and in like manner, if he be killed or wounded with a lance or sword; but if chased with *beagles only*, then he passed to the captor, not to the first pursuer. If slain with a dart, a sling, or a bow, he fell to the hunter, if still in chase, and not to him who might afterwards find and seize him.

Now, as we are without any municipal regulations of our own, and the pursuit here, for aught that appears on the case, being with dogs and hounds of *imperial stature*, we are at liberty to adopt one of the provisions just cited, which comports also with the learned conclusion of Barbeyrac, that property in animals *ferae naturae* may be acquired without bodily touch or manucaption, provided the pursuer be within reach, or have a *reasonable* prospect (which certainly existed here) of taking, what he has *thus* discovered an intention of converting to his own use.

holding ✓

When we reflect also that the interest of our husbandmen, the most useful of men in any community, will be advanced by the destruction of a beast so pernicious and incorrigible, we cannot greatly err, in saying, that a pursuit like the present, through waste and unoccupied lands, and which must inevitably and speedily have terminated in corporal possession, or bodily *seisin*, confers such a right to the object of it, as to make any one a wrongdoer, who shall interfere and shoulder the spoil. The justice's judgment ought, therefore, in my opinion, to be affirmed....

CAROL M. ROSE, POSSESSION AS THE ORIGIN OF PROPERTY
52 U. Chi. L. Rev. 73 (1985).

How do things come to be owned? This is a fundamental puzzle for anyone who thinks about property. One buys things from other owners, to be sure, but how did the other owners get those things? Any chain of ownership or title must have a first link. Someone had to do something to anchor that link. The law tells us what steps we must follow to obtain ownership of things, but we need a theory that tells us why these steps should do the job.

John Locke's view, once described as "the standard bourgeois theory," is probably the one most familiar to American students. Locke argued that an original owner is one who mixes his or her labor with a thing and, by commingling that labor with the thing, establishes ownership of it. This labor theory is appealing because it appears to rest on "desert," but it has some problems. First, without a prior theory of ownership, it is not self-evident that one owns even the labor that is mixed with something else. Second, even if one does own the labor that one performs, the labor theory provides no guidance in determining the scope of the right that one establishes by mixing one's labor with something else. Robert Nozick illustrates this problem with a clever hypothetical. Suppose I pour a can of tomato juice into the ocean: do I now own the seas?

A number of thinkers more or less contemporary to Locke proposed another theory of the basis of ownership. According to this theory, the

John Locke's theory on origin of property

original owner got title through the consent of the rest of humanity (who were, taken together, the first recipients from God, the genuine original owner). Locke himself identified the problems with this theory; they involve what modern law-and-economics writers would call "administrative costs." How does everyone get together to consent to the division of things among individuals?

The common law has a third approach, which shares some characteristics with the labor and consent theories but is distinct enough to warrant a different label. For the common law, possession or "occupancy" is the origin of property. This notion runs through a number of fascinating old cases with which teachers of property law love to challenge their students. Such inquiries into the acquisition of title to wild animals and abandoned treasure may seem purely academic; how often, after all, do we expect to get into disputes about the ownership of wild pigs or long-buried pieces of eight? These cases are not entirely silly, though. People still do find treasure-laden vessels, and statesmen do have to consider whether someone's acts might support a claim to own the moon, for example, or the mineral nodes at the bottom of the sea. Moreover, analogies to the capture of wild animals show up time and again when courts have to deal on a nonstatutory basis with some "fugitive" resource that is being reduced to property for the first time, such as oil, gas, groundwater, or space on the spectrum of radio frequencies.

With these more serious claims in mind, then, I turn to the maxim of the common law: first possession is the root of title. Merely to state the proposition is to raise two critical questions: what counts as possession, and why is it the basis for a claim to title? In exploring the quaint old cases' answers to these questions, we hit on some fundamental views about the nature and purposes of a property regime.

Consider *Pierson v. Post*, a classic wild-animal case from the early nineteenth century. Post was hunting a fox one day on an abandoned beach and almost had the beast in his gunsight when an interloper appeared, killed the fox, and ran off with the carcass. The indignant Post sued the interloper for the value of the fox on the theory that his pursuit of the fox had established his property right to it.

The court disagreed. It cited a long list of learned authorities to the effect that "occupancy" or "possession" went to the one who killed the animal, or who at least wounded it mortally or caught it in a net. These acts brought the animal within the "certain control" that gives rise to possession and hence a claim to ownership.

Possession thus means a clear act, whereby all the world understands that the pursuer has "an unequivocal intention of appropriating the animal to his individual use." A clear rule of this sort should be applied, said the court, because it prevents confusion and quarreling among hunters (and coincidentally makes the judges' task easier when hunters do get into quarrels).

The dissenting judge commented that the best way to handle this matter would be to leave it to a panel of sportsmen, who presumably would have ruled against the interloper. In any event, he noted that the majority's rule would discourage the useful activity of fox hunting: who would bother to go to all the trouble of keeping dogs and chasing foxes if the reward were up for grabs to any "saucy intruder"? If we really want to see that foxes don't overrun the countryside, we will allocate a property right—and thus the ultimate reward—to the hunter at an earlier moment, so that he will undertake the useful investment in keeping hounds and the useful labor in flushing the fox.

The problem with assigning "possession" prior to the kill is, of course, that we need a principle to tell us when to assign it. Shall we assign it when the hunt begins? When the hunter assembles his dogs for the hunt? When the hunter buys his dogs?

Pierson thus presents two great principles, seemingly at odds, for defining possession: (1) notice to the world through a clear act, and (2) reward to useful labor. The latter principle, of course, suggests a labor theory of property. The owner gets the prize when he "mixes in his labor" by hunting. On the other hand, the former principle suggests at least a weak form of the consent theory: the community requires clear acts so that it has the opportunity to dispute claims, but may be thought to acquiesce in individual ownership where the claim is clear and no objection is made.

On closer examination, however, the two positions do not seem so far apart. In *Pierson*, each side acknowledged the importance of the other's principle. Although the majority decided in favor of a clear rule, it tacitly conceded the value of rewarding useful labor. Its rule for possession would in fact reward the original hunter most of the time, unless we suppose that the woods are thick with "saucy intruders." On the other side, the dissenting judge also wanted some definiteness in the rule of possession. He was simply insisting that the acts that sufficed to give notice should be prescribed by the relevant community, namely hunters or "sportsmen." Perhaps, then, there is some way to reconcile the clear-act and reward-to-labor principles.

The clear-act principle suggests that the common law defines acts of possession as some kind of *statement*. As Blackstone said, the acts must be a *declaration* of one's intent to appropriate . . . .

Possession now begins to look even more like something that requires a kind of communication, and the original claim to the property looks like a kind of speech, with the audience composed of all others who might be interested in claiming the object in question . . . .

Possession as the basis of property ownership, then, seems to amount to something like yelling loudly enough to all who may be interested. The first to say, "This is mine," in a way that the public understands, gets the prize, and the law will help him keep it against someone else who says, "No, it is mine." . . .

Why, then, is it so important that property owners make and keep their communications clear? Economists have an answer: clear titles facilitate trade and minimize resource-wasting conflict. If I am careless about who comes on to a corner of my property, I invite others to make mistakes and to waste their labor on improvements to what I have allowed them to think is theirs. I thus invite a free-for-all over my ambiguously held claims, and I encourage contention, insecurity, and litigation—all of which waste everyone's time and energy and may result in overuse or underuse of resources. But if I keep my property claims clear, others will know that they should deal with me directly if they want to use my property. We can bargain rather than fight; through trade, all items will come to rest in the hands of those who value them most. If property lines are clear, then, anyone who can make better use of my property than I can will buy or rent it from me and turn the property to his better use. In short, we will all be richer when property claims are unequivocal, because that unequivocal status enables property to be traded and used at its highest value.

Thus, it turns out that the common law of first possession, in rewarding the one who communicates a claim, does reward useful labor; the useful labor is the very act of speaking clearly and distinctly about one's claims to property. Naturally, this must be in a language that is understood, and the acts of "possession" that communicate a claim will vary according to the audience. Thus, returning to *Pierson v. Post*, the dissenting judge may well have thought that fox hunters were the only relevant audience for a claim to the fox; they are the only ones who have regular contact with the subject matter. By the same token, the mid-nineteenth century California courts gave much deference to the mining-camp customs in adjudicating various Gold Rush claims; the Forty-Niners themselves, as those most closely involved with the subject, could best communicate and interpret the signs of property claims and would be particularly well served by a stable system of symbols that would enable them to avoid disputes.

The point, then, is that "acts of possession" are, in the now fashionable term, a "text," and that the common law rewards the author of that text. But, as students of hermeneutics know, the clearest text may have ambiguous subtexts. In connection with the text of first possession, there are several subtexts that are especially worthy of note. One is the implication that the text will be "read" by the relevant audience at the appropriate time. It is not always easy to establish a symbolic structure in which the text of first possession can be "published" at such a time as to be useful to anyone. Once again, *Pierson v. Post* illustrates the problem that occurs when a clear sign (killing the fox) comes only relatively late in the game, after the relevant parties may have already expended overlapping efforts and embroiled themselves in a dispute. Very similar problems occurred in the whaling industry in the nineteenth century: the courts expended a considerable amount of mental energy in finding signs of "possession" that were comprehensible to whalers from their own customs and that at the same time came early enough in the chase to allow the parties to avoid wasted efforts and the ensuing mutual recriminations.

Some objects of property claims do seem inherently incapable of clear demarcation—ideas, for example. In order to establish ownership of such disembodied items we find it necessary to translate the property claims into sets of secondary symbols that our culture understands. In patent and copyright law, for example, one establishes an entitlement to the expression of an idea by translating it into a written document and going through a registration process—though the unending litigation over ownership of these expressions, and over which expressions can even be subject to patent or copyright, might lead us to conclude that these particular secondary symbolic systems do not always yield widely understood "markings." We also make up secondary symbols for physical objects that would seem to be much easier to mark out than ideas; even property claims in land, that most tangible of things, are now at their most authoritative in the form of written records.

any system of property revolves around costs

It is expensive to establish and maintain these elaborate structures of secondary symbols, as indeed it may be expensive to establish a structure of primary symbols of possession. The economists have once again performed a useful service in pointing out that there are costs entailed in establishing any property system. These costs might prevent the development of any system at all for some objects, where our need for secure investment and trade is not as great as the cost of creating the necessary symbols of possession.

There is a second and perhaps even more important subtext to the "text" of first possession: the tacit supposition that there is such a thing as a "clear act," unequivocally proclaiming to the universe one's appropriation—that there are in fact unequivocal acts of possession, which any relevant audience will naturally and easily interpret as property claims. Literary theorists have recently written a great deal about the relativity of texts. They have written too much for us to accept uncritically the idea that a "text" about property has a natural meaning independent of some audience constituting an "interpretive community" or independent of a range of other "texts" and cultural artifacts that together form a symbolic system in which a given text must be read. It is not enough, then, for the property claimant to say simply, "It's mine" through some act or gesture; in order for the "statement" to have any force, some relevant world must understand the claim it makes and take that claim seriously.

Thus, in defining the acts of possession that make up a claim to property, the law not only rewards the author of the "text"; it also puts an imprimatur on a particular symbolic system and on the audience that uses this system. Audiences that do not understand or accept the symbols are out of luck. For *Pierson*'s dissenting judge, who would have made the definition of first possession depend on a decision of hunters, the rule of first possession would have put the force of law behind the mores of a particular subgroup. The majority's "clear act" rule undoubtedly referred to a wider audience and a more widely shared set of symbols. But even under the majority's rule, the definition of first possession depended on a particular audience and its chosen symbolic context; some audiences win, others lose.

Notes

1. *Interpreting the* Pierson v. Post *Holding*. Professor Rose's article discusses the significance of possession as a "clear act" that sends a signal to third parties regarding the possessor's ownership claim—thus facilitating trade in goods and helping to minimize disputes over control of goods. The court in *Pierson* concludes that Post's acts did not send a sufficiently clear signal to justify a legal determination that Post owned the fox at the time *Pierson* shot it. Do you agree? Exactly what is the majority's holding? Is it accurate to suggest that the majority opinion proposes a "clearer" rule than the dissent? In answering this question, how do you think the majority in *Pierson* would have resolved the dispute under the following scenarios:

(a) Post had shot the fox in the leg before Pierson captured it.

(b) Post had shot the fox in the chest before Pierson captured it.

(c) Post had wounded the fox so severely that it was virtually immobilized when Pierson arrived, put the fox out of its misery, and took possession.

(d) Post had wounded the fox, but darkness intervened to prevent him from capturing it. The next day at dawn, Pierson captured the fox, just minutes before Post returned to continue his pursuit.

Compare Liesner v. Wanie, 156 Wis. 16, 145 N.W. 374 (1914) (awarding wolf to hunter who mortally wounded wolf and continued pursuit) *with Buster v. Newkirk*, 20 Johns. (N.Y.) 75 (1822) (awarding deer to hunter who actually killed deer that other hunter had wounded and pursued).

2. *Public Policy and Empirical Judgments in Judicial Decisionmaking*. In *Pierson v. Post,* the majority and dissenting opinions reach very different conclusions on how best to apply the principle of first possession, likely because (as Rose suggests) different policy objectives motivated each judge. What objectives did the majority seek to advance to justify its conclusion? The dissent? Did each side articulate a rule well-suited to accomplish its objective? What empirical evidence (if any) did the majority and the dissent have to support their conclusions about the likely effect of their respective rules? [Looking at the *Pierson v. Post* case 200 years later, do you think that time justified or disproved the empirical assumptions made by the majority? By the dissent?]

3. *Arbitration as an Alternative to Trial*. Livingston's dissent suggested that the dispute "should have been submitted to the arbitration of sportsmen." Conceivably, Livingston may have meant only that the court should establish the rule of decision by adopting the custom of hunters. Livingston's reference to a "court" of hunters, however, seems to envision a private tribunal for resolving hunting disputes. What are the characteristics of arbitration, and what are the advantages of those characteristics that would make it preferable (in this instance) to judicial trial?

Speed, Lower Costs and Informality. One of the most frequent claims made on behalf of arbitration is that it is faster and cheaper than the courts. Its proponents often focus on the long waiting time for trial in some jurisdictions and the large legal and expert witness fees generated by extensive pre-trial discovery and long, complex trials.…

Informality is praised because it is one of the reasons arbitration can be faster and cheaper than the courts and because it is considered a desirable goal in itself. Although discovery is available in some arbitration systems, it typically is not used as much as in court proceedings. Although evidentiary objections are made in arbitration hearings, most arbitrators do not apply the strict rules of evidence. The practice of filing numerous motions is not widespread in arbitration. The limited review of arbitration awards by courts discourages costly and time consuming appeals. These and other differences between arbitration and traditional litigation create the potential for saving time and money.

It has been argued that adjudication that is less formal also can promote a perception of greater fairness and increase the satisfaction of those who participate in the proceedings. For example, nonlawyers do not normally communicate in a way that consistently satisfies the rules of evidence.… [F]rustration and dissatisfaction result from constraints placed on witnesses' ability to tell their stories in their own way and … they do not understand courts' explanations about why their narratives are unacceptable.… [W]hile disputants prefer giving control of the final decision to a third party, they prefer procedures that give them control over the way evidence is presented.

A More Suitable Decisionmaker. This claim on arbitration's behalf is usually stated in terms of the decisionmaker's expertise. It is helpful to shift the focus somewhat and emphasize the ability of the parties to decide the characteristics desired in the decisionmaker. In one case the parties may want a person with in-depth specialized knowledge—an engineer for instance—to decide a technical issue in a dispute over a construction contract.… In other cases the parties might prefer an arbitrator who knows nothing of the subject matter but has a reputation for good judgment and objectivity. Most commentators believe the ability of the parties to choose the decisionmaker is one of arbitration's principal advantages. It is the best insurance the parties have that the arbitrator not only will make an objective decision based upon the evidence and argument, but will be sensitive to the needs of the parties and their relationship. An arbitrator who consistently fails to satisfy the parties' expectations becomes unacceptable and is not used in future cases. Others view the power to choose the decisionmaker as one of arbitration's principal weaknesses because it encourages arbitrators to make compromise decisions in order to remain acceptable.

Privacy. The arbitration hearing may be conducted in private and the parties have some control over who has access to the arbitrator's opinion and award. This degree of privacy is not typical in the courts. Parties who believe that public access to the hearing or decision might result in competitive or other disadvantages consider arbitration's relative privacy one of its significant advantages.

Party Autonomy. In general, the parties have more control over the handling of their dispute when they arbitrate than when they go to court. As already noted, arbitrating parties have the power to choose the neutral decisionmaker. The parties also may select the substantive standards that govern the arbitrator's decision ... and the procedure for processing the dispute. [Leonard L. Riskin & James E. Westbrook, Dispute Resolution and Lawyers (2d ed. 1993), at 570–72.]

Which of these characteristics seem particularly appropriate as applied to hunting disputes? Why do you think the parties in *Pierson v. Post* did not submit the dispute to an informal panel of hunters? What does this suggest to you, if anything, about the viability or usefulness of arbitration as an alternative to trial once a dispute arises? *Id.* at 526–552 (discussing contractual agreements to arbitrate and their enforceability).

4. *Applying Custom as the Rule of Decision.* As Professor Robert Ellickson explained in his book *Order Without Law: How Neighbors Settle Disputes* (1991), customs often develop because over time, members of a particular culture behave in a fashion that they consider to be efficient or "utility-maximizing." According to Professor Richard Epstein, if the majority in *Pierson v. Post* had used local hunting customs to establish the rule of decision, Post would have won the case, as "it appeared from the record that all hunters in the region regarded hot pursuit as giving rights to take an unimpeded first possession." Richard A. Epstein, *Possession as the Root of Title*, 13 Ga. L. Rev. 1221, 1231 (1979). Assuming that is factually correct, should the court have disregarded this custom? When is it appropriate for courts to adopt (or reject) custom as a basis for allocating property rights? For example, suppose that the San Francisco Giants had attempted to reclaim title to Barry Bonds' 73rd home run ball from the fan that caught it. How should a court resolve that dispute? What information would you consider relevant to the resolution of that dispute?

5. *Capture, Constructive Possession, and First-in-Time.* The fox hunt that provoked *Pierson v. Post* took place on "waste land." Suppose the hunt had taken place upon land that Post actively cultivated and that Pierson had entered Post's land without permission. Under those facts, the court likely would have ruled that even though Post had not physically captured the fox, Post nevertheless "constructively possessed" the fox at the time Pierson shot it, based upon Post's possession of the land in question. In that case, then, the court likely would have held that Post was the first to "possess" the fox and thus had a property claim superior to that of Pierson. *See, e.g., State v. Repp*, 104 Iowa 305, 73 N.W. 829 (1898). Does Professor Rose's article help explain why the law takes this view?

6. *Capture, Constructive Possession, and Escape.* When a captured wild animal escapes and regains its liberty, the captor's claim to possession generally (but not always) lapses, and the animal again becomes an "unowned" object subject to the rule of capture. This rule will not apply, however, if the animal is domesticated or has a habit of returning (*animus revertendi*), or in some instances, when the original possessor is in pursuit of the animal. *See, e.g., Wiley v. Baker*, 597 S.W.2d 3 (Tex. Civ. App. 1980); *Hughes v. Reese*, 144 Miss. 304, 109 So. 731 (1926). What policy reasons support these exceptions to the rule of capture?

Suppose that a siberian tiger escapes from the Busch and Barney Circus. Westbrook, a rancher, shoots the tiger while it is mauling several of his sheep. The Circus asks Westbrook to return the tiger and offers to pay for any damages it caused. Westbrook refuses. The Circus inquires whether it has a claim for the animal or its value. What advice would you offer the Circus? *See E. A. Stephens & Co. v. Albers*, 81 Colo. 488, 256 P. 15 (1927).

7. *Interference with Capture.* Suppose that Barnes owns a commercial hunting tour business in the Rocky Mountain region. Barnes was leading a group of clients on an elk hunt when activists from Animal Freedom began tailing Barnes's group, sounding horns to scare away any elk. This interference has continued for two weeks, reducing the yield from Barnes's hunting parties by 90% over typical levels. Barnes sues Animal Freedom to recover the market value of the lost elk under a conversion theory, asserting constructive possession over the elk. What result should the court reach, and why? Could Barnes successfully proceed under any other legal theory? *See, e.g., Keeble v. Hickeringill*, 11 East 574 (Q.B. 1707) (awarding damages where defendant used loud noise to scare ducks away from plaintiff's commercial decoy pond). Should it matter when Barnes was hunting? Where? What type of game? What if a state statute criminalized Animal Freedom's conduct as "hunter harassment"? *See, e.g., People v. Sanders*, 182 Ill.2d 524, 231 Ill.Dec. 573, 696 N.E.2d 1144 (1998).

Before you conclude that *Pierson v. Post* is a quaint 200-year-old case that is no longer relevant because today nearly everything (other than perhaps wild animals) has an owner already, think again.

POPOV v. HAYASHI

Superior Court of San Francisco County, California.
2002 WL 31833731.

[Editors' Note: On October 7, 2001, at Pacific Bell Park (now renamed SBC Park) in San Francisco, Barry Bonds of the San Francisco Giants hit his 73rd home run of the 2001 baseball season, setting a new Major League Baseball season record. Bonds hit the home run into the arcade, a standing-room area beyond the right field wall. Among the crowd were Alex Popov—who allegedly caught the ball—and Patrick Hayashi, who eventually ended up with the ball. As the ball landed, a melee resulted—captured on videotape by a local news reporter, Josh Keppel. Eventually, Popov sued Hayashi for conversion of the ball.]

McCarthy, J. . . . When the seventy-third home run ball went into the arcade, it landed in the upper portion of the webbing of a softball glove worn by Alex Popov. While the glove stopped the trajectory of the ball, it is not at all clear that the ball was secure. Popov had to reach for the ball and in doing so, may have lost his balance.

Even as the ball was going into his glove, a crowd of people began to engulf Mr. Popov. He was tackled and thrown to the ground while still in the process of attempting to complete the catch. Some people intentionally descended on him for the purpose of taking the ball away, while others were involuntarily forced to the ground by the momentum of the crowd.

Eventually, Mr. Popov was buried face down on the ground under several layers of people. At one point he had trouble breathing. Mr. Popov was grabbed, hit and kicked. People reached underneath him in the area of his glove. Neither the tape nor the testimony is sufficient to establish which individual members of the crowd were responsible for the assaults on Mr. Popov. . . .

Mr. Popov intended at all times to establish and maintain possession of the ball. At some point the ball left his glove and ended up on the ground. It is impossible to establish the exact point in time that this occurred or what caused it to occur.

Mr. Hayashi was standing near Mr. Popov when the ball came into the stands. He, like Mr. Popov, was involuntarily forced to the ground. He committed no wrongful act. While on the ground he saw the loose ball. He picked it up, rose to his feet and put it in his pocket. . . .

Perhaps the most critical factual finding of all is one that cannot be made. We will never know if Mr. Popov would have been able to retain control of the ball had the crowd not interfered with his efforts to do so. Resolution of that question is the work of a psychic, not a judge. . . .

Conversion does not exist . . . unless the baseball rightfully belongs to Mr. Popov. One who has neither title nor possession, nor any right to possession, cannot sue for conversion. The deciding question in this case, then, is whether Mr. Popov achieved possession or the right to possession as he attempted to catch and hold on to the ball. . . .

Mr. Hayashi argues that possession does not occur until the fan has complete control of the ball. Professor Brian Gray suggests the following definition:

> A person who catches a baseball that enters the stands is its owner. A ball is caught if the person has achieved complete control of the ball at the point in time that the momentum of the ball and the momentum of the fan while attempting to catch the ball ceases. A baseball, which is dislodged by incidental contact with an inanimate object or another person, before momentum has ceased, is not possessed. Incidental contact with another person is contact that is not intended by the other person. The first person to pick up a loose ball and secure it becomes its possessor.

Mr. Popov argues that this definition requires that a person seeking to establish possession must show unequivocal dominion and control, a standard rejected by several leading cases. Instead, he offers the perspectives of Professor [Roger] Bernhardt and Professor Paul Finkelman who suggest that possession occurs when an individual intends to take control of a ball and manifests that intent by stopping the forward momentum of the ball whether or not complete control is achieved.

Professors Finkelman and Bernhardt have correctly pointed out that some cases recognize possession even before absolute dominion and control is achieved. Those cases require the actor to be actively and ably engaged in efforts to establish complete control. Moreover, such efforts must be significant and they must be reasonably calculated to result in unequivocal dominion and control at some point in the near future.

This rule is applied in cases involving the hunting or fishing of wild animals or the salvage of sunken vessels. The hunting and fishing cases recognize that a mortally wounded animal may run for a distance before falling. The hunter acquires possession upon the act of wounding the animal—not the eventual capture. Similarly, whalers acquire possession by landing a harpoon, not by subduing the animal.

In the salvage cases, an individual may take possession of a wreck by exerting as much control "as its nature and situation permit." Inadequate efforts, however, will not support a claim of possession. Thus, a "sailor cannot assert a claim merely by boarding a vessel and publishing a notice, unless such acts are coupled with a then present intention of conducting salvage operations, and he immediately thereafter proceeds with activity in the form of constructive steps to aid the distressed party."

These rules are contextual in nature. They are crafted in response to the unique nature of the conduct they seek to regulate. Moreover, they are influenced by the custom and practice of each industry. The reason that absolute dominion and control is not required to establish possession in the cases cited by Mr. Popov is that such a rule would be unworkable and unreasonable. The "nature and situation" of the property at issue does not immediately lend itself to unequivocal dominion and control. It is impossible to wrap one's arms around a whale, a fleeing fox or a sunken ship.

The opposite is true of a baseball hit into the stands of a stadium. Not only is it physically possible for a person to acquire unequivocal dominion and control of an abandoned baseball, but fans generally expect a claimant to have accomplished as much. The custom and practice of the stands creates a reasonable expectation that a person will achieve full control of a ball before claiming possession. There is no reason for the legal rule to be inconsistent with that expectation. Therefore [Professor] Gray's Rule is adopted as the definition of possession in this case.

The central tenet of [Professor] Gray's Rule is that the actor must retain control of the ball after incidental contact with people and things. Mr. Popov has not established by a preponderance of the evidence that he would have retained control of the ball after all momentum ceased and after any incidental contact with people or objects. Consequently, he did not achieve full possession.

That finding, however, does not resolve the case. The reason we do not know whether Mr. Popov would have retained control of the ball is not because of incidental contact. It is because he was attacked. His efforts to establish possession were interrupted by the collective assault of a band of wrongdoers. A decision which ignored that fact would endorse the actions of the crowd by not repudiating them. Judicial rulings, particularly in cases that receive media attention, affect the way people conduct themselves. This case demands vindication of an important principle. We are a nation governed by law, not by brute force.

As a matter of fundamental fairness, Mr. Popov should have had the opportunity to try to complete his catch unimpeded by unlawful activity. To hold otherwise would be to allow the result in this case to be dictated by violence. That will not happen. For these reasons, the analysis cannot stop with the valid observation that Mr. Popov has not proved full possession.

The legal question presented at this point is whether an action for conversion can proceed where the plaintiff has failed to establish possession or title. It can. An action for conversion may be brought where the plaintiff has title, possession or the right to possession.

Here Mr. Popov seeks, in effect, a declaratory judgment that he has either possession or the right to possession. In addition he seeks the remedies of injunctive relief and a constructive trust. These are all actions in equity. A court sitting in equity has the authority to fashion rules and remedies designed to achieve fundamental fairness.

Consistent with this principle, the court adopts the following rule. Where an actor undertakes significant but incomplete steps to achieve possession of a piece of abandoned personal property and the effort is interrupted by the unlawful acts of others, the actor has a legally cognizable pre-possessory interest in the property. That pre-possessory interest constitutes a qualified right to possession which can support a cause of action for conversion.

Possession can be likened to a journey down a path. Mr. Popov began his journey unimpeded. He was fast approaching a fork in the road. A turn in one direction would lead to possession of the ball—he would complete the catch. A turn in the other direction would result in a failure to achieve possession—he would drop the ball. Our problem is that before Mr. Popov got to the point where the road forked, he was set upon by a gang of bandits, who dislodged the ball from his grasp.

Recognition of a legally protected pre-possessory interest vests Mr. Popov with a qualified right to possession and enables him to advance a legitimate claim to the baseball based on a conversion theory. Moreover it addresses the harm done by the unlawful actions of the crowd.

It does not, however, address the interests of Mr. Hayashi. The court is required to balance the interests of all parties.

Mr. Hayashi was not a wrongdoer. He was a victim of the same bandits that attacked Mr. Popov. The difference is that he was able to extract himself from their assault and move to the side of the road. It was there that he discovered the loose ball. When he picked up and put it in his pocket he attained unequivocal dominion and control.

If Mr. Popov had achieved complete possession before Mr. Hayashi got the ball, those actions would not have divested Mr. Popov of any rights, nor would they have created any rights to which Mr. Hayashi could lay claim. Mr. Popov, however, was able to establish only a qualified pre-possessory interest in the ball. That interest does not establish a full right to possession that is protected from a subsequent legitimate claim.

On the other hand, while Mr. Hayashi appears on the surface to have done everything necessary to claim full possession of the ball, the ball itself is encumbered by the qualified pre-possessory interest of Mr. Popov. At the time Mr. Hayashi came into possession of the ball, it had, in effect, a cloud on its title.

An award of the ball to Mr. Popov would be unfair to Mr. Hayashi. It would be premised on the assumption that Mr. Popov would have caught the ball. That assumption is not supported by the facts. An award of the ball to Mr. Hayashi would unfairly penalize Mr. Popov. It would be based on the assumption that Mr. Popov would have dropped the ball. That conclusion is also unsupported by the facts.

Both men have a superior claim to the ball as against all the world. Each man has a claim of equal dignity as to the other. We are, therefore, left with something of a dilemma.

Thankfully, there is a middle ground. The concept of equitable division was fully explored in a law review article authored by Professor R.H. Helmholz in the December 1983 edition of the Fordham Law Review. Professor Helmholz addressed the problems associated with rules governing finders of lost and mislaid property. For a variety of reasons not directly relevant to the issues raised in this case, Helmholz suggested employing the equitable remedy of division to resolve competing claims between finders of lost or mislaid property and the owners of land on which the property was found....

The principle at work here is that where more than one party has a valid claim to a single piece of property, the court will recognize an undivided interest in the property in proportion to the strength of the claim....

Mr. Hayashi's claim is compromised by Mr. Popov's pre-possessory interest. Mr. Popov cannot demonstrate full control.... Their legal claims are of equal quality and they are equally entitled to the ball.

The court therefore declares that both plaintiff and defendant have an equal and undivided interest in the ball. Plaintiff's cause of action for conversion is sustained only as to his equal and undivided interest. In order to effectuate this ruling, the ball must be sold and the proceeds divided equally between the parties....

Notes

1. *The Rest of the Story.* Following this opinion, Popov and Hayashi agreed to sell the ball and split the proceeds evenly. Despite earlier predictions that the ball would fetch between $1 million and $1.5 million at auction, the ball was sold at auction to Todd MacFarlane (creator of the Spawn comics) for only $450,000—a veritable bargain for MacFarlane by comparison to the $3 million he paid for Mark McGwire's then-record 70th home run ball in 1999.

Hayashi's attorney represented him on a contingency fee, receiving a percentage of Hayashi's half of the sale proceeds. Popov, however, retained his lawyer on an hourly fee basis—and by the conclusion of the case, it appears that Popov's legal fees exceeded his share of the sale proceeds. Eventually, when Mr. Popov was unable (or unwilling) to pay his legal bill, his lawyer sued him to collect the unpaid fees. [As a law student and as a prospective lawyer, what strikes you most about the plight of Mr. Popov?]

Keppel sold the videotape, which now plays a central role in the documentary film, "Up for Grabs." The film chronicles the dispute between Popov and Hayashi.

2. *The* Popov *Opinion and First-in-Time.* We will return later in this chapter to the law of finders, and to discuss Professor Helmholz's "equitable division" concept (a concept that courts have rarely used, even to resolve finding disputes). At this point, focus your attention instead on whether the court's decision is consistent with the notion of "first possession." Is "first possession" inherently "win-lose" in nature? If Popov had a "pre-possessory" interest in the ball sufficient to support a conversion claim, how can Hayashi have been the first to possess the ball? Think critically about this opinion: Does Judge McCarthy's opinion reflect reasoned legal analysis, or an inability to make up his mind?

3. *The* Popov *Opinion and Public Policy.* In *Pierson*, the majority justified its rule as appropriate to prevent similar disputes in the future. Is this concern appropriate in a case like *Popov*—and if so, how should that concern influence the analysis of the dispute?

Note that on September 17, 2004, Bonds hit his 700th career home run. As soon as the ball landed in the outfield seats, another melee broke out. Steve Williams emerged from the crowd with the ball, but was later sued for conversion by Timothy Murphy—who alleged that he had secured the ball and that Williams wrested it from him in the melee. Murphy's lawsuit was eventually dismissed, and Williams sold the ball for $804,129 in an online auction. As Bonds approaches and/or passes Hank Aaron's career home run record, can we realistically expect anything other than more melees whenever a landmark home run falls into the seats? Does the court's ruling in *Popov* make such melees more or less likely? What solution(s) might more effectively diminish the risk of such melees?

LAWYERING EXERCISE
(Client Counseling and Fact Investigation)

BACKGROUND: A basic appreciation of interpersonal communication and its shortcomings is critical to developing effective counseling skills:

> Clients often substitute conclusions or judgments for evidentiary detail. Conclusions characterize or judge data rather than describe it. For example, a client characterizes data by saying that "The meeting was a *quick* one;" "Jan spoke in an *angry* tone of voice;" "Hilary *screamed* when her hamster died."
>
> To probe conclusions masking evidentiary detail, simply ask clients to relate the bases for their conclusions. For example, if a client states, "The robber became enraged when the alarm went off," ask what behavior of the robber led the client to that conclusion: "What did the robber do that leads you to say that he became enraged?" Similarly, if a client states, "The meeting was lengthy," you may ask: "How long was it?"
>
> Unless you probe conclusions, you will fill in stories with information drawn from your own experiences. A client may consider a 10 minute meeting to be "lengthy," whereas after a few months of law practice you may regard any meeting of less than an hour as a quickie. And be warned that clients are prone to conclusions. To repeat, very little about everyday social discourse encourages people to describe happenings in great detail. [David A. Binder, Paul Bergman & Susan Price, Lawyers as Counselors 186–87 (1991).]

SITUATION: An irate client, Pushaw, storms into your office and demands that you represent him against Lawless in a suit to recover 3,000 pounds of fish or their value. He relates that he has just come from his boat and that he wants to bring the action because Lawless "stole his fish." Pushaw tells you that he had "trapped" a large school of fish in a cove so that the fish could not escape, when Lawless entered the cove in a small boat and netted most of the fish.

TASK: In advising Pushaw, what additional information do you need to gather before you can evaluate his situation? What additional questions would you ask? *Compare Young v. Hichens*, 1 Dav. & Mer. 592, 6 Q.B. 606, 115 Eng.Rep. 228 (Queen's Bench 1844) *with State v. Shaw*, 67 Ohio St. 157, 65 N.E. 875 (1902).

———————

As the following materials suggest, the law has also applied the "first-in-time" rule as a means of resolving conflicting ownership claims with regard to land. So who was "first" to "possess" the land on the North American continent—European colonizers, or its native inhabitants?

JOHNSON v. M'INTOSH

Supreme Court of the United States.
8 Wheat. 543, 21 U.S. 543, 5 L.Ed. 681 (1823).

Handwritten margin note: procedural notes & case issue

MR. CHIEF JUSTICE MARSHALL delivered the opinion of the Court. The plaintiffs in this cause claim the land, in their declaration mentioned, under two grants, purporting to be made, the first in 1773, and the last in 1775, by the chiefs of certain Indian tribes, constituting the Illinois and the Piankeshaw nations; and the question is, whether this title can be recognised in the Courts of the United States?

Handwritten margin note: Deeds from Indian tribes to non-indian purchasers

[Editors' Note: The lands in question covered a large portion of what later became Illinois and Indiana. The 1773 deed was from the Illinois Indian tribe to a group of non-Indian purchasers and the 1775 deed was from the Piankeshaw Indians to another group of non-Indian purchasers. The 1775 purchasers included Thomas Johnson Jr., who died in 1819, leaving his interest to his son, Joshua Johnson, and grandson, Thomas J. Graham (the plaintiffs). M'Intosh purchased his interest in 1818 from the United States government, which had acquired title to the lands through treaties signed with the Indians sometime after the 1773 and 1775 conveyances.]

Handwritten margin note: Both defendant & plaintiff claim property is theirs.

The facts, as stated in the case agreed, show the authority of the chiefs who executed this conveyance, so far as it could be given by their own people; and likewise show, that the particular tribes for whom these chiefs acted were in rightful possession of the land they sold. The inquiry, therefore, is, in a great measure, confined to the power of Indians to give, and of private individuals to receive, a title which can be sustained in the Courts of this country.

As the right of society, to prescribe those rules by which property may be acquired and preserved is not, and cannot be drawn into question; as the title to lands, especially, is and must be admitted to depend entirely on the law of the nation in which they lie; it will be necessary, in pursuing this inquiry, to examine, not singly those principles of abstract justice, which the Creator of all things has impressed on the mind of his creature man, and which are admitted to regulate, in a great degree, the rights of civilized nations, whose perfect independence is acknowledged; but those principles also which our own government has adopted in the particular case, and given us as the rule for our decision.

Handwritten margin note: Europeans, upon discovery sought to acquire vast land

On the discovery of this immense continent, the great nations of Europe were eager to appropriate to themselves so much of it as they could respectively acquire. Its vast extent offered an ample field to the ambition and enterprise of all; and the character and religion of its inhabitants afforded an apology for considering them as a people over whom the superior genius of Europe might claim an ascendency. The potentates of the old world found no difficulty in convincing themselves that they made ample compensation to the inhabitants of the new, by bestowing on them civilization and Christianity, in exchange for unlimit-ed independence. But, as they were all in pursuit of nearly the same object, it was necessary, in order to avoid conflicting settlements, and consequent war with each other, to establish a principle, which all should acknowledge as the law by which the right of acquisition, which they all asserted, should be regulated as between themselves. This principle was, that discovery gave title to the government by whose subjects, or by whose authority, it was made, against all other European governments, which title might be consummated by possession.

[margin note: original principle of ownership in the U.S.]

The exclusion of all other Europeans, necessarily gave to the nation making the discovery the sole right of acquiring the soil from the natives, and establishing settlements upon it. It was a right with which no Europeans could interfere. It was a right which all asserted for themselves, and to the assertion of which, by others, all assented. Those relations which were to exist between the discoverer and the natives, were to be regulated by themselves. The rights thus acquired being exclusive, no other power could interpose between them.

In the establishment of these relations, the rights of the original inhabitants were, in no instance, entirely disregarded; but were neces-sarily, to a considerable extent, impaired. They were admitted to be the rightful occupants of the soil, with a legal as well as just claim to retain possession of it, and to use it according to their own discretion; but their rights to complete sovereignty, as independent nations, were necessarily diminished, and their power to dispose of the soil at their own will, to whomsoever they pleased, was denied by the original fundamental prin-ciple, that discovery gave exclusive title to those who made it.

[margin note: New comers possessed dominion over native land]

While the different nations of Europe respected the right of the natives, as occupants, they asserted the ultimate dominion to be in themselves; and claimed and exercised, as a consequence of this ultimate dominion, a power to grant the soil, while yet in possession of the natives. These grants have been understood by all, to convey a title to the grantees, subject only to the Indian right of occupancy.

The history of America, from its discovery to the present day, proves, we think, the universal recognition of these principles.... [Edi-tors' Note: The Court gives examples in which Spain, France, Portugal, and Holland relied upon "the rights given by discovery."]

No one of the powers of Europe gave its full assent to this principle, more unequivocally than England. The documents upon this subject are ample and complete. So early as the year 1496, her monarch granted a commission to the Cabots, to discover countries then unknown to *Chris-tian people*, and to take possession of them in the name of the king of England. Two years afterwards, Cabot proceeded on this voyage, and discovered the continent of North America, along which he sailed as far south as Virginia. To this discovery the English trace their title.

In this first effort made by the English government to acquire territory on this continent, we perceive a complete recognition of the principle which has been mentioned. The right of discovery given by this commission, is confined to countries "then unknown to all Christian people;" and of these countries Cabot was empowered to take possession in the name of the king of England. Thus asserting a right to take possession, notwithstanding the occupancy of the natives, who were heathens, and, at the same time, admitting the prior title of any Christian people who may have made a previous discovery....

[Editors' Note: Chief Justice Marshall then considered whether the principle had been accepted by the American states. He concluded, based upon the Louisiana Purchase and other land transactions with European nations, that the American states in fact recognized titles based upon the discovery rule.]

discovery rule accepted by the louisianna purchase

The United States, then, have unequivocally acceded to that great and broad rule by which its civilized inhabitants now hold this country. They hold, and assert in themselves, the title by which it was acquired. They maintain, as all others have maintained, that discovery gave an exclusive right to extinguish the Indian title of occupancy, either by purchase or by conquest; and gave also a right to such a degree of sovereignty, as the circumstances of the people would allow them to exercise.

discovery gave right to extinguish the native's titles

The power now possessed by the government of the United States to grant lands, resided, while we were colonies, in the crown, or its grantees. The validity of the titles given by either has never been questioned in our Courts. It has been exercised uniformly over territory in possession of the Indians. The existence of this power must negative the existence of any right which may conflict with, and control it. An absolute title to lands cannot exist, at the same time, in different persons, or in different governments. An absolute, must be an exclusive title, or at least a title which excludes all others not compatible with it. All our institutions recognise the absolute title of the crown, subject only to the Indian right of occupancy, and recognise the absolute title of the crown to extinguish that right. This is incompatible with an absolute and complete title in the Indians.

Absolute title

We will not enter into the controversy, whether agriculturists, merchants, and manufacturers, have a right, on abstract principles, to expel hunters from the territory they possess, or to contract their limits. Conquest gives a title which the Courts of the conqueror cannot deny, whatever the private and speculative opinions of individuals may be, respecting the original justice of the claim which has been successfully asserted. The British government, which was then our government, and whose rights have passed to the United States, asserted title to all the lands occupied by Indians, within the chartered limits of the British colonies. It asserted also a limited sovereignty over them, and the exclusive right of extinguishing the title which occupancy gave to them. These claims have been maintained and established as far west as the river Mississippi, by the sword. The title to a vast portion of the lands we now hold, originates in them. It is not for the Courts of this country to

Brittish & U.S rights to Indian lands

question the validity of this title, or to sustain one which is incompatible with it.

Although we do not mean to engage in the defence of those principles which Europeans have applied to Indian title, they may, we think, find some excuse, if not justification, in the character and habits of the people whose rights have been wrested from them.

The title by conquest is acquired and maintained by force. The conqueror prescribes its limits. Humanity, however, acting on public opinion, has established, as a general rule, that the conquered shall not be wantonly oppressed, and that their condition shall remain as eligible as is compatible with the objects of the conquest. Most usually, they are incorporated with the victorious nation, and become subjects or citizens of the government with which they are connected. The new and old members of the society mingle with each other; the distinction between them is gradually lost, and they make one people. Where this incorporation is practicable, humanity demands, and a wise policy requires, that the rights of the conquered to property should remain unimpaired; that the new subjects should be governed as equitably as the old, and that confidence in their security should gradually banish the painful sense of being separated from their ancient connexions, and united by force to strangers.

When the conquest is complete, and the conquered inhabitants can be blended with the conquerors, or safely governed as a distinct people, public opinion, which not even the conqueror can disregard, imposes these restraints upon him; and he cannot neglect them without injury to his fame, and hazard to his power.

But the tribes of Indians inhabiting this country were fierce savages, whose occupation was war, and whose subsistence was drawn chiefly from the forest. To leave them in possession of their country, was to leave the country a wilderness; to govern them as a distinct people, was impossible, because they were as brave and as high spirited as they were fierce, and were ready to repel by arms every attempt on their independence.

[handwritten margin note: tribes were savage? had to be dealt with]

What was the inevitable consequence of this state of things? The Europeans were under the necessity either of abandoning the country, and relinquishing their pompous claims to it, or of enforcing those claims by the sword, and by the adoption of principles adapted to the condition of a people with whom it was impossible to mix, and who could not be governed as a distinct society, or of remaining in their neighbourhood, and exposing themselves and their families to the perpetual hazard of being massacred.

[handwritten margin note: reflecting on past experiences of relations w/ Native Americans]

Frequent and bloody wars, in which the whites were not always the aggressors, unavoidably ensued. European policy, numbers, and skill, prevailed. As the white population advanced, that of the Indians necessarily receded. The country in the immediate neighbourhood of agriculturists became unfit for them. The game fled into thicker and more unbroken forests, and the Indians followed. The soil, to which the crown originally claimed title, being no longer occupied by its ancient inhabit-ants, was parcelled out according to the will of the sovereign power, and taken possession of by persons who claimed immediately from the crown, or mediately, through its grantees or deputies.

That law which regulates, and ought to regulate in general, the relations between the conqueror and conquered, was incapable of appli-cation to a people under such circumstances. The resort to some new and different rule, better adapted to the actual state of things, was unavoid-able. Every rule which can be suggested will be found to be attended with great difficulty.

However extravagant the pretension of converting the discovery of an inhabited country into conquest may appear; if the principle has been asserted in the first instance, and afterwards sustained; if a country has been acquired and held under it; if the property of the great mass of the community originates in it, it becomes the law of the land, and cannot be questioned. So, too, with respect to the concomitant principle, that the Indian inhabitants are to be considered merely as occupants, to be protected, indeed, while in peace, in the possession of their lands, but to be deemed incapable of transferring the absolute title to others. However this restriction may be opposed to natural right, and to the usages of civilized nations, yet, if it be indispensable to that system under which the country has been settled, and be adapted to the actual condition of the two people, it may, perhaps, be supported by reason, and certainly cannot be rejected by Courts of justice. . . .

After bestowing on this subject a degree of attention which was more required by the magnitude of the interest in litigation, and the able and elaborate arguments of the bar, than by its intrinsic difficulty, the Court is decidedly of opinion, that the plaintiffs do not exhibit a title which can be sustained in the Courts of the United States; and that there is no error in the judgment which was rendered against them in the District Court of Illinois.

Judgment affirmed, with costs.

Notes

1. *Discovery and the "First in Time" Principle.* Johnson's predeces-sor's claim dated to 1775—well before the U.S. (from whom M'Intosh claimed title) entered a treaty with the Piankeshaw tribe. What reasoning does the Court employ to determine that M'Intosh's title was superior to that of Johnson? Is this decision consistent with the "first in time" principle expressed in *Pierson v. Post*? Chief Justice Marshall asserts that "discovery" gave the discoverer the exclusive right to acquire the soil from the natives. How can property be "discovered" if it is already occupied by someone else?

2. *Absolute Title v. Occupancy.* Chief Justice Marshall states that the Native Americans did not have "absolute title" to the property, but he concedes that they did have "title of occupancy." What is the difference between absolute title and occupancy? What rights are encompassed by

absolute title? What rights are encompassed by occupancy? How can both of these rights co-exist in the same tract of land? Can you think of any modern day examples of property rights that are similar to the Native Americans' title of occupancy?

3. *What Constitutes Possession?* According to Professor Rose, the defendants in *Johnson v. M'Intosh* argued that the Native Americans could not have passed title to Johnson's predecessors because the Native Americans had never undertaken sufficient acts of possession to establish a property right. Would you agree? Consider Professor Rose's analysis:

Professor Rose's analysis on possession ↳

[T]here was indeed something to the argument from the point of view of the common law of first possession. Insofar as the Indian tribes moved from place to place, they left few traces to indicate that they claimed the land (if indeed they did make such claims). From an eighteenth-century political economist's point of view, the results were horrifying. What seemed to be the absence of distinct claims to land among the Indians merely invited disputes, which in turn meant constant disruption of productive activity and dissipation of energy in warfare. Uncertainty as to claims also meant that no one would make any productive use of the land because there is little incentive to plant when there is no reasonable assurance that one will be in possession of the land at harvest time. From this classical economic perspective, the Indians' alleged indifference to well-defined property lines in land was part and parcel of what seemed to be their relatively unproductive use of the earth.

Now it may well be that North American Indian tribes were not so indifferent to marking out landed property as eighteenth-century European commentators supposed. Or it may be that at least some tribes found landed property less important to their security than other forms of property and thus felt no need to assert claims to property in land. But however anachronistic the Johnson parties' (ultimately mooted) argument may now seem, it is a particularly striking example of the relativity of the "text" of possession to the interpretative community for that text. It is doubtful whether the claims of any nomadic population could ever meet the common law requirements for establishing property in land. Thus, the audience presupposed by the common law of first possession is an agrarian or a commercial people—a people whose activities with respect to the objects around them require an unequivocal delineation of lasting control so that those objects can be managed and traded.

But perhaps the deepest aspect of the common law text of possession lies in the attitude that this text strikes with respect to the relationship between human beings and nature. At least some Indians professed bewilderment at the concept of owning the land. Indeed they prided themselves on not marking the land but rather on moving lightly through it, living with the land and with its creatures as members of the same family rather than as strangers who visited only to conquer the objects of nature. The doctrine of first possession, quite to the contrary, reflects the attitude that human beings are outsiders to nature. It gives the earth and its creatures over to those who mark them so clearly as to transform them, so that no one else will mistake them for unsubdued nature.

We may admire nature and enjoy wildness, but those sentiments find little resonance in the doctrine of first possession. Its texts are those of cultivation, manufacture, and development. We cannot have our fish both loose and fast, as Melville might have said, and the common law of first possession makes a choice. The common law gives preference to those who convince the world that they have caught the fish and hold it fast. This may be a reward to useful labor, but it is more precisely the articulation of a specific vocabulary within a structure of symbols approved and understood by a commercial people. It is this commonly understood and shared set of symbols that gives significance and form to what might seem the quintessentially individualistic act: the claim that one has, by "possession," separated for oneself property from the great commons of unowned things. [Carol M. Rose, *Possession as The Origin of Property*, 52 U. Chi. L. Rev. 73, 86–88 (1985).]

4.   *Systemic Subordination—A Critical Race Perspective.* It is clear from Professor Rose's excerpt in note 3 that two different sets of rules and cultures were in conflict in *Johnson v. M'Intosh*. Why does the European concept of property prevail over the customs of the original inhabitants of the land? How does Chief Justice Marshall justify the Court's resolution of the conflicting regimes?

Marshall's opinion suggests that "the character and religion of [the country's original] inhabitants afforded an apology for considering them as a people over whom the superior genius of Europe might claim an ascendency." What bearing does religion or character have upon the determination of property rights? Is Chief Justice Marshall's statement just a relic of an unenlightened time, or is it illustrative of a discriminatory property scheme whose ramifications are still felt today? Consider Professor Singer's observations:

The history of United States law, from the beginning of the nation to the present, is premised on the use of sovereign power to allocate property rights in ways that discriminated—and continue to discriminate—against the original inhabitants of the land.... If those who benefit from this history claim a vested right to its benefits, they should be aware that what they claim is a right to the benefits of a system of racial hierarchy.

Nor is this lesson confined to American Indian nations. Black Americans, torn from Africa, placed in slavery and then "freed," were never given the land, education, and other resources that had been available to other Americans.... We must see the ways in which the rules in force are implicated in the social construction of race. We need to understand the racial context in which property law developed and in which the distribution of wealth has been established and continues to be established....

[P]roperty rights are not self-defining. Rather, the legal system makes constant choices about which interests to define as property. It also determines how to allocate power between competing claimants when interests conflict. And the pattern of protection and vulnerability is a result of a historical and social context which has created different opportunities based on such factors as race, sex, sexual orientation, disability and class. [Joseph William Singer, *Legal Theory: Sovereignty and Property*, 86 Nw. U.L. Rev. 1, 44–45, 47 (1991).]

Can you think of other examples of ways that traditional concepts of property supported (or still support) the subordination of women or racial, ethnic, or religious minorities?

———————

How should the law deal with ownership of natural resources such as air, water, oil and gas, or minerals? Should the principle of "first-in-time" dictate allocation of property rights in such resources—and if so, how? Consider the following materials.

EDWARDS v. SIMS

Court of Appeals of Kentucky.
232 Ky. 791, 24 S.W.2d 619 (1929).

STANLEY, C. This case presents a novel question.

In the recent case of *Edwards v. Lee*, 230 Ky. 375, 19 S.W.(2d) 992, an appeal was dismissed which sought a review and reversal of an order of the Edmonson circuit court directing surveyors to enter upon and under the lands of Edwards and others and survey the Great Onyx Cave for the purpose of securing evidence on an issue as to whether or not a part of the cave being exploited and shown by the appellants runs under the ground of Lee.... It was held that the order was interlocutory and consequently one from which no appeal would lie.

Following that decision, this original proceeding was filed in this court by the appellants in that case (who were defendants below) against Hon. N.P. Sims, judge of the Edmonson circuit court, seeking a writ of prohibition to prevent him enforcing the order and punishing the petitioners for any disobedience of it. It is alleged by the petitioners that the lower court was without jurisdiction or authority to make the order, and that their cave property and their right of possession and privacy will be wrongfully and illegally invaded, and that they will be greatly and irreparably injured and damaged without having an adequate remedy .... It will thus be seen that there are submitted the two grounds upon which this court will prohibit inferior courts from proceeding, under the provisions of section 110 of the Constitution, namely: (1) Where it is a matter in which it has no jurisdiction and there is no remedy through appeal, and (2) where the court possesses jurisdiction but is exercising or about to exercise its power erroneously, and which would result in great injustice and irreparable injury to the applicant, and there is no adequate remedy by appeal or otherwise.

There is no question as to the jurisdiction of the parties and the subject-matter. It is only whether the court is proceeding erroneously within its jurisdiction in entering and enforcing the order directing the

Little authority for the rights of the caves

survey of the subterranean premises of the petitioners. There is but little authority of particular and special application to caves and cave rights. In few places, if any, can be found similar works of nature of such grandeur and of such unique and marvelous character as to give caves a commercial value sufficient to cause litigation as those peculiar to Edmonson and other counties in Kentucky.... In *Cox v. Colossal Cavern Co.*, 210 Ky. 612, 276 S.W. 540, the subject of cave rights was considered, and this court held that there may be a severance of the estate in the property, that is, that one may own the surface and another the cave rights, the conditions being quite similar to but not exactly like those of mineral lands. But there is no such severance involved in this case, as it appears that the defendants are the owners of the land and have in it an absolute right.

a person is entitled to the land above & below his property unless otherwise divided.

Cujus est solum, ejus est usque ad coelum ad infernos (to whomsoever the soil belongs, he owns also to the sky and to the depths), is an old maxim and rule. It is that the owner of realty, unless there has been a division of the estate, is entitled to the free and unfettered control of his own land above, upon, and beneath the surface. So whatever is in a direct line between the surface of the land and the center of the earth belongs to the owner of the surface. Ordinarily that ownership cannot be interfered with or infringed by third persons....

can a person trespass onto anothers property through transcendent power to ascertain the truth in a matter before it

With this doctrine of ownership in mind, we approach the question as to whether a court of equity has a transcendent power to invade that right [of ownership] through its agents for the purpose of ascertaining the truth of a matter before it, which fact thus disclosed will determine certainly whether or not the owner is trespassing upon his neighbor's property.... [T]here can be little differentiation, so far as the matter now before us is concerned, between caves and mines. And as declared in 40 C.J. 947: "A court of equity, however, has the inherent power, independent of statute, to compel a mine owner to permit an inspection of his works at the suit of a party who can show reasonable ground for suspicion that his lands are being trespassed upon through them, and may issue an injunction to permit such inspection."

There is some limitation upon this inherent power, such as that the person applying for such an inspection must show a bona fide claim and allege facts showing a necessity for the inspection and examination of the adverse party's property; and, of course, the party whose property is to be inspected must have had an opportunity to be heard in relation thereto. In the instant case it appears that these conditions were met....

We can see no difference in principle between the invasion of a mine on adjoining property to ascertain whether or not the minerals are being extracted from under the applicant's property and an inspection of this respondent's property through his cave to ascertain whether or not he is trespassing under this applicant's property.

It appears that before making this order the court had before him surveys of the surface of both properties and the conflicting opinions of witnesses as to whether or not the Great Onyx Cave extended under the surface of the plaintiff's land. This opinion evidence was of comparatively little value, and as the chancellor (now respondent) suggested, the controversy can be quickly and accurately settled by surveying the cave .... The peculiar nature of these conditions, it seems to us, makes it imperative and necessary in the administration of justice that the survey should have been ordered and should be made....

The writ of prohibition is therefore denied.

LOGAN, J. (dissenting). The majority opinion allows that to be done which will prove of incalculable injury to Edwards without benefiting Lee, who is asking that this injury be done. I must dissent from the majority opinion, confessing that I may not be able to show, by any legal precedent, that the opinion is wrong, yet having an abiding faith in my own legal judgment that it is wrong.

It deprives Edwards of rights which are valuable, and perhaps destroys the value of his property, upon the motion of one who may have no interest in that which it takes away, and who could not subject it to his dominion or make any use of it, if he should establish that which he seeks to establish in the new suit wherein the survey is sought.

It sounds well in the majority opinion to tritely say that he who owns the surface of the real estate, without reservation, owns from the center of the earth to the outmost sentinel of the solar system. The age-old statement, adhered to in the majority opinion as the law, in truth and fact, is not true now and never has been. I can subscribe to no doctrine which makes the owner of the surface also the owner of the atmosphere filling illimitable space. Neither can I subscribe to the doctrine that he who owns the surface is also the owner of the vacant spaces in the bowels of the earth.

The rule should be that he who owns the surface is the owner of everything that may be taken from the earth and used for his profit or happiness. Anything which he may take is thereby subjected to his dominion, and it may be well said that it belongs to him. I concede the soundness of that rule, which is supported by the cases cited in the majority opinion; but they have no application to the question before the court in this case. They relate mainly to mining rights; that is, to substances under the surface which the owner may subject to his dominion. But no man can bring up from the depths of the earth the Stygian darkness and make it serve his purposes; neither can he subject to his dominion the bottom of the ways in the caves on which visitors tread, and for these reasons the owner of the surface has no right in such a cave which the law should, or can, protect because he has nothing of value therein, unless, perchance, he owns an entrance into it and has subjected the subterranean passages to his dominion.

A cave or cavern should belong absolutely to him who owns its entrance, and this ownership should extend even to its utmost reaches if he has explored and connected these reaches with the entrance. When the surface owner has discovered a cave and prepared it for purposes of exhibition, no one ought to be allowed to disturb him in his dominion over that which he has conquered and subjected to his uses.

It is well enough to hang to our theories and ideas, but when there is an effort to apply old principles to present-day conditions, and they will not fit, then it becomes necessary for a readjustment, and principles and facts as they exist in this age must be made conformable. For these reasons the old sophistry that the owner of the surface of land is the owner of everything from zenith to nadir must be reformed, and the reason why a reformation is necessary is because the theory was never true in the past, but no occasion arose that required the testing of it. Man had no dominion over the air until recently, and, prior to his conquering the air, no one had any occasion to question the claim of the surface owner that the air above him should be subject to his dominion. Naturally the air above him should be subject to his dominion in so far as the use of the space is necessary for his proper enjoyment of the surface, but further than that he has no right in it separate from that of the public at large. The true principle should be announced to the effect that a man who owns the surface, without reservation, owns not only the land itself, but everything upon, above, or under it which he may use for his profit or pleasure, and which he may subject to his dominion and control. But further than this his ownership cannot extend. It should not be held that he owns that which he cannot use and which is of no benefit to him, and which may be of benefit to others.

Shall a man be allowed to stop airplanes flying above his land because he owns the surface? He cannot subject the atmosphere through which they fly to his profit or pleasure; therefore, so long as airplanes do not injure him, or interfere with the use of his property, he should be helpless to prevent their flying above his dominion. Should the waves that transmit intelligible sound through the atmosphere be allowed to pass over the lands of surface owners? If they take nothing from him and in no way interfere with his profit or pleasure, he should be powerless to prevent their passage.

If it be a trespass to enter on the premises of the landowner, ownership meaning what the majority opinion holds that it means, the aviator who flies over the land of one who owns the surface, without his consent, is guilty of a trespass as defined by the common law and is subject to fine or imprisonment, or both, in the discretion of a jury.

If he who owns the surface does not own and control the atmosphere above him, he does not own and control vacuity beneath the surface. He owns everything beneath the surface that he can subject to his profit or pleasure, but he owns nothing more. Therefore, let it be written that a man who owns land does, in truth and in fact, own everything from zenith to nadir, but only for the use that he can make of it for his profit or pleasure. He owns nothing which he cannot subject to his dominion.

In the light of these unannounced principles which ought to be the law in this modern age, let us give thought to the petitioner Edwards, his rights and his predicament, if that is done to him which the circuit

work of, people your into caves is tedious

judge has directed to be done. Edwards owns this cave through right of discovery, exploration, development, advertising, exhibition, and conquest. Men fought their way through the eternal darkness, into the mysterious and abysmal depths of the bowels of a groaning world to discover the theretofore unseen splendors of unknown natural scenic wonders. They were conquerors of fear, although now and then one of them, as did Floyd Collins, paid with his life, for his hardihood in adventuring into the regions where Charon with his boat had never before seen any but the spirits of the departed. They let themselves down by flimsy ropes into pits that seemed bottomless; they clung to scanty handholds as they skirted the brinks of precipices while the flickering flare of their flaming flambeaux disclosed no bottom to the yawning gulf beneath them; they waded through rushing torrents, not knowing what awaited them on the farther side; they climbed slippery steeps to find other levels; they wounded their bodies on stalagmites and stalactites and other curious and weird formations; they found chambers, star-studded and filled with scintillating light reflected by a phantasmagoria revealing fancied phantoms, and tapestry woven by the toiling gods in the dominion of Erebus; hunger and thirst, danger and deprivation could not stop them. Through days, weeks, months, and years—ever linking chamber with chamber, disclosing an underground land of enchantment, they continued their explorations; through the years they toiled connecting these wonders with the outside world through the entrance on the land of Edwards which he had discovered; through the years they toiled finding safe ways for those who might come to view what they had found and placed their seal upon. They knew nothing, and cared less, of who owned the surface above; they were in another world where no law forbade their footsteps. They created an underground kingdom where Gulliver's people may have lived or where Ayesha may have found the revolving column of fire in which to bathe meant eternal youth.

When the wonders were unfolded and the ways were made safe, then Edwards patiently, and again through the years, commenced the advertisement of his cave. First came one to see, then another, then two together, then small groups, then small crowds, then large crowds, and then the multitudes. Edwards had seen his faith justified. The cave was his because he had made it what it was, and without what he had done it was nothing of value. The value is not in the black vacuum that the uninitiated call a cave. That which Edwards owns is something intangible and indefinable. It is his vision translated into a reality.

Then came the horse leach's daughters crying "Give me," "give me." Then came the "surface men" crying, "I think this cave may run under my lands." They do not know they only "guess," but they seek to discover the secrets of Edwards so that they may harass him and take from him that which he has made his own. They have come to a court of equity and have asked that Edwards be forced to open his doors and his ways to them so that they may go in and despoil him; that they may lay his secrets bare so that others may follow their example and dig into the wonders which Edwards has made his own. What may be the result if they stop his ways? They destroy the cave, because those who visit it are they who give it value, and none will visit it when the ways are barred so that it may not be exhibited as a whole.

It may be that the law is as stated in the majority opinion of the court, but equity, according to my judgment, should not destroy that which belongs to one man when he at whose behest the destruction is visited, although with some legal right, is not benefited thereby. Any ruling by a court which brings great and irreparable injury to a party is erroneous. . . .

Notes

1. *The Rest of the Story.* The dispute over the Great Onyx Cave continued for seven additional years, outliving even Lee, who died prior to 1936. The litigation eventually established that one-third of the exhibited cave was located under Lee's land. To this day, the surface property line is marked inside the cave—by a pile of rocks in the upper chamber, and by an earthen dam in the lower chamber. Apparently, following the litigation, these markings identified the spots beyond which the guides were not to take paying customers, so as to avoid having to pay royalties to Lee's estate. Following Lee's death, the courts required Edwards to account to Lee's estate for one-third of the net profits previously obtained by Edwards from exhibition of the entire cave. *Edwards v. Lee's Adm'r*, 265 Ky. 418, 96 S.W.2d 1028 (1936).

2. *The Elusive Meaning of "First Possession."* The *Edwards v. Sims* case is another example of Professor Rose's suggestion that the meaning of "first possession" is extremely elusive. Both parties are essentially claiming a property interest based upon first possession, each informed by fundamentally different theories as to why the law should recognize and protect property rights. Can you explain each party's "first possession" argument and the theory of property rights underlying it?

Many readers find Judge Logan's opinion appealing as a reflection of moral distaste for Lee's actions—*i.e.*, that Lee is somehow getting a windfall profit off the sweat of Edwards's brow. Given the rhetorical force of the maxim that "one should not reap what she has not sown," why does the majority in *Edwards* refuse to grant Edwards ownership (or "sweat equity") in the cave? Does the majority decision persuasively explain why Edwards' labor does not justify allocating to him ownership rights in the cave? In considering this question, go back to note 1 and look carefully at the ultimate remedy in this case—Lee received an accounting for one-third of Edwards's net profits. Does this remedy diminish the rhetorical force of Judge Logan's dissenting opinion in any respect? If so, how?

3. *"Cujus est solum."* Taking the doctrine of *cujus est solum* literally would present some troublesome consequences. For example, suppose Brown sues to enjoin Delta Air Lines from flying directly over his land at 35,000 feet—a height at which jet engines are not audible to the average person on the ground. As Judge Logan notes in his dissent, courts have been unsympathetic to such claims and have not applied the concept of *cujus est solum*

literally in such cases. Can you explain why courts have been unsympathetic? Under what circumstances do you think courts would be sympathetic to a *cujus est solum* argument? Does Judge Logan's dissenting opinion provide a hint? *See* Richard A. Posner, Economic Analysis of Law 36 (4th ed. 1992).

The law often does take a literal view (as does Chancellor Stanley in *Edwards*) of the concept of *cujus est solum* in disputes involving *subsurface* ownership. Why is this so? What arguments can you think of in support of the majority's conclusion? Would the majority's literal view ever present troublesome consequences similar to those presented by oversurface use (such as high-altitude flight)?

4. *Property Rights in "Migratory" Resources: "Cujus est solum" Versus the Rule of Capture.* As *Edwards* suggests, the law has used the *cujus est solum* doctrine to allocate ownership of "fixed" minerals (*e.g.*, coal, rock, gold, etc.) to the owner of the surface of the land immediately above. Other resources are "migratory" in nature, however, such as groundwater or oil and gas. For example, suppose Whitfield and Hunvald own adjacent parcels of land situated atop a small aquifer. If Whitfield drills a well and begins extracting water, this extraction could easily cause water that had been located under Hunvald's land to flow underneath Whitfield's land. If this occurs, has Whitfield taken Hunvald's property?

The migratory nature of these resources makes it conceptually problematic to use a rigid line-drawing rule like *cujus est solum* to allocate property ownership in such resources. For example, consider the law of oil and gas. In some states, courts adopted the *cujus est solum* doctrine to hold that the owner of the surface land was also the owner of the oil and gas located under the surface (the "ownership-in-place" theory). In these states, however, courts also applied a "rule of capture," under which the surface owner lost title to oil and gas drained from beneath her lands by legitimate extraction by the owner of a neighboring parcel. Richard W. Hemingway, The Law of Oil and Gas § 1.3, at 26–32 (3d ed. 1991). Recognizing the fugitive nature of oil and gas, other states held that the surface owner did not actually own oil and gas located under her land until it was actually extracted and reduced to possession (the "nonownership-in-place" theory). *Id.*

Under either approach, however, owners could not obtain certain and indefeasible control over the oil without extracting it—meaning that surface owners had a significant incentive to extract as much oil as possible as quickly as possible. History tells us that the consequences of applying the capture rule to oil and gas (and other migratory resources such as wild animals) has been dramatic:

> On January 10, 1901, near Beaumont, Texas, Captain Anthony F. Lucas and his drilling team struck oil after drilling more than 1,000 feet into the Spindletop salt dome. The "black plume" that shot into the sky rose to twice the derrick height. This initial Spindletop well produced 800,000 barrels of oil in its first nine days, a world record. A hysteria of speculation followed, "with wells being drilled as close together as physically possible." By the end of 1901, 440 wells had been drilled on

the 125–acre hill where Spindletop was located. In 1904, only 100 of the 1,000 wells that had been drilled around Spindletop were producing at least 10,000 barrels per day. When Captain Lucas returned to Spindletop in 1904, he noted, "The cow was milked too hard, and moreover she was not milked intelligently." [Comment, *Of Reservoir Hogs and Pelt Fiction: Defending the* Ferae Naturae *Analogy Between Petroleum and Wildlife*, 44 Emory L.J. 697, 701 (1995).]

The same phenomenon appears with wildlife. In 25 years, the bison population fell from 60 million to fewer than 500. *Id.* at 716–18. Numerous species around the globe have been hunted to the brink of extinction. From the standpoint of developing sustainable common resources under conditions of scarcity, many have argued that the rule of capture has been a dismal failure, illustrating what Garrett Hardin predicted in his seminal article, *The Tragedy of the Commons*, 162 Science 1243 (1968)—the problem of one generation shifting the external costs of its behavior onto the next generation, for which the common resource will have been exhausted. Can you think of more effective ways for the law to internalize the external costs associated with overcapture of common resources? *See* James E. Krier, *The Pollution Problem and Legal Institutions: A Conceptual Overview,* 18 UCLA L. Rev. 429 (1971); *see also* Comment, *Of Reservoir Hogs, supra,* at 726–32 (discussing overdevelopment of oil and gas and overharvesting of wildlife); Todd Wilkinson, "Crowd Control," *National Parks* (July/August 1995), at 36–40 (discussing solutions to problems of excessive crowds at Arches National Park).

In no small part due to these concerns, the modern rules governing the allocation of property claims in surface water and groundwater are extremely complex and vary from state to state. Rather than make sweeping (and probably unhelpful) overgeneralizations, we leave the subject of property rights in water to a later course in Water Law. Those interested in the subject may consult Robert E. Beck, Waters and Water Rights (1991) or David H. Getches, Water Law in a Nutshell (2d ed. 1990).

B. "FIRST–IN–TIME" AND INTANGIBLE PROPERTY

In *Edwards*, the court refused to allocate ownership of the entire cave to Edwards, despite the substantial investment of time, effort, and money that Edwards had made. At first blush, this may seem an outright rejection of the labor theory of property. Does the labor theory possess no normative force as a basis for the allocation of property rights? Or are there reasons for considering the investment of one's time, labor, and money in allocating property rights?

These issues often arise with respect to the recognition and exploitation of property rights in intangibles, such as ideas. Should ideas be treated as property and, if so, what role should "first-in-time" play in allocating control over ideas?

JOYCE v. GENERAL MOTORS CORPORATION

Supreme Court of Ohio.
49 Ohio St.3d 93, 551 N.E.2d 172 (1990).

[Editors' Note: On April 3, 1984, Michael Joyce, a nonsupervisory GM employee, submitted a written suggestion for a procedure to reduce the amount of scrap in the manufacturing and testing of products within his department. As with many companies, GM had a formal suggestion plan under which a committee determined whether suggestions merited awards and made awards for suggestions adopted by GM. Joyce's suggestion was returned the following day with the comment, "[d]uplicate suggestion submitted by another suggester on same day," written on it by the head of the committee—although, according to Joyce, the committee received his suggestion first. The other suggester was Donald Halsey, a supervisory GM employee. According to Joyce, Halsey learned of the idea from Donald Tackett, the supervisor in charge of Joyce's department, who had in turn learned of the idea from Joyce's immediate supervisor, Chuck Guisinger (with whom Joyce had discussed his ideas).

After investigating, the committee adopted Halsey's suggestion and awarded him $12,573.13, because the committee concluded that Halsey's suggestion was the idea that prompted GM's change. The committee apparently also decided that Joyce would not have gotten the award even if the committee had rejected Halsey's suggestion. After receiving the award, Halsey shared $5,000 of the award with Tackett as a gift for Tackett's assistance.

After Joyce unsuccessfully attempted to persuade GM management that Halsey had stolen his idea, that the committee had received Joyce's idea first, and that GM should revoke the award to Halsey, Joyce filed suit against GM, Halsey, and Tackett. The suit alleged that Halsey had wrongfully appropriated his idea and that Halsey and Tackett had conspired to convert the idea to their own benefit. The defendants moved to dismiss the claim for failure to state a valid legal claim. Prior to trial, Joyce voluntarily dismissed GM as a party. At trial, the court entered a directed verdict for Halsey and Tackett, concluding that they had not appropriated any property right of Joyce as there was no protected right in ideas that were not copyrighted, patented or trademarked. The court of appeals reversed, stating that "where a supervisor conspires with a fellow employee to convert the valuable ideas of an hourly employee, a cause of action in conversion must lie. Such a valuable idea, in the form of a suggestion, is a property right which may be the subject of conversion." Halsey and Tackett appealed to the Supreme Court of Ohio.]

Moyer, Chief Justice. . . . [We] consider whether an idea submitted by an employee pursuant to an employee suggestion plan is in itself personal property which may not be converted by another employee.

In *Zacchini v. Scripps–Howard Broadcasting Co.* (1976), 47 Ohio St.2d 224, 226, 1 O.O.3d 129, 130, 351 N.E.2d 454, 456, we held that *conversion* is the wrongful exercise of dominion over property to the exclusion of the rights of the owner, or withholding it from his possession under a claim inconsistent with his rights. Thus, before we reach the issue of conversion, we must first determine whether an "idea" is property protected under the law.

In *Gottschalk v. Benson* (1972), 409 U.S. 63, 67–71, 93 S.Ct. 253, 255–257, 34 L.Ed.2d 273, the United States Supreme Court stated that ideas in themselves are not subject to individual ownership or control. They do not rise to the level of property and are not in themselves protected by law. *See, also,* Anawalt, Ideas in the Workplace (1988) 7–8. The law does not favor the protection of abstract ideas as the property of the originator. "An idea should be free for all to use at least until someone is able to translate such idea into a sufficiently useful form that it may be patented (trademarked) or copyrighted." *Richter v. Westab, Inc.* (C.A. 6, 1976), 529 F.2d 896, 902. In *Puente v. President & Fellows of Harvard College* (C.A. 1, 1957), 248 F.2d 799, 802, the court indicated that an idea which is not in a patented (trademarked) or copyrighted form is not protected "unless it is acquired and used under such circumstances that the law will imply a contractual or fiduciary relationship between the parties." . . .

Appellee's ideas were not expressed in a legally protected manner. They were neither patented, copyrighted, trademarked nor imparted pursuant to a fiduciary or contractual relationship. In fact, they were freely divulged to a third party. Public disclosure of the ideas makes them available to all and operates to deprive appellee of any further rights in them. *Puente, supra,* at 802; *Bonito Boats, Inc. v. Thunder Craft Boats, Inc.* (1989), 489 U.S. 141, 109 S.Ct. 971, 976, 103 L.Ed.2d 118, 132–133. Since the ideas are not property, they are not capable of conversion or appropriation.

For the foregoing reasons, the judgment of the court of appeals is reversed and the judgment of the trial court is reinstated. . . .

[Dissenting opinion omitted.]

Notes

1. *Copying and the Common Law Rule.* The common law rule concerning copying ideas is set down in harsh detail in *Cheney Bros. v. Doris Silk Corp.,* 35 F.2d 279 (2d Cir. 1929). The Doris Silk Corporation sued when Cheney Brothers copied one of its popular dress patterns—and undercut Doris Silk's price—during the 1928 fashion season. When Doris Silk sought an injunction to protect itself against this conduct during the 1928 season, the court responded:

> [T]he reasoning which would justify any interposition at all demands that it cover the whole extent of the injury. A man whose designs come to harvest in two years, or in five, has prima facie as good right to protection as one who deals only in annuals. Nor could we consistently stop at designs; processes, machines, and secrets could have an equal

can copy certain things

claim. The upshot [of Doris Silk's argument] must be that, whenever anyone has contrived any of these, others may be forbidden to copy it. That is not the law. In the absence of some recognized right at common law, or under the statutes—and [Doris Silk] claims neither—a man's property is limited to the chattels which embody his invention. Others may imitate these at their pleasure. [35 F.2d at 280.]

Thus, despite Doris Silk's substantial investment in its dress patterns, it had no property interest in the patterns themselves. Why does the common law refuse to provide innovators like Doris Silk or Michael Joyce with "property" protection of their ideas under the first-in-time rule? Would your analysis of the issues in *Joyce v. General Motors* change if Joyce had spent hundreds of hours and thousands of dollars developing his idea? Should the amount of the financial investment a person makes in an idea determine the extent of the person's entitlement to protection under the principle of first-in-time? Why or why not?

innovation vs. Duplication

2. *Modern Intellectual Property*. There is an apparent tension between society's desire to encourage innovation (by assuring that those who invent new products or come up with new ideas have the incentive of potential profit from their products or ideas) and its desire to promote competition in products or ideas (by encouraging duplication to assure consumers of low-cost access to such products and ideas). As the opinion in *Joyce* suggests, federal and state legislatures have stepped in to balance these competing interests. For example, federal statutes permit persons to register and obtain a *patent* for inventions, processes or machines that incorporate ideas. Broadly speaking, the patent gives the registrant a time-limited (varying in duration, depending upon the type of patent) and exclusive property right in the invention or process (so long as it has social utility and is "novel"). Thus, for example, Samuel Morse was able to patent his specific inventions that eventually resulted in the development of the telegraph, but he could not patent the general use of electromagnetism. Once the applicable patent period expires, the invention becomes part of the "public domain" and anyone may freely use it.

Set limits to Patents

Federal statutes also provide copyright protection for the authors of such works as writings, recordings, art, photographs, and computer software programs. An author can obtain a copyright for the particular manner in which an idea is expressed, but not for the idea itself. For example, John Grisham may have a copyright in the specific words used in the book *The Firm*, but he does not have a copyright in the general story idea about a corrupt law firm trying to kill one of its associates. Generally speaking, copyright protection lasts for the lifetime of the author plus 70 years, after which time the formerly copyrighted material enters the public domain. Are patent and copyright protection solely a function of "desert" (allowing the innovator to recoup its investment and perhaps earn a profit)? Or are there other reasons to allocate monopoly rights to the creator? If so, what reasons?

copyright Protection example

Federal and state laws also provide protection for trademarks, such as Coca–Cola® and the Starship Enterprise.™ In his book *Economic Analysis of Law*, Richard Posner discusses some of the functions of trademark protection:

[handwritten margin notes: purpose of trade marks →; quality as reason for no time limit]

The economic function of trademarks is, by giving assurance of uniform quality, to economize on consumer search costs. Strictly speaking, all a trademark does is identify the *source* of a particular product or service—for example, the General Electric trademark identifies General Electric as the producer of the goods to which the trademark is affixed. But this means the consumer knows whom to blame if his light bulb doesn't work, so trademark law gives producers an incentive to maintain quality, which in turn reduces the need for the consumer to shop as carefully as he would otherwise have to do. Even if the nominal price of a trademarked item is higher because of the producer's investment in advertising and enforcing his mark, the total cost . . . to the consumer may be less because the trademark conveys information about quality that the consumer might find it costly to obtain otherwise. [Richard A. Posner, Economic Analysis of Law 43–44 (4th ed. 1992).]

Based upon these functions, can you explain why trademark protection is not time-limited (in comparison to patent and copyright, which are time-limited)?

Collectively, these property interests generally are described as "intellectual property," and they are the subject of upper level courses you will encounter later in law school. Those interested in intellectual property issues can satisfy their curiosity with Michael A. Epstein, Modern Intellectual Property (3d ed. 1995), or Roger E. Schecter & John R. Thomas, Intellectual Property: The Law of Copyrights, Patents, and Trademarks (2003).

———————

Domain Names and "Cybersquatting." In 1972, the U.S. Defense Information Systems Agency created the Internet Assigned Numbers Authority (IANA), which assigned unique numerical addresses to each computer connected to the Internet. Over time, increased use of the internet created a need for a more user-friendly means of address identification. Researchers and technicians at the University of Wisconsin developed the first "name server" in 1984, which became the basis for the modern system of domain names used today (which allow a user to reach a networked computer by a domain name rather than internet protocol numbers).

Initially, registration of domain names was free, subsidized by the National Science Foundation (NSF) through IANA. In 1992, IANA and the NSF created InterNIC to organize and maintain the growing domain name system, and InterNIC began charging $100 for each two-year registration. In 1998, the Internet Corporation for Assigned Names and Numbers (ICANN) was formed to coordinate the technical management of the Internet's domain name system and to create competition for registry services. ICANN has now accredited a number of private companies (such as Verisign, Network Solutions, and others) licensed to provide domain name registry services. As of 2005, there are an estimated 19 million domain names registered, with 40,000 more registered every day.

Not surprisingly, domain name registration in the generic top-level domains (*i.e.*, .com, .net, .org, .edu, and .gov) is on a first-come, first-served basis. When registration began, "entrepreneurs" quickly began to register domain names using generic terms such as "business.com," "drugs.com," "hotels.com" and the like. Some of the persons who registered these generic domain names in turn sold them for enormous sums of money—for example, the domain name "business.com" was sold to a California company for $8 million.

Also not surprisingly, "entrepreneurs" began to register domain names using the names of celebrities or trademarked products—hoping, of course, to make a profit re-selling the domain name to the celebrity or trademark owner. This practice was quickly dubbed "cybersquatting," and aggrieved celebrities and trademark owners sought relief from Congress in an attempt to protect what they claimed was "theirs."

DAIMLERCHRYSLER v. THE NET INC.

United States Court of Appeals for the Sixth Circuit.
388 F.3d 201 (2004).

KENNEDY, CIRCUIT JUDGE. Plaintiff DaimlerChrysler moved for summary judgment on its Anti–Cybersquatting Consumer Protection Act (ACPA) claim, arguing that there was no genuine issue of material fact with respect to whether the defendants violated the ACPA by their registration of the domain name "foradodge.com." The district court agreed and granted summary judgment to the plaintiff. The district court also permanently enjoined the defendants from any further use of the "foradodge" name, ordered that the "foradodge.com" domain name be transferred to the plaintiff, and struck the defendants' third party claims against the United States in which they alleged that the ACPA provided for an unlawful taking in violation of the Fifth Amendment to the United States Constitution. The defendants appeal from all of the above holdings and orders of the district court. For the following reasons, we AFFIRM. . . .

... In September 1995, DaimlerChrysler registered the domain name 4ADODGE.com with Network Solutions, Inc. and established a website using the 4ADODGE domain name. In late 1996, defendant Maydak, who was incarcerated in federal prison at the time, asked defendant Michael Sussman to register the domain name "foradodge.com" for him. On December 25, 1996, Sussman registered the domain name with Network Solutions Inc. Rather than using his or Maydak's name as the registrant, Sussman listed the registrant as The Net Inc. By the defendants' own admission, however, there is no such corporate entity; rather, The Net Inc. is an "unincorporated association" between defendants Maydak and Sussman. In addition to registering "foradodge.com," Maydak also registered the domain name "foradodge.net." Maydak claims that he planned to use the "foradodge.com" domain name to establish a website that described his "dodging" services such as asset protection, tax and creditor avoidance, and ways to bypass "society's general paradigm."...

... From at least February 1998, and possibly as early as December 1996, to about October 1998, the defendants pointed the "fora-dodge.com" domain name to a website that contained a link to a pornographic website....

In 1999, Congress passed the ACPA as an amendment to the Trademark Act of 1946 ("Lanham Act") to prohibit "cybersquatting." As the district court noted, "cybersquatting" occurs when a person other than the trademark holder registers the domain name of a well known trademark and then attempts to profit from this by either ransoming the domain name back to the trademark holder or by using the domain name to divert business from the trademark holder to the domain name holder. A trademark owner asserting a claim under the ACPA must establish the following: (1) it has a valid trademark entitled to protection; (2) its mark is distinctive or famous; (3) the defendant's domain name is identical or confusingly similar to, or in the case of famous marks, dilutive of, the owner's mark; and (4) the defendant used, registered, or trafficked in the domain name (5) with a bad faith intent to profit.

Because the defendants appeal from the district court's grant of summary judgment only on the grounds that the district court erred when it found that 1) the mark 4ADODGE qualifies as a protected trademark under the ACPA, and 2) the defendants had a bad faith intent to profit when it registered the "foradodge.com" domain name, we need only consider these two arguments, which implicate the first and fifth elements necessary to establish an ACPA claim.

The district court first considered whether plaintiff's DODGE and 4ADODGE marks were entitled to trademark protection. Under the Lanham Act, a trademark is defined as "any word, name, symbol, or device, or any combination thereof ... used by a person ...to identify and distinguish his or her goods, including a unique product, from those manufactured or sold by others and to indicate the source of goods, even if that source is unknown." 15 U.S.C. § 1127.... The district court noted that there is no dispute that plaintiff's DODGE mark is entitled to protection. The DODGE mark has been registered since 1939 and has been in continuous use since 1924. The district court also noted that the plaintiff's registration of the mark entitled it to a presumption that the mark is valid, and that the continuous use of the mark for over five years after registration renders the mark incontestable. The district court then considered whether the plaintiff's 4ADODGE mark, although not registered, is entitled to trademark protection under the ACPA. The district court noted the following:

> This mark, which incorporates plaintiff's incontestable DODGE mark, has been used by the plaintiff to distinguish its automobiles for a number of years. As early as 1994, plaintiff advertised and used

as a toll free telephone number 1–800–4–A–DODGE. Plaintiff has also used the 4ADODGE.COM website since 1995. . . .

Next, we consider the fifth element of the ACPA claim, whether the defendants registered the "foradodge.com" domain name with a "bad faith intent to profit." The ACPA provides a list of nine non-exclusive factors that a court may consider in determining whether a bad faith intent to profit is established. 15 U.S.C. § 1125(d)(1)(B)(i). They are as follows:

(I) the trademark or other intellectual property rights of the person, if any, in the domain name;

(II) the extent to which the domain name consists of the legal name of the person or a name that is otherwise commonly used to identify that person;

(III) the person's prior use, if any, of the domain name in connection with the bona fide offering of any goods or services;

(IV) the person's bona fide noncommercial or fair use of the mark in a site accessible under the domain name;

(V) the person's intent to divert consumers from the mark owner's online location to a site accessible under the domain name that could harm the goodwill represented by the mark, either for commercial gain or with the intent to tarnish or disparage the mark, by creating a likelihood of confusion as to the source, sponsorship, affiliation, or endorsement of the site;

(VI) the person's offer to transfer, sell, or otherwise assign the domain name to the mark owner or any third party for financial gain without having used, or having an intent to use, the domain name in the bona fide offering of any goods or services, or the person's prior conduct indicating a pattern of such conduct;

(VII) the person's provision of material and misleading false contact information when applying for registration of the domain name, the person's intentional failure to maintain accurate contact information, or the person's prior conduct indicating a pattern of such conduct;

(VIII) the person's registration or acquisition of multiple domain names which the person knows are identical or confusingly similar to marks of others that are distinctive at the time of registration of such domain names, or dilutive of famous marks of others that are famous at the time of registration of such domain names, without regard to the goods or services of the parties; and

(IX) the extent to which the mark incorporated in the person's domain name registration is or is not distinctive and famous within the meaning of [the act].

Considering the factors in their entirety, the district court concluded that it is clear that the defendants registered the "foradodge.com" domain name with a bad faith intent to profit. We agree.

All but one of the enumerated factors above support a finding of bad faith. Factor six, which asks whether the person offered to sell the domain name to the mark owner for financial gain, is neutral, as the plaintiff presented evidence that defendant Sussman offered to sell the domain name to it for $30,000 while Sussman avers that it was plaintiff's agent who initially sought to buy the domain name. Although there is a genuine issue of fact on this point, that does not defeat plaintiff's summary judgment since, when considering the factors in their entirety, no reasonable trier of fact could conclude that the defendants did not act in bad faith with intent to profit. After considering the remaining factors, this conclusion is inescapable. For instance, 1) the defendants had no intellectual property rights in the "foradodge" name at the time of registration; 2) the domain name does not contain any variation of the names of the defendants; 3) the defendants have never *actually* used the site in connection with the bona fide offer of goods or services; 4) the defendants never claim that they used the site for any noncommercial or other "fair use;" 5) it can be inferred that the defendants intended to divert customers from the plaintiff's website from the fact that the defendants' "foradodge" domain name is phonetically identical to plaintiff's 4ADODGE mark; 6) the defendants provided misleading contact information as the site's registrant, initially listing the registrant as The Net Inc., of Hewlett, New York, while no such entity exists; 7) the defendants registered multiple sites, such as doj.com, espnet.com, ups. net, which are confusingly similar to names and marks of others; and finally 8) DODGE is a highly distinctive and famous mark.

Accordingly, since we conclude that no rational trier of fact could find that the defendants did not violate the ACPA, we affirm the district court's grant of summary judgment to the plaintiff. . . .

Notes

1. *First-in-Time and Domain Names.* Why does the law allocate control of domain names using a "first-in-time" model of registration? Who do you expect benefitted as a result? Why not instead place domain names up for auction?

2. *First-in-Time and Cybersquatting.* A case like *DaimlerChrysler* is pretty easy as a factual matter. But many cases might be substantially more difficult. Consider the following disputes:

(a) Apple Records is a British record company that began issuing recordings (including those of The Beatles) in the late 1960s. Apple Computer, Inc., the manufacturer of the MacIntosh, was incorporated in California in 1977. If Apple Computer registered for the domain name "apple.com," could Apple Records legitimately assert that it has a superior claim to that domain name?

(b) Wal–Mart Stores, Inc. operates stores under a variety of names (such as Wal–Mart and Sam's Club) throughout the United States. Richard Hatch, a Bangor, Maine, financial consultant, registered the domain name "walmartsucks.com" following an unpleasant confrontation with a

Wal–Mart employee, and began maintaining an anti-Wal–Mart protest site. Can Wal–Mart successfully use the ACPA to prevent Hatch from using its trademarked name within the domain name for his website?

(c) Andruw Jones is the eight-time Gold–Glove winning centerfielder for the Atlanta Braves. Suppose that a high school fan registered the domain name "www.andruwjones.com" and operated it as a "fan site." Could Jones use the ACPA to prevent the fan from operating the website or to force a transfer of the domain name? Now suppose that the person registering the domain name operated it by posting a page that contained only links to baseball-related goods and services (offered by persons other than the registrant). Should Jones be able to use the ACPA to prevent this use?

***

Property Rights in Identity and Celebrity. Should the law recognize a property right in someone's name, likeness, or persona—and if so, why? Consider the case of Bette Midler. In 1985, Ford Motor Company ran an advertising campaign for Lincoln Mercury vehicles featuring TV ad spots that included songs from the 1970s (hoping to appeal to "yuppies"). One of the ads was to feature the song "Do You Want To Dance?," a tune that appeared on Midler's 1973 album *The Divine Miss M.* Ford tried to obtain Midler's consent, but she refused. Ford then hired Ula Hedwig, a former back-up singer for Midler, and had her sing the song for the commercial, instructing her to "sound as much as possible like the Bette Midler record." Hedwig did such a creditable job impersonating Midler's voice that when the advertisement ran, many persons believed the voice was Midler's.

Midler filed a complaint against Ford, asserting that she was entitled to damages based upon two primary theories: (1) that the advertisement violated California Civil Code § 3344, which prohibited the use of another's "name, voice, signature, photograph, or likeness" for commercial purposes without their consent; and (2) that the advertisement violated Midler's common law right of publicity, which permitted her to control the use of her identity or persona for commercial purposes. The trial court granted summary judgment for Ford. The U.S. Court of Appeals for the Ninth Circuit affirmed the grant of summary judgment on Midler's statutory claim, holding that Ford did not use Midler's actual voice. The court reversed the grant of summary judgment on Midler's common law claim, however:

> Why did the defendants ask Midler to sing if her voice was not of value to them? Why did they studiously acquire the services of a sound-alike and instruct her to imitate Midler if Midler's voice was not of value to them? What they sought was an attribute of Midler's identity. Its value was what the market would have paid for Midler to have sung the commercial in person. . . .
>
> . . . A voice is as distinctive and personal as a face. The human voice is one of the most palpable ways identity is manifested. We are

all aware that a friend is at once known by a few words on the phone. At a philosophical level it has been observed that with the sound of a voice, "the other stands before me." D. Ihde, *Listening and Voice* 77 (1976). A fortiori, these observations hold true of singing, especially singing by a singer of renown. The singer manifests herself in the song. To impersonate her voice is to pirate her identity.

We need not and do not go so far as to hold that every imitation of a voice to advertise merchandise is actionable. We hold only that when a distinctive voice of a professional singer is widely known and is deliberately imitated in order to sell a product, the sellers have appropriated what is not theirs and have committed a tort in California. Midler has made a showing, sufficient to defeat summary judgment, that the defendants here for their own profit in selling their product did appropriate part of her identity. [*Midler v. Ford Motor Co.*, 849 F.2d 460, 463–64 (9th Cir. 1988).]

Does granting Midler this type of "property" right in her voice simply result in making her even wealthier than she already is, or are there any socially worthwhile consequences that result from recognizing such a property right? If so, what are they? What limits, if any, should the law place on such property rights? *See* Richard A. Posner, Economic Analysis of Law 43 (4th ed. 1992); George M. Armstrong, Jr., *The Reification of Celebrity: Persona as Property*, 51 La. L. Rev. 443 (1991). Keep these questions in mind as you consider the following case and the examples that follow it.

COMEDY III PRODUCTIONS, INC. v. GARY SADERUP, INC.

Supreme Court of California.
25 Cal.4th 387, 106 Cal.Rptr.2d 126, 21 P.3d 797 (2001).

MOSK, J. A California statute grants the *right of publicity* to specified successors in interest of deceased celebrities, prohibiting any other person from using a celebrity's name, voice, signature, photograph, or likeness for commercial purposes without the consent of such successors. The United States Constitution prohibits the states from abridging, among other fundamental rights, freedom of speech. In the case at bar we resolve a conflict between these two provisions. The Court of Appeal concluded that the lithographs and silkscreened T-shirts in question here received no First Amendment protection simply because they were reproductions rather than original works of art. As will appear, this was error: reproductions are equally entitled to First Amendment protection. We formulate instead what is essentially a balancing test between the First Amendment and the right of publicity based on whether the work in question adds significant creative elements so as to be transformed into something more than a mere celebrity likeness or imitation. Applying this test to the present case, we conclude that there are no such creative elements here and that the right of publicity prevails. On this basis, we will affirm the judgment of the Court of Appeal....

Plaintiff Comedy III Productions, Inc. (hereafter Comedy III), brought this action against defendants Gary Saderup and Gary Saderup, Inc. (hereafter collectively Saderup), seeking damages and injunctive relief for violation of section 990 and related business torts .... [Editors' Note: Section 990, now renumbered as Cal. Civil Code § 3344.1, provides that "Any person who uses a deceased personality's name, voice, signature, photograph, or likeness, in any manner, on or in products, merchandise, or goods, or for purposes of advertising or selling, or soliciting purchases of, products, merchandise, goods, or services," without the prior consent of the personality's survivors or the person to whom the right of publicity was transferred, is liable for damages, including "any profits from the unauthorized use" as well as punitive damages and attorney fees.]

Comedy III is the registered owner of all rights to the former comedy act known as The Three Stooges, who are deceased personalities within the meaning of the statute.

Saderup is an artist with over 25 years' experience in making charcoal drawings of celebrities. These drawings are used to create lithographic and silkscreen masters, which in turn are used to produce multiple reproductions in the form, respectively, of lithographic prints and silkscreened images on T-shirts. Saderup creates the original drawings and is actively involved in the ensuing lithographic and silkscreening processes.

Without securing Comedy III's consent, Saderup sold lithographs and T-shirts bearing a likeness of The Three Stooges reproduced from a charcoal drawing he had made. These lithographs and T-shirts did not constitute an advertisement, endorsement, or sponsorship of any product.

Saderup's profits from the sale of unlicensed lithographs and T-shirts bearing a likeness of The Three Stooges was $75,000 and Comedy III's reasonable attorney fees were $150,000.

On these stipulated facts the court found for Comedy III and entered judgment against Saderup awarding damages of $75,000 and attorney's fees of $150,000 plus costs. The court also issued a permanent injunction restraining Saderup from violating the statute by use of any likeness of The Three Stooges in lithographs, T-shirts, "or any other medium by which [Saderup's] art work may be sold or marketed." The injunction further prohibited Saderup from "Creating, producing, reproducing, copying, distributing, selling or exhibiting any lithographs, prints, posters, t-shirts, buttons, or other goods, products or merchandise of any kind, bearing the photograph, image, face, symbols, trademarks, likeness, name, voice or signature of The Three Stooges or any of the individual members of The Three Stooges." The sole exception to this broad prohibition was Saderup's original charcoal drawing from which the reproductions at issue were made.

Saderup's Charcoal Drawing of the Three Stooges

Saderup appealed. The Court of Appeal modified the judgment by striking the injunction. The court reasoned that Comedy III had not proved a likelihood of continued violation of the statute, and that the wording of the injunction was overbroad because it exceeded the terms of the statute and because it "could extend to matters and conduct protected by the First Amendment . . . ."

The Court of Appeal affirmed the judgment as thus modified, however, upholding the award of damages, attorney fees, and costs. In so doing, it rejected Saderup's contentions that his conduct (1) did not violate the terms of the statute, and (2) in any event was protected by the constitutional guaranty of freedom of speech. . . .

Saderup . . . contends that enforcement of the judgment against him violates his right of free speech and expression under the First Amendment. . . .

The right of publicity is often invoked in the context of commercial speech when the appropriation of a celebrity likeness creates a false and misleading impression that the celebrity is endorsing a product. Because the First Amendment does not protect false and misleading commercial speech, and because even nonmisleading commercial speech is generally subject to somewhat lesser First Amendment protection, the right of publicity may often trump the right of advertisers to make use of celebrity figures.

But the present case does not concern commercial speech. As the trial court found, Saderup's portraits of The Three Stooges are expressive works and not an advertisement for or endorsement of a product. Although his work was done for financial gain, "the First Amendment is not limited to those who publish without charge. . . . [An expressive activity] does not lose its constitutional protection because it is undertaken for profit." *Guglielmi v. Spelling–Goldberg Productions* (1979) 25 Cal. 3d 860, 868, 160 Cal. Rptr. 352, 603 P.2d 454.

The tension between the right of publicity and the First Amendment is highlighted by recalling the two distinct, commonly acknowledged purposes of the latter. First, " 'to preserve an uninhibited marketplace of ideas' and to repel efforts to limit the 'uninhibited, robust and wide-open debate on public issues.' " *Guglielmi, supra*, 25 Cal. 3d at p. 866. Second, to foster a "fundamental respect for individual development and self-realization. The right to self-expression is inherent in any political system which respects individual dignity. Each speaker must be free of government restraint regardless of the nature or manner of the views expressed unless there is a compelling reason to the contrary." *Ibid.*, fn. omitted; see also Emerson, The System of Freedom of Expression (1970) pp. 6–7.

The right of publicity has a potential for frustrating the fulfillment of both these purposes. Because celebrities take on public meaning, the appropriation of their likenesses may have important uses in uninhibited debate on public issues, particularly debates about culture and values. And because celebrities take on personal meanings to many individuals in the society, the creative appropriation of celebrity images can be an important avenue of individual expression. As one commentator has stated:

> Entertainment and sports celebrities are the leading players in our Public Drama. We tell tales, both tall and cautionary, about them. We monitor their comings and goings, their missteps and heartbreaks. We copy their mannerisms, their styles, their modes of conversation and of consumption. Whether or not celebrities are "the chief agents of moral change in the United States," they certainly are widely used—far more than are institutionally anchored elites—to symbolize individual aspirations, group identities, and cultural values. Their images are thus important expressive and communicative resources: the peculiar, yet familiar idiom in which we conduct a fair portion of our cultural business and everyday conversation. [Madow, *Private Ownership of Public Image: Popular Culture and Publicity Rights* (1993) 81 Cal. L. Rev. 125, 128 (Madow).]

As Madow further points out, the very importance of celebrities in society means that the right of publicity has the potential of censoring significant expression by suppressing alternative versions of celebrity images that are iconoclastic, irreverent, or otherwise attempt to redefine the celebrity's meaning. A majority of this court recognized as much in *Guglielmi*: "The right of publicity derived from public prominence does not confer a shield to ward off caricature, parody and satire. Rather, prominence invites creative comment." *Guglielmi, supra*, 25 Cal. 3d at p. 869.

For similar reasons, speech about public figures is accorded heightened First Amendment protection in defamation law. As the United States Supreme Court held in *Gertz v. Robert Welch, Inc.* (1974) 418 U.S. 323, 41 L. Ed. 2d 789, 94 S. Ct. 2997, public figures may prevail in a libel

public figures
Do so voluntarily

action only if they prove that the defendant's defamatory statements were made with actual malice, *i.e.*, actual knowledge of falsehood or reckless disregard for the truth, whereas private figures need prove only negligence. The rationale for such differential treatment is, first, that the public figure has greater access to the media and therefore greater opportunity to rebut defamatory statements, and second, that those who have become public figures have done so voluntarily and therefore "invite attention and comment." *Gertz,* 418 U.S. at pp. 344–345. Giving broad scope to the right of publicity has the potential of allowing a celebrity to accomplish through the vigorous exercise of that right the censorship of unflattering commentary that cannot be constitutionally accomplished through defamation actions.

Nor do Saderup's creations lose their constitutional protections because they are for purposes of entertaining rather than informing. As Chief Justice Bird stated in *Guglielmi*, invoking the dual purpose of the First Amendment:

> Our courts have often observed that entertainment is entitled to the same constitutional protection as the exposition of ideas. That conclusion rests on two propositions. First, "the line between informing and entertaining is too elusive for the protection of the basic right. Everyone is familiar with instances of propaganda through fiction. What is one man's amusement, teaches another doctrine." Second, entertainment, as a mode of self-expression, is entitled to constitutional protection irrespective of its contribution to the marketplace of ideas. "For expression is an integral part of the development of ideas, of mental exploration and of the affirmation of self. The power to realize his potentiality as a human being begins at this point and must extend at least this far if the whole nature of man is not to be thwarted." [*Guglielmi, supra,* 25 Cal. 3d at p. 867, fn. omitted.] . . .

Right of publicity

But having recognized the high degree of First Amendment protection for noncommercial speech about celebrities, we need not conclude that all expression that trenches on the right of publicity receives such protection. The right of publicity, like copyright, protects a form of intellectual property that society deems to have some social utility. "Often considerable money, time and energy are needed to develop one's prominence in a particular field. Years of labor may be required before one's skill, reputation, notoriety or virtues are sufficiently developed to permit an economic return through some medium of commercial promotion. For some, the investment may eventually create considerable commercial value in one's identity." [*Lugosi v. Universal Pictures,* 25 Cal.3d 813, 834–35, 160 Cal.Rptr. 323, 603 P.2d 425 (1979) (dis. opn. of Bird, C. J.).]

The present case exemplifies this kind of creative labor. Moe and Jerome (Curly) Howard and Larry Fein fashioned personae collectively known as The Three Stooges, first in vaudeville and later in movie shorts, over a period extending from the 1920s to the 1940s. The three comic characters they created and whose names they shared—Larry,

Moe, and Curly—possess a kind of mythic status in our culture. Their journey from ordinary vaudeville performers to the heights (or depths) of slapstick comic celebrity was long and arduous. Their brand of physical humor—the nimble, comically stylized violence, the "nyuk-nyuks" and "whoop-whoop-whoops," eye-pokes, slaps and head conks—created a distinct comedic trademark. Through their talent and labor, they joined the relatively small group of actors who constructed identifiable, recurrent comic personalities that they brought to the many parts they were scripted to play. . . .

In sum, society may recognize, as the Legislature has done here, that a celebrity's heirs and assigns have a legitimate protectible interest in exploiting the value to be obtained from merchandising the celebrity's image, whether that interest be conceived as a kind of natural property right or as an incentive for encouraging creative work. Although critics have questioned whether the right of publicity truly serves any social purpose, (see, e.g., Madow, *supra*, 81 Cal. L.Rev. at pp. 178–238), there is no question that the Legislature has a rational basis for permitting celebrities and their heirs to control the commercial exploitation of the celebrity's likeness.

Although surprisingly few courts have considered in any depth the means of reconciling the right of publicity and the First Amendment, we follow those that have in concluding that depictions of celebrities amounting to little more than the appropriation of the celebrity's economic value are not protected expression under the First Amendment. We begin with *Zacchini v. Scripps–Howard Broadcasting Co.* (1977) 433 U.S. 562, 576, 53 L. Ed. 2d 965, 97 S. Ct. 2849 (*Zacchini*), the only United States Supreme Court case to directly address the right of publicity. Zacchini, the performer of a human cannonball act, sued a television station that had videotaped and broadcast his entire performance without his consent. The court held the First Amendment did not protect the television station against a right of publicity claim under Ohio common law. In explaining why the enforcement of the right of publicity in this case would not violate the First Amendment, the court stated: "The rationale for [protecting the right of publicity] is the straightforward one of preventing unjust enrichment by the theft of goodwill. No social purpose is served by having the defendant get free some aspect of the plaintiff that would have market value and for which he would normally pay." *Id.* . . .

To be sure, *Zacchini* was not an ordinary right of publicity case: the defendant television station had appropriated the plaintiff's entire act, a species of common law copyright violation. Nonetheless, two principles enunciated in *Zacchini* apply to this case: (1) state law may validly safeguard forms of intellectual property not covered under federal copyright and patent law as a means of protecting the fruits of a performing artist's labor; and (2) the state's interest in preventing the outright misappropriation of such intellectual property by others is not automatically trumped by the interest in free expression or dissemination of information; rather, as in the case of defamation, the state law interest and the interest in free expression must be balanced, according to the relative importance of the interests at stake.

Guglielmi adopted a similar balancing approach. The purported heir of Rudolph Valentino filed suit against the makers of a fictional film based on the latter's life. *Guglielmi* concluded that the First Amendment protection of entertainment superseded any right of publicity. This was in contrast to the companion *Lugosi* case, in which Chief Justice Bird concluded in her dissenting opinion that there may be an enforceable right of publicity that would prevent the merchandising of Count Dracula using the likeness of Bela Lugosi, with whom that role was identified. *Guglielmi* proposed a balancing test to distinguish protected from unprotected appropriation of celebrity likenesses: "an action for infringement of the right of publicity can be maintained only if the proprietary interests at issue clearly outweigh the value of free expression in this context." *Guglielmi, supra,* 25 Cal. 3d at p. 871.

In *Estate of Presley v. Russen* (D.N.J. 1981) 513 F. Supp. 1339 (*Russen*), the court considered a New Jersey common law right of publicity claim by Elvis Presley's heirs against an impersonator who performed The Big El Show. The court implicitly used a balancing test similar to the one proposed in *Guglielmi.* Acknowledging that the First Amendment protects entertainment speech, the court nonetheless rejected that constitutional defense. "Entertainment that is merely a copy or imitation, even if skillfully and accurately carried out, does not really have its own creative component and does not have a significant value as pure entertainment. As one authority has emphasized: 'The public interest in entertainment will support the sporadic, occasional and good-faith imitation of a famous person to achieve humor, to effect criticism or to season a particular episode, but it does not give a privilege to appropriate another's valuable attributes on a continuing basis as one's own without the consent of the other.' *Russen, supra,* 513 F. Supp. at p. 1360. Acknowledging also that the show had some informational value, preserving a live Elvis Presley act for posterity, the court nonetheless stated: "This recognition that defendant's production has some value does not diminish our conclusion that the primary purpose of defendant's activity is to appropriate the commercial value of the likeness of Elvis Presley." *Ibid.*

On the other side of the equation, the court recognized that the Elvis impersonation, as in *Zacchini,* represented "what may be the strongest case for the 'right of publicity,' involving not the appropriation of the entertainer's reputation to enhance the attractiveness of a commercial product, but the appropriation of the very activity by which the entertainer acquired his reputation in the first place." *Russen, supra,* 513 F. Supp. at p. 1361, quoting *Zacchini, supra,* 433 U.S. at p. 576. Thus, in balancing the considerable right of publicity interests with the minimal expressive or informational value of the speech in question, the *Russen* court concluded that the Presley estate's request for injunctive relief would likely prevail on the merits....

It is admittedly not a simple matter to develop a test that will unerringly distinguish between forms of artistic expression protected by the First Amendment and those that must give way to the right of publicity. Certainly, any such test must incorporate the principle that the right of publicity cannot, consistent with the First Amendment, be a right to control the celebrity's image by censoring disagreeable portrayals. Once the celebrity thrusts himself or herself forward into the limelight, the First Amendment dictates that the right to comment on, parody, lampoon, and make other expressive uses of the celebrity image must be given broad scope. The necessary implication of this observation is that the right of publicity is essentially an economic right. What the right of publicity holder possesses is not a right of censorship, but a right to prevent others from misappropriating the economic value generated by the celebrity's fame through the merchandising of the "name, voice, signature, photograph or likeness" of the celebrity.

Beyond this precept, how may courts distinguish between protected and unprotected expression? Some commentators have proposed importing the fair use defense from copyright law, 17 U.S.C. § 107, which has the advantage of employing an established doctrine developed from a related area of the law. Others disagree, pointing to the murkiness of the fair use doctrine and arguing that the idea/expression dichotomy, rather than fair use, is the principal means of reconciling copyright protection and First Amendment rights.

We conclude that a wholesale importation of the fair use doctrine into right of publicity law would not be advisable. At least two of the factors employed in the fair use test, "the nature of the copyrighted work" and "the amount and substantiality of the portion used," 17 U.S.C. § 107(2), (3), seem particularly designed to be applied to the partial copying of works of authorship "fixed in [a] tangible medium of expression," 17 U.S.C. § 102; it is difficult to understand why these factors would be especially useful for determining whether the depiction of a celebrity likeness is protected by the First Amendment.

Nonetheless, the first fair use factor—"the purpose and character of the use," 17 U.S.C. § 107(1)—does seem particularly pertinent to the task of reconciling the rights of free expression and publicity. As the Supreme Court has stated, the central purpose of the inquiry into this fair use factor

> is to see, in Justice Story's words, whether the new work merely 'supersedes the objects' of the original creation, or instead adds something new, with a further purpose or different character, altering the first with new expression, meaning, or message; it asks, in other words, whether and to what extent the new work is 'transformative.' Although such transformative use is not absolutely necessary for a finding of fair use, the goal of copyright, to promote science and the arts, is generally furthered by the creation of transformative works. [*Campbell v. Acuff–Rose Music, Inc.* (1994) 510 U.S. 569, 579, 127 L. Ed. 2d 500, 114 S. Ct. 1164, fn. omitted.]

This inquiry into whether a work is "transformative" appears to us to be necessarily at the heart of any judicial attempt to square the right of publicity with the First Amendment. As the above quotation suggests, both the First Amendment and copyright law have a common goal of encouragement of free expression and creativity, the former by protecting such expression from government interference, the latter by protecting the creative fruits of intellectual and artistic labor. The right of publicity, at least theoretically, shares this goal with copyright law. When artistic expression takes the form of a literal depiction or imitation of a celebrity for commercial gain, directly trespassing on the right of publicity without adding significant expression beyond that trespass, the state law interest in protecting the fruits of artistic labor outweighs the expressive interests of the imitative artist.

On the other hand, when a work contains significant transformative elements, it is not only especially worthy of First Amendment protection, but it is also less likely to interfere with the economic interest protected by the right of publicity. As has been observed, works of parody or other distortions of the celebrity figure are not, from the celebrity fan's viewpoint, good substitutes for conventional depictions of the celebrity and therefore do not generally threaten markets for celebrity memorabilia that the right of publicity is designed to protect. See *Cardtoons, L.C. v. Major League Baseball Players Association* (10th Cir. 1996) 95 F.3d 959, 974 (*Cardtoons*). Accordingly, First Amendment protection of such works outweighs whatever interest the state may have in enforcing the right of publicity. The right-of-publicity holder continues to enforce the right to monopolize the production of conventional, more or less fungible, images of the celebrity.

Cardtoons, supra, 95 F.3d 959, cited by Saderup, is consistent with this "transformative" test. There, the court held that the First Amendment protected a company that produced trading cards caricaturing and parodying well-known major league baseball players against a claim brought under the Oklahoma right of publicity statute. The court concluded that "the cards provide social commentary on public figures, major league baseball players, who are involved in a significant commercial enterprise, major league baseball," and that "the cards are no less protected because they provide humorous rather than serious commentary." *Cardtoons*, at p. 969. The *Cardtoons* court weighed these First Amendment rights against what it concluded was the less-than-compelling interests advanced by the right of publicity outside the advertising context—especially in light of the reality that parody would not likely substantially impact the economic interests of celebrities—and found the cards to be a form of protected expression. *Cardtoons*, at pp. 973–976. While *Cardtoons* contained dicta calling into question the social value of the right of publicity, its conclusion that works parodying and caricaturing celebrities are protected by the First Amendment appears unassailable in light of the test articulated above....

Another way of stating the inquiry is whether the celebrity likeness is one of the "raw materials" from which an original work is synthesized, or whether the depiction or imitation of the celebrity is the very sum and substance of the work in question. We ask, in other words, whether a product containing a celebrity's likeness is so transformed that it has become primarily the defendant's own expression rather than the celebrity's likeness. And when we use the word "expression," we mean expression of something other than the likeness of the celebrity.

We further emphasize that in determining whether the work is transformative, courts are not to be concerned with the quality of the artistic contribution—vulgar forms of expression fully qualify for First Amendment protection. See, e.g., *Hustler Magazine v. Falwell*, 485 U.S. 46, 99 L. Ed. 2d 41, 108 S. Ct. 876 (1988). On the other hand, a literal depiction of a celebrity, even if accomplished with great skill, may still be subject to a right of publicity challenge. The inquiry is in a sense more quantitative than qualitative, asking whether the literal and imitative or the creative elements predominate in the work.

Furthermore, in determining whether a work is sufficiently transformative, courts may find useful a subsidiary inquiry, particularly in close cases: does the marketability and economic value of the challenged work derive primarily from the fame of the celebrity depicted? If this question is answered in the negative, then there would generally be no actionable right of publicity. When the value of the work comes principally from some source other than the fame of the celebrity—from the creativity, skill, and reputation of the artist—it may be presumed that sufficient transformative elements are present to warrant First Amendment protection. If the question is answered in the affirmative, however, it does not necessarily follow that the work is without First Amendment protection—it may still be a transformative work.

In sum, when an artist is faced with a right of publicity challenge to his or her work, he or she may raise an affirmative defense that the work is protected by the First Amendment inasmuch as it contains significant transformative elements or that the value of the work does not derive primarily from the celebrity's fame....

... [T]he inquiry is into whether Saderup's work is sufficiently transformative. Correctly anticipating this inquiry, he argues that all portraiture involves creative decisions, that therefore no portrait portrays a mere literal likeness, and that accordingly all portraiture, including reproductions, is protected by the First Amendment. We reject any such categorical position. Without denying that all portraiture involves the making of artistic choices, we find it equally undeniable, under the test formulated above, that when an artist's skill and talent is manifestly subordinated to the overall goal of creating a conventional portrait of a celebrity so as to commercially exploit his or her fame, then the artist's right of free expression is outweighed by the right of publicity. As is the case with fair use in the area of copyright law, an artist depicting a celebrity must contribute something more than a "merely trivial variation, [but must create] something recognizably his own," *L. Batlin &*

[handwritten margin note: artists can claim 1st amendment rights when a work contains transformative elements]

Son, Inc. v. Snyder (2d Cir. 1976) 536 F.2d 486, 490, in order to qualify for legal protection.

On the other hand, we do not hold that all reproductions of celebrity portraits are unprotected by the First Amendment. The silkscreens of Andy Warhol, for example, have as their subjects the images of such celebrities as Marilyn Monroe, Elizabeth Taylor, and Elvis Presley. Through distortion and the careful manipulation of context, Warhol was able to convey a message that went beyond the commercial exploitation of celebrity images and became a form of ironic social comment on the dehumanization of celebrity itself. Such expression may well be entitled to First Amendment protection. Although the distinction between protected and unprotected expression will sometimes be subtle, it is no more so than other distinctions triers of fact are called on to make in First Amendment jurisprudence.

Turning to Saderup's work, we can discern no significant transformative or creative contribution. His undeniable skill is manifestly subordinated to the overall goal of creating literal, conventional depictions of The Three Stooges so as to exploit their fame. Indeed, were we to decide that Saderup's depictions were protected by the First Amendment, we cannot perceive how the right of publicity would remain a viable right other than in cases of falsified celebrity endorsements.

Moreover, the marketability and economic value of Saderup's work derives primarily from the fame of the celebrities depicted. While that fact alone does not necessarily mean the work receives no First Amendment protection, we can perceive no transformative elements in Saderup's works that would require such protection.

Saderup argues that it would be incongruous and unjust to protect parodies and other distortions of celebrity figures but not wholesome, reverential portraits of such celebrities. The test we articulate today, however, does not express a value judgment or preference for one type of depiction over another. Rather, it reflects a recognition that the Legislature has granted to the heirs and assigns of celebrities the property right to exploit the celebrities' images, and that certain forms of expressive activity protected by the First Amendment fall outside the boundaries of that right. Stated another way, we are concerned not with whether conventional celebrity images should be produced but with who produces them and, more pertinently, who appropriates the value from their production. Thus, under section 990, if Saderup wishes to continue to depict The Three Stooges as he has done, he may do so only with the consent of the right-of-publicity holder. . . .

Notes

1. *The First Amendment and the Appropriate Limits on the Right of Publicity.* The *Saderup* case demonstrates that a celebrity's common law or statutory right of publicity is not absolute, but is trumped in certain cases by the First Amendment. For example, Nick Nolte cannot recover damages

from a newspaper that ran his now-infamous mug-shot photo following his September 12, 2002, arrest for suspicion of driving under the influence. Even though a newspaper is a for-profit business, Nolte's arrest was a legitimate news event—and the ability of the press to report news would be seriously compromised if persons like Nolte could claim a "property" right to keep their name out of the papers. Another example of how the First Amendment might limit a celebrity's property right is reflected in the concept of "parody." Even if Bette Midler can obtain damages against Ford because it appropriated her identity by using a Midler sound-alike in its advertisements, Midler cannot use her "right of publicity" to prevent NBC from lampooning her in a sketch on the *Saturday Night Live* television show.

Nevertheless, the boundary line between a celebrity's right of publicity and another person's First Amendment rights is not crystal-clear. Saderup, and its adoption of the "transformative" standard, reflects the best effort of the California Supreme Court to provide guidance to future courts faced with similar disputes. Do you agree that Saderup's charcoal drawing violates the Stooges' publicity rights? Suppose that Saderup had done essentially the same charcoal drawing of the Three Stooges, but with the faces appearing to be in relief against a mountain backdrop with the caption "Comedy's Mt. Rushmore." Would commercial sales of that drawing have subjected Saderup to liability under the court's framework in *Comedy III*? Why or why not?

Likewise, consider the following real-life disputes:

(a) An entrepreneur begins marketing portable toilets under the brand name "Here's Johnny." Johnny Carson sues for damages and injunctive relief claiming that the entrepreneur has appropriated Carson's identity based upon the use of Carson's signature Tonight Show introduction. What result? *Carson v. Here's Johnny Portable Toilets, Inc.*, 698 F.2d 831 (6th Cir. 1983).

[handwritten margin note: Carson won injunction]

(b) Following Tiger Woods' first victory in the Masters golf tournament, Rick Rush painted the painting "The Masters of Augusta," which appears on page 128. Rush began marketing limited edition prints of the painting through Jireh Publishing, Inc. (the exclusive publisher of Rush's works). Woods sued Rush and Jireh on the ground that marketing of the prints violated Woods' right of publicity. Do you agree? Can you distinguish this case from *Saderup*? If so, how? *See ETW Corp. v. Jireh Publ'g, Inc.*, 332 F.3d 915 (6th Cir. 2003).

(c) An entertainer begins performing an "Elvis Tribute Show." The estate of Elvis Presley sues for damages and injunctive relief claiming that the entertainer has appropriated Elvis' identity. What result? *Estate of Presley v. Russen*, 513 F.Supp. 1339 (D.N.J. 1981) (granting injunction against impersonator's "Big El Show"). [Given the result in *Russen*, how can you explain all of the Elvis impersonators that remain in business?]

Rick Rush, "The Masters of Augusta"

woods loses

(d) Samsung Electronics ran a print advertising campaign featuring predictions about what various celebrities would be doing in the future. One magazine advertisement involved a photo (right) of a robot standing in front of a game board that looked exactly like the board on the popular game show *Wheel of Fortune*. The robot was wearing a blond wig, jewelry, and a dress similar to those worn on the actual show by *Wheel of Fortune* hostess Vanna White. The caption to the photo read "Longest Running Game Show. 2012 A.D." The ad also contained a photo of a portion of a Samsung VCR, with the following promotional caption:

> The VCR you'll tape it on. 2012 A.D. In the next century, will 'she' still be America's favorite gameshow hostess? You'll have to wait for the answer. But we can tell you about prize VCRs for today and tomorrow: Samsung. Take a look at Samsung's full-featured, high-quality line. And you'll see why Samsung is heading into the future at fast forward. **Samsung. The future of electronics.**

Samsung did not have Vanna's consent for the advertisement. Vanna sued for damages, claiming that the advertisement violated her right of publicity. Samsung argued that its advertisement was protected by the First Amendment, because it was evoking Vanna as a metaphor for the reliability of Samsung products (*i.e.*, we'll be around years from now), rather than as a pitchwoman. What result? *White v. Samsung Elec. Am., Inc.*, 971 F.2d 1395 (1992). Is Samsung's motive/purpose in running the ad clear? Suppose that the evidence indicated that Samsung personnel referred to the advertisement internally as the "Vanna White" ad. Is this relevant to the dispute? Why or why not? *See* David S. Welkowitz, *Catching Smoke, Nailing JELL–O to a Wall: The Vanna White Case and the Limits of Celebrity Rights*, 3 J. Int. Prop. L. 67, 78–79 (1995).

(e) Paramount Productions attempted to capitalize on the popularity of its hit TV series *Cheers* by licensing Host International to operate Cheers-

Vannah White case

Samsung exploited image they know was correlated w/ Vanna White

Created? P. of copyright vrt of Publicity

Cheers case

themed bars in U.S. airports. In these bars, Paramount placed life-sized animatronic figures that moved slightly and spoke recorded messages. The figures did not use the visual likenesses of George Wendt or John Ratzenberger (the actors who played Norm and Cliff on *Cheers*), but one robot was fat and the other was dressed as a mailman. In response, Wendt and Ratzenberger sued Host, claiming that the figures violated their common law right of publicity. Paramount intervened in the litigation, claiming that § 301 of the federal Copyright Act protected its right to create derivative works using its copyrighted *Cheers* characters, and that the Act thus pre-empted the publicity rights of Wendt and Ratzenberger. How do you think this dispute should be resolved? *See, e.g., Wendt v. Host Int'l, Inc.*, 125 F.3d 806 (9th Cir. 1997).

C. "FIRST-IN-TIME" AND FINDING

The preceding cases highlight that the law will protect the expectations of someone who "first" takes "possession" of something that had no previous owner. In the following materials, we focus upon objects that did have a previous owner, but that are no longer in that owner's physical custody because they have been lost, mislaid, stolen or abandoned. To what extent—and against what persons—can someone who finds such objects establish a property claim to them?

ARMORY v. DELAMIRIE

King's Bench.
1 Strange 505 (1722).

The plaintiff being a chimney sweeper's boy found a jewel and carried it to the defendant's shop (who was a goldsmith) to know what it was, and delivered it into the hands of the apprentice, who under a pretence of weighing it, took out the stones, and calling to the master to let him know it came to three-halfpence, the master offered the boy the money, who refused to take it and insisted to have the thing again; whereupon the apprentice delivered him back the socket without the stones. And now in trover against the master these points were ruled:

(1) That the finder of a jewel, though he does not by such finding acquire an absolute property or ownership, yet he has such a property as will enable him to keep it against all but the rightful owner, and consequently may maintain trover . . . .

(3) As to the value of the jewel several of the trade were examined to prove what a jewel of the finest water that would fit the socket would be worth; and the Chief Justice (Pratt) directed the jury, that unless the defendant did produce the jewel, and shew it not to be of the finest water, they should presume the strongest against him, and make the value of the best jewels the measure of their damages: which they accordingly did.

Notes

fair market value is the proper formula for awarding damages)

1. *Valuation and the Measure of Damages for Conversion.* The court in *Armory* applies the standard formula for awarding damages for conversion— the fair market value of the object converted. As an economic matter, the court's measure of damages overcompensates the chimney sweep's boy; can you explain why? [Hint: How much would you pay the boy to acquire his title to the stones?] Is this overcompensation a problem? Why or why not?

2. *Prior Possession, Relativity of Title, and the Jus Tertii Defense.* The *Armory* case teaches an important lesson about the relative nature of ownership (or title) to property. Consider the following hypothetical: *O* (the true owner) loses a necklace. Wells finds the necklace. Wells then loses the necklace. Key then finds the necklace. Upon learning of Key's find, Wells asks Key to return the necklace. Under the holding in *Armory v. Delamirie*, who has the better claim to the necklace, Wells or Key? Are you sure? How would you restate the court's holding in *Armory*?

Would your analysis in the above hypothetical change if you knew that Wells had stolen the necklace from *O*, and that Key had in turn stolen the necklace from Wells? In answering this question, consider the following hypothetical: Pushaw goes onto someone else's land and cuts $2,000 worth of timber. Pushaw decides to ship the timber to a local sawmill using a local trucking company. Before the timber is delivered to the sawmill, however, Henning steals the timber from the truck. Should Pushaw be able to recover the timber from Henning? Should Pushaw be able to recover damages from Henning? *Compare Anderson v. Gouldberg,* 51 Minn. 294, 53 N.W. 636 (1892) ("[B]are possession of property, though wrongfully obtained, is sufficient title to enable the party enjoying it to maintain replevin against a mere stranger, who takes it from him.... Any other rule would lead to an endless series of reprisals in every case where property had once passed out of the possession of the rightful owner.") *with Russell v. Hill,* 125 N.C. 470, 34 S.E. 640 (1900) (in trover case, where plaintiff was wrongful possessor and not the true owner, "it would be manifestly wrong to allow the plaintiff to recover the value of the property; for the real owner may forthwith bring trover against the defendant, and force him to pay the value the second time, and the fact that he paid it in a former suit would be no defense").

jus tertii

In *Russell,* the court allows the second possessor (in our example, Henning) to assert the *jus tertii* defense against the prior possessor (in our example, Pushaw). The *jus tertii* defense allows Henning to assert the rights of the true owner as a defense to an action by Pushaw (*e.g.,* "You aren't the true owner, so you can't recover from me."). In contrast, the court in *Anderson* does not allow the second possessor to assert the *jus tertii* defense. Can you reconcile these decisions? Does the fact that the court knew the identity of the owner of the land in the *Russell* case constitute a meaningful distinction? Does the *Russell* court's concern about double liability arise because we have an action in trover in *Russell* but an action in replevin in

Anderson? Which court's reasoning is more persuasive? Does the *Russell* court's decision truly avoid the risk of double liability?

Richard H. Helmholz, in his article *Wrongful Possession of Chattels: Hornbook Law and Case Law*, 80 Nw. U. L. Rev. 1221 (1986), noted that the *Anderson/Russell* situation of successive wrongdoers rarely arises. Helmholz concluded that in the more common circumstance of disputes between a prior wrongful possessor and an honest subsequent one, courts regularly prefer the latter, suggesting that honesty is a necessary prerequisite for prior possessors seeking to take advantage of the first-in-time rule. *See also* John V. Orth, Russell v. Hill *(N.C. 1899): Misunderstood Lessons*, 73 N.C. L. Rev. 2031 (1995) (arguing that second possessor's ability to raise *jus tertii* defense should be limited to situations where first possessor did not obtain possession in good faith).

Disputes sometimes arise when someone finds an object on land belonging to a person other than the finder or the true owner of the object. When this occurs, both the finder and the landowner may claim prior possession of the object as against the other. How should the law resolve this "finder vs. landowner" dispute? American courts have traditionally drawn a distinction between *lost property, mislaid property,* and *abandoned property* in resolving these cases. Based on the following materials, what instrumental policies does the law serve by drawing such distinctions? Are these distinctions sound?

BENJAMIN v. LINDNER AVIATION, INC.

Supreme Court of Iowa.
534 N.W.2d 400 (1995).

TERNUS, JUSTICE. . . . In April of 1992, State Central Bank became the owner of an airplane when the bank repossessed it from its prior owner who had defaulted on a loan. In August of that year, the bank took the plane to Lindner Aviation for a routine annual inspection. Benjamin worked for Lindner Aviation and did the inspection.

As part of the inspection, Benjamin removed panels from the underside of the wings. Although these panels were to be removed annually as part of the routine inspection, a couple of the screws holding the panel on the left wing were so rusty that Benjamin had to use a drill to remove them. Benjamin testified that the panel probably had not been removed for several years.

Inside the left wing Benjamin discovered two packets approximately four inches high and wrapped in aluminum foil. He removed the packets from the wing and took off the foil wrapping. Inside the foil was paper currency, tied in string and wrapped in handkerchiefs. The currency was predominately twenty-dollar bills with mint dates before the 1960s, primarily in the 1950s. The money smelled musty.

Benjamin took one packet to his jeep and then reported what he had found to his supervisor, offering to divide the money with him. However, the supervisor reported the discovery to the owner of Lindner Aviation, William Engle. Engle insisted that they contact the authorities and he called the Department of Criminal Investigation. The money was eventually turned over to the Keokuk police department.

Two days later, Benjamin filed an affidavit with the county auditor claiming that he was the finder of the currency under the provisions of Iowa Code chapter 644 (1991). Lindner Aviation and the bank also filed claims to the money. The notices required by chapter 644 were published and posted. *See* Iowa Code § 644.8 (1991). No one came forward within twelve months claiming to be the true owner of the money. *See id.* § 644.11 (if true owner does not claim property within twelve months, the right to the property vests in the finder).

Benjamin filed this declaratory judgment action against Lindner Aviation and the bank to establish his right to the property. The parties tried the case to the court. The district court held that chapter 644 applies only to "lost" property and the money here was mislaid property.[1] The court awarded the money to the bank, holding that it was entitled to possession of the money to the exclusion of all but the true owner. The court also held that Benjamin was a "finder" within the meaning of chapter 644 and awarded him a ten percent finder's fee. *See id.* § 644.13 (a finder of lost property is entitled to ten percent of the value of the lost property as a reward).

Benjamin appealed. He claims that chapter 644 governs the disposition of all found property and any common law distinctions between various types of found property are no longer valid. He asserts alternatively that even under the common law classes of found property, he is entitled to the money he discovered. He claims that the trial court should have found that the property was treasure trove or was lost or abandoned rather than mislaid, thereby entitling the finder to the property.

The bank and Lindner Aviation cross-appealed. Lindner Aviation claims that if the money is mislaid property, it is entitled to the money as the owner of the premises on which the money was found, the hangar where the plane was parked. It argues in the alternative that it is the finder, not Benjamin, because Benjamin discovered the money during his work for Lindner Aviation. The bank asserts in its cross-appeal that it owns the premises where the money was found—the airplane—and that no one is entitled to a finder's fee because chapter 644 does not apply to mislaid property. . . .

Benjamin argues that chapter 644 governs the rights of finders of property and abrogates the common law distinctions between types of found property. As he points out, lost property statutes are intended "to encourage and facilitate the return of property to the true owner, and then to reward a finder for his honesty if the property remains un-

---

1. Editor's Note: Chapter 644.6 (which now appears in the Iowa Code at Chapter 556F.6) provides: "If any person shall find any lost goods, money, bank notes, or other things of any description whatever, of the value of five dollars and over, such person shall inform the owner thereof, if known, and make restitution thereof." Chapter 644.7 (now Chapter 556F.7) and other statutory provisions specify the steps that a finder of such property should take when the owner is unknown.

claimed." *Paset v. Old Orchard Bank & Trust Co.*, 62 Ill.App.3d 534, 19 Ill.Dec. 389, 393, 378 N.E.2d 1264, 1268 (1978) (interpreting a statute similar to chapter 644); *accord Flood v. City Nat'l Bank*, 218 Iowa 898, 908, 253 N.W. 509, 514 (1934), *cert. denied*, 298 U.S. 666, 56 S.Ct. 749, 80 L.Ed. 1390 (1936) (public policy reflected in lost property statute is "to provide a reward to the finder of lost goods"); *Willsmore v. Township of Oceola*, 106 Mich.App. 671, 308 N.W.2d 796, 804 (1981) (lost goods act "provides protection to the finder, a reasonable method of uniting goods with their true owner, and a plan which benefits the people of the state through their local governments"). These goals, Benjamin argues, can best be achieved by applying such statutes to all types of found property. . . .

Although a few courts have adopted an expansive view of lost property statutes, we think Iowa law is to the contrary. In 1937, we quoted and affirmed a trial court ruling that "the old law of treasure trove is not merged in the statutory law of chapter 515, 1935 Code of Iowa." *Zornes v. Bowen*, 223 Iowa 1141, 1145, 274 N.W. 877, 879 (1937). Chapter 515 of the 1935 Iowa Code was eventually renumbered as chapter 644. The relevant sections of chapter 644 are unchanged since our 1937 decision. As recently as 1991, we stated that "[t]he rights of finders of property vary according to the characterization of the property found." *Ritz v. Selma United Methodist Church*, 467 N.W.2d 266, 268 (Iowa 1991). We went on to define and apply the common law classifications of found property in deciding the rights of the parties. *Id.* at 269. As our prior cases show, we have continued to use the common law distinctions between classes of found property despite the legislature's enactment of chapter 644 and its predecessors.

The legislature has had many opportunities since our decision in *Zornes* to amend the statute so that it clearly applies to all types of found property. However, it has not done so. When the legislature leaves a statute unchanged after the supreme court has interpreted it, we presume the legislature has acquiesced in our interpretation. *State v. Sheffey*, 234 N.W.2d 92, 97 (Iowa 1975). Therefore, we presume here that the legislature approves of our application of chapter 644 to lost property only. Consequently, we hold that chapter 644 does not abrogate the common law classifications of found property. We note this position is consistent with that taken by most jurisdictions.

Under the common law, there are four categories of found property: (1) abandoned property, (2) lost property, (3) mislaid property, and (4) treasure trove. *Ritz*, 467 N.W.2d at 269. The rights of a finder of property depend on how the found property is classified. *Id.* at 268–69.

A. *Abandoned property.* Property is abandoned when the owner no longer wants to possess it. *Cf. Pearson v. City of Guttenberg*, 245 N.W.2d 519, 529 (Iowa 1976) (considering abandonment of real estate). Abandonment is shown by proof that the owner intends to abandon the property and has voluntarily relinquished all right, title and interest in the property. *Ritz*, 467 N.W.2d at 269; 1 Am.Jur.2d Abandoned Property

§§ 11–14, at 15–20. Abandoned property belongs to the finder of the property against all others, including the former owner. *Ritz*, 467 N.W.2d at 269.

B. *Lost property.* "Property is lost when the owner unintentionally and involuntarily parts with its possession and does not know where it is." *Id.* (citing *Eldridge v. Herman*, 291 N.W.2d 319, 323 (Iowa 1980)); *accord* 1 Am.Jur.2d Abandoned Property § 4, at 9–10. Stolen property found by someone who did not participate in the theft is lost property. *Flood*, 218 Iowa at 905, 253 N.W. at 513; 1 Am.Jur.2d Abandoned Property § 5, at 11. Under chapter 644, lost property becomes the property of the finder once the statutory procedures are followed and the owner makes no claim within twelve months. Iowa Code § 644.11 (1991).

C. *Mislaid property.* Mislaid property is voluntarily put in a certain place by the owner who then overlooks or forgets where the property is. *Ritz*, 467 N.W.2d at 269. It differs from lost property in that the owner voluntarily and intentionally places mislaid property in the location where it is eventually found by another. 1 Am.Jur.2d Abandoned Property § 10, at 14. In contrast, property is not considered lost unless the owner parts with it involuntarily. *Ritz*, 467 N.W.2d at 269; 1 Am.Jur.2d Abandoned Property § 10, at 14; *see Hill v. Schrunk*, 207 Or. 71, 292 P.2d 141, 143 (1956) (carefully concealed currency was mislaid property, not lost property).

The finder of mislaid property acquires no rights to the property. 1 Am.Jur.2d Abandoned Property § 24, at 30. The right of possession of mislaid property belongs to the owner of the premises upon which the property is found, as against all persons other than the true owner. *Ritz*, 467 N.W.2d at 269.

D. *Treasure trove.* Treasure trove consists of coins or currency concealed by the owner. *Id.* It includes an element of antiquity. *Id.* To be classified as treasure trove, the property must have been hidden or concealed for such a length of time that the owner is probably dead or undiscoverable. *Id.*; 1 Am.Jur.2d Abandoned Property § 8, at 13. Treasure trove belongs to the finder as against all but the true owner. *Zornes*, 223 Iowa at 1145, 274 N.W. at 879.

We think there was substantial evidence to find that the currency discovered by Benjamin was mislaid property. In the *Eldridge* case, we examined the location where the money was found as a factor in determining whether the money was lost property. *Eldridge*, 291 N.W.2d at 323; *accord* 1 Am.Jur.2d Abandoned Property § 6, at 11–12 ("The place where money or property claimed as lost is found is an important factor in the determination of the question of whether it was lost or only mislaid."). Similarly, in *Ritz*, we considered the manner in which the money had been secreted in deciding that it had not been abandoned. *Ritz*, 467 N.W.2d at 269.

The place where Benjamin found the money and the manner in which it was hidden are also important here. The bills were carefully tied and wrapped and then concealed in a location that was accessible only by

[handwritten margin note top: money placed there intentionally]

removing screws and a panel. These circumstances support an inference that the money was placed there intentionally. This inference supports the conclusion that the money was mislaid. *Jackson v. Steinberg*, 186 Or. 129, 200 P.2d 376, 378 (1948) (fact that $800 in currency was found concealed beneath the paper lining of a dresser indicates that money was intentionally concealed with intention of reclaiming it; therefore, property was mislaid, not lost); *Schley v. Couch*, 155 Tex. 195, 284 S.W.2d 333, 336 (1955) (holding that money found buried under garage floor was mislaid property as a matter of law because circumstances showed that money was placed there deliberately and court presumed that owner had either forgotten where he hid the money or had died before retrieving it).

The same facts that support the trial court's conclusion that the money was mislaid prevent us from ruling as a matter of law that the property was lost. Property is not considered lost unless considering the place where and the conditions under which the property is found, there is an inference that the property was left there unintentionally. Contrary to Benjamin's position the circumstances here do not support a conclusion that the money was placed in the wing of the airplane unintentionally. Additionally, as the trial court concluded, there was no evidence suggesting that the money was placed in the wing by someone other than the owner of the money and that its location was unknown to the owner. For these reasons, we reject Benjamin's argument that the trial court was obligated to find that the currency Benjamin discovered was lost property.

[handwritten margin note: lost = unintentionally left @ place where found; mislaid = intentional]

We also reject Benjamin's assertion that as a matter of law this money was abandoned property. Both logic and common sense suggest that it is unlikely someone would voluntarily part with over $18,000 with the intention of terminating his ownership. The location where this money was found is much more consistent with the conclusion that the owner of the property was placing the money there for safekeeping. We will not presume that an owner has abandoned his property when his conduct is consistent with a continued claim to the property. Therefore, we cannot rule that the district court erred in failing to find that the currency discovered by Benjamin was abandoned property.

[handwritten margin note: Plaintiff believed it was lost property]

Finally, we also conclude that the trial court was not obligated to decide that this money was treasure trove. Based on the dates of the currency, the money was no older than thirty-five years. The mint dates, the musty odor and the rusty condition of a few of the panel screws indicate that the money may have been hidden for some time. However, there was no evidence of the age of the airplane or the date of its last inspection. These facts may have shown that the money was concealed for a much shorter period of time.

[handwritten margin note left: money was not trove since mint dates put it @ less than 35]

Moreover, it is also significant that the airplane had a well-documented ownership history. The record reveals that there were only two owners of the plane prior to the bank. One was the person from whom the bank repossessed the plane; the other was the original purchaser of the plane when it was manufactured. Nevertheless, there is no indication

[handwritten margin note right: only 2 owners prior to the bank]

that Benjamin or any other party attempted to locate and notify the prior owners of the plane, which could very possibly have led to the identification of the true owner of the money. Under these circumstances, we cannot say as a matter of law that the money meets the antiquity requirement or that it is probable that the owner of the money is not discoverable. . . .

Because the money discovered by Benjamin was properly found to be mislaid property, it belongs to the owner of the premises where it was found. Mislaid property is entrusted to the owner of the premises where it is found rather than the finder of the property because it is assumed that the true owner may eventually recall where he has placed his property and return there to reclaim it.

We think that the premises where the money was found is the airplane, not Lindner Aviation's hangar where the airplane happened to be parked when the money was discovered. The policy behind giving ownership of mislaid property to the owner of the premises where the property was mislaid supports this conclusion. If the true owner of the money attempts to locate it, he would initially look for the plane; it is unlikely he would begin his search by contacting businesses where the airplane might have been inspected. Therefore, we affirm the trial court's judgment that the bank, as the owner of the plane, has the right to possession of the property as against all but the true owner.

Benjamin claims that if he is not entitled to the money, he should be paid a ten percent finder's fee under section 644.13. The problem with this claim is that only the finder of "lost goods, money, bank notes, and other things" is rewarded with a finder's fee under chapter 644. Iowa Code § 644.13 (1991). Because the property found by Benjamin was mislaid property, not lost property, section 644.13 does not apply here. The trial court erred in awarding Benjamin a finder's fee. . . .

SNELL, JUSTICE (dissenting). . . . After considering the four categories of found money, the majority decides that Benjamin found mislaid money. The result is that the bank gets all the money; Benjamin, the finder, gets nothing. Apart from the obvious unfairness in result, I believe this conclusion fails to come from logical analysis.

Mislaid property is property voluntarily put in a certain place by the owner who then overlooks or forgets where the property is. *Ritz v. Selma United Methodist Church*, 467 N.W.2d 266, 268 (Iowa 1991). The property here consisted of two packets of paper currency totalling $18,910, three to four inches high, wrapped in aluminum foil. Inside the foil, the paper currency, predominantly twenty dollar bills, was tied with string and wrapped in handkerchiefs. Most of the mint dates were in the 1950s with one dated 1934. These packets were found in the left wing of the Mooney airplane after Benjamin removed a panel held in by rusty screws.

These facts satisfy the requirement that the property was voluntarily put in a certain place by the owner. But the second test for determining that property is mislaid is that the owner "overlooks or forgets *lost/mislaid/abandoned*

where the property is." *See Ritz*, 467 N.W.2d at 269. I do not believe that the facts, logic, or common sense lead to a finding that this requirement is met. It is not likely or reasonable to suppose that a person would secrete $18,000 in an airplane wing and then forget where it was. . . .

The scenario unfolded in this case convinces me that the money found in the airplane wing was abandoned. Property is abandoned when the owner no longer wants to possess it. *See Ritz*, 467 N.W.2d at 269; *Pearson v. City of Guttenberg*, 245 N.W.2d 519, 529 (Iowa 1976). The money had been there for years, possibly thirty. No owner had claimed it in that time. No claim was made by the owner after legally prescribed notice was given that it had been found. Thereafter, logic and the law support a finding that the owner has voluntarily relinquished all right, title, and interest in the property. Whether the money was abandoned due to its connection to illegal drug trafficking or is otherwise contraband property is a matter for speculation. In any event, abandonment by the true owner has legally occurred and been established.

I would hold that Benjamin is legally entitled to the entire amount of money that he found in the airplane wing as the owner of abandoned property.

Notes

1. *The Lost/Mislaid/Abandoned Framework and the Policies Underlying Finder vs. Landowner Disputes.* When a court must allocate possession of found property between a finder and the owner of the locus in quo, what considerations should be most important? Encouraging finders to be honest? Facilitating the return of found objects to their true owner? Protecting the locus owner's legitimate expectations that he/she can exercise dominion and control over what happens on the land? To what extent do these considerations come into play in *Benjamin*?

Is the lost/mislaid/abandoned test a reasoned approach for courts to use in determining the rights of various parties to a finding dispute? If so, why do the majority and dissent in *Benjamin* disagree as to the proper characterization of the money? Does this suggest the possibility that courts may easily manipulate the lost/mislaid/abandoned test to justify a particular outcome? Consider the view of Justice Wilson, concurring in *Schley v. Couch*, 155 Tex. 195, 284 S.W.2d 333 (1955):

> In so far as money buried or secreted on privately owned realty is concerned, the old distinctions between treasure-trove, lost property, and mislaid property seem to be of little value and not worth preserving. The principal point of distinction seems to be the intent of the true owner who necessarily is not known and not available. Therefore the evidence on his intent will usually be scant and uncontroverted. [284 S.W.2d at 339.]

Are there other reasons that the lost/mislaid/abandoned test may prove troublesome in resolving finding disputes?

2. *The Lost/Mislaid/Abandoned Distinction in Practice.* In trying to classify objects as lost, mislaid, or abandoned, American courts have attached

significance to a variety of factual distinctions concerning the location of the find, the status of the finder, and the object found.

(a) *Location of the Find—"Public" v. "Private" Place.* When an item is found in a more private location (in a private office, or under the ground), courts have often—but not always—awarded it to the landowner. *See, e.g., Allred v. Biegel,* 240 Mo.App. 818, 219 S.W.2d 665 (1949) (awarding boat found in soil to landowner); *but see Danielson v. Roberts,* 44 Or. 108, 74 P. 913 (1904) (awarding money found buried in chicken coop to finders). Conversely, when the finder discovers property in a location accessible to the public (such as the ground's surface or the floor of a room), courts have often—but not always—awarded it to the finder. *See, e.g., McDonald v. Railway Express Agency, Inc.,* 89 Ga.App. 884, 81 S.E.2d 525 (1954) (awarding to finder money found on floor of agency); *but see McAvoy v. Medina,* 93 Mass. 548, 11 Allen 548 (1866) (awarding pocketbook found on barbershop table to shop owner). Why might the location of a find be relevant? What difficulties would a court encounter in applying this distinction?

(b) *Status of Finder—"Employee" or "Trespasser."* When an employee finds an object in the course of her employment, courts have often—but not always—awarded it to the locus owner or the employer. *Compare, e.g., Jackson v. Steinberg,* 186 Or. 129, 200 P.2d 376 (1948) (awarding money found by maid in hotel room dresser drawer to hotel) and *Dennis v. Northwestern Nat'l Bank,* 249 Minn. 130, 81 N.W.2d 254 (1957) (employee of bank finding money in safe deposit inspection room finds it on behalf of bank) *with McDonald v. Railway Express Agency, Inc.,* 89 Ga.App. 884, 81 S.E.2d 525 (1954) (employee who found money on floor of agency found it in individual capacity, not as employee) and *Danielson v. Roberts,* 44 Or. 108, 74 P. 913 (1904) (awarding money found buried in chicken coop to boys hired to clean chicken coop). Likewise, when a trespasser finds an object on someone else's land, courts are more likely to award it to the landowner. *See, e.g., Morgan v. Wiser,* 711 S.W.2d 220 (Tenn. App. 1985); *Favorite v. Miller,* 176 Conn. 310, 407 A.2d 974 (1978). Nevertheless, courts have awarded found property to persons who could have been considered trespassers. *See Willsmore v. Oceola Township,* 106 Mich.App. 671, 308 N.W.2d 796 (1981); *Hendle v. Stevens,* 224 Ill.App.3d 1046, 166 Ill.Dec. 868, 586 N.E.2d 826 (1992). Why might the status of the finder be relevant? What difficulties would a court encounter in applying this distinction?

(c) *Treasure Trove.* Under English common law, the King was entitled to "treasure trove," meaning any money or coin, gold, silver plate, or bullion that had been *intentionally* hidden in the earth, while the finder received any such property that appeared to have been abandoned. Some American jurisdictions recognize "treasure trove" as a separate category of found property and award it to the finder. *See, e.g., Zornes v. Bowen,* 223 Iowa 1141, 274 N.W. 877 (1937); *Zech v. Accola,* 253 Wis. 80, 33 N.W.2d 232 (1948). Other jurisdictions never embraced the treasure trove distinction or have refused to recognize treasure trove as a distinct category of found property. *See Morgan v. Wiser,* 711 S.W.2d 220 (Tenn.

App. 1985); *Willsmore v. Oceola Twp.*, 106 Mich.App. 671, 308 N.W.2d 796 (1981); *Schley v. Couch*, 155 Tex. 195, 284 S.W.2d 333 (1955).

some states have legislation that provides for public notice

3. *Finding Statutes.* Like Iowa, many states have enacted legislation that provides for public notice of found items and permits finders to establish clear title to found property if the true owner fails to reclaim it during a specified period of time. Often, however (as in *Benjamin*), these statutes do not address all of the issues present in a "finder vs. landowner" dispute. Courts have differed in their willingness to incorporate the common law finding rules as "gap-filling" rules in finding statutes. *Compare Hurley v. City of Niagara Falls*, 25 N.Y.2d 687, 306 N.Y.S.2d 689, 254 N.E.2d 917 (1969) (holding that statute abolished distinction between lost and mislaid property and made employer the "finder" of any property found on property by person hired to perform tasks) *with Zech v. Accola*, 253 Wis. 80, 33 N.W.2d 232 (1948) (concluding that statute applies only to lost property and does not apply to "treasure trove"). What do you think of the *Benjamin* court's analysis of the Iowa statute? Do you agree that the Iowa statute preserves the distinction between lost, mislaid, and abandoned objects? Do you think that the legislature intended for this statute to apply to finder vs. landowner disputes at all? What purpose does the statute serve?

4. *The Law as a Win/Lose System of Dispute Resolution.* A pattern emerges from the preceding cases—to the extent that courts apply legal rules based upon the concept of first possession, the resolution of possessory disputes is inevitably "win/lose." Courts rarely, if ever, reach decisions in which the result is "win/win." Is this an inevitable consequence of the concept of "possession"? Of our adversary legal system? Is it impossible to fashion property rules that produce a win/win result? Consider the finding cases. Would the policy goals articulated in finding cases be furthered by having finders and landowners share custody of an item or the value of an item? *See* Richard H. Helmholz, *Equitable Division and the Law of Finders*, 52 Fordham L. Rev. 313 (1983). To what extent does the Iowa finding statute, as interpreted in *Benjamin*, further (or fail to further) these goals?

not often a win/win situation when dealing w/possession

LAWYERING EXERCISE
(Client Counseling and Fact Investigation)

BACKGROUND: As *Hannah, Benjamin* and the cases in note 2 suggest, the application of the rules and principles governing finding disputes is not always certain. A former student of one of the authors once complained about the inconsistencies in the finding cases; this student, like most people, was very uncomfortable with uncertainty and preferred clear and simple rules.

When a lawyer or prospective lawyer raises this concern about uncertainty, one could easily respond flippantly by saying "Don't bite the hand that feeds you." After all, people hire lawyers because they are uncertain of their rights. If the law was crystal clear in every respect, people wouldn't need lawyers—and more lawyers would be looking for jobs as salespersons, cab drivers, short order cooks, or the next coach of the Los Angeles Clippers. But the concern about uncertainty justifies a more serious response. As Professor Carol Rose has observed, certainty (or "crystal") is a legitimate and desirable goal in establishing legal rules, but it is not possible or desirable to fashion rules that would universally apply in every conceivable factual circumstance. Accomplishing justice often requires us to live with some level of uncertainty (or "mud") in legal rules. Carol M. Rose, *Crystals and Mud in Property Law*, 40 Stan. L. Rev. 577 (1988).

You encountered one example of this "crystals and mud" metaphor in *State v. Shack*. Tedesco wanted a "crystal" rule that would permit him to exclude persons like Tejeras and Shack at all times and for any reason. Instead, the court applied a "mud" rule that while Tedesco's right to exclude was broad, it did not permit him to exclude Tejeras and Shack under the circumstances present in that case. "Mud" rules make it more difficult to predict how courts will apply those rules in differing contexts in the future. The presence of "mud" rules, however, is one reason why the marketplace values a lawyer's skills so highly. With careful legal training and the development of keen skills of investigation, counseling, and judgment, lawyers place themselves in a position to assist laypersons by providing predictive judgments about uncertain areas of the law. Therefore, rather than being uncomfortable about uncertainty, you should recognize and appreciate that making these predictive judgments is the lawyer's role. You are preparing to be your clients' guide through uncertain and ever-changing legal waters, in much the same sense that Sam (the young cub pilot in Mark Twain's *Life on the Mississippi*) prepared for a career guiding boats through the ever-changing waters of the Mississippi River.

You must also appreciate, however, that no amount of training and experience on your part can make your judgment *anything other than predictive*. In counseling clients, how do you communicate that you are making a prediction about how the legal system will handle a particular situation—without instilling in your client a false sense of security, and without making yourself appear to be timid or lacking in confidence? This problem is especially troublesome at the conclusion of an initial meeting with a client, at which time the client often unrealistically expects you to produce a definitive and favorable answer. In their book Lawyers as Counselors (West 1991), Professors David A. Binder, Paul Bergman, and Susan C. Price provide the following advice about dealing with "uncertainty" at this point in the lawyer-client relationship:

> Often, you do not have enough information at the conclusion of an initial meeting to fully assess a client's position or give detailed advice. As a result, often you can do little more than provide a tentative assessment and help a client decide whether a matter justifies your services.

> Unfortunately, however, clients sometimes expect definitive answers at the conclusion of initial meetings. Inexperienced clients in particular often believe that the law provides clear answers and that lawyers know which books contain them. Even relatively sophisticat-

ed clients may be unrealistically hopeful of leaving an initial meeting with a firm plan of attack in hand.

If such expectations are overly naive, you nevertheless must respond to them. Ignoring such expectations may damage a client's confidence. Moreover, it is unfair, unprofessional and impolite for you to absorb information like a sponge and give nothing back in return. Clients should leave initial meetings with some insight into possible resolutions. Unless you really cannot give one, a client is entitled to at least a tentative assessment of how things stand.

The issue, then, is how to respond to a client's expectations in a way that both inspires a client's confidence and conveys your need for further information. . . .

Clients who want to sue, or who have been sued, usually have an overwhelming "bottom line" interest in knowing whether they are going to "win." "Do I have a good case?" and "Can I get them to tear down the fence?" are questions of the sort they are likely to ask. . . .

How might you respond when, because you lack either legal or factual knowledge, you are unable to provide even a tentative assessment? That is, while you believe yourself competent to handle a matter, you are too uncertain of applicable legal rules or of facts to assess realistically a client's position. You can neither reassure a client that her or his chances are good, nor warn a client that they are poor.

In such situations, setting forth the legal parameters in which a client's problem arises and explicitly conveying your desire to provide help may maintain a client's confidence without overstating your analysis. . . . [*Id.* at 228–29.]

SITUATION: While playing on wooded land owned by William and Gladys Stevens, four young children (Alma Lopez, Thomas Farrell, Ryan Baassler and Jennifer Moore) discovered approximately $6,000 in cash. About one week later, while babysitting, Lopez told Margaret Lucchetti about the money. Lucchetti called the police, who began an investigation and spoke with each of the children and their parents. In the course of this investigation, the police took possession of the money. After six months, no one has come forward to claim the money other than the Stevenses. The Stevenses concede that they never knew about the money and that it has never been in their physical custody, but the Stevenses filed a claim based upon their ownership of the land.

TASK: The parents of Lopez and Baassler have come into your office seeking advice about whether the four children have a valid claim to the money. How would you conduct an interview? What information would you try to elicit in this interview? Do you see any potential problems with representing the children? What advice would you give regarding the likelihood of recovery?

voluntary bailment situations —▷ clothes to cleaners
checked coat
rent-a-car

142   POSSESSION AND FIRST–IN–TIME   Ch. 2

D. BAILMENTS

A "bailment" is the rightful possession of an object by one who is not the true owner of the item. 9 S. Williston, A Treatise on the Law of Contracts § 1030 (3d ed. 1967). Voluntary bailment relationships are commonplace. Though they frequently arise by express written contract, such as when you rent a car from a car rental agency, they also arise by implication under a variety of common circumstances—for example, when you take your clothes to the dry cleaners, check your coat at a restaurant, or leave your car at the garage for repairs.

Bailment relationships also can arise involuntarily (*i.e.*, other than through the voluntary actions of the true owner). Recall the statement from *Armory* "[t]hat the finder of a jewel, though he does not by such finding acquire an absolute property or ownership, yet he has such a property as will enable him to keep it against all but the rightful owner...." Because a finder has rightful possession, but does not have absolute ownership, a finder is also a bailee.

Why does the existence of a bailment relationship matter? The creation of a bailment imposes certain duties upon the bailee. One such duty is the bailee's duty of care with respect to the object of the bailment. The bailee (the dry cleaner, the restaurant, the mechanic or the finder) assumes a duty of care to maintain the object of the bailment and may be held liable to the bailor for damages caused by the bailee's violation of that duty of care. In some jurisdictions, the bailee must comply with a straightforward negligence standard under which the bailee must exercise the duty of care commensurate with the circumstances. *See, e.g., Christensen v. Hoover*, 643 P.2d 525 (Colo. 1982); *Peet v. Roth Hotel Co.*, 191 Minn. 151, 253 N.W. 546 (1934). In other jurisdictions, the bailee's standard of care may vary depending upon which party derives the most benefit from the bailment arrangement. If the bailment is solely for the benefit of the bailor (*e.g.*, my neighbor keeps my dog while I am on vacation), the bailee has a duty of slight care and will be liable only for damages caused by his gross negligence.[2] Alternatively, if the bailment is solely for the benefit of the bailee (*e.g.*, my neighbor borrows my lawn mower without paying me for its use), the bailee has a duty of great care and will be liable for damage caused by even slight negligence. If the bailment is for the mutual benefit of bailor and bailee (*e.g.*, I take my car to a garage to be repaired for a $250 charge), the bailee has a duty of ordinary care and will be liable for damages caused by ordinary negligence. *See, e.g., Banks v. Korman Assocs.*, 218 N.J.Super. 370, 527 A.2d 933 (1987); Richard H. Helmholz, *Bailment Theories and the Liability of Bailees: The Elusive Uniform Standard of Reasonable Care*, 41 Kan. L. Rev. 97 (1992).

Another duty is the bailee's duty of redelivery once the purpose of the bailment is satisfied. The bailee has an absolute duty to redeliver the

---

2. The law generally treats finders as involuntary bailees, whose act of taking possession creates a bailment solely for the benefit of the bailor.

liable if not returned

object of the bailment to the bailor. If the bailee wrongfully fails to return the object of the bailment, or if the bailee wrongfully delivers the object to a third party, then the bailee is strictly liable for conversion of the object. R. Brown, The Law of Personal Property, § 11.7 (Walter B. Raushenbush 3d ed. 1975).[3]

Notes

1. *The Existence of a Bailment Relationship in Marginal Cases.* By definition, for a bailment to arise, the bailee must have "possession" of the object of the bailment. This can create some difficulty determining whether a bailment arises in marginal cases. For example:

(a) When you park your car in a parking garage, have you created a bailment? How should a court determine whether a bailment exists in such a circumstance? What facts would be relevant to the court's judgment? *Compare Allen v. Hyatt Regency–Nashville Hotel*, 668 S.W.2d 286 (Tenn. 1984) *with Central Parking Sys. v. Miller*, 586 S.W.2d 262 (Ky. 1979). Suppose the garage attendant handed you a ticket that said: "No bailment is created by our parking your car. We are not liable for loss or damage associated with your car." Is there a bailment? Would it matter if you were a lawyer with experience in business transactions? *See Griffin v. Nationwide Moving & Storage Co., Inc.*, 187 Conn. 405, 446 A.2d 799 (1982); *Carr v. Hoosier Photo Supplies, Inc.*, 441 N.E.2d 450 (Ind. 1982); Note, *Bailor Beware: Limitations and Exclusions of Liability in Commercial Bailments*, 41 Vand. L. Rev. 129 (1988).

(b) When you give your coat to a coat check attendant, does that create a bailment of undisclosed items contained in the pocket of your coat? *Compare Shamrock Hilton Hotel v. Caranas*, 488 S.W.2d 151 (Tex. App. 1972) (hotel was bailee of expensive jewelry contained within purse left in dining room) *with Samples v. Geary*, 292 S.W. 1066 (Mo. App. 1927) (dancing school was not bailee of fur piece wrapped inside a checked coat where school was unaware of fur piece). If you represented a client who operated a restaurant, what advice would you give to your client regarding how she should handle the coats, purses, or other personal effects of patrons?

2. *The Bailee's Ability to Recover Damages for Bailed Property.* Suppose Pushaw borrowed Henning's car while Henning was out of the country. While Pushaw was using the car, he was struck by Middleton, who ran a red light. The accident caused $5,000 of damage to Henning's car. Can Pushaw sue Middleton and recover $5,000 in damages? Based upon the analysis in *The Winkfield*, [1902] P. 42 (1901), the answer is yes—a voluntary bailee can recover damages from a tortfeasor. Is that sensible, or should Middleton be able to raise a *jus tertii* defense?

2. jus tertii

Now suppose Henning returns from overseas and, upon learning of the accident, sues Middleton for damages. Can Middleton prevail by arguing that

3. In the case of an involuntary bailee (*e.g.*, a finder), however, courts typically will hold the bailee liable only if he is negligent in giving the item to someone other than the true owner. Why might courts be reluctant to apply a strict liability standard in the case of an involuntary bailment?

he has already paid damages to Pushaw? According to *The Winkfield*, the answer is again yes: "The wrongdoer, having once paid full damages to the bailee, has an answer to any action by the bailor." In light of the earlier discussion of the *jus tertii* principle, does the rule established in *The Winkfield* make sense? Why or why not?

Finally, suppose that the court in *Armory v. Delamirie* had assessed damages of $500 against the goldsmith, and that the goldsmith has paid that judgment to the sweep's boy. Now suppose that the true owner of the jewel shows up and demands that the goldsmith return the jewel. The goldsmith refuses. The true owner asks whether he can sue the goldsmith to recover damages for conversion of the jewel. How would you advise the true owner? Why?

Chapter 3

FIRST POSSESSION AND ESTOPPEL PRINCIPLES

Bona fide Purchase
Adverse Possession

both use estoppel principle to protect reliance of the later possessor

In Chapter 2, we focused upon the significance of "first possession" in determining ownership claims. We now turn to situations in which contrary policies intervene and cause courts and/or legislatures to establish rules that award title to someone other than the "first possessor." These situations—bona fide purchase and adverse possession—share a common denominator. In each situation, the law uses a specific application of the *estoppel* principle to protect the reliance of the later possessor.

A. BONA FIDE PURCHASE

1. *Personal Property*

hard for ownership since no public records

For most items of personal property, there are no public title records—which makes it difficult to establish documentary proof of ownership of personal property. Certainly, sale transactions often involve documentation. In some cases, when a buyer buys goods from a seller, the seller may deliver a *bill of sale* by which the seller purports to transfer its ownership to the buyer. In many transactions, however, the seller does not deliver a formal bill of sale; for example, if the buyer purchases a television from Circuit City, the only written evidence of the transaction may be a receipt that simply identifies the television set and its sale price. More importantly, there is no publicly maintained system of records where a buyer of goods could go to record its bill of sale or its receipt so as to evidence its claim of title.[1] And because many buyers are "organizationally challenged," the buyer may lose or throw away a bill of sale, a receipt, or any other documentary evidence of its ownership.

As a result, for most items of personal property, the best evidence of a person's ownership of an object is that person's possession of the

Best evidence for ownership is possession

---

1. This is not true for automobiles and certain other types of vehicles. For automobiles, each state has a title certification statute, under which a state agency issues a title certificate that purports to recognize a particular person as the owner of a particular automobile. Can you explain why a state might issue title certificates for automobiles but not other kinds of personal property?

object. Typically, the person in possession of an object is in fact that object's true owner. But in some cases, an object that is owned by one person may end up (rightly or wrongly) in the hands of another person. This creates an *ostensible ownership* problem—*i.e.*, third parties may believe that the possessor is the true owner of the object based upon possession, when another unknown person is the real "true owner" of the object. In this section, we explore how the law deals with conflicting title claims that occur due to the ostensible ownership problem.

The principle of *derivative title* states that one cannot transfer greater rights than one possesses.[2] Suppose Thief steals Owner's 1951 Mickey Mantle baseball card, and then sells the card to Buyer for $14,000. Owner can recover the card from Buyer. Why? It is tempting to say that Thief has no rights in the card—but that is inaccurate. Even a thief has a possessory right that is superior to almost everyone else in the world under the principle of relativity of title. But Thief's possessory right is only that of a wrongful possessor, and is subordinate to Owner's right as true owner. Thief can transfer to Buyer only the rights that he possesses. Because Buyer receives Thief's possessory rights—and because Owner can recover possession from Thief—it follows logically that Owner can recover the card from Buyer. Article 2 of the Uniform Commercial Code, which governs the sale of most tangible personal property (such as Owner's card), codifies the derivative title principle in § 2–403(1), which provides that "[a] purchaser of goods acquires all title which his transferor had or had power to transfer . . . ."

There are circumstances, however, in which the law may not allow the true owner to assert the derivative title principle and recover possession of an object from a later purchaser of the object. Suppose that Owner takes a tractor to Mechanic to have it repaired, but Mechanic's assistant mistakenly sells the tractor to Buyer. If Owner sues to recover the tractor from Buyer, should a court apply equitable estoppel—thereby refusing to allow Owner to recover the tractor, despite the derivative title principle?

Traditionally, courts would impose equitable estoppel against a true owner only in exceptional circumstances—where the owner had created a bailment relationship in which the bailee was clothed with "indicia of title." In this example, most courts would have held that the Mechanic's possession of the tractor, by itself, was not a sufficient "indicia of title" to justify an estoppel against Owner's recovery of the tractor. *See, e.g., Zendman v. Harry Winston, Inc.*, 305 N.Y. 180, 111 N.E.2d 871 (1953); *Porter v. Wertz*, 68 A.D.2d 141, 416 N.Y.S.2d 254 (1979). Courts applied equitable estoppel only in those cases in which the true owner was viewed as sufficiently blameworthy for creating the ostensible ownership problem that misled a good faith buyer. For example, suppose that Owner had taken the tractor to Mechanic and said "Creditor has gotten

---

2. Some commentators have referred to this concept as the *nemo dat* principle, from the Latin phrase *nemo dat quod non habet*, meaning "no one may give that which he/she does not have."

a judgment against me and I'm afraid Creditor may try to have the Sheriff take my tractor and sell it to satisfy his judgment. So please take the tractor and pretend it's yours, and here's a fake bill of sale, if anyone asks.'' In that situation, if Mechanic later sold the tractor to Buyer for value, and Buyer knew nothing about Owner's actual claim of ownership, a court might well have equitably estopped Owner from reclaiming the tractor from Buyer.

Today, Article 2 of the Uniform Commercial Code (the "UCC") governs the sale of all tangible, movable personal property ("goods"). In drafting Article 2, the drafters elected not to incorporate the "indicia of title" standard discussed above. Instead, the UCC provides two specific statutory estoppel rules that address this ostensible ownership problem—one dealing with *voidable title*, and the other with *entrustment* of goods to a merchant. The following materials explore the application of these statutory estoppel rules.

a.   *"Voidable Title."* UCC § 2–403(1) begins by codifying the common law's derivative title principle, but then introduces the concept of a "voidable" title. Section 2–403(1) provides:

A purchaser of goods acquires all title that the purchaser's transferor had or had power to transfer.... A person with voidable title has power to transfer a good title to a good-faith purchaser for value. If goods have been delivered under a transaction of purchase, the purchaser has such power even if:

(a) the transferor was deceived as to the identity of the purchaser;

(b) the delivery was in exchange for a check that is later dishonored;

(c) it was agreed that the transaction was to be a "cash sale"; or

(d) the delivery was procured through criminal fraud.

The application of this rule is demonstrated by the following examples:

Example 1. Thief steals Owner's 1951 Mickey Mantle baseball card. When Owner discovers what Thief has done, he demands that Thief return the card. However, Thief has already sold the card to Buyer for $14,000 and has spent the money. Buyer knew nothing about how the card came into Thief's hands. Owner can recover the card or its value from Buyer. Having stolen the card, Thief's title was "void"—*i.e.*, Thief held only the right of a wrongful possessor—and subordinate to Owner's right as prior possessor and true owner of the card. As Buyer received only the rights Thief had, Buyer's interest in the card is likewise subordinate to Owner's.

Example 2. Deadbeat buys Owner's Mickey Mantle card for $12,000, paying with a check. When the check is later dishonored, Owner demands that Deadbeat return the card. Unfortunately, Deadbeat has already sold the card to Buyer for $14,000 and has spent the money. Buyer knew nothing about how the card came into Deadbeat's hands. Owner is estopped from recovering the card or its value from Buyer. Even though Deadbeat paid for the card with a bad check, the transaction between Owner and Deadbeat transferred "voidable" title to Deadbeat, giving Deadbeat the power to convey a good title to Buyer, who purchased the card for value (defined in UCC § 1–204 to include "any consideration sufficient to support a simple contract") and in good faith (defined in UCC § 1–201(b)(20) as "honesty in fact and the observance of reasonable commercial standards of fair dealing").

In Examples 1 and 2, Buyer relies to her detriment on the appearance that her seller has good title to the card, spending $14,000 to acquire the card. Her reliance upon her seller's possession even appears to be reasonable, in the sense that she is unaware of any defect in her seller's title. In Example 1, however, Buyer's reliance does not justify allowing her to retain the card. Owner did nothing in Example 1 to create the mistaken impression that Thief owned the card; Thief simply stole the card. Thus, Owner has done nothing to justify an estoppel that would prevent him from recovering possession of the card based upon his prior possession. By contrast, in Example 2, Owner's own conduct creates the mistaken impression that Deadbeat owned the card. Buyer effectively relies upon Owner's conduct, and thus the law uses the estoppel principle to prevent Owner from recovering the card from Buyer.

> *Example 3.* Same as Example 2, except that when Owner demands return of the card, Deadbeat has already given the card to Donee as a gift. Owner can recover the card or its value from Donee. As in Example 2, Deadbeat held "voidable" title and had the power to transfer good title to the card to a good faith purchaser for value. Donee, however, did not pay value. Donee thus received only Deadbeat's "voidable" title, which is inferior to Owner's right as prior possessor and true owner of the card.

In Example 3, Deadbeat certainly appears to be the owner of the card, and Owner's conduct has helped to create this mistaken impression. Nevertheless, Donee does not rely upon this mistaken impression to her detriment, as she receives the card as a gift. As a general matter, the estoppel principle protects one's reliance only to the extent that it is both reasonable and detrimental; accordingly, the law does not estop Owner from recovering the card from Donee in this context.

> *b.   The Entrustment Rule.* Section 2–403's second "estoppel" rule appears in subsections (2) and (3):
>
> (2) Any entrusting of goods to a merchant that deals in goods of that kind gives the merchant power to transfer all of the entruster's rights to the goods and to transfer the goods free of any interest of the entruster to a buyer in ordinary course of business.[3]

----

3.   UCC § 1–201(b)(9) defines "buyer in ordinary course of business" as "a person   that buys goods in good faith, without knowledge that the sale violates the rights

(3) "Entrusting" includes any delivery and any acquiescence in retention of possession regardless of any condition expressed between the parties to the delivery or acquiescence and regardless of whether the procurement of the entrusting or the possessor's disposition of the goods was punishable under the criminal law.

The application of this rule is demonstrated by the following examples:

Example 4. Dealer sells baseball cards. Dealer is considering buying Owner's Mickey Mantle card. Owner allows Dealer to hold the card while Dealer decides whether to buy it. Dealer places the card in his display. The next day, Owner changes his mind and decides not to sell the card. When Owner asks Dealer to return the card, he learns that Dealer has already sold the card to Buyer for $12,000. Buyer knew nothing about how Dealer acquired the card. Owner is estopped from recovering the card from Buyer. Owner "entrusted" the card to Dealer—a merchant of baseball cards—giving Dealer the power to convey the title of the entruster (Owner) to a buyer in the ordinary course of business. Buyer is a buyer in the ordinary course of business because she bought the card in good faith from a dealer of baseball cards.

Example 5. Thief steals Owner's Mickey Mantle card. Thief takes the card to Dealer (a seller of baseball cards) and asks Dealer to sell it for him. Dealer places the card in his display. When Owner subsequently learns of Thief's actions and demands that Dealer return the card, he discovers that Dealer has already sold it to Buyer for $12,000. Buyer knew nothing about how Thief or Dealer acquired the card. Owner may recover the card from Buyer. Thief entrusted the card to Dealer—a merchant of baseball cards—giving Dealer the power to convey the title of the entruster (Thief) to a buyer in the ordinary course of business. As a buyer in the ordinary course of business, Buyer received Thief's rights in the card, but Thief's rights are subordinate to Owner's rights as the true owner of the card.

In Examples 4 and 5, Buyer purchases the card from Dealer, a merchant of baseball cards, and in each case expects that Dealer has good title (or the power to transfer good title) to the card. [Can you explain the basis for Buyer's expectation?] In Example 4, Owner's own conduct helps to create this mistaken impression, as Owner allowed Dealer to place the card on display before they had agreed on the terms of a sale. Accordingly, § 2–403(2) estops Owner from using the derivative title principle to assert that Dealer did not have good title to the card when he sold it to Buyer. In contrast, in Example 5, Owner does nothing to create this mistaken impression; instead, it is the conduct of Thief that results in Buyer being misled. Accordingly, § 2–403(2) does not estop Owner from asserting the derivative title principle to recover the card.

of another person in the goods, and in the ordinary course from a person, other than a   pawnbroker, in the business of selling goods of that kind...."

estoppel protects the purchaser when he had that *no reason to believe* *seller was* *no* *go over w/people*

Notes

1. *Justifications Underlying the Estoppel Principle.* One of the primary purposes of the estoppel principle is to protect reliance under appropriate circumstances. In the examples in the text, the estoppel principle protects a purchaser in those cases where she has reasonably and detrimentally relied upon the impression that her seller had good title and where the true owner had by his own conduct created or contributed to this problem. Can you see any other purpose that the estoppel principle serves in this context?

2. *Statutory Estoppel under UCC § 2–403—Some Problems.* How would the following examples be resolved under this provision?

(a) Wells takes her watch to Jeweler for repair. One of the sales clerks, believing the watch is part of the store's inventory, sells the watch to Buyer for $200. Can Wells recover the watch from Buyer? Does the fair market value of the watch matter to your analysis? Why or why not?

(b) Liar breaks into Henning's office and is about to steal Henning's laptop computer when Henning returns to his office. Trying to make his conduct appear benign, Liar quickly says to Henning, "I was looking for you because I want to buy your computer for $3,000." Because the computer is worth only $2,000, Henning says, "Fine. Where's my money?" Liar tells Henning, "Peters owes me $3,000; collect it from him." Henning allows Liar to take the computer. Later that day, when Henning attempts to collect from Peters, he learns that Peters owes Liar nothing. When he confronts Liar, Henning learns that Liar has sold the computer to Buyer for $1,500. Can Henning recover the computer from Buyer?

(c) Suppose that in Example 4 (page 149), Owner had allowed Dealer to take possession of the Mantle card, for one week only, to show it to his daughter (allegedly a "big Yankees fan"). Suppose further that Owner did not know that Dealer sold baseball cards, and that the exchange of the card took place at church. Dealer then took the card to his shop, placed it in the display case, and subsequently sold it to Buyer for $12,000. Can Owner recover the card from Buyer? Should it matter that Owner did not know that Dealer was a merchant? Why or why not?

(d) Suppose that in Example 4 (page 149), Buyer purchased the card from Dealer for $12,000, but that the transaction took place at church, not at Dealer's store. In fact, Buyer did not know that Dealer was a merchant in baseball cards, and assumed that instead Dealer was selling the card from his own private collection. Can Owner recover the card from Buyer? Should it matter in this case that Buyer did not know that Dealer was a merchant? Why or why not?

(e) Suppose that Owner takes his car to Lambert's Honda ("Lambert's") for repair. After the repairs are done, Lambert's incompetent employee Uphoff parks the car alongside the used cars held by Lambert's for sale. Before Owner returns to pick up the car, Lambert's sells the car to Buyer for $5,000. Buyer did not know that the car belonged to Owner and that Owner had only brought the car in for repairs. Can Owner recover the car from Buyer? Why or why not? What additional information might be helpful to you?

2. *Real Property*

By contrast to transfers of personal property, transfers of real property typically occur in highly formal transactions. For land transfers, the statute of frauds requires that the owner of the land execute a formal document (called a *deed*) in which the owner (called the *grantor*) purports to transfer title to the land described in the deed to the transferee (called the *grantee*). An example of a typical deed appears on page 152. A transfer of title to the land occurs only after the grantor executes the deed (with the requisite legal formalities) and delivers that deed to the grantee.

Furthermore, by contrast to transfers of personal property, each American county government maintains a public land registry in which an owner of land can *record* its claim. As we will study in greater depth in Chapter 9, a grantee to whom a deed is delivered typically takes the original deed to the local land records office (often called the "Register of Deeds") and presents it to the filing clerk for recording along with the necessary filing fee. The filing clerk stamps the deed, places a copy of the deed into the county records, and places a notation of the deed and its location on the *index*. Third parties interested in acquiring title to a particular parcel of land can then use the index to search for recorded deeds that might affect title to that parcel of land. [We will discuss the indexing and title search processes in greater detail in Chapter 9.]

If the owner of land has properly recorded its deed and the recorder has properly indexed it, it is relatively easy for third parties to discover the owner's claim. However, if an owner fails to properly record her deed, an ostensible ownership problem may exist.

For example, suppose that for a price of $25,000, Barnes delivers to Corrada a deed purporting to convey title to 20 acres of land. Two months previously, however, Barnes had delivered a deed that purported to convey title to the same land to Nice. How should the law prioritize the conflicting claims of Corrada and Nice?

Under the principle of first-in-time, first-in-right, Nice's claim to the land was prior in time to Corrada's claim and would have priority over Corrada's claim. Given the derivative title principle, once Barnes had conveyed all of his title to the land to Nice, he had no remaining title to convey to Corrada. This result seems appropriate, especially if we assume that Corrada either knew or had reason to know that Barnes had previously conveyed his interest to Nice. In that case, Corrada could not have relied *reasonably* on the appearance that Barnes had good title to the land.

WARRANTY DEED

Mail to: Sara Scrivener, Esq.
520 S. Dearborn
Chicago, IL 60604

Send Tax Bills to: Dana Barone
5904 Falstaff Blvd.
Chicago, IL 60618

THE GRANTORS, SAM S. SMITH and JOAN D. SMITH, Husband and Wife, both of the City of Chicago, County of Cook, State of Illinois, for and in consideration of TEN DOLLARS in hand paid, CONVEY AND WARRANT to DANA BARONE of the City of Chicago, County of Cook, State of Illinois, the following described real estate situated in the County of Cook in the State of Illinois, to wit:

> Lot 42 in Block 3 in Irving Park, a Subdivision of the East 1/2 of the West 1/2 of the Southeast 1/4 of Section 14, Township 40 North, Range 13, East of the Third Principal Meridian.

Subject to: general real estate taxes not due and payable at the time of closing; and easements, covenants, conditions and restrictions of record.

Hereby releasing and waiving all rights under and by virtue of the Homestead Exemption Laws of the State of Illinois, TO HAVE AND TO HOLD said premises forever.

Dated this 3rd day of May, 2005

_____
Sam S. Smith

_____
Joan D. Smith

STATE OF ILLINOIS, COUNTY OF COOK

I, the undersigned, a Notary Public in and for said County, in the State of Illinois, DO HEREBY CERTIFY that SAM S. SMITH and JOAN D. SMITH, husband and wife, are personally known to me to be the same persons whose names are subscribed to the foregoing instrument, appeared before me this day in person, and acknowledged that they signed, sealed, and delivered the said instrument as their free and voluntary act, for the uses and purposes therein set forth, including the release and waiver of the right of homestead.

Given under my hand and official seal this 3rd day of May, 2005.

_____
Notary Public

This instrument prepared by: Dora Ryan, Attorney at Law, 300 S. Wacker, Chicago, IL 60604

A. In a warranty deed, the grantor makes a contractual warranty of the quality of the grantor's title. If it later turns out that the grantor's title was defective, the grantee can recover damages from the grantor. By contrast, in a "quitclaim" deed, the grantor makes no contractual warranty of title.

B. This is the deed's *granting clause*. By using the words "CONVEY AND WARRANT," the grantor not only conveys title to the land, but also makes all of the standard deed warranties recognized by the common law (and discussed further in Chapter 9). By statute in Illinois, by using the words "CONVEY AND WARRANT," the grantor can avoid having to spell out each warranty.

C. Note that the deed recites consideration of only $10. Land typically sells at a higher price. In practice, however, parties are reluctant to disclose the actual price paid for the land. Thus, the drafter of the deed typically recites only a modest consideration.

D. The deed must contain a legal description of the land being conveyed. Land is usually described either by "metes and bounds" (courses and distances as determined by a surveyor) or by reference to the government land survey (which is used here). A more extensive summary of land description appears in Chapter 9.

E. This language expresses all of the pertinent exceptions to the title warranties contained in the deed. This means that if any of the listed exceptions exist and constitute a lien or defect in the grantor's title, they are not covered by the grantor's warranty of title. As a result, the grantee would need to make sure that the relevant taxes have been paid, and to review any recorded easements, covenants, and conditions affecting the land to make sure they do not hinder the grantee's intended use of the land. We address conditions in Chapter 5, easements and covenants in Chapter 8, and deed warranties in Chapter 9.

F. Note that only the Grantor signs the deed. As explained in Chapter 4, the Grantee's willingness to accept the terms and conditions of the deed are manifested by the Grantee's acceptance of the deed.

G. The words "TO HAVE AND TO HOLD said premises forever" constitute the deed's *habendum* clause, which indicates what type of estate the deed is conveying to the grantee. We discuss the types of estates in land in greater detail in Chapter 5.

H. To be recorded, a deed must be properly notarized (or "acknowledged") by a notary public. The notarization permits the deed to be admitted into evidence in the event of a later title dispute, without the need to produce witnesses (who would otherwise have to testify that the grantor executed the deed with the requisite intent to transfer the land). If the deed is not properly notarized, it cannot be recorded. Note also that although the deed is dated May 3, 2005, it only becomes effective to transfer title to the land to the grantee once it has been properly executed and delivered to the grantee (as discussed further in Chapter 4). Moreover, as discussed in this section and in Chapter 9, the grantee must record the deed in order to make his or her title claim effective against subsequent purchasers of the land!

[handwritten margin note: if person did not know of prior conveyance]

But what if Corrada did not know or have reason to know of the prior conveyance to Nice, and Nice had not recorded her deed? In such a situation, the equities would favor Corrada, who reasonably concluded that Barnes had good title to convey. To address this situation, each state has a recording statute that creates a statutory estoppel rule in favor of a bona fide purchaser (such as Corrada). For example, consider the Massachusetts statute, which provides as follows:

> A conveyance . . . shall not be valid as against any person, except the grantor or lessor, his heirs and devisees and persons having actual notice of it, unless it . . . is recorded in the registry of deeds for the county or district in which the land to which it relates lies. [Mass. Gen. Laws Ann. ch. 183, § 4.]

The language of this statute makes Nice's prior-in-time deed invalid as against Corrada (who lacked "actual notice" of that deed), because Nice failed to record the deed—and thereby failed to put Corrada on *constructive notice* (or *record notice*) of Nice's prior claim. As a result, the recording statute estops Nice from asserting the prior-in-time rule to establish a superior title claim to Corrada. The result is that Corrada becomes the owner of the land—even though, technically, Barnes had no title to convey to Corrada!

Notes

[handwritten margin note: 3 purposes of recording]

1. *Functions of Real Estate Recording Acts.* All recording acts serve at least three fundamental functions. First, they provide a mechanism (*i.e.*, public recording of documents affecting land interests) whereby owners of land interests can "notify the world" of their rights. Second, by protecting third party reliance, the recording acts provide a reasonably effective means by which a person buying land can investigate the seller's title—thus facilitating the efficient transfer of interests in land. Third, as discussed in note 2, they provide a mechanism for resolving disputes between persons claiming conflicting interests in the same land.

[handwritten margin note: 3 types of recording statutes]

2. *Types of Real Estate Recording Acts.* Each state has its own recording statute, and these statutes fall into three different types—"race" statutes, "notice" statutes, and "race-notice" statutes. To demonstrate the application of each type, assume the following example in which *O*, the owner of Blueacre, purports to sell Blueacre to two different persons in successive transactions. First, *O* conveys Blueacre by deed to *A*, but *A* fails to record his deed. *O* then purports to convey Blueacre by deed to *B*, who lacked any knowledge of *A*'s prior claim. The following day, *A* belatedly records his deed. One week later, *B* records her deed. Finally, a dispute arises between *A* and *B* in which each claims ownership of Blueacre.

A very few states have enacted a "race" statute, which gives priority between conflicting claimants to the claimant that recorded its deed first. In this example, because *A* recorded his deed before *B* recorded her deed, *A* continues to have the superior claim of title to Blueacre based upon the fact that *A*'s claim was prior-in-time. However, if *B* had recorded her deed on the day she received it—in which case she would have recorded before *A*—*B* would have been protected by the recording act and *B*'s claim to possession would have been superior to *A*'s claim. Notice also that under a "race" statute, it would be irrelevant whether *B* had known or had reason to know of *A*'s unrecorded claim at the time *B* purchased Blueacre. If *B* had recorded her deed first, *B* would have been entitled to the protection of the recording act even if *B* knew of *A*'s prior unrecorded claim.

About one-half of the states have adopted a "notice" statute such as the Massachusetts statute quoted in the text. Under a "notice" statute, a subsequent purchaser of land will take priority over a prior claimant of the land, so long as the subsequent purchaser acts without notice (either actual knowledge or constructive notice) of the rights of the prior claimant. In our example, *A*'s unrecorded deed is not effective against *B*, because *B* purchased Blueacre without knowledge or constructive notice of *A*'s unrecorded claim. Thus, in a dispute between *A* and *B*, the court will conclude that *B* is the owner of Blueacre (*i.e.*, *B* has a right to possession that is superior to *A*'s right). If *A* had promptly recorded his deed so that it had appeared on the records at the time *B* purchased Blueacre, then *B* would have had constructive (record) notice of *A*'s prior claim, and thus *A* would have held the superior claim to *B* based upon the fact that *A*'s claim was prior-in-time.

The remaining states have adopted a "race-notice" statute. Under this approach, a subsequent purchaser of land will take priority over a prior claimant only if the subsequent purchaser *both* acts without knowledge or notice of the prior claimant *and* records her deed before the prior claimant records. In our example, *B* is not protected from *A*'s prior claim to Blueacre under a race-notice statute—even though *B* lacked knowledge or constructive notice of *A*'s prior claim at the time *B* purchased Blueacre, *B* did not qualify for the protection of the recording statute because *B* did not record her deed before *A* belatedly recorded his deed. Had *B* recorded her deed immediately upon receiving it—before *A*'s belated recording—she would have qualified for the protection of the recording statute and thus would have been entitled to possession of Blueacre.

How does each type of recording statute reflect the estoppel principles underlying the recording system? Why would a state adopt a pure "race" statute that makes it irrelevant whether the subsequent purchaser knows of a prior unrecorded claim? Which type of recording statute do you think best reflects the policies underlying the estoppel concept?

3. *How Might a Subsequent Purchaser Have "Notice" of a Prior Claim?* When a deed is properly recorded, a subsequent purchaser of the same land is deemed to have notice of the earlier recorded interest, regardless of whether the subsequent purchaser *actually searched* the public records. Such a purchaser "should have known" of the existence of the prior claim, and thus does not deserve the protection of a statutory estoppel rule.

Might a subsequent purchaser have "notice" of a prior *unrecorded* claim? Certainly, a subsequent purchaser that has actual knowledge of an unrecorded claim cannot claim the protection of a recording act that incorporates "notice." Should a purchaser who lacks actual knowledge of an unrecorded claim be deemed to have notice of that claim if that claim was still easily discoverable? For example, in the problem in note 2, assume that although A has not recorded his deed, A did take physical possession of Blueacre and began living there. Should A's physical possession of Blueacre give B "notice" of A's unrecorded claim, and thereby defeat B's ability to raise the recording statute as a defense in a dispute over possession of Blueacre? Why or why not? What additional information might you want to discover? [We return to the concept of "inquiry notice" in greater detail in Chapter 9.]

4. *The Limits of "Constructive" Notice.* The preceding material might imply that the recording system works seamlessly to communicate complete and accurate title information to prospective purchasers. As we will see in Chapter 9, such an implication is inaccurate. Systems for recording and indexing documents often make it difficult to search for claims against a specific parcel of land. For example, most counties have grantor-grantee name indexes that are cumbersome to search, forcing many would-be purchasers to rely upon the services of third-party search experts (such as title insurance companies), at a nontrivial expense. Further, indexing errors may make it impossible for even skilled searchers to find all relevant documents regarding a particular parcel. Moreover, recording statutes only apply to interests that are capable of being recorded. Some interests—such as title by adverse possession, to which we turn next—arise by operation of law, not by means of any document of conveyance. Because title by adverse possession cannot be recorded (at least not without a court decree quieting title first), a recording statute generally does not work a statutory estoppel against a person claiming title by adverse possession.

B. ADVERSE POSSESSION

The concepts of estoppel and bona fide purchaser reflect the idea that one who makes a misstatement (or carelessly allows another to rely upon a misimpression) should bear some legal responsibility to one who reasonably relies to her detriment on the statement or misimpression. In the previous section, we saw how the law will protect the *reasonable* reliance of a later transferee by wresting ownership from a previous true owner who created a misimpression about ownership.

example
LP person dies
& 3rd party takes land w/out any heir

This theme also has a significant influence in the law of adverse possession. Suppose that A, the true owner of Blackacre, dies without leaving a will. After A's death, B (A's distant cousin) simply takes possession of Blackacre—wrongly believing himself to be A's rightful heir[5]—and thereafter continues farming it for 30 years. During this time, none of A's rightful heirs attempt to take possession of Blackacre or assert any claim to the land. If A's rightful heirs showed up after 30 years and sued to recover possession of Blackacre, they would probably

---

5. As you will learn in Chapter 5, when people die without leaving a valid will, title to their property passes to their *heirs* by virtue of an intestate succession statute—a statute that identifies the persons who take the property of someone who dies intestate (*i.e.*, without leaving a valid will).

states have statutes of

lose. Each state has a statute of limitations on possessory actions—*i.e.*, a statute that requires someone suing to recover possession of land to bring that action within a certain number of years after that action accrued (in this example, most likely when *B* first took possession of Blackacre and began farming it). Because the heirs failed to bring their action within that time, the statute of limitations bars them from bringing any action at all. Thus, the law now would recognize *B* as owner of Blackacre, because there is no one else with better title who can legally eject *B*.

At first blush, this may sound "like title by theft or robbery, a primitive method of acquiring land without paying for it." Henry W. Ballentine, *Title by Adverse Possession*, 32 Harv. L. Rev. 135, 135 (1918). Yet the concept of adverse possession has existed, without substantial opposition, for centuries. If *B* takes actual possession of Blackacre, and maintains that possession in a fashion that is hostile, open and notorious, exclusive, and continuous for the relevant statutory period, *B* becomes the new owner of Blackacre. Can you see any resemblance between the principle of estoppel reflected in the doctrine of bona fide purchase and the concept of giving title to one who adversely possesses the land of another? To what extent is the estoppel concept reflected in the justifications Professor Merrill advances for adverse possession law?

THOMAS W. MERRILL, PROPERTY RULES, LIABILITY RULES, AND ADVERSE POSSESSION

79 Nw. U. L. Rev. 1122 (1984).

2 inquiries regarding entitlement

According to Calabresi and Melamed, disputes about legal entitlements necessarily entail two subsidiary inquiries; first, to whom should the entitlement be assigned, and second, what sort of rule should be used to protect this entitlement—a property rule or a liability rule. In this section, I will consider how adverse possession operates as a system for answering the first, or "who," question.

The assignment of entitlements in the period before the statute of limitations runs need not detain us for long. There is no question about who gets the entitlement during this period: courts uniformly and automatically award it to the TO (true owner). The reasons for this are generally the same as those which support a system of private property rights, as opposed to one which recognizes only possessory, *i.e.*, squatter's rights. First, there is a strong economic justification. If the state did not protect title but only the fact of possession, no one would ever be secure in leaving valuable things unattended, or entrusting them to someone else through lease or bailment. The result would undoubtedly be over-investment in security devices, and under-investment in the cultivation and development of natural resources. In addition, there is a derivative justification based upon civic values: cultural diversity, countervailing centers of political power, and independent institutions of scholarly inquiry may require larger accumulations of private wealth than would be possible under a system of mere possessory rights. Finally, and again derivatively, there is a justification based on human personality: accumulated material wealth may be important to an individual's identity and plans for the future, and property rights in material things protect these interests. All of this, with varying degrees of emphasis on different aspects of the justification for property rights, has rarely been a matter of controversy, at least within the Anglo–American legal tradition.

The problem comes in determining who should get the entitlement to the property after the statute of limitations runs. . . . Given the strong case for maintaining a system of property rights, a threshold question is why we are ever justified in shifting the entitlement from the TO to the AP (adverse possessor) after the passage of a number of years. Surprisingly, there is very little systematic discussion of this fundamental issue in the legal literature. Nevertheless, it is possible, with some effort, to glean from that literature four different, and yet essentially complementary, rationales for the institution of adverse possession.

The first justification is one that is invoked in support of statutes of limitations generally—the difficulty of proving stale claims. As time passes, witnesses die, memories fade, and evidence gets lost or destroyed. The statute of limitations recognizes this problem by adopting a conclusive presumption against attempting to prove claims after a certain period of time has elapsed.

[handwritten margin note: as time passes it is harder to prove claims]

The concern about lost evidence is common-sensical. As the quality and quantity of evidentiary material deteriorates over time, the process of fact-gathering and proof becomes more difficult. Surrogate witnesses and documents generally are not as accessible or as reliable as originals; consequently, more resources must be expended in finding them and corroborating their veracity. A rule requiring prompt resolution of claims is thus efficient in that it helps to minimize the costs of litigation and trial. There is also a fairness concern underlying the lost evidence rationale. Requiring that disputes be resolved promptly prevents the plaintiff from unfairly surprising the defendant with a claim that may be difficult or impossible to refute because evidence that would allow the defendant to defeat the claim no longer exists. . . .

A second concern which has frequently been advanced in the literature on adverse possession is the interest in "quieting titles" to property. This objective is related to, yet analytically distinct from, the problem of lost evidence. Imagine a state where lost evidence of title is never a problem—there is a universal recording system, accurate and indestructible boundary markers, and so forth. Nevertheless, if that state has no mechanism for eliminating old claims to property, the information costs, transaction costs, and hold out problems involved in discovering and securing the releases of these claims would very likely impose a significant impediment to the marketability of property. Title examiners would have to trace every deed back to its source; ancient easements, unextinguished spousal rights, grants of future interests, unreleased mortgages or liens could well be discovered; these interests would have to be traced to present-day successors; and releases of these interests would then have to be secured. If the buyer always purchased subject to such claims, no matter how old they might be, he would have to go through a complicated process of fact-gathering and negotiating in order to obtain clear title to the property. The "nuisance" value of these claims could easily lead to holding out or other rent-seeking behavior that would make the process of obtaining clear title even more burdensome.

... Perhaps title insurance would become available to cover this larger set of potentially conflicting claims, but premiums would be much higher than those of today. Thus, whether the buyer incurred the costs of actually securing releases or paid huge insurance premiums, the net effect would be the same: transactions in property would become more costly. The institution of adverse possession is designed to reduce this drag on the market by extinguishing most of the older claims. In the language of takings jurisprudence, adverse possession rests on a collective judgment that the reduction in information and transaction costs (or insurance costs) achieved by wiping these older claims off the books outweighs the "demoralization costs" of eliminating such remote claims.

A third reason commonly advanced in support of a system of adverse possession is that it punishes TO's who "sleep on their rights." Under this view, the shift in entitlement acts as a penalty to deter TO's from ignoring their property or otherwise engaging in poor custodial practices. Since forfeiture is a stiff penalty (frequently deemed unconscionable in other contexts) presumably the objective will be realized in most cases.

At first blush, this rationale seems to rest on a social policy favoring "active" owners of property, who develop or exploit their land, rather than "passive" owners. Such a policy seems dubious, because it ignores the possibility that passive owners, such as land speculators, may perform a valuable social function by preserving the property for use by future generations. Moreover, the notion that a property owner must engage in active exploitation or development or risk losing his property runs counter to the principle that a property owner can do whatever he wants with his property, at least so long as he does not injure others. Why not then let him ignore the property, if by ignoring it he does not injure others?

On closer examination, however, these criticisms overstate what is required of the TO in order to avoid forfeiture. The TO does not have to develop his land or even occupy it; all he has to do periodically is assert his right to exclude others. Moreover, there is at least an arguable economic justification for imposing such an affirmative obligation on the landowner. The passive (and presumably absentee) owner will be harder to negotiate with, if only because he will be harder to locate. When the TO is required to assert his right to exclude, therefore, he is in effect being asked to "flush out" offers to purchase his property, to make a market in the land. On this view, then, the sleeping-owner rationale is again a justification based on the desirability of encouraging market transactions in property rights.

A fourth and final explanation for the system of adverse possession focuses on the possessor, and in particular on the reliance interests that the possessor may have developed through longstanding possession of the property. This justification appears in several different forms. One form, having distinct echoes of a frontier society, invokes the interest in "preserving the peace." After a sufficient period of time has elapsed, so the argument goes, the AP's attachment to the property will be so strong that any attempt by the TO to reassert dominion may lead to violence. In another form, the reliance argument draws upon the personality theory of property rights, and posits that the AP may have developed an attachment to the property which is critical to his personal identity. As Holmes colorfully put it, "[t]he true explanation of title by prescription seems to me to be that man, like a tree in the cleft of a rock, gradually shapes his roots to his surroundings, and when the roots have grown to a certain size, can't be displaced without cutting at his life."

There is also a third, economic version of the reliance theory, grounded in an ex post analysis of the AP's dilemma. The key concept here is that of sunk costs or "quasi-rents." Suppose the AP has built an addition to his house which he thinks is on his own land, but which later turns out to be built on land belonging to the TO. Had the TO and the AP negotiated for the sale of additional land before the structure was built, the TO probably would receive no more than market value for the land, because the AP could always redesign or relocate the addition, or move elsewhere. Now, however, the TO has the AP over a barrel, and may be able to extract not only the value of the land but the full value of the addition as well. In effect, the value of the addition becomes a quasi-rent from the perspective of the TO. This kind of "extortion" is unfair because it creates a disproportionate penalty given the initial "wrong" of the AP (in this case, negligence in failing to procure a survey prior to construction). It is also inefficient, at least if the prospect of appropriating quasi-rents leads to strategic bargaining or other rent-seeking conduct on the part of the parties.

The reliance rationale is troubling, however, at least in any of the foregoing forms, because it seems to ignore a competing reliance-type interest: the interest of the TO and of society generally in preserving the integrity of the set of entitlements grounded in law. Indeed, most modern property theorists, following Bentham, assume that property rights are the creature of law, not of unilateral expectations inconsistent with the law. Thus, a policy of transferring entitlements to individuals in order to protect extra-legal expectations would inevitably undermine the general security of property rights. Arguably, this generalized interest in the security of legal entitlements could outweigh—or at least counterbalance—the expectations of the AP which have grown up through longstanding possession of the property.

There is, however, yet another category of reliance interests that may tip the balance in favor of the institution of adverse possession. So far, the discussion has focused exclusively on the competing claims of the AP and the TO. But there may be third parties who also have an interest in the assignment of [an] entitlement, *i.e.*, vendors, creditors, contractors, tenants, subsequent purchasers of all or part of the property for value. To be sure, public recording acts are designed in part to protect such persons from mistaking an AP for a TO. But it simply is not feasible to expect every interested third party to perform a title search before extending credit to, providing services for, or purchasing an interest from someone who appears to be a TO. The appearance of title—particularly the appearance of title consistently maintained for a long period of time—necessarily becomes a rough and ready substitute for an expensive and time-consuming title search. When we add the expectations of these interested third parties into the mix, there seems to be more than enough justification to invoke "reliance" as a rationale for the institution of adverse possession.

In sum, there are four traditional justifications or clusters of justifications which support transferring the entitlement to the AP after the statute of limitations runs: the problem of lost evidence, the desirability of quieting titles, the interest in discouraging sleeping owners, and the reliance interests of AP's and interested third persons. The important thing to note about these rationales is that, at least at the level of general justification, they are mutually supportive. One can like some and dislike others, or one can subscribe to all four, and the result is still the same—the entitlement should be transferred to the AP after the statute of limitations runs. Indeed, standing alone some of these rationales may appear too weak to overcome the presumption in favor of a system of property rights rather than of possessory rights. But taken together, they represent a rather imposing case for transferring the entitlement to the AP after a significant period of time has elapsed.

Notes

1.   *Efficiency and the Adverse Possession Rule.* Professor Merrill's article sets out in narrative fashion the standard normative justifications for the adverse possession rule. His point can be demonstrated visually by using a graph which reflects the net benefits to be obtained by adherence to a particular rule of allocating property rights (first-in-time or adverse possession) as a function of the passage of time. At time zero, the net benefits of protecting the true owner under first-in-time are quite high, and the net benefits of protecting the adverse possessor using an adverse possession rule are quite low. [Can you explain why?] As time passes, the net benefits of protecting the true owner begin to decrease, and the net benefits of protecting the adverse possessor begin to increase. [Again, can you explain why? Does Prof. Radin's personhood perspective (page 43) have any explanatory value here?]

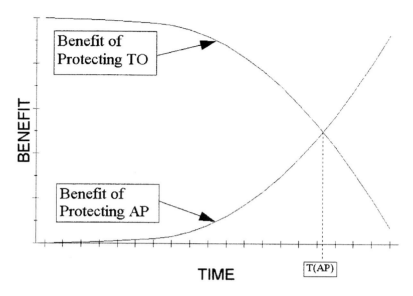

At some point, the net benefit lines intersect—in the graph, at time $T^{(AP)}$. Beyond that point, the net benefits of protecting the adverse possessor begin to exceed the net benefits to be obtained by adhering to the first-in-time rule. One could thus conclude, as a normative matter, that the law would facilitate the greater social good by thereafter protecting the adverse possessor. Do you think this analysis is sufficient to justify the law's refusal to protect the true owner?

2. *The Duration of the Limitations Period.* Even assuming that Merrill's arguments in favor of title by adverse possession are persuasive, they provide no practical guidance in determining *exactly when* title should change hands by adverse possession. It is one thing to demonstrate graphically, in theoretical terms, that over time the benefits of protecting the adverse possessor will eventually exceed the benefits of protecting the true owner. Theoretically, we can even identify that point in time as T^{AP}. In practical terms, however, Merrill's arguments and our graph give us no guidance as to exactly how much real time must pass before we reach T^{AP}.

At one point, most jurisdictions would not protect an adverse possessor unless that possession had continued for 20 or more years. Today, most modern statutes have shortened this period considerably.[6] Why do you think that legislatures have shortened the period for acquiring title by adverse possession? If shorter periods are better, why not have a very short period—such as six months or one year? What considerations should come into play in setting the length of the limitations period? *See* Richard A. Epstein, *Past and Future: The Temporal Dimension in the Law of Property*, 64 Wash.

6. There is considerable variation from state to state—for example, one can acquire title by adverse possession in California in only 5 years, while in Iowa the baseline statutory period is 40 years. For a state-by-

state listing of the statutory requirements for establishing title by adverse possession, see 10 Thompson on Real Property § 87.01, at 75–81 (Thomas ed.1998).

U.L.Q. 667 (1986); Robert C. Ellickson, *Adverse Possession and Perpetuities Law: Two Dents in the Libertarian Model of Property Rights*, 64 Wash. U.L.Q. 723 (1986).

3. *Adverse Possession and the "Tacking" of Successive Possessions.* Suppose that *AP1* has held adverse possession of Blueacre for five years when she purports to convey Blueacre to *AP2* by deed. Thereafter, *AP2* remains in possession of Blueacre for eight years before *TO* brings an action to eject *AP2*. If the jurisdiction's statutory period for adverse possession is 10 years, then *AP2*'s possession is not sufficient by itself to establish title by adverse possession. In this circumstance, however, the law permits *AP2* to "tack" his eight years of adverse possession onto the five–year period of his predecessor *AP1*—thus allowing *AP2* to assert 13 total years of adverse possession (and thereby establish title to Blueacre). *AP2* may "tack" his adverse possession onto *AP1*'s adverse possession because they are in "privity." In general terms, "privity" refers to the nexus or relationship of succession between one possessor to the next. Privity exists, for example, when one person voluntarily transfers land to another person by a sale, gift, inheritance or devise. In this example, the deed from *AP1* to *AP2* establishes privity between them and thus permits *AP2* to use tacking to satisfy the 10–year statutory period. Does it make sense to allow *AP2* to use tacking to satisfy the statutory period? To what extent is the concept of tacking consistent with the rationales underlying adverse possession doctrine (as identified by Prof. Merrill)?

Suppose that on January 1, 1994, *A* takes adverse possession of Blueacre, of which *TO* is the true owner. In 1999, *B* takes adverse possession of Blueacre, forcibly dispossessing *A*. In 2005, *TO* files suit against *B* to recover possession of Blueacre. The applicable statutory period is 10 years. Under English law, *TO*'s action would be time-barred. *See* Robert Megarry and H.W.R. Wade, The Law of Real Property 1036 (5th ed. 1984) ("so long as adverse possession continues unbroken it makes no difference who continues it"). By contrast, under American law, there is no privity between *A* and *B*— and thus *B* cannot tack her possession onto *A*'s possession to satisfy the statutory period. Is this a sensible result? Is this result consistent with the rationales underlying adverse possession doctrine?

4. *Disabilities and Tolling the Statutory Period.* Many states provide that the statute of limitations is "tolled" (*i.e.*, it will not run) against the true owner if he is legally disabled—in other words, not legally capable of taking action to protect his interest—at the time the adverse possession commences. The most common categories of legally disabled persons include minors and those who are mentally incompetent. *See, e.g.*, Miss. Code Ann. § 15–1–13. Some statutes also include prisoners and persons employed overseas in the service of the United States. *See* Ill. Rev. Stat. ch. 735, ¶ 13–112. These statutes generally provide that the statutory period will not begin to run until that disability is removed.[7]

---

7. This means that disabilities may not be "tacked." For example, if *TO* is a minor at the time *AP* takes possession, but *TO* goes to prison at age 15, the typical statute would toll the statutory period only during *TO*'s age disability. The statute would begin to run when *TO* reached the age of majority, even if *TO* remained incarcerated (and thus legally disabled) at that point.

Other state statutes, however, take different approaches to the issue of how much time a true owner has to assert his rights once he is no longer legally disabled. Some states provide that if the statutory period would already have expired but for the true owner's legal disability, then the true owner has a defined period of time to commence an action to recover possession following termination of the disability. A few statutes provide that in no event may a disability toll the statutory period for more than a defined maximum period of time—for example, 21 years in Missouri. Mo. Rev. Stat. § 516.030.

What rationale supports the concept of tolling the statute of limitation for people with a legal disability? Under what circumstances, if any, should an adverse possessor be allowed to argue that the disability statute should not apply to protect a disabled true owner?

Note carefully that many disabilities statutes require that the disability had to exist at the time the adverse possession commenced. Suppose Henning took adverse possession of Pushaw's land in August 1994, three weeks before Pushaw was declared legally insane and committed to a mental institution. Under the typical disability statute, the statutory period continues to run against Pushaw despite his subsequent legal disability. Assuming a ten-year statutory period, if Pushaw attempted to recover possession of the land following his recovery and release in June 2005, Pushaw's attempt would fail. Does this make sense? Why or why not?

5. *Adverse Possession and the Use of "Liability Rules."* Once the statutory period expires, adverse possession doctrine operates to shift title from the former true owner to the adverse possessor. The true owner—formerly protected by a "property" rule that would have permitted him to recover possession—now has no legal protection for his claimed interest. One could imagine a different approach in which adverse possession is treated like a "private taking" with the true owner protected by a liability rule. Under this approach, an adverse possessor might receive title once the statutory period ran, but only if the adverse possessor paid the true owner an amount equal to the fair market value of the land in question (*i.e.,* a forced sale). Why doesn't the law of adverse possession take this approach? Under what circumstances (if any) do you think it would make sense for a court to take this approach? *See* Thomas W. Merrill, *Property Rules, Liability Rules, and Adverse Possession*, 79 Nw. U.L. Rev. 1122, 1145–52 (1984).

6. *Adverse Possession Against the Government.* The traditional common law view was that one cannot adversely possess title to government-owned land. A majority of states continue to apply the traditional view, but a significant minority of states have enacted statutes authorizing adverse possession of some state-owned land. There are significant variations among these statutes. Some require a longer limitations period; some exempt certain types of land (such as school lands or lands used for a public purpose). Some states distinguish between land owned in a "governmental" capacity and land owned for "proprietary" purposes, allowing adverse possession only against the latter. *See* Paula R. Latovick, *Adverse Possession Against the States: The Hornbooks Have It Wrong*, 29 U. Mich. J.L. Reform 939 (1996). Should the law provide the government with greater protection from the consequences of the adverse possession rule than it provides to

private owners of land? Why or why not? Are the policies supporting adverse possession applicable in the context of government-owned land? *See* Paula R. Latovick, *Adverse Possession of Municipal Land: It's Time to Protect This Valuable Asset*, 31 U. Mich. J.L. Reform 475 (1998).

1. *The Basic Elements of Adverse Possession*

Adverse possession claims generally arise in one of two situations. In the first situation, the claimant asserts title by adverse possession to an entire tract of land, typically by virtue of an invalid deed (as in the following case, *Mullis v. Winchester*) or perhaps due to an ambiguity arising from confusion about inheritance (as in the example on page 155). The second situation involves "boundary disputes," or the situation in which an owner of one parcel encroaches upon (and subsequently claims title to) a portion of a neighboring parcel. [The *Norman v. Allison* (page 175) and *Stump v. Whibco* (page 187) cases both involve boundary disputes.]

Although the exact phrasing varies somewhat from case to case, most authorities hold that for possession to ripen into title under adverse possession, that possession must be (1) actual (or constructive), (2) exclusive, (3) continuous, (4) hostile (*i.e.*, under a "claim of right") and (5) "open and notorious"—(6) all for the full duration of the applicable statute of limitations.[8] Throughout the remainder of this chapter, we will focus upon how and why the rationales underlying the adverse possession rule have shaped this legal standard. As you read the following case, consider what facts demonstrate that Mr. Mullis had satisfied each element of the legal standard, and why.

MULLIS v. WINCHESTER

Supreme Court of South Carolina.
237 S.C. 487, 118 S.E.2d 61 (1961).

Moss, Justice. Carl W. Mullis, the respondent herein instituted this action on March 21, 1957 ... to remove a cloud on and quiet title to a tract of land, described in the complaint as containing 310 acres, more or less. The pleadings admit that prior to September 17, 1931, E.C. Winchester had a good fee simple title to this tract of land and that on said date he conveyed same to one R.H. Burns. The said deed is of record in the office of the Clerk of Court for Lancaster County, South Carolina, in Deed Book D, at page 36. It further appears that E.C. Winchester died intestate in the year 1936 and that R.H. Burns died testate. The appellants in this action are either the heirs at law of E.C. Winchester or the devisees of R.H. Burns. It also appears that the taxes on the aforesaid tract of land were not paid and that the sheriff of Lancaster County, South Carolina, pursuant to a tax execution, issued against Mrs. E.C. Winchester, levied upon and sold the said tract of land to one John

8. If it helps you remember these elements, you might remember the mnemonic POACHER: **P**ossession must be **O**pen and notorious, **A**ctual, **C**ontinuous, **H**ostile, and **E**xclusive, all for the **R**equired period of time.

S. Chonis. The defaulting taxpayer having failed to redeem said real estate, the sheriff of Lancaster County conveyed the said tract to John S. Chonis, which said deed is of record in the Clerk of Court's office for Lancaster County, South Carolina, in Deed Book I–3, at page 168. It further appears that John S. Chonis did, by deed dated December 14, 1943, for a consideration of $8,500, convey the said 310 acre tract to Carl W. Mullis, the respondent herein, and this deed was recorded in the office of the Clerk of Court for Lancaster County, South Carolina, on January 3, 1944, in Deed Book J–3, at page 445. The complaint also alleges that the respondent had been in actual, open, hostile, continuous, exclusive and notorious possession of the said tract of land since December 14, 1943, when he purchased same as aforesaid. The answer of the appellants, in so far as this appeal is concerned, denied the allegation of adverse possession contained in the complaint.

This case came on for trial ... on May 12, 1958. It was stipulated that the respondent relied entirely upon adverse possession under color of title. It was further admitted that the tax deed heretofore referred to was invalid.[9] It was agreed also that the only issue for trial was the question of whether the respondent had acquired title to the property in question by adverse possession ...

In order to constitute adverse possession, which results in obtaining title to property, the possession must be actual, open, notorious, hostile, continuous and exclusive for the whole statutory period. It may be stated as a general rule that claimant's possession must be such as to indicate his exclusive ownership of the property. Not only must his possession be without subserviency to, or recognition of, the title of the true owner, but it must be hostile thereto and to the whole world. 1 Am.Jur., Adverse Possession, Section 130.

The respondent alleged in his complaint that he acquired title to the premises in question by adverse possession. We have held in numerous cases that the burden of proof of adverse possession is on the party relying thereon. ...

The issue of title by adverse possession being one of law, our factual review of it is limited to determination of whether there was any evidence reasonably sustaining the verdict ....

The deed of John Chonis to the respondent constituted color of title. This deed contains a minute and definite description of the 310 acre tract of land and there is no doubt as to the identity of the tract of land

---

9. Editors' Note: Unpaid real property taxes constitute a lien upon the land assessed—in other words, the government obtains a proprietary interest in the land that allows the government to sell the land at a public sale and use the proceeds of the sale to satisfy the unpaid tax debt. Before a government-ordered tax sale can extinguish the true owner's interest, however, constitutional limitations upon governmental ac-tion require that the government provide the owner with notice prior to the sale. Often, tax sales are attacked after-the-fact as unconstitutional and therefore invalid, based upon the government's failure to provide effective notice. Although the court in *Mullis* does not explain why the tax sale was invalid, the likely explanation is a defect in notice to the owner.

conveyed. In the case of *Graniteville Co. v. Williams*, 209 S.C. 112, 39 S.E.2d 202, 207, it was said [citations omitted]:

"Color of title" means "any semblance of title by which the extent of a man's possession can be ascertained." It "is anything which shows the extent of [an] occupant's claim." "The object of color of title is not to pass title. In that case it would be title, not color of title. The only office of color of title is to define the extent of the claim and to extend the possession beyond the actual occupancy to the whole property described in the paper. . . . It is by no means necessary that the paper should be in the form of a deed. A bond or even a receipt would be sufficient." Manifestly, an instrument in order to constitute color of title need not be valid as a muniment of title. The extent of the occupant's claim founded on an instrument of writing is not dependent upon the validity of such instrument. A deed may be color of title although the grantor was without interest or title in the land conveyed. "There is a material difference between proving a deed as a part of a chain of title and introducing a paper to show the extent of the party's possession."

Hence, when one enters upon land, under color of title, his actual possession of a portion of the property will be constructively extended to the boundaries defined by his color of title.

It is provided in Section 10–2422, of the 1952 Code of Laws, as follows:

Whenever it shall appear (1) that the occupant or those under whom he claims entered into the possession of premises under claim of title, exclusive of any other right, founding such claim upon a written instrument as being a conveyance of the premises in question or upon the decree of judgment of a competent court and (2) that there has been a continued occupation and possession of the premises, or of some part of such premises, included in such instrument, decree or judgment under such claim for ten years, the premises so included shall be deemed to have been held adversely, except that when the premises so included consist of a tract divided into lots the possession of one lot shall not be deemed a possession of any other lot of the same tract.

Section 10–2423 of the 1952 Code of Laws, provides:

For the purpose of constituting an adverse possession by any person claiming a title founded upon a written instrument or a judgment or decree, land shall be deemed to have been possessed and occupied in the following cases: (1) When it has been usually cultivated or improved; (2) When it has been protected by a substantial enclosure; (3) When, although not enclosed, it has been used for the supply of fuel or of fencing timber, for the purposes of husbandry or for the ordinary use of the occupant; and (4) When a known farm or a single lot has been partly improved the portion of such farm or lot that may have been left not cleared or not enclosed, according to the usual course and custom of the adjoining country, shall be deemed to have been occupied for the same length of time as the part improved and cultivated.

Carl W. Mullis, the respondent herein, owns and operates the Mullis Lumber Company in Lancaster, South Carolina. It was testified that in the course of his business he purchased tracts of land in order to get the timber therefrom and for the future cutting of timber growth thereon. It was further testified that of all the numerous tracts of land purchased by the respondent, all were bought for the purpose of cutting timber therefrom and growing timber thereon, and as to the tract of land here involved, it was used solely for that purpose. The respondent testified that in 1943 when he purchased the 310 acre tract of land, which was during the second World War, he was selling lumber to the government and was trying to keep up his timber reserves by buying as much timber as he was cutting. He found out that the tract of land here involved was for sale and he had the timber thereon cruised and, thereafter, John Chonis was contacted and the respondent succeeded in buying the tract of land from him for $8,500. Chonis executed and delivered to the respondent a deed for said tract of land. Shortly thereafter, Mrs. E.C. Winchester, one of the appellants, was contacted by a representative of the respondent and she was advised that the respondent had purchased the land and desired to obtain from her the plat thereof which was in her possession. She delivered the plat to a representative of the respondent for $10. She did not claim that she and the other appellants owned this tract of land at such time. It then appears that the respondent, with the help of the adjoining landowners, had this tract of land surveyed. Thereafter, the time of which is not definitely fixed in the testimony, the respondent cut all merchantable timber thereon. He cut trees with a diameter greater than ten to twelve inches. The cutting was done by a crew of eight to ten men and the timber cut from said tract was hauled therefrom by three trucks which used woods roads upon said land. The testimony is undisputed that the respondent cut all of the merchantable timber up to the full extent of the boundaries of said tract of land. It was further testified that the best use of this land was for growing timber. The testimony is undisputed that the respondent followed the same cutting practice on this tract as he did on other similar tracts of land owned by him. He testified that he cut infrequently because he considered it good forestry practice to cut only the larger trees. There is testimony that there was a second cutting of timber from this tract of land but such took place after the institution of this action. An estimate of the timber cut from the premises ranges from two hundred thousand to one-half million feet. The testimony is undisputed that the respondent paid all taxes, in his own name, levied and assessed by the County of Lancaster against this tract of land from the year 1944 until the trial of this case. Adjoining landowners and people living in the community testified in behalf of the respondent and corroborated his testimony of the adverse nature of his possession. They also testified that the people in the community considered the property as belonging to the respondent. They testified as to helping the respondent survey the tract of land in question. These same witnesses testified that the tract in question consisted of hilly land and timber growing was the best use to which it could be put. There is testimony that the limbs and tree tops, where such could be done, were sold as pulp wood. All of the foregoing testimony is undisputed, the appellants having offered no evidence.

It is the position of the appellants that the testimony relied on to establish adverse possession proves no continuous use or acts of trespass but only occasional cutting of timber and they assert that this is not sufficient to establish the requisite continuity of possession.

It is true that possession of land to give title by adverse possession must be continuous for the statutory period of ten years. In the case of *Cathcart v. Matthews*, 105 S.C. 329, 89 S.E. 1021, 1025, this Court said:

> The rule requiring continuity of possession does not mean that the person in possession, his tenant or agent, must be actually on the land during the whole of the statutory period. Actual possession, once taken, will continue, though the party taking such possession should not continue to rest with his foot upon the soil, until he be disseised, or until he do some act which amounts to a voluntary abandonment of the possession. [Citations omitted.]

It is, of course, the general rule that in order for adverse possession to ripen into title, it must be continuous and uninterrupted for the full statutory period. The moment the possession is broken it ceases to be effectual because the law immediately restores the constructive possession of the owner. But in determining when possession is broken, the nature and location of the land should be considered and whether the use to which the same has been put comports with the usual management of such property. 76 A.L.R., at page 1492.

It has been held that occasional entries on land to cut a small amount of timber do not constitute a sufficiently continuous use to establish adverse possession. Such was the case of *Bailey v. Irby*, 11 S.C.L. (2 Nott & McC.) 343, where it was held that there was no continuity of possession "with him who enters only occasionally; he commits a petty trespass and disappears without scarcely leaving a mark behind," or where "it may be done so secretly as to elude detection; and it would be monstrous to allow one man to filch away the land of his neighbor without the possibility of guarding himself against it."

Acts of adverse possession, or acts of ownership, with regard to open, wild, unfenced lands, lands not capable of cultivation, are only required to be exercised in such way and in such manner as is consistent with the use to which the lands may be put and the situation of the property admits of without actual residence or occupancy.

In 1 Am.Jur., Adverse Possession, Section 131, at page 866, it is said:

> From what has been stated heretofore, it is evident that in determining what will amount to an actual possession of land, considerable importance must be attached to its nature and to the uses to

which it can be applied, or to which the claimant may choose to apply it. What is adverse possession is one thing in a populous country, another thing in a sparsely settled one, and still a different thing in a town or village.... As a general rule it will be sufficient if the land is so used by the adverse claimant as to apprise the community in its locality that it is in his exclusive use and enjoyment, and to put the owner on inquiry as to the nature and extent of the invasion of his rights; and this is especially true where the property is so situated as not to admit of permanent improvement. In such cases, if the possession comports with the usual management of similar lands by their owners, it will be sufficient. Neither actual occupation, cultivation, nor residence is necessary where neither the situation of the property nor the use to which it is adapted or applied admits of, or requires, such evidences of ownership.

We think the trial Judge was correct in concluding that the acts of adverse possession by the respondent were sufficient to establish requisite continuity of possession for the statutory period of ten years, particularly in view of the use to which this tract of land could be put and the situation of the property. The respondent entered upon this land under color of title and possessed and occupied same for his ordinary use in obtaining timber therefrom and growing timber thereon. Section 10–2423(3), 1952 Code of Laws of South Carolina.

We likewise think that the trial Judge was correct in concluding that the only inference to be drawn from the testimony was that the respondent had made a hostile entry upon the lands in question. His occupation was open, notorious, visible and exclusive. In fact, one of the appellants was notified of the purchase of the land and made no claim of title thereto. In determining what amounts to hostility, the relation which the party claiming adverse possession occupies with reference to the owner is important. As a general rule, the law presumes that the exclusive possession of land by one who is a stranger to the holder of the legal title is adverse. *Knight v. Hilton,* 224 S.C. 452, 79 S.E.2d 871. The respondent here was a stranger to the appellants in this case. There can be no question but what the respondent entered into possession of this land with the intention to dispossess the owners thereof....

We conclude that the trial Judge was correct in holding that the respondent had established title to the premises in question by adverse possession....

Notes

1. *The Elements of Adverse Possession.* The fact that courts traditionally have articulated a six-factor standard for adverse possession can give the mistaken impression that the six elements are fundamentally distinct, mutually exclusive factors. In reality, they overlap significantly, and often confusingly. Over time, courts have fashioned these elements as a shorthand way of describing the character or intensity of possession that is required to

establish adverse possession. In explaining these elements, the *Mullis* court articulates the traditional standard—an adverse possessor must actually or constructively possess the land in a fashion that is as intense as we would expect from a typical or reasonable owner of similar land. Possession of such intensity should place a reasonable owner on notice that someone appears to be asserting a claim of title to the land, and thus should prompt the owner to take legal action to recover possession before the statutory period runs completely.

To understand better how a court evaluates possession in a specific dispute against what a reasonable owner of similar land typically would do, consider the dispute in *Mullis*. Based upon what acts did Mullis take "actual" possession of the land, and when exactly did those acts occur? [On this point, do you think it is relevant that Mullis paid taxes on the land? Why or why not?] How did the court determine that Mullis's possession was "continuous"? On what facts did the court base this conclusion? Did the tree-cutting occur throughout the statutory period or at the beginning, and why might it matter? What facts indicate whether the possession was as exclusive as a reasonable owner's possession would be?

Do the facts on which the court relied demonstrate that Mullis's possession was "open and notorious"? That it was "hostile" and under "claim of right"? There is much more to learn about these two elements, as explained in the notes below and following *Norman v. Allison* (page 175) and *Stump v. Whibco* (page 187).

2. *"Actual" Possession, "Constructive" Possession, and the Role of "Color of Title."* By virtue of the tax sale deed, Mullis held "color of title" to the land in dispute—*i.e.*, Mullis took possession of the land by virtue of an instrument that purported to convey title to the land, but that (unbeknownst to him) was legally ineffective to transfer a good title. The *Mullis* court held that because Mullis entered into possession under color of title, his actual possession of part of the parcel was constructively extended to the full boundaries of the parcel as described in the tax deed. Can you explain why, as a factual matter, Mullis's case may have depended upon his having established possession under color of title?

What limits, if any, should the law place upon the use of "color of title" as a surrogate for actual physical possession? Suppose that Key conveys to Fischer, by deed, a square tract of land containing 240 acres. Fischer builds a home on the five acres in the northeasternmost corner of the tract, and maintains that five acres. He does not maintain any of the other land, however; in fact, he never once sets foot on any of it. After twenty years, Fischer discovers that Key never had good title to the land, which was actually owned by Pushaw. Assume that Fischer has satisfied all of the other requirements for adverse possession of the five acres where he built his home. Does he acquire title to only that five acres, or to the entire 240–acre tract? How can he possibly claim title in the entire 240–acre tract, if he never had actual possession of 235 of those acres? Can you explain why it should be relevant whether Pushaw was actually living on a portion of the remaining 235 acres? [Hint: Is it possible that two or more persons could each claim constructive possession of the same land?] *See Patrick v. Goolsby*, 158 Tenn. 162, 11 S.W.2d 677 (Tenn. 1928). Would your answer be different if the remainder of the 240–acre tract were vacant, but part of it (including all of the five acres possessed by Fischer) was owned by Pushaw, while the remainder of the tract was owned by Henning? If so, why? What if the land was located in South Carolina and Pushaw had previously platted the land into ten 24–acre parcels? [Review the language of the South Carolina statute (page 166) very carefully.] What if the 240 acres described in Fischer's deed consisted of two separate, noncontiguous tracts of land?

A word of warning: students often confuse the terms "color of title" and "claim of right." [The South Carolina statute interpreted in *Mullis* contributes to this confusion by using the term *"claim* of title" instead of the more customary "color of title."] As explained above, "color of title" concerns the existence of some writing (such as a deed) that apparently—but ineffectively—vested title to the land in question in the party claiming adverse possession. In contrast, "claim of right" is an element of adverse possession that is often used interchangeably with the requirement that the possession be "hostile." We will turn specifically to the "claim of right" requirement in the *Norman v. Allison* case (page 175).

3. *Color of Title as a Means of Shortening the Limitations Period.* In a number of states, statutes shorten the limitations period for those possessing land under color of title. *See, e.g.,* Ariz. Rev. Stat. § 12–523 (shortening period from 10 to three years); Tex. Civ. Prac. & Rem. Code Ann. § 16.024 (same). In *Lott v. Muldoon Road Baptist Church,* 466 P.2d 815 (Alaska 1970), the court explained the rationale for Alaska's statute (which shortened the period from 10 years to seven) as "logically attributable to a belief that a person holding land under color of title will be more likely to make improvements and otherwise commit himself to that land." Does this justify shortening the adverse possession period (and if so, how short should it be)?

Suppose that Blueacre is an unoccupied parcel of land that Alexander bought for investment purposes (assume Alexander lives in another state). Robertson pays $100 to his friend Whitfield to have her execute and deliver to him a deed by which Whitfield purports to convey to Robertson title to Blueacre. In fact, as they both know, Whitfield has no ownership claim. Nevertheless, after receiving this deed, Robertson takes possession of Blueacre and builds a home, where he resides for eight years before Alexander files a lawsuit to eject him. Assume that the state's statutory period is 10 years, but reduced to seven years for claimants with color of title. Should Robertson's deed constitute "color of title" so as to qualify him for the shorter seven–year period? *See, e.g., Lott,* 466 P.2d at 818. *See also* Roger A. Cunningham, *Adverse Possession and Subjective Intent: A Reply to Professor Helmholz,* 64 Wash. U.L.Q. 1, 23–25 (1986).

4. *"Continuous" Possession.* The *Mullis* court states that "adverse possession ... must be continuous and uninterrupted for the full statutory period." What must the true owner do in order to interrupt the continuity of an adverse possessor's claim? Clearly, filing a lawsuit to recover possession (traditionally called an action in ejectment) would interrupt an adverse claim if the lawsuit leads to a judgment in favor of the true owner. Can the true owner effectively interrupt an adverse claim without filing a lawsuit? Under the traditional rule, the true owner could interrupt an adverse claim by re-entering the land and taking physical possession of it in a fashion that

effectively ousted the adverse claimant. *See Pierce v. Austin*, 651 S.W.2d 161 (Mo. App. 1983) (interruption where true owner drove stakes into driveway constructed/used by adverse possessor). In some states, however, legislatures have adopted statutes that modify the traditional rule by providing that the true owner's re-entry cannot interrupt an adverse claim unless the true owner remains in possession for some period of time—such as one year in Massachusetts. Mass. Gen. Laws Ann. ch. 260, § 28. Likewise, in some states, statutes require that a true owner's re-entry cannot interrupt an adverse claim unless the true owner brings an ejectment action within a certain period of time after re-entry—such as one year in Pennsylvania. 42 Pa. Cons. Stat. Ann. § 5530(b). Note, however, that the possession of a third party (such as a trespasser) could effectively interrupt the continuity of an adverse possessor's claim even if it continued for less than a year and was not accompanied by an ejectment action. Does it make sense to require the owner to take greater steps than a stranger in order to interrupt the continuity of an adverse possessor's claim? Why or why not?

What about "gaps" in the adverse possessor's occupation of the land, without any physical interference or legal action by the true owner? Consider the following hypothetical: Mr. and Mrs. Frank have a summer vacation home on a canal in upstate Washington. Due to a surveying error, the Franks built their home on the wrong lot, on land in fact owned by a neighbor. The error went undetected for many years, in excess of the limitations period in Washington. Finally, the neighbor attempts to evict the Franks as trespassers on his land. The Franks argue that they have acquired title by adverse possession, but the neighbor argues that their possession was not continuous—after all, they used the home only sporadically, only during the summer months, and in some cases did not use the home at all for several years at a time. Have the Franks established "continuous" possession?

In *Ray v. Beacon Hudson Mountain Corp.*, 88 N.Y.2d 154, 643 N.Y.S.2d 939, 666 N.E.2d 532 (1996), the court elaborated on the meaning of this element:

> The element of continuity will be defeated where the adverse possessor interrupts the period of possession by abandoning the premises, where an intruder's presence renders the possession nonexclusive, or where the record owner acts to eject the adverse possessor. However, the hostile claimant's actual possession of the property need not be constant to satisfy the "continuity" element of the claim.

See also Brown v. Whitcomb, 150 Vt. 106, 550 A.2d 1 (1988). Thus, continuity may be destroyed by the adverse possessor's abandonment of possession (*i.e.*, her absence from the land, under circumstances that reflect her intention to part permanently with the right to possession). In contrast, the possessor's mere absence from the land, without evidence of such intention, is not abandonment. *Compare Kaminski Bros., Inc. v. Grassi*, 237 Pa.Super. 478, 352 A.2d 80 (1975) *with Bruch v. Benedict*, 62 Wyo. 213, 165 P.2d 561 (1946). Consistent with the pervasive "reasonable owner of similar land" standard, the inference of intent to abandon may well depend upon the length of an absence and its reasonableness in view of the nature of the land claimed. Based upon this rationale, should the Franks prevail? *See Howard v. Kunto*, 3 Wash.App. 393, 477 P.2d 210 (1970).

5. *"Open and Notorious" Possession.* Courts and commentators typically treat these two words as if they were synonymous, assuming that openly visible possession is inherently notorious. The use of two terms, however, provides a helpful reminder that two aspects of adverse possession should be apparent to give the owner fair warning: the physical fact of possession (*i.e.*, open possession) and the hostility or adverseness of that possession to the owner's rights (*i.e.*, notorious possession).

Go back to the dispute in *Edwards v. Sims* (page 99). Suppose that Edwards had argued that he had acquired ownership of the portion of the cave under Lee's land by adverse possession. [Assume that Edwards had been exhibiting the cave for longer than the limitations period.] Would Edwards' possession of the cave have been sufficiently "open"? Sufficiently "notorious"? Why or why not? *See Marengo Cave Co. v. Ross*, 212 Ind. 624, 10 N.E.2d 917 (1937).

6. *The "Open Lands" Doctrine—Environmental Issues and the Elements of the Adverse Possession Rule.* The court in *Mullis* follows the general principle that acts of adverse possession must be as intense as those typically engaged in by the reasonable owner of similar land. The court's holding, however, is often referred to as a distinct rule sometimes called the "open lands" doctrine. This doctrine states that on open, wild, unfenced lands, incapable of cultivation, acts of adverse possession need only be exercised "in such way and in such manner as is consistent with the use to which the lands may be put and the situation of the property admits of without actual residence or occupancy" (page 168). Thus, Mullis successfully established title to the land by adverse possession, despite never living on the land or fencing it off so as to exclude others.

Based upon the underlying rationales behind adverse possession doctrine (as articulated by Merrill, page 156), is it good policy to permit adverse possession based on relatively nominal acts for wild, undeveloped land in its natural condition? Why or why not? For a conservationist perspective, including the recommendation that wild lands be exempted from adverse possession law, see John G. Sprankling, *An Environmental Critique of Adverse Possession*, 79 Cornell L. Rev. 816 (1994). Setting aside environmental concerns, might one support Sprankling's proposal by arguing that adverse possession of such lands could not be sufficiently "open and notorious" to give a reasonable owner fair warning that her title is threatened by adverse possession? Why do you think that courts have established the "open lands" rule? How might one establish title to wild lands by adverse possession otherwise? In contrast, what policy (if any) is served by allowing any adverse possession of land that is unsuitable for active possession?

7. *Payment of Taxes.* In many states, one cannot establish a claim of title by adverse possession without paying real property taxes on the property throughout the prescriptive period. *See, e.g.*, Ark. Code Ann. § 18–11–106; Cal. Code Civ. Proc. § 325. In other states, the adverse possessor must pay taxes to take advantage of a shorter statute of limitations. *See, e.g.*, Tex. Civ. Prac. & Rem. Code Ann. § 16.025. Should the law generally

require payment of taxes as a prerequisite to acquisition of title by prescription? In the absence of such a statutory requirement, does payment of taxes strengthen the possessor's claim? Why or why not? Which of Merrill's justifications for adverse possession are served by a payment of taxes requirement?

Notably, with the exception of Florida, Illinois, Indiana and Maine, all of the states that require the adverse possessor to pay taxes are west of the Mississippi River. Almost all imposed the payment of taxes requirement in the late 19th century or early 20th century. What do you think prompted the legislatures in these states to impose a payment of taxes requirement to obtain title to land by adverse possession? *See* Comment, *Payment of Taxes as a Condition of Title by Adverse Possession: A Nineteenth Century Anachronism*, 9 Santa Clara Law. 244–49 (1969). In reflecting on that question, note that Arkansas recently revised its adverse possession statute to require *both* color of title *and* payment of taxes to acquire title by adverse possession in cases not involving boundary disputes. Ark. Code Ann. § 18–11–106. What might have prompted Arkansas to revise its adverse possession statute in this fashion? *See* Legislative Note, *Color of Title and Payment of Taxes: The New Requirements Under Arkansas Adverse Possession Law*, 50 Ark. L. Rev. 489 (1997).

LAWYERING EXERCISE
(Writing/Editing)

BACKGROUND: The *Mullis* court's statement of facts is typical of much legal writing—it is needlessly technical, much too wordy, and fails to limit its presentation to those facts relevant to the issues decided. The court's statement of facts needed a good editing:

> Rewriting is the discipline of exercise and diet that trims a passage down to something easily read and understood. And conciseness is important in legal writing for three reasons. First, concise writing is by nature more clear and often more precise. Second, the typical reader of legal writing has no time to spare and either will resent inflated verbiage or will simply refuse to read it. And third, something about legal work paradoxically creates a temptation to swell a simple expression into something ponderous and pretentious. [Richard K. Neumann, Legal Reasoning and Legal Writing: Structure, Strategy, and Style 208 (4th ed. 2001).]

One of the most important of lawyering skills is the ability to distill a complex situation to its essential facts—to separate relevant information from irrelevant information:

> Facts are relevant or irrelevant in relation to the legal principles at issue. In order to know which facts are relevant, you will need to know what the issue in the problem is. If the issue is whether the client committed a crime, then you must know the elements of that crime. The relevant facts are those that are used to prove or disprove those elements. [Helene S. Shapo, Marilyn R.

Walter & Elizabeth Fajans, Writing and Analysis in the Law 76 (3d ed. 1995).]

TASK: Try your hand at rewriting a more concise statement of the facts in *Mullis*. Use no more than three paragraphs of three to four concise sentences.

2. *Hostility and "Claim of Right"*

The element of "hostile" possession is sometimes called possession under a "claim of right." Functionally, courts have used these two terms interchangeably, each one reflecting a crude definition of the other. What is required to establish "hostility" (*i.e.*, a "claim of right")? When the *Mullis* court referred in its analysis to the hostility of Mullis's actions, what did this mean? Did this mean that Mullis had to be personally hostile (in the everyday emotional sense of that term)? Did this mean Mullis's actual state of mind (*i.e.*, what he actually believed) was relevant to his ability to establish title by adverse possession? Or did it merely mean that Mullis must have acted without the permission of the true owner (*i.e.*, without regard to the true owner's right to exclude him)? In addressing these questions, consider the following materials.

NORMAN v. ALLISON

Missouri Court of Appeals.
775 S.W.2d 568 (1989).

MAUS, JUDGE. Plaintiff–Appellant Jimmie M. Norman holds record title to a 240–acre farm that includes the NE 1/4 NE 1/4 of Section 27, Township 25, Range 26. The defendants-respondents, Charles Allison and Rebecca Allison, hold record title to a farm of approximately 185 acres that includes the NW 1/4 NE 1/4 of that section. The two 40–acre tracts obviously adjoin. By this action appellant sought a declaration that he had acquired title to a triangular tract off the east side of respondents' 40–acre tract by adverse possession.... The circuit court found appellant did not possess ... the triangular tract under a claim of right and denied the appellant relief....

... The Camp Bliss Public Road runs in a northeast-southwest direction through the farms of the appellant and respondents. That road extends diagonally through the SW 1/4 SE 1/4 of Section 22 (owned by respondents) and the SE 1/4 SE 1/4 of Section 22 (owned by appellant). Reproduced below is a sketch (not to scale) of the four quarter-quarter sections to show the boundaries and landmarks mentioned in this opinion.

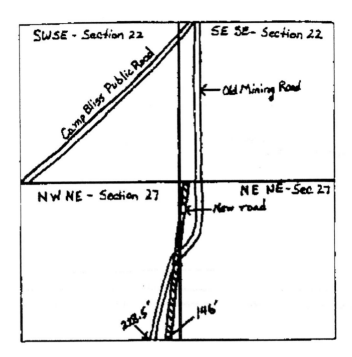

At the time appellant bought his farm in 1972, an old mining road ran south from the Camp Bliss Public Road in NE 1/4 SE 1/4. The old mining road ran south approximately two hundred feet from the west line of the NE 1/4 and SE 1/4 and SE 1/4 SE 1/4 in Section 22. It entered the NE 1/4 NE 1/4 in Section 27 (appellant's adjoining 40) approximately 200 feet east of the northwest corner of that forty. It extended south to approximately the middle of that forty where it turned west and entered the NW 1/4 NE 1/4 in Section 27 (respondents' 40 in question). It then ran in a southwesterly direction and left that 40 approximately 230 feet west of the southeast corner thereof. There it entered the SW 1/4 NE 1/4 in Section 27 (a part of appellant's farm).

In 1972 the land in question was largely covered with trees and brush. The old mining road was indistinct. There were remnants of a fence in trees along the west side of the old road. In March 1974, appellant decided to build a new road to reach his SW 1/4 NE 1/4. The Bunselmeyers then owned respondents' farm. Appellant met with the Bunselmeyers on the NW 1/4 NE 1/4 (then owned by the Bunselmeyers) to show them where the road was to be located. Appellant's testimony included the following:

A.   . . . I went and got them in my car and took them out there.

Q.   And they consented to the fence being built at that particular point?

A.   Yes, and they said they would pay for half of it.

The Bunselmeyers did pay for half of it. The appellant then constructed a new road and fence along the west side of that road. That fence extended from a point nine feet east of the northwest corner of NE 1/4 NE 1/4 (owned by appellant) through the NW 1/4 NE 1/4 (owned by respondents) in a southwesterly direction to a point on the south line of the latter 40, one hundred forty six feet west of the southeast corner thereof. The fence enclosed a triangle off the west side of the NW 1/4 NE 1/4. The fence was completed in June 1974.

The appellant used his farm to run cattle. After constructing the fence, he cleared the area, including the disputed triangle, and sowed it in fescue. Since building the fence, he has continuously used the disputed triangle as part of his farm, until the fence was moved by the respondents in 1984. The use was open and exclusive.

The respondents bought their farm in October 1974. They did not look at the fence in question at the time of their purchase. In 1980, they noticed that the fence was askew. They confirmed their observation by obtaining a photograph of the area from the county ASCS office. Starting late in 1980 or in 1981, they attempted to negotiate with appellant for the relocation of the fence. In 1983 the respondents established the "true line" by a survey. After an earlier attempt to do so, in October 1984 they moved the fence to the true line.

During cross-examination of the appellant, counsel for the respondents inquired concerning the appellant's intention in building the fence. The following is the essence of the appellant's testimony on that subject.

Q. In the building of that fence, you were not going to try to get or you were not claiming property that you did not have a deed for, were you?

A. I was merely building a fence where—

Q. You were not trying to claim property that you did not have a deed for, were you?

A. I was only—are you saying that I—

Q. I asked you a question.

A. I don't know what you want me to say.

Q. Mr. Norman, I am just asking you a question. You did not intend to claim some property that you did not have a deed for but you were just going to build a fence, is that right?

A. Yes, I guess that would be right.

The circuit court made exceptionally thorough Findings of Fact and Conclusions of Law. In doing so, it acknowledged the excellence of counsels' representation of their respective clients. This court has been aided by the outstanding briefs filed by the parties. . . . The circuit court cited and relied upon *Walker v. Walker*, 509 S.W.2d 102 (Mo.1974) and *Maupin v. Bearden*, 643 S.W.2d 860 (Mo.App.1982). It concluded that because appellant "by his own admission made no claim of right to the

Plaintiff didn't intend by building the fence = irrelevant

to gain property

disputed tract or roadway his request for injunctive relief, declaratory judgment vesting title in him and for damages must be denied."

The appellant's first point is that the circuit court erred because "his admission that at the time of the construction of the fence in question the plaintiff did not intend to claim property for which he had no deed ... does not negate plaintiff's claim of right to the property in question...." He argues "it is not necessary for the plaintiff to prove that he had an intention to claim property which was not covered by his deed in order to prevail in his claim of adverse possession." He relies upon the following statement [found in *Walters v. Tucker*, 308 S.W.2d 673, 680 (Mo. 1957)]: "Although the extent of their possession and claim, as indicated by the fence and hedge, originated in mistake as to the location of the true boundary line ..., there was no evidence tending to show or to justify the finding that defendants or their predecessors claimed only to the true line irrespective of the fence and hedge."

The respondents argue that the appellant's admission defeats his claim of adverse possession. They rely upon the following statement [from *Walters v. Tucker*, 308 S.W.2d 673, 676 (Mo. 1957)]: "With respect to a claim of title by adverse possession—although a claimant, upon occupancy under a mistake as to the true boundary, did not intend to take land from the true owner and did not intend to occupy and possess land to which he had no record title, his possession may be hostile and adverse if he intended to occupy and did occupy as the owner."

The intent with which a claimant must possess real property to establish title by adverse possession is an elusive, somewhat ethereal, element. The requirement varies between the states. It has been the subject of numerous texts and articles. Statements concerning the required intent are contained in appellate decisions in this state from its early history to date. Such statements are often dictum. Frequently they are recitations from a prior decision. They vary in their thrust and often are cursorily inconsistent. The cases do contain statements indicating the nature of the claim under which one possesses land is of little consequence. The following is an example. "... It is the intent to possess, and not the intent to take irrespective of his right, which governs...." *Walters v. Tucker, supra,* at 676. *Also see A. Charles Bussen Trust v. Kertz,* 723 S.W.2d 922, 929 (Mo.App.1987) wherein it states "[t]he hostile element is satisfied where the party occupies the land in question intending to occupy it as his own.... Ignorance of the boundary line is irrelevant as an intent to take away from the true owner is not necessary."

Nevertheless, the controlling decisions establish

5 elements of adverse possession

that five elements are essential to acquisition of title by adverse possession under Section 516.010, V.A.M.S. The possession must be (1) hostile, that is, under a claim of right, (2) actual (3) open and notorious, (4) exclusive, and (5) continuous, for ten years prior to commencement of the action to perfect title by adverse possession. [*Walker v. Walker, supra,* at 106.]

The requirement that such possession must be hostile, under a claim of right, is established by a host of cases. The sufficiency of the claim by one in possession is not to be measured by the morality of that claim or the legal efficacy of an instrument under which the claim is made. Nonetheless, it must be an intent to claim to possess the land as the owner. It is not necessary for the disposition of this case to reconcile the cases that deny title to a squatter and the cases that hold a trespasser with no pretext of title may possess the requisite intent.

The required intent is embodied in an often repeated maxim concerning a claim of adverse possession arising from a mistake (or absence of knowledge) concerning the "true" location of a boundary line.

> The rule is that while one's occupancy of an adjoining proprietor's land under a mistake as to the boundary line, and without any intention of claiming beyond the true boundary line, when ascertained, is not adverse possession, yet if he takes and holds possession up to a given point, and claims to be the owner to such point, his possession is adverse, notwithstanding his belief that such point is the true boundary line, when in fact it is not. [*Brown v. Wilson* (Banc), 348 Mo. 658, 666[8], 155 S.W.2d 176, 180 [10, 11] (1941).]

At an early date it was required that one claiming by adverse possession had to establish the "hostile or claim of right" element by affirmative evidence of the requisite intent. *Ware v. Cheek*, 201 S.W. 847, 849 (Mo.1918). That requirement has been relaxed.

> The fact that one encroaches on his neighbor's property by building a fence, or making improvements thereon, thinking the property is his, and that he had no intention of claiming any of his neighbor's property, is not controlling on the question as to whether the possession is adverse. If it were, the protection of the statute would be limited to those who deliberately set out to steal their neighbor's property and to cases where there has been an actual dispute as to the location of the boundary line. In no other case does the occupant intend to claim the land adversely, regardless of legal title. If such were the law, then the man who innocently and inadvertently occupies and improves land beyond his true boundary line or, in other words, one who most needs and deserves the protection of the statute, would be left without protection.

> The better rule on the subject, is embodied in the doctrine that, in the absence of positive proof or unambiguous circumstances showing that a possession is or is not adverse, the exclusive possession and use of land are presumed to be adverse, it is not necessary to show an intention to hold and claim the property in spite of the fact that legal title may be in another. . . . [*Edie v. Coleman*, 235 Mo.App. 1289, 141 S.W.2d 238, 243 (1940), *aff'd, State ex rel. Edie v. Shain*, 348 Mo. 119, 152 S.W.2d 174 (1941).]

"Thus, Missouri has joined other jurisdictions in tempering the harsher rule by announcing that the exclusive possession and use of land is presumed to be adverse, absent positive proof to the contrary." *Schaumburg v. Heafey*, 650 S.W.2d 697, 699 (Mo.App.1983).

In this case the circuit court found there was positive proof that the appellant's possession was not hostile, under a claim of right. The appellant's admission, standing alone, is substantial evidence to support the finding of the circuit court. . . .

Moreover, each claim of adverse possession must be decided upon the basis of its own unique circumstances. The appellant could not have based his claim to the disputed triangle or the right to build the road upon the old mining road. He acknowledged that the old mining road entered the respondents' 40 only at the midpoint of the east line of that quarter-quarter section. The boundary of the disputed triangle is far from coinciding with the boundaries of the old road. Further, the appellant acknowledged that he had asked permission to build the road. In light of these circumstances, the appellant's admission he was "merely building a fence" has greater significance. It is "positive proof" to support the judgment of the circuit court. . . .

Notes

1. *"Hostility" and "Permission."* In defining "hostility," courts initially focus upon whether the possession of the adverse possessor (AP) is permissive, *i.e.*, with the permission of the true owner (TO). If one is in possession of land with the express permission of TO, then that possession cannot be treated as adverse. Based upon what you have learned so far, can you explain why?

What constitutes "permission" sufficient to defeat a claim of hostility? Consider the facts of *Peters v. Juneau–Douglas Girl Scout Council*, 519 P.2d 826 (Alaska 1974). An Alaskan Tlingit tribesman, unfamiliar with the law, had occupied and possessed a parcel of land for a number of years when he approached the true owner's agent (Bez), "seeking a piece of paper, a deed, a title so that he could build a house on the land without fear of losing it." Bez apparently told him "you stay right there, we can't use it no more." On cross-examination, the possessor was asked: "Did [Bez] give you permission to stay there?" The possessor answered "yes." If you represented the possessor, how would you respond to the argument that the possession was permissive and not hostile?

2. *Should Possession of Another's Land Be Presumptively Hostile, or Presumptively Permissive?* Notice that the *Norman* opinion purports to affirm the principle (also stated in *Mullis*) that exclusive possession and use of the land of another is *presumed* to be hostile, absent evidence to the contrary. As a procedural matter, this presumption shifts to TO the burden of coming forward with evidence that AP's possession was permissive; if TO fails to present such evidence, the factfinder may determine that AP's possession was in fact hostile.

Legal presumptions can serve at least two important purposes. First, presumptions can advance the efficient administration of justice by obviating the need for a party to present evidence about a fact that is almost certainly true. For example, in interpreting a sales contract that established a price in "dollars," a court would presume that the parties meant U.S. dollars (at least where the contract was negotiated in the U.S. between two U.S. residents). Second, presumptions may serve a policy goal of advancing justice even though the presumed fact is not demonstrably true. Courts often say that persons are conclusively presumed to "know the law." This presumption prevents a person from pleading ignorance of the law as an excuse to criminal behavior—even if the person was truly ignorant of the law. Sometimes, a presumption may advance both purposes (consider, for example, the presumption that a child of four is incapable of forming the intent to commit a crime).

Consider the presumption that possession of another's land is presumed to be without permission. Does this presumption make good sense? Does the law draw this presumption for evidentiary reasons (because it is true in most cases) or for policy reasons? If the latter, for what reasons?

3. *Judicial Approaches to the "Hostility" or "Claim of Right" Requirement.* Jurisdictions have followed divergent approaches in evaluating whether a claimant's possession is under "claim of right"—sometimes, as *Norman* demonstrates, within the very same opinion! As you read the following material, which approach do you think is preferable? Which is more consistent with the theories and justifications underlying the concept of adverse possession?

(a) *The "Objective" Approach.* Most courts focus not upon AP's state of mind, but upon how an objective observer would evaluate AP's actions. Is AP exercising rights that are in fact inconsistent with the rights held by TO? Would a neutral observer (someone who does not know the true state of the title to the land in question), viewing AP's actions with respect to the land, conclude that AP was the owner of the land based upon AP's conduct? If so, then AP's possession is "under claim of right," even if AP took possession of that land by mistake or misapprehension of the true facts. *See, e.g. Chaplin v. Sanders*, 100 Wash.2d 853, 676 P.2d 431 (1984). England adheres to this objective approach, *see* Robert Megarry & H.W.R. Wade, The Law of Real Property 1034 (5th ed. 1984), as do the majority of American jurisdictions; further, most American scholars consider the objective approach to be the correct view. William B. Stoebuck & Dale A. Whitman, The Law of Property § 11.7, at 857 (3d ed. 2000).

(b) *The "Subjective" Approaches.* Some courts, in contrast, have taken *subjective* approaches to defining "claim of right," under which AP's state of mind is determinative. Courts have taken two different subjective approaches.

(i) *The "Good Faith" Approach.* One set of cases takes what one might call the "good faith" approach:

> A claim of right by a squatter is a false claim. To permit a squatter to assert a claim of right requirement would put a premium on dishonesty. One of the main purposes of the claim of right requirement is to "bar mere squatters from the benefits of adverse possession." [*Carpenter v. Ruperto*, 315 N.W.2d 782, 785–86 (Iowa 1982).]

Under this approach, AP cannot establish title by adverse possession unless she takes possession with the good faith belief that she has valid title.

(ii) *The "Intent to Claim" Approach.* Another set of cases has taken what we call the "intent to claim" approach (some others have called it the "aggressive trespasser" standard). Under this view, AP can acquire adverse possession only if the evidence suggested that the claimant acted with the subjective intent to claim the land possessed, regardless of the location of the proper boundary. The application of this test is reflected in *Miller v. Fitzpatrick*, 418 S.W.2d 884 (Tex. App. 1967). In that case, the claimants asserted possession of a small triangular strip of the neighboring parcel, based upon conduct (by themselves and their predecessors) that included planting and mowing grass, planting flowers, and installing a sprinkler system. When the neighbor discovered this encroachment and an adverse possession claim arose, the claimant's predecessor (Mills) testified that "I was simply claiming it because I thought that was where the line was; I thought it was my property or I wouldn't have been mowing it." *Id.* at 889. The court held that the claimants could not establish title by adverse possession, because the evidence did not establish that Mills possessed the disputed area under claim of right:

> "No matter how exclusive and hostile to the true owner the possession may be in appearance, it cannot be adverse unless accompanied by the intent on the part of the occupant to make it so. The naked possession unaccompanied with any claim of right will never constitute a bar."...

> There is no evidence that Mills ... ever manifested any claim of right to the disputed area by any declaration or verbal assertion of such claim. The acts of mowing the grass, planting flowers, and keeping the land in dispute in the condition in which his grantor kept it did not constitute the character of possession as of itself gave notice of an exclusive adverse possession hostile to the claims of all others. [*Id.* at 889–90 (quoting *Houston Oil Co. v. Stepney*, 187 S.W. 1078, 1084 (Tex. App. 1916)).]

Students should note, however, that courts have not always articulated these two subjective views clearly—or even as mutually exclusive views. Notably, in cases where the claimant knows that the disputed land belongs to someone else, courts purportedly applying the "intent to claim" test have sometimes (but not always) refused to protect the adverse claimant—even if the evidence suggests that the claimant possessed the subjective intent to claim the disputed land as her own.[10] This has created confusion and

10. The case law is sufficiently muddled that leading scholars have disagreed vehemently over the extent to which good faith does (or does not) matter in establishing an adverse possession claim. *See, e.g.,* Richard H. Helmholz, *Adverse Possession and Subjective Intent,* 61 Wash. U.L.Q. 331, 337–39, 342–46 (1983) (asserting possessor's good faith strengthened her likelihood of success); Roger A. Cunningham, *Adverse Possession and Subjective Intent: A Reply to Professor Helmholz,* 64 Wash. U.L.Q. 1 (1986) (asserting that Helmholz's conclusion was flawed and based upon mischaracterization of case law). *See also* Richard H. Helmholz, *More on Subjective Intent: A Response to Professor Cunningham,* 64 Wash. U.L.Q. 65 (1986); Roger A. Cunningham, *More on Adverse Possession: A Rejoinder to Professor Helmholz,* 64 Wash. U.L.Q. 1167 (1986).

inconsistency in opinions that advocate a subjective view of the claim of right standard, and makes generalizing about the cases very dangerous.

To demonstrate the confusion to which some courts have fallen prey, consider the famous case of *Van Valkenburgh v. Lutz*, 304 N.Y. 95, 106 N.E.2d 28 (1952). The Lutzes (owners of Lots 14 and 15 in a subdivision) knowingly built and occupied a small cabin on Lot 19, even though they knew they had no claim of title to Lot 19. The Lutzes also built a garage which they thought was located entirely on their own property, but a portion of the garage actually encroached onto Lot 19 by mistake. Subsequently, the true owner of Lot 19 demanded that the Lutzes remove the cabin and the garage encroachment. The court concluded that Lutzes did not have the requisite "claim of right" to establish title by adverse possession—either as to the cabin (because they knew it was on Lot 19, which did not belong to them) or to the garage encroachment (because they did not know it encroached upon Lot 19 and thus they lacked the specific intent to claim that part of Lot 19 as their own). Under this analysis, under what circumstances would someone be able to acquire title by adverse possession?

(c) *"Hostility" and the* Norman *Case.* Which approach to hostility does the court apply in *Norman*? Focus carefully upon the quoted language of the opinion in *Brown v. Wilson*, 348 Mo. 658, 155 S.W.2d 176 (1941), on which the court relies in *Norman*:

> The rule is that while one's occupancy of an adjoining proprietor's land under a mistake as to the boundary line, and without any intention of claiming beyond the true boundary line, when ascertained, is not adverse possession, yet if he takes and holds possession up to a given point, and claims to be the owner to such point, his possession is adverse, notwithstanding his belief that such point is the true boundary line, when in fact it is not.

Does this distinction make sufficient sense to justify its use as a means of deciding adverse possession cases? Why or why not?

4. *The Agreement to Build a Fence, "Division Fences," and the Doctrine of "Agreed Boundaries."* Should it matter that Norman and the Bunselmeyers agreed to the location of the fence and to share the cost of building it? Consider the following:

(a) A Missouri statute permits landowners to erect a "division fence" to separate their fields from neighboring fields. A landowner seeking to build a division fence can give notice of this desire to the neighbor, who has 90 days to build one-half of the fence. If the neighbor fails to do so, the landowner can obtain a court order allowing her to build the fence and ordering the neighbor to pay one-half of the value of the fence. Thereafter, each adjoining landowner owns one-half of the fence. Mo. Stat. Ann. §§ 272.010 to 272.240. Is this statute relevant to a proper evaluation of the conversation between Norman and the Bunselmeyers? Why or why not?

(b) Decisions in most states recognize the doctrine of "agreed boundaries." Under this doctrine, an express agreement by adjacent landowners as to the location of the boundary line is sufficient to trigger the running of the limitations period for adverse possession if it is later discovered that the agreed-upon boundary line was erroneous. The Missouri Supreme Court has adopted this doctrine. *See Tillman v. Hutcherson*, 348 Mo. 473, 479, 154 S.W.2d 104, 107 (1941). Should the court have applied the agreed boundaries doctrine in *Norman*? Why or why not?

5. *Converting "Permissive" Possession to "Hostile" Possession.* If possession of another's land begins as permissive, the statutory period cannot begin to run unless the possession thereafter becomes hostile. For this conversion to happen, the possessor must take action conspicuous enough to warn the true owner of the nature of the possessor's claim against the land. For example, suppose that Barnes gives Corrada permission to use his Vail condominium as a guest during Corrada's planned two-week vacation. After two weeks, Corrada extends his vacation for an additional two weeks and remains in the condo. After the additional two weeks, Corrada decides to get a job in Vail and decides to remain in the condominium permanently. Is Corrada's possession of the condominium beyond the scope of Barnes' original permission sufficiently hostile for Corrada's claim eventually to ripen into title by adverse possession?

This possibility can arise in a variety of other contexts. For example, suppose that in 1985, Easton builds a fence on what he mistakenly believes is the true boundary line between his land and the neighboring land of Wells. One year later, when Wells discovers the mistake and calls it to Easton's attention, Easton apologizes and offers to buy the encroachment area. Instead, Wells says, "Just leave the fence where it is, as long as you agree that the land belongs to me and you're using it with my permission." Easton agrees, and the fence remains in place. In 1994, Easton conveys his land to Corrada, and in 2001, Wells sells her land to Lazos. At all times, Corrada has continued to maintain the land on his side of the fence, but never speaks with either Wells or Lazos regarding whether the fence is on the true boundary line. If the applicable statutory period is 10 years, has Corrada acquired adverse possession of the encroachment area? Although Easton's use was permissive and not hostile, should the law presume that Corrada's possession is also permissive as against Wells? As against Lazos? Why or why not? *Compare Waltimyer v. Smith*, 383 Pa.Super. 291, 556 A.2d 912 (1989) (permission terminates upon transfer by either true owner or user; continued use thereafter presumed hostile) *with Miller v. Anderson*, 91 Wash.App. 822, 964 P.2d 365 (1998) (continued use remained permissive after sale by original user, but sale by true owner terminated permission).

Likewise, this possibility can arise in situations involving land held in co-ownership, which we study more thoroughly in Chapter 6. In co-ownership, two or more persons hold undivided ownership of land, with each person legally entitled to possess *all* of the land *all* of the time, subject only to the corresponding possessory right of every other co-owner. Thus, the law generally presumes that sole possession by one co-owner is with the permission of all co-owners—in effect, on behalf of all of the co-owners—provided the co-owner in sole possession does not actually exclude any other co-owners or otherwise "oust" them. Because this sole possession is permissive and not hostile, therefore, it could not be the basis for one co-owner to claim title from the other co-owners by adverse possession. In contrast, if the co-owner in sole possession commits an "ouster" of another cotenant, that "ouster" converts the co-owner's possession from permissive to hostile. What actions would you think would be necessary to constitute an ouster? Would the co-owner in possession have to exclude the other co-owners in a physical sense?

Analogous ouster principles also apply to a tenant's possession of the landlord's premises. As we will study in Chapter 7, a tenant presumptively possesses the leased property with the permission of the true owner, the landlord. Thus, the tenant can claim no adverse right without first ousting the landlord so as to overcome the presumption of permissive possession.

6. *Exclusivity of Possession.* What does it mean for a claimant to establish "exclusive" possession? Consider this variation on the facts in *Norman.* Assume that during the nine years after Norman built his fence, the Bunselmeyers had regularly used the disputed area for grazing their cattle (assume the fence included a gate for this purpose). Would this use by the Bunselmeyers prevent Norman from establishing exclusive possession? What additional information might you want to know before reaching a conclusion? *See, e.g., Lilly v. Lynch,* 88 Wash.App. 306, 945 P.2d 727 (1997).

LAWYERING EXERCISE
(Interviewing, Counseling and Ethical Dilemmas)

BACKGROUND: The *Norman* case presents a problem in which the client's state of mind is or may be relevant to the likely legal resolution of the dispute. This situation presents one of the most difficult ethical dilemmas involved in interviewing clients:

> Perhaps the best known ethical dilemma in client interviewing is called the *Anatomy of a Murder* problem, after the novel and movie of the same name. There, a lawyer interviews his client, who is accused of murder. Before asking the client for the facts in detail, the lawyer gives the client a lecture explaining all the defenses to a murder charge. After listening to this, the client describes the facts that would support a defense of temporary insanity. We are left with the impression that if the client had not heard the lecture, he would have told a different story—that the lawyer essentially told the client what the client would have to say in order to escape conviction. [Stefan H. Kreiger & Richard K. Neumann, Jr., Essential Lawyering Skills: Interviewing, Counseling, Negotiation, and Persuasive Fact Analysis 101 (2d ed. 2003).]

If you were Mr. Norman's lawyer, you would have a duty to accurately explain to him the legal standards that apply to the dispute (so that he could make an informed judgment regarding how to proceed). *See* Model Rule of Professional Conduct 1.4(b) (a lawyer "shall explain a matter to the extent reasonably necessary to permit the client to make informed decisions regarding the representation"). Of course, if you explain how the legal standard may depend upon Mr. Norman's state of mind, Mr. Norman may manipulate his testimony to fit the underlying legal standard—and this implicates Model Rule 3.4(b), which provides that a lawyer shall not "falsify evidence, counsel, or assist a witness to testify falsely." So if you explain the legal standard to Mr. Norman, are you providing him with knowledge of the law, or encouraging him to commit perjury to win his case? Consider Professor Steve Pepper's thoughts on this problem:

> In a complex legal environment much law cannot be known and acted upon, cannot function as law, without lawyers to make it accessible to those for whom it is relevant. Thus, in our society lawyers are necessary for much of our law to be known, to be functional. The traditional understanding is that lawyers as professionals act for the client's benefit in providing access to the law. Under this understanding, lawyers do not function as law enforcement officers or as judges of their clients in providing knowledge of the law; the choices to be made concern the client's life and affairs, and they are therefore primarily the client's choices to make.
>
> The limits on the assistance lawyers may provide to their clients have commonly been articulated and thought of as the "bounds of the law." The lawyer may not become an active participant in the client's unlawful activity, and does not have immunity if she becomes an aider and abettor of unlawful conduct. The difficulty arises in deciding whether providing accurate, truthful information about the law—the core function of lawyering—can also be considered active assistance in violation of the law in situations in which the lawyer knows the information may well lead to or facilitate the client's unlawful conduct. The answers or guides to that inquiry are disturbingly unclear. There are no reported cases of civil or criminal liability on the part of the lawyer, or of professional discipline, clearly based only upon providing the client with accurate legal information. On the other hand, the legal limits are not stated in a way to make it clear that providing such advice is within the proper bounds of lawyering. Nor do these limits provide much assistance in knowing when giving the advice is proper and when it is not.... [Stephen L. Pepper, *Counseling at the Limits of the Law: An Exercise in the Jurisprudence and Ethics of Lawyering*, 104 Yale L.J. 1545, 1546–48 (1995).]

TASK: Assume that Mr. Norman is about to enter your office for a fact-gathering interview regarding his dispute with the Allisons. Consider and discuss how you would conduct the interview to avoid (or minimize the risks posed by) this ethical dilemma.

3. *"Open and Notorious" Possession*

Most adverse possession litigation involves boundary disputes, where one neighbor has possessed some land beyond the actual boundary of an adjacent parcel owned by someone else. In these cases, adverse possession claims often confront arguments that the possession was neither hostile nor under claim of right, as in *Norman*, or that the possession was not open and notorious. When is possession sufficiently "open and notorious" in a boundary dispute? If the size of a boundary encroachment is relatively small and the parties are not aware of the true boundary line location, can the encroachment be sufficiently "open and notorious"?

STUMP v. WHIBCO

Superior Court of New Jersey, Appellate Division.
314 N.J.Super. 560, 715 A.2d 1006 (1998).

[Editors' Note: On June 13, 1974, Howard and Catherine Stump bought land along the Maurice River from Paul and Theania Cox, who had operated a boatyard and marina on the land. The Coxes had purchased the parcel in 1948, at which time there was a wire mesh fence that ostensibly delineated the parcel's boundary with the adjoining land. At some point, the Coxes replaced the wire mesh fence with a fence constructed of railroad ties and cable, but without conducting a survey to confirm the true boundary line. Both the Coxes and the Stumps treated the fence as the boundary line. After purchasing the land, the Stumps used the area up to the fence for boat storage until 1981, when they began making substantial improvements, including a concrete walkway, bulkhead, boat ramps, underground conduit and septic systems. In January 1990, a survey revealed that the fence and certain of the improvements encroached onto the adjoining land, owned by Whibco. Upon this discovery, the Stumps sued to establish title to the encroachment area by adverse possession.

The trial court concluded that the Stumps had failed to establish title by adverse possession because they had failed to satisfy New Jersey's 30-year limitations period. The trial court reasoned that the fence (both the wire mesh fence and the railroad tie fence that replaced it) was a minor encroachment that did not satisfy the requirement that possession be "open and notorious":

> The Court concludes as a matter of law that no presumption of knowledge arose from the prior minor and passive encroachments along the common boundary line before 1981. The presence of the fence on [the] Whibco property is concluded by the Court to have been a minor encroachment. The Whibco land is a seven and one-half acre parcel. The fence encroaches by 52 1/2 feet at its widest point and tapers to an encroachment of less than 1 foot as it approaches Fish Factory Road. This case amounts to a minor border encroachment that would call for an on-site survey for the determination of the actual boundary line.

Thus, the court held that the Stumps' possession did not become sufficiently adverse until they began making permanent improvements in 1981. The Stumps appealed.]

KESTIN, J.A.D.   The trial court was correct to posit that "[a]s a general rule, successors in title who continue adverse uses may tack the periods of adverse uses of predecessors to establish the statutory period."

In this connection Whibco contends that the Stumps did not, even with such tacking as may properly be recognized, establish continuous occupancy for thirty years, as is required to prevail on their adverse possession claim. There is a specific contention stemming from the fact that before they took title to the Cox property, the Stumps and their business partner, Ed Borowski, first leased the property from the Coxes. The partners fell out, and Borowski prevented the Stumps from entering the property for at least a year.

The tacking principle is well established in this State. When ownership during the statutory period involves more than one adverse possessor, each owner who acquires title must satisfy all the elements of adverse possession. 7 *Powell on Real Property* § 1014[2], at 91–61 (Dannenberg rev.1990). Tacking is generally permitted "unless it is shown that the claimant's predecessor in title did not intend to convey the disputed parcel." *Id.* at 91–60.

What constitutes continuous possession depends on the nature of the land at issue. Some property is only used seasonally, for example. In general, however, "periodic or sporadic acts of ownership are not sufficient to constitute adverse possession." *Id.* at 91–24. Accordingly,

> The claimant must have affirmatively and consistently acted as if he were the owner, taking into due account the reasonable uses for which the land in question was suitable. It thus suffices if land chiefly timbered is fenced and is cultivated in the areas suitable for cultivation; if land most suitable for seasonal or weekend and holiday use is used for these purposes, even though not during the winter; or if ravined range land is used for the purposes possible in view of its topography. [*Id.* at 91–27.]

The adverse claimant must prove that he or she "has acted towards the land in question as would an average owner, taking properly into account the geophysical nature of the land." *Id.* at 91–44. *Powell on Real Property* lists storage as one of the activities which, if consistently done, meets this standard; and includes fencing—"substantial enclosure"—as one of the two most significant activities. (Paying taxes on the property is the other.) *Id.* at 91–46–47. Abandonment by the adverse possessor breaks the continuity, but departure caused by a "supervening force" does not. *Id.* at 91–28.

When a third party, one who is neither the true owner nor the adverse possessor, interferes with possession, "it seldom constitutes an interruption of possession." *Id.* at 91–26. This is particularly true "when the possessor acts with diligence to protect his possession against such an act." *Ibid.* . . .

In the present case, the partnership relationship between Borowski and Stump adds an unusual element, since through the agency relationship between partners it could be argued that Borowski's acts were attributable to Stump for adverse possession purposes. However, the fact remains that the Coxes, at the time of the Borowski occupancy, were still the owners of the property to which the adverse use attached, and were leasing it out. Thus, the Coxes were using the property in a manner "consistent with acts of possession that ordinary owners of like properties would undertake[; 't]he character of disputed property is crucial in determining what degree of control and what character of possession is required to establish adverse possession'." *Ray* [*v. Beacon Hudson Mountain Corp.*, 88 N.Y.2d 154, 643 N.Y.S.2d 939, 942, 666 N.E.2d 532 (1996)] (citation omitted). The Coxes conducted a marina business on the property; Borowski did the same; and subsequently, the Stumps did the same. The fence remained in place throughout the tenure of each; and the record supports the trial court's finding that, until the 1990 survey showed otherwise, the fence was regarded by all involved as the boundary line of the property.

Thus, the adverse possession of the disputed property was not interrupted during the period of time when Borowski occupied the land and excluded Stump. To the extent that very exclusion might conceivably be taken as evidencing an exercise of dominion over the land by Borowski, it must be seen to have been adverse to the rights of the true owner, Whibco, and its predecessors in interest....

... [T]he question remains whether plaintiffs have made the necessary showing that will enable them to prevail. We conclude, as the trial court did, that plaintiffs have not made the requisite showing and, accordingly, we affirm. We differ with the expressed basis of the trial court's decision, however. The "minor encroachment" rationale employed by the trial judge does not withstand analysis in the light of the record and established rules of law governing that concept. Nevertheless, in the final analysis, plaintiffs have failed to sustain their burden of proving "open and notorious" possession for the requisite period of time....

Those who seek to establish adverse possession bear the burden of proof by a preponderance. However, once evidence is introduced of "an open, continuous, uninterrupted exclusive use for the prescriptive period with the acquiescence of the owner, a presumption arises that the use was adverse except when the land is vacant, unimproved, unenclosed, and the use is casual rather than customary." [*Patton v. North Jersey Dist. Water Supply Comm'n*, 93 N.J. 180, 187, 459 A.2d 1177 (1983).]

Mannillo v. Gorski, [54 N.J. 378, 255 A.2d 258 (1969)], also recognized the minor encroachment exception:

> [T]he occupation or possession [of the land claimed in adverse possession] must be of that nature that the real owner is *presumed to have known* that there was a possession adverse to his title.... However, when the encroachment of an adjoining owner is of a small area and the fact of an intrusion is not clearly and self-evidently apparent to the naked eye but requires an on-site survey for certain disclosure ... [the presumption of adverse use] is fallacious and unjustified. The precise location of the dividing line is then ordinarily unknown to either adjacent owner and there is nothing on the land itself to show by visual observation that a hedge, fence, wall or other structure encroaches on the neighboring land to a minor extent. Therefore, to permit a presumption of notice

to arise in the case of minor border encroachments not exceeding several feet would fly in the face of reality and require the true owner to be on constant alert for possible small encroachments. [54 N.J. at 388, 255 A.2d 258.]

Our disagreement with the trial court that the minor encroachment exception is applicable here is based upon such considerations of quality. A minor encroachment is, by definition, an intrusion so small that it cannot easily be detected without a survey, and thus it cannot be presumed that the true owner is aware of it. *Mannillo* involved an incursion of steps and a concrete walk which intruded fifteen inches onto the land of the true owner. *Mannillo, supra,* 54 N.J. at 382, 255 A.2d 258. In *Maggio* [*v. Pruzansky,* 222 N.J.Super. 567, 573, 537 A.2d 756 (App.Div.1988)], the infringement amounted to slightly more than a foot-long strip of land along a masonry wall; and the supposed acts of dominion consisted of cutting grass and planting flowers on land adjacent to the wall. *Maggio, supra,* 222 N.J.Super. at 573, 537 A.2d 756.

The trial court in evaluating the Stumps' claim herein underemphasized the importance of enclosure—the fencing-in of land—in adverse possession law. The fencing of land by a claimant is evidence of possession and assertion of ownership. "[E]ither of itself or in connection with other acts of dominion it [may] be sufficient" to support an adverse possession claim. 3 Am.Jur.2d Adverse Possession § 36 (1986). Where fencing alone is the evidence on which an adverse possession claim is based,

> it must, to be effective, be complete and so open and notorious as to charge the owner with knowledge thereof. The question ... is whether the inclosure, like other acts of possession, is sufficient to "fly the flag" over the land and put the true owner on notice that the property is held under an adverse claim of ownership. This rule is applicable where a fence or a hedgerow or the like is relied on to delineate the boundaries of the adverse claim. [*Ibid.*] ...

Case law nationwide shows there is a virtual *per se* rule that fences constitute open and notorious possession. [Citations omitted]

Plaintiffs argue, and defendant does not disagree, that the railroad tie and cable fence was generally considered by the community and predecessors in interest to the parties, as the boundary line between the two pieces of land. To the extent there were remnants of an earlier wire mesh fence, they too were considered to establish a boundary, however undefined or invisible in part. In fact, initially Whibco, in 1989, ordered a survey made because of a suspicion that the railroad tie and cable fence was being moved by the Stumps. Although the suspicion appears to have been groundless, the survey made Whibco aware of the fact that the fence was actually located on Whibco's property. ...

Whibco suggests that the old fence, of unknown origin, might have even been constructed by former owners of its property. This argument does not necessarily militate in favor of Whibco. If, in fact, Whibco or a predecessor in title constructed the fence, mistaking the boundary line when it did so, and its error induced the error of the Stumps and their predecessors in title as to the location of the true boundary line, Whibco may be deemed "precluded from disputing the boundary line so fixed." *Keilt v. Lozier,* 7 N.J. Misc. 642, 644, 146 A. 786 (Sup.Ct.1929).

We note also that the disputed parcel is too large to be considered a minor encroachment. *See Mannillo v. Gorski, supra,* 54 N.J. at 382, 388, 255 A.2d 258 (involving a fifteen inch encroachment); *Maggio v. Pruzansky, supra,* 222 N.J.Super. at 573, 537 A.2d 756 (involving an intruding strip slightly more than one foot in width).

We hold, as a matter of law, therefore, that the occupancy depicted herein was not a minor encroachment. We reach this conclusion because of the existence of a true fence and the size of the parcel.

Notwithstanding that the railroad tie and cable fence and the disputed area it separated cannot be considered minor encroachments, the Stumps have not adequately established that their (and their predecessors') occupancy was sufficiently open and notorious for the necessary duration to satisfy that requirement. Their claim is seriously weakened by evidence that when the Cox family first took title to the land, the wire mesh fence was overgrown, indiscernible or non-existent in certain areas. The testimony of Paul Cox, Jr., who was in grammar school at the time his parents purchased the property, was the only evidence on the issue:

> [I]t was an old fence, similar to what they had in those days, which was made out of square wire mesh. And it was covered with bushes and things, so I'm not—you know, I just knew it was there.

As to where the fence began, Cox said:

> [T]he old wire fence that was covered with brush was difficult to tell. I could—you know, I knew there was a fence there ... but I don't know where it [ ] originated and where it terminated.

Manifestly, a fence in the condition described delineates no boundary. So neglected, decrepit, and non-continuous a structure may be adequate to establish that all concerned were under the impression that it signified the approximate location of the property line, but in order to establish dominion over particular property—so essential to a claim of adverse possession—its perimeter, and the adverse claim thereto, must be more well-defined than was the case here when the partially visible wire mesh fence existed during the period of Cox ownership. Plaintiffs, therefore, have not sustained their burden to prove a clear assertion of dominion during that period as an intact fence would.

The Coxes did not maintain the old fence, but after they installed the replacement railroad tie and cable fence, they maintained that structure and kept it clear of brush. The replacement fence was installed when Paul Cox, Jr. was in the Merchant Marines, between 1967 and 1969. That fence in the condition described met the requirements for boundary definition that a claim for adverse possession must of necessity entail. The wire mesh fence clearly did not. In late 1989 or early 1990, the Stumps received a letter from Whibco revealing the results of the 1989 survey, and demanding that the Stumps remove their encroachments upon Whibco's property. This suit was commenced by the Stumps in 1991, and Whibco's counterclaim was filed in 1993. Since, according to the evidence in the record, the existence of the fence as open and notorious, for purposes of presumptive notice to the true owner, cannot be reliably established until sometime between 1967 and 1969, when the old fence was replaced, the plaintiffs have failed to meet the burden of proving thirty years of open and notorious possession by a preponderance of the evidence. . . .

[handwritten margin note: couldn't prove fence was up for 30 yrs]

Notes

1. *"Open and Notorious" Possession in Boundary Disputes.* The *Mannillo* case, addressed by the court in *Stump,* is one of the most infamous decisions in adverse possession law. Ms. Gorski built steps and a concrete sidewalk that encroached onto the neighboring land of the Mannillos (without objection by the Mannillos) by a total of fifteen inches. Many years later, Gorski claimed title to this fifteen-inch strip of land by adverse possession. The *Mannillo* court held that Gorski's possession was insufficiently open and notorious unless the true owners (the Mannillos) had actual knowledge of the true boundary line:

> Generally, where possession of the land is clear and unequivocal and to such an extent as to be immediately visible, the owner may be presumed to have knowledge of the adverse occupancy. . . . However, when the encroachment of an adjoining owner is of a small area and the fact of an intrusion is not clearly and self-evidently apparent to the naked eye but requires an on-site survey for certain disclosure as in urban sections where the division line is only infrequently delineated by any monuments, natural or artificial, such a presumption is fallacious and unjustified. . . . The only method of certain determination would be by obtaining a survey each time the adjacent owner undertook any improvement at or near the boundary, and this would place an undue and inequitable burden upon the true owner. Accordingly we hereby hold that no presumption of knowledge arises from a minor encroachment along a common boundary. In such a case, only where the true owner has actual knowledge thereof may it be said that the possession is open and notorious. [*Mannillo,* 255 A.2d at 263–64.]

The *Mannillo* decision has generated substantial criticism—in fact, courts in other jurisdictions are nearly unanimous that the true owner's knowledge of the adverse claim is not essential to an adverse possession claim, even if the encroachment in question is small or minor. Can you explain why the law has generally rejected the "minor encroachment" test used in *Mannillo*?

In answering this question, consider the following additional questions: How would you expect courts to apply the *Mannillo* test in subsequent cases? Is the *Mannillo* court correct to suggest that a survey is the *only* way of assuring the protection of the proper boundaries? What incentives does the "minor encroachment" test create for landowners regarding the monitoring of their boundary lines? In light of the policies behind adverse possession doctrine, who should bear the risk of an "unknown" small but long-standing encroachment—the encroacher or the true owner? Is the *Stump* court's attempt to distinguish *Mannillo* persuasive?

2. *Adverse Possession of Personal Property.* Suppose that in 1995, Hunvald lost a limited first edition of the book "The Common Law" by Oliver Wendell Holmes when it fell out of his briefcase. Westbrook discovered the book later that day, picked the book up, took it home, and added it to his personal collection of rare books. The book remained there for 11 years, until Westbrook hosted a cocktail party at which Hunvald was a guest. While perusing Westbrook's collection, Hunvald recognized the copy of "The Common Law" as the one he had lost 11 years ago. Has Westbrook acquired title to the book via adverse possession?

As applied to movable personal property like a book, an "open and notorious" test poses a conundrum. On the one hand, Westbrook has possessed and used the book in a fashion typical of a true owner (reading it and displaying it in his personal collection). On the other hand, even though his possession and use is typical, it is not very likely to alert Hunvald as to the fact that Westbrook has possession of the book. For this reason, early decisions held that customary use of personal property was not sufficiently "open and notorious" to justify adverse possession. *See, e.g., Redmond v. New Jersey Historical Soc'y*, 132 N.J. Eq. 464, 28 A.2d 189 (1942).

More recent decisions, however, have adopted a different approach, reflected in the case of *O'Keeffe v. Snyder*, 83 N.J. 478, 416 A.2d 862 (1980). In *O'Keeffe*, Georgia O'Keeffe sued to recover a painting that she claimed had been stolen from her 30 years earlier. The defendant (who apparently was not the thief) asserted that he had acquired title by adverse possession. The trial court concluded that O'Keeffe's action was time-barred because the statute of limitations (six years) began running on the date of the theft. The court of appeals reversed, presumably because the defendant's possession of the painting was not "open and notorious." The New Jersey Supreme Court reversed the court of appeals, articulating the "discovery rule":

> The discovery rule provides that, in an appropriate case, a cause of action will not accrue until the injured party discovers, or by exercise of reasonable diligence and intelligence should have discovered, facts which form the basis of a cause of action....

> [W]e conclude that the discovery rule applies to an action for replevin of a painting.... O'Keeffe's cause of action accrued when she first knew, or reasonably should have known through the exercise of due diligence, of the cause of action, including the identity of the possessor of the paintings. [*O'Keeffe*, 416 A.2d at 869–70.]

In terms of procedure, how does the discovery rule operate differently from the common law adverse possession rule? Under a discovery rule, would Hunvald lose if he had never made any effort whatsoever to locate his book during the previous 11 years? Finally, how would a state finders' statute (note 3, page 139) affect your analysis of the rights of Westbrook and Hunvald with regard to the book?

3. *"Tacking" and "Privity" in Boundary Disputes.* Establishing the "privity" necessary to tack successive periods of possession sometimes proves complicated in boundary disputes, where the possessor lacks color of title. For example, suppose that for six years, Barnes occupies Lot 1 (which he owns), along with a portion of Lot 2 (which Shelton owns) that Barnes fenced in honestly believing it was part of Lot 1. Barnes then sells Lot 1 to Ertman. In preparing the deed to Ertman, Barnes simply copies the description in his original deed (which described only Lot 1); thus, the deed to Ertman did not literally purport to convey the portion of Lot 2 lying inside the fence. Nevertheless, Ertman takes possession of the land (including the fenced-in portion of Lot 2). After six additional years, Shelton obtains a survey that identifies the correct boundary line, and demands that Ertman relocate the fence to the proper position. Ertman argues that she and Barnes have been in successive adverse possession for 12 years (assume the statutory period is 10 years). Shelton argues that Ertman and Barnes cannot tack their periods of possession together—because the deed from Ertman to Barnes described only Lot 1, not the portion of Lot 2 that each adversely possessed. Some courts have accepted this argument, *see, e.g., Moore v. Duran*, 455 Pa.Super. 124, 687 A.2d 822 (1997). However, the weight of authority (and the better view) is reflected by *Shelton v. Strickland*, 106 Wash.App. 45, 21 P.3d 1179 (2001):

> To understand tacking, it is useful to recall the concept of "inchoate title".... Before the statute has run, an adverse possessor has something which, though it is wrongful and cannot stand up against the true owner, is rightful and good against everyone else. This "shadow title," ... is founded in possession; so, it makes sense that it can be transferred by transferring possession. There must be a relationship between the successive adverse possessors, one in which, at a minimum, the prior possessor willingly turns over possession to the succeeding one. This relationship the courts usually call "privity," though, to avoid confusion with the several other meanings of that word, the word "nexus" is better.
>
> The "privity" or "nexus" required to permit tacking of the adverse use of successive occupants of real property does not have to be more than such a reasonable connection between the successive occupants as will raise their claim of right above the status of wrongdoer or trespasser. A formal conveyance between the parties describing some or all of the property is not essential to establish such connection.... "The deed running between the parties purporting to transfer the land possessed traditionally furnishes the privity of estate which connects the possession of the successive occupants." [quoting William B. Stoebuck, *Washington Practice: Real Estate* § 8.18, at 513–14 (1995) and *Howard v. Kunto*, 3 Wash.App. 393, 398–99, 477 P.2d 210 (1970).]

4. *Related Doctrines*

On occasion, an adverse possessor may present a relatively compelling case for legal protection, yet may be unable to demonstrate all of the necessary elements to establish title by adverse possession. In such situations, courts have used a number of alternative theories to protect such claimants. We addressed one such theory—the "agreed boundaries" doctrine—in conjunction with *Norman v. Allison* (page 175). The following materials address several other alternative doctrines that sometimes arise in encroachment cases.

a. *Mutual Recognition and Acquiescence.* As *Norman* and *Stump* demonstrate, neighboring landowners often may be uncertain about the precise location of their boundary lines. In these situations, neighbors may informally treat a particular monument—such as a fence, a line of trees, a power line, or the like—as the boundary line. Some courts have used the doctrine of "mutual recognition and acquiescence" to conclude that the neighbors' long-standing informal recognition of such a boundary results in the relocation of that boundary. To relocate a boundary by mutual recognition and acquiescence, a neighboring landowner must demonstrate:

(1) The line must be certain, well defined, and in some fashion physically designated upon the ground, *e.g.*, by monuments, roadways, fence lines, etc.; (2) In the absence of an express agreement establishing the designated line as the boundary line, the adjoining landowners, or their predecessors in interest, must have in good faith manifested, by their acts, occupancy, and improvements with respect to their respective properties, a mutual recognition and acceptance of the designated line as the true boundary line; and (3) the requisite mutual recognition and acquiescence in the line must have continued for that period of time required to secure property by adverse possession. [*Lamm v. McTighe*, 72 Wash.2d 587, 593, 434 P.2d 565, 569 (1967).]

Courts often refer to mutual recognition and acquiescence as an "alternative" theory to adverse possession. In what sense is this an alternative theory? What purpose(s), if any, does it serve? Can you think of an example in which a possessor would prevail under the theory of mutual recognition and acquiescence but would *lose* under standard adverse possession doctrine? What is the difference (if any) between mutual recognition and acquiescence and the doctrine of agreed boundaries (note 4, page 183)?

b. *Estoppel.* Courts may also use the principle of equitable estoppel to resolve boundary disputes or adjust boundary lines. For example, suppose that Robertson and Whitfield are neighbors who are unsure of the precise location of the boundary line between their respective parcels. Whitfield wants to build extensive landscaping gardens on her parcel, but is concerned that the construction plans (if followed) may result in an encroachment onto Robertson's land. Whitfield shows Robertson where she is planning to build the gardens, and he says "That's your land. I think the boundary is over here (pointing elsewhere)." Whitfield then spends $8,000 installing her gardens. Six months later, Robertson obtains a survey in anticipation of expanding his home, and discovers that Whitfield's gardens encroach on his land by six feet. Robertson immediately files an ejectment action against Whitfield. Whitfield argues that Robertson should be estopped from recovering possession of the disputed land. How should this situation be resolved? Is it appropriate for the court to use estoppel to relocate the boundary line where Whitfield has only been in possession of the land for six months? If not, what relief (if any) should Whitfield obtain?

Would your analysis change if 12 years had passed before Robertson's survey revealed the encroachment? If the statutory period for adverse possession was 10 years, would Whitfield even need to make an estoppel argument, or could she establish title by adverse possession? Can you think of an example in which a possessor would prevail under the theory of estoppel but would *lose* under standard adverse possession doctrine?

c.   The "Good Faith Improver." Suppose that Pushaw builds a home on what he believes to be his lot. Unfortunately, because Pushaw had misread the survey of the land, he actually built the home on a lot owned by Chambers. One year later—long before the 10–year statutory period for adverse possession has run—Chambers sues to eject Pushaw. Chambers still has title to the land; but who owns the home, Pushaw or Chambers? In a similar case, the Supreme Court of New York, Appellate Division, stated:

> The common law doctrine of accession provides that the owner of property is entitled "to all that is added or united to it, either naturally or artificially." That doctrine has been followed in New York, but has been relaxed in limited circumstances: namely, if the mistaken improvement was made in good faith under a claim of title and there is either some misconduct on the part of the owner or a failure to act after the owner knows that the improvement was being made. [*DeAngelo v. Brazauskas*, 210 A.D.2d 989, 620 N.Y.S.2d 692, 692–93 (1994).]

Does this rule make sense? If so, why? To prevail, what sort of evidentiary showing must Pushaw make? If the court found "misconduct" on the part of Chambers and that Pushaw acted in "good faith," what relief should Pushaw obtain? *See* Kelvin H. Dickinson, *Mistaken Improvers of Real Estate*, 64 N.C.L. Rev. 37 (1985).

Many states have enacted statutes (often called "betterments" or "good faith improvement" statutes) to address this problem. Consider the following statute:

> Final judgment shall not be rendered, in any action to recover the possession of land, against any defendant who has, in good faith, believing his title to the land in question absolute, made improvements on the land before the commencement of the action, or whose grantors or ancestors have made the improvements, until the court has ascertained the present value of the improvements and the amount reasonably due the plaintiff from the defendant for the use and occupation of the land. If the value of the improvements exceeds the amount due for use and occupation, execution shall not be issued

until the plaintiff has paid the balance to the defendant or into court for his benefit. If the plaintiff elects to have the title confirmed in the defendant and, upon rendition of the verdict, files notice of the election with the clerk of the court, the court shall ascertain what sum ought in equity to be paid to the plaintiff by the defendant or other parties in interest and, on payment of it, may confirm the title to the land in the parties paying it. [Conn. Gen. Stat. Ann. § 47–30.]

Under this statute, what options would Chambers have in the above hypothetical? What happens if Chambers lacks the money necessary to pay Pushaw for the value of the house? Do you see a problem with this statute?

LAWYERING EXERCISE
(Client Interviewing)

BACKGROUND: As we have noted, most adverse possession cases involve boundary disputes between neighbors. Like the disputes in *Norman* and *Stump*, these disputes usually begin quite innocuously—a fence built in the wrong place, a misread survey, a boundary stake inadvertently moved, or an inadvertent misrepresentation by a previous owner of the property as to the location of the boundary line. Are these disputes better suited for alternative forms of dispute resolution such as negotiation? If so, why, and what consequences does this have for the attorney counseling a client regarding such a boundary dispute? *See* Richard C. Reuben, *The Lawyer Turns Peacemaker*, A.B.A. J., Aug. 1996, at 55.

For an attorney to function effectively as a counselor, the attorney must develop and maintain the ability to interview clients well enough to gather a sufficient understanding of the relevant facts underlying a dispute. This is an acquired skill, but one that you should begin to acquire during law school. Consider the following thoughts about the process of client interviewing:

Your goal during the problem identification stage of the initial interview is to obtain the client's perception of the problem without imposing your own structure on the client. To achieve this goal, begin with an open-ended question or statement that calls for a narrative response from the client....

Once you gain an understanding of the problem as the client sees it and the solution the client wants, you are ready to move to the heart of the interview: the overview.... By overview, we mean you should carefully scrutinize the whole of the client's problem during this stage....

The client's problem identification creates an initial agenda for the overview. Crammed into most clients' ... "short story" answers are many of the key topics you will want to pursue during the primary information-producing portion of the interview. You must first identify the primary topics contained in the client's answer and place them in an order likely to maximize efficient and complete communication of legally relevant information.

[T]opic identification involves determining which events mentioned by the client are significant to solving the client's problem.... Usually the most efficient sequence for the topics is chronological. Such an order facilitates lawyer understanding and aids the client memory. Sometimes, however, the client may signal that a particular topic is so important to his or her perception that it deserves to be taken out of order....

When deciding on the sequence of topics to be pursued, you should avoid starting the inquiry too far into the client's chronology of events. A common interviewing error is zeroing in on some "crucial" sequence of events and, therefore, overlooking less critical but still valuable information....

The primary means of obtaining information during the overview phase of the interview is the posing of a series of questions to the client. Questions, however, can be of various types, each type having different goals. Your inquiries can be broad or narrow, leading or nonleading. In this stage of the interview, you should prefer broad questions to narrow ones, nonleading questions to leading ones. Since your goal ... is to obtain information from the client's perspective, complete with the client's priorities and mental associations, you should avoid tainting the product with narrow, leading questions. Thus you will normally use a funnel technique for the formation of questions. Having selected a topic for inquiry, start at the wide end of the funnel with the broadest question about the issue. As the client responds, move down the funnel toward the narrow end by gradually closing the questions to focus on the specifics of the problem.... [Robert M. Bastress & Joseph D. Harbaugh, Interviewing, Counseling and Negotiating, 93, 97, 99, 101 (1990).]

SITUATION: You are approached by Donna, a local resident who purchased a parcel of four acres of land just outside of the town of Gloryland. Donna had purchased the land from Fred, who had previously inherited it from his mother. After purchasing the land, Donna constructed a home on the land and has lived there ever since. Some time ago, Donna built a play area at the rear of her property for the benefit of her children. Just recently, her neighbor James told her that a new survey had revealed that the play area was on James' land, and that Donna's children did not have permission to play on his land. When Donna's children continued to use the play area, James built a six–foot high fence that prevented Donna's children from reaching the play area. Donna wants to know whether James has the legal right to maintain this fence and prevent her from relocating the play area.

TASK: Conduct an initial client interview of Donna. What questions will you ask Donna to acquire the facts needed to explain to Donna what options (legal or otherwise) she may have?

Chapter 4

TRANSFERRING PROPERTY BY GIFT

Although transferability is not a necessary characteristic of property (as we saw in Chapter 1), an owner can transfer most items of property either by sale or by gift. We reserve more detailed treatment of the transfer of land by sale until Chapter 9, but we take up the transfer of property by gift in this chapter for two reasons. First, the concept of "possession" (explored throughout Chapters 1–3) plays a significant role in the law governing transfers by gift. Thus, the law of gifts provides a logical context for further study of the scope and significance of "possession" in resolving property disputes. Second, the law regarding gifts of land provides a gentle introduction to the means of conveying property (such as deeds, wills, and trusts) and the interpretation of instruments of conveyance. This background should help prepare you for the more difficult material on estates and future interests in land in Chapter 5.

A. INTER VIVOS GIFTS AND THEIR REQUIREMENTS

The most common type of gift (e.g., the typical Christmas, Hanukkah, birthday, or wedding gift) is an *inter vivos* gift—literally, a gift "between the living." For such a gift to be legally effective to transfer ownership, there are three requirements: (1) the donor must have *donative intent* (i.e., the intent to make an immediately effective gift); (2) the donor must *deliver* the object of the gift, and (3) the donee must *accept* the object of the gift.

Most gifts occur in personal and family relationships, and most take place without dispute. In some cases, however, a dispute arises regarding whether a donor made a valid gift. Often, these disputes arise after the donor's death, and they typically involve questions regarding whether the donor made an effective delivery of the object of the gift during the donor's life. Why does the law require delivery of the object of the gift? What purposes does the delivery requirement serve? What actions are (or should be) necessary to constitute an effective delivery?

199

IN RE ESTATE OF EVANS

Supreme Court of Pennsylvania.
467 Pa. 336, 356 A.2d 778 (1976).

NIX, JUSTICE. Appellant, Vivian Kellow, objected to the inventory, proposed schedule of distribution and final accounting of the executor of the estate of Arthur Evans. After appellant finished the presentation of her case, the lower court granted appellees' motion to dismiss appellant's objections. . . . The thrust of her appeal to this Court is that certain contents of a safe deposit box were the subject of an inter vivos gift to her from Arthur Evans, the deceased, and, consequently, should not have been included in his estate.

Appellant, the niece of Arthur Evans' deceased wife, began working for the Evans family when she was 16. For several years she took care of Mrs. Evans who for some years prior to death was an invalid. Appellant cooked meals for the Evanses, cleaned their house, did their laundry and generally cared for Mrs. Evans. She received adequate compensation for performing these needed services. When Mrs. Evans died, appellant continued to cook at least one hot meal a day for Mr. Evans, do his laundry and make sure his house was tidy. After appellant was married, she continued to perform these same services and visited Mr. Evans once a day. In May of 1971, following one of his four hospitalizations, the deceased moved into appellant's home.

Although at times Mr. Evans was confined to his bed because of water in his legs, he frequently took walks, had visits with his lawyers and made trips to his bank. On October 22, 1971, appellant's husband drove Mr. Evans and a friend of his, Mr. Turley, to town so that Mr. Evans might go to the bank. Turley testified that Mr. Evans spent about one hour going through the contents of his safe deposit box. Before leaving the bank, the deceased obtained both keys to the box.

Various witnesses presented by appellant testified to seeing the keys to the safe deposit box beneath appellant's mattress and to statements by Mr. Evans to the effect that the contents of the safe deposit box had been given to appellant. Mr. Evans entered the hospital for the last time on November 5, 1971. During this last hospital stay, Reverend Cunnings visited with him and was told that Mr. Evans was giving the Reverend's church $10,000.00 and that he had given the rest of his possessions and the keys to his safe deposit box to appellant. Mr. Evans expired on November 23, 1971.

Appellant relinquished the keys to the safe deposit box to a bank officer, but not without protesting that the contents of the box were hers. The box revealed a holographic will of Mr. Evans dated September 16, 1965, and approximately $800,000.00 in bonds, preferred and common stock and several miscellaneous items.[1]

---

1. The will was uncontested and under its terms provided for a $1,000.00 bequest to appellant.

The lower court correctly noted that the requirements for a valid inter vivos gift were donative intent and delivery, actual or constructive. With respect to donative intent, the court found: "Turning to the facts of this case, certainly no one can reasonably argue that Arthur Evans lacked sufficient motive to make a gift to Vivian. The record clearly manifests, both by his conduct and his statements, donative intent, the first prerequisite."

Nevertheless, the court ruled that no delivery had been made. This result was predicated upon a finding that the deceased had not divested himself of complete dominion and control over the safe deposit box. After properly noting that constructive delivery is sufficient when manual delivery is impractical or inconvenient, the court reasoned:

> The record contains no evidence of circumstances which were such that it was impractical or inconvenient to deliver the contents of this box into the actual possession or control of Vivian. Arthur Evans, although suffering physical infirmities and apprehensive of death, was nonetheless ambulatory. On October 22, 1971, he appeared at the Nanticoke National Bank in the company of Harold Turley and Leroy Kellow and spent approximately one hour going over the contents of his safe deposit box in a cubicle provided in the bank for that purpose. He left the bank after redepositing the contents and took with him only the keys which independent testimony indicates he delivered to Vivian the next day. There was no manual delivery of the contents. The contents of the box remained undisturbed. The box, and its contents, were registered in the name of the decedent at the date of his death. The objects of the gift were not placed in the hands of Vivian, nor was there placed within her power the means of obtaining the contents.

Appellant now asserts ... that the lower court erred in ruling there was insufficient delivery to sustain the inter vivos gift .... We find these arguments unpersuasive and, therefore, affirm the decision of the lower court. ...

The law in this Commonwealth is well settled concerning the requirements of an inter vivos gift. In *Tomayko v. Carson,* 368 Pa. 379, 385, 83 A.2d 907, 908 (1951) we stated:

> A claim of a gift *inter vivos* against the estate of the dead must be supported by clear and convincing evidence. In order to effectuate an *inter vivos* gift there must be evidence of an intention to make a gift and a *delivery*, actual or constructive, of a nature sufficient not only to *divest* the donor of all dominion over the property but also *invest* the donee with complete control over the subject-matter of the gift. It is claimant's burden to prove by *clear and satisfactory evidence* that a gift in fact was made. [citations omitted]

In the instant case, the controversy focuses on whether there was an adequate delivery. In *Allshouse's Estate*, 304 Pa. 481, 487–488, 156 A. 69, 72 (1931), we elaborated on the requirement of delivery:

> ... In *In re Campbell's Est.*, 7 Pa. 100, 47 Am.Dec. 503, Chief Justice Gibson stated: "A gift is a contract executed; and, as the act of execution is delivery of possession, it is of the essence of the title. It is the consummation of the contract which, without it, would be no more than a contract to give, and without efficacy for the want of consideration." Again, as we stated in *Clapper v. Frederick*, 199 Pa. 609, 613, 49 A. 218, 219: "Without a complete delivery during the lifetime of the donor there can be no valid gift inter vivos. 'Though every other step be taken that is essential to the validity of the gift, if there is no delivery, the gift must fail. Intention cannot supply it; words cannot supply it; actions cannot supply it. It is an indispensable requisite, without which the gift fails, regardless of consequence': Thornt. Gifts, p. 105." The consequence is that no matter how often or how emphatically the desire or intention of the donor to make the gift has been expressed, upon his death before delivery has been completed, the promise or purpose to give is revoked. *Scott v. Lauman*, 104 Pa. 593; 28 Corpus Juris, page 651.

We have recognized that in some cases due to the form of the subject matter of the gift or due to the immobility of the donor actual, manual delivery may be dispensed with and constructive or symbolic delivery will suffice. In *Ream Estate*, 413 Pa. 489, 198 A.2d 556 (1964), for example, the Court found there had been a valid constructive delivery of an automobile where the donor gave the keys to the alleged donee and also gave him the title to the car after executing an assignment of it leaving the designation of the assignee blank. The assignment was executed in the presence of a justice of the peace and the evidence was overwhelming that the name of the donee was to be inserted upon the death of the decedent.[2]

In *Elliott's Estate* 312 Pa. 493, 167 A. 289 (1933), we held there was a valid constructive delivery of the contents of a safe deposit box where the donor turned over to the alleged donee the keys. There, however, just prior to the delivery of the keys a doctor had informed the non-ambulatory donor that death was imminent. Under those circumstances manual delivery was impossible.

Appellant relies heavily on *Leadenham's Estate*, 289 Pa. 216, 137 A. 247 (1927), and *Leitch v. Diamond National Bank*, 234 Pa. 557, 83 A. 416 (1912). These decisions, however, support the Court's finding that there was no delivery in the instant case. In *Leadenham's Estate, supra*, the donor had rented a separate safe deposit box in the name of the intended donee, put the contents of his box into the newly rented one and delivered the keys to it to the donee. On those facts we held that the

---

2. *Ream Estate*, 413 Pa. 489, 198 A.2d 556 (1964), involved an alleged gift causa mortis, however, the requirements for deliv- ery are the same as for a gift inter vivos. *Ream Estate, supra*; *Elliott's Estate*, 312 Pa. 493, 167 A. 289 (1933).

constructive delivery of the keys was sufficient to sustain the inter vivos gift because the donor had divested himself of dominion and control and invested the donee with complete dominion and control.

In *Leitch v. Diamond National Bank*, *supra*, the donor and donee were husband and wife and had lived together harmoniously for many years. The husband had three safe deposit boxes registered in his name and the name of his wife and he designated one of them as his wife's. He gave her the keys to that box. The Court found that she had complete control over that box and that he only entered it with her permission. Since she had complete control over the access to the box the Court found there was a valid delivery of the contents of the box to her.

In both of these cases, the determinative factor was that the donee had complete dominion and control over the box and its contents. In that posture we ruled that giving the keys to the box to the donee was a valid constructive delivery. In the instant case, appellant did not have dominion and control over the box even though she was given the keys to it. The box remained registered in Mr. Evans' name and she could not have gained access to it even with the keys. Mr. Evans never terminated his control over the box, consequently he never made a delivery, constructive or otherwise.

Although appellant suggests that it was impractical and inconvenient for Mr. Evans to manually deliver the contents of his box to her because of his physical condition and the hazards of taking such a large sum of money out of the bank to her home, we need only note that the deceased was obviously a shrewd investor, familiar with banking practices, and could have made delivery in a number of simple, convenient ways. First, he was not on his deathbed. He was ambulatory and not only went to the bank on October 22, 1971, but took walks thereafter and did not enter the hospital until November 5, 1971. On the day he went to the bank he could have rented a second safe deposit box in appellant's name, delivered the contents of his box to it and then given the keys to appellant. He could have assigned the contents of his box to appellant. For that matter, he could have written a codicil to his will.

The lower court noted that the deceased was an enigmatic figure. It is not for us to guess why people perform as they do. On the record before us it is clear that regardless of Mr. Evans' intention to make a gift to appellant, he never executed that intention and we will not do it for him. On these facts, we are constrained to hold that there was not an inter vivos gift to appellant and that the contents of the safe deposit box were properly included in the inventory of Mr. Evans' estate....

ROBERTS, JUSTICE (dissenting). I dissent. The central issue in this case is whether donor made an adequate delivery of the gift to donee. The majority finds that adequate delivery was not made because the safe deposit box was leased solely in donor's name and supports this conclusion by pointing out that there were several alternative means of delivering the gift which would have been adequate. I believe that the inquiry should not be what form of delivery would have been clearly sufficient, but rather whether the delivery made by donor was adequate. I believe that it was.

In *Rynier Estate*, 349 Pa. 471, 32 A.2d 736 (1943), we said that delivery is determined on the facts of each case, with reference to the donor's intent. "As the chief factor in the determination of the question whether a legal delivery has been effected is the intention of the donor to transfer title to the donee, as manifested by his words and actions and by the circumstances surrounding the transaction, it is evident that each case must depend largely upon its own facts." *Id.* at 475, 32 A.2d at 738. . . .

The majority suggests that donor was "obviously a shrewd investor, familiar with banking practices. . . ." From this "familiar[ity] with banking practices," which is nowhere shown on the record, and the absence of a joint lease for the box, it apparently concludes that donor did not intend a gift. There are two reasons why this result is not correct.

First, there is no doubt in this case that donor intended a gift. He told many people that he had given the contents of the box to appellant. In fact, there is competent testimony that donor directed donee to display the keys, hidden under her mattress, to several witnesses.

Second, it is apparent from the record that donor believed undisputed and unconditional delivery of the keys to be sufficient to complete the gift. Most of this Court's cases dealing with inter vivos gifts of the contents of safe deposit boxes turn on the delivery or nondelivery of the keys to the box to the donee. If the key was delivered, the gift was normally upheld; if the key was not delivered, the gift was set aside, whether or not the box was jointly leased. I have found no case which turned on the presence or absence of a joint lease. Given this line of authority, and accepting the majority's conclusion that donor was sophisticated in these matters, it must be concluded that donor believed delivery of the keys to the box completed the gift. If this were not so, why would donor cause donee to take several witnesses into her bedroom to show them that she had the keys and why would he speak in terms that indicated a completed gift—"I *gave* to Vivian . . . the keys and the contents *are* hers." Because it is donor's intention to transfer title which is crucial to a valid delivery, and because this donor intended to transfer title, I dissent from the majority's conclusion.

This record firmly establishes appellant has shown a prima facie gift. I would, therefore, vacate the decree and remand to give the estate an opportunity to present its evidence.

Notes

1. *The Delivery Requirement and the Significance of "Dominion and Control."* The majority opinion in *Evans* concluded that Mr. Evans did not deliver the contents of the box because he neither placed them beyond his "dominion and control" nor invested Ms. Kellow with "dominion and control" over them. This conclusion is typical of many common law decisions

holding that a donor must deliver physical possession of an object to the donee in order to make an effective gift of the object. Simply saying "I want you to have the contents of my safe deposit box" is not enough. Why not? What purpose(s) does it serve for the law to require the donor to make a manual delivery of the object of the gift? *See* Philip Mechem, *The Requirement of Delivery in Gifts of Chattels and of Choses in Action Evidenced by Commercial Instruments*, 21 Ill. L. Rev. 341, 348–49 (1926); W. Lewis Roberts, *The Necessity of Delivery in Making Gifts*, 32 W. Va. L.Q. 313 (1926).

2. *"Constructive" Delivery.* In some cases, actual physical delivery (*i.e.*, handing over) of the object of the gift is impossible. For example, few donors could pick up and hand over a car, a safe, or a heavy article of furniture. Under these circumstances, the common law relaxed the manual delivery requirement and recognized acts sufficient to constitute a "constructive" delivery. For example, suppose that Sara hands her son the keys to her car and says, "I want you to have this car as a gift from me." Although Sara cannot physically hand the car to her son, she can physically hand him the keys, thereby giving him the means to exercise dominion and control over the car in the future. The act of delivering the keys may constitute a sufficient "constructive" delivery of the car to validate Sara's gift.[3]

Mr. Evans gave Vivian the keys to his safe deposit box; why was that not a sufficient constructive delivery of its contents? Why does the majority in *Evans* place such a limit upon the circumstances in which constructive delivery is possible?

3. *"Symbolic" Delivery.* Suppose that Leopold Cohn gives his wife the following note: "I give this day to my wife, Sara K. Cohn, as a present for her (46th) forty-sixth birthday (500) five hundred shares of American Sumatra Tobacco Company common stock. [Signed, Leopold Cohn]." Despite giving his wife the note, Leopold keeps the stock certificates in a safe at his office. Six days later, without ever delivering the actual stock certificates to his wife, Leopold dies. Did Leopold make an effective gift of the shares?

In this situation, Cohn's widow would argue that the note effected a "symbolic" delivery of the shares—*i.e.*, that the law should treat the actual delivery of the note as a symbol of (and a surrogate for) the actual delivery of the stock. Should "symbolic" delivery ever be sufficient to transfer ownership of an object without physical delivery of the object? If so, under what circumstances? *Compare In re Cohn*, 187 A.D. 392, 176 N.Y.S. 225 (1919) (written letter sufficient to transfer ownership of shares of stock) *with Newman v. Bost*, 122 N.C. 524, 29 S.E. 848 (1898) (symbolic delivery ineffective where object is capable of manual delivery). Would it matter if Leopold Cohn had kept possession of the certificates in order to enable him to vote those shares at the annual shareholders' meeting the week following his wife's birthday? Would it matter if the shares were uncertificated (*i.e.*, if the company had not issued certificates evidencing the shares)?

3. A caveat is in order here with respect to cars. In all states today, cars are covered by certificate of title statutes. As a result, in some states, the law may require delivery of the title certificate in order to transfer title to a car. *Compare Johnson v. Daughtridge*, 1979 WL 794 (Ark. 1979) (no gift when alleged donor retained title certificate) *with Smith v. Smith*, 650 S.W.2d 54 (Tenn. App. 1983) (intention of parties, not certificate of title, determines effectiveness of gift of car).

LAWYERING EXERCISE
(Problem Solving: Generating Alternative Strategies)

BACKGROUND: As discussed in the Student Preface to this book, "problem solving" is one of the fundamental lawyering skills identified by the American Bar Association's MacCrate Report:

> In order to effectively develop and evaluate strategies for solving a problem or accomplishing an objective presented by a client ..., a lawyer should be familiar with the skills and concepts involved in problem solving: identifying and diagnosing a problem, *generating alternative solutions and strategies*, developing a plan of action, implementing the plan, and keeping the planning process open to new information and ideas .... [MacCrate Report at 141–42 (emphasis added).]

Effective problem solving often requires the lawyer to discern, develop, and present multiple alternatives, and this requires creative thinking by the lawyer:

> Whether the task at hand is the generation of possible solutions and strategies for solving a client's problem, the formulation of legal or factual theories, or the conceptualization of the subject of a negotiation, competent lawyering requires a person with a creative mind—a person who is willing to look at situations, ideas, and issues in an openminded way; to explore novel and imaginative approaches; and to look for potentially useful connections and associations between apparently unrelated principles, facts, negotiating points, or other factors. [*Id.* at 150.]

SITUATION: Reconsider the hypothetical in note 3 above, and assume that Leopold Cohn had sought your guidance regarding his desire to make a gift of the shares to his wife. Mr. Cohn tells you that he wants to make an effective gift of the shares (and he wants it to be a surprise, of course), but also tells you "I want to be able to vote the shares at the annual shareholders' meeting in two weeks."

TASK: Assuming that your jurisdiction takes a fairly strict view of the delivery requirement, how many possible alternatives can you think of that might enable Mr. Cohn to accomplish his objectives?

B. CAUSA MORTIS AND TESTAMENTARY GIFTS

An *inter vivos* gift takes effect immediately upon the delivery of the object of the gift and acceptance by the donee, and it is generally treated as irrevocable by the donor. [In other words, once the donor has made an effective gift, the donor cannot change his or her mind and "unmake" the gift.] In contrast, a *testamentary gift* is one that the donor intends to take effect only at the time of the donor's death. Traditionally, one had to make a testamentary gift by a *will*—a written instrument that complies with the state's statute governing testamentary gifts. Parliament enacted the original Statute of Wills back in 1536; each American state has its own statute that establishes the requirements for an instrument to constitute a valid will. For example, these statutes generally require that the testator (the maker of the will)[4] must execute the will in the presence of a certain number of disinterested witnesses (*i.e.*, persons to whom the will would not transfer any property interests) and in the presence of a notary public that acknowledges the will.[5] Given the context in which a person executes a will (*i.e.*, in anticipation that it will take effect at a later date, upon the person's death), what purposes do you think that these requirements might serve?

Even if a will is properly executed, witnessed, and acknowledged, that will has no legal effect as long as the testator remains alive. ***A will takes effect (and thus can effect a transfer of property rights) only at the death of the testator.*** While the testator remains alive, she can destroy or revoke the will, or replace it with an entirely new will disposing of her property in a different fashion. Alternatively, the testator may later choose to give away all of her assets by making valid inter vivos gifts. If this occurred, then at the death of the testator, there would be no assets to pass into her "estate" and thus the will (even though technically valid) would not actually effect any transfer of property.

There is a third "intermediate" type of gift called the gift *causa mortis* (literally, a gift in case of death). A gift causa mortis must be made in the context of the donor's expected imminent death (for this reason, these gifts are sometimes called "deathbed gifts"). If a donor makes an effective gift causa mortis, ownership passes to the donee immediately upon delivery and acceptance, even while the donor remains alive. [In this regard, the gift causa mortis is really a special form of inter vivos gift.] The donee's ownership, however, is subject to a *condition subsequent*—*i.e.*, it is subject to the risk of being terminated if one of two conditions later occurs. The first condition is that the donor might change her mind and revoke the gift. The second condition is that the donor might not actually die as a result of the particular peril that placed the donor in contemplation of imminent death. If either condition occurs—if the donor changes her mind or recovers from the brink of

---

4. Traditionally, the law used the term "testator" for a male decedent leaving a valid will and the term "testatrix" for a female decedent leaving a valid will. In the spirit of promoting gender neutrality, the text simply uses the term "testator" as applicable to either gender.

5. A typical acknowledgment for a will might read as follows:

I, the undersigned, an officer authorized to administer oaths, certify that [name of the testator] and [name of the witnesses], whose names are signed to the attached instrument, having appeared together before me and having been first duly sworn, each then declared to me that the testa-

tor signed and executed the instrument as his last will, and that he had willingly signed, and that he executed it as his free and voluntary act for the purposes expressed therein; and that each of the witnesses, in the presence and hearing of the testator, signed the will as witness and that to the best of their knowledge the testator was at that time eighteen (18) or more years of age, of sound mind, and under no constraint or undue influence. In witness of the foregoing, I have hereunto subscribed my name and affixed my official seal this __ day of [month], [year]. [Notary Public's signature] [Notary Public's seal]

imminent death—the gift is revoked.[6] By contrast, if the donor does in fact die as expected and has not expressed any intention to revoke the gift, the gift becomes absolute.

You should be able to see the primary function of the gift causa mortis—it allows a dying person who did not adequately plan for death (*i.e.*, who does not have a valid will) to dispose of her property as she wishes in anticipation of her death.[7] In this regard, the gift causa mortis may seem quasi-testamentary (in the sense that it is motivated by the donor's expected imminent death, and functions as a type of "will substitute"). Yet because the gift causa mortis results in a present transfer of property rights to the donee while the donor remains alive— even if those rights are subject to the two conditions subsequent described above—the gift causa mortis is also a form of inter vivos gift. For that reason, the requirements for a valid gift causa mortis are the same—donative intent (*i.e.*, the intent to make a presently effective causa mortis gift), delivery, and acceptance. Given the context in which disputes over these gifts are likely to occur—*i.e.*, usually, after the donor has died—how stringently should a court interpret the delivery requirement?

SCHERER v. HYLAND

Supreme Court of New Jersey.
75 N.J. 127, 380 A.2d 698 (1977).

PER CURIAM. Defendant, the Administrator ad litem of the Estate of Catherine Wagner, appeals from an Appellate Division decision, one judge dissenting, affirming a summary judgment by the trial court holding that Ms. Wagner had made a valid gift *causa mortis* of a check to plaintiff. We affirm.

6. A donor who recovered could subsequently make the gift over again if she so wished, but would have to comply with the elements for making a new inter vivos gift.

7. As you will see in Chapter 5, if a person dies without having made a valid will, ownership of his/her property passes to the persons identified in the state's *inheritance* or *descent and distribution* statute. Thus, suppose Smith is dying and the statute says that Smith's son would take Smith's assets if Smith died without a will. If Smith wants her son to take her assets, then Smith need not make a valid will or a causa mortis gift—when she dies, her son will become owner of her assets by virtue of the statute. But suppose Smith wants her piano to go to her friend Jones (even though she wants her son to take the rest of her assets). Even if it is too late for a dying Smith to make a valid will, she can make a causa mortis gift of the piano to Jones—and if that gift is effective, the pi-

ano would not become part of Smith's estate at her death (and thus ownership of the piano would not pass to her son under the state's inheritance statute).

There is one other context in which a donor may make a gift causa mortis. Suppose that Smith does have a valid will that disposes of her assets, and that she is comfortable with its terms generally (such that she does not want to revoke it). But suppose that she still wants Jones to have her piano—and, unfortunately, the terms of the will (executed several years earlier) do not provide for Jones to get the piano. On her deathbed, Smith may not have time to have her will modified to reflect her present intent. However, she can make a gift causa mortis of the piano to Jones—taking the piano out of the estate at her death—without affecting the validity of her will (which would remain effective to transfer ownership of all of Smith's other property upon her death).

The facts are not in dispute. Catherine Wagner and the plaintiff, Robert Scherer, lived together for approximately fifteen years prior to Ms. Wagner's death in January 1974. In 1970, the decedent and plaintiff were involved in an automobile accident in which decedent suffered facial wounds and a broken hip. Because of the hip injury, decedent's physical mobility was substantially impaired. She was forced to give up her job and to restrict her activities. After the accident, plaintiff cared for her and assumed the sole financial responsibility for maintaining their household. During the weeks preceding her death, Ms. Wagner was acutely depressed. On one occasion, she attempted suicide by slashing her wrists. On January 23, 1974, she committed suicide by jumping from the roof of the apartment building in which they lived.

On the morning of the day of her death, Ms. Wagner received a check for $17,400 drawn by a Pennsylvania attorney who had represented her in a claim arising out of the automobile accident. The check represented settlement of the claim. Plaintiff telephoned Ms. Wagner at around 11:30 a.m. that day and was told that the check had arrived. Plaintiff noticed nothing unusual in Ms. Wagner's voice. At about 3:20 p.m., decedent left the apartment building and jumped to her death. The police, as part of their investigation of the suicide, asked the building superintendent to admit them to the apartment. On the kitchen table they found the check, endorsed in blank, and two notes handwritten by the decedent. In one, she described her depression over her physical condition, expressed her love for Scherer, and asked him to forgive her "for taking the easy way out." In the other, she indicated that she "bequeathed" to plaintiff all of her possessions, including "the check for $17,400.00 . . . ." The police took possession of the check, which was eventually placed in an interest-bearing account pending disposition of this action.

Under our wills statute it is clear that Ms. Wagner's note bequeathing all her possessions to Mr. Scherer cannot take effect as a testamentary disposition. N.J.S.A. 3A:3–2. A *donatio causa mortis* has been traditionally defined as a gift of personal property made by a party in expectation of death, then imminent, subject to the condition that the donor die as anticipated. Establishment of the gift has uniformly called for proof of delivery.

The primary issue here is whether Ms. Wagner's acts of endorsing the settlement check, placing it on the kitchen table in the apartment she shared with Scherer, next to a writing clearly evidencing her intent to transfer the check to Scherer, and abandoning the apartment with a clear expectation of imminent death constituted delivery sufficient to sustain a gift *causa mortis* of the check. Defendant, relying on the principles established in *Foster v. Reiss*, 18 N.J. 41, 112 A.2d 553 (1955), argues that there was no delivery because the donor did not unequivocally relinquish control of the check before her death. Central to this argument is the contention that suicide, the perceived peril, was one which decedent herself created and one which was completely within her control. According to this contention, the donor at any time before she jumped from the apartment roof could have changed her mind, re-entered the apartment, and reclaimed the check. Defendant therefore reasons that decedent did not make an effective transfer of the check during her lifetime, as is required for a valid gift *causa mortis*. . . .

There is general agreement that the major purpose of the delivery requirement is evidentiary. Proof of delivery reduces the possibility that the evidence of intent has been fabricated or that a mere donative impulse, not consummated by action, has been mistaken for a completed gift. Since "these gifts come into question only after death has closed the lips of the donor," the delivery requirement provides a substantial safeguard against fraud and perjury. *See Keepers v. Fidelity Title and Deposit Co.*, 56 N.J.L. 302, 308, 28 A. 585 (E. & A. 1893). In *Foster*, the majority concluded that these policies could best be fulfilled by a strict rule requiring actual manual tradition of the subject-matter of the gift except in a very narrow class of cases where "there can be no actual delivery" or where "the situation is incompatible with the performance of such ceremony." 18 N.J. at 50, 112 A.2d at 559. Justice Jacobs, in his dissenting opinion (joined by Justices Brennan and Wachenfeld) questioned the reasonableness of requiring direct physical delivery in cases where donative intent is "freely and clearly expressed in a written instrument." *Id.* at 56, 112 A.2d at 562. He observed that a more flexible approach to the delivery requirement had been taken by other jurisdictions and quoted approvingly from *Devol v. Dye*, 123 Ind. 321, 24 N.E. 246, 7 L.R.A. 439 (Sup.Ct.1890). That case stated:

> [G]ifts *causa mortis* . . . are not to be held contrary to public policy, nor do they rest under the disfavor of the law, when the facts are clearly and satisfactorily shown which make it appear that they were freely and intelligently made. *Ellis v. Secor*, 31 Mich. 185. While every case must be brought within the general rule upon the points essential to such a gift, yet, as the circumstances under which donations mortis causa are made must of necessity be infinite in variety, each case must be determined upon its own peculiar facts and circumstances. *Dickeschild v. Bank*, 28 W.Va. 341; *Kiff v. Weaver*, 94 N.C. 274. The rule requiring delivery, either actual or symbolical, must be maintained, but its application is to be militated and applied according to the relative importance of the subject of the gift and the condition of the donor. The intention of a donor in peril of death, when clearly ascertained and fairly consummated within the meaning of well-established rules, is not to be thwarted by a narrow and illiberal construction of what may have been intended for and deemed by him a sufficient delivery . . . .

The balancing approach suggested in *Devol v. Dye* has been articulated in the following manner:

> Where there has been unequivocal proof of a deliberate and well-considered donative intent on the part of the donor, many courts have been inclined to overlook the technical requirements and to hold that a "constructive" or "symbolic" delivery is sufficient to

vest title in the donee. However, where this is allowed the evidence must clearly show an intention to part presently with some substantial attribute of ownership. *Gordon v. Barr*, 13 Cal.2d 596, 601, 91 P.2d 101, 104 (Sup.Ct.Cal.1939).

In essence, this approach takes into account the purposes served by the requirement of delivery in determining whether that requirement has been met. It would find a constructive delivery adequate to support the gift when the evidence of donative intent is concrete and undisputed, when there is every indication that the donor intended to make a present transfer of the subject-matter of the gift, and when the steps taken by the donor to effect such a transfer must have been deemed by the donor as sufficient to pass the donor's interest to the donee. We are persuaded that this approach, which does not minimize the need for evidentiary safeguards to prevent frauds upon the estates of the deceased, reflects the realities which attend transfers of this kind.

In this case, the evidence of decedent's intent to transfer the check to Robert Scherer is concrete, unequivocal, and undisputed. The circumstances definitely rule out any possibility of fraud. The sole question, then, is whether the steps taken by the decedent, independent of her writing of the suicide notes, were sufficient to support a finding that she effected a lifetime transfer of the check to Scherer. We think that they were. First, the act of endorsing a check represents, in common experience and understanding, the only act needed (short of actual delivery) to render a check negotiable. The significance of such an act is universally understood. Accordingly, we have no trouble in viewing Ms. Wagner's endorsement of the settlement check as a substantial step taken by her for the purpose of effecting a transfer to Scherer of her right to the check proceeds. Second, we note that the only person other than the decedent who had routine access to the apartment was Robert Scherer. Indeed, the apartment was leased in his name. It is clear that Ms. Wagner before leaving the apartment placed the check in a place where Scherer could not fail to see it and fully expected that he would take actual possession of the check when he entered. And, although Ms. Wagner's subsequent suicide does not itself constitute a component of the delivery of this gift, it does provide persuasive evidence that when Ms. Wagner locked the door of the apartment she did so with no expectation of returning. When we consider her state of mind as it must have been upon leaving the apartment, her surrender of possession at that moment was complete. We find, therefore, that when she left the apartment she completed a constructive delivery of the check to Robert Scherer. In light of her resolve to take her own life and of her obvious desire not to be deterred from that purpose, Ms. Wagner's failure manually to transfer the check to Scherer is understandable. She clearly did all that she could do or thought necessary to do to surrender the check. Her donative intent has been conclusively demonstrated by independent evidence. The law should effectuate that intent rather than indulge in nice distinctions which would thwart her purpose. Upon these facts, we find that the constructive delivery she made was adequate to support a gift *causa mortis*.

Defendant's assertion that suicide is not the sort of peril that will sustain a gift *causa mortis* finds some support in precedents from other jurisdictions. *E.g., Ray v. Leader Federal Sav. & Loan Ass'n*, 40 Tenn. App. 625, 292 S.W.2d 458 (Ct.App.1953). *See generally* Annot., "Nature and validity of gift made in contemplation of suicide," 60 A.L.R.2d 575 (1958). We are, however, not bound by those authorities nor do we find them persuasive. While it is true that a gift *causa mortis* is made by the donor with a view to impending death, death is no less impending because of a resolve to commit suicide. Nor does that fixed purpose constitute any lesser or less imminent peril than does a ravaging disease. Indeed, given the despair sufficient to end it all, the peril attendant upon contemplated suicide may reasonably be viewed as even more imminent than that accompanying many illnesses which prove ultimately to be fatal. *Cf. Berl v. Rosenberg*, 169 Cal.App.2d 125, 336 P.2d 975, 978 (Dist.Ct.App.1959) (public policy against suicide does not invalidate otherwise valid gift *causa mortis*). And, the notion that one in a state of mental depression serious enough to lead to suicide is somehow "freer" to renounce the depression and thus the danger than one suffering from a physical illness, although it has a certain augustinian appeal, has long since been replaced by more enlightened views of human psychology. *In re Van Wormer's Estate*, 255 Mich. 399, 238 N.W. 210 (Sup.Ct.1931) (melancholia ending in suicide sufficient to sustain a gift *causa mortis*). We also observe that an argument that the donor of a *causa mortis* gift might have changed his or her mind loses much of its force when one recalls that a *causa mortis* gift, by definition, can be revoked at any time before the donor dies and is automatically revoked if the donor recovers.

Finally, defendant asserts that this gift must fail because there was no acceptance prior to the donor's death. Although the issue of acceptance is rarely litigated, the authority that does exist indicates that, given a valid delivery, acceptance will be implied if the gift is unconditional and beneficial to the donee. *See, e.g., Sparks v. Hurley*, 208 Pa. 166, 57 A. 364, 366 (Sup.Ct.1904); *Graham v. Johnston*, 243 Iowa 112, 49 N.W.2d 540, 543 (Sup.Ct.1951). The presumption of acceptance may apply even if the donee does not learn of the gift until after the donor's death. *Taylor v. Sanford*, 108 Tex. 340, 344, 193 S.W. 661, 662 (Sup.Ct. 1912) (assent to gift of deed mailed in contemplation of death but received after grantor's death should be presumed unless a dissent or disclaimer appears). A donee cannot be expected to accept or reject a gift until he learns of it and unless a gift is rejected when the donee is informed of it the presumption of acceptance is not defeated. See *id.* at 344, 193 S.W. at 662. Here the gift was clearly beneficial to Scherer, and he has always expressed his acceptance. . . .

Notes

1. *The Delivery Requirement Revisited.* If the *Scherer* court is correct that the primary function of the delivery requirement is to provide evidence of the donor's intent, then why are intent and delivery *separate* requirements? Does the court in *Scherer* actually treat intent and delivery as separate requirements?

2. *Testamentary Gifts and Causa Mortis Gifts Compared.* Wagner's suicide note did not meet the requirements of most will statutes (which generally require that wills be witnessed); thus, by itself, the note could not have operated to transfer her property to Scherer. Why do you think that will statutes generally refuse to enforce writings such as Wagner's suicide note?

Nevertheless, the court concludes that Wagner made a valid gift causa mortis of the settlement check. Do you think Wagner intended to make a gift causa mortis of the check, or a testamentary gift of the check? What facts would tend to demonstrate the nature of Wagner's intent, and why?

A final question: If the court is correct to award the check proceeds to Scherer, is there any reason not to award him the rest of Wagner's property as well? Could the court treat Wagner's conduct as a sufficient causa mortis gift of all of her assets? If so, what act or acts would constitute "delivery"? Can you explain why the court was unwilling to conclude that Wagner made an effective causa mortis gift of her other assets?

LAWYERING EXERCISE
(Research, Factual Analysis and Advocacy)

BACKGROUND: One of a lawyer's most valuable skills is the ability to organize and present facts in a cogent and persuasive manner. There are a variety of different models that a lawyer might use in organizing facts. One might organize facts by focusing on the legal rules that will be applied to those facts (which Professors Stefan Krieger and Richard Neumann call the "legal elements" model):

> The process of organizing facts in the context of legal rules has three stages. First, you identify the legal elements for a claim or defense. The elements identify the facts the plaintiff must prove to establish a prima facie case (or that the defendant must establish to support an affirmative defense or counterclaim)....
>
> After identifying the applicable elements, restate the elements as "factual propositions." In other words, express each element in the context of the facts of the case....
>
> Finally ... you need to marshal the facts discovered in support of each factual proposition to determine if a prima facie case can be established. [Stefan H. Krieger & Richard K. Neumann, Jr., Essential Lawyering Skills: Interviewing, Counseling, Negotiation, and Persuasive Fact Analysis 137–38 (2003).]

By contrast, one might organize the facts chronologically:

> By focusing on the chronological relationship of facts to each other,
> rather than on the connection of facts to general legal propositions,
> the chronological model provides benefits that are not furnished by
> the [legal elements model]. It locates a particular fact in the context
> of the surrounding circumstances. Moreover, a fact that may not
> appear important standing by itself may have much significance
> when viewed in a chronological sequence. [*Id.* at 145.]

Finally, one might adopt a "story" approach to organizing facts:

> Like the chronological model, the story model often organizes facts
> as a casual sequence of facts. It is not, however, synonymous with
> that model. . . . [N]arrative thinking—structuring the facts in the
> context of stories—strives to endow a sequence of events with
> meaning. It serves this function by highlighting certain facts while
> filtering out others, by focusing on particular details and images
> while downplaying others, by arranging facts and episodes in a
> particular order, or by presenting facts in the context of certain
> images and symbols. A story does more than set out a chronological
> series of events. It tries to make *sense* of those events. [*Id.* at 155.]

SITUATION: Two months ago, Sara Smith died in a local hospital
after a long battle with cancer. The day before her death, Sara made out
a check on her personal bank account (maintained at Bank of America),
payable to the order of her friend Anne Jones, who had cared for Sara
throughout her illness. In the presence of her doctor and two nurses,
Sara handed the check (made out for $60,000) to Anne saying, "I want
you to have this money. Thanks for everything." At that time, Sara's
account had more than $100,000 in it, and there were no outstanding
checks drawn on Sara's account that had not yet been presented for
payment. Further, Sara did not write any other checks during the period
in which she remained alive.

Because she was busy taking care of Sara and was in the process of
moving to a new apartment, Anne did not deposit the check in her own
bank account (maintained at CitiBank) until two days after Sara's death.
When CitiBank presented the check to Bank of America for payment,
Bank of America refused to honor the check because it had received
notification earlier in the day from Tom Davis (the administrator of
Sara's estate) instructing the bank not to honor any checks drawn on
Sara's account that had not been presented for payment prior to her
death. When Anne learned that Bank of America had not honored the
check, she filed suit against Davis as the administrator of Sara's estate,
arguing that Sara had made an effective gift of $60,000. Davis denied
that any effective gift had been made prior to Sara's death, and argued
that all of the money contained in Sara's account should pass to the
three family members named as devisees under the residuary clause in
Sara's will.

Both Tom Davis and Anne Jones have moved for summary judgment. There is no dispute over the above facts, and both parties agree
that Sara's will is valid in all respects. The judge has scheduled a hearing

on the motions and has asked the attorneys for each party to present their respective legal arguments as to whether Sara made a valid gift of the money.

TASK: Prepare a written statement of facts and a written argument in support of the motion of Davis or Jones (as assigned by your instructor). What model (or models) of fact organization should you use in carrying out this task? Would your answer be different if you were representing the other party? Why or why not?

C. GIFTS OF "FUTURE" INTERESTS

Suppose that the current will of Bill Gates provides a specific bequest of his palatial home (Windowsacre) to Freyermuth. This is great news, right? Not as great as it sounds. As discussed earlier, as long as Bill Gates is alive, Freyermuth has no property right whatsoever in Windowsacre. Bill Gates could revoke that will and replace it with one that leaves the land to someone else. Or Bill Gates can sell Windowsacre at some point during his life, so that the words of the will purporting to bequeath Windowsacre to Freyermuth become meaningless. As long as Bill Gates is alive, there is nothing that Freyermuth can do legally to control or limit what Bill Gates may do with his home.

As you will see in more detail in Chapter 5, however, property law does permit an owner of an object to separate ownership of that object temporally—*i.e.*, into present ownership (the present right to possession of the object) and future ownership (the right to possession of the object at a future date). If Bill Gates actually made an effective gift to Freyermuth of a future interest in his home, then Freyermuth would have a property right in the home—and, as discussed further in Chapter 5, this would give Freyermuth substantial "control" rights over the home, even though Bill Gates would still have the present right to possession of the home.

As you read the following two cases—one involving personal property and another involving land—consider how the concept of future interests might influence the way in which donors make gifts. Why should (or should not) Bill Gates grant a future interest in his home (or in some other asset)? And if Bill Gates wanted to grant a future interest in a particular asset, how should he manifest this intent?

GRUEN v. GRUEN

Court of Appeals of New York.
68 N.Y.2d 48, 505 N.Y.S.2d 849, 496 N.E.2d 869 (1986).

SIMONS, JUDGE. Plaintiff commenced this action seeking a declaration that he is the rightful owner of a painting which he alleges his father, now deceased, gave to him. He concedes that he has never had possession of the painting but asserts that his father made a valid gift of the title in 1963 reserving a life estate for himself. His father retained possession of the painting until he died in 1980. Defendant, plaintiff's stepmother, has the painting now and has refused plaintiff's requests that she turn it over to him. She contends that the purported gift was testamentary in nature and invalid insofar as the formalities of a will were not met or, alternatively, that a donor may not make a valid inter vivos gift of a chattel and retain a life estate with a complete right of possession. Following a seven-day nonjury trial, Special Term found that plaintiff had failed to establish any of the elements of an inter vivos gift and that in any event an attempt by a donor to retain a present possessory life estate in a chattel invalidated a purported gift of it. The Appellate Division held that a valid gift may be made reserving a life estate and, finding the elements of a gift established in this case, it reversed and remitted the matter for a determination of value. That determination has now been made and defendant appeals directly to this court, pursuant to CPLR 5601(d), from the subsequent final judgment entered in Supreme Court awarding plaintiff $2,500,000 in damages representing the value of the painting, plus interest. We now affirm.

The subject of the dispute is a work entitled "Schloss Kammer am Attersee II" painted by a noted Austrian modernist, Gustav Klimt. It was purchased by plaintiff's father, Victor Gruen, in 1959 for $8,000. On April 1, 1963 the elder Gruen, a successful architect with offices and residences in both New York City and Los Angeles during most of the time involved in this action, wrote a letter to plaintiff, then an undergraduate student at Harvard, stating that he was giving him the Klimt painting for his birthday but that he wished to retain the possession of it for his lifetime. This letter is not in evidence, apparently because plaintiff destroyed it on instructions from his father. Two other letters were received, however, one dated May 22, 1963 and the other April 1, 1963. Both had been dictated by Victor Gruen and sent together to plaintiff on or about May 22, 1963. The letter dated May 22, 1963 reads as follows:

Dear Michael:

I wrote you at the time of your birthday about the gift of the painting by Klimt.

Now my lawyer tells me that because of the existing tax laws, it was wrong to mention in that letter that I want to use the painting as long as I live. Though I still want to use it, this should not appear in the letter. I am enclosing, therefore, a new letter and I ask you to send the old one back to me so that it can be destroyed.

I know this is all very silly, but the lawyer and our accountant insist that they must have in their possession copies of a letter which will serve the purpose of making it possible for you, once I die, to get this picture without having to pay inheritance taxes on it.

Love, s/Victor.

Enclosed with this letter was a substitute gift letter, dated April 1, 1963, which stated:

Dear Michael:

The 21st birthday, being an important event in life, should be celebrated accordingly. I therefore wish to give you as a present the oil painting by Gustav Klimt of Schloss Kammer which now hangs in the New York living room. You know that Lazette and I bought it some 5 or 6 years ago, and you always told us how much you liked it.

Happy birthday again.

Love, s/Victor.

Gustav Klimt

Schloss Kammer am Attersee II

Plaintiff never took possession of the painting nor did he seek to do so. Except for a brief period between 1964 and 1965 when it was on loan to art exhibits and when restoration work was performed on it, the painting remained in his father's possession, moving with him from New York City to Beverly Hills and finally to Vienna, Austria, where Victor Gruen died on February 14, 1980. Following Victor's death plaintiff requested possession of the Klimt painting and when defendant refused, he commenced this action.

The issues framed for appeal are whether a valid inter vivos gift of a chattel may be made where the donor has reserved a life estate in the chattel and the donee never has had physical possession of it before the donor's death and, if it may, which factual findings on the elements of a valid inter vivos gift more nearly comport with the weight of the evidence in this case, those of Special Term or those of the Appellate Division. The latter issue requires application of two general rules. First, to make a valid inter vivos gift there must exist the intent on the part of the donor to make a present transfer; delivery of the gift, either actual or constructive to the donee; and acceptance by the donee. Second, the proponent of a gift has the burden of proving each of these elements by clear and convincing evidence. . . .

There is an important distinction between the intent with which an inter vivos gift is made and the intent to make a gift by will. An inter vivos gift requires that the donor intend to make an irrevocable present transfer of ownership; if the intention is to make a testamentary disposition effective only after death, the gift is invalid unless made by will.

Defendant contends that the trial court was correct in finding that Victor did not intend to transfer any present interest in the painting to plaintiff in 1963 but only expressed an intention that plaintiff was to get the painting upon his death. The evidence is all but conclusive, however, that Victor intended to transfer ownership of the painting to plaintiff in 1963 but to retain a life estate in it and that he did, therefore, effectively transfer a remainder interest in the painting to plaintiff at that time. Although the original letter was not in evidence, testimony of its contents was received along with the substitute gift letter and its covering letter dated May 22, 1963. The three letters should be considered together as a single instrument (*see, Matter of Brandreth*, 169 N.Y. 437, 440, 62 N.E. 563) and when they are they unambiguously establish that Victor Gruen intended to make a present gift of title to the painting at that time. But there was other evidence for after 1963 Victor made several statements orally and in writing indicating that he had previously given plaintiff the painting and that plaintiff owned it. Victor Gruen retained possession of the property, insured it, allowed others to exhibit it and made necessary repairs to it but those acts are not inconsistent with his retention of a life estate. Furthermore, whatever probative value could be attached to his statement that he had bequeathed the painting to his heirs, made 16 years later when he prepared an export license application so that he could take the painting out of Austria, is negated by the overwhelming evidence that he intended a present transfer of title in 1963. Victor's failure to file a gift tax return on the transaction was partially explained by allegedly erroneous legal advice he received, and while that omission sometimes may indicate that the donor had no intention of making a present gift, it does not necessarily do so and it is not dispositive in this case.

Defendant contends that even if a present gift was intended, Victor's reservation of a lifetime interest in the painting defeated it. . . .

Defendant recognizes that a valid inter vivos gift of a remainder interest can be made not only of real property but also of such intangibles as stocks and bonds. Indeed, several of the cases she cites so hold. That being so, it is difficult to perceive any legal basis for the distinction she urges which would permit gifts of remainder interests in those properties but not of remainder interests in chattels such as the Klimt painting here. The only reason suggested is that the gift of a chattel must include a present right to possession. The application of *Brandreth* to permit a gift of the remainder in this case, however, is consistent with the distinction, well recognized in the law of gifts as well as in real property law, between ownership and possession or enjoyment. Insofar as some of our cases purport to require that the donor intend to transfer both title and possession immediately to have a valid inter vivos gift, they state the rule too broadly and confuse the effectiveness of a gift with the transfer of the possession of the subject of that gift. The correct test is " 'whether the maker intended the [gift] to have *no effect* until after the maker's death, or whether he intended it to transfer *some present interest*.' " *McCarthy v. Pieret*, 281 N.Y. 407, 409, 24 N.E.2d 102, *supra* (emphasis added); *see also*, 25 N.Y.Jur., Gifts, § 14, at 156–157. As long as the evidence establishes an intent to make a present and irrevocable transfer of title or the right of ownership, there is a present transfer of some interest and the gift is effective immediately. Thus, in *Speelman v. Pascal* [178 N.E.2d 728], we held valid a gift of a percentage of the future royalties to the play "My Fair Lady" before the play even existed. There, as in this case, the donee received title or the right of ownership to some property immediately upon the making of the gift but possession or enjoyment of the subject of the gift was postponed to some future time.

Defendant suggests that allowing a donor to make a present gift of a remainder with the reservation of a life estate will lead courts to effectuate otherwise invalid testamentary dispositions of property. The two have entirely different characteristics, however, which make them distinguishable. Once the gift is made it is irrevocable and the donor is limited to the rights of a life tenant not an owner. Moreover, with the gift of a remainder title vests immediately in the donee and any possession is postponed until the donor's death whereas under a will neither title nor possession vests immediately. Finally, the postponement of enjoyment of the gift is produced by the express terms of the gift not by the nature of the instrument as it is with a will. . . .

In order to have a valid inter vivos gift, there must be a delivery of the gift, either by a physical delivery of the subject of the gift or a constructive or symbolic delivery such as by an instrument of gift, sufficient to divest the donor of dominion and control over the property. As the statement of the rule suggests, the requirement of delivery is not rigid or inflexible, but is to be applied in light of its purpose to avoid mistakes by donors and fraudulent claims by donees. Accordingly, what is sufficient to constitute delivery "must be tailored to suit the circumstances of the case." *Matter of Szabo*, [10 N.Y.2d 94, 98, 217 N.Y.S.2d 593 (1961)]. The rule requires that " '[t]he delivery necessary to consummate a gift must be as perfect as the nature of the property and the circumstances and surroundings of the parties will reasonably permit.' " *Id.*

Defendant contends that when a tangible piece of personal property such as a painting is the subject of a gift, physical delivery of the painting itself is the best form of delivery and should be required. Here, of course, we have only delivery of Victor Gruen's letters which serve as instruments of gift. Defendant's statement of the rule as applied may be generally true, but it ignores the fact that what Victor Gruen gave plaintiff was not all rights to the Klimt painting, but only title to it with no right of possession until his death. Under these circumstances, it would be illogical for the law to require the donor to part with possession of the painting when that is exactly what he intends to retain.

Nor is there any reason to require a donor making a gift of a remainder interest in a chattel to physically deliver the chattel into the donee's hands only to have the donee redeliver it to the donor. As the facts of this case demonstrate, such a requirement could impose practical burdens on the parties to the gift while serving the delivery requirement poorly. Thus, in order to accomplish this type of delivery the parties would have been required to travel to New York for the symbolic transfer and redelivery of the Klimt painting which was hanging on the wall of Victor Gruen's Manhattan apartment. Defendant suggests that such a requirement would be stronger evidence of a completed gift, but in the absence of witnesses to the event or any written confirmation of the gift it would provide less protection against fraudulent claims than have the written instruments of gift delivered in this case. . . .

Acceptance by the donee is essential to the validity of an inter vivos gift, but when a gift is of value to the donee, as it is here, the law will presume an acceptance on his part. . . .

Notes

1. *The Aftermath.* The value of Klimt's works have skyrocketed in recent years, and *Schloss Kammer am Attersee II* is no exception. On October 9, 1997, the painting sold at auction at Christie's (London) for £13.2 million ($23.5 million). As of the printing of this book, the Expo-shop.com website indicates that the painting is on display at the Galleria Nazionale d'Arte Moderna in Rome.

2. *Inter Vivos Gifts of a Remainder Compared with Testamentary Transfers.* Be sure to distinguish what Victor did (*i.e.,* make a valid inter vivos gift of a remainder interest in the painting) from the following:

(a) Suppose Victor had written Michael a letter stating "You may have the painting after my death." As the notes following *Scherer* suggested, this would have been an attempted testamentary gift (intended to take effect only at Victor's death), and it would have been invalid for failure to comply with the applicable will requirements. Why does the law strike down such an attempted gift and yet give effect to the gift in *Gruen*?

(b) Suppose that in 1963, Victor made a valid will that devised ownership of the painting to Michael. Suppose further that Victor died in 1980. Between 1963 and 1980, would Michael have a remainder interest (similar to the one he acquired in the actual case)? Why or why not?

3. *The Delivery Requirement Revisited.* Compare the *Gruen* court's articulation of the delivery requirement with that of the majority in *Evans.* Does the *Gruen* court think that delivery is less significant than the majority in *Evans*? Why or why not? In answering this question, consider the following hypotheticals:

(a) Suppose that Victor Gruen had written the same April 1, 1963, letter of gift to his son. Instead of mailing it to his son, however, he attached it to the back of the painting (figuring that his son would discover the letter on the back of the painting after his death). Upon Victor's death, Michael discovers the letter and demands possession of the painting. On these facts, would you decide the case in Michael's favor? Why or why not?

(b) Suppose that Victor Gruen had decided to give his son complete ownership of the painting, without reserving any life interest in himself. Victor sent a letter to Michael at Harvard informing him of the gift, but died before physically delivering the painting. Upon Victor's death, Michael produces the letter and demands possession of the painting. On these facts, would you decide the case in Michael's favor? Why or why not?

LAWYERING EXERCISE
(Counseling)

BACKGROUND: One of the most significant challenges for many lawyers is to learn how to explain legal concepts using language that clients can readily understand (rather than impenetrable legal jargon):

Consider in advance how you will explain legal concepts and terminology. If you try to find the right words off the cuff, they will either be incomprehensible or sound condescending. You want plain words that accurately describe the concept without implying that you are talking down to the client....

Do not talk to a client using words you would say to another lawyer. Clients want you to respect their intelligence but to use words that nonlawyers can understand. This requires careful forethought. Before you sit down with a client, ask yourself what words will most clearly communicate to the client the legal situation. [Stefan H. Krieger & Richard K. Neumann, Jr., Essential Lawyering Skills: Interviewing, Counseling, Negotiation, and Persuasive Fact Analysis 248–49 (2d ed. 2003).]

SITUATION: Assume that you represented Michael Gruen in the *Gruen v. Gruen* dispute, and that the trial judge has just handed down his decision, stating orally from the bench that "Plaintiff Michael Gruen failed to establish any of the elements of an inter vivos gift, and in any event, the purported gift of the painting was invalid because an attempt by a donor to retain a present possessory life estate in a chattel invalidates the gift." The judge did not issue a written opinion.

TASK: Keeping in mind the admonitions of Professors Krieger & Neumann, prepare the words you would use to explain the court's judgment to Michael. Should you explain the judgment to Michael in person, or by letter?

Because land is fixed in place, manual delivery of land is impossible. Accordingly, the law has always recognized some form of constructive or symbolic delivery in order to transfer land. At early common law, this symbolic delivery took place in the form of a ceremony called *livery of seisin*. In this ceremony, the transferor and the transferee physically went onto the land, where the transferor manually handed over to the transferee possession of a twig or a clod of dirt to symbolize the transfer of ownership.

As you will see in Chapter 5, after Parliament enacted the Statute of Uses in 1536, it became possible for a landowner to transfer land by delivery of a written instrument known as a *deed*. As explained in Chapter 3, today the transfer of land must occur by the execution and delivery of a valid deed. Because the grantor must "deliver" a deed in order to transfer title to land, disputes sometimes arise over whether a valid delivery has taken place. What does it mean to "deliver" a deed? Is it necessary that the deed be "handed over" to the grantee, or will something less than manual delivery suffice? And how can one tell whether the grantor's intent is to transfer the present right to possession, as contrasted with a future interest? Consider the following case.

FERRELL v. STINSON

Supreme Court of Iowa.
233 Iowa 1331, 11 N.W.2d 701 (1943).

GARFIELD, JUSTICE. The land in controversy is a farm of 220 acres in Franklin county, Iowa, subject to a mortgage of $2,500. Plaintiff asserts there was no valid delivery of the deed under which defendants claim. In her lifetime, the property was owned by Miss Mary Kamberling, who died on October 2, 1940, in Phoenix, Arizona. She was an only child who had inherited the farm from her parents. She had no near relatives. From early childhood Mary was a cripple who used crutches when she attended school in Iowa Falls, her girlhood home. She developed tuberculosis and about 1917 was taken to Phoenix where she continued to live as an invalid until her death.

In Iowa Falls, Mary formed a most intimate and enduring friendship with Mrs. Esgate, one of the defendants, a daughter of the late Justice Weaver of this court. In 1916 Mrs. Esgate also moved from Iowa Falls to Phoenix and lived there until 1932, when she moved to Washington, D.C. Mary lived with Mrs. Esgate part of that time. After moving to Washington, Mrs. Esgate returned to Phoenix for about six weeks on each of five occasions, during which she did what she could to relieve Miss Kamberling, whose condition grew progressively worse. Miss Kamberling was indebted to Mrs. Esgate and her husband for money loaned her.

The other two defendants who, with Mrs. Esgate, were grantees of the deed, are Brooks Baughman of Cedar Falls, Iowa, a first cousin of the grantor (apparently her nearest living relative), and Mrs. I. W. Stinson of Mason City, Iowa, a distant cousin of Mary and a first cousin of plaintiff Mrs. Ferrell, also a distant cousin of the grantor-testatrix. Miss Kamberling was also attached to these three cousins, defendants Baughman and Mrs. Stinson, and plaintiff Mrs. Ferrell, who visited and assisted her at times.

The deed under which the three defendants claim was executed on December 2, 1939, in Phoenix. Miss Kamberling, bedridden at the time, called in a young lady notary who lived next door, gave her a copy of a quitclaim deed she had filled in with pencil and asked her to copy it on a typewriter. As directed, the notary typed the deed on another form which was duly signed, witnessed by two witnesses and acknowledged. The grantor then handed the executed deed to her housekeeper, Mrs. Orbison, and asked her to put it in a little metal box in a closet opening into her bedroom. The servant did as directed and the deed remained in the box in the closet during the ten months until the grantor's death. The box was not locked and there is no evidence that there was a key for it.

About the time the deed was executed Miss Kamberling talked to the same notary about making a will. The notary, as requested, asked an attorney, Mr. Karz, to get in touch with Miss Kamberling. This attorney prepared a will and it was executed the following day, December 3. The will provides for payment of debts of the testatrix, directs the sale by her executrix of her real estate in Phoenix, describing it, in the event her debts are fully paid from her personal property, leaves two legacies of $400 each and some personal belongings, and bequeaths all the rest and residue of her estate to plaintiff Mrs. Ferrell. Following Miss Kamberling's death the will was admitted to probate both in Arizona and Franklin county, Iowa. Plaintiff claims the farm in question as residuary devisee.

Mrs. Flora Thompson was a close friend of Miss Kamberling who was named in the will as executrix. On December 3, the day the will was made, Miss Kamberling told Mrs. Thompson in substance, "I have made a deed of my Iowa farm to Mrs. I.W. Stinson, Brooks Baughman and Mrs. A.T. Esgate (the defendants), and the deed is placed in the box in the closet with other papers and after I am gone you are to take the deed out of the box and send it to Jane," meaning Mrs. Stinson. In this conversation Mrs. Thompson told testatrix she had always done everything she could for her while alive and would be very glad to do what she could after Miss Kamberling was gone. Mrs. Thompson had frequently seen the box in the closet before that time, but did not see it again till the day after Miss Kamberling's death. Mrs. Thompson then found the deed in the box in the closet, and on October 4, 1940, as directed by the grantor, mailed it to Mrs. Stinson at Mason City, who had it placed of record in Franklin county. When opened by Mrs. Thompson, the box contained the deed, the will, some old canceled mortgages and checks and some tax receipts. The box in which the deed was kept apparently was not used for current papers. The lease to the farm and bills were kept in a folder in a table drawer in the sick room.

There is no doubt that Miss Kamberling desired and intended defendants should have this farm and believed she had effectively conveyed the farm to them. The equity in the Iowa farm is worth approximately three times her other property, her personalty and Arizona real estate. It is plain that she intended to divide her estate in four nearly equal shares between her three cousins and her devoted friend Mrs. Esgate. These four were the principal natural objects of her bounty.

The attorney who drew the will testified without objection:

> At the time she gave me the information with respect to the will she told me she had disposed of her property in Iowa; that she had executed deeds to the people she wanted to have that property, and it would not be necessary to insert it in the will or be bothered with probate proceedings.... She told me specifically at that time she had disposed of the property by deed, and that all had been taken care of long before the will was drawn, that is, the property out of the State of Arizona.

There is competent evidence that Miss Kamberling told the grantees of the making of the deed. She also told intimate friends she had deeded her Iowa farm to the three defendants. Mrs. Smith, an acquaintance of twenty years who wrote letters for the invalid, testified:

> Mary Kamberling had told me what disposition she had made of the Iowa land. . . . Shortly after Mary Kamberling made her will I was at her house and she told me she had made her will which covered her Phoenix property. She said, "Not the farm, the Iowa property," because that was deeded to Mrs. Esgate, her cousin Brooks (Baughman), and Mrs. Stinson; that she deeded it because they might break a will but a deed would secure the property and insure it going to the people she wanted it to go to.

Although the grantor lived ten months after making the deed and will, it fairly appears that she made them in contemplation of impending death. She was in the advanced stages of tuberculosis with many complications and was failing rapidly. There is no evidence she was able to or did leave her bed except to go to the hospital in January or February, 1940, for an operation in an attempt to prolong her life.

It was stipulated upon the trial that, until she died, Miss Kamberling rented the farm, received the rents and controlled its operation.

I. The deed having been duly executed and recorded, plaintiff has the burden of proving its nondelivery by evidence that is clear, satisfactory and convincing. This is true even though the recording was after the grantor's death. Plaintiff does not question the above rule but contends the presumption of delivery has been conclusively rebutted.

II. Delivery is of course essential to the validity of a deed. Our own and other decisions hold that delivery depends very largely upon the intent of the grantor, to be determined by his acts or words or both, and that a manual delivery is not essential if it appears that the grantor intended to relinquish dominion and control over the deed and have it take effect as a present conveyance of title.

We have frequently said that actual manual transfer of the paper is not necessary and that acts and words evincing the grantor's intent to part with the deed and relinquish his right over it is a sufficient delivery. We have declared time and again that the intent of the grantor is the controlling element in the delivery of a deed.

This court has uniformly held that where an unrecorded deed is found in a box belonging to the grantor after his death, without more, there is no presumption of delivery. . . .

We have also frequently held that an effective delivery may be made by placing the deed in the hands of a third person, without reserving the right to recall it and with instructions to deliver to the grantee after the grantor's death. If the conveyance is beneficial to the grantee, the third person is presumed to act as the grantee's agent. The effect of thus placing the instrument with a third person is to reserve a life estate to the grantor with title immediately passing to the grantee but with the latter's right to possession and enjoyment postponed until the grantor's death. . . .

Davis v. John E. Brown College, 208 Iowa 480, 222 N.W. 858, and *Boone Biblical College v. Forrest*, 223 Iowa 1260, 275 N.W. 132, 116 A.L.R. 67, held there was a valid delivery where a deed was placed with a third party, in spite of an expressed reservation of the right to recall the instrument during the grantor's life, provided such reservation was never exercised. These decisions were contrary to the clear weight of authority and to the principles of some of our own cases ... and were overruled in *Orris v. Whipple*, 224 Iowa 1157, 280 N.W. 617, 129 A.L.R. 1....

The trial court's decision in plaintiff's favor here is based entirely on *Orris v. Whipple* upon which plaintiff mainly relies. We are unable to agree that the *Orris* case, with which we are in entire accord, is controlling here. It was a suit at law in replevin by the grantees of an unrecorded deed, which had been executed and placed in the grantor's safety deposit box to which she alone had access. There was, to quote the opinion, "no semblance of a delivery either to the grantees or a third person." No instructions were given to the banker or anyone else to deliver the deed. The only evidence in the *Orris* case having any tendency to show delivery was that the grantor told some others she wanted plaintiffs, or one of them, to have the property and had prepared papers so providing. This court properly held that plaintiffs who had the burden, as the opinion points out, failed to prove delivery.

One important distinction between the case at bar and *Orris v. Whipple* is that here the deed was in the nature of a voluntary settlement among the principal natural objects of the grantor's bounty. In the cited case attention is called to the fact that the grantees were "not even collateral heirs" of the grantor.

The rule that a valid delivery may occur without actual transfer of possession of the deed is particularly true where as here the conveyance is one of voluntary settlement among the objects of the grantor's bounty. In such a case the mere fact that the grantor retains possession of the deed is not conclusive against its validity if there is no circumstance other than its retention to show the deed was not intended to be absolute.

Where there is a good faith voluntary conveyance to those who naturally have a claim upon the grantor's bounty, courts of equity are strongly inclined to uphold the deed and will do so unless impelled to the opposite conclusion by strong and convincing evidence. There is in such a case a high degree of mutual confidence between the parties. In this class of cases courts of equity do not put so much importance in the mere manual possession of the deed as in the intent of the grantor. If his intent to pass title presently to the grantee is satisfactorily shown, equity usually sustains such a conveyance, even where the grantor retained manual possession of the deed....

Mary Kamberling executed this deed when she was in her last illness. By the deed and will she clearly made what she believed was a final and effective disposition of her property among the principal claimants to her bounty. She handed the deed to Mrs. Orbison and instructed her to put it in a box in the closet where it remained. It is a fair inference that the grantor in her weakened condition was physically unable to go to the box during the remainder of her life. The grantor, so far as shown by the evidence, never intended to exercise further control or dominion over the deed. She plainly told Mrs. Thompson where the deed was and would be at her death and asked her to mail it to Mrs. Stinson, giving the address, when the grantor died. Mrs. Thompson at least impliedly promised to do as requested and later made good her promise. The deed was found where the grantor had said it would be.

Miss Kamberling told her attorney that her will was not to include her Iowa property which had been deeded to those she wanted to have it. She later told defendants and others of the deed in a way that clearly shows she believed she had made an effective delivery and intended that what she did would so operate. Evidence of statements by the grantor that he had executed the deed has been "considered a potent factor, in connection with other circumstances, in determining whether or not there has been a delivery." Anno. 129 A.L.R. 11, 27, and cases cited. It is true the belief of the grantor is not sufficient of itself to prove delivery. *Heavner v. Kading*, 209 Iowa 1271, 1274, 228 N.W. 311.

Let us suppose the grantor had handed the deed to Mrs. Thompson when instructing her as to its disposition, that Mrs. Thompson had agreed to do as directed and then herself placed the deed in this same box in the closet. In the light of the evidence in the case there would then clearly have been a valid constructive delivery of this deed under our decisions. Even if the grantor had access to the box, this would not invalidate a previously completed delivery. *Gruber v. Palmer*, 230 Iowa 587, 590, 298 N.W. 926, 927; *Huxley v. Liess*, 226 Iowa 819, 823, 285 N.W. 216; *Foreman v. Archer*, 130 Iowa 49, 106 N.W. 372. Since the controlling consideration is the intent of the grantor, we think the failure to hand the deed to Mrs. Thompson is not fatal to the claim of delivery. Unless we are to sacrifice substance for form, the legal effect of what was done is the substantial equivalent of the supposed case.

Plaintiff relies on one piece of testimony which it is claimed negatives delivery. The housekeeper testified, "After she made a loan on her place of $2,000 she said she had every intention of changing her will or deed, I wouldn't say which, or if she made both, I don't know." On this subject, however, Mrs. Smith, friend and typist, testified:

I was at Mary Kamberling's home every afternoon while the housekeeper was gone. During that time she talked to me about changing her will. She said that the way the will was worded Mrs. Thompson would be unable to give away any of the household furniture or any of her personal things and that there were certain things in the house she wished to go to certain friends, and that was why she felt she should change the will so that Mrs. Thompson would have the privilege of giving those things away. She wanted to make lists of various things in the house to go to certain friends but she never got it done.

In view of Mrs. Smith's testimony about talk of changing the will and under the entire record showing the grantor's complete satisfaction with the deed, we think the housekeeper's uncertain statement does not tend to show the deed was not delivered. We find nothing to indicate that the grantor did not intend the deed to be absolute except its retention in the box in the closet. Under the authorities heretofore cited, where the deed as here is a voluntary settlement, this circumstance is insufficient to establish that the deed was not delivered.

From the standpoint of equity and justice there can be no doubt that defendants are entitled to prevail unless such a decision runs counter to some established rule of law. We think there is no legal principle or no decision of this court which requires an affirmance of the lower court. We hold there was a valid delivery of the deed. . . .

Notes

1. *Conditions Precedent and the Use of Escrow.* Suppose that Grantor (a resident of Missouri) decided to give Blueacre to Grantee (a resident of Colorado) as long as Grantee paid the current real estate taxes due upon Blueacre. Grantor may wish to make sure that Grantee pays the taxes before he delivers a deed to Blueacre; likewise, Grantee may want some assurance that Grantor will actually deliver the deed before she will pay the taxes. The solution to this sort of "chicken-and-egg" problem is for Grantor and Grantee to use an *escrow.* Grantor could execute and deliver a deed to an *escrow agent* (or *escrowee*), who would hold the deed subject to the express instructions that (a) she would not release it until Grantee had paid the taxes on Blueacre and (b) she would release it to Grantee upon receiving evidence that Grantee had indeed paid the taxes.

By using an escrow, Grantor can make a valid delivery that is subject to a condition precedent. In other words, if Grantee pays the taxes and the escrow agent releases the deed to Grantee, the delivery is complete and Grantee holds title to Blueacre. But if Grantee fails to pay the taxes, the deed is ineffective and Grantee does not hold title to Blueacre—even if the escrow agent releases the deed to Grantee anyway—because the escrow instructions demonstrate clearly that Grantor had no intent to pass title to Grantee unless Grantee paid the taxes.

Suppose that Grantor is a trusting sort and simply delivers the deed to Grantee, accompanied with the oral statement "This deed won't be effective unless you pay the taxes." Grantee records the deed and takes possession of Blueacre but does not pay the taxes; Grantor later sues to recover possession of the land. Under the traditional common law rule, Grantor could not recover the land. *See State ex rel. Pai v. Thom*, 58 Haw. 8, 563 P.2d 982 (1977) (delivery upon oral condition effects outright transfer of title even if oral condition unsatisfied); *see also Wells v. Wells*, 249 Ala. 649, 32 So.2d 697 (1947); *Sweeney, Adm'x v. Sweeney*, 126 Conn. 391, 11 A.2d 806 (1940); *but see Martinez v. Martinez*, 101 N.M. 88, 678 P.2d 1163 (1984) (grantor of unconditional deed allowed to offer parol evidence of oral condition). Can you explain the rationale behind the traditional rule? Would it matter if six disinterested witnesses had heard Grantor's statement to Grantee?

2. *Delivery as Evidence of Intent.* The *Ferrell* case expresses the majority view that the grantor may deliver a deed without physically placing the deed in the hands of the grantee. Any act that is sufficient to manifest the grantor's intention to make an immediately effective transfer is considered an effective delivery. Short of manual delivery to the grantee, however, what acts clearly demonstrate the grantor's intention to make an immediately effective transfer? Was Kamberling's act of handing the deed to Orbison, standing alone, sufficient evidence of her intent to make an immediately effective transfer of an interest in the land? If not, what other evidence influenced the court's decision? Is the court treating this transaction as if Kamberling had placed the deed in escrow? Why or why not?

In thinking about these questions, consider this variation on the facts of *Ferrell*. Suppose that one week after Orbison had placed the deed in the box at Kamberling's direction, Kamberling had executed and physically delivered another deed purporting to convey the same land to First Baptist Church, where she had worshiped for 25 years. Would First Baptist Church have any colorable claim of title? If this had actually happened, do you think the *Ferrell* court would have decided the case the same way?

3. *Recording and Delivery.* Note the court's statement that under Iowa law, Esgate's recording of the deed gave rise to a presumption of delivery and that the plaintiff Ferrell thus bore the burden of proving lack of delivery. As explained in Chapter 9, statutes in many states establish a comparable presumption. Can you explain why such a presumption might make sense? Does it makes sense here, where the recording did not occur until after Kamberling's death? Would the court have decided the case the same way if Iowa statutes did not provide that recording established a presumption of delivery?

4. *The* Ferrell *Case—Gifts Causa Mortis and Testamentary Gifts Revisited.* Customarily, someone who wants to create a life estate and a future interest in a parcel of land does so by using language that makes this intention unmistakable. For example, Mrs. Kamberling could have used a deed containing granting language that said "to A.T. Esgate, I.W. Stinson, and Brooks Baughman, subject to a life estate hereby retained by the grantor."

It is not clear from the court's opinion, however, that Mrs. Kamberling's deed expressly retained a life estate. In fact, given the court's opinion, it seems more likely that the deed purported to convey the land to Esgate, Stinson, and Baughman outright—and that the deed said nothing about Kamberling retaining a life estate. This would explain, presumably, why Mrs. Kamberling instructed Orbison to wait until her death to send the deed to the grantees.

So what was Mrs. Kamberling's intent? Was she trying to make a testamentary gift of the Iowa farm? Or was she trying to make an inter vivos gift of a remainder interest in the farm? Does it matter? Consider the following examples:

(a) *X* owned Blueacre, which he wanted his son to have after his death. *X* owned almost no other property, and did not want to bother making a will because he wanted to avoid the time and expense associated with probate. *X* thus executed and delivered to his son a deed purporting to convey title to Blueacre, with the understanding that his son would record the deed only after his death. When *X* died, his son recorded the deed. His daughter (who would inherit Blueacre along with the son if the deed was invalid) wants to sue to have the deed declared testamentary and void. How would you advise her regarding the validity of the deed? *See, e.g., Mueller v. Marshall*, 166 Cal.App.2d 367, 333 P.2d 260 (1958); *First Sec. Bank of Utah v. Burgi*, 122 Utah 445, 251 P.2d 297 (1952).

(b) *A* is on her deathbed. She gives her daughter a deed to Whiteacre and says, "If I die, I want you to have this house." Across town, *B* is also on her deathbed. She gives her neighbor of 40 years a deed to Blackacre and says, "I want you to have this house, unless I manage to recover." How would you decide whether *A* and *B* made testamentary gifts or gifts causa mortis? Should these conveyances be treated differently? If so, why? *Compare In re Nols' Estate*, 251 Wis. 90, 28 N.W.2d 360 (1947) (valid gift cause mortis even though expressed as condition precedent) *with Adams v. Fleck*, 171 Ohio St. 451, 172 N.E.2d 126 (1961) (no valid gift causa mortis where donor's death stated as condition precedent to gift).

5. *Beneficiary or Testamentary Deeds.* By statute, some states now permit a landowner to execute and record a "beneficiary deed"—a deed that does not take effect until the grantor's death. The Missouri statute authorizing beneficiary deeds provides:

> A deed that conveys an interest in real property to a grantee designated by the owner, that expressly states that the deed is not to take effect until the death of the owner, transfers the interest provided to the designated grantee beneficiary, effective on death of the owner, if the deed is executed and filed of record with the recorder of deeds in the city or county or counties in which the real property is situated prior to the death of the owner. A beneficiary deed need not be supported by consideration or be delivered to the grantee beneficiary. [Mo. Stat. Ann. § 461.025(1).]

Is this statute a good idea, or an unfortunate "end run" around the legal formalities for wills? Why do you think that the legislature would enact such a statute? Would such a statute have avoided the problems in *Ferrell* and in the hypothetical in note 4(a)?

6. *Revocation of Deeds.* As stated earlier, inter vivos gifts of personal property are generally considered to be *irrevocable*. Courts have disagreed, however, regarding whether one can make an effective conveyance of land by gift deed and at the same time retain the power to revoke the deed. *Compare St. Louis County Nat'l Bank v. Fielder*, 364 Mo. 207, 260 S.W.2d 483 (1953) (grantor may retain express power to revoke deed) *with Butler v. Sherwood*, 196 A.D. 603, 188 N.Y.S. 242 (1921) (grantor's retention of power to revoke deed prevented valid delivery). Consider the following example, in which Russell Barnes had executed and delivered a deed providing:

I hereby convey to Les Williams, the land and improvements located at 315 Harbison Court, reserving to myself a life estate, with the power to sell, rent, lease, mortgage or otherwise dispose of the land and improvements located at 315 Harbison Court during my lifetime.

Barnes later died, never having attempted to exercise this power during his lifetime. Barnes' will provided that his entire estate should pass to his only living child, Sylvia. Sylvia contacted Williams and informed him that she intended to claim the land and improvements as part of the estate, because the deed was an invalid testamentary transfer. If Williams seeks your advice as to the validity of the deed, what advice would you give? Does Barnes's reservation of those powers (even though he never exercised them) provide evidence that Barnes did not intend to make a presently effective transfer?

LAWYERING EXERCISE
(Counseling)

BACKGROUND: On page 91, we noted one client interviewing and counseling pitfall—the tendency of clients to make conclusory statements that mask the detail of the true facts (*i.e.*, saying "the meeting was quick" instead of stating how long the meeting lasted). In seeking legal assistance, clients sometimes make assumptions or conclusory statements that reflect a misapprehension of the law or of the legal consequences of their actions.

What issues does this pose for the ethical lawyer? The ABA Model Rules of Professional Conduct suggest that "[a] lawyer shall abide by a client's decisions concerning the objectives of representation," but also provide that the lawyer "shall consult with the client as to the means by which [the objectives of representation] are to be pursued." Rule 1.2(a). The Model Rules also provide that "[a] lawyer shall explain a matter to the extent reasonably necessary to permit the client to make informed decisions regarding the representation." Rule 1.4.

TASK: Place yourself in the position of the attorney for Mrs. Kamberling (the owner of the Iowa land in *Ferrell*). She has asked you to prepare her will, and gives you instructions that are consistent with the terms of the will described in the court's decision in *Ferrell*. She says "I've already disposed of my Iowa farm by deeding it to my friend Ann Esgate and two of my cousins. There's no need to deal with that in the will." How would you respond to Mrs. Kamberling's statement?

D. CONDITIONAL GIFTS

Property law generally treats inter vivos gifts as *irrevocable*. If A makes a gift of $2,000 to B, A cannot change her mind one week later and attempt to revoke the transfer and compel B to return the money. Even though inter vivos gifts are irrevocable, however, a donor can make a *conditional* gift—that is, the donor can make a gift that takes effect immediately, but subject to a condition that will, if it occurs, terminate the donee's ownership. For example, A might give B a car, conditioned upon *B*'s graduation from law school in three years or less. If *B* fails to graduate from law school within three years, *B*'s title terminates and *A* may reclaim possession of the car. [One might best call this a gift *subject to a condition subsequent*. Notice that such a gift is still irrevocable; as long as *B* is capable of completing law school in three years or less, *A* cannot simply revoke the gift and demand possession of the car.]

The conditional nature of a gift should pose no problem if the donor and donee have agreed as to the condition in an express writing. As you will see in Chapter 5, for example, courts have generally enforced conditions on ownership of land (called defeasances) when the grantor imposed that condition by means of unambiguous language expressed in the deed to the grantee. Problems tend to occur, however, in cases where there is no written evidence that a gift was conditional in nature, but the donor later claims that the parties understood the gift to be conditional. Perhaps the best example would be a gift of an engagement ring. Is the gift of an engagement ring presumptively conditional on the marriage actually occurring? Can the donor get the ring back if the marriage does not occur? Should it matter who decided to call off the wedding? Or should the law treat the gift of an engagement ring as presumptively unconditional (and require any condition to be expressed in writing)?

LINDH v. SURMAN

Supreme Court of Pennsylvania.
560 Pa. 1, 742 A.2d 643 (1999).

NEWMAN, JUSTICE.... The facts of this case depict a tumultuous engagement between Rodger Lindh (Rodger), a divorced, middle-aged man, and Janis Surman (Janis), the object of Rodger's inconstant affections. In August of 1993, Rodger proposed marriage to Janis. To that purpose, he presented her with a diamond engagement ring that he purchased for $17,400. Rodger testified that the price was less than the ring's market value because he was a "good customer" of the jeweler's, having previously purchased a $4,000 ring for his ex-wife and other expensive jewelry for his children. Janis, who had never been married, accepted his marriage proposal and the ring. Discord developed in the relationship between Rodger and Janis, and in October of 1993 Rodger broke the engagement and asked for the return of the ring. At that time, Janis obliged and gave Rodger the ring. Rodger and Janis attempted to reconcile. They succeeded, and Rodger again proposed marriage, and offered the ring, to Janis. For a second time, Janis accepted. In March of 1994, however, Rodger called off the engagement. He asked for the return of the ring, which Janis refused, and this litigation ensued.

Rodger filed a two-count complaint against Janis, seeking recovery of the ring or a judgment for its equivalent value. The case proceeded to arbitration, where a panel of arbitrators awarded judgment for Janis. Rodger appealed to the Court of Common Pleas of Allegheny County, where a brief non-jury trial resulted in a judgment in favor of Rodger in the amount of $21,200. Janis appealed to the Superior Court, which affirmed the trial court ... [and held] that the ring must be returned regardless of who broke the engagement, and irrespective of the reasons ....

We begin our analysis with the only principle on which all parties agree: that Pennsylvania law treats the giving of an engagement ring as a conditional gift. *See Pavlicic v. Vogtsberger*, 390 Pa. 502, 136 A.2d 127 (1957). In *Pavlicic,* the plaintiff supplied his ostensible fiancee with numerous gifts, including money for the purchase of engagement and wedding rings, with the understanding that they were given on the condition that she marry him. When the defendant left him for another man, the plaintiff sued her for recovery of these gifts. Justice Musmanno explained the conditional gift principle:

> A gift given by a man to a woman on condition that she embark on the sea of matrimony with him is no different from a gift based on the condition that the donee sail on any other sea. If, after receiving the provisional gift, the donee refuses to leave the harbor—if the anchor of contractual performance sticks in the sands of irresolution and procrastination—the gift must be restored to the donor. [*Id.* at 507, 136 A.2d at 130.]

Where the parties disagree, however, is (1) what is the condition of the gift (*i.e.*, acceptance of the engagement or the marriage itself), and (2) whether fault is relevant to determining return of the ring. Janis argues that the condition of the gift is acceptance of the marriage proposal, not the performance of the marriage ceremony. She also contends that Pennsylvania law, which treats engagement gifts as implied-in-law conditional gifts, has never recognized a right of recovery in a donor who severs the engagement. In her view, we should not recognize such a right where the donor breaks off the engagement, because, if the condition of the gift is performance of the marriage ceremony, that would reward a donor who prevents the occurrence of the condition, which the donee was ready, willing, and eagerly waiting to perform.

Janis first argues that the condition of the gift is acceptance of the proposal of marriage, such that acceptance of the proposal vests absolute title in the donee. This theory is contrary to Pennsylvania's view of the engagement ring situation. In *Ruehling v. Hornung*, 98 Pa.Super. 535 (1929), the Superior Court provided what is still the most thorough Pennsylvania appellate court analysis of the problem:

> It does not appear whether the engagement was broken by plaintiff or whether it was dissolved by mutual consent. It follows that in order to permit a recovery by plaintiff, it would be necessary to hold that the gifts were subject to the implied condition that they would be returned by the donee to the donor whenever the engagement was dissolved. Under such a rule the marriage would be a necessary prerequisite to the passing of an absolute title to a Christmas gift made in such circumstances. We are unwilling to go that far, except as to the engagement ring. [*Id.* at 540 (emphasis added).]

This Court later affirmed that "[t]he promise to return an antenuptial gift made in contemplation of marriage *if the marriage does not take place* is a fictitious promise implied in law." *Semenza v. Alfano*, 443 Pa. 201, 204, 279 A.2d 29, 31 (1971) (emphasis added). Our caselaw clearly recognizes the giving of an engagement gift as having an implied condition that the marriage must occur in order to vest title in the donee; mere acceptance of the marriage proposal is not the implied condition for the gift.

Janis' argument that Pennsylvania law does not permit the donor to recover the ring where the donor terminates the engagement has some basis in the few Pennsylvania authorities that have addressed the matter. The following language from *Ruehling* implies that Janis' position is correct:

> We think that it [the engagement ring] is always given subject to the implied condition that if the marriage does not take place either because of the death, or a disability recognized by the law on the part of, either party, or by breach of the contract by the donee, or its dissolution by mutual consent, the gift shall be returned. [*Ruehling*, 98 Pa.Super. at 540.]

Noticeably absent from the recital by the court of the situations where the ring must be returned is when the donor breaks the engagement. Other Pennsylvania authorities also suggest that the donor cannot recover the ring when the donor breaks the engagement. *See* 7 Summary of Pennsylvania Jurisprudence 2d § 15:29, p. 111 ("upon breach of the marriage engagement by the donee, the property may be recovered by the donor"); 17 Pennsylvania Law Encyclopedia, "Gifts," § 9, p. 118 (citing to a 1953 common pleas court decision, "[i]f, on the other hand, the donor wrongfully terminates the engagement, he is not entitled to return of the ring").

This Court, however, has not decided the question of whether the donor is entitled to return of the ring where the donor admittedly ended the engagement. In the context of our conditional gift approach to engagement rings, the issue we must resolve is whether we will follow the fault-based theory, argued by Janis, or the no-fault rule advocated by Rodger. Under a fault-based analysis, return of the ring depends on an assessment of who broke the engagement, which necessarily entails a determination of why that person broke the engagement. A no-fault approach, however, involves no investigation into the motives or reasons for the cessation of the engagement and requires the return of the engagement ring simply upon the nonoccurrence of the marriage.

The rule concerning the return of a ring founded on fault principles has superficial appeal because, in the most outrageous instances of unfair behavior, it appeals to our sense of equity. Where one fiancee has truly "wronged" the other, depending on whether that person was the donor of the ring or the donee, justice appears to dictate that the wronged individual should be allowed to keep, or have the ring returned. However, the process of determining who is "wrong" and who is "right," when most modern relationships are complex circumstances, makes the fault-based approach less desirable. A thorough fault-based inquiry would not only end with the question of who terminated the engagement, but would also examine that person's reasons. In some instances the person who terminated the engagement may have been entirely justified in his or her actions. This kind of inquiry would invite the parties to stage the most bitter and unpleasant accusations against those whom they nearly made their spouse, and a court would have no clear guidance with regard to how to ascertain who was "at fault." The Supreme Court of Kansas recited the difficulties with the fault-based system:

> What is fault or the unjustifiable calling off of an engagement? By way of illustration, should courts be asked to determine which of the following grounds for breaking an engagement is fault or justified? (1) The parties have nothing in common; (2) one party cannot stand prospective in-laws; (3) a minor child of one of the parties is hostile to and will not accept the other party; (4) an adult child of one of the parties will not accept the other party; (5) the parties' pets do not get along; (6) a party was too hasty in proposing or accepting the proposal; (7) the engagement was a rebound situation which is now regretted; (8) one party has untidy habits that irritate the other; or (9) the parties have religious differences. The list could be endless. [*Heiman v. Parrish*, 262 Kan. 926, 942 P.2d 631, 637 (1997).]

A ring-return rule based on fault principles will inevitably invite acrimony and encourage parties to portray their ex-fiancees in the worst possible light, hoping to drag out the most favorable arguments to justify, or to attack, the termination of an engagement. Furthermore, it is unlikely that trial courts would be presented with situations where fault was clear and easily ascertained and, as noted earlier, determining what constitutes fault would result in a rule that would defy universal application.

The approach that has been described as the modern trend is to apply a no-fault rule to engagement ring cases. *See Vigil v. Haber*, 888 P.2d at 455 (N.M.1994). Courts that have applied no-fault principles to engagement ring cases have borrowed from the policies of their respective legislatures that have moved away from the notion of fault in their divorce statutes. As described by the court in *Vigil*, this trend represents a move "towards a policy that removes fault-finding from the personal-relationship dynamics of marriage and divorce." *Vigil*, 888 P.2d at 457. Indeed, by 1986 ... all fifty states had adopted some form of no-fault divorce. Pennsylvania, no exception to this trend, recognizes no-fault divorces. We agree with those jurisdictions that have looked towards the development of no-fault divorce law for a principle to decide engagement ring cases, and the inherent weaknesses in any fault-based system lead us to adopt a no-fault approach to resolution of engagement ring disputes.

Having adopted this no-fault principle, we still must address the original argument that the donor should not get return of the ring when the donor terminates the engagement. Such a rule would be consonant with a no-fault approach, it is argued, because it need not look at the reasons for termination of the engagement; if there is proof that the donor ended the relationship, then he has frustrated the occurrence of the condition and cannot benefit from that. In other words, we are asked to adopt a no-fault approach that would always deny the donor return of the ring where the donor breaks the engagement.

We decline to adopt this modified no-fault position, and hold that the donor is entitled to return of the ring even if the donor broke the engagement. We believe that the benefits from the certainty of our rule outweigh its negatives, and that a strict no-fault approach is less flawed than a fault-based theory or modified no-fault position.[8]

Holding

CAPPY, JUSTICE, dissenting. The majority advocates that a strict no-fault policy be applied to broken engagements. In endorsing this view, the majority argues that it is not only the modern trend but also the approach which will eliminate the inherent weaknesses of a fault based analysis. According to the majority, by adopting a strict no fault approach, we will remove from the courtroom the necessity of delving into the inter-personal dynamics of broken engagements in order to decide which party retains possession of the engagement ring. This view brings to mind the words of Thomas Campbell from The Jilted Nymph: "Better be courted and jilted than never be courted at all." As I cannot endorse this approach, I respectfully dissent.

An engagement ring is a traditional token of the pledge to marry. It is a symbol of nuptial intent dating back to AD 860. The engagement ring was to be of a valued metal representing a financial sacrifice for the husband to be. Two other customs regarding the engagement ring were established in that same century: forfeiture of the ring by a man who reneged on a marriage pledge; surrender of the ring by the woman who broke off an engagement. This concept is consistent with conditional gift law, which has always been followed in Pennsylvania. When the marriage does not take place the agreement is void and the party who prevented the marriage agreement from being fulfilled must forfeit the engagement ring.

The majority urges adoption of its position to relieve trial courts from having the onerous task of sifting through the debris of the broken engagement in order to ascertain who is truly at fault and if there lies a valid justification excusing fault. Could not this theory justifying the majority's decision be advanced in all other arenas that our trial courts must venture? Are broken engagements truly more disturbing than cases where we ask judges and juries to discern possible abuses in nursing homes, day care centers, dependency proceedings involving abused chil-

---

8. Although other "scenarios" related to the consequences of a cancelled wedding can undoubtedly be "envisioned," they are not presented for decision in this case and therefore warrant no comment.

dren, and criminal cases involving horrific, irrational injuries to innocent victims? The subject matter our able trial courts address on a daily basis is certainly of equal sordidness as any fact pattern they may need to address in a simple case of who broke the engagement and why.

I can envision a scenario whereby the prospective bride and her family have expended thousands of dollars in preparation for the culminating event of matrimony and she is, through no fault of her own, left standing at the altar holding the caterer's bill. To add insult to injury, the majority would also strip her of her engagement ring. Why the majority feels compelled to modernize this relatively simple and ancient legal concept is beyond the understanding of this poor man.

Bride left @ alter w/bill

Accordingly, as I see no valid reason to forgo the established precedent in Pennsylvania for determining possession of the engagement ring under the simple concept of conditional gift law, I cannot endorse the modern trend advocated by the majority. Respectfully, I dissent.

CASTILLE, JUSTICE, dissenting. I dissent from the majority's opinion because I do not believe that a no-fault policy should be applied to broken engagements and the issue of which party retains the engagement ring. The Restatement of Restitution, § 58 comment c, discusses the return of engagement rings and states that:

> Gifts made in the hope that a marriage or contract of marriage will result are not recoverable, in the absence of fraud. Gifts made in anticipation of marriage are not ordinarily expressed to be conditional and, although there is an engagement to marry, if the marriage fails to occur without the fault of the donee, normally the gift cannot be recovered. If, however, the donee obtained the gift fraudulently or if the gift was made for a purpose which could be obtained only by the marriage, a donor who is not himself at fault is entitled to restitution if the marriage does not take place, even if the gift was money. If there is an engagement to marry and the donee, having received the gift without fraud, later wrongfully breaks the promise of marriage, the donor is entitled to restitution if the gift is an engagement ring, a family heirloom or other similar thing intimately connected with the marriage, but not if the gift is one of money intended to be used by the donee before the marriage.

I believe that the Restatement approach is superior to the no-fault policy espoused by the majority because it allows equity its proper place in the outcome. Here, it is undisputed that appellee twice broke his engagement with appellant. Clearly, appellant was not at fault in the breaking off of the couple's engagement, and there is no allegation that she fraudulently induced appellee to propose marriage to her twice. Fairness dictates that appellant, who is the innocent party in this couple's ill-fated romantic connection, retain the engagement ring, which was given to her by appellee as an unconditional gift. I would therefore reverse the order of the Superior Court.

Notes

1. *Gifts Subject to Implied Conditions Subsequent.* The majority in *Lindh* concludes that a gift of an engagement ring is subject to an implied condition that the gift will be absolute only if the donor and donee actually marry. On what basis does the court imply this condition where the donor has not expressed it? Can you think of any examples, other than an engagement ring, where a court might treat a gift as being impliedly conditional in nature?

As *Lindh* demonstrates, the law could treat the gift of an engagement ring as being conditioned upon the occurrence of the marriage (such that the donee's title terminates if either party terminates the engagement) or as being conditioned upon the donee's willingness to be married (such that the donee keeps the ring unless the donee terminates the engagement). The majority in *Lindh* took the former approach; on what basis did they reach this conclusion? Do you agree?

Suppose that Rodger had indeed jilted Janis on the wedding day and had left her holding a $15,000 catering bill for the reception that Janis and her parents had scheduled. Is Justice Cappy's dissent correct that the majority decision would leave Janis with no recourse? In that instance, based upon what you have learned so far, what argument would you raise on Janis's behalf?

2. *Gifts Subject to Oral Conditions Subsequent.* Suppose that *A* hands a gold pocket watch to *B* and states, "This is yours, unless you start smoking again." The parties did not reduce this understanding to any writing. Later, when *B* begins smoking again, *A* sues to recover possession of the watch. Should *A* be able to enforce this condition and recover the watch? Why might the law be reluctant to permit this result? Should it matter if the conversation between *A* and *B* occurred in front of four other persons? Why or why not?

3. *Arbitration as a Binding/Nonbinding Alternative to Litigation.* The court in *Lindh* originally directed the dispute between Rodger and Janis to arbitration, and judicial proceedings followed only when Rodger appealed the arbitrator's decision in Janis's favor. You should appreciate that this type of "nonbinding" arbitration is relatively rare. Typically, arbitration is used as a substitute for litigation, the arbitrator's award binds all parties, and judicial review of an arbitrator's award is both rare and extremely limited in nature. The arbitrator's findings of fact are entitled to substantial deference, and a court will not vacate an arbitrator's award merely based upon a mistaken interpretation of law. Indeed, a court generally will not vacate an arbitration award unless the party can demonstrate that the arbitrator was corrupt or that the award was "completely irrational" or a product of "manifest disregard of the law." Leonard L. Riskin, James E. Westbrook, Chris Guthrie, Timothy J. Heinsz, Richard C. Reuben & Jennifer K. Robbennolt, Dispute Resolution and Lawyers 612–16 (3d ed. 2005).

If one party can simply obtain *de novo* judicial review of the arbitrator's award (as it appears that Rodger was able to do in the *Lindh* case), does it make sense for the parties to arbitrate at all? Why or why not?

Chapter 5

PRESENT AND FUTURE
ESTATES IN LAND

In the preceding chapters, you have learned some ways in which a person can acquire an interest in property. The next several chapters examine the nature of the property interest itself—what exactly has the person acquired?

A. INTRODUCTION TO ESTATES AND POSSESSION

When laypersons say they "own" land, they typically mean they hold a bundle of many rights, including basic possessory rights such as the right to be on the land, to use it, and to welcome or exclude others. This collection of rights is called an *estate* in land.

[handwritten margin note: estate in land (1) use (2) be on land (3) exclude others]

Estates are measured in durational terms. Because land theoretically exists forever, its "owner" may have an estate that extends forever. It is possible, however, to create estates of shorter duration. A dying wife, for example, may want to provide her husband with a place to live but ultimately ensure that her home passes to her children from a prior marriage. To do so, her will might give her husband an estate that lasts for the husband's lifetime and give the children the right to possession at the husband's death.

In this latter scenario, the surviving spouse has a ***present possessory estate*** for life and the children hold a future estate or ***future interest***. It is important to keep in mind, however, that both the possessory estate and the future interest are ***present rights***. The holder of the present possessory estate has the present right to immediate possession of the property. The holder of the future interest has the present right to future possession of the property (as compared with a mere hope or expectation of acquiring an interest in the future). Although the children in the scenario described above have no right to possession during the surviving spouse's life, they do have certain presently enforceable rights, such as the right to transfer their future interest even before it becomes possessory and the right to prevent the

[handwritten margin note: both present possessory estate & future interests are present rights]

surviving spouse from engaging in conduct that could harm the children's interest.

You should be able to appreciate why someone might want to separate ownership into rights of present and future possession. Recall the *Gruen* case (page 215), in which Victor Gruen wanted to retain possession of the Klimt painting during his remaining life, but still give his son the right to possession of the painting following his death. Recall also the *Ferrell* case (page 223), in which Ms. Kamberling wanted to retain ownership of the land (and the right to collect rent to provide for her support) during her remaining life, with her friends having the right to possession of the land following her death. In these cases, the court recognized and gave effect to the intentions of Mr. Gruen and Ms. Kamberling, respectively, by separating the present right to possession (a life estate) from the future right to possession (a remainder).

A Brief History Lesson. The elaborate hierarchy of estates and future interests that we recognize today emanates from England's feudal system, created by William the Conqueror after he assumed the throne in 1066. Because society depended on agriculture for the necessities of life, land was the most valuable asset in the kingdom at that time. William used the land to his advantage, systematically distributing large tracts to his most trusted supporters (his "tenants-in-chief") by "grants" of "tenancies" or *tenures*. In exchange, these tenants-in-chief were obligated to provide certain *services* to William.[1] The tenures also were subject to feudal incidents.[2]

The tenants-in-chief further subdivided their large grants among many sub-tenants by the same type of arrangement. These subtenants provided services to their "lords" (*i.e.*, the tenants-in-chief), which gave the tenants-in-chief the wherewithal to meet their service obligations to their "lord" (*i.e.*, William). The sub-tenants further subdivided occupancy of the land into yet another layer of lord-tenant relations, with the sub-sub-tenants receiving the right to occupy and work the land and providing services to their "lords" (*i.e.*, the sub-tenants or "mesne"[3] lords). As a result, this process of subdivision—called *subinfeudation*—created a vast and complex pyramid-like social structure, with the King

---

1. For protection, there developed military tenures such as *knight service* (through which the tenant supplied either personal military service or money with which to pay soldiers). For support, there developed economic tenures such as *socage*, through which the tenant performed various tasks or paid a certain rent to provide subsistence for the lord. For spiritual nurture, there developed the religious tenure called *frankalmoin* tenure, under which land was held by the church, in exchange for services (typically performed by ecclesiastics) that might include the leading of worship or the offering of prayers for the salvation of the lord's soul.

2. Feudal incidents included *aids* (the lord's right to exact financial contributions from his tenants to assist him in meeting financial difficulties); *relief* (the lord's right to extract payment from an heir asserting the right to possession after the tenant's death); *wardship and marriage* (the lord's duty to act as a guardian of a deceased tenant's underage heir, which included the right to arrange a suitable marriage for the ward); and *escheat* (the right to reclaim land if a tenant died without leaving an heir).

3. The term "mesne"—generally meaning *intermediate*, and here referring to intermediate lords in the feudal landholding pyramid—is pronounced like "Maine."

at the top and a host of ordinary folk at the bottom actually working the land or performing other relatively menial tasks.

Not surprisingly, the crucial rules that developed to regulate this social structure focused most centrally upon assuring each lord that he would receive suitable performance of the services owed him by his tenants. The identity, attitude, and talents of the tenant were critical to the lord. This concern was progressively greater the higher a lord stood in the social pyramid. The higher tenures often carried broader and more sweeping services (such as the obligation to provide a battalion of knights for battle) than the lower tenures (under which a tenant himself might agree to be a member of a lord's battalion). As a result, the higher tenures tended to be long-term commitments, with the grantee/tenant "holding of" his grantor/lord by a "freehold" estate.

As is typical of most societies, there also developed a "second-class" tenure known as *villeinage*. Unlike the previously noted "free" tenures (*i.e.,* tenures held not by peasants but by men of power and status), villeinage was "unfree" tenure. The difference is best understood by reference to modern analogues. The villein was similar to the menial servant or the post-Civil War sharecropper—something less than an employee, although not completely a slave. The free tenant, in contrast, was more like "an independent contractor; either he had a set task which he carried out in the way he thought best, or he merely paid a fixed rent in money or in kind." Robert E. Megarry & H.W.R. Wade, The Law of Real Property 24 (3d ed. 1966).

The distinction between "freehold" and "non-freehold" estates centered on the concept of "seisin." The holder of a "freehold" estate was said to be "seised" of the land, which meant that he was entitled to possession but was also responsible for the feudal services and incidents of tenure. The holder of a "non-freehold" interest was not "seised" of the land; he was entitled to occupancy of the land (a lesser right than possession), but did not owe feudal services. As you will see, the concept of seisin was so fundamental to the feudal system that strict rules were enforced to prohibit any gap in seisin (*i.e.,* some person had to be "seised" of the land at all times).

This brief review of the feudal system of landholding is not designed to make you an expert on feudal history.[4] Understanding the historical context, however, should help you appreciate the many categories and distinctions of our modern system of estates. We will return periodically for more historical background as necessary to appreciate our modern rules.

---

4. For more historical detail, *see* Cornelius J. Moynihan & Sheldon F. Kurtz, Introduction to the Law of Real Property (4th ed. 2005); Thomas F. Bergin & Paul G. Haskell, Preface to Estates in Land and Future Interests (2d ed. 1984); James L. Winokur, American Property Law 133–38 (1982).

[handwritten: 6 basic freehold estates, 4 non freehold estates]

B. FREEHOLD ESTATES

Modern law recognizes six basic freehold estates, ranging in duration from the fee simple absolute (which potentially lasts forever) to the life estate (lasting for only the duration of a person's life). There are also four types of "non-freehold" estates, which you will study in greater detail in Chapter 7. For each estate other than a fee simple absolute, there is a corresponding future interest that follows it.

We will discuss each of these estates in turn, but the following charts may help you visualize the relationships between these estates and future interests. As we study the nature of each estate and future interest, you should focus on several main recurring concepts: (a) What is the duration of the estate/interest?; (b) How is it created?; and (c) Is the estate/interest transferable by its holder?

Freehold Estates

Present Possessory Estate	Future Interest (if held by Grantor)	Future Interest (if held by a Third Party)
Fee Simple Absolute	[None]	[None]
Fee Simple Determinable	Possibility of Reverter	
Fee Simple Subject to Condition Subsequent	Right of entry (a.k.a. power of termination)	
Fee Simple Subject to Executory Limitation		Executory Interest
Fee Tail	Reversion	Remainder
Life Estate	Reversion	Remainder

[handwritten down left margin: (1) (2) (3) (4) (5) (6)]

Non-Freehold Estates (Covered in Chapter 7)

Present Possessory Estate	Future Interest (if held by Grantor)	Future Interest (if held by a Third Party)
Tenancy for Years	Reversion	Remainder
Periodic Tenancy	Reversion	Remainder
Tenancy at Will	Reversion	Remainder
Tenancy at Sufferance	Reversion	Remainder

1. The Fee Simple Absolute

The fee simple estate has two basic characteristics. First, it is *potentially infinite in duration*. The humans who own land, however, do not live forever. Accordingly, the second key characteristic of a fee simple estate is that it is freely *alienable, devisable, and inheritable (descendable)*. In other words, the owner has the right to freely transfer the property during the owner's lifetime or at death or, in the absence of such a transfer, the property *descends* to (is *inherited* by) the owner's heirs.[5]

A fee simple estate may be either *absolute* or *defeasible*. A fee simple estate is "absolute" if it is *not subject to any condition or limitation* that

---

5. The right to transfer property while the owner is alive is known as the power to transfer or *alienate* the property. When the owner dies, the owner has the right to direct the distribution of the property by will (*i.e.*, to *devise* the property to a beneficiary or *devisee*). If the owner dies without a valid will, the property *descends* under

might terminate it. The fee simple absolute estate is the highest and best form of ownership in our system of landholding—as close as one can come to "absolute" ownership. In contrast, a fee simple is "defeasible" if it is subject to a condition or limitation that may terminate the estate at some point in the future. [We return to defeasible fee simple estates on page 267.] Most persons owning a freehold estate in land hold it in fee simple absolute.

How is a fee simple absolute created? Suppose that O, the owner of Blackacre, desires to convey a fee simple absolute estate to A. Obviously, O's conveyance would include the words "to A" to identify the person to whom the property is being transferred. The words "to A" are known as *words of purchase.* We also need to know, however, the duration of the estate that O is conveying to A. Accordingly, the conveyance typically includes *words of limitation*—"magic words" that identify the type of estate being granted. The common law had a strict repertoire of "magic words" it recognized for each specific estate. Mastering these words of limitation is crucial to correctly analyzing the possessory estates and their corresponding future interests.

To create a fee simple absolute, the common law required the words "and his heirs" (or, if the grantee were female, "and her heirs"). Thus, O's conveyance would state: "O hereby conveys Blackacre to A and his heirs." The words "to A" are the words of purchase and the words "and his heirs" indicate that A takes a fee simple absolute.

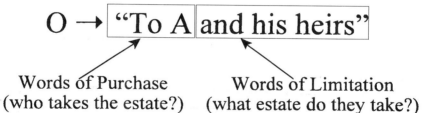

Words of Purchase   Words of Limitation
(who takes the estate?)   (what estate do they take?)

How is it that a conveyance "to A and his heirs" came to create a fee simple absolute in A? The answer is historical. In early feudal times, the fee simple estate was not always inheritable as a matter of right. Land ownership was bound up in the personal relationship of lord and tenant; thus, the lord was under no obligation to accept the tenant's heir (his eldest son)[6] as a substitute tenant following the tenant's death. Customarily, the lord permitted the tenant's heir to inherit the tenant's estate in exchange for the payment of a relief. Over time, the custom became sufficiently established that lords began to show their consent to

the state's intestate succession statute to the owner's heirs.

6. Under the system of primogeniture then in effect, the right of succession extended only to the eldest son—rather than to all surviving sons (or daughters)—as a means of ensuring efficient administration of the feudal services required of the tenancy. *See* Thomas F. Bergin & Paul G. Haskell, Preface to Estates in Land and Future Interests (2d ed. 1984).

accept the tenant's heir by granting land to the tenant "and his heirs." After the 13th century, this custom became a matter of right, inherent in a fee simple estate.

Does a transfer "to *A* and his heirs" mean that *A*'s heirs have a future interest? No. As indicated earlier, the owner of a fee simple absolute can transfer it to whomever the owner desires by an inter vivos conveyance or by a valid will. Thus, *A* may convey the property to *X* while *A* is alive or may devise the property at death to *Z*. In either case, the transfer defeats the ability of *A*'s heirs to inherit the land. At best, *A*'s heirs have a hope or expectation that they might acquire the property if *A* dies without transferring it while alive or by will, but the heirs do not have any legally enforceable future interest. Accordingly, when *O* conveys the land "to *A* and his heirs," *A* acquires a fee simple absolute and *A*'s heirs take nothing.

What if *O*'s conveyance to *A* lacked the magic words "and his heirs"? At common law, the conveyance would give *A* only a *life estate* because it lacked express language to indicate that an inheritable estate was intended. This construction made sense, given that initially estates were not inheritable as a matter of right. But even after fee interests became inheritable of right, the common law continued to require these words anyway. Thus, as a *rule of law* that persisted for centuries, a grantor had to use the words "and his heirs" to create a fee simple estate. These words maintained a technical legal importance; *O*'s actual intent (*i.e.*, whether he had intended to create a fee simple estate) was irrelevant. *See, e.g., Grainger v. Hamilton*, 228 S.C. 318, 90 S.E.2d 209 (1955) ("This is the rule of the common law from which the courts cannot escape.... [I]t has been so long established in this state that the courts cannot now overrule the cases laying it down, without imperiling vested rights.").[7]

Today, all states (including South Carolina, which statutorily over-ruled *Grainger*)[8] have abandoned this strict rule of law, but would consider *O*'s deed to be ambiguous regarding the quantum of the estate created by that deed. To address this problem, most states have adopted modern *rules of construction*, which are statutory or judicial guidelines used to interpret ambiguous language in conveyances. For example, the Tennessee statute provides:

> Every grant ... of real estate, or any interest therein, shall pass all the estate or interest of the grantor..., unless the intent to pass a less estate or interest shall appear by express terms, or be necessarily implied in the terms of the instrument. [Tenn. Code Ann. § 66–5–101.]

7. This is a good example of the rigid technicality of the common law system of estates, bringing to mind Justice Holmes's words: "It is revolting to have no better reason for a rule than that it was laid down in the time of Henry IV. It is still more revolting if the grounds upon which it was laid down have vanished long since, and the rule simply persists from imitation of the past." Oliver Wendell Holmes, *The Path of the Law*, 10 Harv. L. Rev. 457, 469 (1897).

8. S.C. Code Ann. § 27–5–130.

Under this modern rule of construction, the conveyance from *O* "to *A*" (without the magic words "and his heirs") would give *A* a fee simple absolute.

Notes

1. *The Modern Rule Establishing a Preference for Conveyances in Fee Simple.* Think about the modern rule of construction whereby a court would construe a conveyance from *O* "to *A*" to create a fee simple absolute in *A*. Why does this modern rule of construction make sense?

2. *"Heirs," Inheritance, "Issue," and Other Vocabulary.* As you realize by now, the term "heirs" is a legal term of art, *i.e.*, it has a specific meaning in property law. Until Parliament enacted the Statute of Wills in 1540, one could not make a will to transfer property upon death. Instead, at death one's property passed by inheritance to his "heir." Today, laypersons often use the term "heir" to describe a person who receives property under a deceased person's will. That usage, however, is incorrect—a person who would take under a will is a "devisee" or "beneficiary." The term "heirs" applies only to the persons who would take in the absence of a will.

Today, each state has its own statute (called a statute of *descent and distribution* or *intestate succession*) that sets forth how to distribute the assets of a person who dies intestate (*i.e.*, without leaving a valid will). Thus, *A*'s "heirs" are those persons who survive him and who would take his real property under the applicable statute of descent and distribution.

Note several key points about this technical definition. First, "heirs" is not synonymous with "survivors." For example, suppose *A* dies survived by both parents, his wife, and three daughters. *A*'s parents are included among his "survivors" (as that term is commonly used), but in most states they would not be his "heirs." [This is because most descent and distribution statutes specify that if a person dies intestate leaving a spouse and surviving children, the spouse and surviving children would take the decedent's entire estate.] Second, because *A*'s heirs must survive him, *A* has no heirs while he is still alive. At any given time during *A*'s life, those persons who would inherit his land if he died intestate and they survived him may be called "heirs apparent," but this designation does not carry any legal significance.

If *A* dies leaving a valid will, does he have any "heirs"? The answer is yes. *A*'s heirs are the persons who would have taken his property *if he had died without leaving a valid will*. Again, the persons who would take *A*'s property under the terms of his will are not technically referred to as his "heirs"; instead, the law uses the terms "devisees" or "beneficiaries" to describe them. It is possible, of course, that *A*'s "heirs" and the "devisees" under his will could be the same persons—in fact, this happens frequently. Be careful of how you use terminology, however; in that case, they would take the property as *A*'s devisees, not as his heirs.

Sometimes, you will encounter a conveyance that uses the term "issue" (for example, "to *A*, but if *A* dies without issue, then to *B*"). "Issue" refers to a person's *lineal descendants*—*i.e.*, her children, grandchildren, great-grandchildren, etc. It would not include someone's brother, sister, parent, grandparent, aunt, or uncle. Thus, in the above example, suppose that *A* died without ever having had any children, survived by his parents and a brother. *A* would have died "without issue," but *A* would not have died without heirs. Depending upon the state's descent and distribution statute, *A*'s parents (and perhaps also his brother) would be his heirs.

2. *The Life Estate*

a. *Creation of a Life Estate.* The *life estate* is a present possessory estate that lasts only for the lifetime of the person by whose life it is measured. In most cases, the holder of the life estate is also the measuring life; *e.g., O* conveys "to Key for life," under which conveyance Key receives an estate that will terminate at her death. It is possible, however, to create a life estate in one person measured by the life of another; *e.g., O* conveys "to Key for the life of Lawless." By this conveyance, Key receives a life estate *pur autre vie*, one that will terminate upon the death of Lawless.

The limited duration of a life estate forces us to acknowledge the concept of future interests—the reality that two or more persons can simultaneously own substantial interests in the same land. Whenever a life estate is created, at least one future interest (perhaps more) must also exist. For example, what happens when *O*, holder of a fee simple absolute estate, conveys land "to Key for life"? *O* has conveyed an estate of a lesser *quantum* (lesser duration) than *O* held prior to the conveyance; thus *O* has not conveyed all of her interest in the land. Key has a present interest (a life estate), and *O* retains a future interest (the right to possession of the land in the future, after Key's life estate ends). *O*'s future interest is a *reversion* in fee simple absolute; *i.e.,* once Key's life estate is over, the land will revert to *O*, who will thereafter have a present possessory estate in fee simple absolute.

Suppose, alternatively, that *O* had conveyed the land "to Key for life, then to Middleton." *O* has now conveyed a life estate to Key, and has designated that at Key's death, possession of the land should go to Middleton in fee simple absolute. [Recall that the words of limitation "and his heirs" are no longer necessary to indicate an estate in fee simple absolute.] *O* has conveyed a present possessory estate of a lesser quantum than she had, but has also given the rest of her interest to Middleton. Thus, we say that Middleton has a future interest called a *remainder* in fee simple absolute; *i.e.,* once Key's life estate is over, Middleton will thereafter have a present possessory estate in fee simple absolute (and thus ownership will "remain" out of *O*).

By its very nature, a life estate ends at the death of the measuring life. Accordingly, a life estate typically is not inheritable by the life tenant's heirs (if he died intestate) and not devisable by will (if he died testate). A life estate is transferable during the life tenant's lifetime, but under the derivative title rule, the life tenant can convey no more than what the life tenant owned. Thus, if Key holds a life estate and conveys that life estate to Pushaw, Pushaw acquires a life estate *pur autre vie*—a life estate *measured by Key's life*. If Key dies before Pushaw, the life estate will end upon Key's death. If Pushaw dies before Key, the life estate will become part of Pushaw's estate, passing to his heirs (if he died without a will) or one or more beneficiaries (if he had a will) until Key's death.

Dividing the right to possession into present and future estates would seem to give landowners an effective way to share the land among multiple beneficiaries and, most commonly, among successive generations. As the following cases demonstrate, however, the common law governing the relationships between a life tenant and future interest holder(s) severely limits the effectiveness of the life estate as a planning tool.

WHITE v. BROWN

Supreme Court of Tennessee.
559 S.W.2d 938 (1977).

procedural notes

BROCK, JUSTICE. This is a suit for the construction of a will. The Chancellor held that the will passed a life estate, but not the remainder, in certain realty, leaving the remainder to pass by inheritance to the testatrix's heirs at law. The Court of Appeals affirmed.

Mrs. Jessie Lide died on February 15, 1973, leaving a holographic will which, in its entirety, reads as follows:

Lide will

April 19, 1972

I, Jessie Lide, being in sound mind declare this to be my last will and testament. I appoint my niece Sandra White Perry to be the executrix of my estate. I wish Evelyn White to have my home to live in and <u>not</u> to be <u>sold</u>.

I also leave my personal property to Sandra White Perry. My house is not to be sold.

Jessie Lide (Underscoring by testatrix)

Mrs. Lide was a widow and had no children. Although she had nine brothers and sisters, only two sisters residing in Ohio survived her. These two sisters quitclaimed any interest they might have in the residence to Mrs. White. The nieces and nephews of the testatrix, her heirs at law, are defendants in this action.

Mrs. White, her husband, who was the testatrix's brother, and her daughter, Sandra White Perry, lived with Mrs. Lide as a family for some twenty-five years. After Sandra married in 1969 and Mrs. White's husband died in 1971, Evelyn White continued to live with Mrs. Lide until Mrs. Lide's death in 1973 at age 88.

Mrs. White, joined by her daughter as executrix, filed this action to obtain construction of the will, alleging that she is vested with a fee simple title to the home. The defendants contend that the will conveyed only a life estate to Mrs. White, leaving the remainder to go to them under our laws of intestate succession. The Chancellor held that the will

procedural notes

unambiguously conveyed only a life interest in the home to Mrs. White and refused to consider extrinsic evidence concerning Mrs. Lide's relationship with her surviving relatives. Due to the debilitated condition of the property and in accordance with the desire of all parties, the Chancellor ordered the property sold with the proceeds distributed in designated shares among the beneficiaries....

Our cases have repeatedly acknowledged that the intention of the testator is to be ascertained from the language of the entire instrument when read in the light of surrounding circumstances. But, the practical difficulty in this case, as in so many other cases involving wills drafted by lay persons, is that the words chosen by the testatrix are not specific enough to clearly state her intent. Thus, in our opinion, it is not clear whether Mrs. Lide intended to convey a life estate in the home to Mrs. White, leaving the remainder interest to descend by operation of law, or a fee interest with a restraint on alienation. Moreover, the will might even be read as conveying a fee interest subject to a condition subsequent (Mrs. White's failure to live in the home).

In such ambiguous cases it is obvious that rules of construction, always yielding to the cardinal rule of the testator's intent, must be employed as auxiliary aids in the courts' endeavor to ascertain the testator's intent.

In 1851 our General Assembly enacted two such statutes of construction, thereby creating a statutory presumption against partial intestacy.

Chapter 33 of the Public Acts of 1851 (now codified as T.C.A. §§ 64–101 and 64–501) reversed the common law presumption that a life estate was intended unless the intent to pass a fee simple was clearly expressed in the instrument. T.C.A. § 64–501 provides: "Every grant or devise of real estate, or any interest therein, shall pass all the estate or interest of the grantor or devisor, unless the intent to pass a less estate or interest shall appear by express terms, or be necessarily implied in the terms of the instrument."

Chapter 180, Section 2 of the Public Acts of 1851 (now codified as T.C.A. § 32–301) was specifically directed to the operation of a devise. In relevant part T.C.A. § 32–301 provides: "A will ... shall convey all the real estate belonging to (the testator) or in which he had any interest at his decease, unless a contrary intention appear by its words and context."

Thus, under our law, unless the "words and context" of Mrs. Lide's will clearly evidence her intention to convey only a life estate to Mrs. White, the will should be construed as passing the home to Mrs. White in fee. "If the expression in the will is doubtful, the doubt is resolved against the limitation and in favor of the absolute estate." *Meacham v. Graham*, 98 Tenn. 190, 206, 39 S.W. 12, 15 (1897).

Several of our cases demonstrate the effect of these statutory presumptions against intestacy by construing language which might seem to convey an estate for life, without provision for a gift over after the termination of such life estate, as passing a fee simple instead. In *Green v. Young,* 163 Tenn. 16, 40 S.W.2d 793 (1931), the testatrix's disposition of all of her property to her husband "to be used by him for his support and comfort during his life" was held to pass a fee estate. Similarly, in *Williams v. Williams*, 167 Tenn. 26, 65 S.W.2d 561 (1933), the testator's devise of real property to his children "for and during their natural lives" without provision for a gift over was held to convey a fee. And, in *Webb v. Webb*, 53 Tenn.App. 609, 385 S.W.2d 295 (1964), a devise of personal property to the testator's wife "for her maintenance, support and comfort, for the full period of her natural life" with complete powers of alienation but without provision for the remainder passed absolute title to the widow. . . .

Thus, if the sole question for our determination were whether the will's conveyance of the home to Mrs. White "to live in" gave her a life interest or a fee in the home, a conclusion favoring the absolute estate would be clearly required. The question, however, is complicated somewhat by the caveat contained in the will that the home is "not to be sold"—a restriction conflicting with the free alienation of property, one of the most significant incidents of fee ownership. We must determine, therefore, whether Mrs. Lide's will, when taken as a whole, clearly evidences her intent to convey only a life estate in her home to Mrs. White.

Under ordinary circumstances a person makes a will to dispose of his or her entire estate. If, therefore, a will is susceptible of two constructions, by one of which the testator disposes of the whole of his estate and by the other of which he disposes of only a part of his estate, dying intestate as to the remainder, this Court has always preferred that construction which disposes of the whole of the testator's estate if that construction is reasonable and consistent with the general scope and provisions of the will. A construction which results in partial intestacy will not be adopted unless such intention clearly appears. It has been said that the courts will prefer any reasonable construction or any construction which does not do violence to a testator's language, to a construction which results in partial intestacy.

The intent to create a fee simple or other absolute interest and, at the same time to impose a restraint upon its alienation can be clearly expressed. If the testator specifically declares that he devises land to A "in fee simple" or to A "and his heirs" but that A shall not have the power to alienate the land, there is but one tenable construction, *viz.*, the testator's intent is to impose a restraint upon a fee simple. To construe such language to create a life estate would conflict with the express specification of a fee simple as well as with the presumption of intent to make a complete testamentary disposition of all of a testator's property. By extension, as noted by Professor Casner in his treatise on the law of real property: "Since it is now generally presumed that a conveyor intends to transfer his whole interest in the property, it may be reasonable to adopt the same construction, (conveyance of a fee simple) even in the absence of words of inheritance, if there is no language that can be construed to create a remainder." 6 American Law of Property § 26.58 (A. J. Casner ed. 1952).

In our opinion, testatrix's apparent testamentary restraint on the alienation of the home devised to Mrs. White does not evidence such a clear intent to pass only a life estate as is sufficient to overcome the law's strong presumption that a fee simple interest was conveyed.

Accordingly, we conclude that Mrs. Lide's will passed a fee simple absolute in the home to Mrs. White. Her attempted restraint on alienation must be declared void as inconsistent with the incidents and nature of the estate devised and contrary to public policy. *Nashville C. & S.L. Ry. v. Bell*, 162 Tenn. 661, 39 S.W.2d 1026 (1931).

The decrees of the Court of Appeals and the trial court are reversed and the cause is remanded to the chancery court for such further proceedings as may be necessary, consistent with this opinion. Costs are taxed against appellees.

HARBISON, JUSTICE, dissenting. . . . I am unable to agree that the language of the will of Mrs. Lide did or was intended to convey a fee simple interest in her residence to her sister-in-law, Mrs. Evelyn White.

The testatrix expressed the wish that Mrs. White was "to have my home to live in and *not* to be *sold*." The emphasis is that of the testatrix, and her desire that Mrs. White was not to have an unlimited estate in the property was reiterated in the last sentence of the will, to wit: "My house is not to be sold."

The testatrix appointed her niece, Mrs. Perry, executrix and made an outright bequest to her of all personal property.

The will does not seem to me to be particularly ambiguous, and like the Chancellor and the Court of Appeals, I am of the opinion that the testatrix gave Mrs. White a life estate only, and that upon the death of Mrs. White the remainder will pass to the heirs at law of the testatrix.

The cases cited by petitioners in support of their contention that a fee simple was conveyed are not persuasive, in my opinion. Possibly the strongest case cited by the appellants is *Green v. Young*, 163 Tenn. 16, 40 S.W.2d 793 (1931), in which the testatrix bequeathed all of her real and personal property to her husband "to be used by him for his support and comfort during his life." The will expressly stated that it included all of the property, real and personal, which the testatrix owned at the time of her death. There was no limitation whatever upon the power of the husband to use, consume, or dispose of the property, and the Court concluded that a fee simple was intended.

In the case of *Williams v. Williams*, 167 Tenn. 26, 65 S.W.2d 561 (1933), a father devised property to his children "for and during their natural lives" but the will contained other provisions not mentioned in the majority opinion which seem to me to distinguish the case. Unlike the provisions of the present will, other clauses in the *Williams* will contained provisions that these same children were to have "all the residue of my estate personal or mixed of which I shall die possessed or seized, or to which I shall be entitled at the time of my decease, to have and to hold the same to them and their executors and administrators and assigns forever."

Further, following some specific gifts to grandchildren, there was another bequest of the remainder of the testator's money to these same three children. The language used by the testator in that case was held to convey the fee simple interest in real estate to the children, but its provisions hardly seem analogous to the language employed by the testatrix in the instant case.

In the case of *Webb v. Webb*, 53 Tenn.App. 609, 385 S.W.2d 295 (1964), the testator gave his wife all the residue of his property with a clear, unqualified and unrestricted power of use, sale or disposition. Thereafter he attempted to limit her interest to a life estate, with a gift over to his heirs of any unconsumed property. Again, under settled rules of construction and interpretation, the wife was found to have a fee simple estate, but, unlike the present case, there was no limitation whatever upon the power of use or disposition of the property by the beneficiary.

On the other hand, in the case of *Magevney v. Karsch*, 167 Tenn. 32, 65 S.W.2d 562 (1933), a gift of the residue of the large estate of the testator to his daughter, with power "at her demise [to] dispose of it as she pleases . . . ." was held to create only a life estate with a power of appointment, and not an absolute gift of the residue. In other portions of the will the testator had given another beneficiary a power to use and dispose of property, and the Court concluded that he appreciated the distinction between a life estate and an absolute estate, recognizing that a life tenant could not dispose of property and use the proceeds as she pleased. 167 Tenn. at 57, 65 S.W.2d at 569.

In the present case the testatrix knew how to make an outright gift, if desired. She left all of her personal property to her niece without restraint or limitation. As to her sister-in-law, however, she merely wished the latter have her house "to live in," and expressly withheld from her any power of sale.

The majority opinion holds that the testatrix violated a rule of law by attempting to restrict the power of the donee to dispose of the real estate. Only by thus striking a portion of the will, and holding it inoperative, is the conclusion reached that an unlimited estate resulted.

In my opinion, this interpretation conflicts more greatly with the apparent intention of the testatrix than did the conclusion of the courts below, limiting the gift to Mrs. White to a life estate. I have serious doubt that the testatrix intended to create any illegal restraint on alienation or to violate any other rules of law. It seems to me that she rather emphatically intended to provide that her sister-in-law was not to be able to sell the house during the lifetime of the latter—a result which is both legal and consistent with the creation of a life estate. . . .

Notes

1. *The Meaning of "Heirs" and the Mechanics of Wills.* As you have already learned, Jessie Lide's "heirs" were those persons who, under the Tennessee statute of descent and distribution, would take her property if she had died without a valid will. But she left a valid will (even though it was handwritten, it still complied with Tennessee law). So can you explain why Jessie's "heirs" are parties to this lawsuit?

2. *Rules of Construction Revisited.* Both the majority and the dissent rely upon rules of construction to interpret the language of Jessie's will. Upon what rules of construction does the majority rely? Upon what rules of construction does the dissent rely? Which rules of construction do you find more persuasive indicators of Jessie's likely intent?

Notice that the court in *White* characterizes the issue as *what estate Jessie intended* to create—life estate or fee simple absolute. Do you think it makes sense for the court to ask what estate Jessie intended to create (especially if, as may well have been true, Jessie wrote this will without the benefit of any legal advice)? Would it make more sense, in trying to carry out Jessie's intent, to ask a different question? If so, how would you pose the question?

3. *Restraints on Alienation.* In her will, Jessie stated that she was giving her house to Evelyn but that it was "not to be sold." In so doing, the majority concludes that Jessie tried to establish a direct restraint on alienation of the home, but that this restraint was void as "contrary to public policy." Can you explain why? Why shouldn't Jessie Lide be able to give her house to Evelyn, but prevent Evelyn from selling it? *See* Herbert Bernhard, *The Minority Doctrine Concerning Direct Restraints on Alienation*, 57 Mich. L. Rev. 1173, 1179–80 (1959). Are restraints on alienation necessarily contrary to public policy, such that they should never be enforced?

The Restatement (Second) of Property identifies three types of direct restraints on alienation: *disabling* restraints, *forfeiture* restraints, and *promissory* restraints. A disabling restraint ("This is yours, but any attempt to transfer it will be void") purports to deny the grantee any power to alienate the property in the future. Restatement (Second) of Property—Donative Transfers § 3.1. A forfeiture restraint ("This is yours, but if you transfer it, then the property reverts back to me") does not expressly purport to prevent the grantee from transferring the land, but provides for a forfeiture in the event of any such transfer. *Id.* § 3.2. A promissory restraint ("This is yours, and you promise not to transfer it in the future") involves a promise by the grantee not to alienate the land, which promise might be enforced by an action for damages or for an injunction. *Id.* § 3.3. The *White* case involves a disabling restraint, and courts invariably strike down disabling restraints upon a fee simple estate. *See id.* § 4.1. We will return later in this chapter to discuss forfeiture restraints and promissory restraints in greater detail.

Finally, notice that the dissenting judge concluded his argument by suggesting that Jessie intended that Evelyn was not to be able to sell the house during Evelyn's lifetime, and that this intent was "both legal and consistent with the creation of a life estate." Even if the will had created only a life estate, is the dissenting judge correct to suggest that a direct restraint on alienation is consistent with a life estate? Should a direct restraint on the alienation of a life estate be valid? Why or why not? See Restatement (Second) of Property—Donative Transfers §§ 4.1–4.3.

LAWYERING EXERCISE
(Ethics, Client Counseling and Alternatives to Litigation)

BACKGROUND: Several jurisdictions have adopted ethical rules requiring attorneys to inform clients of alternatives to litigation. Colorado's statute, for example, provides as follows:

> In representing a client, a lawyer shall exercise independent professional judgment and render candid advice. In rendering advice, a lawyer may refer not only to law but to other considerations such as moral, economic, social and political factors, that may be relevant to the client's situation. In a matter involving, or expected to involve litigation, a lawyer should advise the client of alternative forms of dispute resolution which might reasonably be pursued to attempt to resolve the legal dispute or to reach the legal objective sought. [Colorado Court Rules of Professional Conduct, Rule 2.1.]

TASK: Assume that at the time of the dispute in *White v. Brown*, Tennessee had imposed a similar ethical rule for attorneys. If you represented one of the parties, what would you do to comply with this rule? What facts about *White v. Brown* might suggest that the dispute was well-suited for alternative dispute resolution? What facts might suggest that the dispute was well-suited for litigation? *See* Frank E.A. Sander & Stephen B. Goldberg, *Fitting the Forum to the Fuss: A User–Friendly Guide to Selecting an ADR Procedure*, Negotiation Journal (January 1994) at 51–59 (evaluating dispute resolution options in light of client goals and impediments to settlement of dispute). Would it help you to know that in 1981, Evelyn White sold the home for only $10,000? *See* Jesse Dukeminier & James E. Krier, Property 228 (5th ed. 2002).

b. *Valuation of a Life Estate.* In *White*, the trial court concluded that Evelyn had a life estate and Jessie's nieces and nephews had a remainder in fee simple absolute. The trial court "ordered the property sold with the proceeds distributed in designated shares among the beneficiaries." For the sake of argument, assume this order had been carried out. The house would have been sold pursuant to court order and the buyer would have received a fee simple absolute title. The proceeds of the sale would have been split, with some of the proceeds paid to Evelyn and the remaining proceeds going to Jessie's nieces and nephews. How should the court go about deciding how to split the proceeds between Evelyn and the heirs?

The goal is to provide the life tenant with the cash equivalent of her right to use, possess and enjoy the property during her lifetime. Thus, there are two key components to determine: (1) the value of the possession; and (2) the potential duration of the possession. With respect to the latter, the duration of possession is not something we can determine with pinpoint accuracy. We can, however, roughly predict a person's life expectancy by using mortality tables similar to those employed by the insurance industry.

Determining the value of the possessory right is a bit more complicated. Once a sale occurs pursuant to the court's order, the life tenant can no longer enjoy possession of the land, so the court must instead place a value on the life tenant's right to enjoy the proceeds of the sale of the land. For example, assume that the property is sold for $100,000. The life tenant would have the right to use that $100,000 during her lifetime, but the remaindermen are entitled to the entire $100,000 upon the life tenant's death. The value of the life estate, then, is the income or interest the money would produce if it were invested. Thus, if the market interest rate is 10%, the life estate is worth $10,000 per year ($100,000 x .10 = $10,000).

We must also recognize, however, that the court will be paying the life tenant for her life estate in a lump sum, rather than in $10,000 installments each year. Accordingly, we must determine the *present value* of the right to receive $10,000 per year into the future. We must similarly discount the remaindermen's interest because they are receiving a lump sum today that represents the present value of their right to receive $100,000 in the future.

Understanding this concept of present value requires an appreciation of the time value of money—*i.e.*, that the value of a dollar in hand today is greater than the promise of receiving a dollar a year from today. The simple explanation is that if you had a dollar today, you could deposit the dollar in a bank (allowing the bank to use the money) and the bank would pay you interest. At 10% interest, the dollar would be worth $1.10 at the end of the year. Conversely, if you needed to pay someone a dollar a year from now, you could invest something less than a dollar today (roughly 91 cents at a 10% interest rate) to ensure that you would have a dollar in a year. For the same reason, the amount we pay the life tenant and remaindermen in our example above must be discounted to reflect the present value of their right to future payment.

Fortunately, the Internal Revenue Service has simplified this process by constructing a set of actuarial tables that factor in both a discount rate[9] and the life expectancy of the life tenant. *See* 26 C.F.R. § 20.2031–7 Table S (2004). Thus, in our example above, if the life

9. The life tenant and remaindermen may disagree about the appropriate discount rate (you should be able to see why—the higher the discount rate, the lower the present value of the future interest). The remaindermen may argue that the court should use an interest rate like the current rate for U.S. Treasury obligations (the least risky type of investment, as it is backed by the full faith and credit of the U.S. government). By contrast, the life tenant may argue for a higher rate (*e.g.*, the rate she might expect to earn by investing the proceeds of the sale in a mutual fund, such as an index fund based on the Standard & Poor's 500). How do you think a court should resolve such a dispute?

tenant is age 50 and discount rate is 10%, the value of the life estate is approximately 88% of the sale proceeds ($88,000) and the remainder is worth 12% ($12,000). If the life tenant were only 20 years old, however, the life estate would be valued at 98% ($98,000) and the remainder only 2% ($2,000).

Now that you know how the life estate and remainder will be valued if they are "cashed out" immediately, does the trial court's order in *White v. Brown* seem appropriate to you? Would the immediate sale and distribution of the proceeds give Jessie's heirs better treatment than they should have received? Does it give the life tenant better treatment than she should have received? What alternatives, if any, are there to cashing out the interests immediately?

c. *Life Estates and the Law of Waste.* As a general rule, a life tenant has the full rights of possession and use of the property during his or her lifetime, including the right to lease the land and collect rent. These rights are not absolute, however; under the law of *waste*, the law limits the life tenant's ability to take actions that would harm the future interest. If the life tenant destroys the home or so poorly maintains it that its value is reduced, the law of waste permits the reversioner or remainderman to recover damages. Recognizing this tort action against the life tenant—based upon a breach of the duty to maintain the property for the benefit of the future interest holder—presents another example of the way that the law attempts to force people to internalize the external costs of their behavior.

Under the traditional view, any substantial change in the property triggered the law of waste, because the person holding the future interest was entitled to receive the property in substantially the same condition as when the life tenant received it (normal wear and tear excepted). Suppose, however, that the home is in poor condition, occupies an area that is rapidly becoming industrialized, and is no longer suitable as a residence. Should the law of waste prohibit the life tenant from tearing down the house and renting the underlying land for storage of industrial equipment and supplies? The answer could depend, at least in part, upon the legal parameters of the term "waste." Keep this in mind as you consider the following materials.

BAKER v. WEEDON

Supreme Court of Mississippi.
262 So.2d 641 (1972).

Procedural Notes

PATTERSON, JUSTICE. This is an appeal from a decree of the Chancery Court of Alcorn County. It directs a sale of land affected by a life estate and future interests with provision for the investment of the proceeds. The interest therefrom is to be paid to the life tenant for her maintenance. We reverse and remand.

John Harrison Weedon was born in High Point, North Carolina. He lived throughout the South and was married twice prior to establishing his final residence in Alcorn County. His first marriage to Lula Edwards resulted in two siblings, Mrs. Florence Weedon Baker and Mrs. Delette Weedon Jones. Mrs. Baker was the mother of three children, Henry Baker, Sarah Baker Lyman and Louise Virginia Baker Heck, the appellants herein. Mrs. Delette Weedon Jones adopted a daughter, Dorothy Jean Jones, who has not been heard from for a number of years and whose whereabouts are presently unknown.

Facts

John Weedon was next married to Ella Howell and to this union there was born one child, Rachel. Both Ella and Rachel are now deceased.

Subsequent to these marriages John Weedon bought Oakland Farm in 1905 and engaged himself in its operation. In 1915 John, who was then 55 years of age, married Anna Plaxco, 17 years of age. This marriage, though resulting in no children, was a compatible relationship. John and Anna worked side by side in farming this 152.95–acre tract of land in Alcorn County. There can be no doubt that Anna's contribution to the development and existence of Oakland Farm was significant. The record discloses that during the monetarily difficult years following World War I she hoed, picked cotton and milked an average of fifteen cows per day to protect the farm from financial ruin.

While the relationship of John and Anna was close and amiable, that between John and his daughters of his first marriage was distant and strained. He had no contact with Florence, who was reared by Mr. Weedon's sister in North Carolina, during the seventeen years preceding his death. An even more unfortunate relationship existed between John and his second daughter, Delette Weedon Jones. She is portrayed by the record as being a nomadic person who only contacted her father for money, threatening on several occasions to bring suit against him.

With an obvious intent to exclude his daughters and provide for his wife Anna, John executed his last will and testament in 1925. It provided in part:

> Second; I give and bequeath to my beloved wife, Anna Plaxco Weedon all of my property both real, personal and mixed during her natural life and upon her death to her children, if she has any, and in the event she dies without issue then at the death of my wife Anna Plaxco Weedon I give, bequeath and devise all of my property to my grandchildren, each grandchild sharing equally with the other.
>
> Third; In this will I have not provided for my daughters, Mrs. Florence Baker and Mrs. Delette Weedon Jones, the reason is, I have given them their share of my property and they have not looked after and cared for me in the latter part of my life.

Subsequent to John Weedon's death in 1932 and the probate of his will, Anna continued to live on Oakland Farm. In 1933 Anna, who had been urged by John to remarry in the event of his death, wed J. E. Myers. This union lasted some twenty years and produced no offspring which might terminate the contingent remainder vested in Weedon's grandchildren by the will.

There was no contact between Anna and John Weedon's children or grandchildren from 1932 until 1964. Anna ceased to operate the farm in 1955 due to her age and it has been rented since that time. Anna's only income is $1000 annually from the farm rental, $300 per year from sign rental and $50 per month by way of social security payments. Without contradiction Anna's income is presently insufficient and places a severe burden upon her ability to live comfortably in view of her age and the infirmities therefrom.

In 1964 the growth of the city of Corinth was approaching Oakland Farm. A right-of-way through the property was sought by the Mississippi State Highway Department for the construction of U.S. Highway 45 bypass. The highway department located Florence Baker's three children, the contingent remaindermen by the will of John Weedon, to negotiate with them for the purchase of the right-of-way. . . .

Until the notice afforded by the highway department the grandchildren were unaware of their possible inheritance. Henry Baker, a native of New Jersey, journeyed to Mississippi to supervise their interests. He appears, as was true of the other grandchildren, to have been totally sympathetic to the conditions surrounding Anna's existence as a life tenant. A settlement of $20,000 was completed for the right-of-way bypass of which Anna received $7500 with which to construct a new home. It is significant that all legal and administrative fees were deducted from the shares of the three grandchildren and not taxed to the life tenant. A contract was executed in 1970 for the sale of soil from the property for $2500. Anna received $1000 of this sum which went toward completion of payments for the home.

There was substantial evidence introduced to indicate the value of the property is appreciating significantly with the nearing completion of U.S. Highway 45 bypass plus the growth of the city of Corinth. While the commercial value of the property is appreciating, it is notable that the rental value for agricultural purposes is not. It is apparent that the land can bring no more for agricultural rental purposes than the $1000 per year now received.

The value of the property for commercial purposes at the time of trial was $168,500. Its estimated value within the ensuing four years is placed at $336,000, reflecting the great influence of the interstate construction upon the land. Mr. Baker, for himself and other remaindermen, appears to have made numerous honest and sincere efforts to sell the property at a favorable price. However, his endeavors have been hindered by the slowness of the construction of the bypass.

Anna, the life tenant and appellee here, is 73 years of age and although now living in a new home, has brought this suit due to her economic distress. She prays that the property, less the house site, be sold by a commissioner and that the proceeds be invested to provide her with an adequate income resulting from interest on the trust invest-

procedural

granted → Anna's claims

ment. She prays also that the sale and investment management be under the direction of the chancery court.

The chancellor granted the relief prayed by Anna under the theory of economic waste.[10] His opinion reflects:

> ... [T]he change of the economy in this area, the change in farming conditions, the equipment required for farming, and the age of this complainant leaves the real estate where it is to all intents and purposes unproductive when viewed in light of its capacity and that a continuing use under the present conditions would result in economic waste.

The contingent remaindermen by the will, appellants here, were granted an interlocutory appeal to settle the issue of the propriety of the chancellor's decree in divesting the contingency title of the remaindermen by ordering a sale of the property.

The weight of authority reflects a tendency to afford a court of equity the power to order the sale of land in which there are future interests. Simes, Law of Future Interests, section 53 (2d ed. 1966), states:

> By the weight of authority, it is held that a court of equity has the power to order a judicial sale of land affected with a future interest and an investment of the proceeds, where this is necessary for the preservation of all interests in the land. When the power is exercised, the proceeds of the sale are held in a judicially created trust. The beneficiaries of the trust are the persons who held interests in the land, and the beneficial interests are of the same character as the legal interests which they formally held in the land.

See also Simes and Smith, The Law of Future Interests, § 1941 (2d ed. 1956).

This Court has long recognized that chancery courts do have jurisdiction to order the sale of land for the prevention of waste. *Kelly v. Neville*, 136 Miss. 429, 101 So. 565 (1924). In *Riley v. Norfleet*, 167 Miss. 420, 436–437, 148 So. 777, 781 (1933), Justice Cook, speaking for the Court and citing *Kelly, supra*, stated: "... The power of a court of equity on a plenary bill, with adversary interest properly represented, to sell contingent remainders in land, under some circumstances, though the contingent remaindermen are not then ascertained or in being, as, for instance, to preserve the estate from complete or partial destruction, is well established."

While Mississippi and most jurisdictions recognize the inherent power of a court of equity to direct a judicial sale of land which is subject to a future interest, nevertheless the scope of this power has not been

---

10. Editors' Note: Do not be misled into concluding that "economic waste" is a recognized legal theory. As explained in note 1 on page 260, the legal doctrine of "waste" involves situations where the party in possession of land has acted (or failed to act) in some fashion that has changed the land in its nature, character, or improvements. As Anna had not acted in such a fashion, Anna had not committed legal "waste" in that traditional sense.

clearly defined. It is difficult to determine the facts and circumstances which will merit such a sale.

It is apparent that there must be "necessity" before the chancery court can order a judicial sale. It is also beyond cavil that the power should be exercised with caution and only when the need is evident. *Lambdin v. Lambdin,* 209 Miss. 672, 48 So.2d 341 (1950). These cases, *Kelly, Riley and Lambdin, supra,* are all illustrative of situations where the freehold estate was deteriorating and the income therefrom was insufficient to pay taxes and maintain the property. In each of these this Court approved a judicial sale to preserve and maintain the estate. The appellants argue, therefore, that since Oakland Farm is not deteriorating and since there is sufficient income from rental to pay taxes, a judicial sale by direction of the court was not proper.

The unusual circumstances of this case persuade us to the contrary. We are of the opinion that deterioration and waste of the property is not the exclusive and ultimate test to be used in determining whether a sale of land affected by future interest is proper, but also that consideration should be given to the question of whether a sale is necessary for the best interest of all the parties, that is, the life tenant and the contingent remaindermen. This "necessary for the best interest of all parties" rule is gleaned from Rogers, Removal of Future Interest Encumbrances—Sale of the Fee Simple Estate, 17 Vanderbilt L. Rev. 1437 (1964); Simes, Law of Future Interest, *supra*; Simes and Smith, The Law of Future Interests, § 1941 (1956); and appears to have the necessary flexibility to meet the requirements of unusual and unique situations which demand in justice an equitable solution.

Our decision to reverse the chancellor and remand the case for his further consideration is couched in our belief that the best interest of all the parties would not be served by a judicial sale of the entirety of the property at this time. While true that such a sale would provide immediate relief to the life tenant who is worthy of this aid in equity, admitted by the remaindermen, it would nevertheless under the circumstances before us cause great financial loss to the remaindermen.

We therefore reverse and remand this cause to the chancery court, which shall have continuing jurisdiction thereof, for determination upon motion of the life tenant, if she so desires, for relief by way of sale of a part of the burdened land sufficient to provide for her reasonable needs from interest derived from the investment of the proceeds. The sale, however, is to be made only in the event the parties cannot unite to hypothecate the land for sufficient funds for the life tenant's reasonable needs. By affording the options above we do not mean to suggest that other remedies suitable to the parties which will provide economic relief to the aging life tenant are not open to them if approved by the chancellor. It is our opinion, shared by the chancellor and acknowledged by the appellants, that the facts suggest an equitable remedy. However, it is our further opinion that this equity does not warrant the remedy of sale of all of the property since this would unjustly impinge upon the vested rights of the remaindermen.

Reversed and remanded.

Notes

1. *Types of Waste.* Courts have identified three basic varieties of waste: *voluntary* (or *affirmative)* waste, *permissive* waste, and *ameliorating* waste. Voluntary waste is an affirmative action by the life tenant that damages the land by changing its nature, character, or improvements to the detriment of the future interest holder. Examples would include tearing down a building, cutting trees, or extracting minerals (subject to a few exceptions we will mention shortly). Permissive waste is damage to the future interest holder that occurs by virtue of the life tenant's failure to maintain and preserve the land and its improvements properly. Examples include the life tenant's failure to pay real estate taxes or her failure to maintain the roof of a building. The future interest holder can recover damages for both voluntary and permissive waste. Further, assuming she can prove an immediate threat of harm, the future interest holder can also obtain injunctive relief to prevent future voluntary waste.

In contrast, ameliorating waste arises when the life tenant changes the nature or character of land or its improvements, but the change *increases* the economic value of the land. Whether the law should provide any remedies for ameliorating waste is a conceptually troublesome question, as the succeeding notes suggest.

2. *The Rationale(s) for the Law of Waste.* If the life tenant takes action that dramatically increases the market value of the land but changes its character, why should that be waste? One can argue that the life tenant, the future interest holder, and society as a whole are better off if the land is put to a more highly valued use. Although this view appears sensible, *Baker v. Weedon* provides a good example of how the rationales underlying the doctrine of waste may actually impede that result.

Because the grandchildren had a remainder in the land, the court refused to order a sale over their objection because the sale would cause the grandchildren to suffer "great financial loss." *Baker,* 262 So.2d at 644. There are two possible rationales underlying this conclusion. One possible rationale focuses upon the grantor's intent in creating a life estate. When a landowner (such as John Weedon) creates a life estate (such as Anna's life estate) and a remainder (such as the remainder in the grandchildren), the law has tended to presume that the landowner intended for the holders of the remainder to eventually take the land in the exact same condition as when the life tenant received it. *See, e.g.,* 8 Thompson on Real Property § 70.08(a), at 334 (Thomas ed. 2005) ("[A] reversioner or remainderman is entitled to obtain possession of the premises in essentially the same condition as when the estate was created . . . ."). The second possible rationale focuses on the economic justification for the law of waste—the problem of externalities and the ability of a life tenant to impose external costs (*e.g.,* economic damage) on the holder of the remainder. The law of waste prevents Anna, as life tenant, from taking action that imposes an unwarranted and unreasonable financial loss on the grandchildren as holders of the remainder.

These two rationales are not mutually exclusive. The "grantor's intent" justification for the law of waste is also related to the problem of externalities—after all, any change presents the potential of harm to the interest or expectations of the future interest holder. Nevertheless, these two rationales might not always justify the same resolution of a particular dispute. Consider the following examples:

(a) *O*, who owns a house in Milwaukee, conveys it to *X* for life, then to *Y*. Over a period of years, the surrounding neighborhood becomes an industrial neighborhood wholly unsuited to residential living. The house cannot rent for enough to pay real estate taxes and ordinary maintenance. *X*, who also owns a brewery next door to the house, tears down the home and expands the brewery. *Y* sues for damages. Result? *See Melms v. Pabst Brewing Co.*, 104 Wis. 7, 79 N.W. 738 (1899).

(b) *O* conveyed a home in Manhattan to *A* for life, then to *B*. The home is worth $300,000, and is surrounded by other residential homes. *A* wants to tear down the home and build apartments that have a projected commercial value of $1,900,000. *B*, who wishes to live in the home following *A*'s death, sues *A* to obtain an injunction against demolition of the home. Result? *See Brokaw v. Fairchild*, 135 Misc. 70, 237 N.Y.S. 6 (1929).

Should these cases lead to different results? Why or why not? When, if ever, should the courts permit a cause of action for ameliorating waste?

3. *Sale of Property Subject to a Life Estate.* A life tenant and the holder(s) of a remainder in fee simple can agree to sell the property and can convey good title, when together they possess all of the relevant ownership interests in the property. Often, however, the life tenant and the holders of future interests cannot agree. In such a case, a sale cannot occur without court approval. The *Baker* court adopts the position typically taken by American courts that the court will not order a sale over the objection of one party, unless the court concludes that the sale is in the best interests of all parties.

In *Baker*, there was no question about harm to Anna, as the farm did not generate enough rental income to support her. The court nevertheless decided that the potential harm to the grandchildren—the loss of the expected appreciation of the land from $168,500 to $336,000 during the ensuing four years—was sufficiently great that a sale was not presently in the best interest of all parties. Do you think the court's decision was correct? Do you think the court properly evaluated the evidence about the land's value, both as of the time of the litigation and its estimated value four years into the future? Why or why not?

One final query: Suppose that Anna and John's grandchildren had agreed to sell the property for $200,000. Could they have conveyed a fee simple title to the purchaser? Based on the language of the will, do you see a problem? If so, what could they do about this problem?

d. *The Legal Life Estate Versus the Trust.* As indicated earlier in this chapter, there are a number of situations in which it would seem desirable to divide property into a life estate and remainder(s), but the *Baker v. Weedon* case illustrates some of the legal and practical limitations of doing so. John Weedon's primary desire was most likely to ensure that the property was used for his widow's financial support, but he failed to anticipate the change in the economy and his widow's physical inability to farm the land as she aged. As it turned out, it was most advantageous for Anna Weedon to sell the property, but she could not do so without the consent of all of the remaindermen (or a finding by a court of equity that a sale would be in the best interest of all parties). Other drawbacks of a life estate include:

- The difficulty in obtaining a mortgage loan on the land (because most lenders would be reluctant to accept only a life estate as security).

- The inability to lease the property for a period that would extend beyond the life tenant's death.

- The limitations placed upon the life tenant's use of the property under the doctrine of waste.

Given these limitations, the creation of a legal life estate and remainder is probably not the most effective device for accomplishing the grantor's goals. The better approach, in most cases, is to use a ***trust***. A trust is a legal device that establishes "a fiduciary relationship in which one person is the holder of title to the property subject to an equitable obligation to keep or use the property for the benefit of another." George T. Bogert, Trusts § 1 (6th student ed. 1987). In John Weedon's case, for example, John could have conveyed title to his property to a trustee in fee simple absolute, subject to the obligation to use the property for the benefit of Anna while she was alive and then for the benefit of Anna's children or John's grandchildren. Thus, the trustee would have held *legal title* to the property (which includes responsibility for administration and management of the property), but the beneficiaries of the trust (Anna and the remaindermen) would have been entitled to the economic benefits as holder of the *equitable title (or beneficial interest)*.[11]

The law recognizes the trustee as the legal "owner" of the property, with the power to sell, lease, mortgage, and otherwise manage the asset. The trustee must exercise these rights, however, solely for the benefit of the trust beneficiaries, whose rights are recognized and enforced as a matter of equity. [In the traditional separation of law and equity (page 54), the rights of trust beneficiaries were enforced by courts of equity. Today, we still speak of "legal" and "equitable" rights and obligations, even though the merger of law and equity means that these rights and obligations are now enforced by the same court.]

---

11. Trusts are the modern outgrowth of a device known in feudal times as a "use," which lawyers employed to circumvent some of the restrictive conveyancing laws of that time. You will learn more about the "use" later in this chapter (page 298).

Because of its flexibility, the trust is one of the most popular tools used in modern estate and financial planning; literally trillions of dollars of wealth are concentrated in trusts. Trusts are frequently used to manage assets for young children, disabled adults, or others who lack the capacity (or desire) to handle their own affairs. Trusts also are an effective tool for avoiding probate, minimizing the federal tax burden (on large estates), and, as appropriate to our study of future interests, managing property for successive beneficiaries or generations of beneficiaries. As Judge Posner observes, "By placing property in a trust, the grantor can split the beneficial interest as many ways as he pleases without worrying about divided ownership. The trustee will manage the property as a unit, maximizing its value and allocating that value among the trust's beneficiaries in the proportions desired by the grantor." Richard Posner, Economic Analysis of Law 84 (5th ed. 1988).

Notes

1. *Trust Advantages.* Based upon the foregoing description of the trust relationship, why would a trust be the better tool to achieve John Weedon's goals than a legal life estate? What problems did the family subsequently encounter that a trust would have avoided? How would a trust avoid some of the other problems associated with the legal life estate?

2. *The Vitality of Legal Life Estates.* Should grantors be *prohibited* from creating legal life estates? England abolished the legal life estate—at least with respect to conveyances of land—by the Law of Property Act of 1925. Pursuant to that act, all life estates became equitable estates; thus, the life tenant was deemed to be holding "a legal fee simple estate as trustee for himself as the beneficial owner of the equitable life estate, and for the future interest conveyees as the beneficial owners of those estates." C. Dent Bostick, *Loosing the Grip of the Dead Hand: Shall We Abolish Legal Future Interests in Land?*, 32 Vand. L. Rev. 1061, 1093–94 (1979).

Should American jurisdictions follow England's lead? From a client's perspective, a legal life estate may be preferable because it is easier and cheaper to create (costing a mere fraction of the legal and trustee fees incurred for a trust) and less cumbersome in operation. Do those concerns offset the problems inherent in a legal life estate?

LAWYERING EXERCISE
(Dispute Resolution—Mediation and Problem–Solving)

BACKGROUND: Mediation is a dispute resolution process in which a neutral party facilitates negotiations between the disputants. "Unlike a judge, the mediator does not have the authority to impose a decision upon the disputants. Instead, the mediator guides the disputants through a discussion of their problem, the issues that need to be resolved, and alternative solutions for the resolution of the dispute." Robert S. Mitchell & Scot E. Dewhirst, The Mediator Handbook (1990). Although the mediator coordinates the negotiation process, it is the disputants themselves who decide whether and how to settle the dispute.

To be effective, therefore, a mediator should anticipate the barriers that might impede the parties' settlement of the dispute. Professors Frank Sander and Stephen Goldberg have suggested that these impediments include:

- The parties are plagued by poor communication.

- The parties need to express their emotions.

- The parties have different views of the relevant facts.

- The parties have different views of the law (*i.e.*, the legal outcome if no settlement is reached).

- One or both parties feels the issue is one of principle.

- One or both parties represents an institution or a group and is subject to "constituency pressures."

- The dispute is linked to other disputes between the parties.

- There are multiple parties involved in the dispute.

- The lawyers and their clients have differing attitudes or interests regarding settlement (*e.g.*, the lawyer may prefer litigation to promote the lawyer's own reputation as a litigator).

- One party has fundamentally overestimated the strength of his or her claim.

Frank E.A. Sander & Stephen B. Goldberg, *Fitting the Forum to the Fuss: A User–Friendly Guide to Selecting an ADR Procedure*, Negotiation Journal (January 1994), at 54–59. Sander and Goldberg also offer suggestions for ways to overcome these impediments.

SITUATION: Bob and Emily Newman were married in 1985, several years after Bob's first wife died from cancer. Bob and Emily did not have any children together, but Bob had two sons, Jeffrey and Michael, from the prior marriage. The brothers were not especially close to Emily, but have never shown any open hostility either.

Bob died in a farming accident in 2000. Prior to his death, he had owned and operated Newman Farms, a 500–acre enterprise that had been in his family for five generations. Bob's will conveyed the farmstead "to my wife, Emily, for her life, then to my sons Jeffrey and Michael and their heirs." Bob also left a sizeable life insurance policy that would allow Emily, who is 69, to live comfortably for the rest of her life.

Emily had worked the farm with Bob throughout their marriage. The operation was too large for her to handle alone after Bob died, however, so she has been leasing about 470 acres of the land to a neighbor for corn and soybean production. Emily continues to live and work on the remaining 30 acres. She has a large vegetable garden and sells the produce at a local farmer's market in the summer. She also raises a small herd of alpacas, which provide fleece that Emily sells to a regional textile merchant.

Several months ago, a real estate agent contacted Emily, Jeffrey, and Michael, to inquire about their willingness to sell Newman Farms.

The real estate agent indicated that a national retailer was interested in their property because of its location just outside the city limits of Murphydale. The company has offered to buy the property for slightly more than its fair market value.

Emily flatly rejected the offer, much to the dismay of Jeffrey and Michael, who were very interested in selling their property rights. Jeffrey, 42, is a carpenter in a neighboring state and has no interest in the family farm. Michael, 44, is now employed as a mechanic in Murphydale. The brothers view the company's offer as a fleeting opportunity, one that is not likely to occur again anytime soon in a town that has been economically depressed since a downturn in the coal industry two decades ago.

Jeffrey and Michael have filed a lawsuit seeking a court order to compel the sale of the land. At the court's request, the parties have agreed to engage in mediation and have sought your assistance as a mediator.

TASK: How would you assess the likelihood that the parties can reach an agreement in mediation? What potential obstacles exist to thwart an agreement? What could you, as the mediator, do to overcome some of these impediments? What practical alternatives would you propose to assist the parties to resolve the dispute without litigation?

3. *The Fee Tail Estate*

Throughout history, landowners have tried to control title to land so as to keep it tied up in the family for future generations. This was particularly true in medieval times, when land was the principal form of wealth. Accordingly, landowners sought to create an estate that would function like an endless series of life estates—each generation of the family would enjoy possession during that generation, but could do nothing to prevent the land from passing to the next generation of the family.

The trick for these medieval landowners was finding language of conveyance (*i.e.*, words of limitation) that would be sufficient to create such an estate. The words "to A and his heirs" did not work, of course; that language created a fee simple absolute, which A could transfer outside of the family. So creative landowners tried the words "to A and the heirs of his body"—meaning A's *lineal descendants*, or A's *issue*. At first, royal courts refused to construe these words to create the desired estate, so influential landowners lobbied for legislation to address the situation. In 1285, Parliament passed the Statute *de Donis Conditionalibus*, which established a rule of construction that enabled landowners to create the "fee tail" estate.

After the Statute *de Donis*, a conveyance by O "to A and the heirs of his body" conveyed a fee tail estate in A, who became the *tenant in tail*. A could use and enjoy the land during his lifetime, but at his death, the land passed to A's issue. A could not transfer the land for longer than his lifetime. Even if A transferred the land to X, X received no better rights than A had to give (the derivative title principle); when A died, the land would pass to A's eldest son, B, who then became the tenant in tail. Thus, by its inherent nature, the fee tail estate was inheritable—indeed, that was its key characteristic—but it was not devisable and could be transferred by inter vivos conveyance only to the same extent as a life estate.[12] If a tenant in tail died without leaving any issue (*i.e.*, lineal descendants), the "tail" ran out, and the fee tail estate ended. In our example, the land would then revert to the grantor, O, who had first created the fee tail estate.

Although the fee tail estate enjoyed great popularity among landowners, it was not popular with the King. Under feudal rules, acts of treason would trigger a forfeiture of the estate, but the treasonous tenant in tail forfeited only his own interest. Thus, when the treasonous tenant in tail died, the land would return to the family. The King, therefore, prevailed upon the judges of the royal court, who in 1472 in *Taltarum's Case* approved the use of a collusive lawsuit to destroy a fee tail estate. Under this lawsuit, a tenant in tail could "cut off" or "disentail" his issue and obtain a court decree awarding him a fee simple estate. This lawsuit (the *common recovery*) limited the fee tail's effectiveness, and its judicial sanction marked the beginning of the law's disfavor with the estate.

Today, the fee tail estate is essentially of only historical significance. England abolished the fee tail estate in 1925; likewise, almost every American jurisdiction has done so as well. Today, one is likely to encounter the fee tail estate only in homemade deeds or wills—written by unsophisticated persons who thought the language "to A and the heirs of his body" sounded good and "legal," but who did not realize what it really meant—or in documents created before the estate was abolished. *See, e.g., Robins Island Pres. Fund, Inc. v. Southold Dev. Corp.*, 959 F.2d 409 (2d Cir. 1992) (dispute involving fee tail estate created in 1734, prior to New York's 1782 abolition of fee tail estate).

Notes

1. *Dynastic Ambitions and Public Policy.* Many landowners still have a strong desire to keep their land within the family for future generations and have sought other mechanisms to accomplish that result (*e.g.*, creating a series of life estates in a dynasty trust). As a matter of policy, is it a good idea to permit landowners to tie up land this way or a bad idea? Why?

2. *Statutes Abolishing the Fee Tail Estate.* In the rare dispute involving a conveyance that would have created a common law fee tail estate, you must be able to determine what became of it when the statute abolishing the

---

12. The fee tail estate could be specially tailored, allowing the grantor to restrict the estate to a select group of lineal descendants. For example, O could limit the estate to "the male heirs of his body" (a *fee tail male*) or to "the female heirs of his body" (a *fee tail female*). It also was possible to create a *fee tail special*, which limited the estate to heirs produced with a particular spouse (*e.g.*, "to A and the heirs of his body by M").

fee tail estate took effect. Suppose that *O* conveyed Greenacre "to *A* and the heirs of her body." *A* recently died without ever having had a child and *A*'s will left all her property to her friend *C*. *O* is also deceased, survived by his son and sole heir, *D*. Who would hold title to Greenacre under the following statutes?

(a) "In cases where, by the common or statute law of England, any person might become seized in fee tail of any lands . . . such person, instead of being seized thereof in fee tail, shall be deemed and adjudged to be, and shall become, seized thereof for his natural life only; and the remainder shall pass in fee simple absolute to the person to whom the estate tail would, on the death of the first grantee, devisee, or donee in tail, first pass according to the course of the common law . . . ." Vernon's Ann. Mo. Stat. § 442.470.

(b) "Each estate, given in fee tail, shall be an absolute estate in fee simple to the issue of the first donee in tail." Conn. Gen. Stat. Ann. § 47–3.

(c) "Estates in fee tail are prohibited; and every estate which, but for this statute, would be an estate in fee tail, shall be an estate in fee simple; but any person may make a conveyance or a devise of lands to a succession of donees then living, and upon the death of the last of said successors to any person or heir." Miss. Code § 89–1–15.

4. *Defeasible Estates: Estates Determinable, Subject to Condition Subsequent, or Subject to Executory Limitation*

A landowner might wish to convey an estate in land in fee simple but make ownership of that estate subject to certain restrictions. Indeed, the landowner may feel so strongly about compliance with these restrictions that she would view forfeiture as the necessary remedy for breach of those restrictions. For example:

- *A grantor might wish to place a restriction upon the land for the benefit of her retained land.* If Bonnie Raitt owns a music store, and Bruce Hornsby approaches her seeking to buy her vacant lot next door, Bonnie might be willing to sell that lot only if she can be sure that nothing built on the lot will compete in any way with her existing music store.

- *A donor of land to charity may have strong feelings that the land be used for specified purposes.* Bill Gates may wish to give land to a university, but only if it is used for a law school.

- *A grantor may wish to control his or her descendants' behavior.* Michael Jordan might want to give land to his children, but only if none of them enroll as students at Duke University.

- *A grantor may wish to keep the land from falling into the hands of certain persons or groups.* Former Ku Klux Klansman David Duke might want to sell land to a developer, but only if the land could never be occupied by non-whites.

Because Bonnie, Bill, Michael, and David otherwise have no practical control over such future events, they might attempt to condition the continued existence of the estate upon compliance with stated restrictions. That way, they could recover the land if the restriction were violated—provided, however, that the restriction is permissible as a matter of public policy (which is not true of some of the restrictions listed above).[13]

The common law generally permitted grantors to create such *defeasible* estates, limiting an estate granted so that it would be *divested* (*i.e.*, terminated), either automatically or at the grantor's option, upon the occurrence of certain future events. Over time, the common law has recognized three forms of defeasible fee simple estates.[14]

The Fee Simple Determinable. The fee simple determinable is an estate in fee simple that terminates automatically once the stated restriction (often called a *special limitation*) is violated. The grantor's future interest, which is called a *possibility of reverter*, automatically becomes a present possessory estate upon breach of the special limitation, without further legal action by the grantor. To create a fee simple determinable estate, the grantor should use language that indicates that the estate will last only until the special limitation is violated. For example, *O* conveys land to the School Board *"for as long as* the land is used for school purposes," or *"until* the land is no longer used as a school," or *"while* the land is used as a school." In each of these examples, *O*'s language suggests a *durational* limit on the estate itself, indicating the grantor's intent that the estate will terminate automatically upon breach of the stated restriction. These words—"so long as," "as long as," "during," "while," "until," or other close synonyms—constitute words of limitation that courts traditionally interpreted to create a determinable estate.

The Fee Simple Subject to Condition Subsequent. Alternatively, a landowner can convey an estate on terms that give the grantor the *optional* right to terminate the estate and recover possession of the land upon violation of a condition. This estate is the fee simple subject to condition subsequent. The occurrence of the condition subsequent does not trigger an *automatic* defeasance; even after the condition is broken, the grantee's estate continues until the grantor exercises her right to terminate the grantee's estate. Until that point, the grantor retains a future interest called a *right of entry* or a *power of termination*, which becomes a present possessory estate only after the grantor exercises that right after the condition is violated. To create a fee simple subject to condition subsequent estate, the grantor should limit the fee simple using language that indicates that breach of the condition gives the

13. Racially restrictive defeasances were common at one time, but a court is unlikely to enforce such restrictions today. *Cf. Shelley v. Kraemer*, 334 U.S. 1, 68 S.Ct. 836, 92 L.Ed. 1161 (1948) (state court's enforcement of a racially restrictive covenant violated the Constitution's Equal Protection Clause). Similarly, as discussed in the notes following *Falls City v. Missouri Pacific*

Railroad Co. (page 286), a court might find that Jordan's attempt to control the personal decisions of his adult children is contrary to public policy.

14. Defeasible estates do not have to be *fee simple* estates; a grantor could create a defeasible life estate or a defeasible term of years. At this point, however, the materials focus upon defeasible fee simple estates.

grantor the right to terminate the estate. For example, *O* conveys land to the School Board "but if the premises are not used as a school, *O* may re-enter and recover the premises," or "provided that, if the premises are not used for school purposes, *O* may re-enter and terminate the estate."

The Fee Simple Subject to Executory Limitation. Prior to 1536, the fee simple determinable and fee simple subject to condition subsequent were the only permitted defeasible estates. A grantor could create a defeasible freehold estate *only if the grantor retained the divesting future interest*—either a possibility of reverter or a right of entry. The grantor could not limit a fee simple estate so that title would pass to a third party upon breach of the limitation. Since 1536, however, as a result of the Statute of Uses, the law has recognized divesting future interests in third parties, called *executory interests*.[15] Thus, a landowner can now create a third defeasible estate, the fee simple subject to executory limitation. To create this estate, the grantor uses language specifying either a special limitation (*e.g.*, "so long as") or a condition subsequent (*e.g.*, "provided that if"), coupled with language clearly indicating that breach of the limitation divests (or "shifts") title from the grantee to an identified third party. For example, *O* conveys land "to the School Board until it ceases using the land as a school, then to *B*," or "to the School Board, but if it ceases using the land as a school, then to *B*." Put very simply, the fee simple subject to executory limitation is virtually identical to the other two defeasible fee estates. The key distinction is that the future interest following the fee simple subject to executory limitation is held by a third party, while the future interest following the other two defeasible fees is held by the grantor.

Although the above rules appear straightforward at first blush, defeasible fee simple estates have generated substantial litigation that demonstrates both (a) the legal and practical pitfalls associated with creating defeasible estates, and (b) the policy implications of allowing persons to use title to land to control or affect either land use or future events, especially by means of forfeiture restrictions.

MAHRENHOLZ v. COUNTY BOARD OF SCHOOL TRUSTEES OF LAWRENCE COUNTY

Appellate Court of Illinois.
93 Ill.App.3d 366, 48 Ill.Dec. 736, 417 N.E.2d 138 (1981).

JONES, JUSTICE. . . . On March 18, 1941, W. E. and Jennie Hutton executed a warranty deed in which they conveyed certain land, to be known here as the Hutton School grounds, to the Trustees of School District No. 1, the predecessors of the defendants in this action. The deed provided that "this land to be used for school purpose only; otherwise to revert to Grantors herein." W. E. Hutton died intestate on

15. We return later in this chapter (page 297) to discuss executory interests in greater detail, as well as their historical origins and the impact that the Statute of Uses had upon the law of conveyancing.

son was only legal heir (handwritten)

July 18, 1951, and Jennie Hutton died intestate on February 18, 1969. The Huttons left as their only legal heir their son Harry E. Hutton.

The property conveyed by the Huttons became the site of the Hutton School. Community Unit School District No. 20 succeeded to the grantee of the deed and held classes in the building constructed upon the land until May 30, 1973. After that date, children were transported to classes held at other facilities operated by the District. The District has used the property since then for storage purposes only. . . .

[Editors' Note: The 1.5 acre school site was located in the middle of a 40–acre farm field. In July 1941, the Huttons conveyed the surrounding farm field to Earl and Madeline Jacqmain. The deed also purported to convey the Huttons' future interest in the Hutton School property. In October 1959, the Jacqmains conveyed these interests to the plaintiffs. On April 9, 1974 (almost one year after the school district stopped holding classes in the building), the plaintiffs filed a complaint in the circuit court to quiet title to the school property in themselves, by virtue of the interests acquired from the Jacqmains.

On May 7, 1977, while the Mahrenholz's action was pending, Harry E. Hutton conveyed to the plaintiffs all of his interest in the Hutton School land. This document was filed in the recorder's office of Lawrence County on September 7, 1977. On September 6, 1977, Harry Hutton purported to disclaim his interest in the school property in favor of the defendants. The document recited that it was made for the purpose of releasing and extinguishing any right Harry E. Hutton may have had in the "interest retained by W. E. Hutton and Jennie Hutton . . . in that deed to the Trustees of School District No. 1, Lawrence County, Illinois dated March 18, 1941, and filed on the same date . . . ." The disclaimer was filed in the recorder's office of Lawrence County on October 4, 1977.

On March 21, 1979, the trial court entered an order dismissing the plaintiffs' complaint, which had asserted title based upon interests received from the Jacqmains and Harry Hutton.]

procedural notes (handwritten)

The basic issue presented by this appeal is whether the trial court correctly concluded that the plaintiffs could not have acquired any interest in the school property from the Jacqmains or from Harry Hutton. Resolution of this issue must turn upon the legal interpretation of the language contained in the March 18, 1941, deed from W. E. and Jennie Hutton to the Trustees of School District No. 1: "this land to be used for school purpose only; otherwise to revert to Grantors herein." In addition to the legal effect of this language we must consider the alienability of the interest created and the effect of subsequent deeds.

language of the deed (handwritten)

The parties appear to be in agreement that the 1941 deed from the Huttons conveyed a defeasible fee simple estate to the grantee, and gave rise to a future interest in the grantors, . . . and that it did not convey a fee simple absolute, subject to a covenant. The fact that provision was made for forfeiture of the estate conveyed should the land cease to be used for school purposes suggests that this view is correct. *Dunne v.*

Minsor (1924), 312 Ill. 333, 143 N.E. 842; *Newton v. Village of Glen Ellyn* (1940), 374 Ill. 50, 27 N.E.2d 821.

The future interest remaining in this grantor or his estate can only be a possibility of reverter or a right of re-entry for condition broken. As neither interest may be transferred by will or by inter vivos conveyance, Ill.Rev.Stat., ch. 30, par. 37b, and as the land was being used for school purposes in 1959 when the Jacqmains transferred their interest in the school property to the plaintiffs, the trial court correctly ruled that the plaintiffs could not have acquired any interest in that property from the Jacqmains by the deed of October 9, 1959.

Consequently this court must determine whether the plaintiffs could have acquired an interest in the Hutton School grounds from Harry Hutton. The resolution of this issue depends on the construction of the language of the 1941 deed of the Huttons to the school district. As urged by the defendants and as the trial court found, that deed conveyed a fee simple subject to a condition subsequent followed by a right of re-entry for condition broken. As argued by the plaintiffs, on the other hand, the deed conveyed a fee simple determinable followed by a possibility of reverter. In either case, the grantor and his heirs retain an interest in the property which may become possessory if the condition is broken. We emphasize here that although [an Illinois statute] provides that rights of re-entry for condition broken and possibilities of reverter are neither alienable or devisable, they are inheritable. *Deverick v. Bline* (1950), 404 Ill. 302, 89 N.E.2d 43. The type of interest held governs the mode of reinvestment with title if reinvestment is to occur. If the grantor had a possibility of reverter, he or his heirs become the owner of the property by operation of law as soon as the condition is broken. If he has a right of re-entry for condition broken, he or his heirs become the owner of the property only after they act to re-take the property.

It is alleged, and we must accept, that classes were last held in the Hutton School in 1973. Harry Hutton, sole heir of the grantors, did not act to legally retake the premises but instead conveyed his interest in that land to the plaintiffs in 1977. If Harry Hutton had only a naked right of re-entry for condition broken, then he could not be the owner of that property until he had legally re-entered the land. Since he took no steps for a legal re-entry, he had only a right of re-entry in 1977, and that right cannot be conveyed inter vivos. On the other hand, if Harry Hutton had a possibility of reverter in the property, then he owned the school property as soon as it ceased to be used for school purposes. Therefore, assuming (1) that cessation of classes constitutes "abandonment of school purposes" on the land, (2) that the conveyance from Harry Hutton to the plaintiffs was legally correct, and (3) that the conveyance was not pre-empted by Hutton's disclaimer in favor of the school district, the plaintiffs could have acquired an interest in the Hutton School grounds if Harry Hutton had inherited a possibility of reverter from his parents.

The difference between a fee simple determinable (or, determinable fee) and a fee simple subject to a condition subsequent, is solely a matter of judicial interpretation of the words of a grant. *Pfeffer v. Lebanon Land Development Corp.* (5th Dist. 1977), 46 Ill.App.3d 186, 4 Ill.Dec. 740, 360 N.E.2d 1115. As Blackstone explained, there is a fundamental theoretical difference between a conditional estate, such as a fee simple subject to a condition subsequent, and a limited estate, such as a fee simple determinable.

A distinction is however made between a *condition in deed* and a *limitation,* which Littleton denominates also a *condition in law.* For when an estate is so expressly confined and limited by the words of its creation, that it cannot endure for any longer time than till the contingency happens upon which the estate is to fail, this is denominated in *limitation*: as when land is granted to a man, *so long as* he is parson of Dale, or *while* he continues unmarried, or *until* out of the rents and profits he shall have made 500£ and the like. In such case the estate determines as soon as the contingency happens (when he ceases to be parson, marries a wife, or has received the 500£) and the next subsequent estate, which depends upon such determination, becomes immediately vested, without any act to be done by him who is next in expectancy. But when an estate is, strictly speaking, upon *condition in deed* (as if granted expressly *upon condition* to be void upon the payment of 40£ by the grantor, or *so that* the grantee continues unmarried, or *provided* he goes to York, etc.), the law permits it to endure beyond the time when such contingency happens, unless the grantor or his heir or assigns take advantage of the breach of the condition, and make either an entry or a claim in order to avoid the estate. (Emphasis in original.) 2 W. Blackstone, Commentaries *155.

A fee simple determinable may be thought of as a limited grant, while a fee simple subject to a condition subsequent is an absolute grant to which a condition is appended. In other words, a grantor should give a fee simple determinable if he intends to give property for so long as it is needed for the purposes for which it is given and no longer, but he should employ a fee simple subject to a condition subsequent if he intends to compel compliance with a condition by penalty of a forfeiture. *School District No. 6 v. Russell* (1964), 156 Colo. 75, 396 P.2d 929.

Following Blackstone's examples, the Huttons would have created a fee simple determinable if they had allowed the school district to retain the property so long as or while it was used for school purposes, or until it ceased to be so used. Similarly, a fee simple subject to a condition subsequent would have arisen had the Huttons given the land upon condition that or provided that it be used for school purposes. In the 1941 deed, though the Huttons gave the land "to be used for school purpose only, otherwise to revert to Grantors herein," no words of temporal limitation, or terms of express condition, were used in the grant.

The plaintiffs argue that the word "only" should be construed as a limitation rather than a condition. The defendants respond that where ambiguous language is used in a deed, the courts of Illinois have expressed a constructional preference for a fee simple subject to a condition subsequent. *Storke v. Penn Mutual Life Ins. Co.* (1954), 390 Ill. 619, 61 N.E.2d 552. Both sides refer us to cases involving deeds which contain language analogous to the 1941 grant in this case.

We believe that a close analysis of the wording of the original grant shows that the grantors intended to create a fee simple determinable followed by a possibility of reverter. Here, the use of the word "only" immediately following the grant "for school purpose" demonstrates that the Huttons wanted to give the land to the school district only as long as it was needed and no longer. The language "this land to be used for school purpose only" is an example of a grant which contains a limitation within the granting clause. It suggests a limited grant, rather than a full grant subject to a condition, and thus, both theoretically and linguistically, gives rise to a fee simple determinable.

The second relevant clause furnishes plaintiffs' position with additional support. It cannot be argued that the phrase "otherwise to revert to grantors herein" is inconsistent with a fee simple subject to a condition subsequent. Nor does the word "revert" automatically create a possibility of reverter. But, in combination with the preceding phrase, the provisions by which possession is returned to the grantors seem to trigger a mandatory return rather than a permissive return because it is not stated that the grantor "may" re-enter the land. *See City of Urbana v. Solo Cup Co.* (4th Dist. 1979), 66 Ill.App.3d 45, 22 Ill.Dec. 786, 383 N.E.2d 262.

The terms used in the 1941 deed, although imprecise, were designed to allow the property to be used for a single purpose, namely, for "school purpose." The Huttons intended to have the land back if it were ever used otherwise. Upon a grant of exclusive use followed by an express provision for reverter when that use ceases, courts and commentators have agreed that a fee simple determinable, rather than a fee simple subject to a condition subsequent, is created. 1 Simes and Smith, The Law of Future Interests (2nd ed. 1956) § 286 n.58. Our own research has uncovered cases from other jurisdictions and sources in which language very similar to that in the Hutton deed has been held to create a fee simple determinable. . . .

Thus, authority from this state and others indicates that the grant in the Hutton deed did in fact create a fee simple determinable. We are not persuaded by the cases cited by the defendants for the terms of conveyance in those cases distinguish them from the facts presented here. . . .

We hold, therefore, that the 1941 deed from W. E. and Jennie Hutton to the Trustees of School District No. 1 created a fee simple determinable in the Trustees followed by a possibility of reverter in the Huttons and their heirs. Accordingly, the trial court erred in dismissing plaintiffs' third amended complaint which followed its holding that the plaintiffs could not have acquired any interest in the Hutton School property from Harry Hutton. We must therefore reverse and remand this cause to the trial court for further proceedings.

We refrain from deciding the following issues: (1) whether the 1977 conveyance from Harry Hutton was legally sufficient to pass his interest in the school property to the plaintiffs, (2) whether Harry Hutton effectively disclaimed his interest in the property in favor of the defendants by virtue of his 1977 disclaimer, and (3) whether the defendants have ceased to use the Hutton School grounds for "school purposes." ...

Notes

1. *Fee Simple Determinable or Fee Simple Subject to Condition Subsequent?* When a deed is ambiguous as to the type of defeasible estate intended by the grantor, courts generally have interpreted the deed to create a fee simple subject to condition subsequent rather than a fee simple determinable. Why have courts adopted this rule of construction? Is this rule of construction designed to carry out the grantor's likely intent?

The *Mahrenholz* court ultimately did not rely on that rule of construction, however. Instead, the court used several other rules of construction to conclude that the deed *unambiguously* created a fee simple determinable. Do you agree with this conclusion? Can you identify the three rules of construction that the court relied upon to distinguish between the two types of defeasible fees?

2. *Fee Simple Absolute or Defeasible Fee?* Suppose that O conveys Greenacre "to A and his heirs, assigns, and successors forever, *it being understood that this grant is made for school purposes only.*" If the deed contains no express reversionary clause, what type of estate does this language create? The Supreme Court of Kansas held that a conveyance with similar language created a fee simple absolute. *Roberts v. Rhodes,* 231 Kan. 74, 643 P.2d 116 (1982). To reach this decision, the court relied upon the modern default rule that a grant will be construed to convey the grantor's entire estate, unless the instrument indicates the grantor's intent to convey a lesser estate. Although the conveyance in *Roberts* was made "for school purposes only," the court found these words insufficient to indicate that a defeasible fee was intended, rather than a fee simple absolute:

> The general rule is well settled that the mere expression that property is to be used for a particular purpose will not in and of itself suffice to turn a fee simple into a determinable fee.... As pointed out in the Restatement, courts have in some cases recognized a special limitation on the interest conveyed which may cause the created interest to automatically expire upon the occurrence of a stated event. Words which are recognized as sufficient to express such automatic expiration include "until," "so long as," or "during," or those conveyances which contain a provision that "upon the happening of a stated event the land is to revert to the grantor." American Law Institute–Restatement of Property § 44, comment 1, p. 128. The conveyances in our present case

contained none of these words limiting the period or term for which the grant was made. [*Id.* at 118.]

Although *Roberts* is typical of decisions from other jurisdictions, a few contrary decisions do exist. *See, e.g., Forsgren v. Sollie,* 659 P.2d 1068 (Utah 1983) (deed that conveyed land "to be used as and for a church or residence purposes only" created a fee simple subject to condition subsequent).

Can you harmonize the *Roberts* decision with the *Mahrenholz* case? What language was present in the *Mahrenholz* deed (but missing in the *Roberts* deed) that would signal that a defeasible fee was intended in the *Mahrenholz* case?

3. *Transferability.* Similar to the fee simple absolute, defeasible fees are transferable, inheritable and devisable—subject to the express conditions attached to the fee. Thus, if *O* conveys "to *A* so long as the property is used for school purposes," *A* can freely transfer the possessory estate to *X*, but *X* must still adhere to the limitation that the property be used for school purposes or risk forfeiture to *O* for violation of the limitation.

In contrast, the *future interests* that follow a defeasible fee were not as freely transferable under the traditional common law. Until 1536, the common law dictated that only the grantor could hold a future interest following a defeasible fee. Accordingly, the courts held that the possibility of reverter and right of entry were not transferable or devisable; they were, however, inheritable by the grantor's heirs. As evident in *Mahrenholz,* Illinois continues to adhere to this traditional view. Most jurisdictions, however, have adopted the modern view that the possibility of reverter and right of entry are transferable, devisable and inheritable.

How did this transferability issue affect the outcome in *Mahrenholz*? Who would have owned the land if Illinois had followed the modern view? Do you understand why the 1959 deed from the Jacqmains to the plaintiffs was void under Illinois law, but the 1977 deed from Harry Hutton to the plaintiffs might have been valid?

4. *Waste and Defeasible Fees.* Earlier in this chapter, you were introduced to the doctrine of waste, which prohibits a possessory estate holder from engaging in conduct that would harm the value of the future interest. The doctrine of waste arises most frequently in the context of life estates and leaseholds because those estates are certain to end at some time in the future (*i.e.,* they are *finite* estates). If you have ever rented property, for example, you already know that tenants are prohibited from making physical changes to the leased premises that would harm the value of the landlord's reversionary interest.

The doctrine of waste also applies in the context of defeasible fees. Some accommodation must be made, however, for the fact that the fee simple defeasible estate could last indefinitely—or at least for many decades or centuries into the future. What factors should a court consider in determining whether to grant an injunction against the holder of a fee simple defeasible? Assume, for example, that the school district in the *Mahrenholz* case was still using the property for classes but also wanted to remove minerals from the land. Could Harry Hutton (or the Mahrenholzes) get an injunction to prevent the mining? Could they get damages for removal of the minerals? *See* Lewis M. Simes & Allan F. Smith, The Law of Future Interests §§ 1664–65 (1956 & Supp. 2004).

5. *Violation of the Limitation.* One of the issues the court did not decide in the *Mahrenholz* case, leaving it for the trial court upon remand, was whether the school district had ceased to use the Hutton School grounds for "school purposes." What arguments would you make on remand if you represented the Mahrenholzes? What arguments would you make if you represented the school district? *See Mahrenholz v. County Bd. of Sch. Trustees (Mahrenholz II)*, 125 Ill.App.3d 619, 80 Ill.Dec. 870, 466 N.E.2d 322 (1984) (addressing the trial court's determination of this issue on remand).

6. *Adverse Possession and Defeasible Fees.* Suppose that in the *Mahrenholz* case, neither Harry Hutton nor the Mahrenholzes had taken any action against the school district until 2005. If the school district began violating the restriction in 1973, would the doctrine of adverse possession bar a suit for recovery of possession of the land, thereby giving the school district a fee simple absolute?

In a purely doctrinal sense, the answer would depend upon whether the conveyance created a fee simple subject to condition subsequent or a fee simple determinable. Can you explain why? [Hint: when would the school district's possession become "hostile" if the school district had a fee simple determinable? When would the possession become "hostile" if the school district held a fee simple subject to condition subsequent?] Nevertheless, courts have not always maintained strict doctrinal purity in deciding such disputes. *Compare Sanford v. Sims*, 192 Va. 644, 66 S.E.2d 495 (1951) (adverse possession statute runs against right of entry from violation of condition subsequent) *with Metropolitan Park Dist. of Tacoma v. Unknown Heirs of Rigney*, 65 Wash.2d 788, 399 P.2d 516 (1965) (adverse possession does not run against unexercised right of entry, but right is lost if not exercised within reasonable time). Which interpretation is more plausible? What policies should govern the resolution of these issues? *See* Thomas Bergin and Paul Haskell, Preface to Estates in Land and Future Interests 61–62 (2d ed. 1984); Lewis Simes, Law of Future Interests 105–09 (2d ed. 1966).

7. *Statutory Limitations on Defeasances.* Several jurisdictions have enacted statutes that provide that a defeasance placed upon a fee simple estate can be enforced for only a specified period of time following its creation. *See* Conn. Gen. Stat. Ann. § 45–97 (thirty years); 765 Ill. Compiled Stat. § 330/4 (forty years). Florida's statute effectively converts a defeasance into a covenant after 21 years. Fla. Stat. Ann. § 689.18. [You will learn more about covenants in the next case.] What reasons justify placing such a limitation upon the grantor's ability to condition a conveyance? One hint: Suppose Henning, owner of Blueacre in fee simple absolute, conveys it "to Temple Beth–El so long as it is used only as a synagogue." Temple Beth–El uses the land as a synagogue for 90 years before deciding to build a new facility elsewhere. If the restriction is valid, what happens to the land at that point?

LAWYERING EXERCISE
(Legal Analysis and Legal Writing)

SITUATION: Oscar, owner of Blueacre in fee simple absolute, conveyed it in 1970 "to Arnold so long as the land is used for residential purposes only, provided that title shall revert if the land is ever used for non-residential purposes, and grantor may enter as of his former estate." In 1985, Arnold opened a business on Blueacre, conspicuously violating the restriction. Oscar was in a nursing home at the time and unaware that Arnold had opened the business.

Oscar died recently, survived by his only heir, Oprah. Oscar's will divided his property equally between Oprah and Oscar's longtime friend, Tony. Tony has asked your law firm to advise him of his rights with respect to Blueacre.

TASK: Your supervising attorney has asked you to analyze Tony's situation under the principles set forth in the *Mahrenholz* case and the notes thereafter. Draft a memorandum to the supervising attorney giving your objective analysis of Tony's claim. Please explain your analysis thoroughly—setting forth the applicable rules of law and the arguments that Tony and opposing parties are likely to make about how those rules apply to the facts of this case. Conclude with your best legal judgment about the strength of Tony's claim.

HUMPHREY v. C.G. JUNG EDUCATIONAL CENTER

United States Court of Appeals for the Fifth Circuit.
714 F.2d 477 (5th Cir.1983).

JOHN R. BROWN, CIRCUIT JUDGE. Very rarely does a Texas trespass to try a title suit disturb the collective consciousness of this court. As diversity jurisdiction sometimes manifests itself in unusual ways, however, we consider such a suit today. By interpreting past decisions, we must probe the psyche of the Texas courts to determine whether those courts would enforce the deed clause in question as a condition subsequent with right of re-entry, and so allow the plaintiffs to claim an undivided one-half interest in an improved lot in the museum district of Houston.[16] Finding the clause to be ambiguous, the district court in a bench trial held that the Texas courts would construe the clause as a mere covenant, and so deny the plaintiffs' claim. Accordingly, the court rendered judgment in favor of the defendants. We agree and affirm.

The Humphreys, appellants here, instituted this suit in September, 1976. The district court rendered summary judgment in favor of the defendants on the ground that the Humphreys' right to reenter the

---

16. Texas alone, among all the states which comprise the Fifth and Eleventh Circuits, does not allow its Supreme Court to answer questions of state law certified to it by the federal courts. In a reverse sort of way, this case illustrates once again the benefits of the certification procedure, which enables such purely state law questions to be answered with certainty and finality by the highest authority on the subject. *See Brown, Certification—Federalism in Action,* 7 Cumb. L. Rev. 455 (1977).

property was barred by the Texas three-year statute of limitations. Tex.Rev.Civ.Stat.Ann. art. 5507 (1958). This Court reversed and remanded the case for further proceedings. *Humphrey v. C.G. Jung Educational Center of Houston*, 624 F.2d 637 (5th Cir.1980).

The case was submitted to the district court for decision on stipulated facts which we briefly summarize. The disputed property is located in Lot F, in Block 8, of the Turner Addition to the City of Houston, on Montrose Boulevard. Block 8 is divided into six lots of approximately equal size, which were sold by the owners, the Trustees of the Hermann Hospital Estate, on March 20, 1919. Each deed contained various restrictions, which expired by their terms on January 1, 1935. Lot F was conveyed to Herbert Humphrey and Robert Caldwell. Herbert and Blanche Humphrey also purchased Lot D, while Robert and Edith Caldwell also purchased Lot A. On February 11, 1920, the Humphreys and Caldwells conveyed Lot F to Tom Randolph. That general warranty deed contains the following provisions:

> It is agreed by the vendee herein, as part of the consideration herein and as a covenant running with the land hereby conveyed, that the said land should be used for residence purposes only, and that no dwelling house shall ever be erected thereon, the original cost of which shall be less than $10,000.00 and that no portion of same, other than galleries and steps, shall be erected nearer than 28 feet to the property line on Montrose Blvd., nor nearer than 15 feet to the property line on 16th Street and that no outhouses shall be erected nearer than 35 feet to any street or avenue line, and no part of same shall ever be conveyed, transferred or demised to any person other than of the Caucasian race, and the vendee covenants that he will not use or permit to be used the property hereby conveyed for the purpose of erecting, establishing or conducting thereon any store or shop for the sale of merchandise or any other commodity, and should the owner of the land hereby conveyed at any time fail to comply with any of the provisions of this covenant, Grantors herein, or any owner of property in Block 8, Turner Addition, may by instituting suit, enforce a compliance therewith, or restrain the further violation thereof, or said land shall revert to the Grantors herein, should they so elect.

Resolution of this suit depends entirely upon the interpretation given to those provisions.

The Caldwells sold Lot A in 1941. The Humphreys sold Lot D in 1942. Neither deed placed any restrictions on the use of the property. None of the Humphreys have owned property in or resided in the Turner Addition since 1942. None of the restrictions set forth in the deed to Lot F were violated prior to August, 1972, when that property was conveyed to Jasper Galleries, Inc. Jasper Galleries demolished the existing residence and built an art gallery building on Lots F and E. The gallery grandly opened in May, 1973. In July, 1975, Jasper Galleries conveyed

Lots F and E to Carolyn Grant Fay.[17] No other lot in Block 8 is still being used for residential purposes. Lots A, B and C are the site of the contemporary Arts Museum, while Lot D is the site of the offices of an architectural firm.

The parties agree that Lot F is being used for nonresidential purposes, in violation of the restrictions contained in the 1920 deed. They differ as to whether under Texas law the Humphreys can enforce those restrictions as conditions subsequent and so reenter the property.

Fay and her tenants argued below that the Texas courts would construe the residential-use-only restriction as a covenant, the remedies for a breach of which would be limited to injunctive relief and damages, rather than as a condition subsequent, the breach of which would allow the plaintiffs to reclaim title to the property. Even if the restrictions were construed as a condition subsequent, they contended that the Texas courts would apply either the doctrine of enhancement of value or the doctrine of change of conditions to bar the enforcement of the condition.

The district court first considered the possible application of the "enhancement of value" doctrine and concluded that the Texas courts would not apply it to this situation. The court analyzed four cases in which the doctrine had been applied to find conditions subsequent unenforceable, and found those cases to be distinguishable from this one. "In each of the four cases," wrote the court, "there was evidence before the trial court that the grantor's intent in imposing conditions on the deeded land was to increase the value of the land the grantor retained, and that the consideration for the conveyance was the increased value of the retained land." No such evidence appears in the present case.

The district court also rejected the argument that the Texas courts would refuse to enforce the condition subsequent because of the changed character of the neighborhood. The court pointed out that some jurisdictions permit a change of conditions to be asserted as a defense to an action at law and will on that basis refuse to give effect to a right of reentry or a possibility of reverter. See *Townsend v. Allen*, 114 Cal. App.2d 291, 250 P.2d 292 (1952); *Letteau v. Ellis*, 122 Cal.App. 584, 10 P.2d 496 (1932); *Cole v. The Colorado Springs Co.*, 152 Colo. 196, 381 P.2d 13 (1962). The district court also recognized that Texas has refused to enforce restrictive covenants in deeds because of changed circumstances. The court found, however, that the Texas courts had never applied the doctrine of changed circumstances to render a condition subsequent unenforceable, and correctly refused to extend the reach of Texas jurisprudence.

The district court concluded, however, that even when a deed contains express language of reverter or reentry, a Texas court may construe the deed restriction as a covenant. Such covenants are enforceable only by injunctive relief or damages, not by forfeiture of the estate.

17. The other appellees, the C.G. Jung Educational Center of Houston and Arch-way Galleries are lessees of Carolyn Grant Fay.

Relying on *W.F. White Land Co. v. Christenson*, 14 S.W.2d 369 (Tex.Civ. App 1928), the court held that the provisions in this deed were ambiguous in their meaning. Citing settled Texas rules of construction, which look with disfavor upon forfeitures, the court then concluded that the Texas courts would resolve that ambiguity in favor of the grantee, Fay, and construe the provisions as covenants. As the plaintiffs sought neither injunctive relief nor damages, they could recover nothing. The court held, moreover, that any recovery under the residential-use covenant would be precluded by the neighborhood's drastic change in character over the years. The court rendered judgment in favor of the defendants.

We consider only the single issue of whether the Texas courts would find these deed provisions to be ambiguous and so construe them as creating mere covenants rather than conditions subsequent enforceable by forfeiture of the estate. As did the district court, we must determine how Texas' courts would resolve this question. While the diagnosis is difficult, we are convinced that the district court's analysis was correct.

Forfeitures are not favored under the law. "If the terms of a contract are fairly susceptible of an interpretation which will prevent a forfeiture, they will be so construed." *Henshaw v. Texas Natural Resources Foundation*, 147 Tex. 436, 216 S.W.2d 566, 570 (1949). "The courts will not declare a forfeiture, unless they are compelled to do so, by language which will admit of but one construction, and that construction is such as compels a forfeiture." *Link v. Texas Pharmacal Co.*, 276 S.W.2d 903, 906 (Tex.Civ.App.—San Antonio 1955 no writ). . . .

The fundamental issue before us, then, is whether the Texas courts would find the language of the 1920 deed to be ambiguous as to whether it creates conditions subsequent with right of reentry or merely a number of covenants. If the courts would consider the language to be at all ambiguous, under Texas law we must decline to enforce the residential-use restriction as a condition subsequent and construe it as a covenant. If there is no ambiguity, however, the Humphreys may reenter and reclaim their share of the property.

We agree with the district court that the Texas courts would find the language in the deed to be ambiguous. . . . In *White Land Company*, the Court of Civil Appeals construed a deed which contained the following two provisions:

> [I]n case the said grantee, or his heirs, as executors, administrators or assigns shall ever violate any one of said conditions contained herein and made a part of the covenants of this deed, the said land and all improvements therein shall immediately revert to and become the property of the grantor herein and its successors or assigns, and it shall be lawful for said grantor and its successors or assigns to re-enter said premises as in its first and former estate. . . .

> [T]he conditions herein contained are intended to and shall run with the land, and . . . should the grantee, his heirs, executors, administrators or assigns, or any person claiming under him, violate

any of the foregoing covenants, then W.F. White Land Company, or its successors, or any owner of any lot conveyed herein, shall have the right to enjoin the doing of same, and in the event the violation has already taken place, . . . then such remedy shall extend to the removal of the improvements placed on said premises in violation of any covenant herein. [14 S.W.2d at 370.]

Although that deed contained express language of both reverter and reentry, the court concluded "that what purported to be conditions subsequent in the deed are merely building restrictions denoting covenants, for the violation of which injunctive relief was provided in the instrument." 14 S.W.2d at 371. The court held that the provision for alternative remedies short of forfeiture and the single reference to the restrictions as "covenants" created ambiguity sufficient to require the court to adopt that interpretation of the instrument.

Recently, in *Malloy v. Newman*, 649 S.W.2d 155, (Tex.App.—Austin 1983, no writ history), a different appellate court construed a deed which also contained language of both covenant and reverter. . . . Holding that the provision should be construed as a covenant, the [*Malloy*] court quoted the Texas Supreme Court's opinion in *Hearne v. Bradshaw*, 158 Tex. 453, 312 S.W.2d 948, 951 (Tex.1958):

> Conditions subsequent are not favored by the courts, and the promise or obligation of the grantee will be construed as a covenant unless an intention to create a conditional estate is clearly and unequivocally revealed by the language of the instrument. In cases where the intention is doubtful, the stipulation is treated as a covenant rather than a condition subsequent with the right to defeat the conveyance. [649 S.W.2d at 159.]

. . . In making their decisions, the courts in both *White Land Company* and *Malloy* relied at least in part on the fact that the restrictions in question were expressly referred to in the deed as "covenants." To both courts, the use of that term rendered the deed less than unequivocal in its meaning. Here, the restrictions are consistently described as a "covenant," and never as a condition. As the district court pointed out, the deed contains neither the customary language of a conditional limitation nor that of a condition subsequent. The use of the language of reversion at the end of the provisions does not dispel the ambiguity inherent in the language of the deed. . . .

The Humphreys argue that the Texas Supreme Court would not follow *White Land Company*. As they point out, the case has been criticized by one commentator. Goldstein, *Rights of Entry and Possibilities of Reverter as Devices to Restrict the Use of Land*, 54 Harv.L.Rev. 248, 260–62 (1940). We have seen no indication, however, that the Texas Supreme Court would disapprove of or decline to follow either *White Land Company* or *Malloy*. Absent a clear signal to that effect, we are bound to follow these decisions of the highest Texas courts which have expressed themselves on this issue.

Once we have determined that the Texas courts would find these deed provisions to be ambiguous, the case is decided. Under Texas law, such ambiguity must be resolved in favor of the grantee, and the provisions construed as mere restrictive covenants enforceable via injunctive relief or suit for damages. The plaintiffs thus cannot regain the estate via forfeiture. As the plaintiffs have asked for neither an injunction nor damages they are entitled to no relief. Moreover, as the district court found, the plaintiffs would in any event be precluded from enforcing the covenants because of the drastically changed character of the neighborhood in which the disputed property is located.

The district court correctly entered judgment for the defendants.

Notes

1. *The Covenant as an Alternative Method of Restraining Land Use.* In the *Mahrenholz* case and the notes thereafter, we saw that a grantor's attempt to restrict use of the land might be interpreted in one of two ways: (1) the grantor had created a defeasible fee and retained a divesting future interest in the land (*i.e.*, a possibility of reverter or right of entry), or (2) the grantor had created a fee simple absolute and retained no interest in the land at all (*i.e.*, the grantor merely expressed a wish, which the grantee could freely disregard).

In *Humphrey*, the court offers a third possibility—treating the use restriction as a *covenant* rather than a defeasance restriction. As *Humphrey* explains, a covenant legally restricts the owner from engaging in certain defined uses of the land, but violation of the restriction does not result in forfeiture of title; instead, a violation subjects the owner to an action for damages caused by the violation or an injunction to force the owner's future compliance with the restriction.[18] What does *Humphrey* suggest about how courts decide whether to interpret a particular limitation or restriction as a condition or a covenant? Is the *Humphrey* court *really* attempting to carry out the likely intent of the original grantor? Why or why not?

2. *Defeasances, Covenants, and the Problem of Changed Circumstances.* As the court's opinion in *Humphrey* illustrates, a court may block enforcement of a covenant when circumstances have so changed since creation of the restriction as to frustrate its purpose. For example, a court might refuse to enforce a covenant restricting the land to residential use when subsequent development leaves that land surrounded by heavy industrial businesses that render it unsuitable for use as a residence. In contrast, as the *Humphrey*

---

18. Defeasances originated early in the feudal period, and the law of defeasances has not experienced major doctrinal changes over the centuries. In contrast, the law governing covenants dates back to the 16th Century, and has experienced major doctrinal changes from the Industrial Revolution to the present. As a result, the law of defeasances and the law of covenants are two notably distinct bodies of law. Because both the defeasance and the covenant are essentially means of regulating land use, some have suggested that the law should unify these two doctrines into one coherent body of law. Gerald Korngold, *For Unifying Servitudes and Defeasible Fees: Property Law's Functional Equivalents*, 66 Tex. L. Rev. 533 (1988). As we will see in Chapter 8, however, common law courts have resisted any such effort, and the new Restatement of Property—Third (Servitudes) likewise continues to treat defeasances and covenants as distinct bodies of law.

case also illustrates, courts generally have declined to apply the changed circumstances doctrine to the law of defeasances. Is there any justification for this distinction? If there is to be a distinction, should it work in reverse—blocking forfeitures more readily in the face of changed circumstances? Why or why not?

3. *Finding Breach of a Land Use Restriction.* The language of the condition itself often will prove critical in resolving the question whether the condition has been breached. Consider the following examples:

(a) In 1934, Cattle Company conveyed nearly 800 acres to the State of Kansas, subject to the conditions that the State use the land "as a public forestry, fish and game preserve and recreational state park" and that the State construct a lake of "at least 150 acres" on the land. The deed provided for an express reverter if these conditions were not satisfied. The State did establish a park and dammed an existing stream to create a lake. The dam was sufficient to create a lake in excess of 300 acres, but due to rainfall and water levels, the lake has not covered 150 acres for many years. As attorney for the State, how would you argue that the State has not breached the restrictions? As attorney for Cattle Company, how would you argue that the State has breached the restrictions? *See Kinney v. Kansas*, 238 Kan. 375, 710 P.2d 1290 (1985).

(b) In 1911, McGuiness conveyed land to Chicory Co., subject to the condition that the land was "to be used for the erection of a kiln for drying chicory roots, and if not used for said purpose, then the title to said land shall revert." Chicory Co. built a kiln and operated it until 1945, when fire accidentally destroyed the kiln. Neither Chicory Co. nor its successors rebuilt the kiln. As attorney for Chicory Co., how would you argue that the company has not breached the restrictions? As attorney for McGuiness, how would you argue that the company did breach the restrictions? *See Flajole v. Gallaher*, 354 Mich. 606, 93 N.W.2d 249 (1958).

LAWYERING EXERCISE
(Problem Solving)

BACKGROUND: One of the fundamental lawyering skills identified in the MacCrate Report is the skill of problem solving—being able to "develop and evaluate strategies for solving a problem or accomplishing an objective presented by a client or other entity that has employed the lawyer's services." MacCrate Report at 141. This skill does not just involve helping your client resolve disputes or problems once they have arisen. It also involves helping your client avoid disputes and conflicts; it involves what Professors Louis Brown and Edward Dauer have called "preventive law":

> The lawyer who is experienced in the practice of preventive law may regard his abilities as intuitive; he is capable of recognizing and resolving problems which have not yet occurred. He can foresee the future legal risks inherent in a course of action, and can guard against them either by taking preventive action now, or by devising

an alternative method for achieving the client's goal. To be successful at this creative task, however, the lawyer's intuitive abilities should rest upon some framework of analysis, even though it may not always be articulated.

Preventive analysis recognizes and takes advantage of the syllogistic structure of all legal reasoning. Its characteristics emerge most clearly when contrasted with nonpreventive legal reasoning.

Most of what is recognized as "law" can be stated in declarative propositions of a conditional form: *"If X, then Y."* For example: *If* the machinery is maintained negligently, *then* the operator will be liable for injuries resulting from the negligent care. . . . In each case *X* is some fact, and *Y* is some result. Nonpreventive legal reasoning, reduced to its bare essentials, takes the facts as given—facts which have already occurred—and subjects them to the operation of a rule of law to achieve a result. . . .

In preventive analysis, this syllogistic framework is also used, not to reach results, but to reach back to facts. That is, when dealing with a problem in preventive law, the lawyer may know the result he wishes to attain. By choosing the appropriate rule of law—the one which results in the desired outcome—the lawyer can then determine the facts which will have to exist if the desired result is to be attained. In preventive analysis, therefore, law is a constant; future results are altered by varying present and future facts.

The word "result," in this context, means the logical outcome of the application of a rule of law to a fact or set of facts; it is an abstraction. However, preventive law focuses on the client, to whom the results of these legal-logical reasonings are usually very unimportant, and who is much more concerned with achieving his goal or purpose. The process of defining this goal is more the business of the nonlegal counselor than the lawyer; however, the lawyer should remember that the client's goal is not always what it is represented to be. The lawyer who fails to ask *why* [the client] wants to achieve his stated purpose runs a substantial risk of solving a problem which has little to do with the client's real intent. [Louis M. Brown & Edward A. Dauer, Preventive Law—A Synopsis of Practice and Theory, The Lawyer's Handbook (ABA, Rev. ed. 1975), *reprinted in* Louis M. Brown & Edward A. Dauer, Planning by Lawyers 270–71 (1978).]

In what ways are the disputes in *Mahrenholz* and *Humphrey* examples of a lawyer's possible failure to appreciate and implement preventive legal reasoning?

SITUATION: Nelson enters your office and makes the following statement: "I own Blueacre, a five-acre parcel of land in Centerville. I want to give Blueacre to the new Holy Family Catholic Church, which has just formed but has not yet built a church building. But I want to make sure that if they stop using it as a church, the land will revert back to me or to my heirs."

TASK: In preparation for further discussion with Nelson, identify the potential ramifications of Nelson's proposed course of action (for Nelson, his heirs, and the Church). Focus both upon the legal issues and "nonlegal consequences":

> Nonlegal consequences ... consist of the likely economic, social, psychological, political, and moral ramifications that may flow from adopting a particular solution. And just as [lawyers] generally have the better data base for predicting legal consequences, a client often has the better data base for predicting nonlegal ones. Clients often know better than you the likely economic effects on their companies when employees have to take time away from their regular duties to participate in discovery and prepare for trial; the likely social effects of suing a defendant that has a high-profile, exemplary reputation in the community; and the likely psychological effects of accepting settlement offers after having previously stated to friends that they would go "all the way to trial." Therefore, [lawyers] often rely on clients to predict nonlegal consequences.

> At the same time, [the lawyer's] own experiences may enable [her] to predict (or at least inquire about) nonlegal consequences. For example, when it comes to recognizing how the business operation of a merchant whose rent is tied to the Consumer Price Index might be affected by fluctuations in the Index, or psychological consequences such as the potential degree of stress that a long trial can create, [the lawyer] may contribute valuable insights to a client's thinking about nonlegal consequences. [David A. Binder, Paul Bergman, & Susan C. Price, Lawyers as Counselors 295 (West 1991).]

To what extent would (or should) you raise any of these nonlegal consequences in advising Nelson?

Defeasances as an Impediment to Alienability. In discussing *White v. Brown*, we saw that although life estates are legally transferable, there is a substantial practical impediment to their alienability. If *X* owns a life estate measured by her life, *X* could die tomorrow, terminating the estate. Potential buyers thus may be unwilling to purchase *X*'s interest (or will substantially discount the price they are willing to pay, to take into account the risk of *X*'s premature death). As a practical matter, this places a substantial limitation on the alienability of *X*'s interest. A similar concern arises when one holds a defeasible fee simple estate. Should divesting restrictions nevertheless be freely enforced, or should the law strike down such restrictions as unreasonable restraints on alienation?

FALLS CITY v. MISSOURI PACIFIC RAILROAD CO.

United States Court of Appeals for the Eighth Circuit.
453 F.2d 771 (1971).

Procedural Notes

ELMO B. HUNTER, DISTRICT JUDGE. This is an appeal from an order of the district court granting summary judgment in favor of the appellee, Missouri Pacific Railroad Company (Railroad), and against the appellant, the City of Falls City, Nebraska (City), thereby quieting title to a certain 33–acre tract of land, which is located outside the City, in the appellee. . . .

[T]he City conveyed, by deed, the land in question to the appellee's predecessor, the Missouri Pacific Railway Company. That deed provided, in part, the following:

Provision of (1) Deed

> title to the . . . land shall remain in the said Railway Co. its successors and assigns as provided in . . . Exhibit "A", as long as the same shall be used for the purposes enumerated therein, and that in case it should be abandoned for such uses according to the terms of said Exhibit "A", then and in that event the title to said land . . . shall revert to the City of Falls City, the donor of said land under the terms aforesaid.

The document referred to in the deed, termed Exhibit "A," was an agreement which had been made earlier between certain citizens of the City and officials of the Railroad. That agreement provided that the Railroad was to construct certain buildings on the land and make certain other improvements to the land. In addition to a recital of the consideration for the agreement and the terms of an escrow arrangement, the agreement further provided that:

Provision (2)

> The intention of this agreement is that the citizens of Falls City agree to furnish to said railway company the ground for a site for said [divisional terminal railway] yards and buildings in consideration of the location of its division headquarters at said point.
>
> It is understood and agreed that the title to said land shall rest in said railway company as long as said ground shall be used for such purposes and in case it is not so used that the title thereto shall revert and rest in the grantors thereof.

It is undisputed between the parties that, following the conveyance, the Railroad constructed the buildings mentioned in the agreement, made the other required improvements, and located its divisional headquarters in Falls City, Nebraska. The divisional headquarters remained in Falls City until at least 1962.

In the district court and on this appeal, the City contends that in 1963 the Railroad moved its divisional headquarters from Falls City, thereby violating the conditions of the deed and causing title to the land to revert to the City. The Railroad conversely urges that the conditions of the conveyance were not breached when its divisional headquarters were relocated in Atchison, Kansas.

The district court, in granting summary judgment, found that, in light of recent Nebraska case law, it was immaterial whether the conditions of the deed had been breached by the Railroad because the reverter clause itself was void and unenforceable.

Under Nebraska law, the conveyance in dispute can be properly characterized as a fee simple determinable with the possibility of reverter in that it creates a fee simple estate and provides that the estate shall automatically expire upon the occurrence of a stated event. *Hiddleston v. Nebraska Jewish Education Society*, 186 Neb. 786, 186 N.W.2d 904, 905 (1971). See also: Restatement, Property § 44 (1936). And, in Nebraska, a reverter clause in a conveyance establishing a defeasible fee simple is enforceable if it is not otherwise invalid as an unreasonable restraint on alienation. *Cast v. National Bank of Commerce, Trust and Savings Association of Lincoln*, 186 Neb. 385, 183 N.W.2d 485, 489 (1971). Thus, although the parties raise numerous contentions involving related collateral matters, the primary question on this appeal, which was resolved adversely to appellant by the district court, is whether, as a matter of Nebraska law, the condition subsequent contained in this particular conveyance is valid and enforceable or invalid and unenforceable as a restraint on alienation.

We find that the recent decision of the Nebraska Supreme Court in *Cast v. National Bank of Commerce, Trust and Savings Association of Lincoln*, 186 Neb. 385, 183 N.W.2d 485 (Neb.1971), is controlling. In *Cast*, the court held, upon rehearing, that a condition attached to a defeasible fee simple is an indirect restraint against alienation "if it materially affects marketability adversely." The court went further to state that a restraint on alienation was void regardless of whether it was direct or indirect:

> A majority of this court, including the writer, has come to the conclusion that the law is the same on direct and indirect restraints on alienation. The authorities are not in accord on the question. While much has been written on the subject, we adopt the following as a proper statement of the law: "As used in this treatise, the expression 'restraint on alienation' refers not merely to the restriction of the legal power of alienation, but also to the restriction of alienability as a practical matter. Any provision in a deed, will, contract, or other legal instrument which, if valid, would tend to impair the marketability of property, is a restraint on alienation. In brief, the law is concerned primarily with practical alienation, not with a theoretical power of alienation." (citations omitted). [183 N.W.2d at page 490.]

Further, in reading the earlier *Cast* decision, including the dissenting opinion, against the majority opinion in the final *Cast* decision, there appears a distinction between those conditions which limit how the property is to be used as opposed to a limitation upon the persons to whom the property may be alienated. If the condition subsequent in the conveyance expressly limits alienation of the property to an impermissibly small number of persons, it is void and unenforceable. Conversely, most use restrictions are valid and enforceable unless they also have the practical effect of "affecting marketability adversely" by unreasonably limiting the class of persons to whom it may be alienated. In that event, under the rationale of *Cast*, such use restrictions are "indirect restraints on alienation" which also are unenforceable.

Holding & Reasoning

Applying the principles enunciated in *Cast* to the conditional limitation presently in issue, it is clear that the reverter clause is unenforceable as an indirect restraint upon alienation. In limiting the use of the property by the Railroad to use as its divisional headquarters only, the City, in practical effect, completely restricted alienation of the land to other grantees. Thus, even though the conditional restriction is couched in terms of the use of the property, like the conditional limitation in *Cast*, it unreasonably affects the marketability of the land adversely by completely restricting alienation. It is therefore void and unenforceable and, under Nebraska law, the Railroad holds an indefeasible estate in fee simple.

Accordingly, the judgment of the District Court granting a summary judgment in favor of the Railroad and against the City is affirmed.

Notes

1. *Use Restrictions and Indirect Restraints on Alienation.* As the court notes in *Falls City,* a land use restriction often effectively operates as a restraint on alienation. Thus, use restrictions are often called *indirect restraints on alienation.* According to the court in *Falls City*, are indirect restraints on alienation necessarily invalid? Under the court's logic, when would a use restraint be enforceable? From your own experience, either as a tenant or homeowner, can you think of a typical, modern-day example of an enforceable use restriction—*i.e.*, one that constitutes a *reasonable* indirect restraint on alienation?

2. *Enforceable Defeasance or Invalid Restraint on Alienation?* The decision in *Falls City* reflects that court's significant distaste for enforcing a defeasance limitation. In contrast, consider the following decisions that enforced restrictions seemingly comparable in scope:

(a) *Johnston v. City of Los Angeles*, 176 Cal. 479, 168 P. 1047 (1917). The grantor conveyed land to the City of Los Angeles on the express condition that the city would use it to erect and maintain a dam, and that the land would revert to the grantor if the city ceased to use it for such purposes. The California Supreme Court held that the condition created a defeasible fee simple estate.

(b) *Dunne v. Minsor*, 312 Ill. 333, 143 N.E. 842 (1924). The Quirks conveyed land to the Bishop of Peoria to be used for the Church of the Visitation in Kewanee, Illinois, as a residence for the local priest, "upon the further condition that the resident priest or the officers of said church shall at all times see that the graves of myself and my said sister, Mary Quirk, and my brother, Peter Quirk, in the Catholic cemetery in Kewanee, Illinois, are cared for and kept in order." The Supreme Court of Illinois held that the conveyance created a fee simple subject to condition subsequent estate—and specifically rejected the Bishop's argument that the restriction was a covenant that entitled the Quirk family to seek only damages or an injunction in case of a violation.

(c) *Merchants Bank & Trust Co. v. New Canaan Historical Soc'y*, 133 Conn. 706, 54 A.2d 696 (1947). A decedent's will devised land to the New Canaan Library Association "upon the condition and provided, however, that if said property shall not be used by said Library Association for the purposes of its organization, this devise shall terminate and the property become a part of my residuary estate." The Supreme Court of Errors of Connecticut held that the will created a fee simple determinable.

What factors do these cases have in common that motivated these courts to tolerate these defeasances, despite their effect on the alienability of the land? Are these factors present in *Falls City*?

Now consider the following examples:

(d) Fred Flintstone conveys land to Bedrock Lodge No. 1, Loyal Order of Water Buffalo, so that Fred, his lodge buddies, and future Water Buffaloes will have a place to socialize in the evenings and plan their occasional public service projects. Fred's deed restricts the land in the following way: "The land may be used only by Bedrock Lodge No. 1, Loyal Order of Water Buffalo, for lodge purposes, and if it ceases to be used in that manner, the land will revert to Fred Flintstone." Is this a valid defeasance provision or an invalid restraint on alienation? *See Mountain Brow Lodge No. 82, Indep. Order of Odd Fellows v. Toscano*, 257 Cal.App.2d 22, 64 Cal.Rptr. 816 (1968).

(e) David gives a parcel of land to his daughter Serena upon her graduation from college, by a deed that provides "to Serena in fee simple, but if Serena should get married, title shall revert to the grantor." Is this a valid defeasance provision or an invalid restraint on alienation? Is David's motive relevant to whether this gift is enforceable? What if the deed instead provided for defeasance only if Serena married someone of the Catholic faith? *See Hall v. Eaton*, 259 Ill.App.3d 319, 197 Ill.Dec. 583, 631 N.E.2d 805 (1994).

3. *The Use of Precedent in* Falls City. In *Falls City*, the court concluded that its holding was a logical extension of the Nebraska Supreme Court's holding in *Cast v. National Bank of Commerce*, 186 Neb. 385, 183 N.W.2d 485 (1971). *Cast* involved the will of William J. Webermeier, who devised his farm to his nephew, Richard Cast, subject to two conditions: (1) that Cast or one of his children move onto and occupy the farm within one year after Webermeier's death, and thereafter occupy the farm as a residence for at least 25 years; (2) that whoever occupies the farm shall, within one year, take legal action to add "Webermeier" to their name. The *Cast* court held, in a 4–3 decision, that the conditions constituted a void restraint on alienation. Does the opinion in *Cast* control the decision in *Falls City* (as Judge Hunter suggests), or can you persuasively distinguish that case? Are there good reasons for the law to be concerned about William Webermeier's intentions—reasons that would not apply in cases like the ones in note 2(a)–2(c)?

LAWYERING EXERCISE
(Counseling—The Proper Scope and/or
Limits of Legal Advice)

BACKGROUND: In your role as a lawyer, is it appropriate to limit your advice solely to legal issues, or can and should you express moral judgment about a client's proposed course of action? Consider the following view:

> Client centeredness assumes that clients are capable of making intelligent and morally acceptable choices. However, these assumptions are less than universally correct. Therefore, when a client makes a decision which you believe is wrong, can you, without violating notions of client centeredness, present your contrary view?
> . . .

> . . . [W]hen a client makes a decision based on value preferences which conflict with yours, you cannot ground your disagreement in a client's illogical thinking. Disagreement asserts, if only implicitly, that your values are more important than a client's. And unless a client's decision violates the law or is clearly immoral, principles of client autonomy suggest that client values prevail.

> Nonetheless, even though a client's decision may be legally valid and not clearly immoral, client centeredness sometimes allows you to express values that conflict with a client's. You do not completely surrender your autonomy by becoming a lawyer. Some clients may even appreciate and benefit from knowing about competing values. However, client centeredness does impact both how often and the way in which you ought to phrase your value preferences.

> With respect to the way in which you voice your views, client autonomy demands that you take care not to state your values so forcefully that you override clients' capacities to make their own decisions. Moreover, as a tactical matter, you must exercise discretion when stating value preferences if you hope to influence a client's decision. . . . [S]ince a client whose values differ from yours is not "wrong," you must often use language that recognizes rather than denigrates a client's values. Only if you recognize the legitimacy of a client's values is a client likely to "hear" you. . . .

> Do you voice personal values whenever clients make decisions which concern you morally? A "yes" response is likely to turn you into something of a "moral know-it-all," regularly converting client dialogues into morality plays. Undoubtedly, few clients want attorneys to conduct regular moral check-ups. Hence, while we have no line by which to measure how frequently you voice moral concerns, we do believe that you should do so sparingly. Moreover, if you do raise moral concerns and a client rejects them, your choice . . . is to accede to the client, to ask a client voluntarily to seek other counsel,

or to withdraw. [David A. Binder, Paul Bergman & Susan C. Price, Lawyers as Counselors 281–84 (West 1990).]

SITUATION: You have a solo law practice in Anytown. Five years ago, you drafted a will for John Davis, and you have done legal work for him on one other occasion. Davis comes to your office and, with a great deal of anger, expresses his displeasure at having just discovered that his grandson Seth is gay. Finally, he hands you his will and says:

> I want you to rewrite this. As it is, it leaves my farm to my son Dan (who is Seth's father). I want you to rewrite the will so that the farm goes to Dan, but that if he ever attempts to give any interest in it to Seth, or even allows Seth to be a guest on the land, the land will be forfeited and will go instead to my daughter Nora.

TASK: Identify how you would respond to John's request. If you think his desire to change his will is motivated by feelings that you consider immoral, would you voice this concern? If so, how? Suppose that you have no moral problems with John's request, but you know that a significant number of people would consider his actions to be immoral. Would you discuss this with John? Can you identify a possible strategy that might permit you to avoid discussing this difficult moral issue (and, if so, should you use that strategy in lieu of having a discussion about the morality of John's proposed action)?

C. FUTURE INTERESTS

A future interest, as you have already learned, is the right to possession of property in the future. With future interests, as with possessory estates, you should focus your attention on several recurring themes: How is the interest created? Is the interest transferable by its holder? What is its duration?

The law recognizes five types of future interests: the possibility of reverter, right of entry, reversion, remainder, and executory interest. You should recognize these interests from the discussion in the previous section about the possessory estates that precede each future interest. In fact, the ability to correctly identify the possessory estate is the first step toward identifying the corresponding future interest. As you proceed through these materials, you might find it helpful to refer back periodically to the chart on page 242 to remind yourself of the future interest linked to each specific possessory estate.

[handwritten margin note: 5 types of future interests]

[handwritten margin note: chart 242]

Keep in mind that each future interest will (or may) take possession at some time in the future. Accordingly, it is important to know what possessory estate the future interest will become, *i.e.,* what is the duration of the estate once it becomes possessory? Assume, for example, that *O* conveys Blackacre "to *A* for life, then to *B* and his heirs." When *A*'s life estate ends, *B*'s future interest becomes a present possessory estate. We can tell from the words of limitation that *O* used to describe *B*'s interest—*"and his heirs"*—that *O* intended for *B* ultimately to have a fee simple absolute. While *A* is still alive, however, we say that *B* has a *remainder in fee simple absolute.*

When *A* is alive:

A = Life Estate	B = Vested Remainder in Fee Simple Absolute

When *A* dies: *A*'s interest expires and *B*'s interest becomes a present possessory estate:

B = Fee Simple Absolute

1. *Future Interests Retained by the Grantor*

Earlier in this chapter, you briefly encountered each of the possible future interests that a grantor can retain. The following is a recap of those interests and their distinctive features.

a. *Reversion.* A *reversion* is the estate that the grantor retains when she (a) conveys a vested estate of a lesser quantum than she has and (b) does not conclusively dispose of her right to take possession of the property at the end of that vested estate. A reversion is a vested interest of the grantor. Accordingly, it is fully alienable, devisable and inheritable.

> *Example 1. O*, who owns Blueacre in fee simple absolute, conveys it "to *A* for life." *A* receives a life estate (an estate of lesser duration than a fee simple absolute). Because *O* has not specified anyone else to take Blueacre at *A*'s death, *O* retains a reversion. [Because *O* will own the land in fee simple absolute when it reverts to him, the full classification of *O*'s interest is a reversion in fee simple absolute.]

The term "quantum," as used in the above definition, refers to the common law hierarchy of estates. The common law organized the system of present estates into a hierarchy based upon the potential duration of those estates. Thus, the fee simple estate (which potentially lasts forever) is of greater quantum than the fee tail estate (which potentially lasts until the grantee's descendants are all dead), which in turn is of greater quantum than the life estate (which will end upon the death of the measuring life).

b. *Possibility of Reverter.* A *possibility of reverter* is the future interest that arises when the grantor (a) conveys a determinable estate (one that ends automatically upon breach of a *special limitation*) of the same quantum as the one she possessed and (b) either specifies that the estate automatically shall revert to her upon breach of the special limitation, or does not specify any third person to take the property upon breach of that limitation.

> *Example 2. O*, who owns Blueacre in fee simple absolute, conveys it "to *A* until the Cubs win the World Series." *A* receives a fee simple determinable estate, an estate of the same quantum as *O* possessed.

Because *O* has not designated any other person to take the estate in the unlikely event the Cubs win the World Series, *O* retains a possibility of reverter in fee simple absolute.

c. *Right of Entry.* A *right of entry* is the future interest that arises when a grantor conveys an estate subject to a condition subsequent and retains for herself a power to take action to terminate the estate if the condition is breached.

Example 3. *O*, who owns Blueacre in fee simple absolute, conveys it "to *A*, provided that, if the Cubs win the World Series, grantor may re-enter the premises and recover the estate." *A* has a fee simple subject to condition subsequent estate. Because *O* has retained the right to take action to recover Blueacre if the Cubs should win the World Series, *O* retains a right of entry in fee simple absolute.

You will recall from *Mahrenholz* that under the traditional common law (still followed in a minority of states), the possibility of reverter and right of entry were inheritable by the grantor's heirs but were not alienable or devisable. Under the modern view, both of these future interests are fully alienable, devisable and inheritable.

2. *Future Interests Created in a Grantee*

a. *Remainder.* A *remainder* is a future interest that is created *in a person other than the grantor* in a conveyance in which the grantor also creates a present possessory estate less than a fee simple—*i.e.*, a life estate, fee tail, or a term of years (leasehold). A remainder follows the *natural* termination of one of these estates; it does not divest another interest.

Example 4. *O*, owner of Blueacre in fee simple absolute, conveys it "to *A* for life, then to *B*." *O* has created a life estate in *A* and a remainder in fee simple absolute in *B* (when *A* dies, *B* is entitled to possession in fee simple absolute).

Example 5. *O*, owner of Blueacre in fee simple absolute, conveys it "to *A* for life." In this example, *O* has created a life estate in *A*, but retains the reversion in fee simple absolute. One year later, *O* conveys "all my right, title, and interest in Blueacre" to *B*. *B* now holds the reversion in fee simple absolute. The conveyance from *O* to *B* does not convert the future interest from a reversion into a remainder.

A remainder can be either *vested or contingent*. A **vested remainder** is one that satisfies two criteria: (1) it must be created in a person who is born and can be *ascertained* (*i.e.*, is in existence and capable of being identified by name) at the time of the conveyance; and (2) it must not be subject to any condition precedent (other than the natural conclusion of the preceding possessory estate). Conversely, a **contingent remainder** is one that is either (1) created in a person who is not yet born or is incapable of being ascertained at the time of the conveyance, or (2) subject to a condition precedent (other than the termination of the preceding estate).

> *Example 6. O*, owner of Blueacre in fee simple absolute, conveys it "to *A* for life, then to *B*." At the time of the conveyance, *B* is an ascertained person and *O*'s conveyance to *B* is not subject to any condition precedent. Thus, *B* has a vested remainder in fee simple absolute.

> *Example 7. O*, owner of Blueacre in fee simple absolute, conveys it "to *A* for life, then when *A* dies, to *B*." *B* has a vested remainder in fee simple absolute. Although the conveyance directs that *B* takes "when *A* dies," this clause is not considered a condition precedent; it merely emphasizes that *B* can take possession upon the natural expiration of the preceding estate.

> *Example 8. O*, who owns Blueacre in fee simple absolute, conveys it "to *A* for life, then, if *B* becomes a judge, to *B*." *B* has a contingent remainder in fee simple absolute. Although *B* is capable of being ascertained at the time of the conveyance, her interest is subject to the condition precedent that she must become a judge.

> *Example 9. O*, who owns Blueacre in fee simple absolute, conveys it "to *A* for life, then to his oldest child then alive." This conveyance creates a contingent remainder in fee simple absolute in *A*'s oldest child alive at *A*'s death. The interest is contingent because the exact recipient cannot be ascertained until *A* dies.

There are three types of vested remainders—the indefeasibly vested remainder, the vested remainder subject to open, and the vested remainder subject to divestment.

(1) ***Indefeasibly vested remainder.*** The indefeasibly vested remainder is one that is not subject to any condition precedent (which would cause the interest not to vest) or any condition subsequent (that would cause the interest to be divested after it had previously vested). In Examples 6 and 7 above, for example, *B* has an indefeasibly vested remainder because *B*'s interest is not subject to any condition at all.

(2) ***Vested remainder subject to open.*** This remainder is one that is conveyed to a group or class of persons and *at least one member of the class is born, ascertained, and not subject to any condition precedent.* The class member who has satisfied these criteria is considered to hold a vested interest, but might have to share his or her interest with other class members who subsequently meet the criteria.[19]

> *Example 10. O*, who owns Blueacre in fee simple absolute, conveys it "to *A* for life, then to *A*'s children." At the time of the conveyance, *A* is alive and has one child, Able. Able has a vested remainder in fee simple absolute (he is born, ascertained and there is no condition

---

19. Because the vested remainderman may end up sharing the interest with other class members, some textbooks and treatises refer to this future interest as a "vested remainder subject to partial divestment."

precedent). But *A* may have additional children; thus, Able's interest is "subject to open" because the class of "children" is still open. You will learn more about class gifts later in this chapter (page 310).

3 *Vested remainder subject to divestment.* A remainder is subject to divestment if the remainder is vested at the time of the conveyance (it is not subject to a condition precedent) but could be completely divested thereafter. Differentiation between a vested remainder of this variety and a contingent remainder is sometimes tricky, and turns upon the subtle distinction between a condition precedent and a condition subsequent. A *condition precedent* is one that must be satisfied before the interest is considered vested.

> *Example 11.* *O*, who owns Blueacre in fee simple absolute, conveys it "to *A* for life, then to *B* if *B* survives *A*, but if *B* does not survive *A*, then to *C*." The grant to *B* is expressly conditioned upon *B* surviving *A*; until that condition precedent is met, *B* has only a contingent remainder in fee simple absolute. *C*'s interest, meanwhile, is subject to the condition that *B* does not survive *A*. Thus, *C*'s interest is also a contingent remainder in fee simple absolute. [These are known as alternative contingent remainders.]

By contrast, a *condition subsequent* is a condition attached to a remainder that is already vested, causing the remainder to be completely divested if the condition occurs. A condition subsequent is easy to spot when the divesting condition is one that could occur only after the remainder takes possession, as in this example:

> *Example 12.* *O*, who owns Blueacre in fee simple absolute, conveys it "to *A* for life, then to *B* so long as *B* continues to farm the land." *B*'s interest is vested, but he could be completely divested in the future if he fails to continue farming the land. Thus, *B* has a vested remainder subject to divestment.[20]

A condition subsequent is slightly more difficult to spot when the condition could occur *before* the remainder takes possession. Compare the following example with Example 11 above:

> *Example 13.* *O*, who owns Blueacre in fee simple absolute, conveys it "to *A* for life, then to *B*, but if B fails to survive *A*, then to *C*." In this conveyance, *B* holds a vested remainder, but it is subject to being divested if he fails to survive *A*. The requirement that *B*

---

20. Astute students might recognize the familiar words of limitation—"so long as"—as giving *B* a vested remainder in a fee simple determinable (and some textbooks and court opinions use such terminology). Similarly, if *O* were to convey "to *A* for life, then to *B*, but if *B* fails to farm the land, then *O* may re-enter and reclaim the land," one might say that *B* has a vested remainder in fee simple subject to condition subsequent. Likewise, if *O* were to convey "to *A* for life, then to *B*, but if *B* fails to farm the land, then to *C*," one might say that *B* has a vested remainder in fee simple subject to executory limitation.

In each of these scenarios, the divestment of *B*'s interest could occur only after *B* takes possession. As you will see in a moment, however, there are other scenarios in which *B*'s interest could be divested *before* *B* takes possession. For the sake of simplicity, we will categorize both situations—divestment *before* or *after* taking possession—as a vested remainder subject to divestment.

survive *A* is a condition subsequent. Thus, *B* has a vested remainder subject to divestment. *C*'s interest will divest *B*'s remainder if *B* predeceases *A*; therefore, *C*'s interest (as you will learn shortly) is an executory interest.

You have no doubt recognized that the condition—surviving *A*—is exactly the same in both Example 11 and Example 13. Why is it called a condition precedent in Example 11 (creating a contingent remainder) and a condition subsequent in Example 13 (creating a vested remainder subject to divestment)?

To appreciate the distinction, it might help to compare the remainder to a ticket to a concert (which gives its holder the right to attend the concert in the future). A contingent remainder is similar to a parent telling a child: "If you do the dishes every night this week, I will give you a ticket to the concert Friday night." The parent holds onto the ticket until the child complies with the conditions; thus, it is a condition precedent to getting the ticket. A vested remainder subject to divestment is similar to the parent telling the child: "Here is a ticket to Friday night's concert, but I will take the ticket back if you do not do the dishes every night this week." In this case, the child has the ticket in hand, but can be divested of it by failing to comply with the condition subsequent.

Still, what difference does it make? In either case, the end result is that the child cannot attend the concert unless the child does the dishes. Similarly, in Examples 11 and 13 above, *B* does not get to take possession of the property if *B* does not survive *A*. So what purpose is served by calling one a contingent remainder and the other a vested remainder subject to divestment?

The answer is largely historical. Under traditional common law, contingent remainders were treated as a lesser estate in a variety of ways. For example, a vested remainder was (and still is) fully alienable, devisable and inheritable. The common law perceived a contingent remainder, however, in much the same way it viewed the possibility of reverter and right of entry—as mere "expectancies," not certain of becoming possessory and thus not capable of being transferred during the remainderman's lifetime. It was, however, devisable and inheritable at the remainderman's death (to the extent permitted by the nature of the contingency). Contingent remainders also were subject to a number of special rules that did not apply to vested remainders—*e.g.*, the Rule of Destructibility of Contingent Remainders, the Rule in Shelley's Case, the Doctrine of Worthier Title, and the Rule Against Perpetuities (all of which you will learn about shortly).

Under the modern view, contingent remainders are alienable, devisable and inheritable (to the extent permitted by the nature of the contingency). In addition, most jurisdictions have abolished many of the special rules that restricted contingent interests. Nonetheless, some of these rules retain vitality today. Accordingly, there can be substantial consequences to creating a contingent, rather than vested, remainder.

Distinguishing between the two types of remainders turns on the form of the conveyance—placement of the condition in the conveyance is crucial. We will address the rules of construction for analyzing conveyances shortly. But first, you must learn about the last type of future interest, the executory interest.

b. *Executory Interest.* An *executory interest* is a future interest that is created in a person other than the grantor and that becomes possessory by divesting another estate (*i.e.*, terminating an estate prior to its natural duration or quantum). Thus, they are distinguishable from remainders because remainders are patient—they become possessory when the preceding estate *naturally* terminates—while an executory interest is predatory (it *divests* a vested interest).

> *Example 14. O*, who owns Blueacre in fee simple absolute, conveys it "to *A*, but if *A* fails to graduate from college by 2015, to *B*." *A* has a fee simple, but the estate can be divested by *B* if *A* fails to graduate by 2015. Thus, *A* has a fee simple subject to an executory limitation and *B* has an executory interest in fee simple absolute.

Historical background. To understand the executory interest, knowledge of its historical development is helpful. Suppose that *O* was a landowner in the 15th century, and that *O* wanted to make the following conveyances of Blackacre and Whiteacre:

#1 Blackacre from *O* "to *X* when *X* becomes 30 years of age." (At the time, *X* is only 20 years of age.)

#2 Whiteacre from *O* "to *X*, but if *X* moves to London, then to *Y*."

Unfortunately for *O*, the common law would not recognize these conveyances. In conveyance #1, *O* was attempting to create a *springing future interest* in *X*. Under the traditional common law, however, *O* could convey land only by the ceremony of livery of seisin, and seisin had to pass to the grantee at the time of the ceremony.[21] Thus, conveyance #1 was impossible, because *O* was trying to convey an interest to *X* without transferring seisin to *X* immediately. The common law simply said that the conveyance to *X* was void.

The common law likewise would have voided conveyance #2 to *Y*, because this was an attempt to create a *shifting future interest* in *Y*. Under the common law, a divesting future interest could be reserved only by a grantor, and the common law would strike down *O*'s conveyance to *Y* as an impermissible attempt by *O* to create a divesting future interest in a grantee. Instead, the law courts would simply hold that *X* received a fee simple absolute.

---

21. In an era when few people could read and write, the livery of seisin ceremony visually commemorated the transfer of possession and title to land. In this ceremony, also called a *feoffment*, the lord and tenant physically went onto the land in the presence of other witnesses. The lord picked up a stick or clod of dirt from the ground and handed it to the tenant, accompanied by words identifying the estate that the lord was granting to the tenant.

Landowners began turning to the equity courts to get around these harsh, inflexible common law conveyancing rules. They did so through a device that came to be known as the "use," as illustrated by the following conveyances:

#1 Blackacre from *O* "to *Z* for the use of *O*, then to the use of *X* when *X* becomes 30 years of age."

#2 Whiteacre from *O* "to *Z* for the use of *X*, but if *X* moves to London, then to the use of *Y*."

The idea was to pass seisin immediately to *Z*—thereby satisfying the rigid seisin rules of the law courts—but for *Z* to hold seisin only in a formal sense, somewhat like the trustee of a modern trust.[24] In conveyance #1, *Z* would hold seisin, but *O* would enjoy the benefit of the land until *X* turned 30, and thereafter *X* would enjoy that benefit. In conveyance #2, *Z* would hold seisin, but *X* would enjoy the benefit of the land unless he moved to London, in which case *Y* would thereafter enjoy the benefit of the land.

The law courts rigidly adhered to rules based upon the significance of seisin and refused to give any legal effect to uses. In conveyance #1, if *Z* failed to allow *X* to enjoy the benefit of the land after *X* turned 30, the law courts would not protect *X*. *X* was not powerless, however. Although most justice was carried out in the law courts, the courts of equity provided an alternative forum, where the Chancellor (the presiding judge in a court of equity) was more concerned with fundamental fairness than rigid adherence to the common law rules. Thus, in conveyance #1, even though *Z* held seisin under the common law rules, the Chancellor would require *Z* to hold the land for the benefit of *O* until *X* turned 30, at which time *Z* would hold the land for the benefit of *X*. As a result, *O* had an "equitable" estate in fee simple subject to *X*'s "equitable" springing future interest. Likewise, in conveyance #2, the Chancellor would require *Z* to hold seisin for the benefit of *X*, until *X* moved to London, at which time *Z* would hold seisin for the benefit of *Y*. *X* would therefore have an equitable estate in fee simple, subject to *Y*'s equitable shifting future interest. These estates were called "equitable" estates because they were recognized only by courts of equity, not the law courts.

By the time of Henry VIII, landowners became quite adept at employing the use as a means of avoiding the feudal incidents. Concerned about the effect of dwindling revenue upon the security of his crown, Henry VIII prevailed upon Parliament to enact the Statute of Uses in 1536. The effect of the Statute of Uses was to give *legal* recognition to shifting and springing future interests by *executing* any use. To demonstrate what this means, consider the examples of *O*'s conveyances above. Visualize the Statute of Uses "red-penciling" the use from these conveyances:

#1 Blackacre from *O* "to ~~Z for the use of O, then to the use of~~ *X* when *X* becomes 30 years of age."

24. The mechanics of the trust were discussed earlier in this chapter at page 262.

#2 Whiteacre from O "to ~~Z for the use of~~ X, but if X moves to London, then to ~~the use of~~ Y."

The Statute "executed" *only the use*, and decreed that seisin (the legal estate) would be taken away from the feoffee to uses (Z) and given to the cestui que uses, the true beneficiary of the use arrangement. The Statute thus converted equitable estates into legal estates. These interests became known as shifting and springing "executory" interests.

Modern status. Today, it is no longer necessary to "raise a use" to create an executory interest; such an interest can be created by deed or will whenever divesting language is used. Moreover, while some textbooks or treatises still distinguish between shifting executory interests and springing executory interests, there appears to be no lingering legal significance for making that distinction today. Accordingly, we will refer to them simply as executory interests.

As you have already observed, executory interests can divest a fee simple estate. [In Example 14 (page 297), for instance, the executory interest follows the fee simple subject to executory limitation.] Executory interests can also divest a remainder. [In Example 13 (page 295), C's interest could divest B's vested remainder; thus C's interest is an executory interest in fee simple absolute.]

Because an executory interest was by its nature subject to a condition precedent, the traditional common law treated the executory interest with the same disfavor given to contingent remainders. Thus, executory interests could not be transferred by inter vivos conveyance, but were devisable and inheritable. Under the modern view, executory interests are fully alienable, devisable, and inheritable.

Notes

1. *Uses and the Development of the Modern Deed.* As mentioned in these materials, land transfer at common law required the ceremony of livery of seisin. If O attempted to sell Blackacre to X using only a written instrument, such as a deed, the law courts would refuse to recognize the conveyance; seisin remained in O until the ceremony of livery of seisin occurred. The Chancellor, however, could use his powers in equity to ensure that O did not escape the bargain he made. Although recognizing that legal title remained in O, the Chancellor would require O to hold the land to the use of X. As a result, the deed gave rise to a use that could be enforced in equity, and X would thus hold an equitable fee simple estate. After the Statute of Uses, X's equitable estate was converted into a legal fee simple estate. Thus, the Statute of Uses made it possible to transfer legal title (*i.e.*, seisin) by deed, without having to engage in the ceremony of livery of seisin.

2. *Uses and the Modern Trust.* Earlier, we suggested that the modern trust is a descendant of the use. Because the Statute of Uses executed uses, thereby converting equitable estates into legal estates, a question arises: How did lawyers develop trusts, if the Statute of Uses converted equitable estates into legal estates?

The answer? Just as all rules seem to have exceptions, there also were exceptions to the Statute of Uses. One exception was that the Statute did not execute a use if the feoffee to uses had some real, active duties to perform on behalf of the cestui que use; in other words, the Statute executed only *passive* uses, not active uses. This exception made sense given the purposes of the Statute—Parliament wanted to prevent the abuse of uses for tax avoidance purposes, but not their utility for permitting land to be managed on behalf of persons incapable of managing it themselves. Because trusts impose active management duties upon the trustee, trusts fell under the exception to the Statute. For further discussion of the exceptions to the Statute of Uses, see John E. Cribbet and Corwin W. Johnson, Principles of the Law of Property 72–76 (3d ed. 1989).

3. *Analyzing Conveyances*

When a conveyance creates both a present possessory estate and one or more future interests, identifying the status of title to the land is a multi-step process and requires careful attention to the precise form and placement of the words of the conveyance. It is critical to classify the interests in the sequence in which they are presented in the conveyance.

Identification of the Present Possessory Estate. The obvious place to start is by identifying the present possessory estate. As you learned earlier in this chapter, there are certain words of limitation (*e.g.,* "and his heirs," "so long as," "and the heirs of his body," "for life") that signal particular types of estates. You also learned some rules of construction to help when a conveyance is ambiguous.

Identification of the Future Interest. There are two components that will help you correctly identify the future interest: (1) knowing which possessory estate it follows; and (2) knowing who holds the interest—the grantor or another person.

Recognizing which estate precedes the future interest is more than half the battle. As you know from the chart on page 242, each possessory estate is linked with a particular future interest. If you have determined that the possessory estate is a life estate or fee tail, the next succeeding future interest *must* be either a reversion or a remainder.

Knowing who holds the future interest will help you distinguish between the reversion and the remainder. It is a reversion if the future interest is retained by the grantor; it is a remainder if the conveyance gives it to someone other than the grantor. Similarly, knowing who holds the interest will help distinguish between the defeasible fee simple estates. If the future interest is held by a person other than the grantor, it must be an executory interest (and, therefore, the possessory estate is a fee simple subject to executory limitation). If the future interest is held by the grantor, the possessory estate is either a fee simple determinable or fee simple subject to condition subsequent.

With remainders, you will need to further determine whether the interest is a contingent remainder, or is indefeasibly vested, vested subject to open, or vested subject to divestment.

Duration of the Future Interest. Once you have determined what type of future interest was created, the next question is: How long does it last? Grantors can create a future interest in every estate available—a remainder, for example, could be in fee simple absolute, in a life estate, in fee tail (where still recognized), or in a defeasible fee—and can stack almost any number of future interests.

> *Example 15.* O, owner of Blueacre in fee simple absolute, conveys it "to A for life, then to B for life, then to C so long as C continues to maintain the property as a nature preserve, but if C does not so maintain the property, then to D." In this conveyance, A has a life estate, B has a vested remainder in a life estate, C has a vested remainder in fee simple subject to executory limitation, and D has an executory interest in fee simple absolute.

Check for Interests Retained by the Grantor. Keep in mind that if the grantor conveys an estate (or series of estates) of lesser quantum than what the grantor had, the grantor retains a future interest. For example, assume that *O,* owning Blackacre in fee simple absolute, conveys "to A for so long as the property is used for farming" but the conveyance is silent about what happens if the property is no longer used for farming. By default, *O* retains the future interest (in this case, a possibility of reverter). If the grantor conveys an estate less than fee simple—a fee tail, life estate or term of years—but does not expressly provide for the future interest, the grantor retains a reversion by default.

The grantor may retain an interest even if the conveyance contains a future interest granted to someone else. Suppose that *O,* owning Blackacre in fee simple absolute, conveys "to A for life, then to B so long as B continues to use the property for farming." Although *O* has created a vested remainder subject to divestment in *B,* *O* has not provided for what happens if *B* breaches the condition. Accordingly, by default, *O* retains the future interest (which, in this case, is a possibility of reverter) following *B*'s remainder. Similarly, *O* retains a reversion whenever the last future interest in a conveyance is a contingent remainder (or alternative contingent remainders), such as in Examples 8, 9, and 11 (pages 294–95).

> *Example 16.* O, owner of Blueacre in fee simple absolute, conveys it "to A for life, then to B if B marries A, but if B does not marry A, then to C." At first glance, it appears that O has conveyed her entire estate because at the end of A's life, we will know whether or not B has married A and, therefore, whether B or C will take the property in fee simple absolute. Under the traditional common law, however, it was possible for A's life estate to terminate prematurely (*e.g.,* it could be forfeited for treason), which would destroy any contingent remainder(s) that had not yet vested. [We discuss this Destructibility Rule in greater detail later in the chapter (page 313).] Thus, if B had not married A by the time A's estate prematurely ended, B and

C's alternative contingent remainders *both* would be destroyed and *O* would take possession under her reversion.

4. *Lookalike Conveyances*

In many cases, analyzing the conveyance is a simple proposition. Lawyers truly earn their fees, however, by knowing how to distinguish (or how to correctly draft) conveyances that are similar in wording but have significantly different consequences. Two scenarios, in particular, are worth additional scrutiny.

   a. *Defeasible Fee Simple Estates.* As illustrated by the *Mahrenholz* case (page 267), it can sometimes be difficult to distinguish between a fee simple determinable and a fee simple subject to condition subsequent. Students also frequently have difficulty distinguishing those two estates from the fee simple subject to executory limitation. The key is to read the conveyance in sequence, comma to comma, and pay attention to who holds the future interest.

   Example 17. O, who owns Blueacre in fee simple absolute, conveys it "to *A* so long as *A* uses the land for farming."

   Example 18. O, who owns Blueacre in fee simple absolute, conveys it "to *A*, but if *A* no longer uses the property for farming, then *O* may re-enter and reclaim the land."

   Example 19. O, who owns Blueacre in fee simple absolute, conveys it "to *A* so long as *A* uses the land for farming, otherwise to *B*."

   Example 20. O, who owns Blueacre in fee simple absolute, conveys it "to *A*, but if *A* no longer uses the property for farming, then to *B*."

In Example 17, the words of limitation "so long as" are in the granting clause, suggesting that *O* created a fee simple determinable. This determination is confirmed by the fact that there is no future interest mentioned in the conveyance, so the grantor retains the future interest (a possibility of reverter in fee simple absolute) by default. Example 19 uses the exact same words of limitation, so—at first glance— it also looks like *O* created a fee simple determinable. Notice, however, that *O* has conveyed the future interest in Example 19 to a third party, *B*. Thus, *B* holds an executory interest in fee simple absolute. *A*'s possessory interest, therefore, is a fee simple subject to executory limitation, rather than a fee simple determinable.

In Example 18, the words of limitation "but if" appear in a separate clause that follows the granting clause and the grantor has expressly retained the right to re-enter if the condition is broken. Accordingly, *A* holds a fee simple subject to condition subsequent and *O* has a right of entry in fee simple absolute. Notice that Example 20 uses similar "but if" language; in this conveyance, however, the grantor has conveyed the future interest to a third party, *B*. Thus, in Example 20, *B* holds an executory interest in fee simple absolute, which makes A's interest a fee simple subject to executory limitation.[23]

b. *Conditions Precedent and Subsequent.* In our discussion of remainders, we noted that it is sometimes difficult to distinguish between a contingent remainder (which is subject to a condition precedent) and a vested remainder subject to divestment (which is subject to a condition subsequent). Here again, the key is to read the conveyance in sequence, comma to comma. If the condition is placed in the granting clause—the clause containing the words of purchase identifying the grantee—or in a clause preceding the granting clause, the courts generally will construe it as a condition precedent. This placement of the condition in the granting clause (or the preceding clause) suggests that the grantor wanted the interest to vest only if the condition is met.

Conversely, if the granting clause makes an unconditional grant, but is followed by a separate clause containing the condition, courts will construe the condition as a condition subsequent. This placement of the condition suggests that the grantor wanted to create a vested interest but divest it if the condition is breached.

> *Example 21.* O, who owns Blueacre in fee simple absolute, conveys it "to A for life, then if B survives A, to B, but if B does not survive A, to C." The condition (that B survive A) appears in a clause preceding the actual grant to B. Therefore, the condition is a condition precedent and B's interest is a contingent remainder in fee simple absolute.

> *Example 22.* O, who owns Blueacre in fee simple absolute, conveys it "to A for life, then to B, but if B does not survive A, to C." Here, reading comma to comma, the conveyance makes an unconditional grant to B, but then appends a *separate clause* containing the condition. Thus, B has a vested remainder in fee simple, but it is subject to divestment because of the condition subsequent.

What interest does C have in Examples 21 and 22? You might be tempted to say that C holds an executory interest in both examples. By definition, however, executory interests can only divest a *vested* interest. That is certainly the case in Example 22, where we concluded that B had a vested remainder subject to divestment. Accordingly, C's interest in Example 22 is an executory interest.

In Example 21, however, B's interest was not vested, it was contingent. Accordingly, C's interest would not divest B's interest, but would merely take effect at the end of A's life estate because the contingency to

---

23. Some writers do not recognize this distinction in terminology. Accordingly, you may see another textbook, study aid, or court opinion classify A's estate as a fee simple determinable in both Example 17 and Example 19, but state that the future interest in Example 17 is a possibility of reverter in the grantor while the future interest in Example 19 is an executory interest in B. Similarly, those writers might classify A's estate in both Example 18 and Example 20 as a fee simple subject to condition subsequent, but identify the future interest in Example 18 as a right of entry in the grantor and the future interest in Example 20 as an executory interest in B.

B's interest failed. In other words, *C*'s interest is a remainder, which is patiently waiting to see if *B*'s interest will vest or not. In fact, by reading comma to comma, we see that the condition ("if *B* does not survive *A*") is in a clause preceding the grant to *C*. Accordingly, *C*'s interest also is a contingent remainder. Thus, *B* and *C* have *alternative contingent remainders*. The following materials examine the significance of distinguishing between these two types of future interests.

KOST v. FOSTER

Supreme Court of Illinois.
406 Ill. 565, 94 N.E.2d 302 (1950).

DAILY, JUSTICE. This is an appeal in behalf of Oscar Durant Kost, one of the plaintiffs and counterdefendant, from a decree for partition entered on the counterclaim of counterplaintiff, Marshall C. Foster, in the circuit court of Fulton County.

The record discloses that on December 11, 1897, John Kost and his wife, Catherine, executed a warranty deed as follows:

> The Grantors, John Kost and his wife Catherine Kost ... Convey and Warrant to their son Ross Kost to have and to hold use and control for and during his natural life only, at his death to his lawful children, the lawful child or children of any deceased lawful child of Ross Kost to have and receive its or their deceased parent's share meaning and intending hereby to Convey to Ross Kost a life estate only the following described real estate, to-wit:

and [the deed] thereinafter describes the real estate in question. The deed was filed for record on September 18, 1909, in the recorder's office of Fulton County.

Ross Kost took possession of the real estate and occupied it until his death on March 8, 1949. The only lawful children ever born to him were Lether Page, Adah Charleroy, Fern Kost Rhodes, Harry L. Kost, Gladys Wilson, Gilbert Kost, Oscar Durant Kost and a child born in 1899, who died thirteen days after birth. Five of the children, including appellant, Oscar Durant Kost, were born prior to the execution of the deed of John and Catherine Kost. The others were born subsequently thereto. All of the children, except the one who died in infancy, are living and were parties plaintiff to the original complaint for partition. . . .

[At issue is the interest of Oscar Durant Kost, who filed for bankruptcy while his father was still alive. On December 29, 1936, the bankruptcy trustee sold Oscar Durant Kost's interest to Marshall C. Foster, defendant and counterplaintiff. After Ross Kost died, his children brought a suit to clear up title to the land. The original complaint alleged that Ross Kosts's seven children—including Oscar Durant Kost—were the sole owners of the real estate. The complaint asked the court to declare the bankruptcy trustee's deed to Foster void and removed as a cloud on the title and to partition the property according to the respective rights and interests of the seven children.]

The principal question involved is whether or not the interest of Oscar Durant Kost was a vested remainder at the time of the purported sale by the trustee in bankruptcy. It is contended that Oscar Durant Kost had but a contingent remainder in the real estate, and that a contingent remainder does not pass to a trustee in bankruptcy of the remainderman.

We have frequently been called upon to define vested remainders and contingent remainders and to distinguish between them. The chief characteristic which distinguishes a vested from a contingent remainder is the present capacity to take effect in possession should the possession become vacant. . . . In the case of a vested remainder, there is a person in being ascertained and ready to take, who has a present right of future enjoyment which is not dependent upon any uncertain event or contingency, while in the case of a contingent remainder the right itself is uncertain. The uncertainty which distinguishes a contingent remainder is the uncertainty of the right and not of the actual enjoyment, for in this regard any remainder may be said to be uncertain, as the remainderman may die without heirs before the termination of the particular estate. *Smith v. Chester*, 272 Ill. 428, 112 N.E. 325, Ann.Cas.1917A, 925, citing 40 Cyc. 1664.

Whether a remainder is vested or contingent depends upon the language employed. If the conditional element is incorporated into the description of or into the gift to the remainderman then the remainder is contingent, but if, after words giving a vested interest, a clause is added making it subject to being divested, the remainder is vested. Thus, on a devise to A for life, the remainder to his children, but if any child dies in the lifetime of A his share to go to those who survive, the share of each child is vested, subject to be divested by its death, but on a devise to A for life, remainder to such of his children as survive him, the remainder is contingent. Gray's Rule against Perpetuities; *Riddle v. Killian*, 366 Ill. 294, 8 N.E.2d 629. . . . [Conversely, with a vested remainder,] the title vests in the remainderman on the delivery of the deed. The title thus vested becomes an estate of inheritance.

The language used by the grantors in the instant case is not conditional in nature. At the time of the execution of the deed there were five lawful children of Ross Kost in being, including the appellant, Oscar Durant Kost, and designated as remaindermen and capable of taking immediate possession upon the termination of the life estate. It is true that each of the estates in remainder was subject to being opened up and diminished in quantity by the birth of other children to the respective life tenants. . . . [Nonetheless, the] estate in remainder vested in the five lawful children of Ross Kost in esse upon the execution and delivery of the deed, and it vested in each of the other lawful children as each of them was born.

The words "at his death," as used in the deed of John and Catherine Kost, are similar in context to the language used in the case of *Dustin v. Brown*, 297 Ill. 499, 130 N.E. 859, 862, wherein we held that the language "after the death" of the life tenant referred to the time when the estate will vest in possession only, and we said

> it has, however, been so many times held in this and other states that the rule may be said to be well established, that the words "after the death of A.," and similar expressions, are to be construed as meaning at the termination (whenever and in whatever manner that may occur) of the particular estate of freehold and as referring to the time when the estate will vest in possession only. The remainder thus created "after the death of A.," is held to be a vested remainder unless there be that in the context which clearly takes it out of the rule.

[handwritten margin note: "after death" creates remainder in A]

It is urged by the appellant that the gift over to the lawful child or children of any deceased lawful child of Ross Kost indicated an intention of the grantors to create a contingent remainder in the children of Ross Kost; since if the remainders were vested it would descend to the issue of any child who might die during the lifetime of Ross Kost, and, therefore, no substitution would have been necessary. However, when we apply the test set forth by Professor Gray as stated above and approved by this court in *Riddle v. Killian*, 366 Ill. 294, 8 N.E.2d 629, and in numerous other decisions, we find that the gift over was in the nature of a condition subsequent, and no conditional limitation was incorporated into the description of or into the gift to the remaindermen. The remainder is subject to being divested on the contingency of one of the children of Ross Kost dying before the life tenant and leaving lawful children.

Nor can we agree with the argument of counsel for appellant that the words "meaning and intending hereby to convey to Ross Kost a life estate only" expressed an intention on the part of the grantors to create a contingent remainder in the lawful children of Ross Kost, so that he would be precluded from the possibility of inheriting any portion of the fee from any child who might predecease him without issue. Had it been the intention of the grantors to create a contingent remainder, the scriveners could have made the gift to the children of Ross Kost conditional upon their surviving him as stated above. They did not elect to do this, and used instead words which created a vested remainder in the children.

[handwritten margin note: created vested remainder in the children]

We have carefully studied the cases cited in the briefs of counsel for appellant and considered the arguments in support of their position, but are forced to the conclusion that the language employed in the deed of John and Catherine Kost meets every test for the creation of a vested remainder in the lawful children of Ross Kost. Since the appellant, Oscar Durant Kost, had a vested remainder, a trustee in bankruptcy could properly convey his interest pursuant to an order of the referee in bankruptcy, and the appellee, Foster, acquired an undivided one-seventh interest in the fee of the real estate, subject to the life estate in Ross Kost. . . .

Notes

1. *Vested vs. Contingent—Classifying Interests in Sequence.* As the *Kost* case illustrates, it is crucial to analyze a conveyance in sequence—reading comma to comma—because the same words, placed in different clauses in the conveyance, can produce substantially different outcomes. *See* John C. Gray, The Rule Against Perpetuities § 108 ("Whether a remainder is vested or contingent depends upon the language employed. If the conditional element is incorporated into the description of, or into the gift to, the remainder-man, then the remainder is contingent; but if, after words giving a vested interest, a clause is added divesting it, the remainder is vested."). Consider the following conveyances:

(a) *O*, owner of Blueacre in fee simple absolute, conveys it "to *A* for life, then to *B*; but if *B* does not survive *A*, then to *C* if *C* survives *A*."

(b) *O*, owner of Blueacre in fee simple absolute, conveys it "to *A* for life, then to *B* if *B* survives *A*; but if *B* does not survive *A*, then to *C* if *C* survives *A*."

Reading comma to comma, conveyance (a) would give *B* a *vested remainder in fee simple subject to divestment* and *C* an executory interest in fee simple absolute. Conveyance (b) would give *B* a *contingent remainder in fee simple absolute* and *C* an alternative contingent remainder in fee simple absolute. In conveyance (a), the description of the gift to *B* (the granting clause) does not contain a condition precedent; after giving *B* a vested interest, the grantor provides a condition subsequent that might divest her vested remainder. In conveyance (b), the condition appears within the granting clause to *B*; therefore, *B*'s gift is conditional on *B* surviving *A*, making it a contingent remainder.

Does this distinction make a difference? Suppose that both *B* and *C* die before *A*. Who will take Blueacre under conveyance (a)? Who will take it under conveyance (b)? [Hint: Notice that *C*'s interest is also conditioned upon surviving *A*.]

2. *The Future Interest Following a Contingent Remainder.* As a rule, whenever the last gift over in a conveyance is a contingent remainder (or alternative contingent remainders as in conveyance (b) in note 1 above), there will always be a reversion in fee simple in the grantor. Why? Because it is always possible that the contingent remainder(s) might fail altogether. Thus, the grantor retains an interest that would become possessory if the contingent remainder fails. The grantor's interest is a reversion in fee simple absolute. [Review the definition of the reversion (page 292). Do you see why the grantor's interest is a reversion?]

3. *Vested or Contingent?—The Significance of this Distinction.* As a historical matter, there were several reasons why it was legally significant that a remainder was classified as either vested or contingent. Some of these reasons are no longer practically or legally significant, but some remain very significant, and the continuing significance of others remains uncertain. For now, it is sufficient to focus upon the following situations in which the classification could make a difference, depending upon the jurisdiction.

(a) *Transferability.* As indicated earlier in this chapter, a vested remainder was fully alienable, devisable and inheritable. As the *Kost* decision demonstrates, however, the common law did not provide the same treatment for contingent remainders. Furthermore, a contingent remainder was not capable of being attached (attachment, or execution, is a type of involuntary transfer whereby certain creditors—such as the bankruptcy trustee for Oscar Kost—can acquire an interest in property to assist them in collecting a debt). Today, almost all American jurisdictions have now rejected the common law approach, and treat both vested and contingent remainders as freely alienable.

(b) *Acceleration of Vested Remainders.* Suppose that Covington dies and his will devises land "to Pushaw for life, then to Fisch." Suppose further that Pushaw, for some reason, decides that he does not want this gift from Covington's will and disclaims (*i.e.,* legally refuses to accept) this interest. Pushaw's action of disclaiming this conveyance operates to terminate his life estate, even though Pushaw is still alive. Because the will devised Fisch a vested remainder in fee simple absolute, his vested remainder will accelerate into possession as soon as Pushaw disclaims the life estate.

The doctrine of acceleration of remainders did not apply, however, while a remainder was still contingent. For example, suppose that Covington's will had devised the land "to Pushaw for life, then, if Fisch becomes a judge, to Fisch." If Pushaw disclaims the life estate, and at that time Fisch has not become a judge, Fisch's remainder (which is still contingent, because it is subject to a condition precedent) cannot be accelerated into possession. [In fact, because the common law would not tolerate an abeyance of seisin, Fisch's contingent remainder would have been destroyed if it had not vested by the time the prior estate ended. We discuss this Destructibility Rule in greater detail later in this chapter (page 313).]

(c) *Prevention of Waste.* Persons holding contingent remainders have more limited rights regarding waste than persons holding vested interests. Although most states would permit a contingent remainderman to obtain an injunction against conduct that would constitute waste, jurisdictions are divided on whether the contingent remainderman can recover damages for waste. *See* J.A. Bryant, Jr., *Right of Contingent Remainderman to Maintain Action for Damages for Waste,* 56 A.L.R.3d 677 (1974). Can you explain why a court might be reluctant to grant damages to a contingent remainderman?

(d) *Common Law Rules Restricting Contingent Future Interests.* The common law established a variety of rules—The Rule in Shelley's Case, The Doctrine of Worthier Title, The Destructibility of Contingent Remainders, and The Rule Against Perpetuities—that did not apply to vested remainders, but voided certain contingent remainders. In most jurisdictions today, only the Rule Against Perpetuities remains a source of significant concern. You will encounter all of these rules in greater detail shortly.

4. *Surviving the Life Tenant—The Constructional Preference for Vested Estates.* Suppose Henning, who owns Blueacre in fee simple absolute, conveys it "to Lawless for life, then to Westbrook." As the *Kost* case and the preceding introductory material suggest, Westbrook has a vested remainder, not a contingent remainder. If Westbrook dies before Lawless, Westbrook's remainder does not fail, but instead passes to the persons so identified in his

will (or to his heirs, if he leaves no valid will). In other words, the law does not imply that Westbrook's survival of Lawless is a condition precedent of his remainder interest.

To a significant extent, this result reflects the common law's traditional constructional preference for interpreting remainders as vested rather than contingent (a preference also manifested in the court's decision in *Kost*). But why have such a preference? As a practical matter, why shouldn't the law imply that Westbrook (as holder of the remainder) must survive Lawless (as life tenant) in order to take the remainder? Do you think that view would be consistent with Henning's likely intent? [In considering this question, ask yourself what would happen to Blueacre if the law treated Westbrook's interest as contingent and both Westbrook and Henning predeceased Lawless.] *See* Thomas F. Bergin & Paul G. Haskell, Preface to Estates in Land and Future Interests 127–32 (2d ed. 1984).

5. *The Deceased Child of Ross Kost.* The court in *Kost* held that Foster, as the assignee of Oscar's vested remainder, had a 1/7 interest in the remainder in common with the other six children of Ross Kost. The court does not address the deceased child of Ross Kost, who died at thirteen days of age in 1899.

Consider Ill. Rev. Stat. ch. 110–1/2, § 2–1, the descent and distribution statute, which provides as follows: "The intestate real and personal estate of a resident decedent . . . shall be distributed as follows . . . (d) If there is no surviving spouse or descendant but a parent, brother, sister, or descendant of a brother or sister of the decedent: the entire estate to the parents, brothers and sisters of the decedent in equal parts . . . ." In light of the facts, is the court's conclusion that Foster has a 1/7 share of the remainder correct under Illinois law? Does it matter whether the deceased child was Ross's sixth, seventh, or eight child?

6. *Pulling It All Together.* Now that you know all of the possessory estates and future interests, take a few moments to synthesize what you have learned. One way to do this is to expand the chart that appears on page 242. For each possessory estate, add a column that lists the "magic words" (words of limitation) typically used to create the estate and another column to indicate whether the estate is alienable, devisable and/or inheritable (under the traditional common law and today). Create a second chart for future interests with a column to identify the language typically used to create the interest, who holds the interest, and whether it is alienable, devisable and/or inheritable.

7. *Review Problems.* At this point, you should be able to classify all of the interests created by the following conveyances. In each case, assume that Henning, owner of a fee simple absolute in Blueacre, makes the indicated conveyance by deed or devise by will, and give the full state of the title to Blueacre immediately after the conveyance or devise. In some instances, the problem sets forth a subsequent conveyance or event, and in those instances, you should identify the full state of the title following the subsequent conveyance or event.

(a) Devise "to Cheever for life, then to Bryan and her heirs if she survives Cheever, otherwise to Nice and her heirs." [Also, what will be the state of the title if Cheever later dies, survived by Bryan?]

(b) Conveyance "to Cheever for life." Cheever then makes a subsequent conveyance "to Bryan for the life of Cheever so long as a restaurant is operated on the premises." [Also, what will be the state of the title if Cheever dies before Bryan? If Bryan dies before Cheever?]

(c) Conveyance "to Cheever for his life." Cheever then makes a subsequent conveyance "to Bryan for her life."

(d) Conveyance "to Cheever for life." Subsequently, Henning conveys "the residue of my title" via quitclaim deed to Nice.

(e) Conveyance "to Nice while she lives on the land."

(f) Conveyance "to Cheever for life, then to such of his living children as graduate from college; if none of his living children graduate from college, then to Nice and her heirs."

(g) Devise "to Cheever for life, then to Nice's children and their heirs." At the time of the devise, Nice has no children. [Also, what will be the state of the title if, one year later, Nice has a child? If that child dies two years later?]

(h) Conveyance "to Cheever for life, then to Bryan for life, then to Nice and her heirs."

(i) Conveyance "to Wells and her heirs until Sam finishes medical school, then to Pushaw and his heirs."

(j) Conveyance "to Key for life, but if Key gets married, then Henning shall have the right to reenter and recover the premises."

5. Class Gifts

A *class gift* is a conveyance to a group or class of persons who share a particular characteristic. In the *Kost* case, for example, the conveyance of the interest to Ross Kost's "children" was a class gift. Other typical classes that you might find in a conveyance include: "descendants," "heirs," "grandchildren," "nieces and nephews," etc. You might even see a (poorly drafted) conveyance to groups such as "employees" or "friends."[24]

Grantors often create class gifts because of their flexibility, *i.e.*, because the class can grow or shrink in size after the conveyance is made.[25] In the *Kost* case, for example, the conveyance was made before some of Ross's children were born. Nonetheless, because the remainder created an interest in Ross's "children," the class naturally expanded to include his later-born children—a result consistent with the grantors' likely desire to benefit all of Ross's children.

---

24. Marilyn Monroe's will, for example, directed her executor to distribute her personal effects to "my friends, colleagues, and those to whom I am devoted."

25. Class gifts can be made of possessory estates as well as future interests. For example, a parent might execute a will leaving his or her estate "equally to my children who survive me." If two or more children survive the parent, the children hold the possessory estate in a *concurrent estate—i.e.,* they each have an equal, undivided interest in the property as a whole. We will discuss the rights and liabilities of co-owners in Chapter 6.

When class gifts are conveyed in a remainder, special care is required to determine whether the remainder is vested or contingent. As you will recall from our discussion of remainders (page 294), a remainder given to a class may be vested subject to open if at least one member of the class is born, ascertained, and not subject to any condition precedent. Conversely, the remainder is contingent if the class members are not yet born, not yet ascertainable, or subject to a condition precedent that no class member has yet satisfied.

> *Example 23.* O, who owns Blueacre in fee simple absolute, conveys it "to A for life, then to A's children." If A has no children at the time of the conveyance, the remainder is contingent because no member of the class has yet been ascertained. If A subsequently has one child, X, the remainder becomes vested in X, but because A is still alive, the class remains open. Therefore, X's interest is a vested remainder subject to open.

> *Example 24.* O, who owns Blueacre in fee simple absolute, conveys it "to A for life, then to A's children who reach age 21." At the time of the conveyance, A has two children: X, who is age 19, and Y, who is age 15. X and Y have a contingent remainder in fee simple absolute.[26] Although there are two members of the class who are alive and ascertainable, neither of them has satisfied the condition precedent of reaching age 21. When X turns 21, X's interest becomes a vested remainder subject to open, *i.e.*, X's interest is vested, but X must share with Y if Y reaches age 21.

A vested remainder subject to open remains open until the class closes. Classes can close in one of two ways: (1) naturally or physiologically; and (2) under the common law's Rule of Convenience. A class closes naturally or physiologically when it is impossible for new members to enter the class. In Examples 23 and 24, the class will close naturally when A dies, because it is then impossible for any additional members to be born into the class of "A's children."

By contrast, a class closes under the Rule of Convenience whenever any member of the class is entitled to demand possession of the land (*i.e.*, at the termination of the preceding estate). Thus, even if the class has not closed naturally, the court will close it administratively.

> *Example 25.* O, who owns Blueacre in fee simple absolute, conveys it "to Able for life, then to the children of Blanche." At the time of the conveyance, Blanche has two children, X and Y. Thus, X and Y hold a vested remainder subject to open. Later, Able dies, but Blanche is still alive. The class has not closed naturally, because Blanche is alive and can have more children. However, the court can close the class under the Rule of Convenience because the life estate has ended and X and Y are now entitled to demand possession. If Blanche later has a third child, Z, application of the Rule of

---

26. You might be tempted to say that the remainder is a "contingent remainder subject to open." However, the "subject to open" language is unnecessary because the remainder is not yet vested.

Convenience would mean that *Z* would not be entitled to a share of Blueacre—because the class closed before *Z* was born.

As its name implies, the Rule of Convenience closes the class because it is inconvenient to wait for the class to close naturally. In Example 25, Blanche might live for several decades, leaving *X* and *Y* in limbo for that period as to the ultimate size of their share. The Rule of Convenience tends to make *X* and *Y*'s estate more marketable because it limits the number of potential class members to those in existence when *X* and *Y* can demand possession.

Notes

1. *A Constructional Preference.* The Rule of Convenience is a "rule of construction" rather than a "rule of law." This means that the court will generally apply the Rule of Convenience unless it concludes that doing so would defeat the grantor's express or apparent intention. For example, suppose Henning, who owns Blueacre in fee simple absolute, conveys it "to Hunvald for life, then to the children of Pushaw." Pushaw currently has three children, and is still alive and capable of having more children. If Hunvald then died, a court would likely apply the Rule of Convenience, close the class, and award possession to Pushaw's three current children in fee simple absolute—cutting off any later-born children of Pushaw. [Do you see why this would carry out Henning's likely intent?]

If, however, Henning had conveyed Blueacre "to Hunvald for life, then to the children of Pushaw, whenever born," the statement "whenever born" demonstrates Henning's intention that *all* of Pushaw's children should share in the gift, not just those who survive Hunvald. Under those circumstances, at Hunvald's death the court would not apply the Rule of Convenience if Pushaw remains alive. In that case, the court would award possession of Blueacre to Pushaw's three living children, who would hold the land in fee simple but would have to share with any subsequently born children of Pushaw.

2. *Review Problems.* Assume that Henning, owner of a fee simple absolute in Blueacre, makes the indicated conveyances by deed. In each case, give the full state of the title to Blueacre immediately after the conveyance, or after the subsequent events identified in the problem.

(a) "To Chambers for life, then to Laughrey for life, then to Lawless's children." At the time of the conveyance, Lawless has one child, Thomas.

(b) "To Chambers's children." [Does it matter whether Chambers had children on the date of the conveyance?]

(c) "To Chambers for life, remainder to Lawless's children who reach age 21." At the time of the conveyance, Chambers and Lawless are alive and Lawless has two children, Thomas (age 19) and Becca (age 15).

(d) Same as (c), then Thomas later dies at age 22.

(e) Same as (d), then Lawless later has a third child, Rachel.

(f) Same as (e), then Chambers later dies.

(g) Same as (f), then Becca later dies at age 20.

(h) Same as (g), then Lawless later has a fourth child, Debbie.

(i) Same as (h), then Rachel later turns 21.

(j) Same as (i), then Debbie later turns 21.

D. SPECIAL RULES GOVERNING FUTURE INTERESTS

1. *The Merger Rule*

The merger rule states that when one person holds a present possessory estate and the *next vested* future interest (*i.e.*, there are no intervening vested future interests held by other persons), the present estate merges into the future interest and is terminated. For example, suppose Henning holds a life estate in Blueacre and Pushaw holds a vested remainder in fee simple absolute. Pushaw then conveys his remainder to Henning by deed. Henning now holds both a life estate and the next vested future interest in Blueacre—and those interests merge together, giving Henning a present fee simple absolute estate. The merger rule (which courts continue to apply today) simply reflects the common sense notion that when one person holds successive interests, there is no compelling reason to continue to treat those successive interests as distinctly separate.

2. *The Destructibility of Contingent Remainders*

Suppose that in the feudal era, *O*, owner of Blueacre in fee simple absolute, conveyed it "to *A* for life, then to *B*'s heirs." *A* later died, with *B* surviving him. Because *B* was still alive, *B*'s heirs were not yet ascertainable (and thus they could not take possession); as a result, the remainder in *B*'s heirs was still contingent. Such an outstanding contingency created several problems. The first problem was a practical one: the land was effectively inalienable until *B*'s death (when *B*'s heirs could be ascertained). The second problem was a doctrinal one—the common law's traditional view that there could never be an abeyance of seisin. In other words, the law had to be able to identify the person who would be seised of the land upon *A*'s death (and thus would be responsible for the feudal services). In this example, because *B*'s heirs could not be ascertained as of the time of *A*'s death, the law held that seisin returned to *O* via reversion. The common law's solution to the "no abeyance of seisin" problem, however, created yet another doctrinal problem. Once seisin had reverted back to *O*, the only way it could pass to *B*'s heirs in the future would be by divesting *O*'s estate—*i.e.*, as a springing future interest. As explained earlier, however (page 297), the common law did not recognize springing future interests.

The common law courts dealt with these problems by adopting the Rule of Destructibility of Contingent Remainders (the "Destructibility Rule"). Under the Destructibility Rule, *a contingent freehold remainder was destroyed if it had not vested at or before the termination of the preceding freehold estate.* The Rule's application is illustrated by the above hypothetical. The remainder in *B*'s heirs had not yet vested at the time of *A*'s death; thus, the remainder in *B*'s heirs was destroyed. Imagine the Destructibility Rule "red-penciling" that remainder: "to *A* for life, then to *B*'s heirs." At *A*'s death, the land reverted to *O* (who retained a reversion) in fee simple absolute. By destroying the contingent remainder in *B*'s heirs, the Destructibility Rule rendered the land immediately alienable at *A*'s death.

The Destructibility Rule applied even if the preceding estate terminated prematurely, which could occur through disclaimer (renunciation) or merger.[27] A disclaimer occurs when the estate or future interest holder refuses or rejects the estate conveyed to her. [Recall from Chapter 4 that a transfer requires acceptance by the grantee.] Merger occurs when the life tenant acquires the next vested interest in the property, which merges into the life estate, terminating it early. Any contingent remainders that had not yet vested at the time of renunciation or merger were destroyed.

> *Example 26. O*, who owns Blueacre in fee simple absolute, conveys it "to *A* for life, then to *A*'s children." If *A* has no children at the time of the conveyance, then *A* has a life estate, *A*'s unborn children have a contingent remainder in fee simple absolute, and *O* has a reversion in fee simple absolute. Suppose that *O* dies, leaving his reversion to *A*. Now, *A* holds two successive vested interests (the life estate and the reversion), which merge together, terminating the life estate. Because the remainder is still contingent (because no children exist), it is destroyed. *A* thereafter holds a fee simple absolute.

Notes

1. *The Present Status of the Destructibility Rule.* Most states have abolished the Destructibility Rule, and no case has actually applied it to defeat a contingent remainder in decades. In the most recent case involving the Destructibility Rule, the New Mexico Supreme Court announced that the rule "is not now and never has been the law in New Mexico." *Johnson v. Amstutz*, 101 N.M. 94, 678 P.2d 1169 (1984).

2. *A Loophole in the Destructibility Rule.* The Destructibility Rule applied only to contingent remainders, not to executory interests. Thus, after the Statute of Uses, landowners could easily circumvent the Destructibility Rule by creating executory interests instead of contingent remainders. [Suppose that *O*, who owned Blackacre in fee simple, wanted to convey to *A* for life and then to *B*'s children who reach age 21. B's children were ages 1 and 2 at the time. What language would you use to create an executory interest in the children?] This loophole was among the pressures that eventually led courts to develop the Rule Against Perpetuities, which applied to all contingent future interests.

3. *A Limitation on Destructibility by Merger.* Under an exception to the common law rule, "a contingent remainder would not be destroyed by

27. At common law, premature termination also occurred under the doctrine of forfeiture, which was used as the penalty for certain crimes, such as treason, or for a "tortious feoffment" (an attempt by a life tenant to transfer a fee simple estate). The doctrine is no longer recognized under modern law.

merger of a life estate and the next vested estate *if the two estates are created simultaneously with the contingent remainder.*" Cornelius J. Moynihan & Sheldon F. Kurtz, Introduction to the Law of Real Property 180 (4th ed. 2005). For example, suppose *O*, who owned Blueacre in fee simple, conveyed it "to *A* for life, then to *B* for life if she gets married, then to *A* and his heirs." The merger rule would not have destroyed *B*'s contingent remainder—even though *A* held a life estate and the next vested estate—because all three interests were created simultaneously in the same instrument. [Why do you think the common law made an exception to the Destructibility Rule in this case?] Suppose, however, that *A* subsequently conveyed both his life estate and his vested remainder in fee simple to *C*, while *B* was still unmarried. Would *B*'s remainder now be destroyed by merger?

3. *The Rule in Shelley's Case*

In feudal times, when a tenant died, the lord did not have to accept the tenant's eldest son as a new tenant, because the lord/tenant relationship was a personal one. Thus, custom developed that the lord would accept the tenant's eldest son as a new tenant if the new tenant paid a "relief" (page 240). If the eldest son did not pay this sum, the eldest son did not inherit the land.

To avoid burdening their eldest sons with the obligation to pay a relief to the lord, creative medieval landowners attempted the following sleight-of-hand: *O*, the landowner, would convey land to *X*, who would in turn reconvey the land "to *O* for life, then to the heirs of *O*." The intent was for the eldest son of *O* to take by *purchase* (*i.e.*, by way of an inter vivos conveyance of a contingent remainder), rather than by inheritance at *O*'s death, thereby avoiding payment of relief.

Law courts closed this tax loophole in *Shelley's Case*, 1 Co. Rep. 93b (1581). The Rule in Shelley's Case provides as follows: if one instrument creates a life estate in a grantee and attempts to create a remainder in the grantee's heirs, and both the life estate and the attempted remainder are legal estates (or both are equitable estates), the remainder in the grantee's heirs is converted (by operation of law) into a remainder in the grantee.

> *Example 27. O*, owner of Blueacre in fee simple absolute, conveys it "to *A* for life, then to *A*'s heirs." The Rule in Shelley's Case applies. In one deed, *O* has created a legal life estate in *A*, and has tried to create a legal remainder in *A*'s heirs. The Rule in Shelley's Case converts the remainder in *A*'s heirs into a remainder in *A*. In other words, by operation of law the deed is rewritten to say "to *A* for life, then to *A*."

Note that in Example 27, the Rule in Shelley's Case does nothing more than to give *A* the remainder that was originally granted to *A*'s heirs. Because *A* is an existing and ascertained person, however, the remainder is now a *vested* remainder in fee simple absolute. Under the doctrine of merger, this vested remainder will merge with *A*'s life estate, giving *A* a fee simple absolute. In this way, the Rule in Shelley's Case assured that if *A*'s heir ever took title, he would take it by inheritance—thereby obligating him to pay a relief—and not by an inter vivos gift from *O*.

To carry out the purpose of the Rule, the common law courts applied the Rule in Shelley's Case as a *rule of law*, not as a rule of construction. Whether or not the grantor wanted the rule to apply was irrelevant—which makes sense, as the very purpose of the rule was to defeat the grantor's intention to avoid the feudal incidents. Still, because of the way the common law courts stated the rule, there quickly developed a number of ways to circumvent the rule. The following example illustrates one of those loopholes.

> *Example 28. O*, owner of Blueacre in fee simple absolute, conveys it "to *A* for life, then to *A*'s children." The Rule in Shelley's Case does not apply. *O* did not try to create a remainder in *A*'s "heirs," but in his children. The Rule would apply only to a remainder created in *A*'s "heirs," meaning those persons who would take by inheritance if *A* died without a will. *A*'s children have a valid remainder.

Notes

1. *Vitality of the Rule in Shelley's Case.* Because there were so many loopholes to the rule, almost all states have abolished the Rule in Shelley's Case, either by statute or by judicial decision. According to the Simes and Smith treatise, the Rule possibly still exists in Arkansas, Colorado, Delaware, and Indiana, see Lewis M. Simes and Allan F. Smith, The Law of Future Interests § 1563 (2d ed. 1956 & Supp. 1991), but it seems questionable that courts in those states would continue to apply the rule in future cases. You should be cognizant of the Rule, however, because statutory abolition of the Rule was typically prospective only. *See, e.g.,* 765 Ill. Comp. Stat. 345/2 (abolished only as to instruments executed after the statute took effect in 1953). As a result, there have been occasional recent decisions applying the Rule to pre-abolition instruments. *See, e.g., In re Estate of Hendrickson*, 324 N.J.Super. 538, 736 A.2d 540 (1999) (interpreting will probated prior to New Jersey's 1934 statutory abolition of Rule).

2. *The Rule in Shelley's Case and Its Effect on Alienability of Land.* The only conceivable remaining justification for the Rule in Shelley's Case is that its application would make land alienable one generation sooner, as Example 27 above demonstrates. Rather than having the land rendered inalienable until *A*'s death, when his heirs could be ascertained, application of the Rule in Shelley's Case renders the land immediately alienable. As you will understand after we consider the Rule Against Perpetuities, however, this "benefit" is no longer considered sufficient to justify the continued application of the rule. [After studying the material on the Rule Against Perpetuities, return to this point, and see if you can explain why this is so.]

LAWYERING EXERCISE
(Legal Analysis, Problem Solving, and Drafting)

BACKGROUND: Assume that you are an attorney in one of the handful of jurisdictions that has not expressly abolished the Rule in

Shelley's Case, either by statute or by judicial decision. A client, Henning, has asked you to draft a will that would devise Henning's property to Henning's son, Bart, for life, then to Bart's heirs.

TASK: Your supervising attorney has asked you to draft the language of the conveyance to accomplish Henning's wishes. How will you proceed? Do you draft the conveyance with the assumption that the Rule in Shelley's Case will be applied to the conveyance at the time Henning dies? Or can you safely assume that your state will join all of the others in abolishing the rule?

If you assume that the Rule in Shelley's Case will be applied to the conveyance, one way of avoiding the rule is to give the gift to Bart's children, rather than his heirs, as suggested in the text above. What drawback(s) do you see with circumventing the rule in that way? Knowing the drawback(s), use your problem-solving skills to carefully analyze the Rule in Shelley's Case and come up with other ways to circumvent the rule. [Hint: what other estates/future interests would roughly accomplish the client's goals?]

4. *The Doctrine of Worthier Title*

The Rule in Shelley's Case thwarted attempts by landowners to create future interests in the heirs of a grantee. The Doctrine of Worthier Title served the same function by preventing a grantor from creating a future interest *in his own heirs*. For example, suppose that Henning, owner of Blueacre in fee simple absolute, conveyed it "to Pushaw for life, then to the heirs of Henning." The Rule in Shelley's Case did not apply, by its terms, to this conveyance. But Henning's underlying intent was the same—if this conveyance was successful in creating a contingent remainder in his own heirs, then his heirs would take the land by purchase, not by inheritance—and the heirs would have no obligation to pay a relief to the lord.

To foil this attempt at tax evasion, the common law courts developed the Doctrine of Worthier Title, which provided as follows: If a grantor conveys a freehold estate to one person, but then conveys a future interest (either a remainder or an executory interest) to the grantor's heirs, the grantor's heirs take nothing by this conveyance. Instead, the grantor retains a reversionary interest.

> *Example 29.* Henning, owner of Blueacre in fee simple absolute, conveys "to Pushaw for life, then to the heirs of Henning." In one document, Henning has created a freehold estate, and has attempted to create a future interest in his own heirs. The Doctrine of Worthier Title applies. The contingent remainder in Henning's heirs is void, and Henning has a reversion in fee simple absolute.

You should visualize the Doctrine of Worthier Title "red-penciling" the invalid remainder: "to Pushaw for life, ~~then to the heirs of Henning~~." Because the contingent remainder is void, and there is no further instruction from Henning as to the disposition of the land following Pushaw's life estate, Henning retains a reversion. Thus, if Henning's heirs ever receive title to Blueacre, they will receive it by inheritance from Henning (and would have to pay the obligatory relief). Thus, you understand the significance of the name of the rule: the Doctrine of *Worthier* Title; in the eyes of the common law, title received by inheritance was *worthier* than title received by purchase (because it was *worthier, i.e., worth more,* to the lord).

Unlike the Destructibility Rule, the Doctrine of Worthier Title also applied to executory interests:

> *Example 30.* Henning, owner of Blueacre in fee simple absolute, conveys it "to Pushaw and his heirs for so long as he abstains from drinking alcoholic beverages, then to the heirs of Henning." In one document, Henning has created a freehold estate (a defeasible fee estate in Pushaw), and has attempted to create an executory interest in his own heirs. The Doctrine of Worthier Title applies. The executory interest in Henning's heirs is void, and Henning retains a possibility of reverter.

Visualize the Doctrine of Worthier Title "red-penciling" the executory interest: "to Pushaw and his heirs for so long as he abstains from drinking alcoholic beverages, then to the heirs of Henning." Because the executory interest in Henning's heirs is void, and Henning has not given further instructions as to who should take title if Pushaw drinks alcohol, Henning retains a possibility of reverter. Thus, if Henning's heirs ever take any interest in the property, they will take it only because they inherited that interest from Henning.

Notes

1. *Rule of Law or Rule of Construction?* At common law, the Doctrine of Worthier Title was a rule of law, applied without regard to the intention of the grantor. In the landmark decision of *Doctor v. Hughes*, 225 N.Y. 305, 122 N.E. 221 (1919), however, Justice (then Judge) Cardozo held that the Doctrine of Worthier Title would be applied in New York as a rule of construction. New York has since abolished the Doctrine, but a series of decisions between the 1930s and the 1960s suggests that the Doctrine may remain valid in a number of states as a rule of construction.

What does this mean? In such a jurisdiction, if a conveyance falls within the terms of the Doctrine, the court would presume that the Doctrine should apply to void the contingent future interest in the grantor's heirs. This presumption could be overcome, however, by evidence that the grantor intended to create a future interest in his own heirs.

To demonstrate how the Doctrine might operate as a rule of construction, consider Example 29. Suppose that Henning's will provided that he was not leaving anything to his heirs, because he had already provided for them during his life by virtue of the conveyance of Blueacre. This would be evidence that he intended for them to take a contingent remainder by virtue of the conveyance. The court might consider this evidence sufficient to overcome the presumption in favor of applying the Doctrine. What result do you think would follow if Henning's will did not specifically address title to

Blueacre, but provided that "all of the rest, residue, and remainder of my property shall go to the American Red Cross"?

2. *Modern Status of the Doctrine of Worthier Title.* The Doctrine of Worthier Title has been abolished by statute or judicial decision in a number of states, including California, Illinois, Maryland, Massachusetts, Nebraska, New York, North Carolina, Texas, West Virginia, and the District of Columbia. The Doctrine survives as a rule of construction in a number of other states.

5. *The Rule Against Perpetuities*

Throughout this chapter, you have encountered how the law of estates and future interests attempts to strike a balance between the desire of landowners to exercise "dead hand control" (*i.e.*, to restrict the ability of future owners to control the use or disposition of the land) and the general policy that land should be freely alienable. Nowhere is this tension more evident than in the venerable Rule Against Perpetuities (RAP). Without any limitation on contingent future interests, one generation could control the alienability of land in perpetuity. Thus, the RAP was adopted as a means of striking "a fair balance between the desires of members of the present generation, and similar desires of succeeding generations, to do what they wish with the property which they enjoy." Lewis Simes, Public Policy and the Dead Hand 58 (1955).

Looking at the language of the RAP, as stated by history's leading perpetuities scholar, you can see the balance to which Simes refers:

No interest is good unless it must vest, if at all, not later than twenty-one years after some life in being at the creation of the interest. [John Chipman Gray, The Rule Against Perpetuities § 201 (4th ed. 1942).]

The RAP allows a grantor to control the alienability of land, but only for a limited period of time—the "perpetuities period," which is defined as the lifetime of some person alive at the time of the conveyance, plus 21 years after that person's death.

a. *Application of the RAP.* The RAP is concerned solely with "remoteness of vesting," or (perhaps more helpfully) *remoteness of the moment when no uncertainty remains as to whether an interest will vest or fail.* Accordingly, the RAP applies only to unvested interests. For purposes of this discussion, we are concerned primarily with the application of the RAP to:

- contingent remainders,
- executory interests, and
- vested remainders subject to open.[28]

28. Wait! If the RAP applies only to unvested interests, why does it apply to the vested remainder subject to open? As you will see later in this chapter (page 325), there is uncertainty about the number of shares into which this type of remainder ultimately will be divided. The RAP requires this uncertainty to be resolved dur-

All of the other estates and future interests you have learned in this chapter were considered vested and, therefore, automatically satisfied the rule.

To understand how the RAP operates in its application, it is helpful to break the rule down into four component parts: (1) no interest is good; (2) unless it must vest, if at all; (3) not later than 21 years after some life in being; (4) at the creation of the interest. The following materials discuss each of these elements in turn, followed by an analysis of several scenarios that commonly present RAP problems, and a reminder to apply the RAP to every future interest in the conveyance.

(1) *"No interest is good."* This part of the rule signals that any interest that violates the RAP is void. Here, as with the prior rules you have learned, use a red-pencil approach to strike the offending interest. In each of the following conveyances, for example, the grantor's intended gift to X violates the RAP:

> #1. Conveyance "to City Hospital, ~~but if the premises are not used as a health care facility, to X~~."
>
> #2. Conveyance "to City Hospital so long as the premises are used as a health care facility, ~~otherwise to X~~."

In each scenario, X was granted an executory interest that violates the RAP. Why? Because X's interest is not *certain* to vest within 21 years of a life in being at the time of the conveyance. X's interest cannot vest until the premises cease to be used as a health care facility. But it is possible that the premises will be used as a health care facility for many decades (perhaps even centuries) into the future—much longer than 21 years after the death of anyone alive at the time the conveyance took effect. Because X's interest might vest too remotely, it must be struck from the conveyance.

Notice that only the offending clause is stricken, which can create two different results in conveyances #1 and #2. In conveyance #1, City Hospital is left with a fee simple absolute. In conveyance #2, however, the grant to City Hospital itself contains a limitation ("so long as the premises are used as a health care facility"). Thus, City Hospital is left with a fee simple determinable and the grantor retains a possibility of reverter.[29]

Under the traditional rule, the offending interest was void from the outset of the conveyance—*i.e.*, the interest is treated as if it never existed. As you will see, some jurisdictions have adopted a modern approach, which "waits to see" if the interest will actually vest too

ing the perpetuities period, or the entire remainder is void.

29. You might be wondering why the interest in X is invalidated by the RAP, but the grantor's possibility of reverter is not. The answer is that future interests held by a grantor were always considered to be vested, and the RAP applies only to unvested interests. Why treat the possibility of reverter (or right of entry) as vested, *especially given that it may never become possessory*? The explanation is pure form over substance: if O had a vested estate in fee simple, then whatever interest O is retaining must also be vested. Thus, O's possibility of reverter would be vested at the moment of its creation and satisfies the RAP—even if the possibility that O's interest will become possessory is remote.

remotely. Under the traditional approach, however, courts were remorseless in striking down any interest that *might possibly* vest too remotely.

(2) *"Unless it must vest, if at all."* This clause tells you that the RAP applies only to unvested interests. The phrase "if at all" means that the interest is not required to vest, but we need to know that it definitely will vest *or definitely will fail* within the perpetuities period. The following examples demonstrate the application of this principle:

> *Example 31. O,* owner of Blueacre in fee simple, conveys it "to *A* for life, then to *A*'s children who survive *A*." The contingent remainder in *A*'s children is valid under the RAP. Immediately upon *A*'s death, the interest in her children will definitely vest (if there are any children who survive *A*) or definitely fail (if there are no children who survive *A*). The interest is valid notwithstanding the fact that it might *fail;* the critical fact for purposes of the RAP is that uncertainty about whether the remainder will vest will be resolved—one way or the other—at the end of *A*'s life (and *A* was alive at the time of the conveyance).

> *Example 32. O,* owner of Blueacre in fee simple, conveys it "to *A* for life, then to *A*'s children who reach 30 years of age." The contingent remainder in *A*'s children is void under the RAP, because the uncertainty of vesting could last for more than 21 years after *A* dies. For example, it is possible that, at the time of her death, *A* could have a child that is age 8 or younger. This child could live for 21 years following *A*'s death, and yet the interest of this child would still be contingent—as the child would not yet have met the condition precedent of reaching 30 years of age. Because it is possible for the interest in *A*'s children to vest too remotely, that interest is void and *O* holds a reversion that will become possessory at the end of *A*'s life estate.

In short, the word "must" means *absolute certainty.* Thus, the RAP is a *possibilities* test. If there is *any* possibility that a series of events *might* cause a contingent future interest to vest too remotely—even if that possibility is a one-in-a-billion chance, more unlikely than winning the lottery—that interest violates the common law RAP. Conversely, the interest is valid if it must vest or must fail within the perpetuities period.

(3) *"Not later than 21 years after some life in being."* A contingent future interest must certainly vest or fail within the lifetime of some person who was alive at the attempted creation of the interest, or within 21 years after that person's death. At first blush, this may seem like an odd formula to use, but it was actually quite practical. This formula allowed a grantor to restrict alienability of land for the lifetime of her known children and then until her grandchildren reached the age of majority—*i.e.,* "to my son *X* for life, then to his children who reach 21." Accordingly, the interest is valid if it has vested (or failed) by the end of *X*'s life or within 21 years after *X* dies.

Applying this formula requires a two-step process: (1) determine what event will cause the interest to vest; and (2) search for a *validating life*—*i.e.*, any person, alive when the interest was created, who can be used to prove that the determining event is *certain to occur* within that person's lifetime or within 21 years afterward. To see this point, reconsider Examples 31 and 32. In Example 31, the remainder is contingent upon surviving A, so the event that causes the interest to vest is A's death. Accordingly, A can be used as the validating life to prove the contingent remainder is valid. She was alive at the time of O's conveyance, and thus is a "life in being." And there is no possibility that the contingent remainder in her children can vest outside the perpetuities period. There are only two possibilities:

- A *dies leaving no children.* In this case, the remainder would fail at the moment of her death.

- A *dies leaving children.* In this case, A's living children have satisfied the condition precedent placed upon their interest—*i.e.*, they have survived A—and their interest vests at the moment of A's death (and they become eligible to take possession). [So we do not even need the additional 21 years to see if the interest will vest; all uncertainties are resolved immediately upon A's death.]

There is *no possible scenario* in which the interest of any child of A could vest more than 21 years after her death.[30] Thus, A is the validating life that proves the contingent remainder in her children is valid.

Compare that example with Example 32, in which A cannot be used as a validating life to prove that the contingent remainder satisfies the RAP. In Example 32, the determining event is not A's death; if A dies leaving children younger than 30 years of age, the interests of those children would still be contingent. Thus, the determining event is A's youngest child reaching 30 after A's death has occurred.[31] At the time of the conveyance by O, it is possible that A could subsequently die leaving a child (Z) who was two years of age and who was born after O's conveyance (meaning that Z was not a "life in being" and thus not a potential measuring life). If this scenario occurs, Z's interest could remain contingent for 28 years following A's death—more than the perpetuities period. Thus, although A is a life in being, she is not a validating life—*i.e.*, her life does not help prove that the interest in her children satisfies the RAP. Similarly, although O is a life in being, the interest in A's children is not *certain* to vest (or fail) within 21 years after O dies.

30. This statement is correct based upon our historically understood limits upon human reproduction. Historically, the law has presumed that women could not have children after their death and that men could not father children (in a genetic sense) after their death. And until very recently, technology did not threaten these presumptions. Today, of course, sperm, eggs, or embryos may be stored so that, genetically speaking, A could have a child years after his death. As you should be able to see, this technological possibility has profound consequences for the application of the RAP to a problem like Example 32.

31. As long as A is still alive, the law presumes that A is capable of having more children. Thus, if A is alive, even if A's youngest living child reaches age 30, this does not eliminate the possibility of remote vesting—as A could later have another child in whom the interest would be contingent.

From these examples, you should recognize that a validating life is a person who was alive at the time the interest was created and whose life or death is *related, by absolute logical necessity, to the moment that the interest vests or fails.* If you can find at least one validating life, your task is done; an interest that is certain to vest or fail within 21 years after that person's death is valid under the RAP. Conversely, if you are unable to identify a validating life, then the interest is void under the RAP.

> *Example 33.* O, owner of Blueacre in fee simple, conveys it "to A so long as the property is used as a hospital; otherwise to B." The executory interest in B is void under the RAP. The condition that determines vesting—the property no longer being used as a hospital—is not *certain* to occur within 21 years after the death of O, A, B, or anyone else alive at the time of the conveyance.

> *Example 34.* O, owner of Blueacre in fee simple, conveys it "to A, but if the property is no longer used as a hospital, then to B if B is then alive." The executory interest in B is valid under the RAP. The condition that determines vesting is B being alive when the property is no longer used as a hospital. Whether B's interest vests or fails is necessarily tied to his own lifetime, and thus B is his own validating life. B's interest must either vest (if the property is not used as a hospital and B is alive) or fail (if B dies before the property ceases to be used as a hospital) no later than the moment of his death.

(4) *"At the creation of the interest."* This part of the RAP instructs us to determine the applicable "lives in being" at the time the interest is created. For purposes of this test, it is critical to realize that interests under a deed are created when the deed is delivered, while interests under a will are created when the testator dies. The date the instrument was actually executed is irrelevant; the critical point is when the instrument becomes operative. As explained in Chapter 4 (and as you will see again in Chapter 9), a deed does not take effect until the grantor delivers the instrument to the grantee. As also explained in Chapter 4, wills are considered "ambulatory"—*i.e.*, they can be amended or destroyed—until the testator's death. Accordingly, a will does not operate to effect a testamentary gift until the testator dies. The discussion of class gifts in the following section demonstrates how the analysis can change significantly depending upon whether the conveyance is by a will or by deed (or other inter vivos conveyance).

(5) *Common RAP Scenarios.* You should be cognizant of potential RAP problems in any conveyance involving an unvested future interest. However, there are several types of conveyances that are especially vulnerable to RAP problems. Be especially wary, therefore, when dealing with conveyances that have one or more of the following characteristics: age contingencies; conditions or events that are not tied to a human life; persons described by a title rather than a name; and class gifts.

Age Contingencies. Grantors commonly desire to postpone the enjoyment of a substantial gift to a time when the recipient is old enough to appreciate and manage it. Accordingly, many future interests are given to recipients "who reach age 21" or some other age of maturity. As you saw in Example 32, however, age contingencies (especially ones greater than 21 years) may cause the conveyance to violate the RAP.

Conditions or Events Not Tied to a Human Life. Many grantors also want to attach certain conditions to a gift ("to the City of Murphydale so long as the property is used for a city park, otherwise to *B*") or make the gift contingent upon a particular event ("to *A* when the mortgage is paid in full"). As you saw in Example 33, however, some future interests created by these types of conditions are likely to violate the RAP because the condition or event *might not occur* within 21 years following the death of a life in being. [Certainly, we expect a mortgage to be paid in full within a person's lifetime, but it is *possible* that the event might not occur within that time frame.] As a result, the future interest that depends upon that condition or event is not *certain* to vest or fail within 21 years following the death of a life in being.

This problem is avoided, of course, if the condition or event is tied to a human life. Examples 19 and 20 (page 302) illustrate this exception: the executory interests in those examples are *valid* under the RAP because the event must occur (or not) within a particular person's lifetime ("to *A* so long as *A* uses the land for farming, otherwise to *B*"). Thus, the named individual (*A*) serves as the validating life.

"Unborn Widows" and Other Persons Described by Title. Conveyances that refer to persons by a title rather than by name pose a similar problem in identifying a validating life. The "unborn widow" is a classic example. Suppose, for example, *O* deeds property into an inter vivos trust that pays income "to *O* for life, then to my widow for life, then to my heirs who survive my widow." A widow, by definition, is the person who was married to the decedent at the time of death. Thus, while *O* is alive, we do not know who *O*'s widow will be and it is *possible* that she was not a life in being at the time of the conveyance. [Even if *O* was married at the time of the conveyance, that spouse may die first and *O* might later marry someone who was born after the conveyance was made—hence the term "unborn widow."] Because "the unborn widow" cannot serve as a validating life, the interest in the heirs is void under the RAP.

Class Gifts. Conveyances to "children," "heirs" and similar groups present one of the most challenging applications of the RAP for several reasons. First, members of an open class generally cannot serve as validating lives, because it is possible that other members may be born into the class after the conveyance is made.

Example 35. *O*, owner of Blueacre in fee simple, conveys it "to *A* for life, then to *A*'s children for their lives, then to *A*'s grandchildren living when *A*'s last child dies." At the time of the conveyance, *A* is alive and has one child, *X*. The contingent remainder in *A*'s grandchildren is void under the RAP. The interest cannot vest until *A*'s last child dies. Because *A* is alive, it is possible for *A* to have another child, Y (who was not a life in being at the time of the conveyance), who could become A's last child to die. Thus, no member of the class of "A's children" can be used as a validating life, because it is possible for the class to include persons who were not alive at the time of the conveyance.

Second, class gifts complicate the RAP analysis because they are not considered "vested" in the class members for purposes of the RAP until the class has closed and the interest of every member of the class has vested. The traditional common law adopted an "all or nothing" rule—if the interest of any member of the class could vest too remotely, the entire class gift was void. Thus, vested remainders subject to open are subject to the RAP, even if one member of the class already has a vested interest at the time of the conveyance.

> *Example 36.* O, owner of Blueacre in fee simple, conveys it "to A for life, then to A's children who reach age 30." Suppose that at the time of the conveyance, A had two children, X and Y, ages 31 and 29. The language purports to grant X a vested remainder subject to open, but the class gift to A's children is void. It is possible that after the conveyance, A could produce a third child, Z, who might then be age 2 when A dies. Although the class closes when A dies, it will be more than 21 years before we know whether or not Z reaches age 30. Thus, Z's interest could vest too remotely. The "all or nothing" rule invalidates the entire class gift—X (and Y) lose out, even though X's interest was vested at the time of the conveyance.

Because of the difficulties presented by class gifts, it is frequently helpful to modify the RAP analysis slightly for conveyances with such gifts.

> Rather than thinking of all the different possible ways that an interest may vest within this time period, approach it from the opposite perspective: If you can conceive of 1 possible scenario that could vest but ONLY AFTER the lives in being plus 21 years, the interest violates the [RAP]. [Peter T. Wendel, A Possessory Estates and Future Interests Primer 156 (2d ed. 2005).]

To perform this analysis, Professor Wendel suggests using a "Create, Kill, and Count" strategy:

- **Create** a person who was not alive at the time of the conveyance but whose life or death can affect vesting of the interest. (In other words, create someone who is not a life in being.)

- **Kill** everyone who was alive at the time of the conveyance. (Kill all of the potential validating lives.)[32]

- **Count** 21 years. (See if the interest is certain to have vested or failed within 21 years after all of the lives in being have died.)

---

32. Do not take this step too literally. You will not be killing off everyone else in the whole world (which would make it impossible for the person you created to have offspring). Instead, you are killing off persons who were alive at the time and could potentially affect vesting of the interest.

Example 37. O, owner of Blueacre in fee simple, conveys it "to A for life, then to O's grandchildren." O is alive and has two children, but no grandchildren. The class of O's grandchildren will remain open until O and all of O's children are dead—at that point, it is impossible for O to have additional grandchildren. Thus, we can create X, a possible after-born child for O who was not alive at the time of the conveyance. Now kill O, O's two children who were alive at the time of the conveyance, and anyone else alive at the time of the conveyance—and then count 21 years. Is it *certain* that X will die (thus closing the class of O's grandchildren) within 21 years after the death of O and O's other two children? No. It is possible that X will live for many decades thereafter. Accordingly, the interest in O's grandchildren is void.

Notice in Example 37 that a relevant life can be someone who is not mentioned in the conveyance. For a gift to O's grandchildren, for example, the relevant lives for vesting purposes are obviously O's children (the persons who can produce the grandchildren).

Finally, when dealing with class gifts, it may be significant to determine when the interest was created—*i.e.*, was the conveyance by a will or by a deed or other inter vivos instrument?—because that determines the applicable "lives in being" at the time the interest is created. Compare the following examples:

#1. O, owner of Blueacre in fee simple, conveys it *by deed* "to O's children for life, then to O's grandchildren who reach 21 years of age."

#2. O, owner of Blueacre in fee simple, devises it *by will* "to O's children for life, then to O's grandchildren who reach 21 years of age."

In example #1, O is alive at the time of the conveyance and can produce additional children (who in turn could produce additional grandchildren of O). Using the "Create, Kill, and Count" approach, we could create a child of O, who we'll call X, then kill everyone else who was alive at the time of the conveyance. Now count 21 years: Is it *certain* that the class of O's grandchildren will be closed such that the interest in O's grandchildren will have either vested or failed? No. We couldn't know all of the potential members of the grandchild class until X dies—and that *might* be longer than 21 years after all of the lives in being are dead.

In example #2, however, O's transfer occurs by a will. By definition, that means that O is dead and cannot produce any more children. Accordingly, the class of O's children is *closed* when the will takes effect and the children, if any, can serve as validating lives. [If you use Professor Wendel's analytical approach, you cannot create any new children for O under the Create, Kill, and Count method.] As a result, the interest in the grandchildren is valid because that interest will definitely vest or fail within 21 years after the last child of O dies.

(6) *Repeat the RAP Analysis for Each Interest in the Conveyance.* Conveyances often have more than one future interest that is subject to the RAP. Therefore, you must systematically apply the RAP analysis to each future interest in any conveyance to determine which ones are valid and which are void.

> *Example 38.* In 1998, *O*, owner of Blueacre in fee simple, conveys it "to *A* for life, then to *A*'s children for their lives, then to *B* if he is still alive, and if not, then to his heirs; provided, however, that if, after the death of *A*'s children, alcoholic beverages are consumed on the premises, then the land shall go to *X*." At the time of the conveyance, *A* has no children. *O* has attempted to convey a life estate to *A*, a contingent remainder for life to *A*'s children (contingent because they cannot be ascertained), a contingent remainder in fee simple to *B* (contingent because he must satisfy the express condition precedent of survival), and an alternative contingent remainder in fee simple in *B*'s heirs. *O* has also attempted to subject the respective interests of *B* and his heirs to an executory interest in fee simple absolute in favor of *X*.
>
> - The contingent remainder in *A*'s children is valid under the RAP. *A* is the measuring life for this interest. If she dies without having had children, the contingent remainder will fail. If she has children, the interest will vest in each child at its birth. In no event could the interest in any child of *A* vest or fail later than the moment of *A*'s death.
>
> - The contingent remainder in *B* is valid under the RAP. *B* is the measuring life for this interest. Either *B* will survive *A*'s children (at which time his interest will vest), or he will not survive them (at which point his interest will fail). Thus, in no event could *B*'s interest vest or fail later than the moment of his death.
>
> - The contingent remainder in *B*'s heirs is also valid under the RAP. Again, *B* is the measuring life for this interest. At his death, the interest of his heirs will either vest (because *B* failed to outlive *A*'s children) or their interest will fail (because *B* did outlive *A*'s children). Again, in no event could their interest vest or fail later than the moment of *B*'s death.
>
> - The executory interest in *X* is void under the RAP. According to the terms of the conveyance, *X*'s interest can vest only when alcoholic beverages are consumed on Blueacre following the death of *A*'s children. At the time of the conveyance, it is *absolutely impossible* to prove with certainty when alcoholic beverages will be consumed on Blueacre. It could happen the next day, or the next year; it could be 500 years; it might never happen. If alcoholic beverages were not consumed on the property until the year 2679, the executory interest would then be vesting in *X* (or more accurately, in the descendants to whom his property passed by will or intestacy) more than 21 years after the death of anyone alive at the time of the conveyance in 1998.

- Thus, the attempted executory interest in X is stricken, as if red-penciled from the conveyance: "to A for life, then to A's children for their lives, then to B if he is still alive, and if not, then to his heirs; ~~provided, however, that if, after the death of A's children, alcoholic beverages are consumed on the premises, then the land shall go to X.~~" The conveyance thus creates a life estate in A, a contingent remainder for life in A's children, a contingent remainder in fee simple in B, an alternative contingent remainder in fee simple in B's heirs, and a reversion in fee simple absolute in O.

Notes

1. *More Problems Applying the RAP.* To test your understanding of the RAP, consider the following examples. In each example, determine the state of the title assuming the common law RAP applies.

(a) Henning, owner of Blueacre in fee simple absolute, conveys it "to Fisch for life, then to Fisch's children who reach 25." At the time of the conveyance, Fisch has a child who is 26 years of age. Is the remainder interest in Fisch's children valid?

(b) Henning, owner of Blueacre in fee simple absolute, conveys it "to Fisch for life, then to Fisch's children for their lives, then to Pushaw's children." At the time of the conveyance, Fisch and Pushaw are alive. Is the remainder interest in Pushaw's children valid?

(c) Henning, owner of Blueacre in fee simple absolute, conveys it "to Fisch for life, then to Fisch's children for their lives, then to the children of Pushaw who are then living." At the time of the conveyance, Fisch and Pushaw are alive. Is the remainder interest in Pushaw's children valid?

(d) Barnes, owner of Blueacre in fee simple absolute, conveys it "to Smith for life, remainder to the first son of Smith who reaches 25 years of age." At the time of the conveyance, Smith is alive and has three teenage sons. [Would it matter if the jurisdiction followed the Destructibility Rule?]

(e) Barnes, owner of Blueacre in fee simple, conveys it "to Bryan for life, then to her children for their lives, then to her grandchildren in fee simple absolute." At the time of the conveyance, Bryan is alive with three unmarried children in their 20s, and no grandchildren.

(f) Winokur, owner of Blueacre in fee simple absolute, conveys it "to Temple Beth–El so long as used for a synagogue, then to Tiffany."

(g) Winokur, owner of Blueacre in fee simple absolute, conveys it "to Temple Beth–El, but if the land ceases to be used for a synagogue, then to Tiffany."

(h) Winokur, owner of Blueacre in fee simple absolute, conveys it "to Pushaw for life, then to Chambers if he attains the age of 50."

b. *Perpetuities Reform.* Now that you have a basic understanding of the RAP, you can appreciate the harsh consequences that resulted from the common law's "remorseless" application of the rule. To mitigate those consequences, many states have adopted one or more of the following types of perpetuities reform:

- *The "wait and see" doctrine.* One of the first reforms was the "wait and see" doctrine, which works just as the name suggests—instead of applying the RAP at the outset to see if there is any possibility the interest might vest too remotely, the wait and see doctrine "waits" to "see" if the interest *actually does vest or fail* within the lifetime of someone who was alive at the time of the conveyance or within 21 years after that person's death.

- *Equitable modification* (also known as *cy pres*). This second early reform allowed courts to modify nonconforming future interests to bring them into compliance with the RAP.

- *Statutory presumptions to resolve particular RAP problems.* A number of jurisdictions have enacted statutes to address the "unborn widow" problem (see page 324) and other remote possibilities that commonly caused future interests to violate the RAP. *See, e.g.,* 765 Ill. Comp. Stat. 305/4(c).

- *Repeal.* A handful of states have enacted statutes abolishing the common law rule in its entirety. *See, e.g.,* R.I. Gen. Laws § 34–11–38; S.D. Cod. Laws § 43–5–8. About a quarter of the states have abolished the rule as it applies to perpetual trusts. *See,* e.g., Mo. Rev. Stat. 456.025.

Our next case, *Merrill v. Wimmer,* illustrates one of these reforms. You should note that the reported decision below is *not* in fact the law in Indiana; as explained in note 4 after the case, the Supreme Court of Indiana reversed this decision on appeal. Nevertheless, the Court of Appeals decision provides a useful backdrop for reviewing how dissatisfaction over the impact of the common law RAP has triggered action by courts and legislatures to ameliorate the RAP's harsh consequences.

MERRILL v. WIMMER

Court of Appeals of Indiana.
453 N.E.2d 356 (1983), *rev'd,* 481 N.E.2d 1294 (1985).

[Editors' Note: This case involves the interpretation of the will of Newell Merrill, who died in 1977. Because the will was very complicated—not to mention *brutally* drafted—we have provided a brief summary in place of the court's recitation of the facts.

In 1970, Newell executed his will. The will made a number of bequests, and then placed the balance of his assets into a trust. Under the terms of the trust, his three children—Judith, Dennis, and Walter—were to receive the income from the trust, in equal shares, reflecting Newell's apparent intent to split the residue of his assets equally among his children. Newell's provisions regarding the termination of the trust and the distribution of the trust's assets, however, were complicated. With regard to two-thirds of the trust's assets, Newell's will provided that the trust would remain in effect until Newell's youngest grandchild turned 25 years of age. At that point, one-third of the trust's assets would be distributed between Judith and her children, with Judith receiving one-half of that amount (or one-sixth of the trust assets) and her children sharing the other one-half equally. Likewise, one-third of the trust's assets would then be distributed between Dennis and his children, with Dennis receiving one-half of that amount and his children sharing the other one-half equally.

With regard to the other one-third of the trust's assets, however, Newell specified that the assets were to remain in trust for Walter for his entire life—regardless of the age of Newell's grandchildren—with Walter continuing to receive the income from that trust during his life. At the time of Walter's death, the trust would terminate as to this one-third of the assets. If Walter died leaving issue of his body, that one-third of the assets would be divided in half, with one-half being shared equally by Walter's issue and the other one-half being shared equally by all of Newell's grandchildren alive at that time (which might also include Walter's children). If Walter died without issue, then that entire one-third of the trust assets was to be distributed equally among Newell's then-living grandchildren.]

CONOVER, PRESIDING JUDGE. Appellants, the majority of beneficiaries under the will of Newell M. Merrill (Newell), appeal the trial court's decision construing Newell's will. . . .

The trial court, adopting the probate commissioner's findings, held the provisions regarding the corpus's distribution to Judith, Dennis and their children were invalid under the rule against perpetuities. It modified the trust by (a) deleting the condition of distribution of the remainder when the youngest grandchild reached 25 years, and (b) awarding one-third of the corpus each to Judith and Dennis outright. It upheld the entire trust provision regarding Walter. . . .

"An interest in property shall not be valid unless it must vest, if at all, not later than twenty-one [21] years after a life or lives in being at the creation of the interest." Ind.Code 32–1–4–1. Under the rule, all vesting must be done during the period of the rule. *Bailey v. Bailey*, (1967) 142 Ind.App. 119, 232 N.E.2d 372. The possibility of vesting after the time of the rule, not only the probability, will void the gift. *Id.*

Here, it is possible the youngest grandchild may reach the age of 25 years more than 21 years after the death of the lives in being, Newell's children, at the creation of the interests. While the youngest grandchild living at the time of trial was sixteen, Newell's children are all still alive. We are required to presume they are still capable of having more children. *Reasoner v. Herman*, (1922) 191 Ind. 642, 134 N.E. 276. Therefore, the class of beneficiaries is not closed.

Such class must close within the period of the rule. L. Simes & A. Smith, The Law of Future Interests § 1265 (2d ed. 1956). Here it may not close until after the period prescribed in the rule. Under the will's terms, it was possible for one or more of Newell's children to outlive him (as they did), and then have a child which would not reach the age of 25 within 21 years of Newell's child's death. Therefore, the possibility exists that grandchild's interest[33] would not vest within the time required by the rule. For that reason, the entire gift fails.

Appellants concede the proposed distribution of two-thirds of the corpus to Judith, Dennis and their children when the youngest grandchild reached 25 violates the rule against perpetuities, Ind.Code 32–1–4–1. They argue, however, the trial court erred by (a) eliminating the provision for payment of the trust's income to Judith and Dennis for life, (b) accelerating the distribution of two-thirds of the corpus to Judith and Dennis, and (c) upholding the entire provision regarding Walter. We agree.

There are several guidelines used by a court when construing a will.

[T]he cardinal and paramount rule is to ascertain the intention of the testator and give it effect as long as it is not prohibited by law or violates public policy. This intention may be ascertained by the language or the words of the will itself and an examination of the entire will or from the four corners thereof. [*Weishaar v. Burton*, (1962) 132 Ind.App. 597, 604, 179 N.E.2d 211, 214–15.]

A will should be construed to prevent intestacy if it can be done without doing violence to the intent of the testator. It is the settled rule that when the striking of an invalid part results in defeat of the main and dominant purpose of the testator, incidental provisions which constitute with it the entire testamentary scheme must fall with it. Conversely it is the settled rule that where the testator's dominant intent is legal and valid, an invalid, separable, incidental provision will be stricken out and the provisions carrying out the dominant intent of the testator will be sustained. [*Sipe v. Merchants Trust Co.*, (1941) 109 Ind.App. 566, 571, 34 N.E.2d 968, 970–71.]

The court may not rewrite the will for the testator. *Szulkowska v. Werwinski*, (1941) 109 Ind.App. 511, 36 N.E.2d 948.

By creating life estates for his children and by providing the corpus was not to be distributed until his youngest grandchild reached 25, Newell made his underlying intent clear, he did not want his property to pass immediately to his children. He wanted the grandchildren to share but only when they reached 25, presumably an age at which he believed they would be mature enough to handle their inheritance wisely. Given this as his intent, the trial court erred by extinguishing the grandchildren's interests and giving a full two-thirds of the corpus immediately to Judith and Dennis. While we try to avoid intestacy, the trial court here has rewritten Newell's will. This it may not do.

---

33. The grandchild's interest may be viewed as an executory interest, which springs into being at a future date and cuts short the prior estate, or a vested remainder subject to open which under these facts is considered contingent, and therefore both are subject to the rule against perpetuities.

We also find the trial court erred by upholding the provision of the trust regarding Walter. While we agree this section does not violate the rule against perpetuities, it was an integral part of Newell's testamentary distribution scheme and may not stand alone. All the specifications for the distribution of the corpus and its income were contained in one section and separated by semi-colons, not periods. The appellees argue Newell intended to create three trusts, one for each child. However, the document itself only refers to "this Trust," singular. Such format demonstrates the testator intended this distribution scheme to be interrelated.

The trial court's construction clearly subverts the testator's intent and cannot stand, but that is not the end of the matter. In an attempt to give effect to both Newell's intent and the rule against perpetuities, we will examine these provisions in light of the doctrine of equitable approximation. . . .

[T]he doctrine of equitable approximation is . . . generally defined in BLACK'S LAW DICTIONARY 632 (rev. 4th ed. 1968), as follows:

> EQUITABLE DOCTRINE OF APPROXIMATION. This doctrine differs from "Cy pres doctrine" in purpose and application. The last mentioned doctrine applies where an apparent charitable intention has failed, whether by an incomplete disposition at the outset or by subsequent inadequacy of the original object, and its purpose is to give a cy pres or proximate application to testator's intention, whereas the "equitable doctrine of approximation" merely authorizes a court of chancery to vary the details of administration, in order to preserve the trust, and carry out the general purpose of the donor. *National Bank of Greece v. Savarika*, 167 Miss. 571, 148 So. 649, 654.

This doctrine has been used frequently in recent years to give effect to a testator's intent when his general purpose, *i.e.* to create a plan for the distribution of his assets after his death, cannot be effectuated due to some other legal principle such as the rule against perpetuities coming into play. *See In re Estate of Chun Quan Yee Hop*, (1970) 52 Hawaii 40, 469 P.2d 183; *Carter v. Berry*, (1962) 243 Miss. 321, 140 So.2d 843; *Berry v. Union National Bank* (W.Va.1980) 262 S.E.2d 766 (referred to as equitable modification). In each of these cases, the supreme courts of the respective states found the time of distribution was the least critical contingent and therefore modified the possible date of distribution from 25 to 21 years after the death of lives in being and thereby saved the trusts. *See also Edgerly v. Barker*, (1891) 66 N.H. 434, 31 A. 900 (where the court reduced the grandchildren's age requirement from 40 to 21 years).

Basically, this doctrine is applied to private trusts in the same manner and for the same policy reasons as the cy pres doctrine is used in regard to charitable trusts. This is a rule designed to help eliminate the harsh effect of the rule against perpetuities.[34] Both the cy pres and equitable approximation doctrines are applied to effectuate the testator's intent to the extent possible. This being the ultimate goal of will construction in Indiana, we adopt this tool to reach that goal to the fullest extent possible under the circumstances.

Contrary to the cases discussed above, we do not believe the time of distribution was the least critical contingent of this trust. We believe the grandchildren's age requirement of 25 years before distribution of the corpus was to be made indicates Newell believed the trust's distributees then would be mature enough to make responsible decisions concerning the property distributed to them. A distribution of Newell's property only to those grandchildren alive at his death seems to be the scheme least disruptive of his apparent intent.

Therefore, we hold the term "grandchild" appearing in the first line of item 3(E) of Newell's will shall be construed to mean "grandchild alive at my death." We believe that construction does the least violence to testator's intent. Under this construction, the class of beneficiaries the will creates closed at the time of Newell's death, and makes the lives of the grandchildren then alive the measuring lives under the rule against perpetuities. Thus, the rule is not violated, and Newell's distribution scheme in the main is saved. This construction most closely approximates the intent of the testator.[35]

Reversed with instructions to enter judgment accordingly.

Notes

1. *Classifying the Interests Created by Newell's Will.* In footnote 33, the court concludes that the interests granted to Newell's grandchildren in his will "may be viewed as an executory interest, which springs into being at a future date and cuts short the prior estate, or a vested remainder subject to open which under these facts is considered contingent, and therefore both are subject to the rule against perpetuities." Can you explain how the future interest might be viewed as a vested remainder subject to open? Can you explain how it might be viewed as an executory interest? [As you will recall from our discussion of executory interests (page 297), an executory interest *divests* a vested interest. What interest would be divested in the *Merrill* case? For a hint, reconsider the materials about trusts following *Baker v. Weedon* (page 262).] Which is it?

2. *"Certainty of Vesting" Revisited—The Common Law's Presumption of Fertility.* In the *Merrill* case, the court stated that it was "required to

---

34. Our decision in this case should not be read as emasculating the rule against perpetuities. On the contrary, we endorse the rule and its purposes. However, under these facts, we are complying with the rule which mandates us to effectuate the testator's intent to the extent possible by applying the doctrine of equitable approximation.

35. While this construction does eliminate any interest of after-born grandchil-

dren, all of Newell's children are in their mid to late 40's. Although we presume they are still able to have children, *Reasoner v. Herman*, (1922) 191 Ind. 642, 134 N.E. 276, the possibility of additional children, without more, does not constitute so grave a harm, we believe, as to offset the benefits of this construction.

presume" that Judith, Dennis, and Walter were capable of having more children. Because it appears that Judith and Dennis each had minor children at the time of Newell's death, this presumption hardly seems outrageous. But the common law drew the same presumption regardless of a person's age. In the infamous case of *Jee v. Audley*, 29 Eng. Rep. 1186 (1787), the court applied the RAP to void an executory interest in the daughters of John and Elizabeth Jee, although John and Elizabeth were *70 years old* at the time of the conveyance.

The court's application of the RAP in *Jee*, colloquially known as the "fertile octogenarian" doctrine, reflects how seriously the common law took the concept that the RAP required *absolute certainty* that an interest would vest in a timely fashion. Even though a 90–year old woman would be significantly more likely to win the lottery than give birth to a child, the common law presumed that she was capable of having a child until the moment of her death. Furthermore, this presumption was conclusive—in other words, the woman could not even prove that conception and birth of a child were impossible because (for example) she was sterile or had undergone surgery to remove her reproductive organs!

Arguably, the presumption that persons are capable of having additional children (regardless of age) makes more sense today than it did when *Jee* was decided. At that time, the law did not treat adopted children as equivalent to natural children, as most state statutes do today. *See* Iowa Code Ann. § 633.223 (adopted children treated identically to natural children for purposes of inheritance); Mich. Comp. Laws § 700.110 (same). Furthermore, technological advances have made it possible for women in excess of 60 to bear children. Nonetheless, a few states have enacted statutes changing the common law's presumption of fertility. *See, e.g.*, N.Y. Est. Powers & Trusts Law § 9–1.3(e) (for purposes of RAP, women over 55 are presumed to be incapable of having children; regardless of age, evidence can be offered to prove fertility or lack thereof).

3. *The Doctrine of "Infectious Invalidity."* The trial court in *Merrill* struck down the provisions of the trust relating to Judith and Dennis, but upheld the provisions relating to Walter. As discussed earlier (page 320), when the RAP is violated, the law typically voids only the offending interest and gives effect to the rest of the conveyance. Under the trial court's holding, Walter would have received his life income interest under the will, but the invalidated trust interests relating to Judith and Dennis would have passed by intestacy to Newell's heirs—in this case, Judith, Dennis, and Walter. The court of appeals held that this result would have done violence to Newell's testamentary scheme and concluded that the trust had to be either enforced or invalidated as a whole. This is an application of the doctrine of infectious invalidity sometimes applied in the law of trusts. Why did the court of appeals consider applying the infectious invalidity doctrine? Why would the court have had to apply this doctrine to invalidate Walter's interest under the trust?

4. *Construing the Language of Newell's Will—"Equitable Approximation" or "Rewriting the Testator's Will"?* The *Merrill* court applied the doctrine of "equitable approximation" to construe Merrill's will so that it did not violate the RAP. The court concluded that the term "grandchildren" was

ambiguous, and thus interpreted the term "grandchildren" to refer only to Newell's living grandchildren, *i.e.*, only those grandchildren already alive at the time of his death. Can you explain how this interpretation avoided a violation of the RAP?

After going to such great pains to suggest that it cannot rewrite Newell Merrill's will for him, did the court of appeals do just that by using the "equitable approximation" doctrine? On appeal, the Indiana Supreme Court thought so, and reversed the court of appeals, rejecting its use of "equitable approximation" as inappropriate:

> The Court of Appeals ... was critical of the trial court for extinguishing the grandchildren's interest in two-thirds (2/3) of the corpus and vesting it immediately in Judith and Dennis, and it referred to this as the trial court's having "rewritten Newell's will." Yet, under the claim of merely construing the will, the Court of Appeals, itself, has rewritten it by changing certain of the beneficiaries from the Testator's grandchildren (regardless of the time of their births) to his grandchildren alive at the time of his death. Its justification for this impermissible action was to avoid intestacy, which results under the will as written. In essence, the Court of Appeals put into effect a testamentary plan that it perceived would have been preferred by the Testator, had he known that his own plan could not be carried out. However, resort may be had to rules of construction only for the purpose of ascertainment of a testator's intent when there is an actual or latent ambiguity.
>
> Here, there is no ambiguity whatsoever in the will, with regard to either the identity of the beneficiaries or the time of termination of the trust. The beneficiaries were the Testator's children and grandchildren, all of them, and the trust was to terminate, as to two-thirds (2/3), when the youngest grandchild attained the age of twenty-five (25) years. What could be more clear?

Merrill v. Wimmer, 481 N.E.2d 1294, 1297–98 (Ind. 1985). When you consider Newell Merrill's likely intent, who do you believe has the better argument here, the Court of Appeals or the Supreme Court? Why? Was the Supreme Court saying that equitable approximation is never appropriate?

5. *Perpetuities Reform—The Cy Pres Doctrine.* As the *Merrill* case notes, the *cy pres* doctrine developed from the law of charitable trusts. Under that doctrine, when property has been conveyed into trust for charitable purposes, but thereafter it becomes impracticable or illegal to carry out the settlor's specific intent, the court may exercise its equitable powers to modify the terms of the trust to give effect to the settlor's general charitable intentions.

At common law, however, *cy pres* was not available to enable courts to reform private instruments of conveyance like deeds or wills. A handful of states—Hawaii, Mississippi, and New Hampshire—have applied equitable reformation as a common law reform to avoid perpetuities violations. William B. Stoebuck & Dale A. Whitman, The Law of Property § 3.22, at 134 n.3 (3d ed. 2000). In most other jurisdictions, however, cy pres reform has come via statute. Some statutes grant broad reformation powers:

When any limitation or provision violates the rule against perpetuities ... and reformation would more closely approximate the primary purpose or scheme of the grantor, settlor or testator than total invalidity of the limitation or provision, ... the limitation or provision shall be reformed, if possible, to the extent necessary to avoid violation of the rule or policy and, as so reformed, shall be valid and effective.

Mo. Stat. Ann. § 442.555(2). Other statutes are more limited, permitting *cy pres* modification of an instrument only for the purpose of reducing any age contingency to 21 years. *See, e.g.,* N.Y. Est. Powers & Trusts Law § 9–1.2. If Indiana had enacted a statute identical to the Missouri statute, would that have permitted the court in *Merrill* to reform the will of Newell Merrill? Are you sure?

6. *Perpetuities Reform—The "Wait and See" Doctrine.* The common law RAP evaluates the contingent future interest at the time of its creation and invalidates it if there is any possibility of remote vesting. In contrast, a "wait and see" approach would not apply the RAP immediately, but would "wait" and "see" whether the interest *actually did vest or fail* within the lifetime of someone who was alive at the time of the conveyance or within 21 years after their death. If so, the interest would satisfy the RAP.

Consider the following example: Assume that Henning, owner of Blueacre in fee simple absolute, conveyed it in 1980 "to Pushaw, but if the Atlanta Braves win the World Series, then to Schmitz." At common law, Schmitz's executory interest would violate the RAP and would be void; in 1980, it would have been impossible to prove with certainty that the Braves would ever win the World Series. Under a "wait and see" approach, however, Schmitz's executory interest would have vested in 1995—only 15 years after its creation, well within the perpetuities period—and thus her interest would be valid.

At present, more than a dozen states have adopted "wait and see" reform that retains the common law perpetuities period of a life in being plus 21 years. William B. Stoebuck & Dale A. Whitman, The Law of Property § 3.22, at 134 nn.1–3 (3d ed. 2000). What are the strengths and weaknesses of the "wait and see" approach as compared with the traditional common law "what might happen" test? Which do you think is preferable, and why?

7. *Perpetuities Reform—The Uniform Statutory Rule Against Perpetuities.* In an effort to encourage perpetuities reform, the National Conference of Commissioners on Uniform State Laws (NCCUSL) promulgated the Uniform Statutory Rule Against Perpetuities (USRAP) in 1986. The USRAP is essentially a hybrid of the common law RAP, "wait and see" reform, and *cy pres* reformation. In pertinent part, the USRAP provides:

§ 1. Statutory Rule Against Perpetuities

(a) A nonvested property interest is invalid unless:

(1) when the interest is created, it is certain to vest or to terminate no later than 21 years after the death of an individual then alive; or

(2) the interest either vests or terminates within 90 years after its creation.

§ 3. Reformation

(a) Upon the petition of an interested person, a court shall reform a disposition in the manner that most closely approximates the transferor's manifested plan of distribution and is within the 90 years allowed by Section 1(a)(2) ... if:

(1) a nonvested property interest ... becomes invalid under Section 1 (statutory rule against perpetuities);

(2) a class gift is not but might become invalid under Section 1 (statutory rule against perpetuities) and the time has arrived when the share of any class member is to take effect in possession or enjoyment; or

(3) a nonvested property interest that is not validated by Section 1(a)(1) can vest but not within 90 years after its creation.

Read the language of the USRAP carefully. As compared to the traditional common law "what might happen" test, how does the USRAP change perpetuities law? As a vehicle for perpetuities reform, do you think it is better or worse than the pure "wait and see" approach discussed in note 6 above? For differing views, compare Lawrence W. Waggoner, *The Uniform Statutory Rule Against Perpetuities: The Rationale of the 90–Year Waiting Period*, 73 Cornell L. Rev. 157 (1988) with Jesse Dukeminier, *The Uniform Statutory Rule Against Perpetuities: Ninety Years in Limbo*, 34 UCLA L. Rev. 1023 (1987). As of 1993, twenty-three states had enacted the USRAP.[36]

8. *More Problems Applying the RAP.* To further test your understanding of the RAP, consider the following examples. In each example, determine the state of the title assuming the common law RAP applies, and alternatively what the state of title would be if the jurisdiction had adopted one of the perpetuities reforms such as "wait and see" or the USRAP. Finally, if the RAP invalidates some portion of the conveyance, explain how you would proceed to carry out the original intention of the grantor (to the maximum extent possible) without violating the RAP.

(a) Barnes, owner of Blueacre in fee simple absolute, dies. His will devises Blueacre "to Dauer for life, then to his widow, if any, for her life, then to his then-living children in fee simple."

(b) Barnes, owner of Blueacre in fee simple absolute, is in poor health and is planning for the eventual disposition of his property. He wishes for ownership of Blueacre to pass to Corrada, but Corrada is also in poor health, and Barnes is concerned that Corrada might die before Barnes does, or before Barnes's estate could be probated following his death. Thus, Barnes instead prepares and delivers a deed conveying Blueacre "to Corrada in fee, from and after the entry of the final order of the

---

36. A warning: Do not be fooled by the title "Uniform" Statutory Rule Against Perpetuities. In an effort to encourage and promote law reform, NCCUSL promulgates a wide range of "uniform" statutes, seeking to promote uniformity in state laws. In some areas, NCCUSL's efforts are spectacularly successful (the best example being the Uniform Commercial Code, which has been adopted in every state except Louisiana, which has even adopted portions of the UCC). In other areas, NCCUSL's efforts have not achieved success, at least to the extent that success is measured by states adopting a proposed uniform statute (for example, zero states have adopted the Uniform Land Transactions Act).

probate court administering my estate, but if Corrada is not alive at that time, then to Bryan."

(c) Barnes, owner of Blueacre in fee simple absolute, dies. His will devises Blueacre "to the youngest of my children alive 25 years after the death of my surviving widow," but makes no other provision regarding title to Blueacre.

(d) Barnes, owner of Blueacre in fee simple absolute, conveys it "to the youngest of my children alive 25 years after the death of my surviving widow."

(e) Nice, owner of Blueacre in fee simple absolute, conveys it "to Bryan for life, and if Bryan's children survive her, to such of her children as reach the age of 25, but if none of her children survive her, then to Chen in fee simple."

(f) Nice, owner of Blueacre in fee simple absolute, conveys it "to the heirs of Bryan's first child." Three years later, Bryan has her first child, Sam. Two years thereafter, Nice conveys "all of the rest and residue of my interest in Blueacre" to Sam.

(g) Chen, owner of Blueacre in fee simple absolute, dies. His will devises Blueacre "to my grandchildren in fee simple." At the time of his death, Chen had no grandchildren, but his wife was pregnant and gave birth four months later to their only child, Mark.[37]

(h) Chen, owner of Blueacre in fee simple absolute, conveys it "to my grandchildren in fee simple." At the time of the conveyance, Chen had no grandchildren, but his wife was pregnant and gave birth four months later to their first child, Mark. Two months later, Chen conveyed "all of the rest and residue of my interest in Blueacre" to Nice.

c. *Other Contingent Property Interests Subject to the RAP*. The preceding materials have focused upon how the RAP applies to contingent remainders, executory interests, and vested remainders subject to open. Courts have also applied the RAP, however, to other contingent property interests, including options to purchase, rights of first refusal, and leases to commence at some unspecified date in the future.

Suppose, for example, Donald Trump is developing a shopping center. To obtain the necessary financing, Trump will probably "prelease" some or all of the center—in other words, he will sign leases with prospective tenants before construction even begins, or while construction is ongoing. Suppose that one such prospective tenant, Kroger, is willing to sign a 20–year lease, but does not want that lease to commence until the construction is completed (for obvious reasons, as Kroger does not want to pay rent until it can occupy the store). Thus, Trump and Kroger sign a lease which states that the lease term will not commence (and thus Kroger will not be entitled to possession) until Trump com-

---

37. For purposes of this problem, you should note that the common law treated children *in utero* as "lives in being" for purposes of applying the RAP. Mark is thus a "life in being" although he had not yet been born as of the time the will took effect.

pletes construction. This seems perfectly sensible. Yet in a jurisdiction that applied the common law RAP, the lease would be void. [Can you explain why?] How would you would address this problem if you were advising Trump?

Options and rights of first refusal are similarly subject to the RAP. An option is a right, given by contract, whereby the optionor (the owner of property) gives the optionee the right to purchase the property at some time in the future. A right of first refusal is a specialized type of option. Typically, it does not give the holder the general right to purchase the property at any time; instead, it gives the holder the first opportunity to purchase the property when the owner decides to sell it, or it prevents the owner from selling the property to a third party without first offering it to the holder on the same terms. If Barnes holds an option to purchase the land of Winokur, and that option is not limited in duration, does the option violate the RAP?

CENTRAL DELAWARE COUNTY AUTHORITY v. GREYHOUND CORP.

Supreme Court of Pennsylvania.
527 Pa. 47, 588 A.2d 485 (1991).

FLAHERTY, JUSTICE. In 1941 and 1950 the Baldwin Locomotive Works conveyed to the Central Delaware County Authority ("Authority") two parcels of land. The Authority paid $5,500 for the parcel conveyed in 1941 and $2,970 for the parcel conveyed in 1950. The deeds in both cases conveyed a fee simple interest subject to a restrictive covenant appearing in the encumbrance clause. The 1941 deed contains the following provision:

> It is specifically covenanted, stipulated, and agreed between the parties hereto that the said tract of land, while in the ownership and possession of the said Central Delaware County Authority and its successors, shall be kept available for and shall be used only for public purposes by the said Central Delaware County Authority and its successor or any other public instrumentality or other agency which may hereafter acquire title to the same. In the event that at any time hereafter said use shall be abandoned so that the said tract shall cease to be used for said public purposes, then and in such event the Baldwin Locomotive Works, its successors and assigns, shall have the right to repurchase, retake and reacquire the same upon the payment, either to the Central Delaware County Authority if owner thereof, or to any successor in right thereto, or to the municipalities for which the said vendee or its successors shall be acting, the sum of fifty-five hundred dollars ($5,500.00) above mentioned and herein provided to be paid therefor; or in the event of dispute, the said sum may be paid into Court in any appropriate proceeding for the benefit of any and all parties entitled to the same. In any such case, vendee shall have the right to remove all improvements.

PROVIDED, HOWEVER, that if the Baldwin Locomotive Works does not pay the sum of fifty-five hundred dollars ($5,500.00) to the said Authority, or otherwise as above provided, within six months after the date when the authority or its successors in title abandons the said property for public purposes, or the date when notified by the Authority of its intention to abandon the property, then and in such event this covenant shall become void and of no effect.

The encumbrance clause of the 1950 deed is substantially the same as that of the 1941 deed, except that ... repurchase is conditioned upon payment of $2,970 instead of $5,500.

The Authority operated a sewage treatment plant on this land for approximately twenty-six years. In 1980, the Authority ceased operation of the sewage treatment facility, but the Authority continues to maintain and possess the land. In 1983, it brought an action to quiet title in the land, alleging that the deed's public use, ownership and repurchase restrictions are void as violative of the rule against perpetuities.

The parties stipulated to evidence on each claim regarding the chain of title of the Baldwin tract and corporate successorship to Baldwin, and, accordingly, to the persons who may assert the right to repurchase. [Editors' Note: Greyhound is a successor to Baldwin's interest.] The trial court found that the restrictions of the deed do not violate the rule and that they are not an unreasonable restraint upon alienation. It concluded that the estates conveyed in the deeds are fee simple interests subject to a condition subsequent. Since a fee simple subject to a condition subsequent creates a present interest in the grantor, the conveyance did not, according to the trial court, violate the rule against perpetuities.

Superior Court, on appeal, held that the restriction in the deed was an option to purchase, not an interest subject to a condition subsequent. 386 Pa.Super. 423, 563 A.2d 139. Since options to purchase are subject to the rule against perpetuities,[38] and since this restriction allowed for the possibility that the option might vest later than twenty-one years after a life in being at the creation of the restriction, Superior Court held that the restrictions violated the rule. Superior Court determined that the restrictions were not invalid, however, on public policy grounds: "were we to find the rule against perpetuities applicable to this particular option contract, we would be creating a climate in which grantors would not freely give their properties for public use." [386 Pa. Super.] At 434, 563 A.2d 139. The Authority petitioned for allowance of appeal and we granted allocatur. The principal issue on this appeal is whether Superior Court erred in determining that the rule against perpetuities did not invalidate the restrictive covenants.

The first question is whether Superior Court was correct in holding that the estate created was a repurchase option rather than an estate subject to a condition subsequent. A fee simple subject to a condition

---

38. An option to purchase is a future interest which may or may not be exercised, *i.e.*, it may or may not vest, within twenty- one years. It is, therefore, subject to the rule against perpetuities.

subsequent arises where the provision is that upon the happening of a certain event, the grantor has the right and power to terminate the conveyed estate. *See Emrick v. Bethlehem Twp.*, 506 Pa. 372, 379, 485 A.2d 736, 739 (1984). This estate is not subject to the rule against perpetuities because the right of reentry or power of termination which it creates is exempt from the rule. However, a repurchase option, as the restriction in the present case was held to be by Superior Court, is subject to the rule, for an option is not a vested estate.

The initial inquiry, then, is whether Superior Court was correct in deciding that the interest in this case was a repurchase option rather than a fee simple subject to a condition subsequent. We concur with Superior Court's analysis. While it is true that the deeds may be read to create a fee simple subject to a condition subsequent (the condition subsequent would be abandonment of public use followed by the payment of certain sums of money), the deeds can also be read to create a repurchase option conditioned upon the termination of public use. Like Superior Court, to resolve this ambiguity, we turn to the Restatement of Property for guidance:

> If the language and circumstances of a conveyance of an estate in fee simple are otherwise reasonably susceptible of two constructions, under one of which it creates either a possibility of reverter or power of termination, ... and under the other of which it creates an option to repurchase, ... the latter of the two constructions is preferred. The fact that the exercise of the reserved privilege requires the parting with money or other consideration, by the reserving conveyor is sufficiently indicative of the intent of the conveyor to create an option.... The finding of the option, under these facts, furthers the protective policy which underlies the rule against perpetuities, and is in accord with the general constructional preference for covenants rather than conditions.

4 Restatement of Property § 394, Comment c (1944). We believe that section 394 accurately reflects the law of this Commonwealth in favoring interpretations of deed restrictions which bring the restriction within the ambit of the rule. *See Barton v. Thaw*, 246 Pa. 348, 364, 92 A. 312, 316 (1914). Superior Court was not in error, therefore, in finding that the interest created was a repurchase option.

It remains to be considered, however, whether Superior Court was correct in also determining that the rule against perpetuities does not apply to the repurchase option on the grounds of public policy, viz., that grantors would not freely give their properties for public use....

... In *Barton v. Thaw*, 246 Pa. 348, 92 A. 312 (1914), this court addressed the policy underlying the rule and the nature of the legal obligation which the rule imposes. In that case, this court voided a covenant in the deed which granted the option to purchase the surface in fee "at any future time whatsoever ... at a price not exceeding one hundred dollars per acre." *Id.* at 350, 92 A. at 313.[39] The court held that the rule against perpetuities applied to this repurchase option which was unlimited in time, and the interest was, therefore, void. The rationale for this holding was that the rule against perpetuities is a "peremptory command of law," and thus is not subject to negation by a countervailing statement of public policy:

> "The rule against perpetuities is not a rule of construction, but a peremptory command of law. It is not, like a rule of construction, a test, more or less artificial, to determine intention. Its object is to defeat intention. Therefore every provision in a will or settlement is to be construed as if the rule did not exist, and then to the provision so construed the rule is to be remorselessly applied." Gray on Rule Against Perpetuities (2nd Ed.), sec 629; Gerber's Est., 196 Pa. 366, 46 A. 497 (1900); Bender v. Bender, 225 Pa. 434, 74 A. 246 (1909). "We must be careful not to strain the law so as to avoid this rule. It is founded upon a sound principle of public policy and should be rigidly enforced." Coggins' App., 124 Pa. 10, 16 A. 579 (1889). [246 Pa. at 354, 92 A. at 314.]

The court described the policy underlying the rule as follows:

> Such an impress on land [one that violates the rule] ought not to be sustained, and it cannot be. It isolates the property. It takes it out of commerce. It removes it from the market. It halts improvements. It prevents the land from answering to the needs of growing communities. No homes can be built or towns laid out on land so encumbered, because the land always remains subject to be taken under the option. It is not a matter which affects the rights of individuals only. The entire community is interested. The welfare of the public is at stake. It is contrary to the well settled public policy of the state that such an option or right to purchase land should be held to be good. It was for the express purpose of destroying such serious hindrances to material and social prosperity and progress that the rule against perpetuities was brought forth. And the rule must be rigidly enforced. [246 Pa. at 364, 92 A. at 316.]

These considerations are as valid today as they were in 1914, when *Barton v. Thaw* was written. Now, as then, economic development and prosperity depends in important part upon the free alienability of land. It is for this reason that the rule against perpetuities is a "peremptory command of law" that "is to be remorselessly applied." The repurchase option is, therefore, void....

39. The language in the *Barton* deed read as follows:

And in case the said parties of the second part, their heirs and assigns, should at any future time whatsoever desire to purchase any of said land in fee simple, then the said parties of the first part, for themselves, their heirs or assigns, hereby covenant and agree to sell and convey the same to the said parties of the second part, their heirs or assigns, at a price not exceeding one hundred dollars per acre.

Notes

1. *Perpetuities Reform Revisited.* Do you agree with the court's rationale in *Greyhound*? Does the use of open-ended options really pose a significant obstacle to land development? By way of contrast, the USRAP has effectively abolished the rule in relation to commercial transactions. *See* USRAP § 4(1) (providing that the statutory rule "does not apply to ... a nonvested property interest ... arising out of a nondonative transfer....""). By its terms, the statute applies only to donative transfers (wills or gifts). In states that have enacted the USRAP, therefore, options, rights of first refusal, leases to commence in the future, and other contingent future interests created in commercial transactions do not violate the RAP, regardless of their duration. Why do you think that USRAP adopted § 4(1)?

2. *Abolition of the Rule for Interests in Trusts.* A number of states recently have enacted statutes that allow the creation of perpetual trusts, essentially abolishing the RAP as applied to trusts. Alaska Stat. § 34.40.110; Del. Code Ann. tit. 25, § 503 (RAP abolished as to personal property held in trust); 765 Ill. Comp. Stat. 305/4; S.D. Codified Laws §§ 43–5–1, 43–5–8 (trust can endure perpetually as long as trustee has power to sell trust assets); Wis. Stat. Ann. § 700.16 (same).

These statutes permit grantors to create "tax-exempt dynasty trusts"— trusts that last for many generations, thereby maximizing the benefits of a $1.5 million exemption from federal estate taxes.[40] Professor Ira Mark Bloom has predicted that repeal of the RAP for perpetual trusts, without some other method of controlling the dead hand, will be "a disaster." Ira Mark Bloom, *How Federal Transfer Taxes Affect the Development of Property Law*, 48 Cleve. St. L. Rev. 661, 676 (2000). He identifies several problems with long-lasting trusts:

- "The wealth that can be amassed from a one million dollar trust after relatively short periods of time, based on an after-tax return of 6%, is startling." *Id.* at 675 n.92 (predicting that the value after 100 years

---

40. Professors Jesse Dukeminier and James E. Krier explain the estate tax benefits as follows:

The federal estate tax, first enacted in 1916, levies a tax on any property interest transferred by will, intestacy, or survivorship to another person, except for transfers to spouses and charities. The tax can be avoided, however, by the use of life estates. At the death of a life tenant, the tenancy ends, leaving no transfer to be taxed. For seventy years, lawyers took advantage of this loophole by creating trusts with successive life estates, which could continue without any estate taxes being levied against succeeding generations until after the termination of the trust. And the trusts themselves could continue until the Rule against Perpetuities, in one or another variant, called a halt.

In 1986 Congress closed this loophole in the tax laws, deciding that a transfer tax is due at the expiration of each generation.... At the same time ..., Congress lightened the taxpayer burden by providing a $1 million exemption from the [Generation Skipping Transfer] tax for each transferor (doubled in the case of married couples). An inflation adjustment in 2002 increased the amount to $1.1 million; it will increase again to $1.5 million in 2004 and ultimately, in gradual steps, to $3.5 million in 2009.... [Thus, a] transferor can create a trust, with $1.1 million ($3.5 million after 2008) as principal, for his children for life, with successive life estates in succeeding generations, for as long as state perpetuities law allows. Thanks to the exemption, no estate tax or GST tax is due until the trust terminates. [Jesse Dukeminier & James E. Krier, *The Rise of the Perpetual Trust*, 50 UCLA L. Rev. 1303 (2003).]

would be $369 million; after 200 years it would be $136.43 billion; after 300 years, the value would be $50.395 trillion).

- The trust will provide significant wealth and power not only to dynasty families but also to the corporate trustees selected to administer the trusts. *Id.*

- Administration of a perpetual trust is likely to become a "nightmare." *Id.* (citing Professor Lawrence W. Waggoner's prediction that "the average settlor will have more than 100 descendants (who are beneficiaries of the trust) 150 years after the trust is created, around 2,500 beneficiaries 250 years after the trust is created, and 45,000 beneficiaries 350 years after the trust is created. Five hundred years after the trust is created, the number of living beneficiaries could rise to an astounding 3.4 million").

Are these valid policy concerns? Can the RAP be justified as a rule that discourages or prevents concentration of wealth? Early commentators attempted to justify the RAP by arguing that no persons in society should have assured incomes and thereby be protected from the economic struggle for subsistence; instead, based upon "survival of the fittest," those who cannot succeed in the market economy ought not survive. Do you think these arguments continue to justify a strict application of RAP? What other reasons might explain the trend towards abolition of RAP? *See* Lewis Simes, Public Policy and the Dead Hand (1955); Joel C. Dobris, *The Death of the Rule Against Perpetuities, or the RAP Has No Friends—An Essay*, 35 Real Prop., Prob. & Tr. J. 601 (2000).

Chapter 6

CONCURRENT OWNERSHIP

Each present and future estate in property may be held by an individual person alone or concurrently by two or more persons. Why did the law choose to recognize concurrent ownership of property? At the risk of (vast) oversimplification, concurrent ownership has satisfied the needs of society's primary collective organizations—families and businesses. Throughout history, the family has served as the primary form of social organization. The terms "family home" and "family farm" demonstrate an understandable human preference for sharing ownership of an object of property in a collective fashion. With the development of market capitalism, most commerce takes place through the operations of business organizations, such as corporations, partnerships, and limited liability companies—entities composed of many persons acting in a collective fashion. By recognizing collective ownership, the law makes it feasible for families and businesses to advance their legitimate objectives.[1]

Chapter 6 focuses primarily upon the consequences of recognizing concurrent ownership of property interests in land. By now, you should be able to predict some of these consequences. Concurrent ownership presents many of the same problems that you encountered studying the problem of the "commons" back in Chapter 2 and some of the problems of consecutive ownership discussed in Chapter 5. Whenever two or more individuals share an identical interest, the potential for conflict and the problem of externalities arise. What happens when one person wants to

---

1. Chapter 6 does not directly address the law of business organizations (agency law, partnership law, corporation law, and the law governing other forms of business entities), which is the subject of later courses in the law school curriculum. Instead, Chapter 6 focuses more narrowly upon the common law forms of concurrent ownership between humans, especially within families. In discussing the problems associated with concurrent ownership in families, however, we will occasionally refer to the law of business organizations and how it has addressed similar problems. Hopefully, these references will allow you to study the law of concurrent ownership with a more critical eye.

In addition, Chapter 6 provides only summary coverage of the laws relating to dissolution of marriage and the distribution of property attendant to dissolution of marriage. We leave more detailed treatment of this subject to a later course in family law.

cut timber and the other does not? What happens when one owner wants to continue farming and the other wishes to develop the land commercially? What happens to the home when a husband and wife decide they cannot live together any longer and obtain a divorce? Before addressing these questions, we begin with an overview of the types of concurrent estates and their distinguishing characteristics.

A. CONCURRENT INTERESTS: THEIR CREATION AND CHARACTERISTICS

1. *Types of Concurrent Ownership*

The common law recognized three types of concurrent ownership that have continuing relevance—the *tenancy in common*, the *joint tenancy*, and the *tenancy by the entirety*.

a. *Tenancy in common.* The tenancy in common is the most basic form of concurrent ownership. Tenants in common have an interest that is "undivided" yet "separate." What does this mean? Two persons share an "undivided" interest as co-owners of a parcel of land if each person simultaneously enjoys the right to possession of that parcel.

> *Example 1.* Barnes, owner of Blueacre in fee simple absolute, conveys it "to Nice and Ertman as tenants in common." As a tenant in common, Ertman has the right to take possession of *every square foot of Blueacre* and use it to the same extent as if she owned it individually. Nice has the exact same right. Neither can take unilateral action to defeat the other's undivided legal right to possession of the whole of Blueacre; Ertman cannot legally exclude Nice from enjoying possession, nor can Nice legally exclude Ertman from enjoying possession.

Nevertheless, although tenants in common share an undivided or "co-equal" right to possession, each also has a "separate" interest. In other words, each tenant in common has a distinct share that belongs to him or her as an individual and can transfer that share by sale, inter vivos gift, or testamentary transfer upon death. Thus, in Example 1, if Ertman later transferred her interest to Key, then Nice and Key would thereafter hold Blueacre as tenants in common.

b. *Joint Tenancy.* A joint tenancy is similar to a tenancy in common in that each co-owner ("joint tenant") holds a separate and undivided right to possession. The joint tenancy differs from a tenancy in common, however, because joint tenants have a right of survivorship; *i.e.*, the right to claim individual ownership of the property as the surviving joint tenant. Where the right of survivorship exists, the death of one co-owner will result in ownership of the land by the surviving co-owners, to the exclusion of the deceased person's heirs or devisees.

> *Example 2.* Barnes, owner of Blueacre in fee simple absolute, conveys it "to Nice, Ertman, and Corrada as joint tenants and not as tenants in common." Ertman later dies, leaving a will that devises

her realty to the American Red Cross. Ertman's death extinguished her interest in Blueacre, and thus Ertman's will does not pass any interest in Blueacre to the Red Cross. As the surviving joint tenants, Nice and Corrada now hold title to Blueacre as joint tenants in fee simple absolute.

At first glance, the right of survivorship resembles a death lottery paying off the co-owner fortunate enough to survive the longest. The right of survivorship, however, was a logical outgrowth of the feudal system of landholding. As explained in Chapter 5, the feudal system established crucial social responsibilities (feudal services) that the tenant performed in exchange for the right to possess land. This relationship of lord and tenant was distinctly personal, with the lord looking directly to his tenant for performance of the services. The idea of co-ownership—under which a group of persons would bear responsibility for the services, rather than just one individual—did not fit easily within this feudal scheme of personal relationships.

Not surprisingly, then, the common law developed doctrines that disfavored co-ownership. One example was the rule of primogeniture, under which only the eldest son inherited the land of his deceased father. This rule prevented the division of feudal service responsibilities among multiple children and allowed the lord to look only to the tenant's eldest son for those services. Furthermore, for those situations when a landowner did create a cotenancy, the courts developed rules of interpretation that favored joint tenancy over tenancy in common. Given the traditional significance of the feudal services, this approach made sense—as joint tenants died off (eventually leaving a sole survivor), the right of survivorship would eliminate the division of responsibility for feudal services. [As explained below, modern law has rejected the ancient constructional preference for joint tenancy over tenancy in common.]

Like tenants in common, joint tenants each hold a separate and undivided interest. How can each joint tenant hold a separate interest, yet also hold that interest subject to the right of survivorship? To explain this form of ownership, the common law established a legal fiction that joint tenants were seised of land *per my et per tout*—by the "share" and by the "whole." In other words, the common law treated each joint tenant as the owner of a distinct share and, at the same time, as the owner of the entire interest. As the owner of a distinct share, a joint tenant thus can transfer her share during her lifetime (as explained below, such a transfer would destroy the joint tenancy and the right of survivorship). If a joint tenant makes no inter vivos transfer of her share, however, then her death extinguishes her "share," and the surviving joint tenant(s)—who all along also owned the entire interest (according to the fiction)—thereafter hold the land.

In adhering to this fiction that joint tenants were seised of the land "by the whole," the law required that each joint tenant had to have an identical interest in the land. The common law articulated this requirement by establishing a rule requiring the presence of "four unities" to create a joint tenancy. These were:

- *Unity of time.* Each joint tenant had to acquire her interest at the same time as her fellow joint tenants.

- *Unity of title.* Each joint tenant had to acquire her interest by virtue of the same instrument that created the interests of her fellow joint tenants.

- *Unity of interest.* Each joint tenant had to hold an interest identical to that of her fellow joint tenants, both as to the size of their respective "shares" and as to the duration (quantum) of the estate held in joint tenancy.

- *Unity of possession.* Each joint tenant had to have an undivided right to possess and enjoy all of the property. [Note that the unity of possession is the only one of the four unities that is also a characteristic of the tenancy in common.]

At common law, if the four unities were not present in a conveyance, no joint tenancy arose and the conveyance instead created a tenancy in common.

> *Example 3.* Barnes, owner of Blueacre in fee simple absolute, conveyed it "to Nice and Ertman as joint tenants, with Ertman holding a 2/3 share and Nice a 1/3 share." Because Barnes did not intend for Nice and Ertman to hold equal shares, there is no unity of interest, and at common law a tenancy in common would result—with Ertman holding a 2/3 share and Nice a 1/3 share—without any right of survivorship.

> *Example 4.* Barnes, owner of Blueacre in fee simple absolute, conveyed a one-half interest in Blueacre to Nice. The following day, Barnes conveyed his remaining one-half interest in Blueacre to Ertman, by virtue of a deed stating that his intent was for Nice and Ertman to hold "as joint tenants and not as tenants in common." Although both Nice and Ertman hold one-half share interests in Blueacre, the unities of time and title are lacking because they received those interests at different times and through different deeds. Thus, Nice and Ertman do not hold Blueacre as joint tenants, but as tenants in common—with each holding an equal share—without any right of survivorship.

Furthermore, the common law maintained that a joint tenancy continued to exist only as long as the four unities remained intact. Thus, any action that destroyed one or more of the four unities had the effect of *severing* the joint tenancy—thereby destroying the right of survivorship and turning the relationship into a tenancy in common.

> *Example 5.* Barnes, owner of Blueacre in fee simple absolute, conveyed it "to Nice and Ertman as joint tenants and not as tenants in common." Nice then conveyed "all of my right, title, and interest in Blueacre" to Corrada. This conveyance by Nice destroyed the unities of time and title; Corrada received his interest at a different time

than Ertman and by virtue of a different instrument of conveyance. Therefore, Corrada and Ertman do not hold Blueacre as joint tenants, but as tenants in common, without the right of survivorship.

As you will see later in the chapter, courts in some jurisdictions no longer require rigid adherence to the "four unities" doctrine, deferring to the clearly expressed intent of the grantor (as to the creation of a joint tenancy) or the co-owners themselves (as to the severance of a joint tenancy). Nevertheless, the requirement continues to retain its significance in many jurisdictions.

The historical justification for the common law's preference for joint tenancy—assurance of the provision of feudal services—no longer justifies such a preference. As a result, statutes in most states now establish a presumption that a conveyance or devise to two or more persons creates a tenancy in common, unless the instrument manifests the clear intention of the grantor/testator to create a joint tenancy with the right of survivorship. *See, e.g.,* 25 Del. Code Ann. § 701; Md. Code Real Prop. § 2–117.

    c.   ***Tenancy by the Entirety.*** While the possibility of a unilateral severance of a joint tenancy might be tolerable in many situations, it might be profoundly undesirable for land co-owned by spouses, such as a family home. [Imagine a wife coming home from work to discover that her husband had conveyed his interest to a complete stranger who would be moving into the house later that evening!]

To allow spouses to avoid this situation, the common law recognized (and many jurisdictions continue to recognize) a special form of co-ownership only possible between spouses—the *tenancy by the entirety.* The common law tenancy by the entirety functioned similarly to the joint tenancy, with each spouse holding a right of survivorship. A tenancy by the entirety, however, required *five* unities—the unities of time, title, interest, possession, and marriage. The common law presumed that any conveyance to husband and wife created a tenancy by the entirety (unless the grantor expressly dictated otherwise).[2] By and large, this presumption continues today, at least in those states that still recognize tenancy by the entirety. [As the next case suggests, a number of states no longer recognize tenancy by the entirety.]

The unique characteristic of the common law tenancy by the entirety was that one spouse could not take unilateral action during the marriage to sever the cotenancy and thereby defeat the other spouse's right of survivorship.[3] Borrowing from the Judeo–Christian conception of

---

   2. Notice that one may create a tenancy by the entirety only by a *conveyance to* a husband and wife. If *W* individually owns a parcel of land before marriage, that remains her individual property during the marriage—it does *not* automatically become entirety property just because *H* and *W* get married.

   3. Accordingly, during the marriage neither tenant by the entirety may unilaterally seek to partition the tenancy. [We discuss partition in greater detail beginning on page 383.]

marriage, the common law deemed that tenants by the entirety were seised *per tout et non per my* ("by the whole and not by the share")—in other words, the husband and wife were literally treated as one person, not two. Neither owned any individual share, and thus neither could take any unilateral action to defeat the other's right of survivorship during the marriage. We will return later in the chapter to discuss some of the practical implications of the protection offered by status as tenants by the entirety.

2. *Interpretation of Ambiguous Conveyances*

When making a conveyance to two or more persons as co-owners, a grantor should state clearly what type of co-ownership he or she intends to create. [Ideally, the grantor should create the form of co-ownership that the grantees prefer—once the grantor has delivered the deed to the grantees and no longer owns any interest in the land, there is typically no reason for the grantor to care about how the grantees hold title.] Examples of relatively unambiguous granting language would include:

- "To *A* and *B* as tenants in common in fee simple absolute."
- "To *A* and *B* as joint tenants with right of survivorship in fee simple absolute, and not as tenants in common."
- "To *H* and *W* as tenants by the entirety in fee simple absolute."

Unfortunately, sometimes a grantor uses language that is too ambiguous to determine precisely what sort of cotenancy was intended. For example, if a grantor deeds Blueacre to *A* and *B* "as joint owners," it is not clear whether *A* and *B* were meant to hold title as tenants in common or as joint tenants.

A similar ambiguity arose in a recent dispute in South Carolina. In June 2000, Joanne Rucker, a woman in her 70s and the owner of a home, married Ernest Smith, a man in his 80s. Rucker wanted to make sure that Smith would get the home if she died before him, so on August 17, 2000, she deeded Smith an undivided one-half interest in her home. The deed's granting clause stated that Smith and Rucker were to hold the land "for and during their joint lives and upon the death of either of them, then to the survivor of them, his or her heirs and assigns forever in fee simple, together with every contingent remainder and right of reversion." A conflict later arose between the Rucker and Smith families. In the wake of this conflict, Smith's son filed a partition action on behalf of Smith (who had become incapacitated). The case was referred to an equitable master. Rucker argued that the deed created a tenancy in common between Smith and Rucker for their lives, with each holding a remainder in fee simple contingent upon surviving the other, and that this remainder interest was not subject to partition. The equitable master granted summary judgment for Smith, holding that the deed created a joint tenancy in fee simple between Rucker and Smith and that this estate was subject to partition. How should a court interpret the language of the deed? Consider the differing approaches of the two appellate courts that heard this dispute.

SMITH v. RUCKER

Court of Appeals of South Carolina.
357 S.C. 532, 593 S.E.2d 497 (2004).

HEARN, C.J.... The deed at hand unquestionably creates survivorship rights. The crux of this case is whether those survivorship rights are paired with a tenancy in common and therefore indestructible or whether they are paired with a joint tenancy, in which case the property would be subject to partition at the whim of either party. We find that the deed created a joint tenancy with rights of survivorship and affirm the master's decision to partition the property.

Section 27–7–40 of the South Carolina Code provides that a joint tenancy with rights of survivorship is conclusively established when a deed grants land to two or more persons "as joint tenants with rights of survivorship, and not as tenants in common." However, this language is not the only means by which joint tenancies are created, but rather is "[i]n addition to any other methods for the creation of a joint tenancy in real estate which may exist by law...." S.C.Code Ann. § 27–7–40 (Supp. 2002).

The common law method of creating a joint tenancy requires a conveyance to have four unities: unity of interest, unity of title, unity of time, and unity of possession. When a joint tenancy is coupled with a right of survivorship, the right of survivorship can, under certain circumstances, be destroyed by one party acting alone. Because survivorship rights often encumber land, our courts require clear, unambiguous, and express language to create a joint tenancy with rights of survivorship and will construe instruments in favor of tenancies in common whenever possible. The reason South Carolina courts favor tenancies in common over joint tenancies is due to "the harsh results of survivorship rights incident to joint tenanc[ies] [which] usually defeated the intention of the grantor." 6 S.C. Jur. *Cotenancies* § 18 (1991). We do not believe this general rule favoring tenancies in common is applicable to cases involving deeds that unequivocally grant rights of survivorship because construing a deed to convey a tenancy in common with a right of survivorship would result in finding an estate that has indestructible survivorship rights and would thereby render the land less rather than more marketable.

Although the deed in the instant case does not contain the language suggested by section 27–7–40, it does satisfy the four unities required to create a joint tenancy: both Husband and Wife have the same interest, created by the same conveyance, which commenced at the same time, and they hold the property in undivided possession. Furthermore, the deed clearly and unambiguously grants the right of survivorship, a distinguishing characteristic of joint tenancies. Thus, we find the language of the deed unambiguously created a joint tenancy with rights of survivorship.

In support of her position that the property is not subject to partition, Wife relies on *Davis v. Davis*, 223 S.C. 182, 75 S.E. 2d 46 (1953), in which our supreme court recognized indestructible survivorship rights attaching to a tenancy in common. However, in that case, the court was called upon to determine what quantum of estate was created by a deed that purported to create a tenancy by the entirety[4] after such estates were no longer recognized in South Carolina. Here, the deed did not purport to create a tenancy by the entirety. Instead, as explained above, Wife's deed created a joint tenancy by satisfying the four unities required under common law and by unambiguously creating a right of survivorship.

Based on the language of the deed and South Carolina's penchant for construing deeds in favor of marketability, we find Wife's deed created a joint tenancy with rights of survivorship. As a joint tenancy, the property is subject to partition .... Accordingly, the master's decision to partition the property is AFFIRMED.

SMITH v. CUTLER

Supreme Court of South Carolina.
623 S.E.2d 644 (2005).

CHIEF JUSTICE TOAL.... Petitioner argues that the deed at issue creates a tenancy in common with an indestructible right of survivorship. We agree.

Although joint tenancies were favored in early common law, they have fallen into disfavor. In South Carolina, documents conveying a shared interest in property have generally been construed in favor of tenancies in common. *Free v. Sandifer*, 131 S.C. 232, 236, 126 S.E. 521, 522 (1925).

However, in 1953, this Court created a shared interest in property referred to as a tenancy in common with a right of survivorship. *Davis v. Davis*, 223 S.C. 182, 191–92, 75 S.E.2d 46, 50 (1953). The Court created the estate of tenancy in common with a right of survivorship because South Carolina did not permit husband and wife to hold property as tenants by the entirety. *Id.* The Court in *Davis* opined that by adding the phrase "and the survivor of them," the parties clearly indicated that upon the death of either of them the absolute estate should vest in the survivor. *Id.* at 191, 75 S.E.2d at 50. The Court stated that while a right of survivorship is not incident to a tenancy in common, the parties may create one if they so desire. *Id.* The Court explained that:

It has been said that great care must be exercised in construing conveyances to two or more persons and to the survivor or survivors

4. ... In *Green v. Cannady*, [77 S.C. 193, 57 S.E. 832 (1907)] the supreme court abolished tenancies by the entirety, finding that the Married Woman's Separate Property Acts and the state constitutions of 1868 and 1895 effectively destroyed the fiction that, upon marriage, a couple merged into one, unified person. Instead, the *Green* court held that property titled to both Husband and Wife created a tenancy in common. *Id.* at 197, 57 S.E. at 834.

of them. If the intention was to create a tenancy in common for life, with cross remainders for life, with remainder in fee to the ultimate survivor, a joint tenancy would not accomplish the purpose because the right of survivorship may be defeated by a conveyance by any joint tenant *but the . . . contingent ultimate remainders are indestructible.* Thus, not all instruments which provide that the survivor of a group will ultimately take the fee in severalty contemplate a joint tenancy; *the intention may be to create a true future interest by way of a remainder or an executory limitation.* [*Davis,* 223 S.C. at 187, 75 S.E.2d at 48 (citation omitted; emphasis added).]

As noted from the excerpt above, the Court held that the future interests created by a tenancy in common with a right of survivorship were indestructible—i.e., not subject to defeat by the unilateral act of one cotenant. *Id.*

In 2000, the legislature created, by statute, the estate of joint tenants with a right of survivorship. The Code directs that:

[i]n addition to any other methods for the creation of a joint tenancy in real estate which may exist by law, whenever any deed of conveyance of real estate contains the names of the grantees followed by the words "as joint tenants with rights of survivorship, and not as tenants in common" the creation of a joint tenancy with rights of survivorship in the real estate is conclusively deemed to have been created. [S.C. Code Ann. § 27–7–40 (Supp. 2004).]

This Court recognizes that the two estates at issue have many similar characteristics. However, unlike a tenancy in common with a right of survivorship, a joint tenancy with a right of survivorship is capable of being defeated by the unilateral act of one joint tenant. Further, property held in joint tenancy is subject to partition. In contrast, a tenancy in common with a right of survivorship cannot be defeated by the act of one tenant absent the agreement of the other tenant.

We note at the outset that § 27–7–40 cited above and relied on by the court of appeals, creating a joint tenancy with a right of survivorship, was not enacted until after the deed in the current case was executed. As a result, the parties to the deed could not have intended to take advantage of the statute creating the estate of joint tenancy with a right of survivorship. However, the estate of joint tenancy still existed in South Carolina, but as previously noted this Court construed documents in favor of tenancies [in common].

In the present case, the language of the deed clearly indicates that the parties intended to create a right of survivorship. However, the question before this Court centers on the type ownership held by both husband and wife and whether the property is subject to partition.

We hold that the use of the phrase "for and during their joint lives and upon the death of either of them, then to the survivor of them" indicates an intention of the parties to share a tenancy in common for life, with cross remainders for life, with remainder in fee to the ultimate survivor. The deed here conveyed a true future interest in the property to the survivor of the two. This is distinct from a joint tenancy, where the full estate is vested immediately and one of the parties could end the joint tenancy. However, with a tenancy in common with a right of survivorship the property will go only to the survivor of the parties and the future interest does not vest until the death of one of the co-owners. We further hold that this conveyance does not unreasonably prevent the alienation of the property because the restriction exists only until the first tenant in common dies.

As a result, the court of appeals erred in holding that the property was subject to partition. . . .

Notes

1. *Joint Tenancy in Fee Simple, or Joint Life Estate with Contingent Remainder in the Survivor?* Compare *Rucker* with the case of *Jones v. Green*, 126 Mich.App. 412, 337 N.W.2d 85 (1983). James Green and Dorothy Jones purchased a home in 1978, receiving a deed conveying the home to them "as joint tenants with full rights of survivorship and not as tenants in common." After three years, Jones sued Green to obtain partition of the home. [We discuss partition beginning on page 383; in essence, Jones, like Smith in the instant case, was asking the court to sell the house and give her one-half of the sale proceeds.] After a trial court order in Jones's favor, the Court of Appeals reversed:

> All land held jointly is generally subject to partition. In *Ames v. Cheyne*, 290 Mich. 215, 287 N.W. 439 (1939), however, the Supreme Court altered this principle, holding that where land is conveyed to parties as "joint tenants and not as tenants in common, and to the survivor thereof" . . . a party to the joint tenancy may not deprive any other party of his right to survivorship and, accordingly, partition may not be granted. In *Ballard v. Wilson*, 364 Mich. 479, 481–484, 110 N.W.2d 751 (1961), the Supreme Court reaffirmed *Ames*, stating:
>
> > . . . Survivorship would follow as a matter of course in any joint tenancy. It is implicit in the concept. Hence, it may be argued per contra, that by the addition of express words of survivorship the grantor intended to create something more than a mere joint tenancy. Thus, it has been held repeatedly in a parallel situation, where a deed ran to "A and B, and the survivor of them, his heirs and assigns," that the intent of the grantor was to convey a moiety [share] to A and B for life with remainder to the survivor in fee, and that neither grantee could convey the estate so as to cut off the remainder. Accordingly, and apparently upon parity of reasoning, we held in *Ames v. Cheyne* that "where property stands in the name of joint tenants with the right of survivorship, neither party may transfer the title to the premises and deprive the other of such right of survivorship" and concluded that "plaintiff may not have partition."
>
> Under the rule of *Ames v. Cheyne* we hold that these parties intended to create and did create joint life estates followed by a contingent remain-

der in fee to the survivor, indestructible by the voluntary act of only one of the life tenants. [*Jones*, 337 N.W.2d at 85–86.]

Some questions for you to consider: First, do you think the decisions in *Ames v. Cheyne* and *Smith v. Cutler* are correct? Why or why not? Taking what you learned about common rules of construction in Chapter 5, how would you argue that both decisions are rightly or wrongly decided? Second, does the decision in *Ames v. Cheyne* appropriately control the result in *Jones v. Green*? Taking what you learned in Chapter 5, on what basis would you argue that the deed in *Jones v. Green* created a joint tenancy in fee simple absolute? [Hint: if the court of appeals in *Jones v. Green* is correct in its interpretation of the deed, what would have happened to the land in the event that Jones and Green had died simultaneously? Why?] Finally, assume that your client wanted to create an indestructible right of survivorship. In light of these cases, what language would you use in the conveyance to achieve that objective?

2. *The "Four Unities" and the Use of "Straw" Conveyances.* At common law, a straw conveyance was necessary for an owner of land to create a joint tenancy between himself and another party. Under such a rule, Wife's deed to Husband in *Smith v. Rucker* would not have created a joint tenancy. Wife already owned her interest in the land before she conveyed a portion of that interest to Husband, so unity of time was lacking; further, Wife originally had acquired her interest in the land by virtue of a different deed than the one in which she attempted to create the joint tenancy, so unity of title was also lacking. Thus, Wife and Husband would have held the land as tenants in common, rather than as joint tenants with the right of survivorship.

Today, almost all jurisdictions that still recognize joint tenancy have enacted statutes that permit a person to create a joint tenancy with another person by direct conveyance, without the need for a straw conveyance. *See, e.g.*, Cal. Civ. Code § 683; Ohio Rev. Code § 5302.18. Even in states without such statutes, courts like *Rucker* have permitted grantors to create a joint tenancy with another person without using a straw conveyance. *See, e.g., Strout v. Burgess*, 144 Me. 263, 68 A.2d 241 (1949); *Therrien v. Therrien*, 94 N.H. 66, 46 A.2d 538 (1946). Do these statutes and court decisions eliminate the unity of time and unity of title requirements for creating a joint tenancy?

Today, it is unlikely that an American court would hold that an attempted conveyance into joint tenancy failed for lack of a straw conveyance. Nevertheless, lawyers in states without statutes like those in California and Ohio often use a straw conveyance in these circumstances. Why do you think these lawyers continue to use the straw conveyance? Are they just set in their ways? Or is there another reason?

One final question about straw conveyances: Suppose that after a grantor had made the straw conveyance, the straw had refused to reconvey the land to the grantor and her joint tenant. Would the grantor be stuck? Based upon the material in Chapter 5, what sort of remedy do you think the grantor would have in this situation?

3. *Classifying Concurrent Estates: Some Examples.* How would you classify the estates created by the conveyances in the following examples?

(a) Suppose that Barnes, owner of Blueacre in fee simple absolute, conveys it "to Nice and Ertman jointly." Nice then dies, leaving a will that devises all of her property to Smith. Who owns Blueacre, and why? *See Montgomery v. Clarkson*, 585 S.W.2d 483 (Mo. 1979).

(b) Suppose that Barnes, owner of Blueacre in fee simple absolute, conveys it "to Nice and Ertman for their lifetime." Nice then dies, having devised all of her property to Smith. Must Ertman allow Smith access to Blueacre prior to Ertman's death? *See Briggs v. Estate of Briggs*, 950 S.W.2d 710 (Tenn. Ct. App. 1997).

(c) Suppose that Barnes, owner of Blueacre in fee simple absolute, conveys it "to Brown and Corrada in equal portions for and during their natural lives, then to their surviving issue." Brown later dies, survived by his children. Must Corrada allow Brown's children access to Blueacre prior to Corrada's death? *See Hollowell v. Hollowell*, 333 N.C. 706, 430 S.E.2d 235 (1993).

(d) Suppose that Barnes, owner of Blueacre in fee simple absolute, conveys it "to Brown and Corrada as tenants by the entirety." At the time of the conveyance, Brown and Corrada are not married. *Compare DeLoatch v. Murphy,* 369 Pa.Super. 255, 535 A.2d 146 (1987) (joint tenancy with right of survivorship) *with Smith v. Stewart*, 268 Ark. 766, 596 S.W.2d 346 (Ct. App. 1980) (tenancy in common).

(e) Pushaw, owner of Rightacre in fee simple absolute, conveys it "to Bob and Elizabeth Dole, husband and wife, and Newt Gingrich." [Would Newt hold a 1/3 share or a 1/2 share, and why?] *See Jenni v. Gamel*, 602 S.W.2d 696 (Mo. Ct. App. 1980).

(f) Lawless, owner of Leftacre in fee simple absolute, conveys it "to Bill and Hillary Clinton, husband and wife, and to Al and Tipper Gore, husband and wife." Would your answer change if the deed instead read "to Bill and Hillary Clinton, husband and wife, and to Al and Tipper Gore, husband and wife, with right of survivorship"? *Compare In re Estate of Michael*, 421 Pa. 207, 218 A.2d 338 (1966) *with Nelson v. Hotchkiss*, 601 S.W.2d 14 (Mo. 1980).

3. *Severance of Joint Tenancies*

As explained previously, the common law provided that a joint tenancy continued to endure for as long as the four unities remained intact. Once any of the four unities was broken, however, this "severed" the joint tenancy and converted it into a tenancy in common. As a result, the very nature of the joint tenancy means that one joint tenant can unilaterally take action to break one of the four unities, sever the joint tenancy, and destroy the right of survivorship.

Should the destruction of one of the four unities be the determinative factor in severing a joint tenancy and destroying the right of survivorship? Why or why not? Consider the approach taken by the courts in the following two cases.

HARMS v. SPRAGUE

Supreme Court of Illinois.

105 Ill.2d 215, 85 Ill.Dec. 331, 473 N.E.2d 930 (1984).

MORAN, JUSTICE. Plaintiff, William H. Harms, filed a complaint to quiet title and for declaratory judgment in the circuit court of Greene County. Plaintiff had taken title to certain real estate with his brother John R. Harms, as a joint tenant, with full right of survivorship. The plaintiff named, as a defendant, Charles D. Sprague, the executor of the estate of John Harms and the devisee of all the real and personal property of John Harms. Also named as defendants were Carl T. and Mary E. Simmons, alleged mortgagees of the property in question. Defendant Sprague filed a counterclaim against plaintiff, challenging plaintiff's claim of ownership of the entire tract of property and asking the court to recognize his (Sprague's) interest as a tenant in common, subject to a mortgage lien. At issue was the effect the granting of a mortgage by John Harms had on the joint tenancy. Also at issue was whether the mortgage survived the death of John Harms as a lien against the property.[5]

The trial court held that the mortgage given by John Harms to defendants Carl and Mary Simmons severed the joint tenancy. Further, the court found that the mortgage survived the death of John Harms as a lien against the undivided one-half interest in the property which passed to Sprague by and through the will of the deceased. The appellate court reversed, finding that the mortgage given by one joint tenant of his interest in the property does not sever the joint tenancy. Accordingly, the appellate court held that plaintiff, as the surviving joint tenant, owned the property in its entirety, unencumbered by the mortgage lien. . . .

Two issues are raised on appeal: (1) Is a joint tenancy severed when less than all of the joint tenants mortgage their interest in the property? and (2) Does such a mortgage survive the death of the mortgagor as a lien on the property?

A review of the stipulation of facts reveals the following. Plaintiff, William Harms, and his brother John Harms, took title to real estate located in Roodhouse, on June 26, 1973, as joint tenants. The warranty

---

5. Editors' Note: The term "lien" refers generally to an interest in property that allows an unpaid creditor to force a sale of that property to repay a debt secured by that lien. A *mortgage* (as involved in *Harms*) is the predominant form of *consensual* lien upon land. But the law recognizes a wide variety of other liens (many nonconsensual) upon land, either by common law or by operation of a statute. These may include, *inter alia*, a judgment lien (an interest securing repayment of a plaintiff's judgment), a tax lien (an interest held by the government securing a tax liability of the property owner), a mechanics' lien (an interest held by a contractor or supplier to secure unpaid bills for labor or supplies used to improve land), or a vendor's or vendee's lien (an interest securing, respectively, the obligations owed by a buyer or seller who breaches a land purchase contract). Differences in the type of lien may affect how the lien comes into existence and its priority relative to other liens, but all liens serve to secure the payment or performance of an obligation.

deed memorializing this transaction was recorded on June 29, 1973, in the office of the Greene County recorder of deeds.

Carl and Mary Simmons owned a lot and home in Roodhouse. Charles Sprague entered into an agreement with the Simmons whereby Sprague was to purchase their property for $25,000. Sprague tendered $18,000 in cash and signed a promissory note for the balance of $7,000. Because Sprague had no security for the $7,000, he asked his friend, John Harms, to co-sign the note and give a mortgage on his interest in the joint tenancy property. Harms agreed, and on June 12, 1981, John Harms and Charles Sprague, jointly and severally, executed a promissory note for $7,000 payable to Carl and Mary Simmons. The note states that the principal sum of $7,000 was to be paid from the proceeds of the sale of John Harms' interest in the joint tenancy property, but in any event no later than six months from the date the note was signed. The note reflects that five monthly interest payments had been made, with the last payment recorded November 6, 1981. In addition, John Harms executed a mortgage, in favor of the Simmonses, on his undivided one-half interest in the joint tenancy property, to secure payment of the note. William Harms was unaware of the mortgage given by his brother.

John Harms moved from his joint tenancy property to the Simmons property which had been purchased by Charles Sprague. On December 10, 1981, John Harms died. By the terms of John Harms' will, Charles Sprague was the devisee of his entire estate. The mortgage given by John Harms to the Simmonses was recorded on December 29, 1981.

Prior to the appellate court decision in the instant case no court of this State had directly addressed the principal question we are confronted with herein—the effect of a mortgage, executed by less than all of the joint tenants, on the joint tenancy. Nevertheless, there are numerous cases which have considered the severance issue in relation to other circumstances surrounding a joint tenancy. All have necessarily focused on the four unities which are fundamental to both the creation and the perpetuation of the joint tenancy. These are the unities of interest, title, time, and possession. The voluntary or involuntary destruction of any of the unities by one of the joint tenants will sever the joint tenancy. *Van Antwerp v. Horan* (1945), 390 Ill. 449, 451, 61 N.E.2d 358.

In a series of cases, this court has considered the effect that judgment liens upon the interest of one joint tenant have on the stability of the joint tenancy. In *Peoples Trust & Savings Bank v. Haas* (1927), 328 Ill. 468, 160 N.E. 85, the court found that a judgment lien secured against one joint tenant did not serve to extinguish the joint tenancy. As such, the surviving joint tenant "succeeded to the title in fee to the whole of the land by operation of law." 328 Ill. 468, 471, 160 N.E. 85. . . . [Editors' Note: At this point, the court considered several previous Illinois cases involving joint tenancy property and a judgment lien against one joint tenant. In summary, these cases demonstrated that obtaining a judgment lien itself did not result in a transfer of title from the joint tenant to the judgment holder. To effect a severance of the joint tenancy, the judgment holder had to force a sale of the property; *i.e.*, have the sheriff execute on the property and sell it to satisfy the judgment. Once such an execution sale became final, then (and only then) would there be a sufficient transfer of title to sever the joint tenancy.]

Clearly, this court adheres to the rule that a lien on a joint tenant's interest in property will not effectuate a severance of the joint tenancy .... It follows, therefore, that if Illinois perceives a mortgage as merely a lien on the mortgagor's interest in property rather than a conveyance of title from mortgagor to mortgagee, the execution of a mortgage by a joint tenant, on his interest in the property, would not destroy the unity of title and sever the joint tenancy.

Early cases in Illinois, however, followed the title theory of mortgages. In 1900, this court recognized the common law precept that a mortgage was a conveyance of a legal estate vesting title to the property in the mortgagee. *Lightcap v. Bradley* (1900), 186 Ill. 510, 519, 58 N.E.2d 221. Consistent with this title theory of mortgages, therefore, there are many cases which state, in dicta, that a joint tenancy is severed by one of the joint tenants mortgaging his interest to a stranger. Yet even the early case of *Lightcap v. Bradley*, cited above, recognized that the title held by the mortgagee was for the limited purpose of protecting his interests. The court went on to say that "the mortgagor is the owner for every other purpose and against every other person. The title of the mortgagee is anomalous, and exists only between him and the mortgagor ...." *Lightcap v. Bradley* (1900), 186 Ill. 510, 522–23, 58 N.E. 221.

Because our cases had early recognized the unique and narrow character of the title that passed to a mortgagee under the common law title theory, it was not a drastic departure when this court expressly characterized the execution of a mortgage as a mere lien in *Kling v. Ghilarducci* (1954), 3 Ill.2d 455, 121 N.E.2d 752. In *Kling*, the court was confronted with the question of when a separation of title, necessary to create an easement by implication, had occurred. The court found that title to the property was not separated with the execution of a trust deed but rather only upon execution and delivery of a master's deed. The court stated:

> In some jurisdictions the execution of a mortgage is a severance, in others, the execution of a mortgage is not a severance. In Illinois the giving of a mortgage is not a separation of title, for the holder of the mortgage takes only a lien thereunder. After foreclosure of a mortgage and until delivery of the master's deed under the foreclosure sale, purchaser acquires no title to the land either legal or equitable. Title to land sold under mortgage foreclosure remains in the mortgagor or his grantee until the expiration of the redemption period and conveyance by the master's deed. [3 Ill.2d 455, 460, 121 N.E.2d 752.]

Kling and later cases rejecting the title theory do not involve the severance of joint tenancies. As such, they have not expressly disavowed the dicta of joint tenancy cases which have stated that the act of mortgaging by one joint tenant results in the severance of the joint tenancy. We find, however, that implicit in *Kling* and our more recent cases which follow the lien theory of mortgages is the conclusion that a joint tenancy is not severed when one joint tenant executes a mortgage on his interest in the property, since the unity of title has been preserved. As the appellate court in the instant case correctly observed: "If giving a mortgage creates only a lien, then a mortgage should have the same effect on a joint tenancy as a lien created in other ways." Other jurisdictions following the lien theory of mortgages have reached the same result. *People v. Nogarr* (1958), 164 Cal.App.2d 591, 330 P.2d 858; *D.A.D., Inc. v. Moring* (Fla.App.1969), 218 So.2d 451; *American National Bank & Trust Co. v. McGinnis* (Okla.1977), 571 P.2d 1198; *Brant v. Hargrove* (Ariz.Ct.App.1981), 129 Ariz. 475, 632 P.2d 978.

A joint tenancy has been defined as "a present estate in all the joint tenants, each being seized of the whole ...." *Partridge v. Berliner* (1927), 325 Ill. 253, 257, 156 N.E. 352. An inherent feature of the estate of joint tenancy is the right of survivorship, which is the right of the last survivor to take the whole of the estate. Because we find that a mortgage given by one joint tenant of his interest in the property does not sever the joint tenancy, we hold that the plaintiff's right of survivorship became operative upon the death of his brother. As such plaintiff is now the sole owner of the estate, in its entirety.

Further, we find that the mortgage executed by John Harms does not survive as a lien on plaintiff's property. A surviving joint tenant succeeds to the share of the deceased joint tenant by virtue of the conveyance which created the joint tenancy, not as the successor of the deceased. *In re Estate of Alpert* (1983), 95 Ill.2d 377, 381, 69 Ill.Dec. 361, 447 N.E.2d 796. The property right of the mortgaging joint tenant is extinguished at the moment of his death. While John Harms was alive, the mortgage existed as a lien on his interest in the joint tenancy. Upon his death, his interest ceased to exist and along with it the lien of the mortgage....

In their petition to supplement defendant Sprague's petition for leave to appeal, the Simmonses argue that the application of section 20–19 of the Probate Act of 1975 (Ill.Rev.Stat.1981, ch. 110 1/2, par. 20–19) to the facts of this case would mandate a finding that their mortgage on the subject property remains as a valid encumbrance in the hands of the surviving joint tenant. Section 20–19 reads in relevant part:

> (a) When any real estate or leasehold estate in real estate subject to an encumbrance, or any beneficial interest under a trust of real estate or leasehold estate in real estate subject to an encumbrance, is specifically bequeathed or passes by joint tenancy with right of survivorship or by the terms of a trust agreement or other nontestamentary instrument, the legatee, surviving tenant or beneficiary to whom the real estate, leasehold estate or beneficial interest is given or passes, takes it subject to the encumbrance and is not entitled to

have the indebtedness paid from other real or personal estate of the decedent. [Ill.Rev.Stat.1981, ch. 110 1/2 , par. 20–19.]

While the Simmonses have maintained from the outset that their mortgage followed title to the property, they did not raise the applicability of section 20–19 of the Probate Act of 1975 at the trial level, and thus the issue is deemed waived. Moreover, because we have found that the lien of mortgage no longer exists against the property, section 20–19 is inapplicable, since plaintiff, as the surviving joint tenant, did not take the property subject to an encumbrance.[6]

For the reasons stated herein, the judgment of the appellate court is affirmed.

MANN v. BRADLEY

Supreme Court of Colorado.
188 Colo. 392, 535 P.2d 213 (1975).

HODGES, JUSTICE. A petition for writ of certiorari was granted to review the opinion of the Colorado Court of Appeals in *Bradley v. Mann*, Colo.App., 525 P.2d 492 (1974). The issue is unique in Colorado case law, and its resolution is significant in the law relating to joint tenancy ownership of real property. Specifically, the issue is whether certain provisions in the divorce property settlement agreement in this case effectuated a termination of a joint tenancy ownership and converted it into a tenancy in common. *Bradley v. Mann*, *supra*, is a well reasoned opinion and correctly holds that the joint tenancy ownership was terminated. We therefore affirm.

The real property involved is a family residence which was in 1954 acquired in joint tenancy by Betty Rea Mann and Aaron C. Mann during their marriage. They were divorced in 1971. In connection therewith, an agreement, which was adopted as an order of the court in the divorce action, was entered into by the parties. Among other things, it provided that the family residence should be sold and that the proceeds equally divided between them upon the occurrence of any one of the three following events: (1) The remarriage of Mrs. Mann; (2) When the youngest child of the couple attains the age of 21; or (3) The mutual agreement of the parties to sell.[7]

Betty Rea Mann continued to reside in the family residence with her children until her death in October of 1972. A short time after her death, Mr. Mann, the petitioner herein, informed his children that the family residence now belonged to him by virtue of the right of survivorship in the joint tenancy ownership with their mother. Thereupon, the adminis-

6. Editors' Note: Look carefully at the quoted language of § 20–19. What do you think the legislature intended to accomplish in enacting § 20–19? How would you evaluate the *Harms* court's interpretation of this language?

7. Editors' Note: If the court was adopting this agreement as an order of the court,

then why didn't the parties' lawyers simply insert a clause in the agreement stating that the divorce terminated their joint tenancy and destroyed the right of survivorship?

tratrix of the estate of Mrs. Mann and the children, the respondents herein, filed an action in the district court of Morgan County to quiet title to the property on the theory that the divorce property settlement agreement had the legal effect of converting the joint tenancy into a tenancy in common with the result that Mrs. Mann's interest passed to the children upon her death. After trial in the district court, judgment was entered quieting title in the children as tenants in common in fee simple of an undivided one-half interest in the family residence. Mr. Mann appealed to the court of appeals which, as indicated previously, affirmed that judgment.

Petitioner argues that the provisions of the agreement demonstrate a clear intent that the property remain in joint tenancy until the occurrence of one of the three contingencies. Since none of these contingencies occurred prior to Mrs. Mann's death, petitioner reasons that the property passed to him by right of survivorship. Under the facts here, this contention has no merit.

The modern tendency is to not require that the act of the co-tenant be destructive of one of the essential four unities of time, title, possession or interest before a joint tenancy is terminated. Comment, 8 Hastings L.J. 294 (1957); Note, 25 Ala.L.Rev. 851 (1973). The joint tenancy may be terminated by mutual agreement, as here, where the parties treated their interests as belonging to them in common. *McDonald v. Morley*, 15 Cal.2d 409, 101 P.2d 690 (1940); 48 C.J.S. Joint Tenancy § 4. An agreement between the joint tenants to hold as tenants in common may be inferred from the manner in which the parties deal with the property. *Thomas v. Johnson*, 12 Ill.App.3d 302, 297 N.E.2d 712 (1973); *Mamalis v. Bornovas*, 112 N.H. 423, 297 A.2d 660 (1972); *Wardlow v. Pozzi*, 170 Cal.App.2d 208, 338 P.2d 564 (1959); *O'Connor v. Dickerson*, 188 So.2d 241 (Miss.1966); *Robertson v. United States*, 281 F.Supp. 955 (N.D.Ala. 1968).

The district court and the court of appeals properly applied these tenets to the facts of this case. The intent of the parties as shown in the property settlement agreement is central to the issue presented. This agreement provided for the ultimate sale of the property and the division of the proceeds, which evinces the intent to no longer hold the property in joint tenancy from the effective date of the agreement. The entire tenor of those provisions of the agreement pertaining to this property is inconsistent with any purpose of the parties to continue the right of survivorship, which is the *sine qua non* of joint tenancy.

Nor does the provision of the agreement which stipulates that the property "shall remain in the joint names of the parties" dictate a different result. This wording is consistent with any form of continued concurrent ownership of the property. *Konecny v. Von Gunten*, 151 Colo. 376, 379 P.2d 158 (1963). In our view, this language in fact strongly supports the proposition that the parties intended to change the ownership from joint tenancy, and that since they were, by the provisions of the agreement, going to sell and divide the proceeds, the property would remain in their joint names, which is precisely the way tenants in common hold property.

When faced with a similar issue in *Wardlow v. Pozzi, supra,* the reviewing court commented: "... it is hard to see how two persons in domestic difficulties, and desirous of settling their domestic problems as well as those relating to property, would have intentionally entered into an agreement such as the one before us which would have left the bulk of his or her estate to the other ...." This statement has salient applicability in this case.

The judgment of the Court of Appeals is affirmed.

Notes

1. *Mortgages—"Title Theory" v. "Lien Theory."* As you probably know from experience—even if that experience only comes from playing Monopoly®—a mortgage is an interest in land given to provide security for repayment of a debt. If the debtor does not repay the debt, the holder of the mortgage (known as the "mortgagee") may sell the land and apply the proceeds of sale to satisfy the debt.

Over time, the law developed two theories to explain the property interest held by the mortgagee. Early common law followed the *title theory* of mortgages. Under this theory, a mortgage constituted a conveyance of the mortgagor's legal title to the mortgagee. This conveyance typically took the form of a fee simple subject to condition subsequent; *e.g.,* "to Lender, but if Borrower repays his debt in a timely fashion, Borrower may re-enter and recover the premises." Under the title theory, the granting of a mortgage by one joint tenant destroyed the unities of time and title, severing the joint tenancy.

Today, fewer than ten states continue to follow the title theory. The vast majority of states now follows the *lien theory* of mortgages. Under this theory, the mortgagee receives only a lien (an interest for security purposes) on the mortgaged land, and this lien can ripen into title only by foreclosure of the lien (*i.e.,* sale of the land) after default by the mortgagor. Grant S. Nelson & Dale A. Whitman, Real Estate Finance Law §§ 4.1, 4.2 (4th ed. 2001). [Query: Why do you think that the law has shifted away from title theory and toward lien theory? Does this have anything to do with the likely expectation of the typical landowner who grants a mortgage?]

Harms v. Sprague demonstrates what happens conceptually when one crosses the lien theory of mortgages with the four unities requirement for joint tenancy—the granting of the mortgage by one joint tenant does not sever the unities of time and title and thus does not sever the joint tenancy. Suppose instead that the dispute in *Harms* had arisen in a title theory jurisdiction like Alabama. Suppose further that while John was still alive, Sprague had repaid the $7,000 promissory note and Simmons had released the mortgage. Who would own the land following John's death? Does it make sense to resolve this issue based upon whether the jurisdiction follows the lien theory or the title theory? Why or why not?

Note that there have been relatively few cases like *Harms v. Sprague* in which courts have had to address whether a mortgage by one joint tenant severed the joint tenancy. Using the concept of preventive lawyering, can you explain why this is so? [Hint: How might the Simmonses have structured the loan and mortgage differently?]

2. *The Four Unities—A Bygone Relic, or a Continuing Requirement?* Is the "four unities" requirement a worthless relic of feudal times—worthy of abandonment—or does it continue to serve a useful purpose? If courts are less inclined to require a straw man to assure the four unities are satisfied in the creation of a joint tenancy, to what extent should the four unities remain a meaningful focus for the severance question?

Perhaps it is easier to consider this question indirectly. *Harms* adopts the position that a joint tenancy will continue to exist until one of the four unities is broken. In contrast, *Mann* suggests that a joint tenant may act to sever a joint tenancy, even without breaking one of the four unities, as long as the joint tenant's act demonstrates that he or she no longer intends to hold the property in joint tenancy. How are these two approaches different? As you think about these questions, consider the following:

(a) Other courts deciding cases with facts similar to *Mann* have reached a contrary result. For example, in *Porter v. Porter*, 472 So.2d 630 (Ala. 1985), *H* and *W*, who owned a home as joint tenants, divorced. Their divorce agreement provided that *W* would have exclusive possession of the home, that *H* would pay all carrying charges and taxes on the home, and that all principal payments on the home would "inure in equal proportion to the parties as joint owners." *H* later remarried. Following *H*'s death, *H*'s second wife sought a partition sale of the home, claiming that the divorce agreement severed the joint tenancy between *H* and *W* and that *H*'s share had passed to her. The court held that the divorce agreement did not sever the joint tenancy between *H* and *W* (recall that Alabama is a title theory state), and that *W* thus owned the home outright as the surviving joint tenant. Does this result make any sense? If so, why?

(b) Suppose that a dispute identical to *Harms* arose in Colorado in 1980, after the *Mann* decision. *Mann* suggests that the key issue would be: "Did John Harms intend to sever the joint tenancy when he granted the mortgage to the Simmonses?" How should the judge analyze this issue? What problems might the judge encounter in the trial of this issue? What ethical issues would the attorney for Mr. Sprague face in counseling her client? *See supra* page 185.

3. *"Secret" Severance.* As suggested in *Harms*, a joint tenant can act unilaterally to sever the joint tenancy, without giving notice to the other joint tenant(s) or obtaining their consent. A classic example is *Riddle v. Harmon*, 102 Cal.App.3d 524, 162 Cal.Rptr. 530 (1980). In *Riddle*, a husband and wife owned land as joint tenants. Secretly, the wife executed a deed that granted her interest as a joint tenant to herself individually, and recited that the intent of the deed was to sever the joint tenancy. In a title dispute following the wife's death, the court held that the deed had effectively severed the joint tenancy and defeated the husband's right of survivorship, so that the wife's share passed to the beneficiaries named in her will. Was this "secret severance" unfair to the husband? Why or why not?

Following the decision in *Riddle v. Harmon*, the California legislature enacted the following statute:

Severance of a joint tenancy of record by deed, written declaration, or other written instrument ... is not effective to terminate the right of survivorship of the other joint tenants as to the severing joint tenant's interest unless one of the following requirements is satisfied:

(1) Before the death of the severing joint tenant, the deed, written declaration, or other written instrument effecting the severance is recorded in the county where the real property is located.

(2) The deed, written declaration, or other written instrument effecting the severance is executed and acknowledged before a notary public by the severing joint tenant not earlier than three days before the death of that joint tenant and is recorded in the county where the real property is located not later than seven days after the death of the severing joint tenant. [Cal. Civ. Code § 683.2(c).]

Why did the legislature bother to enact this statute? What problems does secret severance present that the legislature was attempting to address? See Samuel M. Fetters, *An Invitation to Commit Fraud: Secret Destruction of Joint Tenant Survivorship Rights*, 55 Fordham L. Rev. 173 (1986).

4. *Severance—Some Problems.* The issue of severance can arise in a variety of factual settings. Consider these examples:

(a) Barnes, owner of Blueacre in fee simple absolute, conveys it "to Nice and Ertman as joint tenants and not as tenants in common." Without Ertman's knowledge, Nice signs an agreement leasing the property to Smith for three years. During the lease term, Ertman dies, leaving a will that devised all her property to Chen. What is the state of the title to Blueacre? *Compare Tenhet v. Boswell*, 18 Cal.3d 150, 133 Cal.Rptr. 10, 554 P.2d 330 (1976) (right of survivorship unaffected) *with Alexander v. Boyer*, 253 Md. 511, 253 A.2d 359 (1969) (right of survivorship destroyed). Would the length of the lease term be relevant? Why or why not?

(b) Barnes, owner of Blueacre in fee simple absolute, conveys it "to Nice and Ertman as joint tenants and not as tenants in common." Nice places arsenic in Ertman's lunch and kills her. Ertman's will leaves all of her property to Chen. What is the state of the title to Blueacre? *See Duncan v. Vassaur*, 550 P.2d 929 (Okla. 1976) (murder severed joint tenancy, such that deceased tenant's share passed to his heirs). Is *Duncan* correct as a doctrinal matter? Why or why not? Many states have codified the result in *Duncan*. *See* Uniform Probate Code § 2–803(c)(2).

(c) Barnes, owner of Blueacre in fee simple absolute, conveys it "to Nice, Ertman, and Chen as joint tenants and not as tenants in common." Subsequently, Chen conveys "all my right, title, and interest in Blueacre" to Smith. Should Chen's conveyance have any effect on the right of survivorship between Nice and Ertman? What is the state of title to Blueacre? *See American Nat'l Bank & Trust Co. v. McGinnis*, 571 P.2d 1198 (Okla. 1977).

(d) Barnes, owner of Blueacre in fee simple absolute, conveys it "to Nice and Ertman as joint tenants and not as tenants in common." Later, Nice and Ertman die in a plane crash while on vacation. Nice's will devises her property to Chen; Ertman's will devises her property to the American Red Cross. How should Blueacre be distributed under these circumstances? *See* Uniform Simultaneous Death Act § 24–3.

5. *Joint Tenancy and the "Unity of Possession" Requirement.* To create a joint tenancy, each joint tenant must have an undivided right to possession of the whole of the property. [Actually, the unity of possession is common to all forms of cotenancy.] Consider, then, the following example: Barnes, owner of Blueacre in fee simple absolute, conveys it "to Nice and Ertman as joint tenants and not as tenants in common." Nice and Ertman then sign a written agreement, under which they agree that as between the two of them, Ertman will have the right to exclusive possession of Blueacre. Generally speaking, this does *not* destroy the unity of possession, and Nice and Ertman continue to hold as joint tenants. Can you explain why? *See, e.g., Tindall v. Yeats*, 392 Ill. 502, 64 N.E.2d 903 (1946). Can you think of a situation where an agreement to give one joint tenant exclusive possession *should* cause a severance of the joint tenancy? *See Pike v. Pike*, 208 P.2d 380 (Cal. Ct. App. 1949).

6. *Joint Bank Accounts.* Just as two or more people can concurrently own real property, they may also concurrently own personal property. Joint bank accounts, for example, are often used within families—if one owner of the account dies, the remaining joint owners continue to own all of the funds in the account by right of survivorship. Yet a joint bank account poses some of the same difficulties as concurrent ownership of land—magnified by the fact that the property involved is money. When two or more people are identified as the owners of a joint bank account, each may own a "share" of the funds, but each also has the ability to manage the account—and thus to withdraw all of the money (not just her share). This could pose a problem if (for example) a couple separated and one spouse withdrew the money from the account and secreted it without the other spouse's knowledge or consent. Likewise, if *A* and *B* held a joint bank account, *A*'s creditors could attach all of the funds in the account to satisfy a judgment against *A*—even if *B* has no legal responsibility for *A*'s debt.

7. *Joint Tenancy as "The Poor Man's Will" and Avoidance of Probate.* As you may have guessed by now, one of the primary benefits associated with the right of survivorship is that it permits the survivor to avoid *probate*. Probate is the legal process by which a decedent's estate is administered. The administrator assembles the decedent's assets, pays the decedent's remaining debts and taxes from the assets, and distributes the remaining assets to the beneficiaries named in the decedent's will. [If the decedent left no valid will, the court may appoint someone to identify the decedent's heirs and distribute the decedent's property to those heirs in a similar fashion.] Because the probate process is judicial or quasi-judicial, it can be costly and relatively time-consuming.

The right of survivorship attendant to joint tenancy enables one to avoid probate of joint tenancy property. Under the theory of joint tenancy, no interest passes to the surviving joint tenant, because the survivor already held an undivided interest in the entire property. In this way, joint tenancy can serve as a crude sort of will substitute, making joint tenancy attractive to lay persons looking for an inexpensive alternative to making a will. Is joint tenancy a suitable will substitute, or (based upon what you have learned so far) does a layperson using joint tenancy as a will substitute run unnecessary and unappreciated risks? Consider this question in the context of the following lawyering exercise.

LAWYERING EXERCISE
(Counseling and the Ethics of Soliciting Client Business)

BACKGROUND: The problem of lay persons misunderstanding the law is one that has profound implications for accomplishing justice. What responsibilities does an ethical lawyer have to help educate nonclient lay persons about existing legal rules? Can an ethical lawyer advise a nonclient lay person that he or she needs legal advice and then offer to provide that legal advice? The ABA Model Code of Professional Responsibility (promulgated in the late 1960s and more recently replaced by the Model Rules of Professional Conduct) did not affirmatively forbid an attorney from undertaking representation in the situation posed above. Nonetheless, the Ethical Considerations contained in the Model Code, which expressed "aspirational" norms of conduct, clearly frowned upon this type of "solicitation":

> **EC 2–2** The legal profession should assist lay-persons to recognize legal problems because such problems may not be self-revealing and often are not timely noticed. . . .

> **EC 2–3** Whether a lawyer acts properly in volunteering in-person advice to a layperson to seek legal services depends upon the circumstances. . . . The advice is proper only if motivated by a desire to protect one who does not recognize that he may have legal problems or who is ignorant of his legal rights or obligations. It is improper if motivated by a desire to obtain personal benefit, secure personal publicity, or cause legal action to be taken merely to harass or injure another. A lawyer should not initiate an in-person contact with a non-client, personally or through a representative, for the purpose of being retained to represent him for compensation.

> **EC 2–4** Since motivation is subjective and often difficult to judge, . . . [a] lawyer who volunteers in-person advice that one should obtain the services of a lawyer generally should not himself accept employment, compensation, or other benefit in connection with that matter. However, it is not improper for a lawyer to volunteer such advice and render resulting legal services to close friends, relatives, former clients (in regard to matters germane to former employment), and regular clients.

Today, section 7.3(a) of the ABA Model Rules of Professional Conduct (first promulgated in 1983 and since revised) reflects a slightly different perspective on the tension between educating lay people and soliciting business:

7.3(a) A lawyer shall not by in-person, live telephone or real-time electronic contact solicit professional employment from a prospective client when a significant motive for the lawyer's doing so is the lawyer's pecuniary gain, unless the person contacted: (1) is a lawyer; or (2) has a family, close personal, or prior professional relationship with the lawyer. [ABA Model Rule 7.3(a)]

Comment to Rule 7.3(a)

(1) There is a potential for abuse inherent in direct in-person, live telephone or real-time electronic contact by a lawyer with a prospective client known to need legal services. These forms of contact between a lawyer and a prospective client subject the lay person to the private importuning of the trained advocate in a direct interpersonal encounter. . . . The situation is fraught with the possibility of undue influence, intimidation, and over-reaching.

(2) This potential for abuse inherent in direct in-person, live telephone or real-time electronic solicitation of prospective clients justifies its prohibition, particularly since lawyer advertising and written and recorded communication permitted under Rule 7.2 offer alternative means of conveying necessary information to those who may be in need of legal services. . . .

(4) There is far less likelihood that a lawyer would engage in abusive practices against an individual who is a former client, or with whom the lawyer has close personal or family relationship, or in situations in which the lawyer is motivated by considerations other than the lawyer's pecuniary gain. . . . Consequently, the general prohibition in Rule 7.3(a) . . . [is] not applicable in those situations. . . .

SITUATION: You are attending a reception for a local charitable organization when you encounter Diane, a 60-year-old widow. As you and Diane are conversing with several other guests, the subjects of wills arises. Diane announces: "I don't need a will. My husband died three years ago. After his death, I found a deed book in the library and signed a deed in which I conveyed my house and land to myself and my son, Fred, in joint tenancy with right of survivorship. I also had Fred added as a party to both my checking account and my savings account, so that those accounts are now set up as joint tenancy with right of survivorship. Thus, I have arranged things so that my son, Fred, who is a sophomore in college, will get everything when I die without my having to worry about a will." Several lay persons in the conversation congratulate Diane on her shrewd planning.

TASKS: (1) Based upon what you have learned about co-ownership to this point, what problems do you foresee that might impact upon Diane's plan? Using the concepts you learned in Chapters 4 and 5, what alternatives might better accomplish Diane's goals? (2) Taking into account the ethical considerations discussed above and the language in Model Rule 7.3(a), what (if anything) would you say to Diane and the other persons at the time of her statement? Under what circumstances might you be able to consider representing Diane or another guest (if at all), if Diane or another guest were to ask you to do so?

4. *The Special Status of Tenancy by the Entirety*

As discussed earlier in the chapter, the tenancy by the entirety is a form of co-ownership unique to married couples.[8] The tenancy by the entirety functions as a "joint tenancy plus"—the four unities of the joint tenancy plus the fifth unity of marriage. In all jurisdictions that recognize the tenancy by the entirety, the "plus" factor—the unity of marriage—operates to preclude the ability of either spouse to sever the survivorship interest unilaterally unless one of the spouses terminates the marriage through divorce. As long as the spouses remain married, one spouse cannot unilaterally sever the tenancy and destroy the other's survivorship right. Likewise, as long as the spouses remain married, neither spouse can obtain partition of land held by the entirety. Theoretically, this forces spouses to make joint decisions regarding the use and transfer of entirety property—one might observe that it forces spouses to take their marriage seriously and make their decisions "as one person."

a. *The Impact of Tenancy by the Entirety on Creditors.* If *H* and *W* borrow money to build a home on Blueacre and both sign a mortgage granting Bank a lien upon Blueacre to secure repayment of the loan, Bank can force a sale of Blueacre in the event that *H* and *W* default. But what if only *H* borrows the money, and only *H* signs a mortgage upon Blueacre without the knowledge or authority of *W*? In most jurisdictions, the mortgage is invalid altogether, because as a tenant by the entirety, *H* has no individual interest in Blueacre—rather, *H* and *W* have a collective interest that they can transfer only by collective agreement. In a few states, however, the Bank might still have the ability to attach *H*'s right to survivorship, and perhaps even *H*'s right to possession during the marriage!

To understand these differences, one must place the tenancy by the entirety in a broader historical context—particularly the relationship between the common law estate *jure uxoris* and the Married Women's Property Acts of the late 19th and early 20th centuries. By modern standards, the estate *jure uxoris* is an embarrassing vestige of the common law. At the moment of marriage, wives essentially ceased to be separate individuals in the eyes of the common law and were thus *divested of the ability to make decisions regarding the use and disposition of their own individual property*. Thus, if *W* owned Blackacre in fee simple absolute prior to marriage, her marriage to *H* essentially divested *W* of control over Blackacre during her marriage. Her husband, *H*, became legally entitled to use and occupy Blackacre for the duration of the marriage by virtue of his estate *jure uxoris* ("by the right of the wife"). Because *W* couldn't sue *H* at common law, *H* could basically do whatever he wanted with this estate as long as they remained married. *H* could lease Blackacre to a third party and collect rents—without

---

8. Married couples do not have to hold title to land as tenants by the entirety. However, as discussed on page 349, most states that permit tenancy by the entirety continue to follow the traditional presumption that a conveyance to a husband and wife creates a tenancy by the entirety unless the conveyance provides otherwise.

having to account to *W* for them (as *H* would have had to account to any other cotenant). *H* could sell Blackacre to a third party, who would then get the right to possession of the land for as long as *H* and *W* were still married. *H*'s estate *jure uxoris* did not end until *H* died or *H* and *W* divorced.

Beginning with Mississippi in 1839, state legislatures enacted statutes that came to be known as the Married Women's Property Acts (MWPA). Without question, the MWPA were meant to abolish the estate *jure uxoris* and to remove the legal disabilities that the common law had placed upon married women in dealing with their separate property. What was often not clear is whether the MWPA were meant to affect the tenancy by the entirety (and if so, how). Some courts interpreting their state's statute concluded that it abolished the common law tenancy by the entirety. *Lawler v. Byrne*, 252 Ill. 194, 96 N.E. 892 (1911); *Appeal of Robinson*, 88 Me. 17, 33 A. 652 (1895). In other states, tenancy by the entirety survives, but without consensus regarding the precise impact of the MWPA. If a state's statute was meant to equalize the authority of husband and wife, did it do so by giving wives the same powers that their husbands had under the estate *jure uxoris* (thereby allowing either to act unilaterally with respect to entirety property)? Or did it do so by taking away the husband's powers, such that neither spouse could unilaterally transfer any interest in entirety property? If these questions seem too philosophical, the consequences of how they are resolved is most certainly not—as the following case demonstrates.

SAWADA v. ENDO

Supreme Court of Hawaii.
57 Haw. 608, 561 P.2d 1291 (1977).

MENOR, JUSTICE. This is a civil action brought by the plaintiffs-appellants, Masako Sawada and Helen Sawada, in aid of execution of money judgments in their favor, seeking to set aside a conveyance of real property from judgment debtor Kokichi Endo to Samuel H. Endo and Toru Endo, defendants-appellees herein, on the ground that the conveyance as to the Sawadas was fraudulent.

On November 30, 1968, the Sawadas were injured when struck by a motor vehicle operated by Kokichi Endo. On June 17, 1969, Helen Sawada filed her complaint for damages against Kokichi Endo. Masako Sawada filed her suit against him on August 13, 1969. The complaint and summons in each case was served on Kokichi Endo on October 29, 1969.

On the date of the accident, Kokichi Endo was the owner, as a tenant by the entirety with his wife, Ume Endo, of a parcel of real property situate at Wahiawa, Oahu, Hawaii. By deed, dated July 26, 1969, Kokichi Endo and his wife conveyed the property to their sons, Samuel H. Endo and Toru Endo. This document was recorded in the Bureau of Conveyances on December 17, 1969. No consideration was paid by the grantees for the conveyance. Both were aware at the time of the conveyance that their father had been involved in an accident, and that he carried no liability insurance. Kokichi Endo and Ume Endo, while reserving no life interests therein, continued to reside on the premises.

On January 19, 1971, after a consolidated trial on the merits, judgment was entered in favor of Helen Sawada and against Kokichi Endo in the sum of $8,846.46. At the same time, Masako Sawada was awarded judgment on her complaint in the amount of $16,199.28. Ume Endo, wife of Kokichi Endo, died on January 29, 1971. She was survived by her husband, Kokichi. Subsequently, after being frustrated in their attempts to obtain satisfaction of judgment from the personal property of Kokichi Endo, the Sawadas brought suit to set aside the conveyance which is the subject matter of this controversy. The trial court refused to set aside the conveyance, and the Sawadas appeal.

The determinative question in this case is, whether the interest of one spouse in real property, held in tenancy by the entiret[y], is subject to levy and execution by his or her individual creditors. This issue is one of first impression in this jurisdiction. . . .

[Editors' Note: We have omitted the court's review of the law in other jurisdictions. States that retain tenancy by the entirety take one of two general approaches to the issue. The majority of states hold that an attempted conveyance by one spouse is void and that a creditor of only one spouse may not attach that spouse's interest in the entirety property. A minority of states hold that a creditor of only one spouse may attach that spouse's interest. Some of these states permit the creditor to attach and sell the spouse's interest immediately (subject only to the other spouse's right of survivorship), while a few others permit the creditor to attach only the spouse's contingent right of survivorship.]

Today we join that group of states and the District of Columbia which hold that under the Married Women's Property Acts the interest of a husband or a wife in an estate by the entiret[y] is not subject to the claims of his or her individual creditors during the joint lives of the spouses. In so doing, we are placing our stamp of approval upon what is apparently the prevailing view of the lower courts of this jurisdiction.

Hawaii has long recognized and continues to recognize the tenancy in common, the joint tenancy, and the tenancy by the entirety, as separate and distinct estates. *See Paahana v. Bila*, 3 Haw. 725 (1876). That the Married Women's Property Act of 1888 was not intended to abolish the tenancy by the entirety was made clear by the language of Act 19 of the Session Laws of Hawaii, 1903 (now HRS § 509–1). *See also* HRS § 509–2. The tenancy by the entirety is predicated upon the legal unity of husband and wife, and the estate is held by them in single ownership. They do not take by moieties, but both and each are seized of the whole estate. *Lang v. Commissioner of Internal Revenue*, 289 U.S. 109, 53 S.Ct. 534, 77 L.Ed. 1066 (1933).

A joint tenant has a specific, albeit undivided, interest in the property, and if he survives his cotenant he becomes the owner of a larger interest than he had prior to the death of the other joint tenant. But tenants by the entirety are each deemed to be seized of the entirety from the time of the creation of the estate. At common law, this taking of the "whole estate" did not have the real significance that it does today, insofar as the rights of the wife in the property were concerned. For all practical purposes, the wife had no right during coverture to the use and enjoyment and exercise of ownership in the marital estate. All she possessed was her contingent right of survivorship.

The effect of the Married Women's Property Acts was to abrogate the husband's common law dominance over the marital estate and to place the wife on a level of equality with him as regards the exercise of ownership over the whole estate. The tenancy was and still is predicated upon the legal unity of husband and wife, but the Acts converted it into a unity of equals and not of unequals as at common law. No longer could the husband convey, lease, mortgage or otherwise encumber the property without her consent. The Acts confirmed her right to the use and enjoyment of the whole estate, and all the privileges that ownership of property confers, including the right to convey the property in its entirety, jointly with her husband, during the marriage relation. They also had the effect of insulating the wife's interest in the estate from the separate debts of her husband.

Neither husband nor wife has a separate divisible interest in the property held by the entirety that can be conveyed or reached by execution. *Fairclaw v. Forrest*, 76 U.S.App.D.C. 197, 130 F.2d 829 (1942). A joint tenancy may be destroyed by voluntary alienation, or by levy and execution, or by compulsory partition, but a tenancy by the entirety may not. The indivisibility of the estate, except by joint action of the spouses, is an indispensable feature of the tenancy by the entirety.

In *Jordan v. Reynolds* [66 A. 37 (Md. 1907)], the Maryland court held that no lien could attach against entirety property for the separate debts of the husband, for that would be in derogation of the entirety of title in the spouses and would be tantamount to a conversion of the tenancy into a joint tenancy or tenancy in common. In holding that the spouses could jointly convey the property, free of any judgment liens against the husband, the court said:

> To hold the judgment to be a lien at all against this property, and the right of execution suspended during the life of the wife, and to be enforced on the death of the wife, would, we think, likewise encumber her estate, and be in contravention of the constitutional provision heretofore mentioned, protecting the wife's property from the husband's debts.

> It is clear, we think, if the judgment here is declared a lien, but suspended during the life of the wife, and not enforceable until her death, if the husband should survive the wife, it will defeat the sale here made by the husband and wife to the purchaser, and thereby make the wife's property liable for the debts of her husband. [105 Md. at 295, 66 A. at 39.]

In *Hurd v. Hughes* [109 A. 418 (1920)], the Delaware court, recognizing the peculiar nature of an estate by the entirety, in that the husband and wife are the owners, not merely of equal interests but of the whole estate, stated:

> The estate (by the entiret[y]) can be acquired or held only by a man and woman while married. Each spouse owns the whole while both live; neither can sell any interest except with the other's consent, and by their joint act; and at the death of either the other continues to own the whole, and does not acquire any new interest from the other. There can be no partition between them. From this is deduced the indivisibility and unseverability of the estate into two interests, and hence that the creditors of either spouse cannot during their joint lives reach by execution any interest which the debtor had in land so held. . . . One may have doubts as to whether the holding of land by entiret[y] is advisable or in harmony with the spirit of the legislation in favor of married women; but when such an estate is created due effect must be given to its peculiar characteristics. [109 A. at 419.] . . .

We are not persuaded by the argument that it would be unfair to the creditors of either spouse to hold that the estate by the entirety may not, without the consent of both spouses, be levied upon for the separate debts of either spouse. No unfairness to the creditor is involved here. We agree with the court in *Hurd v. Hughes*: "But creditors are not entitled to special consideration. If the debt arose prior to the creation of the estate, the property was not a basis of credit, and if the debt arose subsequently the creditor presumably had notice of the characteristics of the estate which limited his right to reach the property." 109 A. at 420.

We might also add that there is obviously nothing to prevent the creditor from insisting upon the subjection of property held in tenancy by the entirety as a condition precedent to the extension of credit. Further, the creation of a tenancy by the entirety may not be used as a device to defraud existing creditors. *In re Estate of Wall*, 142 U.S.App. D.C. 187, 440 F.2d 215 (1971).

Were we to view the matter strictly from the standpoint of public policy, we would still be constrained to hold as we have done here today. In *Fairclaw v. Forrest, supra*, the court makes this observation: "The interest in family solidarity retains some influence upon the institution [of tenancy by the entirety]. It is available only to husband and wife. It is a convenient mode of protecting a surviving spouse from inconvenient administration of the decedent's estate and from the other's improvident debts. It is in that protection the estate finds its peculiar and justifiable function." 130 F.2d at 833.

It is a matter of common knowledge that the demand for single-family residential lots has increased rapidly in recent years, and the magnitude of the problem is emphasized by the concentration of the bulk of fee simple land in the hands of a few. The shortage of single-family residential fee simple property is critical and government has seen fit to attempt to alleviate the problem through legislation. When a family can afford to own real property, it becomes their single most important asset. Encumbered as it usually is by a first mortgage, the fact remains that so long as it remains whole during the joint lives of the spouses, it is always available in its entirety for the benefit and use of the entire family. Loans for education and other emergency expenses, for example, may be obtained on the security of the marital estate. This would not be possible where a third party has become a tenant in common or a joint tenant with one of the spouses, or where the ownership of the contingent right of survivorship of one of the spouses in a third party has cast a cloud upon the title of the marital estate, making it virtually impossible to utilize the estate for these purposes.

If we were to select between a public policy favoring the creditors of one of the spouses and one favoring the interests of the family unit, we would not hesitate to choose the latter. But we need not make this choice for, as we pointed out earlier, by the very nature of the estate by the entirety as we view it, and as other courts of our sister jurisdictions have viewed it, "[a] unilaterally indestructible right of survivorship, an inability of one spouse to alienate his interest, and, importantly for this case, a broad immunity from claims of separate creditors remain among its vital incidents." *In re Estate of Wall*, 440 F.2d at 218.

Having determined that an estate by the entirety is not subject to the claims of the creditors of one of the spouses during their joint lives, we now hold that the conveyance of the marital property by Kokichi Endo and Ume Endo, husband and wife, to their sons, Samuel H. Endo and Toru Endo, was not in fraud of Kokichi Endo's judgment creditors. . . .

KIDWELL, JUSTICE, dissenting. . . . The majority reaches its conclusion by holding that the effect of the Married Women's Act was to equalize the positions of the spouses by taking from the husband his common law right to transfer his interest, rather than by elevating the wife's right of alienation of her interest to place it on a position of equality with the husband's. I disagree. I believe that a better interpretation of the Married Women's Acts is that offered by the Supreme Court of New Jersey in *King v. Greene*, 30 N.J. 395, 412, 153 A.2d 49, 60 (1959):

> It is clear that the Married Women's Act created an equality between the spouses in New Jersey, insofar as tenancies by the entirety are concerned. If, as we have previously concluded, the husband could alienate his right of survivorship at common law, the wife, by virtue of the act, can alienate her right of survivorship. And it follows, that if the wife takes equal rights with the husband in the estate, she must take equal disabilities. Such are the dictates of common equality. Thus, the judgment creditors of either spouse may levy and execute upon their separate rights of survivorship.

One may speculate whether the courts which first chose the path to equality now followed by the majority might have felt an unexpressed aversion to entrusting a wife with as much control over her interest as had previously been granted to the husband with respect to his interest. Whatever may be the historical explanation for these decisions, I feel that the resultant restriction upon the freedom of the spouses to deal independently with their respective interests is both illogical and unnecessarily at odds with present policy trends. Accordingly, I would hold that the separate interest of the husband in entirety property, at least to the extent of his right of survivorship, is alienable by him and subject to attachment by his separate creditors, so that a voluntary conveyance of the husband's interest should be set aside where it is fraudulent as to such creditors, under applicable principles of the law of fraudulent conveyances.

Notes

1. *Tenancy by the Entirety and Voluntary Creditors—Three Different Approaches.* Suppose Barnes obtains a judgment against Bill Henning arising out of a contract dispute. Bill Henning owns a home as a tenant by the entirety with his wife, Jeannie. Barnes wishes to have his judgment lien attach to Bill Henning's interest in the house. How will Barnes's rights differ under each of the different approaches to tenancy by the entirety discussed in *Sawada* (page 371?)

2. *Tenancy by the Entirety and Involuntary Creditors.* Justice Menor's opinion highlights that voluntary creditors (such as Barnes in the example in Note 1) are not prejudiced by the *Sawada* court's decision because they should have known how the debtor held title to the land and could have "adjusted"—*i.e.*, taken steps to enlist the cooperation of the non-debtor spouse or to find other security for the debt. *Sawada* presents a situation in which the plaintiffs were *involuntary* creditors. Can such creditors meaningfully adjust? Should a creditor's right to attach entirety property differ depending upon the creditor's status as a voluntary creditor (*e.g.*, a lending bank, or a supplier of trade materials) or an involuntary creditor (*e.g.*, a tort victim)? Why or why not?

3. *Tenancy by the Entirety and "Family" Policy.* Does Justice Menor's articulated concern for "family solidarity" justify his interpretation of the Married Women's Property Acts? Why or why not? In how many different ways does a decision like *Sawada* promote family solidarity? What's so special about marriage that we grant the special protections of a tenancy by the entirety to this relationship and not to other types of partnerships, such as parent-child, aunt-niece, or unmarried couples?

4. *Termination Upon Divorce.* Suppose that *H* and *W*, who have held Blueacre as tenants by the entirety, obtain a divorce. The divorce terminates the unity of marriage and thus terminates the tenancy by the entirety—but the divorce decree itself does not necessarily terminate *H* and *W*'s co-ownership. If there is a property settlement accompanying the divorce decree, the property settlement should specify the disposition of the parties' concurrent interest. But if there is no property settlement, or if the settlement does not specify what happens to the property, some courts have concluded that *H* and *W* would remain joint tenants because the other four unities would remain intact. *See, e.g., Shepherd v. Shepherd*, 336 So.2d 497

(Miss. 1976). In contrast, statutes in a number of states provide that divorce terminates an entirety tenancy and converts it into a tenancy in common. *See, e.g.,* Ark. Code § 9–12–317; Fla. Stat. Ann. § 689.15; Mich. Comp. Laws Ann. § 552–102. Which approach seems more consistent with the likely intent of reasonable parties in the position of *H* and *W*?

LAWYERING EXERCISE
(Planning, Counseling, and Drafting)

SITUATION: Tom and Julie, an unmarried couple who have lived together for two years, have sought your advice in the purchase of a home. They inform you that they have no desire to get married, but would like to hold the home as tenants by the entirety. When you inform them that tenancy by the entirety is available only to legally married couples, Tom responds: "You're a smart lawyer. Can't you figure out how to accomplish the same result legally?"

TASKS: (a) Based on the characteristics of the tenancy by the entirety, what language would you place into the deed that would create in Tom and Julie an estate that would have the same characteristics as a tenancy by the entirety (or as close to that estate as is legally possible)? (b) What advice would you give to Tom and Julie regarding whether they should take title this way (*i.e.*, by a deed containing the granting language you suggested in (a)), rather than another alternative? What problems can you foresee that Tom and Julie may not have considered?

b. ***Tenancy by the Entirety and Federalism.*** As *Sawada* demonstrates, the laws governing tenancy by the entirety vary from state to state—from outright abolition to the highly protective version demonstrated in *Sawada*. Is this nonuniformity a problem about which the law should be concerned? Consider how federal statutes relating to tax liens or civil forfeitures might apply against the background of state law approaches.

UNITED STATES v. CRAFT
Supreme Court of the United States.
535 U.S. 274, 122 S.Ct. 1414, 152 L.Ed.2d 437 (2002).

JUSTICE O'CONNOR delivered the opinion of the Court. This case raises the question whether a tenant by the entirety possesses "property" or "rights to property" to which a federal tax lien may attach. Relying on the state law fiction that a tenant by the entirety has no separate interest in entiret[y] property, the United States Court of Appeals for the Sixth Circuit held that such property is exempt from the tax lien. We conclude that, despite the fiction, each tenant possesses individual rights in the estate sufficient to constitute "property" or "rights to property" for the purposes of the lien, and reverse the judgment of the Court of Appeals.

In 1988, the Internal Revenue Service (IRS) assessed $482,446 in unpaid income tax liabilities against Don Craft, the husband of respondent Sandra L. Craft, for failure to file federal income tax returns for the years 1979 through 1986. When he failed to pay, a federal tax lien attached to "all property and rights to property, whether real or personal, belonging to" him. 26 U.S.C. § 6321.

At the time the lien attached, respondent and her husband owned a piece of real property in Grand Rapids, Michigan, as tenants by the entirety. After notice of the lien was filed, they jointly executed a quitclaim deed purporting to transfer the husband's interest in the property to respondent for one dollar. When respondent attempted to sell the property a few years later, a title search revealed the lien. The IRS agreed to release the lien and allow the sale with the stipulation that half of the net proceeds be held in escrow pending determination of the Government's interest in the property.

Respondent brought this action to quiet title to the escrowed proceeds. The Government claimed that its lien had attached to the husband's interest in the tenancy by the entirety. It further asserted that the transfer of the property to respondent was invalid as a fraud on creditors. The District Court granted the Government's motion for summary judgment, holding that the federal tax lien attached at the moment of the transfer to respondent, which terminated the tenancy by the entirety and entitled the Government to one-half of the value of the property.

Both parties appealed. The Sixth Circuit held that the tax lien did not attach to the property because under Michigan state law, the husband had no separate interest in property held as a tenant by the entirety. It remanded to the District Court to consider the Government's alternative claim that the conveyance should be set aside as fraudulent.

On remand, the District Court concluded that where, as here, state law makes property exempt from the claims of creditors, no fraudulent conveyance can occur. . . .

Both parties appealed the District Court's decision, the Government again claiming that its lien attached to the husband's interest in the entirety property. The Court of Appeals held that the prior panel's opinion was law of the case on that issue.

Whether the interests of respondent's husband in the property he held as a tenant by the entirety constitutes "property and rights to property" for the purposes of the federal tax lien statute is ultimately a question of federal law. The answer to this federal question, however, largely depends upon state law. The federal tax lien statute itself "creates no property rights but merely attaches consequences, federally defined, to rights created under state law." *United States v. Bess,* 357 U.S. 51, 55, 78 S.Ct. 1054, 2 L.Ed.2d 1135 (1958). Accordingly, "[w]e look initially to state law to determine what rights the taxpayer has in the property the Government seeks to reach, then to federal law to determine whether the taxpayer's state-delineated rights qualify as 'property' or 'rights to property' within the compass of the federal tax lien legislation." *Drye v. United States,* 528 U.S. 49, 58, 120 S.Ct. 474, 145 L.Ed.2d 466 (1999).

A common idiom describes property as a "bundle of sticks"—a collection of individual rights which, in certain combinations, constitute property. State law determines only which sticks are in a person's bundle. Whether those sticks qualify as "property" for purposes of the federal tax lien statute is a question of federal law.

In looking to state law, we must be careful to consider the substance of the rights state law provides, not merely the labels the State gives these rights or the conclusions it draws from them. Such state law labels are irrelevant to the federal question of which bundles of rights constitute property that may be attached by a federal tax lien. In *Drye v. United States, supra,* we considered a situation where state law allowed an heir subject to a federal tax lien to disclaim his interest in the estate. The state law also provided that such a disclaimer would "creat[e] the legal fiction" that the heir had predeceased the decedent and would correspondingly be deemed to have had no property interest in the estate. *Id.,* at 53, 120 S.Ct. 474. We unanimously held that this state law fiction did not control the federal question and looked instead to the realities of the heir's interest. We concluded that, despite the State's characterization, the heir possessed a "right to property" in the estate— the right to accept the inheritance or pass it along to another—to which the federal lien could attach. *Id.,* at 59–61, 120 S.Ct. 474. . . .

[Editors' Note: We have omitted the Court's recitation of the history of tenancy by the entirety, which largely duplicates the discussion in *Sawada v. Endo.*]

In determining whether respondent's husband possessed "property" or "rights to property" within the meaning of 26 U.S.C. § 6321, we look to the individual rights created by these state law rules. According to Michigan law, respondent's husband had, among other rights, the following rights with respect to the entiret[y] property: the right to use the property, the right to exclude third parties from it, the right to a share of income produced from it, the right of survivorship, the right to become a tenant in common with equal shares upon divorce, the right to sell the property with the respondent's consent and to receive half the proceeds from such a sale, the right to place an encumbrance on the property with the respondent's consent, and the right to block respondent from selling or encumbering the property unilaterally.

We turn now to the federal question of whether the rights Michigan law granted to respondent's husband as a tenant by the entirety qualify as "property" or "rights to property" under § 6321. The statutory language authorizing the tax lien "is broad and reveals on its face that Congress meant to reach every interest in property that a taxpayer might have." *United States v. National Bank of Commerce,* 472 U.S., at 719–720, 105 S.Ct. 2919. . . . We conclude that the husband's rights in the entiret[y] property fall within this broad statutory language.

Michigan law grants a tenant by the entirety some of the most essential property rights: the right to use the property, to receive income produced by it, and to exclude others from it.... These rights alone may be sufficient to subject the husband's interest in the entiret[y] property to the federal tax lien. They gave him a substantial degree of control over the entiret[y] property, and, as we noted in *Drye*, "in determining whether a federal taxpayer's state-law rights constitute 'property' or 'rights to property,' [t]he important consideration is the breadth of the control the [taxpayer] could exercise over the property." 528 U.S., at 61, 120 S.Ct. 474 (internal quotation marks omitted).

The husband's rights in the estate, however, went beyond use, exclusion, and income. He also possessed the right to alienate (or otherwise encumber) the property with the consent of respondent, his wife. *Loretto,* [*v. Teleprompter Manhattan CATV Corp.,* 458 U.S. 419, 435, 102 S.Ct. 3164, 3176 (1982)] (the right to "dispose" of an item is a property right). It is true, as respondent notes, that he lacked the right to unilaterally alienate the property, a right that is often in the bundle of property rights. There is no reason to believe, however, that this one stick—the right of unilateral alienation—is essential to the category of "property."

This Court has already stated that federal tax liens may attach to property that cannot be unilaterally alienated. In *United States v. Rodgers,* 461 U.S. 677, 103 S.Ct. 2132, 76 L.Ed.2d 236 (1983), we considered the Federal Government's power to foreclose homestead property attached by a federal tax lien. Texas law provided that " 'the owner or claimant of the property claimed as homestead [may not], if married, sell or abandon the homestead without the consent of the other spouse.' " *Id.,* at 684–685, 103 S.Ct. 2132 (quoting Tex. Const., Art. 16, § 50). We nonetheless stated that "[i]n the homestead context ..., there is no doubt ... that not only do *both* spouses (rather than neither) have an independent interest in the homestead property, but that a federal tax lien can at least *attach* to each of those interests." 461 U.S., at 703, n. 31, 103 S.Ct. 2132; cf. *Drye, supra,* at 60, n. 7, 120 S.Ct. 474 (noting that "an interest in a spendthrift trust has been held to constitute 'property for purposes of § 6321' even though the beneficiary may not transfer that interest to third parties").

Excluding property from a federal tax lien simply because the taxpayer does not have the power to unilaterally alienate it would, moreover, exempt a rather large amount of what is commonly thought of as property. It would exempt not only the type of property discussed in *Rodgers*, but also some community property. Community property states often provide that real community property cannot be alienated without the consent of both spouses. Accordingly, the fact that respondent's husband could not unilaterally alienate the property does not preclude him from possessing "property and rights to property" for the purposes of § 6321.

Respondent's husband also possessed the right of survivorship—the right to automatically inherit the whole of the estate should his wife predecease him. Respondent argues that this interest was merely an expectancy, which we suggested in *Drye* would not constitute "property" for the purposes of a federal tax lien. 528 U.S., at 60, n. 7, 120 S.Ct. 474 ("[We do not mean to suggest] that an expectancy that has pecuniary value ... would fall within § 6321 prior to the time it ripens into a present estate"). *Drye* did not decide this question, however, nor do we need to do so here. As we have discussed above, a number of the sticks in respondent's husband's bundle were presently existing. It is therefore not necessary to decide whether the right to survivorship alone would qualify as "property" or "rights to property" under § 6321.

That the rights of respondent's husband in the entiret[y] property constitute "property" or "rights to property" "belonging to" him is further underscored by the fact that, if the conclusion were otherwise, the entiret[y] property would belong to no one for the purposes of § 6321. Respondent had no more interest in the property than her husband; if neither of them had a property interest in the entiret[y] property, who did? This result not only seems absurd, but would also allow spouses to shield their property from federal taxation by classifying it as entiret[y] property, facilitating abuse of the federal tax system. Johnson, After *Drye*: The Likely Attachment of the Federal Tax Lien to Tenancy-by-the-Entirety Interests, 75 Ind. L. J. 1163, 1171 (2000)....

We therefore conclude that respondent's husband's interest in the entiret[y] property constituted "property" or "rights to property" for the purposes of the federal tax lien statute. We recognize that Michigan makes a different choice with respect to state law creditors: "[L]and held by husband and wife as tenants by entirety is not subject to levy under execution on judgment rendered against either husband or wife alone." *Sanford v. Bertrau*, 204 Mich. 244, 247, 169 N.W. 880, 881 (1918). But that by no means dictates our choice. The interpretation of 26 U.S.C. § 6321 is a federal question, and in answering that question we are in no way bound by state courts' answers to similar questions involving state law. As we elsewhere have held, " 'exempt status under state law does not bind the federal collector.' " *Drye v. United States,* 528 U.S., at 51, 120 S.Ct. 474. See also *Rodgers, supra*, at 701, 103 S.Ct. 2132 (clarifying that the Supremacy Clause "provides the underpinning for the Federal Government's right to sweep aside state-created exemptions")....

JUSTICE SCALIA, with whom JUSTICE THOMAS joins, dissenting.... I write separately to observe that the Court nullifies (insofar as federal taxes are concerned, at least) a form of property ownership that was of particular benefit to the stay-at-home spouse or mother. She is overwhelmingly likely to be the survivor that obtains title to the unencumbered property; and she (as opposed to her business-world husband) is overwhelmingly unlikely to be the source of the individual indebtedness against which a tenancy by the entirety protects. It is regrettable that the Court has eliminated a large part of this traditional protection retained by many States.

JUSTICE THOMAS, with whom JUSTICE STEVENS and JUSTICE SCALIA join, dissenting.... The Court does not dispute [Craft's] characterization of Michigan's law with respect to the essential attributes of the tenancy by the entirety estate. However, relying on *Drye v. United States*, 528 U.S. 49, 59, 120 S.Ct. 474, 145 L.Ed.2d 466 (1999) ... the Court suggests that Michigan's definition of the tenancy by the entirety estate should be overlooked because federal tax law is not controlled by state legal fictions concerning property ownership. But the Court misapprehends the application of *Drye* to this case.

Drye ... was concerned not with whether state law recognized "property" as belonging to the taxpayer in the first place, but rather with whether state laws could disclaim or exempt such property from federal tax liability after the property interest was created. *Drye* held only that a state-law disclaimer could not retroactively undo a vested right in an estate that the taxpayer already held, and that a federal lien therefore attached to the taxpayer's interest in the estate. 528 U.S., at 61, 120 S.Ct. 474 (recognizing that a disclaimer does not restore the status quo ante because the heir "determines who will receive the property—himself if he does not disclaim, a known other if he does").
. . .

Extending this Court's "state law fiction" jurisprudence to determine whether property or rights to property exist under state law in the first place works a sea change in the role States have traditionally played in "creating and defining" property interests. By erasing the careful line between state laws that purport to disclaim or exempt property interests after the fact, which the federal tax lien does not respect, and state laws' definition of property and property rights, which the federal tax lien does respect, the Court does not follow *Drye*, but rather creates a new federal common law of property. This contravenes the previously settled rule that the definition and scope of property is left to the States....

That the federal tax lien did not attach to the Grand Rapids property is further supported by the consensus among the lower courts. For more than 50 years, every federal court reviewing tenancies by the entirety in States with a similar understanding of tenancy by the entirety as Michigan has concluded that a federal tax lien cannot attach to such property to satisfy an individual spouse's tax liability. This consensus is supported by the IRS' consistent recognition, arguably against its own interest, that a federal tax lien against one spouse cannot attach to property or rights to property held as a tenancy by the entirety.

That the Court fails to so much as mention this consensus, let alone address it or give any reason for overruling it, is puzzling. While the positions of the lower courts and the IRS do not bind this Court, one would be hard pressed to explain why the combined weight of these judicial and administrative sources—including the IRS' instructions to its own employees—do not constitute relevant authority....

Finally, while the majority characterizes Michigan's view that the tenancy by the entirety property does not belong to the individual spouses as a "state law fiction," our precedents, including *Drye*, 528 U.S., at 58–60, 120 S.Ct. 474, hold that state, not federal, law defines property interests. Ownership by "the marriage" is admittedly a fiction of sorts, but so is a partnership or corporation. There is no basis for ignoring this fiction so long as federal law does not define property, particularly since the tenancy by the entirety property remains subject to lien for the tax liability of both tenants. . . .

Notes

1. *The Majority's Logical Analysis in* Craft. Justice O'Connor notes that whether the interests of a tenant by the entirety are "property or rights to property" is a federal question, but that the answer largely depends upon state law. Yet in analyzing the state law, Justice O'Connor concludes that even though a Michigan tenant by the entirety lacks the unilateral ability to encumber or alienate his interest in the property, he has enough other "sticks in the bundle" to have "property or rights in property"—such that the tax lien can attach to his interest as if he had the ability to unilaterally encumber or alienate the property. Why do you think the Court reached this conclusion?

2. *Valuing a Share of Tenancy by the Entirety Property.* On remand, how should the court determine the value of Mr. Craft's interest in the entirety property? Was Mr. Craft's interest worth 50% of the proceeds of the sale of the land? Does the Court's ruling completely "nullify" (as Justice Scalia suggests) the non-responsible spouse's ability to use tenancy by the entirety as a means of protection from the federal tax debts of the responsible spouse? What if the land had not been sold and was thus still held by the Crafts as tenants by the entirety?

3. *Understanding the Impact (and Limits) of the* Craft *Decision.* In light of the majority opinion in *Craft*, consider the following questions:

(a) Assume that a dispute identical to *Sawada v. Endo* arose after the decision in *Craft*. Would the *Craft* decision dictate a conclusion that the couple's conveyance to their children was a fraudulent conveyance? Why or why not?

(b) Assume the U.S. government is attempting to forfeit property under federal civil or criminal forfeiture statutes relating to drug enforcement against two different defendants—one who lives in Michigan and holds property with her spouse as tenants by the entirety, and one who lives in Ohio (which has abolished tenancy by the entirety) and holds property with his spouse as joint tenants with right of survivorship. How should the state law treatment of property ownership impact the ability of the federal government to seek forfeiture over the objection of the "innocent" spouse, whose interest is not subject to forfeiture under the federal statutes? *See, e.g., United States v. Parcel of Real Prop. Known as 1500 Lincoln Ave.*, 949 F.2d 73 (3d Cir. 1991) (holding that under Pennsylvania law, the government could forfeit only the survivorship interest of the non-innocent spouse). Is this approach different from the approach taken by the majority in *Craft*?

B. RULES GOVERNING THE LEGAL RELATIONSHIP BETWEEN COTENANTS AND THE USE OF COTENANCY PROPERTY

Hornbook property law says that cotenants have an undivided right to possession of the whole of cotenancy property. For the mythical Borg of *Star Trek*® fame, who possess no individualistic tendencies and behave in a purely collective fashion, the concept of an undivided right of possession would present no practical problems. For societies like ours that place a premium upon individual liberties, this "undivided right to possession"—straightforward and understandable on the drawing board—becomes a minefield of potential problems in actual practice.[9]

In an ideal world, cotenants would anticipate the potential problems that arise from shared ownership, consult with attorneys and enter into some type of formal contract that defines their rights and responsibilities with respect to possession, use, expenses, improvements, repairs, rents or profits. In practice, because many cotenancies arise within family groups due to testamentary transfers, such formal contracts often do not exist. As a result, the common law has developed a set of default rules to define the rights and responsibilities of cotenants in the absence of an agreement.

Courts have articulated and applied these default rules in three types of actions between cotenants. The first is *accounting*—an action in which one cotenant (typically a cotenant that is not in possession of the land) seeks to compel another cotenant (typically the cotenant in possession) to share benefits obtained from the leasing or use of the property (*e.g.*, rents, profits, or proceeds). The second is *contribution*—an action in which one cotenant seeks reimbursement from the other cotenant(s) for a pro rata share of expenses that the complaining cotenant has paid (*e.g.*, taxes, mortgage payments, repairs, or improvements). A cotenant can bring an action for an accounting or for contribution without terminating the cotenancy. By contrast, in the third action—*partition*—the complaining cotenant asks the court to terminate the cotenancy and to divide the cotenancy property, either in kind (a physical division of the property) or by sale (with division of the proceeds). As part of the partition action, cotenants frequently ask the court to make equitable adjustments to reflect claims the cotenants otherwise might have asserted in an action for accounting or contribution.

---

9. For example, what implications does the "unity of possession" have for criminal procedure and constitutional law? Suppose that one cotenant refuses a police request to conduct a warrantless search of the co-owned premises, but the other cotenant consents to the search. The Georgia Supreme Court held that in "a situation in which two persons have equal use and control of the premises to be searched, . . . the consent to conduct a warrantless search of a residence given by one occupant is not valid in the face of the refusal of another occupant who is physically present at the scene to permit a warrantless search." *Georgia v. Randolph*, 278 Ga. 614, 604 S.E.2d 835 (2004), *cert. granted*, 125 S.Ct. 1840, 161 L.Ed.2d 722 (2005). Is this a sensible result?

Most litigation between cotenants involves a partition, perhaps because the cotenants have reached a point at which they believe their disagreement prevents them from remaining as cotenants. How does the partition process work?

SCHMIDT v. WITTINGER

Supreme Court of North Dakota.
687 N.W.2d 479 (2004).

SANDSTROM, JUSTICE. Alfred Wittinger appealed from a judgment ordering a partition sale of farmland and awarding compensatory damages to Donald and Kenneth Wittinger. We hold the trial court's finding that a partition in kind could not be made without great prejudice to the co-owners is not clearly erroneous, and we affirm the partition sale of the property. We also hold that the court's award of compensatory damages for loss of federal program payments is not supported by the record evidence, and we therefore reverse that part of the compensatory damages award to Donald and Kenneth Wittinger.

Donald, Kenneth, and Alfred Wittinger are brothers who inherited from their parents undivided equal interests in farmland located in Dunn County. The property was leased by Kevin Schmidt, and Alfred Wittinger was sued by his brothers and Schmidt ... for a partition sale of the property. Donald and Kenneth Wittinger also sued Alfred Wittinger for compensatory damages, asserting that he did not pay his pro rata share of property expenses and taxes and that he refused to sign documents for the parties to receive federal farm program payments. ... [Alfred Wittinger] filed a counterclaim for damages to compensate him for loss of "value, rental payments, government payments, CRP payments and market value."

At the bench trial, Alfred Wittinger neither appeared nor was represented by counsel. After the hearing, the trial court ordered a partition sale of the property with proceeds to be equally divided among the three cotenants. The court also awarded compensatory damages of $2,821.87 to Donald Wittinger and $2,244.50 to Kenneth Wittinger for Alfred Wittinger's failure to pay his share of the farmland expenses and taxes and for his failure to sign federal farm program documents. The court dismissed Alfred Wittinger's counterclaim. ...

On appeal, Alfred Wittinger asserts the trial court erred in ordering a partition sale rather than a partition in kind. Partition of property is available under N.D.C.C. § 32–16–01 when there are cotenants with current possessory interests in the property. *Treiber v. Citizens State Bank,* 598 N.W.2d 96 (1999). Section 32–16–01, N.D.C.C., provides:

> When several cotenants hold and are in possession of real or personal property as partners, joint tenants, or tenants in common, in which one or more of them have an estate or inheritance, or for life or lives, or for years, an action may be brought by one or more of such persons for a partition thereof according to the respective

rights of the persons interested therein and for a sale of such property or a part thereof, if it appears that a partition cannot be made without great prejudice to the owners. Real and personal property may be partitioned in the same action.

Section 32–16–12, N.D.C.C., provides for a partition sale if a partition in kind cannot be made without great prejudice to the owners:

> If it is alleged in the complaint and established by evidence, or if it appears by the evidence without such allegation in the complaint, to the satisfaction of the court, that the property, or any part of it, is so situated that partition cannot be made without great prejudice to the owners, the court may order a sale thereof. Otherwise, upon the making of requisite proof, it must order a partition according to the respective rights of the parties as ascertained by the court and appoint three referees therefor, and must designate the portion to remain undivided for the owners whose interests remain unknown or unascertained.

The law favors partition in kind, and there is a presumption that partition in kind should be made unless great prejudice is shown. *Schnell v. Schnell*, 346 N.W.2d 713, 716 (N.D.1984). "The burden of proving that partition in kind cannot be made without great prejudice is on the party demanding a sale." *Id.* Great prejudice exists when the value of the share of each in case of a partition would be materially less than the share of the money equivalent that each could probably obtain from the whole. *Id.; see also Berg v. Kremers*, 181 N.W.2d 730, 733 (N.D.1970).

On the request for a partition sale of the property, the trial court made the following relevant findings of fact:

> By reason of the existing fence, a partition in kind would necessitate surveying and the construction of a substantial amount of fence, some properties requiring more fencing than others. The river meanders through the property which makes fencing on section lines and boundary lines extremely difficult....

> Portions of the property would not have road access in the event of a partition as all tracts of lands involved do not have access roads due to the river crossing the premises....

> A partition in kind would require the building of fences and the maintaining of fences by adjoining landowners. The Defendant, Alfred Wittinger, has evidenced and demonstrated that he will not discuss or communicate with others and has demonstrated hostility towards the Plaintiffs. It would be extremely difficult to conduct fencing arrangements between Alfred Wittinger and any adjoining property owner....

> Not all tracts or separate parcels of land have a water supply, and thus a partition in kind would result in portions or parts of the property not having water available to it rendering the pasture lands of diminished value or requiring the owner to expend large sums of money for the drilling of wells or constructing dams....

The property is currently being operated and farmed in an efficient manner. In order to partition the land in kind it would require breaking the property up into small tracts of land. Such small tracts typically do not sell for as much per acre as with the larger machinery used by farmers today it is difficult and less efficient to farm smaller tracts of land. . . .

The house that is on the premises appears to be on the section line between Sections 5 and 8 and cannot be partitioned. . . .

The value of the share of each of the Wittingers in case of a partition would be materially less than his share of the money equivalent that could probably be obtained for the whole. . . .

The usefulness of the various tracts of land after partition would be substantially diminished. . . .

A partition in kind would result in great prejudice to the owners. . . .

The trial court's findings in a partition action will not be reversed on appeal unless they are clearly erroneous. *McKechnie v. Berg,* 667 N.W.2d 628 (2003). We conclude the trial court's findings are not clearly erroneous. The plaintiffs have met their burden of proving that a partition in kind could not be made without great prejudice to the owners. We therefore affirm the trial court's grant of a partition sale of the property. . . .

The court also awarded compensatory damages of $2,244.50 to Kenneth Wittinger and $2,821.87 to Donald Wittinger for Alfred Wittinger's "willful refusal and failure to sign various documents required by the U.S. Department of Agriculture and to pay his prorata share of the expenses and taxes." Of the total compensatory damages award, Donald and Kenneth Wittinger each received $2,151.40 for lost Conservation Reserve Program (CRP) payments, because Alfred Wittinger would not sign the necessary federal documents for the owners to continue receiving those payments.

A joint tenant is liable to account to his cotenants for receiving more than a proportionate share of the rents and profits. *American Standard Life & Accident Ins. Co. v. Speros,* 494 N.W.2d 599, 607 (N.D.1993). Generally, cotenants are considered to be in a confidential relationship and must do equity. *See Bartz v. Heringer,* 322 N.W.2d 243, 244 (N.D.1982). Every partition action includes a final accounting for charges, including rents and profits received beyond the cotenant's fractional share, and for credits, including expenditures in excess of the cotenant's fractional share of taxes, insurance, and similar expenses. 7 *Powell on Real Property* § 50.07(6) (2004).

These cotenants were entitled to share equally in the profits from the land, and each had a duty to pay his proportionate share of the taxes and other expenses. It was, therefore, appropriate for the trial court to award Donald and Kenneth Wittinger compensatory damages to account for Alfred Wittinger's share of the farmland taxes and expenses paid on his behalf by Donald and Kenneth Wittinger.

Donald and Kenneth Wittinger, however, have not advanced a legal theory entitling them to receive compensatory damages for loss of CRP payments. This is a voluntary federal program whereby landowners can elect to keep land out of production in exchange for cash payments. 11 Harl, *Agricultural Law* § 91.03[4][e] (2004). Under certain circumstances, participation in the program is a desirable alternative to farming the land. Donald and Kenneth Wittinger, however, have not cited any authority showing that Alfred Wittinger had a duty to participate in the federal CRP program or that his failure to participate in the program constituted a legal breach entitling his cotenants to compensatory damages. We conclude the plaintiffs have failed to present a viable legal theory upon which to justify the court's award of damages for the alleged "loss" of CRP payments, and we reverse that part of the compensatory damages awarded to them. . . .

Notes

1. *Partition as a Matter of Right.* As the New Jersey Court of Chancery pointed out in *Mastbaum v. Mastbaum,* 126 N.J.Eq. 366, 9 A.2d 51 (1939), "[t]wo men cannot plow the same furrow." The concept of undivided ownership of the whole—a concept essential to the common law's conception of co-ownership—does not function well in practice when cotenants cannot agree as to how to use the land. As reflected in *Schmidt,* if cotenants cannot resolve their disagreement, the law provides cotenants with a right to partition as an "out" to deal with the risk of irreconcilable differences.

As *Schmidt* indicates, partition can occur *in kind* or *by sale.* Partition in kind is physical division of the property; the court divides the property into separate tracts, and vests individual title to a divided portion in each of the cotenants based upon each cotenant's respective share.[10] In contrast, partition by sale involves a judicial sale of the entire parcel, followed by a distribution of the sale proceeds to each cotenant in accordance with each cotenant's share.

Early common law established a preference for partition in kind—if one cotenant sought partition in kind, the court would partition the property in kind unless (a) the physical attributes of the land made partition in kind impracticable or inequitable or (b) the interests of all cotenants were better served by partition by sale. *See, e.g., Delfino v. Vealencis,* 181 Conn. 533, 436

---

10. In some cases, it may be difficult to divide the land into physical shares commensurate with the share interests of the parties. For example, suppose that Henning and Dean own Blueacre (a 20–acre parcel) as tenants in common holding equal shares, and Henning seeks partition in kind. Suppose further that based upon the topography and location of Blueacre, the only feasible way to divide the property is to split it into Tract A (suitable for commercial development and worth $150,000) and Tract B (not suitable for commercial use and worth only $100,000). Despite this inequality, a court could still order partition in kind as long as the court accompanies the division with an award of *owelty*—a sum of money that balances the parties' respective shares. In this way, Henning can be awarded Tract A—but only if he pays $25,000 to Dean, so that each receives property with a total value of $125,000. *See, e.g., Clawson v. Silver,* 26 P.3d 209 (Utah 2001).

A.2d 27 (1980) (summarizing earlier Connecticut cases). Today, however, while courts, including the *Schmidt* court, continue to state a preference for partition in kind, courts routinely use partition by sale in many partition actions. Why did the *Schmidt* court opt for partition by sale? Can you offer other reasons why a court might prefer partition by sale?

2. *Restraints on the Right to Partition.* Courts commonly state that partition is available to tenants in common and joint tenants as a matter of right. But may cotenants enter into binding agreements limiting or waiving their respective rights to partition? How should courts view such agreements—as enforceable agreements or as unreasonable restraints on alienation? Consider the following examples:

(a) The agreement between the divorcing spouses in *Mann v. Bradley* (page 361) effectively waived each spouse's ability to seek unilateral partition until Mrs. Mann remarried or their youngest child reached age 21. Should the court enforce this agreement?

(b) Two sisters (Kathryn and Leslie) acquired a home as joint tenants, and signed an agreement that states: (1) if either "decides to permanently vacate the home . . . they must first give a full one year notice" and pay rent to the other during that year; (2) if either party vacated the home, the other had the right to buy out the vacating party's share; and (3) any party that vacates "cannot force the non-vacating party to sell the house just to get her share." When Leslie soon found living with Kathryn to be intolerable, she sued for partition. In light of the agreement, can she obtain it? Would it matter if Leslie was sleeping at her grandmother's, but never moved any of her furniture or personal belongings from the house? *See, e.g., Marchetti v. Karpowich*, 446 Pa.Super. 509, 667 A.2d 724 (1995).

(c) Twenty-one friends who purchased land for investment took title as tenants in common and entered into an agreement that provided: "Any and all decisions relating to said real estate, including decisions to sell or hold part or all of said real estate and relating to the use of said real estate . . . shall be made by majority decision of the co-owners. All of the undersigned agree that all shall be bound by majority decision with respect to said real estate, and that any who are in the minority as to any decision will accept the majority decision. . . ." When a majority of the cotenants voted not to sell the land, one of the dissenting cotenants sued for partition. Should the court grant the petition, or enforce the agreement? Why or why not? What additional information, if any, would you wish to guide your decision? *See, e.g., Raisch v. Schuster*, 47 Ohio App.2d 98, 352 N.E.2d 657 (1975).

3. *Contribution for Carrying Charges.* As discussed in *Schmidt*, if one cotenant pays more than her share of carrying charges of ownership (*i.e.*, real estate taxes, private assessments such as homeowners association charges, and mortgage payments), she has a right of contribution against other cotenant(s) for their pro rata shares of those ownership costs (absent contrary agreement). Thus, without seeking partition, a cotenant who had paid more than her share could pursue a contribution action against her cotenants to recover the amount of carrying charges she has paid in excess of

her share (subject to possible equitable offset for the value of her right to possession, as discussed in the following case and notes).

4. *Partition of Future Interests.* Suppose that Henning, owner of Blue-acre (a 10,000–acre tract) in fee simple absolute, conveys it "to Donald for life, then to his nephews Huey, Louie, and Dewey." Dewey then conveys his interest to his uncle Donald, who wants to use the land to grow and harvest timber. Huey and Louie want to sell the land to Disney, who wants to purchase the land for a new theme park. Can Huey and Louie seek partition while Donald is still alive?

Traditionally, because co-owners of a future interest did not have a present right to possession, they could not maintain a partition action—even if seeking only a partition of their future interest—and a few states still follow this view. *See, e.g., Weed v. Knox*, 157 Fla. 896, 27 So.2d 419 (1946); *Treiber v. Citizens State Bank*, 598 N.W.2d 96 (N.D. 1999). Today, however, many states authorize concurrent owners of a vested future interest to seek partition of that interest. *See, e.g.*, Ark. Code § 18–60–401; N.M. Stat. Ann. § 42–5–1. In a jurisdiction that would permit Huey and Louie to seek partition of the future interest they share with Donald, what would be the state of the title following the partition?

A common dispute among cotenants involves the potential liability of the cotenant in possession to pay rent to the cotenant out of possession and how this potential liability interrelates (if at all) with the liability of the cotenant out of possession to pay carrying charges (such as taxes) incurred by the cotenant in possession. Should a cotenant out of possession be able to collect rent from a cotenant in possession (and, if so, when)? Should a cotenant out of possession have to reimburse the cotenant in possession for a share of expenses incurred with respect to the property (and if so, when)? Should these potential liabilities offset each other (and if so, when)? Consider the following materials.

ESTEVES v. ESTEVES

Superior Court of New Jersey, Appellate Division.
341 N.J.Super. 197, 775 A.2d 163 (2001).

LESEMANN, J.A.D. This appeal deals with the proper division of the proceeds from the sale of a one-family house held by a tenancy in common, with plaintiffs, the parents of defendant, owning one-half of the house and defendant owning the other half.

The trial court held that plaintiffs, who had occupied the house by themselves for approximately eighteen years before it was sold, and had paid all of the expenses relating to the house during that period, were entitled to reimbursement from defendant for one-half of the sums they had paid, without any offset for the value of their occupancy. The net effect of that ruling amounted to a determination that plaintiffs were permitted to occupy the premises "rent free" for approximately eighteen years, while they paid one-half of the costs attributable to the house and defendant paid the other half. The trial court found that such a result was compelled by applicable law. We disagree, and conclude that when plaintiffs sought reimbursement from defendant for one-half of the costs of occupying and maintaining the premises, plaintiffs were required to allow defendant credit for the reasonable value of their occupancy of the house. Accordingly we reverse.

The case involves an unhappy family schism, but the facts, as found by the trial court and not disputed on appeal, are uncomplicated. In December 1980, plaintiffs Manuel and Flora Esteves, together with their son Joao Esteves, bought a house. They took title as tenants in common, with Manuel and Flora owning a one-half interest and Joao owning the other one-half. The purchase price was $34,500. Manuel and Flora paid $10,000 in cash as did Joao, and the parties took a mortgage loan for the remaining $14,500. They then moved into the house, and Joao undertook a considerable amount of work involving repairs and improvements while he lived there with his parents for somewhere between three months and eighteen months after closing. Joao then moved out and for approximately the next eighteen years, until the house was sold on February 26, 1998, Manuel and Flora lived there by themselves. At no time did they rent out any portion of the house.

Sale of the house produced net proceeds of $114,453.18. With the parties unable to agree on distribution of the proceeds, they agreed to each take $10,000 and deposit the remaining $94,453.18 in escrow. They then proceeded to trial, after which the trial court made the following findings and conclusions.

The court found that Manuel and Flora had paid out $17,336 in mortgage payments, including principal and interest; $14,353 for capital expenses; $21,599 for real estate taxes; $3,971 for sewer charges; and $4,633 for homeowners insurance. Those amounts totaled $61,892, and the court found that Joao was obligated to reimburse his parents for one-half that amount. However, the court also found that Joao had supplied labor with a value of $2,000 more than any labor expended by Manuel and Flora, and thus Joao was entitled to a credit for that amount. On the critical issue of credit for the value of plaintiffs' occupancy of the house, the court said this:

> I conclude there being no ouster of the defendant by the plaintiffs that there is no entitlement to the equivalent rent or rental value of the premises where the plaintiffs lived. The defendant could have continued to live there if he wanted to; he chose not to. And the law is clear that that being the case, he's not—there being no ouster, he's not entitled to anything for the rental value or what the rental could have been to the plaintiffs.

Over the years, there have been varying statements by our courts as to the rights and obligations of tenants in common respecting payment for maintenance of the parties' property and their rights and obligations respecting occupancy thereof. *See, e.g., Baker v. Drabik,* 224 N.J.Super.

603, 541 A.2d 229 (App.Div.1988); *Asante v. Abban,* 237 N.J.Super. 495, 568 A.2d 146 (Law Div.1989); and the most frequently cited decision, *Mastbaum v. Mastbaum,* 126 N.J. Eq. 366, 9 A.2d 51 (Ch.1939). While those decisions may not always have been consistent, in *Baird v. Moore,* 50 N.J.Super. 156, 141 A.2d 324 (App.Div.1958), this court, in a comprehensive, scholarly opinion by Judge Conford set out what we conceive to be the most appropriate, fair and practical rules to resolve such disputes. Those principles can be summarized as follows.

First, as a general proposition, on a sale of commonly owned property, an owner who has paid less than his pro-rata share of operating and maintenance expenses of the property, must account to a co-owner who has contributed more than his pro-rata share, and that is true even if the former had been out of possession and the latter in possession of the property.

Second, the fact that one tenant in common occupies the property and the other does not, imposes no obligation on the former to make any contribution to the latter. All tenants in common have a right to occupy all of the property and if one chooses not to do so, that does not give him the right to impose an "occupancy" charge on the other.

Third, notwithstanding those general rules, when on a final accounting following sale, the tenant who had been in sole possession of the property demands contribution toward operating and maintenance expenses from his co-owner, fairness and equity dictate that the one seeking that contribution allow a corresponding credit for the value of his sole occupancy of the premises. To reject such a credit and nonetheless require a contribution to operating and maintenance expenses from someone who (like the defendant here) had enjoyed none of the benefits of occupancy would be patently unfair.

Finally, this court held in *Baird,* that the party seeking the credit for the other's occupancy of the property has the burden of demonstrating the "actual rental value" of the property enjoyed by the occupying co-tenant (*id.* at 172, 141 A.2d 324).[11]

We believe the principles of *Baird* are sound and should be applied here. They support the trial court's conclusions as to defendant's obligation to contribute one-half of the $61,892 expended by his parents respecting the house they all owned. However, against that obligation, the court should offset a credit for the reasonable value of the occupancy enjoyed by the parents over the approximately eighteen years while they, and not their son, occupied the property. The obligation to present

11. The court in *Baird* also said that in any final accounting between the co-tenants, equitable considerations which would weigh against a simple mathematical balancing should be considered and could have an effect. Thus, *e.g.,* in *Baird,* where the co-tenants were brother and sister and the sister had expended extraordinary efforts to maintain the property for their mother and care for their mother in the property, those efforts were to be recognized in considering what if any occupancy credit should be imposed against the daughter. We see no such extraordinary equitable considerations here, but in the hearing which must follow the remand of this case, either party may submit evidence thereof for consideration by the trial court.

evidence of that value, which would normally be represented by rental value of the property, rests on the defendant. Although no such proof was presented at the prior trial, the uncertainty of the law in this area satisfies us that it would be unreasonable to deprive the defendant of the opportunity to do so now. Accordingly, the matter is reversed and remanded to the trial court for further proceedings at which the defendant shall have an opportunity to present evidence related to the value of the plaintiffs' sole occupancy of the property. . . .

Notes

1. *Possessing Cotenant Generally Not Liable for Rental Value Absent Ouster.* The prevailing view (as stated in *Esteves*) is that a cotenant in sole possession does not have to account to cotenants out of possession for their pro rata share of the property's rental value, unless the parties have so agreed or the cotenant in possession has "ousted" the other cotenant(s). Thus, a cotenant out of possession cannot bring an action for accounting for rental value against the cotenant in possession. In contrast, a small minority of courts have held that a cotenant in possession must account for the reasonable rental value of the land, even if she has not ousted her cotenants and is not deriving income from the land. *See, e.g., Modic v. Modic*, 91 Ohio App.3d 775, 633 N.E.2d 1151 (1993). [For a chart reflecting each state's position, see Evelyn Alicia Lewis, *Struggling With Quicksand: The Ins and Outs of Cotenant Possession Value Liability and a Call for Default Rule Reform*, 1994 Wis. L. Rev. 331, 447.] The majority rule effectively places the burden of the default rule on the cotenant out of possession. In other words, Joao Esteves, the cotenant out of possession in *Esteves*, had the burden to "opt out" of the default rule by seeking to get his parents to agree to pay him rent if he wanted to capture his share of the rental value that his parents were enjoying through exclusive possession. Can you explain why most courts have adopted this rule?

2. *Claiming Rent as a Defensive Offset.* As *Esteves* suggests, courts have sometimes struggled to reconcile the cotenant in possession's duty (or lack of duty) to account for her possession and the duty of other cotenants to contribute their share of carrying charges paid by the cotenant in possession. A majority of jurisdictions reconcile this dilemma by following the approach reflected in *Estevez*, giving the cotenants out of possession an "offset" for the fair rental value of the possession enjoyed by the cotenant in possession. Thus, assuming that the fair rental value of the land exceeds the amount of carrying charges incurred, this offset would create a complete defense to an action for contribution by the cotenant in possession. *See, e.g.,* Evelyn Alicia Lewis, *supra* note 1, at 361–62 (discussing cases). Note that consistent with the discussion in note 1, absent ouster or agreement, the cotenants out of possession cannot assert any right to accounting against the cotenant in possession, but may assert rental value only as an offset to contribution liability.

In a minority of jurisdictions, no defensive offset is available against a cotenant in sole possession, absent ouster. *See, e.g., Yakavonis v. Tilton*, 93 Wash. App. 304, 968 P.2d 908 (1998). Which approach do you think makes more sense, and why?

3. *The Sole Possessor's Liability for Rental Value Following Ouster.* Even under the prevailing rule, a cotenant in possession must account for the fair rental value of her possession if she "ousts" the other cotenant(s). Given that each cotenant has a right to possession, on what basis should courts determine whether ouster has occurred? [Hint: Think in terms of how a cotenant in possession would demonstrate an adverse possession claim.] Consider the following examples:

(a) Bob and Alex own a house as cotenants in which Bob resides. Alex wants to sell the house. Bob refuses to sell the house. Has Bob ousted Alex?

(b) *H* and *W* own a house as joint tenants. *W* leaves the house because of repeated domestic abuse by *H*. Has *H* ousted *W* so as to become liable to account for one-half of the home's rental value?

(c) Two sisters, Beth and Anne, inherit a house in which Anne had lived with and cared for their deceased father. Anne continues to occupy the house. When Beth returns to visit the house and take some of her father's personal effects, Anne lets Beth into the house, but Beth feels unwelcome as Anne is constantly hovering nearby. Several weeks later, Beth returns with her boyfriend for more of her father's personal effects. Anne again lets her into the house, but Anne's teenage son (a skinhead) gives Beth's boyfriend a hard time because he is Jewish. When tempers flare, Beth calls the police; when the police arrive, they ask Beth and her boyfriend to leave the premises. Beth subsequently sues for partition and seeks an accounting for rent for the months following her having been "ousted" from the property. How would you advise Anne about her potential liability for rental value? *See Laughon v. O'Braitis*, 360 S.C. 520, 602 S.E.2d 108 (Ct.App. 2004).

4. *Ouster and Adverse Possession.* Notably, in circumstances in which the cotenant in possession has "ousted" the cotenant out of possession, the cotenant in possession is effectively asserting an adverse possession claim. This means that if the ousted cotenant fails to take action for the duration of the statute of limitations in the jurisdiction in which the property is located, the cotenant out of possession risks losing her interest completely (along with any right to obtain an accounting for the period during which she was ousted). With that in mind, assume Mitch, Anthony and Gordon are cotenants of a house and lot. Mitch and Gordon had been sharing possession while Anthony was traveling around the world. Due to a falling out between Mitch and Gordon, Mitch changes the locks on the house and refuses to allow Gordon back into possession (although he does allow Gordon to reclaim his personal belongings). If Gordon comes to you and expresses concern about this situation, how would you advise Gordon? What steps would be sufficient to enable Gordon to prevent losing title by adverse possession? Would Mitch's conduct in relation to Gordon impact in any way the rights Anthony has as a cotenant?

5. *Accounting for Rents Collected from Leasing Co-owned Property.* Absent contrary agreement, a cotenant who leases the cotenancy property to a third party and collects rents on account of that lease must account to the other cotenant(s) for their pro rata share of the rents collected (after deducting any reasonable expenses incurred in leasing the property). The law thus distinguishes between the cotenant who remains in possession

herself and the cotenant who leases the land to a third party—the former is not accountable for rental value (absent ouster), while the latter must account for net rentals received. This rule reflects the influence of partnership law. Under hornbook partnership law, all partners share equally in the net rentals earned from leasing partnership property (absent contrary agreement). Uniform Partnership Act § 18(a). Do you think this distinction makes good sense? If the cotenant in possession can enjoy possession rent-free herself, why should she have to pay one-half of the net rents if she chooses to exercise her right to possession by transferring that right to a tenant under a lease?

In many cases, one cotenant will lease the property with the full knowledge and consent of the other cotenant(s). [Indeed, the lessee should insist that all cotenants join in signing the lease—especially if the property is held in joint tenancy. Can you explain why?] In some cases, however, one cotenant leases the property without the consent or approval of the other cotenant(s). Can the non-consenting cotenant claim that the lease is invalid because he did not sign it or consent to it? No; a lease of land held in joint tenancy or tenancy in common is valid even if only one cotenant signs the lease. *See, e.g., Rogers v. Kelly*, 66 N.C.App. 264, 311 S.E.2d 43 (1984). Because each cotenant has an undivided right to possession of the home, each may transfer that right—but that transfer will not affect the rights of other non-consenting cotenants.

So what options are then available to the non-consenting cotenant? Assume Tom and Nancy, brother and sister, share ownership of a house in which Nancy has resided (as Tom has lived in another city with his wife and two kids). Nancy has an opportunity to travel and leases the house to a friend, Steve, at a below-market rent of $300 per month. [She wants someone in the house to take care of it and is not interested in making money on the deal.] Shortly thereafter, Tom and his wife get a divorce. Tom, needing a place to stay, shows up at the house to find Steve living there. Tom calls you and asks for advice about his options. How do you advise him? Can he move in with Steve? Can he collect half the rent Steve is paying to Nancy? Can he also charge Steve rent (in addition to what Steve is already paying Nancy)? Exactly what steps should Tom take?

6. *Contribution for Repairs and Improvements.* The *Estevez* case involved both capital expenses (improvements) and claims for repairs. Most courts draw no distinctions between repairs and improvements in the context of contribution actions. Absent contrary agreement, if one cotenant unilaterally makes repairs or improvements on the land, she has no right of contribution against the other cotenant(s) for "their respective share(s)" of the cost of those repairs or improvements. Why does the law treat carrying charges differently than repairs and improvements? Why refuse to give the repairing cotenant a right of contribution? *See* 2 American Law of Property §§ 6.17–6.18 (1952); William B. Stoebuck & Dale A. Whitman, The Law of Property § 5.9, at 207–09 (3d ed. 2000).

7. *Repairs and Improvements in the Context of Partition.* Even though the repairing cotenant generally has no legal right of contribution during the cotenancy, courts in an action for partition or accounting typically will adjust the parties' respective shares to account for the reasonable cost of necessary

repairs incurred by one of the cotenants. Can you explain why? [Hint: What is a "necessary" repair, and what effect should such a repair have on the land?]

Courts in partition actions also have adjusted cotenants' shares based upon improvements made by one cotenant. For improvements, however, courts do not award the improving cotenant automatic credit for the *cost* of the improvement, but base an adjustment upon the *effect* of the improvement. Essentially, the improving cotenant "bears the risk" of her improvement. If the improvement increases the value of the property, the court will award the improver a credit for the full increase in the property's value. Likewise, if the improvement actually decreases the value of the property, the court will adjust the improver's share downward, thereby leaving the other cotenants no worse off than they would have been without the "improvement." Does it make sense to treat repairs differently from improvements? Why or why not?

Assume that Tom and Nancy inherit a home from their father, and that Nancy occupies the home. Without Tom's consent, Nancy spends $10,000 remodeling the kitchen. Five years later, Tom and Nancy agree to sell the house. The sale brings a price of $150,000. Tom demands an equal split of the proceeds, but Nancy argues that she should receive $80,000 to account for Tom's half of the cost of the kitchen remodeling. If they cannot settle their dispute, how should a court divide the proceeds of the sale? As Nancy's lawyer, what practical problems would you face in obtaining for Nancy the result she wants? What implications does this problem suggest for a cotenant in sole possession who wishes to engage in a construction or remodeling project?

8. *Accounting for Economic Exploitation of Cotenancy Property.* Just as it requires a cotenant who collects rent from a third party to share the net rental income with her cotenants, the law applies a similar accounting rule when one cotenant extracts natural resources from the land. Suppose that Henning and Pushaw are cotenants of Blueacre, and that Henning cut and sold all of the timber from Blueacre without Pushaw's consent. In its raw, unprocessed form, the timber Henning cut had a value of $20,000; after Henning processed the timber at his sawmill, its value increased to $40,000. Must Henning account for one-half of the raw value of the timber, or one-half of its processed value? Most courts have required the exploiting cotenant to account for net profits based upon raw value, but there are exceptions in cases involving particularly egregious conduct by one cotenant. *Compare Sadler v. Duvall*, 815 S.W.2d 285 (Tex. App. 1991) (raw value) *with White v. Smyth*, 147 Tex. 272, 214 S.W.2d 967 (1948) (processed value). *Cf.* Lawrence Berger, *An Analysis of the Economic Relations Between Cotenants*, 21 Ariz. L. Rev. 1015 (1979). If Henning cuts less than one-half of the timber on Blueacre, should he have to account to Pushaw at all? *See, e.g., Kirby Lumber Co. v. Temple Lumber Co.*, 125 Tex. 284, 83 S.W.2d 638 (1935).

Would you evaluate the Henning/Pushaw situation similarly if Henning were in possession and farmed the land? Should Henning have to account to Pushaw for half of the farming profits? Why or why not? *See Sons v. Sons*, 151 Minn. 360, 186 N.W. 811 (1922) (absent agreement, cotenant in sole possession need not account for profits earned by farming).

9. *Cotenants and Waste.* How does the concept of liability in accounting for economic exploitation square with the concept of "waste" as discussed in Chapter 5? Under the common law rule, an owner holding a fee simple absolute could not be liable for waste. *See* 2 American Law of Property § 6.15 (1952). Does this seem like a sensible rule as applied to co-owned property? A number of states have enacted statutes that allow one cotenant to sue fellow cotenants for damages in waste cases. *See, e.g.,* Mich. Comp. Laws Ann. § 600.2919(2)(a) (cotenant that commits waste without permission of other cotenants is liable to them for double the amount of actual damages). Does the award of multiple damages bestow a windfall on the other cotenants? Why or why not? If the land Pushaw and Henning owned was located in Michigan, Henning stripped the land of all timber as described above, and Pushaw brought both a claim for an accounting and a claim for waste, how would you rule?

Notably, if a statute authorizes a cotenant to sue her fellow cotenant(s) for waste, the complaining cotenant may file that suit without terminating the cotenancy. Absent such a statute, however, a cotenant harmed by such conduct can only recover for that harm in the context of a partition action, by asking the court to equitably adjust the shares of the parties to account for the other cotenant's "wasteful" conduct.

LAWYERING EXERCISE
(Advocacy and Mediation)

BACKGROUND: Most reported cotenancy decisions involve disputes between family members that ended in partition—the dissolution of the co-ownership. In many of these cases, the dissolution of the co-ownership is symbolic of the dissolution of the underlying family relationship—dissolution of a marriage, estrangement between a father and son or between siblings, etc. Many commentators have expressed the view that the benefits of mediation make it superior to litigation for resolution of disputes involving family members.

In her book *Mediation: Principles and Practice*, Kimberlee K. Kovach sets out an illustrative list of factors that suggest a particular dispute may be well-suited to mediation, including:

- the parties want to save time and money in resolving the dispute
- the parties have an ongoing relationship that they wish to maintain
- the parties hope to establish an ongoing relationship through mediation
- the parties seek to avoid a legal precedent
- the parties need to assure confidentiality about the nature of the dispute or its resolution
- the parties need assistance in communicating and exchanging information
- the parties cannot identify or build upon their common interests

- the parties need assistance in negotiating with each other (perhaps because of an imbalance of power in their relationship)
- the parties need help generating creative solutions
- the parties desire to resolve the dispute themselves
- one or both parties have made an unrealistic assessment of their position
- the parties desire to settle the dispute despite their differences.

Id. at 40–41. Which of these factors, if any, are likely present in family disputes? What implications, if any, does this suggest for whether disputes between cotenant family members are well-suited for mediation as an alternative to trial?

Furthermore, disputes between related cotenants often have roots in earlier family conflicts that may have nothing to do with the land. Once the land dispute arises, however, it can become "linked" with earlier family disputes, complicating the dispute exponentially and making resolution of the dispute more difficult without the intervention of a neutral third party such as a mediator. *See, e.g.,* Frank E.A. Sander & Stephen B. Goldberg, *Fitting the Forum to the Fuss: A User–Friendly Guide to Selecting an ADR Procedure,* Negotiation Journal (January 1994), at 57–58.

SITUATION: In 1920, Elbert Smith purchased 640 acres of land eight miles west of the town of Dalcross. For over 80 years, the Smith family has continued to own and operate a farm on this tract, with Elbert's daughter Ann succeeding him following his death in 1977, and Ann's sons Dale and Henry recently succeeding her following her death in 2005.

Dalcross has experienced far more changes than the Smith family farm. Thanks in large part to economic growth fueled by plant relocations by IBM, Honda, and General Mills, the town of Dalcross has grown from a small community to a city of 70,000. With this growth, development has expanded the town's borders to within two miles of the Smith farm. The economy in Dalcross is strong and shows no signs of slowing down soon.

Word around town is that Ford Motor Company may be planning to relocate production of its compact car models to a new plant to be constructed in Dalcross. The Smith family farm, as one of the largest privately held parcels of land near Dalcross, could be an ideal site should Ford Motor Company decide to locate its new plant to Dalcross.

Dale and Henry are interested in working out a cotenancy agreement. Dale and Henry generally agree that Dale will enjoy sole possession of the Smith family farm without having to pay rent to Henry, provided Dale covers all expenses of maintaining the property, including taxes and insurance (at present, there is no mortgage on the property). Dale, who is interested in retiring on the farm if possible, would like Henry to agree not to sell or seek to partition the property for at least 20 years. While generally agreeable with that concept, Henry would like to make sure that he can seek partition if Ford does decide to build a plant near Dalcross and offers a really wonderful price for the Smith family farm property.

TASK: Dale and Henry have not been able to hash out a formal agreement on their own and have agreed to have a mediator help them work through their differences. Please choose to represent either Henry or Dale. Based on your understanding of the types of issues that give rise to disputes in cotenancy situations, prepare a two-page outline of the 10 to 12 things you would want to be sure to have addressed in the cotenancy agreement Henry and Dale will be talking through with the mediator. For each point, briefly explain why it is important to your client.

C. MARITAL INTERESTS

There are a variety of property interests (or potential interests) that arise by virtue of the marital relationship. Earlier in the chapter, we focused upon the tenancy by the entirety, which can exist only within the marital relationship. In that type of cotenancy, however, the spouses collectively own an undivided interest in the property. In this section, we focus briefly on situations in which one spouse can claim a property interest in land or other assets that otherwise belong to the other spouse individually (or are titled in the other spouse's name). We emphasize that the following discussion is not complete. You will study the laws concerning a spouse's elective share in greater detail in an Estates and Trusts course. Likewise, you will encounter more detailed coverage of equitable distribution and community property in Family Law. Here, we provide only a historical overview and a brief summary of marital interests under present law.

1. *The Common Law Estate* Jure Uxoris

As discussed earlier (page 369), the common law provided that upon marriage, the husband (H) acquired an estate *jure uxoris* in all of the land owned by his wife (W) at the time of the marriage. This estate permitted H to exercise dominion and control over W's land throughout the marriage. H could lease the land and collect rents (without obligation to account to W), and could even sell the land to a third party (although, without W's consent to the sale, the purchaser could receive only the right to possession of the land for as long as H and W remained married). In the late 19th and early 20th centuries, the Married Women's Property Acts abolished the estate *jure uxoris* and gave married women full control over their own separate property.

2. *Curtesy*

At common law, H was not an heir of W. If W died intestate and was survived by H, any property owned by W thus would not have passed to H by inheritance. The law presumed that a typical W would not wish for her widower to be left without any means of support during his remaining years, however, and thus provided the surviving *H* with the estate of *curtesy*. This estate entitled *H* to enjoy a life estate in all land that *W* had owned *at any time during their marriage*. *W* could do nothing unilaterally during her life to defeat *H*'s curtesy rights. If, while married to *H*, *W* sold Blackacre to *P*, *P* took the land subject to *H*'s estate of curtesy if *H* survived *W*. [Query: What should a buyer in *P*'s position have insisted upon?]

In performing a title search, you may encounter an old deed in which the grantor is identified as "Jane Smith, an unmarried woman." This may seem odd, but given the estate of curtesy, the reason should be clear—by identifying the grantor as an unmarried woman, the deed communicated to persons subsequently searching the deed records that the grantor had no husband who might claim curtesy rights.

3. *Dower*

Just as *H* was not an heir of *W*, neither was *W* an heir of *H*. Despite the common law's otherwise complete disregard for the rights of women generally, even common law judges could not bear the notion of *W* living out her remaining years without access to the marital home. Thus, the common law gave the surviving widow an estate of *dower*. Not surprisingly, dower was not as good a deal for *W* as curtesy was for *H*. *W*'s estate of dower gave her a one-third interest, for life, in all land in which *H* owned an estate of inheritance at any time during the marriage. During their marriage, *H* could not take unilateral action to defeat *W*'s estate of dower. If *H* transferred Blackacre unilaterally, the grantee took title subject to *W*'s dower right.

4. *Elective Share—The Modern Successor of the Estates of Dower and Curtesy*

Today, statutes in nearly all states have abolished the common law estates of dower and curtesy. Nevertheless, these estates did serve an important purpose—to ensure that one spouse's death did not leave the surviving spouse without any property on which to sustain himself or herself. Today, all states have descent and distribution statutes that make *W* the heir of *H* and vice-versa, which largely solves the inadvertent disinheritance problem. The problem of spiteful conduct remains, however—nothing prevents *W* from making a will that provides nothing for *H*, or vice-versa.

To address this latter problem, nearly all states have replaced dower and curtesy with "forced share" or "elective share" statutes. If *H* dies leaving a will that either (a) devises nothing to *W*, or (b) devises her less property than she would have received as *H*'s heir if *H* had died intestate, then *W* can "elect against" the will. If *W* elects against the will, *W* receives the property that she would have taken as an heir if *H* had died without a valid will. [In other words, for purposes of distribution to *W*, we treat *H* as if he had died without a valid will.] The remainder of *H*'s estate (after *W* gets her elective share) passes under the terms of H's will. Elective share statutes likewise give H the same protection against similar conduct by W.

Caution: The elective share typically applies only to property that would pass by probate transfer (*i.e.*, through the decedent's will)—not "nonprobate transfers" such as life insurance contracts and joint tenant survivorship rights. If H carried a life insurance policy with a death benefit of $1,000,000, with H's son as the beneficiary, W could not obtain a share of that insurance benefit by electing against H's will. Likewise, if H owned Blueacre as a joint tenant with his sister, W could not obtain a share of Blueacre by electing against H's will.

5. *Community Property*

Originally, the common law placed great emphasis on the manner in which persons held title. For example, if H held title in his own name to the home in which he and W lived (*i.e.*, if H was the only grantee on the deed by which he acquired the land), then the home was treated as H's separate property—not the joint property of H and W. Further, because H's earnings during the marriage were treated as his own separate property, and because most family assets were acquired using H's earnings in the single-earner household, the law treated those assets as H's separate property. In short, the common law refused to recognize the marital relationship as a shared enterprise involving shared ownership of assets acquired during the marriage.

By contrast, civil law systems throughout continental Europe adopted the concept of *community property*, which views marriage as an enterprise to which each spouse contributes as an equal of the other. Although each may bring separate property to the marriage (which they would continue to hold as separate property), each spouse's earnings during the marriage are owned equally by the spouses in undivided shares, as "community" property. Furthermore, any assets acquired with those earnings are also community property. Any asset acquired during the marriage is presumed to be community property, unless one spouse can demonstrate that it was acquired with the proceeds of separate property.

How does community property compare with the common law concurrent ownership? During the marriage, neither spouse can act unilaterally to convey his or her share of community property, except to the other spouse. As a result, one spouse cannot take any unilateral action to convert community property to separate property—unlike the common law, where spouses holding as tenants in common or joint tenancy may seek partition as a matter of right. But before you conclude that community property sounds like a common law tenancy by the entirety, realize that *neither spouse has a right of survivorship in community property*. Each spouse has the freedom to transfer his or her share of community property at death. [Each spouse can, of course, voluntarily transfer his or her share of the property to the surviving spouse by will.] In the event of divorce, the community property is distributed evenly between the spouses; in some community property systems, the court can make an unequal distribution if such a distribution is equitable under the circumstances.

Arizona, California, Idaho, Louisiana, Nevada, New Mexico, Texas, Washington and Wisconsin have enacted community property regimes. For additional information about these community property systems, see William Reppy, Jr. & Cynthia A. Samuel, Community Property in the United States (6th ed. 2004).

6. *Equitable Distribution*

Although only a few American jurisdictions have embraced community property as a means of marital ownership, the doctrine has had significant influence in reforming the law that governs the distribution of property upon divorce. In non-community property states, the common law "how is title held?" test has given way to statutes requiring the court to make an equitable distribution of property owned by the divorcing spouses. Under many of these statutes, the court must identify "marital" property (typically defined as property acquired with the earnings of either spouse during the marriage) and then distribute that property between the spouses in an "equitable" or "just" fashion. What is "equitable" or "just" is usually left to the court's discretion,[12] although statutes typically provide some parameters for the court to consider. For example, the Missouri statute provides:

> In a proceeding for dissolution of the marriage or legal separation, or in a proceeding for disposition of property following dissolution of the marriage by a court which lacked personal jurisdiction over the absent spouse or lacked jurisdiction to dispose of the property, the court shall set apart to each spouse his nonmarital property and shall divide the marital property in such proportions as the court deems just after considering all relevant factors including:
>
> (1) The economic circumstances of each spouse at the time the division of property is to become effective, including the desirability of awarding the family home or the right to live therein for reasonable periods to the spouse having custody of any children;
>
> (2) The contribution of each spouse to the acquisition of the marital property, including the contribution of a spouse as homemaker;
>
> (3) The value of the nonmarital property set apart to each spouse;
>
> (4) The conduct of the parties during the marriage; and
>
> (5) Custodial arrangements for minor children. [Mo. Stat. Ann. § 452.330(1).]

Under this statute, could or should a court take into account one spouse's infidelity to increase the other spouse's share of the marital

---

12. A few states require equal division of marital property; other states establish only a presumption that the division should be equal. *See* Thomas J. Oldham, Divorce, Separation, and the Distribution of Property (1989) (providing state-by-state analysis of equitable distribution laws).

property? Could or should the court take into account one spouse's charitable gifts and community involvement (as compared to the other spouse) to increase his or her share? Why or why not?

The philosophy behind equitable distribution is that gender-neutral distributional rules and equitable division of marital property should have the effect of placing divorcing wives in an economic position as good as their husbands—or at least in a better position than the common law left them in upon divorce. There is substantial question, however, whether equitable distribution has accomplished this goal. *See* Lenore J. Weitzman, The Divorce Revolution (1985). Based upon the following case, why would you suggest this is so?

IN RE MARRIAGE OF GRAHAM

Supreme Court of Colorado.
194 Colo. 429, 574 P.2d 75 (1978).

LEE, JUSTICE. This case presents the novel question of whether in a marriage dissolution proceeding a master's degree in business administration (M.B.A.) constitutes marital property which is subject to division by the court. In its opinion in *Graham v. Graham*, Colo.App., 555 P.2d 527, the Colorado Court of Appeals held that it was not. We affirm the judgment.

The Uniform Dissolution of Marriage Act requires that a court shall divide marital property, without regard to marital misconduct, in such proportions as the court deems just after considering all relevant factors. The Act defines marital property as follows:

> For purposes of this article only, "marital property" means all property acquired by either spouse subsequent to the marriage except:
>
> (a) Property acquired by gift, bequest, devise, or descent;
>
> (b) Property acquired in exchange for property acquired prior to the marriage or in exchange for property acquired by gift, bequest, devise, or descent;
>
> (c) Property acquired by a spouse after a decree of legal separation;
>
> (d) Property excluded by valid agreement of the parties. [Section 14–10–113(2), C.R.S.1973.]

The parties to this proceeding were married on August 5, 1968, in Denver, Colorado. Throughout the six-year marriage, Anne P. Graham, wife and petitioner here, was employed full-time as an airline stewardess. She is still so employed. Her husband, Dennis J. Graham, respondent, worked part-time for most of the marriage, although his main pursuit was his education. He attended school for approximately three and one-half years of the marriage, acquiring both a bachelor of science degree in engineering physics and a master's degree in business administration at the University of Colorado. Following graduation, he obtained a job as an executive assistant with a large corporation at a starting salary of $14,000 per year.

The trial court determined that during the marriage petitioner contributed seventy percent of the financial support, which was used both for family expenses and for her husband's education. No marital assets were accumulated during the marriage. In addition, the Grahams together managed an apartment house and petitioner did the majority of housework and cooked most of the meals for the couple. No children were born during the marriage.

The parties jointly filed a petition for dissolution, on February 4, 1974, in the Boulder County District Court. Petitioner did not make a claim for maintenance or for attorney fees. After a hearing on October 24, 1974, the trial court found, as a matter of law, that an education obtained by one spouse during a marriage is jointly-owned property to which the other spouse has a property right. The future earnings value of the M.B.A. to respondent was evaluated at $82,836 and petitioner was awarded $33,134 of this amount, payable in monthly installments of $100.

The court of appeals reversed, holding that an education is not itself "property" subject to division under the Act, although it was one factor to be considered in determining maintenance or in arriving at an equitable property division. . . .

The purpose of the division of marital property is to allocate to each spouse what equitably belongs to him or her. *See* H. Clark, Domestic Relations § 14.8. The division is committed to the sound discretion of the trial court and there is no rigid mathematical formula that the court must adhere to. An appellate court will alter a division of property only if the trial court abuses its discretion. This court, however, is empowered at all times to interpret Colorado statutes.

The legislature intended the term "property" to be broadly inclusive, as indicated by its use of the qualifying adjective "all" in section 14–10–113(2). Previous Colorado cases have given "property" a comprehensive meaning, as typified by the following definition: "In short it embraces anything and everything which may belong to a man and in the ownership of which he has a right to be protected by law." *Las Animas County High School District v. Raye*, 144 Colo. 367, 356 P.2d 237.

Nonetheless, there are necessary limits upon what may be considered "property," and we do not find any indication in the Act that the concept as used by the legislature is other than that usually understood to be embodied within the term. One helpful definition is "everything that has an exchangeable value or which goes to make up wealth or estate." Black's Law Dictionary 1382 (rev. 4th ed. 1968). In *Ellis v. Ellis*, Colo., 552 P.2d 506, this court held that military retirement pay was not property for the reason that it did not have any of the elements of cash surrender value, loan value, redemption value, lump sum value, or value realizable after death. The court of appeals has considered other factors as well in deciding whether something falls within the concept, particularly whether it can be assigned, sold, transferred, conveyed, or pledged, or whether it terminates on the death of the owner. *In re Marriage of Ellis*, 36 Colo.App. 234, 538 P.2d 1347, aff'd, *Ellis v. Ellis, supra.*

An educational degree, such as an M.B.A., is simply not encompassed even by the broad views of the concept of "property." It does not have an exchange value or any objective transferable value on an open market. It is personal to the holder. It terminates on death of the holder and is not inheritable. It cannot be assigned, sold, transferred, conveyed, or pledged. An advanced degree is a cumulative product of many years of previous education, combined with diligence and hard work. It may not be acquired by the mere expenditure of money. It is simply an intellectual achievement that may potentially assist in the future acquisition of property. In our view, it has none of the attributes of property in the usual sense of that term.[13] . . .

Our interpretation is in accord with cases in other jurisdictions. We have been unable to find any decision, even in community property states, which appears to have held that an education of one spouse is marital property to be divided on dissolution. This contention was dismissed in *Todd v. Todd*, 272 Cal.App.2d 786, 78 Cal.Rptr. 131 (Ct.App.), where it was held that a law degree is not a community property asset capable of division, partly because it "cannot have monetary value placed upon it." Similarly, it has been recently held that a person's earning capacity, even where enhanced by a law degree financed by the other spouse, "should not be recognized as a separate, particular item of property." *Stern v. Stern*, 66 N.J. 340, 331 A.2d 257. . . .

The trial court relied on *Greer v. Greer*, 32 Colo.App. 196, 510 P.2d 905, for its determination that an education is "property." In that case, a six-year marriage was dissolved in which the wife worked as a teacher while the husband obtained a medical degree. The parties had accumulated marital property. The trial court awarded the wife alimony of $150 per month for four years. The court of appeals found this to be proper, whether considered as an adjustment of property rights based upon the wife's financial contribution to the marriage, or as an award of alimony in gross. The court there stated that "[i]t must be considered as a substitute for, or in lieu of, the wife's rights in the husband's property . . . ." We note that the court did not determine that the medical education itself was divisible property. The case is distinguishable from the instant case in that here there was no accumulation of marital property and the petitioner did not seek maintenance (alimony). . . .

CARRIGAN, JUSTICE, dissenting. . . . As a matter of economic reality the most valuable asset acquired by either party during this six-year marriage was the husband's increased earning capacity. There is no dispute

---

13. Editors' Note: Based on what you learned in Chapter 1, how satisfying is the *Graham* court's reasoning here? Suppose that five years after Dennis Graham earned his degree, the University of Colorado School of Business faculty purported to revoke that degree based upon unsubstantiated allegations of academic misconduct. Could Dennis raise an argument in this context that the degree was his "property"?

that this asset resulted from his having obtained Bachelor of Science and Master of Business Administration degrees while married. These degrees, in turn, resulted in large part from the wife's employment which contributed about 70% of the couple's total income. Her earnings not only provided her husband's support but also were "invested" in his education in the sense that she assumed the role of breadwinner so that he would have the time and funds necessary to obtain his education.

The case presents the not-unfamiliar pattern of the wife who, willing to sacrifice for a more secure family financial future, works to educate her husband, only to be awarded a divorce decree shortly after he is awarded his degree. The issue here is whether traditional, narrow concepts of what constitutes "property" render the courts impotent to provide a remedy for an obvious injustice.

In cases such as this, equity demands that courts seek extraordinary remedies to prevent extraordinary injustice. If the parties had remained married long enough after the husband had completed his post-graduate education so that they could have accumulated substantial property, there would have been no problem. In that situation abundant precedent authorized the trial court, in determining how much of the marital property to allocate to the wife, to take into account her contributions to her husband's earning capacity. *Greer v. Greer*, 32 Colo.App. 196, 510 P.2d 905 (1973) (wife supported husband through medical school); *In re Marriage of Vanet*, 544 S.W.2d 236 (Mo.App.1976) (wife was breadwinner while husband was in law school).

A husband's future income earning potential, sometimes as indicated by the goodwill value of a professional practice, may be considered in deciding property division or alimony matters, and the wife's award may be increased on the ground that the husband probably will have substantial future earnings. *Todd v. Todd*, 272 Cal.App.2d 786, 78 Cal.Rptr. 131 (1969) (goodwill of husband's law practice); *Golden v. Golden*, 270 Cal.App.2d 401, 75 Cal.Rptr. 735 (1969) (goodwill of husband's medical practice); *Mueller v. Mueller*, 144 Cal.App.2d 245, 301 P.2d 90 (1956) (goodwill of husband's dental lab); *In re Marriage of Goger*, 27 Or.App. 729, 557 P.2d 46 (1976) (potential earnings of husband's dental practice); *In re Marriage of Lukens*, 16 Wash.App. 481, 558 P.2d 279 (1976) (goodwill of husband's medical practice indicated future earning capacity).

Similarly, the wife's contributions to enhancing the husband's financial status or earning capacity have been considered in awarding alimony and maintenance.[14] *Kraus v. Kraus*, 159 Colo. 331, 411 P.2d 240 (1966);

---

14. Editors' Note: Alimony stems from the husband's common law duty to support his wife. Under the traditional law, this duty continued, after a divorce, in the form of alimony payments. More recently, courts and legislatures have described the support obligation as "maintenance" and provide for varying levels of support, such as temporary maintenance (support for a limited period of time), rehabilitative maintenance (support while the ex-spouse seeks the education or training necessary to become self-supporting), or permanent maintenance (support for the ex-spouse's lifetime or until remarriage, as with traditional alimony) as necessary under the circumstances of the case. Permanent maintenance, for example, is generally awarded today only when the ex-spouse is unable to become self-supporting.

Shapiro v. Shapiro, 115 Colo. 505, 176 P.2d 363 (1946). The majority opinion emphasizes that in this case no maintenance was requested. However, the Colorado statute would seem to preclude an award of maintenance here, for it restricts the court's power to award maintenance to cases where the spouse seeking it is unable to support himself or herself. Section 14–10–114, C.R.S.1973.

While the majority opinion focuses on whether the husband's master's degree is marital "property" subject to division, it is not the degree itself which constitutes the asset in question. Rather it is the increase in the husband's earning power concomitant to that degree which is the asset conferred on him by his wife's efforts. That increased earning capacity was the asset appraised in the economist's expert opinion testimony as having a discounted present value of $82,000.

Unquestionably the law, in other contexts, recognizes future earning capacity as an asset whose wrongful deprivation is compensable. Thus one who tortiously destroys or impairs another's future earning capacity must pay as damages the amount the injured party has lost in anticipated future earnings. *Nemer v. Anderson*, 151 Colo. 411, 378 P.2d 841 (1963); Abram, Personal Injury Damages in Colorado, 35 Colo.L.Rev. 332, 338 (1963).

Where a husband is killed, his widow is entitled to recover for loss of his future support damages based in part on the present value of his anticipated future earnings, which may be computed by taking into account probable future increases in his earning capacity. *See United States v. Sommers*, 351 F.2d 354 (10th Cir. 1965); *Good v. Chance*, Colo.App., 565 P.2d 217 (1977). *See also* Colo.J.I. (Civil) 10:3.

The day before the divorce the wife had a legally recognized interest in her husband's earning capacity. Perhaps the wife might have a remedy in a separate action based on implied debt, quasi-contract, unjust enrichment, or some similar theory. *See, e.g., Dass v. Epplen*, 162 Colo. 60, 424 P.2d 779 (1967). Nevertheless, the law favors settling all aspects of a dispute in a single action where that is possible. Therefore I would affirm the trial court's award. . . .

Notes

1. *Alternative Approaches to the "Degree Dilemma."* As the divorce rate has soared, American courts have been forced to struggle with the "degree dilemma"—one spouse supporting the other through school, then claiming an interest in that degree following the parties' later divorce. While *Graham* represents one view, other courts have taken different approaches. Consider, for example, the case of *O'Brien v. O'Brien*, 66 N.Y.2d 576, 498 N.Y.S.2d 743, 489 N.E.2d 712 (1985), where a divorcing wife argued that her husband's medical degree constituted marital property under New York's equi-

table distribution statute. That statute provides that the court must consider "expenditures and contributions and services as a spouse ... to the career or career potential of the other party" in making a distribution of marital property. N.Y. Dom. Rel. Law § 236. The Court of Appeals of New York interpreted this statute in the wife's favor:

> [A]n interest in a profession or professional career is marital property which may be represented by direct or indirect contributions of the non-title-holding spouse, including financial contributions and nonfinancial contributions made by caring for the home and family.... The Legislature has decided, by its explicit reference in the statute to the contributions of one spouse to the other's profession or career ... that these contributions represent investments in the economic partnership of the marriage and that the product of the parties' joint efforts, the professional license, should be considered marital property. [489 N.E.2d at 716.]

In contrast, the New Jersey Supreme Court struck a middle ground in *Mahoney v. Mahoney*, 91 N.J. 488, 453 A.2d 527 (1982). The court refused to characterize a professional degree as marital property, on the ground that its "future monetary value [was] uncertain and unquantifiable." 453 A.2d at 531. The court refused, however, to hold that the supporting spouse had no entitlement on account of the other spouse's degree. Instead, the court held that the supporting spouse should be reimbursed for the contributions made to support the other spouse's education:

> [T]here will be circumstances where a supporting spouse should be reimbursed for the financial contributions he or she made to the spouse's successful professional training. Such reimbursement... should cover *all* financial contributions towards the former spouse's education, including household expenses, educational costs, school travel expenses and any other contributions used by the supported spouse in obtaining his or her degree or license. [453 A.2d at 534.]

Do you find the reasoning of *O'Brien* or *Mahoney* more or less persuasive than the court's reasoning in *Graham*? Which approach—*Graham, O'Brien, or Mahoney*—do you think is preferable:

- in terms of the *ex ante* understandings of parties to a marriage?
- in terms of public policy regarding marriage and family?
- in terms of public policy regarding education?
- in terms of economic efficiency?

Chapter 7

THE LAW OF LANDLORD
AND TENANT

A. THE NATURE OF THE LEASE AND THE
COVENANT OF QUIET ENJOYMENT

1. *The Dual Nature of Modern Leases*

A lease is the property interest often most familiar to new law students. At its simplest, a lease is a conveyance in which the owner of real estate (the landlord or lessor) transfers the right to exclusive possession of land to another person (the tenant or lessee) for some length of time, in return for which the tenant becomes obligated to pay rent. Centuries ago, leased land tended to be unimproved land that the tenant farmed and maintained. In modern times, the leased land is often part or all of a building, perhaps including some surrounding land. The tenant who holds the right to possession has an *estate*—a recognizable possessory interest in the land. While the lease continues, the tenant's *nonfreehold* leasehold estate confers the legal right to exclusive possession of the real estate, which courts will protect as against both the landlord and third parties generally. When the lease terminates, the landlord becomes entitled to exclusive possession of the land; thus, while the lease continues, modern authority would describe the landlord as holding a future interest.[1] Because the lease transfers or conveys an

---

1. In the feudal period, a landlord was considered to have a present fee simple estate, subject to the tenant's nonfreehold estate. Recall from Chapter 5 that in the feudal period, the law drew an important distinction between freehold estates (where the occupier held *seisin*) and nonfreehold estates (where the occupier did not hold seisin). Originally, the law did not treat a lessee as someone who held seisin in the leased premises. This meant that originally a lessee whose possession was interfered with did not have a possessory remedy— *i.e.*, the courts would not order the lessee restored to possession! Over the course of the 13th, 14th, and 15th centuries, however, the law began to recognize a possessory remedy for a lessee whose occupancy was wrongly disturbed. *See, e.g.*, John Forrester Hicks, *The Contractual Nature of Real Property Leases*, 24 Baylor L. Rev. 443 (1972); Hiram H. Lesar, *The Landlord–Tenant Relation in Perspective: From Status to Contract and Back in 900 Years?*, 9 Kan. L. Rev. 369, 370 (1961). Once the law recognized the lessee as having a possessory

estate in land from landlord to tenant, the lease document is an instrument of *conveyance.*

As anyone who has entered into a lease can appreciate, a lease is also a bilateral *contract.* It typically contains mutual promises—the landlord promises not to disturb the tenant's possession; the tenant promises to pay rent; and each party usually makes a number of other promises regarding the condition or use of the land. Because the lease is both a *conveyance* and a *contract,* the landlord-tenant relationship creates the potential for tensions between property law and contract law— many of which we will focus upon in this chapter.

The source of this tension is a distinction between contract law and property law regarding the remedies available for breach of a lease covenant. Under standard contract law, contract covenants (promises in a bilateral contract) are typically considered *dependent* obligations. This means that one party's material failure to carry out its contractual obligation excuses the other party's performance. For example, suppose that a 10-year lease between L and T provides that L is obligated to paint the premises during the third year of the lease term. Standard contract theory would suggest that if L failed to paint the premises as agreed, T's obligation to perform would be excused—thus permitting T to terminate the lease contract or withhold rent payments.

Contract law v. property law

Under property law—which viewed the lease as a conveyance—the essence of the leasehold bargain was rent in exchange for possession of the land; all other aspects of the bargain were secondary. Property law thus treated most of the respective obligations of the landlord and tenant as *independent* obligations. This means that as long as the landlord provided the tenant with the legal right to possession of the land and did not interfere with that possession by evicting the tenant, the landlord performed its part of the bargain and could enforce the tenant's obligation to pay rent—even if the landlord failed to perform some other obligation that the lease imposed on the landlord! In the above example, if L failed to paint the premises as agreed but did not otherwise interfere with T's possession and enjoyment of the premises, property law permitted T to bring an action for damages, *but did not permit T to terminate the lease or stop paying rent* (unless the express terms of the lease specifically permitted the tenant to do so).

This caveat—that T can terminate the lease if the lease expressly so provides—reflects that for the most part, the common law and statutory rules governing the landlord-tenant relationship operate as *default rules,*

default rules

remedy, the lessee's interest came to be considered a real "property" interest—diminishing the practical significance of the idea that the lessee held merely a "nonfreehold" estate. Nevertheless, the law continued to use the term "nonfreehold" as a means to distinguish the leasehold estates.

Today, a landlord's estate is usually termed a "reversion" (*i.e.,* the right to re-cover possession at the natural conclusion of the tenant's leasehold estate). Typically, the landlord will also hold a right of entry (*i.e.,* the right to terminate the lease and recover possession prior to the natural end of the lease term if the tenant breaches a condition subsequent to which the leasehold is subject, such as the payment of rent).

i.e., the rules that govern the parties' relationship on issues not expressly addressed by the terms of the contract. Parties are generally free to contract as they wish, with background rules of landlord-tenant law supplementing the parties' general agreement regarding issues not addressed in their contract.[2] Nearly all leases explicitly state that if the tenant defaults in any of its lease obligations, the landlord can terminate the lease—thus making the landlord's lease obligations dependent upon the tenant's performance. By contrast, most leases do not expressly allow the tenant to terminate the lease in the event of the landlord's breach—which says something about the relative bargaining power of landlords and tenants.

Where the lease does not make particular covenants expressly dependent in nature, should the law "fill the gap" in the parties' agreement by reference to property law (treating the covenants as independent) or contract law (treating them as dependent)? Case study indicates that the question defies a simple answer. The most honest recognition of this fact appears in Justice Lohr's opinion in *Schneiker v. Gordon*, 732 P.2d 603 (Colo. 1987):

> [A]s a result of the dual nature of a lease, neither contract principles nor property principles can be exclusively relied upon to govern the resolution of all issues. One leading authority has described the modern law governing landlord-tenant relationships as follows:
>
> > [T]he present law of leases is a blend of property concepts and of contractual doctrines, made for the service of a wide variety of objectives; agrarian, urban and financial. This historical background makes it clear that we can expect varying proportions of these basic ingredients in the decision of cases litigated now and in the future. Any fixity of proportions would destroy the elasticity of the law, which is, at once, its glory, its challenge and its factor of uncertainty. [2 Powell on Real Property ¶ 221[1], at 187.]
>
> Whether contract principles, property principles, or a blend of both control the resolution of a particular case depends largely on the intent of the parties, the interests of society, and the relative fairness of the results to be achieved through selection among the potentially applicable principles. [732 P.2d at 606–07.]

Is Justice Lohr just waffling, or is this a sensible approach? Consider the following three scenarios:

2. There are limited circumstances where common law and statutory rules of landlord-tenant law operate as immutable rules that the parties may not change by contract. For example, federal and state laws prohibit most landlords from engaging in some forms of discrimination in leasing residential land, a subject we explore beginning on page 537. Likewise, as discussed beginning on page 501, most states have now imposed (either by court decision or statutory enactment) an implied warranty of habitability that obligates residential landlords to keep the leased premises in habitable condition throughout the lease term, even if the lease purports to place on the tenant responsibility for the condition of the premises.

• *Scenario One. L* and *T* enter into a lease for premises in a shopping center, with *T* planning to operate a pharmacy. *L* covenants not to lease any other space in the shopping center for a competing pharmacy, but later breaches this covenant. The lease does not expressly permit *T* to terminate as a remedy for *L*'s breach. Nevertheless, the substantial weight of modern authority would allow T to terminate the lease, on the theory that *L*'s non-competition covenant was part of the essential consideration for the lease such that *T*'s obligation to pay rent was dependent on *L*'s performance of that covenant. *See, e.g., Medico-Dental Bldg. Co. v. Horton & Converse*, 21 Cal.2d 411, 132 P.2d 457 (1942); *University Club v. Deakin*, 265 Ill. 257, 106 N.E. 790 (1914).

[handwritten margin note: essential consideration]

• *Scenario Two. L* and *T* enter into a 15–year lease for a retail store. The lease provides that *T* cannot assign or sublet its right to possession (*i.e.,* transfer its possessory right to another person) without *L*'s prior written consent, but also states that *L* cannot unreasonably withhold its consent. When *L* later breaches this provision, *T* argues that she can terminate the lease, even though the lease did not expressly permit termination as a remedy. Some modern authority would permit *T* to terminate the lease. *See, e.g., Chrysler Capital Corp. v. Lavender*, 934 F.2d 290 (11th Cir. 1991) (applying Alabama law). Substantial case authority, however, holds that *T*'s obligation to pay rent is independent of *L*'s obligation not to unreasonably withhold consent, and that L's breach does not permit *T* to terminate the lease. *See, e.g., Rock County Sav. & Trust Co. v. Yost's, Inc.*, 36 Wis.2d 360, 153 N.W.2d 594 (1967); *Ernst Home Ctr. v. Sato*, 80 Wash.App. 473, 910 P.2d 486 (1996). Which view do you think makes better sense? Is there any additional information that you would like to know that might better inform your judgment?

• *Scenario Three. L* and *T* enter into a 10–year lease for business premises. The lease provides that *L* will repaint the premises every three years during the lease term, but *L* breaches this provision. The lease does not expressly give *T* the right to terminate the lease if *L* breaches. If *T* attempts to use this breach as a basis for terminating the lease, a court would most probably consider *L*'s covenant to paint the premises and *T*'s obligation to pay rent as independent covenants. Can you explain why?

2.　*The Covenant of Quiet Enjoyment*

At its core, the lease is a simple rent-for-possession exchange. In ancient times, when leases were commonly not reduced to writing, the tenant's obligation to pay rent was said to issue directly out of the land:

> Coke says that "rent is reserved out of the profits of the land," and Blackstone says that it is a profit issuing out of the land. These statements presumably mean that . . . rent is in theory part of the actual or possible profits of the land, a theory which is no doubt closely related to another theory, that rent, like any other feudal

service, is something *issuing from and owed by the land itself*, and not by any particular tenant of the land.

> The reservation of rent . . . does not, strictly speaking, involve any *contractual* liability on the part of the lessee. At common law, the *land* was regarded as owing the rent created by the reservation and the lessee owed the rent merely by reason of his tenancy of the land . . . [as] ordinarily expressed [by the term] *"privity of estate."* [1 Herbert T. Tiffany, The Law of Landlord and Tenant, §§ 168, 171 at 1014–15, 1029 (1910) (emphasis added).]

Over time, as leases became commonly reduced to writing, landlords typically began to include in the lease an express covenant to pay rent, thus imposing on the tenant liability to pay rent based upon *privity of contract* as well.

Implicit in the landlord's conveyance of the leasehold estate to the tenant is landlord's recognition and support of tenant's right to exclusive possession. Because the right to possession is the essence of tenant's rights under the lease, the landlord's performance is in some measure complete as soon as the landlord makes an effective conveyance of a leasehold estate. As viewed by the common law, the landlord had no other duties under the lease unless the landlord expressly covenanted otherwise. Nevertheless, the landlord still had (and has) the duty to honor the tenant's possessory estate as promised throughout the lease term—a duty that the law characterized as the landlord's *covenant of quiet enjoyment*. The covenant of quiet enjoyment constitutes a promise to the tenant that neither the landlord, nor anyone acting by or through the landlord, nor anyone holding paramount title to the landlord will interfere with the tenant's possession of the premises.[3] Most modern leases provide an express covenant of quiet enjoyment, and courts will imply such a covenant if the lease is silent on the subject. [Can you explain why?]

If the landlord repudiates or thwarts the tenant's estate so as to deprive the tenant of possession, this constitutes an *eviction*. An eviction can be either rightful (*e.g.*, when *T* fails to pay rent in a timely manner, *L* rightfully terminates the lease in accordance with its terms and retakes possession of the premises after following appropriate common law and statutory procedures) or wrongful (*e.g.*, *L* changes the locks to deny *T* access to the premises even though *T* had made the rent payment). If the landlord's eviction is rightful, the tenant's estate is divested and the tenant has no legal recourse to recover possession.

If a landlord wrongfully evicts a tenant, the landlord's action constitutes a breach of the covenant of quiet enjoyment. As a result of this breach, the tenant has two basic options—either sue to recover possession or terminate the lease. A tenant wrongfully evicted by the landlord can successfully bring an action to recover possession of the land—a

---

3. A paramount title holder is someone whose possessory rights in the land are superior to those of the landlord. Interfer- ence by a paramount title holder is further discussed in note 6 on page 422.

remedy that follows naturally from viewing the lease as a conveyance of an estate in land. If the tenant successfully recovers possession through such an action (traditionally called an ejectment action), the tenant must continue to make the required rent payments to retain that possession. Alternatively, eviction permits the tenant to argue that the lease is terminated and that the termination has extinguished the tenant's liability for rent that otherwise would have accrued in the future.[4] This result again follows logically from the nature of the lease as a rent-for-possession bargain; if the tenant no longer enjoys the possession of the land, the landlord can no longer enforce the tenant's obligation to pay rent. Thus, the covenant of quiet enjoyment effectively constituted an exception to the traditional independence-of-lease-covenants doctrine—the law treated the landlord's covenant of quiet enjoyment and the tenant's obligation to pay rent as dependent covenants.

Constructive Eviction. If the landlord physically excludes the tenant from the premises, there is no doubt that an eviction has occurred. But what happens if there is no actual exclusion? From an early date, American courts extended the concept of eviction to include other conduct by which a landlord or its agents substantially interfered with a tenant's ability to enjoy its bargained-for right of possession. One of the earliest examples of this doctrine—known as *constructive eviction*—is the case of *Dyett v. Pendleton,* 8 Cow. 727 (N.Y. Ct. of Errors 1826). The tenant in *Dyett* leased a portion of a building as a residence, but vacated it during the term because the landlord was conducting a brothel elsewhere in the building. The tenant argued that the "riotous proceedings" that resulted from the operation of a brothel had the same practical effect as if the landlord had "entered in and upon the demised premises, and ejected and put out" the tenant. The court in *Dyett* agreed, holding that the landlord's conduct breached the covenant of quiet enjoyment and rose to the level of a constructive eviction that terminated the lease and excused the tenant from further liability for rent.

Once decisions like *Dyett* held that the landlord could breach the covenant of quiet enjoyment without an actual physical ouster of the tenant, the covenant of quiet enjoyment became a key battleground in landlord-tenant controversies. Courts began to hold that if the tenant can show (1) *active interference* with its possession (or interference that results from the landlord's *inaction in the face of a legal duty to act*), and (2) that this interference is attributable to the landlord, the landlord's agent, or a paramount title holder, then the landlord has breached the covenant of quiet enjoyment. Further, if tenant can show that this interference is sufficiently serious as to deprive the tenant of the benefit of its bargained-for possession, and tenant reasonably promptly departs

---

4. Whether or not the tenant seeks to recover possession of the premises, the tenant may also have a claim against the landlord for compensatory damages suffered by the tenant as a result of the landlord's breach. These compensatory damages might include incidental damages (such as the costs of moving and storing the tenant's personal property during the period of the eviction) and/or lost bargain damages (such as the difference between the stated rental amount and the fair rental value of the premises if the premises have appreciated in value during the lease).

the premises as a consequence, the tenant's departure will escalate the breach into a *constructive eviction*, thereby terminating the leasehold estate and the tenant's liability for future rent.

As you consider the following materials, keep in mind two important points. First, an interference cannot breach the covenant of quiet enjoyment unless it is attributable to the landlord, the landlord's agent, or a paramount title holder. This means that the conduct of third parties not attributable to the landlord cannot breach the covenant of quiet enjoyment (and thus cannot trigger a constructive eviction). Second, not all interferences will justify a constructive eviction (even if they may breach the covenant of quiet enjoyment). The interference must be *intentional* (with intention typically being inferred from the conduct), *substantial*, and *permanent* to support an allegation of constructive eviction. As you read the following case—which involves abortion protestors interfering with a tenant's ability to pursue his gynecology practice—consider whether the landlord is appropriately responsible for the conduct of the protestors and whether the interference should constitute a constructive eviction.

FIDELITY MUTUAL LIFE INS. CO. v. KAMINSKY

Court of Appeals of Texas.
768 S.W.2d 818 (1989).

Murphy, Justice. The issue in this landlord-tenant case is whether sufficient evidence supports the jury's findings that the landlord and appellant, Fidelity Mutual Life Insurance Company ("Fidelity"), constructively evicted the tenant, Robert P. Kaminsky, M.D., P.A. ("Dr. Kaminsky") by breaching the express covenant of quiet enjoyment contained in the parties' lease. We affirm.

Dr. Kaminsky is a gynecologist whose practice includes performing elective abortions. In May 1983, he executed a lease contract for the rental of approximately 2,861 square feet in the Red Oak Atrium Building for a two year term which began on June 1, 1983. The terms of the lease required Dr. Kaminsky to use the rented space solely as "an office for the practice of medicine." Fidelity owns the building and hires local companies to manage it. At some time during the lease term, Shelter Commercial Properties ("Shelter") replaced the Horne Company as managing agents. Fidelity has not disputed either management company's capacity to act as its agent.

The parties agree that . . . they executed a valid lease agreement; . . . Paragraph 35 of the lease contains an express covenant of quiet enjoyment conditioned on Dr. Kaminsky's paying rent when due, as he did through November 1984; Dr. Kaminsky abandoned the leased premises on or about December 3, 1984 and refused to pay additional rent; anti-abortion protestors began picketing at the building in June of 1984 and repeated and increased their demonstrations outside and inside the building until Dr. Kaminsky abandoned the premises.

When Fidelity sued for the balance due under the lease contract following Dr. Kaminsky's abandonment of the premises, he claimed that Fidelity constructively evicted him by breaching Paragraph 35 of the lease. Fidelity apparently conceded during trial that sufficient proof of the constructive eviction of Dr. Kaminsky would relieve him of his contractual liability for any remaining rent payments. Accordingly, he assumed the burden of proof and the sole issue submitted to the jury was whether Fidelity breached Paragraph 35 of the lease, which reads as follows: "*Quiet Enjoyment.* Lessee, on paying the said Rent, and any Additional Rental, shall and may peaceably and quietly have, hold and enjoy the Leased Premises for the said term."

A constructive eviction occurs when the tenant leaves the leased premises due to conduct by the landlord which materially interferes with the tenant's beneficial use of the premises. Texas law relieves the tenant of contractual liability for any remaining rentals due under the lease if he can establish a constructive eviction by the landlord. *Downtown Realty, Inc. v. 509 Tremont Bldg., Inc.*, 748 S.W.2d 309, 312 (Tex.App. 1988); *Ravkind v. Jones Apothecary, Inc.*, 439 S.W.2d 470, 471 (Tex.Civ. App. 1969).

In order to prevail on his claim that Fidelity constructively evicted him and thereby relieved him of his rent obligation, Dr. Kaminsky had to show the following: 1) Fidelity intended that he no longer enjoy the premises, which intent the trier of fact could infer from the circumstances; 2) Fidelity, or those acting for Fidelity or with its permission, committed a material act or omission which substantially interfered with use and enjoyment of the premises for their leased purpose, here an office for the practice of medicine; 3) Fidelity's act or omission permanently deprived Dr. Kaminsky of the use and enjoyment of the premises; and 4) Dr. Kaminsky abandoned the premises within a reasonable period of time after the act or omission.

During oral submission of this case, Fidelity conceded it did not object to an instruction on the four special issues which tracked the foregoing elements. By answering each special issue affirmatively, the jury found that Dr. Kaminsky had established each element of his constructive eviction defense. The trial court entered judgment that Fidelity take nothing on its suit for delinquent rent.

[Fidelity argues] that a tenant cannot complain that the landlord constructively evicted him and breached a covenant of quiet enjoyment, express or implied, when the eviction results from the actions of third parties acting without the landlord's authority or permission. Fidelity insists the evidence conclusively establishes: a) that it did nothing to encourage or sponsor the protestors and; b) that the protestors, rather than Fidelity or its agents, caused Dr. Kaminsky to abandon the premises. Fidelity concludes that reversible error resulted because the trial court refused to set aside the jury's answers to the special issues and enter judgment in Fidelity's favor and because the trial court denied its motion for a new trial. We disagree. . . .

The protests took place chiefly on Saturdays, the day Dr. Kaminsky generally scheduled abortions. During the protests, the singing and chanting demonstrators picketed in the building's parking lot and inner lobby and atrium area. They approached patients to speak to them, distributed literature, discouraged patients from entering the building and often accused Dr. Kaminsky of "killing babies." As the protests increased, the demonstrators often occupied the stairs leading to Dr. Kaminsky's office and prevented patients from entering the office by blocking the doorway. Occasionally they succeeded in gaining access to the office waiting room area.

Dr. Kaminsky complained to Fidelity through its managing agents and asked for help in keeping the protestors away, but became increasingly frustrated by a lack of response to his requests. The record shows that no security personnel were present on Saturdays to exclude protestors from the building, although the lease required Fidelity to provide security service on Saturdays. The record also shows that Fidelity's attorneys prepared a written statement to be handed to the protestors soon after Fidelity hired Shelter as its managing agent. The statement tracked Tex. Penal Code Ann. § 30.05 (Vernon Supp.1989) and generally served to inform trespassers that they risked criminal prosecution by failing to leave if asked to do so. Fidelity's attorneys instructed Shelter's representative to "have several of these letters printed up and be ready to distribute them and verbally demand that these people move on and off the property." The same representative conceded at trial that she did not distribute these notices. Yet when Dr. Kaminsky enlisted the aid of the Sheriff's office, officers refused to ask the protestors to leave without a directive from Fidelity or its agent. Indeed, an attorney had instructed the protestors to remain unless the landlord or its representative ordered them to leave. It appears that Fidelity's only response to the demonstrators was to state, through its agents, that it was aware of Dr. Kaminsky's problems.

Both action and lack of action can constitute "conduct" by the landlord which amounts to a constructive eviction. *E.g., Downtown Realty Inc.*, 748 S.W.2d at 311; 49 Tex.Jur.3d Landlord & Tenant § 288. In *Steinberg v. Medical Equip. Rental Serv., Inc.*, 505 S.W.2d 692 (Tex.Civ.App. 1974) accordingly, the court upheld a jury's determination that the landlord's failure to act amounted to a constructive eviction and breach of the covenant of quiet enjoyment. 505 S.W.2d at 697. Like Dr. Kaminsky, the tenant in *Steinberg* abandoned the leased premises and refused to pay additional rent after repeatedly complaining to the landlord. The *Steinberg* tenant complained that Steinberg placed trash bins near the entrance to the business and allowed trucks to park and block customers' access to the tenant's medical equipment rental business. The tenant's repeated complaints to Steinberg yielded only a request "to be patient." *Id.* Fidelity responded to Dr. Kaminsky's complaints in a similar manner: although it acknowledged his problems with the protestors, Fidelity, like Steinberg, effectively did nothing to prevent the problems.

This case shows ample instances of Fidelity's failure to act in the face of repeated requests for assistance despite its having expressly covenanted Dr. Kaminsky's quiet enjoyment of the premises. These instances provided a legally sufficient basis for the jury to conclude that Dr. Kaminsky abandoned the leased premises, not because of the trespassing protestors, but because of Fidelity's lack of response to his complaints about the protestors. Under the circumstances, while it is undisputed that Fidelity did not "encourage" the demonstrators, its conduct essentially allowed them to continue to trespass. The general rule . . . that a landlord is not responsible for the actions of third parties, applies only when the landlord does not permit the third party to act. *See e.g., Angelo v. Deutser*, 30 S.W.2d 707, 710 (Tex.Civ.App. 1930) ("the act or omission complained of must be that of the landlord and not merely of a third person *acting without his authority or permission*" (emphasis added)). We see no distinction between Fidelity's lack of action here, which the record shows resulted in preventing patients' access to Dr. Kaminsky's medical office, and the *Steinberg* case where the landlord's inaction resulted in trucks' blocking customer access to the tenant's business. We overrule the first point of error. . . .

The challenged special issues establish the first three elements of constructive eviction: intent; act or omission; and permanent deprivation of the premises. In point of error two, Fidelity raises a two-pronged challenge to the factual sufficiency of the evidence to show it intended that Dr. Kaminsky no longer enjoy the leased premises. Fidelity disputes the evidence of its wrongful intent on the grounds that it at least attempted to manage the protestors by drafting the letter threatening the protestors with trespass prosecutions and giving the letter to Dr. Kaminsky to distribute. Fidelity also argues that Dr. Kaminsky acknowledged its lack of "encouragement" or "sponsorship" of the protestors. As we have noted above, the jury was entitled to infer Fidelity's intent from all the circumstances in this case. After reviewing all the evidence on the issue of Fidelity's intent, we conclude that neither Fidelity's having made some effort, nor its lack of sponsorship or encouragement of the protestors, renders the jury's finding so against the great weight and preponderance of the evidence as to be manifestly unjust. We overrule the second point of error.

Fidelity's third point of error disputes the factual sufficiency of the evidence to show that it committed a material act which substantially interfered with Dr. Kaminsky's use and enjoyment of the premises. Here Fidelity essentially raises the same contention we disposed of in its first point of error: that the record unequivocally establishes that Fidelity committed no act which would give rise to a constructive eviction because the protestors committed the acts which caused Dr. Kaminsky to leave. As we have already indicated, the landlord's acts or omissions can form the basis of a constructive eviction. *E.g., Steinberg*, 505 S.W.2d at 697. Special Issue Number Two, to which Fidelity offered no objection, asked whether Fidelity "committed a material act or omission if any, that substantially interfered with" Dr. Kaminsky's use and enjoyment of the premises. Having reviewed all the evidence, both supporting and contrary to the jury's affirmative answer to Special Issue Number Two, we find no basis for Fidelity's argument that the finding was so against the great weight and preponderance of the evidence as to be manifestly unjust. We overrule the third point of error.

In its fourth point of error, Fidelity maintains the evidence is factually insufficient to support the jury's finding that its conduct permanently deprived Dr. Kaminsky of use and enjoyment of the premises. Fidelity essentially questions the permanency of Dr. Kaminsky's being deprived of the use and enjoyment of the leased premises. To support its contentions, Fidelity points to testimony by Dr. Kaminsky in which he concedes that none of his patients were ever harmed and that protests and demonstrations continued despite his leaving the Red Oak Atrium building. Fidelity also disputes whether Dr. Kaminsky actually lost patients due to the protests.

The evidence shows that the protestors, whose entry into the building Fidelity failed to prohibit, often succeeded in blocking Dr. Kaminsky's patients' access to his medical office. Under the reasoning of the *Steinberg* case, omissions by a landlord which result in patients' lack of access to the office of a practicing physician would suffice to establish a permanent deprivation of the use and enjoyment of the premises for their leased purpose, here "an office for the practice of medicine." *Steinberg*, 505 S.W.2d at 697; *accord, Downtown Realty, Inc.*, 748 S.W.2d at 312 (noting jury's finding that a constructive eviction resulted from the commercial landlord's failure to repair a heating and air conditioning system in a rooming house).

Texas law has long recited the requirement . . . that the landlord commit a "material and permanent" act or omission in order for his tenant to claim a constructive eviction. However, as the *Steinberg* and *Downtown Realty, Inc.* cases illustrate, the extent to which a landlord's acts or omissions permanently and materially deprive a tenant of the use and enjoyment of the premises often involves a question of degree. Having reviewed all the evidence before the jury in this case, we cannot say that its finding that Fidelity's conduct permanently deprived Dr. Kaminsky of the use and enjoyment of his medical office space was so against the great weight and preponderance of the evidence as to be manifestly unjust. We overrule the fourth point of error. . . .

Notes

1. *Constructive Eviction—Actions of Third Parties.* As *Kaminsky* makes clear, the covenant of quiet enjoyment does not protect the tenant from eviction—whether actual or constructive—by third parties (other than holders of paramount title) whose actions cannot be attributed to the landlord. Once the lease term commences, if X takes adverse possession from T, and X is not acting on L's behalf or with L's complicity, L has not breached the covenant of quiet enjoyment—unless the lease contains an express covenant by L to protect T against intrusions by trespassers such as X.

In *Kaminsky*, there was no evidence that the protestors acted at Fidelity's request. So why did the court attribute the actions of the protestors to Fidelity?

2. *Constructive Eviction—How Substantial Must the Interference Be?* Are you persuaded by the court's conclusion in *Kaminsky* that the protests constituted such a material and substantial interference to justify termination of the lease? Why or why not? Suppose that instead of abortion protesters, Dr. Kaminsky's complaint was that Fidelity shut off its HVAC (heating, ventilation, and air conditioning) system on weekends, making it uncomfortable (if not dangerous) for him to see patients on Saturday. Would this justify a constructive eviction? *See Barash v. Pennsylvania Terminal Real Estate Corp.*, 26 N.Y.2d 77, 308 N.Y.S.2d 649, 256 N.E.2d 707 (1970). Alternatively, suppose that Dr. Kaminsky's complaint was that Fidelity mispositioned trash dumpsters in the parking lot and refused to move them despite repeated demands, thereby reducing the available parking spaces by 50% (and creating a substantial inconvenience for his patients and staff). Would this justify a constructive eviction? *See RNR Realty, Inc. v. Burlington Coat Factory, Inc.*, 168 Ill.App.3d 210, 119 Ill.Dec. 17, 522 N.E.2d 679 (1988).

As noted in *Kaminsky*, a tenant who claims that an interference is so substantial as to cause a constructive eviction must behave as if she *actually* was evicted—*i.e.*, she must vacate the premises within a reasonable period of time after the interference remains uncured. Many cases have litigated how promptly, and under what circumstances, a tenant must depart the premises to have acted in a reasonably prompt fashion—with quite varied results. What factors would you expect to bear on the amount of time in which the tenant must leave? When would that time commence, in the case of a breach that continues over considerable time? Although there are occasional decisions liberalizing the abandonment requirement for constructive eviction, *e.g.*, *Cox v. Hardy*, 371 S.W.2d 945, 946 (Ky. 1963), the abandonment requirement for constructive eviction continues to have very wide support among courts. Why do you suppose tenant's reasonably prompt vacation of the premises remains important to constructive eviction claims? Should the same requirement apply where the tenant sought damages or injunctive relief due to a breach of the covenant of quiet enjoyment?

3. *Constructive Eviction and Landlord's Violation of Implied Duties.* A constructive eviction is usually triggered because the landlord's breach of an express lease covenant (*e.g.*, a covenant to provide heating and air-conditioning service) creates a condition that substantially deprives the tenant of the benefit of possession. Sometimes, however, the tenant's constructive eviction claim is based upon the assertion that the landlord violated an implied duty—*i.e.*, one not expressly provided in the lease. To what extent (if any) should the law imply duties not expressly assumed by contracting parties? In this regard, consider the following from Judge Richard Posner:

> [C]ontract law has [a function] intimately related to that of preventing opportunistic behavior: filling out the parties' agreement by interpolating missing clauses. This function too is related to the sequential character of contractual performance. The longer performance will take—and bear in mind that in performance we must include the entire

stream of future services that the exchange contemplates—the harder it
will be for the parties to foresee the various contingencies that might
affect performance. Moreover, some contingencies, even though foreseeable in the strong sense that both parties are fully aware that they may
occur, are so unlikely to occur that the costs of careful drafting to deal
with them might exceed the benefits, when those benefits are discounted
by the (low) probability that the contingency will actually occur. It may
be cheaper for the court to "draft" the contractual term necessary to
deal with the contingency if and when it occurs. The two types of
contingency (unforeseen and unprovided for) are closely related. The
less frequent an event is, the less likely it is that the parties thought
about it, their neglect being a rational response to the costs of information relative to the benefits.

The task for a court asked to interpret a contract to cover a
contingency that the parties did not provide for is to imagine how the
parties would have provided for the contingency if they had decided to
do so. Often there will be clues in the language of the contract. But
often there will not be, and then the court may have to engage in
economic thinking—may have to decide what the most efficient way of
dealing with the contingency is. For this is the best way of deciding how
the parties would have provided for it. Each party, it is true, is
interested just in his own profit, and not in the joint profit; but the
larger the joint profit is, the bigger the "take" of each party is likely to
be. So they have a mutual interest in minimizing the cost of performance, and the court can use this interest to fill out a contract along lines
that the parties would have approved at the time of making the
contract. . . .

What about cases in which the parties' intentions, as gleaned from
the language of the contract or perhaps even from testimony, are at
variance with the court's notion of what would be the most efficient
term to interpolate into the contract? If the law is to take its cues from
economics, should efficiency or intentions govern? Oddly, the latter. The
people who make a transaction—thus putting their money where their
mouths are—ordinarily are more trustworthy judges of their self-interest than a judge (or jury), who has neither a personal stake in nor first-
hand acquaintance with the venture on which the parties embarked
when they first signed the contract. So even if the goal of contract law is
to promote efficiency rather than to enforce promises as such . . . ,
enforcing the parties' agreement insofar as it can be ascertained may be
a more efficient method of attaining this goal than rejecting the agreement when it appears to be inefficient. Yet discrepancies between
(apparent) agreement and efficiency can be important clues to the
existence of mistake, incapacity, or other grounds for believing that the
apparent agreement doesn't really promote the parties' joint ends.

Here is an example of how economic analysis can be used to fill in
missing terms in a contract. A buys goods from B, with delivery to take
place in a month, and during the month B's warehouse burns down and
the goods are destroyed. The contract is silent on the allocation of the
risk of loss before delivery. But since B can prevent (or insure against) a
fire in his own warehouse at a lower cost than A can, the parties, if they

had thought about the matter, would have assigned the risk to B, even though he no longer "owns" the goods; and that is the assignment the court should make in the absence of contrary evidence of the parties' intentions. [Richard A. Posner, Economic Analysis of Law 91–93 (4th ed. 1992).]

Consider Posner's analysis as applied to the situation in *Kaminsky.* Is it reasonable to imply on Fidelity a duty to exclude uninvited third parties from the building's common areas? Why or why not? Suppose that the lease had not expressly obligated Fidelity to exclude third parties from the common areas, and that the lease did not expressly obligate Fidelity to provide any building security. If you represented Dr. Kaminsky, how would you use Posner's analysis to construct an argument sufficient to persuade the judge that Fidelity had constructively evicted your client?

4. *Partial Actual Eviction.* Suppose that *T* leases a home and one acre of land from *L.* During the lease term, *L* (who lives on the adjacent parcel) builds a fence that encroaches onto the leased premises by 50 feet, but *L* does not interfere in any way with *T*'s possession of the rest of the premises. While *L*'s fence causes only a partial eviction in a physical sense, this partial eviction nevertheless breaches the covenant of quiet enjoyment, and under the traditional rule—sometimes called the "one-inch" rule, reflecting the idea that depriving the tenant of even one inch of the premises breached the covenant of quiet enjoyment—*T* may (if she wishes) choose to terminate the lease and vacate the premises entirely. What factors might be relevant to *T* in deciding whether to avail herself of this termination remedy? [Hint: Can you envision any scenario in which the agreed-upon rent is higher than the actual value of the premises to *T*?]

Suppose *T* wants to remain in possession of the rest of the land. What liability, if any, does *T* have for rent? Intuitively, one might think that *T* should be liable for rent in a reduced amount (*i.e.*, reduced to account for the proportion of the premises from which *T* has been evicted). Courts traditionally held, however, that a partial actual eviction relieves the tenant of *all* obligations to pay rent during the period the eviction continues (even though all other covenants in the lease remain binding on both parties). *See, e.g., In re Compass Van & Storage Corp.*, 61 B.R. 230 (E.D.N.Y. 1986).[5] Recently, however, a New York intermediate appellate court decision rejected the "one-inch" rule, concluding that "a more realistic remedy than total rent abatement" should be imposed for a minimal partial eviction. *Eastside Exhibition Corp. v. 210 E. 86th St. Corp.*, 801 N.Y.S.2d 568 (App. Div. 2005). Which view do you think makes better sense? Should *T* still be able to get injunctive relief against such an intrusion by *L*?

Even if a court held that *T* had no continuing liability for rent, this does not mean that *T* can remain in possession of the rest of the premises without any obligation to *L.* If *T* chooses to remain in possession of the rest of the premises, *T* will be liable to *L* in quasi-contract for the actual value of that portion of the premises (as distinguished from a proportionate share of the

5. Where the partial actual eviction is by a paramount title holder (rather than the landlord), the tenant's rental abates only in proportion to the actual deprivation of possession. *Fifth Ave. Bldg. Co. v. Kernochan*, 221 N.Y. 370, 117 N.E. 579 (1917).

agreed-upon rental). *See* John E. Cribbet and Corwin W. Johnson, Principles of the Law of Property 245 (3d ed. 1989).

5. *Partial Constructive Eviction?* Suppose that *L* owns a two-story building leased to *T* as a restaurant. City fire codes require sprinklers for fire suppression, and *L* had previously installed the sprinklers on the building's first floor, but not the second floor. Upon discovering the code violation, the city fire marshal orders *T* to shut down the second floor seating area (thereby depriving *T* of one-half of its available seating). *T* continues operating its restaurant on only the first floor, and reduces its rental payments in proportion to the seating area lost, arguing that *L*'s failure to install the sprinklers on the second floor had resulted in a partial constructive eviction. *L* sues to recover the entire rental amount, arguing that there could be no constructive eviction because *T* failed to vacate the premises altogether. How should the court resolve this dispute? *Compare Dennison v. Marlowe*, 106 N.M. 433, 744 P.2d 906 (1987) (allowing partial offset) *with Kenyon v. Regan*, 826 P.2d 140 (Utah Ct. App. 1992) (no partial constructive eviction unless tenant abandons entire premises). Does the court really need to recognize "partial constructive eviction" to protect a tenant in *T*'s position?

6. *Eviction by Paramount Title.* The landlord breaches the covenant of quiet enjoyment if a holder of paramount title interferes with the tenant's possession. A third person holds "paramount title" if, at the time of the lease, she holds rights in the leased premises that may be inconsistent with tenant's rights as purportedly created by the lease, and the landlord cannot terminate the third person's rights by the time tenant is entitled to possession. *See* Restatement (Second) of Property—Landlord & Tenant § 4.1 (1977). These rights could be conflicting possessory rights—for example, where the landlord has previously leased the same land to another person for the same time period. These rights might also be pre-existing non-possessory rights—for example, the landlord may have granted a mortgage on the premises prior to having leased the premises to the tenant, and the mortgagee's enforcement of the mortgage (through a foreclosure sale) could interfere with the tenant's possession.

Once the lease term begins and the tenant is occupying the premises, the mere existence of paramount title does not breach landlord's covenant of quiet enjoyment. Breach occurs only when the paramount title holder interferes with tenant's possessory rights under the lease. *See* Restatement (Second) of Property—Landlord and Tenant § 4.3 (1977). Such interference, regardless of whether it forces tenant from the premises, is often called an "eviction." In which of the following situations is there a breach of the covenant of quiet enjoyment?

(a) *L*, a life tenant, leases Blueacre to *T* for five years. After two years, *L* dies and *A*, the holder of the remainder, enters and takes possession of Blueacre.

(b) *L* leases Whiteacre to *T* for five years, starting February 1. On February 2, *T* discovers that *L* had previously leased the premises to *X*, although *X* has never taken possession.

(c) *L* leases Brownacre to *T* for five years. Brownacre is subject to a prior mortgage in favor of Bank. After *T* enters, *L* defaults on the mortgage and Bank institutes foreclosure proceedings. *P* purchases Brownacre at a foreclosure sale, but has not yet taken possession of Brownacre.

(d) *L* leases a vacant lot to *T*. The lease provides that *T* will use the premises as a parking lot. After taking possession, *T* discovers that *X* holds a prior easement across the lot that entitles *X* to drive her car from the street to her garage located behind the vacant lot.

(e) *L* leases a vacant lot to *T*. The lease says nothing about *T*'s use, but *T* plans to operate a parking lot. After taking possession, *T* is sued by a neighbor, *X*, who claims the premises are subject to a covenant restricting it to residential use only. The court enjoins *T*'s use of the premises as a parking lot.

7. *Holdover Tenants, the Covenant of Quiet Enjoyment, and the Landlord's Duty(?) to Place the Tenant in Actual Possession at the Commencement of the Lease.* Suppose that in July, *L* and *T* sign a three-year lease to commence December 1. When December 1 arrives, however, *T* discovers that the previous tenant, *X*, remains in possession and refuses to leave (even though *X*'s lease expired on October 31). [The law treats *X* as a holdover tenant or a tenant at sufferance, which we discuss further on page 438.] Does the fact that *X* remains in possession mean that *L* has breached the lease—in other words, does *L* have a legal duty to put *T* in actual possession on December 1?

First, you should note that *X*'s holdover *does not breach the covenant of quiet enjoyment.* As discussed in note 1, the covenant of quiet enjoyment does not protect *T* against interference by third parties. By virtue of *T*'s lease, *T* has a superior legal right to possession of the premises, can bring an action to recover possession of the land from *X*, and can recover from *X* for the damages that *T* suffers as a consequence of *X*'s holdover.

Still, *T* certainly expected that he would be able to take possession of the premises on the first day of the lease term. If the lease contains an express promise by *L* that the premises will be empty and ready for *T*'s possession on the first day of the term, then *L* has a contractual duty to place *T* in actual possession on the first day of the term, and *X*'s holdover would constitute a breach of that duty. But what if the lease is silent? Should the law imply this duty on *L*, or should *T* bear the risk associated with *X* holding over? Case authority is divided. Some jurisdictions adopt a position known as the "American rule," under which a landlord has no implied duty to place the tenant in actual possession as long as the tenant has the legal right to possession and the standing to protect its own legal interest:

American Rule

> [I]f the premises are withheld from the possession of the tenant by reason of the wrongful act of a trespasser or of some former tenant who wrongfully holds over, the tenant has a right to recover his damages from such person. . . . It is, of course, true that the tenant will suffer delay in obtaining possession if he is forced to sue for it, but so would the landlord under the same circumstances. It is not, we believe, customary for a person who contracts in respect to any subject to insure the other party against lawsuits. Indeed, both the landlord and tenant have a right to presume that a former tenant will vacate at the end of his term, and that no one will unlawfully prevent the new tenant from going into possession. To sue or be sued is a privilege or misfortune

which may occur to anyone. [*Hannan v. Dusch*, 154 Va. 356, 153 S.E. 824 (1930).]

By contrast, some jurisdictions follow the "English" rule, which provides that a landlord has an implied duty to place the tenant into actual possession on the first day of the lease term:

> Can it be supposed that the [tenant] would have entered into the lease if he had known at the time that he could not obtain possession on the 1st of March, but that he would be compelled to begin a lawsuit, await the law's delays, and follow the case through its devious turnings to an end before he could hope to obtain possession of the land he had leased? Most assuredly not. It is unreasonable to suppose that a man would knowingly contract for a lawsuit, or take the chance of one. Whether or not a tenant in possession intends to hold over or assert a right to future term may nearly always be known to the landlord, and is certainly much more apt to be within his knowledge than within that of the prospective tenant. Moreover, since in an action to recover possession against a tenant holding over, the lessee would be compelled largely to rely upon the lessor's testimony in regard to the facts of the claim to hold over by the wrongdoer, it is more reasonable and proper to place the burden upon the person within whose knowledge the facts are most apt to lie. [*Herpolsheimer v. Christopher*, 76 Neb. 352, 111 N.W. 359 (1907).]

What assumptions do these respective opinions make regarding whether landlord or tenant is better situated to address the problem of a holdover tenant? Can you think of additional reasons why the landlord might be better situated than a tenant to "solve" the holdover tenant problem?

Notwithstanding the "American rule" label, a majority of jurisdictions and the Uniform Residential Landlord and Tenant Act (URLTA) have adopted the English Rule. William B. Stoebuck & Dale A. Whitman, The Law of Property § 6.21, at 270 (3d ed. 2000); URLTA §§ 2.103, 4.102. The Restatement (Second) of Property—Landlord and Tenant strikes a middle ground: it requires the landlord to act to evict the holdover tenant, but provides the landlord is not in breach if it acts to remove the holdover tenant within a "reasonable period." Restatement (Second) of Property—Landlord and Tenant § 6.2. New York, which previously followed the American Rule, has enacted a statute codifying the English rule. N.Y. Real Prop. Law § 233–a.

LAWYERING EXERCISE
(Fact Investigation and Client Counseling)

BACKGROUND: In interviewing a client, the lawyer must know what to ask the client (*i.e.*, what information does the lawyer need to obtain?) and how to formulate questions that will produce that information. When gathering information from a client, the lawyer should (among other things):

- ask the client for facts (not conclusions) and the client's source of knowledge for those facts
- ask the client for details about facts related by the client

- ask for facts that would reveal a potential conflict of interest for the lawyer

- ask for facts that would reveal a statute of limitations or deadline that would affect the client's rights

- ask the client whether there are any pieces of paper (*e.g.*, letters, writings, contracts, documents) or other messages (*e.g.*, e-mail or voice-mail messages) that are related to the client's problem or dispute

- ask questions that would reveal the other side's likely arguments

- ask whether the client has talked with other persons, or other lawyers, about this problem or dispute.

See, e.g., Stefan H. Krieger & Richard K. Neumann, Jr., Essential Lawyering Skills: Interviewing, Counseling, Negotiation, and Persuasive Fact Analysis 94–98 (2d ed. 2003). Moreover, as discussed earlier (page 197), the lawyer should organize questions in a manner that starts with broad questions (designed to elicit larger quantities of information) and gradually moves toward narrower questions (designed to fill in gaps left by previous answers). *Id.* at 98–100.

SITUATION: Ted Lange has made an appointment to obtain your advice regarding a landlord-tenant matter. At present, you know only a few facts: (a) Ted has a lease for apartment 3B in College Arms Apartments; (b) Ted is concerned because the tenants in the apartment next door appear to be selling drugs from their apartment; (c) Ted has complained to the landlord, but to no avail; and (d) Ted wants to move out, but does not want to be liable for any further rent under his current lease.

TASK: Put together a written list of questions that you will ask Ted to obtain the information necessary to advise Ted, and then conduct an interview of Ted.

3. *Distinguishing the Lease from Nonpossessory Interests*

To a layperson, it may be difficult to distinguish between the tenant's right to possession under a lease and certain other interests that may look like possessory interests, but which the law treats as nonpossessory. These nonpossessory interests include *licenses*, *easements*, and *profits*. A *license* is a revocable grant of permission to go onto land in possession of another person for a specific purpose. A typical license would be the right of a person holding a ticket to a movie, concert, or athletic contest to enter the arena and occupy a seat. An *easement* generally permits its holder to enter onto and make a particular use of land in possession of another person. For example, an easement might authorize the utility company to construct and maintain power lines across your land. While licenses and easements may appear similar, there are two important differences. First, licenses are often temporary and short-term in nature, while easements are typically perpetual (although easements can be created for a limited duration and can also be subject to termination in a variety of ways). Second, easements are real property interests—*i.e.,* if the owner of the land violates the easement holder's rights of use, the easement holder is entitled to injunctive relief to prevent such interference in the future. In contrast, licenses are revocable interests, and a licensee typically cannot obtain injunctive relief to prevent the licensor from interfering with or terminating a license (although the licensee may, in appropriate cases, be able to recover damages caused by an interference). Finally, a *profit* is a right to enter onto and remove some part of another person's land or some product of that land, such as the right to cut timber, remove minerals, or engage in hunting or fishing. [We will study easements, licenses, and profits in greater detail in Chapter 8.]

A lease is distinguishable from these other nonpossessory interests because the holder of a leasehold estate holds an "exclusive" right to "possession" of land. This means that the tenant generally has the right to exclude the landlord and third persons from occupying the land. By contrast, the holder of an easement, license, or profit may have extensive rights of use, but not so extensive as to permit the holder to exclude the owner of the affected land from enjoying possession of the land. To appreciate the difficulty of making this distinction in close cases, and to understand the consequences of classifying an interest as a lease, consider the following case.

COOK v. UNIVERSITY PLAZA

Court of Appeals of Illinois.
100 Ill.App.3d 752, 56 Ill.Dec. 325, 427 N.E.2d 405 (1981).

SEIDENFELD, PRESIDING JUSTICE. In this appeal we consider the applicability of the statute providing payment of interest on security deposits to a tenant, Ill.Rev.Stat.1979, ch. 74, pars. 91–93, to particular contracts. The parties to the agreements are the plaintiffs, the residents of University Plaza as a class, who entered into residence hall contracts with University Plaza and its general partners, defendants, a privately owned university dormitory which serves students of Northern Illinois University in DeKalb. Plaintiffs appeal from the dismissal of their class action suit. The defendants' motion [to dismiss] was sustained on the basis that the statute is inapplicable because no tenant-landlord relationship has been created by the contracts and thus that no cause of action was stated.

The individual contracts with the students are entitled "Residence Hall Contract Agreement." The introductory paragraph states that the agreement governs the use of the University Plaza facilities and services by the resident. In Clause I the dormitory agrees to furnish accommodations and services, including basic furniture, carpeting and draperies, local telephone service, cleaning service, social and recreational facilities, and parking facilities. Clause III requires a $50 security deposit and spells out the rights that the resident has in that deposit. University

Plaza reserves the right to cancel the contract for default, although the resident has no right to cancel once it has accepted the agreement. If the resident has not vacated the premises at the end of seven days following a written notice of intent to cancel the contract, University Plaza may take possession of the premises and remove the resident. University Plaza provides meal service for the residents. It also reserves the right to make assignments of space, to authorize or deny room and roommate changes and to require the resident to move from one room to another. There is also a provision that the dormitory is closed and meals are not served during Thanksgiving and spring recess as well as during semester breaks; and that no one is allowed to remain in the residence hall during these stated periods or beyond the established academic year closing date.

Clause IV states:

Notwithstanding anything to the contrary which may herein be contained, expressly, impliedly or otherwise, it is specifically understood and agreed by and between the parties hereto, that it is not the intention of the parties hereto to create a landlord-tenant relationship, and that the intention hereof is strictly contractual in nature; for bed and board, ancillary service, the use of certain recreational facilities, and participation in student social programs promoted at University Plaza, all of which are for the most part in concert with others. The resident may not assign any rights hereunder and may not sublet the room assigned.

Whether a contract is a lease or a license is not to be determined from the language that the parties choose to call it but from the legal effect of its provisions. *Illinois Cent. R. Co. v. Michigan Cent. R. Co.*, 18 Ill.App.2d 462, 473–74, 152 N.E.2d 627 (1958). See, also, *Holladay v. Chicago Arc Light & Power Co.*, 55 Ill.App. 463, 466 (1894).

In *Holladay*, a contract, referred throughout as a lease of the right to run electric wires under the sidewalks of certain buildings, was held not to be a lease but a mere license. In reaching that conclusion, the court reasoned that an instrument which merely gives to another the right to "use premises for a specific purpose; the owner of the premises retaining the possession and control of the premises, confers no interest in the land and is not a lease but a mere license." 55 Ill.App. at 466, 467. In *Illinois Cent. R. Co.*, the court held that an agreement between two railroads to share their track and railroad station rights was a license, not a lease and concluded that where the railroad shared the use of the tracks and terminal areas there was no transfer of exclusive possession sufficient to create a lease. It noted that "a leasehold requires that the lessee's possession be more than merely coextensive with the lessor; it must be exclusive against the world and the lessor." 18 Ill.App.2d at 482, 152 N.E.2d 627. However, "there may be a reservation of a right to possession by the landlord for purposes not inconsistent with the privileges granted to the tenant." 18 Ill.App.2d at 477, 152 N.E.2d 627.

In *In re Application of Rosewell*, 69 Ill.App.3d 996, 387 N.E.2d 866 (1979), the court considered whether agreements between the City of Chicago and certain individuals under which the individuals were permitted to operate city owned parking garages or lots, constituted leases or licenses. The court held that the essence of a lease was transfer of possession[, 69 Ill.App.3d] at 1000–1001, 387 N.E.2d 866[,] while a license is "an agreement which merely entitles one party to use property subject to the management and control of the other party." [69 Ill. App.3d] at 1001, 387 N.E.2d 866. Thus, it concluded that since the City retained the right to control how the parking lots were operated the agreement constituted a license, even though the City surrendered exclusive possession of the lots to the parking lot operators. . . .

While the agreement before us contains certain aspects normally associated with leases, a definite and agreed term and a definite and agreed price of rental and manner of payment, we conclude that it lacks the essential requirement of being a definite agreement as to the extent and bounds of the property to be used. The fact that the students may be moved during the term from room to room at the will of the contracting party is the principal feature of the agreement which we find persuasive in our determination that the parties did not intend to enter into a landlord and tenant relationship since the agreement failed to pass a possessory interest in specific property.

The question remains as to whether the legislature intended the statute on security deposits to apply to dormitories which provide bed and board to students. Paragraph 93 of the statute excludes only public housing units from the application of the act. However, parties are only covered by the statute if the agreement between the residents and the dormitory can be considered a lease. We find nothing in either the legislative history of the act or in its terms which would support the view that the legislature intended to include security deposits paid by students in dormitories in which they reside without reference to whether their agreement is a license or a lease.

We would note that there appears to be no public policy which would prevent the legislature from enacting a statute which would require that interest be paid on deposits made by persons in the class of the plaintiffs or others similarly situated. However, we conclude that the legislature has not done so and that the remedy in these circumstances is within the legislative domain.

The judgment is therefore affirmed.

Notes

1. *"Labels" and the Triumph of Substance Over Form.* Although the label that the parties attach to a relationship provides some evidence of their intent, it does not automatically establish the nature of the legal relationship created. When classifying the interest created by an agreement, courts will look to the effect of the agreement between the parties. If an agreement

creates rights that are effectively equivalent to those of a tenant, a court will treat the agreement as a lease even if the agreement purports to deny that it is a lease. Can you explain why this makes sense and should not be viewed as an unwarranted interference with freedom of contract?

2. Cook *and Security Deposits*. A residential landlord will commonly require a tenant to make a security deposit prior to the commencement of the lease. The lease typically permits the landlord to apply the deposit against any damages that the tenant causes to the premises and/or any rent remaining unpaid upon the expiration or termination of the lease. The amount of the deposit is often a function of the monthly rental amount (*e.g.*, one or two months' rent), but may vary depending upon local customs and practices or the tenant's credit record. Today, statutes in many states (such as the Illinois statute in *Cook*) regulate the collection and application of tenant security deposits.

The court concludes that the students living in University Plaza cannot obtain interest on their security deposits because they are not tenants. Why do you think the legislature enacted the security deposit statute? Do you believe that the legislature intended to exclude students such as those in University Plaza from the protection of the statute? Why or why not?

Note that the Uniform Commercial Code (which applies in all 50 states) provides that "a secured party having possession of collateral ... shall apply money or funds received from the collateral to reduce the secured obligation, unless remitted to the debtor." U.C.C. § 9–207(c)(2). Is this language relevant to the resolution of the dispute in *Cook*? Why or why not? Is a security deposit "collateral" for the tenant's "obligation" such that this section should apply to a landlord collecting a security deposit? *See, e.g.,* R. Wilson Freyermuth, *Are Security Deposits "Security Interests"? The Proper Scope of Article 9 and Statutory Interpretation in Consumer Class Actions*, 68 Mo. L. Rev. 71 (2003).

3. Cook *and Eviction*. Consider the reasoning of *Cook* in the context of the following hypothetical: Susan, a resident of University Plaza, returns from class to find that the building manager has removed her belongings from her assigned room and has ordered her to take her belongings and leave the premises. The building manager tells her that she had violated the building's quiet hours policy by holding a party in her room after hours. In fact, Susan did not hold a party in her room, and she provides proof of this to the building manager (assume her proof would be sufficient to a reasonable person). The building manager nevertheless refuses to readmit her to her room. Susan files a lawsuit, seeking an injunction ordering University Plaza to readmit her to her room. Should the court order University Plaza to let her back in the room? Why or why not? What additional information would you want to gather before making this judgment?

4. *The Effect of Use Restrictions*. Use restrictions on the premises are common in leases. Even though these restrictions constrain the extent to which a tenant enjoys the whole "bundle of rights" that normally comes with the right to possession, most use restrictions typically do not negate the transfer of a possessory interest. *See, e.g., People v. Chicago Metro Car Rentals, Inc.*, 72 Ill.App.3d 626, 28 Ill.Dec. 843, 391 N.E.2d 42 (1979) (lease existed when property was restricted to use as a rent-a-car service). As *Cook*

demonstrates, however, if the transferor retains significant control over the space and how it is used, the transferee might not be deemed to have "possession" sufficient to classify the transfer as a lease. The more control the transferor retains over space and use, the more that the lines between lease, license, and easement begin to blur—and often, the more that the judicial effort to articulate the difference becomes less convincing.

B. TYPES OF LEASEHOLD ESTATES

The common law essentially recognizes four types of leasehold interests: the tenancy for years (fixed term tenancy), the periodic tenancy, the tenancy at will, and the tenancy at sufferance.

The *tenancy for years* is a tenancy for *any* fixed term or duration, whether measured by years, months, or days. A tenancy for years expires on its own at the end of the fixed term, without the need for either party to give notice to terminate the lease (although the tenancy may terminate earlier if it contains a forfeiture or termination provision). The vast majority of residential and commercial leases are tenancies for years.

The *periodic tenancy* is a tenancy that is measured by successive, identical periods of time (such as a year, a month or a week). A periodic tenancy automatically renews for successive periods, unless one of the parties gives proper notice to terminate the tenancy. As a result, parties to a periodic tenancy must be aware of the requirements for giving effective notice of termination, which courts often enforce strictly. The parties may agree between themselves as to the required period of notice to terminate the tenancy. If the lease is silent, however, the common law generally requires that the party seeking to terminate the tenancy must provide notice *at least one period prior* to the date of termination.[6] Further, the effective date of termination must fall at the natural end of a period. Thus, suppose *L* and *T* have a periodic month-to-month tenancy that began on January 1. Assume it is now May 5, and *T* wishes to terminate the lease. Unless the lease provides *T* with the right to terminate at an earlier date, the earliest date on which *T* could terminate the lease would be June 30, so long as *T* gives notice on or prior to May 31 (one month prior to termination).

The *tenancy at will* is a tenancy without a fixed duration and without any defined renewable periods. It lasts as long as both parties wish it to last, and terminates when *either* party demonstrates an intent to discontinue the tenancy. The common law did not require advance notice to terminate a tenancy at will, but most states have now enacted statutes that require some minimal period of notice to terminate a tenancy at will.

You should take care to note that a tenancy that begins as a tenancy at will could in some circumstances (as in the *Selk* case below) become transformed into an *implied* periodic tenancy. For example, if a tenant

---

6. For periodic tenancies with periods of one year or longer, the common law re- quired notice six months in advance of the date of termination.

takes possession of property without agreement as to the duration of the tenancy or the rent due, courts generally treat the resulting tenancy as a tenancy at will. If the tenant begins making monthly rent payments of equal amounts that the landlord accepts, however, a court will likely conclude that the parties' conduct gives rise to an implied month-to-month tenancy.

The *tenancy at sufferance* really is not a tenancy at all. Rather, it is a label given to the situation that arises when a tenant "holds over" in possession after the lease has expired. A tenancy at sufferance lasts only until the landlord evicts the tenant, or until the parties agree expressly or impliedly to create a new tenancy.

At one time or another during the chronology of the following case, each of the four types of tenancies existed between the landlord (David Properties) and the tenant (Mr. Selk). As you read the case, identify each point in the chronology at which the relationship changes to a different type of tenancy and the legal significance of the change.

DAVID PROPERTIES, INC. v. SELK

Florida Court of Appeals.
151 So.2d 334 (1963).

ROGER J. WAYBRIGHT, ASSOCIATE JUDGE. . . . On January 18, 1957 (more than five years before this suit was filed in the circuit court), the plaintiff sold to the defendant a 320–acre tract of land in Volusia County, on which was located a small and simple dwelling. $5,000 of the $50,000 purchase price was presumably paid in cash. A purchase-money mortgage was executed by the defendant to the plaintiff to secure payment of the remaining $45,000, payable in annual installments of $9,000 each. At the time this foreclosure suit was filed, the defendant had paid four annual installments, but was several months overdue in payment of the final $9,000 installment, so that the plaintiff was entitled to foreclose the mortgage. . . .

After he sold the property to the defendant, the plaintiff continued to live on it. While the record is not clear on the point, that continued use of the property by the plaintiff does not seem to have been objectionable to the defendant, and may even have been agreeable to it, up to a point. The plaintiff testified that, when he sold the property, the president of the defendant corporation "says I could stay there as long as I want to." Apparently, after a time, the defendant filed an ejectment suit against the plaintiff, which resulted in the execution by the parties of a written lease agreement. . . . The facts upon which the decision herein must be based are those mentioned below, beginning with execution of the lease.

On October 20, 1959, the parties executed a written lease, in which the defendant leased to the plaintiff "the house and premises heretofore occupied by him and located . . . on the following described tract of land: [describing the 320–acre tract] . . . for a term to end at midnight,

December 31, 1959. The consideration for this lease is the sum of One Dollar ($1.00) the receipt of which is hereby acknowledged by the Lessor. It is expressly agreed by the Lessee that he will vacate the premises subject to this lease and turn over possession of the same to the Lessor at or prior to mid-night, December 31, 1959."

The plaintiff did not vacate by December 31, 1959, but continued to live there from January 1, 1960, until November 27, 1961, a period of almost 23 months after the date set by the lease for him to vacate the property.

On February 17, 1960, about a month and a half after the plaintiff was supposed to vacate the property, the president of the defendant corporation wrote to the plaintiff a letter (with a copy to the attorney who had represented the plaintiff at the sale three years before):[7]

Dear Mr. Selk:

Upon a visible inspection of the property, I find that you are still residing thereon.

In accordance with the terms of a lease dated October 20, 1959, it expressly stated that you would vacate the premises on or before midnight December 31, 1959.

You are hereby instructed to vacate these premises immediately. Your continual occupation shall be at your own risk, and I shall charge rent for the use of these premises at the rate of Three Hundred ($300.00) Dollars per month.

Please advise this office of the date of your departure so that we may make an inspection of the premises at that time.

Upon your departure we shall expect you to leave the premises in a clean condition.

Please govern yourself accordingly.

And a year later, on February 16, 1961, the president of the defendant corporation again wrote to the plaintiff (again with a copy to the attorney who had represented the plaintiff at the sale):

Dear Mr. Selk:

Upon the last two visits to the property ... I found you still occupying these premises.

In accordance with my letter dated February 17, 1960, I am enclosing herein an invoice for rent for the premises from January 1, 1960 through December 31, 1960, and ask that you make payment at this time for the rent, as indicated in my letter of February 17, 1960.

---

7. This fact poses an interesting lawyering dilemma. Assume that you were the attorney who had represented Mr. Selk at the sale, that he had retained you to represent him only in the sale transaction, and that you have never handled any other legal matters for Mr. Selk. When you receive this letter from David Properties, can you simply ignore the letter, or do you have an ethical obligation to contact Mr. Selk?

If you leave the premises, please advise by return mail the date of your departure so that I may accrue the rent to the date of your departure.

This letter shall not in any term or manner be construed as a lease, and you shall occupy this land at your own peril.

Furthermore, you are further instructed to vacate these premises immediately, and notify this office upon the date of your departure.

Your continuing to reside herein shall subject you to rent for the premises at the rate of $300.00 per month.

Please govern yourself accordingly.

With the last letter was enclosed a bill for $3600 for "Rent for 320 acres described as: [legal description] For 12 months, January 1, 1960 through December 31, 1960, at $300.00 per month."

The plaintiff concedes that he received both of those letters, but continued to live on the property until November 27, 1961, a period of almost 23 months after the date set by the lease for him to vacate the property, more than 21 months after he received the first letter, more than 9 months after he received the second letter.

The plaintiff offered no explanation as to why he neither vacated the property, protested against paying $300 per month rent, nor paid the rent. The record is silent on the point.

On February 14, 1962, almost a month after the final $9,000 annual installment was due, the plaintiff wrote the defendant "If you wish to pay that installment, in advance, in the amount of nine thousand dollars ($9,000.00) plus interest at 4 1/2%, I will accept same." [No explanation was offered as to the use of the phrase "in advance" when referring to a payment already overdue.] The defendant replied that it was prepared to pay the $9,000 balance due plus $405 interest, minus $6,600 as rental due the defendant at $300 per month for 22 months, a net amount of $2,805.

A few weeks later the plaintiff filed this suit to foreclose the mortgage. The defendant answered, denying that it was indebted to the plaintiff in the amount claimed because the plaintiff owed the defendant $7,200 plus interest thereon as rent for the property at $300 per month beginning when that first letter of February 17, 1960, was written by the defendant to the plaintiff, and counterclaiming against the plaintiff for the $7,200 plus interest at 6% per annum. The plaintiff replied to the counterclaim, denying any indebtedness for rent.

At the final hearing held before the chancellor on July 27, 1962, the defendant conceded that it owed the plaintiff the final $9,000 installment plus interest, that the payment was overdue and the plaintiff was entitled to foreclose the mortgage. The defendant relied solely upon its contention that the plaintiff owed it rent for the property at the rate of $300 per month from the time it first wrote the plaintiff specifying that amount as rent, plus interest thereon, and that it was entitled to set off that rent against the indebtedness due under the mortgage.

The defendant did not claim that the plaintiff ever expressly agreed to pay that amount as rent, but contended that such an agreement was implied by law. The evidence was that the plaintiff in effect ignored those letters of the defendant, making no reply thereto, neither agreeing to pay the rent demanded, objecting to it, nor vacating the property. The plaintiff offered no reason for his failure to [respond].

The chancellor recited in his final decree that

The so-called "premises" which the Plaintiff occupied was an old shack which the Plaintiff had built with his own hands, and in which this old man (Plaintiff) and his wife lived prior to her death .... There was no sufficient, competent evidence from which the Court might infer that the Plaintiff occupied any of the 320 acres other than a small portion thereof upon which was located the old shack in which the Plaintiff lived .... [T]he evidence does not show that the Defendant was damaged by the occupation of the building, on the 320 acres, nor that the Defendant has been deprived of any income or has suffered any damage by virtue of such occupation.... [S]aid building was no more than a shack, had no rental value, was unsafe and uninhabitable .... [The defendant had no] use or plans for the use, rental or improvement of said building; that actually said building has no value for use or occupation.

The chancellor went on to recite in the final decree that

The evidence shows that the Plaintiff is an old man of approximately 83 years of age, who appeared to the Court to be obviously senile and unable to comprehend what he was doing; and that [the president of the defendant corporation] is a licensed and practicing attorney and certified public accountant in the State of Florida. This Court does not imply that the Defendant nor the said [president of defendant] was guilty of any trickery or fraud; however, if the Court held that the letters sent to the Plaintiff, demanding rent of Three Hundred Dollars ($300.00) per month, were legally and equitably sufficient to set the rental value of the premises at that figure, this Court would itself establish a trick which would almost completely dissipate the balance due this elderly Plaintiff under his note and mortgage. For the Court to so hold would have the effect of this Court operating in an atmosphere of a complete equitable vacuum.

The chancellor found against the defendant with respect to its claim for rent made in its counterclaim, and dismissed that counterclaim. The defendant appealed to this court, contending that the chancellor erred in dismissing its counterclaim....

The plaintiff, who at the final hearing before the chancellor "Stipulated that the premises were occupied up until November 27th, 1961, from the 1st of January, 1960," seeks in his brief in this court to dilute that stipulation, contending that he did not mean to stipulate that the plaintiff occupied all of the 320–acre premises as distinguished from just the house and adjacent area. The context in which the stipulation was made militates against that contention, and in any event "A tenant who without the consent of his landlord retains possession of part of the premises must be considered as holding over as to all." 32 Am.Jur., Landlord and Tenant, § 921 (1941). And see 32 A.L.R.2d 582, 597 (1953). Similarly, the plaintiff cannot now say that he did not mean to stipulate that he occupied the property all of the period.

The primary question presented to the chancellor for his decision, and to this court on appeal, is whether the defendant, having written those letters to the plaintiff setting the rent at $300 per month if the plaintiff continued to live on the property, and having received no reply whatsoever from the plaintiff, who continued to live there, is entitled to that much as rent.

The defendant relies on the principle of law, heretofore apparently not expressed in a decision of any Florida appellate court but well established elsewhere, that is set forth in the annotation in 109 A.L.R. 197–220 at p. 201 (1937) in the language: "It is quite generally held that if a landlord notifies his tenant for a fixed term that in case he holds over beyond the term he must pay a specified increased rental, the tenant will become liable for such rental if he in fact holds over, and either remains silent with reference to the notice, or fails to express his nonassent to the terms thereof." . . .

The plaintiff takes as one of his positions that the most the defendant could possibly have claimed was the "double the monthly rent" that Florida Statutes § 83.06, F.S.A. says a landlord "may" demand of a tenant who "shall refuse to give up possession of the premises at the end of his lease." Ingeniously, the plaintiff reasons that, since the written lease under which the plaintiff held possession until December 31, 1959, provided for rent of $1 for the 70–day term, that statute prevents the defendant from claiming more rent than $2 for each 70 days of the period of almost 23 months that the plaintiff lived on the premises after the lease expired.

The plaintiff concludes that line of thought with the contention that, since the defendant did not demand double rent of the plaintiff in its letters to him, and did not allege a claim under that statute in its answer and counterclaim, the defendant cannot be awarded even that amount of rent, under the holdings in *Painter v. Town of Groveland*, 79 So.2d 765, 767 (S.C.Fla., 1955), and *Central Florida Oil Co. v. Blue Flame*, 87 So.2d 812, 814 (S.C.Fla., 1956). In that final contention the plaintiff is quite correct; those decisions so hold, and the defendant agrees.

The plaintiff then refers, for the rule as to what damages, if any, are recoverable by the defendant "in the absence of any claim for and proof of special damages and of any statutory right to double or treble damages" to 32 Am.Jur., Landlord and Tenant, § 927 (1941):

It seems to be established that where damages may be recovered from a tenant for his failure to surrender premises, he is liable for their reasonable rental value for the time that he retains the possession; or, as it is sometimes expressed, for the fair value of the use of the premises, and in the absence of any claim for and proof of special damages and of any statutory right to double or treble damages, the reasonable rental value for the time possession is withheld, or, in other words, the reasonable value of the use of the premises, is the full measure of recovery. The reasonable rental value may be fixed at a different rate—either greater or less—from that of the rent which the tenant has been paying, although it is proper to consider the stipulated rent in determining the rental value, and it has been said that ordinarily the agreed rent would be evidence of the rental value.

The plaintiff points out that the defendant offered no evidence as to the reasonable rental value of the property, and that the chancellor found that the property had no rental value. The plaintiff argues that, consequently, the defendant is entitled to no damages.

The plaintiff and the defendant agree that no demand was made for double rent under the statute. The statute is, therefore, immaterial, for it comes into play only when such a demand is made.

The apparent conflict between the principle of law contended for by the defendant, and that urged by the plaintiff, dissolves when subjected to analysis.

As was said by the author of the annotation in 32 A.L.R.2d 582–611 at pp. 584–585 (1953):

> There is a difference, although it is not always clearly recognized, between an action for rent accrued during a period of hold-over and for damages for depriving another of the use of property to which he is entitled during such period.

> One situation which generally involves an action for rent as distinguished from an action for damages is that in which the lessor notifies the lessee that upon holding over beyond the expiration of the lease period, the latter will be charged a higher rental. The action in such case is usually upon the implied contract . . . .

> Optionally, a landlord may treat a tenant failing to surrender possession of the leased premises as a trespasser, or he may waive the wrong occasioned by the holding over and treat him as a tenant. [In the instance of the former elected course] the action is one for damages as contrasted to rent, and seeks compensation or indemnity for the wrong occasioned.

In this case, the defendant, as the landlord, had at least several courses of action available when the plaintiff, as the tenant, continued to live on the leased property after expiration of the term of the lease. The defendant could probably have chosen to demand the "double the monthly rent" provided for by the statute; it elected not to do so, and the plaintiff could not force the defendant to do so. The defendant undoubtedly could have treated the plaintiff as trespasser, and sued or counterclaimed against the plaintiff for damages for depriving it of reasonable rental value and any special damages; it elected not to do so, and neither the plaintiff nor the chancellor could force it to do so. The defendant also could waive the wrong occasioned by the holding over and treat the plaintiff as a tenant, demanding an increased rent of the plaintiff if the plaintiff chose to remain on the property; this the defendant elected to do, and neither the plaintiff nor the chancellor could force it to claim damages instead of rent.

When a landlord demands a different rent for continued possession of property it owns, and a tenant receives that demand and thereafter continues on in possession without protest, the tenant impliedly agrees to pay the rent demanded. Those were the facts shown by the evidence in this case, and that rule must be applied to those facts.

If the plaintiff was mentally irresponsible when the demands for rent of $300 per month were received by him, there is no slightest suggestion of it in the pleadings or the evidence. The fact that he appeared to the chancellor to be in that condition when the final hearing was held, about two years and a half after the first demand was received, could not properly form the basis of decision by the chancellor, nor can it on this appeal. No intimation is made as to what effect such a condition of the plaintiff, at the time the demands were received by him, might have, for that point is not before this court for decision.

The chancellor was sitting as a court of equity. This court is also a court of equity. That does not permit the chancellor or this court the luxury of sympathy in deciding cases; each court must follow the evidence. It is sometimes said that courts do not administer justice, but justice under law. In this day, resort may seldom be had to what in an earlier era was called natural law, a sense of what is right and what is wrong, uncontrolled by evidence or by the rules that, through centuries of development since the time of the English ecclesiastical courts, have become nearly as stratified and rigid on the equity side as on the law side. To do so would mean a government not of law but of men.

In this case, to do so would mean ignoring well established rules, on which people are entitled to rely. This court may not do so simply because one party litigant is aged, perhaps now senile, and may need money, while the other party litigant is an artificial entity headed by a lawyer and C.P.A.

There was no element of fraud or trickery here, no claim or evidence that the plaintiff was unable to comprehend the effect of the defendant's demands that he either move from the defendant's property or pay rent of $300 per month.

That part of the chancellor's final decree dismissing the defendant's counterclaim for rent is reversed, with instructions to allow as a setoff against the amount due the plaintiff rent at $300 per month for the period from February 17, 1960, to November 27, 1961, plus interest thereon at the rate of 6% per year. . . .

Notes

1. *The Basis for Implying a Periodic Tenancy.* The court in *Selk* held that "[w]hen a landlord demands a different rent for continued possession of property it owns, and a tenant receives that demand and thereafter continues on in possession without protest, the tenant impliedly agrees to pay the rent demanded." Why does the court reach this conclusion, and is it a sound conclusion? Suppose that instead of $300 per month, the letter had advised Mr. Selk that he would owe rent of *$3,000 per month* if he remained in possession. If he had received that letter but remained in possession without responding, do you think the court would have concluded that he had impliedly agreed to pay rent of $3,000 per month?

Using the various numbers presented in the case, can you figure out why $300 per month might be accepted as reasonable rental value while $3,000 per month might not? If you had been on the court of appeals, and you had wanted to find Mr. Selk liable, would you have joined in this opinion or would you have suggested a different theory? If so, what theory?

2. *Leases and the Statute of Frauds.* Because they convey interests in land, leases are subject to the statute of frauds. In most states, the statute of frauds requires that leases for a term longer than one year are enforceable as to their duration only if they are in writing. Thus, assume that L and T enter into an oral lease for a term of three years at a rent of $500 per month beginning January 1, 2006. T takes possession on January 1, 2006 and L allows T to remain in possession. As the agreement violates the statute of frauds, it does not create a valid tenancy for years, so what type of tenancy do the parties have at that moment? Courts generally conclude that the parties have impliedly entered into a tenancy at will—based upon their conduct, L has agreed to place T in possession and T has taken possession, thereby indicating their intention to be bound as landlord and tenant. As a consequence of the statute of frauds, however, there is no enforceable duration for the tenancy, and accordingly either party can terminate the lease at will (subject to any statutory obligation to provide notice prior to termination). The relationship may change, however, when T begins to make monthly rent payments. To the extent that T pays rent on a monthly basis and L accepts the rent payments each month, this conduct reflects the willingness of the parties to continue to be bound at least upon a monthly basis, as rent is paid by T and accepted by L. Accordingly, courts generally will construe this conduct as having transformed the relationship into an implied monthly periodic tenancy.

Now suppose that T pays the rent each month for three years and then vacates the premises on December 31, 2008, without notice to L, believing that her three-year term is complete. Can L sue T to collect rent for the month of January 2009? Why or why not? What defense might T raise if L files a lawsuit? *See* William B. Stoebuck & Dale A. Whitman, The Law of Property § 10.2 (3d ed. 2000).

3. *Holdover Tenants and the Landlord's Remedies.* Early American decisions held that a landlord faced with a holdover tenant had two options (assuming that the parties could not agree as to the terms of a new lease).

The landlord could treat the holdover as a trespasser and seek to evict him, and could recover damages equal to the reasonable rental value of the premises for the period during which the holdover remained in possession. Alternatively, the landlord could *unilaterally* bind the tenant to a new term (not to exceed one year) upon the same terms and conditions as the expired lease. *See, e.g., Mason v. Wierengo's Estate*, 113 Mich. 151, 71 N.W. 489 (1897). What policies might have justified allowing the landlord to bind the tenant to a new term unilaterally?

Perhaps not surprisingly, courts were reluctant to impose a new one-year term on the holdover tenant, particularly if the tenant's holdover was de minimis or unintended. For example, in a case where a family was less than 10 hours late in vacating a Chicago apartment, the court refused to allow the landlord to hold the tenants liable for an additional year's rent. *Commonwealth Bldg. Corp. v. Hirschfield*, 307 Ill.App. 533, 30 N.E.2d 790 (1940). In another case, the tenant removed all of the contents of his New York apartment before the end of the term, but could not remove his mother for 15 days because she was too ill to move safely. The court characterized the holdover as "involuntary" and refused to allow the landlord to hold the tenant to a new term. *Herter v. Mullen*, 159 N.Y. 28, 53 N.E. 700 (1899).

As indicated in *Selk*, many state legislatures have enacted statutes that permit the landlord to recover double or treble rent from holdover tenants. *See, e.g.*, Fla. Stat. Ann. § 83.06(1) ("double the monthly rent"); Mont. Code Ann. § 70–27–208 (treble rent); Del. Code Ann., tit. 25, § 5509(4)(c) (sum "not to exceed twice the monthly rental" for period in possession). The Restatement takes the view that unless the landlord and tenant validly agree otherwise or the landlord elects to bind the holdover tenant to a new term, the tenant is liable for damages on a daily basis based on the previous rental rate (or on a proven reasonable value, if that differs from the previous rental rate). Restatement (Second) of Property—Landlord and Tenant § 14.5. Should these statutes (or a statute modeled on the Restatement) *supplement* the landlord's common law remedies against holdover tenants—*i.e.*, should the landlord be able to argue that it could still choose to bind the tenant unilaterally to a new term—or should these statutes be interpreted to displace the common law holdover rule?

In advising a tenant, would you ever consciously advise a tenant to hold over? Suppose *L* and *T* had signed a written lease for an office for three years at a rental of $1,000 per month. Early in the third year of the lease, *T* asked *L* to extend the lease for five additional years, but *L* refused. Because relocation would seriously disrupt her business, *T* wants desperately to remain in possession of the premises, and asks if she can simply stay in possession despite her lease expiring. If *T* seeks your advice, how will you respond? What additional information, if any, would you like to know?

4. *Terminating a Periodic Tenancy.* At common law, either landlord or tenant could terminate a periodic tenancy by giving the other party at least one period's notice (or six months' notice in the case of a year-to-year tenancy). Moreover, given the nature of the periodic tenancy, the termination date had to coincide with the natural end of the period. These rules continue to govern the termination of a periodic tenancy, absent an express agreement to the contrary. Accordingly, consider the following problems:

(a) *L* and *T* enter into a month-to-month periodic tenancy on May 1, 2004. *T* subsequently gives notice on December 15, 2005, that he intends to terminate the lease effective January 15, 2006. *L* does not have any other prospective tenants readily available, and wants to know if she can argue that *T*'s notice is simply ineffective to terminate the tenancy. What advice would you give *L*? *See Sage v. Rogers*, 257 Mont. 229, 848 P.2d 1034 (1992); *S.D.G. v. Inventory Control Co.*, 178 N.J.Super. 411, 429 A.2d 394 (1981).

(b) Twelve years ago, *L* and *T* signed a written lease for retail space in a mall for ten years at a monthly rent of $10,750. *T* operated a small discount store. At the conclusion of the term, *T* remained in possession and kept paying *L* $10,750 per month (which *L* accepted). Recently, BigMart (a competitor of *T*) has agreed to lease other space in the mall from *L*, but only if *L* will agree not to permit any other discount stores within the mall. *L* then immediately gave written notice to *T* purporting to terminate *T*'s lease at the end of the following month. *T* seeks your advice as to whether it has any legal basis to remain in possession for more than the following month. How would you advise *T*? What additional information, if any, would you like to know?

5. *Tenancy at Will, or a Freehold Estate?* At common law, either landlord or tenant could terminate a tenancy at will. So what happens if a lease expressly gives one party the right to terminate at will, but is silent regarding the other party? For example, suppose that *L* rents a house to *T* for $100 per month "for as long as *T* lives or until such time as *T* decides to terminate the lease." *L* later conveys his interest in the property to *M*. *M* wants to increase the rent or terminate the lease, but *T* claims she can remain in possession for only $100 per month until her death, if she wishes. Should the court treat this as a tenancy at will? If so, should the court imply that *L* has a right to terminate the lease at will? Or should the court hold that *T* has a life estate? What difference does it make? *See Garner v. Gerrish*, 63 N.Y.2d 575, 483 N.Y.S.2d 973, 473 N.E.2d 223 (1984); *Philpot v. Field*, 633 S.W.2d 546 (Tex. Civ. App. 1982); Restatement (Second) of Property—Landlord and Tenant § 1.6, cmt. g, illus. 7.

6. *Extensions and Renewals.* Often, a lease will expressly provide that the tenant can renew the lease for an additional term or extend it for a defined period after the expiration of the original term. Some case law recognizes a distinction between extensions and renewals—arguing that an extension does not contemplate that the parties will execute a new lease, while a renewal (because it is a "new grant") does contemplate that the parties will execute a new lease. This is an exceedingly fine distinction—and in most cases practically irrelevant—but might prove relevant under certain circumstances.

The ability to extend or renew the lease is a function of the lease's express terms. Sometimes, a lease may provide that the tenant's action of remaining in possession and paying rent following expiration gives rise to an extension or renewal. More frequently, a lease may provide that it will be automatically renewed for an additional term unless the tenant notifies the landlord that she will not renew (typically, by a fixed date during the original lease term). More frequently, by contrast, leases provide that a tenant can extend or renew the lease only by giving effective prior notice to the landlord.

In the negotiation and drafting process, parties should (but sometimes don't) give careful thought to the terms of an extension or renewal clause. Consider the following questions:

- For what reasons might a tenant want the ability to renew or extend the lease?

- For what reasons might a landlord be willing to grant the tenant that ability?

- What economic concerns does extension or renewal present to the landlord, and how can the landlord address these concerns in its negotiation and drafting?

- Under what circumstances, if any, might the landlord reasonably refuse to permit the tenant to renew or extend the lease?

See generally Milton R. Friedman & Patrick A. Randolph, Jr., 2 Friedman on Leasing §§ 14.1–14.4 (5th ed. 2004).

LAWYERING PROBLEM
(Document Review and Drafting)

SITUATION: Local Residential Properties, Inc. (LRP), owns and operates about 1,000 residential apartment units throughout the city. Through networking in the local Chamber of Commerce, you became acquainted with the President of LRP, who has asked you to begin handling all of LRP's legal work.

You asked to see LRP's standard lease form. Upon reviewing it, you discover the following provision:

> Tenant shall have the right to extend the lease for an additional term by giving effective notice to the Landlord in writing. To be effective, notice must be given to the Landlord no later than three months before the date on which the term would otherwise have expired. Tenant may not extend the lease at any time during which Tenant shall be in default of its rental obligations under this Lease.

TASK: Write a letter to LRP that (a) evaluates the quoted provision in terms of the risks it poses to LRP and (b) proposes alternative language that you believe is sufficient to address those risks.

C. SHAPING THE MODERN LEASE: SELECTED PROBLEM AREAS IN NEGOTIATING, DRAFTING AND INTERPRETING LEASES

In this section, we address a variety of problem areas that arise in the negotiation and drafting of a lease agreement. This section does not provide a comprehensive list of legal and practical issues that would arise in the process of lease negotiation. Instead, we focus upon four particular areas—transfer of the leasehold estate, use of the premises, tenant breach, and allocation of responsibility for the physical condition of the premises. These four areas provide a sufficient flavor of the dynamics involved in negotiating and documenting a modern lease.

In the process of studying these areas, you should appreciate the extent to which development of the law in these areas is influenced by the conveyance/contract tension introduced earlier in this chapter. You should also appreciate the problems presented by a lack of specificity in a lease document. Frequently parties enter into leases that do not provide sufficient specificity regarding various aspects of their relationship, and this lack of specificity often results in later disputes. In some cases, this may reflect a lack of sophistication by the parties regarding potential legal or practical consequences; in others, it may be pure oversight. And in some cases, it may reflect a conscious decision by one or both parties not to address an issue in the agreement at all.

Why might a sophisticated party consciously avoid identifying or resolving an issue in advance? This behavior seems odd, as the likelihood of reaching a comprehensive agreement is arguably greatest while the parties are "courting" each other, *i.e.*, seeking to conclude what they perceive to be a mutually advantageous deal. In some cases, though, a particular issue may be so potentially divisive during initial negotia-tions—or one party may perceive it to be so potentially divisive—that the parties may go forward with the deal without resolving that issue, out of fear that attempts to resolve the issue will cause the deal to fall through. In effect, the parties in this situation may make a calculated gamble that the deferred issue will not actually arise. This strategy may be particu-larly attractive to a party who expects her negotiating power to increase as the relationship proceeds, such as where she perceives that the other party will become even more reliant on preserving the arrangement as it unfolds.

Whenever a lease document lacks the foresight or specificity to address a particular issue—for whatever reason—the parties essentially leave the court in the position of establishing and implementing a default rule to resolve that issue. As we have seen, sometimes the court establishes that default rule based upon the characteristics of the lease as a conveyance of an estate in land. In other instances, the court may look to contract law for the default rule, filling the gap in the parties' agreement through the use of implied covenants. As you encounter the issues presented in this section, consider how the conveyance and the contract models of leasing might influence the resolution of a particular dispute. Where these models suggest different results, how should a court resolve the dispute? In particular, pay close attention to whether the rules that courts apply operate as default rules or immutable rules. When, and why, should a court displace freedom of contract principles? Likewise, pay close attention to whether a court defines the rules or applies rules the legislature has defined. When, and why, should the legislature seek to regulate the landlord-tenant relationship? Further, pay close attention to the context in which courts apply rules. Should the same rules apply, for example, both to commercial leases and to residential leases? Finally, pay close attention to the assumptions about the consequences that will result from the application of a given rule. Can those assumptions be justified theoretically or empirically?

1. *Transfer of the Leasehold*

During the lease term, a tenant may conclude that she no longer needs possession of the leased premises. In the case of a residential lease, this often occurs because the tenant has to move suddenly (*e.g.*, a job transfer). In the case of a commercial lease, this may occur because the tenant's business fails, or perhaps instead because the tenant's business is so successful that it has outgrown the existing space. In these situations, the tenant may wish to transfer its leasehold estate—*i.e.*, its right to possession—to another person who needs and wants it.

Unless the lease contains an enforceable covenant against such transfers, the tenant may accomplish this transfer through either an *assignment* or a *sublease*. Generally speaking, if the tenant transfers its entire remaining interest (*i.e.*, the right to possession for the full balance of the lease term), the transfer is an assignment. If the tenant transfers less than its entire remaining interest, the transfer is a sublease. A sublease essentially creates an entirely new landlord-tenant relationship between the sublessor (the original tenant) and the sublessee (the tenant under the sublease).

Understandably, a landlord may have justifiable concerns about the identity and character of the tenant's proposed transferee and about the economic consequences of such a transfer. What risks does such a transfer pose to the landlord? How can the landlord protect itself against these risks in negotiating and documenting the lease in the first instance? From the opposite perspective, how can a tenant protect its interests adequately in negotiating with the landlord regarding the terms of a restriction on the tenant's ability to transfer its estate?

KENDALL v. ERNEST PESTANA, INC.

Supreme Court of California.
40 Cal.3d 488, 220 Cal.Rptr. 818, 709 P.2d 837 (1985).

BROUSSARD, JUSTICE. This case concerns the effect of a provision in a commercial lease that the lessee may not assign the lease or sublet the premises without the lessor's prior written consent. The question we address is whether, in the absence of a provision that such consent will not be unreasonably withheld, a lessor may unreasonably and arbitrarily withhold his or her consent to an assignment. This is a question of first impression in this court.

The allegations of the complaint may be summarized as follows. The lease at issue is for 14,400 square feet of hangar space at the San Jose Municipal Airport. The City of San Jose, as owner of the property, leased it to Irving and Janice Perlitch, who in turn assigned their interest to respondent Ernest Pestana, Inc. Prior to assigning their interest to

respondent, the Perlitches entered into a 25-year sublease with one
Robert Bixler commencing on January 1, 1970. The sublease covered an
original five-year term plus four 5–year options to renew. The rental rate
was to be increased every 10 years in the same proportion as rents
increased on the master lease from the City of San Jose. The premises
were to be used by Bixler for the purpose of conducting an airplane
maintenance business.

Bixler conducted such a business under the name "Flight Services"
until, in 1981, he agreed to sell the business to appellants Jack Kendall,
Grady O'Hara and Vicki O'Hara. The proposed sale included the business and the equipment, inventory and improvements on the property,
together with the existing lease. The proposed assignees had a stronger
financial statement and greater net worth than the current lessee,
Bixler, and they were willing to be bound by the terms of the lease.

The lease provided that written consent of the lessor was required
before the lessee could assign his interest, and that failure to obtain such
consent rendered the lease voidable at the option of the lessor. Accordingly, Bixler requested consent from the Perlitches' successor-in-interest,
respondent Ernest Pestana, Inc. Respondent refused to consent to the
assignment and maintained that it had an absolute right arbitrarily to
refuse any such request. The complaint recites that respondent demanded "increased rent and other more onerous terms" as a condition of
consenting to Bixler's transfer of interest.

The proposed assignees brought suit for declaratory and injunctive
relief and damages seeking, inter alia, a declaration "that the refusal of
ERNEST PESTANA, INC. to consent to the assignment of the lease is
unreasonable and is an unlawful restraint on the freedom of alienation...." The trial court sustained a demurrer to the complaint ...
and this appeal followed. ...

The law generally favors free alienability of property, and California
follows the common law rule that a leasehold interest is freely alienable.
Contractual restrictions on the alienability of leasehold interests are,
however, permitted. "Such restrictions are justified as reasonable protection of the interests of the lessor as to who shall possess and manage
property in which he has a reversionary interest and from which he is
deriving income." Schoshinski, American Law of Landlord and Tenant
(1980) § 8:15, at pp. 578–579. See also 2 Powell on Real Property,
¶ 246[1], at p. 372.97.

The common law's hostility toward restraints on alienation has
caused such restraints on leasehold interests to be strictly construed
against the lessor. Thus, in *Chapman v. Great Western Gypsum Co.*
(1932) 216 Cal. 420, 14 P.2d 758, where the lease contained a covenant
against assignment without the consent of the lessor, this court stated:
"It hardly needs citation of authority to the principle that covenants
limiting the free alienation of property such as covenants against assignment are barely tolerated and must be strictly construed." *Id.*, at p. 426,
14 P.2d 758. This is particularly true where the restraint in question is a

"forfeiture restraint," under which the lessor has the option to terminate the lease if an assignment is made without his or her consent. Civ. Code, § 1442 ("A condition involving a forfeiture must be strictly interpreted against the party for whose benefit it is created.").

Nevertheless, a majority of jurisdictions have long adhered to the rule that where a lease contains an approval clause (a clause stating that the lease cannot be assigned without the prior consent of the lessor), the lessor may arbitrarily refuse to approve a proposed assignee no matter how suitable the assignee appears to be and no matter how unreasonable the lessor's objection. The harsh consequences of this rule have often been avoided through application of the doctrines of waiver and estoppel, under which the lessor may be found to have waived (or be estopped from asserting) the right to refuse consent to assignment.

The traditional majority rule has come under steady attack in recent years. A growing minority of jurisdictions now hold that where a lease provides for assignment only with the prior consent of the lessor, such consent may be withheld only where the lessor has a commercially reasonable objection to the assignment, even in the absence of a provision in the lease stating that consent to assignment will not be unreasonably withheld.

For the reasons discussed below, we conclude that the minority rule is the preferable position. . . .

The impetus for change in the majority rule has come from two directions, reflecting the dual nature of a lease as a conveyance of a leasehold interest and a contract. *See Medico–Dental etc. Co. v. Horton & Converse* (1942) 21 Cal.2d 411, 418, 132 P.2d 457. The policy against restraints on alienation pertains to leases in their nature as conveyances. Numerous courts and commentators have recognized that "[i]n recent times the necessity of permitting reasonable alienation of commercial space has become paramount in our increasingly urban society." [*Schweiso v. Williams,* 150 Cal.App.3d 883, 887, 198 Cal.Rptr. 238 (1984).]

Civil Code section 711 provides: "Conditions restraining alienation, when repugnant to the interest created, are void." It is well settled that this rule is not absolute in its application, but forbids only unreasonable restraints on alienation. *Wellenkamp v. Bank of America* (1978) 21 Cal.3d 943, 948, 148 Cal.Rptr. 379, 582 P.2d 970. Reasonableness is determined by comparing the justification for a particular restraint on alienation with the quantum of restraint actually imposed by it. "[T]he greater the quantum of restraint that results from enforcement of a given clause, the greater must be the justification for that enforcement." *Wellenkamp v. Bank of America, supra,* 21 Cal.3d at p. 949, 148 Cal.Rptr. 379, 582 P.2d 970. In *Cohen v. Ratinoff,* [147 Cal.App.3d 321, 195 Cal.Rptr. 84 (1983)], the court examined the reasonableness of the restraint created by an approval clause in a lease:

Because the lessor has an interest in the character of the proposed commercial assignee, we cannot say that an assignment provision requiring the lessor's consent to an assignment is inherently repugnant to the leasehold interest created. We do conclude, however, that if such an assignment provision is implemented in such a manner that its underlying purpose is perverted by the arbitrary or unreasonable withholding of consent, an unreasonable restraint on alienation is established. [*Id.*, 147 Cal.App.3d at p. 329, 195 Cal. Rptr. 84.] . . .

One commentator explains as follows:

The common-law hostility to restraints on alienation had a large exception with respect to estates for years. A lessor could prohibit the lessee from transferring the estate for years to whatever extent he might desire. It was believed that the objectives served by allowing such restraints outweighed the social evils implicit in the restraints, in that they gave to the lessor a needed control over the person entrusted with the lessor's property and to whom he must look for the performance of the covenants contained in the lease. Whether this reasoning retains full validity can well be doubted. Relationships between lessor and lessee have tended to become more and more impersonal. Courts have considerably lessened the effectiveness of restraint clauses by strict construction and liberal applications of the doctrine of waiver. With the shortage of housing and, in many places, of commercial space as well, the allowance of lease clauses forbidding assignments and subleases is beginning to be curtailed by statutes. [2 Powell, *supra*, ¶ 246[1], at pp. 372.97–372.98, fns. omitted.]

The Restatement Second of Property adopts the minority rule on the validity of approval clauses in leases: "A restraint on alienation without the consent of the landlord of a tenant's interest in leased property is valid, but the landlord's consent to an alienation by the tenant cannot be withheld unreasonably, unless a freely negotiated provision in the lease gives the landlord an absolute right to withhold consent." Rest.2d Property, § 15.2(2) (1977).[8] A comment to the section explains:

The landlord may have an understandable concern about certain personal qualities of a tenant, particularly his reputation for meeting his financial obligations. The preservation of the values that go into the personal selection of the tenant justifies upholding a provision in the lease that curtails the right of the tenant to put anyone else in his place by transferring his interest, but this justification does not go to the point of allowing the landlord arbitrarily and without reason to refuse to allow the tenant to transfer an interest in leased property. [*Id.*, com. a.]

Under the Restatement rule, the lessor's interest in the character of his or her tenant is protected by the lessor's right to object to a proposed

---

8. This case does not present the question of the validity of a clause absolutely prohibiting assignment, or granting absolute discretion over assignment to the lessor. We note that under the Restatement rule such a provision would be valid if freely negotiated.

assignee on reasonable commercial grounds. The lessor's interests are also protected by the fact that the original lessee remains liable to the lessor as a surety even if the lessor consents to the assignment and the assignee expressly assumes the obligations of the lease.

The second impetus for change in the majority rule comes from the nature of a lease as a contract. As the Court of Appeal observed in *Cohen v. Ratinoff, supra,* "... there has been an increased recognition of and emphasis on the duty of good faith and fair dealing inherent in every contract." *Id.,* 147 Cal.App.3d at p. 329, 195 Cal.Rptr. 84. Thus, "[i]n every contract there is an implied covenant that neither party shall do anything which will have the effect of destroying or injuring the right of the other party to receive the fruits of the contract...." *Universal Sales Corp. v. Cal. etc. Mfg. Co.* (1942) 20 Cal.2d 751, 771, 128 P.2d 665. "[W]here a contract confers on one party a discretionary power affecting the rights of the other, a duty is imposed to exercise that discretion in good faith and in accordance with fair dealing." *Cal. Lettuce Growers v. Union Sugar Co.* (1955) 45 Cal.2d 474, 484, 289 P.2d 785. Here the lessor retains the discretionary power to approve or disapprove an assignee proposed by the other party to the contract; this discretionary power should therefore be exercised in accordance with commercially reasonable standards. . . .

Under the minority rule, the determination whether a lessor's refusal to consent was reasonable is a question of fact. Some of the factors that the trier of fact may properly consider in applying the standards of good faith and commercial reasonableness are: financial responsibility of the proposed assignee; suitability of the use for the particular property; legality of the proposed use; need for alteration of the premises; and nature of the occupancy, *i.e.,* office, factory, clinic, etc.

Denying consent solely on the basis of personal taste, convenience or sensibility is not commercially reasonable. Nor is it reasonable to deny consent "in order that the landlord may charge a higher rent than originally contracted for." *Schweiso v. Williams, supra,* 150 Cal.App.3d at p. 886, 198 Cal.Rptr. 238. This is because the lessor's desire for a better bargain than contracted for has nothing to do with the permissible purposes of the restraint on alienation—to protect the lessor's interest in the preservation of the property and the performance of the lease covenants. " '[T]he clause is for the protection of the landlord in its ownership and operation of the particular property—not for its general economic protection.' " *Ringwood Associates v. Jack's of Route 23, Inc.,* [153 N.J. Super. 294, 379 A.2d 508 (1977)], at 512, quoting *Krieger v. Helmsley–Spear, Inc.* (1973) 62 N.J. 423, 302 A.2d 129.

In contrast to the policy reasons advanced in favor of the minority rule, the majority rule has traditionally been justified on three grounds. Respondent raises a fourth argument in its favor as well. None of these do we find compelling.

First, it is said that a lease is a conveyance of an interest in real property, and that the lessor, having exercised a personal choice in the selection of a tenant and provided that no substitute shall be acceptable without prior consent, is under no obligation to look to anyone but the lessee for the rent. This argument is based on traditional rules of conveyancing and on concepts of freedom of ownership and control over one's property.

A lessor's freedom at common law to look to no one but the lessee for the rent has, however, been undermined by the adoption in California of a rule that lessors—like all other contracting parties—have a duty to mitigate damages upon the lessee's abandonment of the property by seeking a substitute lessee. *See* Civ.Code, § 1951.2. Furthermore, the values that go into the personal selection of a lessee are preserved under the minority rule in the lessor's right to refuse consent to assignment on any commercially reasonable grounds. Such grounds include not only the obvious objections to an assignee's financial stability or proposed use of the premises, but a variety of other commercially reasonable objections as well. *See, e.g., Arrington v. Walter E. Heller Int'l Corp.* (1975) 30 Ill.App.3d 631, 333 N.E.2d 50 (desire to have only one "lead tenant" in order to preserve "image of the building" as tenant's international headquarters); *Warmack v. Merchants Nat'l Bank of Fort Smith* (Ark. 1981) 612 S.W.2d 733 (desire for good "tenant mix" in shopping center); *List v. Dahnke* (Col.App. 1981) 638 P.2d 824 (lessor's refusal to consent to assignment of lease by one restauranteur to another was reasonable where lessor believed proposed specialty restaurant would not succeed at that location). The lessor's interests are further protected by the fact that the original lessee remains a guarantor of the performance of the assignee.

The second justification advanced in support of the majority rule is that an approval clause is an unambiguous reservation of absolute discretion in the lessor over assignments of the lease. The lessee could have bargained for the addition of a reasonableness clause to the lease (*i.e.,* "consent to assignment will not be unreasonably withheld"). The lessee having failed to do so, the law should not rewrite the parties' contract for them.

Numerous authorities have taken a different view of the meaning and effect of an approval clause in a lease, indicating that the clause is not "clear and unambiguous," as respondent suggests. As early as 1940, the court in *Granite Trust Bldg. Corp. v. Great Atlantic & Pacific Tea Co.,* 36 F.Supp. 77 [(D. Mass. 1940)], examined a standard approval clause and stated: "It would seem to be the better law that when a lease restricts a lessee's rights by requiring consent before these rights can be exercised, it must have been in the contemplation of the parties that the lessor be required to give some reason for withholding consent." *Id.,* at p. 78.... Again in 1963, the court in *Gamble v. New Orleans Housing Mart, Inc.* (La.App.1963) 154 So.2d 625, stated:

> Here the lessee is simply not permitted to sublet without the written consent of the lessor. This does not prohibit or interdict subleasing. To the contrary, it permits subleasing provided only that the lessee

first obtain the written consent of the lessor. It suggests or connotes that, when the lessee obtains a subtenant acceptable or satisfactory to the lessor, he may sublet.... Otherwise the provision simply would prohibit subleasing. [*Id.*, at p. 627.] ...

In light of the interpretations given to approval clauses in the cases cited above, and in light of the increasing number of jurisdictions that have adopted the minority rule in the last 15 years, the assertion that an approval clause "clearly and unambiguously" grants the lessor absolute discretion over assignments is untenable. It is not a rewriting of a contract, as respondent suggests, to recognize the obligations imposed by the duty of good faith and fair dealing, which duty is implied by law in every contract.

The third justification advanced in support of the majority rule is essentially based on the doctrine of stare decisis. It is argued that the courts should not depart from the common law majority rule because "many leases now in effect covering a substantial amount of real property and creating valuable property rights were carefully prepared by competent counsel in reliance upon the majority viewpoint." *Gruman v. Investors Diversified Services*, [247 Minn. 502, 78 N.W.2d 377 (1956)] at p. 381. As pointed out above, however, the majority viewpoint has been far from universally held and has never been adopted by this court. Moreover, the trend in favor of the minority rule should come as no surprise to observers of the changing state of real property law in the 20th century. The minority rule is part of an increasing recognition of the contractual nature of leases and the implications in terms of contractual duties that flow therefrom. We would be remiss in our duty if we declined to question a view held by the majority of jurisdictions simply because it is held by a majority....

A final argument in favor of the majority rule is advanced by respondent and stated as follows: "Both tradition and sound public policy dictate that the lessor has a right, under circumstances such as these, to realize the increased value of his property." Respondent essentially argues that any increase in the market value of real property during the term of a lease properly belongs to the lessor, not the lessee. We reject this assertion. One California commentator has written:

[W]hen the lessee executed the lease he acquired the contractual right for the exclusive use of the premises, and all of the benefits and detriment attendant to possession, for the term of the contract. He took the downside risk that he would be paying too much rent if there should be a depression in the rental market.... Why should he be deprived of the contractual benefits of the lease because of the fortuitous inflation in the marketplace[?] By reaping the benefits he does not deprive the landlord of anything to which the landlord was otherwise entitled. The landlord agreed to dispose of possession for the limited term and he could not reasonably anticipate any more than what was given to him by the terms of the lease. His reversionary estate will benefit from the increased value from the inflation in any event, at least upon the expiration of the lease. [Miller & Starr, Current Law of Cal. Real Estate (1977) 1984 Supp., § 27:92 at p. 321.]

Respondent here is trying to get more than it bargained for in the lease. A lessor is free to build periodic rent increases into a lease, as the lessor did here. Any increased value of the property beyond this "belongs" to the lessor only in the sense, as explained above, that the lessor's reversionary estate will benefit from it upon the expiration of the lease. We must therefore reject respondent's argument in this regard.[9] . . .

In conclusion, both the policy against restraints on alienation and the implied contractual duty of good faith and fair dealing militate in favor of adoption of the rule that where a commercial lease provides for assignment only with the prior consent of the lessor, such consent may be withheld only where the lessor has a commercially reasonable objection to the assignee or the proposed use. Under this rule, appellants have stated a cause of action against respondent Ernest Pestana, Inc. . . .

LUCAS, JUSTICE, dissenting. I respectfully dissent. In my view we should follow the weight of authority which, as acknowledged by the majority herein, allows the commercial lessor to withhold his consent to an assignment or sublease arbitrarily or without reasonable cause. The majority's contrary ruling, requiring a "commercially reasonable objection" to the assignment, can only result in a proliferation of unnecessary litigation. . . .

Notes

1. *The Interpretation of No–Transfer Clauses.* As *Kendall* notes, the law has generally enforced no-transfer clauses in leases as a reasonable restriction on alienation, given the limited duration of such restrictions and the legitimate purpose they serve (protecting the landlord's interest in the identity and financial wherewithal of the possessor of the leased premises). But because these clauses operate as restraints on alienation, courts have tended to interpret them strictly, sometimes construing ambiguous clauses in a manner that promotes alienability of the leasehold premises. For example, if a lease clause provides only that the tenant cannot "assign" her interest without the landlord's consent, the clause *generally* will not be deemed to prohibit the tenant from subleasing its interest. Likewise, if a clause prohibits only "subleasing," courts *generally* have interpreted it not to prohibit the tenant from assigning its interest. *Compare Serio v. Stewart Invs., Inc.*, 427 So.2d 692 (La. App. 1983) (clause restricting right to sublet

---

9. Amicus Pillsbury, Madison & Sutro requests that we make clear that, "whatever principle governs in the absence of express lease provisions, nothing bars the parties to commercial lease transactions from making their own arrangements respecting the allocation of appreciated rentals if there is a transfer of the leasehold." This princi- ple we affirm; we merely hold that the clause in the instant lease established no such arrangement. [Editors' Note: In 1989, the California legislature enacted Civil Code § 1995.230, which specifically provides that "[a] restriction on transfer of a tenant's interest in a lease may absolutely prohibit transfer."]

also restricted right to assign) *with Krasner v. Transcontinental Equities, Inc.*, 70 A.D.2d 312, 420 N.Y.S.2d 872 (1979) (clause requiring consent to sublease did not apply to assignments).

The no-transfer clause in *Kendall* did not expressly limit the landlord's right to withhold consent. As *Kendall* notes, courts in many jurisdictions have concluded that an unqualified right to withhold consent means that the landlord can withhold consent for any reason, even an arbitrary and purportedly unreasonable one.[10] In a growing minority of jurisdictions, however, courts have embraced the *Kendall* view that landlords may withhold consent only when the landlord has a commercially reasonable objection to the assignment or sublease.

Kendall expressly reserved the question whether its decision applied to residential leases. Does the court's rationale apply with equal force to the transfer of residential leases? For example, suppose that *L* leases an apartment to *T*, a college student, for one year at a monthly rent of $500. The lease provides that *T* may not sublet or assign her interest without the consent of *L*. *L* refuses to consent when *T* proposes to assign the last three months of the lease (May 15–August 15) to another college student. Should the court imply a covenant not to withhold consent unreasonably? [Would it matter if the apartment was a duplex and *L* lived in the other half?] How should the effect and duration of the restraint on alienation imposed by a no-transfer clause affect a court's interpretation of whether to imply a covenant not to withhold consent unreasonably?

2. *What Objections to Transfer Are "Reasonable"?* Sometimes, a lease will require that the tenant obtain the consent of the landlord prior to any transfer of the premises, but will also provide that the landlord may not withhold consent "unreasonably." In such cases, when the landlord refuses to consent and a dispute arises over the landlord's refusal, the court must examine the landlord's justification(s) for withholding consent to determine whether the landlord's decision was reasonable under the circumstances. In other words, the courts generally uphold the validity of the no-transfer clause itself (*i.e.*, the clause is treated as reasonable on its face), but look closely at how the landlord is applying the clause.

What valid purposes does the *Kendall* court suggest a no-transfer clause serves? What improper purposes does the *Kendall* court suggest a no-transfer clause may promote? Consider the following problems:

(a) *L*, a religiously affiliated university, refuses to consent to a proposed assignment of commercial office space to Planned Parenthood. Is *L*'s refusal reasonable? *See American Book Co. v. Yeshiva Univ. Dev. Found., Inc.*, 59 Misc.2d 31, 297 N.Y.S.2d 156 (Sup. Ct. 1969). Now suppose that the office building had been owned by a real estate developer at the time *T* signed its lease, and was subsequently sold to *L*. Would this affect your analysis regarding whether *L*'s refusal was reasonable?

10. The landlord's right to refuse consent still would be subject to the provisions of the Fair Housing Act, discussed beginning on page 539. This would prevent a residential landlord from refusing a proposed transferee on the basis of race, sex, national origin, or other characteristic that identifies a protected class under the statute.

(b) *L* leases a commercial property to *T* for 20 years at a monthly rent of $5,000, subject to an annual adjustment in rent to reflect increases in the cost of living index. The lease provides *T* with an option to renew for an additional 10 years. In Year 15, *L* refuses to consent to a proposed assignment to *T1*, who happens to be an existing tenant of *L* in a different commercial building. Is *L*'s refusal reasonable? *See Krieger v. Helmsley–Spear, Inc.*, 62 N.J. 423, 302 A.2d 129 (1973).

(c) *L* refuses to consent to a proposed sublease without asking about its terms, and subsequently agrees to consent only after *T* agrees to modify the primary lease. Is *L*'s refusal reasonable? *See D.L. Dev., Inc. v. Nance*, 894 S.W.2d 258 (Mo. Ct. App. 1995).

3. *Withholding Consent to Capture Leasehold Bonus Value.* How would you assess the court's analysis of who should capture the increased market value of the leasehold estate? Is it helpful to focus, as the *Kendall* court did, on who is "entitled" to that increase? How else might the court have analyzed this issue? On what bases might a tenant in Bixler's position reasonably have expected the landlord to object to the proposed transfer? [Hint: Why might a landlord of an office building or a shopping center be concerned if one of its tenants is trying to assign/sublet its space?]

Does the following hypothetical provide a useful analogy to the situation in *Kendall*? Suppose that in 1972, Serena took out a 30–year mortgage to purchase her home, at an interest rate of 5%. The mortgage contained a "due-on-sale" clause allowing the lender to accelerate the maturity of the mortgage debt in the event of a sale of the home. In 1982 (when prevailing mortgage interest rates were 17–18% or more), Serena wanted to sell her home to Ben. She sought the lender's consent to the sale and its permission to allow Ben—who was steadily employed and had a higher salary and net worth than Serena—to take over responsibility for the remaining mortgage payments. The lender refused and insisted that if Serena went through with the sale, she would have to pay off the entire balance of the mortgage. Can the lender enforce the due-on-sale clause in this situation? *Compare Wellenkamp v. Bank of Am.*, 21 Cal.3d 943, 148 Cal.Rptr. 379, 582 P.2d 970 (1978) (no) *with Tierce v. APS Co.*, 382 So.2d 485 (Ala. 1979) (yes). In the wake of the savings and loan crisis, Congress adopted the Garn–St. Germain Act, 12 U.S.C. § 1701j–3, which provides that a mortgage lender can exercise a due-on-sale clause notwithstanding contrary state laws such as the *Wellenkamp* decision. Is a mortgage lender's decision to exercise a due-on-sale clause meaningfully different from Pestana's refusal to permit Bixler to transfer his lease? *See* Alex M. Johnson, Jr., *Correctly Interpreting Long–Term Leases Pursuant to Modern Contract Law: Toward a Theory of Relational Leases*, 74 Va. L. Rev. 751 (1988).

As footnote 9 notes, landlords and tenants are free to make express provisions regarding treatment of bonus value in the event of a transfer, and courts will freely enforce such express agreements. These provisions sometimes take the form of "recapture clauses" under which the tenant agrees to pay over some or all of the bonus value (pursuant to a formula established by the lease) in the event of a transfer to which the landlord consents. Alternatively, some leases provide that if the tenant requests that the landlord consent to a proposed transfer, the landlord can terminate the lease and negotiate with the proposed transferee directly. *See, e.g., Carma Developers v. Marathon Dev. Cal., Inc.*, 2 Cal.4th 342, 6 Cal.Rptr.2d 467, 826 P.2d 710 (1992). Which type of provision might a landlord prefer to have in its lease, and why? If you were representing a tenant whose lease contained the latter type of provision, how would you counsel the tenant if she wished to transfer her interest and capture some of the bonus value reflected in the lease?

———

Suppose that *L* and *T* have a 10–year lease with an agreed rental of $1,000/month. *T* then transfers her leasehold estate to *T1*, and *T1* takes possession—but thereafter neither *T* nor *T1* pays rent to *L*. What rights does *L* have in this situation? Certainly, assuming that the lease permits *L* to terminate the lease for failure to pay rent (as leases typically do), *L* may terminate the lease and evict *T1*. But suppose that three months have already passed before *L* can complete an eviction proceeding—and $3,000 of accrued rent remains unpaid. Can *L* recover this amount from *T1*? From *T*?

If the original lease contained an unconditional promise by *T* to pay all rent that accrued during the lease term (as leases typically do), then the lease placed *L* and *T* in *privity of contract* (see page 412). This privity of contract permits *L* to recover the unpaid rent from *T*—even though *T* had already transferred her interest before the rent in question accrued. It does not matter whether *T*'s transfer to *T1* was an assignment or a sublease, nor does it matter whether *L* consented to *T*'s transfer. *T* remains liable to *L* for all rent that accrues during the term of the lease unless *L* expressly releases *T* from liability for rent. [Note that *L*'s consent to *T*'s transfer to *T1* does not impliedly release *T* from liability. Can you explain why?]

Whether *L* can recover the unpaid rent from *T1*, however, depends upon whether *T*'s transfer to *T1* constituted an assignment or a sublease. By virtue of an assignment, the tenant places the assignee in *privity of estate* with the landlord—and while the assignee and the landlord remain in privity of estate, the landlord can hold the assignee personally liable on the covenants expressed in the lease (including the covenant to pay rent). By contrast, a sublease does not place the sublessee and the landlord in privity of estate—and thus a landlord cannot hold a sublessee personally liable on the lease covenants (unless the sublessee expressly agrees to assume such liability).

ERNST v. CONDITT

Court of Appeals of Tennessee.
54 Tenn.App. 328, 390 S.W.2d 703 (1964).

CHATTIN, JUDGE. Complainants, B. Walter Ernst and wife, Emily Ernst, leased a certain tract of land in Davidson County, Tennessee, to Frank D. Rogers on June 18, 1960, for a term of one year and seven days, commencing on June 23, 1960.

Rogers went into possession of the property and constructed an asphalt race track and enclosed the premises with a fence. He also constructed other improvements thereon such as floodlights for use in the operation of a Go–Cart track.

We quote those paragraphs of the lease pertinent to the question for consideration in this controversy:

3.   Lessee covenants to pay as rent for said leased premises the sum of $4,200 per annum, payable at the rate of $350 per month or 15% of all gross receipts, whether from sales or services occurring on the leased premises, whichever is the larger amount. The gross receipts shall be computed on a quarterly basis and if any amount in addition to the $350 per month is due, such payment shall be made immediately after the quarterly computation. All payments shall be payable to the office of Lessors' agent, Guaranty Mortgage Company, at 316 Union Street, Nashville, Tennessee, on the first day of each month in advance. Lessee shall have the first right of refusal in the event Lessors desire to lease said premises for a period of time commencing immediately after the termination date hereof.

5.   Lessee shall have no right to assign or sublet the leased premises without prior written approval of Lessors. In the event of any assignment or sublease, Lessee is still liable to perform the covenants of this lease, including the covenant to pay rent, and nothing herein shall be construed as releasing Lessee from his liabilities and obligations hereunder.

9.   Lessee agrees that upon termination of this contract, or any extensions or renewals thereof, that all improvements above the ground will be moved at Lessee's expense and the property cleared. This shall not be construed as removing or digging up any surface paving; but if any pits or holes are dug, they shall be leveled at Lessors' request.

Rogers operated the business for a short time. In July, 1960, he entered into negotiations with the defendant, A.K. Conditt, for the sale of the business to him. During these negotiations, the question of the term of the lease arose. Defendant desired a two-year lease of the property. He and Rogers went to the home of complainants and negotiated an extension of the term of the lease which resulted in the following amendment to the lease, and the sublease or assignment of the lease as amended to Conditt by Rogers:

By mutual consent of the parties, the lease executed the 18th day of June 1960, between B. Walter Ernst and wife, Emily H. Ernst, as Lessors, and Frank G. Rogers as Lessee, is amended as follows:

1.   Paragraph 2 of said lease is amended so as to provide that the term will end July 31, 1962 and not June 30, 1961.

2.   The minimum rent of $350 per month called for in paragraph 3 of said lease shall be payable by the month and the percentage rental called for by said lease shall be payable on the first day of the

month following the month for which the percentage is computed. In computing gross receipts, no deduction or credit shall be given the Lessee for the payment of sales taxes or any other assessments by governmental agencies.

3.   Lessee agrees that on or prior to April 1, 1961, the portion of the property covered by this lease, consisting of about one acre, which is not presently devoted to business purposes will be used for business purposes and the percentage rent called for by paragraph 3 of the original lease will be paid on the gross receipts derived therefrom. In the event of the failure of the Lessee to devote the balance of said property to a business purpose on or before April 1, 1961, then this lease shall terminate as to such portion of the property.

4.   Lessee agrees to save the Lessor harmless for any damage to the property of the Lessor, whether included in this lease or not, which results from the use of the leased property by the Lessee or its customers or invitees. Lessee will erect or cause to be erected four (4) "No Parking" signs on the adjoining property of the Lessor not leased by it.

5.   Lessor hereby consents to the subletting of the premises to A.K. Conditt, but upon the express condition and understanding that the original Lessee, Frank K. Rogers, will remain personally liable for the faithful performance of all the terms and conditions of the original lease and of this amendment to the original lease.

Except as modified by this amendment, all terms and conditions of the original lease dated the 18th day of June, 1960, by and between the parties shall remain in full force and effect.

In witness whereof the parties have executed this amendment to lease on this the 4 day of August, 1960.

        B. Walter Ernst, Emily H. Ernst   Frank D. Rogers
                    Lessors   Lessee

For value received and in consideration of the promise to faithfully perform all conditions of the within lease as amended, I hereby sublet the premises to A.K. Conditt upon the understanding that I will individually remain liable for the performance of the lease.

This 4 day of Aug, 1960.

        [signed]   Frank D. Rogers

The foregoing subletting of the premises is accepted, this the 4 day of Aug, 1960.

        [signed]   A. K. Conditt.

Conditt operated the Go–Cart track from August until November, 1960. He paid the rent for the months of August, September and October, 1960, directly to complainants. In December, 1960, complainants contacted defendant with reference to the November rent and at that time defendant stated he had been advised he was not liable to them for rent. However, defendant paid the basic monthly rental of $350.00 to complainants in June, 1961. This was the final payment received by complainants during the term of the lease as amended. The record is not clear whether defendant continued to operate the business after the last payment of rent or abandoned it. Defendant, however, remained in possession of the property until the expiration of the leasehold.

On July 10, 1962, complainants, through their Attorneys, notified Conditt by letter the lease would expire as of midnight July 31, 1962; and they were demanding a settlement of the past due rent and unless the improvements on the property were removed by him as provided in paragraph 9 of the original lease; then, in that event, they would have same removed at his expense. Defendant did not reply to this demand.

On August 1, 1962, complainants filed their bill in this cause seeking a recovery of $2,404.58 which they alleged was the balance due on the basic rent of $350.00 per month for the first year of the lease and the sum of $4,200.00, the basic rent for the second year, and the further sum necessary for the removal of the improvements constructed on the property.

The theory of the bill is that the agreement between Rogers, the original lessee, and the defendant, Conditt, is an assignment of the lease; and, therefore, defendant is directly and primarily liable to complainants.

The defendant by his answer insists the agreement between Rogers and himself is a sublease and therefore Rogers is directly and primarily liable to complainants.

The Chancellor heard the matter on the depositions of both complainants and three other witnesses offered in behalf of complainants and documentary evidence filed in the record. The defendant did not testify nor did he offer any evidence in his behalf.

The Chancellor found the instrument to be an assignment. A decree was entered sustaining the bill and entering judgment for complainants in the sum of $6,904.58 against defendant.

Defendant has appealed to this Court and has assigned errors insisting the Chancellor erred in failing to hold the instrument to be a sublease rather than an assignment.

To support his theory the instrument is a sublease, the defendant insists the amendment to the lease entered into between Rogers and complainants was for the express purpose of extending the term of the lease and obtaining the consent of the lessors to a "subletting" of the premises to defendant. That by the use of the words "sublet" and "subletting" no other construction can be placed on the amendment and the agreement of Rogers and the acceptance of defendant attached thereto.

Further, since complainants agreed to the subletting of the premises to defendant "upon the express condition and understanding that the original lessee, Frank D. Rogers, will remain personally liable for the faithful performance of all the terms and conditions of the original lease and this amendment to the original lease," no construction can be placed upon this language other than it was the intention of complainants to hold Rogers primarily liable for the performance of the original lease and the amendment thereto. And, therefore, Rogers, for his own protection, would have the implied right to re-enter and perform the lease in the event of a default on the part of the defendant. This being true, Rogers retained a reversionary interest in the property sufficient to satisfy the legal distinction between a sublease and an assignment of a lease.

It is then urged the following rules of construction of written instruments support the above argument: "Where words or terms having a definite legal meaning and effect are knowingly used in a written instrument the parties thereto will be presumed to have intended such words or terms to have their proper legal meaning and effect, in the absence of any contrary intention appearing in the instrument." 12 Am.Jur., Contracts, Section 238. "Technical terms or words of art will be given their technical meaning unless the context, or local usage shows a contrary intention." 3 Williston on Contracts, Section 68, Sub. S. 2.

As stated in complainants' brief, the liability of defendant to complainants depends upon whether the transfer of the leasehold interest in the premises from Rogers is an assignment of the lease or a sublease. If the transfer is a sublease, no privity of [estate] exists between complainants and defendant; and, therefore, defendant could not be liable to complainants on the covenant to pay rent and the expense of the removal of the improvements. But, if the transfer is an assignment of the lease, privity of [estate] does exist between complainants and defendant; and defendant would be liable directly and primarily for the amount of the judgment. *Brummitt Tire Company v. Sinclair Refining Company*, 18 Tenn.App. 270, 75 S.W.2d 1022; *Commercial Club v. Epperson*, 15 Tenn.App. 649.

The general rule as to the distinction between an assignment of a lease and a sublease is an assignment conveys the whole term, leaving no interest nor reversionary interest in the grantor or assignor. Whereas, a sublease may be generally defined as a transaction whereby a tenant grants an interest in the leased premises less than his own, or reserves to himself a reversionary interest in the term.

The common law distinction between an assignment of a lease and a sublease is succinctly stated in the case of *Jaber v. Miller*, 219 Ark. 59, 239 S.W.2d 760: "If the instrument purports to transfer the lessee's estate for the entire remainder of his term it is an assignment, regardless of its form or of the parties' intention. Conversely, if the instrument purports to transfer the lessee's estate for less than the entire term— even for a day less—it is a sublease, regardless of its form or of the parties' intention."

The modern rule which has been adopted in this State for construing written instruments is stated in the case of *City of Nashville v.*

Lawrence, 153 Tenn. 606, 284 S.W. 882: "The cardinal rule to be followed in this state, in construing deeds and other written instruments, is to ascertain the intention of the parties." . . .

It is our opinion under either the common law or modern rule of construction the agreement between Rogers and defendant is an assignment of the lease.

The fact that Rogers expressly agreed to remain liable to complainants for the performance of the lease did not create a reversion nor a right to re-enter in Rogers either express or implied. The obligations and liabilities of a lessee to a lessor, under the express covenants of a lease, are not in anywise affected by an assignment or a subletting to a third party, in the absence of an express or implied agreement or some action on his part which amounts to a waiver or estops him from insisting upon compliance with the covenants. This is true even though the assignment or sublease is made with the consent of the lessor. By an assignment of a lease the privity of estate between the lessor and lessee is terminated, but the privity of contract between them still remains and is unaffected. Neither the privity of estate or contract between the lessor and lessee are affected by a sublease. 32 Am.Jur., Landlord and Tenant, Sections 356, 413, pages 310, 339.

Thus, the express agreement of Rogers to remain personally liable for the performance of the covenants of the lease created no greater obligation on his part or interest in the leasehold, other than as set forth in the original lease.

The argument that since the agreement between Rogers and defendant contains the words, "sublet" and "subletting" is conclusive the instrument is to be construed as a sublease is, we think, unsound. "A consent to sublet has been held to include the consent to assign or mortgage the lease; and a consent to assign has been held to authorize a subletting." 51 C.J.S. Landlord and Tenant § 36, page 552.

Prior to the consummation of the sale of the Go–Cart business to defendant, he insisted upon the execution of the amendment to the lease extending the term of the original lease. For value received and on the promise of the defendant to perform all of the conditions of the lease as amended, Rogers parted with his entire interest in the property. Defendant went into possession of the property and paid the rent to complainants. He remained in possession of the property for the entire term. By virtue of the sale of the business, defendant became the owner of the improvements with the right to their removal at the expiration of the lease.

Rogers reserved no part or interest in the lease; nor did he reserve a right of re-entry in event of a breach of any of the conditions or covenants of the lease on the part of defendant.

It is our opinion the defendant, under the terms of the agreement with Rogers, had a right to the possession of the property for the entire term of the lease as amended, including the right to remove the improvements after the expiration of the lease. Rogers merely agreed to become personally liable for the rent and the expense of the removal of the improvements upon the default of defendant. He neither expressly, nor by implication, reserved the right to re-enter for a condition broken by defendant.

Thus, we are of the opinion the use of the words, "sublet" and "subletting" is not conclusive of the construction to be placed on the instrument in this case; it plainly appearing from the context of the instrument and the facts and circumstances surrounding the execution of it the parties thereto intended an assignment rather than a sublease. . . .

Notes

1. *Privity of Contract, Privity of Estate, and the Covenant to Pay Rent.* When a landlord and tenant enter into a lease, the law deems them to be in *privity of estate* based upon the lessor-lessee relationship created by the lease. The law also deems them to be in *privity of contract* based upon their mutual promises. To enforce the covenants of a lease against the possessor, the landlord must either be in privity of estate or privity of contract with the possessor. Thus, the Ernsts could have proceeded against Rogers (the original tenant) for the rent, as they never released Rogers from his contractual obligations.

The Ernsts, however, sought to recover rent from Conditt. [Can you explain why?] As Conditt never directly promised the Ernsts to pay them rent, the only way the Ernsts could collect rent from Conditt was to argue that the covenant to pay rent in the lease "ran with the land"—so that Conditt (having received possession by transfer from Rogers) was liable to pay rent as long as he remained in possession of the land. As we will discuss in greater detail in Chapter 8, the burden of a covenant cannot "run with the land" in an action to recover a money judgment unless there is sufficient privity of estate. Thus, Conditt's liability depends upon whether the transfer from Rogers to Conditt placed Conditt in privity of estate with Ernst. By characterizing the transfer as an assignment, the court concludes that Conditt was liable for rent that accrued after the transfer occurred.

2. *Assignment or Sublease? Form, Substance and the Role of "Intent."* Most courts distinguish assignments and subleases by the traditional rule that focuses upon the duration of the tenant's transfer and whether the tenant has retained any interest in the premises. If the tenant transferred its entire remaining interest (measured in duration), the courts treat the transfer as an assignment; if the tenant transferred less than its entire remaining interest (thereby retaining a reversionary interest), then the transfer is a sublease. Suppose that the agreement between Rogers and Conditt had provided as follows: "In the event that Conditt shall fail to perform the terms of this agreement, Rogers may re-enter and terminate Conditt's estate." Would such a right of re-entry constitute a reversionary interest sufficient to make the transfer a sublease? *Compare Rocklen, Inc. v. Radulesco,* 10 Conn.App. 271, 522 A.2d 846 (1987) *with American Cmty. Stores v. Newman,* 232 Neb. 434, 441 N.W.2d 154 (1989).

As *Ernst* suggests, a number of recent decisions conclude that whether a transfer is an assignment or a sublease is governed by "the intent of the parties" as reflected by the language of their agreement. *See, e.g., Jaber v. Miller*, 219 Ark. 59, 239 S.W.2d 760 (1951). Given that Rogers and Conditt characterized the transfer as a "sublease," why doesn't the court treat the agreement as a sublease? Do you think that the term "sublease" was indicative of their intent regarding the nature of the transfer? What might explain why they used the term "sublease" if the document purported to transfer Rogers's right for the remainder of the lease term?

3. *Problems.* To test your understanding of the extent to which the covenant to pay rent "runs with the land," consider the following problems:

(a) *L* rents to *T* for a term of three years, with monthly rental fixed at $500 per month. *T* assigns to *T1*. With one year left on the lease, *T1* assigns to *T2*. For the last four months of the lease the rent goes unpaid. Who has liability to *L* for unpaid rent, and why? Assuming *L* collects from *T*, does *T* have any recourse against *T1*?

(b) *L* rents to *T* for a term of one year, with monthly rental fixed at $500 per month. At the end of one year, *L* and *T* agree that *T* can remain in possession on a month-to-month basis for the same rent. *T* plans to leave for the summer and enters into an agreement with *T1* in which *T* "agrees to sublease and assign to *T1* all its rights and interests" in the property from May 15 until August 15. *T1* agrees with *T* to pay the rent directly to *L*. *T1* subsequently fails to pay the rent. Who has liability to *L* for unpaid rent? Consider the Restatement (Second) of Property, Landlord and Tenant, § 16.1, cmt. c, at 120–21 (1977) (discussing possible third-party beneficiary argument of landlord).

4. *No-Transfer Clauses and Successive Transfers.* Consider the following variation of the facts in *Ernst v. Conditt*. Suppose that six months after the original transfer (from Rogers to Conditt), Conditt assigns the lease to Pushaw (who plans to operate the go-cart business). Because Pushaw has previously experienced several business failures, Ernst objects to the transfer and files suit seeking to terminate the lease for failure to obtain his consent. Conditt argues, however, that under the rule in *Dumpor's Case*, 76 Eng. Rep. 1110 (K.B. 1578), Ernst's approval of the original transfer had operated to waive his right to withhold consent to future transfers. Should Ernst's consent to the original transfer prevent him from objecting to the transfer to Pushaw?

There is some modern authority rejecting the rule in *Dumpor's Case. See, e.g., Boston Props. v. Pirelli Tire Corp.*, 134 Cal.App.3d 985, 185 Cal.Rptr. 56 (1982) ("the rule in Dumpor's Case is not the law in California"). However, there remain recent decisions applying the rule. *See, e.g., Italian Fisherman, Inc. v. Middlemas*, 313 Md. 156, 545 A.2d 1 (1988); *Snow v. Fitian*, 1998 WL 781173 (Mass. Ct. App. 1998). What policy, if any, might justify the rule in *Dumpor's Case*? How might a landlord protect itself from the risk presented by *Dumpor's Case*?

5. *Preventive Lawyering.* Suppose that you had represented the Ernsts at the time of Rogers' proposed transfer to Conditt. What would you have advised the Ernsts to do differently that could have avoided the litigation that ultimately arose?

LAWYERING EXERCISE
(Negotiation and Drafting)

SITUATION: Ten years ago, Jane Smith resigned her job as an accountant and started a business called "The Candy Factory, Inc." in which she made and sold homemade chocolates and other "designer" candies. She originally had operated from her home for two years, but eventually her business needed more space. Thus, she began negotiating with Fred Brown, owner of a large but nearly vacant commercial building on Main Street, to lease a portion of the building. Fred was desperate to get tenants into the building, which was located in an economically depressed area with a number of vacant buildings. Thus, he offered Jane a lease with extremely favorable terms—an initial term of six years at $300 per month rental, with Jane having options to renew the lease for an additional eight years (four additional periods of two years each) at a rent that increased up to $450 per month by the end of the eighth option year. Jane quickly agreed, and the parties signed a written lease that commenced on February 1. The lease provided as follows:

> Tenant may not assign, sublease, or otherwise transfer all or any portion of Tenant's interest in the premises without the prior written consent of Landlord. Landlord shall not withhold consent unreasonably. Should Tenant receive from the proposed transferee rent in excess of the minimum rent provided for in this Lease, Tenant agrees to pay to Landlord as additional rent 75% of the excess amount.

Jane has properly exercised each renewal option to this point. Over the past 10 years, due to a combination of factors, commercial development along Main Street unexpectedly boomed. Nearly 100 new national, regional, and local retailers have opened stores along Main Street within four blocks of the Candy Factory. Fred just recently rented another space in his building (essentially identical in size to the Candy Factory space) for $1,500 per month.

One year ago, however, a national candy retailer opened a store near Jane's Main Street location. Over the next year, this competition cut significantly into the profits Jane's business had been earning, to the point that Jane concluded she would earn more by returning to the practice of accounting. Jane has found a potential buyer for her business—David Jones, a soon-to-be-retired professor. Jane and David have agreed that David will purchase all of the assets of the business (her inventory is worth $5,000; her fixtures and equipment are worth $35,000; and she values the goodwill associated with the "Candy Factory" name at $10,000). David proposes to pay the agreed-upon rent directly to Fred for the duration of the lease, and to pay an additional $1,000 per month to Jane to reflect the market value of the premises. There is exactly one year remaining on the second option period, and two remaining two-year option periods thereafter.

TASK ONE. On behalf of either Jane, David, or Fred (as you are assigned), negotiate the terms of (a) the transfer of the business between Jane and David and (b) Fred's consent to a transfer of the lease. Prepare a memorandum of the agreed-upon terms for execution by the parties.

TASK TWO. Assume that you are representing Fred. Fred has several leases that are about to expire, and he wants you to review his form lease to make sure that it "doesn't need any modifications" before he has new tenants sign it. Review the assignment/subletting clause in his form lease (assume it is identical to the language quoted above), and advise Fred as to what changes (if any) you would suggest that he make to fully protect Fred's legal and economic interests.

2. *Issues Concerning the Use of the Premises*

Generally speaking, a tenant may use the leased premises for any lawful purpose, unless the lease itself contains an express use restriction or such a restriction must be implied. Milton R. Friedman & Patrick A. Randolph, Jr., 3 Friedman on Leases § 27.2, at 27–5 (5th ed. 2004). For a variety of reasons, the landlord may wish to have some control over the tenant's use of the premises, and accordingly leases typically do contain express use restrictions on the tenant's use. In some circumstances, a use restriction may be *prohibitory* in nature—*i.e.*, it may prohibit the tenant from making certain uses of the premises (*e.g.*, forbidding a commercial tenant from selling alcoholic beverages). Alternatively, a use restriction might be *permissive* or *authorizing* in nature, permitting the tenant to make *only* certain defined uses (*e.g.*, an apartment lease that states that the tenant is limited to "residential use only" or a commercial lease permitting the tenant to operate only a restaurant). Can you explain why a landlord might prefer to structure a use restriction one way or the other? *See id.* § 27.3.

The landlord and tenant must take care in negotiating and drafting use restrictions, to ensure that such restrictions are sufficiently clear and neither overbroad nor unduly narrow. For example, suppose that Barnes leases an apartment from Corrada for a two-year period, and that the lease provides that "Tenant shall use the premises for residential purposes only." Barnes moves into the apartment and uses it for his primary residence, but also operates his life insurance sales business from an office set up in a spare bedroom. Has Barnes breached the lease? *Compare Park West Village v. Lewis*, 62 N.Y.2d 431, 477 N.Y.S.2d 124, 465 N.E.2d 844 (1984) *with Galloway v. Ortega*, 61 Misc.2d 539, 305 N.Y.S.2d 546 (Yonkers City Ct. 1969). What additional information, if any, would you want to know about the situation? If a proposed tenant of Corrada wanted to clarify the language of this use restriction, should Corrada agree to be more precise?

Use restrictions appear in nearly all leases, but they are of particular importance in shopping center leases, which commonly restrict the tenant to making particular uses. In this way, a shopping center landlord can better assure that the center has the right "mix" of tenants to best attract customer traffic—and this mix will not be compromised by a tenant changing its use during the lease term. Does a shopping center lease also *require* the tenant to operate throughout the lease term? Or can the tenant choose to leave its leased space empty as long as it pays the agreed-upon rent? Consider the following case, in which two different Georgia courts disagreed.

PIGGLY WIGGLY SOUTHERN, INC. v. HEARD

Court of Appeals of Georgia.
197 Ga.App. 656, 399 S.E.2d 244 (1990).

DEEN, PRESIDING JUDGE. This appeal is from the grant of summary judgment to appellee landlords against appellant Piggly Wiggly Southern (hereinafter "PWS") in which the trial court ruled that PWS had breached an express and implied covenant in a lease contract between the parties. On January 21, 1963, PWS and the landlords' predecessor entered into a lease agreement whereby the landlords constructed a supermarket pursuant to plans and specifications prepared by PWS. The term of the lease was fifteen years with an expiration date of January 31, 1979, at an annual rent of $29,053.60 plus the payment of percentage rent in the amount of one percent of annual gross sales in excess of $2,000,000. The lease was subsequently renewed for an additional seven years, with options to extend the term for two additional periods of three years each at the same basic and percentage rental amounts. PWS exercised its first three-year option and, on June 23, 1988, exercised the second option to extend the lease period to January 31, 1992. When the lease was executed in 1963 the building constructed for PWS was the only one on the property, but by the time the 1979 extension was signed the landlords had built up a small neighborhood shopping center with eight other satellite shops centered around the supermarket as the anchor store.

On March 4, 1989, PWS ceased operating a grocery store at the leased premises after it was acquired by another corporation, which moved the grocery store operations into a supermarket location in a nearby shopping center it owned. Since that time the leased premises have remained vacant and no applications were made for a business license. PWS continued to make the base monthly payments, but no percentage rent has been paid since the closing of the store because there have been no sales. While other competing supermarkets have attempted to lease the property at considerably higher base rents, PWS has refused to sublease the premises to a competitor. The landlords filed the instant suit to recover damages in the form of percentage annual rents from the date operation of the supermarket ceased to the end of the second three-year option; damages for the alleged loss of percentage rent from other leases and diminution of property values in the shopping center; and attorney fees and expenses of litigation. By amendment, the landlords added a claim for punitive damages and sought a declaratory judgment that they were entitled to possession of the premises so that they could lease it to another tenant to operate as a grocery store business. Motions for summary judgment as to various counts of the complaint were filed by both parties. The trial court entered an order granting the landlords' motion on the basis of a breach of the lease contract by PWS and found that they were entitled to damages therefor, the amount to be determined later. It overruled PWS' motion for summary judgment but dismissed the count of the landlords' complaint seeking declaratory judgment. On appeal, PWS contends that the trial court erred in finding that it had breached the lease contract by failing to continuously occupy the premises and operate a business thereon; by denying its motion for summary judgment and failing to find that there was no express or implied covenant requiring it to continuously occupy the premises and operate a business thereon; and in finding that the landlords were entitled to damages based on its payment of past percentage rental.

> The lease provision in controversy provides as follows:
>
> LESSEE is leasing the leased building for use as a supermarket and the other parts of the leased property for parking and other uses incident to a supermarket business, but LESSEE's use of the leased building and the leased property shall not be limited nor restricted to such purposes, and said building and property may be used for any other lawful business, without the consent of LESSOR.

The trial court determined as a matter of law that this language gave rise to both an express and implied covenant on behalf of PWS to continuously conduct business in the leased premises, interpreting the term "any other ... business" as contemplating that some business enterprise must be conducted on the premises. PWS argues that such language permitting the leased premises to be used for certain purposes does not obligate the tenant to actually use the property for any purpose, and that the issues involved are controlled by the recent decisions of this court in *Piggly Wiggly Southern v. Eastgate Assoc., Ltd.*, 195 Ga.App. 10, 392 S.E.2d 337 (1990) and *Kroger Co. v. Bonny Corp.*, 134 Ga.App. 834, 216 S.E.2d 341 (1975), relied on therein.

Neither *Eastgate* nor *Bonny* involved a lease with language requiring that the leased property be used for a lawful *business*, only that the premises be used "in a lawful *manner*." (Emphasis supplied.) Moreover, as found by the trial court in the instant case, the percentage rent paid while the store was being operated under the lease amounted to more than half of the total rent (53 percent) during the lease extension period. Thus the base rent, which was not raised when the lease was extended, did not represent the fair market value of the premises when the first extension was executed. In *Eastgate* no percentage rent was ever paid because the grocery store never opened; in *Bonny* it was stipulated that the base rent represented the fair market rental for the property when the lease was executed and the percentage rent, which was paid in only one year of a 13–year lease, amounted to barely over one percent of the total payments made. Based on those facts it was held that " 'when the rental to be received under a lease is based on a percentage of the gross receipts of the business, with a substantial minimum [or base rent], there is no implied covenant that the lessee will operate its business in the leased premises throughout the term of the lease.' " *Eastgate, supra* 195 Ga.App. at 12, 392 S.E.2d 337.

The trial court found the case most factually similar to this one to be *Fifth Ave. Shopping Center v. Grand Union Co.*, 491 F.Supp. 77 (N.D.Ga.1980). Applying the above Georgia substantive law, the federal district court concluded that "if the parties to a lease contemplate that the amount of rent to be generated by a percentage payment clause will be substantially greater than the minimum rental specified in the contract, it is possible to infer an implied covenant that the lessee will operate its business in the leased premises throughout the term of the lease." *Id.* at 80–81. The *Fifth Ave.* case held that the base rent of only 57 percent of the total rental paid was "substantially below contemplated performance, and was therefore not 'substantial.' " *Id.* at 81. Utilizing this reasoning, the trial court held that in the lease under consideration, the term "business" use of the premises did not contemplate a closed or vacant store; and that the lease contained an affirmative business use obligation that was mandatory as well as retroactive, which meant that in the event PWS decided to cease operating its grocery store in the leased premises, which it could do under the lease, it still had the duty to carry on a business use within the premises so as to generate percentage payments.

We agree and affirm. The lease contract was prepared by PWS and thus, even though it is the tenant, was properly construed against it. *Farm Supply Co. of Albany v. Cook*, 116 Ga.App. 814, 818(2), fn. 2, 159 S.E.2d 128 (1967). The language permitting PWS to use the premises for "any other lawful business," as opposed to using it in "any lawful manner," clearly constitutes a business use covenant giving PWS the option to either use the premises for its supermarket or to use it or sublease it for some other lawful business use which would generate sales or other income. In contradistinction, if the covenant were only to use the premises in a lawful manner, there would be no obligation to operate a business during the term of the lease so long as the base rent was paid. The fact that the base rent of $29,053 a year paid by PWS is not an insubstantial sum standing alone, as it points out, does not negate the fact that when the percentage rent is equal to or greater than the base rent, the base rent is not considered "substantial" in the context of an implied use provision. Indeed, PWS was told when the 1979 extension was negotiated that the landlords would not raise the base rent agreed upon in 1963 because "the percentage rent will take care of inflation and we don't need to draw another lease with a new base rent."

Nor do we agree that if it were PWS's motive to refuse to sublease in order to keep out competition for the benefit of its other store, this could be construed as a business use. "This result would be intolerable and would destroy the good faith reliance among individuals which permits them to act in accordance with their agreements." *Brack v.*

Brownlee, 246 Ga. 818, 820, 273 S.E.2d 390 (1980). Furthermore, this court has previously recognized that the situation in a shopping center differs from that where the leased building stands alone: "Obviously landlord would not want a vacant store in its shopping center even though the original tenant remained solvent and paid the minimum monthly rental." *Buford-Clairmont v. Jacobs Pharmacy Co.*, 131 Ga.App. 643, 647(1), 206 S.E.2d 674 (1974). It follows that the trial court correctly granted summary judgment to the landlords and denied summary judgment to PWS on the issues of express and implied covenant to continuously occupy or sublease the premises and conduct a revenue-producing business therein under the terms of the lease. . . .

PIGGLY WIGGLY SOUTHERN, INC. v. HEARD

Supreme Court of Georgia.
261 Ga. 503, 405 S.E.2d 478 (1991).

HUNT, JUSTICE. . . . We granted the writ of certiorari to determine whether the Court of Appeals was correct in its construction of the parties' lease, and reverse. . . .

We agree with appellant that the lease agreement between the parties does not contain an express covenant of continuous operation. Rather, the language of the agreement is plainly to the contrary, and, therefore, the trial court, the Court of Appeals, and this court are not authorized to construe it otherwise. *Heyman v. Financial Properties Developers, Inc.*, 175 Ga.App. 146, 332 S.E.2d 893 (1985). The language of the agreement expressly negates a requirement of continuous operation: "... LESSEE'S use of the leased building and the leased property shall not be limited nor restricted to such purposes [use as a supermarket, etc.], and said building and property may be used *for any other lawful business*, without the consent of LESSOR" (emphasis supplied). *See Kroger, Co. v. Bonny Corp.*, 134 Ga.App. 834, 216 S.E.2d 341 (1975).

Nor does the lease agreement contain any provision which would create an implied covenant of continuous operation. Rather, the contract, read as a whole, indicates otherwise. The agreement's provision for free assignability by the tenant, without consent of the lessor, weighs strongly against a construction of the contract which would require the tenant to continue its business throughout the term of the lease. *Kroger, Co. v. Bonny Corp., supra* at 836(1), 216 S.E.2d 341. Likewise, the existence of a substantial minimum base rent, in addition to the provision for percentage rental payments, suggests the absence of an implied covenant of continuous operation. *Id.* at 838 to 839(2), 216 S.E.2d 341.

The parties did not agree to nor bargain for appellant's continuous operation of the premises, and we are not authorized to rewrite the contract to create such a provision. *See Coffee System of Atlanta v. Fox*, 227 Ga. 602, 182 S.E.2d 109 (1971). . . .

Notes

1. *Implication of a Continuous Operation Covenant.* As a general rule, there is no requirement that a tenant actually use or occupy the leased premises in the customary fashion. *Stevens v. Mobil Oil Corp.,* 412 F.Supp. 809 (E.D. Mich. 1976). If the tenant wishes to pay the rental stated in its lease but leave its premises empty—as Piggly Wiggly did in the principal case—that is the tenant's prerogative unless the lease otherwise provides. In the real estate industry, the problem in *Piggly Wiggly* is referred to as the problem of the tenant "going dark." Can you explain why a tenant such as Piggly Wiggly would close the store but continue to pay rent, rather than simply allowing the landlord to terminate the lease? Can you explain why a landlord should be concerned about a tenant going dark if that tenant continued to pay rent?

When tenants go dark, the landlord may argue that the tenant's action breaches the lease because the lease impliedly obligates the tenant to operate continuously for the duration of the lease term. In determining whether to imply an "operating covenant" into a lease, courts have taken the following factors into account:

- whether the minimum rent is below the fair market rental for comparable space when the parties executed the lease

- whether the lease provides for percentage rent and whether percentage rental payments are "substantial" in relation to minimum rent payments

- whether the lease is long-term or short-term

- whether the tenant has the right to assign or sublet under the terms of the lease

- whether the tenant has the right to remove and retain fixtures at the end of the lease term

- whether the lease contains a "noncompetition" clause, under which the landlord agrees not to lease space to a business that would compete with the tenant's business

- whether the tenant is an "anchor" tenant (*e.g.*, the primary or largest tenant, such as a supermarket or department store in a neighborhood shopping center)

- whether the tenant or the landlord drafted the lease

Can you explain why each of these factors is or might be relevant to this issue?

A number of courts, like the court of appeals in *Piggly Wiggly*, have demonstrated a willingness to imply a continuous operation covenant into commercial leases. *See, e.g., Columbia East Assocs. v. Bi–Lo, Inc.,* 299 S.C. 515, 386 S.E.2d 259 (Ct. App. 1989); *Ingannamorte v. Kings Super Mkts., Inc.,* 55 N.J. 223, 260 A.2d 841 (1970). But a significant number of courts have expressed a strong unwillingness to imply a duty of continuous operation into commercial leases. *See, e.g., Sampson Invs. v. Jondex Corp.,* 176 Wis.2d 55, 499 N.W.2d 177 (1993) ("[A] commercial lessee is not required to continue operating a business in the absence of a lease which expressly requires continuous operation.''). Do you think that a court should imply a covenant of continuous operation into an anchor tenant shopping center lease? Is the Supreme Court in *Piggly Wiggly* suggesting that it is *never* appropriate for a court to imply a duty of continuous operation into such a lease? If so, why? If not, under what circumstances do you think the court would imply a duty of continuous operation? *Cf. Lagrew v. Hooks–SupeRx, Inc.*, 905 F.Supp. 401 (E.D. Ky. 1995); *Westside Ctr. Assocs. v. Safeway Stores*, 42 Cal.App.4th 507, 49 Cal.Rptr.2d 793 (1996); *Serfecz v. Jewel Food Stores*, 67 F.3d 591 (7th Cir. 1995); Patrick Randolph, *Going Dark Aggressively*, 10 Prob. & Prop. (Nov.-Dec. 1996), at 6.

2. *Remedies for Breach of Operating Covenant.* Suppose that Trump, owner of Trump Plaza Mall, proposes to enter into a 20–year lease with Kerr Drug, which operates a pharmacy. The parties have agreed that the lease will contain an express operating covenant. What remedies can Trump expect to obtain if Kerr Drug breaches that covenant? Why might Trump want a provision allowing him to obtain injunctive relief to enforce the covenant? If the lease contains such a provision, would this provide Trump with sufficient assurance against the risk that Kerr Drug might later go dark? *See, e.g., Madison Plaza, Inc. v. Shapira Corp.*, 180 Ind.App. 141, 387 N.E.2d 483 (1979).

3. *The Structure and Interpretation of Percentage Rental Provisions.* Most reported cases in which courts have implied operating covenants involve leases that obligated the tenant to pay some or all of its rent based upon a specified percentage of some or all of the tenant's sales. Percentage rental provisions come in several varieties, but the most common is reflected in *Piggly Wiggly*, where the lease provides both for a fixed minimum rent and a percentage rent based upon a percentage of tenant's gross sales above a certain level (called the "breakpoint"). Under this approach, the tenant need not pay any percentage rent until its gross sales exceed the breakpoint.

A tenant may prefer a percentage rent clause as a hedge against the risk that the tenant does not meet its business projections. For example, a tenant might project that it will have gross sales of $1 million per year, but not if its primary competitor opens a store in the area. Thus, the tenant might prefer to structure a rental provision whereby it paid a fixed rent of $25,000 per year plus 5% of gross sales over $500,000, rather than a fixed rent of $50,000 per year with no percentage rental obligation. In this way, the tenant could "trade off" the risk of paying more in total rent (if its sales exceed $1 million) against the possibility that it might pay less in rent if its competitor opened a store and drove its sales beneath the projected $1 million mark. Similarly, a landlord may view a percentage rent clause as an indirect investment in the tenant's business, allowing the landlord to capture some benefit from the tenant's success without bearing additional risk (*i.e.*, risk beyond nonpayment of rent) if the tenant's business is not successful.

In other situations—particularly in long-term leases—a percentage rent provision functions as an inflation hedge. If the landlord signs a 20–year lease at a fixed minimum rent of $10,000 per year, and then inflation increases by 5% per year over the period of the lease, the landlord's rental stream (the $10,000 per year) becomes progressively less valuable in real terms, because inflation cumulatively diminishes the purchasing power of that $10,000. But if rent is calculated based upon a percentage of sales, then tenant's total gross sales will likely increase over time (due to the inflationary increases in tenant's prices)—and tenant's total rental obligation will increase accordingly. What other alternatives could you suggest for protecting the landlord against the risks presented by inflation?

The negotiation and drafting of a percentage rental clause presents a number of potential strategic and interpretational questions that the attorney must appreciate. For example, consider the following:

(a) Apu leases land from Smithers and operates a convenience store. The lease obligates Apu to pay percentage rental of 4% of gross sales, defined as "gross receipts of every kind and nature originating from sales and services on the demised premises, whether on credit or for cash, except for rebates and/or refunds to customers, refundable deposits on beverage bottles, and the amount of any sales or other transactions taxes collected and/or paid either directly or indirectly by Lessee to any governmental agency." During 1998, Apu has total gross sales of $1.5 million, including $150,000 from the sale of lottery tickets. Apu sells lottery tickets pursuant to a license from the state lottery commission, which pays him a commission of 3% of every lottery ticket sold. Smithers argues that Apu must pay percentage rent on the full $150,000 in ticket sales, not just the 3% commission. Is he correct? *In re Circle K Corp.*, 98 F.3d 484 (9th Cir. 1996).

(b) Kroger is the anchor tenant in North Hills Shopping Center, operating a grocery store under a 25–year lease requiring percentage rent of 1% of gross sales exceeding $2.5 million per year. Kroger proposes to assign the lease to Sam's Antiques, which plans to open the world's largest antique store. The lease provides that the landlord will not unreasonably withhold consent to a proposed assignment. Can the landlord object to the assignment to Sam's Antiques? Why or why not?

4. *Covenants Not to Compete (Exclusives)—Interpretation and Remedies for Breach.* In some situations, a landlord may agree to protect a commercial retail tenant against potential competitors by granting that tenant either a *true exclusive* or a *limited exclusive*. A true exclusive provision gives the tenant the exclusive right to sell certain products or types of merchandise within a defined area (*e.g.*, a portion of a shopping center or the entire center). By contrast, a limited exclusive gives the tenant the exclusive right to conduct a particular type of business, such as the only grocery store in a shopping center. A limited exclusive usually provides less protection from competition, as other retail tenants might sell food items without actually operating a grocery store. In some cases, these exclusive rights may even extend to other land owned by landlord within a specific geographical area surrounding the center (a "radius restriction"). Courts have generally enforced unambiguous noncompete clauses, treating them as reasonable and rejecting arguments that they constitute an unenforceable restraint on trade. Can you explain why? *National Super Mkts., Inc. v. Magna Trust Co.*, 212 Ill.App.3d 358, 156 Ill.Dec. 469, 570 N.E.2d 1191 (1991); Baum, *Lessors' Covenants Restricting Competition*, 1965 U. Ill. L. F. 228.

Nevertheless, courts have expressed a willingness to construe ambiguous provisions narrowly. For example, in *Almacs Inc. v. Drogin*, 771 F.Supp. 506 (D.R.I. 1991), Almacs operated a grocery store pursuant to a lease that provided "[n]o store in the Shopping Center except that of the Tenant shall ... sell, as the major part of its activity, food and food products, dry groceries, [or] fruit and vegetables." Landlord then signed a lease for unoccupied space within the shopping center with Woolworth's, which planned to open a deep-discount drug store that would carry a significant number of food items, as well as health and beauty aids customarily sold in grocery stores such as Almacs. Almacs sued, alleging that Woolworth's operations would breach the exclusive provisions in Almacs' lease, but the court entered judgment for the landlord, concluding that the provision was ambiguous and that "ambiguity is to be resolved in favor of an unrestricted use." *Id.* at 510. Does this construction make good sense?

Where a tenant has a noncompete clause, the tenant must give careful consideration to the remedies available if landlord breaches the clause. Suppose that Fashion Plate, Inc. is negotiating for a seven-year lease to operate a clothing store in Bronco Acres Shopping Center (owned by Elway). Fashion Plate has asked for, and Elway has agreed to, a clause granting Fashion Plate the exclusive right to sell women's apparel in Bronco Acres, subject only to sales of women's apparel by the existing anchor tenant, BigMart. Elway's form lease provides that if the landlord breaches the lease in any respect, tenant can recover the damages proximately caused by the landlord's breach. How would you attempt to revise Elway's form lease to provide sufficient protection of Fashion Plate's noncompete clause?

5. *Restrictions on the Landlord's Conduct?* Use restrictions in leases typically address concerns about the tenant's use. Nevertheless, a tenant might justifiably be concerned about the landlord's decisions regarding the property. For example, suppose that *L* owns Lincoln Square Shopping Center, located on 200 acres of land at the heart of the area's retail shopping district. In August 2004, the lease of Target (the anchor tenant) expired, and Target decided not to exercise its renewal option. For six months, *L* tried to find a new anchor tenant, but without success (the area was experiencing a high vacancy rate for commercial retail space due to a recent construction boom). Finally, out of desperation, in February 2005, *L* signed a 20–year lease for the space with the Internal Revenue Service, which planned to use the space for two purposes: (a) to install 20 mainframe computers to be used for digital storage of tax returns; and (b) to operate a small customer service office. As soon as *L* announced the signing of the lease with the IRS, Rack Room Shoes filed a lawsuit against *L*. Rack Room is a tenant in Lincoln Square, having signed a 15–year lease back in 2000 for the space next to the anchor tenant. Rack Room's complaint asks for a declaration that its lease (and its obligation for rent) is terminated as a result of the IRS lease, and it also asks for damages from *L*. The lease contains no specific language that addresses this situation. If you were representing Rack Room, what theories would you raise in support of the complaint? What additional information, if any, would you like to know if you were advising Rack Room regarding its likelihood of success?

LAWYERING EXERCISE
(Problem Solving, Negotiation, and Drafting)

BACKGROUND: The issue of whether a retail tenant has a duty to operate demonstrates one instance in which landlords and tenants have (at first blush) seemingly irreconcilable interests. This situation demands effective problem-solving negotiation in which the parties work to develop a variety of possible solutions and attempt to incorporate them into an acceptable deal—what William Ury calls "building a golden bridge" between the parties. William Ury, Getting Past No: Negotiating Your Way from Confrontation to Cooperation 105 (1993). This process requires each party to focus upon the respective interests of both parties and to brainstorm a variety of potential solutions that might meet the unmet needs or economic interests of the respective parties. These solutions may often include "conditional" solutions:

> Another way of dealing with unmet needs is to create conditional solutions. One of the parties in a negotiation might believe that a particular problem will arise in the future but the other disagrees. Instead of arguing over whether this contingency will occur, the parties can frame their agreement to address it. [Stefan H. Krieger & Richard K. Neumann, Jr., Essential Lawyering Skills: Interviewing, Counseling, Negotiation, and Persuasive Fact Analysis 332 (2d ed. 2003).]

SITUATION: You represent Trump, owner of Trump Plaza Mall, a modest indoor regional shopping mall with 58 stores. Trump is currently negotiating with BigMart, the nation's largest discount retailer, about signing a lease for one of the three anchor tenant spaces at Trump Plaza Mall. BigMart has tendered to Trump its proposed lease form, which provides for a 20–year lease term with four five-year renewal options. The lease form expressly disclaims any obligation on the part of BigMart to operate at any time during the lease. In other shopping centers throughout the country, BigMart has demonstrated a willingness to "go dark" for competitive purposes.

TASK: On behalf of either Trump or BigMart (as you are assigned), negotiate and draft an agreement respecting BigMart's obligation to operate and/or Trump's rights in the event that BigMart chooses to cease operations during the lease.

3. Landlord's Remedies for Tenant Breach

a. Introduction. At the beginning of the lease term, both parties typically expect that the tenant will remain in possession and perform her lease obligations until the lease expires naturally (in the case of a tenancy for years) or until one party gives sufficient notice that is effective to terminate the lease (in the case of a periodic tenancy or tenancy at will). Sometimes, however, circumstances frustrate these expectations—for example, a commercial tenant's business may fail, or a residential tenant may have to move because of a job transfer. In these circumstances, the tenant may no longer want or need possession of the land. Yet because the tenant contractually promised to pay the rent for the duration of the lease term, the tenant has no ability to terminate the lease prior to the end of the term, absent an express lease provision to that effect. Such a tenant faces continued liability for the rent as it comes due, even though the tenant no longer wants (or may be incapable of paying for) the benefits of continued possession.

Nevertheless, such a tenant may have several options available to limit her financial liability. If the lease is a periodic tenancy or a tenancy at will, the tenant can terminate her leasehold estate by giving timely notice. Even if the lease is a fixed term tenancy, however, the tenant may be able to minimize its potential liability. First, the tenant might attempt to assign or sublet its estate to someone else who wants or needs possession of the premises. This approach may work readily if the lease permits the tenant to assign or sublet its interest, but may be more difficult if the lease contains an enforceable no-transfer clause. Second, the tenant can negotiate directly with the landlord in an effort to convince the landlord to terminate the lease and release the tenant from future liability for rent. Sometimes, the parties may reach a compromise in which the landlord receives some payment in return for early termination of the lease. If neither of these alternatives are successful, the tenant may simply choose to stop paying rent and abandon the premises altogether (or remain in possession until the landlord brings an eviction proceeding). Although abandoning the premises does not relieve the tenant of its potential liability, this may not practically matter if the tenant is financially distressed. If the tenant is judgment-proof, for example, the landlord may simply let the matter drop and take back possession of the land rather than pay a lawyer to obtain a judgment against a tenant with no assets to satisfy that judgment.

This section focuses upon the legal and practical issues arising when a tenant breaches its lease. First, the materials explore the landlord's options when a tenant breaches its lease but remains in possession. Can the landlord evict the tenant by "self-help" (*i.e.*, without going through court proceedings) or must the landlord resort to the judicial process? Second, the materials discuss the landlord's options when the tenant abandons the premises—*i.e.*, vacates the premises without paying the rent—and evaluates how various landlord responses to abandonment affect the tenant's liability to the landlord. At the conclusion of these materials is a dispute resolution exercise, authored by Professor Dale Whitman, that should help you appreciate some of the practical limitations upon the landlord's ability to pursue its various legal options.

b. *The Defaulting Tenant in Possession.* Assume that *T* fails to pay its rent, but does not voluntarily turn over possession to *L*. What options does *L* have for dealing with this situation?

L could simply choose to leave *T* in possession and sue for the unpaid rent as it comes due. If *T* is Bill Gates, this option may make sense, but it makes little sense if T is judgment-proof. And in some cases, where the market value of the premises has risen since the lease was originally signed, L could now command a higher rent if L could re-lease the premises. In these situations, L will want to recover possession of the premises as quickly as possible so that L can put a more desirable tenant in place.

How can L most efficiently regain possession of the premises following T's breach? Traditionally, a landlord could recover possession either through the judicial proceeding of *ejectment* or by exercising *self-help* to regain possession without judicial process. Landlords preferred self-help—such as by changing the locks to deny the tenant access to the premises—because it was significantly faster and cheaper than the ejectment action, in which tenants could use the rules of civil pleading and procedure to delay eviction and remain in possession without paying rent. Unfortunately, self-help sometimes led to violent confrontations that resulted in serious personal injury, as angry unpaid landlords confronted hard-pressed, desperate tenants being put out of "their homes."

During the 19th century, many states enacted legislation that addressed concerns about the delay associated with the ejectment action and the risk of violence associated with the landlord's exercise of self-help. These statutes, typically designated *forcible entry and detainer* ("FED") statutes, had two principal objectives: (1) to limit the landlord's use of force in self-help eviction, and (2) to provide a more streamlined judicial process for eviction, thereby giving impatient landlords a more appealing alternative to self-help repossession. Based upon similar concerns, all states have now enacted comparable legislation providing a summary, expedited legal procedure through which the landlord can regain possession of the premises following the tenant's breach.

The specifics of these statutes vary somewhat from state to state, but the general structure of the summary eviction procedure is comparable in most states. Essentially, the landlord must give the defaulting tenant a notice of default and a defined number of days to cure the default. If the tenant neither cures the default nor voluntarily vacates the premises, the landlord then files an action seeking an expedited statutory eviction of the tenant. This procedure typically provides the tenant with a relatively short period of time in which to respond to the complaint (via answer or motion to dismiss). The tenant may assert affirmative defenses but typically cannot assert counterclaims[11]—in this

---

11. Thus, if the tenant believed that the landlord had breached the lease and wished to pursue legal action, tenant would have to file a separate lawsuit seeking to enforce its rights under the lease. Under the traditional doctrine of independence of lease covenants, the landlord's breach of a covenant (other than the covenant of quiet enjoyment) was not a defense to tenant's nonpayment of rent. Therefore, the landlord's breach of the lease was not within the ambit of a summary eviction proceeding. Today, however, in those jurisdictions that provide tenants with the right to withhold payment of rent in response to the landlord's breach, summary proceedings have necessarily been broadened to permit a tenant to raise such a breach as a defense to the tenant's failure to pay full rent.

way, summary eviction expedites the eviction process by narrowing the focus of the proceeding to the limited issue of the landlord's right to recover possession. If the tenant does not answer, the landlord receives a default judgment entitling it to possession of the land. If the tenant answers the complaint, the landlord may request a trial date, typically set within a few weeks of the landlord's request. Very limited discovery may be permitted. At trial, if the court awards possession to the tenant (*e.g.*, if the court concludes that tenant is not in default), the tenant may recover damages and attorneys fees if authorized by the statute. If, as is more typical, the court awards possession to the landlord, the tenant may appeal or seek a stay of execution of the judgment (although tenants rarely pursue these unlikely avenues of relief). If the tenant does not leave the premises voluntarily after judgment for the landlord, the landlord may obtain a writ of possession from the court, and the sheriff or other public official may then serve the tenant with a notice to vacate the property. If necessary, the sheriff may forcibly evict the tenant and turn over possession to the landlord after the notice period has expired. For additional background on the summary eviction process, see Randy G. Gerchick, Comment, *No Easy Way Out: Making The Summary Eviction Process a Fairer and More Efficient Alternative to Landlord Self–Help*, 41 UCLA L. Rev. 759, 808–46 (1994).

As one might expect, even this "summary" procedure—while faster than a traditional civil action—can consume significant time, either due to landlord noncompliance with the notice requirements or tenant manipulation of the system to prolong rent-free possession of the premises. Thus, a landlord may still be tempted to pursue self-help, such as by changing the locks to force the tenant out of the premises. What impact, if any, should the availability of a summary eviction procedure have upon the landlord's ability to exercise self-help? Consider the following materials.

GORMAN v. RATLIFF

Supreme Court of Arkansas.
289 Ark. 332, 712 S.W.2d 888 (1986).

HOLT, CHIEF JUSTICE. . . . The appellants, Johnny and Mary Gorman, were tenants of the appellee, Russell Ratliff. The appellants admit that they became delinquent in their rent payments and that the appellee asked them to vacate the premises. Before they did so, Ratliff entered the rental house while the appellants were not at home and removed all of their personal property. Ratliff then stored the property, which included a refrigerator, stove, beds, childrens' toys, a bassinet, personal papers, and other items. The appellants filed suit against Ratliff claiming his actions constitute a wrongful and constructive eviction, and a wrongful conversion of property.

Ratliff filed an answer and counterclaim in which he claimed that appellants had violated the terms of the lease agreement between the parties. Ratliff relied on provisions in the lease permitting him upon nonpayment of rent to enter the property and store all personal property left at the leased premises. The lease also provided that if the charges are still unpaid after 30 days, the stored property can be sold to satisfy the rent arrearage.

In an amended complaint, appellants alleged that Ratliff's actions constitute a forcible entry and detainer. To the extent that appellee's actions were in accordance with the terms of the lease, appellants claim the lease is illegal, unconscionable and against public policy.

The parties stipulated that the lease was entered into on November 30, 1984, that Ratliff and not appellants has had possession of the premises since April 23, 1985, and that Ratliff has had possession of appellants' personal property since then, and that no judicial order has been entered granting possession of the personal property to Ratliff. The trial court ruled, after a preliminary hearing on appellants' motion for relief pendente lite that, pursuant to the lease contract, Ratliff had a right to peaceable repossession of the premises and a lien on the personal property found therein. After a trial, the court denied appellants' claim and awarded Ratliff $528 on his counterclaim, that amount representing unpaid rent and moving, storing, and cleaning expenses. The court further found that the lease conforms to all applicable Arkansas law. We disagree and reverse the trial court's order.

The lease provided in pertinent part:

10. Any violation of any provision of this lease by any of the lessees, or any person on the premises with the lessee's consent, or any failure to pay rent upon the date due, shall result, at the option of the lessor, in the immediate termination of this lease without notice of any kind, and lessor may thereupon enter said premises and take and retain possession thereof and exclude lessees therefrom.

12. If lessees leave said premises unoccupied at any time while rent is due and unpaid, lessor may, if desired, take immediate possession thereof and exclude lessee therefrom, removing and storing at the expense of said lessees all property [] contained therein.

14. The lessor shall have the lien granted by law [upon] all baggage and other property of lessees for their rent, accommodation and services, and the lessees hereby grant to lessor a lien upon all personal property brought into said premises, regardless of any provisions of law or whether or not the apartment is furnished, and lessor may enforce said lien as provided by law or by entering said premises and either taking possession thereof and the belongings contained therein for safekeeping, or by removing said property therefrom and storing the same at the expense of the lessees. Said lien may be enforced whenever rent is due and unpaid and regardless of whether or not a three (3) day notice to pay rent or quit shall have been served, and enforcement of the lien shall not operate to waive any other rights of the lessor in unlawful detainer or otherwise. If rent is still due and unpaid thirty (30) days after the

enforcement of said lien, then the lessor may sell any or all personal property taken possession of as herein provided, and may apply any monies received against the unpaid rent. . . .

In Act 615 of 1981 the legislature revised the statutes describing the cause of action for forcible entry and detainer and unlawful detainer and prescribing the procedure for carrying out the rights and remedies of the affected parties. The legislature did so because it found the former statutes were in need of clarification and revision and it was in the best interest of the people that "an additional procedure be specifically prescribed for the enforcement of the rights of parties. . . ." Ark. Stat. Ann. § 34–1501 (Supp.1985). That additional procedure afforded persons affected by the legislation an opportunity to be heard on legitimate objections to writs of possession. *Id.* At the outset, therefore, the legislature evinced a desire to extend additional protection to parties in possession of property before that property could be taken from them, as well as to provide for procedures to expedite the removal of parties who are unlawfully in possession of property.

Section 34–1503 defines those acts that will constitute a forcible entry and detainer as follows:

> If any person shall enter into or upon any lands, tenements or other possessions and detain or hold the same without right or claim to title, or who shall enter by breaking open the doors and windows or other parts of the house, whether any person be in or not, or by threatening to kill, maim or beat the party in possession or by such words and acts as have a natural tendency to excite fear or apprehension of danger or by putting out of doors or by carrying away the goods of the party in possession, or by entering peaceably and then turning out by force or frightening by threats or other circumstances of terror the party to yield possession, in such cases every person so offending shall be deemed guilty of a forcible entry and detainer within the meaning of this Act.

Included in this list is the action taken by the landlord in this case: "carrying away the goods of the party in possession." Appellee asks us to read this statute as prohibiting only people "without right or claim to title" from carrying away the goods of the party in possession. We do not find his position persuasive however. In this statute, the legislature has embodied guidelines of prohibited conduct, any one of which constitutes a forcible entry and detainer within the meaning of the Act, thus giving protection to appellants.

In addition to delineating prohibited conduct, the legislature provided a remedy for landlords with holdover tenants and others guilty of forcible entry and detainer and unlawful detainer. Once a party is unlawfully in possession of property, the person with a cause of action under this Act may file a complaint and an affidavit in circuit court and the complaint will then be served on the defendant with a notice of intention to issue a writ of possession. § 34–1507. If the defendant does not respond within five days the writ of possession is issued. If the party responds and objects, a hearing will be held. At the hearing, if the court decides the plaintiff is likely to succeed and the plaintiff provides adequate security, the court then orders the clerk to issue the writ. *Id.* For the defendant to retain possession of the property, he must provide adequate security. *Id.*

Although a landlord's use of self-help to evict a holdover tenant is not specifically addressed by the act, § 34–1502 does provide:

> No person shall enter into or upon any lands, tenements, other possessions, and detain or hold the same, but where an entry is given by law, and then only in a peaceable manner.

No entry by a landlord onto property occupied by another is given by Act 615, except by first resorting to legal process. Accordingly, self-help action is prohibited.

This finding is in keeping with the long standing policy behind the forcible entry and detainer statutes, which were first enacted to prevent landlords from retaking their land by force. *Vinson v. Flynn,* 64 Ark. 453, 43 S.W. 146, 46 S.W. 186 (1897). The statutes were designed to restore possession to the tenant until the right to possession could be adjudicated and to compel people "to the more pacific course of suits in court, where the weak and strong stand upon equal terms." *Id., quoting Littell v. Grady,* 38 Ark. 584 [(1882)]....

Other courts addressing this same question have held that, although the real owner of the property may be ultimately entitled to possession of the property, the entry and detainer action is designed to compel the party out of actual possession to respect the present possession of the other party and resort to legal channels to obtain possession. *See e.g., Floro v. Parker,* 205 So.2d 363 (Fla.1968); *Jordan v. Talbot,* 55 Cal.2d 597, 12 Cal.Rptr. 488, 361 P.2d 20 (1961); *Bass v. Boetel & Co.,* 191 Neb. 733, 217 N.W.2d 804 (1974); and *Edwards v. C.N. Investment Co.,* 27 Ohio Misc. 57, 272 N.E.2d 652 (1971).

The Arkansas Legislature through Act 615 has expressed its intention to prohibit landlords from entering premises without statutory authority. Recognizing that landlords, too, have rights with respect to their property, and the problems they face, particularly with holdover tenants, the legislature in the same Act establishes procedures to enable them to expeditiously evict tenants.

Although the terms of the lease agreement clearly permitted Ratliff's actions, the appellants did not waive their rights under the forcible entry and detainer statutes by executing the lease agreement. Section 34–1503 prohibits several kinds of conduct and the appellee is asking us to find that the tenant waived one of them. The provisions of § 34–1503 cannot be isolated so as to permit waiver of a portion of the statute. Nor can the entire statute be waived, since to do so would conceivably permit a person to threaten "to kill, maim or beat the party in possession," actions which are absolutely prohibited.

For these reasons those provisions of the lease authorizing the landlord's self-help remedy are invalid and the trial court's granting of relief to appellee is reversed. . . .

NEWBERN, JUSTICE, concurring. The result reached by the majority is correct. However, I believe the majority opinion does not correctly address the central issue in the case. That issue is whether a lessee, by a provision in a lease contract, may confer upon the lessor the "right" to enter which, according to Ark. Stat. Ann. § 34–1503 (Supp.1985), exempts the landlord from liability for forcible entry.

The majority opinion adequately describes the policies behind the forcible entry and unlawful detainer statutes. However, in applying those policies to invalidating the provisions of the lease which are contrary to them the only discussion is about whether one part of the statute may be "waived" and not the others. If that were the issue, I believe a strong argument could be made that, by contract, the parties might create a landlord's "right" to enter but might not be able to create a right to commit the criminal acts stated disjunctively in § 34–1503.

We should say simply that the General Assembly has stated a strong public policy against forcible entry by a landlord, and a contract by which the parties seek to avoid that policy is invalid. . . . The Arkansas General Assembly has made our public policy clear in the area of landlord-tenant relations. We need not go beyond that policy to find the contract invalid and unenforceable.

Notes

1. *Summary Eviction Statutes and Their Impact upon the Self–Help Remedy.* Traditionally, a landlord could exercise self-help to repossess the premises following a tenant's default as long as the landlord did not "breach the peace" in doing so. Although a few states still follow this approach, most states follow the view expressed in *Gorman* that the adoption of a forcible entry and detainer statute abolished the landlord's common law self-help right. This means that the landlord cannot use self-help without the tenant's consent, even if it can be accomplished without the tenant's knowledge or without an actual breach of the peace. *See* Randy G. Gerchick, Comment, *No Easy Way Out: Making The Summary Eviction Process a Fairer and More Efficient Alternative to Landlord Self–Help*, 41 UCLA L. Rev. 759, 777 (1994).

Why does the *Gorman* court interpret the statute this way? If the statute recognizes that a person may enter upon another's property in a peaceable manner where that right is "given by law," why not interpret the statute to codify the landlord's common law right to enter upon the premises following the tenant's default? Does this seem sensible?

Note that Article 9 of the Uniform Commercial Code allows a creditor holding a security interest in a vehicle to use self-help to repossess the car following the owner's default, so long as the repossession occurs without breaching the peace. *See* U.C.C. § 9–609. This means that the bank with a lien on your car could use self-help to repossess the car from the parking lot while you were at work (assuming you were in default), but that your landlord could not change the locks on your apartment while you were at work. Does this make sense? Should the same rule apply, or does the difference between land and vehicles justify these different rules?

2. *Agreements to Permit Self–Help.* The lease in *Gorman* purported to grant the landlord the right to enter the premises peaceably after default by the tenant. Given that the tenant signed the lease with this provision in it, why doesn't this create a right "given by law" that justifies the landlord's conduct? Why shouldn't the parties be able to agree that the landlord can exercise peaceable self-help after the tenant defaults? Should it matter whether the tenancy is for residential purposes or commercial purposes? *See Rucker v. Wynn*, 212 Ga.App. 69, 441 S.E.2d 417 (1994) (provision permitting self-help in commercial lease is enforceable, but would not be in residential lease); *Bender v. North Meridian Mobile Home Park*, 636 So.2d 385 (Miss. 1994) (provision permitting self-help in residential lease is enforceable). Should it matter whether the tenant was represented by counsel?

Note that even in jurisdictions that permit a landlord to exercise self-help, there is a substantial practical limitation upon the usefulness of the self-help remedy. If the landlord attempts self-help and the tenant raises an objection, most courts hold that the landlord cannot continue its self-help actions in the face of the tenant's objection without breaching the peace. *Cf. Hester v. Bandy*, 627 So.2d 833 (Miss. 1993). Can you explain why?

3. *Repossession of Tenant's Personal Property. Gorman* also demonstrates another pitfall associated with self-help repossession—it typically requires the landlord to assert dominion and control over the tenant's personal property. Ancient common law accorded the landlord the right of *distraint*, which permitted the landlord to seize the chattels of a defaulting tenant located on the leased premises and hold them until the tenant satisfied its unpaid rental obligation. In American states, however, the right of distraint was either never adopted or has been abolished by statute. William B. Stoebuck & Dale A. Whitman, The Law of Property § 6.57, at 365 (4th ed. 2000). Some states have enacted statutes that grant a landlord a lien upon the tenant's personal property located on the leased premises to secure unpaid rental obligations, but most of the statutory liens apply only to growing crops or personal property abandoned by a departing tenant. Thus, a landlord that takes possession of the tenant's personal property during a self-help repossession may well face a complaint that the landlord has converted the tenant's personal property.

Suppose that your client owns a number of residential apartments in a college town. What advice would you give the client to minimize her potential liability for converting the personal property of her tenants when repossessing apartments? Can you satisfactorily address these potential liability concerns in the lease contract itself (and, if so, how)?

4. *Liability for Wrongful Repossession.* What liability (if any) would *L* face for wrongful repossession in the following scenarios?

(a) *L* padlocks *T*'s premises believing that *T* had defaulted in paying rent. In fact, *T* had paid rent, and *L* made a clerical error in its own business records. Prior to repossession, there were five years remaining on the lease term.

(b) *L* padlocks *T*'s premises after *T* defaults in paying rent. *L* moved *T*'s personal property into storage, leaving *T* with express instructions as to where *T* could pick up that property.

(c) *L* padlocks *T*'s premises after *T* defaults in paying rent. *L* leaves *T*'s personal property locked in the premises, refusing to release it until *T* pays the accrued rent.

Note that in addition to facing possible damage claims, landlords in many jurisdictions risk criminal prosecution for violating a forcible entry and detainer statute or an unlawful detainer statute. Gerchick, *supra* note 1, at 779.

c. *Abandonment by the Tenant.* Perhaps the best example of tension between the concept of "lease as conveyance" and "lease as contract" is the case of the tenant that abandons possession of the premises—*i.e.*, vacates the premises *and* ceases to pay rent—prior to the end of the lease term.

Abandonment by the tenant poses two conceptual problems. The first problem is whether the landlord should have any obligation to mitigate the consequences of the tenant's abandonment. If one looks at the lease as a pure conveyance, then the landlord has performed its obligations to the tenant (assuming it does not breach the covenant of quiet enjoyment) once it delivers possession of the premises to the tenant. Thereafter, if the tenant chooses to abandon the premises and let them sit idle, one might argue that this is the tenant's choice as the owner of a leasehold estate. Under this view, the landlord should be able to enforce the lease according to its terms and hold the tenant liable for rent as it comes due, for the duration of the lease term. If one views the lease as a bilateral contract, however, contract law's mitigation principle generally prevents the nonbreaching party from recovering damages that it reasonably could have avoided through mitigation (*i.e.*, by seeking substitute performance or otherwise taking steps to ameliorate the consequences of the breach). Under this view, the landlord should not be able to collect damages equal to the full agreed-upon rent if the landlord made no effort to find another person to occupy the property.[12]

This leads to the second problem posed by tenant abandonment— what impact does the landlord's re-entry and re-letting have on the tenant's rights and obligations under the original lease? Obviously, a

---

12. The mitigation/no-mitigation debate is more significant academically than practically. Leaving the premises vacant and collecting rent as it comes due is often an unappealing (if not entirely useless) remedy for the landlord. If the abandoning tenant is in serious financial difficulty, the right to collect future rent as it comes due may have little or no economic value to the landlord. By contrast, the vacant premises could be generating *some income* if the landlord could re-enter the premises and place a financially responsible third party into pos-session. Further, if the premises sit vacant, they become subject to the risk of vandalism, or the vacancy may send a signal to the marketplace that the premises are undesirable. [For example, would you be enthusiastic to sign a lease to become a tenant in a shopping center if there were already several vacant stores?] As a result, the landlord faced with an abandoning tenant has a significant incentive to re-enter the premises and attempt to "re-lease" or "re-let" them to another party.

landlord would argue that its re-entry *should not extinguish the lease* and the abandoning tenant's liability for rent. This argument, however, presents some logical difficulties attributable to the lingering influence of the "lease as conveyance" model:

- First, how can the landlord have *any authority* to re-let without terminating the lease (and with it, the tenant's liability for rent)? Landlords that have attempted to re-enter and re-let premises often have faced arguments that by exercising dominion over the premises, they impliedly accepted the tenant's surrender—thereby terminating the lease and releasing the tenant from further rental liability. By contrast, the landlord will argue that it is re-entering and re-letting the premises on behalf of the abandoning tenant— *i.e.*, that the tenant's abandonment impliedly authorizes the landlord to assign or sublease the premises on the tenant's behalf— and that the abandoning tenant thus remains ultimately liable to the extent rent is unpaid.

- Second, what happens if the landlord succeeds in re-letting the premises, but at a higher rental or for a longer term than provided in the abandoning tenant's lease? One could argue that by re-letting on terms different from the original lease, the landlord demonstrates that it is acting for its own account and thus has accepted the original tenant's surrender—thereby terminating the lease and relieving the original tenant from further rental liability. Alternatively, if the landlord's re-letting is treated as an implied assignment or sublease on the abandoning tenant's account, this suggests that any excess rent actually collected by the landlord from the replacement tenant may properly belong to the abandoning tenant!

As the following materials demonstrate, courts often have failed to establish predictable rules that clearly delineate the consequences where the landlord re-enters and re-leases the premises following the tenant's abandonment. For this reason, thoughtful negotiation and drafting play a particularly important role in protecting against the risks posed by abandonment.

SCHNEIKER v. GORDON

Supreme Court of Colorado.
732 P.2d 603 (1987).

LOHR, JUSTICE. . . . Sometime before July of 1979, the defendant in this action, Jakob Schneiker (lessee-sublessor), entered into a lease (the primary lease) with the owner of certain property for use of the leased premises as a car wash. The property included a structure and attached equipment. Rent under the primary lease was payable at the rate of $600 per month, and the term of the primary lease was to extend through May of 1983.

On April 1, 1980, the lessee-sublessor entered into a sublease with the plaintiffs, Darrell W. Gordon and Gary F. Peterson (sublessees). The sublease provided for a monthly rent of $1900 and was for a term ending at the same time as that of the primary lease. The sublease specified that the premises were to be operated as a car wash. In addition to containing a provision that the sublessees would keep the premises and equipment in good repair, the sublease also contained a "Repossession" clause which provided:

> The parties agree that in case said premises are left vacant and any part of the rent herein reserved be unpaid, then the Lessor may, without in anyway being obliged to do so, and without terminating this lease, retake possession of said premises, and rent the same for such rent and upon such conditions as the Lessor may think best, making such changes and repairs as may be required, giving credit for the amount of rent so received less all expenses of such changes and repairs, and said Lessee shall be liable for the balance of the rent herein reserved until the expiration of this lease.

After July of 1981, the sublessees ceased making rental payments, and they abandoned the premises in August of 1981. Prior to mid-November of that same year, the sublessees mailed the keys for the car wash to the lessee-sublessor. In November the lessee-sublessor reentered the premises. The equipment was in such a state of disrepair that the property could not be operated as a car wash. The trial court found that the sublessees had breached their obligation to maintain and repair the equipment, that the reasonable cost of repairs was more than $6000, and that the reasonable rental value of the property was less than $600 per month. Being unable to afford to make the necessary repairs, the lessee-sublessor negotiated a surrender of the primary lease with the owner as of February 1982.

The sublessees brought suit against the lessee-sublessor, claiming misrepresentation on the part of the lessee-sublessor concerning the profitability of the car wash business, and requesting compensatory and punitive damages. The lessee-sublessor counterclaimed for damages caused by the sublessees' breach of the sublease and requested the full rent of $1900 per month from the time the sublessees ceased making rental payments, August of 1981, through the expiration of the lease, May of 1983. The case was tried to the court. After presentation of the sublessees' evidence, the trial court dismissed their claim. At the conclusion of the trial, the court awarded the lessee-sublessor partial relief on his counterclaim. The court found that the lessee-sublessor had acted to mitigate his damages by negotiating a surrender of the primary lease and that the lessee-sublessor had intended to hold the sublessees liable for the entire rent payable through the expiration of the sublease. However, the trial court held that the cancellation of the primary lease acted as a surrender and termination of the sublease as a matter of law, and that the lessee-sublessor was therefore entitled only to rent payable up until February 1, 1982, the date the primary lease was terminated by surrender.

The lessee-sublessor appealed the denial of damages for the profits he would have received during the remainder of the original term of the sublease, from February of 1982 through May of 1983. The court of appeals affirmed the judgment of the trial court, holding that the surrender of the primary lease operated as a surrender and termination of the sublease as a matter of law, and that the sublessees' obligation to pay future rent ended when the sublease was terminated since there was no express agreement between the parties that the obligation to pay rent would survive termination of the sublease. The lessee-sublessor then filed a petition for certiorari with this court, and we granted that petition. . . .

The present case directs our attention to the law of landlord and tenant as it relates to abandonment and surrender of a leasehold and the obligation of a lessee for rent following abandonment. Under the common law view of a lease as a conveyance, a tenant's obligation to pay rent was based upon the ownership of the leasehold estate. *See, e.g.*, Love, [*Landlord's Remedies When the Tenant Abandons: Property, Contract, and Leases*, 30 U.Kan.L.Rev. 533 (1982)], at 535. The rent was said to issue from the land. Therefore, so long as the tenant owned the leasehold estate the rental obligation continued, but when the leasehold was extinguished, for whatever reason, the obligation ceased. As a result, if the landlord elected to accept the surrender of the premises upon abandonment by the lessee, the lease was terminated and there was no continuing obligation for rent. *Id.* at 535–36. *See also* 1 American Law of Property, *supra*, § 3.99; 3A G. Thompson & J. Grimes, Thompson on Real Property §§ 1343–45 (1981 repl. vol.); 4 H. Tiffany, The Law of Real Property § 963 (3d ed. 1975). On the other hand, the landlord could decline to accept the offer of a surrender that was implicit in abandonment and could continue to hold the tenant liable for rent as it became due. 3A G. Thompson & J. Grimes, *supra*, § 1345, at 641; Love, *supra*, at 535. Our early cases, reflecting this traditional property law analysis, recognized these two alternatives available to the landlord upon abandonment of the premises by the tenant. *E.g., Ruple v. Taughenbaugh*, 72 Colo. 171, 210 P. 72 (1922); *Carson v. Arvantes*, 10 Colo.App. 382, 50 P. 1080 (1897), *aff'd*, 27 Colo. 77, 59 P. 737 (1899).[13]

Before courts began to recognize that contractual principles are relevant to the determination of a landlord's rights on abandonment by a tenant, a landlord could not rely on the contract doctrine of anticipatory repudiation to recover installments of rent that would have accrued but for the abandonment and surrender. Nor could a tenant successfully maintain that a landlord's right to collect rent accruing after abandonment, in the absence of an acceptance of the tenant's surrender, should be subject to a duty to mitigate damages by using reasonable efforts to

13. The Restatement (Second) of Property, Landlord and Tenant § 12.1 (1977), takes a similar position but also would permit a landlord to relet the premises and hold a tenant liable for the difference in rent regardless of whether the lease contains a provision allowing him to do so, so long as the landlord first notifies the tenant.

secure a substitute tenant. 1 American Law of Property, *supra*, § 3.11, at 203; Love, *supra*, at 535–36.

The traditional emphasis of the courts on the lease as a conveyance, to the exclusion of its contractual characteristics, has generated much criticism by commentators. In recognition of the increasing importance of the covenants found in modern leases, as well as the policy of discouraging economic and physical waste, courts in recent times have begun to look to principles of contract law in analyzing the rights and obligations of a landlord and a tenant upon abandonment of premises by a tenant. . . . [A]cceptance of surrender acts to terminate the privity of estate between the parties but the privity of contract between them is held to be unaffected. Therefore, while a landlord can no longer maintain an action for rent due after termination of the lease in these jurisdictions, he can maintain an action for contract damages caused by the tenant's breach of the lease.

Colorado law in this area, though once exclusively rooted in property law principles, has gradually come to recognize that contract principles can sometimes play a role in resolving landlord-tenant disputes. Our early cases, which viewed a lease as a conveyance and rent as an incident of the tenancy, contain no suggestion that the landlord has any responsibility to mitigate damages by exercising reasonable efforts to find a substitute tenant as a condition to recovering the full amount of rent specified in the lease after a tenant abandons the property. *See, e.g., Ruple v. Taughenbaugh*, 72 Colo. 171, 210 P. 72 (1922); *Carson v. Arvantes*, 10 Colo.App. 382, 50 P. 1080 (1897), *aff'd*, 27 Colo. 77, 59 P. 737 (1899). Nor is there any intimation in those cases that the contract doctrine of anticipatory repudiation might be available to enable a landlord to collect damages caused by the tenant's abandonment, including an amount equal to the rent the landlord would have received had the tenant not breached the lease.

In more recent times, however, we have held that if a lease expressly permits, the landlord may relet the premises abandoned by the tenant on the tenant's account and hold the tenant liable for the difference between the rent required by the original lease and the rent paid by the substitute tenant. *Ruston v. Centennial Real Estate*, 166 Colo. 377, 445 P.2d 64 (1968). In *Ruston*, we stated that "[a] lease, like other contracts, is to be reasonably interpreted according to the apparent intention of the parties." 166 Colo. at 381, 445 P.2d at 66. Then, in *Shanahan v. Collins*, 189 Colo. 169, 539 P.2d 1261 (1975), we noted that at common law the real estate lease developed in the field of real property rather than contract law but that rigid adherence to the law of property to determine the duties and obligations of the parties, implied as well as expressed, was no longer the proper approach in resolving all landlord-tenant disputes. *Id.* at 171, 539 P.2d at 1262. In that case we held, contrary to traditional property law analysis, that a tenant's obligation to pay rent is not independent of a landlord's covenant to make improvements or repairs. *Id.* at 172, 539 P.2d at 1263. As a result, the tenant was entitled to set off against the rent payments the cost of repairs that the landlord had refused to make although required to do so by a covenant in the lease. *Id.* . . .

The case now before us requires us to consider once more the dual nature of a lease as contract and conveyance and to determine the implications of that dual nature for the liability of a subtenant for rent after abandonment. The sublease, in the "Repossession" clause previously referred to, specifically authorized, but did not obligate, the lessee-sublessor to retake possession, make changes and repairs, and rerent, without terminating the lease, after the sublessee departed leaving the premises vacant. The amount of the new rent less the cost of changes and repairs would be credited against the continuing obligation of the sublessee to pay the rent specified in the sublease. Upon examination of the premises after the sublessee's departure, however, it became apparent that the sublessee had left the premises in such a state that the lessee-sublessor would not be able to relet the premises without making substantial repairs. Due to a lack of funds and an inability to borrow, the lessee-sublessor could not afford to make these repairs. The ability of the lessee-sublessor to relet the premises was also adversely affected by the relatively short period of time remaining between the sublessees' departure in August 1981 and the end of the primary term in May 1983. Therefore, the trial court found that the reasonable rental value of the unrepaired premises was less than the $600 monthly rent payable by the lessee-sublessor to the owner-lessor over the remainder of the term of the primary lease.

Had the premises been in a condition permitting rerental on an economic basis, the lessee-sublessor could have elected to pursue his remedy under the "Repossession" clause. *See Ruston v. Centennial Real Estate,* 166 Colo. 377, 380–81, 445 P.2d 64, 66 (1968). However, the terms of the "Repossession" clause implicitly apply only to circumstances in which repair and rerental is physically and economically feasible. Therefore, the actions of the sublessee rendered this remedy unavailable to the lessee-sublessor.[14]

Being unable to make the necessary repairs or to relet the premises at an economically prudent rate, the lessee-sublessor was faced with a difficult choice. Under our early case law, he could have elected to refuse to accept the sublessees' surrender. He then could have continued to pay the $600 per month rent under the primary lease and could have held the sublessees liable for the $1900 per month rent reserved in the sublease as it became due. *See Ruple v. Taughenbaugh,* 72 Colo. 171, 210

---

14. Even had the lessee-sublessor been able to rerent the premises and proceed against the sublessee under the "Repossession" clause, he would not have been required to do so to the exclusion of all other possible remedies. "When a contract describes a remedy for breach without an express or implied limitation making that remedy exclusive, the injured party may seek any other remedy provided by law." *McDonald v. Stockton Metropolitan Transit* *District,* 36 Cal.App.3d 436, 111 Cal.Rptr. 637, 642 (1973). *Accord* A. Corbin, Corbin on Contracts § 1227 (1964). The sublease contains no express or implied provision that the "Repossession" clause is intended to be the exclusive remedy available to the lessee-sublessor upon abandonment of the premises by the sublessee. In fact, the "Repossession" clause expressly states that the lessee-sublessor is under no obligation to proceed under its terms.

P. 72. Rather than pursuing that uneconomic course of action, the lessee-sublessor negotiated a surrender of the primary lease, thereby eliminating the obligation to pay rent on that lease and mitigating the loss resulting from the failure of the sublessees to pay rent to $1300 per month.

Were we to view these facts solely under traditional property law principles, as did the trial court and the court of appeals, we would agree with those courts that the primary lease was extinguished by surrender and acceptance and that the surrender and acceptance of the primary lease was so inconsistent with the continuation of the rights of the lessee-sublessor under the sublease that it constituted an acceptance of the sublessees' surrender of the sublease. Traditionally, surrender and acceptance not only caused the leasehold estate to be absorbed into the lessor's reversion but also terminated the obligation of the lessee for rent that would have accrued subsequent to the surrender. 1 American Law of Property, *supra*, § 3.99; *Ruple*, 71 Colo. at 173, 210 P. at 73. As we said in *Shanahan v. Collins*, however, when faced with an appeal to apply traditional property law principles with respect to the independence of leasehold covenants, "[w]e do not consider this to be the proper approach to the problem presented here." 189 Colo. at 171, 539 P.2d at 1262.

We believe that it is necessary to recognize the dual nature of the lease as contract and conveyance and to analyze the lessee-sublessor's remedy for the sublessees' breach under contract principles in order to achieve a just result consonant with the intent of the parties to this modern commercial lease. A commercial lease, like other contracts, is predominantly an exchange of promises. The covenant to pay rent represents one such promise, and the fairness of requiring fulfillment of that covenant often depends upon the landlord's performance of other covenants contained in the lease. *Shanahan*, 189 Colo. at 171–72, 539 P.2d at 1262–63. We can perceive no reason why the covenant to pay rent should be treated differently than a covenant to pay contained in any other contract. *See* 1 American Law of Property, *supra*, § 3.11 (stating that the covenant to pay rent in a lease is a contractual provision). The parties to a commercial lease are generally sophisticated and aware of the nature of contractual obligations.[15]

Public policy also favors the application of contract principles to these circumstances. Under traditional property law principles a landlord could allow the property to remain unoccupied while still holding the abandoning tenant liable for rent. This encourages both economic and physical waste. In no other context of which we are aware is an injured party permitted to sit by idly and suffer avoidable economic loss and thereafter to visit the full adverse economic consequences upon the party whose breach initiated the chain of events causing the loss.

15. We express no view as to whether our holding today can be applied to leases of all types. On several occasions we have recognized that the parties to a residential lease are not in the same relative position, at least with regard to the equality of bargaining power between them, as are parties to a typical commercial lease. . . .

Furthermore, it is generally in the interests of society that property be put to practical use so far as is economically feasible. Usually, no economic value is obtained from property if a landlord allows it to remain idle. At the same time, the possibility of physical damage to the property through accident or vandalism is increased. The rules for awarding damages in the context of abandonment and breach by the tenant should discourage, rather than encourage, economic and physical waste. We believe that the contract principle of "avoidable consequences" or "duty to mitigate" should be applied in this context to prevent a landlord from passively suffering preventable economic loss, to encourage the productive use of land, and to decrease the likelihood of physical damage to property.[16] Likewise, a landlord should be permitted to maintain an action for contract damages caused by a tenant's wrongful abandonment so that the landlord is able to receive the benefit of his bargain.

The facts of the present case readily lend themselves to analysis under familiar principles of contract law. The lessee-sublessor and the owner-lessor expressly agreed to a surrender of the primary lease on mutually satisfactory terms. At the time, the sublessees had abandoned the premises, so the intent and effect of the surrender of the primary lease was to accomplish a surrender of the sublease as well. This terminated the privity of estate between lessor and lessee-sublessor and between lessee-sublessor and sublessees. However, the lessee-sublessor intended to hold the sublessees liable for rent as parties to a contract, and privity of contract between the parties to the sublease with respect to the covenant to pay rent was not terminated. The sublessees remained under a personal obligation to carry out the terms of the covenant to pay rent contained in the lease.

Prior to surrender of the primary lease, the sublessees not only had abandoned the premises but also had returned the keys and had failed to pay installments of rent that had come due. Viewed in terms of contract law, this was in the nature of an anticipatory repudiation amounting to a total breach of the sublease. We see no reason that the surrender should operate to leave the lessee-sublessor without remedy against the sublessees, for the very purpose of the surrender upon which the sublessees rely was to mitigate damages by eliminating the lessee-sublessor's obligations under the primary lease to pay a higher rental than it could obtain by reletting the premises. Ordinarily, a landlord would be required to exercise reasonable efforts to procure a substitute tenant in order to fulfill his duty to mitigate. This course of action was not available to the lessee-sublessor in this case because of the actions of the sublessee. The necessity of the surrender was in essence forced upon the

16. Language in several of our cases would permit a landlord to refuse to accept a tenant's surrender, to make no effort to obtain a substitute tenant, and to continue to hold the tenant liable for rent while allowing the premises to remain idle. To the extent that these cases so hold and are inconsistent with our holding today that a landlord must mitigate damages upon abandonment of the premises by the tenant, we overrule them.

lessee-sublessor in order to minimize the economic loss, and the lessee-sublessor therefore fulfilled his duty to mitigate damages.

We must now determine the proper measure of damages in this case. This requires nothing more than application of established principles of contract law. The measure of damages is the amount it takes to place the landlord in the position he would have occupied had the breach not occurred, taking into account the landlord's duty to mitigate. *See Taylor v. Colorado State Bank*, 165 Colo. 576, 440 P.2d 772 (1968). Usually this will be the difference between the rent reserved in the lease and the reasonable rental value of the premises for the duration of the term of the lease, plus any other consequential damages caused by the breach. However, if the landlord is unable to secure a substitute tenant after making reasonable efforts to do so or if the premises have been rendered unmarketable, the landlord is entitled to an amount equal to the full amount of rent reserved in the lease, plus any other consequential damages. If the landlord has avoided any cost by not having to perform, that cost should be deducted from his recovery in order to place him in the position he would have occupied had the tenant performed.

Under the circumstances of the present case, we conclude that the sublessees are obligated to the lessee-sublessor in the amount of $1900 per month for the entire term remaining on the sublease after the last rental payment made by the sublessees, less the $600 per month rental under the primary lease subsequent to surrender of that lease, as the damages actually suffered by the lessee-sublessor for the sublessees' breach of the covenant to pay rent in the sublease by anticipatory repudiation.

We remand this case to the court of appeals for return to the trial court for entry of judgment consistent with the views expressed in this opinion.

Notes

1. *Tenant Abandonment: The Landlord's Options.* As *Schneiker* suggests, the common law held that a landlord had three options when faced with an abandoning tenant: (a) allow the premises to remain vacant and collect rent from the tenant as it accrues; (b) accept the tenant's surrender and thereby terminate the lease (and the tenant's liability for rent), with any re-letting occurring on the landlord's behalf; or (c) re-enter and re-let the premises for the tenant's account, with the tenant remaining liable for rent (and thus responsible for any deficiency between the stated rent and the amount collected from the third party). In a jurisdiction that follows *Schneiker*, which of these options does the landlord retain? Why?

2. *Accepting the Tenant's Surrender—Impact on the Lease.* If the landlord accepts the tenant's surrender, this terminates the lease and thus terminates the tenant's liability for *future rent*. [The tenant still remains liable for all rent that had accrued prior to landlord's acceptance of the surrender.] Thus, if a landlord wants to hold the tenant liable for future rent—*i.e.*, if the landlord wants to preserve its ability to pursue either option

(a) or option (c) as identified in note 1—the landlord must ensure that it neither expressly nor impliedly accepts the tenant's surrender. The landlord's problem is this: what can the landlord do with the premises without triggering an implied acceptance of surrender?

Whether an acceptance of surrender has occurred is a question of fact. If a landlord allows the premises to remain vacant and takes no steps to re-let them, a court will likely conclude that there is no acceptance of the tenant's surrender, even if the landlord has asserted some level of control over the premises (such as by retaining the keys or taking other action to secure the premises). *See, e.g., Klosterman v. Hickel Inv. Co.*, 821 P.2d 118 (Alaska 1991). By contrast, if the landlord makes serious alterations to the premises, or re-lets the premises for a period longer than the original lease term, a court would more likely conclude that the landlord's conduct constituted an implied surrender. *See, e.g., Guaranty Bank & Trust Co. v. Mid–State Ins. Agency*, 383 Mass. 319, 418 N.E.2d 1249 (1981); *Bonsignore v. Koondel*, 134 Misc. 344, 235 N.Y.S. 453 (Mun. Ct. 1929). On this continuum, there is a huge "middle ground" of potential cases where implied acceptance of surrender is more debatable. This demonstrates the need for a landlord to be explicit in its communication with an abandoning tenant. If the landlord wishes to preserve the tenant's liability for rent under the lease—but also wants to clean or repair the premises and show it to potential new tenants—the landlord should first communicate to the tenant (a) exactly what steps the landlord plans to take, (b) that by taking those steps, landlord is not terminating the lease, and (c) that any re-letting of the premises would be on the tenant's behalf.

To protect against a tenant's defense of implied acceptance of surrender, landlords frequently include *survival clauses* in their leases. A survival clause purports to grant the landlord the right to re-enter and re-let the premises to a third party on the tenant's behalf, without terminating the original lease and the tenant's residual rental liability thereunder. A well-drafted survival clause should be very explicit with respect to potential risks, as courts have often tended to construe survival clauses strictly against the landlord. *Compare Pinkerton, Inc. v. Palmer, Inc.*, 113 Ga.App. 859, 149 S.E.2d 859 (1966) (survival clause did not authorize re-letting beyond original term) *with Weingarten/Ark., Inc. v. ABC Interstate Theatres, Inc.*, 306 Ark. 64, 811 S.W.2d 295 (1991) (survival clause with express right to alter premises did permit landlord to convert theater into two retail stores without terminating original lease).

3. *The Tenant's Liability for Damages When Landlord Accepts the Tenant's Surrender.* The landlord's acceptance of the tenant's surrender does terminate the lease and extinguish the tenant's liability for rent, but does it also extinguish all liability that the tenant might have for *damages* the landlord suffers because the tenant breached its contract? *Schneiker* suggests that the proper answer is no. The tenant's abandonment is an anticipatory repudiation of the lease—and thus permits the landlord to terminate the lease and take immediate action to recover the damages it incurs due to tenant's abandonment. These damages would include an amount equal to the present value of the agreed rental that would have come due under the tenant's covenant to pay rent over the rest of the term, reduced by the present fair rental value of the premises (the amount that the

landlord could recover by mitigating its damages by finding a substitute tenant) over that same period. For example, suppose T abandons the premises (and that L accepts T's surrender) with three years left on a lease under which T agreed to pay $1,000 per month in rental. The fair rental value of the premises at the time of the abandonment is only $800 (assume that market rents have declined since T signed the lease).[17] T's abandonment damages L to the extent of $200/month (the $1,000/month agreed rent, less the $800/month L can obtain by re-letting)—a total of $7,200 over what would have been the final three years of the lease. Under the doctrine of anticipatory repudiation, L can immediately recover this amount, but the award would be reduced to present value (to take account for the fact that L would be collecting it in a lump sum now, rather than on a monthly basis over the ensuing three years). Milton R. Friedman & Patrick A. Randolph, Jr., 2 Friedman on Leasing § 16:3.3, at 16–51 to 16–55. *See also, e.g., United States Nat'l Bank of Or. v. Homeland, Inc.*, 291 Or. 374, 631 P.2d 761 (1981). This approach recognizes the dual nature of the lease as both contract and conveyance.

Unfortunately, courts often have struggled to understand the proper consequences of the lease's dual nature as conveyance and contract, and cases occasionally have produced bizarre results. For example, some courts have held (or at least suggested) that the landlord's express or implied acceptance of a tenant's surrender not only terminates the lease but also releases the tenant of all liability for future rent or damages. A few courts have taken this view even though they also impose on the landlord a duty to mitigate damages caused by the tenant's abandonment! *See, e.g., Signal Mgmt. Corp. v. Lamb*, 541 N.W.2d 449 (N.D. 1995); *Maney v. Parker*, 1995 WL 577805 (Tenn. Ct. App. 1995); *Roosen v. Schaffer*, 127 Ariz. 346, 621 P.2d 33 (Ct. App. 1980).

An attorney advising a landlord must draft pleadings carefully when pursuing judicial remedies against an abandoning tenant. If the landlord's complaint seeks to recover unpaid rent, the complaint may be dismissed if the court concludes that the landlord had accepted the tenant's surrender. Thus, a prudent landlord might well choose to plead in the alternative—for damages on account of the tenant's breach (in case the court concludes that landlord accepted tenant's surrender) or for unpaid rent (in case the court concludes that landlord's re-entry did not terminate the original lease).

4. *The Landlord's Re-letting Options.* If landlord has a prospective replacement for an abandoning tenant, which re-letting option should landlord pursue? Should landlord accept the surrender of the premises and re-let them for its own account, or should landlord re-enter and re-let the premises for the account of the abandoning tenant? What difference does it make, and to what extent does the answer to this question vary with the circumstances? In considering these questions, consider the following examples:

---

17. For purposes of this hypothetical, we are simply assuming the fair rental value of the premises is $800. In fact, if L sues T for damages, the court will have to establish the fair rental value of the premises at the time of T's abandonment. This may be a hotly contested issue on which the court may have to evaluate conflicting evidence presented by the parties. What facts would you consider relevant to a determination of the fair rental value of the premises?

(a) *L* and *T* have a five-year lease of commercial office space with rent set at $1,000 per month. With 30 months remaining on the lease, *T* abandons the premises and returns the keys to *L*. *L* has another prospective tenant, *T1*, who would rent the premises (with a few slight renovations) at a rent of $1,200 per month. How would you advise *L* to proceed? What additional information, if any, would you want to know before advising *L*? *See, e.g., Maney v. Parker*, 1995 WL 577805 (Tenn. Ct. App. 1995); *Mesilla Valley Mall Co. v. Crown Indus.*, 111 N.M. 663, 808 P.2d 633 (1991); *Weingarten/Ark., Inc. v. ABC Interstate Theatres, Inc.*, 306 Ark. 64, 811 S.W.2d 295 (1991); *McNeil Real Estate Mgmt., Inc. v. Seiler*, 1995 WL 420008 (Tenn. Ct. App. 1995).

(b) Same as situation (a), but now the prospective tenant *T1* is willing to rent the premises for only $800 per month. How would this change your advice to *L*?

5. *Issues Regarding the "Duty" to Mitigate.* Does it make good sense to impose a duty to mitigate upon the landlord? Would such a duty reflect the unexpressed intentions of the typical landlord and tenant? Would it reflect sound policy? The American Law Institute rejected any mitigation requirement for landlords, concluding that "[a]bandonment of property is an invitation to vandalism, and the law should not encourage such conduct by putting a duty of mitigation of damages on the landlord." Restatement (Second) of Property—Landlord and Tenant § 12.1(3), cmt. i. Is this persuasive?

(a) *The Modern Status of the Duty to Mitigate.* Today, a majority of jurisdictions require (either by statute or court decision) that a residential landlord must mitigate the harm caused by a tenant's abandonment. Milton R. Friedman & Patrick A. Randolph, 2 Friedman on Leasing, Appendix 16A. The Friedman treatise notes that there are 22 jurisdictions in which common law decisions have recognized a duty to mitigate in commercial leases as well. Several recent decisions, however, have reaffirmed the common law position that landlords in commercial leases have no duty to mitigate and can recover full rent from the abandoning tenant without making any effort to find a replacement tenant. *See, e.g., Stonehedge Square Ltd. P'ship v. Movie Merchs., Inc.*, 552 Pa. 412, 715 A.2d 1082 (1998) (dictum suggesting no duty to mitigate in residential leases either); *Holy Props. Ltd. v. Kenneth Cole Prods., Inc.*, 87 N.Y.2d 130, 637 N.Y.S.2d 964, 661 N.E.2d 694 (1995). Why do you suppose that these courts reject the duty to mitigate damages? Should the law draw a distinction between residential and commercial leases? Why or why not?

(b) *Can Tenant Waive Landlord's Duty to Mitigate?* Several jurisdictions allow the landlord to contract out of any duty to mitigate the consequences of tenant's abandonment. *See, e.g., Austin Hill Country Realty, Inc. v. Palisades Plaza, Inc.*, 948 S.W.2d 293 (Tex. 1997) (no distinction between residential and commercial leases); *Carisi v. Wax*, 192 N.J.Super. 536, 471 A.2d 439 (1983) (commercial tenants can waive landlord's duty, but not residential tenants). Does it make sense to allow tenants to waive the "duty" to mitigate? Is there a significant distinction between residential and commercial leases in this respect? Based on your reading of the *Schneiker* case, do you think that the Colorado courts would permit the parties to contract out of the landlord's duty to mitigate?

(c) *Effect of Landlord's Failure to Mitigate*. Suppose that in a jurisdiction that imposes a duty to mitigate, Henning leases Blueacre to George for a five-year term, at a rent of $500 per month. After two years, George abandons the premises. If Henning makes no effort whatsoever to mitigate his damages, should Henning be able to recover any amount from George? Should it matter whether reasonable efforts to re-let would have succeeded? *Compare St. George Chicago, Inc. v. George J. Murges & Assocs.*, 296 Ill.App.3d 285, 230 Ill.Dec. 1013, 695 N.E.2d 503 (1998) *and Whitehorn v. Dickerson*, 419 S.W.2d 713 (Mo. Ct. App. 1967) (tenant's liability reduced by amount that landlord reasonably could have recovered through re-letting) *with Finish Line, Inc. v. Jakobitz*, 557 N.W.2d 914 (Iowa Ct. App. 1996) *and* Uniform Residential Landlord and Tenant Act § 4–203 (landlord's failure to use reasonable efforts to mitigate damages extinguishes tenant's liability altogether).

(d) *Satisfying the Duty to Mitigate and Carrying the Burden of Proof.* Exactly what steps must the landlord take to satisfy its duty to mitigate damages? Furthermore, who should carry the burden of proof regarding whether landlord has satisfied this duty? *Compare St. George Chicago, Inc. v. George J. Murges & Assocs.*, 296 Ill.App.3d 285, 230 Ill.Dec. 1013, 695 N.E.2d 503 (1998) and *Finish Line, Inc. v. Jakobitz*, 557 N.W.2d 914 (Iowa Ct. App. 1996) (landlord bears burden of proof) *with Austin Hill Country Realty, Inc. v. Palisades Plaza, Inc.*, 948 S.W.2d 293 (Tex. 1997) and *Hilliard v. Robertson*, 253 Neb. 232, 570 N.W.2d 180 (1997) (tenant bears burden of proof). If you represented a tenant, how would you go about proving that the landlord has failed to mitigate its damages? If you represented a landlord, how would you go about proving that the landlord did satisfy its obligation to mitigate damages? *See* Dennis M. Horn, "Duty to Mitigate Damages," *reprinted in* The Commercial Property Lease 177, 183–85 (A.B.A. 1993).

6. *Rental Acceleration Clauses.* At common law, a landlord had no right upon the tenant's default to accelerate the due date of future rent payments absent an express "rent acceleration clause" in the lease permitting the landlord to do so. Without a rent acceleration clause, a landlord faced with an abandoning tenant would have only two relatively unappealing options— either to sue the tenant each rental period as the rental for that period accrued, or wait until the expiration of the lease and sue for all accrued but unpaid rent. For this reason, many leases contain rental acceleration provisions that authorize the landlord to demand the immediate payment of all future rent payments provided in the lease upon tenant's default. Authority is divided on whether acceleration clauses are enforceable. A significant number of courts have enforced acceleration clauses generally, reasoning that nothing prevents the parties from negotiating that the tenant should pay all rent in advance. *See, e.g., Jimmy Hall's Morningside, Inc. v. Blackburn & Peck Enters., Inc.*, 235 So.2d 344 (Fla. Dist. Ct. App. 1970). Some courts, however, have refused to enforce acceleration clauses on the ground that they constitute an unenforceable penalty rather than a valid measure of liquidating the landlord's damages. *See, e.g., Ricker v. Rombough*, 261 P.2d 328 (Cal. Super. 1953). Can you explain why a rent acceleration clause might

constitute a penalty, or provide the landlord with a recovery in excess of its actual damages? [Hint: How would the enforcement of an acceleration clause operate differently than a landlord's action for damages for anticipatory repudiation as discussed in note 3?]

Suppose that *L* purports to exercise a rental acceleration clause and obtains a judgment against *T* for the full accelerated rental balance. Can *L* thereafter re-let the premises? If *L* does re-let the premises, can L keep the rent paid by the new tenant for its own account, or must it be applied to the balance of the judgment against *T*? Does it matter whether or not *L* has a duty to mitigate? *See Hi Kai Inv., Ltd. v. Aloha Futons, Beds & Waterbeds,* 84 Haw. 75, 929 P.2d 88 (1996) (allowing eviction along with recovery of damages for future rent, reduced by mitigation); *Reid v. Mutual of Omaha Ins. Co.,* 776 P.2d 896 (Utah 1989) (court retains jurisdiction over claim to account for mitigation obligation); Roberta Kwall, *Retained Jurisdiction in Damage Actions Based on Anticipatory Breach: A Missing Link in Landlord—Tenant Law,* 37 Case W. Res. L. Rev. 273 (1986).

LAWYERING EXERCISE
(Document Review and Drafting)

SITUATION: Your client is a landlord that owns numerous commercial properties in a jurisdiction that imposes no duty to mitigate in case of tenant abandonment. Your client has asked you to review its standard lease form and evaluate whether that form provides the landlord with sufficient flexibility and leverage in dealing with problems associated with tenant abandonment. The form lease provides:

On the occurrence of any material default by Tenant, Landlord may, at any time thereafter:

(a) Terminate Tenant's right to possession of the premises by any lawful means, in which case this Lease shall terminate and Tenant shall immediately surrender possession of the premises to Landlord. In such event, Landlord shall be entitled to recover from Tenant any and all damages incurred by Landlord by reason of Tenant's default;

(b) Maintain Tenant's right to possession, in which case this Lease shall continue in effect whether or not Tenant has abandoned the premises. In such event, Landlord shall be entitled to enforce all of Landlord's rights and remedies under this Lease, including the right to collect rent as it accrues; or

(c) Pursue any other remedy now or hereafter available to Landlord under the laws or judicial decisions of the state in which the premises are located.

TASK: Prepare a memorandum in which you advise your client whether this provision is sufficient to protect her ability to act to re-let the premises without releasing the Tenant from liability. Revise the quoted provision as needed to protect your client against the risks that you have identified in the preceding materials.

LAWYERING EXERCISE
(Negotiation/Dispute Resolution)

Adapted from "The Missing Tenant," by Professor Dale A. Whitman

BACKGROUND: Professor Melvin Eisenberg has argued that when lawyers attempt to negotiate a settlement to a dispute, their training as lawyers inevitably influences the settlement process and the resulting resolution:

> Because of their training, and the fact that they typically become involved only when formal litigation is contemplated, lawyers are likely to negotiate on the basis of *legal* principles, rules, and precedents. When these two elements are combined, the result is that [lawyer vs. lawyer negotiation] is strikingly similar to a formal adjudicative unit in terms of both input and output. [Melvin A. Eisenberg, *Private Ordering Through Negotiation: Dispute–Settlement and Rulemaking*, 89 Harv. L. Rev. 637, 664–65 (1976).]

Professor Carrie Menkel–Meadow has argued that this effect has overall negative societal consequences:

> Negotiators too often conclude that they are limited to what would be available if the court entered a judgment. To the extent that court resolution of problems results in awards of money damages and injunctions, negotiators are likely to limit their crafting of solutions to those remedies. To the extent that a court would not allow a particular remedy such as barter, exchange, apology, or retributory action, negotiators may reject or not even conceive of these solutions.

> Similarly, because courts often declare one party a winner and the other a loser, negotiators often conceive of themselves as winners and losers, and in court games, the result is usually "winner take all." . . . [T]he more common structure of court resolution of disputes, such as "plaintiff wins $25,000" or "defendant acquitted," tends to narrow the conceptions of negotiation solutions since all solutions are judged against what the court is likely to do. Negotiations, therefore, proceed as an earlier version of court resolution, without the judge.

> One of the strengths of the legal system—definitive, precedential rulings to promote clarity, certainty, and order—may actually be dysfunctional for the creation of innovative and idiosyncratic solutions to problems that may never reach judicial resolution. To the extent that negotiations in the shadow of the court are limited by conceptions of what the court would do, negotiation may present no real, substantive alternative to trial. Lawyers may prefer this limited conception because it makes evaluation of possible outcomes clearer and easier, especially when discussing alternatives with clients. If this is so, then the large number of settlements can only be explained by the lower cost and relative speed of completion,

rather than the superior substantive justice that is done. . . . [Carrie Menkel–Meadow, *Toward Another View of Legal Negotiation: The Structure of Problem Solving*, 31 UCLA L. Rev. 754, 789–91 (1984).]

SITUATION: Frank Lawrence is the owner of a small commercial building near the University's football stadium. He has owned it for 10 years, and for most of that time it was rented to various retail and restaurant establishments. However, it has been vacant for the past year.

About three months ago, Lawrence was approached by Adam Turner, a local entrepreneur, who inquired about leasing the building for a new restaurant. Turner said that he had acquired a franchise from the nationally famous "Red Devil Dog" chain, and intended to set up a Red Devil Dog fast-food restaurant. After considerable discussion, Lawrence and Turner signed a written lease for the building. The lease was properly executed and complied with all legal formalities. In pertinent part, it read as follows:

LEASE

Frank Lawrence agrees to lease to Adam Turner the land and building located at [legal description]. Turner will use the property for a Red Devil Dog Restaurant, and for no other purpose. This lease shall commence 60 days from the date of its execution, and shall continue for five years. Turner shall pay as rental $1,000 per month, and in addition shall pay three percent (3%) of gross sales for the previous month. Turner shall also pay all property taxes, shall insure the property against fire and other casualty in the amount of $100,000 at Turner's own expense, and shall perform all necessary maintenance and repairs on the property during the continuance of this lease.

[signed]   Frank Lawrence

[signed]   Adam Turner

Date: _____

The lease was dated 90 days prior to the date of your negotiation. Turner gave Lawrence a security deposit of $2,000 at the time the lease was signed, although the lease itself did not mention the deposit.

The building was somewhat run-down and dilapidated as a consequence of its having been unoccupied for the last year. Turner advised Lawrence that the roof needed to be reinforced to hold the large "Red Devil Dog" sign which Turner planned to install. He also asked Lawrence to replace the existing front windows with much larger windows, as are customary in Red Devil Dog restaurants. These items were not mentioned in the lease, but Lawrence was willing to provide them without additional charge. During the next month, Lawrence made these modifications at a cost to himself of $2,500.

After these modifications were made to the building, Turner began acquiring the necessary restaurant equipment: a large grill for cooking, booths, counters, barstools, and the like. Even though the lease term had not yet commenced, Turner needed a place to store these items. At his request, Lawrence gave Turner permission to store them in the vacant building. They were not unpacked, and remain there at this time in their original shipping cartons and crates. Turner spent $9,000 of his own funds to buy these items.

One week before the lease term was to commence, Turner read in the *Wall Street Journal* that the "Red Devil Dog" chain had filed for bankruptcy, was hopelessly insolvent, and could not be expected to carry on its normal advertising and promotional activities in the future. Turner felt that he could not possibly make a profit in his new restaurant without the support of the national franchise. He immediately telephoned Lawrence and advised him that: "The lease is off. I can't rent your building." Lawrence merely replied that he would have to talk with his attorney about the matter.

Lawrence, however, did not discuss the case with his attorney at that time. Instead, he sent a letter to Turner which accused Turner of breaching the lease, and which demanded that Turner immediately pay to Lawrence:

- $60,000, representing the fixed rent that would have accrued over the lease term of five years.

- $18,000, representing an estimate of the percentage rent that would have accrued over the lease term.

- $2,500, representing the cost of the modifications Lawrence made to the building in anticipation of Turner leasing it.

The letter also advised Turner that the locks had been changed on the building and that Turner would not be allowed to gain access to it (either to remove his equipment or to begin doing business) until Turner had given Lawrence adequate assurances that he would meet his legal responsibilities, either to pay the sums demanded in the letter or to actually open for business as a "Red Devil Dog" restaurant. The parties have had no further direct communication, but each has retained counsel and the attorneys have arranged to meet.

TASK ONE. Assume a role as attorney for one of the parties (as assigned by your instructor). Prepare to negotiate this dispute with opposing counsel by preparing a brief memorandum that assesses the strengths and weaknesses of your case. What is your best alternative to a negotiated agreement (*i.e.,* what's the best result you can expect if you were to litigate the matter?) What is your worst alternative to a negotiated agreement? Knowing these parameters, what would you reasonably desire to achieve in negotiation? What matters are so essential that you will walk away from the negotiations if you cannot achieve them?

TASK TWO. Negotiate a resolution to the dispute with opposing counsel.

TASK THREE. Evaluate the extent to which the results of your negotiation were dictated by each party's respective legal position.

4. *The Physical Condition of the Leased Premises*

a. *Habitability—From Caveat Lessee to Implied Warranty.* Often, a tenant will find that she cannot fully enjoy the benefit of possession of the premises because of defects in the physical condition of the premises. In some cases, these conditions may be so egregious that they effectively deprive the tenant of getting any benefit from the right to possession. At common law, however, such conditions did not permit the tenant to raise a constructive eviction claim, unless the landlord had made express covenants in the lease regarding the condition of the premises (and the interference resulted from the landlord's breach of those covenants). At common law, courts used the doctrine of *caveat lessee*—in reliance upon the conveyance model—to place upon the tenant all responsibility for the condition of the premises during the tenancy, except in those cases where the landlord expressly contracted to bear responsibility.

Caveat lessee essentially equated the tenant with any other buyer of an interest in land—someone presumed fully capable of evaluating and repairing the physical condition of the property. Only in a few limited circumstances did the common law place any implied obligation upon the landlord regarding the condition of the premises:

- If the property suffered from latent defects of which the landlord knew or should have known, and which the tenant could not be expected to notice by inspection, the landlord was obligated to disclose such defects. *See Service Oil Co., Inc. v. White,* 218 Kan. 87, 542 P.2d 652 (1975).

- The landlord was responsible for maintaining the physical condition of common areas under the landlord's control. *See Nayman v. Tracey,* 599 So.2d 604 (Ala. 1992)*; Cappaert v. Junker,* 413 So.2d 378 (Miss. 1982).

- If the landlord contractually agreed to perform any repairs, the landlord was obligated to perform that agreement. *See Jordan v. Savage,* 88 Ill.App.2d 251, 232 N.E.2d 580 (1967); *Bartlett v. Taylor,* 351 Mo. 1060, 174 S.W.2d 844 (1943).

- If the lease was a short-term lease for the rental of furnished premises, the landlord was responsible for the physical condition of the premises. *See Ingalls v. Hobbs,* 156 Mass. 348, 31 N.E. 286 (1892).

- If the parties entered into a lease for a building under construction, the courts concluded that the lease contained an implied covenant by the landlord that the premises, when completed, would be fit for the purposes for which the tenant entered into the lease. *See Levitz Furniture Co. v. Continental Equities, Inc.*, 411 So.2d 221 (Fla. Dist. Ct. App. 1982).[18]

In these limited circumstances, landlords had some obligation to warrant, repair, or maintain the premises. Nevertheless, the law considered even these limited obligations to be independent of the tenant's obligation to pay rent. Thus, if the landlord breached this duty, the tenant could not withhold rent and terminate the lease unless either (a) the lease specifically provided the tenant with a termination right or (b) the landlord's breach resulted in conditions that were so serious as to justify a constructive eviction. Otherwise, the tenant was obliged to continue paying rent and could enforce the landlord's obligation only by seeking damages for the landlord's breach of the lease contract.

The doctrine of *caveat lessee* made sense when the typical tenancy was an agricultural lease of rural land. The land itself was the primary focus of such a lease, and the agricultural tenant was fully capable of making the repairs needed to the typical farm structures. Over time, however, the urban residential tenancy began to replace the rural agricultural tenancy as the "typical" tenancy. In the urban residential tenancy, the focus of the bargain was not the underlying land itself, but the individual apartment unit within the building. Further, the typical urban residential tenant did not necessarily have the skills or aptitude to make all repairs necessary to keep the premises in habitable condition, and in multi-unit buildings usually lacked access to critical building systems (heat, water heating, elevators, etc.) that might require maintenance. Nevertheless, throughout the late 19th and early 20th centuries, caveat lessee continued to hold sway as the default rule for residential leases. Because of the inadequate supply of residential rental housing as urban populations boomed, landlords did not need to invest substantial sums to make residential apartments "livable" to lease those apartments—many tenants effectively had to take whatever apartment they could find, regardless of its condition.

The condition of the nation's rental housing stock (especially in large cities) had its most profound consequences for the daily life of low-income tenants. Slum tenants found themselves paying relatively high urban rents (or at least high in relation to their ability to pay), yet occupying apartments with substandard heating, faulty wiring, leaking or inoperable plumbing fixtures, broken windows or window locks, and other conditions that compromised the ability of those tenants to enjoy their legal right to possession. Further, these tenants lacked sufficient market power to bargain for a lease that obligated the landlord to maintain the premises in a safe, healthy, and clean fashion. As a result, this convergence of economic circumstance and *caveat lessee* left an entire economic class of persons living in conditions that were at best undesirable and at worst unhealthy and unsafe. In this sort of world, the strict *caveat lessee* doctrine seems anachronistic. Over time, the doctrine

---

18. Can you explain why each of these exceptions was consistent with the philoso-phy underlying the doctrine of *caveat lessee*?

of *caveat lessee* became subject to intense criticism by editorialists, activists, and scholars—most of whom argued that the doctrine of *caveat lessee* unfairly and inefficiently placed responsibility for the condition of the premises upon tenants rather than landlords.

Early Reform—The Development of Housing Codes. In the late 19th and early 20th centuries, beginning with the New York Tenement House Law of 1867, legislatures began to respond to the widespread notoriety of slum housing conditions by enacting housing codes to govern the construction and operation of multi-unit residential properties. Housing codes were designed to protect the public health by ensuring the safety and cleanliness of housing stock, and did so by providing minimum standards governing the four basic aspects of building or operating rental housing: structural integrity (*e.g.*, walls, roofs, floors), nonstructural fixtures (*e.g.*, toilets, sinks, doors and door locks, windows and window locks), services (*e.g.*, heat, water, sewer, garbage, elevators), and occupancy (*e.g.*, limiting numbers of occupants per dwelling). Typically, legislatures entrusted enforcement of the housing codes to public officials, who inspected rental properties (either based upon official's own initiative or in response to tenant complaints) and who had authority to sanction violations through fines or orders to bring substandard properties up to code requirements.

Housing codes provided a significant impetus for the broader reform movement aimed at improving the quality of the nation's housing stock. For several reasons, however, the adoption of housing codes did not provide an effective solution to the plight of residential tenants. First, housing codes were not universal in scope; they did not become widespread until the late 1960s and early 1970s; even today, small-population counties may lack comprehensive housing codes. Second, tenants who complained to housing officials often discovered that at the conclusion of the lease, the landlord would not renew their leases. This sort of retaliatory conduct by landlords had the obvious effect of discouraging tenant complaints.[19] Third, housing code enforcement has been too sporadic to effect a systematic improvement in housing conditions.

---

19. As discussed earlier, at common law landlords had virtually unfettered power to terminate periodic tenancies and tenancies at will, and had equally unfettered power to refuse to renew an expired tenancy for years. The landlord's malevolence or spitefulness was irrelevant—the conveyance model of leasing accorded the landlord this power as an incident of the landlord's reversionary interest in the land. Of course, if landlords could use this power to retaliate against tenants who complained about housing code violations, this would seriously compromise the potential effectiveness of housing codes.

As a result, courts and legislatures have developed the doctrine of *retaliatory eviction* to forbid such retaliatory action by landlords. In most states recognizing the doctrine, if the landlord attempts to terminate a lease and evict the tenant within some period of time following a tenant's good faith complaint about housing code violations or the habitability of the premises, a rebuttable presumption arises that the landlord's action is retaliatory. Should a tenant also be able to use retaliatory eviction to forbid the landlord from refusing to renew an expired lease? If so, why? *See Building Monitoring Sys., Inc. v. Paxton*, 905 P.2d 1215 (Utah 1995).

Although retaliatory eviction doctrine provides tenants with a potential useful source of leverage in dealing with the landlord, many tenants are still hesitant to report violations or pursue legal action for fear of retaliation by the landlord. Can you explain why?

Traditionally, enforcement authority rested only with public officials; tenants could not bring private actions for housing code violations (unless the landlord expressly covenanted to maintain the premises up to housing code standards—which, of course, landlords typically never did!). But housing authorities were traditionally understaffed and inspectors were often overworked, poorly trained, or subject to corruption. As a result, tenant complaints to housing officials often resulted in no corrective action.

Judicial Reform—The "Illegal Lease" Doctrine. As criticism of *caveat lessee* widened and legislative efforts failed to address the problem of slum housing in an effective fashion, public interest lawyers turned their reform efforts toward courts. One early victory came with the District of Columbia Court of Appeals decision in *Brown v. Southall Realty Co.*, 237 A.2d 834 (1968), in which the court adopted the "illegal lease" doctrine. In *Brown*, a tenant signed a lease for premises that the landlord knew were in substantial violation of D.C.'s housing code. When the landlord failed to correct these violations, the tenant refused to pay rent and vacated the premises. The court concluded that the violations rendered the property unhealthy and unsafe, and concluded that the lease was void and that the landlord could not enforce it.

The direct impact of the illegal lease doctrine upon housing conditions was blunted by the doctrine's own limitations. The most significant limitation was that a lease was illegal (and thus unenforceable by the landlord) only if the premises violated the housing code *at the time the lease commenced*. The illegal lease doctrine did not impose on the landlord any *continuing duty to maintain* the premises in compliance with the housing code during the lease term. Thus, if the premises satisfied the housing code at the beginning of the term, but later fell into violation—a common scenario—the tenant could not raise the illegal lease doctrine as a defense to the tenant's obligation to pay rent. *Saunders v. First Nat'l Realty Corp.*, 245 A.2d 836 (D.C. App. 1968). In addition, the illegal lease doctrine presented a practical dilemma for the tenant. If a tenant successfully raised the doctrine, this defense did relieve the tenant from any further obligation to pay rent. Unfortunately, it also meant that the tenant could no longer claim the legal right to possession, as the lease was of no legal effect—and this gave the landlord a basis for claiming the ability to recover possession of the premises. Thus, tenants who wanted to retain possession of the premises (rather than endure the hassle of finding new places to live) often chose not to assert the illegal lease doctrine for fear of being evicted. In this regard, the doctrine was primarily useful only to those tenants who were ready to abandon the premises anyway.[20]

20. In this way, the illegal lease doctrine created something of a conundrum—exactly what was the status of a "tenant" who successfully asserted the illegal lease doctrine yet stayed in possession of the premises? The D.C. courts eventually concluded that such a person was a statutory tenant at sufferance, who was not liable for the rent stated in the lease but was liable in quasi-contract for the reasonable rental value of the premises in their existing condi-

Judicial Reform—The Implied Warranty of Habitability. The foregoing limitations on the illegal lease doctrine meant that the doctrine did not (and really could not) have a significant impact by itself upon housing conditions generally. Instead, the doctrine's true significance was as a harbinger of later and more aggressive judicial reforms. The illegal lease doctrine reflected the increasing willingness of courts to look to principles of contract law as a basis to re-evaluate the legitimacy of *caveat lessee* as a model for understanding the residential landlord-tenant bargain. This process of re-evaluation came to fruition with two significant reforms. First, courts began to adopt in widespread fashion an *implied warranty of habitability*—a covenant by the landlord, implied by law into residential leases, that the landlord will maintain the premises in a habitable condition throughout the duration of the lease. Second, courts concluded that the tenant's obligation to pay rent was *dependent* upon the landlord's compliance with the implied warranty of habitability. As the following materials demonstrate, these two changes fundamentally shifted the balance between residential landlords and tenants, greatly increasing the tenant's leverage in dealing effectively with problems concerning the condition of the leased premises. As you consider the following materials, consider why the law has chosen to imply such a warranty. Is it a function of public policy, or does it carry out the likely *ex ante* expectations of the typical landlord and tenant?

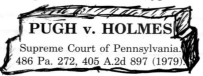

PUGH v. HOLMES

Supreme Court of Pennsylvania.
486 Pa. 272, 405 A.2d 897 (1979)

month to month Lease   *Pugh LL*

LARSEN, JUSTICE. Eloise Holmes, appellee, had been, pursuant to an oral month-to-month lease, renting a residential dwelling in Chambersburg in Franklin County at the rate of $60.00 per month from November, 1971 until recently. Her landlord, appellant J.C. Pugh, instituted two separate landlord-tenant actions against appellee before a justice of the peace, the first resulting in a judgment for unpaid rent (for the period from September, 1975 through June, 1976) and the second resulting in a judgment for unpaid rent (for the period from June, 1976 through August, 1976) and for possession of the premises. Following Mrs. Holmes' appeals to the Court of Common Pleas of Franklin County, appellant filed separate complaints, the first seeking unpaid rent and the

tion. *William J. Davis, Inc. v. Slade*, 271 A.2d 412 (D.C. App. 1970).

To demonstrate the difficulties created by this doctrine, consider the case of *Robinson v. Diamond Housing Corp.*, 150 U.S. App. D.C. 17, 463 F.2d 853 (1972). In this case, a tenant successfully asserted the illegal lease doctrine in response to an action for unpaid rent. Shortly thereafter, the landlord gave the tenant written notice to vacate, in compliance with the requirements of the D.C. statutes for recovering possession from a tenant at sufferance. When the landlord thereafter sued to evict the tenant, the tenant argued that the landlord was retaliating against the tenant for reporting housing code violations and that the landlord's eviction was thus illegal. The court agreed, and refused to allow the eviction unless the landlord could prove that it was going out of the rental housing business or was acting without a retaliatory motive. Exactly how could the landlord establish lack of retaliatory motive?

second seeking both unpaid rent and possession. In both actions, appellee filed answers asserting a defense of the landlord's alleged breach of an implied warranty of habitability. Additionally, in the second action, appellee asserted a setoff due in an amount which she claimed she had spent to repair a broken lock after having given appellant notice and a reasonable opportunity to repair the lock. Appellee also filed a counterclaim for the cost of repairing other allegedly defective conditions of which she had given appellant notice. Appellant filed preliminary objections to the answer and counterclaim which the Court of Common Pleas sustained finding that appellee's answer failed to set forth a legal defense to the landlord's actions, and that the counterclaim failed to set forth a legal cause of action.

On appeal, the Superior Court, by opinion of President Judge Jacobs, reversed and remanded. The Superior Court abolished the doctrine of *caveat emptor* as applied to residential leases and held that a warranty of habitability by the landlord will be implied in all such leases, which implied warranty would be mutually dependent upon the tenant's obligation to pay rent. By order dated July 20, 1978, this Court granted appellant's petition for allowance of appeal.

I. *Doctrine of Caveat Emptor Abolished/Implied Warranty of Habitability Adopted.* The doctrine of *caveat emptor* comported with the needs of the society in which it developed. However, we find that the doctrine of *caveat emptor* has outlived its usefulness and must be abolished, and that, in order to keep in step with the realities of modern day leasing, it is appropriate to adopt an implied warranty of habitability in residential leases. . . .

As stated by appellee, "times have changed. So has the law." Today, the doctrine of the implied warranty of habitability has attained majority status in the United States, the doctrine having been embraced by the appellate courts and/or the legislatures of some 40 state jurisdictions and the District of Columbia. The warranty recognizes that the modern tenant is not interested in land, but rather bargains for a dwelling house suitable for habitation.

Functionally viewed, the modern apartment dweller is a consumer of housing services. The contemporary leasing of residences envisions one person (landlord) exchanging for periodic payments (rent) a bundle of goods and services, rights and obligations. The now classic description of this economic reality appears in *Javins v. First National Realty Corp.*, 138 U.S.App.D.C. 369, 428 F.2d 1071, 1074, *cert. denied*, 400 U.S. 925, 91 S.Ct. 186, 27 L.Ed.2d 185 (1970) (footnote omitted). When American city dwellers both rich and poor, seek "shelter today, they seek a well known package of goods and services—a package which includes not merely walls and ceilings, but also adequate heat, light and ventilation, serviceable plumbing facilities, secure windows and doors, proper sanitation, and proper maintenance." [*Commonwealth v. Monumental Properties, Inc.*, 459 Pa. 450, 467–68, 329 A.2d 812, 820–21 (1974) (holding Unfair Trade

Practices and Consumer Protection Law applicable to residential leases.)]

Moreover, prospective tenants today can have vastly inferior bargaining power compared with the landlord, as was recognized in *Reitmeyer v. Sprecher*, 431 Pa. 284, 243 A.2d 395 (1968). In *Reitmeyer* this Court stated:

> Stark necessity very often forces a tenant into occupancy of premises far from desirable and in a defective state of repair. The acute housing shortage mandates that the average prospective tenant accede to the demands of the prospective landlord as to conditions of rental, which, under ordinary conditions with housing available, the average tenant would not and should not accept. No longer does the average prospective tenant occupy a free bargaining status and no longer do the average landlord-to-be and tenant-to-be negotiate a lease on an "arm's length" basis. [*Id.* at 289–90, 243 A.2d at 398.]

The Superior Court correctly observed that to join the trend toward an implied warranty of habitability would not be a complete and sudden break with the past, but would be the "next step in the law which has been developing in the Commonwealth for a number of years." 384 A.2d at 1239. Pennsylvania courts have held that a tenant's obligation to pay rent was mutually dependent on *express* covenants of a landlord to repair and that a material breach of the landlord's covenant to repair relieved a tenant from his obligation to pay rent. *McDanel v. Mack Realty Company*, 315 Pa. 174, 172 A. 97 (1934). In *Reitmeyer v. Sprecher, supra*, recognizing the contractual nature of modern leasing and the severe housing shortage resulting in unequal bargaining power, this Court adopted § 357 of the Restatement (Second) of Torts and imposed liability on a landlord who had breached a covenant to repair a dangerous condition on the premises, which breach resulted in injury to the tenant. In *Elderkin v. Gaster*, 447 Pa. 118, 288 A.2d 771 (1972), we abolished *caveat emptor* and adopted an implied warranty of habitability in sales of new homes to buyers by vendors/builders. . . .

More recently we held that a lessee of commercial property is relieved from the obligation to pay rent when the leased premises are destroyed by fire. *Albert M. Greenfield & Co., Inc. v. Kolea*, 475 Pa. 351, 380 A.2d 758 (1977). This Court stated

commercial obligation void when premises destroyed by fire

> In reaching a decision involving the landlord-tenant relationship, too often courts have relied on outdated common law property principles and presumptions and have refused to consider the factors necessary for an equitable and just conclusion. . . . Buildings are critical to the functioning of modern society. When the parties bargain for the use of a building, the soil beneath is generally of little consequence. Our laws should develop to reflect these changes. [*Id.* at 356–57, 380 A.2d at 760.]

Given the foregoing considerations and authority, we affirm the Superior Court's holding that a lease is in the nature of a contract and is to be controlled by principles of contract law. The covenants and warranties in the lease are mutually dependent; the tenant's obligation to pay rent and the landlord's obligation imposed by the implied warranty of habitability to provide and maintain habitable premises are, therefore, dependent and a material breach of one of these obligations will relieve the obligation of the other so long as the breach continues.

II. *Adoption of Implied Warranty of Habitability: A Proper Judicial Function*. Appellant does not argue that an implied warranty of habitability does not comport with current understanding of the landlord-tenant relationship. In light of the overwhelming authority in favor of the warranty, he would be hard pressed to do so. Rather, the thrust of appellant's argument is that the establishment of an implied warranty of habitability is the setting of social policy, which is a function of the legislature. Specifically, appellant maintains that, because the legislature has acted in the field via the Rent Withholding Act, Act of January 24, 1966, P.L. 1534, *as amended*, 35 P.S. § 1700–1 (1977), the courts are prohibited from further development of common law solutions to landlord-tenant/habitability problems. We cannot accept this position. . . .

[Editors' Note: The Rent Withholding Act permitted a tenant to deposit its rent payments into an escrow account if housing officials certified the premises as "unfit for human habitation," until such conditions were cured. Once the premises were certified as fit for human habitation, the escrowed rents were to be released to landlord; if not cured within six months, they were to be paid to the tenant (or the tenant could use them to cure the uninhabitable conditions). While the conditions persisted, the landlord could not evict the tenant for nonpayment of rent so long as the tenant deposited the rent into escrow.]

The Act does not purport to be the exclusive tenant remedy for unsavory housing, nor does it attempt to replace or alter certain limited and already existing tenant remedies such as constructive eviction. *Kelly v. Miller*, 249 Pa. 314, 94 A. 1055 (1915). The Act's silence as to constructive eviction could not be construed, without more, as a legislative abolition of that doctrine. Neither can mere enactment of the Rent Withholding Act signal a legislative intent to remove from the courts the authority to fashion new remedies where appropriate in the landlord-tenant field.

Caveat emptor was a creature of the common law. *Elderkin v. Gastner*, *supra* at 123, 288 A.2d at 774. Courts have a duty "to reappraise old doctrines in the light of the facts and values of contemporary life—particularly old common law doctrines which the courts themselves have created and developed." *Javins v. First National Realty Corp.*, *supra*, 138 U.S.App.D.C. at 372, 373, 428 F.2d at 1074, *quoted in Albert M. Greenfield & Co., Inc. v. Kolea*, *supra* at 357, 380 A.2d at 760. And when a rule has been duly tested by experience and found inconsistent with the sense of justice or the social welfare there should be little hesitation in "frank avowal and full abandonment." Cardozo, The Nature of the Judicial Process, 150–51 (1921), *cited [in] Griffith v. United Airlines, Inc.*, 416 Pa. 1, 23, 203 A.2d 796, 806 (1964). . . .

In reappraising antiquated laws, it is entirely proper to seek guidance from policies underlying related legislation. . . . The purpose of the Act is to restore substandard housing to a reasonable level of habitability as swiftly as possible and to deter landlords from allowing their property to deteriorate into a condition unfit for habitation. *Newland v. Newland*, 26 Pa.Cmwlth. 519, 364 A.2d 988 (1976) and *Palmer v. Allegheny County Health Department*, 21 Pa.Cmwlth. 246, 345 A.2d 317 (1975). The adoption of the implied warranty of habitability is consistent with this policy.

Appellate courts of other jurisdictions have considered and rejected the argument that a state's rent withholding act or other statutory remedies precluded judicial adoption of the implied warranty of habitability. . . . We conclude, therefore, that the Rent Withholding Act is not the exclusive tenant remedy for a landlord's failure to maintain the leased premises in a habitable state nor does it preclude judicial development of common law landlord and tenant obligations, rights and remedies. To the contrary, the Act supports the adoption of the implied warranty of habitability.

III. *Breach of the Implied Warranty of Habitability*. Appellant also asserts that the Superior Court erred by failing to establish definite standards by which habitability can be measured and breach of the warranty ascertained. We disagree—the parameters of the warranty were adequately defined by the Superior Court.

The implied warranty is designed to insure that a landlord will provide facilities and services vital to the life, health, and safety of the tenant and to the use of the premises for residential purposes. This warranty is applicable both at the beginning of the lease and throughout its duration.

[margin note: Duty of landlord]

In order to constitute a breach of the warranty the defect must be of a nature and kind which will prevent the use of the dwelling for its intended purpose to provide premises fit for habitation by its dwellers. At a minimum, this means the premises must be safe and sanitary. Of course, there is no obligation on the part of the landlord to supply a perfect or aesthetically pleasing dwelling. *Pugh v. Holmes*, 384 A.2d at 1240. "Materiality of the breach is a question of fact to be decided by the trier of fact on a case-by-case basis." *Id.* Several factors (not exclusive) are listed by the Superior Court as considerations in determining materiality, including the existence of housing code violations and the nature, seriousness and duration of the defect. *Id.*

[margin note: factors]

We believe these standards fully capable of guiding the fact finder in his determination of materiality of the breach. Further, these standards are flexible enough to allow the gradual development of the habitability doctrine in the best common law tradition. This finds support in *Elderkin v. Gaster, supra*, wherein we declined to establish rigid standards for determining habitability and its breach in the builder/vendor vendee context and, instead, defined habitability in terms of "contemporary community standards" and breach of the warranty as whether the defect prevented the use of the dwelling for the purposes intended—habitation. 447 Pa. at 128, 288 A.2d at 777. In that case, we held that lack of a potable water supply to the home prevented its use as habitation and, accordingly, found the implied warranty of habitability to have been breached.

Additionally, we agree with the Superior Court that, to assert a breach of the implied warranty of habitability, a tenant must prove he or she gave notice to the landlord of the defect or condition, that he (the landlord) had a reasonable opportunity to make the necessary repairs, and that he failed to do so.

Appellant would require that a determination of breach of the implied warranty be dependent upon proof of violations of the local housing codes. We decline to accept this argument as it would unnecessarily restrict the determination of breach. The Supreme Court of Massachusetts was asked to define their implied warranty of habitability by reference to a housing code of statewide applicability, but declined to do so. [*Boston Housing Authority v. Hemingway*, 293 N.E.2d 831 (Mass. 1973).] . . .

Other courts have likewise concluded that the existence of housing code violations is only one of several evidentiary considerations that enter into the materiality of the breach issue. *E.g., Foisy v. Wyman*, 83 Wash.2d 22, 515 P.2d 160 (1973); *King v. Moorehead*, 495 S.W.2d 65 (Mo.App.1973); *Mease v. Fox*, 200 N.W.2d 791 (Iowa 1972). This reasoning is even more persuasive in Pennsylvania where there is no statewide housing code and where many municipalities have not promulgated local housing regulations.

In this case, appellee alleged ten specific defective conditions including a leaky roof, lack of hot water, leaking toilet and pipes, cockroach infestation and hazardous floors and steps. If proven on remand, these conditions would substantially prevent the use of the premises as a habitable dwelling place and could justify a finding by the trier of fact that a breach of the implied warranty of habitability had occurred.

IV. *Remedies for Breach of Implied Warranty of Habitability*. As the adoption today of the implied warranty of habitability creates new legal rights and obligations, it is essential for this Court to outline and clarify some of the available remedies and the manner in which these remedies are to be implemented. The tenant may vacate the premises where the landlord materially breaches the implied warranty of habitability—we have held analogously where the landlord materially breaches express covenants to repair or to maintain the leasehold in a habitable state. *See McDanel v. Mack Realty Co., supra*, 315 Pa. at 174, 172 A. 97. Surrender of possession by the tenant would terminate his obligation to pay rent under the lease. *Lemle v. Breeden*, 51 Haw. 426, 462 P.2d 470 (1969).

Where the tenant remains in possession, and the landlord sues for possession for unpaid rent, the implied warranty of habitability may be asserted as a defense. Virtually all courts addressing the issue of breach of this warranty as a defense concur with this view. *See e. g.,* cases cited by the Superior Court at 384 A.2d 1240 and *Rome v. Walker,* 38 Mich.App. 458, 196 N.W.2d 850 (1972); *Fritz v. Warthen,* 298 Minn. 54, 213 N.W.2d 339 (1973); *see* Restatement (Second) of Property, Landlord and Tenant, § 11.1 (Rent Abatement). If the landlord totally breached the implied warranty of habitability, the tenant's obligation to pay rent would be abated in full—the action for possession would fail because there would be no unpaid rent. *Pugh v. Holmes, supra,* 384 A.2d at 1241, *citing Javins v. First National Realty Corp., supra,* 138 U.S.App.D.C. at 380–81, 428 F.2d 1082–83. If the landlord had not breached the warranty at all, no part of the tenant's obligation to pay rent would be abated and the landlord would be entitled to a judgment for possession and for unpaid rent. *Id.* If there had been a partial breach of the warranty, the obligation to pay rent would be abated in part only. In such case, a judgment for possession must be denied if the tenant agrees to pay that portion of the rent not abated; if the tenant refuses to pay the partial rent due, a judgment granting possession would be ordered. *Id.*

Appellant urges that the failure of the Superior Court to require a method of escrowing unpaid rent monies is "the most glaring defect" in the Superior Court's decision below. This Court is in favor of an escrow procedure, but is not inclined to make such procedure mandatory. Rather, the decision whether a tenant should deposit all or some of the unpaid rents into escrow should lie in the sound discretion of the trial judge or magistrate. The tenant may retain his rent, subject to the court's discretionary power to order him, following a hearing on the petition of the landlord or tenant, to deposit all or some of the rent with the court or a receiver appointed by the court. This is the approach taken by a majority of the courts which permit the tenant to withhold rent pending the outcome of litigation in which the defense of the implied warranty of habitability is asserted. Restatement (Second) of Property, Landlord and Tenant § 11.3, Reporter's note 2 (1970), *citing, e.g., Javins v. First National Realty Corp., supra* and *Hinson v. Delis,* 26 Cal.App.3d 62, 102 Cal.Rptr. 661 (1972). Factors to be considered include the seriousness and duration of the alleged defects, and the likelihood that the tenant will be able to successfully demonstrate the breach of warranty. *Id.*

Also at issue in this case is the availability of the "repair and deduct" remedy. Appellee, after allegedly giving notice to the landlord and a reasonable opportunity to repair, repaired a broken door lock and deducted $6.00 from her rent for the month of May, 1975. We have held that, where a landlord fails to perform a lease covenant, the tenant may perform it at his own expense (if reasonable) and deduct the cost of his performance from the amount of rent due and payable. *McDanel v. Mack Realty Co., supra,* 315 Pa. at 177, 172 A. 97 (landlord failed to perform covenant to supply heat; tenant could have provided heat and deducted reasonable costs from rent). Similarly, the repair and deduct remedy is appropriate for breaches of the implied warranty of habitability. This remedy has been approved in other jurisdictions, *Marini v. Ireland,* 56

N.J. 130, 265 A.2d 526 (1970); *Garcia v. Freeland Realty Co.*, 63 Misc.2d 937, 314 N.Y.S.2d 215 (1970) and by the Restatement (Second) of Property, Landlord and Tenant § 11.2. Section 11.2 provides "[i]f a tenant is entitled to apply his rent to eliminate the landlord's default, the tenant, after proper notice to the landlord, may deduct from his rent reasonable costs incurred in eliminating the default." "Proper notice" in this instance is one that describes the default and specifies what steps will be taken by the tenant to correct it if the landlord has not eliminated the defective condition within a reasonable time. The use of the repair and deduct remedy is not, of course, unlimited. Repairs must be reasonably priced and cannot exceed the amount of the rent available to apply against the cost, i.e., the amount of rent owed for the term of the lease. Further the tenant runs the risk of an adverse court finding on the necessity of the repairs—if the court finds that the repairs were not needed to render the premises habitable, the court must find the rent deduction unreasonable. In such event, the landlord could obtain a judgment for the amount of rent deducted. Or if the repairs were needed but the cost was excessive, the landlord could recover the difference between the actual cost and what would have been the reasonable cost of repairs.

Appellant also asserted a counterclaim for $25.00 for repairs allegedly made at various times to the heating system, the bathroom floor and to replace a broken window pane. In principle, we see little difference between the counterclaim for repairs and the "repair and deduct" remedy. The counterclaim can be utilized to recover damages from already paid rents based upon expenses incurred in making repairs of defective conditions after failure of the landlord to repair within a reasonable time following proper notice. *See Marini v. Ireland, supra* and *Garcia v. Freeland Realty Co., supra, Pines v. Perssion*, 14 Wis.2d 590, 111 N.W.2d 409 (1961). The limitations applicable to the repair and deduct remedy are applicable here as well—the cost of the repairs must be reasonable and the maximum amount which the tenant may expend is the amount of rent owed for the term of the lease. However, the counterclaim is not available where the tenant has not paid his rent for the period in which the repairs are made and the cost of the repairs do not exceed the rent owed for that period. In that case, there are no damages as the tenant has already been compensated for the cost of repairs by not paying rent.

Finally, since the lease is a contract, other traditional contract remedies such as specific performance are available to enforce the implied warranty of habitability. *Javins, supra* 138 U.S.App.D.C. at 380, at 428 F.2d 1082, n.61; *see* Uniform Residential Landlord and Tenant Act § 4.101(b) (1972) *and* Blumberg and Robbins, Beyond URLTA: A Program for Achieving Real Tenant Goals, 11 Harv.Civ.Rts.-Civ. Lib.L.Rev. 1 (1976). As with other contracts, however, specific performance is an equitable remedy not available as a matter of course but only in unique situations. 11 S. Williston, Contracts § 1418A (3d ed. 1968).

V. *Measure of Rent Abated*. The Superior Court held, where the tenant claims the breach of warranty of habitability as a defense or counterclaim, "the monthly rent past and future (until the dwelling is returned to a habitable state) may be reduced by the difference between the agreed upon rent and the fair rental value of the apartment in its present condition." It is urged that this Court adopt the "percentage reduction of use" method of calculating damages for breach of the implied warranty rather than the "fair rental value" approach suggested by the Superior Court. We hold that the "percentage reduction in use" method is the correct manner of determining the amount by which the obligation to pay rent is abated.

The "fair market value" approach suffers from two drawbacks. The first is that it assumes there is a *fair market* for the defective premises. This assumption is questionable given the housing crisis which exists today. *Reitmeyer v. Sprecher, supra* 431 Pa. at 289–90, 243 A.2d at 398 (1968). Because of the housing shortage, "Premises which, under normal circumstances, would be completely unattractive for rental are now, by necessity, at a premium." *Id.* at 290, 243 A.2d at 398. As one author phrased it "it seems questionable whether in asserting damages in this situation cognizance should be taken of a 'fair' market value of noncomplying housing—such a market could be regarded as an illegal 'black market' existing only by violation of law." Note, 84 Harv.L.Rev. 729, 737 (1971).

The second flaw is a practical one. The determination of the fair market value of the defective dwelling would in all probability require some type of market survey, statistical evidence, or expert testimony from realtors or appraisers familiar with the local rental market. See, Moskovitz, The Implied Warranty of Habitability: A New Doctrine Raising New Issues, 62 Calif.L.Rev. 1444, 1467–68 (1974). "The cost of obtaining such evidence or testimony would simply be prohibitive to many litigants, especially low-income tenants." *Id.*

Under the "percentage reduction in use" approach, the rent is to be abated "by a percentage reflecting the diminution [in] the value of the use and enjoyment of leased premises by reason of the existence of defects which gave rise to the breach of habitability." *McKenna v. Begin*, 325 N.E.2d 587 (1975).

This method of evaluation better achieves the goal of returning the injured party (the tenant) to the position he would have been in if performance had been rendered as warranted. The tenant bargains for habitable premises and the rental price reflects the value placed on those premises by the parties. Therefore, where the premises are rendered uninhabitable, in whole or in part, the contract price (fixed by the lease) is to be reduced by the percentage which reflects the diminution in use for the intended purpose. Another advantage of the percentage reduction method is that the need for expert testimony is greatly reduced as the determination in "percentage of reduction in use" of a residential dwelling is a matter within the capabilities of the layman....

Accordingly, on remand, if breach of the implied warranty of habitability is proven, the trial court is to apply the "percentage reduction in use" formula to determine the percentage by which the use and enjoyment of the premises had been diminished. . . .

Notes

1. *The Underlying Basis for Implying a Warranty of Habitability.* What does the *Pugh* case suggest about why courts and legislatures have embraced the implied warranty of habitability? Have they done so purely because of concerns of public health and safety (*i.e.*, to assure a minimum and safe quality of housing)? Or have they done so because a reasonable landlord and a reasonable tenant, if they had equal bargaining power, would agree that the landlord would bear such a warranty? In terms of how the implied warranty is applied in particular cases, why does it matter what the warranty's underlying rationale is?

2. *The Mechanics of the Implied Warranty of Habitability.* As the *Pugh* case suggests, implementing the implied warranty of habitability requires the resolution of a number of issues, either by courts or legislatures (a significant number of states have adopted statutory regimes governing habitability in residential leases, many of those regimes based upon the provisions of the Uniform Residential Landlord and Tenant Act). These issues include:

(a) *What Types of Residential Units Should Be Covered?* Does the implied warranty of habitability apply to all residential units? Only to multi-family units? Only to residential units in urban areas? *Compare Glasoe v. Trinkle*, 107 Ill.2d 1, 88 Ill.Dec. 895, 479 N.E.2d 915 (1985) (applies to all leases of residential real estate) *with Zimmerman v. Moore*, 441 N.E.2d 690 (Ind. Ct. App. 1982) (does not apply to leases of single-family homes). What did the *Pugh* court say about this question?

(b) *What Problems Should Result in a Breach of the Warranty?* Like *Pugh*, most states have concluded that the implied warranty does not depend upon the existence of a housing code. *See, e.g.,* Me. Rev. Stat. Ann. § 6021(2), (3) (condition that renders dwelling unit unfit for human habitation constitutes breach even in absence of housing code).

Where a housing code exists, it is relatively clear that a significant or serious violation of the housing code—*i.e.*, one that renders the premises unsafe or unfit for the purposes of habitation, such as nonfunctional plumbing or broken door/window locks—will violate the implied warranty of habitability. But what is the impact of landlord's compliance with the code? *Compare Boston Hous. Auth. v. Hemingway*, 363 Mass. 184, 293 N.E.2d 831, 844 n.16 (1973) (warranty may be violated by condition despite compliance with code) *with Jack Spring, Inc. v. Little*, 50 Ill.2d 351, 280 N.E.2d 208 (1972) (warranty is satisfied by "substantial compliance with the pertinent provisions of the Chicago building code"). Further, would all code violations place the landlord in breach of the implied warranty? For example, suppose that Tenant argues Landlord has breached the implied warranty of habitability because of repeated failures to repair a central air conditioning system. Does lack of air conditioning constitute a breach of the implied warranty of habitability? *Park Hill Terrace Assocs. v. Glennon*, 146 N.J.Super. 271, 369 A.2d 938 (1977).

(c) *Should Tenants Be Permitted to Waive the Warranty?* Suppose that Tenant signs a lease that states "Landlord and Tenant expressly agree that Landlord shall have no duties with respect to the condition of the premises. Tenant hereby waives the protection of any warranty of habitability implied by law. Tenant expressly agrees that it shall be solely and completely responsible for the condition and maintenance of the premises." Should a court enforce this provision against Tenant? Should it matter whether the agreed rental in fact approximates the actual rental value of the premises in their substandard condition? Should it matter whether the Tenant is sophisticated and/or well-educated (for example, should law students be able to waive the implied warranty)? Should it matter if the landlord is not someone typically in the business of leasing property? Why or why not? *Compare* Vt. Stat. Ann. tit. 9, § 4457 (waiver is void as contrary to public policy) *with* Me. Rev. Stat. Ann. § 6021(5)-(6) (tenant may agree to accept certain conditions in violation of implied warranty of habitability in exchange for reduction in rent).

(d) *What Must the Tenant Do to Place the Landlord in Breach?* As *Pugh* suggests, the tenant cannot effectively place the landlord in breach of the implied warranty of habitability unless the tenant has first given the landlord notice of the defect and a reasonable time to make the necessary repairs. *See* Uniform Residential Landlord and Tenant Act §§ 2.104, 4.101, 4.103, 4.104.

3. *Remedies for Breach of the Implied Warranty of Habitability.* Because of the ostensibly contractual basis of the implied warranty of habitability, most courts (like *Pugh*) have agreed that in the case of breach, the tenant may choose between the traditional contract remedies. The tenant may rescind the contract and terminate the lease, as the tenant's obligation to pay rent is dependent upon the landlord's performance of the implied warranty. To terminate the lease (and all future liability for rent), however, the tenant must vacate the premises. Alternatively, the tenant may remain in possession and continue to remain liable for rent, although the tenant's ultimate liability for rent may be diminished by virtue of the landlord's breach. If the tenant remains in possession, the tenant may withhold rent and raise habitability violations either as a defense to the landlord's action for unpaid rent or in an action by the tenant for damages resulting from the landlord's breach.

(a) *Rent Withholding and Rent Escrowing.* As *Pugh* explains, a number of courts allowed tenants to withhold rent in the face of the landlord's breach of the implied warranty of habitability, beginning with the landmark decision in *Javins v. First Nat'l Realty Corp.*, 138 U.S. App. D.C. 369, 428 F.2d 1071 (1970). As a practical matter, withholding rent is a superior remedy for the tenant because it provides leverage to force the landlord to make repairs without the necessity of filing a lawsuit. If the landlord sues for eviction based upon unpaid rent, the tenant can raise the implied warranty of habitability as an affirmative defense—*i.e.*, the tenant can assert that the breach has either satisfied or reduced the tenant's rent obligation.[21]

---

21. In these jurisdictions, how does the implied warranty of habitability alter the dynamics of the summary eviction process? Traditionally, jurisdictions limited the scope

The remedy of rent withholding may present some risk for the tenant, however. If the court concludes either that the landlord had not breached its warranty or that the tenant withheld more rent than the actual damages tenant suffered, the landlord may then be able to terminate the lease for the tenant's nonpayment of rent properly due (thereby extinguishing tenant's right to possession). [Recall that constructive eviction presented the tenant with the same dilemma.] Therefore, a tenant pursuing rent withholding might act more prudently by paying the stated rent into an escrow account, held either by the court or a third party identified by the court. In this way, the court could require application of these funds to the tenant's ultimate rental liability as determined by the court. Like *Pugh*, many judicial decisions suggest that the judge has the discretion to provide for escrowing of rent. Furthermore, a few state statutes require the tenant to escrow rental payments in certain habitability disputes. *See, e.g.*, Wash. Rev. Code Ann. § 58.18.115 (tenant must deposit withheld rent into escrow following certification by local authority that premises are not habitable).

(b) *Calculation of Damages (or Amount of Rent Withholding)*. Consider the following hypothetical: Tenant agrees to pay Landlord $600 per month in rent. The premises fall into disrepair to an extent that violates the implied warranty of habitability. Assume that in their defective condition, the premises were worth $600—*i.e.*, there are other persons who would pay $600/month to occupy the premises even in their present condition. Tenant argues that if the premises had been in full compliance with the implied warranty of habitability, they would have been worth $750 per month. How much can Tenant recover (for any prior months for which Tenant has paid the full stated rent) or withhold from future rental payments?

Courts have adopted one of three distinct measures of damages for breach of the implied warranty of habitability.

- One is the traditional "benefit of the bargain" measure generally applied for breaches of other lease covenants, *i.e.*, the fair value of the premises as warranted (*i.e.*, habitable premises) less the value of the premises in their defective condition. Under this approach, typified by the decision in *Hilder v. St. Peter*, 144 Vt. 150, 478 A.2d 202 (1984), Tenant could recover or withhold $150/month in damages. [Under this measure, notice that damages could actually exceed the total rent agreed on by the parties; if a jury found that the premises were so bad as to be worth zero, the landlord's liability would be $750/month even though the tenant had only agreed to pay $600/month.]

of summary eviction proceedings so that the only issue was the landlord's right to possession; under this narrow view, the tenant could not raise the landlord's conduct as a defense. Many jurisdictions now allow the tenant to raise the habitability of the premises as a defenses to a summary eviction proceeding (although many do not allow the tenant to assert counterclaims for damages in such proceedings). As a result, the summary eviction proceeding is no longer per-

ceived as being very "summary" in many jurisdictions. How might a summary eviction statute protect the tenant's right to address habitability issues without permitting tenant abuse of the eviction process? *See* Randy G. Gerchick, Comment, *No Easy Way Out: Making The Summary Eviction Process A Fairer And More Efficient Alternative To Landlord Self-Help*, 41 UCLA L. Rev. 759 (1994).

- By contrast, the court in *Pugh* measured the tenant's damages as a function of the percentage diminution in the usefulness of the premises resulting from the breach. Under this view, if Tenant could demonstrate that the habitability violations reduced the usefulness of the premises below the habitability standard by 50%, Tenant could recover or withhold $300/month (the $600 rent paid/agreed x 50% diminution in usefulness).

- Finally, a number of courts have measured the tenant's damages by reference to the agreed rental specified in the lease. Under this view, typified by the decision in *Kline v. Burns*, 111 N.H. 87, 276 A.2d 248 (1971), a tenant could recover damages equal to the agreed rent less the value of the premises in their defective condition. *See also Berzito v. Gambino*, 63 N.J. 460, 308 A.2d 17 (1973). Under this approach, Tenant would recover no damages so long as the jury concludes that the agreed rent of $600/month accurately reflects the fair market value of the premises in their defective condition.

Which of these three measures would a tenant prefer and why? Can you articulate the strengths and weaknesses of each measure of damages? Given the policies for implying a warranty of habitability, which measure best advances those policies?

(c) *"Repair and Deduct."* Statutes in a number of states authorize tenants to exercise self-help to remedy a breach of the implied warranty of habitability through the use of the "repair and deduct" mechanism. This allows the tenant to satisfy its rental obligation, in whole or in part, by undertaking the repairs itself. Can you explain why this is such a useful remedy? Do you see why landlord might view this as a potentially dangerous remedy? Where permitted, should "repair and deduct" be limited to certain maximum amounts or types of repairs? Should a group of tenants be able to "pool" repair and deduct rights to address building-wide problems (*e.g.*, defects in a central heating system)? Most of these statutes place a limit upon the total rental obligation that a tenant may satisfy using the repair and deduct remedy, *see* Calif. Civil Code § 1942 (one month's rent). Should a court permit a tenant to use repair and deduct even if there is no statute authorizing its use? *See Pines v. Perssion*, 14 Wis.2d 590, 111 N.W.2d 409 (1961).

4. *The Condition of Commercial Premises—Caveat Lessee, or Implied Warranty of Fitness?* Do the justifications for implying the warranty of habitability in the residential context carry over into the realm of commercial relationships? For example, suppose that Barnes signs a three-year lease of a building in which he plans to operate a restaurant. Two weeks after the lease commences, the building floods following a heavy rain due to extensive roof leakage. If the lease did not specifically address the condition of the roof and its effect on the lease, can Barnes terminate the lease? Although there are a few decisions that have recognized an implied warranty of fitness in commercial leases, *see, e.g., Davidow v. Inwood North Prof'l Group—Phase I*, 747 S.W.2d 373 (Tex. 1988) (implying warranty of fitness into lease for medical office space), the vast weight of authority has refused to extend any implied warranty of fitness into commercial leases. *See, e.g., Knapp v. Simmons*, 345 N.W.2d 118 (Iowa 1984); *Mobil Oil Credit Corp. v. DST*

Realty, Inc., *689 S.W.2d 658 (Mo. Ct. App. 1985). Can you explain why?* See generally *Note,* The Unwarranted Implication of a Warranty of Fitness in Commercial Leases—An Alternative Approach, *41 Vand. L. Rev. 1057 (1988).*

5. *Habitability and the Covenant of Quiet Enjoyment.* Not all jurisdictions have adopted an implied warranty of habitability. *See, e.g., Blackwell v. Del Bosco,* 191 Colo. 344, 558 P.2d 563 (1976) (adoption of warranty is more properly a legislative function). In such a jurisdiction, can a tenant turn to the covenant of quiet enjoyment for comparable protection? For example, consider the facts of *Bedell v. Los Zapatistas, Inc.,* 805 P.2d 1198 (Colo. Ct. App. 1991). In *Bedell,* the tenant leased a home on a month-to-month basis, but encountered significant problems with malfunctioning heating and plumbing systems and collapsing ceilings. When the tenant did not pay rent, the landlord sued to recover the unpaid rent, and the tenant counterclaimed for damages based upon the diminished value of the premises in their existing condition. The court held that while there was no implied warranty of habitability, the landlord had constructively evicted the tenant and thus the tenant had no obligation for rent for the premises following her departure. The court also remanded the case, however, for a new trial on the tenant's claim for damages (including the period while the tenant remained in possession). Does the covenant of quiet enjoyment, as previously explored, support this conclusion?

Alternatively, consider the commercial context, where most jurisdictions have rejected any implied warranty of fitness. Suppose that Monahan signs a five-year lease for ground floor office space in a building. During the first year of the lease, Monahan discovers that the ground floor offices flood during heavy rains because water running off of an adjacent driveway seeps through the building foundation. During the second year, Monahan is negotiating with landlord to rent additional space in the building. In the context of these negotiations, Monahan asks landlord to make the repairs necessary to prevent flooding of the ground floor office areas, and landlord agrees (as an inducement to convince Monahan to sign a new lease covering both the original space and the additional space). The flooding continues, and eventually is so frequent and severe that Monahan vacates the premises and argues constructive eviction. How would your analysis of this situation differ if Monahan argues (a) breach of the implied warranty of fitness, as opposed to (b) breach of the covenant of quiet enjoyment and constructive eviction? *See, e.g., Reste Realty Corp. v. Cooper,* 53 N.J. 444, 251 A.2d 268 (1969).

b. *Allocating Responsibility for Damage or Destruction of the Premises.* As discussed in the preceding section, the common law did not require the landlord to warrant the condition of the premises or to repair the premises if damage or destruction occurred during the lease term (unless the lease contained the landlord's personal covenant to make repairs). This view continues to hold sway as between commercial landlords and tenants in the majority of states that refuse to imply any warranty of fitness into commercial leases.

As a result, landlords and tenants must be particularly alert to the issues associated with repair of the premises necessitated by ordinary wear and tear, obsolescence, deferred maintenance, casualty, or intervening governmental regulation. Among the issues that the parties must address include: (1) What impact does casualty damage to the premises have upon the tenant's obligation to pay rent? (2) What duties, if any, does the tenant have with respect to maintaining the property and/or making routine repairs? (3) When extraordinary problems plague the premises, what duties, if any, does the tenant have with respect to rebuilding the property or making extraordinary repairs? (4) How might lease provisions be used to protect each party's interests regarding responsibilities related to the condition of the premises?

HADIAN v. SCHWARTZ

Supreme Court of California, In Bank.
8 Cal.4th 836, 35 Cal.Rptr.2d 589, 884 P.2d 46 (1994).

ARABIAN, J. . . . On April 14, 1984, plaintiff Rose Hadian and defendant Edward Schwartz signed a lease agreement involving commercial property at 2906 Sunset Boulevard in the Silver Lake district of Los Angeles. Hadian owned the building, constructed of unreinforced masonry, and Schwartz intended to lease it for use as a combined bar and cabaret. The term of the lease was three years at a monthly rental of $650, with an option to renew for an additional five years at a rental of $800 a month. The lease agreement itself took the form of a preprinted "fill-in-the-blank" document entitled "Standard Industrial Lease—Net" published by the American Industrial Real Estate Association, several features of which the parties amended prior to signing it. *[handwritten: 3yr lease]*

Among other amendments to the form lease, the parties struck by lining through two subsections of both the "compliance with law" and "condition of premises" provisions. The first of these stricken provisions consisted of a warranty by the lessor that the premises did not violate applicable building codes, regulations or ordinances in effect at the commencement of the term; in the second, the lessor warranted the condition of the plumbing, lighting, heating and similar building systems. Both stricken provisions would have required the lessor to correct promptly any breach of the warranties. The parties also struck a provision requiring the lessee to pay the real property taxes (and added a provision requiring the lessee to pay only any increase in property taxes occurring during the term of the lease) and made additional changes— none of which are pertinent here—by attaching a typewritten addendum to the form lease. *[handwritten: Lessor should have been req'd to correct promptly]*

As modified and signed by the parties, the lease required the lessee to "comply promptly with all applicable statutes, ordinances, rules, regulations, orders, covenants and restrictions of record, and requirements in effect during the term or any part of the term hereof, regulating the use by the lessee of the premises . . . ." In addition, the lessee agreed to accept the building "in [its] condition existing as of the lease commencement date or earlier, subject to all applicable zoning, municipal, county and state laws, ordinances, and regulations governing and regulating the use of the Premises . . . ." The document also required the lessee to "keep in good order, condition and repair the Premises and every part thereof, structural and nonstructural (whether or not such portion of the Premises requiring repair . . . occurs as a result of Lessee's use, any prior use, the elements or the use of such portion of the Premises) including . . . all . . . walls (interior and exterior), foundation, ceiling, roofs (interior and exterior), floors . . . ." Finally, the lease provided that "Lessor [shall] have no obligation, in any manner whatsoever, to repair and maintain the Premises nor the building located thereon nor the equipment therein, whether structural or nonstructural, which obligation is intended to be that of the lessee under [the maintenance and repair provision] hereof." Lessor remained obligated to pay the premiums for casualty insurance on the building.

In a letter to Hadian dated October 1, 1986, Schwartz exercised his option to renew the lease for an additional five years at the increased rent, the new term to commence on July 24, 1987, the date on which the initial three-year term expired. On March 4, 1987—five months after Schwartz exercised the renewal option and almost five months before the initial three-year term ended—Hadian received a letter from City of Los Angeles officials advising her that the unreinforced masonry construction of the Sunset Boulevard building made it susceptible to substantial structural damage in the event of an earthquake. The letter explained that, under a so-called "earthquake hazard reduction" program enacted by the city in 1981, Hadian, as the building's owner, was required to arrange for a structural survey of the property to determine its susceptibility to earthquake damage and was liable for the cost of any quake-proofing (or "seismic retrofitting") indicated by the survey results; accompanying the letter was an "Earthquake Hazard Reduction Compliance Order" directing Hadian, as the building owner, to meet minimum earthquake standards for a structure of that type within a specified time.

Discussions between Hadian and Schwartz then took place, intended to resolve liability between the parties for the required seismic alterations. After failing to reach an agreement with her lessee, who denied any responsibility for the cost of the quake-proofing work, Hadian authorized and paid the costs of a survey and redesign of the building, followed by the actual work itself—an extensive undertaking requiring the complete reconstruction of the building's frame and the installation of a new roof—at a cost totaling $34,450.26.

Following completion of the seismic upgrade work and issuance of a certificate of completion by the city, Hadian filed this breach of contract action against Schwartz to recover the cost of the alterations. Her complaint alleged in substance that Schwartz had agreed through a provision of the lease to bear the cost of complying with any alterations ordered by municipal authorities, that the seismic retrofit so qualified, and that Schwartz, having refused to pay the cost himself, was liable to her by way of indemnity. At the conclusion of a bench trial, the superior court ruled in favor of Hadian. Schwartz appealed.[22]

In an unpublished opinion, the Court of Appeal affirmed the judgment of the trial court. It reasoned that such a result was "impelled" by our opinion in [*Glenn R. Sewell Sheet Metal, Inc. v. Loverde,* 70 Cal.2d 666, 75 Cal.Rptr. 889, 451 P.2d 721 (1969)], because the terms of the lease in issue, like the lease in *Sewell*, obligated the lessee to assume the duty of keeping the building in repair and complying with all applicable laws. In addition, the court reasoned that, as in *Sewell*, the lessor had assumed no obligation of repair or compliance with laws; nor had the lessor made any representations respecting the condition of the property. Although pointing out that its judgment required Schwartz to pay, in effect, for capital improvements to the building and that such a result was "arguably unfair" because the improvements would benefit primarily the lessor, the Court of Appeal felt compelled by the rule of *Auto Equity Sales, Inc. v. Superior Court* (1962) 57 Cal.2d 450, 455 [20 Cal.Rptr. 321, 369 P.2d 937], to follow what it perceived to be our analysis in *Sewell*. We granted the lessee's ensuing petition for review and now reverse. . . .

As we explain in greater detail in *Brown v. Green*, [8 Cal.4th 812, 35 Cal.Rptr.2d 598, 884 P.2d 55 (1994)], also filed today, our opinion in *Sewell, supra,* 70 Cal.2d 666, "is apt to be misinterpreted as one which, in the search for the parties' intent, exalts a text-bound logic over a close consideration not only of the terms of the lease but of the circumstances surrounding its making." *Brown v. Green, supra,* at p. 825. The defining feature of *Sewell*—the characteristic of the lease transaction that drove our result in that case—was the fact that the lessee's use of the property was both different from the lessor's prior use and one that led to the government-ordered alteration at issue.

Our opinion pointed out that a change in use that invokes government-ordered alterations is one of the principal ways by which a lessee may be deemed to have assumed the cost of compliance. *Sewell, supra,* 70 Cal.2d at p. 674. Indeed, we went so far as to observe that anyone using leased property for the purpose of operating a trailer park "must know that laws respecting and regulating such facilities [*i.e.*, waste disposal] would be of primary importance . . . and would be those most obviously included in a clause requiring compliance with all applicable laws." *Id.* at p. 676.

As we conclude in *Brown v. Green, supra,* 8 Cal.4th at page 825, these considerations are decisive in distinguishing *Sewell, supra,* 70 Cal.2d 666, from cases in which the use is not one that provokes the government order at issue. The distinction is, moreover, consistent with both common sense and a reasonable construction of the lease provision.

---

22. Counsel for Mrs. Hadian argues that the trial court's conclusion that the parties intended to place liability for the cost of the seismic upgrade on the lessee is based on "observations of the parties." The opinion of the Court of Appeal, however, relied entirely on our opinion in *Sewell,* *supra,* 70 Cal.2d 666, and it is clear that the trial court's conclusion was one of law based on undisputed facts. We may thus properly review de novo both that court's and the Court of Appeal's construction of the lease.

After all, a lessee who, like the one in *Brown v. Green*, undertakes the retail sale of furniture on leased property is hardly likely to anticipate that such a use will trigger a municipal demand that asbestos laden fireproofing material coating the building's structural frame be removed at a cost of roughly a quarter of a million dollars. Nor is the government's cleanup demand in such a case one that lies within the reach of a compliance with laws provision confined to laws or orders "regulating the lessee's use" of the property. *See Brown v. Green, supra, ante*, at p. 824.

Like the compliance with laws clause at issue in *Brown v. Green, supra*, 8 Cal.4th 812, the compliance clause in the lease here is drawn to obligate the lessee to "comply promptly with all applicable statutes [etc.] ... *regulating the use* by the lessee of the premises ...." (Italics added.) The provision, in other words, is not one that on its face obligates the lessee to comply with—and bear the expense of—"requirements that would be applicable to *any* occupancy." 2 Friedman on Leases (3d ed. 1990) Compliance with Laws, ¶ 11.1, p. 689 and cases cited at fn. 8, italics added; *see also Brown v. Green, supra, ante*, at p. 825. Nor, in agreeing to such a provision, is a lessee who intends to operate a bar/cabaret on the property likely to have in mind that his use will provoke a municipal demand that he bear the substantial cost of a virtual reconstruction of the building as a means of strengthening it against the contingency of an earthquake.

We cannot, in other words, endorse the Court of Appeal's view that the text of the compliance with laws clause itself supports the straightforward application of our analysis in *Sewell, supra*, 70 Cal.2d 666, and the conclusion that the lessee assumed responsibility for compliance with "all applicable laws." ...

A compliance with laws provision that is limited to requiring the lessee to obey or comply with laws, orders and other governmental demands regulating the lessee's use of the leased property does not, by its literal terms, obligate the lessee to comply with laws, regulations, et cetera, that do not purport to regulate the use. *See, e.g., Wolf v. 2539 Realty Associates* (1990) 161 A.D.2d 11 [560 N.Y.S.2d 24]. It is no answer to reason, as the Court of Appeal appeared to do in this case, that the lessee is responsible for the cost of compliance because the failure to comply might otherwise lead to the destruction of the leasehold; were that the law, there would be no limit on the lessee's liability for governmental demands, even those demonstrably of benefit solely to the property owner. ...

Because the lessee's use here, like that in *Brown v. Green, supra*, 8 Cal.4th 812, differs from the use in *Sewell, supra*, 70 Cal.2d 666, in being unrelated to the property condition that led to the government's compliance order, it follows that the city's order here lies outside the literal scope of the compliance with laws clause of the lease. In light of the resulting uncertainty as to the intention of the parties regarding the duty to comply with laws, regulations, etc., directed at conditions unrelated to the lessee's use, we may properly have recourse both to the overall provisions of the lease and the circumstances surrounding its making. *See Brown v. Green, supra,* at pp. 826, 829. As in *Brown v. Green,* we adopt a two-part analysis in resolving that question.

Naturally, the analysis begins with the language of the lease itself. The literal text of the agreement—even so-called preprinted "form" leases—is presumptively controlling in determining the intent of the parties, always the paramount question in contract cases. If, as in both this case and *Brown v. Green, supra,* 8 Cal.4th 812, the language of the lease appears to place the duty of compliance on the lessee, the court then takes the second analytical step. It examines the lease terms in light of a handful of judicially developed circumstantial factors as a means of confirming that the allocation of risk suggested by the text of the lease accurately reflects the probable intent of the parties and leads to a reasonable construction of the lease terms.

If, on balance, these factors reinforce the conclusion suggested by an examination of the text of the lease, the court will conclude that the obligation to make alterations to comply with the law or regulation at issue falls on the lessee. If, however, the assessment is inconsistent with the lease provisions and points to the conclusion that the parties intended that the lessor shoulder the burden of compliance, the court will conclude that the actual agreement of the parties deviates from the literal text of the lease and construe and enforce the agreement accordingly. . . .

As noted, the lease is self-characterized as being a "net" lease,[23] a type of agreement often used in commercial leases of entire buildings, a defining characteristic of which is the virtually complete transfer of the incidents of ownership from landlord to tenant. *See Brown v. Green, supra,* 8 Cal.4th at pp. 827–828. As in *Brown,* the preprinted form used by the parties here not only bears the title "Standard Industrial Lease—Net," but the word "net" appears at the foot of each page. As we remark in *Brown,* however, these facts "[are] not alone decisive. What is persuasive is a consideration of the provisions of the lease agreement as a whole . . . ." *Id.* at p. 828. As explained in our opinion in *Brown,* chief among these provisions are the life of the lease and the extent to which the incidents of full ownership of the property are transferred to the lessee. Although the terms of the lease in this case do exhibit some features characteristic of a true net lease (*e.g.,* a virtually unqualified covenant to keep the property in repair and a provision purporting to

23. [Editors' Note: The term *net lease* or *triple net lease* generally refers to a lease arrangement whereby the tenant bears responsibility not only for the stated rental, but also for (1) the real estate taxes accruing on the premises, (2) the cost of insuring the premises, and (3) the cost of maintaining the premises. The term "net" thus refers to the fact that the lease allows the landlord to collect the agreed rent *net of* these expenses of ownership. In some cases, the landlord actually pays the tax, insurance, and maintenance bills and then "passes through" those costs to the tenant pursuant to a provision of the lease that obligates the tenant to pay these "pass-through" expenses. In other cases, with a financially strong and sophisticated tenant, the landlord may agree to allow the tenant to pay these expenses directly.]

negate any obligation on the part of the lessor to maintain the property), other features—more central to the transfer of ownership issue—suggest the opposite conclusion.

The life of the lease, for example—three years with an option to renew for an additional five years—makes the lease one for a comparatively short term. In addition, the lessor agreed both to pay all but a small yearly increment in property taxes and to obtain and pay the premiums for casualty insurance on the building, obligations that suggest her intention to retain the major benefits and burdens of ownership and which thus tend to negate the conclusion that the parties intended a true "net" lease. Cf. *Brown v. Green, supra,* 8 Cal.4th at pp. 827–828. Moreover, in the typewritten addendum to the preprinted form, the parties agree that the lessor continues to own all the "fixtures, operating systems and other improvements" in the building, "including the bar, freezer, lighting fixtures, bar cabinets, bar mirrors ...," an acknowledgment of continuing ownership that also tends to undermine the view that the parties intended a true net lease.

On balance, these features lead us to conclude that, despite the form characterization of the lease as "net," the lessor did not intend to "forego[] the speculative advantages of ownership in return for the agreed net rental," nor was the lessee "gambl[ing] on the continued value of the location and the improvement ... and assum[ing] all risk in connection therewith." Van Doren, Some Suggestions for the Drafting of Long Term Net and Percentage Leases (1951), 51 Colum. L.Rev. 186; *see also Brown v. Green, supra,* 8 Cal.4th at p. 826. ...

In addition to concluding from the text of the lease that the parties did not intend to negotiate a true net lease, we apply to the lease and the circumstances surrounding its making the six factors enumerated in *Sewell, supra,* 70 Cal.2d at page 674, footnote 10, factors which we said "reflect a court's determination whether or not the parties to a lease agreed that the lessee assumed certain risks, despite the use of unqualified language." Applying these criteria to the lease and the circumstances surrounding its execution in *Brown v. Green, supra,* 8 Cal.4th 812, we concluded that the lessees agreed to accept responsibility for the cost—there, totaling over $250,000—of replacing asbestos laden insulation material applied to steel members supporting the roof of a 45,000–square-foot building leased for a term of 15 years. Applying the same factors to the virtually identical form lease at issue here yields the opposite result, reinforcing our conclusion that the parties intended that the lessor would be responsible for complying with laws unrelated to the particular use made of the property by the lessee.

(1) *The relationship of the cost of the curative action to the rent reserved.* As noted, the initial three-year term of the lease called for a monthly rental of $650. The total rent reserved over the life of the initial term was thus $23,400. Expressed as a percentage, the cost of compliance with the city's order is almost one and one-half times (145 percent) the cost of the entire rent reserved over the three-year life of the lease.

Thus, using the initial lease term as a benchmark, the cost of the curative action fairly dwarfs the total rent reserved.

Even if we add to the initial term the five years of the option, renewed by Schwartz some nine months before the end of the initial term and several months before the city's compliance order was served on Hadian, the relationship is still one of significant imbalance. In *Brown v. Green, supra*, 8 Cal.4th 812, we point out that although the cost of complying with the county's asbestos abatement order there— over $250,000—was high as an absolute number, it represented less than 5 percent of the total rent reserved over the 15–year life of the lease, "an expression of value," we said, "that throws a different light on the relative financial magnitude (and hardship) of the undertaking." *Id.* at p. 830. Here, of course, these comparative values are inverted. Instead of compliance costs of less than 5 percent of the aggregate rent, the cost of earthquake-proofing the Sunset Boulevard property is roughly half of the total rent payable by the lessee over the combined eight years of the term, or 49 percent.[24]

(2) *The term for which the lease was made*. Although the question of the length of a lease term is irreducibly relative, most would agree that a term of three years qualifies as "short"; neither do we think that the addition of the five-year renewal option changes the result. The parties agreed to a lease for a term of three years with the option for an additional five years. In assessing the life of the lease for purposes of determining the intent of the parties with respect to the issue of complying with governmental orders affecting the property, we accord somewhat less weight to the option term than we would to an initial lease of, say, eight years. Under the circumstances here, we conclude that a lease of three years with a five-year option qualifies as a short rather than a long term lease.

As our opinion in *Brown v. Green, supra*, 8 Cal.4th 812, points out, courts are reluctant to construe a repair or compliance clause literally where the term of the lease is short, the lessee has little time in which to amortize the cost of repairs over the life of the lease, and the cost of repair or compliance represents a substantial percentage of the aggregate rent over the term. "Where the term of the lease is short," we noted, "it is highly unlikely that the lessee would have expected to assume responsibility for the cost of alterations that are, in effect, capital improvements to the property that will benefit primarily the owner." *Id.* at p. 831. As one commentator has observed, under such circumstances, "there is a virtual refusal of the courts to construe this language literally." 1 Friedman on Leases, *supra*, Repair, ¶ 10.601, p. 656.

(3) *The relationship of the benefit to the lessee to that of the reversioner*. Here again, it is plain that, as the Court of Appeal itself pointed

---

24. A percentage arrived at by multiplying the monthly rent ($650 and $800) times the two terms (the initial three years and the five-year option to renew) and dividing the cost of the seismic upgrade ($34,000) by the resulting sum ($69,600) to yield a figure of 49 percent.

out, the primary benefit of the seismic work will inure to Hadian, the building's owner. Although the record does not inform us of the estimated useful life of the building, it is safe to assume that its substantial reconstruction and "hardening" against earthquake damage will last for more than the five years remaining on the lease. The record here, we conclude, unlike that in *Brown v. Green, supra, ante,* is sufficient to support the conclusion that the work will primarily benefit the lessor. The record is also clear that the earthquakeproofing reconstruction ordered by the city resulted from the classification of the building itself as being of a type—unreinforced masonry—that is especially susceptible to severe damage during an earthquake. The city's compliance order was not the result of activity on the property or prompted by the lessee's particular use. Thus, this factor as well points to the building owner as the party responsible for compliance costs.

(4) *Whether the curative action is structural or nonstructural in nature.* Little argument is needed to establish both the substantiality and structural nature of the seismic retrofit required at the Sunset Boulevard building. As the record confirms, the upgrade entailed the insertion of a new steel frame into the core of the building, the installation of plywood shear walls and foundation anchors, and the construction of a new roof—work that literally qualifies as "structural."

(5) *The degree to which the lessee's enjoyment of the premises will be interfered with while the curative action is being undertaken.* The record is unfortunately silent on this aspect of the analysis. We may, however, surmise that the substantial reconstruction of the building's structural frame and the addition of a new roof were not unintrusive, and conclude that application of this factor does not, at least, favor the lessor.

(6) *The likelihood that the parties contemplated the application of the particular law or order involved.* A negative answer to this query favors the case for the lessee: responsibility for the consequences of events affecting leased property that are truly unanticipated is likely to be that of the lessor, who generally has the financial resources and long-term investment interest to respond to such events. Yet here again, the record is not definitive. Although it is common knowledge that southern California is "earthquake country," the extent to which the parties were aware of a city code program designed to upgrade unreinforced buildings and that that eventuality could have been contemplated by both or either at the time the lease was signed are questions not clearly answered by the record before us.

The record does include copies of letters to Mrs. Hadian from the city's department of building and safety dated September 20, 1967, and July 31, 1968, ordering the removal of building parapets along the Sunset Boulevard side and the anchorage of exterior walls to the roof frame, and subsequently acknowledging the completion of those changes. These alterations were ordered as part of the city's code program of removing building parapets that might pose a threat to pedestrians in the event of an earthquake. It is also likely that Hadian, as the owner of a building constructed of unreinforced masonry, was more likely than her lessee to be aware of the city's earthquake hazard reduction program, enacted in 1981, some three years before the lease commenced. On balance, it appears fair to charge the owner with at least a general awareness, based on past experience, of the possibility that the ownership of property within an earthquake zone might entail government demands that the building be renovated in particular ways.

Perhaps the most that can be said of this factor is that it does not tip decidedly in favor of either party.

Although the uses by the lessees in neither *Brown v. Green, supra,* 8 Cal.4th 812, nor this case fell within the text of the compliance with laws clauses or triggered the government orders at issue, a comparison of the circumstances relevant to determining compliance responsibility in the two cases leads us to conclude that, unlike the case in *Brown v. Green,* the probable intent of the parties here was that the lessor would bear the cost of complying with orders not arising from the lessee's particular use of the property. The material features of the lease and surrounding circumstances in this case and those in *Brown v. Green* differ with respect to almost every controlling factor: Differences in the amount of the monthly rent ($28,500 versus $800), the life of the lease (fifteen years versus three years, with a five-year option), the cost of compliance alterations as a percentage of the aggregate rent (less than 5 percent versus 49 percent), prior notice of the potential for compliance problems (written notice in *Brown v. Green,* none in this case) and the extent of the alterations entailed by compliance (removing fireproofing material sprayed on beams supporting the roof versus a virtual reconstruction of the building, including steel framing and reroofing), support that conclusion, leading us to reverse the judgment of the Court of Appeal.

We also are carried to our conclusion by the manifest unfairness of the result reached by the Court of Appeal, a fact that court acknowledged. Although the Court of Appeal regarded itself as constrained by the duty of deference owed to a prior decision of this court, we have concluded that it construed our opinion in *Sewell, supra,* 70 Cal.2d 666, as one imprisoned by its own logic. We now correct that misreading, confident that our reasoning in *Sewell* was never intended to produce the result reached by the courts below....

The judgment of the Court of Appeal is reversed and the cause is remanded with directions to vacate the judgment of the trial court and to enter judgment in favor of defendant.

Notes

1. *The Effect of Casualty Upon the Lease and the Tenant's Rental Obligation—The Default Rule.* Under the traditional default rule, the destruction of the leased premises did not relieve the tenant of the obligation to pay rent (unless the lease itself provided to the contrary). This view was the logical extension of the conception of the lease as conveyance—because

the landlord had already performed by conveying to the tenant the leasehold estate in the premises, the tenant was bound to perform regardless of casualty damage by paying its rental obligation for the duration of the lease term.

The trend of recent decisions, however, has established a modern default rule that total destruction of the leased premises terminates the lease and relieves the tenant of liability for future rent. For example, in *Albert M. Greenfield & Co. v. Kolea*, 475 Pa. 351, 380 A.2d 758 (1977), the tenant leased two parcels—one containing a building and the other a vacant lot—for purposes of operating an automobile sales and service business. After the lease commenced, the building was destroyed by fire. Declaring that the fire had terminated the leases, the court noted:

> It is no longer reasonable to assume that in the absence of a lease provision to the contrary the lessee should bear the risk of loss in the event of total destruction of the building. Where the parties do not expressly provide for such a catastrophe, the court should analyze the facts and the lease agreement as any other contract would be analyzed. Following such an analysis, if it is evident to the court that the parties bargained for the existence of a building, and no provision is made as to who bears the risk of loss if the building is destroyed, the court should relieve the parties of their respective obligations when the building no longer exists. [380 A.2d at 760.]

In *Kolea*, the court referred to the doctrines of impracticability and frustration of purpose, which are defined in the *Restatement (Second) of Contracts* as follows:

> Where, after a contract is made, a party's performance is made impracticable without his fault by the occurrence of an event the non-occurrence of which was a basic assumption on which the contract was made, his duty to render that performance is discharged, unless the language or the circumstances indicate the contrary. [§ 261.]

> Where, after a contract is made, a party's principal purpose is substantially frustrated without his fault by the occurrence of an event the non-occurrence of which was a basic assumption on which the contract was made, his remaining duties to render performance are discharged, unless the language or the circumstances indicate the contrary. [§ 265.]

What is the difference in these two doctrines? Which do you think applied in *Kolea*? Should it matter, for purposes of applying these doctrines, whether the casualty was easily foreseeable (such as the fire in *Kolea*), and thus could have been insured against by the tenant? *See, e.g., Williams v. Whitehead*, 854 S.W.2d 895 (Tenn. Ct. App. 1993); *Wichita Props. v. Lanterman*, 6 Kan.App.2d 656, 633 P.2d 1154 (1981); *Kel Kim Corp. v. Central Mkts., Inc.*, 70 N.Y.2d 900, 524 N.Y.S.2d 384, 519 N.E.2d 295 (1987). *See also West Los Angeles Inst. for Cancer Research v. Mayer*, 366 F.2d 220 (9th Cir. 1966); Restatement (Second) of Contracts § 261 cmt. b (the fact that an event "was foreseeable, or even foreseen, does not necessarily compel a conclusion that its nonoccurrence was not a basic assumption" on which the contract was made). Should it matter, for purposes of applying these doctrines, whether the lease was a triple net lease that imposed upon the tenant the burden of insuring the premises?

Few cases like *Kolea* arise today, because most commercial leases typically contain extensive provisions that allocate the risks of casualty loss.

2. *When Must a Tenant Maintain, Repair, or Rebuild?* In the absence of an express covenant to repair, the tenant's only duty with respect to the condition of the premises is *to avoid committing waste.* If the tenant commits affirmative waste, the tenant has a duty to repair the damage caused by such acts. *Rumiche Corp. v. Eisenreich,* 40 N.Y.2d 174, 386 N.Y.S.2d 208, 352 N.E.2d 125 (1976). Absent a contrary agreement, the tenant is not an insurer of the condition of the premises. Therefore, the tenant is not liable for "ordinary wear and tear"—*i.e.,* deterioration typical of that experienced when an owner uses the premises in a fashion typical of the reasonable owner. Likewise, if a casualty destroyed the premises through no fault of the tenant (*i.e.,* the destruction was not actionable waste), the tenant had no duty to rebuild the premises.

The traditional default rule is arguably sub-optimal, as it places no repair duty on the landlord and a very limited repair duty on the tenant. This could lead to the eventual deterioration of the property through ordinary wear and tear, and potential dispute and litigation over whether particular deterioration is "ordinary wear and tear" or "permissive waste." As a result, most leases include very specific lease covenants regarding the parties' respective repair duties. The most common sort of provision is a *general repair* clause:

> Lessee agrees to maintain the premises and all parts thereof in the same condition as when received at all times during the term of the lease, and to make all repairs necessary to maintain the premises in this fashion.

This provision would not only require the tenant to make repairs necessitated by waste, but also to conduct any maintenance necessary to avoid ordinary wear and tear. Often, such a general repair clause is accompanied by a *redelivery* clause under which the tenant agrees to return the premises at term's end in the same condition as at the term's beginning.

In more sophisticated leases, especially for multi-tenant commercial buildings, the lease commonly divides specific repair duties between the landlord and the tenant. For example, the lease may obligate the landlord to maintain the "exterior" of the premises and/or to make "structural" repairs of the premises, with the tenant obligated to maintain the "interior" and/or to make "nonstructural" repairs. In addition, in multi-tenant developments, the lease will typically obligate the landlord to provide maintenance services for the common areas of the development (*e.g.,* hallways, elevators, parking lots, lighting in public areas). Net leases often allow the landlord to pass through a proportionate cost of this maintenance to the tenant in the form of additional rent or "CAM" (common area maintenance) payments. Frequently, the allocation of these responsibilities are topics of intense negotiation between the parties. If you were representing a tenant in such negotiations, what reasoning might you use to persuade landlord to undertake responsibility for these expenses?

3. *The Tenant's Duty to Repair or Rebuild Under a "Net Lease."* In a well-drafted lease, the parties will define the parties' respective maintenance and repair obligations in detail to minimize the possibility of disputes regarding responsibility for future repairs. Unfortunately, sometimes parties

fail to draft with sufficient specificity, either intentionally or through over-sight; in *Hadian*, for example, the parties never anticipated the possibility of a government order requiring seismic retrofitting of the premises. Such oversights will happen from time to time; only hindsight is perfect. But why might the parties intentionally agree upon a lease that would not specify the parties' maintenance and repair obligations in detail?

For example, suppose that Royal Crown Bottling Co. leased a building for use as a soft drink bottling and distribution facility, under a 25–year lease that the parties agreed would be a "triple net" lease. The executed lease agreement provided the following general repair clause: "Lessee will, at its cost and expense and without deduction from the rental payments, make all repairs necessary to keep the leased premises in good repair." Ten years into the lease term, Lessor discovers that the roof is structurally unsound and that replacing the roof would be no more expensive than structural repair. Must the tenant pay to replace the roof? To what extent does it matter that the lease is a "net" lease? In this regard, compare *Hadian* with *Washington Univ. v. Royal Crown Bottling Co. of St. Louis*, 801 S.W.2d 458 (Mo. Ct. App. 1990) (lease containing above-quoted language required tenant to bear cost of structural repairs to roof). Would it matter if the roof replacement becomes necessary in year 24 of the 25–year lease?

Was the lease in *Hadian* a true net lease? Why should this matter in terms of how the court interprets a repair clause?

4. *Compliance with Laws.* Often, governmental regulatory agencies may require that all property of a particular character, or used in a particular way, must comply with certain regulatory standards, codes, or ordinances designed to protect public health or safety. The seismic retrofit-ting in *Hadian* is an example; other common regulatory compliance issues include installation and maintenance of sprinkler systems, exhaust systems, and/or fire suppression devices.

Ordinarily, the burden of regulatory compliance of this nature falls on the "owner" of the property. In the landlord-tenant context, absent contrary agreement, this burden would fall upon the landlord. *E.g., Petroleum Collections, Inc. v. Swords*, 48 Cal.App.3d 841, 122 Cal.Rptr. 114 (1975); *Cherberg v. Peoples Nat'l Bank*, 88 Wash.2d 595, 564 P.2d 1137 (1977). Leases commonly include a covenant by the tenant (often called a *compliance with laws* provision), however, that shifts this burden to the tenant in whole or in part. Are you persuaded by the *Hadian* court's interpretation of the compli-ance with laws clause in Schwartz's lease? Why or why not?

LAWYERING EXERCISE
(Document Review, Counseling, and Drafting)

BACKGROUND: An attorney representing a commercial landlord in a lease negotiation with a large, sophisticated tenant must appreciate the dynamic in such negotiations. In the typical residential lease or a commercial lease involving a small tenant, the landlord usually has superior bargaining position. As a result, there may be little or no negotiation of the lease terms, with the tenant largely having to "take it or leave it." Large and sophisticated commercial tenants, however, have significantly greater bargaining power because their presence in a shopping center development might predictably make the remaining space in the development more valuable to other tenants (and thus to the landlord, who can command higher rents from other tenants).

The landlord negotiating with sophisticated tenants cannot insist upon a one-sided, landlord-favorable lease; if it does, the tenant may simply refuse to negotiate with the landlord and instead approach landlords operating competing projects. To attract a prime commercial tenant—and thus to maximize the chances of having a fully occupied, vibrant premises—the landlord may have to agree to a lease structured less favorably than one it would insist upon receiving from a smaller, less financially secure tenant. In this context, an attorney representing a landlord must learn to distinguish carefully between suggested amendments that are essential—*i.e.*, without which the lease would present an unacceptable legal or business risk for the landlord—and those that would be desirable but not essential.

SITUATION: You represent Trump, who is negotiating with Big-Mart over the terms of a 20–year lease with four five-year renewal options for anchor space in Trump Plaza Mall. Trump purchased the Mall with the proceeds of a loan he acquired from East Virginia Life Insurance Company, which holds a mortgage on the Mall. BigMart has proposed a draft lease containing the following provisions:

> Lessee agrees to carry all risk coverage insurance on the Premises for an amount providing coverage for the fair market value of the Premises. Lessor agrees to pay for any increase in the cost of insuring the Premises if such increase is due to Lessor's activities in the Mall (*e.g.*, storage of harmful or explosive materials, failure to make repairs that present a risk of harm to the public). Notwithstanding anything to the contrary, as long as Lessee's net worth shall exceed $50,000,000, Lessee shall have the right to self-insure.

> In the event of destruction of the Premises, Lessee shall have the right, at its option, to terminate this Lease upon providing written notice of termination to Lessor within ten (10) days of such destruction. If the Lessee does not exercise its right to terminate the Lease, then Lessor shall promptly rebuild or restore the Premises to as nearly as possible its condition immediately prior to such destruction, such work to be commenced sixty (60) days from the time of the destruction and thereafter to be undertaken with due diligence until such rebuilding or restoration is complete. If, for any reason except delays caused by Lessee, Lessor should fail to commence and complete the rebuilding or restoration in accordance with the previous sentence, Lessee shall have the option of terminating this Lease by giving written notice to Lessor within thirty (30) days of Lessor's failure.

> All rent shall be abated during the period that the Premises is damaged and untenantable and for a period of thirty (30) days after

the date rebuilding or restoration is completed, or until the date the Lessee shall reopen for business, whichever is earlier.

TASK: Trump has asked you to review the lease and to recommend changes as necessary to address any unacceptable risks posed by the lease. Prepare a memorandum that identifies the provisions that you believe pose unacceptable legal or business risks for Trump. If you need additional background information to make a judgment regarding any of the provisions, identify what information you would need, and how it would influence your analysis.

c. *The Landlord's Tort Liability Due to Property Conditions.* Suppose that Landlord leases premises to Tenant, and upon moving in, Tenant discovers that the premises are infested with rodents. During the middle of the night, Tenant is bitten by a rat and becomes ill, incurring $3,000 in medical expenses. The rats also destroy $1,000 worth of clothing and food belonging to Tenant. Can Tenant recover damages from the Landlord for the losses caused by the rodents? Would the Tenant's recovery be in any way related to the amount of rent Tenant had agreed to pay?

Traditionally, the general rule was that landlords were not liable in tort for personal injuries suffered by tenants or third parties on the premises, or for damage to the tenant's personal property, occurring as a result of the condition of the premises. This also followed from the traditional *caveat lessee* rule—as landlord had no responsibility for the condition of the premises, landlord had no duty to protect the tenant or third parties from such personal injury and/or property damage. Only in the limited circumstances where landlord had some maintenance duty (page 497) did the law impose tort liability upon the landlord for personal injuries and/or property damage resulting from the landlord's failure to satisfy that duty. *Borders v. Roseberry*, 216 Kan. 486, 532 P.2d 1366 (1975).

Widespread adoption of the implied warranty of habitability does not, by itself, require the expansion of tort liability for landlords who breach that warranty. Contract law generally serves to protect a party from economic loss due to breach of a contract. In this regard, the implied warranty of habitability is meant to protect the benefit of the tenant's bargain—*i.e.*, to protect the tenant from the loss occasioned by the devaluation of the tenancy by uninhabitable conditions. Contract law traditionally did not protect parties against such noneconomic losses as personal injury and property damage. Over the past several decades, however, as the states have adopted the implied warranty of habitability into residential leases, courts have shown increasing willingness to impose upon landlords a general tort-based duty of care to protect tenants and third parties from dangerous or uninhabitable conditions. *See, e.g., Sargent v. Ross*, 113 N.H. 388, 308 A.2d 528 (1973); *Pagelsdorf v. Safeco Ins. Co. of Am.*, 91 Wis.2d 734, 284 N.W.2d 55 (1979). What is the appropriate limit of these duties, and can the parties bargain over allocation of these risks? Consider the following materials.

RANSBURG v. RICHARDS

Court of Appeals of Indiana.
770 N.E.2d 393 (2002).

BARNES, JUDGE. . . . In May 1995, Richards leased an apartment at Twin Lakes. The written lease agreement provided that Twin Lakes would "gratuitously" maintain the common areas. The lease agreement further provided that Richards' use of the Twin Lakes facilities, including the parking lot, would be at "[her] own risk." In addition, the lease agreement provided that Twin Lakes was not liable for damages to persons or property even if such damages were caused by Twin Lakes' negligence. Specifically, the lease contained the following clause:

> Lessor shall not be liable for damages to person or property sustained by the Lessee, his family, servants, agents or visitors, due to the building or any of the appurtenances being out of repair or arising from leakage or stoppage of gas, plumbing, steam, water, sewer pipes or from defective wiring or from defective construction of any of the aforesaid. It is agreed that the common areas and grounds, on which the demised premises are located, recreational facilities, laundry rooms and equipment, hallways, walkways, stairways, *parking lots,* lawns and all other areas and equipment to be used in common by all occupants of the apartment building and grounds, are provided and maintained gratuitously by Lessor, and that their use is not appurtenant to the premises hereby leased; and *the Lessee hereby expressly agrees that [if] the same shall be made use of [by] Lessee, his family, servants, agents or visitors, such use shall be at his, or their own risk, and that the Lessor shall, in no event, be, or become liable thereby for any loss, or damage, to persons or property,* whether such property be contained in the storerooms, in the common areas, in the leased premises or in any other portion of said building and grounds, *even though such loss or damage shall be caused by the negligence of Lessor,* or its agents, servants, or employees.

In the early morning hours of January 28, 1999, it snowed approximately two inches. When Richards left her apartment that morning, she noticed that the sidewalk had been cleared. It also appeared that the parking lot had been plowed and cleared. As Richards walked across the parking lot to her car, she slipped and fell on snow-covered ice.

Richards subsequently filed a negligence action against Ransburg. Ransburg responded with a summary judgment motion wherein she alleged that because of the non-liability clause in the lease, Richards had "waived any right that she ha[d] to complain of injuries or damages. . . ." The trial court denied Ransburg's motion. . . .

Ransburg argues that the trial court erred in denying her summary judgment motion because Richards waived any claim to damages. . . . In support of her argument, she relies on basic contract principles and

Indiana's recognition of the validity of exculpatory clauses, where parties are allowed to agree in advance that one is under no obligation of care for the benefit of the other and shall not be liable for the consequences of negligent conduct. She maintains that in the absence of legislation to the contrary, it is not against public policy to enter into an agreement that exculpates one from the consequences of her own negligence. . . .

Resolving the question of whether this lease provision is void as against public policy turns on fairly balancing the parties' freedom to contract against the policy of promoting responsibility for damages caused by one's own negligent acts. Indiana courts have long recognized and respected the freedom to contract. *Trotter v. Nelson,* 684 N.E.2d 1150, 1152–53 (Ind. 1997). We recognize a "very strong presumption of enforceability of contracts that represent the freely bargained agreement of the parties." *Id.* (quoting *Continental Basketball Assoc. v. Ellenstein Enter., Inc.,* 669 N.E.2d 134, 139 (Ind.1996)). However, in certain circumstances a court may declare an otherwise valid contract unenforceable if it contravenes the public policy of Indiana. . . .

[*Trotter*] categorized three situations where courts have refused to enforce private agreements on public policy grounds: "(i) agreements that contravene statute; (ii) agreements that clearly tend to injure the public in some way; and (iii) agreements that are otherwise contrary to the declared public policy of Indiana." We further noted that, depending on the category, we must approach the analysis in different manners. If an agreement is in direct contravention of a statute, "then the court's responsibility is to declare the contract void." If, however, the agreement falls into the more amorphous category of "otherwise contrary to the declared public policy of Indiana," then the court must balance five relevant factors: (i) the nature of the subject matter of the contract; (ii) the strength of the public policy underlying the statute; (iii) the likelihood that refusal to enforce the bargain or term will further that policy; (iv) how serious or deserved would be the forfeiture suffered by the party attempting to enforce the bargain; and (v) the parties' relative bargaining power and freedom to contract. The case before us falls in the "amorphous" category of "otherwise contrary to the declared public policy of Indiana," and, therefore, we must consider the five factors in evaluating this provision of the lease.

Indiana recognizes the general validity of exculpatory clauses. *Marsh v. Dixon,* 707 N.E.2d 998, 1000 (Ind.Ct.App.1999), *trans. denied.* We have stated:

> Parties are permitted to make such contracts so long as they are knowingly and willingly made and free from fraud. No public policy exists to prevent such contracts. However, exceptions exist where the parties have unequal bargaining power, the contract is unconscionable, or the transaction affects the public interest such as utilities, carriers, and other types of businesses generally thought to be suitable for regulation or which are thought of as a practical

necessity for some members of the public. [*General Bargain Ctr. v. American Alarm Co.*, 430 N.E.2d 407, 411–12 (Ind.Ct.App. 1982).]

Exculpatory clauses are generally enforced and are not void on public policy grounds unless one of the exceptions noted is present.

Franklin Fire Ins. Co. v. Noll, 115 Ind.App. 289, 58 N.E.2d 947 (1945), is an example where many years ago we found a clause in a commercial lease releasing the lessor from liability to be binding, enforceable, and not void as an unconscionable contract. In that case, the lessee signed a lease releasing the landlord from liability for leaking water. The lessee sued for damages resulting from water damage caused by leaky pipes. In affirming the trial court's judgment in favor of the landlord, we held:

> Stipulations between a landlord and tenant, determining which shall bear a loss arising from nonrepair or misrepair of the tenement, and which shall be immune, are not matters of public concern. Moreover, the two stand upon equal terms; neither the one nor the other is under any form of compulsion to make the stipulations; either may equally well accept or refuse entry into the relationship of landlord and tenant. We think it clear that public policy does not condemn the immunity clause voluntarily agreed upon by the parties. [*Id.* at 951.]

Ransburg argues that *Franklin Fire* is still the law in Indiana and must be applied to this case, which would result in the non-liability clause in the lease absolving Ransburg from any liability for the incident.

The facts of the *Franklin Fire* case are clearly distinguishable from those before us. The dispute in that case involved a commercial lease. To that end, the parties were of equal bargaining power because they were both corporate entities, and the lessee was not seeking a basic necessity of life, namely shelter. The damages for which the lessee sought to recover were for the loss of commercial inventory, not for personal injuries. Our supreme court has more recently held a release in a commercial lease enforceable and not against public policy, but emphasized that the lease concerned a commercial matter. . . . *Fresh Cut, Inc. v. Fazli*, 650 N.E.2d 1126, 1130 (Ind.1995). . . .

The rationale underlying the argument for enforceability of such clauses has often been based upon the doctrine of freedom of contract and the view that lease terms are a purely private matter. . . . However the application of these principles in all contexts is not warranted. As stated by the Supreme Court of Wisconsin:

> The unconsidered application of the principle of freedom of contract, even when accompanied by the rules of strict construction, is not always justified where there are extenuating circumstances which may affect the degree to which that freedom actually exists. Therefore, we are of the opinion that the better view is that which takes into account the actual effect of the particular clause in question and the facts and circumstances attendant upon the creation of the

landlord-tenant relationship. [*College Mobile Home Park & Sales v. Hoffmann*, 72 Wis.2d 514, 519, 241 N.W.2d 174, 177 (1976).]

A growing number of states have held similar exculpatory clauses to offend public policy concerns and to be unenforceable.

In 1971, the Supreme Court of Washington held that a lease provision exculpating the landlord of a multifamily dwelling complex from liability for injury to lessee or anyone entering the premises was void against public policy. [McCutcheon v. United Homes Corp., 79 Wash.2d 443, 486 P.2d 1093 (1971)]. In so holding, the court found:

> In the landlord-tenant relationship it is extremely meaningful to require that a landlord's attempt to exculpate itself, from liability for the result of its own negligence, not fall greatly below the standard of negligence set by law. As indicated earlier, a residential tenant who lives in a modern multi-family dwelling complex is almost wholly dependent upon the landlord for the reasonably safe condition of the "common areas." However, a clause which exculpates the lessor from liability to its lessee, for personal injuries caused by lessor's own acts of negligence, not only lowers the standard imposed by the common law, it effectively destroys the landlord's affirmative obligation or duty to keep or maintain the "common areas" in a reasonably safe condition for the tenant's use.

> When a lessor is no longer liable for the failure to observe standards of affirmative conduct, or for any conduct amounting to negligence, by virtue of an exculpatory clause in a lease, the standard ceases to exist. In short, such a clause destroys the concept of negligence in the landlord-tenant relationship. Neither the standard nor negligence can exist in abstraction. [*Id.* at 447–48, 486 P.2d at 1096.]

The court further reasoned:

> Furthermore, one must ignore present day realities to say that such an exculpatory clause, which relieves a lessor of liability for personal injuries caused by its own negligence, is purely a "personal and private affair" and "not a matter of public interest."

> We no longer live in an era of the occasional rental of rooms in a private home or over the corner grocery. In the relatively short span of 30 years the public's use of rental units has expanded dramatically. . . . It takes no imagination to see that a business which once had a minor impact upon the living habits of the citizenry has developed into a major commercial enterprise directly touching the lives of hundreds of thousands of people who depend upon it for shelter. Thus, we are not faced merely with the theoretical duty of construing a provision in an isolated contract specifically bargained for by one landlord and one tenant as a purely private affair. Considered realistically, we are asked to construe an exculpatory clause, the generalized use of which may have an impact upon thousands of potential tenants. Under these circumstances, it cannot be said that such exculpatory clauses are "purely a private affair" or that they

are "not a matter of public interest." [*Id.* at 449–50, 486 P.2d at 1096–97 (footnotes omitted).] . . .

Other courts have emphasized the unequal bargaining power between residential landlords and tenants. As one judge put it:

A tenant must live somewhere. The tenant has no meaningful choices. He can accept this landlord or go to another landlord who charges the same rent and asks the tenant to sign the same standard form lease. In other words, the modern standard form lease is in essence an adhesion contract. A reasonable person with equal bargaining power would not accept a term whereby they or their children may be injured or killed, and they would have no recourse against the guilty party. [*Taylor v. Leedy & Co.,* 412 So.2d 763, 766 (Al.1982) (Faulkner, J. concurring specially).] . . .

We agree with the reasoning in these cases. We also point out that an exculpatory clause of this type contravenes the long established common law rules of tort liability. At common law in Indiana, the landlord has a duty of reasonable care that the common ways and areas are maintained in a reasonably fit and safe condition. Exculpatory clauses are inconsistent with this principle of tort law. Exculpatory clauses discourage residential landlords from meeting the duty imposed on them by law for the protection of society. Tort law imposes liability for unsafe products, unsafe food, and unsafe premises. "It makes little sense for us to insist, on the one hand, that a workman have a safe place in which to work, but, on the other hand, to deny him a reasonably safe place in which to live." *McCutcheon,* 79 Wash.2d at 450, 486 P.2d at 1097. The best way to promote the exercise of due care is to hold residential landlords liable for their own negligence. Permitting landlords to insulate themselves from potential liability for negligently maintaining common areas serves only to encourage those landlords who are irresponsible, however few they may be, not to take reasonable steps to maintain their properties. It can hardly be in anyone's interest to sanction poor maintenance that can easily cause dangerous conditions in common areas. Tenants are not the only people at risk on poorly maintained premises. Any member of the public may enter the premises and be injured as a result of a landlord's failure to exercise due care. The public has an interest in protecting itself from such injury.

With these thoughts in mind, we conclude that the five factors outlined [in *Trotter*] weigh in favor of not enforcing this type of clause in residential leases. . . . Given the vast number of people clauses like these affect, the inequality of bargaining power caused by the need for housing, the fact that people who are not parties to the contracts could suffer as a result of such clauses, and the desire to promote responsible maintenance by landlords to avoid personal injuries by tenants and third parties, we find that the factors weigh in favor of public policy. Based on the foregoing, we conclude that the exculpatory clause in this residential lease is contrary to public policy insofar as it seeks to immunize Ransburg against damages caused by her negligence, if any, in maintaining common areas. Therefore, Ransburg was not entitled to judgment as a matter of law, and the trial court properly denied her summary judgment motion. . . .

Najam, Judge, dissenting. I respectfully dissent. The majority opinion nullifies a valid private agreement, rewrites the lease, and reallocates the exchange of costs and benefits between the parties. The majority declares that the exculpatory clause in question is void and unenforceable because it "contravenes long established common law rules of tort liability" and "offends the public policy of the state." In making this new rule the majority assumes what it seeks to prove, namely, that the law of negligence and the law of contract occupy mutually exclusive spheres and cannot be reconciled on these facts, notwithstanding a body of Indiana law to the contrary. The majority ignores the plain meaning of the exculpatory clause and violates the well-settled common law right of the parties to make such a provision and to have it enforced according to its terms. In so doing, the majority has unilaterally altered the economic equation in countless residential leases across the state. . . .

The majority acknowledges this state's "strong presumption of enforceability of contracts that represent the freely bargained agreement of the parties," and that "exculpatory clauses are generally enforced and are not void on public policy grounds. . . ." But the majority then discards these principles and declares instead that the question of whether a residential lease, which insulates the landlord from his own negligence, is unconscionable and therefore void as against public policy "has never been specifically addressed in Indiana." By phrasing the question in this manner, the majority attempts to distinguish residential leases from other types of leases or contracts in which exculpatory provisions have been upheld.

There is no such distinction. It has long been the law in Indiana that a lease is to be construed in the same manner as any other contract. This principle applies to commercial leases. *See Loper v. Standard Oil Co.,* 138 Ind.App. 84, 211 N.E.2d 797, 800 (1965). And Judge Darden, writing for our court, recently reaffirmed that this principle also applies to residential leases. *See Smyrniotis v. Marshall,* 744 N.E.2d 532, 534 (Ind.Ct.App.2001) (citing *Stout v. Kokomo Manor Apartments,* 677 N.E.2d 1060, 1064 (Ind.Ct.App.1997)).

Further, the issue of whether residential apartment leases are adhesion contracts and unconscionable and, therefore, void as against public policy has already been decided by this court. In *Nylen v. Park Doral Apartments,* 535 N.E.2d 178, 184 (Ind.Ct.App.1989), *trans. denied,* we acknowledged our supreme court's opinion in *Weaver,* that a contract may be declared unenforceable due to unconscionability when there is a great disparity in bargaining power which leads the party with the lesser power to sign a contract unwillingly and unaware of its terms. But the contract must be one that no sensible person not under delusion, duress or in distress would make, and one that no honest and fair person would accept. *Id.* In *Nylen* we held that a standardized residential lease agreement signed by three college students was not unconscionable. We stressed that contracts are not unenforceable simply because one party enjoys an advantage over the other. *Id.* at 185. The fact that the lease in *Nylen* contained terms favorable to the landlord did not render that lease unconscionable. *Id.*

Here, neither does the fact that the exculpatory clause benefits Ransburg more than Richards render that provision unenforceable. The majority points to no evidence that Richards signed the lease under compulsion or duress. The majority also fails to demonstrate why residential lessees, such as Richards, are so disadvantaged that they deserve special "immunity" from exculpatory clauses—a protection this court has never bestowed upon a particular class of lessees.

Richards entered this lease agreement after having been trained as a paralegal. She renewed her year-to-year lease in May 1995, and she fell in January 1997. Richards had an opportunity to terminate or renegotiate the lease terms, but she renewed the lease, even after Ransburg had informed her that the monthly rent would be increased by more than $100 per month. These facts neither suggest a great disparity of bargaining power nor that Richards was unwilling and unaware of its terms when she signed the contract on at least two occasions. . . .

Finally, the majority usurps the role of the legislature when it invokes "public policy" to justify its opinion. The flaw in the majority's reliance on "public policy" is underscored by recent legislation. The 2002 session of the Indiana General Assembly enacted a bill that regulates residential leases, House Bill 1013, which becomes effective July 1, 2002. The new legislation was enacted some twenty-six years after landlord-tenant legislation was first introduced in the General Assembly and is the best evidence of the public policy of our state on this issue. It is significant that the Senate Committee on Judiciary deleted from House Bill 1013 as introduced a provision that would have created a tenant's cause of action against a landlord for "any damages for personal injuries," and would have made any attempt to waive such an action, by contract or otherwise, void. If enacted, the provision would have modified the common law and, in its operation and effect, would have prohibited exculpatory clauses in residential leases. Now, the majority opinion has invoked "public policy" to accomplish by judicial decree precisely what the General Assembly has declined to do.[25]

---

25. The majority contends that this point is a "mischaracterization" of the statute. The majority also asserts that its opinion is "consistent with the statute as enacted," in that the statute imposes a duty on a landlord to "make all reasonable efforts to keep common areas of a rental premises in a clean and proper condition," which cannot be waived. The majority insists that this language "specifically precludes" landlords from disclaiming their own negligence. But the majority errs when it equates "all reasonable efforts" with "all non-negligent efforts." And the majority ignores the fact that our legislature considered and rejected a provision that would have given tenants a right to recover for "personal injuries"—a statutory remedy that undoubtedly contemplated a negligence cause of action. It is just as important to recognize what a statute does not say as it is to recognize what it does say. The legislative history is clear. Had the legislature wanted to prohibit landlords from disclaiming their own negligence, it would have included such a provision in the statute. It did not.

Our supreme court supports the traditional precaution against the reckless use of public policy as a means of invalidating contracts and has emphasized that the power of the courts to declare a contract void for being in contravention of sound public policy is a very delicate and undefined power. *Hogston v. Bell,* 185 Ind. 536, 112 N.E. 883, 885 (1916); *Straub v. B.M.T. by Todd,* 645 N.E.2d 597, 599 n. 3 (Ind.1994). Our courts should not invoke "public policy" to nullify an otherwise valid private agreement, except as a last resort, and then only where the legal justification is clear, compelling and unavoidable. We tinker with private contracts at great peril. In so doing we jeopardize the freedom our citizens enjoy to make agreements by which they voluntarily allocate their respective rights, risks and responsibilities. . . .

Notes

1. *The Landlord's Tort Liability.* If the Landlord has any duties of general care toward tenants and third parties, what is the appropriate limit of these duties? Consider the following examples:

(a) *L* leases an apartment to *T,* whose son is killed when he is struck in the parking lot by two boys racing their bikes. The parking lot is owned by *L,* used by tenants, and contains no speed bumps nor warning signs. Is *L* liable to *T* for the death of *T*'s son? *See Jackson v. Ray Kruse Constr. Co.,* 708 S.W.2d 664 (Mo. 1986). What if the accident occurs on the adjacent public street, which *T*'s son was able to reach because *L* did not build a fence around the apartments? *See Udy v. Calvary Corp.,* 162 Ariz. 7, 780 P.2d 1055 (Ct. App. 1989); *Brooks v. Eugene Burger Mgmt. Corp.,* 215 Cal.App.3d 1611, 264 Cal.Rptr. 756 (1989).

(b) *L* leases an apartment to *T,* who parks her car in a parking lot owned by *L* and used by its tenants. One evening, while getting out of her car, *T* was assaulted and robbed by three unidentified men. Is *L* liable for *T*'s injuries? *See Kline v. 1500 Mass. Ave. Apt. Corp.,* 141 U.S. App. D.C. 370, 439 F.2d 477 (1970); *Gulf Reston, Inc. v. Rogers,* 215 Va. 155, 207 S.E.2d 841 (1974). Would it matter if the assailants were also tenants of *L*? *Miller v. Whitworth,* 193 W.Va. 262, 455 S.E.2d 821 (1995).

2. *Exculpatory Clauses.* Why does the court in *Ransburg* refuse to enforce the exculpatory clause? Are you persuaded by the court's public policy justifications? To what extent do (or should) the facts and circumstances matter in evaluating the enforceability of an exculpatory clause? Consider the following questions:

(a) Suppose that Ransburg had not bothered to plow the parking lot at all. If Richards slips on ice covered by the newly fallen snow, should a court enforce the exculpatory clause? Is there a meaningful difference between "active" and "passive" negligence? *See, e.g., Walston v. Birdnest Apts.,* 395 So.2d 45 (Ala. 1981).

(b) Suppose that the exculpatory provision in *Ransberg* said merely: "Lessor shall not be liable to tenant for personal injury or damage to property occurring on the premises or due to the condition thereof. Tenant agrees to hold the Landlord harmless from any claims for such injury or damage." How would this affect the analysis of the Richards's claim, if any? *See, e.g., Peacock's, Inc. v. Shreveport Alarm Co.*, 510 So.2d 387 (La. Ct. App. 1987); *Galligan v. Arovitch*, 421 Pa. 301, 219 A.2d 463 (1966).

(c) Suppose that the accident in *Ransburg* happened when Richards slipped in the shower and was injured when the sliding glass shower door shattered (assume that the door contained non-shatterproof glass unsuitable for use in showers). With respect to the enforceability of the exculpatory clause, should it matter that the condition is within the demised premises (as contrasted with a common area)? Should it matter if the applicable housing code required non-shatterproof glass in showers? *See Cappaert v. Junker*, 413 So.2d 378 (Miss. 1982) (exculpatory clause invalid as contrary to public policy); *McCutcheon v. United Homes Corp.*, 79 Wash.2d 443, 486 P.2d 1093 (1971) (exculpatory clause could be enforceable if specifically bargained for in exchange for reduced rent).

(d) Suppose that instead of a being a tenant in a multi-tenant apartment building, Richards had been leasing one-half of a duplex from Ransburg. Should it matter that Ransburg is not a "typical" commercial landlord? Why or why not?

D. DISCRIMINATION IN LEASING

The traditional model of lease as conveyance suggested that the landlord—as owner of an estate in land—could exercise complete discretion in choosing its tenants. At common law, the landlord generally could choose to lease (or not to lease) to any tenant for any reason. Such discretion was considered a "necessary" component of the right to exclude—the essence of "property" ownership.

The common law's recognition of absolute discretion in the landlord's choice of tenants resulted in widespread racial, ethnic, and religious discrimination in the leasing of land. In previous sections, we discussed how the ascendancy of contract theory enabled courts to use principles of contract law to ameliorate some of the harsh consequences of existing common landlord-tenant law. But because this discrimination was the product of deliberate conduct by landlords designed to carry out their own individual preferences, the law of private contract provided scant help in addressing the problem, as landlords could merely communicate their discriminatory preferences in an express fashion.

In a legal sense, issues of racial discrimination in the sale or lease of housing should have been resolved by the passage of the Civil Rights Act of 1866, enacted in the wake of the Civil War to dismantle slavery. Section 2 of that act, 42 U.S.C. § 1982, provided that "[a]ll citizens of the United States shall have the same right, in every State and Territory, as is enjoyed by white citizens thereof to inherit, purchase, lease, sell, hold, and convey real and personal property." This statute, however, did little to prevent attempts by state and local governments to promote racial segregation in housing. First, despite its broad language, the statute was initially understood to reach only discriminatory conduct by public officials, not private parties. Further, as Richard Sander has noted, enforcement of the statute was problematic:

> The federal courts could only invalidate those statutes and ordinances that were litigated. No administrative agency was charged with responsibility for enforcing Section 1982, and the likelihood that individual blacks would challenge racial zoning laws in the interwar years was predictably small. Consequently, cities continued to pass laws mandating or encouraging segregation. Although blacks occasionally (and successfully) challenged the laws, the statutes did not fade away until the 1940s. By that time, they were moot: Black segregation was an accomplished fact. [Comment, *Individual Rights And Demographic Realities: The Problem Of Fair Housing*, 82 Nw.U.L. Rev. 874 (1988).]

Furthermore, despite the clear language of 42 U.S.C. § 1982, the federal government's own housing policies nevertheless actively promoted racial segregation. For example, consider the impact of the policies of the Federal Housing Administration (referred to in the excerpt below as the "FHA," but not to be confused with the Fair Housing Act discussed later in these materials). The Federal Housing Administration was established in 1934 to promote the availability of home mortgage financing and more widespread home ownership—but did so in a way that overtly reinforced existing patterns of racial segregation:

> The role of FHA was not to make mortgage loans, but to insure them.... Because FHA insured lenders against loss, lenders were willing to make loans on terms that were acceptable to FHA; and the terms that FHA set made homeownership affordable to middle-income people for the first time.
>
> FHA focused its mortgage insurance on "new residential developments on the edges of metropolitan areas, to the neglect of core cities." FHA insurance required appraisals of the property, the borrower, and the neighborhood, and FHA instructed its underwriters that the characteristics of existing city neighborhoods made insuring housing in those neighborhoods unacceptably risky.
>
> The final important FHA policy was reflected in the appraisal standards. The FHA Underwriting Manual specifically instructed that the presence of "inharmonious racial or nationality groups" made a neighborhood's housing undesirable for insurance. The Underwriting Manual explicitly recommended racially restrictive covenants, and warned: "If a neighborhood is to retain stability, it is necessary that properties shall continue to be occupied by the same social and racial classes...." [Florence Wagman Roisman, *Teaching About Inequality, Race, and Property*, 46 St. Louis U.L.J. 665, 677–78 (2002) (*quoting* Kenneth T. Jackson, Crabgrass Frontier: The Suburbanization of the United States (1985)).]

During the period from the end of World War II through the 1960s, advocacy groups began aggressive campaigns to challenge racial discrimination in housing in the judicial and legislative settings. On the judicial front, this campaign eventually culminated with the June 1968 decision in *Jones v. Alfred H. Mayer Co.*, 392 U.S. 409, 88 S.Ct. 2186, 20 L.Ed.2d 1189, which held that Section 1982 "bars all racial discrimination, private as well as public, in the sale or rental of property." On the legislative front, initial success came in state legislatures. As Professor Robert Schwemm explains:

> The California experience is illustrative. In 1959, California passed the Unruh Act, which provided for equal accommodations and services in all business establishments. The Hawkins Act followed and prohibited discrimination in publicly assisted housing.... Finally, in 1963, the Rumford Fair Housing Act prohibited racial discrimination in the sale or rental of any private dwelling containing more than four units. [Robert G. Schwemm, Housing Discrimination: Law and Litigation § 3.5, at 3–11 (1990).]

California's legislation served as a blueprint for similar legislative enactments in other states. By 1968, nearly one-half of the states had enacted fair housing legislation. In April 1968, shortly after the assassination of Dr. Martin Luther King, Jr., Congress enacted the federal Fair Housing Act ("FHA"), which banned discrimination in housing based upon race, color, religion and national origin. Subsequent amendments have extended the FHA's prohibitions to encompass discrimination based upon gender, familial status, and handicapped status.[26]

An excerpt from several key sections of the FHA appears below. Note that in enacting the FHA, Congress did not repeal the Civil Rights Act of 1866; thus, someone asserting a claim of racial discrimination in housing could pursue their claim under either Section 1982 or the FHA (or both), while someone asserting a claim based upon familial status discrimination could proceed only under the FHA. Likewise, while Section 1982 provides no exceptions, the FHA contains a number of statutory exceptions limiting its scope.

FAIR HOUSING ACT (Title VIII of the Civil Rights Act of 1968)

42 U.S.C.A. § 3602. Definitions.

As used in this subchapter—

(a) "Secretary" means the Secretary of Housing and Urban Development.

(b) "Dwelling" means any building, structure, or portion thereof which is occupied as, or designed or intended for occupancy as, a residence by one or more families, and any vacant land which is offered for sale or lease for the construction or location thereon of any such building, structure, or portion thereof.

(c) "Family" includes a single individual.

---

26. Note that the FHA does not include "age" as a protected class. Can you explain why?

(d) "Person" includes one or more individuals, corporations, partnerships, associations, labor organizations, legal representatives, mutual companies, joint-stock companies, trusts, unincorporated organizations, trustees, trustees in cases under Title 11, receivers, and fiduciaries.

(e) "To rent" includes to lease, to sublease, to let and otherwise to grant for a consideration the right to occupy premises not owned by the occupant.

(f) "Discriminatory housing practice" means an act that is unlawful under section 3604, 3605, 3606, or 3617 of this title. . . .

(h) "Handicap" means, with respect to a person—

(1) a physical or mental impairment which substantially limits one or more of such person's major life activities,

(2) a record of having such an impairment, or

(3) being regarded as having such an impairment, but such term does not include current, illegal use of or addiction to a controlled substance (as defined in section 802 of Title 21). . . .

(k) "Familial status" means one or more individuals (who have not attained the age of 18 years) being domiciled with—

(1) a parent or another person having legal custody of such individual or individuals; or

(2) the designee of such parent or other person having such custody, with the written permission of such parent or other person. The protections afforded against discrimination on the basis of familial status shall apply to any person who is pregnant or is in the process of securing legal custody of any individual who has not attained the age of 18 years. . . .

42 U.S.C.A. § 3603. Effective dates of certain prohibitions

(a) *Application to certain described dwellings.* Subject to the provisions of subsection (b) of this section and section 3607 of this title, the prohibitions against discrimination in the sale or rental of housing set forth in section 3604 of this title shall apply . . .

(2) After December 31, 1968, to all dwellings except as exempted by subsection (b) of this section.

(b) *Exemptions.* Nothing in section 3604 of this title (other than subsection (c)) shall apply to—

(1) any single-family house sold or rented by an owner: *provided,* That such private individual owner does not own more than three such single-family houses at any one time: . . . *provided further,* That such bona fide private individual owner does not own any interest in, nor is there owned or reserved on his behalf, under any express or voluntary agreement, title to or any right to all or a portion of the proceeds from the sale or rental of, more than three such single-family houses at any one time: *provided further,* That after December 31, 1969, the sale or rental of any such single-family house shall be excepted from the application of this subchapter only if such house is sold or rented (A)

without the use in any manner of the sales or rental facilities or the sales or rental services of any real estate broker, agent, or salesman, or of such facilities or services of any person in the business of selling or renting dwellings, or of any employee or agent of any such broker, agent, salesman, or person and (B) without the publication, posting or mailing, after notice, of any advertisement or written notice in violation of section 3604(c) of this title; but nothing in this proviso shall prohibit the use of attorneys, escrow agents, abstractors, title companies, and other such professional assistance as necessary to perfect or transfer the title, or

(2) rooms or units in dwellings containing living quarters occupied or intended to be occupied by no more than four families living independently of each other, if the owner actually maintains and occupies one of such living quarters as his residence.

(c) *Business of selling or renting dwellings defined.* For the purposes of subsection (b) of this section, a person shall be deemed to be in the business of selling or renting dwellings if—

(1) he has, within the preceding twelve months, participated as principal in three or more transactions involving the sale or rental of any dwelling or any interest therein, or

(2) he has, within the preceding twelve months, participated as agent, other than in the sale of his own personal residence in providing sales or rental facilities or sales or rental services in two or more transactions involving the sale or rental of any dwelling or any interest therein, or

(3) he is the owner of any dwelling designed or intended for occupancy by, or occupied by, five or more families.

42 U.S.C.A. § 3604. Discrimination in the sale or rental of housing and other prohibited practices

As made applicable by section 3603 of this title and except as exempted by sections 3603(b) and 3607 of this title, it shall be unlawful—

(a) To refuse to sell or rent after the making of a bona fide offer, or to refuse to negotiate for the sale or rental of, or otherwise make unavailable or deny, a dwelling to any person because of race, color, religion, sex, familial status, or national origin.

(b) To discriminate against any person in the terms, conditions, or privileges of sale or rental of a dwelling, or in the provision of services or facilities in connection therewith, because of race, color, religion, sex, familial status, or national origin.

(c) To make, print, or publish, or cause to be made, printed, or published any notice, statement, or advertisement, with respect to the sale or rental of a dwelling that indicates any preference, limitation, or discrimination based on race, color, religion, sex, handicap, familial status, or national origin, or an intention to make any such preference, limitation, or discrimination.

(d) To represent to any person because of race, color, religion, sex, handicap, familial status, or national origin that any dwelling is not available for inspection, sale, or rental when such dwelling is in fact so available.

(e) For profit, to induce or attempt to induce any person to sell or rent any dwelling by representations regarding the entry or prospective entry into the neighborhood of a person or persons of a particular race, color, religion, sex, handicap, familial status, or national origin....

42 U.S.C.A. § 3607. Exemption

(a) *Religious organizations and private clubs.* Nothing in this subchapter shall prohibit a religious organization, association, or society, or any nonprofit institution or organization operated, supervised or controlled by or in conjunction with a religious organization, association, or society, from limiting the sale, rental or occupancy of dwellings which it owns or operates for other than a commercial purpose to persons of the same religion, or from giving preference to such persons, unless membership in such religion is restricted on account of race, color, or national origin. Nor shall anything in this subchapter prohibit a private club not in fact open to the public, which as an incident to its primary purpose or purposes provides lodgings which it owns or operates for other than a commercial purpose, from limiting the rental or occupancy of such lodgings to its members or from giving preference to its members.

(b) *Numbers of occupants; housing for older persons; persons convicted of making or distributing controlled substances.*

(1) Nothing in this subchapter limits the applicability of any reasonable local, State, or Federal restrictions regarding the maximum number of occupants permitted to occupy a dwelling. Nor does any provision in this subchapter regarding familial status apply with respect to housing for older persons.

(2) As used in this section, "housing for older persons" means housing—

(A) provided under any State or Federal program that the Secretary determines is specifically designed and operated to assist elderly persons (as defined in the State or Federal program); or

(B) intended for, and solely occupied by, persons 62 years of age or older; or

(C) intended and operated for occupancy by persons 55 years of age or older, and—

(i) at least 80 percent of the occupied units are occupied by at least one person who is 55 years of age or older....

JANCIK v. DEPARTMENT OF HOUSING & URBAN DEVELOPMENT

United States Court of Appeals, Seventh Circuit.
44 F.3d 553 (1995).

ROVNER, CIRCUIT JUDGE. Stanley Jancik petitions for review of a decision of the Department of Housing and Urban Development ("HUD"), which found that he discriminated in the rental of an apartment on the basis of both race and family status in violation of section 804(c) of the Fair Housing Act ("FHA"), 42 U.S.C. § 3604(c). He also petitions for review of an order awarding attorney fees to the Leadership Council for Metropolitan Open Communities. We affirm....

Stanley Jancik owns Building No. 44 in King Arthur's Court, a large housing complex in the Chicago suburb of Northlake. King Arthur's Court houses people of all ages, including children, and although all of the apartments in Jancik's building have only one bedroom, they are large enough to house more than one occupant under local codes. The claims in this case arise out of Jancik's conduct in the rental of an apartment in that building. On August 29, 1990, Jancik placed this ad in a local suburban newspaper: "NORTHLAKE deluxe 1 BR apt, a/c, newer quiet bldg, pool, prkg, mature person preferred, credit checked. $395...." Suspecting that the request for a "mature person" might reflect a violation of the Act, the Leadership Council's Investigations Manager Glenn Brewer decided to "test" the property. In that process, "testers" bearing fictitious identities pose as potential renters in order to check for discriminatory practices. In this instance, Brewer chose to use volunteer testers Cindy Gunderson, who is white, and Marsha Allen, who is African American, for the task.

Gunderson spoke with Jancik by telephone on the evening of September 7, 1990. She subsequently related that after asking Gunderson her age and learning that she was 36, Jancik told her "that was good— he doesn't want any teenagers in there." Jancik also asked Gunderson her name and, upon hearing it, inquired "what kind of name" it was. Learning that the name was Norwegian, Jancik asked whether "that's white Norwegian or black Norwegian" and repeated the question a second time after Gunderson failed to answer. Gunderson asked Jancik whether he was inquiring as to her race and, after he responded affirmatively, told him that she was white. Gunderson then asked to view the apartment and the two arranged for her to do so the following morning.

Marsha Allen spoke with Jancik two hours later the same evening. Jancik asked Allen her occupation, income, age, marital status, race and whether she had any children or pets. Allen did not reveal her race, but in response to that question asked Jancik why he needed this information. He responded, in her words, "that he had to screen the applicants because the tenants in the building were middle-aged and he did not want anyone moving in who was loud, made a lot of noise and had children or pets." When Allen told Jancik that she did not have any children or pets he said "wonderful," and the two arranged for Allen to see the apartment the next morning. Both testers arrived the next morning at approximately 10:00, and Jancik's rental manager separately informed each that the apartment had been rented earlier that morning.

Based on the reports filed by Gunderson and Allen, the Leadership Council filed an administrative complaint with HUD on May 22, 1991. The Council charged that Jancik had violated section 804(c) of the FHA, 42 U.S.C. § 3604(c). The Leadership Council claimed that Jancik's print advertisement violated the section by indicating a preference based on family status and that his interviews with the testers violated the section by indicating a preference based on both race and family status. After HUD's General Counsel issued a "Determination of Reasonable Cause and Charge of Discrimination," the matter was set for hearing before Administrative Law Judge ("ALJ") William C. Cregar, as provided by 42 U.S.C. § 3612(b). With the Council and Marsha Allen as intervenors, the ALJ conducted a two-day hearing in early June of 1993 and issued a 21–page Initial Decision and Order on October 1, 1993, which found that Jancik had violated section 3604(c). The ALJ awarded damages to the Leadership Council ($21,386.14) and to Marsha Allen ($2,000), assessed a civil penalty of $10,000, and enjoined Jancik from engaging in further acts of discrimination, all as authorized by 42 U.S.C. § 3612(g)(3). The ALJ's decision became final on October 31, 1993. See 42 U.S.C. § 3612(h). The Leadership Council subsequently filed a petition requesting $23,842.50 in attorney's fees. Although Jancik did not raise any factual objections to the fee petition, which was supported by affidavits, he did request a hearing on the fees issue. In a February 10, 1994 order, the ALJ denied that request and granted the fees petition for the full amount requested. Jancik now seeks review of both of the ALJ's orders. . . .

Section 3604(c) prohibits the making or publishing of any statement or advertisement that "indicates" any preference or limitation based on, among other factors, race or family status. Whether a given statement or advertisement "indicates" such a preference is therefore central to our analysis. Although we have not previously dealt with the "indicates" aspect of section 3604(c), the circuit courts that have done so have employed a relatively straightforward approach, which we also find appropriate. First, every circuit that has considered a claim under section 3604(c) has held that an objective "ordinary reader" standard should be applied in determining what is "indicated" by an ad. Thus, "the statute [is] violated if an ad for housing suggests to an ordinary reader that a particular [protected group] is preferred or dispreferred for the housing in question." *Ragin v. New York Times Co.*, 923 F.2d 995, 999 (2d Cir.), *cert. denied*, 502 U.S. 821, 112 S.Ct. 81, 116 L.Ed.2d 54 (1991);[27] *see also United States v. Hunter*, 459 F.2d 205, 215 (4th Cir.), *cert. denied*, 409 U.S. 934, 93 S.Ct. 235, 34 L.Ed.2d 189 (1972); *Housing*

---

27. *Ragin* further explained that "an ordinary reader is neither the most suspicious nor the most insensitive of our citizenry." 923 F.2d at 1002.

Opportunities Made Equal, Inc. v. Cincinnati Enquirer, Inc., ["HOME"], 943 F.2d 644, 646 (6th Cir.1991). In applying the "ordinary reader" test, courts have not required that ads jump out at the reader with their offending message, but have found instead that the statute is violated by "any ad that would discourage an ordinary reader of a particular [protected group] from answering it." *Ragin*, 923 F.2d at 999–1000.

Significantly, no showing of a subjective intent to discriminate is therefore necessary to establish a violation of the section. *HOME*, 943 F.2d at 646; *Ragin*, 923 F.2d at 1000. At the same time, however, evidence of such intent is not irrelevant. Evidence that the author or speaker intended his or her words to indicate a prohibited preference obviously bears on the question of whether the words in fact do so. *See, e.g., Soules* [*v. HUD*, 967 F.2d 817, 825 (2d Cir.1992)]; *Ragin v. Harry Macklowe Real Estate Co.*, 6 F.3d 898, 907 (2d Cir.1993). Thus, if such proof exists, it may provide an alternative means of establishing a violation of the section. *See, e.g., HOME*, 943 F.2d at 646; *Soules*, 967 F.2d at 824.

In view of these guidelines, the ALJ's finding that Jancik's advertisement and statements expressed a preference based on family status in violation of section 804(c) was certainly supported by substantial evidence. First, Jancik told Allen that he did not want any families with children and told Gunderson that he did not want any teenagers in the building. In our view, both of these statements quite clearly would suggest to an "ordinary" listener that Jancik had a preference or limitation based on family status. The advertisement indicating his preference for a "mature person" was similarly problematic. Not only do we view that term as suggesting an unlawful preference to an ordinary reader,[28] the term is noted in the implementing regulation as being among "those most often used in residential real estate advertising to convey either overt or tacit discriminatory preferences or limitations." 24 C.F.R. § 109.20(b)(7). Of course, as Jancik points out, use of the listed terms does not violate the Act per se, but it does "indicate a possible violation of the act and establish a need for further proceedings on the complaint, if it is apparent from the context of the usage that discrimination within the meaning of the act is likely to result." *Id.* Here, the context of the usage, which included explicit verification of Jancik's preference to each of two prospective tenants who responded to the ad, makes clear that the usage was meant to convey an unlawful preference.[29]

And, although we have no doubt that the Act has been violated based solely on this objective analysis, the record was also replete with evidence of Jancik's subjective intent to discriminate against families

---

28. *Cf. Hunter*, 459 F.2d at 215 (to the ordinary reader, the term "white home" indicates a racial preference and therefore violates section 3604(c)).

29. Jancik cites *Soules* for the proposition that questions about children may sometimes be asked for legitimate reasons, such as local zoning ordinances that limit the number of permitted occupants or conditions in the neighborhood that are dangerous to children. Not only is the record here completely devoid of evidence suggesting that Jancik's questions were asked for any such permissible reasons, it makes clear that his reasons were impermissible.

with children. For example, Jancik admitted at the hearing that he had told prospective tenants with children that there was no school in the area, when there was in fact a high school located on adjacent property and an elementary school within one mile. Jancik also told the HUD investigator that he had previously turned away a single parent with a ten-year-old child.

Although the question of whether Jancik violated section 3604(c) by asking Gunderson and Allen about their race is somewhat more difficult, the ALJ's determination in that regard is also supported by substantial evidence. Unlike his comments regarding family status, Jancik did not expressly indicate a preference based on race, but merely asked the testers about their race. In the only case that has commented on the issue, the Second Circuit has indicated by way of dicta in *Soules* that questions about race standing alone are sufficient to violate the section because "[t]here is simply no legitimate reason for considering an applicant's race." 967 F.2d at 824. We need not decide that question here, however, because the context of the questions makes clear they did indicate an intent to discriminate on the basis of race. First, each question came in the midst of conversations in which Jancik was expressing other impermissible preferences. Hearing an inquiry about race immediately after being asked about children and told that applicants with children were undesirable, would, in our view, suggest to an ordinary listener that the racial question was part of the same screening process. Indeed, when Allen asked Jancik the purpose of his question about her race, he admitted that he was, in her words, "screening the applicants." Jancik's unlawful purpose was similarly revealed in his conversation with Gunderson by the pointedness of his inquiry. After asking the origins of the Gunderson name and learning that it was Norwegian, he twice inquired whether Gunderson was "white Norwegian or black Norwegian" and subsequently admitted, in answer to her question, that he was inquiring as to her race. It is unlikely that if the inquiry had been merely conversational, as Jancik has contended, he would have pursued it with such determination. In addition, the fact that Jancik had never rented to an African American tenant before the Leadership Counsel filed its complaint in this case further bolsters the ALJ's conclusion that Jancik's question reflected an intent to exclude tenants on the basis of race. . . .

For the foregoing reasons, we find that each of the ALJ's orders is both in accordance with law and supported by substantial evidence. Jancik's petitions for review are therefore DENIED.

Notes

1. *Applying and Interpreting the Fair Housing Act and Its Exceptions.* If the purpose of the Fair Housing Act is to address the problem of leasing decisions driven by discriminatory motives, what is the rationale behind the exemptions set out in §§ 3603 and 3607? Why not simply apply the prohibitions of § 3604 to all leasing decisions? Exactly what is the purpose of the Fair Housing Act?

Using the language of the Civil Rights Act of 1866 and the excerpts from the Fair Housing Act, consider the following problems:

(a) The Hansens own a duplex, living in one side and renting the other. They want to place an ad in the paper stating: "2 bdrm., 2 bth., perfect for mature individual or couple." They want to know whether the ad presents any legal problems. How would you advise them?

(b) Assume the Hansen's ad reads as follows: "2 bdrm., 2 bth, a/c and garage; $500, incl. util." Do you see any legal problems in the following situations?

    i) A couple with two children respond to the ad. The Hansens do not want children living next to them. Thus, they tell the couple that they already have rented the unit to someone else, though this is a lie. If the Hansens ask you whether the statement poses any risk of liability for discrimination, how would you advise them? What other information would you need to gather to advise them?

    ii) Same as i), except that an African–American couple responds to the ad, and the Hansens lie because they do not want to have African–Americans living next to them.

(c) The Garcias own a four-unit apartment building and want to provide affordable housing to Hispanic families. They want to place the following ad in the paper: "2 bdrm., 2 bth. apt., a/c, $400, not incl. utils. Prefer Spanish-speaking tenants." If they ask you whether the ad or a decision to rent only to Hispanic tenants would pose any risk of liability, how would you advise them? *See Shaare Tefila Congregation v. Cobb*, 481 U.S. 615, 107 S.Ct. 2019, 95 L.Ed.2d 594 (1987); *Holmgren v. Little Vill. Cmty. Reporter*, 342 F.Supp. 512 (N.D. Ill. 1971).

(d) Mr. Smith owns an eight-unit apartment complex, and resides in one of the units. While showing a vacant apartment to a young couple, Smith discovers that they are unmarried. Smith, who is morally opposed to cohabitation by unmarried persons, informs the couple that he will not rent to them unless they are married. The couple asks whether they have a valid discrimination claim. How would you advise them? *Compare Foreman v. Anchorage Equal Rights Comm'n*, 779 P.2d 1199 (Alaska 1989) (violation of state and local housing acts) *with State by Cooper v. French*, 460 N.W.2d 2 (Minn. 1990) (no violation of state housing act given landlord's legitimate interest in religious freedom).

(e) Jane owns a small condominium and is seeking a roommate. She places the following ad in the paper: "Female owner of 2 bdrm., 2 bath home seeks female roommate. $300/mo. plus ½ utils. Call 375–8120." Has Jane violated the Fair Housing Act?

(f) The Forshays own and manage a 16–unit apartment complex in which they live. The Forshays are showing an apartment to two men when they learn that the men are gay, and that one of them has AIDS. The next day, they call the men and tell them the apartment has been rented to someone else, even though that is a lie. Have the Forshays violated the Fair Housing Act?

(g) Mary owns a two-story apartment building. Because of safety issues associated with the balconies of the second floor units, Mary wants to refuse to rent the second floor units to families with small children, instead directing them to ground floor units. Due to complaints about noise, Mary also wants to institute a new rule: "Children will not be allowed to play or run around inside the building area at any time because of disturbance to other tenants or damage to building property." Would Mary's decisions violate the Fair Housing Act? *See Fair Hous. Cong. v. Weber*, 993 F.Supp. 1286 (C.D. Cal. 1997).

2. *Fair Housing Legislation: Shield or Sword?* After nearly four decades, it is evident that the Fair Housing Act has not produced a society with fully integrated living patterns. Was the Fair Housing Act intended merely to combat discrimination in housing? Or was it affirmatively intended to promote racial integration in housing? Does it matter? Why or why not?

Consider the following hypothetical. Anytown is a community of 100,000 residents—75% white, 20% African–American, and 5% Hispanic–American. There is very little racial integration in the Anytown housing market. Wells, who considers herself very progressive, recently won a $125 million lottery jackpot. She wants to use this money to promote integration in housing by creating the "model integrated community" in Anytown. She plans to purchase a local 1000–unit apartment complex, and she plans to lease the units so as to maintain a complex that racially reflects the composition of Anytown. Can she do so, or would this violate federal housing laws? How would you advise her? *Compare United States v. Starrett City Assocs.*, 840 F.2d 1096 (2d Cir. 1988), *cert. denied*, 488 U.S. 946, 109 S.Ct. 376, 102 L.Ed.2d 365 (1988) *with Otero v. New York City Hous. Auth.*, 484 F.2d 1122 (2d Cir. 1973).

3. *Legal and Evidentiary Issues in Proving Discrimination.* The Fair Housing Act is aimed at landlords who act with discriminatory motives in making leasing decisions. Unfortunately, not all instances of discriminatory motive are as transparent as the acts of the hapless Mr. Jancik. Recognizing that plaintiffs may have a difficult burden if forced to prove subjective discriminatory motive, courts have held that a plaintiff need only prove *discriminatory effect* or *disparate treatment* to establish a prima facie case. This might include, for example, a landlord denying an apartment to a qualified minority applicant and thereafter leasing it to another party or allowing it to remain vacant. *See* James A. Kushner, *The Fair Housing Amendments Act of 1988: The Second Generation of Fair Housing*, 42 Vand. L. Rev. 1049, 1074–75 (1989). Once the plaintiff establishes a prima facie case, the defendant must then "justify the action ... [as] one taken pursuant to a rational and necessary business purpose." *Id.* If the defendant provides a neutral justification for the decision, the burden then shifts back to the plaintiff to demonstrate that the stated justification was "pretextual," *i.e.*, just a neutral excuse used to enable the defendant to engage in discrimination on illegal grounds. In light of this procedure, consider the following lawyering problem regarding fact investigation.

LAWYERING EXERCISE
(Fact Investigation)

BACKGROUND: Fact investigation plans provide attorneys with a structured approach for gathering the evidence needed to prove or disprove a claim. The first place to start in developing a fact investigation plan is by identifying the elements of the relevant cause of action, defense, remedy, or counterclaim. The lawyer must then determine what facts to gather to prove or disprove each element on the list.

A fact investigation chart, like the one that appears below,[30] can be quite helpful in developing a thorough investigation strategy. The chart forces the lawyer to systematically link the rules of law with the factual evidence that the lawyer has in hand or needs to gather. The chart then fosters strategic brainstorming about where to get the information and what tools the lawyer will use to get it.

Elements of the Cause of Action, Defense, Remedy, Counterclaim	Facts 1. True facts 2. Believed true 3. Hoped true	Source(s) Witnesses, Exhibits, etc.	Discovery Method 1. Formal 2. Informal

What Facts are Needed to Prove Each Element? Once the elements are listed on the chart, the lawyer can systematically analyze what specific facts are required to prove each element of the claim. This step forces the lawyer to think about development of the evidence, rather than merely factual conclusions. To reach the conclusion that a defendant was negligent, for example, the lawyer must develop evidentiary facts such as: the defendant was intoxicated; the defendant was driving above the speed limit; the defendant was tailgating.

Sources of Proof. After identifying the critical facts, the next step is to determine the source from which that information should be sought. The client will be a source of information, but the lawyer will need to consider what additional witnesses and exhibits will corroborate contested facts. Other potential witnesses to consider include:

- Witnesses to the event or transaction

- Opposing parties

- Persons who have no direct knowledge but may have useful circumstantial information

- Experts/consultants to assist with interpretation of specialized or complex material

Similarly, physical evidence may come from a wide range of sources. The lawyer may begin by identifying places or physical objects that were

---

30. Adapted from Paul J. Zwier & Anthony J. Bocchino, *Fact Investigation: A Practical Guide to Interviewing, Counsel-* ing, and Case Theory Development 77 (NITA 2000); Thomas A. Mauet, *Pretrial* (Aspen Law & Bus. 5th ed. 2002).

involved in the event or transaction, such as the scene of an accident and the vehicles involved in it. Other potential exhibits to consider are:

- Photographs
- Medical records
- Police reports
- Business records
- Transaction documents
- Diaries, appointment books, or other personal records
- Other documents relevant to the transaction or event

To develop the possible sources of evidence, it may be helpful to "visualize the possible conduct of the party in question and then think of records that may have been created in the course of that conduct." Lawrence Dessem, *Pretrial Litigation: Law, Policy and Practice* 67 (1991).

SITUATION: You have been approached by Harrison, an African–American law student. Harrison recently applied for an apartment at College View Apartments, but was told that his application was denied because (a) "we don't rent to students," (b) "we don't rent to lawyers," and (c) he did not meet the complex's income qualification, which requires a monthly income at least four times the monthly rent. Harrison believes that College View Apartments has discriminated against him based on his race, and wants you to represent him in pursuing a claim under the Civil Rights Act of 1866 and the Fair Housing Act.

TASK: Develop a fact investigation plan for how you will gather the information needed to advise Harrison whether he can establish a valid discrimination claim.

Chapter 8

NONPOSSESSORY PRIVATE LAND USE ARRANGEMENTS: SERVITUDES

A. INTRODUCTION

In this chapter we study *servitudes*, a group of related private property interests that confer nonpossessory rights in land possessed by others. The catalogue of servitudes includes *easements* (both affirmative and negative), profits, licenses, *real covenants* (affirmative and negative) and *equitable servitudes*.

The earliest servitudes recognized in our legal system were easements. Most easements are *affirmative easements*—i.e., they confer upon the holder the right to make some limited affirmative use of land possessed by another, such as crossing over it to gain access to an adjacent tract of land or running pipes or wires across it. In contrast, *negative easements* involve a very limited catalogue of limitations on the use of another's land—easements preventing a neighbor from obstructing light, air, or view, from blocking an artificial stream, or from removing a building's support (such as by excavation or removal of a supporting wall).

Closely related to easements are *profits* (more formally called *profits a prendre*)—the right to detach and remove something (*e.g.*, timber, minerals, ice) inherently attached to the land of another. The holder of a profit typically also has an easement to enter the land from which she may take the profit. *Licenses* also closely resemble easements, except that a true license is *revocable* by the servient owner (except in rare circumstances discussed later on page 581), while an easement is generally an irrevocable property right.[1]

Promissory servitudes are enforceable promises between a land owner and someone else. Promissory servitudes are often *negative covenants, i.e.*, promises that restrict the owner of land from making certain

---

1. An easement may have a limited duration, after which it terminates by *expiration, not* revocation.

uses of the servient estate (such as a restriction permitting land to be used for residential purposes only). Some promissory servitudes are *affirmative covenants* that obligate the promisor to undertake affirmative acts (such as a covenant requiring a landowner to pay a neighborhood subdivision association assessment). For reasons to be discussed later in this chapter, the law gives promissory servitudes a different label depending upon the remedy that is sought for breach of the promise. For example, suppose that Whitfield owns Blueacre, subject to a promissory servitude that restricts use of the land to residential purposes only. If Whitfield opens a business in breach of the restriction, and a neighbor benefitted by the restriction sues Whitfield for damages, the law characterizes the restriction as a *real covenant.* By contrast, if the neighbor sues for an injunction to stop Whitfield from further violation of the restriction, the law characterizes the restriction as an *equitable servitude.*

The term "servitudes" reflects our legal system's early bias against recognizing and enforcing these arrangements because they were seen primarily as burdening a parcel of land—often termed the *servient estate* or the *burdened estate*. In a typical easement, for example, the servient estate must "suffer" the burden of allowing the easement holder to enter onto and cross the servient estate to obtain access to adjacent land. The servient estate generally remains burdened by the servitude even after the owner of that estate transfers it to a successor. In other words, the *burden* of the servitude *"runs with the land"*—or more precisely, the burden of the servitude *runs with the servient estate*.[2]

Many servitudes also benefit land (and owners of that land). Consider these examples:

- The owner of Lot A holds an easement allowing her to cross a driveway located on Lot B, to access Lot A from the only nearby road. This easement benefits Lot A (and its owner) even though it burdens Lot B (and its owner).

- Each lot in Shady Acres subdivision is subject to a covenant (or promissory servitude) restricting each lot to "residential use only." This covenant benefits the adjacent lots in the subdivision by preventing nonresidential uses that—except for the restriction—might reduce the attractiveness of the subdivision as a residential community.

The benefitted land—Lot A or any other parcel in the residential-use-only subdivision, respectively—is called the *dominant estate*.

If a servitude benefits a parcel of land, property law designates the servitude as *appurtenant* (or *real*). By contrast, a servitude that is not appurtenant—*i.e.*, one that benefits someone without regard to her

---

2. At this point, a caveat is useful. While the burden of an easement will almost always run with the servient estate, it is not clear that the burden of a promissory servitude will always run with the servient estate. We will return to this subject in addressing promissory servitudes later in the chapter (page 615).

ownership of any parcel of land—is purely personal to its holder and is thus termed as a servitude *in gross.*

Is There a Unified Law of Servitudes? Easements and covenants (promissory servitudes) developed as two distinct bodies of law. As a result, even though easements and covenants serve similar purposes— facilitating private land use by tying rights and duties to ownership of land—the law of easements and covenants developed separately and in ways that were not internally consistent. For example, while the holder of an easement in gross can continue to enforce that easement after a transfer of the servient estate, the common law held that a person holding the benefit of a covenant in gross could not do so.

Recently, however, courts and commentators began to question whether the common law rules of easements and covenants—as traditionally articulated and as defended in the first Restatement of Property, published in 1944—were ideally suited to modern development patterns. A century ago, most landowners had little or no means to control undesired land uses by their neighbors (other than the minimal limitations imposed by the common law of nuisance). Over the past 75 years, however, most residential development (and a substantial amount of commercial development as well) has occurred in various forms of *common interest communities* such as residential subdivisions, condominiums, and planned unit developments. These developments have made increasing (and, in some cases, increasingly intrusive) use of covenants as a form of land use control. These changes eventually led the American Law Institute to an "overhaul" of the law of servitudes, with the new Restatement (Third) of Property: Servitudes (hereafter "Restatement of Servitudes") promulgated in 2000.

The Restatement of Servitudes overtly attempts to modernize the law of servitudes in an integrated and coherent fashion:

> [The Restatement's goal is] to present[] servitudes law as an integrated body of doctrine encompassing the rules applicable to profits, easements, and covenants. The draft reflects the modern analytical perception that all the servitude devices are functionally similar, and that for the most part they are, or should be, governed by the same rules. Only in the relatively few instances where there are real differences among the servitude devices are different rules justifiable. Treating all the servitude devices together, rather than dividing the subject into a division for each, not only avoids substantial repetition of identical rules, but also promotes thoughtful consideration of the reasons why different rules may be required.... [Restatement of Servitudes, Tentative Draft No. 1 (April 5, 1989).]

The new Restatement has proved influential in sparking substantial academic and practical commentary about the law of servitudes. It remains to be seen, however, whether courts will follow the Restatement in a way that will systematically integrate the law of easements and promissory servitudes—or whether courts will continue to adhere to the historical distinctions and the traditional judicial limitations upon the enforceability of servitudes. As a result, the materials that follow address easements and promissory servitudes separately, setting out the traditional historical rules and using the provisions of the Restatement of Servitudes to evaluate and critique those rules.

B. EASEMENTS

In its typical form, an easement is a nonpossessory interest in land that gives its holder the right to use land owned by another person. In other words, the easement holder does not get the full rights of possession, but merely the right to use another's land (the "servient estate," "servient tenement" or "servient land") for a particular purpose. This type of easement is known as an *affirmative* easement. A *negative* easement, by comparison, gives the holder the right to *restrict* the use of land owned or possessed by another person. As explained more fully below, property law historically recognized only a limited number of negative easements. The refusal to recognize a wider range of such easements ultimately gave rise to a different type of servitude—the promissory servitude—as a means of restricting activities on land owned by another.

Easements are either *appurtenant* or *in gross*. An appurtenant easement "attaches" to the ownership of an estate in land (the "dominant estate," "dominant tenement" or "dominant land"), and provides the owner of the dominant land with the right to use (or restrict the use of) the servient land. In contrast, the benefit of an easement in gross is not "attached" to ownership of an estate in land. Rather, an easement in gross gives its holder rights in the servient land regardless of the holder's ownership of any other parcel of land.[3]

1. *Negative Easements*

To the extent that the law recognizes such a right, a *negative* easement gives its holder the right to restrict the possessor of the servient land from making some use of that land. For example, suppose that Smith owns 500 acres of land, on which he has built a home with a commanding view of Mount Rogers. Suppose further that Smith conveys 200 acres of the land to Bowman, subject to a deed that says "subject to an easement across the land hereby conveyed to preserve to grantor (and his heirs, successors and assigns) an unobstructed view of Mt. Rogers." If Bowman subsequently begins constructing a 20–story office tower that would block Smith's view of Mt. Rogers from his home, this easement would permit Smith to obtain an injunction to prevent this interference. *See, e.g., Petersen v. Friedman*, 162 Cal.App.2d 245, 328 P.2d 264 (1958) (easement for unobstructed view of San Francisco Bay).

---

3. A "profit" is a special type of easement that allows its holder to enter the servient land and remove something from it (*e.g.*, timber, stone, minerals, or other natural resources). For purposes of determining the rights of the parties, profits are governed by the law of easements.

kinds of neg easements

English law recognized only a few kinds of negative easements, principally easements to prevent interference with: (a) the flow of light or air; (b) the support of a building; or (c) the flow of an artificial stream. English courts refused to recognize other types of negative easements, in large part because of a concern that recognition of negative easements would unreasonably burden the alienability of land. Early English law strictly applied the *caveat emptor* doctrine—a purchaser of land took title subject to all existing servitudes, regardless of whether the purchaser had notice of them. This meant that purchasers of land had the burden of trying to discover whether a previous owner had conveyed any nonpossessory interests in the land. Unfortunately, because early 19th-century England had no effective system for recording land interests, buyers of land could not discover the existence of negative easements by searching public land records (as buyers of land commonly do today). This "discoverability" problem made English courts reluctant to recognize new types of negative easements and thus increase the title investigation burden on buyers of land.

Because American states have always maintained recording systems that make it possible for buyers of land to discover most prior interests, one might have predicted that American courts would have been more willing to recognize new forms of negative easements. But other than the occasional decision recognizing easements for preserving scenic views (such as *Petersen v. Friedman* cited above), American courts have not recognized additional categories of negative easements (further encouraging the development of the law of promissory servitudes).

There is one additional type of negative easement that frequently arises—the conservation easement. A conservation easement imposes limits on the use of the servient land so as to preserve its availability for forest, recreational, or agricultural use; to protect natural resources, maintain or enhance air or water quality; or to preserve historically or culturally significant land. Although courts were initially reluctant to recognize conservation easements, legislatures in most states enacted enabling statutes that provided express authority for the creation of conservation easements. Due to both tax policy (taxpayers can deduct the value of conservation easements donated to charitable organizations) and heightened sensitivity to the perceived benefits of conservation and preservation, the past several decades have seen a significant increase in the number of conservation easements granted.

Although a conservation easement could be granted for a defined period of time, most conservation easements are perpetual in nature (either by their express terms, or because they are treated as such by default, absent a specific duration). Thus, a conservation easement has the potential to prevent the development of the servient land forever. Is this sound policy? *See, e.g.,* Eric Freyfogle, *Ethics, Community, and Private Land*, 23 Ecology L.Q. 631 (1996); John Sprankling, *The Anti-wilderness Bias in American Property Law*, 63 U. Chi. L. Rev. 519 (1996); Jeffrey A. Blackie, *Conservation Easements and the Doctrine of Changed Circumstances*, 40 Hastings L.J. 1187 (1989); Gerald Korngold,

Privately Held Conservation Servitudes: A Policy Analysis in the Context of In Gross Real Covenants and Easements, 63 Tex. L. Rev. 433 (1984).

2. *Affirmative Easements*

An *affirmative* easement gives the easement holder the right to enjoy some specified use of the servient tenement, such as a right of way for access across the servient land or the right to run a utility line across the servient land. Because of judicial reluctance to expand the catalogue of negative easements, nearly all modern easements are affirmative in nature.

The following sections discuss the issues that most commonly give rise to disputes regarding affirmative easements. These include: whether the easement is appurtenant or in gross; whether a deed or other instrument of conveyance uses language sufficient to create an express easement; whether (in the absence of an express grant or reservation) an easement arises by implication, prescription, or as an extension of a license; whether the easement holder or the owner of the servient estate is responsible for maintaining the easement; whether the use is subject to change or is transferable (which manifests itself generally in disputes regarding the scope of the easement); and what circumstances trigger termination of an easement.

a. *Creation by Express Grant or Reservation.* Because they are interests in land, easements generally are subject to the statute of frauds. To assure the validity of an easement, the grantee of an easement should have the grantor memorialize it in writing, using the standard formalities for the execution and conveyance of a deed. An express easement can be created in one of two ways:

- By *grant,* when the grantor (the owner of the servient land) executes and delivers to the grantee an instrument conveying an easement over the servient land, or

- By *reservation,* when the grantor executes and delivers a deed conveying a possessory estate in the servient land to the grantee, but "reserves" or retains in herself an easement over the servient land.

Because most easements arise by express grant or express reservation, problems involving the statute of frauds rarely arise. Nevertheless, due to careless drafting, questions can arise regarding whether an easement is appurtenant or in gross, or whether the parties intended to create an easement at all (as opposed to some other interest in land). Consider the following materials.

ALFT v. STEWART

Tennessee Court of Appeals.
1995 WL 412876 (1995).

GODDARD, P.J. The controversy giving rise to this appeal had its genesis in a certain warranty deed dated August 14, 1989, whereby Charles N. Clayton conveyed to Gracie P. Alft a tract of land in the Third District of Bledsoe County. The specific issue presented is whether the deed also conveyed a right-of-way appurtenant to the property conveyed, as was held by the Chancellor, or was personal and, as such, a right-of-way in gross.

The warranty deed in question contained the following paragraphs referred to in the Chancellor's opinion as paragraphs three and four:

[3.] Also conveyed herein is the right of egress and ingress over a dam and the Charles Clayton driveway, connecting said tract with a gravel road.

[4.] The Grantee herein, Gracie P. Alft and her husband, Harold Alft, have the right of access and use of the lake referred to above as long as the Grantee owns the above described property. This right is personal to Gracie P. Alft and husband, Harold Alft, and may not be leased, conveyed or assigned, and upon the sale of the above described property or the death of Gracie P. Alft and Harold Alft, this right shall terminate.

The case was tried upon stipulated facts and agreed exhibits which, as to the stipulation, is set out in the Chancellor's memorandum opinion as follows:

1. The Alfts are owners of property located in the Third Civil District of Bledsoe County, Tennessee. 2. The Alfts purchased a parcel of wooded property from the defendant, Mr. Clayton ("Grantor").[4] A copy of the Deed was attached to the Complaint and there is no issue as to its authenticity. 3. The Alfts cleared the property and put a 16 x 80 foot mobile home on the property. It is now not moveable. They added a 16 x 24 foot living room in 1990, a 10 x 16 foot porch, a basement and reroofed the entire house. 4. The Alfts occasionally put gravel across the dam. 5. Mr. Clayton has never placed gravel across the dam. 6. Mr. Alft purchased a culvert and it was installed using Mr. Clayton's equipment. 7. Mr. Clayton owns 20 feet of property east of the high water mark of the lake which abuts the Alfts' property. 8. The Alfts have planted and still have flowers planted on Mr. Clayton's 20 foot of property on the east side of the lake. 9. Mr. Clayton has two or three out buildings or shops approximately 40 feet from said driveway or easement containing various equipment and tools.

---

4. This statement is in error. The stipulated deed shows the property was conveyed to Mrs. Alft only.

Based upon the stipulated facts, the Chancellor made the following conclusions of law with which we concur:

The paragraph at issue in the deed states: "Also conveyed herein is the right of egress and ingress over a dam and the Charles Clayton driveway, connecting said tract with a gravel road." It is the plaintiff's contention that the right of egress and ingress over the dam and the Charles Clayton driveway is an easement appurtenant that runs with the land and can be conveyed, assigned or otherwise transferred to a third party. It is defendants' position that this is a personal easement, or easement in gross, that cannot be leased, conveyed or assigned to a third party. In construing an easement clause under Tennessee law, the construction of a clause creating an easement appurtenant, rather than an easement in gross, is favored. An easement will never be presumed to be a personal right when it can fairly be construed to be appurtenant to some other estate. It is a settled rule in Tennessee that in the absence of ambiguity or irreconcilable conflict in the provisions of a deed, parol evidence is not admissible to contradict, add to, or explain the provisions of a deed. In this case, the Deed is not ambiguous or irreconcilable and thus, the court will determine the conveyance by examining the Deed from its four corners and by determining the intention of the parties. The four corners of the Deed evidence the Grantor's intention to grant an easement appurtenant. In reaching this conclusion, the court defines the words in the Deed by their usual and appropriate meaning. In so doing, the Court finds that immediately after conveying a tract of land in the Deed, Mr. Clayton "also conveyed" the right of egress and ingress over a dam and the Charles Clayton driveway. "Conveyed" is defined by Black's Law Dictionary as "to pass or transmit the titled property from one to another." It is apparent from the four corners of the Deed that it was Mr. Clayton's intent to "also convey" the right of egress and ingress over a dam and the Charles Clayton driveway, connecting said tract with the gravel road. This language clearly evidences the conveyance of an easement appurtenant that runs with the land and that can be conveyed, assigned or transferred to third parties when they purchase the property described in the deed. This intent of the Grantor is further evidenced by the explicit language of the Deed when one compares the language in Paragraph 4 of the Deed with the language used in Paragraph 3. It is undisputed that the language used in Paragraph 4 creates an easement in gross which is personal to the Alfts and cannot be transferred, leased or conveyed by them to a third party. Paragraph 4 explicitly states that the right of access and use of the lake is "personal" and "may not be leased, conveyed or assigned, and upon the sale of the above described property or the death of Gracie P. Alft and Harold Alft, this right shall terminate." Contrasting this language to the language used in Paragraph 3, conveying an easement appurtenant, highlights the different intentions of the grantor concerning the different easements. In addition,

Grantor own 20 ft strk of prop

in construing the Deed by looking at its four corners, it is apparent that the Grantor owns a 20 foot strip of property between the lake and the Alfts' property. As such, the Grantor intended to grant the Alfts the "right of access" over this 20 foot piece of property in order to use the lake, such use being granted as an easement in gross conveyed in Paragraph 4 of the Deed. The Defendant's contention that this "right of access," refers to the use of the Clayton driveway and the road over the dam and should be interpreted as an easement in gross misconstrues the language of the Deed and is without merit.

P3 = appurtena

In conclusion, and upon construing and interpreting the Deed entered into between the parties within its four corners, "the right of egress and ingress over a dam and the Charles Clayton driveway," conveyed in Paragraph 3 of the Deed, is an easement appurtenant that runs with the property that can be leased, conveyed, or assigned by the plaintiffs to a third party. As a property right, the right of egress and ingress over a dam and the Charles Clayton driveway shall not be interfered with by the Defendant or any other third person.

Although not mentioned in the Chancellor's memorandum opinion, we think it is significant that the deed conveyed the "wooded property" and the right-of-way mentioned in paragraph three to Gracie P. Alft alone, and the right of access mentioned in paragraph four was granted to both Mr. and Mrs. Alft, which would suggest that different rights were intended to be transferred.

For the foregoing reasons the judgment of the Chancellor is affirmed and the cause remanded for collection of costs below. Costs of appeal are adjudged against Mr. Clayton and his sureties.

Notes

1. *The Rest of the Story.* Although the court's opinion does not disclose the fact, Gracie Alft and Charles Clayton were siblings. According to Harold Alft, this dispute arose when Gracie and Harold decided to sell the land and move to Florida. The Alfts retained a real estate agent, but when the agent would attempt to show the home, Charles (allegedly) would stand in the driveway and inform prospective buyers that he would not allow them to use his driveway to reach the home. Gracie filed the lawsuit to obtain a declaration of the nature of her easement rights.

Although he lost the lawsuit, Clayton allegedly continued to interfere with efforts to sell the land. A few months after the decision (and after Gracie and Harold had moved to Florida), the Alft home was destroyed by fire. Gracie and Harold collected the insurance proceeds (after satisfying the insurance company that they had not set the fire themselves). Ultimately, they sold the land to Clayton's son-in-law.

2. *Easement Appurtenant or Easement in Gross?* A well-drafted easement should state clearly whether it is appurtenant, but sometimes—especially with easements prepared by laypersons—the language creating an easement is not sufficiently explicit. In such cases, almost all jurisdictions

apply a rule of construction, suggested in *Alft*, favoring an easement appurtenant over an easement in gross.[5] Why should the law adopt a presumption of appurtenance? Consider the following problems:

(a) Ziegler, owner of Blackacre, holds an easement to install and use a sewer line across the adjacent Whiteacre, to connect Blackacre to the city's sewer system. The document creating the easement does not specify whether the easement is appurtenant to Blackacre. A few years later, after installing the sewer line, Ziegler conveys Blackacre to Wells via a deed that makes no mention of the easement. Shortly thereafter Marsh, the owner of Whiteacre, approaches Wells and demands that she pay a fee for continued use of the sewer line across Whiteacre. Should Marsh's claim fail? Does the substance of the original agreement suggest that the parties intended the easement to be appurtenant or in gross? Would it matter if the easement had a defined duration (say, either 50 or 100 years)?

(b) Ziegler, owner of Blackacre, holds an easement to visit the beautiful gardens located on Whiteacre. The document creating the easement does not specify whether the easement is appurtenant to Blackacre. A few years later, Ziegler conveys Blackacre to Wells via a deed that does not mention the easement. Shortly thereafter Marsh, the owner of Whiteacre, approaches Wells and demands that she pay for the continued right to visit the gardens. Should Marsh's claim fail? Does the substance of the original agreement suggest that the parties intended the easement to be appurtenant or in gross? Would it matter if the easement had a defined duration (say, either 50 or 100 years)?

(c) Chen is considering buying land on the northwest corner of Main and Fifth Streets. The current owner of that land, Bryan, had previously granted an easement by an instrument that contains the following language: "I hereby convey to the First Episcopal Church an easement on my property located on the northwest corner of Main and Fifth for automobile parking during church hours." The First Episcopal Church was located on the southwest corner of Main and Fifth when Bryan granted the easement. Recently, the First Episcopal Church moved to a new location on the other side of town and an evangelical nondenominational church bought the property at the southwest corner of Main and Fifth. Chen wants to know whether the easement still burdens the land he wants to buy. How would you advise him? Does the quoted language create an easement appurtenant or an easement in gross? What other information would you like to gather to assist you in advising your client properly? *See Willard v. First Church of Christ, Scientist*, 7 Cal.3d 473, 102 Cal.Rptr. 739, 498 P.2d 987 (1972).

(d) Reconsider the *Alft* court's conclusions in light of the facts reported in note 1 above. The court concluded that paragraph [3] of the deed "clearly evidences the conveyance of an appurtenant easement." Do you agree? Does it matter that Charles Clayton and Gracie Alft were

5. Interestingly, Connecticut law provides that if the language of the instrument does not mention the "heirs and assigns" of the grantee, the presumption favors construing the easement as an easement in gross. *Stiefel v. Lindemann*, 33 Conn.App. 799, 638 A.2d 642 (1994). Does this seem sensible in light of what you learned in Chapter 5 about the modern rules regarding the use of the term "heirs"?

siblings? Would it make a difference to you if this deed had been drafted by Mr. Clayton personally? By his lawyer?

3. *Appurtenant or In Gross?* Under the traditional common law, the transferability of an easement depended upon whether the easement was appurtenant or in gross. Because an appurtenant easement benefitted ownership of the dominant estate, the benefit of an appurtenant easement automatically transferred with (or "ran with") ownership of the dominant estate. The transferability of an easement in gross, however, generally depended upon whether the easement was commercial or noncommercial in nature. As indicated in *Alft*, a noncommercial easement in gross was personal to its holder (and thus nontransferable); by contrast, the holder of a commercial easement in gross could freely transfer that easement right. [Can you explain why?]

The new Restatement of Servitudes takes a slightly different definitional approach. Section 1.5 maintains the traditional appurtenant/in gross distinction: a servitude is "appurtenant" if its rights or obligations "are tied to ownership or occupancy of a particular unit or parcel of land," and "in gross" if its rights or obligations are "not tied to ownership or occupancy of a particular unit or parcel of land." But under the Restatement, this characterization does not dictate the transferability of the easement. Instead, the Restatement suggests that transferability depends upon whether the party creating the easement intended for it to be "personal." Under § 1.5(3), a servitude benefit is "personal" (and thus nontransferable) if the parties did not intend for that benefit to run with a parcel of land—*even if that benefit is otherwise tied to ownership of that parcel of land so as to be appurtenant*. Thus, under the Restatement, an easement could be (a) appurtenant and not personal; (b) appurtenant and personal; (c) in gross and not personal; or (d) in gross and personal. In which categories would you place the two easements in *Alft*? Does Restatement § 1.5 effectively moot the traditional common law constructional preference for appurtenance? Why or why not?

4. *Creating Easements in Third Parties (Persons Other than the Grantor or Grantee).* At common law, an owner of land could create an easement for herself by reservation, but could not reserve an easement for a "stranger" to the conveyance. Thus, *O* could not transfer a possessory estate to *A* and, in the same deed, reserve an easement over the same land in favor of *B*. *See, e.g., Tripp v. Huff*, 606 A.2d 792 (Me. 1992); *Estate of Thomson v. Wade*, 69 N.Y.2d 570, 516 N.Y.S.2d 614, 509 N.E.2d 309 (1987). The doctrinal explanation for this rule was that *B*, unlike the grantor, did not hold a property interest at the time of the conveyance and, therefore, the grantor could not be said to have *reserved* an easement for *B*.

Today, there is a significant amount of modern authority that permits a grantor to use one deed to convey a possessory estate to one grantee and an easement to another (*e.g., O* conveys "to *A* and his heirs, subject to an easement in favor of *B*"). *See, e.g., Willard v. First Church of Christ, Scientist, supra* note 2; Restatement of Servitudes § 2.6(2). Nevertheless, as *Tripp* and *Estate of Thomson* suggest, the common law rule appears to remain effective in some states. In Maine or New York, what would *O* have to do to convey Blueacre to *A*, subject to an easement in favor of *B*?

5. *Railroad Rights of Way.* As transportation patterns have changed, railroad companies permanently ceased using many no-longer-needed railroad corridors. When that occurs, what happens to the underlying strip of land? The answer depends upon what type of interest the railroad held:

- If the railroad held title to the corridor in fee simple absolute, the railroad continues to own the corridor (often, railroads transfer no-longer-needed corridors to state and local governments, which use them to establish recreational trails).

- If the railroad held title to the corridor by a defeasible fee estate, the railroad's cessation of use may terminate the railroad's title, with possession then shifting to the person(s) who held the future interest (most likely—but not necessarily—the owners of the adjacent parcels from whom the corridor was originally acquired).

- If the railroad held only an easement over the corridor, the railroad's cessation of use may constitute an abandonment that terminates the easement. [We discuss abandonment in greater detail on page 605.]

Ideally, the documents creating a rail corridor would clearly articulate the consequences that would follow if the railroad permanently ceased using the corridor. Often, however, the documents are ambiguous. For example, suppose the original owner of Blueacre had deeded to Railroad "a strip of land for a right-of-way one hundred (100) feet wide [across Blueacre], to have and to hold said strip of land unto said Railroad for a right of way, its successors and assigns forever." Seventy years later, Railroad ceases using the corridor, removes its tracks (salvaging the steel), and proposes to convey the land (and all other parcels in the corridor) to the state's government as part of a "rails-to-trails" program. Can the owner of Blueacre argue that the deed created only an easement that Railroad has now abandoned? Why or why not? *Compare Grill v. West Va. R.R. Maint. Auth.*, 188 W.Va. 284, 423 S.E.2d 893 (1992) *and Maberry v. Gueths*, 238 Mont. 304, 777 P.2d 1285 (1989) (fee simple estate) *with Jordan v. Stallings*, 911 S.W.2d 653 (Mo. Ct. App. 1995) (easement). Can you think of a good reason to establish a rule of construction preferring an easement, rather than an estate in fee simple, in railroad right-of-way cases? *See* Richard A. Posner, Economic Analysis of Law 76 (4th ed. 1992).

b. *Implied Easements.* Most easements are express easements (like the driveway and lake easements in *Alft v. Stewart*). In some circumstances, however, the law will imply an easement in favor of one of the parties to a deed even though the deed itself fails to create an express easement. Easements may be implied from subdivision plats, from necessity following severance of a common parcel, or from pre-existing use following severance of a common parcel.

(1) *Easements Implied from Subdivision Plats.* Assume Davis subdivides a parcel of land into 50 building lots for a new residential subdivision called Shady Acres. Davis prepares a plat (a map) showing the location of each lot and all neighborhood streets. Davis shows this map to prospective purchasers, including Monahan, who purchases Lot 1. Davis delivers Monahan a deed that conveys fee simple title to Lot 1, but creates no express easement across the neighborhood streets to reach Lot 1. In this situation, a court will imply an appurtenant easement over the neighborhood streets in favor of Lot 1. This reflects the presumed (if unexpressed) intention of Davis as developer and

Monahan as the buyer of Lot 1—Monahan bought her lot in reliance upon the plat's implicit representation that she could legally use the neighborhood streets to reach her lot. *See, e.g.,* Restatement of Servitudes § 2.13; *Shear v. Stevens Bldg. Co.,* 107 N.C.App. 154, 418 S.E.2d 841 (1992); *Clearwater Realty Co. v. Bouchard,* 146 Vt. 359, 505 A.2d 1189 (1985); *Cleveland Realty Co. v. Hobbs,* 261 N.C. 414, 135 S.E.2d 30 (1964).

(2) *The Implied Easement of Necessity.* Assume that Key owns Blueacre, which is bounded to the north, east, and west by other privately owned land and to the south by a public highway. Key then subdivides Blueacre, keeping the southern portion (Parcel A) and conveying the northern portion (Parcel B) to Wells. Because Parcel B will be "landlocked" as a result of this conveyance—*i.e.,* because Wells will lack any means of legal access to reach Parcel B from the public road—Wells would be ill-advised to acquire Parcel B without ensuring the deed creates an express easement to cross Parcel A. However, assume that the deed to Wells does not contain such an express easement because the parties did not realize it was necessary. Should the law imply into the deed an easement across Parcel A to provide Wells with access to Parcel B?

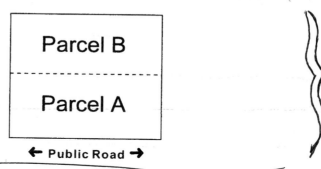

In this situation, a court is likely to recognize an *implied easement of necessity* in favor of Parcel B, which will permit Wells (and successor owners of Parcel B) to cross Parcel A to reach the public road. An implied easement of necessity can arise only when the owner of one parcel of land conveys part of the land, landlocks the parcel conveyed or the parcel retained, and fails to create an express easement for a right of way to the landlocked parcel. Notably, the requisite necessity must exist at the time the two parcels are first severed from common ownership. If someone purchases a parcel of property to which she has legal access at the time of purchase, but which subsequently becomes landlocked, the purchaser has no claim to a common law easement of necessity across the property of the grantor or anyone else. *See, e.g., Jackson v. Nash,*

109 Nev. 1202, 866 P.2d 262 (1993); *Schwab v. Timmons*, 224 Wis.2d 27, 589 N.W.2d 1 (1999).

One might argue that recognizing an implied easement of necessity is good public policy—it would seem dubious to allow subdivision of land to render a portion of that land inaccessible (thereby limiting its potential use/development). However, if public policy alone were a sufficient justification, the law would presumably imply an easement in favor of any landlocked parcel, no matter when or how it became landlocked. Thus, public policy alone cannot justify the implied easement of necessity. Instead, the law bases implication of this easement upon the presumed intention of the parties to the deed that severed the common parcel (in our example, Key and Wells). The law assumes that reasonable persons in the position of Key and Wells must have assumed that Parcel B would have access over Parcel A—otherwise, Wells would have been irrational to purchase Parcel B—and that the deed conveying Parcel B failed to include an express easement due to oversight or lack of sophistication (rather than a conscious intent to landlock Parcel B). Is this a reasonable assumption? What facts related to the transaction would help us understand whether this is a reasonable assumption in a specific case?

(3) *The Implied Easement Based Upon Pre-existing Use ("Quasi–Easement").* A deed that subdivides a parcel of land may sometimes fail to address the rights and obligations of the parties with respect to uses of that land that occurred prior to subdivision. For example, suppose that Key had built and occupied a residence on the northern portion of Blueacre and had constructed a driveway across the southern portion that she used to reach her home from the public road. [Assume in this situation that Key also has a means of legal access to Blueacre from the north.] Suppose that Key then conveyed the southern portion of Blueacre (Parcel A) to Wells—but that the deed from Key to Wells did not say anything about whether Key could continue to use the driveway across Parcel A to reach Parcel B from the public road. Should the law imply into the deed an easement that would permit Key to continue this use? Consider the following materials.

BOB'S READY TO WEAR, INC. v. WEAVER

Court of Appeals of Kentucky.
569 S.W.2d 715 (1978).

PARK, JUDGE. This litigation is the result of the construction of a chain link fence along a portion of the common boundary line between owners of commercial property. The plaintiffs-appellants (the Parmans) are the owners of Bob's Ready to Wear Store located on Main Street within the city of London. The defendants-appellees, Drew and Betty Jane Weaver, own and operate a restaurant on a lot adjacent to Bob's Store. In addition, the Weavers own a lot at the rear of Bob's Store and the Weaver restaurant. This lot is rented to the city as a municipal parking lot. The Weavers constructed a chain link fence which prevented

[handwritten margin note: construction of chain link fence]

[handwritten note at bottom: lot rented as municipal parking lot]

any access between the parking lot and an entrance at the rear of Bob's Store.

The Parmans filed an action in the Laurel Circuit Court seeking an injunction requiring the removal of the fence and enjoining the Weavers from any further interference with access between Bob's Store and the parking lot. The Parmans asserted that they owned an easement by . . . implication or equitable estoppel. Following a trial before the court, judgment was entered denying the injunction and dismissing the complaint. The Parmans appeal. . . .

The property in question was originally part of a commercial block owned by the Eversole family. This block was bounded by Main Street on the east, Sixth Street on the north and Broad Street on the west. The Weaver family had conducted a restaurant in the building (A, B, H, G) at the corner of Main and Sixth Streets since 1940. Beginning in 1953, the Parmans had operated Bob's Store, a retail clothing business, in a building (G, I, K, J) adjacent to the Weaver restaurant fronting on Main Street. Immediately to the rear of the restaurant and store was a vacant lot extending along Sixth Street to Broad Street. In 1965, the Eversole family leased the lot to the city of London. The city installed parking meters, and the city has operated the property (C, N, M, L) as a municipal parking lot.

In 1971, the Weavers and the Parmans purchased from the Eversole family the buildings presently occupied by the respective parties. In addition to the property previously occupied by Bob's Store, the Parmans purchased a portion of the building which had been a part of the Weaver Restaurant (D, E, H, G). The building originally occupied as Bob's Store extended back from Main Street approximately 100 feet. The building originally occupied by the Weavers extended back a distance of only 80 feet. In order to make the rear property lines (C, F, I, L) straight, the conveyance from the Eversole family to the Parmans included a small paved lot (E, F, I, H) approximately 20 feet square at the rear of that portion of the building that had previously been released to the Weavers. A similar paved area (B, C, F, E) approximately 20 feet square was included in the conveyance from the Eversole family to the Weavers.

At the time of the conveyances by the Eversole family in 1971, there were no physical barriers between the paved parking lot leased to the city and the paved area at the rear of Bob's Store and the Weaver restaurant. Shortly after acquiring title to their respective buildings, the Parmans and the Weavers both made significant structural and decorative improvements to the rear entrances of their respective buildings. The Parmans installed display windows and a new door (point X) which opened onto the 20 foot plot acquired with the building by the deed from the Eversole family.

The municipal parking lot was used by customers as a means of access to the rear entrances to Bob's Store and to the Weaver's restaurant. In addition, trucks used the parking lot as a means of access to the rear of Bob's Store for the purpose of making deliveries or picking up refuse. In 1976, the Eversole family conveyed the parking lot property to the Weavers. The city continues to maintain a municipal parking lot on the property, but only as a tenant from month to month. Following their purchase of the parking lot property in 1976, the Weavers closed off the rear entrance to Bob's Store by erecting a chain link fence (E, F, I) along the two open sides of the 20 foot plot at the rear of their building. At the present time, the only functional purpose of the fence is to block access between Bob's Store and the municipal parking lot. . . .

The Parmans . . . argue that an easement by implication resulted from the sale of the Bob's Store building by the Eversole family to the Parmans in 1971. When finding an easement by implication, courts in effect infer an unarticulated intention by the owner of property that a particular use of one portion of the property for the benefit of another portion be continued although one or both segments of the whole are conveyed away. Necessarily, the use sought to be imposed upon the servient tract for the benefit of the dominant tract must have been initiated when both tracts were the property of a common owner. Once common ownership is established and the particular use is found to have been initiated prior to severance, the determination whether the creation of an easement was intended will depend upon a number of factors. 2 American Law of Property § 8.31 (A. J. Casner, ed. 1952). Until 1971, the Eversoles owned the property occupied by the commercial building fronting on Main Street and the adjacent property to the rear which was used as a parking lot. During the entire period of their ownership prior to the severance of the commercially improved portion of the property, the Eversoles permitted free access from the parking lot to the rear exits of the building. Therefore, the Parmans have satisfied the two threshold prerequisites to a finding of an implied easement.

Among the factors bearing upon the intention of the grantor and grantee are the following: (1) whether the claimant is the grantor or the grantee of the dominant tract; (2) the extent of necessity of the easement to the claimant; (3) whether reciprocal benefits accrue to both the grantor and grantee; (4) the manner in which the land was used prior to conveyance; and (5) whether the prior use was or might have been known to the parties to the present litigation. *Knight v. Shell*, 313 Ky. 852, 233 S.W.2d 973 (1950); 5 Restatement of the Law of Property § 476 (1944); Note, Implied Easements of Necessity Contrasted with those Based on Quasi–Easements, 40 Ky.L.J. 324 (1952).

[margin note: Factors looked @ to interpn intent of grantor]

Courts imply an easement more readily in favor of a grantee than a grantor. The Parmans claim an easement by implication as grantees from the Eversole heirs, the original owners of all the property. For many years prior to the 1971 conveyance, the parking lot had been openly and continuously used as a means of access to the rear entrances of the buildings fronting on Main Street. While they were tenants of the Eversole heirs, the Weavers had enjoyed free access to the rear entrance of their business across the parking lot. Following the 1971 sales, both the Weavers and the Parmans continued to use the parking lot as a means of access to the rear of their buildings. One of the Eversole heirs testified that she specifically advised the Weavers prior to the 1976 sale of the lot that the Parmans had a right of access to and from the parking lot. All of these factors favor finding an easement by implication in favor of the Parmans.

When the question of necessity is considered, the facts are less clear. The main entrance to Bob's Store is from Main Street, the main thoroughfare in the city. Recently, the Parmans have opened an entrance leading to Fifth Street through other property. There is no showing of absolute necessity for access to the parking lot. However, absolute necessity is not required. The fact that the Parmans have other access to their store is not an automatic bar to their claim to an easement by implication to the parking lot. *Irvine v. McCreary*, 108 Ky. 495, 56 S.W. 966 (1900). All that is required is that the easement be "reasonably necessary." *Knight v. Shell, supra*, 313 Ky. 852, 233 S.W.2d at 975. Without access to the parking lot which opened on Broad and Sixth Streets, the recently developed rear entrance to Bob's Store becomes landlocked. The 20 foot plot at the rear of Bob's Store becomes virtually useless if the Weavers are permitted to cut off all access to the parking lot. The trial judge specifically found that the Parmans had suffered and would in the future suffer monetary damages from the maintenance of the chain link fence.

[margin note: no absolu necessity however not req'd must only be reasonably necessary]

The last factor to be considered is whether reciprocal benefits accrue to both the grantor and the grantee if an easement is implied as a part of the 1971 conveyance from the Eversole heirs to the Parmans. The benefit to the Parmans is obvious if customers may use the rear entrance to Bob's Store only a few feet from the parking lot. Access to the public parking lot at the rear of the building can only have enhanced the purchase price paid by the Parmans to the Eversoles. In turn, Bob's Store would attract customers to the parking lot thereby enhancing the value of that property. Unfortunately, an easement by implication would be of mutual benefit to grantors and grantees only so long as a public parking lot was maintained on the property to the rear of Bob's Store. The existence of an easement from Broad Street across the lot to the rear of Bob's Store would be an extremely heavy burden impeding any future development of this valuable city property.

Giving consideration to the relative nature of the necessity for an easement of access to the parking lot and the possible future burden to the Weavers, we conclude that the evidence was not so overwhelming as to require the trial judge to find that an easement by implication existed. Balancing the interests of both parties, we conclude that the trial judge did not err in refusing to adjudge the Parmans an easement by implication. . . .

Notes

1. *Easements Implied from Pre-existing Use.* The party claiming an implied easement from pre-existing use must prove that, at the time the would-be dominant and servient parcels were severed from common ownership, the common owner had been using the allegedly servient portion to benefit the allegedly dominant portion. In addition, the claimant must show that the use was "apparent" and "continuous" at the time of the severance, and that the continuation of the use was "reasonably necessary" for the enjoyment of the would-be dominant parcel. Courts have often struggled, however, to apply these standards in a predictable way.

(a) *Implied Grants vs. Implied Reservations.* The *Bob's* case involves a potential easement by implied grant; *i.e.*, the Parmans are arguing that the deed by which they took title to the Bob's store parcel also impliedly *granted* them an easement across the parking lot (which the Eversoles retained). By contrast, the hypothetical on page 563 involves a potential easement by implied reservation; in that example, Key is arguing that the deed by which she conveyed Parcel A to Wells impliedly *reserved* to Key an easement to cross Parcel A using the existing driveway.

Bob's suggests that courts may be *less* willing to imply easements by reservation than by grant. Some courts, for example, have held a party claiming by implied reservation must make a greater showing of necessity to establish a successful easement claim. *See, e.g., Adams v. Cullen*, 44 Wash.2d 502, 268 P.2d 451 (1954). Other courts have held that the same degree of "necessity" is required to justify any implied easement from pre-existing use, regardless of whether by grant or reservation. *See, e.g., Jack v. Hunt*, 200 Or. 263, 264 P.2d 461 (1953). Should this distinction matter? Why or why not?

(b) *The Algebra of the "Apparent," "Continuous" and "Necessary" Requirements.* What purposes do these elements serve? How would you demonstrate the existence of these elements as of the time of severance? Consider the following problems:

(1) Stan claims an implied easement across three lots he had previously conveyed, for the benefit of his retained lot, for the purpose of connecting the home on his lot to the public sewer system via a sewer line crossing the three conveyed lots. What facts would lead you to believe that such an easement was apparent, continuous, and reasonably necessary? *Otero v. Pacheco,* 94 N.M. 524, 612 P.2d 1335 (Ct. App. 1980).

(2) Golden Properties conveys a portion of a shopping center and claims an implied easement to allow delivery trucks to cross the conveyed parcel to make deliveries to a portion of the shopping center retained by Golden Properties. What facts would lead you to believe that such an easement was apparent, continuous, and reasonably necessary? *Granite Props. Ltd. P'ship v. Manns,* 117 Ill.2d 425, 111 Ill.Dec. 593, 512 N.E.2d 1230 (1987).

(3) Frank conveys Parcel B to Jane, retaining Parcel A. The deed to Jane provides that "Jane shall have a license to use the driveway across Parcel A to reach the highway while she owns Parcel B." If Frank later attempts to revoke the license, could Jane argue that she had an easement implied from a pre-existing use? What facts would lead you to believe that an implied quasi-easement was (or was not) apparent, continuous, and reasonably necessary? *Condry v. Laurie,* 184 Md. 317, 41 A.2d 66 (Ct. App. 1945).

(c) *The "Reciprocal Benefits" Test.* Why should it matter whether implication of the easement would involve reciprocal benefits to the owners of the dominant and servient parcels? What form would this "reciprocal benefit" need to take? The *Bob's* court concluded that implication of the easement would provide a reciprocal benefit to the parking lot parcel only so long as the parcel continued to be used as a parking lot. Is this necessarily true? How else might the implication of an easement have reciprocally benefitted the Eversoles? Given that the other factors cited by the *Bob's* court seemed to cut in favor of the Parmans, do you think the court was justified in refusing to imply an easement?

Section 2.12 of the Restatement of Servitudes provides that the court should imply an easement from prior use when, upon severance of the parcels, "the parties had reasonable grounds to expect that the conveyance would not terminate the right to continue the prior use." Whether "reasonable grounds" existed is a function of the following factors: (a) whether the prior use "was not merely temporary or casual"; (b) whether its continuance was "reasonably necessary" to enjoyment of the benefitted parcel; (c) whether its existence was "apparent or known to the parties"; and (d) whether the use was "for underground utilities serving either parcel." The "reciprocal benefits" standard used in the old Restatement no longer appears as a specific factor. Does this mean that the potential reciprocal benefits that might arise from implication of an easement are irrelevant? How do you think a court applying § 2.12 would decide the dispute in *Bob's?*

2. *Implied Easements of Necessity—What Degree of "Necessity" Is Required?* All courts agree that mere convenience is not a sufficient basis for implying an easement of necessity. Courts have disagreed, however, over how to apply the "necessary" standard. For example, suppose that Parcel B

is technically adjacent to a public road on its western boundary, but that Wells could not reach the public road without spending $40,000 to bridge a creek that runs along the entire western boundary of Blueacre. Is an implied easement across Parcel A "necessary" under these circumstances? *See, e.g., Hitchman v. Hudson*, 40 Or. App. 59, 594 P.2d 851 (1979) *and Jackson v. Nash*, 109 Nev. 1202, 866 P.2d 262 (1993) (using "reasonable" necessity standard); *Condry v. Laurie*, 184 Md. 317, 41 A.2d 66 (Ct. App. 1945) (using "strict" necessity standard).

3. *Duration of an Implied Easement.* An implied easement of necessity lasts only for as long as it is needed to provide access to the landlocked parcel; it terminates when the necessity disappears (*i.e.*, if the owner of that parcel later acquires another means of legal access). *See, e.g., Cordwell v. Smith*, 105 Idaho 71, 665 P.2d 1081 (Ct. App. 1983). By contrast, courts treat implied easements based upon pre-existing use as unlimited in duration. Can you explain this distinction in light of the respective rationales for the two types of implied easements?

4. *Private Condemnation of a Right of Way.* Some states have addressed the problem of "landlocked" parcels by enacting statutes that allow the owner of a landlocked parcel to condemn an easement over neighboring lands. These statutes require the owner of the landlocked parcel to pay the servient land owner to acquire this easement (with the court establishing the price if the parties cannot agree). In comparison, the recipient of an implied easement of necessity *does not* have to compensate the owner of the servient land (because it is assumed that the parties already must have factored the benefit and burden of the easement into the purchase price). *See, e.g.,* Ariz. Rev. Stat. § 12.1202; Wash. Rev. Code § 8.24.010.

The availability of a private condemnation statute presents some interesting legal questions. Should a landlocked owner be able to use the statute *only* if she cannot legally establish an implied easement of necessity under common law? *Compare Brown v. McAnally*, 97 Wash.2d 360, 644 P.2d 1153 (1982) *with Bickel v. Hansen*, 169 Ariz. 371, 819 P.2d 957 (Ct. App. 1991). Should the availability of such a statute *prevent* a party from claiming a common law implied easement of necessity (*i.e.*, does the statute abolish the common law implied easement of necessity)? How should a court decide on the path for the right of way—by maximizing convenience for the landlocked owner, or minimizing inconvenience to the servient owner(s)? *Compare Solana Land Co. v. Murphey,* 69 Ariz. 117, 210 P.2d 593 (1949) (condemnor's proposed path will be upheld absent bad faith, oppression or abuse of power) *with Stair v. Miller,* 52 Md.App. 108, 447 A.2d 109 (1982) ("way of necessity should be located so as to be the least onerous to the owner of the servient estate while, at the same time, being of reasonable convenience to the owner of the dominant estate"). Finally, a practical question: If a landlocked party had the choice of claiming a common law implied easement of necessity or pursuing the statutory condemnation remedy, would you ever advise them to choose the statutory remedy (given that it requires compensation to the servient landowner)? Why or why not?

c. *Prescriptive Easements.* Sometimes one or more persons may make use of another's land without having the benefit of an express or implied easement. If such use continues for a sufficiently long period of time, it may ripen into a *prescriptive easement* (or an easement by prescription).

Though English law had long recognized prescriptive rights, some early American decisions justified the prescriptive easement by adopting the *theory of the lost grant.* Courts applied this theory to protect uses of land that had continued with the acquiescence of the true owner for a very long time. In these cases, courts presumed that the servient owner's acquiescence was consistent with the idea that the servient owner must have conveyed an express easement at some time in the past, by virtue of a "lost grant"—*i.e.,* a grant of which there no longer was any tangible evidence other than the continued use and the servient owner's long acquiescence. *See, e.g.,* William B. Stoebuck, *The Fiction of Presumed Grant,* 15 Kan. L. Rev. 17 (1966).

Today, the "lost grant" theory has largely fallen out of favor. Courts recognize prescriptive easements, but typically do so based upon the notion of longstanding *adverse* use. In Chapter 3, we discussed the doctrine of adverse possession. The law of prescriptive easements provides an analogue for use—where one person makes an actual, open, hostile, and continuous use of another's land that continues for a period exceeding the statutory period of limitations for an action to prevent that use, the user obtains a prescriptive easement.

In Chapter 3, you learned that the law typically presumes that possession of another's land is hostile (thereby placing the burden on the true owner to demonstrate a grant of permission). Is a similar presumption appropriate for *use* of another's land? If two neighbors (*A* and *B*) share the use of a driveway located on *A*'s land, should the law presume that *B*'s use of *A*'s land is hostile or permissive?

MELENDEZ v. HINTZ

Idaho Court of Appeals.
111 Idaho 401, 724 P.2d 137 (1986).

SWANSTROM, JUSTICE. Michael and Kathryn Melendez brought this action against their neighbor James Hintz after Hintz blocked a driveway on his property which the Melendezes or their predecessors had used for twenty years. The Melendezes claimed they had acquired a prescriptive easement by adverse use of the driveway. The district court agreed. Hintz has appealed. Upon a record of undisputed facts we are asked to decide whether, as a matter of law, the Melendezes' use of the driveway was adverse to Hintz or permissive. Holding that the use was adverse, we affirm.

The properties involved are shown in the following illustrative sketch. The easement granted by the district court is the "Y" shaped shaded area.

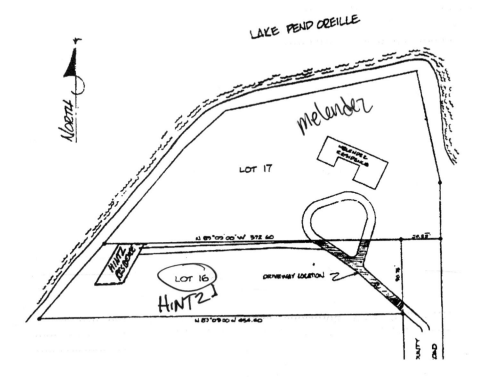

Hintz did not acquire his property until 1981. What we refer to as Hintz's home and driveway were constructed by a predecessor on Lot 16 prior to August 1962. His driveway leaves a county road on the east end of his lot, angles to the north boundary and follows the north side of the lot to his home at the west end of his lot.

The Melendezes' home was constructed by their predecessors in 1963 on Lot 17 lying north of Lot 16. A platted county road running north along the east ends of several lots deadends against the south line of Lot 17. While the facts are not clear on this point, testimony indicates that the road was not well-established on its northern end. For a time during construction of the Melendez home there was a direct access to Lot 17 from the platted right-of-way. Then a county official who owned property on the east side of the roadway claimed ownership of part of the right-of-way and erected a barrier, preventing further use of that route. Melendezes' predecessors then began using a part of the Hintz driveway for access to Lot 17. They added a new section of driveway, branching off from the Hintz driveway, yet still on the Hintz property, to reach Lot 17. They constructed a loop drive on their lot which connected with the Hintz driveway at two different places. Thus, the Melendezes' predecessors began using a "Y" shaped section of driveway on Lot 16. The lower stem and left branch of the "Y" they used jointly with Hintz's predecessor. The right branch has not been used by Hintz or his predecessor. The owners of Lot 17 used the driveway continuously since 1963 as did the

Melendezes after they purchased Lot 17 in 1982. The use was not disputed until 1983 when Hintz decided that he no longer wanted the Melendezes to use the driveway across his property.

A claimant, in order to acquire a prescriptive easement in Idaho, must present reasonably clear and convincing evidence of open, notorious, continuous, uninterrupted use, under a claim of right, with the knowledge of the owner of the servient estate for the prescriptive period. *State ex rel. Haman v. Fox*, 100 Idaho 140, 594 P.2d 1093 (1979); *West v. Smith*, 95 Idaho 550, 511 P.2d 1326 (1973); *Kaupp v. City of Hailey*, 110 Idaho 337, 715 P.2d 1007 (Ct.App.1986). The prescriptive period in Idaho is five years. I.C. § 5–203. A prescriptive right cannot be obtained if use of the servient estate is by permission of the owner. *Haman*, 100 Idaho at 143, 594 P.2d at 1096.

Here, there was no evidence of how the use began, other than what we have summarized. At the time of trial, the persons who built the Melendez home were deceased. Two witnesses who testified by depositions had no personal knowledge about whether the initial use of the Hintz driveway by the owners of Lot 17 was permissive or not. The general rule in Idaho is:

> [P]roof of open, notorious, continuous, uninterrupted use of the claimed right for the prescriptive period, without evidence as to how the use began, raises the presumption that the use was adverse and under a claim of right. The burden is then on the owner of the servient tenement to show that the use was permissive, or by virtue of a license, contract, or agreement. [*West v. Smith,* 95 Idaho at 557, 511 P.2d at 1333.]

This rule has been repeatedly upheld. One exception to this rule—not applicable here—occurs when the servient land is wild, unenclosed, or unimproved. Then the presumption is that the use was permissive. *West*, 95 Idaho at 557 n.32, 511 P.2d at 1333 n.32. *See e.g., Christle v. Scott*, 110 Idaho 829, 718 P.2d 1267 (Ct.App.1986). Our Supreme Court has also recognized that the general rule has another exception which is applicable in the absence of evidence as to whether the use began adversely or with permission of the servient owner. In *Simmons v. Perkins*, 63 Idaho 136, 144, 118 P.2d 740, 744 (1941) the Court said:

> The rule would seem to be that where the owner of real property constructs a way over it for his own use and convenience, the mere use thereof by others which in no way interferes with his use will be presumed to be by way of license or permission.

Other states which currently recognize this rule include Colorado, Nevada, Oregon, and Utah....

Hintz argues that the driveway was established by the former owner of Lot 16; that the driveway was jointly used by the owners of Lots 16 and 17; and therefore it should be presumed that use of the driveway by Melendezes' predecessors was with permission of the owner of Lot 16. The Melendezes argue that the *Simmons* rule or exception is no longer favored in Idaho. They point particularly to our Supreme Court's opinion in *West v. Smith, supra,* where *Simmons* was mentioned. 95 Idaho at 557 n.28, 511 P.2d 518 n.28. However, *West v. Smith* was not a "joint use" case, and the Supreme Court did not there in any way address the joint use exception stated in *Simmons.* The Supreme Court disavowed only the language in *Simmons* which suggested that proving an owner of the servient property "acquiesced" in the use of his property by another was equivalent to proof that the owner had given his consent or permission. The Court in *West* said that proving "mere inaction and passive acquiescence" is not sufficient to establish that the use "was with the permission of the owner of the servient estate." *Id. Accord, Feldman v. Knapp,* 196 Or. 453, 250 P.2d 92 (1952).

Before *West* was decided the Idaho Supreme Court had one occasion to again recognize and apply the *Simmons* rule. *See Cusic v. Givens,* 70 Idaho 229, 231, 215 P.2d 297, 298 (1950). No reported Idaho cases since *Simmons* give any indication that the Idaho Supreme Court has disavowed, or would disavow, the "joint use" rule recognized in *Simmons.* Although *Simmons* has often been cited for other principles we can find no other case where its joint use rule has been applicable.[6]

To establish a prescriptive right in a roadway it is essential that the use of the way must constitute some actual invasion or infringement of the right of the owner. *Cox v. Cox,* 84 Idaho 513, 521, 373 P.2d 929, 934 (1962); *Simmons v. Perkins, supra.* If the use is with permission of the owner of the property no invasion or infringement of the owner's rights occurs. Adverse use is some actual invasion or infringement that is made without permission of the owner. As we have noted, mere proof that the owner "acquiesced" in the use is not proof that the use was with the owner's consent or permission. *West v. Smith, supra.*

Understanding the basis for the *Simmons* rule helps to determine the limits of its application. There should be no presumption that the use originated adversely to the owner unless the use itself constitutes some invasion or infringement upon the rights of an owner. Where one person merely uses a roadway in common with his neighbor, without damage to the roadway, without interfering with the neighbor's use of the roadway, and where the neighbor has established and maintained the roadway on his own property for his own purposes, only the most minimal intrusion is made into the owner's dominion over his property. Logically, a use which is not in fact adverse to the owner provides no basis for the presumption that the use is adverse. However, where the use made of the property for the prescriptive period is shown to consti-

6. *Sinnett v. Werelus,* 83 Idaho 514, 365 P.2d 952 (1961), was a case involving a claimed prescriptive easement in a driveway used by two neighbors. The Court discussed the general rule presuming the origin of the use to be adverse. *Simmons* is not mentioned. However, *Sinnett* is in a different category of joint use cases. There two owners jointly constructed and used a driveway which straddled their common boundary. The Court held that after mutual use of the common driveway for the prescriptive period neither owner can obstruct or close the part which is on his land. Mutual use of the whole of the way will be considered adverse to a separate or exclusive use by either owner.

tute some infringement or invasion of the owner's rights, it is more appropriate to apply the general rule, presuming the use to be adverse, that is, without permission of the owner.

Here, the trial judge found that the Melendezes' predecessors created their own driveway system which branches off the Hintz driveway and serves as access to Lot 17. Their usage of this added portion of the driveway, on Lot 16, is not in common with the owners of Lot 16. The court concluded that the creation and maintaining of this portion of the driveway serving only Lot 17 constitutes an actual invasion or infringement on the rights of the owner of Lot 16. We agree. *See Feldman v. Knapp, supra*. This branch was an additional burden on the Hintz property which had no benefit to Hintz. In effect, the Melendezes' predecessors appropriated this part of the Hintz property for their own purposes.

Moreover, there is evidence that such infringement occurred at the outset, when the Melendezes' predecessors first began using part of the Hintz driveway. Therefore, we believe the district judge was correct in applying the general rule presuming that when this use originated it was adverse to the owners of Lot 16. We also agree that such adverse use extends to all parts of the driveway on Lot 16 which have been used in common by the parties.

Hintz also challenges the scope of the prescriptive easement. As we have noted, the circular driveway on the Melendez lot connects with the two prongs of the "Y" on the Hintz lot. Hintz argues that if an easement by prescription has been established it should be limited to one prong of the "Y" only. He contends that because the Melendezes can have full access to their property over the prong nearest to the county road there is no "necessity" for the circular drive.

It has been said that prescription acts as a penalty against a landowner and thus the rights obtained by prescription should be closely scrutinized and limited by the courts. Nevertheless, the extent of a prescriptive easement is determined not by what is strictly necessary but by the use made during the prescriptive period. Here, the district judge found that both prongs of the driveway had been regularly used as the sole vehicular access to the Melendez home since 1963. He found that this use was open, notorious, continuous and uninterrupted for more than the prescriptive period. Therefore, the Melendezes were entitled to the presumption that such use was adverse. Hintz then had at least the burden to "burst the bubble" of this presumption by producing some evidence "to show that the use was permissive, or by virtue of a license, contract or agreement." *West v. Smith*, 95 Idaho at 557, 511 P.2d at 1333. He produced no such evidence.

Accordingly, the judgment of the district court was correct and is affirmed.

Notes

1. *The Theoretical Justification for Prescriptive Easements—Of Hostility, Acquiescence and the Theory of the "Lost Grant."* Some of the justifications advanced by Professor Merrill to defend the doctrine of adverse possession (page 157) apply with comparable force to prescriptive easements. A person making an uninterrupted adverse use over time develops an expectation that she has the right to continue the use. Based upon the servient landowner's disinterest—as manifested by his failure to grant permission or object to the use for the applicable limitations period—the law of prescription determines that the adverse user's continued use merits legal protection via a property rule, and that society should no longer protect the servient landowner's right to exclude the longstanding user.

By contrast, the "lost grant" theory was premised upon the servient owner's knowledge of and acquiescence to a longstanding use. The different premise presents a potential doctrinal tension for the law of easements. As you might imagine, the same facts that could tend to prove the servient owner's acquiescence to a longstanding use (and thus that would justify a prescriptive easement under a "lost grant" theory) could also serve as evidence that the servient landowner had impliedly permitted the use (which would defeat a prescriptive easement under traditional "hostility" analysis). For this reason, most commentators have argued that "lost grant" analysis should no longer have any place in American law, *see, e.g.*, William B. Stoebuck & Dale A. Whitman, The Law of Property § 8.7, at 452 (3d ed. 2000), and courts rarely presume a lost grant in modern prescription cases. Instead, most modern cases adopt a general presumption that use of another's land is hostile.

Nevertheless, some courts occasionally apply the "lost grant" concept, and this has practical consequences in terms of the steps that the true owner must take to interrupt the prescriptive period. For example, consider the situation in *Sparling v. Fon du Lac Twp.*, 319 Ill.App.3d 560, 253 Ill.Dec. 537, 745 N.E.2d 660 (2001). Prior to 1983, the owner of Lot 226 had granted the city an express easement to maintain a drainage pipe along the southern five feet of the lot. In 1983, however, the city moved the drainage pipe three feet further onto Lot 226, outside the boundary of the express easement. In 1993, Gray purchased Lot 226, and sent a letter to the city identifying the encroachment and requesting that the city return the pipe to its proper location within the easement. The city took no action. In 1996, when Sparling purchased Lot 226 from Gray, Sparling likewise sent a letter to the city objecting to the location of the pipe, but to no avail. Finally, in May 1999, Sparling sued in ejectment, seeking to compel the removal of the pipe; the city responded claiming a prescriptive easement (assume that the relevant statutory period is 15 years). The court held that the city lacked a prescriptive easement, because the 1993 and 1996 letters from Gray and Sparling manifested their knowledge and nonacquiescence to the pipe encroachment. How would a court resolve this lawsuit under the more modern "adverse use" theory implicit in cases like *Melendez v. Hintz*? In light of the reasons behind prescription doctrine (as discussed in Chapter 3), do you think it makes sense to use the "lost grant" theory in this situation?

2. *Proving a Prescriptive Easement—The Burden of Proof and Presumptions.* The law generally employs a presumption that the claimant's use of another's land is hostile, thus placing upon the servient landowner the burden of establishing that the use was permissive.

Nevertheless, while recognizing that Idaho law follows the general rule, the *Melendez* court also notes an exception involving shared use by the dominant and servient owners: if there is no evidence as to the original nature of the use (*i.e.*, whether it was hostile or permissive), and the use does not interfere with the servient landowner's use, the claimant's use is presumed to be permissive, and the claimant must then present evidence to prove the use was adverse. *See* R. Powell, The Law of Real Property § 413, at 34–118 n.24 (1981) (noting that some—but not all—jurisdictions consider use shared with servient owner to be presumptively permissive). In light of the policies underlying prescription, is this presumption appropriate? Do you think that the ability of the Melendezes to continue using the driveway should have depended upon their construction and use of what the court calls the "Y" portion of the loop driveway? Do you think their case would be less compelling if they had merely shared the main part of the driveway, without building the "loop"?

To help understand how the burden of proof and presumptions can dictate the outcome of a prescriptive easement claim, consider the "shared driveway" problem referenced in footnote 6 in *Melendez*. How should the law of prescriptive easements apply in the following problem?

> Fifteen years ago, Sarah and her then-neighbor Ted mutually agreed to construct a common driveway along the border of their respective parcels, with roughly half of the driveway on each side of the boundary line. For the last fifteen years, both of them have used the driveway and shared the cost of maintaining it. Recently, Ted sold the property. The new neighbor casually mentioned to Sarah that he intended to put a fence up on the boundary line this weekend, making future use of the driveway impossible. Sarah wants to know whether she can prevent her new neighbor from obstructing the driveway. How would you advise Sarah whether she can assert a claim for a prescriptive easement? What information would you like to gather from her? From Ted? From her new neighbor?

Compare Altieri v. Dolan, 423 A.2d 482 (R.I. 1980) (finding no prescriptive easement because claimant failed to satisfy burden of proving that use was hostile when evidence indicated use over 30 years had been on a neighborly, mutually agreeable basis) *with Fischer v. Grinsbergs*, 198 Neb. 329, 252 N.W.2d 619 (1977) (finding prescriptive easement with respect to common driveway because use is presumed to be under a claim of right and owner of servient tenement failed to rebut presumption by offering proof that use was permissive).

3. *Prescriptive Easements and Open Lands.* The *Melendez* court also indicates that a use is presumed to be permissive when the servient land is wild, unenclosed, or unimproved. How should the status of the servient property (enclosed or unenclosed) affect whether the use is viewed as permissive or adverse? Does it make sense to draw a distinction between enclosed and unenclosed parcels? Would the status of the property (enclosed

or unenclosed) have mattered if the issue was whether someone was claiming title by adverse possession? *See Weihl v. Wagner,* 210 Ill.App.3d 894, 155 Ill.Dec. 297, 569 N.E.2d 297 (1991); *Behen v. Elliott,* 791 S.W.2d 475 (Mo. Ct. App. 1990).

4. *Exclusive Use, Shared Use and Public Easements.* Not surprisingly, given the similar rationales behind adverse possession and prescriptive easements, the elements of a prescriptive easement resemble the elements of adverse possession. Perhaps because of this similarity, some courts go so far as to require that the claimant prove that her use was exclusive. What do courts mean when they talk about a claimant making an "exclusive" use of the property?

> Although several of the cases continue to mention exclusive use as an essential element to the acquisition of an easement by prescription, most agree that the term is not to be given the meaning which is given to it in the acquisition of title by adverse possession. It simply means that exercise of the right shall not be dependent upon a similar right in others. The use may be shared with the owner of the servient estate.

White v. Wheatland Irrigation Dist., 413 P.2d 252, 260 (Wyo. 1966); *accord Gilman v. McCrary,* 97 N.M. 376, 640 P.2d 482 (1982) *and* Restatement (Third) of Property: Servitudes §§ 2.16–2.17 (exclusive use not an element required to establish prescriptive easement). *But see* R. Powell, The Law of Real Property § 413, at 34–118 n.24 (1981) (noting that some jurisdictions consider a use shared with the owner of the servient estate to be presumptively permissive). Under the logic of *White,* does it make sense to call the use "exclusive" at all?

What happens when a use is shared by many members of the public at large? A public prescriptive easement is possible, although courts may be sympathetic to landowners by employing the presumption that the use of unenclosed land by the public at large is permissive. *Compare Leu v. Littell,* 2 Neb.App. 323, 513 N.W.2d 24 (1993) (finding public prescriptive easement in trail road) *with Public Lands Access Ass'n, Inc. v. Boone & Crockett Club Found., Inc.,* 259 Mont. 279, 856 P.2d 525 (1993) *and Cleland v. Westvaco Corp.,* 314 S.C. 508, 431 S.E.2d 264 (Ct. App. 1993) (finding no public prescriptive easement across unenclosed property).

d. *Licenses and "Easement by Estoppel*" Once granted, an easement is not revocable by the servient owner (unless the express terms of the easement permit its revocation). The easement is a property right—if the servient owner wants to extinguish the easement, the servient owner must re-acquire the easement from its holder by transfer.

As discussed in Chapter 7, not all rights to use or occupy another person's land create property rights. A *license* is a contractual or permissive right to use or occupy the land of another. Licenses are generally revocable. This means that if the licensor revokes the license, the licensee generally cannot obtain an injunction to prevent the licensor from excluding the licensee (although the licensee may have the ability to recover damages for breach of contract in appropriate cases).

Nevertheless, in some cases, a licensee may incur substantial expenses in reliance upon the continued ability to use the license. For example, suppose that *A* owns a lake and grants *B* permission to boat on the lake. To facilitate her boating, *B* spends $10,000 constructing a dock to allow her to moor the boat without having to remove it from the water. If *A* later attempts to revoke the license, can *B* argue that a court should estop *A* from terminating the license in the face of *B*'s reliance? Is *B*'s reliance sufficiently reasonable to justify the intervention of estoppel?

Now reconsider the facts in the *Bob's Ready-to-Wear Case* (page 564). Recall that the court held that the Parmans did not have either an express or implied easement to use the parking lot parcel for customer parking and customer access to the rear entrance of the Bob's store. As a result, the court treated continued use of the parking lot by the Parmans after their purchase of the Bob's store parcel as permissive. The Parmans argued that if they had only a license, the Weavers should be estopped from revoking it given all of the store improvements that the Parmans made upon buying the store. How should the court have addressed this estoppel argument?

BOB'S READY TO WEAR, INC. v. WEAVER

Court of Appeals of Kentucky.
569 S.W.2d 715 (1978).

PARK, JUDGE. . . . [The facts of the case appear beginning on page 564.]

The Parmans assert that the Weavers are estopped to sever access between the rear entrance of Bob's Store and the municipal parking lot by construction of the chain link fence. Not having an easement for access across the parking lot to the rear of the Bob's Store, the Parmans had only a license to use the parking lot. As a general rule, a license is revocable at the will of the owner of the property subject to the license. However, an owner may be estopped to revoke the license when, with the knowledge of the owner, the licensee makes valuable improvements in reliance upon the continued existence of the license. *Holbrook v. Taylor*, Ky., 532 S.W.2d 763 (1976).

Following the purchase of their building in 1971, the Parmans made valuable improvements to the rear entrance to Bob's Store. These improvements were made with the knowledge of both the Eversole heirs and the Weavers. The only purpose for the new rear entrance was as a means of access to and from the municipal parking lot. The value of the improvements would be destroyed if access to the parking lot were blocked. The city of London continues to maintain a municipal parking lot on the property leased from the Weavers. The only purpose of the chain link fence is to revoke the Parmans' license by obstructing access to the parking lot. There is detriment to the Parmans and no benefit to the Weavers. Under these circumstances, we conclude that the Weavers are estopped to revoke the Parmans' license for access between the rear entrance to Bob's Store and the parking lot.

Even if the Weavers are estopped to revoke the Parmans' license across the parking lot, it does not follow that the Parmans have, in effect, an unlimited easement of access across that tract. The duration of a license may be limited even though the licensor is estopped to revoke the license:

> Since the estoppel to terminate a license arises out of action taken in reliance upon representations as to duration of the license, the extent of the estoppel is measured, in part at least, by the extent of the action taken. The fact that a licensor is estopped to revoke or terminate a license altogether does not necessarily mean that the license constitutes an irrevocable privilege in accordance with its terms. It means that it is irrevocable to the extent necessary to prevent the licensee from being unfairly deprived of the fruits of expenditures made by him. It may still be possible to terminate at will some though not all of the privileges created by the license. [Restatement of the Law of Property § 519, Comment G. (1944).]

The improvements made by the Parmans to the rear entrance to Bob's Store were substantial. Nevertheless, the expenditures were not so substantial that the Parmans were entitled to assume that the property subject to the license would be maintained as a public parking lot forever.

We conclude that the Parmans could reasonably rely upon the continuation of the license only so long as the property was maintained as a public parking lot. Clearly, the Parmans have no right to compel the Weavers to maintain the property as a public parking lot. When a landowner grants a license for a limited purpose, licenses which are irrevocable because of estoppel should not be extended beyond their original purpose to additional uses. *Smallwood v. Diz, Ky.,* 245 S.W.2d 439 (1952). In this case, the primary purpose of the license is a means of access between Bob's Store and the municipal parking lot. If the Weaver property should cease to be used as a parking lot open to members of the public, then the Parmans' license should also cease. In this way, the improvements made by the Parmans in reliance upon the existence of the license may be balanced against the right of the Weavers to devote their property to a more profitable use. Of course, any decision on the part of the Weavers to terminate the use of the property as a public parking lot must be made in good faith and not merely for the purpose of denying the Parmans their rights established by this litigation. *Wilson v. Irwin,* 144 Ky. 311, 138 S.W. 373 (1911). . . .

The judgment of the circuit court is reversed with directions to enter a judgment enjoining the Weavers from obstructing or interfering with access between the rear entrance of Bob's Ready to Wear Store and the parking lot property owned by the Weavers, for so long as the Weavers' property shall be maintained as a parking lot open to the public.

1. *The Court's Analysis in* Bob's *and the Nature of Licenses.* The court in *Bob's* states that a license cannot be extended beyond its purpose to additional uses. This statement is correct because it reflects the inherent nature of a license, which authorizes a particular use. If Smith gives Key permission to use his driveway, Key's occupation of Smith's home is not within the scope of that permission and constitutes a trespass.

The court in *Bob's*, however, uses this statement to justify its dictum that the Weavers could terminate the license as soon as they ceased operating the land as a parking lot. [This statement was unnecessary, as the Weavers had not stopped operating the land as a parking lot.] Why did the court make this statement if it was unnecessary? Moreover, does the court's conclusion logically follow from the premise? Would the Parmans be extending their license beyond its original purpose to an additional use?

2. *Licenses, Easements, and the Statute of Frauds.* What happens when a landowner intends to create an express easement, but fails to do so in writing? Under the statute of frauds, the intended easement would be invalid because of the lack of a writing. If the landowner thereafter allows the "grantee" of the invalid easement to use the land, the law typically will characterize the user as a licensee. [Query: Can you explain why implied easements based upon pre-existing use and implied easements of necessity do not violate the statute of frauds?]

3. *The Rationale for Treating a License as Irrevocable.* As *Bob's* suggests, the rationale for the irrevocable license stems from estoppel theory. If the user incurs expenses in reasonable reliance on statements or conduct of the owner of the "servient" land, and such statements/conduct led the user to expect that the servient owner would not revoke the license, the court may refuse to allow the owner of the servient land to revoke the license to the extent necessary to protect the licenseholder from irreparable or unjust injury. To illustrate this point, consider the following examples:

(a) Fisch asks Guthrie for the right to use a roadway across Guthrie's land, for access to Fisch's land for the purpose of delivering supplies to build Fisch's house. Guthrie responds: "Sure, that sounds okay." Fisch proceeds to build the house on his land, using the roadway across Guthrie's land. Later Guthrie threatens to obstruct the roadway unless Fisch compensates Guthrie for the use of the roadway. *See Holbrook v. Taylor*, 532 S.W.2d 763 (Ky. 1976).

(b) George asks Henning for the right to use a roadway across Henning's land to provide access for trucks to reach George's warehouse. Henning responds: "Sure, but you can use it only for the next three months. After that you will have to find some other means of access." George proceeds to invest $100,000 renovating the warehouse. Four months later Henning informs George that further use will be considered a trespass.

How would you evaluate the claims of Fisch and George? Should Fisch and George be entitled to prevent revocation of each license? Why or why not? *Compare Zivari v. Willis*, 416 Pa.Super. 432, 611 A.2d 293 (1992) *with Closson Lumber Co. v. Wiseman*, 507 N.E.2d 974 (Ind. 1987).

4. *Irrevocable License and Easement by Estoppel—Property Rules and Liability Rules Revisited.* Is it accurate to say that once a licensor loses the right to revoke a license, the license becomes an easement? On this issue, consider the following questions: What did the *Bob's* court identify as the duration of the easement by estoppel? For how long should the licensor lose the right to revoke? As counsel for a licensee, on what basis would you argue that the license should be permanently irrevocable? As counsel for a licensor, on what basis would you argue that the license should be of limited duration? What duration would you suggest? *See* Restatement of Servitudes § 4.3(5) (duration of servitude by estoppel is "indeterminate"). Under what circumstances should the licensor be allowed to terminate a license that a court has held to be irrevocable? *See, e.g., Lee Highway & Assocs., L.P. v. Pryor Bacon Co., Inc.*, 1995 WL 619941 (Tenn. Ct. App. 1995).

3. *Scope of Easements*

An easement creates the potential for a wide variety of conflicts between the easement holder and the owner of the servient land. What limits, if any, constrain the easement holder's ability to use the servient land? Must the easement holder bear any costs associated with maintaining the easement? Is the easement holder limited to the original authorized use, or may the easement holder make different uses or more intensive uses of the servient estate as time passes? Can the holder of the easement relocate it to a different portion of the servient estate? Can the holder of an appurtenant easement expand the dominant estate by acquiring adjacent land?

As a general matter, disputes over the scope of an easement will be governed by the intention of the parties at the creation of the easement. For example, suppose Winokur grants an easement to Ziegler to permit him to hunt on Winokur's land and that the easement by its terms limits Ziegler to hunting only with shotguns. If Ziegler thereafter hunts with a high-powered rifle, Ziegler would exceed the scope of his easement and Winokur could obtain an injunction against such conduct—in this instance, the easement terms demonstrate Winokur's intent regarding the permissible scope of the easement.

Commonly, however, persons who create an express easement are not sufficiently specific regarding the intended scope of the easement. In such cases, how should a court interpret the language of the easement, and to what extent should the court consider extrinsic evidence regarding the intent of the parties who created the easement? The evolving approach is reflected in the decision in *Lazy Dog Ranch v. Telluray Ranch Corp.*, 965 P.2d 1229, 1235 (Colo. 1998), in which the Colorado Supreme Court described the standards governing the court's inquiry:

> Circumstances relevant to interpreting the language of a servitude include: the location and character of the properties burdened and benefited by the servitude, the use made of the properties before and after creation of the servitude, the character of the surrounding area, the existence and contours of any general plan of development for the area, and consideration paid for the servitude. *Id.* . . .

... In some cases the intentions of the parties regarding a particular matter may be difficult to determine, even after reference to all the relevant circumstances. In these cases, courts have developed a system of "default rules" that supply necessary terms of the easement. These rules, in large part, determine the rights of the respective landowners according to a reasonableness standard because it is presumed that, absent clear authorization in the written instrument for the particular use, the parties to the original instrument did not intend unreasonable use of the easement. ...

Unless the intentions of the parties are determined to require a different result, the owner of the servient estate may make any use of the burdened property that does not unreasonably interfere with the enjoyment of the easement by its owner for its intended purpose.... Conversely, the owner of the easement may make any use of the easement (including maintenance and improvement) that is reasonably necessary to the enjoyment of the easement, and which does not cause unreasonable damage to the servient estate or unreasonably interfere with the enjoyment of the servient estate. [965 P.2d at 1235–38.]

The *Lazy Dog Ranch* opinion states what has been called the "rule of reason" in interpreting the rights and obligations attendant to easements. To what extent does this rule manifest itself in the disputes that follow?

a. *Maintenance of Easements*

SCHLUEMER v. ELROD

Court of Appeals of Missouri.
916 S.W.2d 371 (1996).

CROW, JUDGE. This is a dispute about a "roadway easement." Plaintiffs, William E. Schluemer and Elizabeth L. Schluemer, own the servient estate; Defendants, B. Russell Elrod and Frances Elrod, own the dominant estate. ...

In 1983, Defendants purchased two parcels of land in Maries County from W.H. Stratman and Katherine Stratman: a 5.36–acre tract adjacent to Highway 42 and a .46–acre tract abutting the Gasconade River. No public road reaches the smaller tract.

The Stratmans retained ownership of a farm between Defendants' two tracts. To enable Defendants to reach the smaller tract, the Stratmans granted Defendants [a] "roadway easement." ... [The deed creating this easement provided, in pertinent part:

Grantees *shall pay* to the record owners of the land where the easements are located the sum of One Hundred Dollars per year starting July 1, 1983, and each and every July 1 thereafter, as long as grantees shall have the use of the easements described above, to be used to help maintain the roadways located on said easements.]

The easement (part of which is forty feet wide and part of which is thirty feet wide) begins at Highway 42 adjacent to Defendants' larger tract and proceeds across the Stratman farm approximately one and one-fourth miles to Defendants' smaller tract.

Defendants reside on their larger tract. Because that tract abuts Highway 42, Defendants do not use the easement for access to the highway. When Defendants go from their larger tract to their smaller tract, they enter the easement at a point where it abuts their larger tract behind their house.

On November 5, 1984, the Stratmans conveyed their farm—the servient estate—to Plaintiffs.

Defendants presented evidence that Plaintiffs thereafter failed to maintain the road over the easement in good enough condition for Defendants to reach their smaller tract by motor vehicle. Defendants admitted they never paid Plaintiffs the $100 per year required by [the deed], but claimed they paid for gravel and performed labor on the road in an effort to maintain it in usable condition. According to Defendants' evidence, those expenses and labor totaled $825. Defendants insisted they were entitled to a setoff against the sum claimed by Plaintiffs ... ($1,000 at time of trial).

The trial court made no finding regarding the expenditures allegedly made by Defendants or the value of the labor allegedly performed by them in maintaining the road. Instead, the trial court resolved ... that Defendants, as owners of the dominant estate, "have an obligation to maintain the easement roadway." Therefore, reasoned the trial court, Defendants are not entitled to a setoff against the $100 per year they must pay Plaintiffs pursuant to [the deed]. Consistent with that analysis, the trial court ... entered judgment for Plaintiffs ... for $1,000.

Defendants begin the argument under their first point by acknowledging *Stotzenberger v. Perkins*, 332 Mo. 391, 58 S.W.2d 983, 987 (1933), which states that where a roadway easement is created by deed, the owner of the dominant estate has the right to maintain the roadway in a condition for passage, and the owner of the servient estate is under no obligation to maintain or repair.

However, Defendants call our attention to *McDonald v. Bemboom*, 694 S.W.2d 782 (Mo.App.W.D.1985), where owners of the dominant estate and owners of the servient estate each used a road across an easement on a regular and continuing basis. *Id.* at 783. In *McDonald*, the appellate court held:

> A respectable body of authority in other jurisdictions holds that apportionment of the cost of repairs and maintenance of a private roadway between the owners of the dominant and servient tenements is fair and just, even though the agreement creating the easement is silent with respect thereto, where the owners of both the dominant and servient tenements regularly use the private roadway. [*Id.* at 786 (citations omitted).]

McDonald affirmed a judgment in favor of the owners of the dominant estate against the owners of the servient estate for the latters' proportionate share of repair and maintenance costs for the roadway.

In the instant case, the trial court found Plaintiffs "generally use the road for access to their fields, pastures and to the Gasconade River."

Plaintiffs do not dispute the above finding. Plaintiffs concede they "conduct a farming operation on the servient estate and use the roadways on the easement to access various parts of the servient estate as well as for placing cattle feeders." Additionally, explain Plaintiffs, some parts of the servient estate can be accessed only by use of the roadways on the easement because of the terrain.

Inasmuch as the easement was created by [the deed], we first look to it to determine the parties' obligations regarding maintenance of the roadway. *Rollins v. Schwyhart*, 587 S.W.2d 364, 366 (Mo.App.S.D.1979). The only provision in [the deed] regarding maintenance ... requires Defendants to pay "the record owners" of the servient estate $100 per year "to be used to help maintain the roadways located on said easements." ...

In 1979, at the request of W.H. Stratman, a surveyor prepared a survey of the Stratmans' land (which then included the land now owned by Plaintiffs and the two tracts now owned by Defendants). The survey shows Tract A [the Elrods' smaller tract], the north side of which abuts the Gasconade River. The survey also shows four other tracts abutting the river, designated as Tracts B, C, D and E. They lie side-by-side, east of tract A. The easement roadway is shown on the survey, abutting the south sides of all five tracts. The survey recites that all five tracts shall have a "non-exclusive easement for roadway purposes ... over the present roadway which ... connects with Missouri Highway No. 42."

Plaintiff William E. Schluemer testified that when he bought the servient estate, the Stratmans told him they "had platted lots along the river" and gave him the survey. Mr. Schluemer conceded the survey described a nonexclusive roadway easement for each of the platted lots.

... [E]xcept for Tract A, the Stratmans sold none of the platted lots before conveying the servient estate to Plaintiffs. The deed from the Stratmans to Plaintiffs excepts Tract A, but does not mention Tracts B, C, D or E. As we comprehend the deed, the land comprising the latter four tracts is included in the metes and bounds description of the servient estate.

Defendants argue that the provision in [the deed] regarding maintenance of the roadway is unambiguous. According to Defendants, the provision unequivocally assigns the duty of maintaining the roadway to the owners of the servient estate alone, and Defendants' only obligation is to pay the servient owners $100 per year to help defray maintenance expenses. However, add Defendants, if the provision in [the deed] is ambiguous, parol evidence may be considered in determining the parties' intent. Defendants assert that the evidence set forth in the five paragraphs immediately preceding this one demonstrates that the Stratmans and Defendants intended that the owners of the servient estate alone must maintain the roadway, and that the owners of the dominant estate must pay the servient owners $100 per year.

Plaintiffs contend [the deed] is ambiguous and can be construed to place the maintenance obligation on Defendants. Consequently, say Plaintiffs, the trial court properly denied Defendants' prayer for a setoff.

We shall assume, arguendo, that [the deed] is ambiguous, hence parol evidence may be considered in ascertaining the parties' intent.

Had the Stratmans, instead of selling the servient estate to Plaintiffs, sold Tracts B, C, D and E to sundry buyers, inserting a provision similar to the one in [the deed] in the deeds to those buyers, we doubt the Stratmans could have successfully argued that the duty of maintaining the easement roadway was to be shared by all buyers. Assigning five sets of property owners the duty of maintaining an easement used by all, with no method of determining each one's share of the obligation, would likely result in quarrels and chaos. It is inferable that the Stratmans understood this and intended to bear the responsibility of maintaining the roadway, collecting an annual sum from each property owner to defray the cost.

However, that scenario never eventuated. The year after selling Defendants Tract A and the tract abutting Highway 42, the Stratmans conveyed all of the servient estate to Plaintiffs. We thus have a situation where only Defendants and Plaintiffs (and their invitees) have a right to use the roadway. Although Plaintiffs argue that Defendants use the roadway more than Plaintiffs, the trial court made no finding on that issue.

Because Defendants and Plaintiffs (and their invitees) use the roadway, one could argue that *McDonald*, 694 S.W.2d 782, should apply, producing a holding that the duty of maintaining the roadway must be borne equally by Defendants and Plaintiffs. However, in *McDonald* the document creating the easement was silent regarding maintenance. Here, [the deed] addressed that subject....

The above principles caution us that inasmuch as [the deed] in the instant case assigned Defendants the duty of paying the owners of the servient estate $100 per year "to be used to help maintain the roadways," but assigned Defendants no other duty, [the deed] should not be construed to place the obligation for maintaining the roadway on Defendants. Furthermore, the evidence regarding the 1979 survey showing Tracts B, C, D and E and the nonexclusive easement for access to those tracts from Highway 42 indicates that when Defendants acquired Tract A and the tract where they reside from the Stratmans, neither Defendants nor the Stratmans intended that Defendants maintain the roadway.

For the reasons in the preceding paragraph, we hold the trial court erred in finding that Defendants have an obligation to maintain the roadway. We hold as a matter of law that [the deed] assigns the duty of maintaining the roadway to the owners of the servient estate (currently Plaintiffs), and that the only obligation of the owners of the dominant estate (currently Defendants) is to pay the servient owners $100 every July 1.

However, as explained in *Stotzenberger*, 58 S.W.2d at 987, the owners of the dominant estate have the right to maintain the roadway in a condition such that it can be traversed. Consequently, if Plaintiffs fail to maintain the roadway in that condition, Defendants may do so. If that becomes necessary, Defendants shall have a claim against Plaintiffs for the necessary and reasonable expenses incurred by Defendants, which Defendants can assert as an offset against the $100 per year they must pay Plaintiffs.

We do not imply that Plaintiffs must pave the roadway and maintain it in turnpike condition. The record indicates Defendants were aware of the condition of the roadway when they acquired their two tracts from the Stratmans in 1983, and that the roadway was usable at that time. That should be the standard by which Plaintiffs' maintenance obligation shall be measured.

We recognize future disputes may arise about maintenance. However, there is no way to judicially eliminate that possibility. If Defendants alone had the maintenance obligation and disdained it, Plaintiffs would have to shoulder the burden if they wanted to continue using the roadway. In that event, Plaintiffs, if they chose, could seek redress from Defendants.

If the maintenance obligation were assigned to the parties equally, the same possibility for disputes would exist.

As noted earlier, the trial court made no finding regarding the reasonableness and necessity of the expenses allegedly incurred by Defendants and the value of the labor allegedly performed by them in maintaining the roadway after Plaintiffs' acquisition of the servient estate in 1984. Consequently, the case must be remanded to the trial court for a determination of the amount of the offset, if any, to which Defendants are entitled. . . .

Notes

1. *General Responsibility to Maintain a Right of Way.* The common law developed (and the new Restatement retains) two default rules regarding the maintenance of easements. Under these default rules, if the servient owner does not use the easement, then the easement holder is responsible for maintaining the easement. *Raksin v. Crown–Kingston Realty Assocs.*, 254 A.D.2d 472, 680 N.Y.S.2d 265 (1998). If the servient owner also uses the easement along with the easement holder, however, they both share the responsibility and expense associated with maintaining the easement.

As *Elrod* highlights, the parties to an express easement are free to assign the responsibility for maintaining the easement. What facts were most significant in persuading the *Elrod* court that the servient landowner was responsible for maintaining the easement? What does *Elrod* suggest regarding the remedies available to an easement holder when the party responsible for maintaining the easement fails to fulfill its responsibilities?

In light of the rules described above, reconsider the facts of *Melendez v. Hintz* (page 571). If the parties were in dispute regarding maintenance of the driveway, how should a court resolve the dispute?

2. *Maintenance and Trees.* Commonly, utility companies will trim or cut trees to keep the growth from interfering with utility lines. Questions sometimes arise regarding whether the utility was excessive in its efforts to trim or chop down trees. *See, e.g., Branson West, Inc. v. City of Branson*, 980 S.W.2d 604 (Mo. Ct. App. 1998) (city not entitled to clear-cut entire 60–foot easement, but could cut trees only to extent reasonably necessary to facilitate installation of sewer); *Larew v. Monongahela Power Co.*, 199 W.Va. 690, 487 S.E.2d 348 (1997) (applying rule of reason to trimming of trees by utility and contractor).

b. *Change and Expansion of Use*

Over time, the holder of an easement may begin using the easement in a fashion that effectively increases the burden of the easement upon the servient estate. For example, suppose that when Pham's ancestors purchased their farm in the 1870s, they acquired an easement for access across the neighboring farm. The easement did not specify the precise means of access, but at the time, Pham's ancestors used this easement for pedestrian and horse-drawn cart access. Now, Pham wants to build and pave a road sufficient to support modern farm vehicles and automobile traffic. Would this be a reasonable use of the easement, or an unreasonable use that the servient owner can enjoin? Likewise, suppose that Wells owns a 40–acre parcel of land benefitted by an appurtenant access easement over the adjoining land of Lawless. If Wells divides the dominant estate into 10 different 4–acre parcels, does each of those parcels now have an appurtenant easement over Lawless's land? Or can Lawless argue that the subdivision of the dominant estate would create an excessive burden on the servient estate?

Consider these questions as you read the following case, *Henley v. Continental Cablevision of St. Louis County*. The *Henley* case involves two different yet related scope problems. The first is whether the holder of a utility easement granted in the 1920s for telephone service can now use the easement to provide cable television service. The second is whether the utility company holding the easement may divide it—*i.e.*, use it themselves, but also license other utility companies to use it as well. Recall that the law traditionally considered easements in gross to be nontransferable, but generally permitted the transfer of profits in gross and commercial easements in gross. [Can you explain why the parties creating a profit in gross or a commercial easement in gross might well intend for these interests to be transferable?] If the holder of a commercial easement or profit in gross can transfer that easement to another party, can the holder also divide that easement or profit—*i.e.*,

can they retain the easement or profit but also authorize additional parties to share in using it?

HENLEY v. CONTINENTAL CABLEVISION OF ST. LOUIS COUNTY, INC.

Missouri Court of Appeals.
692 S.W.2d 825 (1985).

GAERTNER, JUDGE. Plaintiffs, as trustees of University Park subdivision, appeal from an order dismissing their petition for failure to state a claim in an action against defendant Continental Cablevision of St. Louis County, Inc. We affirm.

The facts essential to a resolution of this matter are not in dispute. Pursuant to an indenture recorded on April 8, 1922, plaintiffs' predecessors as trustees, were expressly granted the right to construct and maintain electric, telephone and telegraphic service on or over the rear five feet of all lots in the subdivision, and to grant easements to other parties for the purposes of creating and maintaining such systems. In July, 1922 and August, 1922, respectively, the trustees conveyed an easement to Southwestern Bell Telephone Company to "construct, reconstruct, repair, operate and maintain its lines for telephone and electric light purposes" and similarly to Union Electric to "keep, operate and maintain its lines consisting of cables, manholes, wires, fixtures and appurtenances thereto." Subsequently, in 1981 and 1982, defendant exercised licenses acquired from both utilities to enter upon these easements, and erected cables, wires and conduits for the purpose of transmitting television programs.

Plaintiffs filed an action for an injunction on December 29, 1983, seeking not only to enjoin a continuing trespass and compel the removal of defendant's wires and cables, but also seeking $300,000 in damages and the reasonable value of the use of plaintiffs' property for defendant's profit based upon quantum meruit. Defendants then filed a motion to dismiss for failure to state a cause of action, which was supported by both the affidavit of defendant's chief executive officer and copies of the easements granted by plaintiffs' predecessors to Southwestern Bell Telephone Company and Union Electric. Said motion was sustained by the trial court on July 30, 1984 and this appeal ensued with plaintiffs contending in effect that the easements granted the utilities were not apportionable and did not authorize the right to run television cables over the property in question.

Both parties agree that the subject easements are easements in gross, i.e., easements which belong to the owner independently of his ownership or possession of other land, and thus lacking a dominant tenement. See Three-o-Three Investments, Inc. v. Moffitt, 622 S.W.2d 736 (Mo. App. 1981); 3 Powell, The Law of Real Property 34–22 (1984). The dispositive issue here is whether or not these easements are exclusive and therefore apportionable by the utilities to, in this case, defendant Continental Cablevision.

We believe the very nature of the 1922 easements obtained by both utilities indicates that they were intended to be exclusive and therefore apportionable. It is well settled that where the servient owner retains the privilege of sharing the benefit conferred by the easement, it is said to be "common" or non-exclusive and therefore not subject to apportionment by the easement owner. Conversely, if the rights granted are exclusive of the servient owners' participation therein, divided utilization of the rights granted are presumptively allowable. This principle stems from the concept that one who grants to another the right to use the grantor's land in a particular manner for a specified purpose but who retains no interest in exercising a similar right himself, sustains no loss if, within the specifications expressed in the grant, the use is shared by the grantee with others. On the other hand, if the grantor intends to participate in the use or privilege granted, then his retained right may be diminished if the grantee shares his right with others. Thus, insofar as it relates to the apportionability of an easement in gross, the term "exclusive" refers to the exclusion of the owner and possessor of the servient tenement from participation in the rights granted, not to the number of different easements in and over the same land. Powell at 344–224–25.

Here, there is no claim that plaintiffs' predecessors had at the time the easements were granted, any intention to seek authority for, or any interest whatsoever in using the five-foot strips for the construction and maintenance of either an electric power system or telephone and telegraphic service. Moreover, at no time during the ensuing sixty-three years have the trustees been authorized to furnish such services by any certificate of convenience and necessity issued by the Public Service Commission pursuant to §§ 392.260 and 393.170, RSMo.1978. Accordingly, the easements granted to Southwestern Bell and Union Electric were exclusive as to the grantors thereof and therefore apportionable.

Plaintiffs also argue defendant could acquire no rights from the utilities since their easements did not mention television cables, and that the cable attachments themselves constituted an extra burden on the property. We disagree. The owner of an easement may license or authorize third persons to use its right of way for purposes not inconsistent with the principal use granted. *Eureka Real Estate and Investment Company v. Southern Real E. and F. Company*, 355 Mo. 1199, 200 S.W.2d 328, 332 (1947). The 1922 easements granted to Union Electric expressly provided the right of ingress and egress by Union Electric, its successors and assigns, to "add to the number of and relocate all wires, cables, conduits, manholes, adding thereto from time-to-time...." Similarly, the easement conveyed to Southwestern Bell expressly contemplated the construction and maintenance of "all poles, cables, wires, conduits, lateral pipes, anchor guys and all other fixtures and appurtenances deemed necessary at anytime by [Southwestern Bell], its successors and assigns...." It can hardly be said that the addition of a single coaxial cable to the existing poles for the purpose of transmitting television images and sound by electric impulse increases the burden on the servient tenement beyond the scope of the intended and authorized use....

Although this is a case of first impression in Missouri, courts in other jurisdictions have addressed the legal effect of adding coaxial cables for television transmission to existing electric and telephone poles erected on easements without the consent of the owners of the fees. These courts have uniformly rejected arguments identical to those made by plaintiffs herein and have reached a conclusion similar to ours.

In *Jolliff v. Hardin Cable Television Co.*, 26 Ohio St.2d 103, 269 N.E.2d 588 (1971), an easement granted to a power company for the transmission of electric power, including telegraph or telephone wires, was held to be an apportionable easement in gross by reason of the express language of the conveyance authorizing the grantee to lease some portion of its interest to third parties. In addressing the question of an additional burden on the servient tenements, the court noted that the attachment of a television coaxial cable to existing poles constituted no more of a burden than would installation of telephone wires, a burden clearly contemplated at the time of the grants. *Id*. 269 N.E.2d at 591....

In *Hoffman v. Capitol Cablevision System, Inc.*, 52 A.D.2d 313, 383 N.Y.S.2d 674 (1976), the court concluded that the rights granted to two utilities were exclusive vis a vis the landowner, and were, therefore apportionable by the grantees. The addition of cable and equipment to already existing poles was held to constitute no additional burden since the defendant was doing only what the utilities were enabled to do. *Id*. 383 N.Y.S.2d at 677. The court noted the general rule that easements in gross for commercial purposes are particularly alienable and transferable. *See* 5 Restatement of the Law, Property § 489. For these reasons, the court held the failure to foresee and specifically refer to cable television in the grant was of no consequence. *Id*.

The reasoning of the *Hoffman* court has recently been found persuasive by the California court in *Salvaty v. Falcon Cable Television*, 165 Cal.App.3d 798, 212 Cal.Rptr. 31 (1985). The court stated:

> In the case at bench, the addition of cable television equipment on surplus space on the telephone pole was within the scope of the easement. Although the cable television industry did not exist at the time the easement was granted, it is part of the natural evolution of communications technology. Installation of the equipment was consistent with the primary goal of the easement, to provide for wire transmission of power and communication. We fail to see how the addition of cable equipment to a pre-existing utility pole materially increased the burden on appellant's property. [*Id*. 212 Cal.Rptr. at pages 34–35.]

The unsurprising fact that the drafters of the 1922 easements did not envision cable television does not mandate the narrow interpretation of the purposes of the conveyance of rights and privileges urged by plaintiffs. The expressed intention of the predecessors of plaintiff trustees was to obtain for the homeowners in the subdivision the benefits of electric power and telephonic communications. Scientific and technological progress over the ensuing years have added an unforeseen dimension to such contemplated benefits, the transmission by electric impulse of visual and audio communication over coaxial cable. It is an inescapable conclusion that the intention of plaintiffs' predecessors was the acquisition and continued maintenance of available means of bringing electrical power and communication into the homes of the subdivision. Clearly, it is in the public interest to use the facilities already installed for the purpose of carrying out this intention to provide the most economically feasible and least environmentally damaging vehicle for installing cable systems.

Accordingly, the judgment of the trial court dismissing plaintiffs' petition for failure to state a claim is affirmed.

Notes

1. *Transferability of Easements in Gross.* As you learned in *Alft v. Stewart*, because the common law historically treated easements in gross as "personal" to the holder, it held them to be generally nontransferable. *See, e.g., Maw v. Weber Basin Water Conservancy Dist.*, 20 Utah 2d 195, 436 P.2d 230 (1968) (shooting privileges nonassignable). Profits and commercial easements in gross, however, generally have been held to be assignable. *See, e.g., Crane v. Crane*, 683 P.2d 1062 (Utah 1984) (prescriptive easement to drive cattle across trail was commercial and therefore assignable). Does this distinction make sense? Why or why not?

The Restatement of Servitudes rejects the traditional approach, viewing the question of an easement's transferability as distinct from its characterization as appurtenant or in gross. Under the new Restatement, any servitude (even an in gross easement) is transferable unless it is separately characterized as "personal" (*i.e.*, if the language creating the servitude or the circumstances surrounding its creation indicate that the parties did not intend for the servitude's benefits to be assignable, either outright or in conjunction with a benefitted parcel of land). Restatement of Servitudes §§ 1.5(3), 4.6.

2. *Divisibility of Easements in Gross.* You should distinguish the *divisibility* of an easement in gross from its *transferability*. Transferability focuses on the easement holder's right to substitute a new easement holder in its place; by contrast, divisibility focuses on the easement holder's right to allow additional parties to share in the easement holder's use of the servient land. *Henley* presents a divisibility question.

Divisibility issues often arise with respect to profits, and often turn on whether the profit is exclusive in nature. For example, in *Stanton v. T. L. Herbert & Sons*, 141 Tenn. 440, 211 S.W. 353 (Tenn. 1919), a former owner of land had conveyed it by a deed that reserved to him the right to remove sand from that property. The court held that he could not assign to other contractors the right to remove sand as well because he had reserved only a nonexclusive (and thus not divisible) profit. In another early case, *Miller v. Lutheran Conference & Camp Ass'n*, 331 Pa. 241, 200 A. 646 (1938), the court ruled that an exclusive right to boat and fish on a private lake was assignable and divisible. The court also ruled, however, that once this right was divided, each owner of the divided rights was subject to the "one stock" rule, *i.e.*, the owners must act in concert (or as one person) to avoid overburdening the easement. Do the materials on concurrent ownership in Chapter 6 provide any additional insight into the rationale for the "one stock" rule?

Should the easement in *Henley* be viewed as exclusive or nonexclusive? Assume that after the decision in *Henley*, the subdivision trustees voted to purchase a satellite television system and to provide satellite television to all neighborhood residents (with the residents agreeing to pay a monthly fee to the trustees). The trustees plan to install the necessary wiring and cabling over the five-foot strip at the rear of each subdivision lot (the easement area described in the 1922 easements). Cablevision sues for an injunction to prevent the trustees from doing so. How should the court rule? Does it matter that the 1922 subdivision indenture granted the trustees the right to construct utility lines and provide service? Does it matter that the trustees never actually provided any utility services? Why or why not? Should it matter that the trustees granted easements to *both* Southwestern Bell and Union Electric?

3. *Changes in the Use of an Easement or the Servient Estate.* When an easement is expressly limited to a particular use, any change involving a new unauthorized use is excessive and the holder of the servient estate can enjoin it. If the easement's language is not sufficiently specific, however, disputes can arise regarding whether a contemplated change is permitted (*i.e.*, within the scope of the easement) or excessive (*i.e.*, outside the scope of the easement). Consider the following questions:

(a) In *Henley*, why does the court conclude that providing cable service (or licensing Cablevision to do so) was within the scope of the 1922 easements granted to the utility companies? Is it reasonable to think that the original trustees of the subdivision could have anticipated cable television service at a time two decades before broadcast television? Should that matter?

(b) Your client, Harrison, wants to develop a 1,000–acre ranch into a 200–lot residential subdivision. The only access to the ranch is by a road easement crossing the adjacent land of Smith. Harrison needs to be able to assure each lot purchaser that he or she can use the easement to cross Smith's land to reach their lot. How you would advise Harrison regarding his right to expand the use of the easement? What facts would lead you to conclude that the proposed change in use was reasonable? That it was unreasonable? Would it matter whether the easement was an express easement, an implied easement or an easement by prescription? Why or why not? *Compare Mueller v. Hoblyn*, 887 P.2d 500 (Wyo. 1994) *and Jordan v. Worthen*, 68 Cal.App.3d 310, 137 Cal.Rptr. 282 (1977) *with Wright v. Horse Creek Ranches*, 697 P.2d 384 (Colo. 1985) *and Gibbens v. Weisshaupt*, 98 Idaho 633, 570 P.2d 870 (1977). *See also* Restatement of Servitudes § 4.10 ("The manner, frequency, and intensity of the use may change over time to take advantage of developments in technology and to accommodate normal development of the dominant estate or enterprise benefited by the servitude.").

(c) Your client, Reese, holds an easement for access via a gravel road crossing the adjacent land of Tiffany. Reese wants to know whether he can pave the road. Would it matter whether the easement was an express easement, an implied easement or an easement by prescription? *Compare Beck v. Mangels*, 100 Md.App. 144, 640 A.2d 236 (1994) *with Davis v. Bruk*, 411 A.2d 660 (Me. 1980) *and Brock v. B & M Moster Farms, Inc.*, 481 N.E.2d 1106 (Ind. Ct. App. 1985).

(d) Your client, Nice, holds an easement across the land of Ertman that Nice uses to reach her summer cabin via an existing dirt road. She would like to add utilities so that the cabin can be turned into a year-round home. How you would advise Nice regarding her ability to use the easement to provide utilities to the cabin? What information would you seek to discover before advising Nice? Would it matter whether the easement was an express easement, an implied easement or an easement by prescription? Why or why not? *See* Restatement of Servitudes § 4.10 cmt. d. *Compare Bivens v. Mobley*, 724 So.2d 458 (Miss. Ct. App. 1998) *and Kelly v. Schmelz*, 439 S.W.2d 211 (Mo. Ct. App. 1969) *with Wendy's of Fort Wayne, Inc. v. Fagan*, 644 N.E.2d 159 (Ind. Ct. App. 1994) *and Kuras v. Kope*, 205 Conn. 332, 533 A.2d 1202 (1987).

(e) Your client, Barnes, wishes to expand his home. The proposed expansion would require Barnes to relocate his driveway, which Barnes shares with his neighbor Corrada pursuant to an easement. Corrada has objected to Barnes's plan to relocate the driveway. Barnes wants to know whether he can relocate the easement over Corrada's objection. How you would advise Barnes? What facts, if any, would you seek to discover before advising him? Would it matter whether the easement was an express easement, an implied easement or an easement by prescription? Why or why not? *Compare Sakansky v. Wein*, 86 N.H. 337, 169 A. 1 (1933) (owner of servient land may not unilaterally relocate express easement with defined location) *with Lewis v. Young*, 92 N.Y.2d 443, 682 N.Y.S.2d 657, 705 N.E.2d 649 (1998) (owner of servient estate can relocate easement so long as servient owner bears expense and relocation does not frustrate the parties' intent or decrease the utility of the right of way) *and Umphres v. J.R. Mayer Enters.*, 889 S.W.2d 86 (Mo. Ct. App. 1995) (owner of servient land may unilaterally relocate clearly defined access easement obtained by prescription, but is liable for damages to owner of dominant land resulting from relocation of easement). *See* Restatement of Servitudes § 4.8(3).

Suppose that Chambers owns Lot B and Peters owns neighboring Lot A. Lot B has the benefit of an appurtenant access easement over Lot A. Chambers then purchases 10 acres of land adjacent to Lot B and uses the access easement over Lot A to reach both Lot B and the additional 10 acres. Is this an unreasonable expanded use of the easement?

BROWN v. VOSS

Supreme Court of Washington.
105 Wash.2d 366, 715 P.2d 514 (1986).

BRACHTENBACH, JUSTICE. The question posed is to what extent, if any, the holder of a private road easement can traverse the servient estate to reach not only the original dominant estate, but a subsequently acquired parcel when those two combined parcels are used in such a way that there is no increase in the burden on the servient estate. The trial court denied the injunction sought by the owners of the servient estate. The Court of Appeals reversed. *Brown v. Voss*, 38 Wash.App. 777, 689 P.2d 1111 (1984). We reverse the Court of Appeals and reinstate the judgment of the trial court. . . .

In 1952 the predecessors in title of parcel A granted to the predecessor owners of parcel B a private road easement across parcel A for "ingress to and egress from" parcel B. Defendants acquired parcel A in 1973. Plaintiffs bought parcel B on April 1, 1977 and parcel C on July 31, 1977, but from two different owners. Apparently the previous owners of parcel C were not parties to the easement grant.

When plaintiffs acquired parcel B a single family dwelling was situated thereon. They intended to remove that residence and replace it with a single family dwelling which would straddle the boundary line common to parcels B and C.

Plaintiffs began clearing both parcels B and C and moving fill materials in November 1977. Defendants first sought to bar plaintiff's use of the easement in April 1979 by which time plaintiffs had spent more than $11,000 in developing their property for building.

Defendants placed logs, a concrete sump and a chain link fence within the easement. Plaintiffs sued for removal of the obstructions, an injunction against defendant's interference with their use of the easement and damages. Defendants counterclaimed for damages and an injunction against plaintiffs using the easement other than for parcel B.

The trial court awarded each party $1 in damages. The award against the plaintiffs was for a slight inadvertent trespass outside the easement.

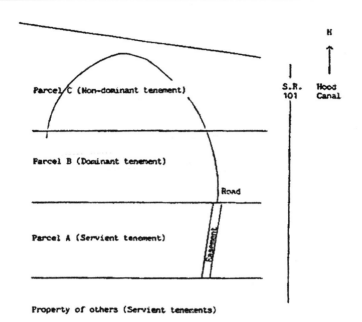

The trial court made the following findings of fact:

VI.   The plaintiffs have made no unreasonable use of the easement in the development of their property. There have been no complaints of unreasonable use of the roadway to the south of the properties of the parties by other neighbors who grant[ed] easements to the parties to this action to cross their properties to gain access to the property of the plaintiffs. Other than the trespass there is no evidence of any damage to the defendants as a result of the use of the easement by the plaintiffs. There has been no increase in volume of travel on the easement to reach a single family dwelling whether built on tract B or on Tracts B and C. There is no evidence of any increase in the burden on the subservient estate from the use of the easement by the plaintiffs for access to parcel C. . . .

VIII.   If an injunction were granted to bar plaintiffs access to tract C across the easement to a single family residence, Parcel C would become landlocked; plaintiffs would not be able to make use of their property; they would not be able to build their single family residence in a manner to properly enjoy the view of the Hood Canal and the surrounding area as originally anticipated at the time of their purchase and even if the single family residence were constructed on parcel B, if the injunction were granted, plaintiffs would not be able to use the balance of their property in parcel C as a yard or for any other use of their property in conjunction with their home. Conversely, there is and will be no appreciable hardship or damage to the defendants if the injunction is denied.

IX.   If an injunction were to be granted to bar the plaintiffs access to tract C, the framing and enforcing of such an order would be impractical. Any violation of the order would result in the parties back in court at great cost but with little or no damages being involved.

X. Plaintiffs have acted reasonably in the development of their property. Their trespass over a "little" corner of the defendants' property was inadvertent, and de minimis. The fact that the defendants counterclaim seeking an injunction to bar plaintiffs access to parcel C was filed as leverage against the original plaintiffs' claim for an interruption of their easement rights, may be considered in determining whether equitable relief by way of an injunction should be granted.

Relying upon these findings of fact, the court denied defendant's request for an injunction and granted the plaintiffs the right to use the easement for access to parcels B & C "as long as plaintiffs' properties (B and C) are developed and used solely for the purpose of a single family residence."

The Court of Appeals reversed, holding:

In sum, we hold that, in denying the Vosses' request for an injunction, the trial court's decision was based upon untenable grounds. We reverse and remand for entry of an order enjoining the use of the easement across parcel A to gain access to a residence any part of which is located on parcel C, or to further the construction of any residence on parcels B or C if the construction activities would require entry onto parcel C. [*Brown v. Voss, supra* at 784–85, 689 P.2d 1111.]

The easement in this case was created by express grant. Accordingly, the extent of the right acquired is to be determined from the terms of the grant properly construed to give effect to the intention of the parties. *See Zobrist v. Culp*, 95 Wash.2d 556, 561, 627 P.2d 1308 (1981); *Seattle v. Nazarenus*, 60 Wash.2d 657, 665, 374 P.2d 1014 (1962). By the express terms of the 1952 grant, the predecessor owners of parcel B acquired a private road easement across parcel A and the right to use the easement for ingress to and egress from parcel B. Both plaintiffs and defendants agree that the 1952 grant created an easement appurtenant to parcel B as the dominant estate. Thus, plaintiffs, as owners of the dominant estate, acquired rights in the use of the easement for ingress to and egress from parcel B.

However, plaintiffs have no such easement rights in connection with their ownership of parcel C, which was not a part of the original dominant estate under the terms of the 1952 grant. As a general rule, an easement appurtenant to one parcel of land may not be extended by the owner of the dominant estate to other parcels owned by him, whether adjoining or distinct tracts, to which the easement is not appurtenant.

Plaintiffs, nonetheless, contend that extension of the use of the easement for the benefit of nondominant property does not constitute a misuse of the easement, where as here, there is no evidence of an increase in the burden on the servient estate. We do not agree. If an easement is appurtenant to a particular parcel of land, any extension thereof to other parcels is a misuse of the easement. As noted by one court in a factually similar case, "[I]n this context this classic rule of property law is directed to the rights of the respective parties rather than the actual burden on the servitude." *National Lead Co. v. Kanawha Block Co.*, 288 F.Supp. 357, 364 (S.D.W.Va.1968), *aff'd*, 409 F.2d 1309 (4th Cir.1969). Under the express language of the 1952 grant, plaintiffs only have rights in the use of the easement for the benefit of parcel B. Although, as plaintiffs contend, their planned use of the easement to gain access to a single family residence located partially on parcel B and partially on parcel C is perhaps no more than technical misuse of the easement, we conclude that it is misuse nonetheless.

However, it does not follow from this conclusion alone that defendants are entitled to injunctive relief. Since the awards of $1 in damages were not appealed, only the denial of an injunction to defendants is in issue. Some fundamental principles applicable to a request for an injunction must be considered. (1) The proceeding is equitable and addressed to the sound discretion of the trial court. (2) The trial court is vested with a broad discretionary power to shape and fashion injunctive relief to fit the particular facts, circumstances, and equities of the case before it. Appellate courts give great weight to the trial court's exercise of that discretion. (3) One of the essential criteria for injunctive relief is actual and substantial injury sustained by the person seeking the injunction. *Washington Fed'n of State Employees v. State*, 99 Wash.2d 878, 665 P.2d 1337 (1983); *Port of Seattle v. International Longshoremen's Union*, 52 Wash.2d 317, 324 P.2d 1099 (1958).

The trial court found as facts, upon substantial evidence, that plaintiffs have acted reasonably in the development of their property, that there is and was no damage to the defendants from plaintiffs' use of the easement, that there was no increase in the volume of travel on the easement, that there was no increase in the burden on the servient estate, that defendants sat by for more than a year while plaintiffs expended more than $11,000 on their project, and that defendants' counterclaim was an effort to gain "leverage" against plaintiffs' claim. In addition, the court found from the evidence that plaintiffs would suffer considerable hardship if the injunction were granted whereas no appreciable hardship or damages would flow to defendants from its denial. Finally, the court limited plaintiffs' use of the combined parcels solely to the same purpose for which the original parcel was used—*i.e.*, for a single family residence.

Neither this court nor the Court of Appeals may substitute its effort to make findings of fact for those supported findings of the trial court. Therefore, the only valid issue is whether, under these established facts, as a matter of law, the trial court abused its discretion in denying defendants' request for injunctive relief. Based upon the equities of the case, as found by the trial court, we are persuaded that the trial court acted within its discretion. The Court of Appeals is reversed and the trial court is affirmed.

Dore, Justice (dissenting). The majority correctly finds that an extension of this easement to nondominant property is a misuse of the easement. The majority, nonetheless, holds that the owners of the servient estate are not entitled to injunctive relief. I dissent.

The comments and illustrations found in the Restatement of Property § 478 (1944) address the precise issue before this court. Comment e provides in pertinent part that "if one who has an easement of way over Whiteacre appurtenant to Blackacre uses the way with the purpose of going to Greenacre, the use is improper even though he eventually goes to Blackacre rather than to Greenacre." Illustration 6 provides:

> 6. By prescription, A has acquired, as the owner and possessor of Blackacre, an easement of way over an alley leading from Blackacre to the street. He buys Whiteacre, an adjacent lot, to which the way is not appurtenant, and builds a public garage one-fourth of which is located on Blackacre and three-fourths of which is located on Whiteacre. A wishes to use the alley as a means of ingress and egress to and from the garage. He has no privilege to use the alley to go to that part of the garage which is built on Whiteacre, and he may not use the alley until that part of the garage built on Blackacre is so separated from the part built on Whiteacre that uses for the benefit of Blackacre are distinguishable from those which benefit Whiteacre.

The majority grants the privilege to extend the agreement to nondominant property on the basis that the trial court found no appreciable hardship or damage to the servient owners. However, as conceded by the majority, any extension of the use of an easement to benefit a nondominant estate constitutes a misuse of the easement. Misuse of an easement is a trespass. *Raven Red Ash Coal Co. v. Ball*, 185 Va. 534, 39 S.E.2d 231 (1946); *Selvia v. Reitmeyer*, 156 Ind.App. 203, 295 N.E.2d 869 (1973). The Brown's use of the easement to benefit parcel C, especially if they build their home as planned, would involve a continuing trespass for which damages would be difficult to measure. Injunctive relief is the appropriate remedy under these circumstances.... Thus, the fact that an extension of the easement to nondominant property would not increase the burden on the servient estate does not warrant a denial of injunctive relief.

The Browns are responsible for the hardship of creating a landlocked parcel. They knew or should have known from the public records that the easement was not appurtenant to parcel C. *See Seattle v. Nazarenus*, 60 Wash.2d 657, 670, 374 P.2d 1014 (1962). In encroachment cases this factor is significant. As stated by the court in *Bach v. Sarich*, 74 Wash.2d 575, 582, 445 P.2d 648 (1968): "The benefit of the doctrine of balancing the equities, or relative hardship, is reserved for the innocent defendant who proceeds without knowledge or warning that his structure encroaches upon another's property or property rights."

In addition, an injunction would not interfere with the Brown's right to use the easement as expressly granted, *i.e.*, for access to parcel B. An injunction would merely require the Browns to acquire access to parcel C if they want to build a home that straddles parcels B and C. One possibility would be to condemn a private way of necessity over their existing easement in an action under RCW 8.24.010. *See Brown v. McAnally*, 97 Wash.2d 360, 644 P.2d 1153 (1982).

I would affirm the Court of Appeals decision as a correct application of the law of easements. If the Browns desire access to their landlocked parcel they have the benefit of the statutory procedure for condemnation of a private way of necessity.

Notes

1. *The Permissible Scope of an Appurtenant Easement.* One might argue (using "rule of reason" analysis) that if the actual use of the easement does not change in nature or intensity, then the expansion of the dominant estate does not unreasonably interfere with the servient landowner's enjoyment of her estate. Nevertheless, the *Brown* court states—and seemingly accepts—the traditional common law rule that the holder of an appurtenant easement cannot unilaterally expand the dominant parcel, *i.e.*, cannot use the easement to benefit land other than the original dominant parcel. Such an expansion is treated as a *per se* unreasonable burden on the owner of the servient land. *See* Restatement of Servitudes § 4.11; *Riddell v. Ewell*, 929 P.2d 30 (Colo. Ct. App. 1996).

So if Voss had a "property right" to exclude the Browns from expanding the dominant parcel in this way, why didn't the court award Voss an injunction as a matter of right? Is it appropriate for the court to permit the Browns to use Voss's land in a manner not permitted by the easement simply because an injunction would impose a greater hardship on the Browns? Can you articulate a defensible alternative theory for the court's refusal to grant an injunction to Voss? How would the availability of a statutory easement of necessity (as cited by the dissent) impact your analysis of these questions?

2. Brown v. Voss—*The Rest of the Story.* After teaching the *Brown* case for several years, Professor Elizabeth Samuels contacted the parties to learn the post-litigation history of their dispute. Her research revealed that:

Today there is no longer an easement across the Vosses' Parcel A providing access to the Browns' Parcels B and C. The Browns never built their house. Before the supreme court of Washington issued its decision in March 1986, the Browns had forfeited Parcel B for failure to make payments on the land installment contract they entered into with the original owner, Mrs. Christensen. The Browns had also lost Parcel C before the decision of the supreme court, in a tax sale conducted by Mason County in January 1986, as a consequence of their failure to pay taxes on the property for a period of more than three years. Thus Parcels B and C were no longer in common ownership. Shortly after the supreme court of Washington's decision, the Vosses bought Parcel B from Mrs. Christensen, thereby merging Parcel A and Parcel B into common ownership, terminating the bitterly contested easement. The Browns had left behind on Parcel B stacks of cedar shake shingles and old tires, which Mr. Voss sold and which helped defray his litigation expenses, as well as new power lines, a deep new well, and a new structure. The Browns' victory in the seven-year legal contest had conferred no practical benefit on them. The outcome reminds one of Abraham Lincoln's admonitions: "Discourage litigation. Persuade your neighbors to compromise whenever you can. Point out to them how the nominal winner is often a real loser—in fees, expenses, and waste of time. As a peacemaker the lawyer has a superior opportunity of being a good man. There will still be business enough."

Elizabeth J. Samuels, *Stories Out of School: Teaching the Case of* Brown v. Voss, 16 Cardozo L. Rev. 1445, 1463–65 (1995). Why do you think that the parties litigated this dispute all the way to the Supreme Court of Washington?

LAWYERING EXERCISE
(Document Review and Drafting)

SITUATION: Your client, Jones, is interested in acquiring Blueacre, a parcel of undeveloped agricultural land owned by Sweeney. Because Blueacre is landlocked, Jones needs an easement across Sweeney's adjacent land to reach Blueacre. Sweeney's attorney has prepared the document below, and Jones has asked you to review it.

TASKS: (1) Based on the preceding materials, identify the additional issues (if any) that the proposed easement does not sufficiently address, and any additional information that you need from Jones before you can advise him as to what amendments are necessary. (2) Revise the document as you believe necessary to protect Jones's interest in this transaction.

EASEMENT

This DEED made _____, 20__, by Steve Sweeney ("Grantor"), to Jane Jones ("Grantee").

Grantor, for and in consideration of Five Dollars ($5.00) paid by Grantee, the receipt of which is hereby acknowledged, grants to Grantee an easement over the following parcel of land:

[Here, the easement provides a legal description of Sweeney's land. You may assume for purposes of this exercise that this legal description is sufficient.]

IN WITNESS WHEREOF, Grantor has executed this deed on the date first above written.

_____
Grantor

4. *Termination of Easements*

Easements may be terminated in a variety of ways, including:

- *Written Conveyance or Release.* The holder of the easement may deliver a writing to the owner of the burdened land indicating that the burdened land is released from the burden of the easement. Restatement of Servitudes § 7.3. [Can you explain why a writing is required?]

- *Merger.* The "merger" of the dominant and servient estates (*i.e.*, when both estates are owned by the same person) terminates an easement. *Id.* § 7.5. Can you explain why the easement is terminated under these circumstances? [Hint: recall why an easement implied from a pre-existing use was called a quasi-easement prior to severance of title.]

- *Prescription.* If the owner of the servient parcel occupies it in a fashion that wrongfully interferes with the easement, and maintains this interference adversely to the holder of the easement for the statutory period for prescription, the easement is extinguished. *Id.* § 7.7.

- *Abandonment.* Courts will terminate an easement when the holder of the easement has abandoned it. But what does it mean to abandon an easement? Does abandonment require more than mere nonuse?

GRAVES v. DENNIS

Supreme Court of South Dakota.
691 N.W.2d 315 (2004).

KONENKAMP, JUSTICE: Gary W. and Patricia A. Graves, plaintiffs, brought a declaratory judgment action against defendants, Thomas R. and Carla Sue Dennis. Plaintiffs sought an order determining their rights on a road easement granted in 1981. Specifically, they wanted defendants to remove obstructions on the road. After the action began, plaintiffs learned that a separate 1978 easement existed. They amended their complaint to seek a ruling on both easements. After a bench trial, the circuit court ruled that defendants had obstructed plaintiffs' use and enjoyment of the 1981 easement. Defendants were required to repair the road. However, the court found that the 1978 easement was abandoned. On appeal, we affirm both rulings because the creation and exclusive use of the 1981 easement coupled with the nonuse of the 1978 easement constituted an effective abandonment of the earlier easement.

In November 1982, plaintiffs purchased a piece of real property near Rapid City, South Dakota. The property, referred to as Lot 1, is described in two parcels, north and south, because at one point each parcel had a different owner. In February 2002, defendants acquired Lot 11, an abutting piece of land. . . .

Plaintiffs' predecessors in interest were William R. and Nelva C. Blenner. Before plaintiffs purchased the property, the Blenners made two easement agreements: the first was in 1978; the second in 1981. The 1978 easement was made when the Blenners owned both Lot 11 and the

Express Easement

Blenners sold Lot 11 to Vaughn

south portion of Lot 1. The easement granted ingress and egress across Lot 11 to Elson J. and Anna L. Leavitt and Rita S. Larson, the owners of the north portion of Lot 1. The easement ran from the north parcel of Lot 1 through Lot 11 to provide access to the main road, Pine Tree Drive. There is no evidence that this easement was ever used.

Subsequently, the Blenners sold Lot 11 to Thomas C. Vaughn. At that point, the Blenners owned only the south portion of Lot 1. However, following the sale of Lot 11 to Vaughn, the Blenners became the outright owners of both the north and south portions of Lot 1. The Blenners then obtained an easement from Vaughn, running from the south portion of Lot 1 across Vaughn's Lot 11. In sum, although the Blenners had created an easement running from the north portion of Lot 1 through Lot 11 with Leavitt and Larson in 1978, an easement which was apparently never used, the Blenners subsequently entered into the 1981 easement with Vaughn, and used the 1981 easement exclusively for access to Pine Tree Drive.

In 1982, the Blenners sold all their interest in Lot 1 to plaintiffs. Like the Blenners, plaintiffs used the 1981 easement. They never used the 1978 easement. They were unaware of its existence, although it was of record with the Pennington County Register of Deeds. While plaintiffs and Vaughn were neighbors, Vaughn built a two-stall garage on his property. The garage was located directly on the 1978 easement. Before constructing the garage, Vaughn conferred with plaintiffs and inquired whether there were any problems with the garage's location. Plaintiffs did not object to the placement of the garage at the time nor did they express any problems with Vaughn after he built it.

In February 2002, Vaughn sold Lot 11 to defendants. Beginning in the spring of 2003, plaintiffs and defendants had several disputes over the 1981 road easement. Most, if not all, of the disputes concerned the manner in which the road was used. Defendants called the police many times to complain about the rate of speed that plaintiffs, their family members, and their guests drove on the access road. On one occasion, defendants sought law enforcement help to disperse a crowd outside their residence when a visitor's vehicle became incapacitated on the easement road. To slow down traffic, defendants created two speed dips on the road. These obstructions impaired plaintiffs' access to their property.

Plaintiffs sued for damages and a declaratory judgment on their rights to the 1981 easement. After the action began, plaintiffs learned that the earlier 1978 easement existed. They amended their complaint to include the 1978 easement, seeking a ruling on both easements. The court found that the speed dips defendants had constructed on the road hindered or restricted plaintiffs' use of the 1981 easement and ordered them removed. The court also found that a portion of a retaining wall located within the thirty-foot easement had to be relocated.

As for the 1978 easement, the court ruled that it had been effectively abandoned when the 1981 easement was created. Defendants do not appeal any of the court's rulings, but plaintiffs complain that they are entitled to maintain both the 1978 and 1981 easements. . . .

Plaintiffs believe the trial court erred when it found that the 1978 easement had been abandoned, thereby extinguishing it. Since Vaughn and the Blenners did not discuss the 1978 easement when they agreed to the 1981 easement, and since plaintiffs were unaware of the 1978 easement, plaintiffs contend there is no evidence of intent to abandon the 1978 easement. South Dakota has a statute specifically dealing with extinguishment of servitudes. SDCL 43–13–12 provides: "A servitude is extinguished by the performance of any act upon either tenement, by the owner of the servitude, or with his assent, which is incompatible with its nature or exercise."

Under this statute, "there must be an affirmative act of abandonment on the part of the owner of the easement to extinguish the easement. Mere nonuse of an easement, created by grant, is insufficient to satisfy this requirement." *Hofmeister v. Sparks,* 2003 SD 35, ¶ 13, 660 N.W.2d 637, 641 (citing *Clark v. Redlich,* 147 Cal.App.2d 500, 305 P.2d 239, 244 (1957)). However, a substituted access may serve as evidence of abandonment, but that by itself is not dispositive. *Id.* Use of a substitute road may be evidence of an abandonment of the old road; however, "[t]he mere use of a new right-of-way will not extinguish the old. There must also be an abandonment by non-use of the old right-of-way." *Id.* (quoting *Shippy v. Hollopeter,* 304 N.W.2d 118, 122 (S.D.1981)). Those claiming abandonment carry the burden of showing by clear and convincing evidence an intent to abandon the easement. *Cleveland* [*v. Tinaglia*], 1998 SD 91, ¶ 26, 582 N.W.2d at 725; *see Mueller v. Bohannon,* 256 Neb. 286, 589 N.W.2d 852, 859 (1999).

There is no evidence that the 1978 easement has ever been used since it was created two and a half decades ago. The only roadway shown in the photographs admitted in evidence is the one reflecting the 1981 easement. According to the Restatement, "[a] servitude benefit is extinguished by abandonment when the beneficiary relinquishes the rights created by a servitude." Restatement (Third) of Property § 7.4 (2000). "A finding of abandonment is usually based on circumstantial evidence rather than on direct expressions of intent. . . ." *Id.* § 7.4 cmt. a.

Failure to take advantage of a servitude benefit, even for a lengthy period, is seldom sufficient to persuade a court that abandonment has occurred. Some additional action on the part of the beneficiary inconsistent with continued existence of the servitude is normally required, although the amount of additional evidence required tends to diminish as the period of nonuse grows longer. In cases where a very long period of time has passed, abandonment may be found even without other evidence of intent. *Id.* § 7.4 cmt. c.

We conclude that the elements necessary for abandonment of the 1978 easement are present here: exclusive use of the new right of way and nonuse of the old right of way. After the Blenners gained ownership of both the north and south parcels of Lot 1, they obtained a new easement in 1981. They never used the old easement nor, apparently, did the previous owners. Thus, the Blenners had two easements, both to Lot 1 and both allowing access from the same main road at the same point. After plaintiffs purchased Lot 1 from the Blenners, they never used the 1978 easement. Furthermore, plaintiffs and Vaughn had discussed the construction of a two-stall garage on Lot 11. Although neither Vaughn nor plaintiffs were aware of the 1978 easement, the placement of the garage was directly on that easement.

In sum, the 1978 easement had never been used, and, in fact, no road had ever been created for that easement. Although separate easements might have been necessary when the north and south portions of Lot 1 had different owners, for more than twenty-five years both portions have had the same owner. Both easements provide access to Lot 1, and both converge before intersecting with Pine Tree Drive. We conclude that the trial court did not err in finding that the 1978 easement was abandoned and extinguished.

Affirmed.

Notes

1. *Abandonment of Easements.* In deciding whether an easement has been abandoned, courts generally focus on the intent of the easement holder, rather than the expectations of the owner of the servient tenement. Courts have traditionally required "clear and convincing evidence" of the easement holder's intent to abandon the easement—typically in the form of an affirmative act by the easement holder that demonstrates her intent to abandon the easement. As the *Graves* opinion suggests, courts have universally held that mere non-use (regardless of its duration) is insufficient to extinguish an easement. Should non-use for a long period of time (*e.g.*, the statutory period for acquiring prescriptive rights) give rise to a presumption of abandonment? Is it unreasonable to require the holder of the easement to make occasional use of the easement or otherwise signal a continuing intention to use it? Why hasn't the law traditionally imposed such a burden on the easement holder? *See, e.g.*, 7 Thompson on Real Property § 60.08(b)(3), at 482.

2. *Abandonment and Termination by Prescription Compared.* If the servient landowner engages in sufficiently open and notorious acts adverse to the easement that continue for longer than the statute of limitations for acquiring prescriptive rights, the easement is terminated by prescription. In this circumstance, whether the easement holder intended to abandon the easement is irrelevant. *See, e.g., Hickerson v. Bender*, 500 N.W.2d 169 (Minn. Ct. App. 1993). If the interference has continued for a long time—but not for the full prescriptive period—should the court treat the easement holder's non-use and failure to object as sufficient evidence of abandonment? In the *Graves* case, should it matter that the Graveses did not object to the garage being built on the 1978 easement because they were unaware that easement existed? Can a person abandon a property interest that she doesn't know she owns?

Assume that your client, Smith, seeks your advice regarding an easement claimed by her neighbor Jones. Jones claims that he holds a right of access across Smith's property over a 15–foot easement conveyed by Smith's predecessor in 1920. Smith advises you of the following facts: (a) prior owners of nearby land state that the easement has not been used since 1941; (b) in the late 1930s, the county opened a road, which Jones and her predecessors have used for access to the Jones parcel; (c) Smith's predecessor built a garden shed in 1973 that encroaches by about two feet onto the easement; (d) over the past 50 years, several trees have grown in the path of the easement, making access across the easement impossible (at least without removal of the trees). Smith wants to know whether she can successfully claim that the easement has been abandoned. How would you advise her? What other information would you like to gather? *See Witt v. McKenna*, 600 A.2d 105 (Me. 1991); *Iorfida v. Mary Robert Realty Co.*, 372 Pa.Super. 170, 539 A.2d 383 (1988); *Skvarla v. Park*, 62 N.C.App. 482, 303 S.E.2d 354 (1983).

C. PROMISSORY SERVITUDES: REAL COVENANTS AT LAW AND EQUITABLE SERVITUDES

1. *Introduction*

a. *English Resistance to Negative Easements.* As discussed in Part B (page 554), the common law permitted parties to create a limited set of *negative easements*, such as the right to prohibit a neighbor from restricting access to the flow of light or air, the right to prohibit interference with the support of a building, or the right to prohibit interference with an artificial stream. The common law's refusal to recognize a greater variety of negative easements profoundly shaped our modern law of covenants and equitable servitudes.

Throughout the 19th century, people in and near urban areas faced increased commercialization, industrialization and population density. As people became aware of the negative consequences of living next to certain types of commercial and industrial facilities, they began to search for new ways to protect investments in residential land. Before investing a significant sum in developing a residence, for example, a landowner reasonably might want her neighbors to agree that they would not use their land in a way that would impose external costs on her and thereby diminish the value of her land. Conceptually, the law of easements could have allowed for the creation of an individual or reciprocal right to restrict the use of land. For example, adjoining landowners each might have made the following arrangement: "I hereby grant *X* an easement across [description of land] to prevent use of the land as a factory."

Unfortunately, 19th-century English courts resisted recognizing new negative easements for two reasons—one practical and one conceptual. From a practical standpoint (as discussed in Part B), English judges were concerned that the lack of recording systems made it difficult for buyers of land to discover negative easements, even though such easements would be binding on those buyers. As a result, English courts feared that recognition of new negative easements would unreasonably burden transferability and development of land. Conceptually, English courts also were constrained by the notion that a landowner could create an express easement only by a grant of "tangible" property rights. This presented no problem with affirmative easements, which are by nature sufficiently visible and tangible to appear like "property" in an age when prevailing thought was most comfortable with tangible rights: *e.g.*, "I hereby grant you the right to cross my land to access your land." By contrast, a negative easement involves the servient landowner forgoing some use of her land—and thus involves rights more invisible and intangible in nature. English courts had trouble conceptualizing such an arrangement as the subject of a grant of an interest in land; however phrased, an arrangement to forgo uses more closely resembled a promise, covenant, or contract than a "property" right like an easement.

b. ***The Development of Covenants Running With Land.*** Because of these practical and conceptual stumbling blocks, English courts limited the types of enforceable negative easements to those mentioned above. Thus, landowners turned to contract law. Unfortunately, in the early part of the 19th century, the law generally considered contract rights as non-assignable. Thus, contract law would enforce a promissory use arrangement only as between the original contracting parties, not as between their successors in ownership of the land involved. Because the long-term utility of the restriction depended upon its enforceability against subsequent owners, a land use restriction could not remain effective if the landowner could circumvent it merely by transferring the land in question to a successor owner.

There was an exception to the general rule of non-assignability, however—situations in which the parties stood in privity of estate. This exception arose in the 16th century, in *Spencer's Case*, 5 Coke 16a, 77 Eng. Rep. 72 (1583). The case involved a lease of land for a term of 21 years. The lessee covenanted to build a brick wall on the land. Subsequently, the lessee assigned his leasehold estate. The lessor eventually sued the assignee for breach of the covenant to build the wall. *Spencer's Case* is generally understood to have set forth three requirements for such a covenant to bind successors in ownership of the burdened land: that the covenantor demonstrate the covenanting parties' *intent* to bind successors, that the covenant *"touch and concern"* the land, and that there be *privity of estate* between the covenanting parties.

Following *Spencer's Case*, courts could have applied the concept of privity of estate in contexts beyond landlord-tenant law. In *Keppell v. Bailey*, 2 My. & K. 517, 39 Eng. Rep. 1042 (1834), however, the Chancery Court narrowly defined the "privity of estate" required by *Spencer's Case* to encompass only the relationship between landlords and tenants entering into covenants as part of a lease. *Keppell* involved a dispute between shareholders of a railroad and the owners of an ironworks. The preceding owners of the ironworks had entered into a covenant to purchase limestone from a given quarry and transport it to the ironworks by means of the Trevil Railroad, which would receive a stated toll for such transportation. Upon obtaining title to the ironworks, the new owners wished to obtain limestone from a new source and transport it by a different railway. The shareholders of the Trevil Railroad sought an injunction requiring the iron works to continue using the old quarry and railroad. In refusing to issue the injunction, the *Keppell* court limited enforceability of a "real covenant" against an assignee to cases where the original contracting parties stood in a landlord-tenant relationship when they first made the covenant. The court's language reflects the deep suspicion that courts harbored for attempts to create promissory servitudes that could bind successors:

> [G]reat detriment would arise and much confusion of rights if parties were allowed to invent new modes of holding and enjoying real property, and to impress upon their lands and tenements a peculiar character, which should follow them into all hands, however remote. Every close, every messuage, might thus be held in a several fashion; and it would hardly be possible to know what rights the acquisition of any parcel conferred, or what obligations it imposed.... [I]f one man may bind his ... land to take lime from a particular kiln, another may bind his to take coals from a certain pit, while a third may load his property with further obligations to employ one blacksmith's forge, or the members of one corporate body, in various operations on the premises, besides many other restraints as infinite in variety as the imagination can conceive;... there can be no ... support of the covenant in question which would not extend to every covenant that can be devised. [39 Eng. Rep. at 1049.]

By requiring a landlord-tenant relationship to establish privity of estate, *Keppell* effectively precluded neighboring fee simple landowners, or grantors and grantees of fee title, from creating land use restrictions that could be enforced against subsequent owners of the land.

Just over a decade later, however, in *Tulk v. Moxhay*, 2 Phil. 774, 41 Eng. Rep. 1143 (1848), the Chancery Court laid the most important stone in the legal foundation for the enforcement of contractual land use restrictions against successor landowners. *Tulk* involved a dispute over Leicester Square (now in the heart of the Theatre District in London). The former owner of Leicester Square, Tulk—who also owned several other buildings surrounding the square—had conveyed the property to Elms subject to the following covenant:

> That Elms, his heirs, and assigns, should, and would from time to time, and at all times thereafter at his and their own costs and charges, keep and maintain the said piece of ground and Square garden, and the iron railing round the same in its then form, and in sufficient and proper repair as a Square Garden and Pleasure Ground, in an open state, uncovered with any buildings, in neat and ornamental order; and that it should be lawful for the inhabitants of Leicester Square, tenants of the plaintiff, on payment of a reason-

able rent for the same, to have keys at their own expense and the privilege of admission therewith at any time or times into the said Square Garden and Pleasure Ground.

Subsequently, Elms's interest passed to Moxhay, who took the land with knowledge of the quoted covenant. When Moxhay expressed interest in developing the property, Tulk sought and received an injunction against breach of the covenant. Affirming the grant of the injunction, the Chancery Court chose to ignore the precedents expressed in *Spencer's Case* and *Keppell*, instead holding that the arrangement created a persisting "equity" (which later came to be called an "equitable servitude") that bound the covenantor's land even after its transfer to a successor:

> It is said that, the covenant being one which does not run with the land, this court cannot enforce it; but the question is, not whether the covenant runs with the land, but whether a party shall be permitted to use the land in the manner inconsistent with the contract entered into by his vendor, and with notice of which he purchased. Of course, the price would be affected by the covenant, and nothing could be more inequitable than that the original purchaser should be able to sell the property the next day for a greater price, in consideration of the assignee being allowed to escape from the liability which he had himself undertaken.
>
> That the question does not depend upon whether the covenant runs with the land, is evident from this, that if there was a mere agreement and no covenant, this court would enforce it against a party purchasing with notice of it; for if an equity is attached to the property by the owner, no one purchasing with notice of that equity can stand in a different situation from the party from whom he purchased. . . .
>
> With respect to the observations . . . in *Keppell v. Bailey*, . . . [the court] never could have meant to lay down, that this court would not enforce an equity attached to land by the owner, unless under such circumstances as would maintain an action at law. If that be the result of [the *Keppell* court's] observations, I can only say that I cannot coincide with it.

2. *Covenants Running With Land in American Law*

American courts have generally followed the principles set forth in *Spencer's Case* and *Tulk v. Moxhay* as a framework for deciding when a covenant should run with the land. Thus, to enforce a covenant against a successor at law (*i.e.*, in an action for monetary damages), American courts generally have required that

- the original covenanting parties intended to bind successor owners to the restriction,
- the restriction "touched and concerned" the land,
- the original covenanting parties stood in "privity of estate," and

● the successor took the land with notice of the restriction.[7]

Likewise, to enforce a covenant against a successor in equity (*i.e.*, in an action for specific performance or an injunction), American courts generally have discarded the privity requirement, requiring only that

● the original covenanting parties intended to bind successor owners to the restriction,

● the restriction "touched and concerned" the land, and

● the successor took the land with notice of the restriction.

In evaluating most covenants, the "intent to bind successors" and "notice" requirements pose little analytical difficulty. If a covenant is intended to run with the land to bind successors, this intent is typically reflected by express language indicating that the covenant binds the covenanting parties and their "heirs, successors, and assigns." Likewise, if the document creating a covenant is properly recorded in the public land records, the recording will give constructive notice of the covenant to all subsequent purchasers of the land (as discussed in Chapter 3 and again in Chapter 9).

By contrast, covenant disputes more frequently involve the "privity of estate" and "touch and concern" requirements. The following sections focus upon these requirements as traditionally applied by American courts, exploring the purposes served by these requirements. In the process, the materials also highlight the potential impact of the new Restatement of Servitudes on these two requirements.

a. *Privity of Estate.* Unlike *Keppell v. Bailey*, American courts have extended privity of estate beyond the landlord-tenant relationship. Nevertheless, as the following case demonstrates, even this broader view of privity of estate can be quite limited.

BREMMEYER EXCAVATING, INC. v. McKENNA

Court of Appeals of Washington.
44 Wash.App. 267, 721 P.2d 567 (1986).

GROSSE, JUDGE. . . . On January 29, 1980, Bremmeyer Excavating, Inc. (Bremmeyer) and Gerald Parks entered into a written agreement whereby Bremmeyer was to provide labor and materials to fill a parcel of property owned by Parks. Paragraph 7 of the agreement provided as follows:

Bremmeyer is hereby given the exclusive right, to be exercised at its option, for a period of five years from the date of this agreement, to perform on the subject property the following: (a) all the hauling

---

7. Although *Spencer's Case* did not articulate "notice" of the restriction as a requirement, American law requires notice as a consequence of the recording acts—discussed in Chapter 9 beginning at page 731—which require that interests in land must be recorded in the public land records to make them effective against subsequent good-faith purchasers of the land.

onto or from the subject property all fill material of any nature; (b) all the work for the installation of any and all water and sewer utilities on the subject property, including but not limited to digging, trenching, installation, refilling and surcharging. If Bremmeyer exercises its right to perform any of the above-mentioned work, Bremmeyer agrees to meet the lowest competitive price obtained by Parks for such work from a responsible contractor.

Sometime thereafter Parks sold the property to John McKenna and John Pietromonaco. McKenna and Pietromonaco filled the property without Bremmeyer's services. Bremmeyer filed suit against McKenna and Pietromonaco alleging breach of the fill contract and claiming that the contract created a covenant that runs with the land. . . .

The requisites for a covenant running with the land are set forth in *Leighton v. Leonard*, 22 Wash.App. 136, 589 P.2d 279 (1978).

(1) [T]he covenants must have been enforceable between the original parties, such enforceability being a question of contract law except insofar as the covenant must satisfy the statute of frauds; (2) the covenant must "touch and concern" both the land to be benefited and the land to be burdened; (3) the covenanting parties must have intended to bind their successors in interest; (4) there must be vertical privity of estate, *i.e.*, privity between the original parties to the covenant and the present disputants; and (5) there must be horizontal privity of estate, or privity between the original parties. (Footnotes omitted.) (Citations omitted.) [*Leighton*, at 139, 589 P.2d 279.]

The contract at issue here fails to satisfy the second and fifth of these prerequisites.

[The court's discussion of whether the covenant "touched and concerned" land is omitted.]

A recent decision of this court, *Feider v. Feider*, 40 Wash.App. 589, 699 P.2d 801 (1985), illustrates the failure of this agreement to satisfy the fifth requisite of a running covenant, that of horizontal privity of estate. In that case, the Court of Appeals held that horizontal privity did not exist for a right of first refusal to purchase land because the right of first refusal "did not pass *with an estate in land* or relate to coexisting or common property interests." *Feider*, at 593, 699 P.2d 801. Although during oral argument on the instant case appellant's counsel stated that the property subject to the fill contract had been acquired by respondents' predecessor in interest from the appellant, we can find no support for this in the record. Indeed, the allegation in the original complaint suggests that the fill contract was entered into subsequent to the agreement for purchase and sale. In any event, the record before this court lacks evidence that the fill contract passed between the original parties in conjunction with an estate in land or that the fill contract relates to coexisting or common property interests. Absent such proof, horizontal privity does not exist. . . .

Notes

1. *Privity of Estate in American Law.* To better understand the vocabulary used in *McKenna*, consider the following diagram and how it distinguishes between the two sides of a promissory servitude (*i.e.*, the burden to one party and the benefit to another):

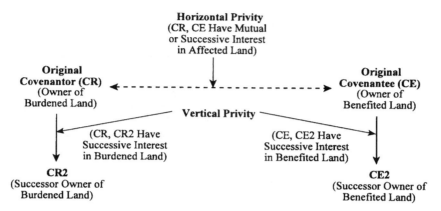

As the diagram indicates, privity of estate has two components—*horizontal privity* and *vertical privity*. Horizontal privity focuses on the relationship between the original parties to the covenant. The first Restatement of Property provided that horizontal privity exists if the original parties to the covenant have either a *mutual* interest (sometimes called a *simultaneous* interest) or *successive* interests (sometimes called a *succession of interest*) in the affected land at the time they enter into the covenant:

- A *mutual interest* exists when each party has some interest in a given parcel of land, such as when CR owns fee title and CE has an easement appurtenant across CR's land, or when CE owns fee title and CR has an easement appurtenant across CE's land.

- A *succession of interest* exists when the parties make the covenant as a part of a grant of an estate from one to the other, thereby standing in a grantor-grantee relationship, such as when CR conveys an estate to CE, or when CE conveys an estate to CR.

Thus, one must determine at the time CR and CE enter into a covenant whether CR and CE stand in horizontal privity.

In contrast, vertical privity focuses upon succession to the interests of the original parties to the covenant—*i.e.*, either a transfer of the burdened parcel by CR, a transfer of the benefitted parcel by CE, or perhaps both—at some point after CR and CE enter into the covenant. In its most familiar definition, vertical privity requires that the successor owner succeed to the entire estate of the predecessor.

2. *What Type of Privity Is Required for a Burden or a Benefit of a Covenant to Run with the Land?—The First Restatement.* The result in *McKenna* is consistent with the provisions of the first Restatement of

Property—which required both horizontal and vertical privity before a covenantee or her successor (CE or CE2) could enforce the *burden* of a covenant *against a successor to the covenantor* (CR2). Restatement of Property §§ 534, 535 (1944). Although McKenna and Pietromonaco (CR2) stood in vertical privity with Parks (CR), there was no horizontal privity between Bremmeyer Excavating (CE) and Parks (CR). Thus, the court held that the burden of the covenant (the obligation to use Bremmeyer to fill the lot) did not run with the land when Parks sold the land to McKenna and Pietromonaco.[8]

With respect to the running of the *benefit* of a covenant, however, the common law relaxed the privity requirement. Neither horizontal privity nor vertical privity was required if a successor owner of the benefitted parcel (CE2) sought to enforce the covenant against the original covenantor (CR). *Id.* §§ 547, 548. Thus, suppose McKenna and Pietromonaco had requested Bremmeyer to perform the contract and Bremmeyer had refused. The first Restatement suggests that McKenna and Pietromonaco could have recovered damages against Bremmeyer for breach of the covenant. Would such a result make sense? Why or why not?

3. *Understanding the Consequences of the Horizontal Privity Requirement.* Assume that Andrew and Bob own adjacent parcels of land on which they plan to build homes. Andrew and Bob mutually agree to restrict their land to residential use in a writing in which they declare their intention to bind themselves and their successors and assigns. Later:

(a) Andrew sells his parcel to Chris, who builds a home. Bob thereafter opens a restaurant on his parcel. Chris wants to recover damages from Bob for violating the covenant. How do you advise him? What information would you want to gather before offering your advice?

(b) Bob builds a home. Andrew thereafter sells his land to Chris, who promptly builds a restaurant on the land. Bob wants to recover damages from Chris for violating the covenant. How do you advise him? What information would you want to gather before offering your advice?

(c) Bob builds a home. Andrew thereafter sells his land to Chris, and Chris informs Bob of his intent to open a restaurant on the land. Bob wants to get an injunction to prevent Chris from violating the covenant. How do you advise him?

4. *Understanding the Consequences of the Vertical Privity Requirement.* Assume that Frances, who owns a parcel of land in fee simple, sells a portion of that parcel to Gail. In the deed, both parties agree, for themselves and their successors and assigns, to refrain from selling liquor on their respective parcels of property.

(a) Assume that Frances leases her remaining land to Edith. Edith opens a restaurant and begins selling liquor. Gail indicates that she intends to

---

8. These sections of the first Restatement were subject to withering criticism by Judge Charles Clark, who argued in a leading treatise that there should be no horizontal privity required for the burden of a covenant to run at law. Charles Clark, Real Covenants and Other Interests Which "Run With Land" (2d ed. 1947). Although courts in some states have not required horizontal privity in damages actions against successors, the weight of judicial authority is consistent with the first Restatement and with *McKenna.*

bring an action for damages and an injunction against Edith. How would you advise Edith regarding her liability for damages for breach of the covenant and her ability to continue to operate the restaurant? How would your advice change, if at all, if Edith informed you that instead of selling liquor, she intends to offer every patron a complimentary alcoholic beverage?

(b) Assume that Harriet begins adversely possessing Gail's land, and after several years, opens a liquor store on the land. Frances wants to bring an action for damages and an injunction against Harriet. How would you advise Frances regarding her ability to recover damages or her ability to obtain an injunction against Harriet?

5. *Liability of Covenantor Upon Transfer of Burdened Estate.* In Chapter 7, you learned that a tenant's assignment of its leasehold estate did not relieve the tenant of its contractual liability for rent that accrued following the assignment. Courts have typically held that this type of continuing contractual liability does not exist with respect to covenants entered into outside of the landlord-tenant context. For example, assume that Wilbur conveys a portion of his land to Charlotte, subject to a restriction limiting use of the land to single-family residential purposes. Charlotte in turn conveys her property to Isolde, who immediately opens a restaurant on the land. Although Wilbur could obtain an injunction or damages against Isolde, Wilbur will be unable to obtain damages against Charlotte. Can you explain why? *See Waikiki Malia Hotel, Inc. v. Kinkai Props. Ltd. P'ship,* 75 Haw. 370, 862 P.2d 1048 (1993); Restatement of Property § 538 (1944); Restatement of Servitudes § 4.4(1).

6. *The Restatement of Servitudes and Its "Abolition" of the Privity Requirement.* The horizontal privity requirement prevents certain types of agreements from being enforceable at law against successors to the original covenanting parties. For example, suppose that two neighboring landowners (A and B) acquired their interests in unrelated transactions years ago and do not share any mutual interests in each other's land. A and B agree to place a reciprocal restriction on their respective lots whereby each agrees not to construct any buildings other than a single-family residence. There may be good reasons to enforce such a restriction freely—the restriction would enable A and B (and their successors) to invest in the land for residential purposes without fear of adjacent nonresidential uses. Unfortunately, neither A nor B could enforce the restriction in an action for damages against subsequent transferees, because horizontal privity does not exist between A and B. [Can you explain how A and B could have documented their agreement to address this problem?]

Not surprisingly, therefore, American courts followed the lead of *Tulk v. Moxhay* by recognizing equitable servitudes as interests in land enforceable in equity, even in the absence of privity. To be entitled to an injunction against a successor of B, A would need to demonstrate only that A and B intended for the covenant to bind successors and assigns, that the covenant touches and concerns the land, and that the successor has notice of the covenant—the lack of privity is legally irrelevant. Further, because most parties typically seek to enforce such covenants by injunction rather than damages (can you explain why?), the presence or absence of privity is practically irrelevant in most litigated disputes. As a result, scholars have questioned the wisdom of retaining any privity requirement for the enforcement of covenants (at least with respect to covenants outside of the landlord-tenant context).

The Restatement of Servitudes purports to dispose of the privity requirement, because judicial acceptance of running covenants as "property interests" indicates that there is no need to rely on privity to enforce covenants against third parties under a contract theory. Section 2.4 states that horizontal privity is not necessary to create an enforceable servitude. Section 5.2 rejects vertical privity, providing that appurtenant benefits and burdens generally run with the land to bind subsequent owners of the benefitted and burdened land. The Restatement then provides specific rules that address enforcement of a covenant when one of the parties is a lessee [§ 5.3], life tenant [§ 5.4], or adverse possessor that has not yet established title [§ 5.5]. Whether American courts will follow the new Restatement and abandon the privity requirement remains to be seen, but commentary regarding abolition of the privity requirement is uniformly positive.

b. *The "Touch and Concern" Requirement at Common Law.*
In tracing the development of the law of promissory servitudes, we noted the judicial concern in earlier centuries, articulated in *Keppell v. Bailey*, that land not be subjected to long-term "restraints as infinite in variety as the imagination can conceive." Accordingly, English courts decided early on that even where the original covenanting parties intended for a covenant to bind successors, that covenant was enforceable against successors only when its subject matter was sufficiently bound up with the use of the land. As the court articulated in *Spencer's Case*, 17 Eng. Rep. 77 (1583) (emphasis added): "If the covenant 'be *merely collateral to the land*, and *doth not touch or concern* the thing demised in any sort' it will not be enforceable as between successors in ownership to the original parties to the covenant."

Courts have had little difficulty applying the "touch and concern" requirement to negative covenants restricting land use. For example, consider a covenant restricting land to "single-family residential use only." Without question, such a covenant would "touch and concern" the land—both with respect to the burden of that covenant (as it would prohibit the covenantor or her successor from using the land for other purposes) and with respect to the benefit of that covenant (as the covenantee or her successor would be protected against harm potentially posed by nonresidential use).

Courts have had greater difficulty applying the touch and concern requirement to evaluate affirmative covenants—*i.e.*, covenants that purport to require an owner of land to perform some affirmative act (such as to pay money). English courts simply refused to enforce affirmative covenants against successors, either as real covenants (at law) or equitable servitudes (in equity). In American decisions, affirmative covenants have met divergent fates. For example, in the *McKenna* case (page 610), the court concluded that the covenant between Parks and Bremmeyer (requiring use of Bremmeyer's services to fill the land in question) did not "touch and concern" the land and could not be enforced against Parks's successors. By contrast, in the following landmark decision, the Court of Appeals for New York interpreted the touch and concern standard to permit enforcement of a residential subdivision homeowners' assessment—a critically important precedent that paved the way for modern common interest community development. What do these decisions suggest about the purpose underlying the "touch and concern" requirement?

NEPONSIT PROPERTY OWNERS' ASS'N, INC. v. EMIGRANT INDUSTRIAL SAVINGS BANK

Court of Appeals of New York.
278 N.Y. 248, 15 N.E.2d 793 (1938).

LEHMAN, JUDGE. The plaintiff, as assignee of Neponsit Realty Company, has brought this action to foreclose a lien upon land which the defendant owns. The lien, it is alleged, arises from a covenant, condition or charge contained in a deed of conveyance of the land from Neponsit Realty Company to a predecessor in title of the defendant. The defendant purchased the land at a judicial sale. The referee's deed to the defendant and every deed in the defendant's chain of title since the conveyance of the land by Neponsit Realty Company purports to convey the property subject to the covenant, condition or charge contained in the original deed. [The lower court and appellate court denied defendant's motion for judgment on the pleadings and granted plaintiff's motion to dismiss defendant's counterclaim and affirmative defenses. Defendant appealed.]

It appears that in January, 1911, Neponsit Realty Company, as owner of a tract of land in Queens county, caused to be filed in the office of the clerk of the county a map of the land. The tract was developed for a strictly residential community, and Neponsit Realty Company conveyed lots in the tract to purchasers, describing such lots by reference to the filed map and to roads and streets shown thereon. In 1917, Neponsit Realty Company conveyed the land now owned by the defendant to Robert Oldner Deyer and his wife by deed which contained the covenant upon which the plaintiff's cause of action is based.

That covenant provides:

> And the party of the second part for the party of the second part and the heirs, successors and assigns of the party of the second part further covenants that the property conveyed by this deed shall be subject to an annual charge in such an amount as will be fixed by the party of the first part, its successors and assigns, not, however exceeding in any year the sum of four ($4.00) Dollars per lot 20x100 feet. The assigns of the party of the first part may include a Property Owners' Association which may hereafter be organized for the purposes referred to in this paragraph, and in case such association is organized the sums in this paragraph provided for shall be payable to such association. The party of the second part for the

party of the second part and the heirs, successors and assigns of the party of the second part covenants that they will pay this charge to the party of the first part, its successors and assigns on the first day of May in each and every year, and further covenants that said charge shall on said date in each year become a lien on the land and shall continue to be such lien until fully paid. Such charge shall be payable to the party of the first part or its successors or assigns, and shall be devoted to the maintenance of the roads, paths, parks, beach, sewers and such other public purposes as shall from time to time be determined by the party of the first part, its successors or assigns. And the party of the second part by the acceptance of this deed hereby expressly vests in the party of the first part, its successors and assigns, the right and power to bring all actions against the owner of the premises hereby conveyed or any part thereof for the collection of such charge and to enforce the aforesaid lien therefor.

These covenants shall run with the land and shall be construed as real covenants running with the land until January 31st, 1940, when they shall cease and determine.

Every subsequent deed of conveyance of the property in the defendant's chain of title, including the deed from the referee to the defendant, contained, as we have said, a provision that they were made subject to covenants and restrictions of former deeds of record.

There can be no doubt that Neponsit Realty Company intended that the covenant should run with the land and should be enforceable by a property owners association against every owner of property in the residential tract which the realty company was then developing. The language of the covenant admits of no other construction. Regardless of the intention of the parties, a covenant will run with the land and will be enforceable against a subsequent purchaser of the land at the suit of one who claims the benefit of the covenant, only if the covenant complies with certain legal requirements. These requirements rest upon ancient rules and precedents. The age-old essentials of a real covenant, aside from the form of the covenant, may be summarily formulated as follows: (1) It must appear that grantor and grantee intended that the covenant should run with the land; (2) it must appear that the covenant is one "touching" or "concerning" the land with which it runs; (3) it must appear that there is "privity of estate" between the promisee or party claiming the benefit of the covenant and the right to enforce it, and the promisor or party who rests under the burden of the covenant. Clark on Covenants and Interests Running with Land, p. 74. Although the deeds of Neponsit Realty Company conveying lots in the tract it developed "contained a provision to the effect that the covenants ran with the land, such provision in the absence of the other legal requirements is insufficient to accomplish such a purpose." *Morgan Lake Co. v. New York, N. H. & H. R. R. Co.*, 262 N.Y. 234, 238, 186 N.E. 685, 686. In his opinion in that case, Judge Crane posed but found it unnecessary to decide many of the questions which the court must consider in this case.

The covenant in this case is intended to create a charge or obligation to pay a fixed sum of money to be "devoted to the maintenance of the roads, paths, parks, beach, sewers and such other public purposes as shall from time to time be determined by the party of the first part [the grantor], its successors or assigns." It is an affirmative covenant to pay money for use in connection with, but not upon, the land which it is said is subject to the burden of the covenant. Does such a covenant "touch" or "concern" the land? These terms are not part of a statutory definition, a limitation placed by the State upon the power of the courts to enforce covenants intended to run with the land by the parties who entered into the covenants. Rather they are words used by courts in England in old cases to describe a limitation which the courts themselves created or to formulate a test which the courts have devised and which the courts voluntarily apply. *Cf. Spencer's Case*, Coke, vol. 3, part 5, 16a; *Mayor of Congleton v. Pattison*, 10 East 130. In truth such a description or test so formulated is too vague to be of much assistance and judges and academic scholars alike have struggled, not with entire success, to formulate a test at once more satisfactory and more accurate. "It has been found impossible to state any absolute tests to determine what covenants touch and concern land and what do not. The question is one for the court to determine in the exercise of its best judgment upon the facts of each case." Clark, op. cit. p. 76.

Even though that be true, a determination by a court in one case upon particular facts will often serve to point the way to correct decision in other cases upon analogous facts. Such guideposts may not be disregarded. It has been often said that a covenant to pay a sum of money is a personal affirmative covenant which usually does not concern or touch the land. Such statements are based upon English decisions which hold in effect that only covenants, which compel the covenanter to submit to some restriction on the use of his property, touch or concern the land, and that the burden of a covenant which requires the covenanter to do an affirmative act, even on his own land, for the benefit of the owner of a "dominant" estate, does not run with his land. *Miller v. Clary*, 210 N.Y. 127, 103 N.E. 1114, L.R.A.1918E, 222, Ann.Cas.1915B, 872. In that case the court pointed out that in many jurisdictions of this country the narrow English rule has been criticized and a more liberal and flexible rule has been substituted. In this State the courts have not gone so far. We have not abandoned the historic distinction drawn by the English courts. So this court has recently said:

> Subject to a few exceptions not important at this time, there is now in this state a settled rule of law that a covenant to do an affirmative act, as distinguished from a covenant merely negative in effect, does not run with the land so as to charge the burden of performance on a subsequent grantee [citing cases]. This is so though the burden of such a covenant is laid upon the very parcel which is the subject-matter of the conveyance. [*Guaranty Trust Co. of New York v. New York & Queens County Ry. Co.*, 253 N.Y. 190, 204, 170 N.E. 887, 892, opinion by Cardozo, Ch. J.]

Both in that case and in the case of *Miller v. Clary, supra,* the court pointed out that there were some exceptions or limitations in the application of the general rule. Some promises to pay money have been enforced, as covenants running with the land, against subsequent holders of the land who took with notice of the covenant. Cf. *Greenfarb v. R. S. K. Realty Corp.,* 256 N.Y. 130, 175 N.E. 649; *Morgan Lake Co. v. New York, N. H. & H. R. R. Co., supra.* It may be difficult to classify these exceptions or to formulate a test of whether a particular covenant to pay money or to perform some other act falls within the general rule that ordinarily an affirmative covenant is a personal and not a real covenant, or falls outside the limitations placed upon the general rule. At least it must "touch" or "concern" the land in a substantial degree, and though it may be inexpedient and perhaps impossible to formulate a rigid test or definition which will be entirely satisfactory or which can be applied mechanically in all cases, we should at least be able to state the problem and find a reasonable method of approach to it. It has been suggested that a covenant which runs with the land must affect the legal relations—the advantages and the burdens—of the parties to the covenant, as owners of particular parcels of land and not merely as members of the community in general, such as taxpayers or owners of other land. Clark, op. cit. p. 76. Cf. Professor Bigelow's article on The Contents of Covenants in Leases, 12 Mich.L.Rev. 639; 30 Law Quarterly Review, 319. That method of approach has the merit of realism. The test is based on the effect of the covenant rather than on technical distinctions. Does the covenant impose, on the one hand, a burden upon an interest in land, which on the other hand increases the value of a different interest in the same or related land?

Even though we accept that approach and test, it still remains true that whether a particular covenant is sufficiently connected with the use of land to run with the land, must be in many cases a question of degree. A promise to pay for something to be done in connection with the promisor's land does not differ essentially from a promise by the promisor to do the thing himself, and both promises constitute, in a substantial sense, a restriction upon the owner's right to use the land, and a burden upon the legal interest of the owner. On the other hand, a covenant to perform or pay for the performance of an affirmative act disconnected with the use of the land cannot ordinarily touch or concern the land in any substantial degree. Thus, unless we exalt technical form over substance, the distinction between covenants which run with land and covenants which are personal, must depend upon the effect of the covenant on the legal rights which otherwise would flow from ownership of land and which are connected with the land. The problem then is: Does the covenant in purpose and effect substantially alter these rights?
. . .

Looking at the problem presented in this case . . . and stressing the intent and substantial effect of the covenant rather than its form, it seems clear that the covenant may properly be said to touch and concern the land of the defendant and its burden should run with the land. True, it calls for payment of a sum of money to be expended for "public purposes" upon land other than the land conveyed by Neponsit Realty Company to plaintiff's predecessor in title. By that conveyance the grantee, however, obtained not only title to particular lots, but an easement or right of common enjoyment with other property owners in roads, beaches, public parks or spaces and improvements in the same tract. For full enjoyment in common by the defendant and other property owners of these easements or rights, the roads and public places must be maintained. In order that the burden of maintaining public improvements should rest upon the land benefited by the improvements, the grantor exacted from the grantee of the land with its appurtenant easement or right of enjoyment a covenant that the burden of paying the cost should be inseparably attached to the land which enjoys the benefit. It is plain that any distinction or definition which would exclude such a covenant from the classification of covenants which "touch" or "concern" the land would be based on form and not on substance.

Another difficulty remains. Though between the grantor and the grantee there was privity of estate, the covenant provides that its benefit shall run to the assigns of the grantor who "may include a Property Owners' Association which may hereafter be organized for the purposes referred to in this paragraph." The plaintiff has been organized to receive the sums payable by the property owners and to expend them for the benefit of such owners. Various definitions have been formulated of "privity of estate" in connection with covenants that run with the land, but none of such definitions seems to cover the relationship between the plaintiff and the defendant in this case. The plaintiff has not succeeded to the ownership of any property of the grantor. It does not appear that it ever had title to the streets or public places upon which charges which are payable to it must be expended. It does not appear that it owns any other property in the residential tract to which any easement or right of enjoyment in such property is appurtenant. It is created solely to act as the assignee of the benefit of the covenant, and it has no interest of its own in the enforcement of the covenant.

The arguments that under such circumstances the plaintiff has no right of action to enforce a covenant running with the land are all based upon a distinction between the corporate property owners association and the property owners for whose benefit the association has been formed. If that distinction may be ignored, then the basis of the arguments is destroyed. How far privity of estate in technical form is necessary to enforce in equity a restrictive covenant upon the use of land, presents an interesting question. Enforcement of such covenants rests upon equitable principles, *Tulk v. Moxhay*, 2 Phillips, 774; *Trustees of Columbia College v. Lynch*, 70 N.Y. 440, 26 Am.Rep. 615; *Korn v. Campbell*, 192 N.Y. 490, 85 N.E. 687, 37 L.R.A., N.S., 1, 127 Am.St.Rep. 925, and at times, at least, the violation "of the restrictive covenant may be restrained at the suit of one who owns property or for whose benefit the restriction was established, irrespective of whether there were privity either of estate or of contract between the parties, or whether an action at law were maintainable." *Chesebro v. Moers*, 233 N.Y. 75, 80, 134 N.E. 842, 843, 21 A.L.R. 1270. The covenant in this case does not fall exactly within any classification of "restrictive" covenants, which have been enforced in this State, *[c]f. Korn v. Campbell*, 192 N.Y. 490, 85 N.E. 687, 37 L.R.A.,N.S., 1, 127 Am.St.Rep. 925, and no right to enforce even a restrictive covenant has been sustained in this State where the plaintiff did not own property which would benefit by such enforcement so that some of the elements of an equitable servitude are present. In some jurisdictions it has been held that no action may be maintained without such elements. *But cf. VanSant v. Rose*, 260 Ill. 401, 103 N.E. 194, 49 L.R.A.,N.S., 186. We do not attempt to decide now how far the rule of *Trustees of Columbia College v. Lynch, supra,* will be carried, or to formulate a definite rule as to when, or even whether, covenants in a deed will be enforced, upon equitable principles, against subsequent purchasers with notice, at the suit of a party without privity of contract or estate. *Cf.* "Equitable Rights and Liabilities of Strangers to a Contract," by Harlan F. Stone, 18 Columbia Law Review, 291. There is no need to resort to such a rule if the courts may look behind the corporate form of the plaintiff.

The corporate plaintiff has been formed as a convenient instrument by which the property owners may advance their common interests. We do not ignore the corporate form when we recognize that the Neponsit Property Owners' Association, Inc., is acting as the agent or representative of the Neponsit property owners. As we have said in another case: when Neponsit Property Owners' Association, Inc., "was formed, the property owners were expected to, and have looked to that organization as the medium through which enjoyment of their common right might be preserved equally for all." *Matter of City of New York, Public Beach, Borough of Queens*, 269 N.Y. 64, 75, 199 N.E. 5, 9. Under the conditions thus presented we said: "It may be difficult, or even impossible to classify into recognized categories the nature of the interest of the membership corporation and its members in the land. The corporate entity cannot be disregarded, nor can the separate interests of the members of the corporation" [*Id.* at 73, 199 N.E. 8]. Only blind adherence to an ancient formula devised to meet entirely different conditions could constrain the court to hold that a corporation formed as a medium for the enjoyment of common rights of property owners owns no property which would benefit by enforcement of common rights and has no cause of action in equity to enforce the covenant upon which such common rights depend. Every reason which in other circumstances may justify the ancient formula may be urged in support of the conclusion that the formula should not be applied in this case. In substance if not in form the covenant is a restrictive covenant which touches and concerns the defendant's land, and in substance, if not in form, there is privity of estate between the plaintiff and the defendant....

The order should be affirmed, with costs, and the certified questions answered in the affirmative.

Notes

1. *Identifying the* Neponsit *"Touch and Concern" Test.* In *Neponsit*, the court phrases the touch and concern test in two distinct ways. First, the court states that a covenant "touches and concerns" the land when it "affect[s] the legal relations—the advantages and burdens—of the parties to the covenant, *as owners of particular parcels of land and not merely as members of the community in general, such as taxpayers or owners of other land.* . . . The test is based on the effect of the covenant rather than on technical distinctions." Second, the court suggests that the test is whether "the covenant impose[s], on the one hand, a burden upon an interest in land, which on the other hand increases the value of a different interest in the same or related land." Is the latter statement of the touch and concern standard useful in helping to identify whether a particular covenant should run with the land?

2. *The Decision to Litigate in* Neponsit. At the time of the litigation in *Neponsit*, the covenant in question had only a few years left to run, and the total amount at stake was relatively small. So why did Emigrant Bank decide to litigate the case all the way to the Court of Appeals of New York? What do you think was the Bank's objective in this litigation? *See* Stewart E. Sterk, *Neponsit Property Owners' Association v. Emigrant Industrial Savings Bank*, Property Stories 301–22 (2004).

3. *Who Can Enforce? Owners' Associations and the Role of "Privity."* In modern subdivision development today, the governing documents authorize enforcement of covenants both by the owners' association and by any individual owner. This dual authorization is useful because it makes clear that any owner could enforce a restrictive covenant against another unit owner even if the owners' association itself refused to take enforcement action. *Neponsit* further demonstrates why this dual authorization is prudent. The developer in *Neponsit* did not transfer ownership of any common areas to the owners' association—thus, technically, one might question (as did Emigrant Bank) whether the association had sufficient privity of estate to enforce the covenant. The *Neponsit* court permitted the association to enforce the covenant as the agent of the lot owners, ignoring any technical lack of vertical privity between the developer and the association. Can you explain how the court's analysis in *Neponsit* foreshadows the analysis by which the new Restatement has rejected the privity requirement?

4. *Secured Monetary Obligations as Enforceable Servitudes.* Was the court correct to focus upon whether there was sufficient privity in *Neponsit*? The Association in *Neponsit* sought to enforce a *lien* securing the assessment obligation. Was this assessment covenant, by its terms, backed by a lien? Does the presence of a lien to secure the monetary obligation render servitude law irrelevant to the outcome of the case? *Cf. University Gardens Prop. Owners Ass'n v. Steinberg*, 40 Misc.2d 816, 244 N.Y.S.2d 208 (1963). For example, suppose Cheever borrowed money from Bank to pay for his daughter's college expenses. Cheever signed a promissory note to Bank and further granted Bank a mortgage to secure repayment of the loan. Under *Neponsit*, would Cheever's promise to repay Bank be "a promise to pay for something to be done in connection with the promisor's land"? Even if not,

does it matter? Under mortgage law, wouldn't the mortgage lien securing repayment of Cheever's loan be enforceable against Cheever's successors?

Sometimes, covenants are created in conjunction with business transactions that may have only an indirect relation to the burdened land. For example, suppose that Wells conveys Blueacre to Monahan, but subject to a covenant that provides "neither grantee nor her heirs, successors, or assigns shall use Blueacre for the purposes of operating a grocery store." Wells places the restriction on Blueacre because she does not want the owner of Blueacre to compete with the grocery store that Wells operates in the same neighborhood. Does this covenant sufficiently "touch and concern" land so as to be binding against successors to Blueacre? Is there a risk of substantial harm if this type of covenant is allowed to run with title to land?

CAULLETT v. STANLEY STILWELL & SONS, INC.

Superior Court of New Jersey, Appellate Division.
67 N.J.Super. 111, 170 A.2d 52 (1961).

FREUND, J.A.D. This is an action in the nature of a bill to quiet title to a parcel of land in the Township of Holmdel. Defendant appeals from the entry of summary judgment in favor of plaintiffs.

Defendant, a developer, by warranty deed conveyed the subject property, consisting of a lot approximately one acre in size, to the plaintiffs for a consideration of $4,000. The deed was delivered on January 13, 1959. Following the collapse of negotiations directed towards agreement on the construction by defendant of a dwelling on the transferred premises, the present suit was instituted.

The focal point of the action is a recital in the deed, inserted under the heading of "covenants, agreements and restrictions," to the effect that: "(i) The grantors reserve the right to build or construct the original dwelling or building on said premises." The item is one of those designated in the instrument as "covenants running with the land ... (which) shall bind the purchasers, their heirs, executors, administrators and assigns."

In support of their motion for summary judgment, plaintiffs set forth that no contract exists or ever did exist between the parties for the construction of a dwelling or building on the premises. The principal officer of the defendant corporation, in a countering affidavit, stated that one of the foremost considerations in fixing the price of the lot, and one of the primary conditions of the sale as it was effected, was the understanding that when the purchasers declared themselves ready and able to build, defendant would act as general contractor.

The trial judge held that the provision in question was unenforceable and should properly be stricken from the deed. He granted plaintiffs the relief demanded in their complaint, namely, an adjudication that (1) defendant has no claim, right or interest in and to the lands by virtue of the clause in question; (2) defendant has no interest, right or cause of action against plaintiffs by virtue of the covenant; and (3) the clause in question is stricken from the deed and declared null, void and of no further force and effect.

The central issue argued on the appeal is whether the recital constitutes an enforceable covenant restricting the use of plaintiffs' land. Defendant urges that it comprises an ordinary property restriction, entered into for the benefit of the grantor and his retained lands. Plaintiff maintains that the clause is too vague to be capable of enforcement and that, in any event, it amounts to no more than a personal covenant which in no way affects or burdens the realty and has no place in an instrument establishing and delimiting the title to same.

While restrictive covenants are to be construed realistically in the light of the circumstances under which they were created, counter considerations, favoring the free transferability of land, have produced the rule that incursions on the use of property will not be enforced unless their meaning is clear and free from doubt. Thus, if the covenants or restrictions are vague or ambiguous, they should not be construed to impair the alienability of the subject property. . . .

Approached from a direction compatible with the constructional principles set forth above, it is clear that the deed item in question is incapable of enforcement and is therefore not restrictive of plaintiffs' title. The clause is descriptive of neither the type of structure to be built, the cost thereof, or the duration of the grantees' obligation. While it might conceivably have been intended to grant to defendant a right of first refusal on construction bids on the property, this is by no means its palpable design. What, for example, would be its effect were plaintiffs to erect a structure by their own hands?

It must be remembered that a restrictive covenant is in its inception a mere contract, subject to the interpretative doctrines of contract law which focus on the parties' mutual purpose. *See* 3 Williston, Contracts (rev. ed. 1936), § 620, pp. 1787–88, nn. 5 and 6. A purported contract so obscure that no one can be sure of its meaning is incapable of remedy at law or equity for its alleged breach, and therefore cannot constitute a valid impediment to title.

Moreover, assuming *arguendo* that the clause is sufficiently definite to give defendant a primary option to build whenever plaintiffs should decide to construct a dwelling or building on the premises, it still cannot operate either as a covenant running with the land at law, or as an equitable servitude enforceable against the original grantee and all successors, having notice, to his interest.

In the first place, it is clear to us that the item in question does not satisfy the primary requirement of covenants directly restrictive of title to land—that they "touch and concern" the subject property. To constitute a real rather than a personal covenant, the promise must exercise direct influence on the occupation, use or enjoyment of the premises. It must be a promise "respecting the use of the land," that is, "a use of identified land which is not merely casual and which is not merely an incident in the performance of the promise." 5 Restatement, Property, Scope Note to Part III, pp. 3147–48 (1944).... In substantial accord with the Restatement analysis are *Dunn v. Ryan*, 82 N.J.Eq. 356, 88 A. 1025, 49 L.R.A.,N.S., 1015 (E. & A. 1913), and *Butterhof v. Butterhof*, 84 N.J.L. 285, 86 A. 394 (E. & A. 1913), holding that the breach of deed provisions, to the effect that the grantee would provide support and maintenance for the grantor during the latter's natural life, does not affect the fee conveyed but at most gives rise to an action for damages for failure to perform a collateral covenant.

Thus, to qualify as a covenant properly affecting the subject property, the deed provision must define in some measurable and reasonably permanent fashion the proscriptions of and limitations upon the uses to which the premises may be put. Typical provisions, some of them included in the deed of the parties herein, limit the property to residential purposes, provide minimum setback and acreage requirements, proscribe certain architectural forms, and limit the number of and set the minimum cost of future dwellings to be constructed on the land.

The provision here in issue is not of the variety described above. It pertains to the use of plaintiffs' land only in the very incidental fashion that refusal to allow defendant to build the original structure would seemingly preclude plaintiffs from constructing at all. This is at best a personal arrangement between the two parties, designed to insure defendant a profit on the erection of a dwelling in return, allegedly, for a comparatively low sales price on the land. While there is nothing in our law precluding such an arrangement, as a contract *inter partes*, this form of contract, contemplating a single personal service upon the property, does not affect the title. And the stipulation between the parties in their instrument to the effect that this was a covenant running with the land cannot override the inherently personal nature of their arrangement under established legal principles.

We note, in addition, that even if the deed clause were to be construed as directly restricting plaintiffs' use of their land, *i.e.*, prohibiting erection of a structure until such time as the owner shall permit such construction to be performed by the grantor, the clause would nonetheless comprise neither a legal restriction nor an equitable servitude upon the estate. This is so because whatever the effect of the burden of the covenant, its benefit is clearly personal to the grantor, securing to him a mere commercial advantage in the operation of his business and not enhancing or otherwise affecting the use or value of any retained lands.

Generally prerequisite to a conclusion that a covenant runs with the land at law is a finding that both burdened and benefited properties exist and were intended to be so affected by the contracting parties. Where, however, the *benefit* attaches to the property of one of the parties, the fact that the *burden* is in gross, *i.e.*, personal, does not preclude the covenant from running with the land conveyed. *National Union Bank at Dover v. Segur*, 39 N.J.L. 173 (Sup.Ct.1877). There is no public policy opposed to the running of a benefit, since a continuing benefit is presumed to help rather than hinder the alienability of the property to which it is attached. 5 Powell, Real Property, § 675, p. 173; 5 Restatement, Property, supra, § 543, comment (c), pp. 3255–56. When, however, as here, the *burden* is placed upon the land, and the *benefit* is personal to one of the parties and does not extend to his or other lands, the burden is generally held not to run with the land at law. The policy is strong against hindering the alienability of one property where no corresponding enhancement accrues to surrounding lands. *See* 5 Restatement, Property, *supra*, § 537, pp. 3218–24; 2 American Law of Property, § 9.13, pp. 373–76 (1952).

Nor can the covenant be enforced as an equitable servitude where the benefit is in gross and neither affects retained land of the grantor nor is part of a neighborhood scheme of similar restrictions. Purporting to follow the case of *Tulk v. Moxhay*, 2 Phil. 774, 41 Eng.Rep. 1143 (Ch.1848), our courts have consistently enforced the covenantal rights of an owner of benefited property against a successor, with notice, to the burdened land, even though the covenant did not run with the land at law. However, the right to urge enforcement of a servitude against the burdened land "depends primarily on the covenant's having been made for the benefit" of other land, either retained by the grantor or part of a perceptible neighborhood scheme. *Hayes v. Waverly & Passaic R.R. Co.*, 51 N.J.Eq. 345, 348, 27 A. 648 (Ch.1893). Where the benefit is purely personal to the grantor, and has not been directed towards the improvement of neighboring properties, it cannot pass as an incident to any of his retained land and therefore is not considered to burden the conveyed premises but only, at best, to obligate the grantee personally. See 2 Tiffany, Real Property, § 399, pp. 1441–42 (1920).

The latter doctrine has recently come under considerable criticism, see 2 American Law of Property, supra, § 9.32, pp. 428–30, and has even been rejected in some jurisdictions, thus permitting attachment of an equitable servitude even though the benefit is in gross. *See, e.g., Pratte v. Balatsos*, 99 N.H. 430, 113 A.2d 492 (Sup.Ct.1955). But the law in this jurisdiction, as last authoritatively declared, is that "from the very nature of the equitable restriction arising from a restrictive covenant," the "existence of the dominant estate is . . . essential to the validity of the servitude granted . . . ." *Welitoff v. Kohl*, 105 N.J.Eq. 181, 189, 147 A. 390, 393, 66 A.L.R. 1317 (E. & A. 1929).

We therefore conclude that the clause in question, even were we to assume both its clarity and its direct operation upon the use of plaintiffs' land, cannot comprise an impairment of plaintiffs' title, because of the indisputably personal nature of the benefit conferred thereby. An intention to dispense broader land use benefits, in the form of a neighborhood scheme, cannot here be found, as in effect conceded by defendant and as expressly stipulated in the parties' deed. . . .

Notes

1. Caullett *and the Common Law's Treatment of "Personal" Covenants*. The court in *Caullett* concludes that the covenant established a tying arrangement (*i.e.*, tying acquisition of the land to the use of Stilwell & Sons construction services), and that this tying arrangement created only a personal benefit to Stilwell & Sons. In declaring the covenant unenforceable, the *Caullett* case articulated the traditional rule that *if the benefit of a covenant is in gross (personal), the burden of that covenant will not run with the land to bind a successor to the covenantor.*

But why refuse to enforce such arrangements against successors? A covenant like the one in *Caullett* raises two potentially related (and yet also potentially distinct) sets of concerns. The first concern is the potential impact of covenant enforcement on the alienability of land. Decisions like *Caullett* reflected the traditional judicial belief that courts should not burden the free alienability of land by enforcing against successors covenants that are related to the person or entity owning the land, rather than being *inherently related to the land itself*. As a practical matter, would the enforcement of this covenant have a substantial impact upon Caullett's ability to transfer the land? [Hint: If you were considering buying the lot from Caullett, how would the covenant affect your decisionmaking?] Did the court *really* evaluate whether the enforcement of the covenant would unreasonably restrain the alienation of the land? Should it have?

The second concern is whether a covenant that is concededly "land-related" might still offend some *other public policy*—for example, by restricting competition in a free market, by imposing upon customers practices perceived as predatory, or by restricting transfers based upon racial classification or other form of invidious discrimination. Is there any compelling public policy that would justify refusing to allow developers like Stilwell & Sons to "tie" lot sales and general contracting services? What additional information would you like to know in reaching a conclusion?

A final question about *Caullett*: given that Caullett was the original covenantor, whether the covenant ran with the land was irrelevant to the question of his own liability on the covenant. So why did the court even discuss whether the covenant "touched and concerned" the land?

2. *Other Forms of "Business" Restrictions.* A commonly used form of business covenant is the covenant not to compete. For example, consider the non-compete covenant described on page 623 before *Caullett*. Under the rule established in early decisions, Wells could not have enforced the covenant against a successor owner of Blueacre; many such courts concluded that the benefit of a non-compete covenant was personal to the covenantee. *See, e.g., Norcross v. James*, 140 Mass. 188, 2 N.E. 946 (1885). As explained in Chapter 7, however, courts generally have enforced covenants not to compete in the landlord-tenant context, especially as the use of such covenants has become more pervasive. Not surprisingly, then, the weight of recent authority has enforced covenants not to compete against successors to the burdened land. *See, e.g., Whitinsville Plaza, Inc. v. Kotseas*, 378 Mass. 85, 390 N.E.2d 243 (1979) (overruling *Norcross*). Can this result be reconciled

with the *Caullett* court's discussion of the "touch and concern" doctrine? If so, how?

Courts also have struggled with other types of tying arrangements. In the early 20th century, gasoline companies would sell land to a prospective gas station proprietor and require the proprietor (and successors) to purchase all gasoline sold at the site from the grantor/gasoline company. [Today, gas companies handle such tie-ins through franchising arrangements.] For example, suppose that Barnes and Chen decide to dissolve their partnership of gas stations. In the dissolution, Barnes conveys his interest in five of the stations to Chen, pursuant to a deed that explicitly obligates Chen and his successors to purchase all of the gas sold in those stations from Barnes (who has an agency relationship with Conoco). Chen later sells one of the stations to Whitfield, who begins purchasing her gas from Exxon. Barnes sues Whitfield for damages for breach of the gas-purchase covenant and seeks an injunction to compel Whitfield to perform the covenant. Should the court enforce this covenant against Whitfield? *Compare Montgomery v. Creager*, 22 S.W.2d 463 (Tex. Ct. App. 1929) (no) with *Bill Wolf Petroleum Corp. v. Chock Full of Power Gasoline Corp.*, 41 A.D.2d 950, 344 N.Y.S.2d 30 (1973) (yes). Would your analysis be different if the duration of the gas-purchase covenant was one year? 20 years? Perpetual?

c. ***Will "Touch and Concern" Survive?—Law Reform and the Restatement of Servitudes.*** Many scholars have long argued that the "touch and concern" requirement as applied by American courts is too amorphous and too easily manipulated analytically—and that this prevents the law from achieving meaningful predictability about the extent to which courts will enforce servitudes. This uncertainty is evident in the split of authority regarding the enforceability of "business" covenants like non-compete covenants and tying arrangements.

As Professor Lawrence Berger has argued, the touch and concern requirement should function as a means of effectuating the presumed intention of the community regarding the enforceability of a covenant—thus permitting a court to invalidate restrictions that would be out of step with the "normal, usual or probable understandings of the community." Lawrence Berger, *A Policy Analysis of Promises Respecting the Use of Land*, 55 Minn. L. Rev. 167, 208–09 (1970). Berger rejected the notion that a covenant was either "personal" or "touched and concerned" land—though he acknowledged that covenant law traditionally took this dichotomy as a given. Instead, he argued that a covenant should be viewed as either (a) "bound up with an interest in land," (b) personal, or (c) both. *Id.* at 211. In category (c), for example, Berger placed the non-compete covenant—arguing that in many circumstances, reasonable parties would have understood it to be *both* personal to the covenantee (benefiting the covenantee's business) *and* intended to run with the land (so as to prevent the burdened land from being used to compete with the covenantee). Berger suggested that in cases of doubt or ambiguity, a jury (which "theoretically represents the judgment and knowledge of the intelligent members of the community") could appropriately resolve doubt about the intended nature of a covenant. However, the law traditionally treated the question whether a covenant touched and concerned land as a question of law for judicial determination. Perhaps not surprisingly, then, the "touch and concern" standard has proved sufficiently "manipulable" that differing judges can use the same rhetoric either to enforce or invalidate the same type of covenant.

Another vocal critic of the touch and concern standard is Professor Susan French, who served as the Reporter for the new Restatement of Servitudes. Professor French has argued that while courts nominally identified "touch and concern" as a requirement for the creation of a covenant running with the land, courts effectively used the touch and concern standard as a doctrine for terminating servitudes:

> Throughout the 19th and early 20th centuries, the touch-or-concern doctrine played an important role in servitudes law by providing courts with a flexible, discretionary power to disallow and terminate servitudes. The doctrine was particularly useful in that era because it permitted courts to invalidate servitudes they found unwise or pernicious without articulating the policy reasons for their decisions, and it permitted them to terminate obsolete and unwise servitudes without explicitly developing termination doctrines, or acknowledging what they were doing. The vagueness of the doctrine's content afforded a wide range of judicial discretion in policing servitudes. . . .
>
> In the 20th century, the need for the touch-or-concern doctrine decreased markedly as other, more satisfactory doctrines became available, and as increasing experience with servitudes brought more discriminating understanding of the problems presented by various servitude arrangements. Courts began addressing directly the problems created by restraints on trade and competition and restraints on alienation, both direct and indirect. More recently, they have begun applying the unconscionability doctrine, developed in commercial law, to servitudes as well as to other contracts. These doctrines provide courts with a comprehensive means of policing servitude arrangements for abuses that would have been dealt with by the touch-or-concern doctrine in the 19th century. Twentieth century courts have also had available the changed-conditions doctrine, and increased flexibility in remedies, which permit them to address the questions whether enforcement should be available and, if so, whether damages or injunctive relief is appropriate, at the point of relief, rather than as a consequence of factors present at creation of the servitude. [Restatement of Servitudes § 3.2, cmt. b.]

Consistent with these critiques, the Restatement of Servitudes purports to reject the "touch and concern" standard. While it concedes that some legal limitation is needed to protect against the social harms that servitudes may inflict, the Restatement concluded that the "touch and concern" approach had proven over-inclusive in some circumstances (*i.e.*, invalidating servitudes that ought to be enforced) and under-inclusive in others (*i.e.*, enforcing servitudes that ought not bind successors). In place of the "touch and concern" standard, the Restatement advocates a "public policy" limitation on enforceability and offers a series of subject-matter limitations intended to focus judicial attention on precisely *why* a particular covenant either advances or contravenes public policy.

RESTATEMENT (THIRD) OF PROPERTY: SERVITUDES

§ 3.1 GENERAL RULE. A servitude ... is valid unless it is illegal or unconstitutional or violates public policy. Servitudes that are invalid because they violate public policy include, but are not limited to:

(1) Servitudes that are arbitrary, spiteful, or capricious;

(2) Servitudes that unreasonably burden fundamental constitutional rights;

(3) Servitudes that impose unreasonable restraints on alienation . . . .

(4) Servitudes that impose unreasonable restraints on trade or competition . . . , and

(5) Servitudes that are unconscionable . . . .

Comment:

a. *Historical Note and Rationale.* This section applies the modern principle of freedom of contract to creation of servitudes. . . .

e. *Servitudes that violate public policy.* . . . Traditional approaches to protecting the public welfare from servitudes have included blanket prohibitions on whole categories of potential servitudes like those that are not for the benefit of adjacent land (prohibition on benefits in gross, requirement that both burden and benefit touch or concern the land), or affirmative burdens, or burdens that do not touch or concern the land. These kinds of prohibitions were apparently based on assumptions that, as a group, servitudes with these characteristics posed unacceptable risks of social harm. Because the assumptions were not articulated, however, they became very difficult to apply when it became apparent that at least some of the prohibited servitudes created significant social value. Other rules that invalidate servitudes based on the degree of an identified harm they cause have been much more successful. Targeting servitudes that create unreasonable restraints on alienation, or servitudes that are unconscionable, instead of servitudes that fail to touch or concern the land, for example, avoids problems of both over-and under-inclusion. . . .

Instead of attempting to limit allowable servitudes to those that are unlikely to pose threats to the general welfare, or to those where the threat can be avoided by applying established rules against restraints on alienation and competition, or attempting to anticipate all the servitudes that might threaten the social harm, this section states the overarching principle that lies behind all the particular rules that invalidate servitudes and other property arrangements because of the risks they pose to the general welfare. . . .

g. *Arbitrary, spiteful, and capricious servitudes are invalid.* Servitudes found to be arbitrary, spiteful, or capricious are invalid. Arbitrary normally means that the purpose is not legitimate, or that the means adopted have no reasonable relationship to accomplishment of the purpose. Spiteful means that the primary purpose of the servitude was to cause harm to another, rather than to secure a benefit to the creating party or parties. Capricious generally means that no legitimate purpose for creating the servitude is discernible. Servitudes created out of spite or malice, or merely to satisfy a whim of the grantor, are probably invalid even between the original parties, but if valid between the original parties, are certainly invalid as servitudes. Most arbitrary and capricious servitudes will negatively affect the value of the land and may be invalidated as unreasonable indirect restraints on alienation under § 3.5. Even if they have no effect on marketability of the property, however, they are invalid because using the legal system to enforce arbitrary and capricious arrangements violates public policy. Courts should be reluctant to find a servitude that has little impact on outsiders, and was agreed upon in an exchange for value, arbitrary or capricious because the parties are usually the best judge of what makes sense to them and for their property. In donative transfers, particularly where the transfer is at the death of the transferor, courts may be less reluctant to find invalidity because there are no market checks on the servitude's utility or effect on the value of the property....

i. *Resolving public policy claims requires balancing interests.* Resolving claims that a servitude violates public policy requires assessing the impact of the servitude, identifying the public interests that would be adversely affected by leaving the servitude in force, and weighing the predictable harm against the interests in enforcing the servitude. Only if the risks of social harm outweigh the benefits of enforcing the servitude is the servitude likely to be held invalid. The policies favoring freedom of contract, freedom to dispose of one's property, and protection of legitimate-expectation interests nearly always weigh in favor of the validity of voluntarily created servitudes. A host of other policies, too numerous to catalog, weigh in the other direction. Policies favoring privacy and liberty in choice of lifestyle, freedom of religion, freedom of speech and expression, access to the legal system, discouraging bad faith and unfair dealing, encouraging free competition, and socially productive uses of land have been implicated by servitudes. Other policies that become involved may include those protecting family relationships from coercive attempts to disrupt them, and protecting weaker groups in society from servitudes that exclude them from opportunities enjoyed by more fortunate groups to acquire desirable property for housing or access to necessary services.

The balancing process involved in determining whether a servitude should be invalidated is necessarily imprecise. Often the court must weigh several conflicting policies to determine whether an overriding interest of society outweighs the interests supporting validity of the servitude. In addition to identifying and assessing the relative strength of the policies involved, courts must also assess the extent to which the challenged servitude is likely to have an adverse impact on the societal interests involved. In assessing the likely adverse impact, the possibility that a ruling validating a servitude will encourage developers and others to use similar servitudes should be taken into account. The likely duration of a servitude is often an important factor in assessing its potential for long-term harm. The ease with which it could be modified or terminated is an important factor in determining its likely duration and potential for harm. . . .

§ 3.2 **TOUCH–OR–CONCERN DOCTRINE SUPERSEDED**. Neither the burden nor the benefit of a covenant is required to touch or concern land in order for the covenant to be valid as a servitude. Whether a servitude is valid is determined under the general rule stated in § 3.1 and the particular rules stated in §§ 3.4 through 3.7.

Comment: . . .

b. *Historical note and rationale.* . . . Although courts still use the rhetoric of touch or concern, they increasingly determine the validity of servitudes on the basis of the rules stated in this Chapter. They look to the legitimacy and importance of the purposes to be served by the servitude in the particular context, the fairness of the arrangement, its impact on alienability and marketability of the property, its impact on competition, and the degree to which it interferes with the fundamental rights and expectations of property owners. In modern law there is no need to use the obsolete and confusing rhetoric of touch or concern to determine whether the parties were successful in creating an interest that runs with the land. . . .

e. *Affirmative burdens.* . . . The reluctance [to allow landowners to attach affirmative burdens to their land] may also be explained by the additional risks confronting the landowner whose property is subject to an affirmative covenant. If the obligation is monetary, or can be converted to a monetary obligation, it may be enforceable by a lien, which may result in loss of the land. Since the obligation is also enforceable by damages, the landowner's potential losses extend to other assets reachable in satisfaction of a money judgment. Another concern is that the obligation may become so significant in relation to the value of the land that marketability may be seriously affected.

Although these concerns remain significant, the clear utility of affirmative servitude burdens in modern land-development practice has led to elimination of all categorical restrictions on their use. Affirmative obligations to pay dues to property-owners associations, to maintain commonly owned facilities, to trim vegetation to protect views, to maintain facades of historic buildings, and the like are widespread. Affirmative obligations that should not be permitted as servitudes can be invalidated under the rules stated in §§ 3.5 through 3.7; those which should be modified or terminated can be dealt with adequately under the rules stated in Chapters 7 and 8.

§ 3.4 DIRECT RESTRAINTS ON ALIENATION. A servitude that imposes a direct restraint on alienation of the burdened estate is invalid if the restraint is unreasonable. Reasonableness is determined by weighing the utility of the restraint against the injurious consequences of enforcing the restraint.

§ 3.5 INDIRECT RESTRAINTS ON ALIENATION.

(1) An otherwise valid servitude is valid even if it indirectly restrains alienation by limiting the use that can be made of property, by reducing the amount realizable by the owner on sale or other transfer of the property, or by otherwise reducing the value of the property.

(2) A servitude that lacks a rational justification is invalid.

Comment:

a. *Rationale.* Many servitudes indirectly affect the alienability of property by limiting the numbers of potential buyers or by reducing the amount the owner might otherwise realize on a sale of the property. If the servitude is validly created ... and is not otherwise invalid under the rules stated in this Chapter, the fact that the servitude results in some diminution in return to the owner, or some reduction in the potential market for the property, is not sufficient justification for refusing to give effect to the intent of the parties to create the servitude. Many economic arrangements for spreading the purchase price of property over time and for allocating risk and sharing profit from property development can be attacked as indirect restraints on alienation. If such arrangements are not unconscionable and do not otherwise violate public policy, there is usually no reason to deny the parties freedom of contract. The parties are usually in a better position than judges to decide the economic trade-offs that will enable a transaction to go forward and enhance their overall value....

The purpose of this section is to reject the rule that a servitude must be reasonable. If the servitude is not otherwise invalid because it is illegal, unconstitutional, or against public policy, it need not be reasonable. The only requirement is that there be a rational justification for creating it as a servitude. The fact that the servitude limits the market for property by limiting its use or reducing its value or requires the seller to share sale proceeds with another is irrelevant in determining its validity, so long as there is some rational justification for creation of the servitude. The fact that there may be a rational justification for the obligation is not sufficient; there must be a rational justification for imposing the obligation as a servitude that runs with the land. If there is no rational justification for the servitude, it should not be enforced because there is no real trade-off for the resulting decrease in the value of the land, and the legal system should not be used to enforce irrational arrangements against unwilling participants....

b. *Servitudes lacking rational justification.* Servitudes created in commercial transactions seldom lack rational justification. However, those imposed in connection with donative transfers may be the result of personal caprice on the part of a donor or testator, since the creator of the servitude will not suffer the financial consequences of the servitude. . . .

d. *Use restrictions.* Use restrictions on property are valid even though they severely reduce the value of the property, so long as there is some rational justification for the restriction. Use of property for open space, protection of views, historic preservation, and conservation of habitat for plants and animals provides a rational justification for restrictions that severely limit the value and potential market for property. Limitations on use of property to serve various governmental and charitable purposes are also generally valid so long as the limitations are rationally related to serving a legitimate purpose.

§ 3.6 UNREASONABLE RESTRAINTS ON TRADE OR COMPETITION. A servitude that imposes an unreasonable restraint on trade or competition is invalid.

§ 3.7 UNCONSCIONABILITY. A servitude is invalid if it is unconscionable.

Notes

1. *Some Problems in Applying the "Touch and Concern" Standard and the New Restatement.* Consider how a court should evaluate the following covenants under the traditional "touch and concern" standard and under the standards articulated in the new Restatement. Assume that in each case, the covenant appears in a deed that is effective to convey Blueacre to Chen, and that the deed expressly states the intention of the parties that the covenant will run with the land to bind Chen's successors.

(a) A covenant requiring the owner of Blueacre to provide piano lessons to the owner of the adjoining land (Whiteacre) for a period of 50 years.

(b) A covenant requiring the owner of Blueacre to change his or her name to "Webermeier" and to refrain from consuming alcohol on the land.

(c) A covenant prohibiting the owner of Blueacre from operating a grocery store that would compete with the grantor's nearby store.

(d) A covenant requiring the owner of Blueacre to pay to the grantor 25% of any profit earned on future sales of the land.

(e) A covenant requiring the owner of Blueacre to pay a monthly membership fee for a health and fitness club located within the neighborhood in which Blueacre is located. *Compare Streams Sports Club, Ltd. v. Richmond,* 99 Ill.2d 182, 75 Ill.Dec. 667, 457 N.E.2d 1226 (1983) *with Raintree Corp. v. Rowe,* 38 N.C.App. 664, 248 S.E.2d 904 (1978). Should it matter whether the club was operated for profit and allowed people outside the subdivision to join?

(f) A covenant requiring the owner of Blueacre to contribute 1% of the proceeds of any resale of the land to Habitat for Humanity to fund the construction of low-income housing within the community.

(g) A covenant requiring the owner of Blueacre to purchase water to be supplied by the grantor. [Assume that the current owner of Blueacre has constructed a well and no longer wishes to purchase water from the grantor.] Does it matter that the water is no longer needed? Does it matter whether the covenant was time-limited or perpetual? Would your analysis be different if the grantor was refusing to provide water and the owner of Blueacre was suing to enforce the covenant? *See Eagle Enters. v. Gross*, 39 N.Y.2d 505, 384 N.Y.S.2d 717, 349 N.E.2d 816 (1976).

2. *Rights of First Refusal and Repurchase Options.* Assume that Greta sells land to Jane, and inserts a provision in the deed stating: "Grantee hereby agrees, for itself, its heirs and assigns, that Grantor shall have the right to purchase the premises for $100,000 in the event Grantee should determine to sell the premises." Jane then dies, leaving a will that devises the premises to Fred. Fred attempts to sell the premises. Can Greta enforce her right to purchase the premises? What other information would you like to have to advise Greta? *Compare Drayson v. Wolff*, 277 Ill.App.3d 975, 214 Ill.Dec. 632, 661 N.E.2d 486 (1996) (right of first refusal to purchase at market price for a defined period touches and concerns land) *with Low v. Spellman*, 629 A.2d 57 (Me. 1993) (perpetual right of first refusal to purchase at fixed price did not bind successors because it violated Rule Against Perpetuities and constituted an unreasonable restraint on alienation). [Note that under § 3.3 of the Restatement of Servitudes, the Rule Against Perpetuities does not apply to servitudes; thus, the Restatement suggests that courts should evaluate options and rights of first refusal under the standards governing the enforceability of indirect restraints on alienation.]

LAWYERING EXERCISE
(Oral Advocacy)

BACKGROUND: Effective lawyers develop excellent oral advocacy skills and the ability to bring those skills to bear in both nonjudicial settings (e.g., negotiation) and judicial settings (oral argument). As Professor Richard Neumann explains, the lawyer approaches oral argument with three goals in mind:

> First, you want to engage the judges' attention by getting them *interested* in your case and *motivated* to rule in your favor. They will hear many other arguments on the same day, and they will read many other briefs in the week they read yours. They will forget your theory of the appeal unless you touch their natural desire to do the right thing.

> Second, you want to focus the judges' attention on *the few aspects of your case that are most determinative*: the one or two issues that are fundamental, the facts that are most prominent in your theory, the rule or rules for which a decision in your favor would become precedent, and the policy considerations that most compel the result for which you argue. . . .

> Third, you want *access to the court's thinking*. Ideally, you want to discover each doubt the judges have about your theory and every

confusion they entertain about any part of your case—all so you can satisfy doubt and clear up confusion. And you want to learn which issues the judges think are most important: if those are profitable issues for you, you can concentrate on them, and if they are the wrong issues, you can try to persuade the court of that. [Richard K. Neumann, Jr., Legal Reasoning and Legal Writing: Structure, Strategy, and Style 399 (4th ed. 2001) (emphasis in original).]

SITUATION: In 1996, your client David Rosenshein bought a parcel of land ("Lot A") in Peabody for $775,000. Shortly thereafter, he began negotiating to buy the adjoining parcel from Willowdale Realty Trust (the "Willowdale parcel"). Rosenshein planned to combine the two parcels into one parcel large enough to develop as a mall. However, Rosenshein was unable to reach an agreement to buy the Willowdale Parcel.

In 1997, Rosenshein sold Lot A to North Shore Auto Brokers, Inc. ("North Shore") for $1,250,000, subject to a covenant that provided as follows:

> This conveyance is made on the express condition and Grantee covenants for the benefit of Grantor [Rosenshein] that neither Grantee nor its successors or assigns shall at any time hereafter develop, directly or indirectly, the land described above and conveyed by this deed [Lot A] together with the [Willowdale parcel].

In 1999, North Shore sold Lot A to Smith, subject to the restriction, for $1,675,000. Smith eventually defaulted on his mortgage, and in 2001, the mortgagee foreclosed and took title to Lot A. The mortgagee attempted to sell Lot A, but several sales fell through when buyers objected to the covenant. Finally, in January 2004, the mortgagee sold Lot A to William Garland for $550,000.

Last month, Garland entered into an agreement with Willowdale Realty Trust to combine Lot A and the Willowdale parcel into one parcel suitable for a new Wal–Mart Supercenter. Rosenshein demanded a $200,000 payment to release his covenant rights. Garland refused to pay and filed a lawsuit seeking a declaration that the covenant was invalid and did not bind him. The applicable state statute provides that a promissory servitude may be enforced only if it "is at the time of the proceeding of actual and substantial benefit to a person claiming rights of enforcement." The trial judge granted summary judgment for Garland, holding that the covenant was personal and not of "actual and substantial benefit" to Lot A. Rosenshein has appealed, and the case is now pending before the state's supreme court.

TASK: In light of the preceding materials, prepare the argument you would make on Rosenshein's behalf seeking a reversal of the trial court's judgment.

3. *Promissory Servitudes in Residential Servitude Regimes: The Modern Common Interest Community*

a. *Introduction.* Although promissory servitudes are used in a wide variety of settings, they appear most frequently in residential developments often called "Common Interest Communities" (CICs). The basic element of all CICs is separate ownership of individual homes or units combined with common ownership (directly or indirectly) of common areas. CICs have emerged in three different forms: condominiums,[9] cooperatives,[10] and residential subdivisions with homeowners' associations (HOAs).[11] [Gradually, these three forms of CICs are coming to be seen as substantively the same, even though their original legal forms were distinct.]

The typical CIC is administered by an owners' association, which serves a number of related functions critical to community life. The owners' association is responsible for regulating potentially conflicting or undesired uses within the community by enforcing the community's restrictive covenants. In many cases, the association is also responsible for managing and maintaining the community's common assets (which might include streets, parks, recreational facilities, and any other common areas). In these circumstances, the association is empowered to establish and collect assessments—thereby spreading among all owners the costs of constructing and maintaining the community's common facilities.

The remainder of this chapter looks at the law of promissory servitudes through the prism of the CIC. We will begin by discussing the technical aspects of how a developer creates a CIC servitude regime, highlighting how the law has developed implied servitude doctrines in cases where developers failed to take the appropriate technical steps. We will then discuss how CICs finance their operations (page 641) and how they regulate land use and day-to-day life within the community (page 648). We conclude by considering termination and amendment of servitudes, considering the extent to which the law can and should permit CICs to adapt to changed circumstances within the community over time (page 676).

b. *Creating a CIC Servitude Regime*. CICs typically are structured around a promissory servitude regime, established by means of a written instrument typically called a "declaration." Either the declara-

---

9. In the condominium form of ownership, each interior unit is held in fee simple by its owner, while the underlying land, exterior walls, and common areas are owned collectively by the unit owners. Ownership of these interests (the fee simple interest in the unit and the cotenancy interest in the common areas) cannot be separated—*e.g.*, an owner cannot transfer fee title to her unit but retain her cotenancy interest in the common areas.

10. In the cooperative form of ownership, the entire building and underlying land is held in fee simple by an entity (such as a corporation or trust) that manages the operation of the building, acting as a landlord to all residents. Each occupant of the

cooperative building purchases an interest in the ownership entity *and* executes a lease for her/his respective unit. Thus, each occupant is necessarily both a tenant of the ownership entity (the landlord) and a part-owner of that entity. Ownership of these interests (the leasehold estate and the ownership interest in the cooperative entity) cannot be separated.

11. The term "community association" is often used to describe the owners' association in any of these three settings: *i.e.*, this term includes both a condominium association, an HOA or property owners association (POA) in a residential subdivision, or the cooperative governing entity.

tion or a separate document will set forth so-called "Covenants, Conditions and Restrictions" (often referred to as "CC & Rs" or "CCRs").[12] The developer of a CIC prepares the declaration and CCRs with the help of an attorney, usually in conjunction with a map or plat indicating the proposed development as subdivided into lots or units. By their terms, the CCRs are stated as reciprocal restrictions and obligations, burdening each lot covered by the declaration for the reciprocal benefit of every other lot. The developer then records the declaration and CCRs in the county land records before selling any of the lots or units. In this way, when the developer finally sells a lot or unit, the buyer will have record notice of the CCRs and will take the lot subject to all enforceable obligations and restrictions contained in the CCRs. *See, e.g., Citizens for Covenant Compliance v. Anderson*, 12 Cal.4th 345, 47 Cal.Rptr.2d 898, 906 P.2d 1314 (1995).

Sadly, developers have not always established promissory servitude regimes in this careful fashion. For example, suppose that Dave Developer subdivides a parcel into 40 lots. Dave does not file a plat map or a declaration; instead, each time Dave sells a lot, he instead inserts into the deed an identical set of restrictions (including a "residential use only" restriction) purporting to bind the lot owner and her heirs, successors and assigns. Dave then sells the lots in numerical order. When Dave deeds Lot 1 to Buyer 1, Buyer 1 takes Lot 1 subject to the burden of the covenants contained in the deed. In turn, these covenants benefit Dave as the owner of the remaining Lots 2–40. Thus, if Buyer 1 begins to construct a gas station on Lot 1, Dave can enforce the benefit of the covenants in Buyer 1's deed (and can obtain an injunction against Buyer 1's conduct).

When Dave then sells Lot 2 to Buyer 2—with the same restrictions in the deed to Buyer 2—what does Buyer 2 receive? Buyer 2 receives fee simple title to Lot 2, and also receives the benefit of the covenant affecting Lot 1, because that benefit is appurtenant to Lot 2 (as well as Lots 3–40) and thus "runs with" ownership of that lot. Thus, if Buyer 1 begins constructing a gas station on Lot 1, Buyer 2 can now enforce the benefit of the residential-use-only covenant in Buyer 1's deed and can obtain an injunction against Buyer 1's conduct.

Because the deed to Buyer 2 contains the same set of restrictions, Buyer 2 also takes the land subject to those restrictions. But who has the benefit of (*i.e.*, the right to enforce) the restrictions in Buyer 2's deed? The covenant in the deed is a promise between Buyer 2 and Dave. Thus, if Buyer 2 starts constructing a gas station on Lot 2, Dave (as the owner of Lots 3–40) may obtain an injunction against Buyer 2's conduct. But

---

12. Though this terminology is in widespread use, the use of the term "conditions" is erroneous. As explained in Chapter 5, the law traditionally used the term "condition" to describe a restriction upon a possessory estate that, when breached, triggered the divestment or potential divestment of that estate. Modern CIC declarations, however, typically do not provide for forfeiture of title as a sanction for violation of the CCRs.

suppose that Dave fails to act. Can Buyer 1—alarmed at the possibility of a gas station next door—obtain an injunction?

In a purely technical sense, the answer should be no. The covenants in Buyer 2's deed burden Buyer 2 for the benefit of the grantor of the deed, *i.e.*, Dave Developer. But Dave had previously sold Lot 1 to Buyer 1; thus, the covenants in the deed to Buyer 2 do not technically appertain to Lot 1 (which Dave no longer owns). Furthermore, Buyer 1 was not a party to the deed between Dave and Buyer 2, and thus lacks the privity of contract typically required to enforce contractual promises contained in that deed. This creates a "lack of mutuality" problem—Buyer 1 could not enforce the residential-use-only restriction in Buyer 2's deed against Buyer 2—but Buyer 2 can legally enforce the identical restriction in Buyer 1's deed against Buyer 1!

This result would be an unwelcome surprise to Buyer 1, who certainly assumed that the restrictions would benefit every lot in the neighborhood. Buyer 1 would rightly feel hoodwinked by Dave Developer's sloppiness. Thus, under these circumstances—where Dave Developer established a common scheme for developing and marketing the lots as a residential neighborhood—Buyer 1 might ask the court to ***imply*** a reciprocal residential-use-only servitude over Lot 2 in favor of Lot 1. Courts have responded to such arguments in one of three ways.

- A few courts have taken a relatively strict view of the statute of frauds and have refused to imply reciprocal servitudes. *See, e.g., Riley v. Bear Creek Planning Comm.*, 17 Cal.3d 500, 131 Cal.Rptr. 381, 551 P.2d 1213 (1976); *Werner v. Graham*, 181 Cal. 174, 183 P. 945 (1919). Under this view, if the deed to Lot 2 does not expressly state that it also benefits the owner of Lot 1, the covenants in that deed can be enforced only by the grantor (Dave) or his successors—not the owner of Lot 1, who is simply stuck. Why might a court take such a strict view of the statute of frauds?

- Some courts have concluded that the residential-use-only restriction in the deed for Lot 1 (from Dave to Buyer 1) should be interpreted as a reciprocal restriction, *i.e.*, that it also subjected Dave's remaining lots (Lots 2–40) to the identical restriction. Under this view, the deed created an *implied negative reciprocal servitude* over Lots 2–40, benefiting the owner of Lot 1—and thus allowing Buyer 1 to obtain an injunction against Buyer 2's gas station. The leading case accepting this argument and recognizing the implied negative reciprocal servitude is *Sanborn v. McLean*, 233 Mich. 227, 206 N.W. 496 (1925), where the court stated:

  > If the owner of two or more lots, *so situated as to bear the relation*, sells one with restrictions of benefit to the land retained, the servitude becomes mutual, and, during the period of restraint, the owner of the lot or lots retained can do nothing forbidden to the owner of the lot sold. . . . It runs with the land sold by virtue of express fastening and abides with the land retained until loosened by expiration of its period of service or

by events working its destruction. . . . Such a scheme of restrictions must start with a common owner; it cannot arise and fasten upon one lot by reason of other lot owners conforming to a general plan. [206 N.W. at 497 (emphasis added).]

Which lots are "so situated as to bear the relation"? Courts recognizing an implied negative reciprocal servitude have uniformly required that the party seeking to enforce such a servitude demonstrate the existence of a "common scheme" of restrictions that existed at the time of the original severance of the dominant and servient parcels. In light of the requirements for the enforcement of a promissory servitude (page 609), what elements would seem to support a finding of such a "common scheme"? Can you explain why a "common scheme" (and the timing of its existence) is so important?

- Some courts would allow Buyer 1 to enforce the covenants contained in Buyer 2's deed—even though Buyer 1 was not a party to that deed or a named beneficiary of the restrictions contained in it—under *third-party beneficiary* theory. Under contract law, a non-party to a contract may enforce that contract in limited circumstances in which that non-party can demonstrate that she was an intended beneficiary of the contract. In the "sloppy developer" situation, Buyer 1 will typically argue that the covenants contained in Buyer 2's deed were intended to benefit not only Dave Developer (as owner of the remaining lots), but also Buyer 1. Some courts have allowed prior purchasers (like Buyer 1) to enforce the covenants against later purchasers (like Buyer 2) based upon third-party beneficiary doctrine—as long as the prior purchasers can demonstrate the covenants were part of a "scheme" of uniform development at the time the developer subdivided the parcels. *See, e.g., Snow v. Van Dam*, 291 Mass. 477, 197 N.E. 224 (1935).

Does it make any practical difference which of these two theories—the "implied reciprocal servitude" theory or "third-party beneficiary" theory—a court uses to support mutual covenant enforcement in these "sloppy developer" cases?

Notes

1. *The Developer's Right to Modify Restrictions.* Suppose that in the deed conveying Lot 1 to Buyer 1, Dave Developer inserted the following statement: "Developer retains the right and power to modify the restrictions imposed upon any lots retained by Developer for future sale." Would this provision negate the existence of a scheme and thus prevent the implication of a reciprocal negative servitude over the Developer's retained lots? Why or why not? *Nelle v. Loch Haven Homeowners' Ass'n, Inc.*, 413 So.2d 28 (Fla. 1982). Would it make a difference if the statement authorized the Developer to remove all restrictions upon any lots retained by Developer for future sale? How do you think the new Restatement would evaluate a restriction

that permitted the Developer to remove all restrictions upon any lots retained by Developer for future sale?

2. *The "Scheme" of Development and Notice to Later Purchasers.* Warren and Faye Smith recently purchased half of a platted lakefront lot in a residential subdivision from the developer. The other half of the lot is owned by Donald and Arlene Webb, who previously built a home that they occupy as their primary residence. The deed to the Smiths did not contain a provision purporting to restrict their ability to build a home upon their portion of the lot. When the Smiths began building a home, the Webbs objected that each lot was subject to a restriction that "not more than one building shall be used for dwelling purposes on each lot" as shown on the original subdivision plat. The Smiths continued building their home, taking the position that because the developer deeded them the land without reference to this restriction, it did not bind their lot. The Webbs then filed suit against the Smiths, arguing that the home violated an implied reciprocal servitude binding the lot and seeking an injunction to require the Smiths to remove the house. Should the court grant the relief sought by the Webbs? Why or why not? If you believe that you need additional information, what additional information do you need, and how would it affect your analysis of the problem? *See, e.g., Webb v. Smith*, 224 Mich. App. 203, 568 N.W.2d 378 (1997).

c. *Financing a CIC Regime.* Increasingly, nearly all residential housing development occurs in CICs. Several factors account for this phenomenon. Some CICs (particularly condominiums) shift maintenance responsibilities for some portions of homes, lots, and common areas from the lot owners to the association; as a result, many purchasers perceive these communities as "carefree living." Other purchasers may desire homes with uniformly restricted appearances, believing this will promote secure property values or protect their aesthetic preferences. Of course, it is expensive for the association to provide these maintenance services and to regulate the community through enforcement of the servitude regime. For their viability, CICs thus require efficient and enforceable assessment mechanisms that are sufficient to fund the efficient and timely provision of services and maintenance of common facilities—in much the same way that local governments depend upon efficient and enforceable real property taxation regimes.

Generally, the declaration establishes the initial and maximum amounts of assessments, procedures for increasing assessments or levying special assessments, allocation of reserves for future capital needs, and collection and enforcement mechanisms. As *Neponsit* suggested, where the declaration provides for assessments for community facilities and services, courts generally have enforced residents' assessment obligations as covenants that run with the land. Courts typically conclude that a landowner is personally liable for assessments imposed during the landowner's ownership of land within the community. Furthermore, the declaration typically provides that unpaid lot assessments constitute a lien against that lot, enabling the association to sell a lot in the event that the lot owner cannot (or refuses to) pay the assessments. This framework theoretically provides the community association with the fiscal strength necessary to satisfy its responsibilities to provide services and maintain common facilities.

The structure of CIC financing has become even more important during the past two decades, as local governments have begun to use CICs as a means to shift financial responsibility for public services to the private sector. In many localities, public officials require that developers who want approval to build new CICs must provide (and finance some or all of the cost of!) substantial and expensive public facilities and services. These services may include greenspace, lighting, water/sewer, recreational facilities, street repair, trash collection/disposal, and snow removal. [Further, except in gated communities, facilities like roads and open spaces may even be used by some portion of the public at large.] The initial costs of these facilities and services are financed by the developer and passed through to the purchasers who buy homes, who in turn pay assessments to support the continued provision of these services. Because local governments traditionally provided many of these essential services, some have argued that local governments have adopted this "load-shedding" of fiscal responsibility onto CICs as a conscious strategy for relieving the strain on the public treasury. Mark Weiss & John Watts, *Community Builders and Community Associations: The Role of Real Estate Developers in Private Residential Governance*, Residential Community Associations: Private Governments in the Intergovernmental System 95, 100–02 (1989). To the extent that local governments are engaged in this "load-shedding" process, it ratchets up the need for developers to ensure that a CIC's assessment structure is sufficient to ensure the CIC's ability to perform its obligations.

Because the developer usually drafts the declaration in anticipation of marketing lots, the developer may set the parameters of the association's assessment powers hoping to make its lots competitive in the broader market for residential land. As a result, the developer may establish an assessment threshold based upon the developer's perception of what the market will bear, rather than upon a realistic judgment of the amount that might be necessary in the future to provide the promised and required facilities and services. For example, many early CIC regimes provided for voluntary rather than mandatory assessments, based in part upon perceived concern that prospective buyers would balk at buying land subject to a mandatory assessment obligation. Even in new CIC development—where mandatory assessments are the norm—a developer may place unrealistic or inappropriate limits upon the association's ability to increase assessment levels in order to better market lots to potentially skittish buyers. [It does not help, of course, that the developer's primary goal is selling its lots as quickly as possible—once the developer has sold its lots and turns over management of the CIC to the association, the developer may no longer care very much about whether the assessment structure is sufficient to fund future community needs.] *See generally* James L. Winokur, *Critical Assessment: The Financial Role of Community Associations*, 38 Santa Clara L. Rev. 1135 (1998).

When required facilities and services costs later increase, or unanticipated maintenance or capital needs arise, the association's board may face difficult choices. In the following case, an owners' association faced its financial crisis by voting to convert from voluntary assessments to mandatory assessments. Should this be permissible without unanimous consent of all lot owners within the CIC?

EVERGREEN HIGHLANDS ASSOCIATION v. WEST

Supreme Court of Colorado.
73 P.3d 1 (2003).

JUSTICE RICE. . . . Petitioner Evergreen Highlands Association, a Colorado non-profit corporation ("Association"), is the homeowner association for Evergreen Highlands Subdivision—Unit 4 ("Evergreen Highlands") in Jefferson County. The subdivision consists of sixty-three lots, associated roads, and a 22.3 acre park area which is open to use by all residents of the subdivision. The Association holds title to and maintains the park area, which contains hiking and equestrian trails, a barn and stables, a ball field, a fishing pond, and tennis courts. The park area is almost completely surrounded by private homeowners' lots, with no fence or other boundary separating the park area from the homes. Respondent Robert A. West owns one of the lots bordering directly on the park area, and has used the facilities there to play tennis, fish, and walk his dog.

Evergreen Highlands Subdivision was created and its plat filed in 1972. The plat indicated that the park area was to be conveyed to the homeowners association. Protective covenants for Evergreen Highlands were also filed in 1972, but did not require lot owners to be members of or pay dues to the Association. The Association, however, was incorporated in 1973 for the purposes of maintaining the common area and facilities, enforcing the covenants, paying taxes on the common area, and determining annual fees. The developer conveyed the park area to the Association in 1976. Between the years of 1976 and 1995, when the modification of the covenants at issue in this case occurred, the Association relied on voluntary assessments from lot owners to pay for maintenance of and improvements to the park area. Such expenses included property taxes, insurance for the park area and its structures, weed spraying, tennis court resurfacing, and barn and stable maintenance.

Article 13 of the original Evergreen Highlands covenants provides that a majority of lot owners may agree to modify the covenants, stating in relevant part as follows:

> [T]he owners of seventy-five percent of the lots which are subject to these covenants may release all or part of the land so restricted from any one or more of said restrictions, *or may change or modify any one or more of said restrictions,* by executing and acknowledging an appropriate agreement or agreements in writing for such purposes

and filing the same in the Office of the County Clerk and Recorder of Jefferson County, Colorado.

Protective Covenants for Evergreen Highlands—Unit 4, art. 13 (Nov. 6, 1972) (emphasis added) (hereinafter "modification clause"). In 1995, pursuant to the modification clause, at least seventy-five percent of Evergreen Highlands' lot owners voted to add a new Article 16 to the covenants. This article required all lot owners to be members of and pay assessments to the Association, and permitted the Association to impose liens on the property of any owners who failed to pay their assessment. Assessments were set at fifty dollars per year per lot.

Respondent purchased his lot in 1986 when membership in the Association and payment of assessments was voluntary, a fact that Respondent contends positively influenced his decision to purchase in Evergreen Highlands. Respondent was not among the majority of home-owners who approved the 1995 amendment to the covenants, and he subsequently refused to pay his lot assessment. When the Association threatened to record a lien against his property, Respondent filed this lawsuit challenging the validity of the 1995 amendment. The Association counterclaimed for a declaratory judgment that it had the implied power to collect assessments from all lot owners in the subdivision, and accordingly sought damages from West for breach of the implied contract. The district court ruled in favor of the Association on the ground that the amendment was valid and binding; therefore, it never reached the merits of the Association's counterclaims.

The court of appeals reversed, finding that the terms "change or modify" as set forth in the modification clause of the covenants did not allow for the addition of a wholly new covenant, but only for modifications to the existing covenants. . . . The court of appeals did not address the issue of whether the Association had the implied power to collect assessments from lot owners, and therefore whether Respondent was in breach of an implied contract. We granted certiorari and now reverse and remand. . . .

[Editors' Note: The court first held that the covenant had been properly modified under the terms of the modification provision. We return to address the community's power to amend covenants on page 695.]

The Association additionally argues that, even in the absence of an express covenant imposing mandatory assessments, it has the implied power to collect assessments from its members. To this end, the Association brought a counterclaim against West for breach of an implied contract obligating him to pay a proportionate share for repair, upkeep, and maintenance of the common area. The Association now argues that, based on West's breach of the implied contract, it is entitled as a matter of law to collect the unpaid assessments from Respondent.

We agree. Our review of case law from other states, the Restatement of Property (Servitudes), and the declarations for Evergreen Highlands in effect when West purchased his property, as supported by our understanding of the purpose of the Colorado Common Interest Ownership Act ("CCIOA"), convinces us that such an implied power exists in these circumstances. We therefore hold that Evergreen Highlands is a common interest community by implication, and that the Association has the implied power to levy assessments against lot owners to provide for maintenance of and improvements to common areas of the subdivision.

This being a question of first impression in Colorado, we first examine case law from other jurisdictions and find it largely in concurrence with our holding. When faced with this issue, a substantial number of states have arrived at the conclusion that homeowner associations have the implied power to levy dues or assessments even in the absence of express authority. *See, e.g., Spinnler Point Colony Ass'n, Inc. v. Nash,* 689 A.2d 1026, 1028–29 (Pa.Commw.Ct.1997) (holding that where ownership in a residential community allows owners to utilize common areas, "there is an implied agreement to accept the proportionate costs for maintaining and repairing these facilities."); *Meadow Run & Mountain Lake Park Ass'n v. Berkel,* 409 Pa.Super. 637, 598 A.2d 1024, 1026 (1991) (same); *Seaview Ass'n of Fire Island, N.Y., Inc. v. Williams,* 69 N.Y.2d 987, 517 N.Y.S.2d 709, 510 N.E.2d 793, 794 (1987) (holding that when lot purchaser has knowledge that homeowners association provides facilities and services to community residents, purchase creates an implied-in-fact contract to pay a proportionate share of those facilities and services); *Perry v. Bridgetown Cmty. Ass'n, Inc.,* 486 So.2d 1230, 1234 (Miss.1986) ("A landowner who willfully purchases property subject to control of the association and derives benefits from membership in the association implies his consent to be charged assessments and dues common to all other members."). *But see Popponesset Beach Ass'n, Inc. v. Marchillo,* 39 Mass.App.Ct. 586, 658 N.E.2d 983, 987–88 (1996) (holding that where lot owner had no notice in his chain of title of assessments and had not used the common areas, there existed no implied-in-fact contract to pay past and future assessments).[13]

Reflecting this considerable body of law, the newest version of the Restatement of Property (Servitudes) provides that "a common-interest community has the power to raise the funds reasonably necessary to carry out its functions by levying assessments against the individually owned property in the community...." Restatement of Servitudes § 6.5(1)(a) (2000). In addition, as explained in a comment to that section, the power to levy assessments "will be implied if not expressly granted by the declaration or by statute." *Id.* at § 6.5 cmt. b; *see also* Wayne S. Hyatt, *Condominium and Homeowner Association Practice: Community Association Law* 36 (1981) ("The assessment is not equivalent to membership dues or some other discretionary charge.... As long as legitimate expenses are incurred, the individual member must bear his or her share.").

---

13. We note that in contrast to *Marchillo,* testimony in this case showed that West had, in fact, availed himself of the benefits of the park area.

We find the Restatement and case law from other states persuasive in analyzing the issue before us today. In addition, these authorities are in harmony with the legislative purpose motivating the enactment of CCIOA. *See, e.g.,* § 38–33.3–102(1)(b), 10 C.R.S. (2002) ("That the continuation of the economic prosperity of Colorado is dependent upon the strengthening of homeowner associations . . . through enhancing the financial stability of associations by increasing the association's powers to collect delinquent assessments"); § 38–33.3–102(1)(d) ("That it is the policy of this state to promote effective and efficient property management through defined operational requirements that preserve flexibility for such homeowner associations").

Respondent, however, argues that the implied power to mandate assessments can only be imputed to "common interest communities," which both CCIOA and the Restatement define as residential communities in which there exists a mandatory obligation or servitude imposed on individual owners to pay for common elements of the community. Respondent therefore contends that because the original covenants did not impose such a servitude, Evergreen Highlands is not a common interest community, and accordingly cannot have the implied power to levy assessments against its members pursuant to these authorities.

Respondent's argument, however, relies on the assumption that the servitude or obligation to pay which would have defined Evergreen Highlands as a common interest community was required to have been made express in the covenants or in his deed. This assumption is incorrect. CCIOA provides only that the obligation must arise from the "declarations," which are defined as "any recorded instruments however denominated, that create a common interest community, including any amendments to those instruments and also including, but not limited to, plats and maps." § 38–33.3–103(13), 10 C.R.S. (2002); *see also* Restatement of Servitudes § 6.2(5)(2000) (" 'Declaration' means the recorded document or documents containing the servitudes that create and govern the common-interest community.").

The declarations in effect for Evergreen Highlands in 1986 incorporated all documents recorded up to that date, and included not only: (1) the covenants, but also; (2) the 1972 plat, which noted that the park area would be conveyed to the homeowners association; (3) the 1973 Articles of Incorporation for the Association stating that the Association's purposes were to "own, acquire, build, operate, and maintain" the common area and facilities, to pay taxes on same, and to "determine annual membership or use fees"; and (4) the 1976 deed whereby the developer quit-claimed his ownership in the park area to the Association.

At the time Respondent purchased his lot in 1986, the Evergreen Highlands' declarations made clear that a homeowners association existed, it owned and maintained the park area, and it had the power to impose annual membership or use fees on lot owners. These declarations were sufficient to create a common interest community by implication. As explained by the Restatement:

An implied obligation may ... be found where the declaration expressly creates an association for the purpose of managing common property or enforcing use restrictions and design controls, but fails to include a mechanism for providing the funds necessary to carry out its functions. When such an implied obligation is established, the lots are a common-interest community within the meaning of this Chapter.

Restatement (Third) of Property: Servitudes § 6.2 cmt. a (2000); *see also id.* at illus. 2 (citing an example virtually identical to that of Evergreen Highlands and finding it a common interest community by judicial decree).

We accordingly adopt the position taken by the Restatement and many other states, and hold that the declarations for Evergreen Highlands were sufficient to create a common interest community by implication. The Association therefore has the implicit power to levy assessments against lot owners for the purpose of maintaining the common area of the subdivision. Respondent, as a lot owner, has an implied duty to pay his proportionate share of the cost of maintaining and operating the common area. We therefore remand the case to the court of appeals with orders to return it to the trial court to calculate Petitioner's damages in a manner consistent with this opinion....

Notes

1. The *Power to Levy Assessments.* Are you persuaded by the *West* court's analysis that a CIC has the implied power to levy assessments? Do you believe that a reasonable purchaser in West's position would have appreciated the possibility of the future adoption of mandatory assessments? Would West's position be more reasonable if the declaration had not been amendable, and the association had been relying solely on its (alleged) implied power to impose mandatory assessments?

In considering this question, compare the situation in *West* with the following hypothetical. Shady Acres is the only neighborhood in the area without a playground. At a meeting of the Shady Acres HOA, 47 of the 63 lot owners in Shady Acres voted to have the HOA spend $100,000 to build a playground on part of the existing greenspace (featuring state-of-the-art playground equipment and bathrooms) and to impose mandatory assessments on all lot owners to finance the project. Pushaw (one of the 16 dissenting owners) files a lawsuit arguing that the HOA lacks the power to do this. Does the analysis in *West* mean that the HOA would prevail? Why or why not? What additional information, if any, would you want to ascertain in making your judgment?

2. *Collection of Assessments.* When association assessments go unpaid, the uncollected share of community expenses falls upon the remaining neighbors in one of two potentially destructive ways. First, the association may choose to maintain its existing level of services and simply pass the costs on to the remaining reliable owners. This makes it more difficult for the remaining owners to meet their own community obligations, perhaps

increasing their risk of default on the increased assessment burden. The remaining owners may also discover that their land value decreases as a result of those assessment increases (can you explain why?), thus threatening their investment and cutting off their ability to readily escape from the increased community burdens. [Note, however, that in some cases the declaration may contain an expense ceiling that effectively blocks associations from passing on all losses due to defaults.] Second, the association may choose to reduce its expenses by deferring or decreasing maintenance or eliminating services. The association cannot productively maintain this strategy for a long period, however, because it accelerates the deterioration of community facilities and may inevitably lower the value of land within the community.

Does it sufficiently address these concerns if the declaration provides that unpaid assessments constitute a lien upon affected land? Why or why not?[14] Suppose that X fails to pay his homeowners' assessments for two years due to financial difficulties caused by losing his job following an accident. As a result, the association chooses to mow subdivision common areas less frequently rather than to enforce a lien against X's residence. If another community resident challenges the association's decision, do you expect that such a challenge would be successful? Why or why not?

d. *Managing Daily Life Within CICs.* As the prior section suggests, CICs increasingly resemble local governments in the sense that they provide "community services" paid for by the imposition of "community taxes" (assessments). CIC servitude regimes typically place a variety of contractual land use restrictions on lots within the community as a means of protecting community members from uses that might potentially threaten their financial investment or aesthetic values. In this regard, CICs also resemble local governments—which commonly use zoning powers, public nuisance laws, and other police powers to regulate life within public communities. *See generally* Robert C. Ellickson, *Cities and Homeowners Associations*, 130 U. Pa. L. Rev. 1519 (1982).

As residential CICs proliferate, disputes inevitably arise between neighbors over certain uses of land—uses that some may consider undesirable or inconsistent with the community as defined in the CCRs, yet others may think desirable or at least permitted by the CCRs. When such disputes arise, what role should courts play in applying the community's declaration and CCRs? For example, should courts interpret a "residential-use-only" restriction to prohibit someone from operating a freelance website design business within their home or from providing day care for some neighborhood children whose parents work outside the home? Even if a covenant might be so interpreted based upon its

---

14. Some states (primarily those that have adopted the Uniform Common Interest Ownership Act) provide for a statutory lien to secure assessment obligations. Under UCIOA, this lien has "super-priority"— *i.e.*, priority over pre-existing liens and mortgages—to the extent of up to six months' worth of delinquent assessments.

For analysis of this legislation, and explanation of enforcement of assessment liens, see generally James L. Winokur, *Meaner Lienor Community Associations: The "Super Priority" Lien and Related Reforms Under the Uniform Common Interest Ownership Act*, 27 Wake Forest L. Rev. 353 (1992).

language and context, should there be limits on the community's authority to regulate the conduct of its residents, especially if that involves infringement upon the residents' privacy? What if the conduct being regulated has no impact outside the particular resident's own home? Does constitutional law or public policy provide any basis for blocking enforcement of some covenants? To what extent may these problems be avoided by careful drafting? Consider the following materials.

NAHRSTEDT v. LAKESIDE VILLAGE CONDOMINIUM ASS'N, INC.

Supreme Court of California.
8 Cal.4th 361, 33 Cal.Rptr.2d 63, 878 P.2d 1275 (1994).

KENNARD, JUSTICE. . . . Lakeside Village is a large condominium development in Culver City, Los Angeles County. It consists of 530 units spread throughout 12 separate 3–story buildings. The residents share common lobbies and hallways, in addition to laundry and trash facilities.

The Lakeside Village project is subject to certain covenants, conditions and restrictions (hereafter CC & Rs) that were included in the developer's declaration recorded with the Los Angeles County Recorder on April 17, 1978, at the inception of the development project. Ownership of a unit includes membership in the project's homeowners association, the Lakeside Village Condominium Association (hereafter Association), the body that enforces the project's CC & Rs, including the pet restriction, which provides in relevant part: "No animals (which shall mean dogs and cats), livestock, reptiles or poultry shall be kept in any unit."[15]

In January 1988, plaintiff Natore Nahrstedt purchased a Lakeside Village condominium and moved in with her three cats. When the Association learned of the cats' presence, it demanded their removal and assessed fines against Nahrstedt for each successive month that she remained in violation of the condominium project's pet restriction.

Nahrstedt then brought this lawsuit against the Association, its officers, and two of its employees, asking the trial court to invalidate the assessments, to enjoin future assessments, to award damages for violation of her privacy when the Association "peered" into her condominium unit, to award damages for infliction of emotional distress, and to declare the pet restriction "unreasonable" as applied to indoor cats (such as hers) that are not allowed free run of the project's common areas. Nahrstedt also alleged she did not know of the pet restriction when she bought her condominium. The complaint incorporated by reference the grant deed, the declaration of CC & Rs, and the condominium plan for the Lakeside Village condominium project.

The Association demurred to the complaint. In its supporting points and authorities, the Association argued that the pet restriction furthers the collective "health, happiness and peace of mind" of persons living in

15. The CC & R's permit residents to
keep "domestic fish and birds."

close proximity within the Lakeside Village condominium development, and therefore is reasonable as a matter of law. The trial court sustained the demurrer as to each cause of action and dismissed Nahrstedt's complaint. Nahrstedt appealed.

A divided Court of Appeal reversed the trial court's judgment of dismissal. In the majority's view, the complaint stated a claim for declaratory relief based on its allegations that Nahrstedt's three cats are kept inside her condominium unit and do not bother her neighbors. According to the majority, whether a condominium use restriction is "unreasonable," as that term is used in section 1354, hinges on the facts of a particular homeowner's case. Thus, the majority reasoned, Nahrstedt would be entitled to declaratory relief if application of the pet restriction in her case would not be reasonable. . . .

On the Association's petition, we granted review to decide when a condominium owner can prevent enforcement of a use restriction that the project's developer has included in the recorded declaration of CC & Rs. . . .

When restrictions limiting the use of property within a common interest development satisfy the requirements of covenants running with the land or of equitable servitudes, what standard or test governs their enforceability? In California . . . our Legislature has made common interest development use restrictions contained in a project's recorded declaration "enforceable . . . *unless unreasonable*." § 1354, subd. (a), italics added.

In states lacking such legislative guidance, some courts have adopted a standard under which a common interest development's recorded use restrictions will be enforced so long as they are "reasonable." *See Riley v. Stoves* (1974) 22 Ariz.App. 223, 228, 526 P.2d 747, 752 (asking whether the challenged restriction provided "a reasonable means to accomplish the private objective"). Although no one definition of the term "reasonable" has gained universal acceptance, most courts have applied what one commentator calls "equitable reasonableness," upholding only those restrictions that provide a reasonable means to further the collective "health, happiness and enjoyment of life" of owners of a common interest development. Others would limit the "reasonableness" standard only to those restrictions adopted by majority vote of the homeowners or enacted under the rulemaking power of an association's governing board, and would not apply this test to restrictions included in a planned development project's recorded declaration or master deed. Because such restrictions are presumptively valid, these authorities would enforce them regardless of reasonableness. . . .

In *Hidden Harbour Estates v. Basso* (Fla.Dist.Ct.App.1981) 393 So.2d 637, the Florida court distinguished two categories of use restrictions: use restrictions set forth in the declaration or master deed of the condominium project itself, and rules promulgated by the governing board of the condominium owners association or the board's interpretation of a rule. *Id.* at p. 639. The latter category of use restrictions, the court said, should be subject to a "reasonableness" test, so as to "somewhat fetter the discretion of the board of directors." *Id.* at p. 640. Such a standard, the court explained, best assures that governing boards will "enact rules and make decisions that are reasonably related to the promotion of the health, happiness and peace of mind" of the project owners, considered collectively. *Id.*

By contrast, restrictions contained in the declaration or master deed of the condominium complex, the Florida court concluded, should not be evaluated under a "reasonableness" standard. *Hidden Harbour Estates v. Basso, supra*, 393 So.2d at pp. 639–640. Rather, such use restrictions are "clothed with a very strong presumption of validity" and should be upheld even if they exhibit some degree of unreasonableness. *Id.* at pp. 639, 640. Nonenforcement would be proper only if such restrictions were arbitrary or in violation of public policy or some fundamental constitutional right. *Id.* at pp. 639–640. . . .

Indeed, giving deference to use restrictions contained in a condominium project's originating documents protects the general expectations of condominium owners "that restrictions in place at the time they purchase their units will be enforceable." Note, Judicial Review of Condominium Rulemaking (1981) 94 Harv.L.Rev. 647, 653; Ellickson, Cities and Homeowners' Associations (1982) 130 U.Pa.L.Rev. 1519, 1526–1527 (stating that association members "unanimously consent to the provisions in the association's original documents" and courts therefore should not scrutinize such documents for "reasonableness."). This in turn encourages the development of shared ownership housing—generally a less costly alternative to single-dwelling ownership—by attracting buyers who prefer a stable, planned environment. It also protects buyers who have paid a premium for condominium units in reliance on a particular restrictive scheme. . . .

. . . As mentioned earlier, under subdivision (a) of section 1354 the use restrictions for a common interest development that are set forth in the recorded declaration are "enforceable equitable servitudes, unless unreasonable." In other words, such restrictions should be enforced unless they are wholly arbitrary, violate a fundamental public policy, or impose a burden on the use of affected land that far outweighs any benefit.

This interpretation of section 1354 is consistent with the views of legal commentators as well as judicial decisions in other jurisdictions that have applied a presumption of validity to the recorded land use restrictions of a common interest development. *Noble v. Murphy* (1993) 34 Mass.App.Ct. 452, 612 N.E.2d 266, 270; *Hidden Harbour Estates v. Basso, supra*, 393 So.2d 637, 639–640; Note, Judicial Review of Condominium Rulemaking, *supra*, 94 Harv.L.Rev. 647, 653. As these authorities point out, and as we discussed previously, recorded CC & Rs are the primary means of achieving the stability and predictability so essential to the success of a shared ownership housing development. In general, then, enforcement of a common interest development's recorded CC &

Rs will both encourage the development of land and ensure that promises are kept, thereby fulfilling both of the policies identified by the Restatement. See Rest., Property, § 539, com. f, p. 3230.

When courts accord a presumption of validity to all such recorded use restrictions and measure them against deferential standards of equitable servitude law, it discourages lawsuits by owners of individual units seeking personal exemptions from the restrictions. This also promotes stability and predictability in two ways. It provides substantial assurance to prospective condominium purchasers that they may rely with confidence on the promises embodied in the project's recorded CC & Rs. And it protects all owners in the planned development from unanticipated increases in association fees to fund the defense of legal challenges to recorded restrictions.

How courts enforce recorded use restrictions affects not only those who have made their homes in planned developments, but also the owners associations charged with the fiduciary obligation to enforce those restrictions. When courts treat recorded use restrictions as presumptively valid, and place on the challenger the burden of proving the restriction "unreasonable" under the deferential standards applicable to equitable servitudes, associations can proceed to enforce reasonable restrictive covenants without fear that their actions will embroil them in costly and prolonged legal proceedings. Of course, when an association determines that a unit owner has violated a use restriction, the association must do so in good faith, not in an arbitrary or capricious manner, and its enforcement procedures must be fair and applied uniformly.

There is an additional beneficiary of legal rules that are protective of recorded use restrictions: the judicial system. Fewer lawsuits challenging such restrictions will be brought, and those that are filed may be disposed of more expeditiously, if the rules courts use in evaluating such restrictions are clear, simple, and not subject to exceptions based on the peculiar circumstances or hardships of individual residents in condominiums and other shared-ownership developments.

Contrary to the dissent's accusations that the majority's decision "fray[s]" the "social fabric," we are of the view that our social fabric is best preserved if courts uphold and enforce solemn written instruments that embody the expectations of the parties rather than treat them as "worthless paper" as the dissent would. Our social fabric is founded on the stability of expectation and obligation that arises from the consistent enforcement of the terms of deeds, contracts, wills, statutes, and other writings. To allow one person to escape obligations under a written instrument upsets the expectations of all the other parties governed by that instrument (here, the owners of the other 529 units) that the instrument will be uniformly and predictably enforced.

The salutary effect of enforcing written instruments and the statutes that apply to them is particularly true in the case of the declaration of a common interest development. As we have discussed, common interest developments are a more intensive and efficient form of land use that greatly benefits society and expands opportunities for home owner-ship. In turn, however, a common interest development creates a com-munity of property owners living in close proximity to each other, typically much closer than if each owned his or her separate plot of land. This proximity is feasible, and units in a common interest development are marketable, largely because the recorded declaration of CC & Rs assures owners of a stable and predictable environment.

Refusing to enforce the CC & Rs contained in a recorded declaration, or enforcing them only after protracted litigation that would require justification of their application on a case-by-case basis, would impose great strain on the social fabric of the common interest development. It would frustrate owners who had purchased their units in reliance on the CC & Rs. It would put the owners and the homeowners association in the difficult and divisive position of deciding whether particular CC & Rs should be applied to a particular owner. Here, for example, deciding whether a particular animal is "confined to an owner's unit and cre-ate[s] no noise, odor, or nuisance" is a fact-intensive determination that can only be made by examining in detail the behavior of the particular animal and the behavior of the particular owner. Homeowners associa-tions are ill-equipped to make such investigations, and any decision they might make in a particular case could be divisive or subject to claims of partiality.

Enforcing the CC & Rs contained in a recorded declaration only after protracted case-by-case litigation would impose substantial litiga-tion costs on the owners through their homeowners association, which would have to defend not only against owners contesting the application of the CC & Rs to them, but also against owners contesting any case-by-case exceptions the homeowners association might make. In short, it is difficult to imagine what could more disrupt the harmony of a common interest development than the course proposed by the dissent . . . .

Under the holding we adopt today, the reasonableness or unreason-ableness of a condominium use restriction that the Legislature has made subject to section 1354 is to be determined not by reference to facts that are specific to the objecting homeowner, but by reference to the common interest development as a whole. As we have explained, when, as here, a restriction is contained in the declaration of the common interest devel-opment and is recorded with the county recorder, the restriction is presumed to be reasonable and will be enforced uniformly against all residents of the common interest development unless the restriction is arbitrary, imposes burdens on the use of lands it affects that substantial-ly outweigh the restriction's benefits to the development's residents, or violates a fundamental public policy.

Accordingly, here Nahrstedt could prevent enforcement of the Lake-side Village pet restriction by proving that the restriction is arbitrary, that it is substantially more burdensome than beneficial to the affected properties, or that it violates a fundamental public policy. For the reasons set forth below, Nahrstedt's complaint fails to adequately allege any of these three grounds of unreasonableness.

We conclude, as a matter of law, that the recorded pet restriction of the Lakeside Village condominium development prohibiting cats or dogs but allowing some other pets is not arbitrary, but is rationally related to health, sanitation and noise concerns legitimately held by residents of a high-density condominium project such as Lakeside Village, which includes 530 units in 12 separate 3–story buildings.

Nahrstedt's complaint alleges no facts that could possibly support a finding that the burden of the restriction on the affected property is so disproportionate to its benefit that the restriction is unreasonable and should not be enforced. Also, the complaint's allegations center on Nahrstedt and her cats (that she keeps them inside her condominium unit and that they do not bother her neighbors), without any reference to the effect on the condominium development as a whole, thus rendering the allegations legally insufficient to overcome section 1354's presumption of the restriction's validity....

[Editors' Note: The court also rejected Nahrstedt's argument that the California Constitution's right of "privacy," Cal. Const., art. I, § 17, accorded her the right to keep cats within the confines of her residence.]

ARABIAN, JUSTICE, dissenting.

> *"There are two means of refuge from the misery of life: music and cats." [Albert Schweitzer]*

I respectfully dissent. While technical merit may commend the majority's analysis, its application to the facts presented reflects a narrow, indeed chary, view of the law that eschews the human spirit in favor of arbitrary efficiency....

As explained below, I find the provision known as the "pet restriction" contained in the covenants, conditions, and restrictions (CC & Rs) governing the Lakeside Village project patently arbitrary and unreasonable within the meaning of Civil Code section 1354. Beyond dispute, human beings have long enjoyed an abiding and cherished association with their household animals. Given the substantial benefits derived from pet ownership, the undue burden on the use of property imposed on condominium owners who can maintain pets within the confines of their units without creating a nuisance or disturbing the quiet enjoyment of others substantially outweighs whatever meager utility the restriction may serve in the abstract. It certainly does not promote "health, happiness [or] peace of mind" commensurate with its tariff on the quality of life for those who value the companionship of animals. Worse, it contributes to the fraying of our social fabric....

Under the majority's construction of Civil Code section 1354, the pet restriction is unreasonable, and hence unenforceable, if the "burdens [imposed] on the affected land ... are so disproportionate to the restriction's beneficial effects that the restriction should not be enforced." What, then, is the burden at issue here?

Both recorded and unrecorded history bear witness to the domestication of animals as household pets. Throughout the ages, dogs and cats have provided human beings with a variety of services in addition to their companionship—shepherding flocks, guarding life and property, hunting game, ridding the house and barn of vermin. Of course, the modern classic example is the assist dog, which facilitates a sense of independence and security for disabled persons by enabling them to navigate their environment, alerting them to important sounds, and bringing the world within their reach. Emotionally, they allow a connection full of sensation and delicacy of feeling.

Throughout the ages, art and literature, as well as mythology, depict humans in all walks of life and social strata with cats and dogs, illustrating their widespread acceptance in everyday life. Some religions have even incorporated them into their worship. Dogs and cats are also admired for the purity of their character traits. Closer to home, our own culture is populated with examples of the well-established place pets have found in our hearts and homes.

In addition to these historical and cultural references, the value of pets in daily life is a matter of common knowledge and understanding as well as extensive documentation. People of all ages, but particularly the elderly and the young, enjoy their companionship. Those who suffer from serious disease or injury and are confined to their home or bed experience a therapeutic, even spiritual, benefit from their presence. Animals provide comfort at the death of a family member or dear friend, and for the lonely can offer a reason for living when life seems to have lost its meaning. In recognition of these benefits, both Congress and the state Legislature have expressly guaranteed that elderly and handicapped persons living in public-assistance housing cannot be deprived of their pets. 12 U.S.C. § 1701r–1; Health & Saf.Code, § 19901. Not only have children and animals always been natural companions, children learn responsibility and discipline from pet ownership while developing an important sense of kindness and protection for animals. Single adults may find certain pets can afford a feeling of security. Families benefit from the experience of sharing that having a pet encourages. While pet ownership may not be a fundamental right as such, unquestionably it is an integral aspect of our daily existence, which cannot be lightly dismissed and should not suffer unwarranted intrusion into its circle of privacy.

... Pets that remain within the four corners of their owners' condominium space can have no deleterious or offensive effect on the project's common areas or any neighboring unit. Certainly, if other owners and residents are totally unaware of their presence, prohibiting pets does not in any respect foster the "health, happiness [or] peace of mind" of anyone except the homeowners association's board of directors, who are thereby able to promote a form of sophisticated bigotry. In light of the substantial and disproportionate burden imposed for those who must forgo virtually any and all association with pets, this lack of benefit renders a categorical ban unreasonable under Civil Code section 1354.

The proffered justification is all the more spurious when measured against the terms of the pet restriction itself, which contains an exception for domestic fish and birds. A squawking bird can readily create the very kind of disturbance supposedly prevented by banning other types of pets. At the same time, many animals prohibited by the restriction, such as hamsters and the like, turtles, and small reptiles, make no sound whatsoever. Disposal of bird droppings in common trash areas poses as much of a health concern as cat litter or rabbit pellets, which likewise can be handled in a manner that avoids potential problems. Birds are also known to carry disease and provoke allergies. Neither is maintaining fish without possible risk of interfering with the quiet enjoyment of condominium neighbors. Aquarium water must be changed and disposed of in the common drainage system. Leakage from a fish tank could cause serious water damage to the owner's unit, those below, and common areas. Defendants and the majority purport such solicitude for the "health, sanitation and noise concerns" of other unit owners, but fail to explain how the possession of pets, such as plaintiff's cats, under the circumstances alleged in her complaint, jeopardizes that goal any more than the fish and birds expressly allowed by the pet restriction. This inconsistency underscores its unreasonableness and discriminatory impact.

From the statement of the facts through the conclusion, the majority's analysis gives scant acknowledgment to any of the foregoing considerations but simply takes refuge behind the "presumption of validity" now accorded all CC & Rs irrespective of subject matter. They never objectively scrutinize defendants' blandishments of protecting "health and happiness" or realistically assess the substantial impact on affected unit owners and their use of their property. As this court has often recognized, "deference is not abdication." *People v. McDonald* (1984) 37 Cal.3d 351, 377, 208 Cal.Rptr. 236, 690 P.2d 709. Regardless of how limited an inquiry is permitted under applicable law, it must nevertheless be made.

Here, such inquiry should start with an evaluation of the interest that will suffer upon enforcement of the pet restriction. In determining the "burden on the use of land," due recognition must be given to the fact that this particular "use" transcends the impersonal and mundane matters typically regulated by condominium CC & Rs, such as whether someone can place a doormat in the hallway or hang a towel on the patio rail or have food in the pool area, and reaches the very quality of life of hundreds of owners and residents. Nonetheless, the majority accept uncritically the proffered justification of preserving "health and happiness" and essentially consider only one criterion to determine enforceability: was the restriction recorded in the original declaration? If so, it is "presumptively valid," unless in violation of public policy. Given the application of the law to the facts alleged and by an inversion of relative interests, it is difficult to hypothesize any CC & Rs that would not pass muster.[17] Such sanctity has not been afforded any writing save the commandments delivered to Moses on Mount Sinai, and they were set in stone, not upon worthless paper.

Moreover, unlike most conduct controlled by CC & Rs, the activity at issue here is strictly confined to the owner's interior space; it does not in any manner invade other units or the common areas. Owning a home of one's own has always epitomized the American dream. More than simply embodying the notion of having "one's castle," it represents the sense of freedom and self-determination emblematic of our national character. Granted, those who live in multi-unit developments cannot exercise this freedom to the same extent possible on a large estate. But owning pets that do not disturb the quiet enjoyment of others does not reasonably come within this compromise. Nevertheless, with no demonstrated or discernible benefit, the majority arbitrarily sacrifice the dream to the tyranny of the "commonality."

Our true task in this turmoil is to strike a balance between the governing rights accorded a condominium association and the individual freedom of its members. To fulfill that function, a reviewing court must view with a skeptic's eye restrictions driven by fear, anxiety, or intolerance. In any community, we do not exist *in vacuo*. There are many annoyances which we tolerate because not to do so would be repressive and place the freedom of others at risk.

In contravention, the majority's failure to consider the real burden imposed by the pet restriction unfortunately belittles and trivializes the interest at stake here. Pet ownership substantially enhances the quality of life for those who desire it. When others are not only undisturbed by, but completely unaware of, the presence of pets being enjoyed by their neighbors, the balance of benefit and burden is rendered disproportionate and unreasonable, rebutting any presumption of validity. Their view, shorn of grace and guiding philosophy, is devoid of the humanity that must temper the interpretation and application of all laws, for in a civilized society that is the source of their authority. As judicial architects of the rules of life, we better serve when we construct halls of harmony rather than walls of wrath....

Notes

1. *Revisiting the "Touch and Concern" Standard and the Restatement of Servitudes.* Professor French defended the Restatement's decision to discard the "touch and concern" standard by arguing that courts "increasingly determine the validity of servitudes on the basis of the rules [set forth in the Restatement]." Restatement of Servitudes § 3.2, cmt. b. Review the rules reflected in the new Restatement (pages 630–34). Does the decision in *Nahrstedt* support her thesis? Why or why not?

17. Under the facts of this case, the majority do more than simply accord the restriction a presumption of reasonableness. They encourage and endorse the enforcing body to disregard the privacy interests of law-abiding property owners. If pets are maintained in the manner alleged in plaintiff's complaint, then only snoopers are in a position to claim a violation of the restriction.

2. *The Presumptive Reasonableness of Condominium Restrictions.* The *Nahrstedt* court treats condominium restrictions as presumptively reasonable. Does this presumption seem appropriate? Why or why not? Should this presumption apply with equal force in a common interest community where the housing units were less densely situated (*i.e.*, detached single-family homes)?

3. *Assent to Servitudes: Constructive or Actual?* Do you think that when she purchased her unit, Mrs. Nahrstedt actually understood that the covenant would prevent her from keeping an indoor cat? Traditional doctrine characterizes the purchase of land subject to a recorded servitude regime as a manifestation of consent to that regime. *See, e.g.,* Richard Epstein, *Notice and Freedom of Contract in the Law of Servitudes*, 55 S. Cal. L. Rev. 1353 (1982). Others have criticized this view:

> Typically, the developer draws up subdivision restrictions prior to any sales of restricted lots. This excludes the participation of the lot owners who will occupy the lots upon completion of the development. To allow neighbors to enforce the agreement, the restrictions must be conceived as part of a common development plan, entailing uniform restrictions applicable to all servitude-restricted lots. Thus, by the time prospective owners consider purchasing restricted parcels or units, the prospective purchasers' options upon reviewing the servitudes are simply to take them or leave them.

> Furthermore, as more and more residential properties are bound by servitude regimes, and standard forms proliferate, the option to reject the model(s) of servitude regimes prevailing in a given area becomes less realistic for substantial segments of the real estate market, particularly for those buyers who wish to enjoy either suburban or condominium living. What might be objectionable in one set of restrictions will increasingly be contained in restrictions of other area subdivisions. This standardization of documentation throughout, and even beyond, entire residential markets is increased by government regulatory oversight, either by state real estate agencies or by federal secondary mortgage agencies. Rather than fight bureaucratic tastes, developers regularly lift servitude language from government forms.

> Most prospective owners do not intelligently review the restrictions to which they subject themselves upon acceptance of a deed to land burdened by servitudes. The documentation typically makes long, boring reading for laypersons, who rarely retain counsel to review the documentation involved in home purchases. Even those who read the restrictions in advance may miscalculate their own future attitudes toward servitude restrictions, perhaps inaccurately expecting that friendly relations with neighbors will eliminate hostile disagreements between residents. Such optimistic expectations are often disappointed.... [James L. Winokur, *The Mixed Blessings of Promissory Servitudes: Toward Optimizing Economic Utility, Individual Liberty, and Personal Identity*, 1989 Wis. L. Rev. 1, 56–62.]

See also Gregory Alexander, *Freedom, Coercion, and the Law of Servitudes*, 73 Cornell L. Rev. 883 (1988).

4. *Restrictions Against Leasing or Transfer.* In some cases, CIC declarations absolutely prohibit unit owners from leasing their units (or allowing them to be occupied by persons other than the owner and the owner's immediate family). What might justify such an absolute restriction? Is this a reasonable and enforceable restriction? Could an owners' association or a neighboring owner enforce a no-leasing restriction without regard to the identity or creditworthiness of the proposed tenant? Why or why not? *See, e.g., Flagler Fed. Sav. & Loan Ass'n v. Crestview Towers Condo. Ass'n,* 595 So.2d 198 (Fla. Dist. Ct. App. 1992) (upholding absolute prohibition on leasing); *Worthinglen Condo. Unit Owners' Ass'n v. Brown,* 57 Ohio App.3d 73, 566 N.E.2d 1275 (1989) (same).

Some CIC declarations do not prohibit leasing absolutely, but create rules designed to limit or eliminate potential negative impacts of leasing activity within the community. One approach is to permit leasing only in specifically defined situations. For example, courts have upheld rules that prohibited leases of short duration (*e.g.,* three months or less) or that permitted each owner only a certain number of leases (*e.g.,* no more than two per year). *See, e.g., Beachwood Villas Condo. v. Poor,* 448 So.2d 1143 (Fla. Dist. Ct. App. 1984). Another approach is to prohibit any leasing without prior board approval. *See, e.g., Le Febvre v. Osterndorf,* 87 Wis.2d 525, 275 N.W.2d 154 (1979). Which approach do you think makes most sense—an absolute prohibition on all leasing, clear rules prohibiting certain types of leases, or having the association address proposed leases on a case-by-case basis?

In some CICs, the declaration goes beyond restricting leasing, and prohibits a unit owner from making *any transfer*—even a fee simple absolute—without the prior consent of the owners' association. Suppose that your client owns a condominium unit subject to such a restriction in a posh beach resort. Because your client's business responsibilities prevent her from using the unit except during the spring, she finds three other individuals willing to purchase 1/4 shares in the unit (assume that the four will hold title as tenants in common). When your client seeks the approval of the homeowners' association, the association refuses and attempts to obtain an injunction against the proposed transfers. Can the association legitimately refuse to consent to your client's proposed transfer? Why or why not? *See, e.g., Laguna Royale Owners Ass'n v. Darger,* 119 Cal.App.3d 670, 174 Cal.Rptr. 136 (1981). Should a court view such a direct restraint on alienation more stringently than indirect restraints (such as use restrictions)? *See* Restatement of Servitudes § 3.4. How would it influence your advice if the CCRs also contained a leasing restriction that prohibited leases for periods less than 90 days without the approval of the association?

5. *Promissory Servitude Enforcement: Original Declaration vs. Association Rules.* For certain community issues, a declaration may not provide a specific rule in the CCRs, but instead may authorize the association's governing board to adopt and implement rules in the future. Courts often have applied different standards of review to association enforcement decisions depending upon whether the association is enforcing a servitude contained in the CCRs or a rule subsequently promulgated by the association (or its governing board). For example, in *Beachwood Villas Condo. v. Poor,* 448 So.2d 1143, 1144 (Fla. Dist. Ct. App. 1984), the court held that when the

association is enforcing a restriction contained in the original declaration, the reviewing court should presume that the restriction is valid; by contrast, when evaluating an association-promulgated rule, the reviewing court should uphold the rule only if "the board acted within its scope of authority" and only if "the rule reflects reasoned [as opposed to] arbitrary and capricious decision making." What might justify heightened scrutiny of board-promulgated rules?

LAWYERING EXERCISE
(Counseling, Creating a Dispute Resolution Process)

SITUATION: You represent Smith, who is developing a new 400–unit residential development called Tidy Acres. Smith wants to implement viable community governance procedures and reasonable use restrictions throughout Tidy Acres, so as to make Tidy Acres an attractive place to live (thereby encouraging lot sales). Smith wants to make sure Tidy Acres has effective pet controls. He says: "Should the CCRs simply prohibit pets, or instead let the board adopt rules regulating pets? And if disputes about pets arise, would it make sense to have the board litigate those disputes, or instead have a panel of homeowners that would make binding decisions?"

TASKS: For each question, based upon the prior materials, identify for Smith the benefits and detriments of each approach.

———————

The no-pet covenant in *Nahrstedt* was unambiguous. Nahrstedt could not argue that the terms of the covenant did not prohibit her conduct; at best, she could only challenge the enforceability of the covenant. By contrast, consider the "residential use only" covenant, which is ubiquitous in modern residential CIC development. Exactly what does "residential use" mean? Must the owner live there? Can the owner hold garage sales? Could the owner run a home-based business?

GABRIEL v. CAZIER
Supreme Court of Idaho.
130 Idaho 171, 938 P.2d 1209 (1997).

JOHNSON, JUSTICE. This is a restrictive covenant case. We conclude that the covenant prohibiting a business in a subdivision is ambiguous in the context of the covenant, and that it should not be construed to prohibit swimming lessons conducted by a homeowner's children for profit during the summer months. . . .

The Caziers and the Gabriels live across the street from each other in a subdivision. A declaration of protective restrictions and covenants applies to the subdivision. Under the title "NUISANCES," the declaration provides:

No business or trade or offensive or noxious activity shall be carried on upon any lot in the Subdivision, nor shall anything be done thereon which may become an annoyance or a nuisance to the neighborhood by unreasonably interfering with the use and enjoyment of other property within the Subdivision, nor shall any residence be utilized for public purposes or services including public worship or church services. Weeds shall be kept cut and portions of any lot not in use for lawn or otherwise shall be kept trimmed and in a neat and orderly condition.

Another portion of the declaration provides that "toilet facilities shall be located inside the dwelling ... and shall be connected ... with ... a septic tank ...."

The Caziers' children taught swimming lessons at their backyard pool in the subdivision during the summer months from 1988 through 1995. Each summer, they conducted eighteen lessons four or five days a week for ten weeks, earning approximately $10,000. These lessons resulted in a substantial increase in traffic and parking in the neighborhood. The Caziers maintained a portable chemical toilet outside their home near the swimming pool for the convenience of the swimming students.

The Gabriels sued the Caziers, alleging that the Caziers violated the declaration by operating a business within the subdivision and by creating a nuisance and annoyance that unreasonably interfered with the Gabriels' use and enjoyment of their property. The Gabriels sought a permanent injunction against the swimming lessons, general damages, together with reasonable attorney fees and costs. In addition, the Gabriels sought to have the portable chemical toilet removed.

Following a court trial, the trial court found:

1. at least two other families in the subdivision conduct swimming lessons at their pools;

2. the Caziers do not employ anyone outside the family for the lessons;

9. the Gabriels are the only residents of the subdivision that have a complaint about the Caziers' swimming lessons;

10. the increase in traffic is well within the capacity of the streets in the subdivision;

11. the parking does not constitute a disturbance to the Gabriels;

12. the swimming lessons are not unduly noisy or disturbing to neighbors;

13. the Gabriels conduct part of their real estate business from their home, have operated a mail-order business from their home, have raised farm animals in their backyard, and have sold these animals.

The trial court ruled that the Caziers' activity is not a "business" as used in the declaration because it is an occasional or seasonal activity, and that the declaration has been interpreted by those in the subdivision to allow swimming lessons for at least fifteen years without complaint.

Therefore, the trial court concluded that the declaration has been abandoned as it applies to swimming lessons offered by a homeowner's children during a limited period of time. The trial court also ruled that the lessons are not a nuisance, but that the portable chemical toilet violates the declaration. The trial court awarded the Caziers judgment, except it said the Caziers shall not use a portable chemical toilet in connection with the swimming lessons. The Gabriels appealed. . . .

The Gabriels assert that the swimming lessons were a "business" prohibited by the declaration. We conclude that, in the context of the declaration, the term "business" is ambiguous, and that there is substantial and competent evidence to support the trial court's finding that the swimming lessons are not a business. We first address the ambiguity of the term "business" in the context of the declaration. In order to determine whether a provision of a restrictive covenant is ambiguous, we must determine whether the provision is reasonably susceptible to conflicting interpretations. *Brown v. Perkins*, 129 Idaho 189, 193, 923 P.2d 434, 438 (1996).

The declaration states that "no business or trade or offensive or noxious activity shall be carried on upon any lot in the Subdivision." "Business" can be reasonably interpreted to include the swimming lessons at issue in this case, as well as other activities, including home offices. "Business" can also reasonably be interpreted to include only permanent commercial enterprises like shops, restaurants, and office buildings. Therefore, we conclude that, in the context of the declaration, the term "business" is ambiguous, requiring construction.

If a restrictive covenant is subject to conflicting interpretation, it is ambiguous, and its construction is a question of fact to be interpreted according to the following principles:

> If an ambiguity is found in the restrictive covenant, the Court is to determine the intent of the parties at the time the instrument was drafted. The interpretation of the restrictive covenants intended by the drafters can be ascertained from the language of the covenants, the existing circumstances at the time of the formulation of the covenants, and the conduct of the parties. Additionally, the mutual interpretation of the restrictive covenants afford cogent evidence of their meaning. [*Brown* at 193, 923 P.2d at 438 (citations omitted).]

We are also constrained in our interpretation by the principle that "When 'construing a restrictive covenant, which is in derogation of the common law right to use land, restrictions are not to be extended by implication to include any restrictions not expressed clearly and doubts are to be resolved in favor of the free use of land.'" *Id.* at 192, 923 P.2d at 437 (quoting *Post v. Murphy*, 125 Idaho 473, 475, 873 P.2d 118, 120 (1994)).

The trial court heard evidence by the writer of the declaration who stated that the prohibition on businesses was intended to prohibit activities such as opening automobile repair shops and animal kennels. In addition, the trial court found that at least two other families in the subdivision conduct swimming lessons from their backyard pools. One family has conducted lessons for over fifteen years. The trial court also found that with the exception of the Gabriels, no other resident of the subdivision has registered any complaints about the lessons. This evidence supports the finding that the term "business" as used in the declaration was not intended nor interpreted by the owners of lots in the subdivision to prohibit swimming lessons conducted by a homeowner's children in their own backyard during a limited time in the summer....

We affirm the judgment of the trial court....

SCHROEDER, JUSTICE, concurring. I concur in the result but do so on the basis that it is clear, as the district court determined, that the declaration of restrictions has been abandoned as it applies to swimming lessons of the type conducted by the respondent's children. The Court's decision goes too far in using evidence of conduct within the neighborhood to interpret the meaning of the restriction. That evidence clearly establishes abandonment but should not be used to say that this commercial activity is not a business. If this activity had been challenged shortly after the subdivision was developed it would seem almost certain that there would be a finding that this was a business. However, the neighborhood has abandoned objection to this commercial activity. Even those who now object have conducted business on their property.

Notes

1. *Rules of Construction for Interpreting Covenants.* The *Gabriel* court applies the rule of construction traditionally applied to conveyances—ambiguous restrictions should be construed narrowly (*i.e.,* in the least restrictive fashion) so as to promote the general alienability of land. Is this a sensible approach? Consider the view expressed in the new Restatement:

> (1) A servitude should be interpreted to give effect to the intention of the parties ascertained from the language used in the instrument, or the circumstances surrounding creation of the servitude, and to carry out the purpose for which it was created.

> (2) Unless the purpose for which the servitude is created violates public policy, and unless contrary to the intent of the parties, a servitude should be interpreted to avoid violating public policy. Among reasonable interpretations, that which is more consonant with public policy should be preferred. [Restatement of Servitudes § 4.1.]

The comments highlight the Restatement's shift to an intent-based determination:

> The rule that servitudes should be interpreted to carry out the intent of the parties and the purpose of the intended servitude departs from the often expressed view that servitudes should be narrowly construed to favor the free use of land. It is based in the recognition that servitudes are widely used in modern land development and ordinarily play a valuable role in utilization of land resources. The rule is supported by modern case law. [*Id.* cmt. a.]

Does this comment suggest that property law should no longer care about facilitating the "free use" or alienability of land? Why or why not? How should a court resolve the dispute in *Gabriel* under the new Restatement?

2. *Defining "Single–Family Residence."* Disputes regarding the interpretation of single-family residence covenants generally have arisen in one of three contexts. The first—is a use residential or commercial?—raises questions similar to those presented in the *Gabriel* case.

The second is whether "single-family residential use" permits only detached homes or instead allows for the construction of multiple residential units that each contained only a single family within each unit. Should a "single-family residential use only" covenant prevent the owner from constructing a duplex? Why or why not? *See, e.g., Stolba v. Vesci,* 909 S.W.2d 706 (Mo. Ct. App. 1995).

The third is whether "single-family residential use" includes residential use by unrelated individuals. This latter issue has arisen most commonly in disputes involving group homes. Though most courts have reached the conclusion that group homes are not inconsistent with "single-family" classification, *see, e.g., Hill v. Community of Damien of Molokai,* 121 N.M. 353, 911 P.2d 861 (1996); *Gregory v. Department of Mental Health, Retardation and Hospitals,* 495 A.2d 997 (R.I. 1985), at least one court has found that a group home violated a single-family residence covenant. *See Mains Farm Homeowners Ass'n v. Worthington,* 121 Wash.2d 810, 854 P.2d 1072 (1993). How might the exact phrasing of the covenant impact the result in a given case? Would it matter if the covenant defined "single-family" to include only those related by blood or marriage? Under the new Restatement, how should a court interpret the term "single-family" as applied to a group home?

Consider how you would advise your client regarding whether a covenant restricting use "for single-family residential purposes only" would prohibit the following activities. What additional information would you like to gather to advise your client properly?

(a) Your client proposes to use his residence as a day-care facility. *Compare Metzner* v. *Wojdyla,* 125 Wash.2d 445, 886 P.2d 154 (1994) *and Walton v. Carignan,* 103 N.C.App. 364, 407 S.E.2d 241 (1991) *with Beverly Island Ass'n v. Zinger,* 113 Mich.App. 322, 317 N.W.2d 611 (1982).

(b) Your client wants to construct a parking lot on her land to serve an adjacent parcel that is not subject to a restriction. *Compare Dierberg v. Wills,* 700 S.W.2d 461 (Mo. Ct. App. 1985) *with Morgan v. Matheson,* 362 Mich. 535, 107 N.W.2d 825 (1961).

(c) Your client wants to build a little league practice field on the lot adjacent to his house. *See Bagko Dev. Co. v. Damitz,* 640 N.E.2d 67 (Ind. Ct. App. 1994).

(d) Your client wants to conduct a garage sale and conduct a series of "sales parties" for Pampered Chef® kitchen goods.

Now that information technology has made "telecommuting" a reality, how should courts interpret "residential use only" covenants with respect to writers, consultants, painters, craftspersons and manufacturer's sales representatives working out of their homes? Is this solely a matter of importance to residents of the affected subdivision? Does that matter?

3. *Building Restrictions vs. Use Restrictions.* Restrictive covenants often limit the physical types and features of structures on lots within a CIC, and these restrictions often give rise to disputes. Should application of *building* restrictions be reviewed under a different standard than application of *use* restrictions? Are these two types of restrictions clearly distinguishable? For example, suppose that the declaration for Shady Acres subdivision provides that: "No structure of a temporary character, trailer, tent, shack, barn, or other outbuilding shall be placed on any lot and used as a residence at any time." Henning, owner of a lot in Shady Acres, purchases a mobile home and places it on his lot on a permanent foundation (so that it is no longer readily movable). Can the homeowners' association require Henning to remove the home? *Compare Timmerman v. Gabriel*, 155 Mont. 294, 470 P.2d 528 (1970) *and Newman v. Wittmer*, 277 Mont. 1, 917 P.2d 926 (1996) with *Hussey v. Ray*, 462 S.W.2d 45 (Tex. Civ. App. 1970) *and Kinchen v. Layton*, 457 So.2d 343 (Miss. 1984). How might the developer of Shady Acres have drafted the restriction to address the risk of such improvements with greater effectiveness and less uncertainty?

4. *The Fair Housing Act (FHA).* The FHA provides a significant basis for asserting challenges that a covenant is inconsistent with public policy and thus unenforceable. For example, in *Shelley v. Kraemer*, 334 U.S. 1, 68 S.Ct. 836, 92 L.Ed. 1161 (1948), the Supreme Court held that enforcement of a racially restrictive covenant in state court violated the Constitution's equal protection clause. Today, racially restrictive covenants also violate the FHA, and thus a court could strike down a racially restrictive covenant without having to rely upon the *Shelley* case.

Can a facially neutral restriction violate the FHA? Review the provisions of the FHA (page 539) in light of the following facts: Assume that a restricted subdivision limits lots to use only for a "single-family residence," but the covenant does not specifically define "single-family residence." Assume further that a local church purchases a three-bedroom home in the subdivision and begins operating a hospice for three AIDS patients. The patients pay rent, and church members provide a variety of services (including in-home health care, meal preparation, and companionship). Several neighbors seek your advice regarding whether they can enforce the single-family residence covenant to enjoin the church from operating the hospice. How would you advise them? What information would you want to gather? Can you think of circumstances in which neighbors could enforce a single-family residence restriction to prevent a group home without running afoul of the FHA?

Another common set of restrictions that exist in many subdivisions concern minimum square footage requirements and other aesthetic obligations. Does the FHA provide a means for contesting restrictions such as minimum square footage restrictions? How difficult would it be to prove an FHA claim based on minimum square footage requirements?

Management of daily life within a CIC depends upon the exercise of judgment by the association board (or some other authorized decision-making group). For example, many modern residential CICs have CCRs that prohibit lot owners from building a new home or modifying an existing one without obtaining prior approval of the building plans and specifications (either by the association board or an architectural control committee). An association board might have to make a decision between relying upon neighborhood residents to volunteer to mow grass in common areas or to expend association funds to hire a private contractor to perform the job.

People of good will often disagree regarding how to govern or regulate life within CICs. If a lot owner disagrees with a board's decision, should the law respond by deferring to the board's judgment as a product of the community's democratic process? Or should lot owners have recourse to judicial review—and, if so, what standard should govern that review?

LAMDEN v. LA JOLLA SHORES CLUBDOMINIUM HOMEOWNERS ASS'N

Supreme Court of California.
21 Cal.4th 249, 87 Cal.Rptr.2d 237, 980 P.2d 940 (1999).

WERDEGAR, J. . . . Plaintiff Gertrude M. Lamden owns a condominium unit in one of three buildings comprising the La Jolla Shores Clubdominium condominium development (Development). Over some years, the Board of Governors (Board) of defendant La Jolla Shores Clubdominium Homeowners Association (Association), an unincorporated community association, elected to spot treat (secondary treatment), rather than fumigate (primary treatment), for termites the building in which Lamden's unit is located (Building Three).

In the late 1980's, attempting to remedy water intrusion and mildew damage, the Association hired a contractor to renovate exterior siding on all three buildings in the Development. The contractor replaced the siding on the southern exposure of Building Three and removed damaged drywall and framing. Where the contractor encountered termites, a termite extermination company provided spot treatment and replaced damaged material.

Lamden remodeled the interior of her condominium in 1990. At that time, the Association's manager arranged for a termite extermination company to spot treat areas where Lamden had encountered termites.

The following year, both Lamden and the Association obtained termite inspection reports recommending fumigation, but the Association's Board decided against that approach. As the Court of Appeal explained, the Board based its decision not to fumigate on concerns about the cost of fumigation, logistical problems with temporarily relocating residents, concern that fumigation residue could affect residents' health and safety, awareness that upcoming walkway renovations would include replacement of damaged areas, pet moving expenses, anticipated breakage by the termite company, lost rental income and the likelihood that termite infestation would recur even if primary treatment were utilized. The Board decided to continue to rely on secondary treatment until a more widespread problem was demonstrated.

In 1991 and 1992, the Association engaged a company to repair water intrusion damage to four units in Building Three. The company removed siding in the balcony area, repaired and waterproofed the decks, and repaired joints between the decks and the walls of the units. The siding of the unit below Lamden's and one of its walls were repaired. Where termite infestation or damage became apparent during this project, spot treatment was applied and damaged material removed.

In 1993 and 1994, the Association commissioned major renovation of the Development's walkway system, underpinnings of which had suffered water and termite damage. The $1.6 million walkway project was monitored by a structural engineer and an on-site architect.

In 1994, Lamden brought this action for damages, an injunction and declaratory relief. She purported to state numerous causes of action based on the Association's refusal to fumigate for termites, naming as defendants certain individual members of the Board as well as the Association. Her amended complaint included claims sounding in breach of contract (viz., the governing Declaration of Restrictions [Declaration]), breach of fiduciary duty and negligence. She alleged that the Association, in opting for secondary over primary treatment, had breached Civil Code section 1364, subdivision (b)(1)[18] and the Declaration[19] in failing adequately to repair, replace and maintain the common areas of the Development....

After both sides had presented evidence and argument, the trial court rendered findings related to the termite infestation affecting plaintiff's condominium unit, its causes, and the remedial steps taken by the Association. The trial court found there was "no question from all the evidence that Mrs. Lamden's unit ... has had a serious problem with termites." In fact, the trial court found, "The evidence ... was overwhelming that termites had been a problem over the past several years." The court concluded, however, that while "there may be active infestation" that would require "steps [to be] taken within the future years," there was no evidence that the condominium units were in imminent structural danger or "that these units are about to fall or something is about to happen."

---

18. As discussed more fully below, "In a community apartment project, condominium project, or stock cooperative ... unless otherwise provided in the declaration, the association is responsible for the repair and maintenance of the common area occasioned by the presence of wood-destroying pests or organisms." (Civ.Code, § 1364, subd. (b)(1).)

19. The Declaration, which contained the Development's governing covenants, conditions, and restrictions (CC & R's), stated that the Association was to provide for the management, maintenance, repair and preservation of the complex's common areas for the enhancement of the value of the project and each unit and for the benefit of the owners.

The trial court also found that, "starting in the late '80's," the Association had arranged for "some work" addressing the termite problem to be done. Remedial and investigative work ordered by the Association included, according to the trial court, removal of siding to reveal the extent of damage, a "big project ... in the early '90's," and an architect's report on building design factors. According to the court, the Board "did at one point seriously consider" primary treatment; "they got a bid for this fumigation, and there was discussion." The court found that the Board also considered possible problems entailed by fumigation, including relocation costs, lost rent, concerns about pets and plants, human health issues and eventual termite reinfestation.

As to the causes of the Development's termite infestation, the trial court concluded that "the key problem came about from you might say a poor design" and resulting "water intrusion." In short, the trial court stated, "the real culprit is not so much the Board, but it's the poor design and the water damage that is conducive to bringing the termites in."

As to the Association's actions, the trial court stated, "the Board did take appropriate action." The court noted the Board "did come up with a plan," viz., to engage a pest control service to "come out and [spot] treat [termite infestation] when it was found." The trial judge opined he might, "from a personal relations standpoint," have acted sooner or differently under the circumstances than did the Association, but nevertheless concluded "the Board did have a rational basis for their decision to reject fumigation, and do what they did." Ultimately, the court gave judgment for the Association, applying what it called a "business judgment test." Lamden appealed.

Citing *Frances T. v. Village Green Owners Association* (1986) 42 Cal.3d 490, 229 Cal.Rptr. 456, 723 P.2d 573 (*Frances T.*), the Court of Appeal agreed with Lamden that the trial court had applied the wrong standard of care in assessing the Association's actions. In the Court of Appeal's view, relevant statutes, the governing Declaration and principles of common law imposed on the Association an objective duty of reasonable care in repairing and maintaining the Development's common areas near Lamden's unit as occasioned by the presence of termites. The court also concluded that, had the trial court analyzed the Association's actions under an objective standard of reasonableness, an outcome more favorable to Lamden likely would have resulted. Accordingly, the Court of Appeal reversed the judgment of the trial court. . . .

The Association would have us decide this case through application of "the business judgment rule." As we have observed, that rule of judicial deference to corporate decisionmaking "exists in one form or another in every American jurisdiction." (*Frances T., supra*, 42 Cal.3d at p. 507, fn. 14, 229 Cal.Rptr. 456, 723 P.2d 573.)

"The common law business judgment rule has two components— one which immunizes [corporate] directors from personal liability if they act in accordance with its requirements, and another which insulates from court intervention those management decisions which are made by directors in good faith in what the directors believe is the organization's best interest." (*Lee v. Interinsurance Exchange* (1996) 50 Cal.App.4th 694, 714, 57 Cal.Rptr.2d 798.) A hallmark of the business judgment rule is that, when the rule's requirements are met, a court will not substitute its judgment for that of the corporation's board of directors. . . . According to the Association, uniformly applying a business judgment standard in judicial review of community association board decisions would promote certainty, stability and predictability in common interest development governance. Plaintiff, on the other hand, contends general application of a business judgment standard to board decisions would undermine individual owners' ability, under Civil Code section 1354, to enforce, as equitable servitudes, the CC & R's in a common interest development's declaration. Stressing residents' interest in a stable and predictable living environment, as embodied in a given development's particular CC & R's, plaintiff encourages us to impose on community associations an objective standard of reasonableness in carrying out their duties under governing CC & R's or public policy. . . .

. . . The precise question presented, then, is whether we should in this case adopt for California courts a rule—analogous perhaps to the business judgment rule—of judicial deference to community association board decisionmaking that would apply, regardless of an association's corporate status, when owners in common interest developments seek to litigate ordinary maintenance decisions entrusted to the discretion of their associations' boards of directors.

Our existing jurisprudence specifically addressing the governance of common interest developments is not voluminous. While we have not previously examined the question of what standard or test generally governs judicial review of decisions made by the board of directors of a community association, we have examined related questions.

Fifty years ago, in *Hannula v. Hacienda Homes* (1949) 34 Cal.2d 442, 211 P.2d 302, we held that the decision by the board of directors of a real estate development company to deny, under a restrictive covenant in a deed, the owner of a fractional part of a lot permission to build a dwelling thereon "must be a reasonable determination made in good faith." Sixteen years ago, we held that a condominium owners association is a "business establishment" within the meaning of the Unruh Civil Rights Act, section 51 of the Civil Code. (*O'Connor v. Village Green Owners Association* (1983) 33 Cal.3d 790, 796, 191 Cal.Rptr. 320, 662 P.2d 427.) And 10 years ago, in *Frances T., supra*, 42 Cal.3d 490, 229 Cal.Rptr. 456, 723 P.2d 573, we considered "whether a condominium owners association and the individual members of its board of directors may be held liable for injuries to a unit owner caused by third-party criminal conduct." (*Id.* at p. 495, 229 Cal.Rptr. 456, 723 P.2d 573.)

In *Frances T.*, a condominium owner who resided in her unit brought an action against the community association, a nonprofit corporation, and the individual members of its board of directors after she was raped and robbed in her dwelling. She alleged negligence, breach of contract and breach of fiduciary duty, based on the association's failure to install sufficient exterior lighting and its requiring her to remove additional lighting that she had installed herself. The trial court sustained the defendants' general demurrers to all three causes of action. (*Frances T., supra*, 42 Cal.3d at p. 495, 229 Cal.Rptr. 456, 723 P.2d 573.) We reversed. A community association, we concluded, may be held to a landlord's standard of care as to residents' safety in the common areas, and the plaintiff had alleged particularized facts stating a cause of action against both the association and the individual members of the board. The plaintiff failed, however, to state a cause of action for breach of contract, as neither the development's governing CC & R's nor the association's bylaws obligated the defendants to install additional lighting. The plaintiff failed likewise to state a cause of action for breach of fiduciary duties, as the defendants had fulfilled their duty to the plaintiff as a shareholder, and the plaintiff had alleged no facts to show that the association's board members had a fiduciary duty to serve as the condominium project's landlord. . . .

More recently, in *Nahrstedt v. Lakeside Village Condominium Assn.* (1994) 8 Cal.4th 361, 375, 33 Cal.Rptr.2d 63, 878 P.2d 1275 (*Nahrstedt*), we confronted the question, "When restrictions limiting the use of property within a common interest development satisfy the requirements of covenants running with the land or of equitable servitudes, what standard or test governs their enforceability?"

In *Nahrstedt*, an owner of a condominium unit who had three cats sued the community association, its officers and two of its employees for declaratory relief, seeking to prevent the defendants from enforcing against her a prohibition on keeping pets that was contained in the community association's recorded CC & R's. In resolving the dispute, we distilled from numerous authorities the principle that "[a]n equitable servitude will be enforced unless it violates public policy; it bears no rational relationship to the protection, preservation, operation or purpose of the affected land; or it otherwise imposes burdens on the affected land that are so disproportionate to the restriction's beneficial effects that the restriction should not be enforced." Applying this principle, and noting that a common interest development's recorded use restrictions are "enforceable equitable servitudes, unless unreasonable" (Civ.Code, § 1354, subd. (a)), we held that "such restrictions should be enforced unless they are wholly arbitrary, violate a fundamental public policy, or impose a burden on the use of affected land that far outweighs any benefit."

In deciding *Nahrstedt*, we noted that ownership of a unit in a common interest development ordinarily "entails mandatory membership in an owners association, which, through an elected board of directors, is empowered to enforce any use restrictions contained in the project's declaration or master deed and to enact new rules governing the use and occupancy of property within the project." "Because of its considerable power in managing and regulating a common interest development," we observed, "the governing board of an owners association must guard against the potential for the abuse of that power." We also noted that a community association's governing board's power to regulate "pertains to a 'wide spectrum of activities,' such as the volume of playing music, hours of social gatherings, use of patio furniture and barbecues, and rental of units."

We declared in *Nahrstedt* that, "when an association determines that a unit owner has violated a use restriction, the association must do so in good faith, not in an arbitrary or capricious manner, and its enforcement procedures must be fair and applied uniformly." Nevertheless, we stated, "Generally, courts will uphold decisions made by the governing board of an owners association so long as they represent good faith efforts to further the purposes of the common interest development, are consistent with the development's governing documents, and comply with public policy." . . .

[H]aving reviewed the record in this case, and in light of the foregoing authorities, we conclude that the Board's decision here to use secondary, rather than primary, treatment in addressing the Development's termite problem, a matter entrusted to its discretion under the Declaration and Civil Code section 1364, falls within [this pronouncement from] *Nahrstedt*. . . . Moreover, our deferring to the Board's discretion in this matter, which, as previously noted, is broadly conferred in the Development's CC & R's, is consistent with *Nahrstedt*'s holding that CC & R's "should be enforced unless they are wholly arbitrary, violate a fundamental public policy, or impose a burden on the use of affected land that far outweighs any benefit."

Here, the Board exercised discretion clearly within the scope of its authority under the Declaration and governing statutes to select among means for discharging its obligation to maintain and repair the Development's common areas occasioned by the presence of wood-destroying pests or organisms. The trial court found that the Board acted upon reasonable investigation, in good faith, and in a manner the Board believed was in the best interests of the Association and its members.

Contrary to the Court of Appeal, we conclude the trial court was correct to defer to the Board's decision. We hold that, where a duly constituted community association board, upon reasonable investigation, in good faith and with regard for the best interests of the community association and its members, exercises discretion within the scope of its authority under relevant statutes, covenants and restrictions to select among means for discharging an obligation to maintain and repair a development's common areas, courts should defer to the board's authority and presumed expertise. . . .

Our conclusion also accords with our recognition in *Frances T.* that the relationship between the individual owners and the managing association of a common interest development is complex. On the one hand, each individual owner has an economic interest in the proper business management of the development as a whole for the sake of maximizing the value of his or her investment. In this aspect, the relationship between homeowner and association is somewhat analogous to that between shareholder and corporation. On the other hand, each individual owner, at least while residing in the development, has a personal, not strictly economic, interest in the appropriate management of the development for the sake of maintaining its security against criminal conduct and other foreseeable risks of physical injury. In this aspect, the relationship between owner and association is somewhat analogous to that between tenant and landlord. Relying on *Frances T.*, the Court of Appeal held that a landlord-like common law duty required Association, in discharging its responsibility to maintain and repair the common areas occasioned by the presence of termites, to exercise reasonable care in order to protect plaintiff's unit from undue damage.... [But] *Frances T.* involved a common interest development resident who suffered "physical injury, not pecuniary harm...." Plaintiff here, by contrast, has not resided in the Development since the time that significant termite infestation was discovered, and she alleges neither a failure by the Association to maintain the common areas in a reasonably safe condition, nor knowledge on the Board's part of any unreasonable risk of physical injury stemming from its failure to do so. Plaintiff alleges simply that the Association failed to effect necessary pest control and repairs, thereby causing her pecuniary damages, including diminution in the value of her unit. Accordingly, *Frances T.* is inapplicable.

Plaintiff warns that judicial deference to the Board's decision in this case would not be appropriate, lest every community association be free to do as little or as much as it pleases in satisfying its obligations to its members. We do not agree. Our respecting the Association's discretion, under this Declaration, to choose among modes of termite treatment does not foreclose the possibility that more restrictive provisions relating to the same or other topics might be "otherwise provided in the declaration[s]" (Civ.Code, § 1364, subd. (b)(1)) of other common interest developments. As discussed, we have before us today a declaration constituting a general scheme for maintenance, protection and enhancement of value of the Development, one that entrusts to the Association the management, maintenance and preservation of the Development's common areas and confers on the Board the power and authority to maintain and repair those areas. Thus, the Association's obligation at issue in this case is broadly cast, plainly conferring on the Association the discretion to select, as it did, among available means for addressing the Development's termite infestation. Under the circumstances, our respecting that discretion obviously does not foreclose community association governance provisions that, within the bounds of the law, might more narrowly circumscribe association or board discretion....

Finally, plaintiff contends a rule of judicial deference will insulate community association boards' decisions from judicial review. We disagree. As illustrated by *Fountain Valley Chateau Blanc Homeowner's Assn. v. Department of Veterans Affairs* (1998) 67 Cal.App.4th 743, 754–

755, 79 Cal.Rptr.2d 248 (*Fountain Valley*), judicial oversight affords significant protection against overreaching by such boards.

In *Fountain Valley*, a homeowners association, threatening litigation against an elderly homeowner with Hodgkin's disease, gained access to the interior of his residence and demanded he remove a number of personal items, including books and papers not constituting "standard reading material," claiming the items posed a fire hazard. The homeowner settled the original complaint, but cross-complained for violation of privacy, trespass, negligence and breach of contract. The jury returned a verdict in his favor, finding specifically that the association had acted unreasonably.... [T]he Court of Appeal held that, in light of the operative facts found by the jury, it was "virtually impossible" to say the association had acted reasonably. The city fire department had found no fire hazard, and the association "did not have a good faith, albeit mistaken, belief in that danger." In the absence of such good faith belief, the court determined the jury's verdict must stand, thus impliedly finding no basis for judicial deference to the association's decision....

Common sense suggests that judicial deference in such cases as this is appropriate, in view of the relative competence, over that of courts, possessed by owners and directors of common interest developments to make the detailed and peculiar economic decisions necessary in the maintenance of those developments. A deferential standard will, by minimizing the likelihood of unproductive litigation over their governing associations' discretionary economic decisions, foster stability, certainty and predictability in the governance and management of common interest developments. Beneficial corollaries include enhancement of the incentives for essential voluntary owner participation in common interest development governance and conservation of scarce judicial resources.

For the foregoing reasons, the judgment of the Court of Appeal is reversed.

Notes

1. *The Enforceability of Assessments for Community Facilities/Services and the Quality of Services Provided.* Suppose that a subdivision's HOA generally provides snow removal services, but fails to do so on two occasions during the year—and that as a result, several residents in a low-lying area of the development are unable to get to work. May those residents withhold some or all of their assessment payments? The majority view suggests that the answer is no; each landowner's assessment obligation is independent (*i.e.*, without regard to the association's performance of those services or her satisfaction with that performance). *See, e.g., Kay v. Via Verde Homeowners' Ass'n, Inc.*, 677 So.2d 337 (Fla. Dist. Ct. App. 1996) *and Panther Lake Homeowners' Ass'n v. Juergensen*, 76 Wash.App. 586, 887 P.2d 465 (1995) (denying offsets); *but see Kirktown Homes Ass'n v. Arey*, 812 S.W.2d 198 (Mo. Ct. App. 1991) (allowing offset). Some states protect association finances in this setting by statute. *See, e.g.*, Ga. Code Ann. § 44–3–80(d). Can

you explain why the law should view the landowner's assessment obligation as independent? To what extent should the language of the declaration control this determination?

2. *Judicial Review of Association Decisions—"Reasonableness" vs. "Business Judgment."* When an owner raises a challenge to a board decision or action, courts have applied one of two standards of review: the "business judgment" rule, applied by analogy in *Lamden*, or the "reasonableness" standard typified by *Hidden Harbour Estates, Inc. v. Basso*, 393 So.2d 637 (Fla. Dist. Ct. App. 1981). In *Basso*, a couple sought permission to drill a well on their lot. The board of the Hidden Harbor Estates owners' association denied their request because of concerns that the proposed well might (a) increase the salinity of two existing wells that supplied water to unit owners, (b) result in staining of sidewalks and other common areas, and (c) cause a proliferation of wells by other unit owners. When the Bassos drilled a well anyway, the board sued to enjoin its operation. The trial court denied an injunction, and the appellate court affirmed. The court admitted that the board's stated reasons for denial were "legitimate objectives which would have promoted the aesthetic appeal of the condominium development." 393 So.2d at 640. The court nevertheless concluded that the board had failed to demonstrate that its denial was reasonable:

> The requirement of "reasonableness" in these instances is designed to somewhat fetter the discretion of the board of directors. By imposing such a standard, the board is required to enact rules and make decisions that are reasonably related to the promotion of the health, happiness and peace of mind of the unit owners. . . . [W]here the decision to allow a particular use is within the discretion of the board, the board must allow the use unless the use is demonstrably antagonistic to the legitimate objectives of the condominium association, *i.e.*, the health, happiness and peace of mind of the individual unit owners. [*Id.*]

Do you think that Ms. Lamden would have prevailed under this standard? Why was the court in *Lamden* willing to provide such strong deference to the Association's judgment as to how to address the termite infestation problem? Are you persuaded by the court's explanation? If you were representing Ms. Lamden, what facts (if true) might strengthen her case that the board's decision breached its duty to her as a lot owner?

Note that the language of *Lamden* addresses judicial review of a very wide variety of potential board actions. Examine the court's discussion of the appropriate standard(s) of judicial review in the series of precedents it discusses: *Frances T.*, *Hannula*, *O'Connor*, *Nahrstedt* and *Fountain Valley*. In which of these decisions does *Lamden* consider the business judgment rule to apply? In which does *Lamden* consider the reasonableness review to be applicable? In particular, which rule would you characterize *Nahrstedt's* "broad deference" to embody? Do the distinctions applied in California case law, as summarized in *Lamden*, seem appropriate to you? Why or why not?

LAWYERING EXERCISE
(Fact Investigation and Negotiation)

SITUATION: A dispute has arisen concerning a restrictive covenant in the high-end development of Lincoln Heights in the town of Murphydale. Lincoln Heights was developed in 1985 on a 200–acre tract of farm ground. There are 50 homes in the development, ranging in price from $600,000 to more than $3 million. Lincoln Heights has an extensive list of covenants, conditions and restrictions (CCRs), which were recorded in 1984 before the development was built. Many of the covenants are common to those in the typical residential development (*e.g.*, single family residences only; no sheds or other outbuildings), but some are more controversial, such as:

6. No pets of any kind are allowed.

8. Exteriors: All homes must have cedar shake roofs and natural cedar siding, which may be stained only in neutral grays and earth tone colors. Yards must be neatly landscaped with natural shrubbery, flowers and plants. No artificial yard ornaments are permitted.

13. No outdoor sports facilities are permitted. The prohibition includes, but is not limited to basketball hoops, backstops, and soccer goals. Swingsets and jungle gyms may be installed only if made of wood and other high-quality components authorized by the board of directors. In-ground swimming pools also are permitted.

14. No businesses of any kind are permitted, which includes for-profit day care; music lessons, swimming lessons, or other types of instruction on the premises; garage/yard sales; or any other for-profit enterprise that would invite customers or patrons to the premises.

15. Vehicles owned by homeowners or regularly parked on the premises must be black, white, gray, beige, or gold to blend in with the surrounding natural environment. No bright colors are permitted. Vehicles are limited to automobiles, vans, and other passenger vehicles. No trucks, all-terrain vehicles, or motorcycles are permitted.

With respect to termination and amendment, the Declaration provides:

33. These covenants shall run with the land and continue until January 1, 2014, after which time they shall be automatically extended for successive periods of five years, unless an instrument signed by a majority of the then owners of said land shall have been recorded in the office of the County Clerk of Washington County, agreeing to change the covenants in whole or in part.

Eugene Basanta, a transactional attorney with a medium-sized law firm in Murphydale, recently purchased one of the high-end homes in Lincoln Heights. Basanta owns a bright yellow Cooper Mini. Shortly after

Basanta moved into his home in January, one of the neighbors filed a complaint with the homeowners association's Board of Directors alleging that Basanta's car violated CCR No. 15. The Board has agreed to meet with Basanta (and his attorney) in an attempt to negotiate a settlement of the matter.

TASK: On behalf of either the Board or Basanta (as assigned by your instructor), negotiate an acceptable settlement to the dispute, and explain how the parties will document that settlement.

e. *Termination and Amendment of Servitudes.* As CICs proliferate, servitude law must address the financial and regulatory challenges involved when the original CCRs prove insufficient to address changed circumstances. In large part, servitude regimes are designed to promote stability over time and typically remain binding for many decades. Yet in drafting a servitude regime, no one can foresee the changes that will occur over long periods of time.

As we have already seen, a developer may establish an assessment mechanism that proves inadequate if community maintenance needs dramatically increase over time. Likewise, as circumstances change, community residents may change their views about ideal uses or community governance within the subdivision, for any number of reasons. The association may realize that the community's lack of recreational facilities (in comparison to other communities) has adverse effects on home values within the community. The residents may conclude that some of their covenants or enforcement procedures are unworkably strict or lax. Board positions may remain unfilled due to apathy, or to the "negative experience" of prior board members who became involved in earlier conflicts.[20] [Consider whether you would have agreed to serve as a board member of the La Jolla Shores Clubdominium Association after the *Lamden* case!] Changes surrounding the subdivision may change the uses that some residents wish to permit (or forbid) within the subdivision, such as the palette of permissible exterior paint colors or minimum square footage requirements for buildings. A covenant that requires wood-shake shingle roofs—highly valued 25 years ago for its aesthetic appeal—may today be viewed as suboptimal (because such roofs are more difficult and expensive to maintain, often require more frequent replacement, and present an increased fire risk).

Likewise, market valuation of competing land uses may affect the utility of a covenant. Even the most fundamental of typical CIC restrictions—the "residential use only" restriction—may trigger this problem:

---

20. These negative consequences can be financial as well as emotional. In one noteworthy case, *Riss v. Angel*, 131 Wash.2d 612, 934 P.2d 669 (1997), the association board exercised its discretion to reject architectural plans for a lot owner's new home. The court concluded that the plans complied with the applicable CCRs, that the association's decision was unreasonable and unenforceable, *and that the individual association members who participated in or ratified that decision were jointly and severally liable for damages!*

Perhaps the original prohibition of commercial uses reflected an accurate judgment that operation of a grocery store or pharmacy within the restricted area would, on balance, impose harmful externalities on surrounding properties. Over time, however, the market may come to consider isolation from all commercial services an even more onerous burden than the harmful spillovers traditionally associated with commercial uses in residential areas. As the drafting of servitudes becomes increasingly detailed and restrictive, the likelihood grows that changing circumstances and preferences will render the servitudes obsolete, and the obsolescence concern obviously grows over time. Unless the drafters of the servitude regime included workable provisions for modifying restrictions, property owners seeking to moderate the neighborhood's isolation from commercial services will face one of two often prohibitive options: either obtain unanimous agreement of all neighbors to a servitude change or litigate the continued enforceability of restrictions on the basis of changed circumstances. Where servitudes are part of a common development plan for large subdivisions, overwhelming transaction costs will often prevent any modification not provided for in advance by the servitude drafter. [James L. Winokur, *The Mixed Blessings of Promissory Servitudes: Toward Optimizing Economic Utility, Individual Liberty, and Personal Identity*, 1989 Wis. L. Rev. 1, 34–36.]

Accordingly, servitude law may be unable to preserve the value-protecting or value-enhancing effects of promissory servitudes without providing the flexibility necessary to terminate or modify servitudes as future circumstances warrant. One fundamental question is whether this flexibility should be external or internal to the servitude regime. In other words, should the law permit (or encourage) courts to freely modify or terminate servitudes as circumstances change? Or should the law permit modification or termination of servitudes only in accordance with the terms of the declaration itself? Further, should legislatures *require* that CCRs contain provisions that will easily facilitate future changes?

The next two cases focus upon the way in which courts have traditionally dealt with old or obsolete servitudes using judicial doctrines regarding modification or termination of servitudes. After these cases, the materials then address the processes that permit a CIC to amend its declaration. How effectively have developers built flexibility into servitude regimes? To what extent should (or should not) servitude law dictate the parameters of amendment processes?

FINK v. MILLER

Utah Court of Appeals.
896 P.2d 649 (1995).

ORME, PRESIDING JUDGE. . . . Plaintiff C.W. Fink and defendant Shannon Miller purchased lots in Maple Hills Subdivision No. 3, Plat D, located in the east bench area of Bountiful, Utah. Both parties received copies of the Agreement for Protective Covenants, recorded in Davis County by the developer of Maple Hills in 1978. One of the covenants recites that "[w]ood shingles ... shall be required on the exterior roofs of all structures." Also, prospective home builders, as well as owners intending to improve or alter existing structures, must submit all plans and specifications, including proposed exterior colors and materials, to the Community Development Committee for its approval before commencing construction.

Sometime prior to 1985, Committee members received a copy of the Agreement with a handwritten addition to the roofing materials provision, so that the restriction read "wood shingles or bar tile." Consequently, prior to 1985 the Committee approved plans calling for tile roofs. In 1985 it learned that the covenant had not, in fact, been thus amended. Meanwhile, six homes were built with fiberglass/asphalt shingle roofs without Committee approval. By the end of 1985, twenty-nine homes had been completed in Maple Hills. Eight homes had wood shingle roofs, while twenty-one homes had either tile or fiberglass/asphalt shingle roofs.

Nevertheless, subsequent to 1985, the Committee has sought to enforce the covenant restricting roofing materials to wood shingles and has refused to approve plans that included tile or fiberglass/asphalt shingle roofs. In 1990, the Committee approved plans submitted by defendants Shannon Miller and her husband, Jim Miller, which called for a wood shingle roof. One year later, the Millers requested approval to change the originally specified roofing material from wood shingles to fiberglass shingles. After the Committee denied the change, the Millers nonetheless commenced installation of fiberglass shingles.

In November 1991, Fink commenced this action and filed an *ex parte* motion seeking injunctive relief to prevent the installation of fiberglass shingles on the Millers' home. . . .

. . . On February 2, 1994, the trial court issued its final order . . . denying a permanent injunction. The court, noting in its factual findings that as of July 1993 the subdivision's eighty-one completed homes included fifty-eight homes with wood shingle roofs and twenty-three homes with non-wood roofs, concluded that the covenants still validly restricted the color and quality of materials, but could not restrict roofing materials by type. The court opined that the Committee must approve any roofing materials of adequate quality that blend "harmoniously with the current neighborhood." Fink now appeals from this order. . . .

Fink's arguments focus on two issues: (1) whether the trial court erred in concluding, as a matter of law, that the covenant restricting roofing materials to wood shingles cannot be enforced and (2) whether there existed disputed material facts which should have precluded the court's grant of summary judgment in favor of the Millers. . . .

As a general proposition, property owners who have purchased land in a subdivision, subject to a recorded set of restrictive covenants and conditions, have the right to enforce such restrictions through equitable relief against property owners who do not comply with the stated restrictions. *See Crimmins v. Simonds*, 636 P.2d 478, 480 (Utah 1981) (noting property owners' protectable interest in enforceability of covenants). *See generally* Roger A. Cunningham et al., The Law of Property §§ 8.32, 8.33 (1984). However, as explained below, property owners may lose this right if the specific covenant they seek to enforce has been abandoned, thereby rendering the covenant unenforceable. . . .

In the instant case, the trial court, as well as the parties, relied upon *Crimmins v. Simonds*, 636 P.2d 478 (Utah 1981), in analyzing the enforceability of the covenant restricting roofing materials. In *Crimmins*, the Utah Supreme Court examined a restriction forbidding the operation of a trade or business within a subdivision and held that a restrictive covenant is unenforceable if a change in circumstances in the neighborhood is "so great that it clearly neutralizes the benefits of the restriction to the point of defeating its purpose, or . . . renders the covenant valueless." *Id.* at 479. This analysis is useful in the context of restrictions that are closely related to the use of the affected property, such as a covenant that forbids commercial operations or limits land use to agricultural activities. Repeated violations of such covenants may directly affect the nature and character of a particular area or neighborhood, thereby producing a discernible change in circumstances. The Court in *Crimmins* determined that most of the property owners operating existing businesses in the subdivision did so out of their homes, *i.e.*, they were residents whose business activities were secondary to their residential activities. *Id.* at 480. Accordingly, the predominantly residential character of the neighborhood had not changed so dramatically as to render the prohibition on commercial activities valueless. *Id.*

However, unlike the covenant at issue in *Crimmins*, the covenant in the instant case restricts not the use of the property itself, but merely the selection of certain building materials for aesthetic purposes. Violations of this sort of covenant would not produce obvious changes in the fundamental nature of the Maple Hills subdivision—its upscale residential character remains unchanged.[21] Instead, a more appropriate test to determine abandonment of such a covenant requires the party opposing enforcement to prove that existing "violations are so great as to lead the mind of the average [person] to reasonably conclude that the restriction in question has been abandoned." *Tanglewood Homes Ass'n v. Henke*, 728 S.W.2d 39, 43 (Tex.App.1987). In simplest terms, this test is met when the average person, upon inspection of a subdivision and knowing

---

21. Utilization of the *Crimmins* test put the trial court in the awkward position of determining whether the visual qualities of the nonconforming roofs caused a change in aesthetic circumstances. The court, after viewing the subdivision, noted that "those that had the worst appearance as far as the aesthetics, were the wood shingle shake roofs because of all the bleaching and the different colors." Joining the debate at this level, Fink implied that the trial court could not have made an accurate observation of the roofs of Maple Hills because they were wet from a rainstorm during the court's tour, and thus the differences were not as apparent as they would have been during drier conditions. The essentially objective test which we adopt obviates the need for courts to make such subjective judgments.

of a certain restriction, will readily observe sufficient violations so that he or she will logically infer that the property owners neither adhere to nor enforce the restriction.

In applying this test, courts consider the " 'number, nature, and severity of the then existing violation[s], any prior acts of enforcement of the restriction, and whether it is still possible to realize to a substantial degree the benefits intended through the covenant.' " *Id.* at 43–44 (quoting *New Jerusalem Baptist Church, Inc. v. City of Houston*, 598 S.W.2d 666, 669 (Tex.App.1980)). *See also Lakeshore Property Owners Ass'n v. Delatte*, 579 So.2d 1039, 1043 (La.App.) ("abandonment of a restriction depends upon the character, materiality and number of violations and their proximity to the objecting residents"), *cert. denied*, 586 So.2d 560 (La.1991); *Tompkins v. Buttrum Constr. Co.*, 99 Nev. 142, 659 P.2d 865, 867 (1983) (abandonment of restriction will be found if "general and substantial violations" existed).

To maximize the benefits of the essentially objective quality of this test, courts applying it should first analyze violations as to their number, nature, and severity. If these elements alone are sufficient to lead the average person to believe the covenant has been abandoned, it is not necessary to go further. However, if abandonment is still in doubt, courts should then consider the other two factors—namely, prior enforcement efforts and possible realization of benefits—to resolve the abandonment question. . . .

We now consider whether, employing the above test, the existing violations of the Maple Hills roofing covenant demonstrate that it has been abandoned. . . .

We may readily ascertain the actual "number, nature, and severity" of violations of the roofing materials covenant by merely looking at the undisputed facts. Twenty-three out of eighty-one houses in Maple Hills have roofs which do not conform to the wood shingle restriction. A plain reading of the covenant shows that permitted exterior roofing materials are limited to wood shingles only. *See Gosnay v. Big Sky Owners Ass'n*, 205 Mont. 221, 666 P.2d 1247, 1250 (1983) (interpreting covenants according to plain language contained therein). Fink incorrectly attempts to characterize the houses with tile roofs that were erroneously approved by the Committee as somehow less in violation of the covenant than the houses with fiberglass/asphalt shingles that were not approved by the Committee. The circumstances under which property owners obtained approval for tile roofing materials cannot mask the simple fact that there are twenty-three houses, a substantial number of the total houses in the subdivision, not conforming with the restrictive covenant.[22]

---

22. Because the covenant mandates use of a specific roofing material, wood shingles, we need not address the severity of each individual violation—a structure either has the required type of roof or it does not. Other restrictions may not be so clear-cut. For example, in the case of a covenant that mandates certain set back distances, a de minimis violation of a few inches may be accorded less significance than a flagrant violation of ten feet. *See Tanglewood Homes Ass'n v. Henke*, 728 S.W.2d 39, 43 (Tex.App.1987).

Accordingly, violations of the wood shingle restrictive covenant are sufficiently widespread that it must be concluded, as a matter of law, that the restriction has been abandoned and is unenforceable.....

Because objective analysis of the number and nature of the violations demonstrates the covenant has been abandoned, we need not extend our inquiry to the remaining factors discussed above. We briefly touch upon them only to aid future judicial application of the test adopted in this opinion.

First, the property owners' overall record of enforcement of the covenant is problematic. While there has been a fairly consistent pattern of enforcement since 1985, there was little or no enforcement between 1978 and 1985. Indeed, by 1985 only eight of the twenty-nine existing houses conformed with the wood shingle requirement. Fink attempts to minimize this fact by claiming the Committee inadvertently used a copy of the Agreement that appeared to allow houses with tile roofs. As we see it, however, the Committee's unquestioning reliance on a handwritten note of unknown origin only underscores the laxity of the Committee's enforcement approach during the 1978–85 period.

Next, we consider whether, notwithstanding the existing violations, it is possible to realize the benefits intended by the covenant. In so doing, we read the entire Agreement as a whole, and do not read a single covenant in isolation, in order to determine the intent of the restriction at issue. *Gosnay*, 666 P.2d at 1250. The Agreement plainly states its purposes: to maintain the natural environment; to promote uniform development; and to maintain property values. Given the significant number of houses with nonconforming roofing materials in Maple Hills, uniformity of development—at least with respect to that particular design element—cannot be accomplished by belated enforcement of the covenant. However, property owners can still enforce other restrictions related to architectural design,[23] such as the provision requiring approval of color and quality of materials, with colors limited to earth tones.[24]

23. The trial court made three conclusions of law:

1. Although the Covenants are still enforceable with regard to the color and quality of roofing materials so as to blend harmoniously into the natural environment, they are no longer enforceable as to material, provided the color and quality of the material is such that it blends harmoniously with the character and environment of the subdivision.

2. The protective covenant restricting roofing materials is not binding except with regard to color and quality.

3. The Community Development Committee may approve defendants' plans for roofing material as to color and quality if it blends harmoniously with the current neighborhood environment, but the Community Development Committee may not reject tile or high density fiberglass/asphalt [shingles] as long as color and quality standards are met to blend harmoniously with the current neighborhood environment.

While the first two conclusions are beyond reproach, we agree with Fink's contention that the trial court incorrectly instructed the Committee as to what action it must take regarding the Millers' plans and how it must apply the covenants. The Committee was never a party to this proceeding, and the trial court exceeded the bounds of its authority by directing the actions of a nonparty. Therefore, we vacate the court's third conclusion of law insofar as it purports to direct or limit the actions of the Committee.

24. Thus, property owners may still benefit from the stated purposes of the

Abandonment of one covenant does not suggest abandonment of other, albeit similar, covenants in the agreement. *See Tompkins v. Buttrum Constr. Co.*, 99 Nev. 142, 659 P.2d 865, 867 (1983) (violations of other covenants have no effect on covenant at issue). . . .

Fink contends that the affidavits submitted to the trial court present conflicting issues of material fact which the court "weighed" in reaching its findings on diminution of value and the Committee's approval of, or acquiescence in, plans calling for tile or fiberglass/asphalt shingle roofs. While there were conflicting facts among the profusion of affidavits presented by both parties, none of the disputed facts were material, so as to preclude summary judgment. Given our conclusion of unenforceability due to abandonment of the covenant, it does not matter whether the tile or fiberglass/asphalt shingle roofs were approved, approved in error, or disapproved by the Committee or other property owners. The single pivotal fact, which is not disputed by either party, is that twenty-three of eighty-one houses have roofs not in compliance with the covenant limiting roofing materials to wood shingles. As a matter of law, the twenty-three violations demonstrate abandonment of the wood shingle requirement, thereby rendering that part of the covenant unenforceable. Therefore, we affirm the trial court's grant of summary judgment in favor of the Millers.

WEST ALAMEDA HEIGHTS HOMEOWNERS ASS'N v. BOARD OF COUNTY COMMISSIONERS

Supreme Court of Colorado.
169 Colo. 491, 458 P.2d 253 (1969).

DAY, J. The West Alameda Heights Homeowners Association and certain individual homeowners, representatives in a class action for persons who reside in West Alameda Heights Subdivision, are here assigning error to the decree of the Jefferson County district court, declaring null and void restrictive covenants on a number of lots in certain blocks in the subdivision.

As plaintiffs below they brought an action to enjoin the construction of two large shopping facilities on the subject property by the F.W. Woolworth Company and Safeway Stores, Inc. to be financed by Bankers Life Insurance Company. The three Newtons are made defendants as owners of the property. George Newton was the original developer of the subdivision who in 1947 filed the plat and created the covenants contained therein. The subdivision is bounded on the north by West First Avenue; on the east by Wadsworth Boulevard; on the south by West Alameda; and on the west by Cody Street. Outside of the subdivision,

Agreement by enforcing other covenants that have the effect of restricting building materials and styles to those that harmonize with the environment, maintain the overall value of the homes in the subdivision, and promote uniform development. Of course, an architectural committee's decisions made in the course of the approval or denial of prospective house plans and specifications "must be reasonable and made in good faith and must not be arbitrary or capricious." *Rhue v. Cheyenne Homes, Inc.*, 168 Colo. 6, 449 P.2d 361, 363 (1969) (en banc).

particularly to the east and to the southeast, there has been extensive commercial development, and both Wadsworth Boulevard and West Alameda are major four-lane highways.

The plat contains protective covenants restricting the use of the lands in the subdivision. Each covenant provides that, except as noted, all lots shall be Residential 1. The significance in our determination is the fact that the subdivision is large and almost fully developed as planned, consisting primarily of single family residences. There are over 350 lots comprising the tract. Only 80 to 85 of these have not been developed. The only commercial uses presently situated in the subdivision are a service station and a garden center located on land originally reserved for commercial use in the plat. Apartments have been constructed on other land set aside for commercial purposes. The major portion of three blocks—numbers 13, 14 and 15—proposed to be used for the shopping facilities was platted as residential property and restricted to such use by the covenants which have never been amended. The original covenants provide that they would be in force until June 30, 1965 and automatically extended for successive ten-year periods unless the owners of a majority of the lots by vote change the covenants in whole or in part. There has been no attempt to amend or change them, no election has been called or held, and the present extension of the covenants does not expire until June 30, 1975.

The factor which precipitated this action was an application by George Newton to re-zone a portion of the blocks retained by him to permit the building of a Safeway Store and a Woolco Department Store. This property still owned by George Newton fronts on West Alameda and extends northward approximately 600 feet to an area zoned for single family homes. It was planned to erect a buffer consisting of a masonry wall not less than five feet nor more than six feet in height between the commercial enterprises and the residential property to the north.

The writ of error here involves only plaintiffs' fourth claim for relief which relates to the restrictive covenants. In this claim the plaintiffs, after setting out the existence and nature of the covenants, aver that the purchasers of the lots in the subdivision relied on restrictive and protective covenants which were designed for the protection of the neighborhood and of the property; and that the restrictions are applicable not only to the property in the development which has been sold but also to the property retained by the defendant George Newton for future sales. They allege they have invested large sums of money in lots and homes in the subdivision in reliance on the covenant.

In entering judgment against the homeowners on this claim, the trial court made the following findings, *inter alia*:

10. The character of this neighborhood has changed considerably since the West Alameda Heights was created. The subject land borders on West Alameda Avenue, a short distance from the intersection of Wadsworth Avenue. At the time of the imposition of the

covenants, Alameda was mainly a residential avenue. Now it is a heavily traveled thoroughfare and the area is developing as a commercial area. Villa Italia Shopping Center is at the intersection of Alameda and Wadsworth.

11. The subject land is not suitable for residential use and is suitable only for commercial use. Plaintiffs will suffer no damage by commercial use. To deprive the defendants Newton of the right to use the property would not be equitable and if the restrictive covenants are enforced, they would be deprived of the right to use their property. The enforcement of the restrictive covenants would impose an oppressive burden on defendants Newton without any substantial benefit.

The court declared the restrictive covenants to be null and void as to the subject property.

QUESTION TO BE DETERMINED: *DO THE FACTS OF THIS CASE AND THE LAW APPLICABLE THERETO JUSTIFY THE TRIAL COURT IN RULING THAT THE COVENANTS RESTRICTING TO RESIDENTIAL USE BLOCKS 13, 14 AND 15 NO LONGER APPLY?*

We answer the question in the negative and hold that the covenants are valid and enforceable.

The pertinent rule of law applicable to this case is most recently set out in *Zavislak v. Shipman*, 147 Colo. 184, 362 P.2d 1053, wherein this court adopted the language of *McArthur v. Hood Rubber Co.*, 221 Mass. 372, 109 N.E. 162, as follows:

> When the purpose for which the restriction was imposed has come to an end, and where the use of the tract of land for whose benefit it was established has so utterly changed that no party to the bill could be heard to enforce it in equity or would suffer any damage by its violation, . . . a proper case is made out for equitable relief. . . .

Parties plaintiffs and defendants all rely on our pronouncement in *Zavislak*. The court, in striking down the covenants, attempted to apply the same rule of law. We hold, however, that the court misconceived and misapplied the rule to changes and developments outside of and beyond the subdivision itself. This is made evident by the court's reference to the changed traffic patterns on Wadsworth and Alameda and the development of Villa Italia Shopping Center and other developments east of the Alameda and Wadsworth intersection.

The true test here, however, as to whether the purpose of the restrictions has come to an end, is the development of the subdivision which is the subject of the covenants subsequent to their creation. Thus the courts look to whether the original purposes of insuring maintenance of residential character for the subdivision has been abandoned or changed by acquiescence or passiveness of the subdivision residents.

Newton, in planning the property with the restrictions which he imposed, intended to insure the maintenance of the residential character for the subdivision. That purpose has continued to the present time, and the effect of it is demonstrated by what has happened to land outside of its perimeter over which the West Alameda Heights residents had no control. It is undisputed that in the subdivision wherein the covenants did control no change of the use contemplated when the plat was filed has occurred. Only the property originally platted for use of commercial enterprises thereon has been occupied as such.

Another test announced in the *Zavislak* case is whether the parties would suffer any damage by the removal of the covenant. Touching on this phase the testimony of the individual plaintiffs was that their property would be subject to substantial decrease in value. One of plaintiffs' witnesses—a professional land planner—depicted the foreseeable increase in traffic to and from the proposed shopping facility with concomitant increase in noise, fumes, and hazard to children. The Traffic and Safety Engineer for Jefferson County stated that although he probably could control increased traffic through the residential area by the use of traffic signals and one-way streets, he candidly admitted that such a traffic pattern would inconvenience the homeowners as much as it might deter shoppers from driving through the area. There was testimony as to the present pleasant aspects of the neighborhood, undisturbed by the commercial activity beyond the borders.

Contrariwise, the defendants did not prove that the purpose of the protective covenants had come to an end; that the land use within the tract had changed from what it was intended to be at the time the plat was filed; and that no person would suffer any damage by its violation. The evidence therefore is contrary to the court's finding that plaintiffs will suffer no damage from commercial use of the subject property.

Cases are numerous from other jurisdictions wherein covenants have been sought to be removed because subject lands would be more valuable for commercial than for residential purposes, and wherein there were conditions such as the presence of commercial uses nearby, heavy street traffic on the perimeter of the tract, and some commercial property within a primarily residential subdivision. But the weight of authority supports the view that *changes outside* of the tract will not warrant the lifting of restrictive covenants affecting property within the subdivision if the covenants are still a benefit to the owners of the property under the restrictions.

Normal growth and change and the possibility of encroachment of commercial uses, we can infer, were contemplated when the covenants and the master plan of development were created by the original owner and platter. There would be no need for the covenants to protect the subdivisions from inroads of commercial expansion if it were not expected that such might take place. As long as the original purpose of the covenants can still be accomplished and substantial benefit will inure to the restricted area by their enforcement, the covenants stand even though the subject property has a greater value if used for other purposes.

A comment in *Cowling v. Colligan,* 158 Tex. 458, 312 S.W.2d 943, appeals to us:

> The reasoning of the courts is that if because of changed conditions outside the restricted area one lot or tract were permitted to drop from under the protective cover of residential-only restrictions, the owner of the adjoining lot would then have an equal claim on the conscience of the court, and, in due course, all other lots would fall like ten-pins, thus circumventing and nullifying the restriction and destroying the essentially residential character of the entire area.

In the case of protective covenants, it has sometimes been held that changes within the affected area may result in modification or removal of the covenant because the changes were within the control of those entitled to enforce the covenant. In other words, the doctrines of abandonment, estoppel and waiver are applicable. *See Thodos v. Shirk,* 248 Iowa 172, 79 N.W.2d 733; *Mechling v. Dawson,* 234 Ky. 318, 28 S.W.2d 18; *Greer v. Bornstein,* 246 Ky. 286, 54 S.W.2d 927; *Tull v. Doctors Bldg. Inc.,* 255 N.C. 23, 120 S.E.2d 817. However, as to changes in conditions occurring outside the area restricted, the parties affected have no control whatever, and the doctrines of waiver, abandonment and estoppel are not applicable. Here, the problem presents itself as to whether the outside conditions affect the entire subdivision in a way that the restrictive purposes of the protective covenants would be defeated. As stated in *Thodos v. Shirk, supra:*

> In both cases the factual situation largely governs as to whether or not equity will refuse to enforce the restrictions for the reason that by so doing the result would be oppressive and inequitable without any appreciable value to other property in the restricted area. It has been said that in order for this equitable defense of change of conditions to arise, there must be a change in the character of the surrounding neighborhood sufficient to make it impossible any longer to secure in substantial degree the benefits sought to be realized through the performance of the building restriction.

The construction of Villa Italia Shopping Center and of other commercial properties outside of West Alameda Heights, but in close proximity to it, have not changed the residential character of the subdivision. If the changed conditions outside the tract have made the particular property held by the owner since the original platting less desirable for residential use than it previously was, this is not to say that the whole tract has been made unfit for residential use. On the contrary, the evidence shows that the subdivision is a residential area of high quality, with expensive homes and quiet streets. The construction of commercial facilities nearby are all the more reason why the covenants for West Alameda Heights must be strictly enforced. The covenants have no meaning if external forces and pressures result in their removal.

The judgment is reversed and the cause remanded to the trial court with directions to enter a permanent injunction as prayed for in the complaint.

Notes

1. *Termination of Promissory Servitudes.* Like easements, promissory servitudes may be terminated in a variety of ways. These include: written release, Restatement of Servitudes § 7.3; merger of the benefitted and burdened parcels, *id.* § 7.5; prescription (wrongful interference with the servitude for the prescriptive period), *id.* § 7.7; and abandonment, *id.* § 7.4. In addition, promissory servitudes can be terminated as a result of changed circumstances, *id.* § 7.10.

2. *Abandonment (or Waiver) of Promissory Servitudes.* Which facts were most important to the court's conclusion that the covenant had been abandoned in *Fink*? Does/should the court focus on the perceptions of the owner of the burdened land, the perceptions of potential buyers of subdivision lots, or the intent of the beneficiaries of the covenant? *Compare Gibbs v. Cass*, 431 S.W.2d 662 (Mo. Ct. App. 1968) (four of eight lots had been re-subdivided without objection; court held covenant against re-subdivision had been abandoned/waived) *with Marquess v. Bamburg*, 188 So.2d 721 (La. Ct. App. 1966) (residents could enjoin use of home for commercial beauty salon, even though other lot owners used their home addresses for business correspondence and performed certain job tasks in their homes—including employee of optical company who ground lenses and housewife who gave piano lessons) *and Western Land Co. v. Truskolaski*, 88 Nev. 200, 495 P.2d 624 (1972) (even if use of one home as painting contractor's office and another home as day-care violated residential-use-only covenant, violations were "too distant and sporadic" to constitute waiver of covenant). Would you expect courts to be receptive to finding waiver or abandonment of servitudes? Would it matter whether membership in the association had changed frequently during the alleged period of waiver?

3. *Abandonment of Easements vs. Abandonment of Promissory Servitudes.* How would you compare and contrast the law governing abandonment of easements (as manifested in *Graves v. Dennis*, page 602) with the analysis reflected in *Fink v. Miller*? Are the differences substantive, or do they merely reflect differences in terminology? Is non-use of an easement analytically similar to non-enforcement of a promissory servitude? Why or why not? Are the policy concerns relevant to abandonment of easements identical to those relevant to promissory servitudes?

4. *The Changed Circumstances Doctrine.* Compare the abandonment doctrine applied in *Fink* with the changed circumstances doctrine applied in *West Alameda*. What policy rationales justify the "changed circumstances" doctrine? How do the policy rationales for the doctrine influence its application? Does it make sense to focus on changed circumstances "inside" the area subject to the covenants—as the court does on the facts in *West Alameda*—rather than changed circumstances "outside" the community (*i.e.*, in the area surrounding the land subject to the covenant)? Is the court suggesting that changed circumstances "outside" the community can never justify termination of a servitude? If not, under what circumstances might a court grant relief from a servitude based upon "outside" changed circumstances?

What is the relationship between CCRs and local zoning regulations? Suppose that the local zoning board had approved Newton's re-zoning application and had re-zoned the land to permit commercial uses. Would this re-zoning decision have dictated a result in favor of Newton? No; courts can and have enforced promissory servitudes even when applicable zoning laws permit uses prohibited by such servitudes. *See, e.g., Western Land Co. v. Truskolaski*, 88 Nev. 200, 495 P.2d 624 (1972) (zoning board resolution indicating willingness to re-zone parcel did not compel invalidation of residential-use-only covenant). Can you explain why? To what extent, then, should the court be willing to consider the zoning board's action?

Finally, the *West Alameda* case raises interesting questions about the enforcement remedies available to the owner(s) of the benefitted parcel(s). Effectively, the court's decision protects the homeowners using a property rule; if Newton wants to proceed with his development project, he will have to negotiate a release of the restriction from every owner within the community. [What roadblocks might he encounter in this process?] Could (or should) the court instead conclude that given the surrounding commercial development, Newton should be allowed to breach the covenant and proceed with his development, as long as he pays damages to each owner benefitted by the covenant? Why or why not? Based upon the court's language in *West Alameda*, what problems might a court face in determining damages?

5. *Changed Circumstances—Easements and Promissory Servitudes Compared.* Courts traditionally have rejected arguments by a servient owner that changed circumstances alone justify termination of an easement. *See, e.g., Witt v. McKenna*, 600 A.2d 105 (Me. 1991) (mere fact that easement holder had obtained and used an alternative means of access did not constitute abandonment of easement). Should courts be able to terminate burdensome easements when changed circumstances reduce or eliminate the easement's benefit to its holder? Is there any other doctrinal argument potentially available to a servient owner seeking termination of an easement? Can you explain why the common law developed the "changed circumstances" doctrine only with respect to promissory servitudes and not with respect to easements (other than implied easements of necessity, which terminate when the necessity ends)? Does this distinction make sense? *Cf.* Restatement of Servitudes § 7.10 (applying changed circumstances doctrine to all servitudes).

6. *The Aftermath of* West Alameda. When it opened in 1966, Villa Italia was one of the premier regional malls in the West—the largest (at that time) indoor, air-conditioned shopping center between Chicago and California. Obviously, it was the commercial center of Lakewood—a community that had no other defined "downtown" area. In *West Alameda*, the developer argued that the scope of the 100–acre Villa Italia and surrounding commercial development demonstrated a sufficient change of circumstance to justify judicial termination of the residential-use-only servitude.

In an ironic twist, Villa Italia closed its doors on July 15, 2001, a victim of evolving patterns in residential and commercial development. During recent years, most of the stores in Villa Italia had closed, causing Lakewood's sales tax revenues to plunge dramatically. Beginning in fall 2001, Villa Italia was torn down to make way for a proposed $500 million mixed-use development—designed in the "new town" model typical of many recent "smart growth" projects. The development will include shops, offices, entertainment, and residences and will be designated as Lakewood's "downtown" district. *See* "Villa Italia Closes Up Shop," Denver Post, Sunday, July 15, 2001.

LAWYERING EXERCISE
(Dispute Resolution and Problem Solving)

SITUATION: You represent the Board of Trustees for the Shady Acres Homeowners Association, the governing board of Shady Acres (which contains 120 single-family homes). The recorded CCRs for Shady Acres require that all homes must have cedar shake roof shingles. Over the past five years, six homeowners within Shady Acres have installed noncompliant roofs. Two of the noncompliant roofs are made of Italian slate (substantially more expensive than cedar shake), while the other four are asphalt shingles. None of these six homeowners sought Board approval for their noncompliant roofs. At no time during this period did the Board of Trustees take any action against any of the six homeowners.

Last month, at the annual Homeowners Association election meeting, all five of the incumbent members of the Board of Trustees were defeated and replaced with new board members. Each of the new members wants to preserve the enforceability of the Shady Acres CCRs, including the cedar shake roofing covenant. They have asked you to advise them regarding the most effective way to do so—even if that means filing a lawsuit to enforce the covenant against the six noncompliant homeowners (one of whom was a former Board member).

TASK: Prepare a memorandum that sets forth the strategy that you would suggest to accomplish the Board's stated objective. If you recommend litigation, explain why this is preferable to some other form of dispute resolution. By contrast, if you recommend some form of negotiated settlement, explain how the Board could document an acceptable settlement that would preserve its ability to enforce the cedar shake roofing covenant in the future.

Throughout this chapter, the materials have stressed the "stability vs. flexibility" trade-off the developer faces in establishing a CIC—the need to balance reliance of individual owners on the original declaration with the community's need to adapt when faced with changed circumstances. *See generally* Stewart Sterk, *Foresight and the Law of Servitudes*, 73 Cornell L. Rev. 956 (1988). On the one hand, stability can serve a value-preserving function; the community benefits from the continued enforcement of efficient restrictions, and thus community residents may find it appealing to have a stable covenant regime that is not easily changed. On the other hand, today's efficient, value-preserving restriction may become the next decade's suboptimal, value-detracting or downright unwise restriction. Indeed, some restrictions may be poorly conceived from the start.

To strike the proper balance, developers often include a provision in the declaration that permits future changes in the declaration based upon either a majority or super-majority vote. Should an amendment provision permit a majority or super-majority of residents to make any changes? Could they adopt new covenants over the objection of dissenting lot owners? Consider the following materials.

BOYLES v. HAUSMANN

Supreme Court of Nebraska.
246 Neb. 181, 517 N.W.2d 610 (1994).

WHITE, JUSTICE. This appeal arises from an action filed by appellants, Larry R. Boyles and Olga J. Boyles, seeking to declare that a restrictive covenant on their real property is invalid. After a bench trial the district court entered an order declaring the covenants valid. The Nebraska Court of Appeals reversed the decision of the district court. *Boyles v. Hausmann*, 2 Neb.App. 388, 509 N.W.2d 676 (1993). We modify and affirm the decision of the Court of Appeals.

On August 14, 1977, appellants purchased Lot 18 of the Pioneer Hills Subdivision. The Pioneer Hills Subdivision is located at Section 7, Township 17 North, Range 12 East of the 6th P.M. in Washington County, Nebraska. At the time of the purchase, there were covenants on the subdivision lots which restricted the use of the land. These covenants had been established by the original owners of the lots within the subdivision.

Generally, the covenants address the following: (1) limiting residential buildings to one single-family residence per lot; (2) limiting the size and number of attached garages or carports; (3) prohibiting the building of a residence on a plot smaller than the original lot size; (4) prohibiting noxious or offensive activities; (5) prohibiting trailers, tents, shacks, junk cars, or other temporary structures on a lot; (6) setting minimum size of ground floor living space in residences; (7) restricting the extent of grading the land; (8) restricting type and number of various animals permitted on a lot; (9) limiting the use, size, and number of outbuildings on a lot; (10) prohibiting preconstructed dwellings' being moved to a lot; and (11) requiring preapproval of all construction plans.

The covenants also provided that

[t]hese covenants, restrictions and conditions shall run with the land and continue until January 1, 1983, after which time they shall be automatically extended for successive periods of five years, unless an instrument signed by a majority of the then owners of said land shall have been recorded in the office of the County Clerk of Washington County, Nebraska, agreeing to change same in whole or in part.

In February 1984, the original covenants were amended by a majority of the lotowners. Appellants voted in favor of these changes. The following covenants were changed at that meeting: (5), permitting recreational vehicles to be parked on lots on which the resident resides; (8), changing the type and number of animals which may be kept on the lots; (9), changing the size of outbuildings permitted on lots of a particular size; (10), excepting new factory-built homes from the prior restriction; and (11), requiring that all building plans be submitted and approved by Pioneer Hills Association officers.

According to the February 1984 amending instrument, the covenants were to continue until January 1, 1988, after which time they shall be automatically extended for successive periods of five years, unless an instrument signed by a majority of the then owners of said land shall have been recorded in the office of the County Clerk of Washington County, Nebraska, agreeing to change same in whole or in part.

Amendments were made again in February 1990. Appellants also voted in favor of these amendments. The amendments included the following: (2), changing the restriction on garages and carports; (6), changing square-foot minimum for residential ground floor space; and (9), changing size limitations on outbuildings. The document also included "Water Use Regulations." These regulations generally involve defining the interests of some lot owners in a jointly owned water system, establishing the fees associated with such interests, providing insurance for the system, regulating the maintenance of the system, and outlining the permissible uses of water from the system.

Finally, the February 1990 instrument provided that

[t]hese covenants, water use regulations, restrictions and conditions shall run with the land and continue until January 1, 1995, after which time they shall be automatically extended for successive periods of five years, unless an instrument signed by a majority of the then owners of said land shall have been recorded in the office of the County Clerk of Washington County, Nebraska, agreeing to change same in whole or in part.

On August 24, 1990, a majority of the landowners changed the covenants to include the covenant which is the source of the present dispute. The disputed covenant prohibits the building of residences or other buildings within 120 feet of Pioneer Hills Road (the county road which runs through the subdivision). This covenant was added to an existing covenant, which prohibited residential structures "on any building lot which is smaller in area than the original plotted number on which it is erected." Appellants did not agree to the disputed covenant and did not sign the new instrument.

Appellants filed a declaratory judgment action seeking to have the district court declare the August 1990 covenant invalid. In their petition, appellants contend that as a result of the new covenant, the value of their lot has substantially decreased. Appellants state that because of the size of Lot 18 and an existing pipeline and easement across the lot, the disputed covenant makes the lot unsuitable for building.

After a bench trial, the district court found generally for appellees. Appellants timely filed an appeal to the Court of Appeals.

In the Court of Appeals, appellants argued that the covenants should be declared invalid because (1) although existing covenants could be changed, new covenants could not be added; (2) appellants detrimentally relied on the fact that when they purchased Lot 18, no setback restriction existed; and (3) the 120–foot setback does not apply uniformly to all of the lots in the subdivision.

The Court of Appeals, finding plain error in the record, examined the February 1990 covenant and found that it did not authorize any changes until after 1995. Accordingly, the Court of Appeals held that the August 1990 covenant was invalid and reversed the decision of the district court. We granted appellees' petition for further review. . . .

Appellees contend that the Court of Appeals erred in interpreting the covenant agreement and finding that the covenant agreement could not be amended until 1995. Appellees contend that the covenant provision which permits changes is ambiguous and that the action must be remanded for further proceedings in the district court.

Restrictive covenants are to be construed so as to give effect to the intention of the parties at the time they agreed to the covenants. *Breeling v. Churchill*, 228 Neb. 596, 423 N.W.2d 469 (1988). If the language is unambiguous, the covenant shall be enforced according to its plain language, and the covenant shall not be subject to rules of interpretation or construction. *Baltes v. Hodges*, 207 Neb. 740, 301 N.W.2d 92 (1981); *Lakeland Prop. Owners Ass'n v. Larson*, 121 Ill. App.3d 805, 77 Ill.Dec. 68, 459 N.E.2d 1164 (1984). *See, also, Ross v. Newman*, 206 Neb. 42, 291 N.W.2d 228 (1980). An ambiguity exists when the instrument at issue is susceptible of two or more reasonable but conflicting interpretations or meanings. Moreover, the fact that the parties have suggested opposing meanings of the disputed instrument does not necessarily compel the conclusion that the instrument is ambiguous. *Baker's Supermarkets v. Feldman*, 243 Neb. 684, 502 N.W.2d 428 (1993) (quoting *Crowley v. McCoy*, 234 Neb. 88, 449 N.W.2d 221 (1989)).

The relevant covenant provision provides that "[t]hese covenants, water use regulations, restrictions and conditions shall run with the land and continue until January 1, 1995, after which time they shall be automatically extended for successive periods of five years, unless an instrument signed by a majority of the then owners of said land shall have been recorded in the office of the County Clerk of Washington County, Nebraska, agreeing to change same in whole or in part."

Appellees contend that the word "unless" causes the provision to be susceptible of at least three conflicting meanings. On the contrary, we find that the word "unless" does not render the provision ambiguous. The "unless" clause modifies the immediately preceding clause regarding automatic extension. Thus, the only reasonable reading of the provision is that the term will be automatically extended unless changes are made by a majority.

After thorough review of the decision rendered by the Court of Appeals and our own independent review of the record and the relevant law, we find that the analysis and conclusion of the Court of Appeals are correct with regard to the meaning of the plain language of the covenant agreement. We therefore find it unnecessary to restate the discussion of the Court of Appeals. *See Boyles v. Hausmann*, 2 Neb.App. 388, 509 N.W.2d 676 (1993).

However, we do find it necessary to consider whether the Court of Appeals should have addressed the primary issue raised by appellants: whether a majority of the lotowners may adopt covenants which are new and different from the existing covenants and which are binding on all of the lotowners. . . .

Restrictive covenants are to be construed in connection with the surrounding circumstances at the time that the covenants were made to give effect to the intention of the parties. . . . When asked to consider a restrictive covenant, a court should keep in mind that restrictive "covenants which restrict the use of land are not favored by the law, and, if ambiguous, they should be construed in a manner which allows the maximum unrestricted use of the property." *Knudtson v. Trainor*, 216 Neb. 653, 655, 345 N.W.2d 4, 6 (1984). . . . If the language is unambiguous, the covenant should be enforced according to its plain language. . . . If a restrictive covenant agreement also contains a provision which provides for future alteration, the language employed determines the extent of that provision. *Larson, supra.* Further, under no circumstances shall restrictions on the use of land be extended by mere implication. . . .

In light of the principles set forth above, we find that the unambiguous language of this provision authorizes a majority of the lotowners to make changes to existing covenants, but the provision does not authorize a majority to add new and different covenants. In the covenant agreement, the change provision follows the itemization of the land-use covenants, and the provision refers to "these covenants" and provides that "they" shall be automatically extended, unless the majority changes the "same." The references throughout this provision refer only to the previously listed covenants. We find that there is no other reasonable reading of this provision and that the provision does not authorize a majority of lotowners to bind all lotowners to new and different covenants which restrict the use of land. *See, Larson, supra* (discussing a provision nearly identical to that presented in this case); *Caughlin Homeowners Ass'n [v. Caughlin Club*, 849 P.2d 310 (Nev. 1993)] (adopting the rationale of *Larson*). . . .

The issue then becomes whether the disputed covenant constitutes a new and different covenant when compared with the existing covenants.

The disputed covenant provides that no building may be erected within 120 feet of Pioneer Hills Road. This covenant was added to an existing covenant, which prohibited residential structures from being built "on any building lot which is smaller in area than the original plotted number on which it is erected." The existing covenant to which the disputed covenant was added did not address where on the lot a building could be erected or how far from the lot boundaries a building could stand. We find that compared with this existing covenant, the disputed covenant is new and different.

Similarly, the disputed covenant is new and different from the other covenants which existed when the disputed covenant was adopted. The other covenants involved the size of a residence and the size of its floor plan, limited the size of garages, prohibited nuisances, prohibited temporary shelters, restricted the type and number of animals, limited the number of outbuildings, and required preapproval of construction plans. We find that none of these existing covenants involved setbacks, nor did such covenants restrict in any way the location of a building on a lot.

The law will not subject a minority of landowners to unlimited and unexpected restrictions on the use of their land merely because the covenant agreement permitted a majority to make changes to existing covenants. Although we will enforce those restrictions of which a landowner has notice, we will not hold that a property owner is bound to that of which he does not have notice. There is nothing in the existing covenants which would have put appellants on notice that their land would one day be subject to a setback limit.

Finally, we address appellees' estoppel argument. Appellees appear to offer two different theories that appellants are estopped from challenging the disputed covenant. First, appellees argue that appellants, by their previous actions, are estopped from challenging the validity of the "covenant which provides for amendment by majority action." Brief for appellees at 3. Broadly accepting appellees' estoppel argument, we find that its premise is flawed. Appellants do not challenge the validity of the covenant provision which permitted changes; rather, appellants challenge the extent of the changes permitted pursuant to that provision. As stated above, we acknowledge the validity of a provision which permits change; however, we hold that the disputed covenant exceeded the extent and scope of the changes permitted by the covenant agreement.

Second, appellees contend that appellants accepted the 1984 and 1990 changes to the original covenant agreement, and thus, appellants waived their right to challenge the validity of the disputed covenant. This theory is similarly flawed. Unlike the disputed covenant, the prior changes did not constitute new and different covenants. The changes made by a majority of the lotowners in 1984 and 1990 were changes made to existing covenants, not the addition of new covenants restricting the use of the land.

In summary, we find that (1) the provision of the February 1990 covenant agreement did not authorize changes by a majority of the lotowners until after January 1, 1995; (2) although a majority could adopt changes to the original covenants, a majority did not have the authority to adopt new and different covenants which restricted the use of the land; and (3) appellants were not estopped from asserting their right to challenge the validity of the disputed covenant....

Notes

1. *Considering* Boyles. Why do you think that the majority of residents in *Boyles* sought to add the setback restriction to the covenants? What function would a 120–foot setback restriction serve? Would it serve a different function than a 50–foot setback restriction? A 10–foot setback restriction? Should this matter in terms of the court's willingness to uphold the setback restriction? Why or why not? What is the significance of the fact that the covenant would render the Boyles's lot unsuitable for building? To what extent do you think that this fact influenced the court's evaluation of the attempted setback covenant?

2. *Modification of a Covenant or Addition of a New Covenant.* Not all courts have agreed with *Boyles* that a covenant authorizing a majority of owners to "modify" CCRs does not permit a majority of owners to adopt new covenants. *Evergreen Highlands Association v. West* (page 643) provides a contrary example. Recall that the Evergreen Highlands CCRs permitted a majority of the owners to "change or modify" the covenants, and that a majority of the owners signed an agreement amending the covenants to impose mandatory lot assessments. A dissenting homeowner challenged the validity of the amendment, arguing that the mandatory lot assessment was a "new" covenant requiring unanimous consent. The Colorado Supreme Court disagreed:

> [F]rom a linguistic standpoint, [the] conclusion that "change or modify" can only apply to the alteration of existing covenants, and not the addition of new and different ones, is not well-founded. Webster defines "change" as "to make different." *Webster's Third New International Dictionary* 373 (1986). Applying this definition to the language at issue, covenants could certainly be changed or made different either by the addition, subtraction, or modification of a term. Confining the meaning of the term "change" only to the modification of existing covenants, then, seems illogically narrow.

> ... In those cases where courts disallowed the amendment of covenants, the impact upon the objecting lot owner was generally far more substantial and unforeseeable than the amendment at issue here.

> In contrast, [other cases], like this case, all specifically considered— and allowed—the amendment of covenants in order to impose mandatory assessments on lot owners for the purpose of maintaining common elements of a subdivision. We accordingly find [these cases] more applicable to the situation here. This interpretation also avoids the absurd result that could follow from application of the [*Boyles*] reasoning; Evergreen Highlands would be unable to adopt a mandatory-assessment covenant when its original covenants were silent on the subject, yet could adopt such a covenant if its original covenants had expressly prohibited a mandatory-assessment covenant. [*Evergreen Highlands Ass'n v. West*, 73 P.3d 1, 6–7 (Colo. 2003).]

Linguistically, which court—*Boyles* or *West*—has the better of this argument? Was the *Boyles* court overly influenced by the purpose and effect of the setback covenant? Under the *West* approach, how could someone considering buying a home within a CIC intelligently account for the possibility of new covenants in her purchasing decision?

Finally, suppose that an amendment provision either expressly permits (or is interpreted to permit) a majority of owners to impose new covenants. Would all new covenants be permissible, regardless of content? For example, consider the fact pattern involved in *West Alameda* (page 682). If neighborhood residents had voted by 76% to 24% to amend the covenants to relieve Lots 13–15 of the burden of the residential-use restriction—while preserving that restriction on all other lots—would the amendment be enforceable? Why or why not? *See, e.g., Maatta v. Dead River Campers, Inc.*, 263 Mich.App. 604, 689 N.W.2d 491 (2004).

3. *Should "Amendability" Be Mandatory?* As *Boyles* suggests, courts traditionally have held that if a servitude regime does not contain a provision authorizing change by majority or super-majority vote, any change to the regime requires unanimous consent. However, recent legislation in some states establishes a presumption that a CIC servitude regime can be amended unless the declaration expressly provides to the contrary. *See, e.g.,* La. Civ. Code art. 780 (if declaration is silent regarding amendability, building restrictions that have been in place for more than 15 years may be amended or terminated by agreement of owners of one-half of affected land area, and building restrictions that have been in place for more than 10 years may be amended or terminated by agreement of owners of two-thirds of affected land area and two-thirds of landowners within affected area). Should the law permit a developer to explicitly make a regime unamendable except by unanimous consent? Would you expect developers to insert such clauses into declarations?

4. *Timing of Amendments.* The *Boyles* decision also emphasizes that the procedures for amending covenants may limit the time periods during which amendment may take place. In a similar case, *Kauffman v. Roling*, 851 S.W.2d 789 (Mo. Ct. App. 1993), the Missouri Court of Appeals interpreted a covenant very similar to the one in *Boyles*, but which provided for a rolling 25–year duration (rather than the rolling five-year period in *Boyles*). The court held that the original covenants were not subject to amendment, except by unanimous consent of all landowners, during the first 25 years following their recording. *See also In re Wallace's Fourth Southmoor Addition to the City of Enid*, 874 P.2d 818 (Okla. Ct. App. 1994) (amendment not effective until next renewal period). *But see Hill v. Rice*, 505 So.2d 382 (Ala. 1987) (amendment effective immediately even though in middle of renewal term). Does it make sense to treat a covenant regime as unamendable (except by unanimous consent) for a fixed period of time? Is 25 years too long?

5. *Voting Rights and Developer Control.* Assume that a declaration contains the following amendment provision: "These restrictive covenants may be modified, changed or amended, and new covenants may be added, when such modifications, changes, amendments or new covenants are approved in writing by the owners of 67% of the lots within the development."

The development has 100 lots and developer has sold only 23 of the lots. You represent the developer, who believes that the market for smaller homes is better and thus wants to amend the covenants to reduce the minimum square footage requirement from 2200 square feet to 1600 square feet. The developer wants to know whether she unilaterally can amend the covenants, given that she still owns more than 67% of the lots. How do you advise her? Does she get one vote (one vote per owner) or seventy-seven votes (one vote per lot)? *Compare Cieri v. Gorton*, 179 Mont. 167, 587 P.2d 14 (1978) (amendment provision requiring approval by "a majority of then owners of lots affected thereby" meant majority of property owners and not majority of lots) *with Diamond Bar Dev. Corp. v. Superior Court*, 60 Cal.App.3d 330, 131 Cal.Rptr. 458 (1976) (amendment provision requiring approval by "70% of the then owners . . . of property then covered" by the covenants meant 70% of lots, not 70% of owners). What equitable factors might influence how a court interprets such a provision? How would your advice change if the covenants reserved to the developer an express right to modify existing covenants or add new covenants? *Compare Johnson v. Three Bays Props. #2, Inc.*, 159 So.2d 924 (Fla. Dist. Ct. App. 1964) (developer had right to make modest changes in building restrictions by virtue of express reservation of such right) *with Wright v. Cypress Shores Dev. Co., Inc.*, 413 So.2d 1115 (Ala. 1982) ("the reservation of the right to annul, cancel, amend or modify the restrictive covenants could only be exercised . . . in a reasonable manner consistent with" the general scheme or plan of development; canceling residential use restrictions to permit the construction of a convenience store was unreasonable).

Chapter 9

THE LAND TRANSFER TRANSACTION

A. INTRODUCTION

In this chapter, we address the negotiation, formation, performance, and enforcement of a land purchase and sale contract, as well as the typical "due diligence" investigation that a prudent purchaser undertakes when acquiring an interest in land.

In complex transactions such as the purchase of land, there is a significant time gap—often 30 to 90 days or more—between the time that the parties bind themselves by signing a purchase and sale contract and the time of "closing" when the parties actually perform their contractual obligations. This "executory interval" or "gap period" allows the parties an opportunity to make important preparations in anticipation of the closing, including (but not limited to):

- investigating and assuring the quality of the seller's title;
- arranging the financing that the buyer will use to purchase the land; and
- investigating the land and improvements (by physical examination or otherwise) to assure that the buyer will receive what the buyer thinks he or she bargained for.

Sometimes during the gap period, one of the parties will reconsider whether to perform the transaction—a situation often called "buyer's remorse" or "seller's remorse." This remorse may occur because a party's individual circumstances change (*e.g.*, the buyer may become unemployed during the gap period), or because the local real estate market changes (leading one of the parties to think that he can strike a better bargain), or for a variety of other reasons. Generally speaking, the real estate purchase and sale contract is designed to fix the parties' legal positions during the gap period, thereby binding the parties to perform the transaction notwithstanding such "remorse."

This chapter begins with a general overview of the various stages in a typical residential real estate transaction and the variety of legal and practical issues that can arise in even the most basic land transfer transaction. The remainder of Chapter 9 discusses many of these issues in greater depth.

A.B.A. SPECIAL COMMITTEE ON RESIDENTIAL REAL ESTATE TRANSACTIONS: THE PROPER ROLE OF THE LAWYER IN RESIDENTIAL REAL ESTATE TRANSACTIONS

3-14 (1974).

A HYPOTHETICAL HOME PURCHASE TRANSACTION

A. *The Brokerage Contract.* Initially a seller will enter into a brokerage contract with a real estate agent. In all or virtually all jurisdictions this contract is not subject to the statute of frauds and may be [oral].... A special peril faced by sellers who have not had the advantage of legal counsel is that they may employ more than one broker and, in the absence of a clear understanding concerning the conditions under which the brokerage fee is earned, the seller may become liable to pay more than one such fee. In practice a high percentage of brokerage contracts are in writing. A common assumption is that the contract is simple and standardized. In fact, a properly drawn contract will anticipate a number of legal problems of some complexity, such as the right of the seller to negotiate on his own behalf, the effect of multiple listings, the disposition of earnest money if the buyer defaults, the rights of the broker if the seller is unable to proffer a marketable title, the duration of any exclusive listing and, as already brought out, the point at which the brokerage fee is earned.... [A]ny person signing such a contract should have it approved by his attorney before he attaches his signature. He should have his attorney explain its meaning and be on hand to see that it is properly executed. (It is presumed that if he consults an attorney he will be advised against entering into any [oral] agreement.)... The broker needs similar services at one time or another and receives them from his own attorney as needed. But in routine transactions he is sufficiently familiar with the details to be able to handle the matter himself without resort to professional assistance.

B. *The Preliminary Negotiations.* When the broker has found a potential buyer, negotiations between the buyer and the seller will begin, with the broker acting in the role of intermediary. In some cases the seller will leave to the broker all the work of negotiation and will merely ratify the agreement reached with the buyer. It is generally thought that neither the buyer nor the seller needs a lawyer in the course of the negotiations. In theory this assumption is correct because neither party is bound until a written sales contract is signed. In fact, a great deal of trouble can be avoided if both the buyer and the seller have their own attorneys at their elbows during the course of the dickering. If they are to make a proper bargain they must know what to bargain about. Aside from the question of price, which seems paramount in the minds of both parties, they should consider such problems as the mode of paying the purchase price and the tax consequences resulting therefrom, the status of various articles as fixtures or personal property, the time set for occupancy and the effect of loss by casualty pending the closing. They can make whatever agreement they want. But they should anticipate all important questions and be certain a complete understanding has been reached. If they fail to do so in the preliminary negotiations they may find, at the time for signing a contract, they will have to start negotiations all over again. Worse, they may enter into a contract highly disadvantageous to one or the other, so uncertain as to require litigation to determine its meaning, or void for indefiniteness.

C. *The Commitment for Financing.* Before entering into a sales contract, it would be desirable for the buyer, if he can, to obtain as much of a commitment as possible for any necessary financing. Otherwise, the buyer may find himself forced to default or to obtain a loan on disadvantageous financing terms.

Sometimes the same broker will present the buyer with a package consisting of a purchase and sale agreement and an application to a financial institution for a loan, both containing provisions on which the buyer should have the advice of his lawyer. Many sellers make no attempt to provide the buyer with financing references, many lenders refuse to make the necessary inspections, appraisals and credit investigations until the buyer can exhibit a signed purchase and sale agreement, and many buyers are reluctant to risk losing the property to a higher offer by deferring the execution of the purchase and sale agreement. All of this leads to the common practice of including in the agreement a "subject to financing" clause. The drafting of an acceptable and binding provision is difficult. Where the buyer cannot obtain financing prior to entering into an agreement to purchase, an appropriate clause should be drafted only by counsel. If the draftsman is not already the attorney for the buyer the buyer should insist that his legal representative give approval before the contract is signed.

Finding a willing lender is not part of a lawyer's professional duties. In practice a lawyer may be able to render this service simply because he is a man of affairs. Where he exercises legal expertise is when he advises the buyer about problems he should anticipate in coming to terms with the lender. By way of illustration, the buyer will seldom have any understanding of the potential effect of anticipation or acceleration clauses. He may find one or the other acceptable, but he should know what he is doing and what the legal and practical consequences will be. The buyer should also be cautioned to obtain a binding statement of the closing costs he will have to pay the lender and should consult his attorney as to the legitimacy of all items found in the statement.

The commitment contract between the lender and buyer will probably be drafted by the lender's attorney, but before it is signed, the buyer's attorney should assure him that it properly anticipates all important contingencies, comports with the oral agreement previously reached and binds the lender.

The inequality of bargaining power between the buyer and lender is a matter of notoriety. What is less understood is that normally the lender has much greater expertise. This advantage may not have been of as much importance formerly as it is today, but the financing of homes has in many instances become so complex as to defy the understanding of anyone not thoroughly versed in property law and practice. For this reason, when dealing with the lender the buyer is in peculiar need of assistance from his own lawyer.

The lender, by contrast, will generally employ a form contract drafted by its counsel. In ordinary transactions it will not require additional legal services at this point.

D. *The Contract of Sale.* Once an informal agreement has been reached, the buyer and the seller will enter into a formal contract of sale. The importance of this document cannot be overestimated. As one observer has warned,

> The contract makes the law of the case for the parties. It is their charter and, for one of them, perhaps a straitjacket. This is true where the contract has been thoroughly negotiated. It is equally true where the contract is in the form of a binder, torn off a broker's pad and signed at the seller's back door.

Because each bargain is unique, in theory a special contract should be drafted for each sale. The interested parties are the broker, the buyer and the seller. The broker wants assurance he will receive his commission. Both the buyer and the seller want assurance that the writing reflects their prior understanding. If they have not received legal advice during the preliminary negotiations they will need to know what questions should have been anticipated and whether firm and advantageous provisions are found in the document. When the instrument is executed their attorneys should be on hand to assure that the proper formalities are observed to make it binding. Here again the parties need legal services in the form of drafting, advice, and representation. This need is not avoided by the use of forms. Even if we accept the dubious assumption that the form is properly drawn, the printed portion may not adequately express the particular agreement made between the parties, or the words used in filling in blanks may hopelessly distort its effectiveness. At this point the statement previously made about the use of "simple," standardized forms should be reiterated. In theory all such forms are objectionable. In practice, in some instances they may serve a useful purpose. The Committee recommends that local bar associations draft these standard forms of sales agreements. Even if very well drafted forms are used, any insertion should be carefully checked by the buyer's and seller's attorneys. If standard forms must be used, they should include the phrase "subject to the approval of the attorneys for the parties" which would make clear that the contract contemplates further negotiations between the parties. The broker may be well able to take care of himself. But the buyer and the seller will generally be unaware of what the contract means, what they should anticipate, and what steps are needed to make the instrument binding. They cannot look to the broker for unbiased assistance and should be advised by legal counsel loyal to themselves.

At the time the contract is signed the buyer and the seller require detailed advice about the effect of the doctrine of equitable conversion. They may or may not be aware of the need to anticipate the question, who bears the loss of damage to or destruction of buildings on the premises between the time the contract is signed and the time of closing. However, they will almost inevitably be ignorant of the existence of such problems as whether the contract so changes the interest of the seller as to void insurance policies; whether either the buyer or seller, or both, should execute new wills; whether their liability for the payment of inheritance taxes, in case of death, will be changed; whether joint tenancies or tenancies by the entireties will be affected; and the like.

E. *Establishing Title.* After the contract is executed the state of the seller's title must be established to the satisfaction of both the buyer and the lender. This is generally the most important and most expensive legal work connected with the transaction. The initial examination will be made by the attorney for the buyer, the lender, or the title insurer, relying in any case upon the official land title records or an abstract thereof, or by a title insurance company which maintains its own title plant.... [E]ither the lender or the buyer, or both, may demand additional protection in the form of a title insurance policy.

Whoever makes the examination, the buyer should be told by his own counsel what limitations, if any, impair the title he is getting. He should also receive formal protection by a written opinion from his attorney, an owner's title insurance policy, or both. If he applies for title insurance, his attorney should negotiate the provisions to be included or excluded from the policy. The attorney should also make clear to the buyer what the policy means. In particular, all of the exceptions to coverage contained in Schedule B should be explained. The use of standardized exceptions is common to all forms of insurance. The standardized exceptions contained in Schedule B of a title insurance policy are generally more complex and more restrictive than those of other insurance policies and are frequently unintelligible to the layman. Even if they are not, Schedule B is unique in that it contains additional exceptions peculiar to each individual title. The buyer must first be made aware of the existence of these exceptions and must then be made to understand them. If the exception is to a $10,000 mortgage and the buyer sees the provision he will probably not mistake its meaning. But if the exception is to "all of the conditions and restrictions found in deed of X to Y, recorded in the office of the clerk of the court of County, in Deed Book 309 at page 873," he will not ... realize that the exception is important, or, if he does, will not understand its meaning without assistance from his own lawyer....

F. *The Survey.* ... At some time prior to the approval of title the buyer, the lender, or the title insurance company may demand a survey.

The primary purpose of the survey will be to find whether the legal description of the land conforms to the lines laid down on the ground. An additional purpose may be to determine whether structures on the premises violate restrictive covenants or zoning ordinances or constitute an encroachment. When the survey has been completed the parties should have their attorneys advise them about any legal implications of the surveyor's findings.

G. *Curative Action.* In some cases routine curative action, such as the recording of affidavits, is needed to make titles marketable. Any such curative action should be carried out by an attorney for the seller, the buyer, or the lender. If the curative action is carried out by the attorney for the seller it should be checked for sufficiency by the attorneys for the buyer and lender; if by the attorney for the buyer, by the attorney for the lender; and if by the attorney for the lender, by the attorney for the buyer.

H. *Termite Inspection.* In a few jurisdictions an examination for termites must be made and a certificate turned over to the buyer. Such an examination is not legal work but may be ordered by the attorney for any one of the parties.

I. *Drafting Instruments.* Before closing, a lawyer must draft the deed and mortgage and, in most instances, the bond or note secured by the mortgage. This drafting is everywhere conceded to be legal work. As a matter of convenience it is most commonly performed by the mortgagee's attorney, although the representative of either of the other parties is equally qualified. Whoever does the work, the product should be examined by lawyers for each of the other two parties and the title insurance company, and they should be advised whether the instruments are effective and create the interests intended. The drafting of these instruments is sometimes considered merely routine work. Nothing could be further from the truth. For example, the description of the parties must be so phrased as to prevent confusion, and the description of the land must be complete and accurate. The importance of the form of warranties is often overlooked. By way of illustration, if the title is encumbered by equitable covenants or utility easements, either or both may be acceptable to the buyer and lender. But they should be excepted from the warranty. How title is to be taken should have been provided in the initial contract between the buyer and the seller, and the buyer should be advised as to the tax and other effects of the manner in which title is taken. Whether it was or not, the deed should conform to the needs and understanding of the parties. Of equal importance are other special agreements reached earlier in the transaction. The law says that the deed supersedes prior understandings and if they are not embraced in the writing they are nullified. Each deed or mortgage must therefore be examined to determine whether it carries out what has been agreed upon.

J. *Incidental Paper Work.* The Real Estate Settlement Procedures Act of 1974 places upon the lender the preparation of a complex settlement statement in virtually all residential real estate transactions. In addition, the Truth–In–Lending form must be filled in and executed. If the mortgage loan is to be insured by FHA, VA or by a private mortgage insurance company, more paper work is required. The required documents are standardized and can be completed without resort to legal expertise. They are part of the financing, rather than the legal aspects of the sale and mortgage. Nevertheless, lawyers are very frequently called upon by their clients to do this work. With a few exceptions, the government has taken the position that whoever performs these services shall receive no compensation therefor. This demand for unpaid labor is not peculiar to any one branch of the government and has done much to increase the irritation marking the closing costs controversy.

K. *Obtaining Title Insurance.* Where a title insurance policy for the buyer is based on the certificate of an independent attorney, the attorney may make an application for the initial binder, and, after closing, send in a final certificate and procure a policy for his client. . . .

L. *Closing.* A closing statement is generally prepared prior to final closing. The statement may take various forms but is designed to indicate the allocation of debits and credits to the various parties. In some cases it is drawn up by a layman, in others by a lawyer. The buyer's and seller's attorneys should make sure their clients understand the nature and amount of all closing costs. Much of the disenchantment of the buyer and seller of real estate stems from their misunderstanding of the specific items constituting closing costs. . . .

Unless either the closing attorney or an escrow company acts as an escrow agent a further check of title should be made immediately prior to closing. If this check is not made, it is possible that the parties will be unaware that the title has been impaired between the time of the original examination and the closing date. This further check will generally be carried out by the attorney, abstracter or title insurance company certifying or insuring title.

The closing is the proceeding at which the parties exchange executed instruments, make required payments and conclude the formal aspects of the transaction. At this point the buyer, the seller, and the lender should be represented by their own lawyers. They require advice and may need representation if a disagreement arises. They should be assured that the legal documents they exchange create the interests intended, that they are receiving the protection they need, and that correct payments have been made to those entitled to receive them.

M. *Post-Closing Procedures.* At or immediately following closing, arrangements must be made for insurance, taxes, and other incidents of ownership. Instruments must be recorded and a final check of title carried out. Disbursements must be made and documents distributed to the parties entitled to receive them. Title insurance policies, where called for, must be procured. Theoretically, there can be dispute about which of these various activities constitutes legal work. Practically, the closing lawyer generally handles all or virtually all of the post-closing details.

The ABA report expresses the view that an attorney should participate in any land transfer transaction. This opinion is widely shared among lawyers, but not universally so. Some critics have argued that many residential real estate transactions are sufficiently "routine" that the parties can avoid hiring lawyers altogether. These critics contend that the parties can protect themselves without the additional expense of lawyers if they use a real estate broker (who is familiar with the problems that parties might face), standardized forms (which reflect the accumulated wisdom of previous transactions), and an institutional mortgage lender (who is unlikely to make a mortgage loan if there are problems with title to the land or with the physical condition of the improvements). Indeed, in many states, thousands of real estate transfers occur every day without a lawyer representing either buyer or seller. As you study the remaining materials in this chapter, we encourage you to reflect on whether the involvement of a lawyer in all real estate transfer transactions is a justifiable caution or an unwarranted expense. We also encourage you to think critically about those aspects of the transaction in which legal assistance remains prudent and those aspects in which legal assistance is frequently unnecessary.

B. ISSUES IN CONTRACT FORMATION

Many real estate transactions begin with securing a real estate agent or "broker" to assist one or both of the parties in marketing or finding a property and negotiating an agreement for the sale of the property—which is then memorialized in a written contract. The following materials highlight some of the issues that arise in contracting with the broker and in the ultimate contract for sale between the parties.

1. *The Real Estate Broker*

Real estate brokers typically perform two separate functions. The first is the "listing" function—*i.e.*, entering into a brokerage contract with the seller to list the property (typically in exchange for a commission ranging from 5–10% of the purchase price) and thereafter advertising the property for sale by placing the property into the broker's own promotional materials and onto an area's multiple listing service. The second is the "selling" function—*i.e.*, displaying the home to potential buyers and facilitating negotiation and contract formation between the seller and prospective buyers. In some cases, the "listing" and "selling" are done by the same individual broker; in other cases, the "listing" and "selling" agents may be different agents who work for the same real estate brokerage firm.[1] In the typical transaction, however, both the "listing" agent and the "selling agent" serve as an agent of the seller.

Nonetheless, even though the selling broker may legally represent only the seller, the selling broker works closely with both parties, often assisting both parties in preparing the written contract (typically using a form agreement approved by the local association of brokers, such as the one on pages 792–97). Indeed, during the negotiation and formation of the agreement, the selling broker may be the only real estate "professional" involved in the process. In many cases, a lawyer may not see the contract until the parties have already executed it—by which time it may be too late for a lawyer to give advice about how the agreement might better have protected a party's interests.

The selling broker's involvement with both parties can lead to misunderstanding about the nature of the broker's role. An uninformed buyer who works closely with the broker may believe that the broker also works for the buyer as well.[2] For example, suppose Buyer, after viewing a number of houses with Broker over several days, asks for advice about the listing price on a particular home: "Is that a fair price, or can I do better?" Clearly, the question places Broker in a conflict of interest. Broker wants to be helpful; if Buyer purchases the home, Broker earns a commission, and Buyer may be more likely to employ Broker if Buyer later decides to sell the home. Nevertheless, Broker is the agent of the seller, and her commission will be calculated as a percentage of the selling price—so if Broker tells Buyer "the house is overpriced; you should bid lower," Broker would not only effectively reduce her own commission, but also might breach the duty of loyalty she owes to the seller. If Buyer does not understand clearly that Broker represents the seller, Buyer may make a decision that she might not have made alone or with the advice of a more independent agent (sometimes referred to as a "buyer's agent").[3] This potential for misunderstanding and conflicting interests helps to enliven the debate about

---

1. In some cases, the "listing" and "selling" agents may even work for different brokerage firms altogether, which may necessitate some additional contractual agreement between those firms regarding how the listing agent will divide the commission with the selling agent.

2. An influential survey of consumers in the early 1980s reflected that the potential for misunderstanding was significant. Where the "listing" and "selling" agents were different individuals, 74% of the buyers actually believed that the selling agent represented the buyer; only 8% of the buyers correctly believed that the selling agent represented the seller. *See* Gerard R. Butters, *Consumers' Experiences with Real Estate Brokers: A Report on the Consumer Survey of the Federal Trade Commission's*

Residential Real Estate Brokerage Investigation 24–25 (Nov. 1983), *in* L.A. Reg'l Office Staff, Fed. Trade Comm'n, The Residential Real Estate Brokerage Industry (Dec. 1983).

3. This is an empirical question, of course, and the empirical data is mixed. The conventional wisdom is that a buyer that uses a buyer's broker would be able to obtain a lower price for the same house than a buyer who works solely with a "selling" broker. However, one empirical study suggested that there was no statistically significant difference in prices where buyers' brokers were used. Harold W. Elder et al., *Buyer Brokers: Do They Make a Difference? Their Influence on Selling Price and Search Duration*, 28 Real Est. Econ. 337 (2000).

whether persons can safely buy land without being represented by a lawyer at some or all of the stages of the process.

Buyers are not the only persons who may misunderstand the legal implications of a broker's involvement in a real estate transaction. Consider the seller's situation in the following case.

DRAKE v. HOSLEY

Supreme Court of Alaska.
713 P.2d 1203 (1986).

MOORE, JUSTICE. . . .

On March 5, 1984, Paul Drake signed an exclusive listing agreement[4] with The Charles Hosley Company, Realtors (hereafter "Hosley"). The agreement authorized Hosley to act as Drake's agent until March 30, 1984, to sell some land Drake owned in North Pole, Alaska. The agreement provided for payment of a ten percent commission if, during the period of the listing agreement, 1) Hosley located a buyer "willing and able to purchase at the terms set by the seller," or 2) the seller entered into a "binding sale" during the term set by the seller.

Hosley found a group of three buyers, Robert Goldsmith, Dwayne Hofschulte and David Nystrom (hereafter "buyers"), who were interested in the property. On March 23, 1984, Drake signed a purchase and sale agreement, entitled "earnest money receipt," in which he agreed to sell the land to the buyers at a specified price and terms. The buyers also signed the agreement. It provided that closing would occur "within 10 days of clear title" and "ASAP, 1984." A typed addendum stated that Drake agreed to pay Hosley a commission of ten percent of the price paid for the property. Both Drake and Hosley signed the addendum.

On April 3, 1984, Hosley received a preliminary commitment for title insurance. The title report listed a judgment in favor of Drake's ex-wife as the sole encumbrance on the title. The next day Hosley called Drake's attorney, Tom Wickwire, to ask about the judgment. Wickwire stated that the judgment would be paid with the cash received at closing.

Two or three days later, attorney Wickwire called Hosley and stated that his client (Drake) wanted the sale closed by April 11. Wickwire explained that he had negotiated a discounted settlement with Drake's ex-wife that required payment by April 11. Wickwire claims that Hosley

---

4. Editors' Note: The vast majority of listing or brokerage arrangements today are "exclusive" arrangements. These "exclusive" arrangements come in two basic types—the "exclusive agency" and the "exclusive right to sell." In the "exclusive agency" arrangement, the owner may not use another agent's efforts to sell the home during the effective period of the listing agreement; however, the owner may sell the property through her own efforts without incurring liability for a brokerage commission. In the "exclusive right to sell" arrangement, the broker has the exclusive right to facilitate sales of the property, even as against the property owner; if the property owner sold the property during the period of the listing agreement, the broker would earn a commission even if the broker's efforts did not facilitate the sale in any way. Which type of arrangement was involved in *Drake v. Hosley*?

agreed to close by April 11. Hosley disagrees, and claims that he merely stated that he would try to close as quickly as possible.

When Hosley became concerned that the buyers would not be able to close on April 11, he telephoned the attorney for Drake's ex-wife and learned that the April 11 deadline for payment of the judgment had been extended until the end of the month.

On April 11, Wickwire called Hosley to set up the closing. Hosley told Wickwire that the buyers could not close that day because they did not have the money and would not have it before May 1. Wickwire indicated that he would advise Drake to call off the sale because the buyers had refused to perform.[5] Wickwire mailed a letter to Hosley, dated April 11, stating that Drake's offer to sell was withdrawn. Hosley received the letter on approximately April 18. On April 12, Drake sold his property through another broker to different buyers.

On April 12, Hosley went to Wickwire's office to close the sale and submitted checks from the buyers totaling $33,000 for the down payment. Wickwire refused the checks, stating that another buyer already had purchased the property.

Hosley filed a complaint, alleging he had fulfilled the terms of the exclusive listing agreement and was entitled to payment of a commission. The parties filed cross-motions for summary judgment. The trial court granted Hosley's motion and denied Drake's. Drake appeals....

AS 08.88.361 provides that "[a] commission is earned when the real estate broker fulfills the terms of a written personal services contract." The exclusive listing agreement between Drake, as seller, and Hosley, as broker, provided that a ten percent commission would be paid to Hosley if one of three conditions occurred: a) if a property is sold or a *binding sale or lease agreement is entered into by Seller* during the term set by seller; or b) if during the term of this Agreement [Hosley] *finds a buyer willing and able to purchase* at the terms set by Seller; or c) if a buyer located by [Hosley] enters into a binding sale or lease agreement within 120 days after the expiration of this Agreement. (Emphasis added.)

It is undisputed that during the term of the agreement, Hosley found a group of three buyers, and that Drake entered into a purchase and sale agreement ("earnest money receipt") with the buyers. The earnest money agreement signed by Drake stated: "I hereby approve and accept the above sale for said price and on said terms and conditions and agree to consummate the same as stated." A typed addendum to the earnest money agreement provided: "Seller agrees to pay a Realtors' commission in the amount of 10% of price to be paid by partial assignment of the deed of trust at the rate of $1,000/month."

---

5. In his brief, Hosley suggests that Wickwire responded in this way because he was confused about which party Hosley represented. Since Wickwire was not involved in the transaction when the listing and earnest money agreements were signed, Hosley suggests that Wickwire may have assumed that Hosley was acting for the buyers.

On the basis of these facts, the trial court concluded that Hosley had performed the terms of his agreement with Drake. The court found that, within the terms of the listing agreement, Hosley located a group of buyers who entered into a binding sale agreement with Drake. The court ruled that Hosley therefore was entitled to his commission.

Drake invites this court to adopt the reasoning of *Ellsworth Dobbs, Inc. v. Johnson,* 50 N.J. 528, 236 A.2d 843 (1967), and hold that a real estate broker does not earn a commission unless the contract of sale is performed.

The traditional rule followed by a majority of jurisdictions is that a broker is entitled to a commission when he produces a buyer ready, willing and able to purchase the property on the seller's terms, even if the sale is not completed. *Sowash v. Garrett,* 630 P.2d 8, 12 (Alaska 1981). The rationale for concluding that a potential purchaser is deemed "willing and able" the instant the purchaser signs a contract with the seller is explained in *Kopf v. Milam,* 60 Cal.2d 600, 35 Cal.Rptr. 614, 617, 387 P.2d 390, 393 (1963):

> When a vendor enters a valid unconditional contract of sale with a purchaser procured by a broker, the purchaser's acceptability is conclusively presumed because the vendor is estopped to deny the qualifications of a purchaser with whom he is willing to contract.

Drake suggests that the rule of *Dobbs* is better reasoned because it emphasizes that a broker has not produced a ready, willing and able buyer if the buyer refuses or is unable to perform at closing. *Dobbs,* 236 A.2d at 853. In a practical world the true test of a willing buyer is not met at the time a purchase agreement is signed, but at the time of closing of title. *Id.* Since the broker's duty to the owner is to produce a buyer who is financially able to pay the purchase price, it is reasonable to allow the owner to accept the buyer and enter into a sales contract without becoming liable for a broker's commission unless the sale is consummated. *Id.*

The *Dobbs* court also noted that when an owner of property lists it for sale with a broker, the owner usually expects that money for payment of a commission will come from the sale proceeds. *Id.* at 854. For these reasons, the *Dobbs* court concluded that "public policy requires the courts to read into every brokerage agreement or contract of sale a requirement that barring default by the seller, commissions shall not be deemed earned against him unless the contract of sale is performed." *Id.* at 857.

We find such reasoning persuasive. We also note that several jurisdictions recently have adopted the *Dobbs* rule, or modified versions of it. *See* Annot., 12 A.L.R. 4th 1083, 1088, 1094–1103 (1982). However, adoption of the rule does not assist Drake in this case. The *Dobbs* court specifically held that "in the *absence of default by the seller,* the broker's right to commission ... comes into existence only when his buyer performs in accordance with the contract of sale." *Dobbs,* 236 A.2d at 855 (emphasis added). A broker still is entitled to a commission if "improper or frustrating conduct" by the owner prevents title from passing. *Id.* at 853.

Drake claims that there is a genuine issue of fact regarding whether the buyer or seller refused to perform. In particular he argues that there is a material factual dispute "whether Hosley, acting for the buyers, first agreed with Wickwire to close the sale on April 11, 1984, then . . . refused to close on that day. . . ." Drake is correct that the existence of an agreement is disputed. However, there is no genuine issue as to whether Hosley was acting for the buyers. Other than a bare allegation in Drake's pleadings, the record is devoid of any evidence that Hosley was representing the buyers. Hence, the buyers could not be bound whether or not an agreement to expedite closing was made by Hosley and Wickwire.

Drake points to the fact that Hosley told Drake's attorney that the buyers could not close on April 11 because they did not have the money. The fact that Hosley communicated a message from the buyers does not make him their agent. Further, the affidavit of Drake's attorney, Wickwire, does not state that Hosley ever claimed or intimated that he was acting in any role other than as Drake's broker.

In short, Drake failed to make any showing that Hosley was the buyers' agent and had authority to modify their contract. In the absence of such evidence, any agreement between Drake's attorney and Drake's broker could not modify the contractual obligations of the buyers. Since Hosley's right to a commission does not turn on whether he and Drake's attorney agreed to expedite closing, the disputed agreement was not a material fact that would preclude summary judgment.

Under the terms of the earnest money agreement, the buyers were required to close within ten days after evidence of clear title was furnished. Hosley stated that he received a report from the title insurance company on April 3. The report carried a typist's date of April 2. We agree with the trial court that the buyers met the terms of the earnest money agreement by submitting checks for the down payment to Drake's agent on April 12—which was within ten days of either the April 2 or April 3 date. Thus, it was not the buyers who prevented the sale from going through.

We also reject a second argument raised by Drake. He contends the earnest money agreement was ambiguous, that the sale was not consummated because of the ambiguities, and that Hosley, who prepared the form, should be held responsible. The document included three provisions relating to time of performance. It provided for closing "within 10 days of clear title" and "ASAP, 1984." It also stated that "time is of the essence of this contract." We find these terms neither ambiguous nor inconsistent. Further, we find no merit in Drake's suggestion that the contract could be interpreted to allow Drake to select any day prior to the end of the ten-day period for closing.

Finally, Drake asserts that Hosley is not entitled to a commission because he breached his fiduciary duty to act in the best interests of his principal and to disclose any conflicts of interest. *See* AS 08.88.391. Drake claims Hosley breached this duty by representing the buyers in selecting a closing date and communicating their position to Drake. This claim is without merit. As we have noted, there is no evidence that Hosley ever acted for the buyers. . . .

To summarize, Hosley found a group of buyers who were willing and able to perform in accord with the terms set by the seller, but they were prevented from doing so by the seller's frustrating conduct. The buyers tried to perform by tendering checks for the down payment "within 10 days of clear title," as required by the earnest money agreement. The sale did not take place because the seller, Drake, sold the property to a third party during the ten-day closing period. Thus, even under the *Dobbs* rule, Hosley is entitled to his commission. . . .

Notes

1. *The Common Law "Ready, Willing, and Able" Standard.* Courts traditionally took the position that a broker earns her commission when she obtains a buyer that is "ready, willing, and able" to purchase the property. Most courts interpreted this language to mean that the broker earned her commission once the parties signed the contract. As the *Drake* case suggests, the rationale behind this position was that having agreed to contract with the buyer, the seller was "estopped" to deny that the buyer was "ready, willing, and able." Is this a sensible use of the concept of estoppel? Why or why not? Why do you think the court in *Dobbs* refused to use the concept of estoppel and instead held that the broker could not collect its commission unless the sale actually closed?

Despite the fact that a number of jurisdictions have adopted the approach taken in *Dobbs*, the common law "ready, willing, and able" test is still applied in a substantial number of jurisdictions as a default rule in cases where the seller's listing agreement does not provide a contrary provision. *See, e.g., Hallmark & Johnson Props., Ltd. v. Taylor*, 201 Ill.App.3d 512, 147 Ill.Dec. 141, 559 N.E.2d 141 (1990); *Blackman De Stefano Real Estate, Inc. v. Smith*, 157 A.D.2d 932, 550 N.Y.S.2d 443 (1990); *Bennett Realty, Inc. v. Muller*, 100 N.C.App. 446, 396 S.E.2d 630 (1990).

2. *The* Dobbs *Rule Applied in Cases When No Closing Occurs.* A broker still can collect his commission, even under the *Dobbs* rule, if the seller's "improper" or "frustrating" conduct breaches the contract. Suppose that Broker helps Buyer and Seller prepare a contract in which Buyer offers to pay Seller $140,000 for a two-story home. Just prior to closing, however, the parties discover that Seller's title is unmarketable and Buyer decides not to complete the sale. When the sale falls through, Broker demands that Seller pay her $9,800, claiming that she is entitled to the 7% commission in her brokerage contract with Seller. Should Broker be able to recover her commission from Seller? Why or why not? Suppose, instead, that Seller had good title, but Buyer had breached the contract (assume that she had found another home she liked better) and refused to perform. Under the *Dobbs* rule, Broker could not recover the commission from Seller. Should she be able to recover anything from Buyer, and if so, under what legal theory—

contract, tort, or something else? *See, e.g., Bailey v. Montgomery*, 31 Ark. App. 1, 786 S.W.2d 594 (1990).

3. *Buyers' Agents and Dual Agency.* Although the traditional practice has been for brokers to serve as the seller's agent, it is possible for buyers to employ their own broker (*buyer's agent*). However, the source of the broker's compensation may become an issue:

> Obviously, most buyers are not eager to pay these brokers direct commissions; they assume that a "full" commission is already built into the price of the house and will be paid by the seller. On the other hand, listing brokers have no obligation to split their commissions with buyers' brokers, since the latter are not subagents of the listing broker. They may or may not split their commissions voluntarily. [Grant S. Nelson & Dale A. Whitman, Real Estate Transfer, Finance and Development: Cases and Materials 13 (6th ed. 2003).]

Assume that a seller's brokers are willing to split their commission with the buyer's agent. Do you see any problems with that arrangement? Can you think of an alternative method of compensating the buyer's agent?

Some states also have enacted statutes permitting brokers to serve as the agent of both parties, a concept known as a *dual agency*, provided both parties give their informed consent. The Illinois statute, for example, requires both parties to sign a written form specifying what a dual agent can or cannot do for them, as follows:

WHAT A LICENSEE CAN DO FOR CLIENTS WHEN ACTING AS A DUAL AGENT

1. Treat all clients honestly.

2. Provide information about the property to the buyer or tenant.

3. Disclose all latent material defects in the property that are known to the Licensee.

4. Disclose financial qualification of the buyer or tenant to the seller or landlord.

5. Explain real estate terms.

6. Help the buyer or tenant to arrange for property inspections.

7. Explain closing costs and procedures.

8. Help the buyer compare financing alternatives.

9. Provide information about comparable properties that have sold so both clients may make educated decisions on what price to accept or offer.

WHAT LICENSEE CANNOT DISCLOSE TO CLIENTS WHEN ACTING AS A DUAL AGENT

1. Confidential information that Licensee may know about a client, without that client's permission.

2. The price the seller or landlord will take other than the listing price without permission of the seller or landlord.

3. The price the buyer or tenant is willing to pay without permission of the buyer or tenant.

4. A recommended or suggested price the buyer or tenant should offer.

5. A recommended or suggested price the seller or landlord should counter with or accept.

225 Ill. Comp. Stat. 454/15–45. Do dual agencies solve the problems discussed in the introduction to this section regarding conflicts of interest and misunderstandings by the parties?

LAWYERING EXERCISE
(Counseling and Drafting)

BACKGROUND: The traditional common law rule and the *Dobbs* rule are default rules that apply when the seller and the broker do not specifically agree upon the moment when the broker becomes entitled to her commission. If the parties' agreement specifies otherwise, that agreement controls.

TASK: Suppose that you are in a jurisdiction that follows the "ready, willing, and able" test. You learn that Janet (a wealthy and valued client) is considering selling her home and retiring in Monaco, and plans to list the home for sale with her friend Clyde, a successful broker in the area. Would it be sufficient if Janet included a provision in her listing agreement with Clyde that stated that Clyde's commission "will be paid from the proceeds available at closing"? *Compare Realty Assocs. of Sedona v. Valley Nat'l Bank*, 153 Ariz. 514, 738 P.2d 1121 (App. 1987) *with Chamberlain v. Porter*, 562 A.2d 675 (Me. 1989). If not, draft the language that you would encourage Janet to include in her listing agreement with Clyde to protect her from the risk of litigation similar to *Drake v. Hosley*.

2. *The Form of the Contract*

All states have enacted a statute of frauds, which requires that transfers of land—and contracts for such transfers—must be in writing to be enforceable. Missouri's statute is typical:

> No action shall be brought ... upon any contract made for the sale of lands, tenements, hereditaments, or an interest in or concerning them, or any lease thereof, for a longer time than one year, or upon any agreement that is not to be performed within one year from the making thereof, unless the agreement upon which the action shall be brought, or some memorandum or note thereof, shall be in writing and signed by the party to be charged therewith, or some other person by him thereto lawfully authorized.... [Mo. Rev. Stat. § 432.010.]

How complete does this writing have to be? Does a party have any recourse if an agreement fails to satisfy the statute of frauds? Consider these questions in the context of the following case.

HICKEY v. GREEN

Appeals Court of Massachusetts.
14 Mass.App.Ct. 671, 442 N.E.2d 37 (1982).

CUTTER, JUSTICE.... Mrs. Gladys Green owns a lot (Lot S) in the Manomet section of Plymouth. In July, 1980, she advertised it for sale. On July 11 and 12, Hickey and his wife discussed with Mrs. Green purchasing Lot S and "orally agreed to a sale" for $15,000. Mrs. Green on July 12 accepted a deposit check of $500, marked by Hickey on the back, "Deposit on Lot ... Massasoit Ave. Manomet.... Subject to Variance from Town of Plymouth." Mrs. Green's brother and agent "was under the impression that a zoning variance was needed and [had] advised ... Hickey to write" the quoted language on the deposit check. It turned out, however, by July 16 that no variance would be required. Hickey had left the payee line of the deposit check blank, because of uncertainty whether Mrs. Green or her brother was to receive the check and asked "Mrs. Green to fill in the appropriate name." Mrs. Green held the check, did not fill in the payee's name, and neither cashed nor endorsed it. Hickey "stated to Mrs. Green that his intention was to sell his home and build on Mrs. Green's lot."

"Relying upon the arrangements ... with Mrs. Green," the Hickeys advertised their house on Sachem Road in newspapers on three days in July, 1980, and agreed with a purchaser for its sale and took from him a deposit check for $500 which they deposited in their own account.[6] On July 24, Mrs. Green told Hickey that she "no longer intended to sell her property to him" but had decided to sell to another for $16,000. Hickey told Mrs. Green that he had already sold his house and offered her $16,000 for Lot S. Mrs. Green refused this offer.

The Hickeys filed this complaint seeking specific performance. Mrs. Green asserts that relief is barred by the Statute of Frauds contained in G.L. c. 259, § 1. The trial judge granted specific performance. Mrs. Green has appealed.

The present rule applicable in most jurisdictions in the United States is succinctly set forth in Restatement (Second) of Contracts, § 129 (1981). The section reads, "A contract for the transfer of an interest in land may be specifically enforced notwithstanding failure to comply with the Statute of Frauds if it is established that the party seeking enforcement, *in reasonable reliance on the contract* and on the continuing assent of the party against whom enforcement is sought, *has so changed his position that injustice can be avoided only by specific enforcement*" (emphasis supplied).[7] The earlier Massachusetts decisions laid down

6. On the back of the check was noted above the Hickeys' signatures endorsing the check "Deposit on Purchase of property at Sachem Rd. and First St., Manomet, Ma. Sale price, $44,000."

7. Comments a and b to § 129, read (in part): "a.... This section restates what is somewhat strict requirements for an estoppel precluding the assertion of the Statute of Frauds. *See, e.g., Glass v. Hulbert*, 102 Mass. 24, 31–32, 43–44 (1869). Frequently there has been an actual change of possession and improvement of the transferred property, as well as full payment of the full purchase price, or one or more of these elements.

It is stated in Park, Real Estate Law, § 883, at 334, that the "more recent decisions . . . indicate a trend on the part of the [Supreme Judicial C]ourt to find that the circumstances warrant specific performance." This appears to be a correct perception. *See Fisher v. MacDonald*, 332 Mass. 727, 729, 127 N.E.2d 484 (1955), where specific performance was granted upon a showing that the purchaser "was put into possession and . . . [had] furnished part of the consideration in money and services." . . .

The present facts reveal a simple case of a proposed purchase of a residential vacant lot, where the vendor, Mrs. Green, knew that the Hickeys were planning to sell their former home (possibly to obtain funds to pay her) and build on Lot S. The Hickeys, relying on Mrs. Green's oral promise, moved rapidly to make their sale without obtaining any adequate memorandum of the terms of what appears to have been intended to be a quick cash sale of Lot S. So rapid was action by the Hickeys that, by July 21, less than ten days after giving their deposit to Mrs. Green, they had accepted a deposit check for the sale of their house, endorsed the check, and placed it in their bank account. Above their signatures endorsing the check was a memorandum probably sufficient to satisfy the Statute of Frauds. . . . At the very least, the Hickeys had bound themselves in a manner in which, to avoid a transfer of their own house, they might have had to engage in expensive litigation. No attorney has been shown to have been used either in the transaction between Mrs. Green and the Hickeys or in that between the Hickeys and their purchaser.

There is no denial by Mrs. Green of the oral contract between her and the Hickeys. This, under § 129 of the Restatement, is of some significance.[8] There can be no doubt (a) that Mrs. Green made the

widely known as the 'part performance doctrine.' Part performance is not an accurate designation of such acts as taking possession and making improvements when the contract does not provide for such acts, but such acts regularly bring the doctrine into play. The doctrine is contrary to the words of the Statute of Frauds, but it was established by English courts of equity soon after the enactment of the Statute. Payment of purchase-money, without more, was once thought sufficient to justify specific enforcement, but a contrary view now prevails, since in such cases restitution is an adequate remedy. . . . Enforcement has . . . been justified on the ground that repudiation after 'part performance' amounts to a 'virtual fraud.' A more accurate statement is that courts with equitable powers are vested by tradition with what in substance is a dispensing power based on the promisee's reliance, *a discretion to be exercised with caution* in the light of all the circumstances. . . ." [emphasis supplied]

"b. . . . Two distinct elements enter into the application of the rule of this Section: first, the extent to which the evidentiary function of the statutory formalities is fulfilled by the conduct of the parties; second, the reliance of the promisee, providing a compelling substantive basis for relief in addition to the expectations created by the promise."

8. Comment d of Restatement (Second) of Contracts, § 129, reads "d. . . . Where specific enforcement is rested on a transfer of possession plus either part payment of the price or the making of improvements, it

promise on which the Hickeys so promptly relied, and also (b) she, nearly as promptly, but not promptly enough, repudiated it because she had a better opportunity. The stipulated facts require the conclusion that in equity Mrs. Green's conduct cannot be condoned. This is not a case where either party is shown to have contemplated the negotiation of a purchase and sale agreement. If a written agreement had been expected, even by only one party, or would have been natural (because of the participation by lawyers or otherwise), a different situation might have existed. It is a permissible inference from the agreed facts that the rapid sale of the Hickeys' house was both appropriate and expected. These are not circumstances where negotiations fairly can be seen as inchoate. *Compare Tull v. Mister Donut Development Corp.*, 7 Mass. App. 626, 630–632, 389 N.E.2d 447 (1979).

We recognize that specific enforcement of Mrs. Green's promise to convey Lot S may well go somewhat beyond the circumstances considered in the *Fisher* case, 332 Mass. 727, ... where specific performance was granted. It may seem (perhaps because the present facts are less complicated) to extend the principles stated in [*Cellucci v. Sun Oil Co.*, 2 Mass.App. 722, 728, 320 N.E.2d 919 (1974)]. We recognize also the cautionary language about granting specific performance in comment a to § 129 of the Restatement (see note 6, *supra*). No public interest behind G.L. c. 259, § 1, however, in the simple circumstances before us, will be violated if Mrs. Green fairly is held to her precise bargain by principles of equitable estoppel, subject to the considerations mentioned below.

Over two years have passed since July, 1980, and over a year since the trial judge's findings were filed on July 6, 1981. At that time, the principal agreed facts of record bearing upon the extent of the injury to the Hickeys (because of their reliance on Mrs. Green's promise to convey Lot S) were those based on the Hickeys' new obligation to convey their house to a purchaser. Performance of that agreement had been extended to May 1, 1981. If that agreement has been abrogated or modified since the trial, the case may take on a different posture. If enforcement of that agreement still will be sought, or if that agreement has been carried out, the conveyance of Lot S by Mrs. Green should be required now.

The case, in any event, must be remanded to the trial judge for the purpose of amending the judgment to require conveyance of Lot S by Mrs. Green only upon payment to her in cash within a stated period of the balance of the agreed price of $15,000. The trial judge, however, in her discretion and upon proper offers of proof by counsel, may reopen the record to receive, in addition to the presently stipulated facts, a stipulation or evidence concerning the present status of the Hickeys'

is commonly said that the action taken by the purchaser must be unequivocally referable to the oral agreement. But this requirement is not insisted on *if the making of the promise is admitted or is clearly proved. The promisee must act in reasonable reliance on the promise, before the promisor has* *repudiated* it, and the action must be such that the remedy of restitution is inadequate. If these requirements are met, *neither taking of possession nor payment of money nor the making of improvements is essential....*" (emphasis supplied)

apparent obligation to sell their house. If the circumstances have changed, it will be open to the trial judge to require of Mrs. Green, instead of specific performance, only full restitution to the Hickeys of all costs reasonably caused to them in respect of these transactions (including advertising costs, deposits, and their reasonable costs for this litigation) with interest. The case is remanded to the Superior Court Department for further action consistent with this opinion. . . .

Notes

1. *The Statute of Frauds as Evidentiary Assurance.* Historical wisdom defends the statute of frauds as a means of ensuring that when one party seeks to enforce an "agreement," that "agreement" actually reflects a mutual understanding as to the essential terms of the alleged bargain. What are those essential terms? Most statutes of frauds are silent as to the exact content of the writing, but courts typically require that the writing identify the parties, describe the land, state the purchase price, and be signed by the party to be charged. *See* 3 American Law of Property § 11.5 (1952). Courts also have recognized that the writing need not be in a particular form; a letter, note, or other informal memo may suffice. *Id.* Given this background, can you make an argument that the Hickeys' check constituted a sufficient writing in the *Green* case? Why or why not?

2. *Exceptions to the Statute of Frauds—The Doctrine of Part Performance.* If a primary purpose of the statute of frauds is to provide evidentiary assurance of agreement, it should not be surprising that courts occasionally have dispensed with the statute of frauds in cases where one party presented compelling evidence of an agreement. For instance, in appropriate cases, courts have considered acts taken in performance of an oral agreement—such as the payment of money, together with either the transfer of possession of the land or the construction of improvements (or both)—as a sufficient evidentiary substitute for a written document. Based upon these acts of "part performance," courts have justified enforcement of an oral agreement in equity despite the lack of compliance with the statute of frauds.

Relying upon "part performance" to avoid the statute of frauds is problematic, however, because courts often have held that sufficient acts of part performance must be "unequivocally referable" to the existence of an oral agreement—in other words, there must be no other plausible explanation for those acts. One of the best known and most egregious "part performance" cases is *Burns v. McCormick*, 233 N.Y. 230, 135 N.E. 273 (1922). In *Burns*, an elderly widower told some of his relatives that if they gave up their home and business, moved in with him, and cared for him during his life, then his house, lot, equipment, and furniture would be theirs upon his death. These relatives did as the widower asked and cared for him until his death, but the widower never executed a deed to them, nor did he leave a will that provided anything for them. When the relatives sought specific performance of this oral agreement, they argued that their acts of part performance—selling their home and business, moving in with the widower, and caring for him until his death—provided sufficient proof of the oral agreement. The trial court refused to enforce the agreement for noncompliance with the statute of frauds, and the New York Court of Appeals affirmed, holding that the relatives' behavior was not "unequivocally referable" to an agreement to convey the land. Why not? What other plausible explanation existed for the relatives' behavior? Is the "unequivocally referable" test too stringent to be of any practical use?

3. *Exceptions to the Statute of Frauds—Estoppel.* The *Hickey* case demonstrates an alternative exception to the statute of frauds—one grounded in the equitable estoppel principle with which you are already familiar. The Hickeys relied to their detriment (by agreeing to sell their home) upon Green's oral promise to sell her home. If a party seeking to enforce an oral agreement can demonstrate (a) reasonable and detrimental reliance on the oral agreement, and (b) the necessity for specific enforcement of the agreement to avoid injustice or irreparable injury, the court can estop the other party from asserting the statute of frauds as a defense. As *Hickey* demonstrates, in such cases the courts will not require partial payment, the transfer of possession, or the making of improvements. Do you think that the Hickeys' reliance upon their oral agreement with Green was reasonable reliance? Do you think it was detrimental reliance? Why or why not?

4. *Criticism of the Statute of Frauds.* Several scholars have questioned whether the statute of frauds effectively accomplishes its ostensible objectives, and some have called for its repeal. Consider the following criticism:

> Because the statute of frauds is satisfied by a memorandum that contains only a sketchy reference to the agreement it memorializes, compliance with the statute actually does little to prevent fraud, perjury, or misrecollection. Moreover, there are many reasons for putting an agreement in writing that are independent of the statute of frauds. These reasons include: (1) Written agreements are more certain than oral ones; (2) they are not as open to misinterpretation; (3) only written agreements can take advantage of certain other statutes and legal rules, such as the parole evidence rule and the recordation and registry laws; (4) the discipline of a writing requires the parties to think through their agreement in more detail than they might otherwise; and (5) the ceremony of a writing encourages the parties to take their understanding seriously, thus increasing the likelihood of voluntary performance. These reasons are compelling enough that parties likely would use written agreements even if no statute of frauds existed. [Michael Braunstein, *Remedy, Reason, and the Statute of Frauds: A Critical Economic Analysis*, 1989 Utah L. Rev. 383, 385–86.]

Do you agree with Prof. Braunstein that these arguments justify repeal of the statute of frauds?

3. *Land Descriptions*

As suggested in the previous section, the statute of frauds requires the real estate contract to contain an adequate description of the land being sold. Most courts are fairly lenient with this requirement and do not require a formal legal description at this stage of the proceedings. Instead, it is generally enough to give the street address, tax identification number, or some other description specific enough to identify the land with reasonable certainty. Problems can arise when the description is ambiguous, such as "forty acres of my farm" (when the seller owns a 100–acre farm) or "the property known as the Copper Dragon Brewery." [Why is the latter ambiguous?] Nonetheless, courts usually will allow extrinsic evidence to clarify an ambiguous description. They will not permit such evidence, however, to supply a description when one is completely missing from the contract.

By contrast, most courts require the deed of conveyance to contain a full legal description. [Some jurisdictions also require the full legal description in the real estate contract itself. *See, e.g., Key Design Inc. v. Moser,* 138 Wash.2d 875, 983 P.2d 653 (1999).] Accordingly, property lawyers should have some rudimentary understanding of the three primary methods of land description: metes and bounds, government survey, and plat. A typical legal description today is likely to use a combination of these methods.

Metes and bounds. The earliest form of land description, the metes and bounds method, describes the land in relation to natural monuments (*e.g.,* rivers, rocks and trees) or artificial monuments (bridges, roads, fences, stakes, pins, or posts). The description begins at some easily identifiable corner of the property and then traces the boundary lines of the property by using distances, compass point headings, and monuments until the description "closes" by returning to the point of beginning. Thus, an overly simplified description by metes and bounds might look like this:

> Beginning at a metal post at the northeast corner of the intersection of Robertson Road and Whitfield Way, run thence north 600 feet, thence run east 250 feet, thence run south 600 feet, thence run west 250 feet to the point of beginning.

It is not uncommon, however, for metes and bounds descriptions to be much longer and more complicated in their details.

Government survey. The government survey, also known as the rectangular survey system, was established by Congress in 1785 as a standardized way of describing all lands conveyed to or acquired by the federal government. This survey was a remarkable feat, ultimately encompassing Illinois, Wisconsin, Indiana, Michigan, Ohio, Alabama, Mississippi, Florida, and all states west of the Mississippi River (excluding Texas).

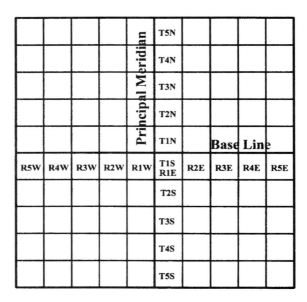

Figure 1

To decipher a legal description based upon the government survey, it is necessary to understand how the survey was conducted. In each region to be surveyed, surveyors began by establishing a starting point at the intersection of two perpendicular lines. The north-south line was called the principal or prime meridian, and the east-west line was called the base line. Next, parallel north-south lines (range lines) were established at six-mile intervals on each side of the principal meridian. Similarly, parallel east-west lines (township lines) were established at six-mile intervals on each side of the baseline. This matrix of lines formed a checkerboard of squares known as townships, as illustrated in Figure 1.[9] Townships are numbered in relation to their location north or south of the baseline and east or west of the principal meridian. The townships in the first row north of the baseline are known as Township 1 North; townships in the second row are known as Township 2 North; townships in the first row south of the baseline are Township 1 South; and so on. They are further delineated by their range lines east and west of the principal meridian. Townships in the first row east of the principal meridian are known as Range 1 East, townships in the first row west of the principal meridian are known as Range 1 West. Thus, the township located five rows north of the baseline and three rows to the west of the baseline is designated as Township 5 North, Range 3 West (T5N, R3W).

9. These townships are different from the local governmental units known by the same name in some states. Although some governmental townships have the same boundaries as the surveyor's township, others do not.

Townships were further divided into 36 squares, known as sections. Each section encompasses one square mile, or roughly 640 acres. The sections are numbered consecutively, beginning with section 1 at the northeast corner and proceeding west to section 6; then reversing direction, starting with section 7 directly underneath section 6 and ending with section 12 directly under section 1; the next row reverses direction again, and so on back and forth with each tier, until reaching section 36 in the southeast corner, as illustrated in Figure 2.

6	5	4	3	2	1
7	8	9	10	11	12
18	17	16	15	14	13
19	20	21	22	23	24
30	29	28	27	26	25
31	32	33	34	35	36

Figure 2

Finally, each section may be subdivided in halves and quarters and even smaller parcels. These smaller units are designated by their geographic location within the section. Thus, if a section is divided into quarters, the units are designated as the northwest, northeast, southwest, and southeast quarters. If divided in half, the units are designated as the north half and the south half. Examples of these divisions and their corresponding acreage are illustrated in Figure 3.

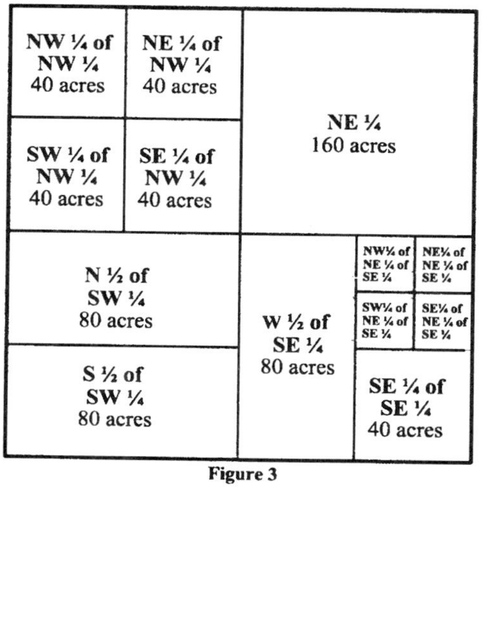

NW ¼ of NW ¼ 40 acres	NE ¼ of NW ¼ 40 acres	NE ¼ 160 acres		
SW ¼ of NW ¼ 40 acres	SE ¼ of NW ¼ 40 acres			
N ½ of SW ¼ 80 acres		W ½ of SE ¼ 80 acres	NW¼ of NE ¼ of SE ¼	NE¼ of NE ¼ of SE ¼
			SW¼ of NE ¼ of SE ¼	SE¼ of NE ¼ of SE ¼
S ½ of SW ¼ 80 acres			SE ¼ of SE ¼ 40 acres	

Figure 3

Combining all of these components, a simple description based upon the government survey might look like this:

> All of that land lying in the southeast quarter of the northwest quarter of section 15, Township 78 north, Range 39 west of the 5th Prime Meridian, Shelby County, Iowa.

Plat. The third method of describing land, commonly used when a larger tract is divided into a number of small parcels (lots and blocks), is by reference to a recorded plat or map. The boundaries of the large tract are initially described by either a metes and bounds or government survey. A surveyor then prepares a plat illustrating the consecutively numbered lots and describing them by metes and bounds. The survey plat is recorded in the county's land records and becomes part of the legal description as in this example:

> Lot No. 42, in Block No. One (1), of the CYPRESS GARDENS SUBDIVISION, an addition to Williamson County, Illinois, according to the established map and plat of record in Volume 6, Page 267 of the Plat Records of Williamson County, Illinois.

C. TITLE INVESTIGATION AND ASSURANCE

The investigation and assurance of the seller's title is often the most significant aspect of any land transfer transaction. This process typically involves several steps.

Contractual Provisions. The parties' contract usually provides—either expressly or impliedly—that the seller will provide title of a certain quality. Most often, the contract uses the term "marketable" title. You will discover shortly that this term is difficult to define precisely, but it generally requires the seller to convey title that is free from encumbrances or interests held by third parties that would affect the ability of the buyer to re-sell the property.

Title Investigation. Next, the contract typically provides the buyer with some period of time to investigate whether the seller's title meets the stated standard. The buyer may conduct its own search of the public records to establish the seller's "chain of title" (*i.e.*, the series of deeds by which the seller acquired title from preceding owners). Alternatively, the buyer may rely upon a *title abstract* (a summary of each prior transaction affecting title to the land, prepared by an attorney or a title abstracting service) or a *title insurance commitment* provided through a licensed title insurance company. If investigation reveals that the seller's title may be defective, the seller may be given an opportunity to cure any defects; if the seller cannot cure them, the buyer may choose to rescind the contract, seek enforcement of the contract with a price reduction for the title defect, or (in some cases) seek to recover damages resulting from the seller's inability to convey title as promised. If the investigation reveals that the seller's title is acceptable, the parties will proceed toward the closing.

Title Assurance. Although the title investigation process gives the buyer some assurance that the seller has good title, some defects may not be discovered in a title search. Accordingly, buyers typically desire some additional protection against the existence of outstanding rights and claims of third parties. The seller may provide such assurance in the form of a warranty deed, which gives the buyer a contractual remedy against the seller if the buyer discovers a defect in the title after closing. A second alternative is for the buyer to obtain title insurance, by which a title insurance company agrees to indemnify the buyer against future losses due to latent defects in the title. The following subsections focus in greater detail on each step in the process of title investigation and assurance.

1. *The Contract of Sale—Provisions Regarding the Quality of Seller's Title*

The typical buyer of land enters into the transaction expecting to receive a fee simple absolute estate. It is unlikely, however—if not impossible—that the seller will have a *perfect* and *unencumbered* fee simple absolute title. Utility companies may have easements across the land to provide the land with utility services. Neighbors may have the benefits of restrictive covenants enforceable at law or in equity. The local county or municipality may have zoning ordinances that dictate permissible uses for the land. A neighbor's fence may encroach onto the land by a few inches. To what extent may a buyer properly object to the seller's title—and thus escape any obligation to perform the contract—because others hold such interests, restrictions, or encroachments?

Unless the contract provides otherwise, the law implies that the seller must deliver a title that is "marketable." [In some communities, the words "good and marketable" or "merchantable" are substitutes, with no difference in meaning.] Most standard agreement forms make this obligation explicit, as the form contract on pages 792–97 demonstrates. The law developed this requirement to protect the expectations of the typical buyer of land, who expects to receive a fee simple absolute estate subject to neither (a) outstanding third-party property rights in the land that might interfere with buyer's (or any successor owner's) use of the land nor (b) reasonable doubt that such outstanding rights may exist. Such doubts or colorable claims generally are termed "clouds" on title:

> [Marketable title is] a title not subject to such reasonable doubt as would create a just apprehension of its validity in the mind of a

reasonable prudent and intelligent person; one that persons of reasonable prudence and intelligence, guided by competent legal advice, would be willing to take and pay the fair value of the land for.... It is further defined as "not perfect title, but rather title reasonably secure against litigation or flaws decreasing market value." [*Sinks v. Karleskint*, 130 Ill.App.3d 527, 85 Ill.Dec. 807, 474 N.E.2d 767, 769 (1985).]

The concept of "marketability" seems simple enough, but as the above definition suggests, the law must still distinguish factually between those matters that create "reasonable doubt" as to the seller's title and those that do not. How should the law make such distinctions? As you consider this question, keep in mind that the buyer (and often the seller) typically approach the negotiation of the purchase and sale contract for land without any specific knowledge regarding the quality of the seller's title. Thus, a sound contract should permit the buyer to rescind the contract or to recover damages if the seller's title fails to meet the specified standard.

LOHMEYER v. BOWER

Supreme Court of Kansas.
170 Kan. 442, 227 P.2d 102 (1951).

PARKER, JUSTICE. [Editors' Note: Lohmeyer entered into a contract to purchase Lot 37 in Berkley Hills Addition in the city of Emporia from Bower. After execution of the agreement, he discovered that the house on the real estate was located within 18 inches of the north line of the lot in violation of the city ordinances providing that no frame building should be erected within three feet of a side or rear lot line. He also discovered that the one-story house was in violation of the Dedication of the Berkley Hills Addition, which requires that only a two-story house should be erected on the lot. Lohmeyer sued Bower to rescind the contract, in which Bower had agreed to convey the property

> by Warranty Deed with an abstract of title, certified to date showing good merchantable title or an Owners Policy of Title Insurance in the amount of the sale price, guaranteeing said title to party of the second part, free and clear of all encumbrances except special taxes subject, however, to all restrictions and easements of record applying to this property, it being understood that the first party shall have sufficient time to bring said abstract to date or obtain Report for Title Insurance and to correct any imperfections in the title if there be such imperfections....]

... [T]he all decisive issue ... is whether such property is subject to encumbrances or other burdens making the title unmerchantable and if so whether they are such as are excepted by the provision of the contract which reads "subject however, to all restrictions and easements of record applying to this property."

. . . [Lohmeyer] makes no complaint of the restrictions contained in the declaration forming a part of the dedication of Berkley Hills Addition nor of the ordinance restricting the building location on the lot but bases his right to rescission of the contract solely upon presently existing violations thereof. This . . . must necessarily be his position for we are convinced, although it must be conceded there are some decisions to the contrary, the rule supported by the better reasoned decisions, indeed if not by the great weight of authority, is that municipal restrictions of such character, existing at the time of the execution of a contract for the sale of real estate, are not such encumbrances or burdens on title as may be availed of by a vendee to avoid his agreement to purchase on the ground they render his title unmerchantable. . . .

On the other hand there can be no question the rule respecting restrictions upon the use of land or the location and type of buildings that may be erected thereon fixed by covenants or other private restrictive agreements, including those contained in the declaration forming a part of the dedication of Berkley Hills Addition, is directly contrary to the one to which we have just referred. Such restrictions, under all the authorities, constitute encumbrances rendering the title to land unmerchantable. . . .

[T]here still remains the question whether, under the stipulated facts, the restrictions imposed by such ordinance and/or the dedication declaration have been violated and if so whether those violations make the title to such property unmerchantable. . . .

[W]e are convinced a fair construction of [the parties' stipulation] compels the conclusion that on the date of the execution of the contract[,] the house on the real estate in controversy was a one story frame dwelling which had been moved there in violation of section 2 of the dedication restrictions providing that any residence erected on Lot 37 should be of the height of a two story residence and that it had been placed within 18 inches of the side or rear lot line of such lot in violation of [the ordinance] prohibiting the erection of such building within three feet of such line.

There can be no doubt regarding what constitutes a marketable or merchantable title in this jurisdiction. This court has been called on to pass upon that question on numerous occasions. See our recent decision in *Peatling v. Baird*, 168 Kan. 528, 213 P.2d 1015, 1016, and cases there cited, wherein we held:

> A marketable title to real estate is one which is free from reasonable doubt, and a title is doubtful and unmarketable if it exposes the party holding it to the hazard of litigation.

> To render the title to real estate unmarketable, the defect of which the purchaser complains must be of a substantial character

and one from which he may suffer injury. Mere immaterial defects which do not diminish in quantity, quality or value the property contracted for, constitute no ground upon which the purchaser may reject the title. Facts must be known at the time which fairly raise a reasonable doubt as to the title; a mere possibility or conjecture that such a state of facts may be developed at some future time is not sufficient.

Under the rule just stated, and in the face of facts such as are here involved, we have little difficulty in concluding that the violation of . . . the ordinances of the city of Emporia as well as the violation of the restrictions imposed by the dedication declaration so encumber the title to Lot 37 as to expose the party holding it to the hazard of litigation and make such title doubtful and unmarketable. It follows, since, as we have indicated, the appellees had contracted to convey such real estate to appellant by warranty deed with an abstract of title showing good merchantable title, free and clear of all encumbrances, that they cannot convey the title contracted for and that the trial court should have rendered judgment rescinding the contract. This, we may add is so, notwithstanding the contract provides the conveyance was to be made subject to all restrictions and easements of record, for, as we have seen, it is the violation of the restrictions imposed by both the ordinance and the dedication declaration, not the existence of those restrictions, that renders the title unmarketable. The decision just announced is not without precedent or unsupported by sound authority. . . .

See, also, *Hebb v. Severson*, 32 Wash.2d 159, 201 P.2d 156, which holds, that where a contract provided that building and use restrictions general to the district should not be deemed restrictions, the purchaser's knowledge of such restrictions did not estop him from rescinding the contract of purchase on subsequent discovery that the position of the house on the lot involved violated such restrictions. At page 172 of 32 Wash.2d, at page 162 of 201 P.2d it is said:

> Finally, the fact that the contract contains a provision that protective restrictions shall not be deemed encumbrances cannot aid the respondents. It is not the existence of protective restrictions, as shown by the record, that constitutes the encumbrances alleged by the appellants; but, rather, it is the presently existing violation of one of these restrictions that constitutes such encumbrance, in and of itself. The authorities so hold, on the rationale, to which we subscribe, that to force a vendee to accept property which in its present state violates a building restriction without a showing that the restriction is unenforceable, would in effect compel the vendee to buy a lawsuit.

Finally appellees point to the contract which, it must be conceded, provides they shall have time to correct imperfections in the title and contend that even if it be held the restrictions and the ordinance have been violated they are entitled to time in which to correct those imperfections. Assuming, without deciding, they might remedy the violation of the ordinance by buying additional ground the short and simple answer to their contention with respect to the violation of the restrictions imposed by the dedication declaration is that any changes in the house would compel the purchaser to take something that he did not contract to buy.

Conclusions heretofore announced require reversal of the judgment with directions to the trial court to cancel and set aside the contract and render such judgment as may be equitable and proper under the issues raised by the pleadings. . . .

Notes

1. *Elements of Seller's Contractual Title Obligation.* There are several distinct elements of the seller's title obligation under the contract, including: (a) what *quality* of title must the seller provide to the buyer (*e.g.,* "marketable" title; "insurable" title; "record" title, "satisfactory" title); (b) what type of *evidence* of title must the seller provide to the buyer, if any (*e.g.,* the official land records; a title insurance commitment; a title abstract); (c) by what *time/date* must the seller produce title that meets the applicable quality standard; and (d) by what *type of deed* must seller convey title? How are these issues addressed in section 6 of the form contract printed on page 793?

2. *Quality of Title.* Unless the contract of sale provides to the contrary, it is implied that the seller will furnish marketable title. The two most common alternatives to the marketable title standard are:

- *Marketable record title*, title evidenced and provable by conveyances or other instruments that are all duly entered in the public land records. Marketable record title is considered more rigorous because it is intended to exclude titles based upon adverse possession and to ensure that there are no gaps in the chain of title because of unrecorded conveyances; and

- *Insurable title*, title that a title insurance company would approve and insure. Insurable title is generally considered to be a more lenient standard because (1) title insurance policies contain many exclusions and exceptions from their coverage; and (2) title insurance companies may be willing to "insure over" (provide coverage for) a known risk.[10]

Suppose you were the attorney for the buyer in the *Lohmeyer* case. Would you advise your client to proceed with the transaction if the title insurance company was willing to provide coverage for the violations of both the ordinance and the restrictive covenant?

3. *Title Exceptions.* In some cases, as in *Lohmeyer,* the seller will propose to convey marketable title "subject to easements and restrictions of record." The seller may wish to condition its obligation in this way because

---

10. In some cases, however, the "insurable title" provision may be *more* protective of the buyer because some courts have held that insurable title is satisfied only when the title company insures title "unconditionally and without exception." *Laba v. Carey,* 29 N.Y.2d 302, 327 N.Y.S.2d 613, 277 N.E.2d 641 (1971); *see also Beacher v. Madera,* 226 N.Y.S.2d 227 (Sup. Ct. 1962) (purchaser not required to accept title insurance policy with restrictions, encroachments, and other defects that were not provided for in the contract of sale).

the seller knows that certain encumbrances (such as utility easements or restrictive covenants) exist that the seller cannot remove and that the buyer simply will have to accept if buyer wishes to purchase the land. Unless buyer has *already* done a title investigation, however, the buyer cannot know for certain whether it would be willing to accept title subject to all recorded encumbrances. If the buyer thus signs a contract stating that seller must provide marketable title "subject to easements and restrictions of record," has the buyer waived the ability to object to the content of any recorded easements and restrictions? [Hint: Suppose that there were no actual violations of the ordinance or restrictive covenants in the *Lohmeyer* case. Could the buyer seek rescission based solely on the fact that the ordinance and restrictive covenants exist?]

Assume a seller proposes to deliver title "subject to easements and restrictions of record." How should a buyer seek to modify this language to protect the buyer sufficiently against title matters that are recorded but as-yet unknown?

4. *What Makes Title Unmarketable?* It is impossible to list all of the potential defects that might make title unmarketable. However, they generally fall into one of three categories: (1) some flaw in the seller's title, suggesting the seller does not actually own the estate to be conveyed; (2) the existence of encumbrances—liens, easements, and other rights of third parties in the land; and (3) events that have deprived the seller of title, such as the government's exercise of eminent domain. William B. Stoebuck & Dale A. Whitman, The Law of Property § 10.12, at 779 (3d ed. 2000).

Suppose that the buyer in *Lohmeyer* had conducted a title search and failed to find any record indicating conveyance of the land to the sellers. Would the sellers still have marketable title if they presented uncontroverted evidence that they have been in actual, open, hostile, exclusive, and continuous possession of the land for more than 27 years—enough time to satisfy the state's statute of limitations on actions to recover possession of land? *Compare Tri–State Hotel Co. v. Sphinx Inv. Co.*, 212 Kan. 234, 510 P.2d 1223 (1973) (buyer entitled to rescission; title by adverse possession is not marketable title) *with Conklin v. Davi*, 76 N.J. 468, 388 A.2d 598 (1978) (buyer not entitled to rescission if seller can prove acquisition of title by adverse possession). How could a buyer draft a contract that would avoid the result in *Conklin*?

5. *Title vs. Non–Title Defects.* In defining marketable title, courts often focus on whether there are "outstanding rights" in the land that might interfere with its use. Accordingly, physical defects in the land or improvements—such as termite infestation, for example—normally do not constitute *title* problems, even if they present substantial practical problems for a buyer. Why did the *Lohmeyer* court conclude that the existence of public restrictions on land, such as zoning ordinances, does not affect marketability of the land, but that a violation of the ordinance would make title unmarketable? Would you agree that violation of a zoning ordinance constitutes a *title* problem? *See Voorheesville Rod & Gun Club, Inc. v. E.W. Tompkins Co.*, 82 N.Y.2d 564, 606 N.Y.S.2d 132, 626 N.E.2d 917 (1993) (seller's violation of village regulations regarding subdivision of land did not make title unmarketable).

In contrast with its analysis of the zoning ordinance, *Lohmeyer* suggests that the mere existence of *private* restrictions (covenants) would make title unmarketable. Does it make sense to treat private restrictions differently from public restrictions? *See Caselli v. Messina*, 148 Misc.2d 671, 567 N.Y.S.2d 972 (Sup. Ct. 1990) (holding that the mere existence of covenants restricting the use of land does not make title unmarketable if the buyer's intended use would not violate the covenant).

The distinction between title and non-title defects can be difficult to discern. Consider the following hypothetical: Henning agrees to buy a home, Greenacre, from Laughrey, under an agreement obligating Laughrey to provide "marketable title." Which of the following defects, if any, would render Laughrey's title unmarketable, and why?

(a)   A neighbor's garage encroaches onto Laughrey's property by five feet. *Compare Bethurem v. Hammett*, 736 P.2d 1128 (Wyo. 1987) (title unmarketable where fence encroached onto dedicated city street by 17 feet) *with Mertens v. Berendsen*, 213 Cal. 111, 1 P.2d 440 (1931) (two-inch encroachment onto street frontage did not make title unmarketable).

(b)   Laughrey has no legal means of access to the parcel. Since building the home, Laughrey has gained access to the home across the land of her neighbor, Wells, pursuant to an express license that by its terms is revocable if Laughrey chooses to sell her home. Does it matter whether Henning knows of the lack of access at the time of the contract? *Compare Sinks v. Karleskint*, 130 Ill.App.3d 527, 85 Ill.Dec. 807, 474 N.E.2d 767 (1985) *with Barasky v. Huttner*, 210 A.D.2d 367, 620 N.Y.S.2d 121 (1994).

(c)   East Virginia Power Company has an easement across Greenacre for the purpose of transmitting power across Greenacre on high-voltage transmission lines. *Compare Waters v. N.C. Phosphate Corp.*, 310 N.C. 438, 312 S.E.2d 428 (1984) (recorded, obvious transmission line easement rendered title unmarketable) *with Thompson v. Shaw Real Estate, Inc.*, 210 Va. 714, 173 S.E.2d 812 (1970) (recorded, obvious transmission line easement did not render title unmarketable where easement of reasonable width).

(d)   Henning discovers that Greenacre is contaminated with toxic PCBs in violation of federal and state environmental statutes. Removal of the PCBs will cost tens of thousands of dollars. *See Vandervort v. Higginbotham*, 222 A.D.2d 831, 634 N.Y.S.2d 800 (1995) (presence of hazardous materials does not render title unmarketable; marketable title is "concerned with one's right to 'unencumbered ownership and possession' of property, not with its value."). Would this analysis change if the applicable environmental law gave the government the power to impose a lien on the land to secure the owner's financial obligation to clean up the contamination? Would it change if the government had in fact already imposed such a lien?

6.   *The Timing of the Seller's Obligation to Deliver Marketable Title.* Suppose that a buyer has contracted to purchase a fee simple absolute but discovers, during the gap period, that the seller has only a life estate in the property. Can the buyer immediately declare the seller to be in breach of the

contract? Probably not—a seller generally has until the closing date to clear up any title defects and tender marketable title. Until that time, she is not yet in breach unless the contract itself obligates her to demonstrate marketable title prior to closing, or unless it appears impossible for Seller to obtain the required title in time for the closing. *Wright v. Bryan*, 226 Va. 557, 311 S.E.2d 776 (1984).

The timing of seller's obligation to deliver marketable title can impose a special hardship in transactions involving an installment land contract (or "contract for deed"). Under this arrangement, the buyer contracts to purchase the property by making monthly "installment" payments to the seller. Although the buyer takes immediate possession of the land, the buyer typically does not receive a deed until the full purchase price is paid.[11] Suppose that the buyer discovers a title defect several years into a 20–year installment land contract. Can the buyer declare the seller to be in breach and stop making payments? No; unless the contract specifies otherwise, the seller must deliver marketable title at closing, and in the context of an installment contract, that means when the buyer makes his final payment and the seller must deliver the deed. Until that time, the buyer will have to continue making installment payments to comply with his obligations! Given this result, what advice would you give to someone planning to purchase land using an installment contract?

2. *Title Searching and the Recording System*

In conducting its title investigation, how does the buyer reach a conclusion as to the state of the seller's title? Before title insurance became the dominant form of title assurance, the buyer's investigation often took the form of an *abstract of title*—a report, prepared by a title abstractor based upon a review of the public land records, that listed and described each recorded instrument affecting title to the land in question. Alternatively, the buyer's investigation often took the form of an attorney's legal opinion as to the quality of the seller's title (which the opining attorney would base either upon the title abstract or the attorney's own search of the public land records).

Today, title insurance has largely replaced abstracting and opinion letters in residential transactions (although opinion letters may be used in commercial transactions where larger sums are at stake). Thus, the buyer typically does not conduct his own title investigation, but instead obtains a *title insurance commitment*—the promise of a title insurance company that it will, upon payment of a risk premium, protect the buyer against loss due to unknown and undisclosed title problems that may not become evident until after closing. The title insurance commitment discloses to the buyer all recorded claims or interests affecting the title (such as easements or covenants) and specifically "excepts" those matters from insurance coverage—meaning that if the buyer proceeded to purchase the land, the buyer could not expect the title insurer to compensate the buyer for any loss resulting from those matters. Thus,

---

11. Installment land contracts are discussed in more detail beginning on page 821.

the buyer typically uses the information contained in the title insurance commitment to conclude whether the seller's title is "marketable" or otherwise complies with the seller's obligation under the terms of the contract.

Each method of title investigation requires an understanding of how the local recording system works and how to search that system to ascertain all relevant information about potential conflicting claims to or encumbrances upon the seller's land. The following materials provide background about American recording systems and the rules governing both the searching of title and the land claimant's obligation to place evidence of its claim on record. [You should also review the introductory material on priorities and recording acts in Chapter 3, pages 151–55.]

a. *Recording Acts.* Suppose that Oliver, the owner of Blueacre, delivers Alice a deed to Blueacre on Monday. Then, two days later, Oliver delivers Bob a deed to the same property.[12] Who owns Blueacre? Under the common law, the answer is simple. Conflicting claims of title were decided under the "first-in-time, first-in-right" principle. When Oliver conveys Greenacre to Alice, Oliver no longer has title to Blueacre and thus (under the derivative title principle) cannot subsequently transfer title to Blueacre to Bob. But how would Bob know that Oliver no longer had clear title to the property? Even the most thorough investigation would not necessarily reveal the prior conveyance to Alice.

Today's modern recording system eliminates many of the risks posed by the common law rule. Each state has a mechanism through which purchasers like Alice can record their deeds, thereby providing notice of the transaction to subsequent purchasers like Bob (who can search those records before buying to identify prior claimants). Conversely, if Alice fails to record, most recording acts protect subsequent purchasers like Bob by giving them priority if they take without notice of the prior transaction. In other words, Alice risks losing her interest in Blueacre if she fails to record her deed promptly.

There are three basic types of recording acts in the United States. The earliest type of recording act was the ***pure race*** statute, which remains in effect only in North Carolina and Louisiana. The North Carolina statute provides:

> No (i) conveyance of land, or (ii) contract to convey, or (iii) option to convey, or (iv) lease of land for more than three years shall be valid to pass any property interest as against lien creditors or purchasers for a valuable consideration from the donor, bargainor or lessor but

---

12. Students often find it difficult to believe that multiple transfers of this sort happen with any frequency in real life. Spend a summer in a real estate practitioner's office, however, and you will soon discover that such transactions are quite common—either as a result of outright fraud or, more benignly, when the grantor forgets that he has made a prior conveyance (particularly when the conveyance is of a mortgage, easement, or some other interest less than a fee simple) or when the grantor dies and his executor/administrator is unaware of the prior conveyance.

from the time of registration thereof in the county where the land lies ... [N.C. Gen. Stat. § 47–18(a).]

Under a pure race statute, if one grantor purports to sell land to two different grantees, the grantee who records her deed first will prevail over the other grantee in a title dispute—even if the grantee who records first has actual knowledge of the other grantee's claim!

Problem 1. Henning, owner of Blueacre in fee simple absolute, conveys Blueacre to Pushaw. Pushaw does not record his deed. Henning subsequently conveys Blueacre to Laughrey, who pays valuable consideration, with full knowledge of Pushaw's unrecorded deed. Laughrey promptly records her deed. Under a pure race statute, Pushaw's failure to record his deed renders that deed ineffective against Laughrey. Laughrey's knowledge of Pushaw's unrecorded deed is irrelevant. Laughrey now owns Blueacre.

Problem 2. Henning, owner of Blueacre in fee simple absolute, conveys Blueacre to Pushaw. Pushaw does not record his deed. Henning subsequently conveys Blueacre to Laughrey, who pays valuable consideration, without knowledge of Pushaw's unrecorded deed. Pushaw then records his deed shortly before Laughrey records her deed. Under a pure race statute, Pushaw now owns Blueacre. Laughrey cannot claim the benefit of the recording statute because she failed to record her deed prior to Pushaw's recording.

Before moving forward, take special notice of two key points that are critical for a proper understanding of the application of recording statutes:

- *A deed does not have to be recorded to be effective against the grantor of the deed.* In Problem 1, Henning's conveyance to Pushaw was valid even though Pushaw had not recorded the deed. If the later transfer to Laughrey had not arisen, Henning could not have recovered possession of Blueacre based upon Pushaw's failure to record. At first, this seems inconsistent with the language of the quoted "pure race" recording act, which appears to say the conveyance is not valid until it is recorded. But notice the language carefully: "[no] conveyance of land ... shall be valid to pass any property interest *as against ... purchasers for a valuable consideration ...* but from the time of registration thereof." In other words, lack of compliance with the recording act affects the validity of Pushaw's claim against future third party purchasers, but not against the grantor Henning.

- *In applying a recording statute, you should always ask whether the **later purchaser** may claim the benefit of the recording statute's protection*—in other words, whether the later purchaser meets the statute's requirements for elevating her claim above its lower status under the common law first-in-time principle. In Problem 2, for example, you may be tempted to say that Pushaw's title is valid because he was first to record—and thus that Pushaw qualifies for the protection of the recording statute and therefore prevails over Laughrey. But remember that Pushaw's claim was already prior-in-time to Laughrey's claim—thus, Pushaw will prevail under the common law first-in-time rule unless Laughrey can successfully assert the benefit of the recording statute. Pushaw prevails because he was first in time and because, by recording, he prevented subsequent purchasers like Laughrey from qualifying for the protection of the recording act.

In contrast to North Carolina and Louisiana, most American jurisdictions have adopted recording acts that protect subsequent purchasers[13] only if they are "bona fide" purchasers for value (or "BFPs")—that is, *only if they do not have notice of prior unrecorded claims.*[14] Because recording acts function as statutory estoppel rules, the incorporation of a "notice" principle makes some sense conceptually. If a later purchaser of land knows or should know of another party's prior unrecorded deed, then how can that purchaser have reasonably relied upon the absence of any adverse conveyances in the public records (recall that reasonable reliance is a necessary predicate for establishing equitable estoppel)—and thus why should the law elevate the later purchaser in priority over the prior purchaser?

Approximately half of the states have adopted ***pure notice*** recording acts, such as the Massachusetts recording statute:

> A conveyance of an estate in fee simple, fee tail or for life, or a lease for more than seven years from the making thereof, or an assignment of rents or profits from an estate or lease, shall not be valid as against any person, except the grantor or lessor, his heirs and devisees and persons having actual notice of it, unless it ... is recorded in the registry of deeds for the county or district in which the land to which it relates lies. [Mass. Gen. Laws Ann. ch. 183, § 4.]

Under a pure notice statute, if one grantor sells land to two separate grantees but the first grantee fails to record his or her deed, the second grantee will prevail over the first, if the second grantee has no actual knowledge or other reason to know of the first grantee's claim.

---

13. When we use the term "purchaser," we do not mean to equate it with the term "buyer." In this context, we are using the term "purchaser" in its precise historical sense, to refer to one who takes an interest via conveyance (containing "words of purchase," as discussed on page 243). As a result, a "purchaser" in this context could include not only someone who takes a simple interest by deed or by will, but also a mortgagee, a tenant, or a person holding the benefit of an easement or servitude. Thus, someone who received a gift of land by deed or by will may be considered a "purchaser" in this traditional sense; she would not be a purchaser *for value*, howev-

er, and thus could not qualify for the protection of most recording acts.

14. Note that "BFP" is an inherently *relative* term. Someone purchasing rights in land could take those rights as a protected BFP relative to an earlier unrecorded interest, but not relative to a different prior interest of which she did have notice. Furthermore, keep in mind that in a priority controversy between two conflicting interests, only the later purchaser can be a BFP; the earlier purchaser could not have had "notice" of an interest not yet in existence! Again, the earlier purchaser will prevail under the common law first-in-time rule unless the recording statute protects the later purchaser as a BFP.

Problem 3. Henning, owner of Blueacre in fee simple absolute, conveys Blueacre to Pushaw. Pushaw does not record his deed. Henning subsequently conveys Blueacre to Laughrey, who pays valuable consideration, without knowledge of Pushaw's deed. Under a pure notice statute, Pushaw's failure to record his deed renders that deed ineffective against Laughrey. Laughrey now owns Blueacre.

Problem 4. Henning, owner of Blueacre in fee simple absolute, conveys Blueacre to Pushaw. Pushaw does not record his deed. Henning subsequently conveys Blueacre to Laughrey, who pays valuable consideration, with full knowledge of Pushaw's unrecorded deed. Under a pure notice statute, Pushaw's failure to record his deed does not render that deed ineffective against Laughrey, because she knew of Pushaw's claim. Pushaw now owns Blueacre.

Under a pure notice statute, the subsequent purchaser may claim the benefit of the recording statute against a prior claimant *even if the subsequent purchaser has not recorded her deed.* In Problem 3, for example, Laughrey prevails over Pushaw—even though the problem does not state whether Laughrey has recorded her deed. [Of course, if Laughrey fails to record, she runs the risk of having her claim cut off by a subsequent purchaser who lacks notice of her claim.[15]]

The remaining states have adopted ***race-notice*** recording acts:

> Every conveyance of real property or an estate for years therein, other than a lease for a term not exceeding one year, is void as against any subsequent purchaser or mortgagee of the same property, or any part thereof, in good faith and for a valuable consideration, whose conveyance is first duly recorded. . . . [Cal. Civ. Code § 1214.]

Under a race-notice statute like California's, if one grantor sells land to two different grantees but the first grantee fails to record his deed, the second grantee will prevail over the first only if the second grantee has no actual knowledge or reason to know of the first grantee's claim *and* the second grantee records her deed before the first grantee finally records.

Problem 5. Henning, owner of Blueacre in fee simple absolute, conveys Blueacre to Pushaw. Pushaw does not record his deed. Henning subsequently conveys Blueacre to Laughrey, who pays valuable consideration, without knowledge of Pushaw's deed. Laughrey records her deed. Under a race-notice statute, Laughrey's recording of her deed combined with Pushaw's failure to record his

---

15. Students (and some courts) sometimes ask whether, in a given situation, a party has a "duty" to record. Use of the word "duty" is misleading and blurs the significance of recording. In Problem 3, for example, Laughrey has no legal duty to record. But by recording—and thereby giving notice of her rights to later claimants—Laughrey eliminates the risk that her interest may become inferior to the claim of a later bona fide purchaser.

deed renders Pushaw's deed ineffective against Laughrey. Laughrey now owns Blueacre.

Problem 6. Henning, owner of Blueacre in fee simple absolute, conveys Blueacre to Pushaw. Pushaw does not record his deed. Henning subsequently conveys Blueacre to Laughrey, who pays valuable consideration, with full knowledge of Pushaw's unrecorded deed. Laughrey records her deed. Under a race-notice statute, Pushaw's failure to record his deed does not render that deed ineffective against Laughrey because she knew of Pushaw's claim. Pushaw now owns Blueacre.

Problem 7. Henning, owner of Blueacre in fee simple absolute, conveys Blueacre to Pushaw. Pushaw does not record his deed. Henning subsequently conveys Blueacre to Laughrey, who pays valuable consideration, without knowledge of Pushaw's unrecorded deed. Laughrey does not record her deed. Subsequently, Pushaw finally records his deed. Under a race-notice statute, Pushaw's initial failure to record his deed does not render that deed ineffective against Laughrey, because she failed to record her deed. Pushaw now owns Blueacre.

Notes

1. *The Rationale for the Various Types of Recording Acts.* Can you articulate the rationale behind each type of recording act? What are the benefits and shortcomings of each? Should courts interpret recording acts with a focus on fairness between parties to a specific conflict, or on making the market for land transfer more efficient as a whole? Why do you think that so few states have pure race statutes? *See generally* 6A Powell, The Law of Real Property ¶ 905[1] (rev. ed. 1992) (discussing types of recording acts generally); Taylor Mattis, *Recording Acts: Anachronistic Reliance,* 25 Real Prop., Prob. & Tr. J. 17 (1990) (arguing that notice statute is preferable); Francis S. Philbrick, *Limits of Record Search and Therefore of Notice* (pt. 1), 93 U. Pa. L. Rev. 125 (1944) (critiquing introduction and expansion of notice concepts into recording acts).

2. *Persons Protected by the Recording Acts.* Assume the following examples arise in a state with a recording act identical to the Massachusetts statute (page 733):

(a) Telephone Company holds a recorded easement over Henning's land and has installed underground telephone lines pursuant to this easement. Henning contracted with Borison to plant azaleas in his yard. While digging, Borison (who was unaware of the location of the telephone lines) accidentally cut the lines. Telephone Company sues Borison for damages, claiming that Borison should have known of the underground lines because of the recorded easement. What result? *See Mountain States Tel. & Tel. Co. v. Kelton,* 79 Ariz. 126, 285 P.2d 168 (1955) (recording provides notice only to subsequent purchasers).

(b) Henning, owner of Blueacre in fee simple, conveys Blueacre to Cimini, who fails to record her deed. Two weeks later, Middleton obtains a judgment against Henning for damages suffered in a car accident caused by Henning's negligence. Middleton's judgment constitutes a lien upon all of Henning's land within the county. Can Middleton claim the benefit of the recording act—in other words, can Middleton claim that the lien of his judgment attaches to Blueacre because Cimini's unrecorded deed is ineffective against him? Some recording acts, such as the North Carolina statute (page 731), expressly protect "lien creditors" like Middleton. But other recording acts, like the California statute (page 734), protect only purchasers and mortgagees, not judgment lien creditors like Middleton. Can you explain why a recording statute either should (or should not) protect lien creditors? *See Texas Am. Bank/Levelland v. Resendez*, 706 S.W.2d 343 (Tex. App. 1986).

(c) Same as problem (b), but assume that Middleton asks the court to order an execution sale of the land to satisfy his judgment lien, and further assume that the court (unaware of Cimini's title claim) orders the sale. At the sale, Laughrey purchases the land without knowledge of Cimini's unrecorded deed. What result? *See Valley Nat'l Bank v. Avco Dev. Co.*, 14 Ariz.App. 56, 480 P.2d 671 (1971).

(d) Henning, owner of Blueacre in fee simple, conveys Blueacre to Pushaw, who fails to record his deed. Two weeks later, Henning purports to convey Blueacre to Dean as a birthday gift. Who owns Blueacre, Pushaw or Dean? *Compare Fritz v. Mazurek*, 156 Conn. 555, 244 A.2d 368 (1968) *and Bagwell v. Henson*, 124 Ga.App. 92, 183 S.E.2d 485 (1971) (recording act does not protect donees) *with Eastwood v. Shedd*, 166 Colo. 136, 442 P.2d 423 (1968) (recording act interpreted to protect donees). If the recording acts create a statutory estoppel rule, should they be interpreted to protect donees? Why or why not?

3. *The "Shelter Principle."* The protection of a recording act extends not only to the bona fide purchaser, but also to grantees who take from that person. For example, suppose that Osman, owner of Blueacre in fee simple, conveys Blueacre to Anderson, who fails to promptly record her deed. Osman later conveys Blueacre to Basanta, who had no knowledge of the prior conveyance to Anderson, and Basanta promptly records his deed. The "shelter principle" permits Basanta to convey a good title to a grantee even if that grantee had actual knowledge of Osman's unrecorded deed to Anderson or otherwise failed to qualify as a bona fide purchaser. Do you understand why this rule is necessary to protect Basanta's rights under the recording act? *See Sun Valley Land & Minerals, Inc. v. Burt*, 123 Idaho 862, 853 P.2d 607 (Ct. App. 1993) (discussing and applying the "shelter" principle).

There are some grantees, however, who cannot take advantage of the "shelter principle." Under the preceding facts, for example, the "shelter principle" would not permit Osman to reacquire title from Basanta free of Anderson's interest. Do you understand why?

4. *Review Problem.* Consider the following problem to test your understanding of the operation of the various types of recording acts: Henning, owner of Blueacre in fee simple, conveys Blueacre to Ziegler, who does not record. Henning subsequently conveys Blueacre to Key, who purchases in good faith for valuable consideration. Key likewise fails to record her deed.

Later, Ziegler records his deed and conveys Blueacre to Chambers, who purchases in good faith and for valuable consideration. Key finally records her deed only a few moments before Chambers records his deed. Who prevails under a pure race statute? A pure notice statute? A race-notice statute?

b. *The Mechanics of Recording and Title Searching.* As each purchaser brings his or her deed to the recording office, the clerk date-stamps the document and places it sequentially into a record book. By the end of the year (or the end of the month in urban areas!), the record book contains hundreds of deeds, appearing in order from the first filed to the most recently filed. So how does a title searcher find the deeds relating to a particular parcel of land? Searching through each document one at a time would require an immense undertaking. Accordingly, some form of indexing is required.

The following excerpt discusses the two most common indexing systems—the tract index and the grantor-grantee index—and explains how a typical title search is conducted.[16]

GRANT S. NELSON & DALE A. WHITMAN, REAL ESTATE TRANSFER, FINANCE AND DEVELOPMENT

214–220 (6th ed. 2003).

All privately-held land titles (except those derived from accretion or adverse possession) can be traced back through a chain of owners to some original conveyance from a sovereign, typically the federal government or a state. Let us invent a simple chain of title which we can use as the basis for illustration of title search problems. . . .

---

16. A third method of indexing, the Torrens system, is a title registration system similar to the registration of vehicle titles. Under this system, a government agency issues a certificate of title that identifies the current title holder(s) and lists all easements, covenants, liens, mortgages, and other encumbrances on the title. Although this system was lauded by most scholars and is available in a handful of jurisdictions (*e.g.*, Chicago and Cook County, Illinois, and Hawaii), the concept was not widely embraced by homeowners, largely because of the cost of initial registration. (Registration in Torrens is voluntary and requires the applicant to prove ownership through a judicial or quasi-judicial proceeding, with notice to all parties having a potential interest in the land). Accordingly, the Torrens system has been abandoned in most jurisdictions.

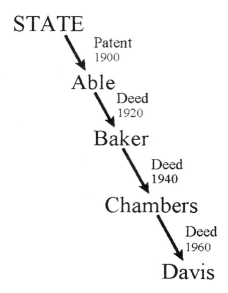

The patent is merely a grant of title by the state. The present owner of the land is Davis, and we will assume that he proposes to sell it to your client, who has asked you to search and examine the title. When you receive this assignment, you know nothing about the prior title history of the land; you are merely told its legal description, (Lot 4, Block G, Suburban Acres) and the fact that Donald Davis presently claims to own it.

How will you proceed? The answer depends on the type of indexing which is employed by the recorder in your jurisdiction. From the searcher's viewpoint, indexing by tract or parcel is by far the better method. This approach allocates a separate page or set of pages in the index books to each parcel of land, or perhaps to each tract ... even though it might contain several parcels. As each instrument is brought into the courthouse for recordation, an entry is made on the appropriate page for the parcel which the instrument affects. . . .

Parcel Index					
Lot 3, Block L, Eastlawn Estates Subdivision					
Type of Instrm't	Grantors, etc.	Grantees, etc.	Doc. No.	Date Filed	Book & Page
[Note: for prior instruments, see SE¼ of NW¼, T4N,R2E.]					
Subdiv. Plat	Eastlawn Devel. Co.	....	45872	9-15 1949	34-17 Plat Bk
Deed of Trust	Eastlawn Devel. Co.	Fourth State Bank	47339	10-10 1949	117-667
Reconv.	Fourth State Bank	Eastlawn Devel. Co.	48960	5-12 1950	119-88
Deed	Eastlawn Devel. Co.	Shaw, Harry & Betty	48961	5-12 1950	119-89
Deed of Trust	Shaw, Harry & Betty	Last Federal Sav. & Loan	48962	5-12 1950	119-90
Lis Pen.	Shaw, Harry & Betty	Gotcha, George	53964	8-30 1952	124-733

This particular page represents the title history of the land commencing at the time it was subdivided by the filing of an approved plat. The reference at the top of the page shows where the same land's pre-subdivision records would be indexed. You should be able to follow the imposition and later satisfaction of the construction loan deed of trust given by the developer, the deed to the first owners of the house which the developer built on the land, and their deed of trust to the lender who made the loan with which they bought the house. Finally, you can see that they apparently had a dispute concerning title to their land, and were sued in connection with it by George Gotcha in 1952. With this sort of index, the construction by the searcher of a chain of title is relatively easy, for all of the information is on a single page. Of course, it may be necessary to consult other records in other offices (e.g., for wills, intestacies, judgments, property taxes, etc.), but in most cases the chain can be determined without much trouble. The searcher must then pull the books from the shelves and examine the actual copies of the instruments themselves to see if they appear to be regular and indeed affect the land in question. The references in the last column on the right in the index book tell the searcher where each document will be found. If any prior owner has made an "adverse conveyance"—one which impairs the present quality of the title or makes it unmarketable—that fact will also be easy to see. The lis pendens would be considered such an adverse conveyance unless it had been removed later or a statute of limitations had cut it off.

The tract index is very convenient for searchers, but it does require a reasonable amount of skill on the part of the recording office personnel, since they must read every instrument with some care to determine what land it affects, so that it can be properly indexed. This is not hard when the legal description is based on a recorded subdivision plat as in our example, but it can be formidable with descriptions based on natural monuments (e.g., "to the old white oak tree," etc.). Perhaps for this reason, only a few American states provide in their recording statutes for the maintenance of tract or parcel indexes. In the great majority of states, the only official indexes available to searchers in the courthouse are "name" indexes—those based on the names of the parties to a given instrument. They are easier to construct and maintain, but much harder to search in. There is little pressure from any organized group—recorders, lawyers, title companies, or the public—for reform. Hence there is only modest movement toward the establishment of public tract indexes in this country. The overall advantages of the tract index are attested by the fact that virtually every privately-owned set of title records ("title plant") in the nation employs tract indexing! . . .

Suppose you are not fortunate enough to practice in a state with an official tract index. (Ironically, in those states few lawyers perform searches in the public records.) Instead, you find that you must search in the name indexes in your courthouse. How can you construct a chain of title to the land your client wishes to buy from Davis? There are dual sets of name indexes; one set is arranged alphabetically by the name of the grantee(s) to each instrument, and the other alphabetically by the name of the grantor(s). You will begin your work in the grantee index, which might take a form like this:

Grantee Index Year 1960						
Grantee's Names beginning with Da						
Type of Instrm't	Grantee's Name	Grantor's Name	Doc. No.	Date Filed	Book & Page	Brief Legal Description
Release of Easm't	Davis, Abner	Voltzman Elect. Power Co.	2243	5–22 1960	344–221	Lt. 14, Block B Ridge Estates
Mech's Lien	Damion Plumbing & Heating	Fish, Frederick	4322	8–16 1960	346–132	E ½ of SE ¼ Sec. 22, R2E T3N
Deed	Davis, Donald	Chambers, Elaine	2089	8–19 1960	346–367	Lot 4, Block G Suburban Acres
Lease	Dalton's Men's Wear	Watson Real Estate, Inc.	4531	8–28 1960	346–451	Lots 3–4, Brown's Addition No. 2

There are several interesting features of the grantee index page above. The grantee's names are not in exact alphabetical order, since they are entered on the page (this one is labeled "Da") as they come into the office for recordation. In some sophisticated offices, a computer program may be used to resort and reprint the pages periodically in accurate alphabetical order. Note that all entries are during the year 1960. In large urban counties, a new set of index books is generally made up each year; if this were not done, the books would soon become so large as to be physically unmanageable. In rural counties with few transactions, the indexes might be allowed to accumulate over a five-year or even ten-year period before a new set is begun.

Now, to search Donald Davis' title, we must begin by looking for his name in the grantee index, since if he owns the land he must have been a grantee under a deed at some past time. Unless we can get a copy of Davis' deed from him or he tells us when he acquired the land, we will not know in which of the (possibly yearly) grantee books to check, so we must start with the present year and work our way backwards, looking for Davis' name as a grantee. When we finally get to 1960 and read the page reproduced above, we will find him. Scanning across to the "Brief Legal Description" column will verify that the entry does in fact affect the land we are searching. (Unfortunately, in some states there is no such column, and we would have to look up in the actual record books each deed which is indexed with Davis as a grantee to see what land is covered. If Davis had bought a good deal of real estate in the county, this could become exceedingly tedious. Even where the indexes carry this column, there may be a serious but rarely litigated question as to whether a searcher can safely rely upon it; as a practical matter, searchers obviously do so.)

We must now look for the next link (going backward in time) in the chain of title. We do so by looking for Elaine Chambers' name in the grantee index, since the entry which we found under Davis' name told us that Chambers was Davis' grantor. We assume that Chambers received title to the land prior to the time she deeded it to Davis (although this need not always be true under the doctrine of estoppel by deed), and begin looking for her name as a grantee in 1960. Searching back year by year, we will find her as a grantee from Baker in 1940. We then search for Baker as a grantee, and so on, until we come back to the original patent from the state in 1900.

We now have a complete chain of title to the land, but that is only the first of three major steps in searching the record title. The second step involves determining whether any of the owners we have identified has made any adverse conveyances. Suppose, for example, that Able (who obtained the land in 1900) granted an easement to Zoller in 1910. You might wish to pencil in such a grant on the diagram of the chain. We would certainly want to advise our client that the easement exists. How can we discover such conveyances? We must use the other set of name indexes, those arranged alphabetically by the name of the grantor. A part of a typical page might look as follows:

| Grantor Index Year 1910 | | | | | | |
| Grantor's Names beginning with Aa through Ac | | | | | | |
Type of Instrm't	Grantor's Name	Grantee's Name	Doc. No.	Date Filed	Book & Page	Brief Legal Description
Mortg.	Ackerman, Alan	Third Nat'l Bank	2276	1-14 1910	22-889	Pt. of N ½ Sec. 5 R3E T6S
Grant of Easement	Able, Abner	Zoller, Charles	2298	2-21 1910	22-970	Lot 4, Block G Suburban Acres
Assign. of Mtg.	Abbott Mortgage Co.	Philadelphia Soc. for Savings	2375	4-12 1910	23-29	Lot 18, Summit Ridge Add'n
Release of Mtg.	Abbott Mortgage Co.	Weller, Frank & Martha	2418	7-7 1910	23-445	S ½ of NE ¼ Sec. 12, R3E T5S

We will begin with Able's name. Since he acquired the land in 1900 and deeded it away to Baker in 1920, we will look for any conveyances with Able as a grantor during that period.... Again we check year by year, this time in the grantor index. The page reprinted above shows that in 1910 Able was a grantor to Zoller of an easement. Unless we subsequently find a release of the easement by Zoller (which we can find by looking in the grantor index under his name), we will conclude that the easement still exists and will report it to our client as affecting the current state of the title. Of course, some off-record circumstances, such as a stone wall which has blocked the path of the easement for 30 years, might convince us that despite the records the easement is no longer viable but has been terminated by prescription.

We must check the grantor index in a similar fashion for Baker, Chambers, and Davis to see if any of them made adverse conveyances. We are very likely to find, for example, that one or more of them gave mortgages or deeds of trust on the land. We must then use the grantor index to trace any further transfers or releases of these interests in order to determine whether they still affect the title today....

We have now completed the second major step in the search process, checking for adverse conveyances. We're ready to proceed to the third step, which requires that we look at the full copies of each of the instruments we have thus far identified. We will check them for the necessary formalities, consistency of legal descriptions, etc., and we will also be alert for any references in them to unrecorded documents or interests. Assuming that no problems develop in this area, we will check for adverse interests in relevant sources outside the county land records, such as tax and assessment liens, bankruptcies, judgment liens, and so on. Finally, we are ready to prepare an opinion of title for transmission to our client. Since we have only performed a search in the records, we cannot negate the possible existence of some off-record claims, such as those of parties in possession, undisclosed spouses of prior owners, etc. Many careful lawyers use "boilerplate" language in their title opinions to exclude such matters from coverage.

Notes

1. *Limitations of the Traditional Grantor–Grantee Index System.* As you might surmise from the foregoing discussion, the traditional grantor-grantee index system was less than optimal. Tracing a chain of title was (and in many places, still is) a time-consuming process, requiring a painstaking search through several books of records. Moreover, the name-based system presented a number of opportunities for error—both in the recording process and in the search itself. For example, how would the clerk record a deed that conveyed a contingent future interest to an unascertained person (*e.g.*, "to Schmitz for life, then to Schmitz's children who survive her")? You may also recall that there was some debate in Chapter 8 (page 561) regarding a grantor's ability to reserve an easement for a "stranger" to the conveyance. Assume, for example, that *O* conveys Blackacre in fee simple to *A*, but

includes a clause attempting to reserve an easement for *B*. *A*'s name would appear as grantee in the index, but *B*'s name likely would not. As you proceed through this chapter, you will encounter a number of other problems inherent in this system.

2. *Computerized Title Records.* During the past several decades, a growing number of jurisdictions have begun keeping their title records in computerized databases.

> To service this new demand, several commercial firms are providing software (and as needed, hardware) to permit recorders to accept electronic documents, record them in a quasi-automated fashion, and make them searchable by the public via the internet. A few recorders' offices have already made this shift, and others are seriously considering it. Thus, it seems possible that within a few years, a truly modern system of public land title records will be available in much of the United States. [Grant S. Nelson & Dale A. Whitman, Real Estate Transfer, Finance & Development 216 (2003).]

Computerized databases present many advantages to the traditional grantor-grantee index system. For example, less time will be required to conduct a title search because the searcher can simply type in a name (or parcel identification number), rather than flipping through the grantor-grantee index books. Moreover, to the extent the records are searchable through the internet, attorneys can conduct a search from their own offices, rather than traveling to the county courthouse.

In many jurisdictions, however, computerized records are available only for documents recorded after installation of the computerized system. Thus, the computerized records have not completely eliminated the former grantor-grantee indexes; instead, a title searcher must use both systems to conduct a complete title search.[17] Can you see any other potential drawbacks to a computerized system?

LAWYERING EXERCISE
Internet Title Search

(Exercise Created by Professor Dale Whitman)

SITUATION: During the mid–1990s, David and Sheila McClung owned a house on Lot 73 of the Sunrise Acres subdivision in Boone County, Missouri. You have been asked to verify certain information relating to the property based upon the records in the county recorder's office.

TASK: Answer the questions below by using the records that are available through the internet at http://www.showmeboone.com/record-

---

17. In jurisdictions with marketable title acts (see page 764), the need to use both sets of records will theoretically decline during the next several decades. Marketable title acts generally protect an unbroken chain of title that exists for a statutory period, typically 30 to 40 years. Thus, to the extent that a title searcher can rely on the most recent records, title searches in those jurisdictions eventually will become limited to the computerized database. *But see* page 765 for notable exceptions that limit the effectiveness of marketable title acts.

er/. Note that "recording information" means the Book and Page Numbers at which the document was recorded in the Boone County Recorder's Office. You will not be doing a complete title search, but the assignment will allow you to become familiar with some of the work done by title examiners.

1. The purchase of the property:

   (a) What is the recording date of the deed by which the McClungs acquired the property? (b) Who sold the property to them? (c) Recording information for the deed? (d) Who made the purchase-money loan? (e) How much did the McClungs borrow? (f) Recording information for the deed of trust? (g) Recording information for the subdivision plat?

2. Additional financing on the property:

   (a) Who else made a loan to the McClungs? (b) What was the amount of this loan? (c) What type of loan was it? (d) When was the deed of trust recorded? (e) What was the priority of the deed of trust? (f) Recording information for the deed of trust?

3. Refinancing the property:

   (a) Who made the refinancing loan? (b) What was the amount of this loan? (c) Was the interest rate fixed or adjustable? (d) What was the initial interest rate? (identify releasing party, date of release, and recording data for release (e) When was the deed of trust recorded? (f) Recording information for the deed of trust? (g) Was the prior purchase-money deed of trust released at this time? (h) When was the release recorded? (i) Recording information for the release? (j) Who gave the release? Why?

4. The resale of the property:

   (a) What is the recording date of the deed by which the McClungs resold the property? (b) Who were the purchasers? (c) Recording information for the deed? (d) The first deed of trust released at that time? (identify releasing party, date of release, and recording data for release) (e) The second deed of trust released at that time? (identify releasing party, date of release, and recording data for release) (f) How did the purchaser take title? Why? (g) Did the purchaser obtain new financing? (h) Who made the new loan? (i) What was the amount of the new loan? (j) Date deed of trust was recorded? (k) Recording information for the deed of trust?

---

   c. Constructive Notice. As you learned earlier in this chapter, most recording acts protect subsequent purchasers only if they lack notice of the prior transaction. There are three ways in which a purchaser might have acquired such notice:

   • *Actual notice*—where the purchaser has actual knowledge of the transaction, such as through an express statement or direct observation.

- *Constructive notice (record notice)*—where knowledge is imputed to the purchaser by the recording system. Thus, if *A* records her deed from *O*, the recording provides constructive notice to the entire world, regardless of whether a subsequent purchaser has actually looked at the public records.
- *Constructive notice (inquiry notice)*—where knowledge obtainable from a reasonable investigation is imputed to the purchaser. Thus, a subsequent purchaser is presumed to have notice of a prior transaction that a diligent investigation would reveal.

The following materials focus on constructive notice, examining whether such notice exists when there are defects in the recorded instruments, errors in the recording process, or off-record facts and circumstances indicating the existence of a prior claim.

(1) *Defects in Instruments as Recorded.* For the recording system to provide notice to third parties in effective fashion, deeds must be executed and recorded accurately so that title searchers can find them in the records and evaluate their validity and their impact upon title. Unfortunately, many types of mistakes can easily occur. For example, the party preparing a deed may misspell the name of the grantor or grantee, or may use the grantor's new name (*i.e.*, a different name than the grantor had at the time the grantor acquired the land), thus leading the recorder to enter a name in the grantor-grantee indexes that is incorrect or not easily discovered. Such mistakes may make it impossible for even a prudent title searcher to locate the deed in the records. When such mistakes occur—and a title dispute results because the error misleads an innocent purchaser—how should the law choose to allocate the loss as between the conflicting title claimants? And what consequences will that allocation have for the title search process?

As you consider these questions more fully, return to the mechanics of searching land titles and think carefully about how different mistakes would affect the title search process. For example, suppose that your client is considering the purchase of a parcel of land from William Elliott. When you perform a record title search, can you limit the search of the indexes to the name "William Elliott"? Do you need to worry about alternative spellings, like Elliot or Eliot? What about middle initials? If William Elliott had in fact conveyed the land earlier, by a recorded deed that identified him as "Bill Eliott," would your client have constructive notice of that deed?

NATIONAL PACKAGING CORPORATION
v. BELMONT

Court of Appeals of Ohio.
47 Ohio App.3d 86, 547 N.E.2d 373 (1988).

DOAN, JUDGE.... The record reveals that the plaintiff, National Packaging Corporation ("NPC"), sued Michael Bolan, d.b.a. Trade Packaging, in the Franklin County Court of Common Pleas. On November 25,

1983, NPC obtained a judgment for $3,331.76 plus interest; and, at a later time, it certified the judgment in Hamilton County, with Bolan's name incorrectly spelled "B–O–L–E–N" in the docket book. At the time the judgment was certified, Michael Bolan owned property in Hamilton County at 8107 Camargo Road and 815 Indian Hill Road.

Bolan's ex-wife, Elaine (now Elaine Belmont), brought a foreclosure action against the property located at 815 Indian Hill Road to collect overdue child-support payments. The property was sold in a sheriff's sale to L. Michael and Elaine Belmont (Bolan's ex-wife and her new husband). Because NPC's judgment was filed under an incorrect spelling of Bolan's name, NPC did not receive notice of the sheriff's sale and was unable to protect its interest in the property.

The Belmonts subsequently sold the Indian Hill Road property to Richard E. and Vera DeCamp. It was only after this second conveyance that NPC brought its own foreclosure action, asserting the certified judgment from Franklin County against both the Indian Hill Road property and the Camargo Road property.

The Belmonts moved to dismiss NPC's complaint in a filing that the trial court treated as a motion for summary judgment. The DeCamps then moved for summary judgment against NPC and the Belmonts. NPC responded with its own motion for summary judgment against the Belmonts and the DeCamps. On April 30, 1987, the trial court overruled NPC's motion for summary judgment, entered summary judgment for the DeCamps and the Belmonts against NPC and held that the De-Camps' motion for summary judgment against the Belmonts was moot.... [T]his appeal followed.

In its single assignment of error, NPC asserts that the trial court erred to its prejudice by overruling its motion for summary judgment. Relying upon the doctrine of *idem sonans*, it argues that the certified judgment filed under a similar sounding but incorrect spelling of the debtor Bolan's name, retaining the same initial letters as the correctly spelled name, should have been held to give rise to a valid lien for the benefit of NPC and to provide the appropriate constructive notice to title searchers.

The doctrine of *idem sonans* was adopted by the Ohio Supreme Court in *Lessee of Pillsbury v. Dugan's Administrator* (1839), 9 Ohio 117. There the court held that Mrs. Pillsbury was on sufficient notice that her one-eighth interest in certain real estate was being adjudicated, even though the petition for partition listed her as "Pillsby." Its reasoning was expressed in these terms:

> In adjudicating upon transactions occurring in the early settlement of our state, we must never forget the absence of precedents and system, the different usages introduced by people emigrating from every part of the country, the want of knowledge or neglect of technical learning, and the risk of loss of evidence from the lapse of

time. Hence errors of form have always been overlooked, where the acts of a court are manifest, and its jurisdiction established....

. . . It is not every mistake in names which will invalidate an instrument or proceeding. *This effect will follow where the person can not be identified*, or where the error is such as to describe another. But words are intended to be spoken; and where the sound is substantially preserved, bad spelling will not vitiate.... [*Id.* at 119–120 (emphasis added).]

The petition in *Pillsbury* otherwise identified Mrs. Pillsbury by reference to her father, who died seized of the subject real estate, and to her apparent siblings and in-laws. Further, the petition correctly identified the real estate. Thus, she could be identified in spite of her misspelled name....

NPC cites *Rauch v. Immel* (1936), 55 Ohio App. 71, and *Horton v. Matheny* (1943), 72 Ohio App. 187, as the basis for validation of its claimed error. We note, however, that in *Rauch* the doctrine was applied to a misnomer in a notice of a lawsuit, and in *Horton* it was applied to a misspelling in a deed description. In these two cases, as in *Pillsbury*, ... the error did not involve misspellings in a name index.

The case of *Gleich v. Earnest* (1930), 36 Ohio App. 326, 173 N.E. 212, is NPC's best authority because it is factually analogous to the instant matter. In *Gleich*, the court held that *idem sonans* validated the assertion of a mechanic's lien against the purchaser of the property at a foreclosure sale, even though the foreclosure suit did not name the lienholder. The lienholder had filed its lien against "C.C. Ernest," when in fact the property was held in the name of "Chester C. Earnest." The court's decision upholding the lienholder's position rested upon the testimony of two abstractors who testified that they would have searched the records under both "Ernest" and "Earnest."

. . . [T]hree experts have given affidavits stating that the doctrine of *idem sonans* should not be applied today as a standard for determining the marketable title of real estate on the basis of irregularities in last names or surnames, and that by custom it is not applied by abstractors in southwestern Ohio.

We hold that the doctrine of *idem sonans* is inapplicable to names that are misspelled in judgment-lien name indexes. We are not a frontier society of pioneers with little education or an absence of precedent and system. Since the Supreme Court issued its opinion in *Pillsbury* in 1839, we have experienced a tremendous growth in the population and the economy, and those developments have spawned countless real estate sales and a volume of litigation resulting in an abundance of indexed judgment liens. In modern society we cannot overlook matters of form by continuing to indulge the outmoded premises of our societal infancy. To impose rigidly the doctrine of *idem sonans* to name indexes now maintained for judgment liens would tax all land abstractors beyond reasonable limits and require them to be poets, phonetic linguists, or multilingual specialists. The additional time necessary to examine name indexes under such a stringent doctrine would make the examinations financially prohibitive.

The appellees, in their brief, demonstrate the difficulty in applying the doctrine of *idem sonans* to the range of spellings implicated in the instant case: Bolan, Bolen, Bolin, Bowlin, Bowlan, Bowlen, Bolun; the addition of double "l," "ein," and "ien" spellings does not even exhaust all conceivable spelling possibilities. The impossibility of the task created by the doctrine of *idem sonans* is further illustrated by the fact that we, as a society and state, are no longer a small homogeneous population primarily of European abstraction. Since our infancy, we have added Asian, African, South American, Oriental and Arabic surnames. The spelling, sound, and pronunciation of our population's surnames create an insurmountable burden for an abstractor to face in appreciating all the possible variations. Under all the circumstances, a strict application of the doctrine today would leave a real estate purchaser with a lingering fear that misspelled lienholders, either negligently or deliberately, might be lurking under the *idem sonans* doctrine in the judgment-debtor indexes.

We further conclude that the misspelling of Bolan as "B-o-l-e-n," does not rise to being "otherwise identifiable." Unlike many states that statutorily require land descriptions with lien filings, Ohio's indexes merely require a name.

Finally, with the exception of *Gleich*, the courts have not strictly applied *idem sonans*. We find instead a conditional application, which includes as a factor whether the individual is otherwise identified, and in only one case has the doctrine been applied to listings in a judgment-lien name index. We cannot, in sum, find any authority mandating strict application of the *idem sonans* doctrine. . . .

Notes

1. *The Current Status of the "Idem Sonans" Doctrine.* The impact of the *idem sonans* doctrine upon the title searcher is described in 4 American Law of Property § 17.18, at 593–94 (1952):

> [A] purchaser from a record owner "Cheffey" will not be expected to look in the grantor's index under the letter "S," and accordingly is not affected by the record of a prior conveyance made by his vendor under the name of "Sheffey." There is no constructive notice when the two names, even though pronounced alike, begin with a different letter. In fact, the record of any instrument recorded and indexed in any name, which so materially differs from that in which the title is held that a careful search would be unlikely to disclose it, is not considered as being in the regular chain of title and does not impart constructive notice. However, there is a general presumption that names in successive transfers refer to the same person when the pronunciations are alike or substantially alike, and that they afford constructive notice so long as they begin with the same letter. . . .

The doctrine of *idem sonans* adds uncertainty and expense into the process of searching land titles. Which person can avoid or solve this problem with the least burden—the prior claimant (by recording under the correct name) or the subsequent title searcher (by searching under predictable alternative spellings)? In light of these comparative burdens, do you think it makes sense to retain the *idem sonans* doctrine? Does your answer depend upon whether a jurisdiction maintains only paper indexes (searchable only manually) or instead maintains computerized indexes? [Is there any reason why the search method might make a difference?]

2. *Name Changes and Their Effect on the Recording System's Ability to Provide Notice.* Confirming the names of the grantor and grantee seems like a simple task, and yet the problem of name changes presents a potential trap. In many states, statutes provide for the notation of a legal name change on the public land records, thereby signaling the change to future searchers. *See, e.g.,* Wis. Stat. Ann. § 786.36 (judicial order effecting an individual name change "shall be entered at length upon the records of the court and a certified copy of the record shall be recorded in the office of the register of deeds of the county, who shall make an entry in a book to be kept by the register").

What happens if the record owner of land changes his, her, or its name, but does not file any instrument on the public records to signify this change? Consider the following examples:

(a) Chris Jackson owns Blueacre in fee simple absolute. Shortly after graduating from college, he borrows a substantial sum of money from First Bank, granting First Bank a mortgage on Blueacre and signing the mortgage "Chris Jackson." First Bank properly records his mortgage. A few years later, Chris becomes a convert to Islam and changes his name to Mahmoud Abdul–Rauf. He later conveys Blueacre to Bob and Betty Buyer, using a deed that describes him with the name "Mahmoud Abdul–Rauf." The Buyers pay value and have no actual knowledge of Mahmoud's prior name or First Bank's mortgage on Blueacre. Under these circumstances, should the Buyers take title to the land free of First Bank's mortgage? Why or why not?

(b) Chris Jackson owns Blueacre in fee simple absolute. Shortly after graduating from college, Chris becomes a convert to Islam and changes his name to Mahmoud Abdul–Rauf. He then borrows a substantial sum of money from First Bank, granting First Bank a mortgage on Blueacre and signing the mortgage, "Mahmoud Abdul–Rauf." First Bank properly recorded this mortgage. After several years, Chris becomes disenchanted with Islam and resumes using the name Chris Jackson. He later conveys Blueacre to Bob and Betty Buyer, who pay value and have no actual knowledge of the mortgage Jackson executed under the name Mahmoud Abdul–Rauf. Under these circumstances, should the Buyers take title to the land free of First Bank's mortgage? Why or why not?

3. *"Gaps" in Title Due to Inheritance or Devise.* Suppose that Henning, owner of Blueacre in fee simple, dies intestate and survived by his sole heir, Dean. In most states, Dean would not have to record any evidence of his inheritance in the public land records. Inheritance takes effect by operation of law under the applicable intestacy statute, and neither heirs nor devisees

must record their interests to make those interests effective against subsequent purchasers. 11 Thompson on Real Property § 92.07(h) (Thomas ed. 1994). Thus, if Dean later attempts to convey Blueacre to Key, Key would find no evidence in the grantee index of any instrument under which Dean acquired title to Blueacre. Looking solely in the public land records, then, Key could not reconstruct the chain of title to Blueacre sufficiently to conduct a thorough title search.

If Henning's estate has been judicially administered, a record of that administration will appear in another public office (such as the office of the probate clerk), and Key could verify Dean's title by searching the probate records (which would be indexed under Henning). But suppose that Henning's estate had never been judicially administered. If Key seeks your advice about purchasing Blueacre from Dean, what advice would you give to Key?

4. *Defects Rendering a Deed Invalid*. Certain defects in execution of a deed, such as *forgery*, may render the deed void; a forged deed conveys no title to the grantee—even if he pays value in good faith and without knowledge of the forgery. Similarly, the grantee under a forged deed cannot convey good title to a subsequent purchaser. The purchaser's rights are derivative of the original grantee, who acquired a void title.

Likewise, a deed cannot validly transfer title unless the grantor *delivers* the deed to grantee in a legally sufficient manner. Suppose that Nice, owner of Blueacre in fee simple absolute, decides to make a gift of Blueacre to Corrada. Nice executes a deed of the property and sets it on top of her desk. Nice is killed in a car accident and, therefore, never actually delivers the deed. Shortly after the funeral, Corrada discovers the deed on Nice's desk, records it, and immediately thereafter conveys Blueacre to Key, who took the deed for value, in good faith and without actual knowledge of how Corrada obtained the deed. A few weeks later, Nice's heirs bring an action to quiet title against Key on the ground that the deed from Nice to Corrada was void for lack of delivery. How would a court evaluate whether the deed was effectively delivered? If Nice did not validly deliver the deed, should this prevent Key from asserting the benefit of the recording act?

Courts generally hold that the recording of a deed raises a rebuttable presumption that the deed was validly delivered. *See, e.g., Gross v. Gross*, 239 Mont. 480, 781 P.2d 284 (1989); *Myers v. Key Bank, N.A.*, 68 N.Y.S.2d 744, 506 N.Y.S.2d 327, 497 N.E.2d 694 (1986). Is this a logical presumption? Would the presumption be of any benefit to Key in the hypothetical described above? Why or why not? In some states, this presumption of delivery is conclusive. *See* Mass. Gen. Laws Ann. ch. 183, § 5. Why would the legislature make this presumption conclusive? Do you think a conclusive presumption is a good idea? Would a conclusive presumption necessitate a judgment in favor of Key in the hypothetical above?

5. *Defective Acknowledgment of a Deed*. Some defects affect the *recordability* of a deed rather than its validity. The best example is a deed that bears a defective acknowledgment. All states require that the grantor authenticate the deed prior to its recordation; this authentication usually involves the grantor acknowledging the execution of the deed before a notary

public and/or witnesses. For example, for a deed to be recorded in Missouri, statutes require the deed to bear the following form of acknowledgment:

> On this ___ day of _____, ___, before me personally appeared _____, to me known to be the person described in and who executed the foregoing instrument, and acknowledged that he [she] executed the same as his [her] free act and deed.

_____

Notary Public

Suppose, however, that the grantor of a deed does not personally appear before the notary public and the notary public completes the acknowledgment without the grantor being present. If the grantor subsequently hands the deed to the grantee and it is accepted by the recorder of deeds—which would not be surprising, as the recorder would likely be unaware of the defective acknowledgment—what effect does the defective acknowledgment have upon the effectiveness of the deed? As between the grantor and the grantee, there is no effect; the deed is effective. But given that the deed was not legally sufficient to be recorded, should that deed give constructive notice to subsequent third party purchasers? *Compare Hildebrandt v. Hildebrandt*, 9 Kan.App.2d 614, 683 P.2d 1288 (1984) (recorded deed provided constructive notice when defect in acknowledgment was not apparent from the face of the instrument) *with Messersmith v. Smith*, 60 N.W.2d 276 (N.D. 1953) (recorded deed did not provide constructive notice even though defect in acknowledgment was undiscoverable from the face of the instrument).

In many states, legislatures have enacted "curative" statutes to address the problem of recorded instruments with defective acknowledgments. Under these statutes, a deed that bears a defective acknowledgment but has been recorded is "deemed" valid after the passage of a certain time period. *See* Iowa Code § 589.3 (10 years).

_____

(2) *"Chain of Title" Problems.* As Professors Nelson and Whitman described (page 738), the term "chain of title" describes the series of recorded documents by which a person holds title to land. If a grantee properly records her deed "within the chain of title"—*i.e.*, in a manner in which subsequent purchasers conducting a competent search of the record can find it using the indexes—then the deed gives constructive notice of its contents to such searchers. If the grantee records her deed, but does not do so "within the chain of title," this substantially increases the risk that conflicting title claims may arise, because subsequent purchasers of the land may be unable to locate the deed in the records. But what does it mean to record a deed "within the chain of title"? "Chain of title" problems commonly arise in one of three different contexts—the "wild deed," the deed recorded too late or too early, and multiple chains of title arising from a common owner. Each is discussed briefly below.

"Wild deeds." Suppose that Blueacre is an undeveloped parcel of land that Stein purchased in the 1960s as an investment. In 1980, Stein conveyed Blueacre to Randolph, but Randolph failed to record the deed. In 1985, Randolph conveyed Blueacre to Cameron. Cameron immediately recorded his deed, but did not take possession of Blueacre. In 2000, upon Stein's death, Stein's administrator—unaware that Stein had conveyed Blueacre—conveyed Blueacre to Key, who paid value and took possession of Blueacre without knowledge of Cameron's prior claim. A dispute subsequently arises between Key and Cameron. Did Cameron's deed—which does appear in the public records—give constructive notice of his claim to Key, such that Cameron can eject Key from Blueacre?

The answer is no, because Cameron's deed is a "wild deed"—*i.e.*, it is not properly connected to the chain of title and thus is practically undiscoverable by a purchaser in Key's position. Because Randolph never recorded his deed, there is a "missing link" in Cameron's chain of title. When Key searches the grantor index for adverse conveyances under the name "Stein" (her apparent predecessor in title), she will not find any recorded instrument by which Stein purported to convey title to Blueacre. She will assume that title remained with Stein until his death and may therefore decide to complete the purchase believing Stein's administrator can deliver marketable title to Blueacre. Courts have uniformly ruled that a "wild deed" does not give constructive notice to subsequent purchasers like Key. *See, e.g., Board of Educ. of City of Minneapolis v. Hughes*, 118 Minn. 404, 136 N.W. 1095 (1912). This means that Cameron's deed was not ***duly*** "recorded"—even though he took it to the recorder, tendered the proper recording fee, and had the recorder accept and index the deed![18]

The best explanation for this rule is that as between Cameron (the prior-in-time claimant) and Key (the subsequent purchaser), Cameron was more responsible (more "at fault," if you will) for the fact that the recording system broke down in terms of its ability to give effective notice. When Cameron bought Blueacre from Randolph, he should have realized from a search of the grantee index that there was no recorded instrument indicating that Randolph owned Blueacre. Further inquiry of Randolph would have revealed that Randolph held an unrecorded deed from Stein (the record owner). Thus, Cameron could have solved the problem by insisting that Randolph record his deed first—thereby establishing the chain of title of record—before Cameron completed the purchase and recorded his own deed. By contrast, once the broken chain of title existed, a prudent buyer in Key's possession would have had no effective way to discover Cameron's improperly recorded deed. [Had Cameron taken possession of the land, however, his possession might have given Key inquiry notice of his claim, as discussed beginning on page 757.]

Deeds recorded too late or too early. To see the "recording too late" problem, suppose that in 1980, Wells conveys Blueacre to Reuben,

---

18. If the jurisdiction had a tract index, the "missing link" in the chain of title would not matter. The recorder would have placed Cameron's deed on the index page for Blueacre, and thus Key (in a subsequent search of that index page) should have discovered Cameron's prior claim.

but Reuben fails to record his deed. [Again, assume that at all times, Blueacre is undeveloped and unoccupied land held for investment.] In 1985, Wells (realizing Reuben has not recorded his deed) makes a gift of Blueacre to Monahan, who records her deed. In 1990, Reuben belatedly records his deed. Then in 2000, Monahan contracts to sell Blueacre to Lawless. Should Reuben's belatedly recorded deed give constructive notice of his prior claim to Lawless?

If you consider the situation from the position of Lawless, you can see the problem. A search of the grantor index for adverse conveyances, under the name Wells, will first reveal the 1985 deed to Monahan. If Lawless kept looking in the grantor index under the name Wells, he would also eventually discover Wells's prior deed to Reuben (which would appear *later* in the index because Reuben was late in recording it). But after finding the 1985 deed to Monahan, Lawless might well stop looking in the grantor index under Wells—thinking Wells has now conveyed her interest—and instead begin looking under Monahan to see if Monahan has made any adverse conveyances. Lawless might not think to search the grantor index under Wells after 1985, because he would not likely expect that Wells might have made a previous conveyance that the grantee was late in recording.

Courts have split regarding the efficacy of the too-late-recorded deed. Some courts have held that such a deed does give constructive notice to subsequent purchasers. *See, e.g., Angle v. Slayton*, 102 N.M. 521, 697 P.2d 940 (1985). This rule would require a searcher in Lawless's position to search the grantor index for adverse conveyances by Wells all the way up to the present date (not just through 1985 when she appeared to convey her title). This extra search burden would take more time to complete (and thus presumably more expense). By contrast, other courts hold the late-recorded deed does not give constructive notice to subsequent purchasers like Lawless. *See, e.g., Rolling "R" Constr., Inc. v. Dodd*, 477 So.2d 330 (Ala. 1985). Which approach do you think is more sound? Who was in the better position to have avoided this problem: Reuben (by timely recording) or Lawless (by extending his search)?

The "too early recording" problem occurs more rarely. Suppose that Easton's father (who owns 1500 acres of wilderness land in Alaska) is about to die, and Easton expects to inherit the land. In 2000, in anticipation of his father's death, Easton purports to deed the land to Lee by warranty deed, which Lee records. A few years later, Easton's father dies, and Easton inherits the land. Under the doctrine of after-acquired title (or estoppel by deed),[19] Easton's title immediately passes by operation of law to Lee. But now suppose that in 2005, Easton conveys the same land to Allgire, who pays value and has no knowledge of Lee's prior claim of title. Would Lee's "too early recorded" deed provide constructive notice to Allgire? Again, you should be able to see the problem. Allgire is likely to begin searching the grantor indexes for

---

19. You will learn more about this doctrine on page 770.

adverse conveyances under the name Easton, starting with the date Easton apparently obtained title—when his father died. If Allgire searches forward in the grantor index from that point, she will not find Easton's deed to Lee; she will find that deed only if she searched *backwards* in the grantor index. But Allgire is unlikely to search backwards, as it might not occur to her that Easton might have purported to convey the land before he had acquired it in the first place!

By contrast to the "too late" problem, most courts have held that the too-early-recorded deed does not provide constructive notice to subsequent purchasers. *See, e.g., Sabo v. Horvath*, 559 P.2d 1038 (Alaska 1976).[20] Does this result seem sound? Who was in the better position to have avoided this problem: Lee (by timely recording) or Allgire (by extending her search)?

Multiple chains of title from a common owner. To see this problem, suppose that prior to 1981, Hunvald owned 25 acres of land. In 1981, he conveyed three acres of this land to Henning, by virtue of a deed that contained a restrictive covenant requiring that any house built on Hunvald's remaining land had to be a two-story home containing at least 2,500 square feet. In 1985, Hunvald deeded a different three acres of the parcel to Dean. Dean's deed did not contain a comparable restrictive covenant, and Dean had no knowledge that the 1981 deed to Henning created a restrictive covenant burdening this land. When Dean later began construction of a ranch-style home only 1,800 square feet in size, Henning sued him to enforce the covenant. Did Dean have constructive notice of the restrictive covenant contained in the deed from Hunvald to Henning?

Here, there is no real question about Dean's ability to find the deed containing the restriction. If Dean searches the grantor index for adverse conveyances under the name Hunvald, here is what Dean might find:

Grantor Index Year 1981						
Grantor's Names beginning with Hu						
Type of Instrm't	Grantor's Name	Grantee's Name	Doc. No.	Date Filed	Book & Page	Brief Legal Description
Deed	Hunvald, Edward	Henning, William	259232	3/26/81	25/397	

When Dean realizes this index entry contains no legal description of the land, he has to go look at Book 25, Page 397, to read the deed—because

20. Note that the "too early" and "too late" deeds would pose no problems if the jurisdiction had a tract index, because any such deeds would nevertheless appear on the index page for that tract and thus would give effective notice to subsequent purchasers of the tract.

he has to make sure that deed did not convey to Henning the same land Dean now plans to buy (if it did, that would be an adverse conveyance!). If Dean actually reads that deed, he should also see that it not only conveyed Henning title to three acres, but that it also placed a covenant on Hunvald's remaining land—and thus that Dean would take the three-acre parcel subject to the burden of that covenant. Because the system should readily allow Dean to find this deed, many courts would hold that the deed was recorded in Dean's chain of title and thus gave him constructive notice of the covenant. *See, e.g., Guillette v. Daly Dry Wall, Inc.*, 367 Mass. 355, 325 N.E.2d 572 (1975). Nevertheless, some courts would hold that the Hunvald-to-Henning deed was not in Dean's chain of title—because it involved a different tract of land—and thus would not give constructive notice of the covenant to Dean. *See, e.g., Witter v. Taggart*, 78 N.Y.2d 234, 573 N.Y.S.2d 146, 577 N.E.2d 338 (1991). As a policy matter, which approach do you think is preferable?[21]

Is the *Taggart* approach more defensible in a county where the recorder of deeds includes a "brief description" or "parcel description" column in the index? For example, suppose that the relevant page of the grantor index had read as follows:

Grantor Index Year 1981						
Grantor's Names beginning with Hu						
Type of Instrm't	Grantor's Name	Grantee's Name	Doc. No.	Date Filed	Book & Page	Brief Legal Description
Deed	Hunvald, Edward	Henning, William	259232	3/26/81	25/397	Lot 1, Hunvald Tract

In this situation, if Dean has contracted to buy Lot 2 of the Hunvald Tract, Dean might look at this index entry and conclude "I don't need to look at that deed, because it doesn't affect title to Lot 2." Is that a prudent conclusion for Dean to reach?

(3) *Errors by the Recording Office—Lost Documents and Misindexing.* Even if the parties to a transaction present a properly executed deed for recording, errors by the recorder can compromise the recording system's effectiveness. The recording clerk may misplace the deed prior to indexing it, such that the deed is never indexed. Alternatively, the recording clerk could erroneously index (or "misindex") the

---

21. Going back to Chapter 8, how should Hunvald have documented the creation of the covenant in a way that would have obviated this whole "chain of title" mess?

deed. For example, suppose that Pratt, owner of Blueacre in fee simple absolute, conveys Blueacre to Ziegler by warranty deed. The deed spells their names correctly, and Ziegler promptly presents the deed to the recorder for recording, but the recording clerk mistakenly enters the deed into the grantor index under the name "Bratt." Several years later, Pratt purports to convey Blueacre to Key, who pays value and accepts the deed without actual knowledge of the earlier deed to Ziegler. Is Ziegler's deed sufficient to give constructive notice to Key and thus to prevent her from asserting the protection of the recording act?

The traditional rule is that a deed provides constructive notice to subsequent purchasers even if the recorder misindexes it. *See, e.g., First Citizens Nat'l Bank v. Sherwood*, 583 Pa. 466, 879 A.2d 178 (2005) (misindexed mortgage gave constructive notice to subsequent purchaser of mortgaged land). One might defend this view by arguing that a grantee in Ziegler's position should not bear a loss due to a mistake by the recorder of deeds. In contrast, some courts have held that a misindexed deed does not provide constructive notice to subsequent purchasers. *See, e.g., Waicker v. Banegura*, 357 Md. 450, 745 A.2d 419 (Ct. Spec. App. 2000); *Howard Savings Bank v. Brunson*, 244 N.J.Super. 571, 582 A.2d 1305 (1990). Which approach is preferable? Is there a reason to place the risk of misindexing on Ziegler rather than Key (or vice-versa)? Is either Ziegler or Key in a better position to have avoided this risk? Would your analysis of this problem change if the recorder's office had entered the deed into the grantor index under the name "Pratts"? What if the recorder's office had simply lost Ziegler's deed before indexing it?

(4) *"Inquiry" or "Off-Record" Notice.* The purchase of land is usually a significant event for the buyer, and buyers usually visit and inspect the property personally before going forward with a purchase. In the process of inspecting the property, the buyer could discover potential defects in the seller's title. Such defects might include the presence of someone in possession under an unrecorded claim of title, the presence of tenants claiming under a lease from the seller, an encroachment by a neighboring landowner, or the existence of a reciprocal servitude implied from a common scheme of development. Not all purchasers of land make a careful visual inspection, however, and someone purchasing land for investment purposes might never actually visit the property personally. Should a buyer of land be deemed to have constructive (or "inquiry") notice of title defects that they would have (or should have) discovered had they conducted a careful personal inspection of the land? What types of facts should provide notice of adverse claims to a prudent purchaser? How suspicious must the surrounding facts be to justify imputing notice of an adverse claim?

SCHWALM v. DEANHARDT

Court of Appeals of Kansas.
21 Kan.App.2d 667, 906 P.2d 167 (1995).

JERRY G. ELLIOTT, PRESIDING JUDGE: Plaintiffs Maurice and Ann Schwalm appeal the trial court's granting of defendant Gary Deanhardt's motion for involuntary dismissal of plaintiffs' quiet title action. We reverse.

This is, factually, a rather bizarre case. The Schwalms owned a rental home they wished to sell. On January 28, 1993, they agreed with Michael Eddins to sell the house to Eddins in the name of the G.E. Trust No. PV 16–40 Trust (Trust). Eddins was to place $5,000 in escrow to cover foundation repairs, and plaintiffs were to carry the purchase price at 7% interest.

The next day, plaintiffs signed a quitclaim deed in favor of the Trust and Eddins signed a mortgage as trustee. Plaintiffs gave Eddins the deed and the mortgage; the parties do not agree what Eddins was to do next. Regardless of plaintiffs' intent, Eddins recorded only the deed on January 29, 1993.

That same day, Eddins approached Gary Deanhardt with an investment opportunity—invest $38,500 in the Schwalm property for an annualized return of 20%. Eddins represented that he owned the property, that there were no existing loans against the property, and that Deanhardt's security for the investment would be a first mortgage on the property.

Deanhardt balked at the opportunity, so Eddins sweetened the pot by shortening the payout on the "loan"—thereby raising the rate of return.

Without any investigation into Eddins, the property, or the recorded ownership of the property, Deanhardt, on February 5, 1993, gave Eddins his personal check. At Eddins' request, the check was made payable to Eddins personally, rather than to the Trust. In return, Eddins gave Deanhardt a note and mortgage, both in the name of the Trust and both dated January 29, 1993.

After receiving Deanhardt's check, Eddins recorded both the Schwalm mortgage and the Deanhardt mortgage. Unfortunately for the Schwalms, the Deanhardt mortgage was recorded 0.7 seconds before theirs.

The Schwalms obtained a judgment against Eddins, reconveying the property to them; they then brought this quiet title action against Deanhardt. At the close of plaintiffs' evidence in the bench trial, the court granted Deanhardt's motion for involuntary dismissal.

On appeal, plaintiffs stipulate to the trial court's findings of fact and also to the truth of Deanhardt's testimony and all documents supporting Deanhardt's mortgage interest in the house. Accordingly, the question of whether Deanhardt had notice of the Schwalms' mortgage becomes one of law.

Among the trial court's conclusions of law were: Deanhardt took Eddins' mortgage without notice of the Schwalm mortgage, under either the common law or K.S.A. 58–2223; Deanhardt had no duty to investigate, and even if the duty were there, a reasonable investigation would not have revealed the Schwalm mortgage.

"Actual notice," as used in K.S.A. 58–2223 and its predecessors, has long been understood to mean either express or implied notice. " 'It is implied when it consists of knowledge of facts so informing that a reasonably cautious person would be prompted to further inquiry, which further inquiry would inform him of the outstanding unrecorded conveyance.' " *Lane v. Courange*, 187 Kan. 645, 648, 359 P.2d 1115 (1961) (quoting *Edwards v. Myers*, 127 Kan. 221, Syl. P 2, 273 P. 468 (1929)).

Among other things, actual notice includes knowledge of circumstances to enable reasonably prudent persons to investigate and ascertain the ultimate facts. *Lane*, 187 Kan. at 648, 359 P.2d 1115. *See Pope v. Nichols*, 61 Kan. 230, 236, 59 P. 257 (1899).

No one disputes that Deanhardt did not have express actual notice of plaintiffs' mortgage. The question is whether a duty arose for Deanhardt to inquire further and whether that inquiry would have revealed the Schwalms' mortgage. If so, he may be charged with constructive/implied knowledge of that mortgage.

The trial court ruled Deanhardt had no duty to investigate matters. But Deanhardt is charged with constructive notice of the quitclaim deed from plaintiffs to the Trust, because that deed was recorded. *See* K.S.A. 58–2222. The deed was recorded the same day Eddins first approached Deanhardt with the investment opportunity. Other circumstances surrounding the investment were at least suspicious: the extremely high rate of return offered; Eddins' claim he did not like banks because they did not move fast enough; and Eddins' request for a check made personally to him, even though the property, note, and mortgage were all in the name of the Trust. . . .

In the present case, the Schwalms rented their property, and it was occupied at pertinent times. . . . Deanhardt was under a duty to at least inquire as to the tenants' interest in the property. Whether this would have led to any meaningful information is another question.

Further, Deanhardt had more than mere knowledge of a note, as in *Lane*. He knew he was offered a high rate of return, which Eddins voluntarily increased; he knew he paid Eddins personally, even though the Trust owned the property; and he is charged with the knowledge Eddins received and recorded a quitclaim deed from the Schwalms just the day before the investment opportunity was offered to him.

Perhaps more compelling than what Deanhardt knew is what he chose not to know: He did not visit the property, other than to drive by, and, therefore, did not know the city had posted a condemnation sign on the front door; he did not search the recorded instruments; he did not order a title search; he did not inquire into Eddins' background, financially or otherwise; he did not request an appraisal; he did not inquire into the validity of the Trust; and he did not request proof of property insurance.

The circumstances surrounding Deanhardt's "investment" should cause a reasonably prudent person to investigate. Deanhardt had a duty to further inquire into Eddins' right to mortgage the property.

The trial court erred in ruling no duty existed. Although the trial court erred in this ruling, the error could be harmless if such an inquiry would be futile. *See Lane*, 187 Kan. at 650, 359 P.2d 1115. On this issue, the trial court ruled that investigation would have provided no notice of the Schwalms' mortgage. . . .

. . . Deanhardt at least should have checked into recorded instruments and should have inquired of the tenants in possession, neither of which he did. These inquiries, however, would not have turned up evidence of the Schwalms' mortgage.

The question here is whether something in the quitclaim deed gave rise to a duty to further investigate. The quitclaim deed was to the Trust and was recorded the same day Eddins first proposed the instrument to Deanhardt.

In *Johnson v. Williams*, 37 Kan. 179, 182–83, 14 P. 537 (1887), the court held:

> We would think that in all cases, however, where a purchaser takes a quitclaim deed he must be presumed to take it with notice of all outstanding equities and interests of which he could by the exercise of any reasonable diligence obtain notice from *an examination of all the records affecting the title to the property*, and from *all inquiries which he might make of persons in the possession of the property*, or *of persons paying taxes thereon*, or *of any person who might, from any record or from any knowledge which the purchaser might have, seemingly have some interest in the property*. In nearly all cases between individuals where land is sold or conveyed, and where there is no doubt about the title, a general warranty deed is given; and it is only in cases where there is a doubt concerning the title that only a quitclaim deed is given or received; hence, when a party takes a

quitclaim deed, he knows he is taking a doubtful title and is put upon inquiry as to the title. The very form of the deed indicates to him that the grantor has doubts concerning the title; and the deed itself is notice to him that he is getting only a doubtful title. Also, as a quitclaim deed can never of itself subject the maker thereof to any liability, such deeds may be executed recklessly, and by persons who have no real claim and scarcely a shadow of claim to the lands for which the deeds are given; and the deed may be executed for a merely nominal consideration, and merely to enable speculators in doubtful titles to harass and annoy the real owners of the land; and speculators in doubtful titles are always ready to pay some trifling or nominal consideration to obtain a quitclaim deed. This kind of thing should not be encouraged." (Emphasis added.)

In short, the holder of a quitclaim deed is not a BFP with respect to adverse equities discoverable by reasonable diligence. 37 Kan. at 183, 14 P. 537. The steps required by *Johnson* would have led Deanhardt to the Schwalms. *Johnson* was followed in *Pope v. Nichols*, 61 Kan. 230, 234–35, 59 P. 257 (1899), but since then, the *Johnson* rule has been diluted. . . .

Deanhardt is charged with knowing Eddins had title only by a quitclaim deed, and he relied on Eddins' first mortgage as security for his "investment." Accordingly, Deanhardt must be presumed to have taken the mortgage with notice of all outstanding equities of which he could have obtained notice with reasonable diligence. Further, the quitclaim deed should have opened Deanhardt's eyes for facts and for clues as to the apparent title.

Had Deanhardt conducted a reasonably diligent search, he would have been led to the Schwalms as the last owners with a clean title; he should then have inquired of plaintiffs why they conveyed with only a quitclaim deed.

The trial court erred in ruling a reasonable investigation would not have led Deanhardt to information concerning the Schwalms' mortgage. . . .

Notes

1. *The Concept of Inquiry Notice.* The doctrine of inquiry notice establishes that where a purchaser of land knows (or should know) of information that would cause a prudent purchaser to be suspicious of the seller's title, the purchaser will be deemed to have notice of any adverse interest that an investigation would have revealed. *See, e.g., Miller v. Hennen,* 438 N.W.2d 366 (Minn. 1989); *Williston Co-op. Credit Union v. Fossum,* 459 N.W.2d 548 (N.D. 1990). Thus, a prudent purchaser will inquire about the rights of parties in possession as well as the rights of any claimants he may learn of

through other sources of information (such as recorded deeds or other parties).

The court in *Schwalm* makes a great deal of the fact that Deanhardt did not inspect the land, make any inquiry of the Schwalms' tenants, or conduct a title search. If an inquiry of Schwalm's tenants and a search of the title records would not have revealed the Schwalm's unrecorded mortgage, does Deanhardt's inattentiveness or laziness matter? What facts should have triggered Deanhardt to inquire further? Of whom should he have inquired?

2. *The Rights of Parties in Possession.* Courts have struggled to define clearly the circumstances under which there is sufficient "possession" to trigger inquiry notice, and whether possession by someone other than the grantor should always cause a reasonable purchaser to inquire further. Consider the following examples:

(a) Rosalie purchases Blueacre as a home, but has the grantor execute the deed to her son Jimmy, as grantee, to avoid creditors. [Assume that under this jurisdiction's law, because Rosalie provided the purchase price and did not intend to make a presently effective gift, Rosalie is the true equitable owner of Blueacre and Jimmy thus holds legal title as a trustee for her.] Jimmy later purports to convey Blueacre to Deborah, who pays value in good faith and without actual knowledge of Rosalie's equitable interest in the land. What facts would be relevant in determining whether Deborah will take title to Blueacre free of Rosalie's interest? *See, e.g., Diamond v. Wasserman*, 14 Misc.2d 781, 178 N.Y.S.2d 91 (Sup. Ct. 1958) (husband occupying home titled in wife's name); *Yancey v. Harris*, 234 Ga. 320, 216 S.E.2d 83 (1975) (mother-in-law sole occupant of home titled in son-in-law's name).

(b) Trump owns Trump Plaza Shopping Center. One tenant, Fred's Bar and Grill, operates in the shopping center pursuant to an unrecorded seven-year lease. Trump contracts to sell the shopping center to Walton, who is unaware of Fred's tenancy—Walton has never seen Trump Plaza (he lives in another state) and Trump inadvertently omitted Fred's lease from the package of leases that it gave Walton to review. Thus, Walton incorrectly assumed that the space in which Fred's was operating was vacant. After closing, Walton discovers Fred's in possession and sues to evict Fred's, because Walton has lined up a new tenant willing to pay higher rent. Can Walton evict Fred's by claiming that it purchased Trump Plaza without notice of Fred's lease? *See, e.g., Grand Island Hotel Corp. v. Second Island Dev. Co.*, 191 Neb. 98, 214 N.W.2d 253 (1974).

(c) Wells, owner of Jayhawk Place (a 100–unit apartment complex), agrees to sell the apartments to Peters. Wells provides Peters with the original leases, all of which provide for rent of $500/month. Based upon his review of the leases, Peters purchased the complex for $2 million. Shortly after closing, Peters received rent checks from 50 tenants in the amount of $400, and upon investigating, discovered that Wells had entered into oral agreements with each of those tenants, reducing their rent to $400/month. [All of the applicable leases were for less than one year.] How much can Peters collect from these tenants in rent? *See, e.g., Grosskopf Oil, Inc. v. Winter*, 156 Wis.2d 575, 457 N.W.2d 514 (Ct. App. 1990); *Vitale v. Pinto*, 118 A.D.2d 774, 500 N.Y.S.2d 283 (1986).

3. *Inquiry Notice from Deed References*. Suppose that Henning conveys Blueacre to Pushaw, who builds a chain link fence around Blueacre. Pushaw's neighbor, Key, sues Pushaw for an injunction to force him to remove the fence, claiming that the fence violates a "no chain-link-fencing" restrictive covenant benefitting Key's land. Henning's predecessor in title (Fischer) had agreed to the restrictive covenant with Key's predecessor (Wells) back in 1972, but the instrument creating the covenant was never recorded. The recorded deed from Fischer to Henning had conveyed Blueacre to Henning "subject to restrictions in favor of Wells," but did not specify what those restrictions were. In many jurisdictions, Pushaw would have inquiry notice of the fencing covenant based on the reference in the deed from Fischer to Henning. *See, e.g., Harper v. Paradise*, 233 Ga. 194, 210 S.E.2d 710 (1974). In other states, this reference alone would not give Pushaw inquiry notice because the instrument creating the covenant was not recorded. *See, e.g.,* Colo. Rev. Stat. Ann. § 38–35–108. Which approach appears more sound?

4. *Quitclaim Deeds and Inquiry Notice*. Citing an 1887 decision, the court in *Schwalm* held that one taking land by a quitclaim deed takes the land subject to "all outstanding equities of which he could have obtained notice with reasonable diligence." But if there are no facts indicating the existence of adverse conveyances other than the existence of a quitclaim deed, why should the mere fact that the grantor is delivering a quitclaim deed cause the grantee to be suspicious? [Note: *Schwalm* is a distinct minority position, with which the vast majority of courts have disagreed. *See, e.g., Miller v. Hennen*, 438 N.W.2d 366 (Minn. 1989); *Sabo v. Horvath*, 559 P.2d 1038 (Alaska 1976). Why have most courts rejected the position that a grantee by quitclaim cannot be a BFP? Are the inferences one can draw from the use of a quitclaim deed the same in 1995 as they were in 1887? Why or why not?]

5. *The Utility of Inquiry Notice*. The concept of inquiry notice certainly brings a great deal of uncertainty into title searching. Is it worth it? Why or why not?

LAWYERING EXERCISE
(Preventive Lawyering, Legal Research, and Drafting)

BACKGROUND: When a real estate transaction involves the sale of leased premises, it is common for a buyer or lender to insist that the tenant(s) complete an estoppel certificate (also known as a tenant estoppel letter).

> Purchasers and lenders base their business decisions, in large part, on the rent roll of a property, and they do not want any surprises after the transaction has closed. Representations in a purchase and sale agreement or mortgage are only as good as the

knowledge, honesty and assets of the seller/landlord. If the landlord misrepresents facts concerning the leases, whether due to honest mistake or fraud, the lender or purchaser could be seriously harmed. For example, a landlord might fail to disclose that there is an amendment to the lease, extending the term at below-market rents, or that the tenant has various offsets or defenses to the payment of rent, or that it had prepaid a significant amount of rent.

Therefore, prudent purchasers and lenders require estoppel certificates from tenants so that, even if the landlord fails to disclose the relevant facts, the tenant does so in a manner that precludes the tenant making a contrary claim in the future. . . . [Jonathon Hoffman, *Estoppel Certificate Pitfalls of Which Tenants Should Be Aware*, Com. Leasing L. & Strategy 8 (Nov. 1998).]

Estoppel certificates set forth basic information about the landlord-tenant relationship, such as the lease term, amount of the rent, a description of the leased premises, confirmation that neither party is in default, and confirmation that the lease has not been modified, altered, assigned, or amended in any respect. They are not contracts, but they can provide the buyer or lender with the basis for an estoppel or waiver claim if the tenant attempts to later contradict the contents of the certificate. *See* Brent C. Shaffer, *Using Tenant Estoppel Letters to Cut to the Chase*, Prob. & Prop., Nov.-Dec. 2001, at 38.

TASK 1: Assume that you are advising Walton in his planned purchase of the Trump Plaza Shopping Center (as discussed in note 2(b) following *Schwalm v. Deanhardt*). Walton has reviewed all of the leases for the shopping center and is prepared to pay a purchase price of $10 million, so long as he is certain that he can enforce the leases according to the terms contained in the original lease files that he reviewed. Draft an estoppel certificate that would provide Walton with the assurances he needs. There is no need to completely reinvent the wheel, however; use your research skills on Westlaw to find form documents that you can modify to suit your needs. You may find it helpful to combine provisions from several forms. [Caution: In using any form, be sure that you understand the meaning and purpose of each provision in the form; never insert language just because it sounds "legal."]

TASK 2: Assume that you represent Fred, the owner of Fred's Bar and Grill, which is located in the Trump Plaza Shopping Center. To facilitate a sale of the shopping center to Walton, Trump has asked Fred to execute an estoppel certificate. Knowing that the certificate would bind Fred to his assertions, what advice would you give him about completing the document? *See* Hoffman, *supra*, at 8; David E. Vieweg, *Tips for Reviewing and Revising Estoppel Certificates*, Comm. Leasing L. & Strategy 8 (Nov. 1995).

d. *Marketable Title Acts.* Suppose that *F* is seeking to acquire title to Blueacre from its current possessor, *E*. As explained on pages 737–43, *F* can search title to land back to a grant from the original owner, thereby assembling the complete chain of title to Blueacre. In many states, this process would require a search covering 150 years or more. Such expansive searches are cost-inefficient: not only are they expensive to conduct, but in most cases the likelihood of an "ancient" title defect is remote.

To streamline the process of title searching, roughly one-third of American states have adopted marketable title acts, many of which derive from the Model Marketable Title Act (1960) or the more recent Uniform Marketable Title Act (1990). The Prefatory Note to the UMTA states its objective: "The basic idea of the Marketable Title Act is to codify the venerable New England tradition of conducting title searches back not to the original creation of title, but for a reasonable period only. The Model Act is designed to assure a title searcher who has found a chain of title starting with a document at least 30 years old that he need search no further back in the record."

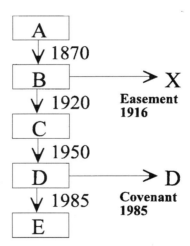

As applied to the hypothetical illustrated above, the UMTA would permit *F* to search no further back in the public records than the 1950 deed from *C* to *D*—this conveyance would constitute the statutory "root of title" from which *F* would search for adverse conveyances in the grantor index. UMTA § 1(14). Under UMTA §§ 3(a) and 4,[22] *E* would have a "marketable record title" to Blueacre subject only to the restric-

---

22. UMTA § 3(a) provides "A person who has an unbroken record chain of title to real estate for 30 years or more has a marketable record title to the real estate, subject only to the matters stated in Section 4." In turn, UMTA § 4(3) provides that this marketable record title is subject to "all interests arising out of title transactions recorded after the effective date of the root of title, and which have not been previously extinguished. . . ."

tive covenant rights reserved by *D* in 1985 (which arose after *E*'s 1950 root of title). Under UMTA § 5(b), *E*'s marketable record title would be free and clear of the 1916 easement over Blueacre, assuming neither *X* (nor *X*'s successors or assigns) had re-recorded the easement during the 30–year period following *E*'s root of title (1950–1980). In other words, if *X*'s easement was not re-recorded by 1980, the UMTA would extinguish *X*'s easement; in contrast, if *X* had re-recorded that easement in 1955, then *E*'s title would still be subject to that easement. UMTA § 6(a).

Notes

1. *The Burden of Re–Recording.* As a practical matter, you should be able to see that a marketable title act such as the UMTA places a burden upon those claiming an interest in land to re-record evidence of their claim every 30 years to avoid the possible future extinguishment of that claim. Is it appropriate to impose this burden on persons holding such interests? Do you think most property owners are aware of the need to re-record their interests to preserve them under a marketable title act?

2. *The Effectiveness of Marketable Title Acts.* In theory, marketable title acts can significantly reduce the cost of title searching. In practice, however, marketable title acts have fallen short of this goal because they typically except certain interests from their coverage and provide that the owner need not re-record to preserve those interests. Some of these exceptions are common-sense; for example, the UMTA does not apply to "a use or occupancy inconsistent with the marketable record title, to the extent that the use or occupancy would have been revealed by reasonable inspection or inquiry." UMTA § 7(2). Thus, an owner who had acquired land 50 years ago but had not re-recorded evidence of her claim of title would not have her claim extinguished so long as she remained in possession of the land; her possession would provide inquiry notice to any future purchasers attempting to establish an adverse marketable record title claim. Likewise, the UMTA does not extinguish the rights of a person whose name has appeared on the real property tax rolls as the owner of the land during the previous three years, assuming the tax rolls are accessible to the public. UMTA § 7(3).

Other exceptions, however, are more controversial, such as claims to as-yet unexercised oil, gas, and mineral rights; claims of the federal government, state and local governments; and utility and railroad easements. Litigants also have asked courts to create judicial limitations upon the marketable title acts. These exceptions defeat the title-clearing function of the act because they require the title searcher to look beyond the act's root of title to ensure that excepted interests do not exist.

3. *Post–Closing Title Assurance—Deed Warranties and Title Insurance*

By now, you can appreciate that the title search process is not perfect. Even the buyer who conducts a careful title search bears some residual risk that the grantor conveyed a defective title.

By tradition, buyers used (and continue to use) deed warranties—warranties of title made by the grantor in the deed itself—to provide post-closing title protection. Today, however, because there are significant legal and practical limitations upon the usefulness of deed warranties, most grantees commonly seek to protect against this risk by obtaining title insurance. The following materials discuss these two approaches to title assurance.

a. *Deed Warranties (or Title Covenants)*

WILLIAM B. STOEBUCK & DALE A. WHITMAN, THE LAW OF PROPERTY

905–906, 907–910 (3d ed. 2000).

The law does not generally read into a deed a representation or promise that it conveys any title, or title of any particular quality. Often the grantor will wish to exclude any such promise quite expressly, and hence will employ the term "quitclaim" or similar language to indicate that no covenants as to title are being made. However, it is customary in most areas of the nation for the grantor in an ordinary sale transaction to include covenants regarding the title. A deed containing such covenants is conventionally termed a "warranty deed"....

Deed covenants of title are not a highly effective means of title assurance. They depend on the covenantor's continued solvency and availability for suit, and recovery under them is seriously limited.... Most grantees rely on additional modes of title assurance, such as examination of public records under the recording system and the purchase of title insurance. Yet deed covenants remain important, and continue to form the basis of suits, both by disappointed grantees and by their title insurers, with the latter acting under their right of subrogation after indemnifying insured grantees for their losses....

American law generally recognizes six distinct types of title covenants in deeds. In many areas it is customary to spell them out in detail on the face of the deed, but some states have statutes which impose certain of the covenants whenever specific words, such as "grant," "convey and warrant," or the like are used in a deed. A grantor may also use express words to limit the coverage of the covenants. For example, it is common in some areas for grantors to give a full set of covenants, but to limit their application to title defects caused or created by the grantor personally, and not those created by his or her predecessors in title. Such a deed is sometimes loosely termed a "special warranty deed." It is also common to list in the deed, as exceptions to the covenants, any specific encumbrances that the grantee has agreed to accept. Examples might include a mortgage which the grantee is assuming, a recorded declaration of use restrictions, or an existing easement for utility lines. Such a listing is very desirable, for it avoids any subsequent dispute as to whether such matters were intended to be within the coverage of the covenants.

The six traditional title covenants may be used separately or together in any combination the parties agree upon. The first three are known as "present" covenants, and the latter three as "future" covenants.... The basic coverage of each covenant is as follows.

Seisin. The medieval notion of seisin connoted possession, and a few jurisdictions today simply treat this covenant as promising that the grantor is in possession of the land, whether that possession is legal or wrongful. In most states, however, the covenant of seisin is in substance a promise that the grantor owns the estate in the land that the deed purports to convey....

Right to Convey. In most cases, the covenants of seisin and right to convey are virtually synonymous, but there can be differences, at least theoretically. For example, a grantor who owned land subject to a valid restraint on alienation might satisfy the covenant of seisin but not the right to convey....

Against Encumbrances. An encumbrance is some outstanding right or interest in a third party which does not totally negate the title which the deed purports to convey. Typical encumbrances include mortgages, liens, easements, leases, and restrictive covenants. In general, the principles which define encumbrances in the context of the marketable title concept ... apply equally to deed covenants against encumbrances....

Warranty and Quiet Enjoyment. These two covenants are usually identical in their coverage. While not technically promising that the grantee is receiving good and unencumbered title, they have much the same practical effect, for they obligate the grantor to indemnify the grantee for any loss resulting from an "eviction" or disturbance of the grantee due either to an absence of title to all or part of the land, or to an outstanding encumbrance. They include an obligation on the grantor's part to defend against any legal attack on the grantee's title or possession.

Further Assurances. This is a promise by the grantor to execute any additional documents that may be needed in the future to perfect the title which the original deed purported to convey. It is the only one of the six standard covenants that can be enforced by specific performance as well as damages. In most cases a grantor's after-acquired title will inure to the grantee automatically and no further instrument is needed, so this covenant is not asserted very frequently.

Notes

1. *Types of Deeds.* As the Stoebuck and Whitman excerpt suggests, there are three types of deeds generally used in the United States: the *general warranty deed*, the *special warranty deed*, and the *quitclaim deed*. What circumstances might suggest that the grantor should use a special warranty deed rather than a general warranty deed? What circumstances might suggest that a quitclaim deed is most desirable?

Stoebuck and Whitman also refer to statutes, enacted in some states, that prescribe acceptable short forms for the three types of deeds. These statutory forms permit the use of specific expressions—*e.g.*, "convey and warrant," "grant, bargain, or sell," or "convey and quitclaim"—as a short-hand method of creating a particular type of deed without spelling out all of the title covenants. *See, e.g.,* 765 Ill. Comp. Stat. §§ 5/8 to 5/10.

2. *"Present" and "Future" Covenants—Timing Issues.* The primary difference between the present and future covenants is the *timing* of when the covenant is breached. The grantor breaches the present covenants, *if at all*, at the time the grantor delivers the deed—either the grantor's title is defective (whether or not the parties are aware of it), or the grantor's title is sound. In contrast, the future covenants are not breached until the holder of an encumbrance or paramount title actually disturbs the grantee's possession.

The case of *Brown v. Lober,* 75 Ill.2d 547, 27 Ill.Dec. 780, 389 N.E.2d 1188 (1979), demonstrates why this distinction can be important. The Browns purchased 80 acres of land from the Bosts via warranty deed in 1957. In 1974, the Browns agreed to transfer subsurface coal rights to Coal Company for the sum of $6,000, believing they had clear title to these rights. Subsequently, however, the Browns discovered that a prior owner of the land had reserved a two-thirds interest in all subsurface mineral rights. Upon this discovery, the Browns amended their contract with Coal Company, which agreed to pay $2,000 for the Browns' remaining one-third interest. The Browns then filed suit against the executor of the estate of Faith Bost (recently deceased) seeking damages of $4,000 due to the existence of the reserved mineral rights.

The court concluded that the Browns could not recover on the deed's present covenants. Although the existence of the reserved mineral rights did breach the covenant of seisin, the court concluded that the Browns' cause of action for this breach arose in 1957 (upon delivery of the warranty deed) and that Illinois's 10–year statute of limitations barred the Browns' cause of action. [Thus, when title defects manifest themselves many years after a conveyance by warranty deed, the statute of limitations will often bar any action on the present covenants.]

The Browns also argued that the reserved mineral rights constituted a breach of the future covenant of quiet enjoyment, and that this breach occurred when they discovered the defect and renegotiated their contract with Coal Company in 1974. The court rejected the Browns' argument, however, pointing out that "the mere existence of paramount title in one other than the covenantee is not sufficient to constitute a breach of the covenant of warranty or quiet enjoyment: '[T]here must be a union of acts of disturbance and lawful title, to constitute a breach of the covenant for quiet enjoyment, or warranty....'" *Id.* at 1191–92, quoting *Barry v. Guild,* 126 Ill. 439, 446, 18 N.E. 759, 761 (1888). Because the owner of the reserved mineral rights had not yet asserted those rights in a way that interfered with the Browns' enjoyment of the land, the court concluded that the Browns had not demonstrated an actual or constructive eviction and that accordingly there had been no breach of the future covenant of quiet enjoyment. [Note the consistency of this position with the interpretation of the covenant of quiet enjoyment in landlord-tenant law (pages 411–25).]

Brown v. Lober demonstrates a significant practical limitation upon the usefulness of deed covenants. The Browns sued Bost's executor, who was in the process of closing Bost's estate. In most states, parties holding a claim against a deceased person have only a limited period of time to assert those claims, after which time the executor will satisfy valid claims and then dispose of the rest of the decedent's property in accordance with the decedent's will (or intestacy laws). Notice the "bind" that this rule placed upon the Browns. By the time the holder of the mineral rights might have asserted those rights—thereby breaching the covenant of quiet enjoyment— the period for filing claims against Bost may have expired and Lober may have distributed all of Bost's assets!

3. *Liability to Remote Grantees.* Suppose that O conveys to A by a general warranty deed and A later conveys to B by a quitclaim deed. Does B have any recourse if it turns out that someone else has paramount title? Obviously, B cannot pursue an action against A under the quitclaim deed. Can B recover from O under the general warranty deed given to A? Here again, the distinction between a present covenant and a future covenant is significant. In a majority of states, a remote grantee (like B) cannot sue the original grantor (O) for breach of a present covenant. A present covenant is breached, if at all, when the deed is delivered; thus, A would have a cause of action against O, but under the traditional common law, causes of action were not assignable. In contrast, future covenants do run with the land to the grantee's successors. Thus, while B is prohibited from recovering from O under the present covenant of seisin, B may recover from O under the future covenants of warranty/quiet enjoyment—provided, of course, that (a) the title defect actually existed at the time O conveyed the warranty deed and (b) the paramount title holder actually asserts its rights against B to trigger the violation of the future covenant, as discussed in note 2 above.

4. *Calculation of Damages for Breach of Deed Warranties.* The method by which the common law calculates damages for breach of deed warranties constitutes the most significant practical limitation upon the usefulness of deed covenants as a method of title assurance. For example, suppose that in 1986, Jones (posing as Brown, the owner of Blueacre) delivered to Smith a general warranty deed to Blueacre for a payment of $20,000. The following year, Smith conveyed Blueacre to Davis by warranty deed for a payment of $22,000. Then, in 1991, the state built a freeway adjacent to Blueacre—at which point Blueacre became suitable for commercial purposes and increased in value to $300,000. In 1995, the real Brown successfully prosecuted a lawsuit against Smith to quiet title to the land. Davis then filed a suit against Smith for breach of the future covenants of warranty and quiet enjoyment, seeking damages in the amount of $300,000.

Although Davis may have suffered an economic loss of $300,000, Davis cannot recover from Smith an amount greater than the purchase price Smith received when he made the deed warranties—in this case, $22,000. *See, e.g., Forrer v. Sather*, 595 P.2d 1306 (Utah 1979). [Some courts instead limit the covenantor's liability to the value of the land at the time the warranty deed was delivered, with the purchase price received taken as evidence of the land's value. *See, e.g., Bridges v. Heimburger*, 360 So.2d 929 (Miss. 1978).] Why limit the grantor's liability in this fashion? What justification, if any, exists for placing the loss due to future appreciation upon Davis rather than Smith?

Suppose that Smith had given Blueacre to Davis as a wedding gift. Would Davis be able to recover anything from Smith? *Compare Smith v. Smith*, 243 Ga. 56, 252 S.E.2d 484 (1979) (donee may recover from remote grantor) *with Ragsdale v. Ragsdale*, 172 S.W.2d 381 (Tex. App. 1943) (donee may not recover from immediate donor/grantor). What advice would you give to someone planning to make a gift of land? To someone receiving a gift of land?

5. *Calculation of Damages in a Partial Breach.* Suppose that Archibald conveyed Parcel A (purportedly 300 feet in width) to Hillsboro Cove, Inc. for $60,000 via warranty deed. Two years later, it was discovered that due to a surveying error, a 30–foot strip of land that Archibald had purported to convey to Hillsboro Cove was in fact part of Parcel B. Hillsboro Cove paid $49,850.61, plus surveying costs of $3,385.00, to acquire the 30–foot strip, as needed to construct a condominium development it had planned. Hillsboro Cove then sued Archibald for breaching the covenant of seisin and sought to recover the entire cost of purchasing the 30–foot strip. Archibald instead contended that the proper measure of damages was $60,000 (the purchase price) times 10% (the percentage of Parcel A as to which Archibald's title was defective), or $6,000. What result? *See Hillsboro Cove, Inc. v. Archibald*, 322 So.2d 585 (Fla. Dist. Ct. App. 1975).

6. *Accepting a Warranty Deed with Knowledge of an Encumbrance.* Suppose that *A* agrees to sell Blueacre to *B*. *B* knows that *A*'s neighbor *C* has an easement to use a portion of *A*'s driveway (*A* disclosed this to *B* during their negotiations). The contract is silent about the existence of the easement and at closing, *A* delivers a general warranty deed to *B* that takes no exception for the easement. Has *A* breached the covenant against encumbrances? *Compare Jones v. Grow Inv. & Mortgage Co.*, 11 Utah 2d 326, 358 P.2d 909 (1961) (open prescriptive easement violated covenant against encumbrances if not expressly excluded) *with Merchandising Corp. v. Marine Nat'l Exch. Bank*, 12 Wis.2d 79, 106 N.W.2d 317 (1960) (open prescriptive easement did not violate covenant against encumbrances).

7. *"Further Assurances" and After–Acquired Title.* As the excerpt from Stoebuck and Whitman noted, grantees rarely assert the covenant of further assurances because of the doctrine of "after-acquired title" or "estoppel by deed." Suppose, for example, that Henning purports to convey Blueacre to Pushaw in fee simple absolute by warranty deed. At the time, however, Henning owns no estate in Blueacre. Subsequently, Henning purchases Blueacre from its former owner. Can Henning argue that the earlier deed to Pushaw was void because he had no title to Blueacre at that time?

> The law's response to this situation is to deny to the grantor the right, as against the grantee and his or her successors, to assert the title thus acquired. The theory is estoppel: if the grantor, by language in the deed, represents to the grantee that title of a certain quality is being conveyed, the grantor is estopped to deny later that such title has passed to the grantee. [William B. Stoebuck & Dale A. Whitman, The Law of Property § 11.5, at 841 (3d ed. 2000).]

Under estoppel by deed, title passes to Pushaw (the earlier grantee) immediately when Henning acquires it. [Thus, courts often refer to estoppel by deed as the doctrine of "after-acquired title."] The estoppel prevents Henning from denying the validity of his earlier deed to Pushaw. Moreover, the estoppel "attaches to the land" to prevent any successor to Henning from denying the validity of that deed. Thus, if Henning later purports to convey the land to Dean, Pushaw's title is valid as against Dean, unless Dean can claim the protection of the recording act as a subsequent bona fide purchaser for value. [Can you see why Dean might qualify for the protection of the recording act?]

Assume, however, that Henning conveyed the property to Pushaw through a *quitclaim* deed. In that case, estoppel by deed is not applicable, as Stoebuck & Whitman explain:

> This theory [estoppel by deed] is sensible only if the deed does in fact make a representation about the quality of the title it conveys; not all deeds do so. Older cases often distinguished between warranty and quitclaim deeds on this score. But that approach can be misleading, for language of warranty may really represent nothing (e.g., "I hereby warrant whatever title I may have at this time, if any") while a quitclaim deed may assert that title of a certain quality is being conveyed (e.g., "I hereby set over and quitclaim a fee simple absolute."). The modern trend is simply to look for language in the deed which fairly constitutes an assertion about the title's quality; if it is found, estoppel by deed will operate. The ordinary warranty deed will nearly always be sufficient, and most quitclaims will not. [*Id.* at 841.]

LAWYERING EXERCISE
(Legal Analysis and Memo Writing)

SITUATION: In 1992, Henning delivered a general warranty deed to Blueacre to Pushaw for a price of $25,000. In 1993, Pushaw delivered a special warranty deed to Blueacre to Abrams, who paid $26,000. In 1994, Abrams delivered a general warranty deed to Blueacre to Key, who paid $24,000. In 1995, Key delivered a quitclaim deed to Blueacre to Wells, who paid $30,000. In 2005, Wells is evicted by the true owner of Blueacre, Heinsz. [In fact, Henning committed fraud and never had title.] Assume that at the time Wells is evicted, Blueacre is worth $40,000.

TASK: Using the knowledge you have acquired about deed covenants from the preceding materials, prepare a memo to your supervising attorney to explain whether Wells can recover from any of her predecessors in title under the deed warranties (and if so, in what amount).

FRIMBERGER v. ANZELLOTTI

Appellate Court of Connecticut.
25 Conn.App. 401, 594 A.2d 1029 (1991).

LAVERY, JUDGE. . . . In 1978, the defendant's brother and predecessor in title, Paul DiLoreto, subdivided a parcel of land located in Old Saybrook for the purpose of constructing residences on each of the two resulting parcels. The property abuts a tidal marshland . . . .

DiLoreto built a bulkhead and filled that portion of the subject parcel immediately adjacent to the wetlands area, and then proceeded with the construction of a dwelling on the property. On February 21, 1984, DiLoreto transferred the subject property to the defendant by quitclaim deed. On December 31, 1985, the defendant conveyed the property to the plaintiff by warranty deed, free and clear of all encumbrances but subject to all building, building line and zoning restrictions as well as easements and restrictions of record.

During the summer of 1986, the plaintiff decided to perform repairs on the bulkhead and the filled area of the property. The plaintiff engaged an engineering firm which wrote to the state department of environmental protection (DEP) requesting a survey of the tidal wetlands on the property. On March 14, 1986, working with the plaintiff's engineers, the DEP placed stakes on the wetlands boundary and noted that there was a tidal wetlands violation on the property. In a letter to the plaintiff dated April 10, 1986, the DEP confirmed its findings and indicated that in order to establish the tidal wetlands boundary, as staked for regulatory purposes, the plaintiff must provide DEP with an A–2 survey of the property. At some point after April, 1986, and before March, 1988, the plaintiff engaged a second group of engineers who met with DEP officials and completed an A–2 survey.

On March 28, 1988, members of the DEP water resources unit met with the plaintiff's new engineers to stake out the wetlands boundary again. On April 13, 1988, as confirmation of that meeting, Denis Cunningham, the assistant director of the DEP water resources unit, wrote to the plaintiff to advise him that the filled and bulkheaded portion of the property, and possibly the northwest corner of the house were encroaching on the tidal wetlands boundary, thereby creating a violation of General Statutes § 22a–30. This letter suggested that to correct the violation, the plaintiff would have to submit an application to DEP demonstrating the necessity of maintaining the bulkhead and fill within the tidal wetlands. Instead of filing the application, the plaintiff filed the underlying lawsuit against the defendant, claiming damages for breach of the warranty against encumbrances. . . .

The trial court determined that the area had been filled without obtaining the necessary permits required under General Statutes § 22a–32. The court found that the defendant had breached the warranty against encumbrances and had innocently misrepresented the condition of the property by allowing the plaintiff to purchase the property in reliance on the defendant's warranty against encumbrances. The court awarded the plaintiff damages and costs in the amount of $47,792.60, a figure that included the costs to correct the wetlands violation as well as the diminution of value of the property caused by the wetlands violation. The defendant brought the present appeal.

This appeal turns on a determination of whether an alleged latent violation of a land use statute or regulation, existing on the land at the time title is conveyed, constitutes an encumbrance such that the conveyance breaches the grantor's covenant against encumbrances. An encumbrance is defined as "every right to or interest in the land which may subsist in third persons, to the diminution of the value of the land, but consistent with the passing of the fee by the conveyance." H. Tiffany, Real Property (1975) § 1002; *Aczas v. Stuart Heights, Inc.*, 154 Conn. 54, 60, 221 A.2d 589 (1966). All encumbrances may be classed as either (1) a pecuniary charge against the premises, such as mortgages, judgment liens, tax liens, or assessments, or (2) estates or interests in the property less than the fee, like leases, life estates or dower rights, or (3) easements or servitudes on the land, such as rights of way, restrictive covenants and profits. H. Tiffany, *supra*, §§ 1003–1007. It is important to note that the covenant against encumbrances operates in praesenti and cannot be breached unless the encumbrance existed at the time of the conveyance. *Id.*

The issue of whether a latent violation of a restrictive land use statute or ordinance, that exists at the time the fee is conveyed, constitutes a breach of the warranty deed covenant against encumbrances has not been decided in Connecticut. There is, however, persuasive and authoritative weight in the legal literature and the case law of other jurisdictions to support the proposition that such an exercise of police power by the state does not affect the marketability of title and should not rise to the level of an encumbrance. *See, e.g., Domer v. Sleeper*, 533 P.2d 9 (Alaska 1975) (latent building code violation not an encumbrance); *McCrae v. Giteles*, 253 So.2d 260, 261 (Fla.App.1971) (violation of housing code noticed and known by vendor not an encumbrance); *Monti v. Tangora*, 99 Ill.App.3d 575, 54 Ill.Dec. 732, 425 N.E.2d 597 (1981) (noticed building code violations not an encumbrance); *Silverblatt v. Livadas*, 340 Mass. 474, 164 N.E.2d 875 (1960) (contingent or inchoate lien which might result from building code violation not an encumbrance); *Fahmie v. Wulster*, 81 N.J. 391, 408 A.2d 789 (1979) (discussed *infra*); *Woodenbury v. Spier*, 122 App.Div. 396, 106 N.Y.S. 817 (1907) (a lis pendens filed to enforce housing code violations after conveyance not an encumbrance); *Stone v. Sexsmith*, 28 Wash.2d 947, 184 P.2d 567 (1947).

Of the cases cited from other jurisdictions, *Fahmie v. Wulster, supra*, provides the closest factual analogue to the case before us. In *Fahmie*, a closely held corporation that originally owned certain property requested permission from the New Jersey bureau of water to place a nine foot diameter culvert on the property to enclose a stream. The bureau required instead that a sixteen and one-half foot diameter culvert should be installed. The corporation went ahead with its plan and installed the nine foot culvert.

The property was later conveyed to Wulster, the titular president of the corporation, who had no knowledge of the installation of the nine foot culvert. Nine years after the installation of the culvert, Wulster conveyed the property, by warranty deed, to Fahmie.

In anticipation of the subsequent resale of the property, Fahmie made application to the New Jersey economic development commission, division of water policy and supply, to make additional improvements to the stream and its banks. It was then that the inadequate nine foot culvert was discovered, and the plaintiff was required to replace it with a sixteen and one-half foot diameter pipe. Fahmie sued Wulster for the cost to correct the violation claiming a breach of the deed warranty against encumbrances.

The New Jersey Supreme Court concluded that it was generally the law throughout the country that a claim for breach of a covenant against encumbrances cannot be predicated on the necessity to repair or alter the property to conform with land use regulations. By so doing, the *Fahmie* court refused to expand the concept of an encumbrance to include structural conditions existing on the property that constitute violations of statute or governmental regulation. The court concluded that such a conceptual enlargement of the covenant against encumbrances would create uncertainty and confusion in the law of conveyancing and title insurance because neither a title search nor a physical examination of the premises would disclose the violation. The New Jersey court went on to state that "[t]he better way to deal with violations of governmental regulations, their nature and scope being as pervasive as they are, is by contract provisions which can give the purchaser full protection [in such situations]." *Id.*, 408 A.2d 789.

The case before us raises the same issues as those raised in *Fahmie*. Here, the court found that in 1978 the wetlands area was filled without a permit and in violation of state statute. The alleged violation was unknown to the defendant, was not on the land records and was discovered only after the plaintiff attempted to get permission to perform additional improvements to the wetlands area.

Although the DEP first advised the plaintiff of the alleged violation in 1986, it did not bring any action to compel compliance with the statute. Rather, it suggested that the violation may be corrected by submitting an application to DEP. As of the date of trial, the plaintiff had not made such an application, there had been no further action taken by the DEP to compel compliance, and no administrative order was ever entered from which the plaintiff could appeal. Thus, the plaintiff was never required by DEP to abate the violation or restore the wetlands.

Our Supreme Court has stated that for a deed to be free of all encumbrances there must be marketable title that can be sold "at a fair price to a reasonable purchaser or mortgaged to a person of reasonable prudence as a security for the loan of money." *Perkins v. August*, 109 Conn. 452, 456, 146 A. 831 (1929). To render a title unmarketable, the defect must present a real and substantial probability of litigation or loss at the time of the conveyance. *Frank Towers Corporation v. Laviana*, 140 Conn. 45, 53, 97 A.2d 567 (1953). Latent violations of state or municipal land use regulations that do not appear on the land records, that are unknown to the seller of the property, as to which the agency charged with enforcement has taken no official action to compel compliance at the time the deed was executed, and that have not ripened into an interest that can be recorded on the land records do not constitute an encumbrance for the purpose of the deed warranty. *Monti v. Tangora*, 99 Ill.App.3d 575, 581–82, 54 Ill.Dec. 732, 425 N.E.2d 597 (1981). Although, under the statute, DEP could impose fines or restrict the use of the property until it is brought into compliance, such a restriction is not an encumbrance. *Silverblatt v. Livadas*, 340 Mass. 474, 479, 164 N.E.2d 875 (1960); *Gaier v. Berkow*, 90 N.J.Super. 377, 379, 217 A.2d 642 (1966).

Because the plaintiff never actually filed the application, any damages that he may have suffered were speculative. The court based its assessment of damages on a proposed application and the anticipated costs of complying with that proposed application. The fact that the alleged violation was first noted by DEP only after the plaintiff made requests to rework the bulkhead and filled area, leads us to the conclusion that no litigation or loss was imminent. This position is confirmed by the fact that, as of the date of trial, no order was entered by DEP to compel the plaintiff to rectify the violative condition and no application was made by the plaintiff to gain approval of existing conditions.

We adopt the reasoning of *Fahmie v. Wulster, supra*, and hold that the concept of encumbrances cannot be expanded to include latent conditions on property that are in violation of statutes or government regulations. To do so would create uncertainty in the law of conveyances, title searches and title insurance. The parties to a conveyance of real property can adequately protect themselves from such conditions by including protective language in the contract and by insisting on appropriate provisions in the deed. As the Illinois Appellate Court held in *Monti v. Tangora, supra*, 99 Ill.App.3d at 582, 54 Ill.Dec. 732, 425 N.E.2d 597,

> [t]he problem created by the existence of code violations is not one to be resolved by the courts, but is one that can be handled quite easily by the draftsmen of contracts for sale and of deeds. All that is required of the law on this point is that it be certain. Once certainty is achieved, parties and their draftsmen may place rights and obligations where they will. It is the stability in real estate transactions that is of paramount importance here.

The plaintiff in this case is an attorney and land developer who had developed waterfront property and was aware of the wetlands requirement. He could have protected himself from any liability for wetlands violation either by requiring an A–2 survey prior to closing or by inserting provisions in the contract and deed to indemnify himself against potential tidal wetlands violations or violations of other environmental statutes. . . .

The judgment is reversed. . . .

Notes

1. *The "Marketable Title" Standard and the Doctrine of Merger.* Suppose that Karen purchased a parcel of land on which she planned to construct an office building. The contract contained the following provision: "The Seller further represents and warrants that water, sewer and electric service are presently available at the property line or lines of the premises with sufficient capacity to accommodate a 45,000 sq.ft. office/warehouse building." After closing, however, Karen discovered that water and sewer connections were not available at the property line as warranted, and that she would have to pay more than $25,000 to extend the utility lines to obtain service. Would the contract warranty remain in effect after the closing and permit Karen to rescind the contract or recover damages?

Traditionally, the common law rule was that all covenants in a sale contract "merged" into the deed upon delivery. Once the grantee had accepted the deed, the grantee could no longer enforce the covenants of the sale contract, but only those covenants that appeared in the deed itself—and typically deeds contain only covenants for title, not covenants regarding "nontitle" matters such as utility services. Such a rule seems outrageous in its failure to give effect to the expectations of the grantee, and today most courts have abandoned or narrowed the merger concept:

> Where a provision of a contract to sell land is not performed or satisfied by the execution and delivery of the deed, "[t]he rule that acceptance of a deed tendered in performance of a contract to convey land merges or extinguishes the covenants and stipulations contained in the contract does not apply...." It is said that "[i]n such case, the delivery of the conveyance is merely a part performance of the contract, which remains binding as to its further provisions."

> The continued efficacy, then, of collateral agreements which are not usually included in the terms of a deed is not affected by the merger rule. Such collateral agreements call for acts by the seller which go beyond merely conveying clear title and placing the purchaser in possession of the property. [*American Nat'l Self Storage, Inc. v. Lopez–Aguiar*, 521 So.2d 303, 305 (Fla. Dist. Ct. App. 1988).]

The doctrine of merger of covenants is not entirely dead, however. Where a warranty in the sale contract pertains to title—such as any express or implied warranty that title is marketable—the merger doctrine still applies. The seller's warranty of marketable title in the contract will merge into the deed (and out of existence as a basis for recovery) upon delivery of the deed; thus, after closing the grantee may no longer rescind the contract but may only sue for breach of any deed warranties. *See, e.g., Stephan v. Brown*, 233 So.2d 140 (Fla. Dist. Ct. App. 1970) (contract warranty that land would be free of encumbrances not enforceable after purchaser accepted deed without such warranty).

Frimberger demonstrates the potential consequences of this doctrine. Suppose Frimberger had discovered the tidal wetlands violation prior to closing. Based upon this discovery, could Frimberger have rescinded the contract based upon the unmarketability of Anzellotti's title? In answering this question, should it matter that, if forced to perform, Frimberger would have no recourse against his predecessors in title to compensate him for the economic loss occasioned by the tidal wetlands violation?

2. *Preventive Lawyering.* Given that the tidal wetlands violation did not constitute an encumbrance protected by the covenant against encumbrances, how should Frimberger protect himself against the risk of having to accept title subject to "unknown" risks like this tidal wetlands violation? Would title insurance provide any potential protection for Frimberger? Consider this question after the materials in the following section on title insurance.

LAWYERING EXERCISE
(Problem–Solving and Alternatives to Litigation)

BACKGROUND: Because case analysis remains a predominant method of teaching law, law students often focus on litigation as the primary model of resolving a client's problem. Litigation, however, is not always the optimal approach. It can be expensive and fraught with delay (with simple cases costing thousands of dollars and taking years to resolve). More fundamentally, the judicial process has only a limited range of remedies at its disposal; accordingly, the outcome of a lawsuit may be less-than-satisfying—even for the victor. Effective lawyers, therefore, must be problem-solvers and consider alternatives to litigation, as suggested in this excerpt from the MacCrate Report:

A lawyer should be familiar with the skills and concepts involved in developing a plan of action with the client, including:

a. Identifying the full range of possible plans of action;

b. Evaluating the comparative efficacy and desirability of the alternative possible plans of action, comparing and ranking them on the basis of:

   (i)   The extent to which each plan of action is likely to achieve the client's objectives and satisfy his or her priorities and preferences;

   (ii) The benefits and costs of each plan of action;

   (iii) The probabilities of successful implementation of each plan of action;

   (iv) The likely consequences of unsuccessful implementation of each plan of action (including those of both total and partial failure);

   (v)   The extent to which each plan of action is consistent with the financial resources which the client is able and willing to devote;

   (vi) The extent to which each plan of action is consistent with a timetable which is strategically desirable and which satisfies the client's wishes and needs. . . . [MacCrate Report at 144–45.]

TASK: Given the court's holding in *Frimberger*, the "investment" in litigation clearly was a poor allocation of Frimberger's resources. Assuming Frimberger had won, can you envision circumstances in which the "investment" in the litigation still would be viewed as a wasted effort? How might you have advised Frimberger differently if you were representing him? Based upon the facts given in the decision, make a list of other possible plans of action that were available to him. Try to weigh the relative costs and benefits of those alternatives, as compared with pursuing litigation. [Assume that the attorney's legal fee is $150 per hour and that litigation to the appellate court level would cost about $10,000 (a conservative estimate).]

---

b. *Title Insurance.* With increasing prevalence, grantees commonly seek additional post-closing title assurance through the use of title insurance. In exchange for payment of a one-time risk premium by or on behalf of the insured party, the insurance company agrees to indemnify that party against covered losses arising out of that party's ownership of the land. [Note that when a person acquires land using a mortgage, the company will issue two separate policies—an "owner's" policy insuring the owner's fee simple interest, and a "lender's" policy insuring the lender's interest under the mortgage—and assess two separate premiums.] If an insured party suffers a loss due to an insured title defect, the title insurance company must reimburse the insured party for the loss, up to the agreed-upon policy limits.

Title insurance is not the panacea that a layperson might expect because it does not cover all title defects. There are two major categories of uninsured title defects: *exclusions* and *exceptions. Exclusions* are title matters that the title company's *standard policy form* never agrees to insure against, regardless of the type of land involved—such as zoning ordinances or building codes. Looking at the exclusions listed in the standard policy (pages 780–81), can you explain why the title insurer's standard policy will not insure against any of these defects?

Exceptions are title matters that are specific to the insured parcel of land. The title insurer conducts its own search of the publicly recorded documents. In many states, title insurers maintain copies of these documents in a private "title plant" that the insurer establishes with its own tract index.[23] In a few states, the title insurer must rely upon a title opinion from an attorney who has conducted a search of the public records herself. The insurer lists on Schedule B of the policy all outstanding rights it discovers through this search. Thus, if the search

---

23. One or more title companies will bear the expense of establishing and maintaining a title plant. Not surprisingly, there are sometimes errors in duplicating all of the public records into the title plant. Errors in a title plant have no impact upon the legal rights of landowners—a grantee who properly records her deed on the public records is protected against later takers even if a title insurer failed to include that deed within its title plant. The significance of title plant errors is that they may cause the title insurer to err in setting the limits of its coverage.

indicates that the land is subject to an easement in favor of SBC, the title insurer will "except," or refuse to indemnify the insured party against, any losses that might occur because SBC or its successor later asserts its rights under that easement. Likewise, if the search indicates that the land is subject to a covenant that restricts the land to residential use only, the title insurance company will list that covenant as an exception and refuse to indemnify against losses that might occur if another party obtains an injunction to prevent the insured party from operating a business on the land.

Once the insurer issues its preliminary title report, one or more parties may negotiate to get the insurer to remove an exception altogether or to narrow its scope—perhaps arguing that the exception creates no valid property right or poses no serious risk to the insurer. [Negotiated changes in coverage may also be manifested in policy "endorsements" that "insure over" certain risks excluded or excepted from the basic policy form. Title insurers often have a standard price list for such endorsements.][24] Thus, an insurer will often remove exceptions—either for a fee or, in some cases, for free—when the insurer concludes that the exception poses only an acceptable risk.

Below, we have included a portion of the 1992 Standard Owner's Policy of Title Insurance approved by the American Land Title Association. As you review the policy, pay attention to the following fundamental questions:

- What types of title problems does this policy protect against? What types does it *not* protect against?

- What type of remedies can the insured party demand upon discovery of a covered title defect?

- Must the title insurer indemnify the insured party for its entire economic loss due to a covered title defect?

- Who is protected by the policy? The Buyer? The Buyer's mortgage lender? Someone who later acquires the land from Buyer?

POLICY OF TITLE INSURANCE

Issued by FIRST AMERICAN TITLE INSURANCE COMPANY

SUBJECT TO THE EXCLUSIONS FROM COVERAGE, THE EXCEPTIONS FROM COVERAGE CONTAINED IN SCHEDULE B AND THE CONDITIONS AND STIPULATIONS, FIRST AMERICAN TITLE

---

24. This negotiation pressure may come from the buyer's broker—who wants to ensure that the buyer will accept the seller's title so that the deal will close, the seller will get its purchase price, and the broker will earn its commission. This negotiation pressure may also come from a mortgage lender (who may want to place a mortgage loan that it views as favorable) or an attorney for one of the parties (who may want to improve his or her reputation as a dealmaker and not a dealbreaker). Because title insurers receive much of their business from referrals from real estate professionals, insurers have significant incentive to be cooperative in such negotiations in order to obtain "repeat business."

INSURANCE COMPANY, a California corporation, herein called the Company, insures, as of Date of Policy shown in Schedule A, against loss or damage, not exceeding the Amount of Insurance stated in Schedule A, sustained or incurred by the insured by reason of:

1. Title to the estate or interest described in Schedule A being vested other than as stated therein;

2. Any defect in or lien or encumbrance on the title;

3. Unmarketability of the title;

4. Lack of a right of access to and from the land.

The Company will also pay the costs, attorneys' fees and expenses incurred in defense of the title, as insured, but only to the extent provided in the Conditions and Stipulations.

EXCLUSIONS FROM COVERAGE

The following matters are expressly excluded from the coverage of this policy and the Company will not pay loss or damage, costs, attorneys' fees or expenses which arise by reason of:

1. (a) Any law, ordinance or governmental regulation (including but not limited to building and zoning laws, ordinances, or regulations) restricting, regulating, prohibiting or relating to (i) the occupancy, use, or enjoyment of the land; (ii) the character, dimensions or location of any improvement now or hereafter erected on the land; (iii) a separation in ownership or a change in the dimensions or area of the land or any parcel of which the land is or was a part; or (iv) environmental protection, or the effect of any violation of these laws, ordinances or governmental regulations, except to the extent that a notice of the enforcement thereof or a notice of a defect, lien or encumbrance resulting from a violation or alleged violation affecting the land has been recorded in the public records at Date of Policy.

(b) Any governmental police power not excluded by (a) above, except to the extent that a notice of the exercise thereof or a notice of a defect, lien or encumbrance resulting from a violation or alleged violation affecting the land has been recorded in the public records at Date of Policy.

2. Rights of eminent domain unless notice of the exercise thereof has been recorded in the public records at Date of Policy, but not excluding from coverage any taking which has occurred prior to Date of Policy which would be binding on the rights of a purchaser for value without knowledge.

3. Defects, liens, encumbrances, adverse claims or other matters:

(a) created, suffered, assumed or agreed to by the insured claimant;

(b) not known to the Company, not recorded in the public records at Date of Policy, but known to the insured claimant and not disclosed in writing to the Company by the insured claimant prior to the date the insured claimant became an insured under this policy;

(c) resulting in no loss or damage to the insured claimant;

(d) attaching or created subsequent to Date of Policy; or

(e) resulting in loss or damage which would not have been sustained if the insured claimant had paid value for the estate or interest insured by this policy.

4. Any claim, which arises out of the transaction vesting in the Insured the estate or interest insured by this policy, by reason of the operation of federal bankruptcy, state insolvency, or similar creditors' rights laws, that is based on:

(a) the transaction creating the estate or interest insured by this policy being deemed a fraudulent conveyance or fraudulent transfer; or

(b) the transaction creating the estate or interest insured by this policy being deemed a preferential transfer except where the preferential transfer results from the failure:

(i) to timely record the instrument of transfer; or

(ii) of such recordation to impart notice to a purchaser for value or a judgment or lien creditor.

SCHEDULE A

(File No.) Policy No. _____

Amount of Insurance $_____

Premium $_____

Date of Policy _____ (at ___ a.m./p.m.)

1. Name of Insured:

2. The estate or interest in the land which is covered by this policy is:

3. Title to the estate or interest in the land is vested in:

4. The land referred to in this policy is described as follows:

[legal description of land is inserted here]

SCHEDULE B

EXCEPTIONS FROM COVERAGE

This policy does not insure against loss or damage (and the Company will not pay costs, attorneys' fees or expenses) which arise by reason of:

[Editors' Note: At this point, the Title Insurer will include a list of all easements, restrictions, covenants, or other title matters of record—at least those that the Title Insurer has discovered—such that the policy, when issued, will not protect the policy holder from loss due to those items. In addition, the Title Insurer will also list an exception for governmental liens on account of real estate taxes that are not due and payable until after the policy date. Further, the Title Insurer will often include a standard "survey" exception that excepts coverage for "encroachments, overlaps, boundary line disputes, or other matters that would be disclosed by an accurate survey or inspection of the premises." Typically, the Title Insurer will agree to remove this exception only if it receives, reviews, and approves a new survey of the premises. Finally, the Title Insurer also may include an exception for the rights of "parties in possession" of the premises or other exceptions based upon local customs. In some situations, however, the Insurer will agree to remove this or other exceptions for "business reasons"—either for payment of an additional fee, or to help the referring broker or attorney complete the transaction without "hitches" in order to retain the favor of the referring broker or attorney. Indeed, some title insurers will readily agree to remove some of the standard exceptions upon request (even without a fee).]

CONDITIONS AND STIPULATIONS

1. DEFINITION OF TERMS. The following terms when used in this policy mean:

(a) "insured": the insured named in Schedule A, and, subject to any rights or defenses the Company would have had against the named insured, those who succeed to the interest of the named insured by operation of law as distinguished from purchase including, but not limited to, heirs, distributees, devisees, survivors, personal representatives, next of kin, or corporate or fiduciary successors.

(b) "insured claimant": an insured claiming loss or damage.

(c) "knowledge" or "known": actual knowledge, not constructive knowledge or notice which may be imputed to an insured by reason of the public records as defined in this policy or any other records which impart constructive notice of matters affecting the land.

(d) "land": the land described or referred to in Schedule A, and improvements affixed thereto which by law constitute real property. The term "land" does not include any property beyond the lines of the area described or referred to in Schedule A, nor any right, title, interest, estate or easement in abutting streets, roads, avenues, alleys, lanes, ways or waterways, but nothing herein shall modify or limit the extent to which a right of access to and from the land is insured by this policy.

(e) "mortgage": mortgage, deed of trust, trust deed, or other security instrument.

(f) "public records": records established under state statutes at Date of Policy for the purpose of imparting constructive notice of matters relating to real property to purchasers for value and without knowledge. With respect to Section 1(a)(iv) of the Exclusions From Coverage, "public records" shall also include environmental protection liens filed in the records of the clerk of the United States district court for the district in which the land is located.

(g) "unmarketability of the title": an alleged or apparent matter affecting the title to the land, not excluded or excepted from coverage, which would entitle a purchaser of the estate or interest described in Schedule A to be released from the obligation to purchase by virtue of a contractual condition requiring the delivery of marketable title.

2. CONTINUATION OF INSURANCE AFTER CONVEYANCE OF TITLE. The coverage of this policy shall continue in force as of Date of Policy in favor of an insured only so long as the insured retains an estate or interest in the land, or holds an indebtedness secured by a purchase money mortgage given by a purchaser from the insured, or only so long as the insured shall have liability by reason of covenants of warranty made by the insured in any transfer or conveyance of the estate or interest. This policy shall not continue in force in favor of any purchaser from the insured of either (i) an estate or interest in the land, or (ii) an indebtedness secured by a purchase money mortgage given to the insured. . . .

6. OPTIONS TO PAY OR OTHERWISE SETTLE CLAIMS; TERMINATION OF LIABILITY. In case of a claim under this policy, the Company shall have the following additional options:

(a) To Pay or Tender Payment of the Amount of Insurance.

(i) To pay or tender payment of the amount of insurance under this policy together with any costs, attorneys' fees and expenses incurred by the insured claimant, which were authorized by the Company, up to the time of payment or tender of payment and which the Company is obligated to pay.

(ii) Upon the exercise by the Company of this option, all liability and obligations to the insured under this policy, other than to make the payment required, shall terminate, including any liability or obligation to defend, prosecute, or continue any litigation, and the policy shall be surrendered to the Company for cancellation.

(b) To Pay or Otherwise Settle With Parties Other than the Insured or With the Insured Claimant.

(i) To pay or otherwise settle with other parties for or in the name of an insured claimant any claim insured against under this policy, together with any costs, attorneys' fees and expenses incurred by the insured claimant which were authorized by the Company up to the time of payment and which the Company is obligated to pay; or

(ii) To pay or otherwise settle with the insured claimant the loss or damage provided for under this policy, together with any costs, attorneys' fees and expenses incurred by the insured claimant which were authorized by the Company up to the time of payment and which the Company is obligated to pay.

Upon the exercise by the Company of either of the options provided for in paragraphs (b)(i) or (ii), the Company's obligations to the insured under this policy for the claimed loss or damage, other than the payments required to be made, shall terminate, including any liability or obligation to defend, prosecute or continue any litigation.

7. DETERMINATION, EXTENT OF LIABILITY AND COINSUR-ANCE. This policy is a contract of indemnity against actual monetary loss or damage sustained or incurred by the insured claimant who has suffered loss or damage by reason of matters insured against by this policy and only to the extent herein described.

(a) The liability of the Company under this policy shall not exceed the least of:

(i) the Amount of Insurance stated in Schedule A; or,

(ii) the difference between the value of the insured estate or interest as insured and the value of the insured estate or interest subject to the defect, lien or encumbrance insured against by this policy.

(b) In the event the Amount of Insurance stated in Schedule A at the Date of Policy is less than 80 percent of the value of the insured estate or interest or the full consideration paid for the land, whichever is less, or if subsequent to the Date of Policy an improvement is erected on the land which increases the value of the insured estate or interest by at least 20 percent over the Amount of Insurance stated in Schedule A, then this Policy is subject to the following:

(i) where no subsequent improvement has been made, as to any partial loss, the Company shall only pay the loss pro rata in the proportion that the amount of insurance at Date of Policy bears to the total value of the insured estate or interest at Date of Policy; or

(ii) where a subsequent improvement has been made, as to any partial loss, the Company shall only pay the loss pro rata in the proportion that 120 percent of the Amount of Insurance stated in Schedule A bears to the sum of the Amount of Insurance stated in Schedule A and the amount expended for the improvement.

The provisions of this paragraph shall not apply to costs, attorneys' fees and expenses for which the Company is liable under this policy, and shall only apply to that portion of any loss which exceeds, in the aggregate, 10 percent of the Amount of Insurance stated in Schedule A.

(c) The Company will pay only those costs, attorneys' fees and expenses incurred in accordance with Section 4 of these Conditions and Stipulations. . . .

9. LIMITATION OF LIABILITY.

(a) If the Company establishes the title, or removes the alleged defect, lien or encumbrance, or cures the lack of a right of access to or from the land, or cures the claim of unmarketability of title, all as insured, in a reasonably diligent manner by any method, including litigation and the completion of any appeals therefrom, it shall have fully performed its obligations with respect to that matter and shall not be liable for any loss or damage caused thereby.

(b) In the event of any litigation, including litigation by the Company or with the Company's consent, the Company shall have no liability for loss or damage until there has been a final determination by a court of competent jurisdiction, and disposition of all appeals therefrom, adverse to the title as insured.

(c) The Company shall not be liable for loss or damage to any insured for liability voluntarily assumed by the insured in settling any claim or suit without the prior written consent of the Company.

10. REDUCTION OF INSURANCE; REDUCTION OR TERMINATION OF LIABILITY. All payments under this policy, except payments made for costs, attorneys' fees and expenses, shall reduce the amount of the insurance pro tanto. . . .

15. LIABILITY LIMITED TO THIS POLICY; POLICY ENTIRE CONTRACT.

(a) This policy together with all endorsements, if any, attached hereto by the Company is the entire policy and contract between the insured and the Company. In interpreting any provision of this policy, this policy shall be construed as a whole.

(b) Any claim of loss or damage, whether or not based on negligence, and which arises out of the status of the title to the estate or interest covered hereby or by any action asserting such claim, shall be restricted to this policy. . . .

Notes

1. *The Usefulness of Title Insurance.* After the exceptions and exclusions, what good is a title insurance policy? What risks *does* it cover? Based upon your review of the standard form policy, can you explain why someone should obtain title insurance, and the specific ways in which title insurance would provide the grantee with greater protection than the title covenants in a deed? *See* Quintin Johnstone, *Title Insurance*, 66 Yale L.J. 492 (1957). Specifically, would a standard owner's policy have protected the following persons (and, if so, how):

(a) Mr. Lohmeyer in the *Lohmeyer v. Bower* case (page 724)?

(b) Key, who purchased Blueacre without knowledge of Ziegler's previously recorded but misindexed deed (page 756)?

(c) The Belmonts in the *National Packaging Corp. v. Belmont* case (page 745)? [Keep in mind that the Belmonts won. So what benefit, if any, would they have received from their title insurance policy?]

2. *Title Insurance Forms, Loan Policies, and Owner's Policies.* In most states, title insurance companies can use any form they wish to issue title insurance policies. As a practical matter, however, most title companies actually issue policies that comply with the standard form policy approved by the American Land Title Association (ALTA). Two related reasons explain this phenomenon. First, most institutional mortgage lenders generally require that the borrower obtain and pay for a "loan policy" of title insurance insuring the lender's mortgage lien. Second, institutional mortgage lenders often sell their mortgages on the secondary mortgage market operated by quasi-governmental entities like Fannie Mae or Freddie Mac. To sell a

mortgage on the secondary market, however, the mortgage must be covered by a loan policy of title insurance issued upon an approved form.

3. *Liability to Remote Grantees.* Revisit the hypothetical in note 3 following the materials on deed warranties (page 769). As we noted there, the original grantor may be liable to a remote grantee for breach of a future covenant. Assume that the original grantor had purchased an owner's title insurance policy. Would that policy cover the claim by a remote grantee? *See* Conditions and Stipulations, ¶ 2, of the Standard Owner's Title Insurance Policy printed above.

4. *Do Title Insurers Have a "Duty" to Search Title?* As indicated earlier in this chapter, many buyers do not conduct their own title search but instead rely upon the title insurance commitment to determine if the seller has marketable title at closing. What recourse does the buyer have if the title company's search is defective? Clearly, if the buyer obtains a title policy and the defect is a covered risk, the title company is liable for the buyer's loss up to the policy limit. But suppose that by the time the buyer became aware of the defect, the buyer's land was worth $100,000 more (due to market appreciation) than the policy limit (which was based on the value of the land at the time of buyer's purchase). Can the buyer recover the additional $100,000 loss from the title company on a tort theory (*i.e.*, that the company negligently searched the title)? There is a split of authority on this issue. Some courts have concluded that the title insurer has no duty in tort:

> Although we recognize that an insured expects that a title company will conduct a reasonable title examination, the relationship between the company and the insured is essentially contractual. The end result of the relationship between the title company and the insured is the issuance of the policy. To this extent, the relationship differs from other relationships conceivably sounding in both tort and contract, such as the relationship between physician and patient.... Although the relationship between physician and patient is contractual in its origins, the purpose of the relationship is to obtain the services of the physician in treating the patient. The patient reasonably expects the physician to follow the appropriate standard of care when providing those services. By contrast, the title company is providing not services, but a policy of insurance. That policy appropriately limits the rights and duties of the parties.... [*Walker Rogge, Inc. v. Chelsea Title & Guar. Co.*, 116 N.J. 517, 540, 562 A.2d 208, 220 (1989).]

In contrast, courts in other jurisdictions have concluded that the insured party does have a reasonable expectation that the title company will exercise due care in searching the title and that this expectation justifies the imposition of a tort duty upon title insurers.

> Although title insurance applicants are interested in obtaining insurance coverage, their primary interest is in what the examination discloses. For this they rely on the title companies to tell them of any risks. Risks usually covered by title insurance policies include errors in the title examination, including the negligent failure to note a title defect. A title company, as insurer, owes its clients the duty of conducting a title

search with reasonable care. [*Lipinski v. Title Ins. Co.*, 202 Mont. 1, 10, 655 P.2d 970, 974 (1982).]

Should the law permit an insured to recover on a tort theory? As between the rationales expressed in *Walker Rogge* and *Lipinski*, which do you find more compelling? Would your answer depend upon the context in which the transaction arose or the characteristics of the buyer?

LAWYERING EXERCISE
(Counseling and Explaining Risk to Clients)

SITUATION: Jane is planning to purchase Greenacre, and her mortgage lender (First Bank) has required the issuance of a loan policy of title insurance as a condition of making a loan to Jane. Jane asks "Why do I need a separate owner's policy when I'm already having to pay for First Bank's policy? If the title is defective, the insurer would pay off the mortgage. Doesn't that provide me with sufficient protection?"

TASK: How would you respond to Jane, and why? Identify one or more specific risks that Jane would face if she does not obtain a separate owner's policy.

CAMP v. COMMONWEALTH LAND TITLE INS. CO.

United States Court of Appeals, Eighth Circuit.
787 F.2d 1258 (1986).

JOHN R. GIBSON, CIRCUIT JUDGE. . . . Camp purchased a new home for $51,000 cash in the Pinewood Subdivision in Pine Bluff, Arkansas, in November 1978. Commonwealth issued a title policy insuring her as owner against loss or damages sustained by reason of the unmarketability of title. The property was subject to a series of recorded restrictive covenants, one of which, Restrictive Covenant No. 5, provided in part: "Top of floor joist or minimum grade of floor slab of each house to be a minimum of one foot above flood plain elevation as shown on plat." A second restrictive covenant, Restrictive Covenant No. 7, permits any person owning land in the subdivision to bring suit to secure an injunction or damages against any other owner in the subdivision who violates or attempts to violate the restrictive covenants. Camp brought this action under the title policy claiming her property was unmarketable, as it was built below the minimum elevation and was in violation of this covenant.

In response to Commonwealth's motion for summary judgment, Camp filed affidavits establishing that the living room floor slab and the carport were constructed in gross violation of the restrictive covenant. Camp also submitted affidavits from two title examiners stating that violation of the restrictive covenants rendered the property unmarketable. Camp stated in her affidavit that she has listed the house for sale and has received no offers for it.

The district court reasoned that under Arkansas law, Camp had a valid claim only if the breach of the restrictive covenant amounted to a cloud on the title, and thereby impaired marketability. The court concluded that the breach reduced the value of the property, but did not affect Camp's title to the property. Since the breach did not extinguish Camp's title to the property, or raise any reasonable doubt as to the validity of her title, the title was not unmarketable, the risk against which Commonwealth insured.[25]

On appeal Camp argues that the district court erred in finding that there was no question of material fact as to the marketability of her title. She points to the affidavits attesting that the house was built in violation of the restrictive covenant and is unmarketable, and to her statements that it is not habitable and has been listed for sale several times without offers. She contends, moreover, that she cannot sell the house or live on the property without violating the restrictive covenant, and therefore is exposed to suit to bring the property into compliance with the restrictive covenants for money damages. She argues that the district court erred in determining that she had failed to demonstrate that the title was unmarketable.

Summary judgment should be granted only when no genuine issue of material fact is present in the case and the moving party is entitled to judgment as a matter of law. *Mandel v. United States*, 719 F.2d 963, 965 (8th Cir.1983). The party against whom judgment was entered must be given the benefit of every doubt and every favorable inference that may be drawn from the record. *Buford v. Tremayne*, 747 F.2d 445, 447 (8th Cir.1984). This case is before us by virtue of the diversity of the parties, and Arkansas law governs. In diversity cases, the district court's interpretation of the law of the state in which it sits is entitled to great weight or deference. *Shidler v. All American Life and Financial Corp.*, 775 F.2d 917, 920 (8th Cir. 1985); *Pyle v. Dow Chemical Co.*, 728 F.2d 1129, 1130 (8th Cir. 1984).

We are satisfied that the experienced district judge thoroughly examined the issues under prevailing Arkansas law and did not err in granting summary judgment. The purpose of title insurance is to protect a buyer of real estate from any damage or loss arising through defects clouding his title. *Bourland v. Title Insurance Co.*, 4 Ark.App. 68, 73, 627 S.W.2d 567, 570 (Ark.Ct.App.1982). The Arkansas Supreme Court has held that marketable title "is one which imports such ownership as enables and ensures to the owner the peaceable control and use of the property as against everyone else." *Holt v. Manuel*, 186 Ark. 435, 437, 54 S.W.2d 66, 66–67 (1932). To be marketable, title need only be free from reasonable doubt, not "ultimately prove impervious to assault." *Id.* at 437, 54 S.W.2d at 67. Reasonable doubt affecting marketability is said to exist where " 'there is uncertainty as to some defects appearing in the course of its deduction, and the doubt must be such as affects the value

---

25. The district court expressly reserved the question whether Camp could recover under the title policy when and if she found a buyer for the property who refused to close on the grounds that the breach of the restrictive covenant raised reasonable doubts as to her ability to pass marketable title. In the present posture of the case, we have no reason to address this issue.

of the land, or will interfere with its sale.' " *Id.* at 437–38, 54 S.W.2d at 67 (quoting *Griffith v. Maxfield*, 63 Ark. 548, 551, 39 S.W. 852, 853 (1897)).[26]

A violation of a restrictive covenant which results from a construction flaw in the property does not introduce a defect in the title. It creates no lien on the property or adverse interest in any other person. See *Davis v. St. Joe School District*, 225 Ark. 700, 284 S.W.2d 635 (1955). Although the breach undoubtedly affects the value of the land, and interferes with its salability, it is not as a result of any doubt as to who holds title to the property.

We think this case is governed by the Arkansas Supreme Court's decision in *Davis v. St. Joe School District*, 225 Ark. at 701, 284 S.W.2d at 637. There the court was required to determine the interest passed by a deed which conveyed the fee simple, subject to a restriction on the use of the property. The court held that the deed passed a fee simple absolute with a covenant binding the grantee to the specified use of the property. The court added that a breach of the covenant might give rise to an action for damages but would not extinguish the grantee's title. (*citing Bain v. Parker*, 77 Ark. 168, 90 S.W. 1000 (1905)).

Although the covenant in *Davis* involved a use restriction, and the present case involves a construction restriction, the former would seem to pose a greater threat to the marketability of title.

The district court did not err in its conclusion that Camp's title was not unmarketable within the meaning of the insurance policy. We affirm the judgment of the district court.

Notes

1. *Application/Extension of Existing Precedent.* In the *Davis* case, on which *Camp* relies, the court had to decide whether the original deed to the school district created a defeasible fee simple estate (terminable upon the land no longer being used for school purposes) or a fee simple subject to a restrictive covenant binding the land to use for school purposes. Is the *Camp* court correct to conclude that *Davis* is controlling precedent? Why or why not?

2. *"Unmarketability" of Title.* Based upon what you learned earlier in this chapter, do you agree with the court's conclusion that Mrs. Camp's title is marketable? Why or why not? Is it crucial to the court's conclusion that the covenant in question was part of a uniform set of reciprocal restrictions applicable to all homes in this subdivision? If Mrs. Camp later signs a contract to sell the property to Clinton, how would you advise Clinton regarding his obligation to close once he learns of the problems with the house? Compare the result in the *Camp* case with the court's decisions in

---

26. Camp argues that affidavits of the title examiners suggesting that the title is not marketable are sufficient to raise a reasonable doubt as to marketable title. The Arkansas Supreme Court has squarely rejected this contention. *See Holt,* 186 Ark. at 437, 54 S.W.2d at 67.

Lohmeyer (page 724) (violation of zoning ordinance and restrictive covenant breached marketability provision in real estate contract) and *Frimberger* (page 771) (latent violation of wetlands law did not violate deed warranty against encumbrances). Should the "marketability" standard vary according to whether the issue is raised pre-closing in the context of the real estate contract or post-closing in the form of deed covenants or title insurance?

LAWYERING EXERCISE
(Document Review and Legal Writing)

SITUATION: Fred and Wilma Flintstone were expecting a new baby and needed to move out of the small bungalow that they had inherited from Fred's parents. Although they had sentimental attachment to the house because it had been built by Fred's father when Fred was a child, they really needed more space for the new baby and their rambunctious dog, Dino. Fred and Wilma contacted Mr. Peebles, the local realtor, to help them sell the bungalow. Peebles agreed to list the home for them and had Fred and Wilma sign a standard listing agreement. Fred and Wilma also signed a Residential Real Estate Disclosure Form, which indicated that they were unaware of any defects in the home or property.

Peebles brought Barney and Betty Rubble to see the house and they immediately signed a standard real estate contract to purchase it. At the closing, the Flintstones gave the Rubbles a Special Warranty Deed to the property and the Rubbles secured title insurance through Murphydale Title and Abstract Company.

Several years later, Barney and Betty adopted a baby, BamBam. Barney then decided to have the property surveyed so that he could put up a fence for BamBam to play in the back yard. The survey showed that the attached garage (which had been built at the same time as the house in 1960) was in violation of a subdivision covenant which stated that "[n]o building shall be placed closer to the front property line than 30 feet and shall be no closer than 10 feet to the side and rear property lines." The garage was within four feet of the side property line.

TASK: Barney and Betty have come to you for advice. Draft a letter that explains to the Rubbles what their rights are against the Flintstones, Murphydale Title and Abstract Company, and any other parties under this set of facts. Assume that the title insurance policy is the same as the ALTA Policy on pages 779–85 and the real estate contract is the same as the contract on pages 792–97.

D.   OTHER PITFALLS IN NEGOTIATING LAND PURCHASE AND SALE CONTRACTS

In the following section, we discuss a sampling of the issues that can arise in the course of a land purchase transaction. Many of these issues have produced significant litigation, largely because parties did not sufficiently take a preventive approach to a transaction—*i.e.*, they failed to anticipate foreseeable risks or problems, and thus failed to address those risks or problems in advance in their contract.

Many of the problems we will encounter in this section—such as the risk of casualty loss during the "gap period," the physical condition of the land and the improvements, and the remedies available following breach by one of the parties—are the more obvious problems that a buyer could appreciate going into a transaction. In fact, these issues have produced enough litigation in past transactions that standard form contracts now address these issues in relatively thorough fashion. Because drafting a new contract of sale from scratch in every land transaction would be time-consuming, professionals often use standard form contracts as a starting point—particularly in the residential context, where brokers encourage the use of standard form contracts approved by the local or state board of realtors. An example of such a form appears on pages 792–97.

As you encounter the various subjects in this section, you should refer back to this standard form contract. Does it provide sufficient protection of the buyer's interests? The seller's interests? Does it sufficiently address the specific problem areas that follow in this section? Based on its protections, can the buyer prudently enter into the agreement using this form contract without the advice of an attorney, or should the buyer have an attorney review even standard form agreements before executing them? To what extent, and when, should a party—or the party's lawyer—insist upon deviating from the language contained in a standard form contract? When might deviating from the standard language be unjustified?

MISSOURI ASSOCIATION OF REALTORS®
Working for Missouri's REALTORS®

Contract for Sale of Residential Real Estate
This document has legal consequences. If you do not understand it, consult your attorney.

This Contract is made between _____ ("**Seller**") and
_____, ("**Buyer**"). The
"**Effective Contract Date**" shall be the date of final acceptance hereof, as indicated by the date adjacent to the signature of the last party to sign this Contract and the Counter Offer attached hereto (if any).

1. **PROPERTY TO BE CONVEYED.** In consideration of the mutual obligations being assumed by Seller and Buyer as set forth herein, Seller agrees to sell and convey to Buyer and Buyer agrees to purchase from Seller, upon and subject to the terms and conditions stated in this Contract, the following described real estate (legal description on Seller's title to govern):

_____ _____ _____ _____ _____
Street Address   City   State   Zip   County

2. **INCLUSIONS AND EXCLUSIONS.** *(Note: This Contract, and not the Seller's Disclosure Statement, the MLS, or other promotional material, provides for what is to be included in this sale. To avoid any misunderstanding, the parties are urged to list as "included" or "excluded" any items which may be subject to question.)*   The purchase price includes all existing improvements on the property and appurtenances, fixtures and equipment (**which Seller guarantees to own free and clear**) including but not limited to the following, if any:

- All Keys and Remote Entry Controls	- Trash Compactors	- Tacked Down & Wall to Wall Carpet
- Electric Garage Door Openers & Controls	- Garbage Disposals	- Attached Shelving & Closet Organizers
- Exterior Gas or Electric Lights	- Ovens/Ranges and Attachments	- Shades, Curtain & Drapery Hardware
- Landscaping and Mailbox	- Built-in Microwave Ovens	- Blinds, Shutters, Storm Windows, Sashes and Doors, Screens, Awnings
- Sprinkler Systems and Controls	- All Built-in Heating, Cooling, Electrical and Plumbing Equipment and Fixtures/Systems	- Burglar Alarms
- Fences (including invisible pet systems and controls)	- Radiator Shields	- Fire and Smoke Alarms
- Built-in Gas Fired Barbecue Grills	- All Window Air Conditioning Units	- Attached Fireplace Equipment and Doors (including gas logs)
- Attached TV Antennas (excluding satellite dishes)	- Ventilation and Exhaust Fans	- Central Vacuum Systems & Attachments
- All Lighting Fixtures	- Propane Tanks	- All manuals and written warranties pertaining to any of the foregoing
- Attic and Ceiling Fans	- Water Heaters	- Articles Now Provided for Tenant Use Only (as set forth below)
- Attached Mirrors & all Bathroom Mirrors	- Water Softeners and Sump Pump	
- Dishwashers	- Humidifier (if attached)	- Outbuildings, Silos, Crops (as set forth below)
	- Attached Floor Coverings	

The following items are also **included** in the sale: _____
_____

The following items are **excluded** from the sale: _____
_____

3. **PURCHASE PRICE.** The purchase price for said property shall be $_____, to be paid by Buyer as follows: $_____ as "**Earnest Money**" in the form of *(check one)* ☐personal check ☐cashier's check ☐other _____ at the time of the delivery of this Contract, the receipt of which is hereby acknowledged by Seller and which shall be deposited within _____ days *(ten (10) banking days if none stated)* after the Effective Contract Date with _____ ("**Escrow Agent**") in an escrow account. The Escrow Agent may retain any interest earned on such deposit. If sale is closed, Earnest Money to apply toward the purchase price. Upon delivery of the deed, Buyer shall pay the balance of the purchase price to Seller in cash, cashier's check or by other form of certified funds acceptable to Closing Agent.

4. **CLOSING.** This Contract will be closed (meaning the exchange of the deed for the purchase price) at the office of _____ ("**Closing Agent**") in _____, _____, on or before _____, 20__, or at such other place as the parties may mutually agree.
          City   State   Date

Possession and all keys will be delivered to Buyer at *(check one)* ☐ closing or ☐ other _____.

(Note: If possession is on a day other than day of closing or if the property is tenant occupied, then the parties should complete an appropriate Rider.)

5. **FINANCING.** *(Check applicable box)*

    ☐ **A. Not contingent upon financing.** Buyer reserves, however, the right to finance any portion of the purchase price.

    ☐ **B. Assumption.** See attached Rider.

    ☐ **C. Seller Financing.** See attached Rider.

    ☐ **D. Government Financing.** See attached Rider.

    ☐ **E. Conventional Financing.** Buyer agrees to apply for a loan, as described below, within _____ days *(7 days if none stated)* after the Effective Contract Date. If Buyer does not apply within that time for the loan described below, Buyer shall be deemed to have waived this financing contingency. Buyer agrees to do all things necessary, including but not limited to the execution of a loan application and other instruments, and to cooperate fully in order to obtain the financing necessary to complete this transaction. If Buyer does not provide written notice to Seller of Buyer's inability to obtain a loan commitment on the terms as described below by 5:00 p.m. on _____, 200_____, then this contingency shall be deemed to have been waived and this Contract shall thereafter not be contingent upon financing. If Buyer has complied with the terms of this paragraph and has timely provided written notice to Seller of Buyer's inability to obtain the loan commitment, this Contract shall be terminated with Earnest Money to be returned to Buyer.

Loan amount: _____% of the purchase price or $ _____.

Initial interest rate: _____%. Amortization term _____ years.

Type *(check one)*: ☐ Fixed Rate ☐ Adjustable Rate ☐ Other: _____

Other terms: _____

6. **TITLE AND SURVEY.** Seller shall transfer marketable title to Buyer by general warranty deed, subject to the following: (a) Zoning regulations; (b) Leases and other occupancy of tenants existing on the date Contract is executed by Buyer, and disclosed to Buyer in writing before execution of Contract by Buyer; (c) General taxes payable in the current year and thereafter; (d) Any lien or encumbrance created by or assumed by Buyer in writing and any easement accepted by Buyer in writing; (e) Subdivision, use and other restrictions, rights of way and utility easements, all of record.

If Buyer disapproves of the zoning, subdivision, use or other restrictions, rights of way or utility easements, or any other document or encumbrance whatsoever of record, then Buyer shall have _____ days *(10 days if none stated)* after the Effective Contract Date to terminate this Contract by delivering written notice to Seller, in which case the Earnest Money is to be returned to Buyer.

Within *(check one)* ☐ 5 days or ☐ _____ days after the Effective Contract Date *(check applicable box below)*:

    ☐ **A.** Seller shall deliver to Buyer, at Seller's cost, a commitment to issue, at Seller's cost, an owner's policy of title insurance.

    ☐ **B.** Seller shall deliver to Buyer an abstract of title to the property certified to date, at Seller's cost, by a competent abstracter.

    ☐ **C.** Seller shall deliver to Buyer, at Seller's cost, a commitment to issue, at Buyer's cost, an Owner's policy of title insurance.

    ☐ **D.** Buyer shall deliver a copy of the executed Contract to a company authorized to issue title insurance with an order to issue, at Buyer's cost, a commitment for an owner's policy of title insurance (also at Buyer's cost).

Buyer may, at Buyer's expense, obtain a Boundary and Improvement Survey ("**stake survey**") of the property to determine if there are any defects, encroachments, overlaps, boundary line or acreage discrepancies, or other matters that may be disclosed by a stake survey. Buyer acknowledges that a Surveyor's Real Property Report ("**spot survey**"), is the minimum report usually required by a lender, is not a "stake" survey and may not disclose all defects. A title insurance company may require a "stake" survey in order to provide full survey coverage to Buyer.

Buyer shall have _____ days *(10 days if none is stated)* after receipt of commitment (or abstract) to state to Seller in writing any title or survey defects that (1) are not listed in lines 55-58 above; (2) cause a failure of marketable title; and (3) are unacceptable to Buyer. "Marketable title" shall have the meaning contained in Title Standard 4 of the Title Examination Standards of The Missouri Bar. It is also agreed that if the title insurance commitment (or abstract) discloses any encumbrance or defect which is within the scope of any of the Title Standards of The Missouri Bar, then such encumbrance or defect will not constitute a valid objection by Buyer if Seller furnishes the affidavits or other documentation described in the applicable Title Standard to remove said encumbrance or defect. It is further agreed that any existing lien(s) may be paid out of the purchase price proceeds. Failure by Seller to receive such objections to title or survey within such time will constitute a waiver by Buyer of any such objections. If Buyer does timely object, Seller has five (5) days from receipt of Buyer's notice of objection(s) to agree in writing to correct defects prior to closing at Seller's expense. If Seller does not so agree, then this Contract shall automatically terminate unless Buyer, within two (2) additional days, agrees in writing to accept the title "as is." If the Contract is terminated under this subparagraph, then the Earnest Money is to be refunded to Buyer, and Seller shall be liable for survey and title examination charges. Seller shall be liable for clearing any defects that arise between the Effective Contract Date and closing. Unless otherwise provided in this Contract, the owner's title policy will include mechanic's lien and inflation coverage. Buyer is responsible for the cost of any lender's policy of title insurance to be issued.

7. **INSPECTIONS, DISCLAIMERS AND WARRANTIES.** Buyer may, at Buyer's option and expense, obtain written inspection reports from any independent qualified inspector(s) of the property and improvements as deemed necessary by Buyer, including, but not limited to, environmental hazards; stachybotrys mold; termite and wood-destroying insect infestation and damage; plumbing, including water well, sewer, septic and waste-water treatment systems; roof and other structural improvements; heating and air conditioning systems and equipment; electrical systems and equipment; swimming pools and equipment; chimneys, flues and gas lines; basement leaks and exterior drainage; mechanical equipment, including appliances; school district; and square footage. Buyer

shall furnish a complete copy of the written inspection report(s) to Seller with a written list of unacceptable condition(s) within _____ days (*10 days if none stated*) after the Effective Contract Date (the "**Inspection Period**"). (*For zoning, subdivision, use and other restrictions see Section 6.*)

If Seller has not received written notice of the results of any inspection by the end of the Inspection Period, Buyer shall be deemed to be satisfied with the results of such inspection(s). Failure to obtain any inspection shall constitute a waiver by Buyer and acceptance of any condition the inspection may have disclosed. If timely inspection notice is given, it shall state whether (1) Buyer is satisfied with all the inspections; (2) Buyer intends that any unacceptable conditions are to be satisfied by Seller; or (3) Buyer is terminating the Contract with Earnest Money to be returned to Buyer.

If this Contract is not terminated as provided above, Seller shall have _ days (*7 days if none stated*) (the "**Initial Response Period**") to respond in writing to Buyer's requests for repairs. The parties shall have an additional _____ days (*3 days if none stated*) after the end of the Initial Response Period to reach an agreement in writing as to who will complete and pay for the correction of the defects, or as to a monetary adjustment at closing in lieu of correction of the defects, or the Contract is to be deemed to be automatically terminated and the Earnest Money shall be returned to Buyer; provided, however, that either a written commitment by Seller to correct those items submitted by Buyer for correction during the Inspection Period at Seller's expense, or a written commitment by Buyer to accept the property without correction of unacceptable conditions, shall constitute an "agreement" for purposes of this subparagraph, even after earlier negotiation failed to produce an agreement. *(Note: A monetary adjustment may affect the terms of Buyer's loan, e.g., down payment, interest rate and private mortgage insurance, and may also affect Buyer's ability to obtain an occupancy permit, where applicable).*

The parties acknowledge that neither Selling Broker or licensees, nor Listing Broker or licensees, have any responsibility and make no warranties, guarantees or representations, express or implied, as to any matters regarding the property, including but not limited to: (1) the working order of any components of the property; (2) the condition or repairs of any of the buildings or improvements situated upon the property; (3) the title of said property; (4) any discrepancies that a survey may reveal; (5) the tax consequences of the sale; or (6) whether high risk or serious sex offenders or other convicted criminals may reside in the area (*contact local law enforcement officials for information pertaining to item 6*). The parties understand that the real estate licensee(s) may be present during inspections; however, such presence shall only serve to assist in the coordination of and compliance with the terms of this Contract and shall not in any way be interpreted as providing the licensee(s) with a special knowledge or understanding of the inspection results. Therefore, the parties hereby acknowledge that they will rely only upon the written inspection results received directly from the appropriate expert(s).

Buyer acknowledges: (1) that neither Selling Broker or licensees, nor Listing Broker or licensees, have any expertise or responsibility in determining any defects that may be disclosed by any inspections, warranties, or services; (2) that Buyer will not rely upon Selling Broker or licensees, nor Listing Broker or licensees, in any way as to the selection of a particular company for any inspections, warranties and services; (3) that any inspections, warranties and services may be offered by more than one company and that the determination to select a particular company and the completeness and satisfaction of any said inspection, warranty or service is the sole responsibility of Buyer; and (4) that when choosing an inspector, warranty, service company, title company, lender, repair company or any other service provider, Buyer should consider, but not be limited by, the existence of errors and omissions insurance, liability insurance, business and professional licensure membership in professional associations and years of experience.

8. EARNEST MONEY. In the event of a dispute over any Earnest Money being held by Escrow Agent, the parties agree that Escrow Agent shall continue to hold said Earnest Money in its escrow account until Escrow Agent has a written release from all parties consenting to its disposition or until a civil action is filed to determine its disposition, at which time payment of the Earnest Money may be made into the court less any attorney fees, court costs and other legal expenses incurred by Escrow Agent in connection with such dispute. If Escrow Agent initiates an interpleader action, its attorney's fees, court costs and other legal expenses incurred by Escrow Agent shall likewise be deducted from the Earnest Money at the time of filing the interpleader. In any reference in this Contract (including any Rider(s) attached hereto) to the return of the Earnest Money to Buyer, Buyer agrees that (1) any expenses incurred by or on behalf of Buyer may be withheld by the Escrow Agent and paid to the service provider to whom expenses were incurred; and (2) the abstract, if any, shall be returned to Seller. *(Note: An escrow agent who is not a licensed real estate broker or salesperson is not bound by the Missouri statutes and regulations which apply to earnest money deposits. If the Escrow Agent is not a licensed broker or salesperson, then the parties are urged to have the Escrow Agent agree in writing to be bound by the provisions of this Contract before being named as the escrow agent.)*

9. LOSS. Risk of loss to the improvements on the property shall be borne by Seller until title is transferred. If any improvements covered by this Contract are damaged or destroyed, Seller shall immediately notify Buyer in writing of the damage or destruction, the amount of insurance proceeds payable, if any, and whether Seller intends, prior to closing, to restore the property to its condition at the time of the Effective Contract Date. If Seller restores the property to its prior condition before scheduled closing, Buyer and Seller shall proceed with closing. If the property is not to be restored to its prior condition by the Seller before closing, Buyer may either (1) proceed with the transaction and be entitled to all insurance money, if any, payable to Seller under all policies insuring the improvements, or (2) rescind the Contract, and thereby release all parties from further liability hereunder, in which case the Earnest Money shall be returned to Buyer. Buyer shall give written notice of Buyer's election to Seller within ten (10) days after Buyer has received written notice of such damage or destruction and the amount of insurance proceeds payable, and closing will be extended accordingly, if required. Failure by Buyer to so notify Seller shall constitute an election to rescind this Contract. A rescission hereunder does not constitute a default by Seller. If Buyer accepts the insurance proceeds and closes this Contract and Seller has agreed to finance a part of the purchase price, then Buyer must use the insurance proceeds to restore the improvements, or Seller, at Seller's election, can terminate this Contract.

10. TIME IS OF THE ESSENCE. Time is of the essence in the performance of the obligations of the parties. All references to a specified time shall mean Central Time.

11. ADJUSTMENTS AND CLOSING COSTS. Adjustments, charges, and closing costs are agreed to be paid by the parties as of the date of closing (subject to current FHA and VA regulations and except as may otherwise be expressly set forth herein or in any Rider hereto) as follows:

Buyer shall pay for (where applicable):
- hazard insurance premium(s);
- flood insurance premium if required by lender;
- survey, subject to paragraph 6;
- title company charges (including closing, recording and escrow fees) customarily paid by Buyer, subject to paragraph 6;
- any charges imposed by lender, for example: appraisal and credit report fees, loan discount (points), loan origination fees, funding fees and other loan expenses, unless specifically agreed to be paid by Seller;
- building, termite, environmental and any other inspections ordered by Buyer;
- special taxes, special subdivision, home owners association and/or condominium assessments levied after closing;
- the value of any propane gas left in the propane tank (if any) at the property (based on fair market value according to current charges of supplier); and
- agreed upon repairs.

Seller shall pay for (where applicable):
- existing loans on property (if not assumed by Buyer);
- any expenses of Buyer's loan agreed to by Seller in paragraph 5, if any;
- title company charges (including closing, releasing and escrow fees) customarily paid by Seller, subject to paragraph 6;
- any required municipal, conservation district and fire district inspection fees, if any;
- special taxes, special subdivision, home owners association and/or condominium assessments levied before closing;
- real estate commission to listing broker per agreement; Seller authorizes selling portion of commission to be paid directly to selling broker; and
- agreed upon repairs.

Buyer and Seller shall have prorated and adjusted between them on the basis of thirty (30) days to the month as of the date of closing (Seller to pay for last day):
- current rents (Seller to receive rent for day of closing). Rents which are delinquent over thirty (30) days to be collected by Seller and not adjusted. All security deposits and advance rents (if any) will be paid by Seller to Buyer at closing;
- general taxes (based on assessment and rate for current year, if both are available; otherwise based on previous year);
- subdivision upkeep assessments and monthly condominium fee;
- interest (when Buyer assumes existing loan);
- flat rate utility charges (including water, sewer and trash); and
- boat dock fees.

12. FRANCHISE DISCLOSURE. Although one or more of the Brokers participating in this transaction may be a member of a franchise, the franchise is not responsible for the acts of said Broker(s).

13. ASSIGNABILITY. This Contract is assignable by Buyer, but not without the written consent of Seller if **(a)** Seller is taking back a note and deed of trust as part of the purchase price, or **(b)** Buyer is assuming the existing note. Assignment does not relieve the parties from their obligations under this Contract.

14. BINDING EFFECT. This Contract shall be binding on and for the benefit of the parties and their respective heirs, personal representatives, executors, administrators, successors and assigns.

15. GOVERNING LAW. This Contract shall be considered a contract for the sale of real property and shall be construed in accordance with the laws of the State of _____ (*Missouri, if not otherwise stated*), including the requirement to act in good faith.

16. ENTIRE AGREEMENT. This Contract and the Rider(s) attached hereto (if any) constitute the entire agreement between the parties hereto. There are no other understandings, written or oral, relating to the subject matter hereof. This Contract may not be changed, modified or amended, in whole or in part, except in writing signed by all parties.

17. SALES INFORMATION. Permission is hereby granted by Seller and Buyer for the involved Broker(s) to provide sales information of this transaction, including purchase price and property address, to any multi-listing service, local Association or Board of REALTORS®, its members, member's prospects, appraisers and other professional users of real estate data. Permission is also hereby specifically granted by Seller and Buyer for the involved Broker(s) to obtain and retain copies of both Buyer's and Seller's closing statements as required by 4 CSR 250-8.150.

18. REMEDIES UPON DEFAULT. If either party defaults in the performance of any obligation of this Contract, the party claiming a default shall notify the other party in writing of the nature of the default and the party's election of remedy. The notifying party may, but is not required to, provide the defaulting party with a deadline for curing the default.

If the default is by Buyer, Seller may either accept the Earnest Money as liquidated damages (it being agreed that Seller's actual damages would be difficult, if not impossible, to ascertain and that the Earnest Money represents the parties' best estimate as to what the amount of said actual damages might reasonably be) and release Buyer from this Contract (in lieu of making any claim in court), or pursue any remedy at law or in equity.

If the default is by Seller, Buyer may either release Seller from liability upon Seller's release of the Earnest Money and reimbursement to Buyer for all direct costs and expenses, as specified in Buyer's notice of default (in lieu of making any claim in court), or may pursue any remedy at law and in equity, including enforcement of sale. Buyer's release of Seller does not relieve Seller of his liability to brokers under the Seller's listing contract.

In the event of litigation between the parties, the prevailing party shall be entitled to recover, in addition to damages or equitable relief, the cost of litigation including reasonable attorney's fees. This provision shall survive closing.

19. SELLER'S DISCLOSURE STATEMENT. *(check one)*

☐ **A.** Buyer confirms that before signing this offer to purchase, Buyer has read a copy of the Seller's Disclosure Statement for this property. The Seller's Disclosure Statement is not a substitute for any inspection that Buyer may wish to obtain, and Buyer is advised to address any concerns Buyer may have about information in the Seller's Disclosure Statement by use of contingencies in this Contract. Buyer has reviewed and signed the Seller's Disclosure Statement.

☐ **B.** Seller agrees to provide Buyer with a Seller's Disclosure Statement within one (1) calendar day after the Effective Contract Date. Buyer shall have three (3) calendar days after the Effective Contract Date to review and sign said disclosure and elect to declare in a writing delivered to Seller that this Contract is terminated, in which case the Earnest Money shall be returned to Buyer. Otherwise, this contingency shall be deemed to have been waived by Buyer.

☐ **C.** No Seller's Disclosure Statement will be provided by Seller.

Seller confirms that the information in the Seller's Disclosure Statement is accurate as of the Effective Contract Date. Seller will fully and promptly disclose in writing to Buyer any new information pertaining to the property that is discovered at any time prior to closing.

NOTE: The Seller's Disclosure Statement is not in any way incorporated into the terms of this Contract.

20. LEAD-BASED PAINT DISCLOSURE. Buyer has reviewed and signed, if required by law, the Disclosure of Information of Lead-Based Paint and/or Lead-Based Paint Hazards form.

21. ACCESS AND FINAL WALK-THROUGH. Seller agrees to permit inspections of the property by building inspectors, contractors, termite inspectors, engineers and appraisers selected by Buyer as provided for in the Contract, and/or inspections required by Buyer's lender, upon reasonable advance notice to Seller. Listing Broker and Selling Broker may each also be present during all inspections and the "walk through."

Seller also grants Buyer and any inspector whose report prompted a request for repairs the right to enter and "walk through" the property and the right to have the utilities transferred to Buyer within four (4) days prior to closing. This right is not for the purpose of conducting a new building inspection, but only for the Buyer to confirm (1) that the property is in the same general condition as it was on the Effective Contract Date, and (2) that repairs agreed upon (if any) are completed in a workmanlike manner. Seller will arrange, at Seller's expense, to have all utilities turned on during the Inspection Period and during this "walk-through", unless utilities have been transferred to Buyer. Waiver of property and improvement inspections does not waive the right to a "walk through" prior to closing. The closing does not relieve Seller of Seller's obligation to complete improvements and repairs required by this Contract.

22. LIMITED WARRANTY OR SERVICE AGREEMENT. Seller and Buyer acknowledge that a limited warranty or service agreement may be available for purchase regarding the above-described property.

23. FACSIMILE SIGNATURES. "Facsimile signatures," as that term is commonly used with reference to facsimile machines used in transmitting documents, signatures, photocopies, etc., will be and hereby are declared by all parties to this Contract to be the same as an original signature to this Contract. A facsimile of this Contract, including the signature portion thereof, will be treated and relied upon by all parties hereto as an authentic signature with the same legal effect as though the facsimile were an original document to which a genuine signature has been affixed.

24. CONSTRUCTION. The terms "Seller" and "Buyer" may be either singular or plural masculine, feminine or neuter gender, according to whichever is evidenced by the signatures below. Paragraph captions in this Contract are intended solely for convenience of reference and will not be deemed to modify, place any restriction upon, or explain any provisions of this Contract. If any one or more provisions contained in this Contract shall for any reason be held to be invalid, illegal or unenforceable in any respect, then such invalidity, illegality or unenforceability shall not be deemed to terminate this Contract or to affect any other provision hereof, but rather this Contract shall, to the fullest extent permitted by law, remain in full force and effect and be construed as if such invalid, illegal or unenforceable provision(s) had never been contained herein; provided, however, that such provision(s) may be referred to in order to determine the intent of the parties.

25. NOTICES For purposes of this Contract, any notice to be delivered to Seller shall be deemed to have been delivered to Seller upon delivery thereof to the Broker (or any of its affiliated licensees or "salespersons") working for Seller as a limited agent pursuant to a listing contract, or upon delivery to the designated agent (if any) acting on behalf of Seller, or to a dual agent. Likewise, any notice to be delivered to Buyer shall be deemed to have been delivered to Buyer upon delivery thereof to the Broker (or any of its affiliated licensees or "salespersons") working for Buyer as a limited agent pursuant to a buyers agency agreement, or upon delivery to the designated agent (if any) acting on behalf of Buyer, or to a dual agent. No notice delivered to a transaction broker shall be deemed to constitute delivery of such notice to the Buyer or Seller (as the case may be) unless and until such notice is delivered to such party.

26. RIDERS. The following Riders are attached hereto and incorporated herein as part of this Contract:

☐ Financing Agreements (Form RES-2010)   ☐ Arbitration (Form RES-2030)

☐ Contract Contingencies (Form RES-2020)   ☐ Other _____

27. PRINCIPAL(S) INVOLVED. *(check one, none or both, if and as may be applicable)*

☐ Seller   ☐ Buyer is a licensed real estate broker or salesperson and is a principal party in this transaction.

28. COMPENSATION.   Any real estate commission or other compensation due Brokers will be paid by _____ no later than closing. The parties authorize the selling portion of the commission (*if any*) to be paid by Listing Broker directly to Selling Broker.

29. BROKERAGE RELATIONSHIP DISCLOSURE. Buyer and Seller confirm that they have received and read the Broker Disclosure Form prescribed by the Missouri Real Estate Commission and that disclosure of the licensee's relationship, as required by law or regulation, was made to the Seller and Buyer or their respective agents, by said agents and/or any transaction broker, no later than the first showing of the property, upon first contact, or immediately upon the occurrence of any change to the relationship.

Licensee assisting Seller is a: *(Check appropriate box)*

☐ **Buyer's Limited Agent:** Licensee is acting on behalf of the Buyer.

☐ **Seller's Limited Agent:** Licensee is acting on behalf of the Seller.

☐ **Dual Agent:** Licensee is acting on behalf of both Seller and Buyer.

☐ **Designated Agent:** Licensee has been designated to act on behalf of the Seller.

☐ **Transaction Broker Assisting Seller:** Licensee is not acting on behalf of either Seller or Buyer.

Licensee assisting Buyer is a: *(Check appropriate box)*

☐ **Buyer's Limited Agent:** Licensee is acting on behalf of the Buyer.

☐ **Seller's Limited Agent:** Licensee is acting on behalf of Seller.

☐ **Dual Agent:** Licensee is acting on behalf of both Buyer and Seller.

☐ **Designated Agent:** Licensee has been designated to act on behalf of the Buyer.

☐ **Transaction Broker Assisting Buyer:** Licensee is not acting on behalf of either Buyer or Seller.

☐ **Subagent of Seller:** Licensee is acting on behalf of Seller

By signing below, the licensees confirm making timely disclosure of the brokerage relationship to the appropriate parties.

_____   _____
Selling Broker's Firm   **Listing Broker's Firm**

By (*Signature*)_____   By (*Signature*)_____

Licensee's Printed Name: _____   Licensee's Printed Name:_____

Date _____   Date_____

Offer to automatically expire at: _____ o'clock ___. m. on _____, 200___, if not accepted by Seller or withdrawn by Buyer before then.

_____   _____
BUYER   **DATE**   **SELLER**   **DATE and TIME**

_____   _____
BUYER   **DATE**   **SELLER**   **DATE and TIME**

By signing above, Seller indicates that Seller has accepted this Contract.

Seller (*check one*)   ☐ rejects   ☐ counter offers (Counter Offer form RES-2040, which amends the terms of this Contract, is attached and incorporated into this Contract).

1. *The Condition of the Land and Improvements*

The buyer typically goes into a transaction expecting the land and improvements will be in a certain condition or in compliance with certain legal standards such as environmental laws or building codes. If the land and improvements turn out not to be in compliance, the buyer's expectations may be profoundly frustrated. How is the law to deal with this frustration, and how should attorneys advising the parties best negotiate and document the transaction to avoid such frustrated expectations?

Recall from Chapter 7 that in residential transactions, landlord-tenant law has shifted from the traditional *caveat lessee* rule toward the more modern position that the landlord has a duty to maintain the premises in a certain physical condition. Likewise, the law governing sales of land has experienced a similar (although not identical) reform movement. Traditionally, in disputes concerning the physical condition of land under a sale contract, the common law applied the *caveat emptor* rule—the seller of land was not liable for defective conditions, except in cases where the seller made an express warranty that the premises were free of defects or the seller committed fraud by *affirmatively misrepresenting* the condition of the premises. Similarly, in the absence of an express warranty, builders of structures generally possessed no contractual liability for defects in the construction of the premises. In recent years, however, some courts have re-analyzed the *caveat emptor* doctrine and, to some extent, have rejected it in the context of residential real estate purchase and sale transactions. Does this reform seem appropriate, or are there reasons to treat real estate sales differently from leases?

JOHNSON v. DAVIS

Supreme Court of Florida.
480 So.2d 625 (1985).

ADKINS, JUSTICE.... In May of 1982, the Davises entered into a contract to buy for $310,000 the Johnsons' home, which at the time was three years old. The contract required a $5,000 deposit payment, an additional $26,000 deposit payment within five days and a closing by June 21, 1982. The crucial provision of the contract, for the purposes of the case at bar, is Paragraph F which provided:

> F. Roof Inspection: Prior to closing at Buyer's expense, Buyer shall have the right to obtain a written report from a licensed roofer stating that the roof is in a watertight condition. In the event repairs are required either to correct leaks or to replace damage to facia or soffit, seller shall pay for said repairs which shall be performed by a licensed roofing contractor.

The contract further provided for payment to the "prevailing party" of all costs and reasonable fees in any contract litigation.

Before the Davises made the additional $26,000 deposit payment, Mrs. Davis noticed some buckling and peeling plaster around the corner of a window frame in the family room and stains on the ceilings in the family room and kitchen of the home. Upon inquiring, Mrs. Davis was told by Mr. Johnson that the window had had a minor problem that had long since been corrected and that the stains were wallpaper glue and the result of ceiling beams being moved. There is disagreement among the parties as to whether Mr. Johnson also told Mrs. Davis at this time that there had never been any problems with the roof or ceilings. The Davises thereafter paid the remainder of their deposit and the Johnsons vacated the home. Several days later, following a heavy rain, Mrs. Davis entered the home and discovered water "gushing" in from around the window frame, the ceiling of the family room, the light fixtures, the glass doors, and the stove in the kitchen. Two roofers hired by the Johnsons' broker concluded that for under $1,000 they could "fix" certain leaks in the roof and by doing so make the roof "watertight." Three roofers hired by the Davises found that the roof was inherently defective, that any repairs would be temporary because the roof was "slipping," and that only a new $15,000 roof could be "watertight."

The Davises filed a complaint alleging breach of contract, fraud and misrepresentation, and sought rescission of the contract and return of their deposit. The Johnsons counterclaimed seeking the deposit as liquidated damages.

The trial court entered its final judgment on May 27, 1983. The court made no findings of fact, but awarded the Davises $26,000 plus interest and awarded the Johnsons $5,000 plus interest. Each party was to bear their own attorneys' fees.

The Johnsons appealed and the Davises cross-appealed from the final judgment. The Third District found for the Davises affirming the trial court's return of the majority of the deposit to the Davises ($26,000), and reversing the award of $5,000 to the Johnsons as well as the court's failure to award the Davises costs and fees. Accordingly, the court remanded with directions to return to the Davises the balance of their deposit and to award them costs and fees. . . .

We . . . agree with the district court's conclusions under a theory of fraud and find that the Johnsons' statements to the Davises regarding the condition of the roof constituted a fraudulent misrepresentation entitling respondents to the return of their $26,000 deposit payment. In the state of Florida, relief for a fraudulent misrepresentation may be granted only when the following elements are present: (1) a false statement concerning a material fact; (2) the representor's knowledge that the representation is false; (3) an intention that the representation induce another to act on it; and, (4) consequent injury by the party acting in reliance on the representation. *See Huffstetler v. Our Home Life Ins. Co.*, 67 Fla. 324 (1914).

The evidence adduced at trial shows that after the buyer and the seller signed the purchase and sales agreement and after receiving the $5,000 initial deposit payment the Johnsons affirmatively repeated to the Davises that there were no problems with the roof. The Johnsons subsequently received the additional $26,000 deposit payment from the Davises. The record reflects that the statement made by the Johnsons was a false representation of material fact, made with knowledge of its falsity, upon which the Davises relied to their detriment as evidenced by the $26,000 paid to the Johnsons.

The doctrine of caveat emptor does not exempt a seller from responsibility for the statements and representations which he makes to induce the buyer to act, when under the circumstances these amount to fraud in the legal sense. To be grounds for relief, the false representations need not have been made at the time of the signing of the purchase and sales agreement in order for the element of reliance to be present. The fact that the false statements as to the quality of the roof were made after the signing of the purchase and sales agreement does not excuse the seller from liability when the misrepresentations were made prior to the execution of the contract by conveyance of the property. It would be contrary to all notions of fairness and justice for this Court to place its stamp of approval on an affirmative misrepresentation by a wrongdoer just because it was made after the signing of the executory contract when all of the necessary elements for actionable fraud are present. Furthermore, the Davises' reliance on the truth of the Johnsons' representation was justified and is supported by this Court's decision in *Besett v. Basnett*, 389 So.2d 995 (1980), where we held "that a recipient may rely on the truth of a representation, even though its falsity could have been ascertained had he made an investigation, unless he knows the representation to be false or its falsity is obvious to him." *Id.* at 998.

In determining whether a seller of a home has a duty to disclose latent material defects to a buyer, the established tort law distinction between misfeasance and nonfeasance, action and inaction must carefully be analyzed. The highly individualistic philosophy of the earlier common law consistently imposed liability upon the commission of affirmative acts of harm, but shrank from converting the courts into an institution for forcing men to help one another. This distinction is deeply rooted in our case law. Liability for nonfeasance has therefore been slow to receive recognition in the evolution of tort law.

In theory, the difference between misfeasance and nonfeasance, action and inaction is quite simple and obvious; however, in practice it is not always easy to draw the line and determine whether conduct is active or passive. That is, where failure to disclose a material fact is calculated to induce a false belief, the distinction between concealment and affirmative representations is tenuous. Both proceed from the same motives and are attended with the same consequences; both are violative of the principles of fair dealing and good faith; both are calculated to produce the same result; . . . both essentially have the same effect.

Still there exists in much of our case law the old tort notion that there can be no liability for nonfeasance. The courts in some jurisdictions, including Florida, hold that where the parties are dealing at arms's length and the facts lie equally open to both parties, with equal opportunity of examination, mere nondisclosure does not constitute a fraudulent concealment. *See Ramel v. Chasebrook Construction Co.*, 135 So.2d 876 (Fla. 2d DCA 1961). The Fourth District affirmed that rule of law in *Banks v. Salina*, 413 So.2d 851 (Fla. 4th DCA 1982), and found that although the sellers had sold a home without disclosing the presence of a defective roof and swimming pool of which the sellers had knowledge, "[i]n Florida, there is no duty to disclose when parties are dealing at arms length." *Id.* at 852.

These unappetizing cases are not in tune with the times and do not conform with current notions of justice, equity and fair dealing. One should not be able to stand behind the impervious shield of caveat emptor and take advantage of another's ignorance. Our courts have taken great strides since the days when the judicial emphasis was on rigid rules and ancient precedents. Modern concepts of justice and fair dealing have given our courts the opportunity and latitude to change legal precepts in order to conform to society's needs. Thus, the tendency of the more recent cases has been to restrict rather than extend the doctrine of caveat emptor. The law appears to be working toward the ultimate conclusion that full disclosure of all material facts must be made whenever elementary fair conduct demands it.

The harness placed on the doctrine of caveat emptor in a number of other jurisdictions has resulted in the seller of a home being liable for failing to disclose material defects of which he is aware. This philosophy was succinctly expressed in *Lingsch v. Savage*, 213 Cal.App.2d 729, 29 Cal.Rptr. 201 (1963):

> It is now settled in California that where the seller knows of facts materially affecting the value or desirability of the property which are known or accessible only to him and also knows that such facts are not known to or within the reach of the diligent attention and observation of the buyer, the seller is under a duty to disclose them to the buyer.

In *Posner v. Davis*, 76 Ill.App.3d 638, 32 Ill.Dec. 186, 395 N.E.2d 133 (1979), buyers brought an action alleging that the sellers of a home fraudulently concealed certain defects in the home which included a leaking roof and basement flooding. Relying on *Lingsch*, the court concluded that the sellers knew of and failed to disclose latent material defects and thus were liable for fraudulent concealment. *Id.* 32 Ill.Dec. at 190, 395 N.E.2d at 137. Numerous other jurisdictions have followed this view in formulating law involving the sale of homes.

We are of the opinion, in view of the reasoning and results in *Lingsch, Posner* and the aforementioned cases decided in other jurisdictions, that the same philosophy regarding the sale of homes should also be the law in the state of Florida. Accordingly, we hold that where the seller of a home knows of facts materially affecting the value of the property which are not readily observable and are not known to the buyer, the seller is under a duty to disclose them to the buyer. This duty is equally applicable to all forms of real property, new and used.

In the case at bar, the evidence shows that the Johnsons knew of and failed to disclose that there had been problems with the roof of the house. Mr. Johnson admitted during his testimony that the Johnsons were aware of roof problems prior to entering into the contract of sale and receiving the $5,000 deposit payment. Thus, we agree with the district court and find that the Johnsons' fraudulent concealment also entitles the Davises to the return of the $5,000 deposit payment plus interest. . . .

Notes

1. *The Rationale for Requiring Disclosure.* At first blush, one might conclude that the problem in *Johnson* is that the Johnsons lied about the leaking roof when the Davises inquired about it before making the second $26,000 deposit specified in the contract. But by that point, the Davises had already signed the contract—and there was no evidence that the Davises had asked (or been lied to) about the roof before signing the contract. Thus, the real problem is whether the Johnsons should have disclosed the leaking roof prior to the signing of the contract. As a policy matter, why should the law adopt this duty of disclosure?

2. *The Judicial Parameters of the Seller's Duty to Disclose.* The overwhelming majority of states has adopted—either by judicial decree or legislative action—some variant of the seller's duty to disclose "material" facts that are known to the seller but that are not "readily observable" by the buyer. Katherine A. Pancak, Thomas J. Miceli, & C.F. Sirmans, *Residential Disclosure Laws: The Further Demise of Caveat Emptor,* 24 Real Est. L.J. 291 (1996). Today, most litigation of these disputes does not involve whether the seller should have a duty to disclose defects generally, but instead whether a particular defect is "material" and "not readily observable" to the buyer (so that it must be disclosed). Consider the following problems, and assume that in each case, Buyer has sued Seller to rescind the contract and obtain restitution of the purchase price:

(a) Seller did not disclose to Buyer that the previous owner committed suicide in the home. Is this information "material"? *See, e.g., Reed v. King,* 145 Cal.App.3d 261, 193 Cal.Rptr. 130 (1983) (seller required to disclose that home was site of murder 10 years earlier); *Stambovsky v. Ackley,* 169 A.D.2d 254, 572 N.Y.S.2d 672 (1991) (seller required to disclose that house was reputed to be possessed by poltergeists).

(b) Seller did not disclose to Buyer that the home was the scene of a violent rape, although Seller was aware that Buyer has teenaged daughters. Is this information material? *See Van Camp v. Bradford,* 63 Ohio Misc.2d 245, 623 N.E.2d 731 (Com. Pl. 1993).

(c) Seller did not disclose to Buyer that the roof leaks following heavy rains. A professional contractor walking on the roof would have discovered that certain of the shingles had been installed improperly, creating an increased risk of leaks. Buyer did not physically get on the roof, and did not see the installation problem in viewing the roof from the ground. Is this defect "readily observable"? Should the law hold Buyer to a low threshold (think "Homer Simpson") and conclude that this defect was not readily observable? A higher standard (think "Bob Vila") and conclude that it was readily observable? Most courts have applied a "reasonable buyer" standard; would a reasonable buyer discover this defect? Why or why not? What other information would be useful to you in making this judgment?

(d) Seller did not disclose to Buyer that there is a landfill nearby that causes odor problems depending upon prevailing winds. Is this information "material"? Is it "readily observable"? Should Seller have a duty to disclose it? *Compare Hanlon v. Thornton*, 218 Ga.App. 500, 462 S.E.2d 154 (1995) *with Strawn v. Canuso*, 140 N.J. 43, 657 A.2d 420 (1995).

3. *Legislative Parameters of the Seller's Duty to Disclose.* In a number of states, statutes require that the seller provide written disclosure statements and mandate that the statements take a particular form. These forms vary depending upon the state. All of them require disclosure of information about known structural defects in any buildings. Many also require the disclosure of other known defects: soil or drainage problems; underground storage tanks; violations of zoning ordinances, building codes, or building permitting requirements. California's statutory form even requires disclosure of "neighborhood noise problems or other nuisances." For a complete list of statutory disclosure requirements, see Katherine A. Pancak, Thomas J. Miceli, & C.F. Sirmans, *supra* note 2, at 300–03.

In a few states, legislatures also have enacted statutes specifying that the seller *need not disclose* certain information about the land. For example, consider the following Missouri statute:

1. The fact that a parcel of real property, or any building or structure thereon, may be a psychologically impacted real property, or may be in close proximity to a psychologically impacted real property shall not be a material or substantial fact that is required to be disclosed in a sale, exchange or other transfer of real estate.

2. "Psychologically impacted real property" is defined to include:

(1) Real property in which an occupant is, or was at any time, infected with human immunodeficiency virus or diagnosed with acquired immune deficiency syndrome, or with any other disease which has been determined by medical evidence to be highly unlikely to be transmitted through the occupancy of a dwelling place; or

(2) Real property which was the site of a homicide or other felony, or of a suicide.

3. No cause of action shall arise nor may any action be brought against any real estate agent or broker for the failure to disclose to a buyer or other transferee of real estate that the transferred real property was a psychologically impacted real property. [Mo. Ann. Stat. § 442.600.]

What do you think is the purpose of this statute? Does it make sense for the legislature to enact a statute that deems a fact as not "material" if market experience tells us that many purchasers would consider it important? Why or why not?

4. *"As Is" and "Non-reliance" Clauses.* Some sellers have attempted to obtain the benefit of the caveat emptor rule by including "as is" clauses in the real estate contract, *e.g.*, "This property is being purchased 'as is' and neither seller nor agent or broker(s) makes or implies any warranties regarding the condition of the premises." Courts generally have declined to enforce "as is" clauses against a buyer's claim of fraud or misrepresentation; they are divided, however, as to whether such clauses preclude actions based upon mere nondisclosure of defects. *See* Florrie Young Roberts, *Let the Seller Beware: Disclosures, Disclaimers, and "As Is" Clauses,* 31 Real Est. L.J. 303 (Spring 2003).

Some legislatures have allowed sellers to opt out of statutory disclosure requirements through "as is" clauses and similar disclaimers. *See, e.g.* Va. Code Ann. § 55–519(A)(1). Did the Illinois legislature intend to permit such disclaimers under the following language in the Illinois Residential Real Property Disclosure Report?

Notice: The purpose of this report is to provide prospective buyers with information about material defects in the residential real property. This report does not limit the parties' right to contract for the sale of residential real property in "as is" condition....

The prospective buyer is aware that the parties may choose to negotiate an agreement for the sale of the property subject to any or all material defects disclosed in this report (as is). [765 Ill. Comp. Stat. § 77/35.]

See Bauer v. Giannis, 359 Ill.App.3d 897, 296 Ill.Dec. 147, 834 N.E.2d 952 (2005) ("We see nothing in the 'as is' provisions of the disclosure form that may be read as allowing a seller to contract out of its disclosure obligations.").

A close cousin to the "as is" clause is the "non-reliance" clause, which states that the buyer has not relied upon any representations by the seller. The effectiveness of a "non-reliance" clause depends upon its specificity. A general, or boilerplate, "non-reliance" clause will not preclude a fraud or misrepresentation claim; a "non-reliance" clause that identifies specific statements or matters, however, may effectively bar claims that relate to those statements or matters. *See Slack v. James*, 364 S.C. 609, 618, 614 S.E.2d 636, 641 (2005).

5. *The Use of "Inspection" Contingencies.* The buyer can obtain assurance about the physical condition of land and buildings by using an "inspection contingency," *i.e.*, by conditioning the buyer's obligation to complete the purchase upon the satisfactory completion of a physical inspection. The use of "contingencies" permits the buyer to protect itself against a variety of unknown facts and circumstances that might affect the buyer's willingness to complete the transaction.

Negotiating and drafting an effective contingency provision requires the drafter to appreciate the need for protection against both imprudent risks and opportunistic behavior by buyer or seller. Reconsider the language that the parties used in *Johnson v. Davis*, quoted on page 798. If you had been advising the Davises in the negotiation of that contract, what problems would you have brought to their attention concerning this language? How would you have recommended revising the language?

6. *The Implied Warranty of Quality/Fitness.* Buyers can avoid the *caveat emptor* principle by securing an express warranty from the seller that the property is free from defects. In the case of residential property, most states have gone even further, recognizing an *implied* warranty of quality or fitness for newly constructed homes. *See, e.g., Lane v. Trenholm Bldg. Co.*, 267 S.C. 497, 500, 229 S.E.2d 728, 729 (1976) (when a "new building is sold there is an implied warranty of fitness for its intended use which springs from the sale itself"). Courts have justified this departure from the *caveat emptor* principle on the theory that a buyer is incapable of making a proper inspection of the house before the building is complete and, even when the

home is completed, many buyers lack the expertise to evaluate the quality of the builder's performance; thus, the buyer must depend upon the skill and integrity of the builder-vendor. *See Petersen v. Hubschman Constr. Co.,* 76 Ill.2d 31, 27 Ill.Dec. 746, 389 N.E.2d 1154 (1979).

Cases recognizing an implied warranty of quality have adopted three different theoretical justifications for permitting the homebuyer to recover: implied warranty in contract, negligence in tort, and strict liability in tort. The theory propounded by the court will dictate the scope of the warranty, particularly with respect to the following questions:

(a) Is the claim available only to the initial purchaser (under a privity of contract theory) or also to a subsequent purchaser (under a tort theory)?

(b) Can a homebuyer waive the claim? (Is this more likely under a contract theory or a tort theory?)

(c) What type of damages can the buyer recover (*i.e.,* "economic" loss as compared to damage for personal injury)?

(d) What statute of limitations applies to the claim?

While a few courts have extended the implied warranty of quality to commercial buildings, *e.g., Hodgson v. Chin,* 168 N.J.Super. 549, 403 A.2d 942 (1979), most courts have refused to extend this warranty beyond the sale of new dwellings. *E.g., Dawson Indus., Inc. v. Godley Constr. Co.,* 29 N.C.App. 270, 224 S.E.2d 266 (1976). Do you think that the average business owner or landlord is better able to protect herself than the average home buyer?

LAWYERING EXERCISE
(Client Interviewing and Counseling)

SITUATION: Barbara was tired of city life. She wanted to move to a quiet country town and open a small bed and breakfast. She contacted a real estate agent, Dan, in the small town of Quayle Roost. Dan informed Barbara that a local resident, George, had just listed a moderately sized home for $140,000. Dan told Barbara: "The house would work for your purposes, I think, and it is a good bargain at that price. I think it is underpriced."

While showing the house to Barbara, George said: "This is a wonderful home. I hate to sell it, but my wife got a job in Los Angeles and we have to move away." He also said: "The property is in good shape, as far as I know, but you should get your own inspection done." Barbara looked around and didn't notice any problems. She contacted First Bank about obtaining a loan to purchase the property. First Bank was eager to loan her the money because it held George's mortgage and George was in default.

Barbara completed the purchase and began renovations. She went to visit a local decorator, Marilyn, about curtains. When Barbara gave Marilyn the address, Marilyn was shocked and said: "Didn't you know about that house?" Marilyn explained that both of George's sons had died within the past six months from AIDS. Marilyn said: "You'll have to find someone else. I won't go near the place, and none of the locals will, either."

A few days later, several pipes in the home began leaking. When Barbara investigated, she discovered that Bill, the contractor, had used substandard pipes. Within a few months, Barbara had leaks in nearly every pipe in the house.

Tired of all these problems, Barbara decided to sell the house. When she contacted another real estate agent, however, the agent expressed concern that no one would buy the house, even if the price was reduced below $100,000.

TASK: Barbara has come to your office. Barbara wants to know if she can sue George, First Bank, Dan, or Bill. Based on the cases and materials you have read regarding the condition of the property, how would you advise Barbara? What additional information do you need to obtain?

LAWYERING EXERCISE
(Document Review and Drafting)

SITUATION: Sam Seller has listed his two-story Victorian home with a local real estate agent. The house has been on the market for several months, which has caused some anxiety for Seller because he has recently built a new home and cannot juggle two mortgages for long. The real estate agent finally brought Seller an offer from a prospective buyer yesterday. The offer contains the following inspection provision:

10. *Property Disclosure and Inspection.* On or before [specified date], Seller agrees to provide Buyer with a Seller's Property Disclosure form completed by Seller to the best of Seller's current actual knowledge.

a.   Inspection Objection Deadline. Buyer shall have the right to have inspection(s) of the physical condition of the Property, at Buyer's expense. If the physical condition of the Property is unsatisfactory in Buyer's subjective discretion, Buyer shall, on or before [specified date]

  1.   notify Seller in writing that this contract is terminated, or

  2.   provide Seller with a written description of any unsatisfactory physical condition which Buyer requires Seller to correct (Notice to Correct).

  If written notice is not received by Seller on or before [specified date], the physical condition of the Property shall be deemed satisfactory to Buyer.

b.   Resolution Deadline. If a Notice to Correct is received by Seller and if Buyer and Seller have not agreed in writing to settlement thereof on or before [specified date], this contract shall terminate one calendar day following [such specified date], unless before such termination Seller has received Buyer's written withdrawal of the Notice to Correct.

TASK: Sam has asked you to review the inspection clause and revise it to better protect his interests. To help you analyze the provision, consider what would happen under the clause in the following scenarios:

(a) Buyer gives a timely Notice to Correct complaining that the Property is located in a school district that Buyer considers undesirable. What would be the effect of such notice?

(b) Buyer gives a timely Notice to Correct complaining of the age and degree of wear of the roof, all of which Seller had disclosed to Buyer prior to the contract (both orally and in the Seller's Property Disclosure form), and the color of trim paint used on the house. What would be the effect of such notice?

(c) What happens to the contract if Seller refuses to address these conditions? Must Seller return the Buyer's earnest money deposit if Buyer so demands? Is Seller liable for damages if Buyer seeks to enforce the contract?

(d) If there is no limit on the reasonableness of the Buyer's objections, can Seller argue that the contract was unenforceable because the Buyer's promises were illusory? Why or why not?

2.   *Remedies for Breach of Purchase and Sale Contract*

MAHONEY v. TINGLEY

Supreme Court of Washington, En Banc.
85 Wash.2d 95, 529 P.2d 1068 (1975).

BRACHTENBACH, JUSTICE. Plaintiff seeks against defendants damages arising out of the breach of an earnest money agreement, those damages being in excess of an amount stipulated in a liquidated damages clause.

The parties entered into an earnest money agreement in which the plaintiff agreed to sell residential property to the defendants. The price, originally fixed in the agreement at $21,500, was later reduced to $20,250 in order to conform to a Veterans Administration appraisal. Defendants deposited $50 as earnest money with the real estate broker and, subsequently, deposited $150 as additional earnest money. The agreement contained the following clause: "If title is so insurable and purchaser fails or refuses to complete purchase, the earnest money shall be forfeited as liquidated damages unless seller elects to enforce this agreement."

At defendants' request, the plaintiff moved from the premises, but the defendants did not move in. Instead, upon being notified that the transaction was ready for closing, the defendants indicated that they did not intend to complete the purchase. Defendants' attorney wrote to the plaintiff's realtor and stated that the defendants wished to cancel the agreement. Plaintiff's attorney responded that cancellation was not justified and demanded that defendants complete the transaction. Defendants did not respond to that letter, and the plaintiff sold the property to a third party for $19,000.

On the basis of the defendants' breach, plaintiff sued, alleging damages totaling $3,141.44. The defendants answered the complaint with a general denial and prayed for dismissal of the suit. On the day set for trial, the trial judge met with counsel in chambers. During that conference, the trial judge determined that the case turned upon the effect to be given the liquidated damages clause. Accordingly, the judge decided to treat the matter as one in which summary judgment was appropriate. After hearing argument relating to the liquidated damages clause, the court ruled that plaintiff was entitled only to the stipulated amount and entered an order for summary judgment in favor of defendants.

The Court of Appeals reversed the summary judgment. . . .

The liquidated damages clause at issue here provided an option to the plaintiff once there was failure or refusal by defendants to complete the purchase. Plaintiff could elect to sue for specific performance of the earnest money agreement, or she could retain the earnest money as liquidated damages. The potential remedy of specific performance was, of course, foreclosed upon sale of the property to a third party. Plaintiff now seeks to avoid the limitation imposed by the provision for stipulated damages.

Plaintiff first argues that the alternative remedies provided by the earnest money agreement are not exclusive, and cites *Reiter v. Bailey*, 180 Wash. 230, 39 P.2d 370 (1934), for the proposition that a vendor may forego declaring a forfeiture of earnest money and elect, instead, to sue for actual damages. *Reiter* involved a real estate contract in which it was provided that, upon failure of the purchaser to make any payment

> [T]he seller *may* elect to declare a forfeiture and cancellation of this contract and upon such election being made, . . . any payments theretofore made hereunder by the purchaser shall be retained by the seller in liquidation of all damages sustained by reason of such failure. (Italics ours.) [*Reiter v. Bailey, supra* at 231, 39 P.2d at 370.]

This court interpreted the clause to mean that the seller had reserved the options of seeking specific performance, liquidated damages or actual damages upon the buyer's default. Where parties expressly provide for such alternatives, there can be no objection to the seller's choice of one remedy from among those contemplated in the agreement. However, where an earnest money agreement provides that, upon the purchaser's failure or refusal to complete the transaction, the earnest money *shall* be forfeited as liquidated damages unless the seller chooses specific performance (as does the clause in the present case), we have clearly held that the seller cannot pursue a third remedy of unliquidated damages which is not written into the agreement. *Underwood v. Sterner*, 63

Wash.2d 360, 367, 387 P.2d 366 (1963). In this case the liquidated damages clause, if enforceable, will limit plaintiff's recovery to that amount stipulated in the earnest money agreement.

Plaintiff's principal contention is that the liquidated damages clause constitutes a penalty and is, therefore, unenforceable. However, no penalty is involved here. A penalty exists where there is an attempt to enforce an obligation to pay a sum fixed by agreement of the parties as a *punishment* for the failure to fulfill some primary contractual obligation. 5 S. Williston, Contracts § 770, at 641 (3d ed. 1961). In this case, it is not the party in default who seeks relief from an excessively high liquidated damages provision. Rather, the provision operates to limit the recovery of the party who incurred a loss as a result of the other parties' breach. There being no element of punishment involved, it cannot be said that plaintiff is being penalized in any sense.

There is some authority to support the view that where a stipulated amount of damages is substantially below the actual damage, the limitation will be found to be unenforceable. There is, however, contrary authority. For example, in *City of Kinston v. Suddreth*, 266 N.C. 618, 146 S.E.2d 660 (1966), the argument was made that a liquidated damages clause, which stipulated an amount less than actual damages, was a penalty and unenforceable. The court refused even to consider the nature of the clause at issue, holding that an injured party cannot recover damages beyond the amount stipulated in a liquidated damages clause. We believe that the view expressed by the North Carolina court is the better one.

The precise issue raised in this case, whether a seller can avoid the consequences of a liquidated damages clause which proves insufficient, has not previously been considered by this court, but the law relating generally to the enforceability of liquidated damages provisions is summarized in *Jenson v. Richens*, 74 Wash.2d 41, 47, 442 P.2d 636, 640 (1968), where it is stated: "Unless it be demonstrated that provisions for liquidated damages are actually a penalty or are . . . otherwise unlawful, this court will sustain them."

Also, in addition to a background of case law which suggests that provisions for liquidated damages will ordinarily be upheld by the courts, there are practical considerations which lend further support to our decision that such provisions under these circumstances are binding upon the seller. We must assume that the seller considered the certainty of a liquidated damages clause to be preferable to the risk of seeking actual damages in the event of the purchasers' breach. We must also assume that the purchasers understood and relied upon the liability limitation stipulated in the agreement. Furthermore, it cannot be ignored that the seller, in making an earnest money agreement, can simply demand more protection—a larger deposit of earnest money—or even dispense with a liquidated damages provision altogether. Except where extraordinary circumstances are involved such as fraud or serious overreaching by the purchaser, a seller who chooses to utilize the device of liquidated damages in an earnest money agreement, with its attendant features of certainty and reliance upon the limitation, cannot avoid the effect of that agreement. . . .

Notes

1. *The Traditional "Benefit of the Bargain" Measure of Damages.* The plaintiff's argument in *Mahoney* hints at the traditional "expectation" or "benefit of the bargain" measure of damages awarded for breach of real estate contracts. In a case like *Mahoney*, in which the buyer breaches the contract, the seller typically may recover damages equal to the contract price less the fair market value of the premises at the time of the buyer's breach. William B. Stoebuck & Dale A. Whitman, The Law of Property, § 10.3, at 724 (3d ed. 2000). If the seller resells the land within a reasonable period of the buyer's breach, the court often will consider the resale price as persuasive evidence of the land's value on the date of breach. Likewise, if the seller breaches, the buyer may recover damages in the amount by which the fair market value of the land at the time of the seller's breach exceeds the contract price.

2. *The Remedy When Seller's Title Is Defective.* Approximately half of American jurisdictions abandon the "expectation" measure of damages in cases where the seller cannot perform because its title is unmarketable or otherwise defective, assuming the seller acted in good faith in this regard. [The seller would act in "bad faith" if seller knew of the defect prior to contracting but failed to disclose it, or if the seller failed to take steps during the gap period to cure a curable defect. In these cases, the buyer could recover expectation damages.] Under this so-called "English rule," the buyer is limited to restitution (*i.e.*, a return of the buyer's purchase money or deposit) from a good-faith seller. Why such a limitation?

> The English principle developed because of the uncertainties of title due to the complexity of the rules governing title to land during the eighteenth and nineteenth centuries. At that time the only evidence of title was contained in deeds which were in a phrase attributed to Lord Westbury, "difficult to read, disgusting to touch, and impossible to understand." [*Donovan v. Bachstadt*, 91 N.J. 434, 453 A.2d 160, 164 (1982) (rejecting the English rule in favor of the American rule).]

Why would this concern justify using restitution as the buyer's remedy rather than expectation damages?

The remaining jurisdictions have adopted the "American rule," under which the buyer may recover benefit-of-the-bargain damages in all cases of seller breach. Which rule do you think is justified? Do you think it is really *that hard* for the seller to ascertain whether it has good title or not prior to entering into a contract for sale? Why might a seller make this investigation before contracting for the sale of land?

3. *Consequential Damages.* Subject to the basic limitations of contract law, the nonbreaching party always can recover "consequential" or "out-of-pocket" damages to compensate her for expenses incurred as a result of the breach. For the seller, these would include costs of resale (advertising, attorney fees, etc.); for the buyer, they might include expenses incurred for

title examination, property inspections, and loan application charges. Would the following be permissible "consequential" damages?

(a) Buyer spent $800 for airfare to travel to the meeting at which she negotiated the contract, which Seller subsequently breached. Should Buyer recover the $800? Why or why not? *See Fountain v. Mojo*, 687 P.2d 496 (Colo. Ct. App. 1984).

(b) After Seller's breach, Buyer (who had already sold her former home) signed a month-to-month lease at $500/month to have quarters while finding a suitable new home to buy. In addition, Buyer incurred $1,000 worth of moving expenses in moving her belongings to the premises she leased. How would you advise the Buyer concerning her ability to recover the $500/month in rent? The $1,000 in moving expenses? *See Gorzelsky v. Leckey*, 402 Pa.Super. 246, 586 A.2d 952 (1991).

(c) Buyer breached its contract to purchase Seller's home. After three months, Seller managed to resell the home. During that three months, Seller incurred $250 in additional property taxes, $1,200 in mortgage interest, $200 in utilities, and $500 in repairs when a tree fell on the roof during a storm. Should the Seller recover the $250 in property taxes? The $1,200 in mortgage interest? The $200 in utilities? The $500 in repairs? Why or why not? *See Allen v. Enomoto*, 228 Cal.App.2d 798, 39 Cal.Rptr. 815 (1964).

(d) Buyer breaches its contract to purchase Seller's home. Under the "ready, willing, and able" rule, however, Seller's broker was entitled to a $5,000 commission notwithstanding buyer's breach. When Seller resells the property three months later, Seller's broker earns another commission. Can Seller recover the $5,000 for the first commission? Can Seller recover the amount of the second commission? *See Mueller v. Johnson*, 60 Wash.App. 683, 806 P.2d 256 (1991).

(e) Seller breaches his contract with Buyer. Buyer had secured financing at 7%. Two months later, Buyer finds another suitable home. During the intervening two months, however, interest rates have jumped significantly, and Buyer can only borrow at 9%. This increase means that during the five years of the loan, Buyer will pay approximately $3,000 per year more in interest than Buyer would have paid on a 7% loan. Can Buyer recover damages from Seller in the amount of the interest differential? *Compare Wall v. Pate*, 104 N.M. 1, 715 P.2d 449 (1986) *with Appollo v. Reynolds*, 364 N.W.2d 422 (Minn. Ct. App. 1985).

4. *Liquidation of Damages.* Often, as in *Mahoney*, real estate contracts will provide that in the event that buyer breaches, seller can retain the buyer's earnest money deposit as liquidated damages for buyer's breach. In some areas, earnest money deposits are relatively small—in Missouri, for example, deposits of $1,000–$2,000 are common. In other areas, such as New York, the customary deposit is 10% of the purchase price—a significant sum when the purchase price exceeds six figures.

Not surprisingly, most liquidated damages disputes arise when the seller attempts to retain a deposit amount that greatly exceeds the seller's actual damages. For example, consider *Covington v. Robinson*, 723 S.W.2d 643 (Tenn. Ct. App. 1986). Covington agreed to purchase 1,567 acres of land for a total price of $2,010,675. Covington made a deposit of $100,000, but later refused to complete the purchase. The Robinsons resold the land two months later for $2,000,000, and retained all of Covington's earnest money deposit as liquidated damages. Covington then sued, claiming that the liquidated damages provision was an unenforceable penalty.

The traditional standard applied to liquidated damages provisions is set out in Restatement (Second) of Contracts § 356(1), which provides:

> (1) Damages for breach by either party may be liquidated in the agreement but only at an amount that is reasonable in the light of the anticipated or actual loss caused by the breach and the difficulties of proof of loss. A term fixing unreasonably large liquidated damages is unenforceable on grounds of public policy as a penalty.

The comments to § 356 provide the following guidance as to characterizing the liquidated amount as a "penalty":

> [T]wo factors combine in determining whether an amount of money fixed as damages is so unreasonably large as to be a penalty. The first factor is the anticipated or actual loss caused by the breach. The amount fixed is reasonable to the extent that it approximates the actual loss that has resulted from the particular breach, even though it may not approximate the loss that might have been anticipated under other possible breaches.... Furthermore, the amount fixed is reasonable to the extent that it approximates the loss anticipated at the time of the making of the contract, even though it may not approximate the actual loss.... The second factor is the difficulty of proof of loss. The greater the difficulty either of proving that loss has occurred or of establishing its amount with the requisite certainty ..., the easier it is to show that the amount fixed is reasonable. To the extent that there is uncertainty as to the harm, the estimate of the court or jury may not accord with the principle of compensation any more than does the advance estimate of the parties. A determination whether the amount fixed is a penalty turns on a combination of these two factors. If the difficulty of proof of loss is great, considerable latitude is allowed in the approximation of anticipated or actual harm. If, on the other hand, the difficulty of proof of loss is slight, less latitude is allowed in that approximation. If, to take an extreme case, it is clear that no loss at all has occurred, a provision fixing a substantial sum as damages is unenforceable.

Under § 356(1), as explained in the comments, do you believe that the court should enforce the liquidated damages provision in *Covington*?

In contrast, the *Mahoney* case is less typical, because the *buyer* is attempting to force the *seller* to accept liquidated damages when the seller's actual damages exceed the liquidated sum. Should the seller ever be permitted to make the argument that the liquidated damages provision is unenforceable? *See* Restatement (Second) of Contracts § 356, cmt. a.; *Community Dev. Serv., Inc. v. Replacement Parts Mfg., Inc.*, 679 S.W.2d 721 (Tex. App. 1984). If you had been advising the seller in *Mahoney*, how would you have drafted the contract to provide the appropriate protection for the seller?

Finally, consider the following contract provision: "If Buyer fails to perform the Contract within the time specified, the deposit made by Buyer may be retained by the Seller as liquidated damages in full settlement of any claims; alternatively, Seller, at its option, may proceed at law to recover its actual damages or in equity to specifically enforce the Contract." Suppose that Buyer breaches and Seller attempts to retain the deposit even though Seller did not suffer any actual damages. Does the Seller's retention of an option to seek actual damages render the liquidated damages provision unenforceable? *Compare Lefemine v. Baron*, 573 So.2d 326 (Fla. 1991) (yes) *with Hoelscher v. Schenewerk*, 804 S.W.2d 828 (Mo. Ct. App. 1991) (no). On what basis could it be treated as unenforceable?

5. *Specific Performance and "Uniqueness."* Upon request, courts may grant specific performance of a contract as an alternative remedy in cases where damages would be inadequate to compensate the nonbreaching party. Restatement (Second) of Contracts § 359. Traditionally, courts have demonstrated a willingness to grant specific performance of real estate contracts on the grounds that each parcel of land is "unique," rendering damages inadequate to compensate the nonbreaching party. Can you explain why the "uniqueness" of a parcel of land justifies a conclusion that damages are not an adequate remedy (and thus that specific performance should be granted)?

Rarely, if ever, have courts challenged the presumed "uniqueness" of land. Perhaps the most famous example is *Centex Homes v. Boag*, 128 N.J.Super. 385, 320 A.2d 194 (1974), where the seller sought specific performance after the buyer breached a contract to purchase a condominium unit. The *Centex Homes* court refused to grant specific performance to the seller, noting that there were numerous available units in the condominium project that were identical to or similar in design and size to the unit in question. Why might these facts suggest that specific performance is unjustified (*i.e.*, why do they suggest that damages is an adequate remedy)? Why aren't damages *always* adequate to compensate a nonbreaching seller? If the seller in *Mahoney* had sought specific performance, should it have been granted? Why or why not? If the parties' contract provides that the seller is entitled to specific performance upon the buyer's breach, should courts nevertheless evaluate whether damages would provide an adequate remedy before deciding whether to grant specific performance?

Should the rationale of *Centex Homes* apply if the **buyer** is seeking specific performance? Assume that the Boags had been seeking specific performance of the contract in *Centex Homes*. Would evidence that the units were identical to other available units be sufficient to justify denying the Boags' claim and according them only damages? Why or why not? *See Pruitt v. Graziano*, 215 N.J.Super. 330, 521 A.2d 1313 (1987) (buyer may enforce contract for sale of condominium without proof of uniqueness); *Giannini v. First Nat'l Bank of Des Plaines*, 136 Ill.App.3d 971, 91 Ill.Dec. 438, 483 N.E.2d 924 (1985) (same). What if the Boags were buying the condo solely for investment purposes? Would that justify denying them specific performance? Why or why not? *See Watkins v. Paul*, 95 Idaho 499, 511 P.2d 781 (1973).

Finally, consider California Civil Code section 3387:

It is to be presumed that the breach of an agreement to transfer real property cannot be adequately relieved by pecuniary compensation. In the case of a single-family dwelling which the party seeking performance intends to occupy, this presumption is conclusive. In all other cases, this presumption is a presumption affecting the burden of proof.

What is the logic of this provision? Are houses more "unique" than commercial, industrial, or agricultural property?

6. *Specific Performance and Other Remedies.* If the seller cannot perform the contract completely—for example, if the seller's title is unmarketable due to an encumbrance that the seller cannot remove—the buyer can choose not to rescind the contract, but instead to seek specific performance with an abatement of the purchase price (to take into account the reduction in the land's value due to the encumbrance). *See Burk v. Hefley*, 32 Ark.App. 133, 798 S.W.2d 109 (1990); *Rosenthal v. Sandusky*, 35 Colo.App. 220, 533 P.2d 523 (1975).

Likewise, a party who obtains specific performance can also recover any foreseeable consequential damages suffered as a result of the party's breach. *See, e.g., Bravo v. Buelow*, 168 Cal.App.3d 208, 214 Cal.Rptr. 65 (1985) (buyer who contracted for unimproved lot to build home entitled to recover damages for increases in construction costs due to seller's delay in performance).

3. *Financing the Purchase of Land*

The buyer usually pays for its purchase of land using funds borrowed under a mortgage loan,[27] often obtained from an institutional lender such as a bank or mortgage company. Because the lender expects the buyer/borrower to repay this loan (according to the terms specified in the promissory note that evidences the loan), the lender will investigate the buyer/borrower's financial condition and personal credit history to assure the buyer/borrower's capacity for repaying the loan.

Even if the buyer/borrower is creditworthy, however, the lender will also require the buyer/borrower to grant the lender a mortgage lien against the land, thereby providing security for the buyer/borrower's obligation to repay the mortgage loan. If the buyer/borrower cannot or does not repay the loan according to its terms, the lender can enforce its lien by selling the land at a foreclosure sale and applying the sale proceeds toward the mortgage debt. Because the land thus may constitute the primary source of recovery if the borrower defaults, a prudent lender will not approve a mortgage loan unless the land's value exceeds the mortgage loan balance by at least a specified amount (*e.g.*, the loan amount must be no more than 80% or 90% of the land's value). This "equity cushion" increases the likelihood that the lender will be able to recover the full amount of the mortgage loan even if the buyer/borrower defaults.

Often, the buyer has not obtained a mortgage loan before signing a contract to purchase land. As a result, the buyer will often seek to make

27. Mortgage loans may also finance expenses other than the purchase of land (*e.g.*, a child's college education); the discussion in the text also applies to these mortgage loans (often called "home equity" loans).

its obligation contingent upon obtaining the necessary financing to complete the purchase.

PROCTOR v. HOLDEN

Court of Special Appeals of Maryland.
75 Md.App. 1, 540 A.2d 133 (1988).

ALPERT, JUDGE. This is an appeal by John P. and Deborah Proctor, and Freeman & Kagan, Inc. from a jury verdict entered in favor of Michael and Deborah Holden in the Circuit Court for Talbot County. Count I of appellees' Complaint alleged breach of contract by the Proctors for their failure to return the $20,000 deposit despite appellees' inability to obtain the financing provided for in the contract. . . .

The material facts, which are not in dispute, follow. In April 1985, appellees Michael and Deborah Holden decided to relocate from Ocean City, Maryland to the Mid–Shore area in order to be closer to their families in Baltimore and Annapolis. The Holdens contacted Charlotte Valliant, a real estate agent associated with appellant Freeman & Kagan, Inc., a real estate brokerage in Easton. For more than a month, Valliant showed the Holdens homes in the Talbot County area, some listed with Freeman & Kagan and some listed with other brokers. Also, on a weekly basis Valliant sent appellees a list of new properties, as well as information about properties which had not yet been listed, but of which she had knowledge. During this period, Valliant was actively seeking a home for appellees. . . .

On May 24, 1985, Valliant showed Michael Holden a home located on Edgeview Road, near Royal Oak, which the then owner, Howard Gillellan, had just listed with Freeman & Kagan at a price of $169,500. Upon Valliant's urging that the house was a "tremendous buy" and that it was "grossly under-priced," Michael Holden submitted a contract offer in the amount of $170,000 cash, the only contingency being that Deborah Holden be allowed to inspect the property prior to noon the next day. Because the Holdens could not make the trip to Freeman & Kagan's office that day to sign a contract, their offer was submitted by telegram, the text of which was dictated by Tim Kagan.

In exhorting appellees to submit an offer, Valliant related to the Holdens that there was strong interest in the Gillellan property, and that any delay could mean the loss of the property. In fact, Mr. Holden was told that another full-price contract had been submitted by another client of Freeman & Kagan. In a phone conversation with Kagan and Valliant, Michael Holden specifically requested that either Valliant or Kagan personally sponsor, present, and urge their offer upon Mr. Gillellan, the owner. Nevertheless, only the listing agent, Marshall Bailey, presented both contracts. Gillellan accepted the other contract submitted by appellant Deborah Proctor. According to Bailey, Gillellan accepted the Proctor contract, at least in part because of his fear of losing both offers if he waited for Mrs. Holden's inspection and approval of the home. The

Proctor contract was for $169,500 and was subject to a financing contingency.

Although apparently losing the Gillellan home, appellees remained in contact with Charlotte Valliant during the months of June and July, 1985. On July 14, 1985, Valliant called and informed the Holdens that they could buy the Gillellan property from the Proctors for $203,000. Almost immediately Michael Holden contacted Delphine Amrhun, Office Manager at Magnet Mortgages, a mortgage company located in Ocean City, about obtaining a $150,000, 30–year term loan for the property.

On July 24, 1985, the Proctors signed a 24–hour listing agreement with Freeman & Kagan. Later that same day Michael and Deborah Holden visited the property where they met and spoke directly with Deborah Proctor for the first time. Asked about the possibility of owner-financing, Deborah Proctor responded that she would not hold any financing, and in addition she wanted settlement within 30 days. Michael Holden responded that even though he had already submitted a mortgage application to Magnet Mortgages 60 days was needed; after some discussion Proctor agreed.

Thereafter, at the Freeman & Kagan office, Valliant prepared for the Holdens' signature a standard fill-in-the-blanks contract then in use by the Talbot County Board of Realtors. $210,000 was inserted in the blank for the purchase price.[28] In addition, a mortgage contingency clause was completed, which is set out in full infra. The contract also stated: "Time is of the essence of this agreement." The Holdens tendered a $20,000 deposit with their contract, to be held in an interest bearing account by the broker, Freeman & Kagan.

The Proctors accepted the contract on July 26, 1985. On approximately August 1, 1985, Delphine Amrhun of Magnet Mortgages telephoned Michael Holden to advise him that he would not qualify for a $150,000 30–year loan; moreover, she intimated that no lender employing standard FNMA/FHLMC guidelines would qualify him for such a loan because of his high debt to earnings ratio. Amrhun later confirmed this in a letter to Holden dated August 8, 1985. Holden then submitted a mortgage application to Second National Building & Loan on August 9th, which similarly was rejected on August 12th.

Michael Holden also approached the Talbot Bank for a loan. Mr. Jeffrey Hefflebower, a senior vice president of the bank, testified, however, that Talbot did not offer long-term fixed rate mortgages. It was Hefflebower's understanding that Holden was seeking a short-term loan that would be paid off from the proceeds of the sale of a business. Hefflebower also stated that although the property was appraised and the application was ready for the Committee's decision, the bank took no final action and neither accepted nor rejected Holden's application. Holden testified that he assumed the bank's silence meant the loan was rejected.

---

28. The asking price was raised by the Proctors from $203,000 to $210,000, appar-ently to cover Freeman & Kagan's $7,000 commission.

At the request of the realtors, Mr. Talbot Roe of United Mortgage contacted Holden. Mr. Roe stated that he could help the Holdens obtain a loan through a group of investors "who didn't care what the risk was." Holden testified that he was not interested in Roe's offer on the basis of his being told by two reputable banks that he could not afford the loan.

Holden notified Charlotte Valliant by letter of his inability to obtain financing and requested the return of his $20,000 deposit. In response, Tim Kagan of Freeman & Kagan, in a letter dated August 20, 1985, informed the Holdens that the Proctors had agreed to finance the purchase pursuant to the adjustable rate terms stated in the contract. Specifically, in a letter addressed to Mr. Kagan, the Proctors expressed their willingness to finance the Holdens' purchase with a $150,000 mortgage at an initial 10% interest rate, the interest rate to be adjusted annually by no more than 2% up or down and a 4% lifetime cap. Three points were to be paid the Proctors by the Holdens. The Proctors also requested that the Holdens forward a financial statement and credit references. The Holdens rejected this offer of owner financing and again requested a refund of their deposit. The Proctors refused. Accordingly, Freeman & Kagan did not release the funds, and the Holdens filed suit against the Proctors to compel release of their deposit ....

The essence of appellants' argument is that the Holdens forfeited their right to the return of their deposit by not fulfilling their obligation under the financing clause. Specifically, appellants assert that appellees breached the contract (1) by not applying for a mortgage within five days of acceptance of the contract, and (2) by rejecting the Proctors' offer of owner financing. We disagree with both assertions.

The specific contract language underlying this dispute is paragraph 7, the "Financing Contingency," which reads:

FINANCING CONTINGENCY—This contract is contingent upon the Buyer obtaining a Purchase Money Loan as follows:

Amount borrowed at least *$150,000.00*. Interest rate not greater than *11%*. Period of amortization *30* years. Payments made on a *monthly* basis. Payoff of mortgage in *30* years. Required mortgage points paid by *buyer*. Adjustable rate mortgage starting at *10%* interest with a *4%* life cap. Buyer agrees to apply for said mortgage within five days of acceptance and to pay the normal closing costs in obtaining same. Buyer to receive mortgage commitment and approval on or before *Sept. 7, 1985*. Should Buyer be unable to obtain said mortgage and Buyer so notifies the Seller or his agent on said date this contract will be null and void of no force or effect, all deposits returned and all parties to this contract released of all liability hereunder.

Thus, the clause provides for both a fixed rate conventional mortgage and an adjustable rate mortgage. Appellants argue that the clause should be read in the disjunctive despite the omission of language to that effect. We see no error in the trial judge's determination that the financing contingency is ambiguous inasmuch as the terms are obviously inconsistent. Clearly the Holdens were not agreeing to obtain a mortgage with both a fixed rate and an adjustable rate. If read in the disjunctive, the terms of the mortgage are unclear: Does the language "Period of amortization *30* years. Payments made on a *monthly* basis. Payoff of mortgage in *30* years. Required mortgage points paid by *buyer*" sandwiched between the two types of mortgages apply to both, or only to the fixed rate mortgage? The court did not err in admitting extrinsic evidence to determine the parties' intent. *See Admiral Builders Savings & Loan Ass'n v. South River Landing, Inc.*, 66 Md.App. 124, 502 A.2d 1096 (1986). Thus, the next step, to determine whether the Holdens took bona fide, prompt and reasonable actions to procure financing, was a question properly presented to the jury.

(1) *Five Day Requirement.* Next, appellant alleges that the "time is of the essence clause" superimposed upon the financing contingency compelled performance in the five day period following the contract's acceptance. According to appellants, the Holdens' mortgage application with Magnet Mortgages, originating before the Proctors accepted the contract, does not comply with the five-day requirement in the financing contingency. We disagree. . . .

The contingency at bar does contain a time limitation: "within five days of acceptance." The contract sets only an outside limit of five days for the buyer to make application. We do not construe this to mean that the application may not be initiated prior to acceptance of the contract. The purpose of the time limitation is to prevent a delay that jeopardizes the agreement. A buyer who delays in applying for a mortgage puts the settlement at risk. Setting an outside limit on the time for making a mortgage application protects the seller who is taking his house off the market. It also gives both parties peace of mind that the buyer is qualified and that settlement will take place on the stated date. *See* W.B. Raushenbush, Problems and Practices With Financing Conditions in Real Estate Purchase Contracts, 1963 Wis.L.Rev. 566, 577. In the absence of specific language to the contrary, we cannot justify penalizing a buyer who acts responsibly by initiating the financing process in anticipation of making an offer to purchase property. *Cf. Bushmiller v. Schiller*, 35 Md.App. 1, 368 A.2d 1044 (1977) (contract purchaser's cancellation of mortgage application filed one day before the contract's acceptance and failure to apply elsewhere evidenced a lack of good faith efforts to obtain a mortgage). Indeed, Holden approached Magnet Mortgages three days after being told the Proctors had decided to sell. He testified, ". . . I initiated an application for a $150,000 loan. And my intention was to try to speed up the loan process in the event that we came to some kind of a deal on the house."

Moreover, the record indicates that Holden told Mrs. Proctor that he had applied for a loan at the time the two were negotiating a settlement date. . . . [W]e perceive no possible advantage to either party, and no greater chance of success had the Holdens filed their application after, instead of before, the execution of the contract. Indeed, after learning that their application had been rejected, the Holdens applied to Second

National Building & Loan and were again rejected because of their debt/income ratio. Inasmuch as most banks follow the same guidelines, it was Holden's "understanding ... that [he and his wife] would not qualify for any mortgage with any of those banks." The Holdens also followed up a lead from Ms. Valliant and contacted Miss Heath at Eastern Shore Mortgage. She too stated her bank would not approve the loan. . . .

(2) *Sellers' Offer to Finance.* On August 12th the Holdens sent Ms. Valliant a copy of their rejection letter from Magnet Mortgages. On the 13th, they did the same with their rejection from Second National and requested the return of their deposit. Thereafter, in a letter from Tim Kagan dated August 20th, the Holdens were informed that the Proctors were willing to finance the purchase. Kagan forwarded the Proctors' letter offering a $150,000 loan subject to the following terms:

> [W]e will provide a thirty (30) year (monthly payment of principal, interest, taxes and insurance) adjustable rate mortgage with an initial interest rate of 10%. The interest rate will be adjusted annually; any increase or decrease in the annual rate will not exceed two (2) percentage points. The rate will never be greater or less than four (4) percentage points above or below the initial (10%) rate. Three (3) points will be paid by purchasers at the time of settlement; and, the adjustable rate note will specify that it may not be assumed. Except as set forth in this paragraph, the adjustable rate note will follow the format and contain the conditions in Loyola Federal Savings and Loan Association's standard adjustable rate note.

The Holdens rejected this offer and the appellants now argue that this rejection breached the financing contingency. Appellants cite no law to support their contention that the appellees were required, as a matter of law, to accept owner financing. Instead, appellants argue again only that the contract was unambiguous and, therefore, the court erred in admitting appellees' evidence that the parties did not contemplate owner financing at the time of contract.[29] Inasmuch as we have already held that the financing clause was ambiguous, this argument has no merit.

The evidence supports the Holdens. Prior to submitting their contract, Mr. Holden asked Mrs. Proctor if she would hold the mortgage. Mrs. Proctor refused. Furthermore, in Interrogatory No. 12 Mrs. Proctor was asked: "State when you first decided to offer owner financing to the

---

29. A home purchaser may prefer an institutional loan over owner financing for several reasons. Among the more commonly stated reasons are:

(1) A buyer may want to buy only if the judgment of a particular lender as to the property's value concurs with his own; (2) A buyer may want to borrow only from a lender whose practices in the event of default are known to be patient and reasonable; and (3) Lender's practices in permitting rapid pre-payment of loans vary widely, and a buyer might want to borrow only from a lender he knew would not seek to penalize pre-payment.

Raushenbush, *supra*, at 576; *Kovarik v. Veseley*, 3 Wis.2d 573, 89 N.W.2d 279, 285–86 (1958) (Fairchild, J., dissenting).

[appellees]." She responded: "Approximately Thursday, Friday or Saturday, August 15, 16 or 17, 1985."

While there is no mention of owner financing in the contract, that fact alone is not decisive. There may be cases where owner financing, while not mentioned in the contract, may have been contemplated and indeed may be required. Under the facts of this case, we agree with the appellees that appellants were attempting "to force on him financing of the type that he did not desire or originally contemplate." *Tieri v. Orbell*, 192 Pa.Super. 612, 162 A.2d 248, 250 (1960). *See also Lach v. Cahill*, 138 Conn. 418, 85 A.2d 481 (1951). *But cf. Kovarik v. Veseley*, 3 Wis.2d 573, 89 N.W.2d 279 (1958) (source of loan was not material part of financing clause and buyer must accept seller's offer). We hold that the jury could reasonably conclude the appellees fulfilled their obligation under the financing clause by making reasonable efforts to secure a $150,000 fixed rate mortgage through an institutional lender.[30] . . .

Notes

1. *The Financing Contingency.* Because most buyers of land do not have the funds to pay the purchase price in cash, the financing contingency is encountered in most modern real estate contracts. Obviously, it serves to protect the buyer against having to perform in cases where the buyer's inability to obtain financing would render buyer's performance difficult or impossible. Suppose, however, that Debbie (who receives $1 million per year as a recent Lotto winner) wishes to purchase Redacre. Why might Debbie propose a financing contingency as part of the contract, even if she is financially able to pay without regard to her ability to obtain financing? Does the ability to obtain a commitment for a mortgage loan from a financial institution provide any information that Debbie might find useful in deciding whether to complete the proposed purchase?

The drafting of a financing contingency is difficult, and the cases are replete with examples of poorly drafted contingency provisions. For example, in the case of *Gildea v. Kapenis*, 402 N.W.2d 457 (Iowa App. 1987), the contract provided that buyer's obligation was "subject to buyer obtaining suitable financing interest rate no greater than 12¾%." What does "suitable" financing mean? Suppose that the buyer could obtain a 30–year mortgage at 13½% or a 15–year mortgage at 12%. Should the court then order the buyer to perform, or should the court allow the buyer to argue that the 15–year mortgage is not "suitable"? Should the court order the buyer to perform if the seller offers to provide financing on a 30–year note bearing 12% interest? *See Woods v. Austin*, 347 So.2d 897 (La. Ct. App. 1977).

The parties should also carefully consider the precise impact of the buyer's inability to obtain financing. Consider the following examples:

(a) If buyer cannot obtain financing (at an interest rate not to exceed 9% for a term of 30 years), this contract shall become null and void.

---

30. We also note that the Proctor financing absolutely required the payment of "[t]hree (3) points . . . by the purchasers at the time of settlement" whereas the Holdens may not have been required to pay any points upon obtaining an adjustable rate mortgage. . . .

(b) If buyer cannot obtain financing (at an interest rate not to exceed 9% for a term of 30 years), this contract shall become null and void at the option of the buyer.

Do these two provisions create conditions precedent to the buyer's obligation? Does either of them create a *condition subsequent*? How is a condition subsequent different from a condition precedent? Why would it matter whether the provision was interpreted to be a condition precedent or a condition subsequent? See Calamari & Perillo, Contracts § 11–5 (2d ed. 1977).

2. *Timing Concerns—Addressing the Risk of Opportunistic Behavior.* The provision in the *Proctor* case specified that the buyer had to seek financing within a certain number of days and had to obtain its commitment by a fixed date prior to closing. [Can you explain why the Seller may have negotiated for these provisions?] In contrast, many financing contingencies do not provide such specific requirements; the poorly drafted contingency in *Gildea* (quoted in note 1 above) is an unfortunately typical example, and some are even more cursory (*e.g.*, "This contract is subject to financing."). Under such a cursory provision, consider the following questions:

(a) Does the buyer have an obligation to perform the contract, or is the buyer's promise unenforceable? [And, if so, on what basis?] *Compare Gildea*, *supra* note 1, *with Perkins v. Gosewehr*, 98 Wis.2d 158, 295 N.W.2d 789 (Ct. App. 1980). If the agreement specifies that "This contract is subject to financing," is it possible to sufficiently ascertain the intention of the parties?

(b) Suppose that the buyer never bothered to apply for a mortgage loan, or applies only on such borrower-favorable terms that no mortgage lender will approve buyer's application. Can the buyer then cancel the contract under the mortgage contingency? Does it matter that the contract does not expressly place any duty upon the buyer to apply for a loan? *See Phillipe v. Thomas*, 3 Conn.App. 471, 489 A.2d 1056 (1985) (contract impliedly obligates buyer to use good faith efforts to obtain financing). Why would a court imply upon the buyer a duty to seek financing?

In most real estate purchases, the buyer will rely upon "conventional" financing, *i.e.,* a mortgage loan provided by a bank or other institutional lender. Occasionally, however, a buyer may have poor credit or otherwise lack the financial resources to obtain a conventional loan. As an alternative to the conventional mortgage, the buyer may enter into an installment land contract—also known as a "contract for deed"—in which the seller finances the transaction by permitting the buyer to pay the purchase price in a series of monthly installments. During the contract period, the buyer has possession of the property, but the seller generally retains legal title and does not deliver a deed to the land until the final payment is made.

Most installment contracts contain a forfeiture clause, which typically provides that if the buyer defaults—*e.g.*, by failing to make timely payments—the seller has the right to terminate the contract, immediately regain possession without legal process, and retain all of the previous payments as liquidated damages. At early common law, courts regularly enforced such clauses against the hapless buyer, who stood to lose a substantial investment, particularly if the forfeiture occurred near the end of the contract term. More recently, courts and legislatures have shown a greater willingness to protect the buyer through a variety of judicial and legislative means.

DAUGHERTY CATTLE CO. v. GENERAL CONSTRUCTION CO.

Supreme Court of Montana.
254 Mont. 479, 839 P.2d 562 (1992).

WEBER, JUSTICE. . . . On February 13, 1981, Meyer Construction Company, a predecessor company of defendant General Construction Company (General), and the plaintiffs Daugherty Cattle Co., . . . entered into a written contract for deed for the sale and purchase of real property located on the outskirts of Billings in Yellowstone County, Montana. The purchase price of the property was $1,195,000.00 plus interest at the rate of nine percent per annum. . . .

[When General failed to make its scheduled payments in 1989, Daugherty sent a written notice of default. On January 8, 1990, General offered to convey back to Daugherty an 85–acre portion of the property (approximately 47% of the land covered by the contract) together with payments already made totalling $1,273,290.00, in return for termination of the contract and retention of the remaining 53% of the land. Daugherty rejected the offer and sent a termination notice dated July 18, 1990.]

General refused to execute special warranty deeds to reconvey the property to Daugherty and refused to deliver possession to Daugherty to effect the termination of the contract. Daugherty filed this action to quiet title and to obtain possession of the property.

The District Court granted Daugherty's motion for summary judgment on the quiet title and ejectment claims, rejected General's claim that termination and forfeiture were not enforceable remedies under the contract and allowed Daugherty to retain all monies previously paid by General and its predecessor. The District Court refused to apply Montana's anti-forfeiture statute, § 28–1–104, MCA, because General's tender of a portion of the property did not constitute "full compensation" as required by the statute. From this judgment, General appeals.

. . . The appellant, General, contends that there are genuine issues of fact and that evidence relating to these factual issues should have been introduced into evidence at a trial. Specifically, General claims that a clause included in the parties' contract requires the court to determine the relationship between payments retained and actual damages suffered by Daugherty and to determine whether the retention of contract payments constitutes a penalty rather than damages. The pertinent clause is [italicized] in the following excerpt from Paragraph 5 of the contract for deed:

(1) If Buyer fails to cure such default or breach within the aforesaid 30 day period, the Seller may then declare the outstanding balance of the purchase price together with all other unpaid obligations of the Buyer undertaken in this contract due and payable within an additional 30 days. If the outstanding balance of the purchase price together with all other unpaid obligations of the Buyer are not paid within the second 30 day period, the Seller may either:

(a) declare this contract terminated. In the event of such termination, Buyer agrees on demand to surrender possession of the property, and any improvements thereon immediately and peaceably, and to execute and deliver such instruments as Seller may require to evidence of record the termination of this contract and Buyer's interest in the contract and real property, and Seller may retain all payments made hereunder *as reasonable rental for the use of the property and as liquidated damages* . . . .

General claims there is no evidence that the damages Daugherty recovered have any relationship to the actual damages suffered by Daugherty. General has made payments of principal and interest totalling $1,242,447.50 on the original contract amount of $1,195,000.00. The amounts applied to principal total $857,000.00, leaving a principal balance of $338,000.00. General further claims that liquidated damages must bear a reasonable relationship to the actual damages or such damages will constitute an invalid penalty. Daugherty contends that the language quoted above from Paragraph 5 of the contract is neither ambiguous nor uncertain in any sense and maintains that to accept General's argument would essentially convert the contract from a purchase agreement to a lease, as noted by the District Court.

We agree with the District Court's assessment relating to the result which would ensue if we were to depart from longstanding interpretation of land sale contract provisions. In effect, the result would be to rescind the contract at the whim of the defaulting purchaser whose wrongdoing caused the vendor to terminate the contract.

Long ago, in *Cook-Reynolds Co. v. Chipman* (1913), 47 Mont. 289, 133 P. 694, the defendant made a similar argument against a forfeiture of a contract for deed. This Court noted that in an action to terminate the contract for breach, "the remedies afforded by the contract will be enforced unless they impinge upon other rules of equity or law." *Cook-Reynolds,* 133 P. at 697. In *Cook-Reynolds,* and subsequent forfeiture cases, this Court has consistently upheld contract provisions such as the clause in Paragraph 5 which allows the seller to retain all payments "as reasonable rental for the use of the property and as liquidated damages."

. . .

At the time of contracting, Daugherty and General's predecessor agreed that the payments already made under the contract terms at the time of a default by the purchaser would be reasonable rental and proper liquidated damages. General contends that Erickson [v. First Nat'l Bank of Minneapolis, 697 P.2d 1332, 1338 (Mont. 1985)], requires a court to hear evidence of a reasonable relationship between the actual damage suffered and the liquidated damage claimed. In *Erickson,* the trial court found that the reasonable rental of the property was $114,750.00. The purchaser had paid only $154,751.67 on an $800,00.00 contract and had been in possession of the property for over a year and a half. The trial court found that the amount forfeited was reasonable, a finding this Court affirmed, noting that, "[s]urely Starhaven did not intend that it should remain in possession for so long and pay nothing for the use of the property." *Erickson,* 697 P.2d at 1338. *Erickson,* however, does not require a judicial determination that the amount forfeited was a reasonable rental.

Section 28–2–721, MCA, allows parties to a contract to agree to damages in advance of a breach:

> *When provision fixing liquidated damages valid....*
>
> (2) The parties to a contract may agree therein upon an amount which shall be presumed to be an amount of damage sustained by a breach thereof when, from the nature of the case, it would be impracticable or extremely difficult to fix the actual damage.

General argues that this statute, when applied to the facts of this case, clearly shows that the actual damages have no relationship to the liquidated damages and therefore the contract terms should be invalidated. The District Court ruled that plaintiff was not required to return to the defendant the difference, if any, between the amount paid by the defendant and what evidence would show the reasonable rental value of the land to have been. In pertinent part the District Court stated:

> The later Montana case of *Burgess v. Shiplet,* 230 Mont. 387, 750 P.2d 460 (1988) involved a default by a purchaser in contract payments. The Montana Supreme Court ordered forfeiture of all amounts paid by the purchaser and termination of the contract. There was no consideration of a reasonable rental value during the period of the buyer's holding of the property.... The court stated at 230 Mont. 390 [750 P.2d 460]: "When a purchaser enters into a contract for deed with a seller, he or she runs the risk of defaulting on the required payments and facing the consequences of losing the property along with forfeiting the amount already paid. If this produces a harsh or unwanted result, it is for the legislature to remedy and not the job of this Court to change the plain meaning of the contract."...

We hold that the District Court did not err by refusing to hear evidence relating to the reasonable rental value of the property subject to the land contract for purposes of computing damages.

Does Montana's anti-forfeiture statute, § 28–1–104, MCA, apply to prohibit the seller from declaring a forfeiture when the purchaser tenders a portion of the property back to the seller as "full compensation" for the balance owing on the contract?

Section 28–1–104, MCA, provides:

Relief from forfeiture. Whenever by the terms of an obligation a party thereto incurs a forfeiture or a loss in the nature of a forfeiture by reason of his failure to comply with its provisions, he may be relieved therefrom upon making full compensation to the other party, except in case of a grossly negligent, willful, or fraudulent breach of duty.

In order for § 28–1–104, MCA, to apply, the party requesting relief from forfeiture must tender *full compensation* to the vendor as a condition precedent to relief. *Sun Dial Land Co. v. Gold Creek Ranches, Inc.* (1982), 198 Mont. 247, 251, 645 P.2d 936, 939.

General contends that its offer to reconvey 47 percent of the land to Daugherty, at a time when General was in default and during a period which was a 60–day extension of the time to cure the default, constituted "full compensation" as required by § 28–1–104, MCA. . . . We have repeatedly required the defaulting party under a contract for deed to tender the entire outstanding principal balance in order to obtain relief from forfeiture in equity. . . . General's tender of 47 percent of the property in exchange for Daugherty's cancellation of the remainder owed on the contract was at best an offer to modify the contract—an offer not accepted by Daugherty. It falls short of the full compensation required under § 28–1–104, MCA, which is the entire principal balance plus interest. . . .

Notes

1. *The Nature of an Installment Land Contract.* Earlier in this chapter, you were introduced to the executory contract for the sale of land, known as an "earnest money contract," a "binder,"or a "marketing contract." What is the difference between the earnest money contract and an installment land contract?

[The earnest money contract] is simply an executory contract for the sale of land and does not serve a mortgage function; rather, it governs the rights and liabilities of the parties during the short period between the time of its signing and the closing of the transaction. At the closing, a deed is delivered to the purchaser, who usually executes and delivers a purchase money mortgage to an institutional lender, or in some situations, to the vendor. [Grant S. Nelson, *The Contract for Deed as a Mortgage: The Case for the Restatement Approach*, 1998 BYU L. Rev. 1111, 1112.]

In contrast, an installment contract functions both as a purchase agreement and financing instrument. It governs the parties throughout the life of the debt, which may be for as long as 20 years or more. While the buyer has possession of the property during the contract, the seller typically does not deliver the deed until the purchase price is paid in full. 1 Grant S. Nelson & Dale A. Whitman, Real Estate Finance Law § 3.26, at 93 (4th ed. 2002).

2. *Conventional Mortgages Compared.* A conventional mortgage is accomplished through two instruments. First, the borrower executes a promissory note, which is a promise to repay the loan. The borrower then signs a second instrument, the mortgage. At early common law, the mortgage transferred legal title to the lender (the *mortgagee*), roughly in the form of a defeasible fee—*i.e.*, the title was subject to a condition subsequent that the lender would reconvey title when the loan was paid in full. If the borrower (the *mortgagor*) defaulted on the loan, however, the lender owned the property in fee simple absolute (no matter how much of the loan the mortgagor had repaid).

To ameliorate the harshness of this situation, courts of equity permitted the mortgagor to redeem the property by paying the full balance of the loan. To cut off this right of redemption—known as the equity of redemption—the lender had to seek foreclosure. Initially, this proceeding took the form of a *strict foreclosure*, in which the mortgagor was ordered to pay the debt within a certain period or be forever barred from doing so (thus leaving the mortgagee with fee simple title). Today, while strict foreclosure is still theoretically available in a few states, the primary method of foreclosure is through a *foreclosure sale* of the property.

> There are two main types of sale foreclosure used in the United States today. The most common type is judicial foreclosure where a public sale results after a full judicial proceeding in which all interested persons must be made parties. In many states this is the sole method of foreclosure. It is time-consuming and costly. The other method of foreclosure is by power of sale. Under this method, after varying types and degrees of notice to the parties, the property is sold at a public sale, either by some public official such as a sheriff, by the mortgagee, or by some other third party. No judicial proceeding is required in a power of sale foreclosure. It is generally available only where the mortgage instrument authorizes it. [1 Grant S. Nelson & Dale A. Whitman, Real Estate Finance Law § 1.4, at 9 (4th ed. 2002).]

If a foreclosure sale produces a price that exceeds the unpaid balance of the debt, the mortgage lender must return the surplus proceeds to the borrower. Conversely, if the sale proceeds are insufficient to repay the debt, the lender can obtain a deficiency judgment against the borrower for the balance. Some states, however, have enacted anti-deficiency statutes to protect some borrowers from deficiency judgments. *Id.* § 8.3 at 741–71.

Many states have codified the foreclosure procedures by statute. Some grant even further protection to mortgagors, giving them a statutory right to redeem the property by buying back the property even *after* the foreclosure sale. *See, e.g.,* Tenn. Code. Ann. § 66–8–101.

3. *Modern Approaches to Installment Land Contracts.* The discussion in note 2 demonstrates why a seller financing the purchase price for the buyer might prefer an installment contract rather than delivering legal title and taking back a "purchase money" mortgage on the land. Under the forfeiture clause in the installment land contract, the seller could cancel the contract, recover possession of the land, and retain the payments previously made by the buyer—even if the buyer had paid 90% of the purchase price! By contrast, a mortgage required the seller to conduct a costly and time-

consuming foreclosure sale and to return surplus proceeds from that sale to the buyer.

Under modern statutes and judicial decisions, forfeitures are not as readily available as they once were. Viewing installment contracts as economically equivalent to mortgages, some state legislatures have included installment contracts under the statutory foreclosure rules. *See, e.g.,* 735 Ill. Comp. Stat. 5/15–1106(2). Similarly, courts in some jurisdictions have refused to permit the installment seller to declare a forfeiture and instead require the seller to conduct a foreclosure sale. *See, e.g., Skendzel v. Marshall,* 261 Ind. 226, 301 N.E.2d 641 (1973). Section 3.4 of the Restatement (Third) of Property: Mortgages takes the same approach.

A number of jurisdictions still treat the installment contract as a "contract" rather than a mortgage and permit the installment seller to terminate the contract and recover possession upon the buyer's breach. Many of these jurisdictions mollify the harsh consequences of forfeiture through a variety of means, such as allowing the defaulting buyer to obtain specific performance (if the buyer can pay off the entire contract balance) or to seek restitution to the extent that the seller's retention of the buyer's prior installment payments would exceed the seller's actual damages incurred as a result of the buyer's breach. What approach does the court employ in *Daugherty?*

4. *Risk of Loss*

SANFORD v. BREIDENBACH

Court of Appeals of Ohio.
111 Ohio App. 474, 173 N.E.2d 702 (1960).

HUNSICKER, JUDGE. On January 14, 1959, James R. Sanford and Bianchi R. Sanford, his wife, herein known as "Sanford," agreed in writing to sell to Frederic (herein impleaded as "Frederick") R. Breidenbach, herein known as "Breidenbach," certain lands in the village of Hudson, Summit County, Ohio, upon which lands was an 8–room, 1-1/2 story, house and separate outbuilding. The agreed purchase price was $26,000. According to the terms of the contract, possession of the premises was to be delivered on transfer of the title, although Breidenbach did receive two keys to the house prior to its destruction by fire. He did enter the house with certain others, preparatory to having the heating system changed from oil heat to gas, to plan the location of furniture, and to show the new home to friends. Breidenbach also checked the oil tank to see if there was fuel to heat the house.

The written contract to purchase these premises had, on the reverse side thereof, the following provisions: ... "1. A proper legal agreement signed by all owners concerned shall be furnished by the sellers giving permanent permission to use of the present septic system by the purchasers and their successors and assigns." ...

On February 16, 1959, while the papers necessary to a transfer of title were being prepared, the 8–room house on the lands was totally destroyed by fire. Breidenbach immediately instructed the Evans Savings Association, that was to loan him a part of the money needed to buy the home, not to file the deed for record. This deed, transferring the premises from Sanford to Breidenbach, had been prepared and placed in escrow with the Evans Savings Association pending a title search.

When Breidenbach executed the contract of purchase, he secured from Northwestern Mutual Insurance Company a policy of insurance to protect him against loss in the event the 8–room house was destroyed by fire. The amount of this insurance was $22,000.

Sanford had maintained insurance on these premises in the sum of $20,000. The agent from whom Sanford purchased insurance, in accord with standing instructions from Sanford, renewed this insurance coverage on December 26, 1958. On learning that the premises were being sold, this agent, through his employee, cancelled this policy without authority from Sanford, and without notice to Sanford. There seems to be no great question herein that the terms of such policy were in full force and effect at the time of the fire.

On April 29, 1959, Sanford brought an action in the Common Pleas Court of Summit County, Ohio, against Breidenbach, Northwestern Mutual Insurance Company, and Hudson Village Real Estate Co., Inc. Breidenbach had deposited, with the real estate company, $12,000 as a partial payment for the premises. This sum has been, by arrangement of the parties, placed in escrow with a third party, and the real estate company is to all intents and purposes no longer involved herein. The principal relief sought by this action was specific performance of the contract to purchase the lands of Sanford.

Breidenbach, by way of cross-petition, brought Insurance Company of North America into the action by alleging that such company had insured the Sanford home against fire, and that such company should be made responsible for the loss suffered by Sanford, or, if the premises are decreed to be the property of Breidenbach, then his interest in the proceeds of the policy should be declared. . . .

After a trial of the issues herein, the court determined that Sanford was not entitled to specific performance, but that he should recover from each insurance company for the loss of the premises.

The judgment against Northwestern Mutual Insurance Company is $11,523.81 being 22/42 of the loss, and the judgment against Insurance Company of North America is $10,476.19, being 20/42 of the loss. The court added the amounts of the two policies, and then proportioned the loss in accord with the ratio which each policy bears to such total. . . .

We shall first direct our attention to the question of whether Sanford is entitled to specific performance, and shall therein consider whether Breidenbach was, under the doctrine of equitable conversion, the owner of the premises at the time the house was destroyed by fire. After a disposition of those questions, we shall then pass to the matter of the liability of the two insurance companies.

"A decree for the specific performance of a contract is not a matter of right, but of grace, granted on equitable principles, and rests in the sound discretion of the court." 37 Ohio Jurisprudence, Specific Performance, Section 20, at pp. 24 and 25, and authorities there cited.

The rule above set out is so well known that no authorities need be cited and it is such rule that must be applied in the instant case. We have a contract herein for the sale and purchase of real property, which made definite mention of a septic tank easement. The easement is, by the language used by the parties, an essential part of the contract. At the time of trial, August 3, 1959, a satisfactory septic tank easement had not been submitted to the purchaser, Breidenbach. The septic tank agreement submitted in May, 1959, provided that under certain conditions the right to use this facility terminated, whereas the provision of the contract made no such exception.

It is apparent, therefore, that at the time when specific performance was sought in the trial court, one of the material parts of the agreement had not been complied with, and hence we had an uncompleted contract. . . .

We therefore determine that specific performance cannot be decreed under the facts of this case.

Sanford insists that, even though specific performance may not lie, Breidenbach is to be considered in equity the owner of the premises; and, under the doctrine of equitable conversion, the loss, if any has ensued as a result of the destruction of the house by fire, must be placed upon Breidenbach and his insurer, Northwestern Mutual Insurance Company.

There are few cases in Ohio in which, in contracts for the sale and purchase of real property, the doctrine of equitable conversion has been discussed. Counsel have brought to our attention *Gilbert & Ives v. Port*, 28 Ohio St. 276; and *Oak Building and Roofing Co. v. Susor*, 32 Ohio App. 66, 166 N.E. 908; in which latter case the court, in following the pronouncement in *Gilbert & Ives v. Port, supra*, said: "Where contract for exchange of real estate contained no provision as to who should bear the loss in case any building on either of properties should be destroyed before deeds were executed, the purchaser must be regarded as equitable owner of property and loss by reason of fire destroying building before execution of deed falls on him.". . . [Editors' Note: *Gilbert & Ives* was an 1876 decision of the Supreme Court of Ohio applying the doctrine of equitable conversion in a risk-of-loss context.]

In general, the rule under the doctrine of equitable conversion is that a contract to sell real property vests the equitable ownership of the property in the purchaser; and thus, where there is any loss by a destruction of the property through casualty during the pendency of the contract (neither party being guilty of causing the destruction), such loss must be borne by the purchaser.

We do not find herein that possession had been given to Breidenbach. The incidental checking of the oil level in the heating system, and the acceptance of the key to the premises, do not constitute a surrender of possession to the purchaser in this case.

The courts of Ohio have spoken with reference to the rights of a vendor and purchaser where the purchaser has gone into possession of the premises agreed to be conveyed, for in the case of *Coggshall v. Marine Bank Co.*, 63 Ohio St. 88, at pages 96 and 97, 57 N.E. 1086, at page 1088, Judge Spear cites with approval the statement from *Jaeger v. Hardy*, 48 Ohio St. 335, 27 N.E. 863—". . . to the effect that a vendor's interest before conveyance 'is the legal title and a beneficial estate in the lands to the extent of the unpaid purchase money,' while that of the vendee is 'an equitable estate in the land equal to the amount of the purchase money paid by him, and which, upon full payment, may ripen into a complete equity entitling him to conveyance of the legal title according to the terms of the contract,' " and then says:

> This language cannot be reconciled with the proposition that the purchaser is the full owner and the vendor a mere naked trustee, and if we adhere to the principle above quoted, as we must, the latter proposition must fail. Every just right of the vendee is protected by the rule that his ownership extends to the amount of the purchase money paid, and the right to receive a deed upon payment of the balance of the purchase money in compliance with the contract. Possession by the purchaser gives notice of his right to all the world, and of nothing more . . . .

The better rule in cases such as that now before us, we believe, is that equitable conversion by the purchaser, in a contract to convey real property, does become effective in those cases in which the vendor has fulfilled all conditions and is entitled to enforce specific performance, and the parties, by their contract, intend that title shall pass to the vendee upon the signing of the contract of purchase. The case before us does not meet any of these requirements.

In 4 Pomeroy's Equity Jurisprudence (5 Ed.), Section 1161a, the author, quoting from "Chafee and Simpson, Cases on Equity," gives five rules concerning the risk of loss in contracts for the sale of real estate.

One of such rules, which we believe sustains our position herein, is stated by the author as follows: "That the risk of loss should be on the vendor until the time agreed upon for the conveyance of the legal title, and thereafter on the purchaser, unless the vendor is then in such default as to be unable specifically to enforce the contract." *See, also, Coolidge & Sickler, Inc. v. Regn*, 7 N.J. 93, 80 A.2d 554, 27 A.L.R.2d 437, at page 443.

It is hence our judgment that, since Sanford could not specifically enforce the contract of sale, and there was no intention expressed in the contract of purchase that the risk of loss should be on the vendee when the contract was executed by the parties, there is no basis to claim that equitable conversion existed, thereby placing the burden of loss by fire upon Breidenbach.

We now pass to the question of the liability of the respective insurance companies. As we have heretofore stated, Sanford had fire loss coverage in the amount of $20,000, with Insurance Company of North America as the insurer; Breidenbach, in order to protect whatever interest he had in such premises, secured a policy with a fire loss coverage of $22,000 with Northwestern Mutual Insurance Company.

It is our heretofore stated judgment that the policy of Insurance Company of North America is a valid and subsisting contract to indemnify Sanford for the loss he might sustain, if, as a result of fire, the house described in the policy was destroyed. This contract of insurance was not cancelled by the unilateral action of the agent for Insurance Company of North America.

At the time of the loss, Sanford was the owner of the premises, and hence the risk of loss must, in this case, fall upon him. With this view of the matter, it follows naturally that his insurer must respond under the terms of the policy for the face amount thereof.

Since we have determined that Sanford and not Breidenbach was the owner of the premises at the time of the fire, what, if any, interest did Breidenbach have in these premises?

It is true that he could have waived any defect in the title or a failure to give a septic tank agreement and insisted that the contract of sale be completed by a delivery to him of a deed to the lands. He did not, however, choose this course of action, but, since the subject matter of the contract was destroyed, he refused to accept delivery of a deed to the land. We have said, in effect, that he had a legal right to take this position.

Up to the moment when Breidenbach refused to complete the contract of purchase, he had an insurable interest in the premises. The contract of insurance with Northwestern Mutual Insurance Company insured Breidenbach and his legal representatives for loss by fire and other casualty; it did not insure Sanford or any other person except those "named in the policy." This policy which Breidenbach purchased was for his protection in the event he suffered a loss. Breidenbach did not suffer a loss: first, because all of the money he deposited in escrow, as a part of the purchase price for the premises, has been, or will be, returned to him under an agreement to that effect, made by the parties and Hudson Village Real Estate Company, Inc., the realtor herein; and, second, because by the judgment of this court he is not required to perform his contract. Inasmuch as Breidenbach suffered no indemnifiable loss in this matter, his insurer need not respond by way of money payment under the policy of insurance. . . .

Notes

1. *The Theoretical Basis for the Doctrine of Equitable Conversion.* During the gap period, the question "who is the owner—the vendor or the purchaser?" may arise in a number of different situations. In *Sanford,* the

question arises in the context of a casualty loss during the gap period. Generally, the "owner" of an item of property bears the risk of loss or damage to that property—a perfectly commonsense notion. But during the gap period, which party is the "owner"? In addressing the question of "ownership" during the gap period, courts have often (but not exclusively) turned to the doctrine of equitable conversion to help resolve disputes turning upon "ownership," both in casualty loss cases like *Sanford* and in other contexts as well. Consider the following examples involving situations other than casualty loss:

(a) Ziegler signs a contract to purchase Blueacre from Cheever. During the gap period, the local municipality announced the proposed formation of a new local sewer district. By statute, only the "owner" of land within the proposed district has standing to protest the formation of the district. How should a court decide whether Ziegler or Cheever is the "owner"? *See Committee of Protesting Citizens v. Val Vue Sewer Dist.*, 14 Wash. App. 838, 545 P.2d 42 (1976).

(b) Ziegler signs a contract to purchase Blueacre (located in Boone County) from Cheever. During the gap period, Zaranka obtains a judgment in Boone County District Court against Cheever for damages Zaranka suffered in an automobile accident. Under state law, a judgment constitutes a lien against all real property of the defendant located in the county where the judgment is docketed. Does Zaranka have a judgment lien against Blueacre? *Compare Mooring v. Brown*, 763 F.2d 386 (10th Cir. 1985) (yes, under Colorado law) *with Cannefax v. Clement*, 818 P.2d 546 (Utah 1991) (no). If Zaranka does have a judgment lien against Blueacre, how would you advise Ziegler about whether he has an obligation to perform the contract?

(c) Ziegler signs a contract to purchase Blueacre from Cheever for $100,000. During the gap period, Cheever dies. Cheever's will devised all of his real property to Ritchie, and all of his personal property to Ricketson. On the closing date, when Ziegler tenders the $100,000 purchase price, who is entitled to that money, Ritchie or Ricketson? *See In re Hills' Estate*, 222 Kan. 231, 564 P.2d 462 (1977).

(d) Ziegler signs a contract to purchase Blueacre from Cheever for $100,000. During the gap period, the state condemns Blueacre as part of a highway construction project. The judicially determined condemnation award is $120,000. What happens to the condemnation proceeds? *See County of San Diego v. Miller*, 13 Cal.3d 684, 119 Cal.Rptr. 491, 532 P.2d 139 (1975). What if the award had been only $80,000?

Based upon your reading of *Sanford* and your understanding of "equitable" interests, can you articulate the legal concept underlying the doctrine of equitable conversion? Under what circumstances may the court apply the doctrine of equitable conversion? Why does the *Sanford* court conclude that equitable conversion did not occur?

2. *Equitable Conversion as a Method for Allocating Risk of Loss.* The doctrine of equitable conversion often operates to shift the risk of a casualty loss during the gap period to the purchaser. Do you think this is the way that the typical parties to a real estate contract would choose to allocate the risk of loss if they considered the issue at the time of contracting? Does it

matter whether the contract is an earnest money contract as compared to an installment land contract? Consider the rationale advanced for the "equitable conversion" rule:

> There is no warranty or condition in the contract between [seller and buyer] that the property should be in the same condition when the transaction was completed as it was when the contract was made; [seller] did not guarantee that its then existing condition would continue until the legal title had passed, nor is such guaranty to be implied; neither did the loss occur on account of any negligence or wrongful act of his. It was purely an accident, and in such case equity places the loss upon the vendee, the equitable owner of the property. [*Maudru v. Humphreys*, 83 W.Va. 307, 98 S.E. 259, 261 (1919).]

3. *The "Massachusetts Rule."* Massachusetts rejects equitable conversion in the casualty loss context and instead imposes the risk of pre-closing loss upon the seller:

> [W]hen, as in this case, the conveyance is to be made of the whole estate, including both land and buildings, for an entire price, and the value of the buildings constitutes a large part of the total value of the estate, and the terms of the agreement show that they constituted an important part of the subject matter of the contract,... the contract is to be construed as subject to the implied condition that it no longer shall be binding if, before the time for the conveyance to be made, the buildings are destroyed by fire. The loss by the fire falls upon the vendor, the owner; and if he has not protected himself by insurance, he can have no reimbursement of this loss; but the contract is no longer binding upon either party. If the purchaser has advanced any part of the price, he can recover it back.... If the change in the value of the estate is not so great, or if it appears that the building did not constitute so material a part of the estate to be conveyed as to result in an annulling of the contract, specific performance may be decreed, with compensation for any breach of agreement, or relief may be given in damages. [*Libman v. Levenson*, 236 Mass. 221, 128 N.E. 13 (1920).]

Note that the Massachusetts rule contemplates the possibility of specific performance despite a casualty. In the quoted statement, to what do the words "compensation" and "damages" refer? If a buyer wishes to complete a purchase after a significant casualty, would a court ever deny performance if the seller objects? Would the amount of "compensation" sought by the buyer be relevant in resolving this question?

Which approach—equitable conversion or the Massachusetts rule—do you think is more consistent with the probable expectations of the parties as to their rights? In choosing between these approaches, does it matter which party is better able to oversee the property and guard against loss? Does it matter which party is more likely to carry insurance against the property?

After re-reading *Sanford*, would you characterize Ohio as an "equitable conversion" state? A "Massachusetts rule" state? Something else? Exactly when, under the court's analysis in *Sanford*, would the risk of loss shift from buyer to seller? Suppose that the Sanfords had obtained the septic easement required by the contract between the casualty and the time of closing. What advice would you have given Breidenbach regarding his obligation to perform the contract? Would this advice change if they had obtained the easement prior to the casualty?

4. *Statutory Reform—The Uniform Vendor and Purchaser Risk Act.* In response to criticism of the equitable conversion rule in risk of loss cases, the National Conference of Commissioners on Uniform State Laws enacted the Uniform Vendor and Purchaser Risk Act (the "UVPRA"), now adopted in 13 states. Section 1 of the UVPRA provides that, unless the contract expressly provides otherwise:

> (a) If, when neither the legal title nor the possession of the subject matter of the contract has been transferred, all or a material part thereof is destroyed without fault of the purchaser or is taken by eminent domain, the vendor cannot enforce the contract, and the purchaser is entitled to recover any portion of the price that he has paid;

> (b) If, when either the legal title or the possession of the subject matter of the contract has been transferred, all or any part thereof is destroyed without the fault of the vendor or is taken by eminent domain, the purchaser is not thereby relieved from a duty to pay the price, nor is he entitled to recover any portion thereof that he has paid.

What is the rationale underlying the UVPRA's allocation of risk? As a default rule, do you think the UVPRA rule is superior to the equitable conversion rule?

5. *Insuring Against the Risk of Loss.* The party that bears the risk of loss during the gap period obviously should obtain insurance against an unexpected casualty loss. But what if the party who bears the risk of loss fails to have coverage, either through inadvertence, neglect, or lack of awareness? For example, suppose that Ziegler contracts to purchase Blueacre from Cheever for $100,000, and that during the gap period Blueacre is damaged by fire, reducing its value to $10,000. Also, suppose that Blueacre is located in an "equitable conversion" jurisdiction (such that Ziegler has the risk of loss) and that while Ziegler is uninsured, Cheever continued making payments under the insurance policy he had prior to signing the sale contract. Can Cheever's insurer refuse to pay under the policy on the ground that Cheever has not suffered any loss, or on the ground that he has no insurable interest in Blueacre? *Compare Wolf v. Home Ins. Co.,* 100 N.J.Super. 27, 241 A.2d 28 (1968) (seller's insurer liable when fire occurred prior to closing and parties performed contract with no adjustment in purchase price) *with Westfall v. American States Ins. Co.,* 43 Ohio App.2d 176, 334 N.E.2d 523 (1974) (seller's insurer not liable when fire destroyed buildings that purchaser planned to demolish anyway and seller received full contract price at closing despite fire).

Suppose that Cheever's insurer does pay $90,000 to Cheever on account of the fire damage. Does Ziegler have any legal claim against those insurance proceeds? Could Cheever keep the proceeds and get a judgment against Ziegler for specific performance of Ziegler's obligation to pay the purchase price? *See Raplee v. Piper,* 3 N.Y.2d 179, 164 N.Y.S.2d 732, 143 N.E.2d 919 (1957); *Dubin Paper Co. v. Insurance Co. of N. Am.,* 361 Pa. 68, 63 A.2d 85 (1949).

LAWYERING EXERCISE
(Preventive Lawyering and Drafting)

BACKGROUND: You should recognize that all of the risk of loss rules—equitable conversion, the "Massachusetts rule," and the UVPRA—are merely default rules that govern in the absence of express contractual provisions. Because a "gap period casualty" is a foreseeable risk, any well-drafted contract will contain an express allocation of the risk of casualty loss during the gap period.

TASK: Your firm represents Bob Buyer, who is negotiating for the purchase of an antebellum home located in the city's historic district. The seller has proposed using the form purchase and sale contract on pages 792–97. What advice would you offer Buyer about signing a contract containing the risk of loss provision in that form? Do you see any potential problems? If so, what alternative would you propose?

E. THE ROLE OF LAWYERS

Now that you are familiar with some of the issues that arise in real estate transactions, it is time to revisit the questions we raised at the outset of this chapter relating to the attorney's role in the transaction. Is the American Bar Association correct in asserting that attorneys should be involved in *all* land transactions, as suggested in the ABA's report (pages 699–705)? Are there aspects of the transaction that constitute the practice of law such that only those persons with a law license may perform them?

Because the contract establishes the blueprint for the entire transaction, legal advice may well be effective only if it comes at the contract formation stage. Accordingly, in most major commercial real estate transactions, both parties are typically represented by their own counsel during contract negotiations. In residential real estate transactions, by contrast, most contracts are completed on pre-printed forms that are filled in by the real estate agent and signed by the buyer and seller without consulting an attorney. Although the agreement is typically binding upon its execution, some documents contain attorney approval clauses that permit review by an attorney after the fact. Consider the effectiveness of such clauses as you read the following case.

HUBBLE v. O'CONNOR

Appellate Court of Illinois, First District.
291 Ill.App.3d 974, 225 Ill.Dec. 825, 684 N.E.2d 816 (1997).

ZWICK, JUSTICE. . . . The facts of this case revolve around a common real estate transaction involving the purchase of a condominium. The written contract at issue contained an attorney review provision which allowed the contract to be voided if either sellers' or purchasers' attorney gave written notice of disapproval within 5 business days after formation of the contract. Although the agreement was signed and tendered by defendant-purchaser Paul O'Connor to seller-plaintiff Ron Hubble, the parties continued to discuss modifications to the agreement past the disapproval period. Two weeks after the disapproval period had expired, purchasers' attorney gave notice that he was invoking the disapproval clause. The parties filed cross-motions for summary judgment and, on February 28, 1996, the circuit court entered judgment in favor of the purchasers and against the sellers.

The contract is a standardized real estate sales agreement widely used in the Chicago area. The agreement was executed on June 8, 1993. The attorney disapproval clause within the agreement states in pertinent part:

> This contract is contingent upon the approval hereof as to form by the attorney(s) for Buyer and Seller within 5 Business days after Seller's acceptance of this contract. Unless written notice of disapproval is given within the time period specified above, then this contingency shall be deemed waived and this contract will remain in full force and effect.

> If written notice of disapproval is given within the time period specified above, this contract shall be null and void and the earnest money shall be returned to the Purchaser.

The contract also provides that notice of disapproval may be given or accepted by either of the parties' attorneys.

Although the attorney disapproval clause expired by its own terms on June 15, 1993, the parties agreed on that day to extend the disapproval period to June 22, 1993.... [From June 17, 1993, to June 30, 1993, the parties' attorneys exchanged several proposals for modifying the contract, but never finalized the documents.] On July 6, 1993, in a letter written to sellers' attorney, purchasers' attorney summarily stated he had "withdrawn attorney approval." He requested that the sellers return to his clients their earnest money....

In seeking summary judgment, sellers asserted that the purchasers had not exercised the attorney disapproval clause in a timely manner, and that the attempt to exercise it on July 6, 1993, was designed simply to exculpate purchasers from their binding contractual obligation to purchase the property. Sellers noted that purchasers conceded during discovery that part of their motivation in having their attorney withdraw his approval for the agreement was because defendant Paul O'Connor had a business opportunity to relocate from Chicago to Budapest, Hungary....

... [T]he record establishes that the purchasers submitted an offer to buy the sellers' condominium, promising to pay $330,000. The offer contained a condition subsequent, *i.e.*, if either attorney disapproved of the contract within a certain period, the contract would become void. Sellers accepted the offer on June 8, 1993. Clearly then, at this point in time, a binding contract was formed subject only to a condition subsequent. "[A]n offer that states that it is 'subject' to the approval of the attorneys of both parties creates a contract the moment it is accepted.'' *Corbin on Contracts,* Rev. Ed., Sec. 3.7, p. 336. The essential terms of the contract were that Ron and Barbarann Hubble would sell unit number 9 at 1616 N. Hudson, Chicago, for $330,000, to be paid by Lynda Simon and Paul O'Connor at closing. . . .

Recognizing the clear nature of written terms of the June 8 agreement, purchasers suggest that the parties essentially had an implied covenant that the contract would not become binding until the rider was executed. None of the writings or testimony, however, supports such a conclusion. Moreover, such an implied covenant would directly contradict the express covenant in the attorney disapproval clause that the contract would remain in full force and effect if timely notice of disapproval was not given. Express covenants abrogate the operation of implied covenants, so the allegation of an implied covenant is not permitted to overrule or modify the express agreement of the parties. . . . In addition, purchasers are precluded from offering testimony to contradict the terms of the written agreement because, where contract terms are clear and unambiguous, the terms of the written agreement must be given their ordinary and natural meaning, and parol evidence cannot be considered to vary that meaning. . . .

Once the contract came into existence on June 8, 1993, the only question regarding its enforceability was whether one of the attorneys would disapprove it within the stated disapproval period. The disapproval clause is unambiguous and we agree with sellers: purchasers' attorney never timely disapproved.

The first letter from purchasers' attorney after the contract was signed and delivered by defendant Paul O'Connor, was dated June 17, 1993. It stated:

> I have enclosed for your review and comment a proposed Rider to the above-captioned contract. Please give me a call to discuss after you have had a chance to review it.
>
> Thank you for your help.

Clearly, this letter did not invoke the attorney disapproval clause. It served merely to request changes to what was, at that time, a binding agreement.

After most of his suggested changes had been made to the agreement in the form of a proposed rider, purchasers' attorney, on the last day of the attorney disapproval period, June 22, 1993, again drafted a letter to the sellers. This letter stated:

> I would like to propose a final additional provision to the Rider which I previously submitted to you for discussion purposes.
>
> I would like to add a provision which allows for the earnest money to be paid in the form of a promissory note to your clients in lieu of an actual cash payment during the mortgage contingency period. . . .

I realize that this request is somewhat out of the ordinary, but is necessitated by tax concerns that my clients have. . . .

I emphasize that the purchasers have applied for the mortgage and have received indications that they will be receiving a positive outcome. The sole reason I am raising this is because of the tax concerns.

I appreciate your consideration of this. Please give me a call to discuss as soon as it is convenient.

Again, this letter hardly constitutes "disapproval" of the agreement. It does not clearly and unambiguously state that the contract would be disapproved and thereby voided unless the sellers agreed to the proposed modifications.

In any case, if there is doubt as to what was intended by the purchasers' actions, that doubt is resolved in favor of avoiding a forfeiture of the contract. *McElvain v. Dorris,* 298 Ill. 377, 379, 131 N.E. 608 (1921); see also *Restatement (Second) of Contracts,* Sec. 227, comment b ("when it is doubtful whether or not the agreement makes an event a condition of an obligor's duty, an interpretation is preferred that will reduce the risk of forfeiture"). This is because conditions subsequent such as attorney disapproval clauses operate to deny vested rights. . . .

The contract in this case specifically stated that "unless written notice of disapproval is given . . . the contract will remain in full force and effect." Unquestionably, the option to disapprove the agreement is a powerful right and basic fairness requires that any communication invoking the disapproval right be made clearly and unambiguously. Only after the sellers have notice of disapproval are they free to list the property for re-sale. Correspondingly, were the sellers to invoke the disapproval provision, it would be only after the purchasers had received unambiguous disapproval that they would be able to consider making offers on other residences. It would be fundamentally unfair, in our view, to allow one party to give ambiguous disapproval so as to play both sides of the fence, *i.e.,* to argue that a binding contract exists or that no contract exists, depending upon the development of subsequent events. . . .

Summarizing, we find that the writings here did not fairly inform the sellers that the contract would be voided under the attorney disapproval clause if the sellers failed to agree to the purchasers' suggested changes. We therefore find the contract became irrevocable when the attorney disapproval period ended on June 22, 1993. . . .

Notes

1. *The Unauthorized Practice of Law.* Are there aspects of the real estate transaction that constitute the practice of law, requiring that they be performed only by a lawyer? Suppose that Guthrie, after spending 20 years as a paralegal assisting a real estate attorney in conducting real estate closings, decides to open a business in which he will provide "closing

services"—including ordering and preparing title reports, coordinating communication between buyer and seller over title objections and other matters, preparing and filing deeds, mortgages and other closing documents, and coordinating the closing. May Guthrie legally provide these services, or is he subject to prosecution for engaging in the unauthorized practice of law?

Most authorities agree that drafting the deed, mortgage, and similar "legal documents" constitutes the practice of law. Under a *"pro se"* exception to this rule, however, a non-lawyer who is a party to the transaction (*e.g.*, the grantor or lender) may draft documents on that party's own behalf. *See, e.g. King v. First Capital Fin. Servs. Corp.*, 215 Ill.2d 1, 293 Ill.Dec. 657, 828 N.E.2d 1155 (2005) (lender was permitted to prepare its own loan documents, but it was unauthorized practice of law for non-lawyer and non-party to prepare loan documents without attorney supervision); *cf. Chicago Bar Ass'n v. Quinlan & Tyson, Inc.*, 34 Ill.2d 116, 214 N.E.2d 771 (1966) (non-lawyer real estate agent may fill in the blanks on contract form prepared by an attorney but may not fill in the blanks on deeds, mortgages, and "other legal instruments").

Beyond this point, there is disagreement regarding other aspects of the real estate transaction. *Compare, e.g., In re UPL Advisory Opinion 2003–2*, 277 Ga. 472, 588 S.E.2d 741 (2003) (unauthorized practice for non-lawyer to conduct real estate closing) *with Countrywide Home Loans, Inc. v. Kentucky Bar Ass'n*, 113 S.W.3d 105 (Ky. 2003) (real estate closing by non-lawyer is not unauthorized practice of law). Is it *essential* to have a licensed attorney perform certain functions as a means of protecting consumers against unknown or unappreciated risks? Or can non-lawyer real estate professionals adequately deliver those services when armed with standard form documentation and an awareness of the "typical" risks involved in most transactions?

2. *Personal Representation of the Parties.* As mentioned in the introduction to this section, most buyers and sellers complete residential real estate transactions without hiring their own attorneys. The real estate agent can help them fill in the blanks on a standardized form contract and, if an institutional mortgage is required, the lender will prepare the loan documents and oversee the procurement of title insurance as a means of protecting the lender's own interests. The lender or title company's attorney can prepare the deed and other closing documents and oversee the closing. So what value, if any, is there for sellers and buyers to have their own attorneys? *Compare* Michael Braunstein, *Structural Change and Inter–Professional Competitive Advantage: An Example Drawn From Residential Real Estate Conveyancing*, 62 Mo. L. Rev. 241 (1997) *with* Peter J. Birnbaum, *Illinois Real Estate Lawyers and the Battle to Control Residential Closings*, 84 Ill. B.J. 132 (1996).

Homeowners increasingly have turned to lower-cost options for selling their homes, whether through discount brokerage services or "for sale by owner," and frequently have taken advantage of the internet to reach a much broader audience. *See, e.g.*, Jeff Bailey, *Owners' Web Gives Realtors Run for Money*, N.Y. Times, Jan. 3, 2006, at A–1; Kristen M. Bolt, *A New Player in Real Estate Market with Home Sales and Commissions Climbing, Sellers Taking More Notice of Discount Brokerages*, Seattle Post–Intelligencer, Dec. 15, 2005, at A–1. Might attorneys have a more important role to play in these types of transactions, given that the homeowners are less likely to have the services of a realtor or relationships with a lender or mortgage broker? In which aspects of the transaction might attorneys be most likely to "add value?"

3. *Attorney Approval Clauses.* The *Hubble* case illustrates some of the issues that arise with the use of attorney approval clauses. First, the court concluded in *Hubble* that the attorney approval clause created a condition subsequent. What difference, if any, would it have made if the court had concluded the provision created a condition precedent?

Second, the language used in drafting the clause is critical. Suppose the parties used the following language from the standard form approved by the New Jersey State Bar and the New Jersey Association of Realtor Boards: "This is a legally binding contract that will become final within three business days. During this period you may choose to consult an attorney who can review and cancel the contract." Consider the following questions:

(a) Is this clause a condition precedent or condition subsequent? What happens if the client never consults an attorney after signing the form?

(b) What is the scope of the attorney's review under this clause? May the attorney cancel the contract because the purchase price is too high or the client gets cold feet?

(c) Is the attorney *required* to propose modifications that would cure the attorney's objections to the contract? Conversely, is the attorney *permitted* to propose modifications and, if so, what is the legal effect of the proposal—does it constitute a rejection, a counteroffer, or simply a suggestion? Without knowing the answer to this question, an attorney might inadvertently cancel a contract by proposing slight modifications that were not critical to the client's goals.

Are consumers helped or hindered by the use of attorney approval clauses? Should legislatures require that such clauses be included in all form contracts used by real estate agents? *See* Alice M. Noble–Allgire, *Attorney Approval Clauses in Residential Real Estate Contracts—Is Half a Loaf Better Than None?*, 48 Kan. L. Rev. 339 (2000).

4. *The "Cooling–Off" Provision.* A few states have enacted consumer protection statutes that give certain real estate buyers a time-limited right to cancel the contract. Consider the following Florida statute:

Any contract for the sale of a residential unit or a lease thereof for an unexpired term of more than 5 years shall contain: (a) The following legend in conspicuous type: THIS AGREEMENT IS VOIDABLE BY BUYER BY DELIVERING WRITTEN NOTICE OF THE BUYER'S INTENTION TO CANCEL WITHIN 15 DAYS AFTER THE DATE OF EXECUTION OF THIS AGREEMENT BY THE BUYER, AND RECEIPT BY BUYER OF ALL OF THE ITEMS REQUIRED TO BE DELIVERED TO HIM BY THE DEVELOPER UNDER SECTION 718.503, FLORIDA STATUTES. BUYER MAY EXTEND THE TIME FOR CLOSING FOR A PERIOD OF NOT MORE THAN 15 DAYS AFTER THE BUYER HAS RECEIVED ALL OF THE ITEMS REQUIRED. BUYER'S RIGHT TO VOID THIS AGREEMENT SHALL TERMINATE AT CLOSING. [Fla. Stat. Ann. § 718.503(1).]

Is this legislation a good idea? How does its protection for buyers differ from an attorney approval clause? Note that this statute applies only to sales of condominiums; why hasn't Florida extended this statute to all land sales? Would you expect sellers and real estate brokers to be inclined to use a form containing this language? Why or why not?

5. *Conflicts of Interest.* On occasion, the two parties to a real estate transaction will seek one attorney to "handle the transaction" for both, believing that this will save attorney fees while making sure that the "legalities" are followed. In many cases, these parties believe they have agreed on the essential aspects of the anticipated transaction and see the lawyer as primarily a scrivener who can simply handle the technical details of documenting the transfer. Although sometimes tempting—especially as a service to existing clients—representation of multiple parties is very often unwise, and dangerous for both the clients and their shared attorney.

Contemplating the need for limits on multiple representation, the ABA Model Rules of Professional Conduct provide:

(a) Except as provided in paragraph (b), a lawyer shall not represent a client if the representation involves a concurrent conflict of interest. A concurrent conflict of interest exists if:

    (1) the representation of one client will be directly adverse to another client; or

    (2) there is a significant risk that the representation of one or more clients will be materially limited by the lawyer's responsibilities to another client, a former client or a third person or by a personal interest of the lawyer.

(b) Notwithstanding the existence of a concurrent conflict of interest under paragraph (a), a lawyer may represent a client if:

    (1) the lawyer reasonably believes that the lawyer will be able to provide competent and diligent representation to each affected client;

    (2) the representation is not prohibited by law;

    (3) the representation does not involve the assertion of a claim by one client against another client represented by the lawyer in the same litigation or another proceeding before a tribunal; and

    (4) each affected client gives informed consent, confirmed in writing. [2004 ABA Model Rules of Professional Conduct, Rule 1.7.]

Consistent with this rule, under what circumstances could an attorney represent both buyer and seller in a residential real estate transaction?

LAWYERING EXERCISE
(Counseling, Negotiation and Drafting)

SITUATION: W.Y. Whitfield owns a single family residence at 219 E. Front Street, Carbondale, Illinois. She recently put "for sale by owner" signs in the yard and advertised the property in the local newspaper. A married couple, Gerry and Cindy Buys, visited the property and have expressed interest in purchasing it.

The Whitfield home was built in 1990 and has an ultra-modern design. It is a tri-level with four bedrooms upstairs and a spacious recreation room in the basement. Its amenities include a great room with sliding glass doors leading to a deck that wraps around three sides of the house, wood-burning fireplaces in the recreation room and great room, a hot tub on the deck, a built-in dishwasher and garbage disposal in the kitchen, and a water garden in the backyard.

Whitfield and the Buyses have reached agreement for the Buyses to purchase the Whitfield home for $180,000. This price includes the house, one acre of land upon which the house is located, and all fixtures in the home. Whitfield has completed a copy of the statutory Residential Real Property Disclosure Report, indicating that to her knowledge, there are no material defects in the physical condition of the house or land.

The Buyses are currently in the process of selling their own home, which is located at 1743 Main Street, Carterville, Illinois. They have accepted an offer for the home and are hoping to close within the next month. They intend to use the proceeds of that sale to pay the balance of the mortgage loan on that property. They also hope to have at least $5,000 left over for the downpayment on the Whitfield property. They will need to secure a new loan for the balance of the purchase price on the Whitfield property.

TASK 1: The Buyses and Whitfield have contacted your law firm for assistance in executing a real estate sales contract. They are confident that they have worked out all of the major details and simply need to have their agreement memorialized. At your request, the Buyses and Whitfield have come to your office for a meeting. How will you proceed? Under what circumstances, if any, would it be appropriate for you to represent both parties in this transaction? To appreciate the complexities of this question, be prepared to address the following issues during the meeting with the parties:

(a) What will you need to do to comply with Model Rule 1.7? What information do you need from the Buyses and Whitfield to determine whether you can represent both parties in memorializing the agreement? What information do you need to communicate to the Buyses and Whitfield to ensure that you would have their *informed* consent?

(b) Assume that you would use the form contract on pages 792–97 as a template for the Buys–Whitfield contract. How will you gather the information you need to complete the document? What advice will you give them about how the contract should be drafted?

(c) Which of these issues should you approach first? Suppose that you started by getting the parties' consent and then proceeded to conduct a detailed review of the form contract. How will you respond if the Buyses or Whitfield ask questions about their respective rights or obligations under various provisions of the contract? How will you respond if one of the parties asks you to change a provision and the other party objects? Do the answers to these questions help you rethink how you would fulfill your obligations under Model Rule 1.7?

TASK 2: Assume, for purposes of this task, that the Buyses and Whitfield each hired an attorney to represent them in finalizing the real estate sales contract. You are the attorney for one of the parties (as assigned by your instructor). Schedule a meeting with both attorneys and their clients present to complete the negotiations. Use the form contract on pages 792–97 as a template and modify its terms, as needed, to accomplish the clients' objectives. [Your instructor may give the clients additional information relevant to the negotiations.]

Chapter 10

GOVERNMENTAL LAND USE CONTROLS: JUDICIAL DOCTRINES AND LEGISLATIVE REGULATION

Conflicts frequently arise regarding how land is used or how society may want land to be used. The law of servitudes (as discussed in Chapter 8) sometimes operates to avoid and/or resolve these disputes, but only in circumstances where owners have created contractual servitudes. Chapter 10 explores *public* land use controls as reflected in the common law of public and private nuisance, the regulatory structure of zoning, and the government's ability to use its police powers to regulate land use.

A. THE LAW OF NUISANCE

1. *What Is a Nuisance?*

There is perhaps no more impenetrable jungle in the entire law than that which surrounds the word "nuisance."... There is general agreement that it is incapable of any exact or comprehensible definition. Few terms have afforded so excellent an illustration of the familiar tendency of the courts to seize upon a catchword as a substitute for analysis of a problem; the defendant's interference with the plaintiff's interests is characterized as a "nuisance," and there is nothing more to be said. [William L. Prosser, Handbook of the Law of Torts 549 (1st ed. 1941).]

As discussed in Chapter 8, neighbors often rely upon servitudes to reconcile in advance potentially incompatible land uses in neighborhoods. But what happens when conflict about appropriate and permissible land uses arises between neighbors in the absence of any servitude regime or other consensual private arrangements? Long before the law of servitudes evolved, courts developed the law of *nuisance* to regulate such conflicts, and to define when one landowner could face liability for—or could be enjoined from engaging in—conduct that interfered with another's use and enjoyment of her land.

Courts frequently cite, as a principle deeply imbedded in our law, the Latin maxim *sic utere tuo ut alienum non laedas*—roughly translated "one must so use her property as not to injure that of another." The law of nuisance provides that although each landowner has the general right to make use of her land as she wishes, no landowner has the right to use her land in a way that unreasonably interferes with her neighbors' enjoyment of their possessory rights in their land. As a practical matter, *A*'s use of the 10 feet of land on her side of a common boundary line with *B* almost inevitably affects *B*'s enjoyment of the adjoining land on his side of the boundary. But while we all must accept *reasonable* interferences with our use and enjoyment of land, we should not have to accept *unreasonable* interferences. The difficulty arises in trying to distinguish between reasonable and unreasonable interferences.

The Restatement (Second) of Torts employs an explicit balancing test to determine whether one landowner's conduct should be considered a nuisance.

§ 821. Significant Harm. There is liability for a nuisance only to those to whom it causes significant harm, of a kind that would be suffered by a normal person in the community or by property in normal condition and used for a normal purpose.

§ 822. General Rule. One is subject to liability for a private nuisance if, but only if, his conduct is a legal cause of an invasion of another's interest in the private use and enjoyment of land, and the invasion is either

(a) intentional and unreasonable, or

(b) unintentional and otherwise actionable under the rules controlling liability for negligent or reckless conduct, or for abnormally dangerous conditions or activities.

§ 825. Intentional Invasion—What Constitutes. An invasion of another's interest in the use and enjoyment of land or an interference with the public right, is intentional if the actor

(a) acts for the purpose of causing it, or

(b) knows that it is resulting or is substantially certain to result from his conduct.

§ 826. Unreasonableness of Intentional Invasion. An intentional invasion of another's interest in the use and enjoyment of land is unreasonable if

(a) the gravity of the harm outweighs the utility of the actor's conduct, or

(b) the harm caused by the conduct is serious and the financial burden of compensating for this and similar harm to others would not make the continuation of the conduct not feasible.

§ 827. Gravity of Harm—Factors Involved. In determining the gravity of the harm from an intentional invasion of another's interest in the use and enjoyment of land, the following factors are important:

(a) the extent of the harm involved;

(b) the character of the harm involved;

(c) the social value that the law attaches to the type of use or enjoyment invaded;

(d) the suitability of the particular use or enjoyment invaded to the character of the locality; and

(e) the burden on the person harmed of avoiding the harm.

§ 828. Utility of Conduct—Factors Involved. In determining the utility of conduct that causes an intentional invasion of another's interest in the use and enjoyment of land, the following factors are important:

(a) the social value that the law attaches to the primary purpose of the conduct;

(b) the suitability of the conduct to the character of the locality; and

(c) the impracticability of preventing or avoiding the invasion.

§ 829. Gravity vs. Utility—Conduct Indecent or Malicious. An intentional invasion of another's interest in the use and enjoyment of land is unreasonable if the harm is significant and the actor's conduct is

(a) for the sole purpose of causing harm to the other; or

(b) contrary to common standards of decency.

§ 829A. Gravity vs. Utility—Severe Harm. An intentional invasion of another's interest in the use and enjoyment of land is unreasonable if the harm resulting from the invasion is severe and greater than the other should be required to bear without compensation.

The following materials demonstrate that stating the maxim is far easier than understanding exactly when *A*'s use of her land legally constitutes a nuisance. Determining whether something is a nuisance requires the balancing of a multitude of factors—something that might be a nuisance in one situation might not be a nuisance in another situation. Hence, Professor Prosser's description of nuisance as an "impenetrable jungle."

CARPENTER v. THE DOUBLE R CATTLE CO., INC.

Supreme Court of Idaho.

108 Idaho 602, 701 P.2d 222 (1985).

BAKES, JUSTICE.... Plaintiff appellants are homeowners who live near a cattle feedlot owned and operated by respondents. Appellants filed a complaint in March, 1978, alleging that the feedlot had been expanded in 1977 to accommodate the feeding of approximately 9,000 cattle. Appellants further alleged that "the spread and accumulation of manure, pollution of river and ground water, odor, insect infestation, increased concentration of birds, ... dust and noise" allegedly caused by the feedlot constituted a nuisance. After a trial on the merits a jury found that the feedlot did not constitute a nuisance. The trial court then also made findings and conclusions that the feedlot did not constitute a nuisance.

Appellants assigned as error the jury instructions ... that in the determination of whether a nuisance exists consideration should be given to such factors as community interest, utility of conduct, business standards and practices, gravity of harm caused, and the circumstances surrounding the parties' movement to their locations. On appeal, appellants chose not to provide an evidentiary record, but merely claimed that the instructions misstated the law in Idaho.

The case was assigned to the Court of Appeals which reversed and remanded for a new trial. The basis for this reversal was that the trial court did not give a jury instruction based upon subsection (b) of Section 826 of the Restatement (Second) of Torts. That subsection allows for a finding of a nuisance even though the gravity of harm is outweighed by the utility of the conduct if the harm is "serious" and the payment of damages is "feasible" without forcing the business to discontinue.

This Court granted defendant's petition for review. We hold that the instructions which the trial court gave were not erroneous, being consistent with our prior case law and other persuasive authority. We further hold that the trial court did not err in not giving an instruction based on subsection (b) of Section 826 of the Second Restatement, which does not represent the law in the State of Idaho.... Accordingly, the decision of the Court of Appeals is vacated, and the judgment of the district court is affirmed....

The Court of Appeals, without being requested by appellant, adopted the new subsection (b) of Section 826 of the Second Restatement partially because of language in *Koseris v. J.R. Simplot Co.*, 352 P.2d 235 (Idaho 1960), which reads: "We are constrained to hold that the trial court erred in sustaining objections to those offers of proof [evidence of utility of conduct], since they were relevant as bearing upon the issue whether respondents, in seeking injunctive relief, were pursuing the proper remedy; nevertheless, on the theory of damages which respondents had waived, the ruling was correct." 352 P.2d at 239. The last phrase of the quote, relied on by the Court of Appeals, is clearly dictum, since the question of utility of conduct in a nuisance action for damages was not at issue in *Koseris*. It is very doubtful that this Court's dictum in *Koseris* was intended to make such a substantial change in the nuisance law. When the isolated statement of dictum was made in 1960, there was no persuasive authority for such a proposition. Indeed, no citation of authority was given. The [two] cases from other jurisdictions which the Court of Appeals relied on for authority did not exist until 1970. *See Boomer v. Atlantic Cement Co.*, 257 N.E.2d 870 (N.Y. 1970); *Jost v. Dairyland Power Co-op.*, 172 N.W.2d 647 (1970).... The Second Restatement, which proposed the change in the law by adding subsection (b) to Section 826, was also not in existence until 1970. Therefore, we greatly discount this Court's dictum in the 1960 *Koseris* opinion as authority for such a substantial change in the nuisance law. The case of *McNichols v. J.R. Simplot Co.*, 262 P.2d 1012 (Idaho 1953) should be viewed as the law in Idaho that in a nuisance action seeking damages the interests of the community, which would include the utility of the conduct, should be considered in the determination of the existence of a nuisance. The trial court's instructions in the present case were entirely consistent with *McNichols*. A plethora of other modern cases are in accord.

The State of Idaho is sparsely populated and its economy depends largely upon the benefits of agriculture, lumber, mining and industrial development. To eliminate the utility of conduct and other factors listed by the trial court from the criteria to be considered in determining whether a nuisance exists, as the appellant has argued throughout this appeal, would place an unreasonable burden upon these industries. We see no policy reasons which should compel this Court to accept appellant's argument and depart from our present law. Accordingly, the judgment of the district court is affirmed and the Court of Appeals decision is set aside.

BISTLINE, JUSTICE, dissenting.... The majority today continues to adhere to ideas on the law of nuisance that should have gone out with the use of buffalo chips as fuel. We have before us today homeowners complaining of a nearby feedlot—not a small operation, but rather a feedlot which accommodates 9,000 cattle. The homeowners advanced the theory that after the expansion of the feedlot in 1977, the odor, manure, dust, insect infestation and increased concentration of birds which accompanied all of the foregoing, constituted a nuisance. If the odoriferous quagmire created by 9,000 head of cattle is not a nuisance, it is difficult for me to imagine what is. However, the real question for us today is the legal basis on which a finding of nuisance can be made.

The Court of Appeals adopted subsection (b) of § 826 of the Restatement (Second) of Torts. The majority today rejects this Restatement section, reasoning that the Court of Appeals improperly relied upon dictum in *Koseris v. J.R. Simplot Co.*, 352 P.2d 235 (Idaho 1960). Instead, the majority holds that the 1953 case of *McNichols v. J.R. Simplot Co.*, 262 P.2d 1012 (Idaho 1953) espoused the correct rule of law for Idaho: in a nuisance action seeking damages, the interests of the community, which includes the utility of the conduct, should be considered in determining the existence of a nuisance. I find nothing immediately wrong with this statement of the law and agree wholeheartedly that the interests of the community should be considered in determining the existence of a nuisance. However, where this primitive rule of law fails is in recognizing that in our society, while it may be desirable to have a serious nuisance continue because the utility of the operation causing the nuisance is great, at the same time, those directly impacted by the serious nuisance deserve some compensation for the invasion they suffer as a result of the continuation of the nuisance. This is exactly what the more progressive provisions of § 826(b) of the Restatement (Second) of Torts addresses. Clearly, § 826(b) recognizes that the continuation of the serious harm must remain feasible. What § 826(b) adds is a method of compensating those who must suffer the invasion without putting out of business the source or cause of the invasion. This does not strike me as a particularly adventuresome or far-reaching rule of law. In fact, the fairness of it is overwhelming.

The majority's rule today overlooks the option of compensating those who suffer a nuisance because the interests of the community outweigh the interests of those afflicted by the nuisance. This unsophisticated balancing overlooks the possibility that it is not necessary that one interest be ignored when the community interest is strong. We should not be adopting a rule of preference which suggests that if the community interest is preferred any other interest must be disregarded. Instead, § 826(b) accommodates adverse interests by contemplating continuation of the facility which creates the nuisance while compensating those who suffer the direct impact of the nuisance—in the instant case the homeowners who live in the vicinity of the feedlot.

The majority's rule today suggests that part of the cost of industry, agriculture or development must be borne by those unfortunate few who have the fortuitous luck to live in the immediate vicinity of a nuisance producing facility. Frankly, I think this naive economic view is ridiculous in both its simplicity and its outdated view of modern economic society. The "cost" of a product includes not only the amount it takes to produce such a product but also includes the external costs: the damage done to the environment through pollution of air or water is an example of an external cost. In the instant case, the nuisance suffered by the homeowners should be considered an external cost of operating a feedlot and producing beef for public consumption. I do not believe that a few should be required to pay this extra cost of doing business by going uncompensated for a nuisance of this sort. If a feedlot wants to continue, I say fine, providing compensation is paid for the serious invasion (the odors, flies, dust, etc.) of the homeowner's interest. My only qualification is that the financial burden of compensating for this harm should not be such as to force the feedlot (or any other industry) out of business. The true cost can then be shifted to the consumer who rightfully should pay for the entire cost of producing the product he desires to obtain.

The majority today blithely suggests that because the State of Idaho is sparsely populated and because our economy is largely dependent on agriculture, lumber, mining and industrial development, we should forego compensating those who suffer a serious invasion. If humans are such a rare item in this state, maybe there is all the more reason to protect them from the discharge of industry. At a minimum, we should compensate those who suffer a nuisance at the hands of industry and agriculture. What the majority overlooks is that the cost of development should not be absorbed by few, but rather should be spread out and paid by all. I am not convinced that agriculture or industry will be put out of business by requiring compensation for the nuisance they generate. Let us look at the case before us. The owners of the feedlot will not find themselves looking for new jobs if they are required to compensate the homeowners for the stench and dust and flies attendant with 9,000 head of cattle. Rather, meat prices at the grocery store will undoubtedly go up. But, in my view it is far better that the cost of the nuisance be carried by the consumer of a product than by the unfortunate homeowners currently suffering under adverse conditions. Some compensation should be paid the homeowners for suffering the burden from which we all benefit....

Notes

1. *Property Rules, Entitlements and the Restatement's Balancing Test— When Is a Nuisance Not a Nuisance?* Decisions in nuisance cases basically involve the allocation of an entitlement. What are the consequences for the plaintiffs after the court's conclusion that operation of the cattle feedlot was not a nuisance? If the plaintiffs want to stay on their land, but be free from the "interferences" attributable to the feedlot, what will they need to do?

In some cases factually similar to *Carpenter*, courts have enjoined the operation of animal feedlots or cement plants as a nuisance. *See, e.g., Valasek v. Baer*, 401 N.W.2d 33 (Iowa 1987) (granting injunction against spreading of wastes from hog confinement facility within a few hundred feet of plaintiffs' homes); *Morgan County Concrete Co. v. Tanner*, 374 So.2d 1344 (Ala. 1979) (granting injunction against operator of ready-mix concrete plant due to dust and noise). What is the consequence of the issuance of an injunction in such a circumstance? If the defendant wants to continue to engage in the desired conduct, what will the defendant have to do?

Sections 826(a), 827, and 828 explicitly integrate the relative social utility of each landowner's conduct in determining whether a nuisance exists. As a result, an otherwise significant interference with one landowner's use and enjoyment of her land may not be a nuisance if the offending landowner's conduct is of significant social utility. *Carpenter* highlights one consequence of applying this balancing test in certain circumstances: a landowner located adjacent to an activity of great social utility arguably must accept greater interference with the use and enjoyment of her land than a landowner located adjacent to an activity of lesser social utility. At least one scholar has noted that courts concerned about the consequences of injunctive relief if a nuisance is found tended to conclude that conduct that caused significant harm did not constitute a nuisance, even though the landowner engaged in the conduct could have absorbed the costs associated with diminishing the harm to neighboring owners. *See* Robert Ellickson, *Alternatives to Zoning: Covenants, Nuisance Rules, and Fines as Land Use Controls*, 40 U. Chi. L. Rev. 681 (1973).

2. *The Restatement's Balancing Test Revisited—Sections 826(b) and 829A.* Read Justice Bistline's dissent carefully. Do you think Justice Bistline is correct that the balancing test (as reflected in sections 826(a), 827, and 828) makes little sense from the standpoint of economic efficiency because it fails to encourage defendants to internalize external costs? Why or why not? How do sections 826(b) and 829A adjust the framework of the Restatement's balancing test?

3. *Entitlements and Economic Efficiency Revisited.* Some economics scholars (most notably Ronald Coase) question the appropriateness of requiring the defendant to internalize external costs. Coase argues that nuisance problems present a 'joint cost' or 'reciprocal cost' conundrum. While many view a factory (or feedlot) as imposing external costs on neighboring homeowners, one could just as easily say that homeowners are imposing external costs on neighboring landowners who want to use their land for a feedlot. Giving the feedlot the right to pollute imposes external costs on the neighboring homeowners, but giving the homeowners the right to be free from pollution imposes external costs on the feedlot. Coase suggests that no clear justification exists to impose on the feedlot (rather than the homeowners) the obligation to internalize external costs. Coase further suggests that in the absence of transaction costs, it does not matter to whom the law awards the entitlement. Regardless of who possesses the initial entitlement (*i.e.*, the right to engage in certain conduct, or the right to prevent it), market forces will produce negotiations that will reallocate the entitlement if reallocation would lead to a more efficient result (assuming the parties have perfect information and can bargain freely). Under this view, it should not matter whether a facility has the "right" to pollute or the neighboring landowners have the "right" to be free from pollution. Either way, the party who places the greater value on its use has the ability to bargain to accomplish what it believes is in its best interest. In other words, if the facility has the "right" to pollute, but the neighbors place a greater value on being free from pollution than the facility places on its right to pollute, the neighbors can pay the facility for the "right" to be free from pollution. Conversely, if the neighbors have the "right" to be free from pollution, but the facility places a greater value on having the "right" to pollute, the facility can buy this right from the neighbors. *See, e.g.*, Ronald Coase, *The Problem of Social Cost*, 3 J. L. & Econ. 1 (1960).

From a practical standpoint, are there any holes in this theory? What problems can hinder the parties in their efforts to reach an efficient result? Even if the parties can reallocate the entitlement to reach an efficient result, does that necessarily mean that how the law initially allocates that entitlement does not matter? *See* Frank Michelman, *Pollution as a Tort: A Non–Accidental Perspective on Calabresi's Costs*, 80 Yale L. J. 647 (1971); Ellickson, *supra* note 1; Ward Farnsworth, *Do Parties to Nuisance Cases Bargain After Judgment? A Glimpse Inside the Cathedral*, 66 U. Chi. L. Rev. 373 (1999) (in set of nuisance cases involving a small number of parties, none of the parties engaged in further negotiation after the judgment assigning the entitlement).

4. *Proof Problems—Causation and Extent of Harm.* A landowner complaining that a neighbor's conduct unreasonably interferes with her use and enjoyment of her land must show that such conduct is the proximate cause of that interference. Causation may be clear in some cases, *e.g.,* where distinct loud noises interfere with someone's use and enjoyment of her land. *See, e.g., Maykut v. Plasko,* 170 Conn. 310, 365 A.2d 1114 (1976) (use of corn cannon to scare birds held a nuisance); *Sakler v. Huls,* 183 N.E.2d 152 (Ohio Ct. Com. Pl. 1961) (drag strip constituted nuisance). In some cases, however, background sources of noise or pollution may make it difficult to prove that the targeted defendant is "causing" the unreasonable interference. *See, e.g., Karpiak v. Russo,* 450 Pa.Super. 471, 676 A.2d 270 (1996) (noise from landscaping business not nuisance given limited impact and other sources); *Bove v. Donner–Hanna Coke Corp.,* 236 A.D. 37, 258 N.Y.S. 229 (1932) (dust, soot and noise from industrial facility in industrial region of city not nuisance). The plaintiff also may find it difficult to prove that the conduct resulted in a significant interference with use and enjoyment. *See, e.g., Leaf River Forest Prods., Inc. v. Ferguson,* 662 So.2d 648 (Miss. 1995) (paper mill's discharge of dioxin-containing wastewater did not constitute nuisance to residents miles downstream); *State of New York v. Fermenta ASC Corp.,* 166 Misc.2d 524, 630 N.Y.S.2d 884 (Sup. Ct. 1995) (release of chemical contaminant into groundwater did not constitute nuisance at concentrations found in groundwater); *Langan v. Bellinger,* 203 A.D.2d 857, 611 N.Y.S.2d 59 (1994) (church bells not a nuisance).

5. *First-in-Time and "Coming to the Nuisance."* Should it matter whether the landowner had been engaged in the allegedly offensive conduct long before a neighbor began his competing use? As we have seen repeatedly, property law often allocates entitlements based upon the "first-in-time, first-in-right" principle. Sometimes, as we saw in Chapter 3, property law reallocates those entitlements despite the first-in-time principle. When should the law of nuisance allow a prior use to continue, even though it may result in an unreasonable interference with a neighbor's subsequent use? Should someone who "comes to a nuisance" be foreclosed from bringing suit? Section 840D of the Restatement (Second) of Torts suggests that "coming to the nuisance" is not determinative, but is simply a factor in deciding whether an alleged nuisance is actionable.

For example, suppose that Organ Scrap Metal, Inc. has owned and operated an automobile shredding facility for 30 years. At the time Organ began operating, there were two persons residing within one mile of the facility. Ten years later, this number had grown to six; after 10 more years, it had grown to 15. Now there are 35 neighbors living within one mile of Organ's facility, all of whom bring a nuisance action against Organ complaining of the explosions, noise, and emissions coming from the facility. Assuming that Organ's operation significantly interferes with the neighbors' use and enjoyment of their land, should the neighbors necessarily prevail? Are the arguments of all the neighbors equally compelling? *See Hoffman v. United Iron & Metal Co.,* 108 Md.App. 117, 671 A.2d 55 (1996).

6. *"Coming to the Nuisance" and "Right-to-Farm Statutes".* Suburban growth has produced increasing tension between farmers (who wish to continue their agricultural life) and nonfarmers (who wish to pursue metropolitan life but seek to reside in "the country" while they do so). Acting to preserve the agricultural communities near growing metropolitan centers, many state legislatures have passed "right-to-farm" statutes legislating that certain agricultural activities cannot constitute a nuisance under certain circumstances—generally if they have been in operation for a year or more. *See, e.g.,* Jacqueline P. Hand, *Right-to-Farm Laws: Breaking New Ground In The Preservation of Farmland,* 45 U. Pitt. L. Rev. 289 (1984); Margaret R. Grossman & Thomas G. Fischer, *Protecting the Right to Farm: Statutory Limits on Nuisance Actions Against the Farmer,* 1983 Wis. L. Rev. 95.

Livestock feedlot disputes like those reflected in *Carpenter* have reemerged in recent years with the development of confined animal feeding operations ("CAFOs") in the hog and poultry industries. For example, pork producers have constructed large automated facilities that house tens of thousands of hogs in elevated pens. The floors are rinsed on a regularly scheduled basis, with wastewater pumped to on-site "lagoons." After temporary retention in the lagoons, the wastewater is applied to surrounding agricultural land as fertilizer. Many of these facilities have encountered frequent problems with releases of wastewater that have resulted in fish kills. More significant for many neighboring landowners, however, is the odor that results from such a large concentration of animals generating so much waste. These situations continue to prompt nuisance actions, as well as other types of enforcement actions under environmental statutes. *See, e.g., Sierra Club v. Wayne Weber LLC,* 689 N.W.2d 696 (Iowa 2004).

LAWYERING EXERCISE
(Counseling Amidst Uncertainty)

SITUATION: Suppose that Westbrook seeks your advice about the operation of a cement plant located three-quarters of a mile from his residence. Westbrook complains that the dust from this plant is so bad that he must remain indoors and cannot work in his yard without a special mask for breathing.

TASK: How would you advise Westbrook regarding the value of investing in a nuisance action? What costs would you need to make him aware of in helping him decide whether to invest in a nuisance action? What would you tell Westbrook about his likelihood of success if he wanted to obtain injunctive relief?

2. *Determining the Appropriate Remedy*

A plaintiff may pursue damages, an injunction, or both when bringing a nuisance action. After concluding that a nuisance exists, courts frequently look to the Restatement's balancing test in deciding whether to protect the plaintiff using a property rule (injunction), a liability rule (damages), or some combination of the two. What does the following case suggest about the circumstances in which each remedy is most appropriate?

P sought injunction
Drums cement plant

BOOMER v. ATLANTIC CEMENT CO.

Court of Appeals of New York.
26 N.Y.2d 219, 309 N.Y.S.2d 312, 257 N.E.2d 870 (1970).

BERGAN, JUDGE. Defendant operates a large cement plant near Albany. These are actions for injunction and damages by neighboring land owners alleging injury to property from dirt, smoke and vibration emanating from the plant. A nuisance has been found after trial, temporary damages have been allowed; but an injunction has been denied.

The public concern with air pollution arising from many sources in industry and in transportation is currently accorded ever wider recognition accompanied by a growing sense of responsibility in State and Federal Governments to control it. Cement plants are obvious sources of air pollution in the neighborhoods where they operate.

But there is now before the court private litigation in which individual property owners have sought specific relief from a single plant operation. The threshold question raised . . . is whether the court should resolve the litigation between the parties now before it as equitably as seems possible; or whether, seeking promotion of the general public welfare, it should channel private litigation into broad public objectives.

A court performs its essential function when it decides the rights of parties before it. Its decision of private controversies may sometimes greatly affect public issues. Large questions of law are often resolved by the manner in which private litigation is decided. But this is normally an incident to the court's main function to settle controversy. It is a rare exercise of judicial power to use a decision in private litigation as a purposeful mechanism to achieve direct public objectives greatly beyond the rights and interests before the court.

Effective control of air pollution is a problem presently far from solution even with the full public and financial powers of government. In large measure adequate technical procedures are yet to be developed and some that appear possible may be economically impracticable.

It seems apparent that the amelioration of air pollution will depend on technical research in great depth; on a carefully balanced consideration of the economic impact of close regulation; and of the actual effect on public health. It is likely to require massive public expenditure and to demand more than any local community can accomplish and to depend on regional and interstate controls.

A court should not try to do this on its own as a by-product of private litigation and it seems manifest that the judicial establishment is neither equipped in the limited nature of any judgment it can pronounce nor prepared to lay down and implement an effective policy for the elimination of air pollution. This is an area beyond the circumference of one private lawsuit. It is a direct responsibility for government and should not thus be undertaken as an incident to solving a dispute between property owners and a single cement plant—one of many—in the Hudson River valley.

The cement making operations of defendant have been found by the court of Special Term to have damaged the nearby properties of plaintiffs in these two actions. That court, as it has been noted, accordingly found defendant maintained a nuisance and this has been affirmed at the Appellate Division. The total damage to plaintiffs' properties is, however, relatively small in comparison with the value of defendant's operation and with the consequences of the injunction which plaintiffs seek.

The ground for the denial of injunction, notwithstanding the finding both that there is a nuisance and that plaintiffs have been damaged substantially, is the large disparity in economic consequences of the nuisance and of the injunction. This theory cannot, however, be sustained without overruling a doctrine which has been consistently reaffirmed in several leading cases in this court and which has never been disavowed here, namely that where a nuisance has been found and where there has been any substantial damage shown by the party complaining an injunction will be granted.

The rule in New York has been that such a nuisance will be enjoined although marked disparity be shown in economic consequence between the effect of the injunction and the effect of the nuisance.

The problem of disparity in economic consequence was sharply in focus in *Whalen v. Union Bag & Paper Co.*, 101 N.E. 805 (N.Y. 1913). A pulp mill entailing an investment of more than a million dollars polluted a stream in which plaintiff, who owned a farm, was "a lower riparian owner." The economic loss to plaintiff from this pollution was small. This court, reversing the Appellate Division, reinstated the injunction granted by the Special Term against the argument of the mill owner that in view of "the slight advantage to plaintiff and the great loss that will be inflicted on defendant" an injunction should not be granted. *Id.* at 805. "Such a balancing of injuries cannot be justified by the circumstances of this case," Judge Werner noted. *Id.* He continued: "Although the damage to the plaintiff may be slight as compared with the defendant's expense of abating the condition, that is not a good reason for refusing an injunction." *Id.* at 806.

Thus the unconditional injunction granted at Special Term was reinstated. The rule laid down in that case, then, is that whenever the damage resulting from a nuisance is found not "unsubstantial," viz., $100 a year, injunction would follow. This states a rule that had been followed in this court with marked consistency. *McCarty v. Natural Carbonic Gas Co.*, 81 N.E. 549 (N.Y. 1907); *Strobel v. Kerr Salt Co.*, 58 N.E. 142 (N.Y. 1900).

. . . Thus if, within *Whalen v. Union Bag & Paper Co., supra* which authoritatively states the rule in New York, the damage to plaintiffs in these present cases from defendant's cement plant is "not unsubstantial," an injunction should follow.

Although the court at Special Term and the Appellate Division held that injunction should be denied, it was found that plaintiffs had been damaged in various specific amounts up to the time of the trial and damages to the respective plaintiffs were awarded for those amounts. The effect of this was, injunction having been denied, plaintiffs could maintain successive actions at law for damages thereafter as further damage was incurred.

The court at Special Term also found the amount of permanent damage attributable to each plaintiff, for the guidance of the parties in the event both sides stipulated to the payment and acceptance of such permanent damage as a settlement of all the controversies among the parties. The total of permanent damages to all plaintiffs thus found was $185,000. This basis of adjustment has not resulted in any stipulation by the parties.

This result at Special Term and at the Appellate Division is a departure from a rule that has become settled; but to follow the rule literally in these cases would be to close down the plant at once. This court is fully agreed to avoid that immediately drastic remedy; the difference in view is how best to avoid it.[1]

One alternative is to grant the injunction but postpone its effect to a specified future date to give opportunity for technical advances to permit defendant to eliminate the nuisance; another is to grant the injunction conditioned on the payment of permanent damages to plaintiffs which would compensate them for the total economic loss to their property present and future caused by defendant's operations. For reasons which will be developed the court chooses the latter alternative.

If the injunction were to be granted unless within a short period— *e.g.,* 18 months—the nuisance be abated by improved methods, there would be no assurance that any significant technical improvement would occur.

The parties could settle this private litigation at any time if defendant paid enough money and the imminent threat of closing the plant would build up the pressure on defendant. If there were no improved techniques found, there would inevitably be applications to the court at Special Term for extensions of time to perform on showing of good faith efforts to find such techniques.

Moreover, techniques to eliminate dust and other annoying by-products of cement making are unlikely to be developed by any research the defendant can undertake within any short period, but will depend on the total resources of the cement industry nationwide and throughout the world. The problem is universal wherever cement is made.

For obvious reasons the rate of the research is beyond control of defendant. If at the end of 18 months the whole industry has not found a

1. Respondent's investment in the plant is in excess of $45,000,000. There are over 300 people employed there.

technical solution a court would be hard put to close down this one cement plant if due regard be given to equitable principles.

On the other hand, to grant the injunction unless defendant pays plaintiffs such permanent damages as may be fixed by the court seems to do justice between the contending parties. All of the attributions of economic loss to the properties on which plaintiffs' complaints are based will have been redressed.

The nuisance complained of by these plaintiffs may have other public or private consequences, but these particular parties are the only ones who have sought remedies and the judgment proposed will fully redress them. The limitation of relief granted is a limitation only within the four corners of these actions and does not foreclose public health or other public agencies from seeking proper relief in a proper court.

It seems reasonable to think that the risk of being required to pay permanent damages to injured property owners by cement plant owners would itself be a reasonable effective spur to research for improved techniques to minimize nuisance.

The power of the court to condition on equitable grounds the continuance of an injunction on the payment of permanent damages seems undoubted. *See, e.g.,* the alternatives considered in *McCarty v. Natural Carbonic Gas Co., supra,* as well as *Strobel v. Kerr Salt Co., supra.*

The damage base here suggested is consistent with the general rule in those nuisance cases where damages are allowed. "Where a nuisance is of such a permanent and unabatable character that a single recovery can be had, including the whole damage past and future resulting therefrom, there can be but one recovery." 66 C.J.S. Nuisances § 140, p. 947. It has been said that permanent damages are allowed where the loss recoverable would obviously be small as compared with the cost of removal of the nuisance. *Kentucky-Ohio Gas Co. v. Bowling,* 95 S.W.2d 1 (Ky. 1936). . . .

. . . [I]t seems fair to both sides to grant permanent damages to plaintiffs which will terminate this private litigation. The theory of damage is the "servitude on land" of plaintiffs imposed by defendant's nuisance. *See United States v. Causby,* 328 U.S. 256, 261, 262, 267 (1946) where the term "servitude" addressed to the land was used by Justice Douglas relating to the effect of airplane noise on property near an airport.

The judgment, by allowance of permanent damages imposing a servitude on land, which is the basis of the actions, would preclude future recovery by plaintiffs or their grantees. *See Northern Indiana Public Serv. Co. v. W.J. & M.S. Vesey,* 200 N.E. 620 (Ind. 1936).

This should be placed beyond debate by a provision of the judgment that the payment by defendant and the acceptance by plaintiffs of permanent damages found by the court shall be in compensation for a servitude on the land.

Although the Trial Term has found permanent damages as a possible basis of settlement of the litigation, on remission the court should be entirely free to re-examine this subject. It may again find the permanent damage already found; or make new findings.

The orders should be reversed, without costs, and the cases remitted to Supreme Court, Albany County to grant an injunction which shall be vacated upon payment by defendant of such amounts of permanent damage to the respective plaintiffs as shall for this purpose be determined by the court.

JASEN, JUDGE (dissenting). I agree with the majority that a reversal is required here, but I do not subscribe to the newly enunciated doctrine of assessment of permanent damages, in lieu of an injunction, where substantial property rights have been impaired by the creation of a nuisance.

It has long been the rule in this State, as the majority acknowledges, that a nuisance which results in substantial continuing damage to neighbors must be enjoined. To now change the rule to permit the cement company to continue polluting the air indefinitely upon the payment of permanent damages is, in my opinion, compounding the magnitude of a very serious problem in our State and Nation today.

In recognition of this problem, the Legislature of this State has enacted the Air Pollution Control Act, Public Health Law, Consol.Laws, c. 45, §§ 1264 to 1299–m, declaring that it is the State policy to require the use of all available and reasonable methods to prevent and control air pollution.

The harmful nature and widespread occurrence of air pollution have been extensively documented. Congressional hearings have revealed that air pollution causes substantial property damage, as well as being a contributing factor to a rising incidence of lung cancer, emphysema, bronchitis and asthma.

The specific problem faced here is known as particulate contamination because of the fine dust particles emanating from defendant's cement plant. The particular type of nuisance is not new, having appeared in many cases for at least the past 60 years. *See Hulbert v. California Portland Cement Co.*, 118 P. 928 (Cal. 1911). It is interesting to note that cement production has recently been identified as a significant source of particulate contamination in the Hudson Valley. This type of pollution, wherein very small particles escape and stay in the atmosphere, has been denominated as the type of air pollution which produces the greatest hazard to human health. We have thus a nuisance which not only is damaging to the plaintiffs, but also is decidedly harmful to the general public.

I see grave dangers in overruling our long-established rule of granting an injunction where a nuisance results in substantial continuing damage. In permitting the injunction to become inoperative upon the payment of permanent damages, the majority is, in effect, licensing a continuing wrong. It is the same as saying to the cement company, you may continue to do harm to your neighbors so long as you pay a fee for it. Furthermore, once such permanent damages are assessed and paid, the incentive to alleviate the wrong would be eliminated, thereby continuing air pollution of an area without abatement.

It is true that some courts have sanctioned the remedy here proposed by the majority in a number of cases, but none of the authorities relied upon by the majority are analogous to the situation before us. In those cases, the courts, in denying an injunction and awarding money damages, grounded their decision on a showing that the use to which the property was intended to be put was primarily for the public benefit. Here, on the other hand, it is clearly established that the cement company is creating a continuing air pollution nuisance primarily for its own private interest with no public benefit.

This kind of inverse condemnation, *Ferguson v. Village of Hamburg*, 5 N.E.2d 801 (N.Y. 1936), may not be invoked by a private person or corporation for private gain or advantage. Inverse condemnation should only be permitted when the public is primarily served in the taking or impairment of property. *Matter of New York City Housing Auth. v. Muller*, 1 N.E.2d 153, 156 (N.Y. 1936); *Pocantico Water Works Co. v. Bird*, 29 N.E. 246, 248 (N.Y. 1891). The promotion of the interests of the polluting cement company has, in my opinion, no public use or benefit.

Nor is it constitutionally permissible to impose [a] servitude on land, without consent of the owner, by payment of permanent damages where the continuing impairment of the land is for a private use. *See Fifth Ave. Coach Lines v. City of New York*, 183 N.E.2d 684, 686 (N.Y. 1962); *Walker v. City of Hutchinson*, 352 U.S. 112 (1956). This is made clear by the State Constitution, art. I, § 7, subd. (a), which provides that "[p]rivate property shall not be taken for *public* use without just compensation." (Emphasis added.) It is, of course, significant that the section makes no mention of taking for a private use.

In sum, then, by constitutional mandate as well as by judicial pronouncement, the permanent impairment of private property for private purposes is not authorized in the absence of clearly demonstrated public benefit and use.

I would enjoin the defendant cement company from continuing the discharge of dust particles upon its neighbors' properties unless, within 18 months, the cement company abated this nuisance.

It is not my intention to cause the removal of the cement plant from the Albany area, but to recognize the urgency of the problem stemming from this stationary source of air pollution, and to allow the company a specified period of time to develop a means to alleviate this nuisance.

I am aware that the trial court found that the most modern dust control devices available have been installed in defendant's plant, but, I submit, this does not mean that *better* and more effective dust control devices could not be developed within the time allowed to abate the pollution.

Moreover, I believe it is incumbent upon the defendant to develop such devices, since the cement company, at the time the plant commenced production (1962), was well aware of the plaintiffs' presence in the area, as well as the probable consequences of its contemplated operation. Yet, it still chose to build and operate the plant at this site.

In a day when there is a growing concern for clean air, highly developed industry should not expect acquiescence by the courts, but should, instead, plan its operations to eliminate contamination of our air and damage to its neighbors.

Accordingly, the orders of the Appellate Division, insofar as they denied the injunction, should be reversed, and the actions remitted to Supreme Court, Albany County to grant an injunction to take effect 18 months hence, unless the nuisance is abated by improved techniques prior to said date.

Notes

1. *The Rest of the Story and the Appropriateness of the* Boomer *Remedy.* After the remand, all but one of the plaintiffs settled with Atlantic Cement. The nonsettling plaintiff received a verdict for $175,000. In total, Atlantic Cement paid the plaintiffs in excess of $700,000 to avoid an injunction against its operations. It also invested over $1.6 million in additional efforts to reduce emissions from its plant. *Boomer v. Atlantic Cement Co., Inc.,* 72 Misc.2d 834, 340 N.Y.S.2d 97 (Sup. Ct. 1972); *Atlantic Cement Co. v. Fidelity & Cas. Co.,* 91 A.D.2d 412, 459 N.Y.S.2d 425 (1983), *aff'd,* 63 N.Y.2d 798, 481 N.Y.S.2d 329, 471 N.E.2d 142 (1984). What do these developments suggest about whether the *Boomer* court selected the proper remedy in granting a conditional injunction? How would you describe the protection afforded the plaintiffs in *Boomer?* Does the *Boomer* court protect the plaintiffs' entitlement to be free from unreasonable interferences with the use and enjoyment of their land through a property rule or a liability rule?

2. *Property Rules, Liability Rules and Entitlements—Further Travels in the Impenetrable Jungle.* Although *Boomer* never discussed sections 826(b) and 829A of the Restatement of Torts (the decision predated the revision that adopted those sections), it embraced the principles reflected in those sections. In his article, Boomer *and the American Law of Nuisance: Past, Present, and Future,* 54 Alb. L. Rev. 189, 234–35 (1990), Jeff Lewin labeled Restatement section 826(a) the "defendant-centered balance of utilities test," and sections 826(b) and 829A the "plaintiff-centered compensation principle." [You can infer how Lewin derived these labels by comparing the results in *Carpenter* and *Boomer.*] Lewin summarized the state of nuisance law as it relates to sections 826(a) and 826(b) as follows:

> Thus, as of 1990, at most fifteen states have adopted the Restatement's definition of unreasonableness as set forth in section 826. Of these fifteen states, eight have adopted or endorsed the plaintiff-centered

compensation principle expressed in sections 826(b) and 829A as an alternative to the defendant-centered balance of utilities test. The other seven states can be said to employ the balance of utilities test as the primary criterion for the determination of nuisance liability. In none of these states, however, has a court had an opportunity to consider adoption of the compensation principle.

In virtually all the remaining thirty-six jurisdictions, the courts continue to employ some form of reasonableness test that reflects an unresolved and often unarticulated tension between the plaintiff-centered and defendant-centered perspectives on nuisance law. These courts ask whether the defendant's conduct and/or the plaintiff's damages are unreasonable "under all of the circumstances." In balancing the "rights" or "interests" of the parties, these courts usually consider the utility of the defendant's conduct as one of many pertinent factors, giving no clear indication as to its relative importance. The uncertain weight accorded to the utility of the defendant's conduct under these general reasonableness tests represents a middle ground between the balance of the utilities test and the compensation principle: under the former, the utility of the defendant's conduct is a primary and often determinative factor; under the latter, it may be irrelevant.

Consider carefully the language of sections 826(b) and section 829A. Do these two sections provide identical—or even consistent—guidance to courts? If not, how should a court reconcile the two sections? *See* Lewin, *supra*, at 224–29.

Lewin's summary suggests the law of nuisance remains a morass. Still, based on the language of the Restatement and the decisions in *Carpenter* and *Boomer*, how would you differentiate the circumstances in which plaintiffs likely will receive no relief, likely will be entitled to damages, and likely will be entitled to an injunction?

3. *Environmental Regulation and Nuisance.* Not long after the *Boomer* decision, both Congress and state legislatures enacted a wave of environmental statutes addressing air and water pollution problems. If a factory's emissions comply with the permit conditions mandated under the federal Clean Air Act, the Clean Water Act, or the Resource Conservation and Recovery Act, should its owner be per se immune from common law nuisance liability? Why or why not? Do you think the federal regulatory structure was designed to address the unique situation in which specific aggrieved landowners may find themselves? *See, e.g., Gutierrez v. Mobil Oil Corp.,* 798 F.Supp. 1280 (W.D. Tex. 1992) (while compliance with applicable regulations reasonably should preclude injunctive relief, compliance with permit should not immunize defendant from liability for private nuisance).

4. *Prospective Injunctive Relief and Nuisance.* Nuisance actions frequently seek to prevent commencement of an activity neighboring owners deem objectionable. Courts generally will not grant injunctive relief prospectively, however, unless the alleged conduct constitutes a "nuisance *per se*"— *i.e.,* either 1) the challenged conduct would be a nuisance in any location, or 2) it will constitute a nuisance in the particular location regardless of any measure that the actor could take to minimize the impact on surrounding landowners. *Compare Vickridge First & Second Addition Homeowners Ass'n,*

Inc. v. Catholic Diocese of Wichita, 212 Kan. 348, 510 P.2d 1296 (1973) (refusing to enjoin construction of gymnasium and athletic fields, given school's agreement to fence land, revise plans to minimize drainage impacts, and not install floodlights and public address system) *and Demont v. Abbas*, 149 Neb. 765, 32 N.W.2d 737 (1948) (refusing to enjoin construction of rendering plant in agricultural area) *with Sharp v. 251st St. Landfill, Inc.*, 925 P.2d 546 (Okla. 1996) (enjoining construction of landfill that could not be operated without likelihood of contaminating groundwater).

5. *Of Nuisance and Trespass.* Over the last few decades, plaintiffs concerned about pollution have frequently brought actions claiming both nuisance (interference with use and enjoyment) and trespass (a direct physical invasion of their land in violation of their right to exclude). *See, e.g., Martin v. Reynolds Metals Co.*, 221 Or. 86, 342 P.2d 790 (1959), *cert. denied*, 362 U.S. 918, 80 S.Ct. 672, 4 L.Ed.2d 739 (1960) (intrusion of particulate and gaseous flouride toxins generated by defendant's aluminum reduction operation constituted trespass). Reflect on the above discussion of nuisance law in comparison with the discussion of trespass as raised in *Jacque v. Steenberg Homes, Inc.* (page 12) in Chapter 1. In terms of proving a case and obtaining a desired remedy, why might a plaintiff wish to pursue a trespass claim rather than a nuisance claim, to the extent that the facts support an argument that there has been a direct invasion of land?

Assume that the neighbor of a large manufacturing facility seeks to enjoin emissions of dust and other particulate matter from the facility on the ground that these emissions constitute a trespass on the neighbor's land. As judge, how might you rule on the claim for injunctive relief? On what basis might you conclude that the facility was not trespassing? On what basis might you conclude that the facility was trespassing, but that the neighbor was not entitled to injunctive relief? As you begin to move down this slippery slope, at what point do the concepts of nuisance and trespass begin to merge? *Compare Borland v. Sanders Lead Co.*, 369 So.2d 523 (Ala. 1979) *with Adams v. Cleveland–Cliffs Iron Co.*, 237 Mich.App. 51, 602 N.W.2d 215 (1999).

LAWYERING EXERCISE
(Negotiation and Document Drafting)

SITUATION: When a court speaks of a cement company having a "servitude" on its neighbors' land, this should bring to mind for you the concepts we discussed in Chapter 8. In *Boomer*, the servitude involved the Atlantic Cement Company's right to continue to release dust at the levels authorized by the court's opinion in exchange for the agreed-upon payments to each of the plaintiffs. What concerns should each party have with respect to the language of the servitude? In memorializing this "servitude," what practical problems might arise in trying to come up with language that reflects the plaintiffs' desire to limit the impact of the cement company's operations so that they are no worse than that authorized by the court? What practical problems might arise in drafting language that is readily enforceable and yet allows the cement company to have enough flexibility that it can modernize and expand its operation (provided the impact on neighbors is not increased)?

TASK: Choose to represent either one of the plaintiffs or Atlantic Cement Company. Prepare a short memorandum that outlines the key issues you need to have addressed in the memorialization of the "servitude" and also identifies the issues you anticipate the other side will want to address in developing the language for the servitude. With this memorandum in mind, prepare sample language for the "servitude" and then sit down with a student representing the other side and negotiate the language of the servitude.

LAWYERING EXERCISE
(Client Counseling Exercise)

SITUATION: You have been asked to represent People United to Reclaim the Environment ("PURE"), a loosely affiliated band of rural citizens impacted by a recent expansion of a confined animal feeding operation (CAFO) near their homes. You also have been asked to represent several individual members of PURE. These individuals have differing perspectives on the CAFO operation. Jim Close, who is very wealthy and lives closest to the facility, wants to do whatever it takes to shut the facility down. Mark Farmer, a neighboring landowner who quit hog farming because his costs prevented him from being competitive with CAFOs, also would like to see the facility shut down. Bob Wilsell, a nearby resident disturbed by odor from the CAFO, is ready to retire and would be happy to sell his land to the CAFO to provide a nest egg for retirement. Martha Windfall, who occasionally suffers from odor problems depending upon the prevailing winds, is willing to sell but wants the CAFO to pay "a premium" for the problems it has caused her with respect to the use and enjoyment of her land. PURE and each of the individuals want you to represent them in a nuisance action against the CAFO.

TASK: In light of the cases and materials you have read so far, prepare a short outline of the information you would want to gather before opining on the likelihood of PURE succeeding in a nuisance action. Then write up a short explanation of why a court might find that such a facility does not constitute a nuisance, and why, even if the court were to find that such a facility constitutes a nuisance, your clients may not receive their respectively desired remedies. Your memorandum also should discuss whether you would want to have the case heard by a jury rather than a judge and how that might impact the availability of your clients' desired remedies. Finally, your memorandum should explore whether you can represent both PURE and the individuals in one nuisance action.

3. *Comparing Public Nuisance and Private Nuisance*

Section 821B(1) of the Restatement of Torts defines a "public nuisance" as "an unreasonable interference with a right common to the general public" (such as a right to unpolluted air). Conduct might be unreasonable if it (a) involves a significant interference with public health, safety, peace, comfort or convenience; (b) violates a statute, ordinance, or administrative regulation; or (c) is of a continuing nature or has permanent effects and the defendant knows or should know of the conduct's significant effect upon the public right. *Id.*

You should note that a landowner's conduct could constitute both a public nuisance and a private nuisance, depending upon the scope of the harm. For example, a confined animal feeding operation might constitute a private nuisance with respect to an adjacent landowner and a public nuisance to the extent that odors cause public health problems. A decision by local authorities to pursue a public nuisance action would not prevent the adjacent landowner from seeking relief in a private nuisance action.

Courts generally have been reluctant to grant private landowners standing to pursue public nuisance actions unless the private landowner suffers an injury different in kind from that suffered by the public or has been delegated authority to pursue litigation by a public official. Thus, the plaintiff in a public nuisance action most frequently will be a public official seeking an injunction against the conduct on behalf of the general public. Although the Restatement broadens the range of circumstances in which private citizens have standing to sue on behalf of the general public (which may be important if a local public official refuses to take action), *id.* § 821C(2)(c), most jurisdictions continue to be chary in authorizing private landowners to pursue public nuisance actions. *See* Denise E. Antoloni, *Modernizing Public Nuisance: Solving the Paradox of the Special Injury Rule,* 28 Ecology L.Q. 755 (2001).

B. THE LAW OF ZONING

Although nuisance law provides a legal mechanism for resolving conflicting uses of land among neighbors, nuisance law has limited value as a land use planning tool for several reasons. First, nuisance law is essentially a "mud rule," in Professor Rose's terminology (pages 139–40), because it requires a case-by-case, fact-intensive analysis. As a result, proving a nuisance is often difficult and expensive. Second, even if neighbors succeed in proving that conduct constitutes a nuisance, they might obtain only damages rather than injunctive relief if the utility of the conduct outweighs the gravity of the harm it causes. Thus, given the transaction costs involved in nuisance litigation and the uncertain likelihood of success, many genuinely aggrieved landowners may resign themselves to suffer a nuisance rather than pursue litigation.

The widespread development of private servitude regimes has been somewhat helpful in addressing these use conflicts prospectively (with mixed success as discussed in Chapter 8). In many circumstances, however—particularly in the urban centers where development first took place on a lot-by-lot basis largely in the absence of servitude regimes—servitudes have been less helpful. [Can you explain why?]

The most systematic and pervasive form of American public land use control has been zoning regulation, originally based on a plan that allocates different land uses—*e.g.*, residential, commercial, and industrial uses, with different intensities of each type—to separate areas or "zones" within a community. This type of zoning rests upon an increasingly debated (and debatable) premise—that different types of land uses are inherently "incompatible" with other types and thus should be geographically segregated.

Planning and zoning begins legislatively, with the state legislature enacting a zoning enabling act (discussed *infra* at pages 875–78) to empower cities and counties to develop their own zoning regimes. The city council or county commission then adopts (a) a comprehensive land use plan for the community and (b) the associated zoning ordinances to implement that plan.[2] The plan, frequently accompanied by a map, identifies the locations in which the community would like to see or to limit different types of development. The zoning ordinances then describe the types of buildings and uses allowed within each district. Frequently, a planning and zoning commission may serve to advise the city council or county commission on land use matters.

1. *The Validity of Zoning*

With the rise of zoning regulations came litigation regarding its validity as a tool for controlling land use. *Village of Euclid v. Ambler Realty Co.*, presented below, was the U.S. Supreme Court's first statement on the validity of comprehensive zoning. To understand the question the Court had to decide, however, it is essential to understand the zoning system that was at issue, which was a classic example of a typical early zoning regime.

In the 1920s, the village of Euclid, Ohio, a suburb of Cleveland, consisted of an area of roughly 13 square miles, with a population between 5,000 and 10,000. Most of the city consisted of farms or otherwise unimproved land. The city had three main east-west roads—Euclid Ave. on the south, St. Clair Ave. through the middle and Lake Shore Blvd. on the north. Two railroads also ran east and west between Euclid Ave. and St. Clair Ave, largely parallel to those roads.

The village enacted a *cumulative zoning* ordinance, which was the predominant approach of most early 20th century zoning ordinances. Think of a "cumulative" zoning scheme as an inverted pyramid. At the bottom of the inverted pyramid, the city places the zone it wants to protect the most from other uses—generally a single-family residence zone. As you move up the pyramid, each zone allows increasing numbers of additional, more intensive uses. Thus, a change in zoning that expands the uses available generally is described as "upzoning" while a

---

2. Does a community have to adopt a plan before it can enact a zoning ordinance? Several jurisdictions have concluded that a separate "plan" is not necessary because the ordinance itself can serve as the "plan." *See, e.g., State ex rel. Chiavola v. Village of Oakwood*, 886 S.W.2d 74 (Mo. Ct. App.

1994); *Iowa Coal Mining Co. v. Monroe County*, 494 N.W.2d 664 (Iowa 1993). Other jurisdictions require a separate document that represents the comprehensive plan. *See, e.g.*, 30–A Me. Rev. Stat. § 4352; Or. Rev. Stat. § 215.050.

change in zoning to a more restrictive classification is generally described as "downzoning."

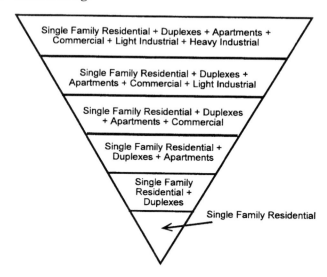

In the Village of Euclid, for example, the U–1 zone permitted only single-family residences, some farming activities, parks, water towers and railway lines. [The area south of Euclid Avenue was largely U–1.] The U–2 classification allowed all of the uses permitted in U–1, plus duplexes. The U–3 zone also permitted apartment houses, churches, schools, hotels and other public gathering places, such as museums and libraries. U–4 added a variety of commercial uses. [The area north of Euclid Avenue but south of the railroads was largely U–2 but also included lands in U–1, U–3 and U–4.] U–5 added some more intensive commercial uses and some industrial uses. U–6 added the heaviest types of industrial use. [The area between the railroads, and on either side of the railroads for the entire width of the village, was exclusively U–5 and U–6.] Thus, the zoning scheme separated Euclid's heaviest industrial uses from the single-family residential areas south of Euclid Ave. by means of a buffer zone of multi-family and commercial uses.

The village ordinance also contained height and area limitations. The height limitations varied from 35 feet in the H–1 district to 50 feet in the H–2 district to 80 feet in the H–3 district (with exceptions for church steeples and water towers). The area restrictions mandated minimum lot sizes for corner lots and other lots, which ranged from as much as 4,000–5,000 feet in the A–1 district to as little as 700–900 feet in the A–4 district. The ordinance also contained various setback provisions defining the distance between the property boundary and any buildings in the front, side and back yards. The ordinance included a zone map, which showed the location and limits of the various use, height, and area districts, each of which overlapped to some extent.

The ordinance entrusted enforcement of the zoning scheme to the inspector of buildings, under rules and regulations of the board of zoning appeals. Under the ordinance, any person claiming adverse effect from the inspector's decision could appeal that decision to the board of zoning appeals. The ordinance also gave the board power, in specific cases of practical difficulty or hardship, to interpret the ordinance in harmony with its general purpose and intent—to ensure the public health, safety and general welfare and secure substantial justice. The ordinance further provided that the board should conduct its meetings in public and maintain minutes.

VILLAGE OF EUCLID v. AMBLER REALTY CO.

Supreme Court of the United States.
272 U.S. 365, 47 S.Ct. 114, 71 L.Ed. 303 (1926).

Mr. Justice Sutherland delivered the opinion of the Court.... Appellee is the owner of a tract of land containing 68 acres, situated in the westerly end of the village, abutting on Euclid avenue to the south and the Nickel Plate Railroad to the north. Adjoining this tract, both on the east and on the west, there have been laid out restricted residential plats upon which residences have been erected....

Appellee's tract of land comes under U–2, U–3 and U–6. The first strip of 620 feet immediately north of Euclid avenue falls in class U–2, the next 130 feet to the north, in U–3, and the remainder in U–6. The uses of the first 620 feet, therefore, do not include apartment houses, hotels, churches, schools, or other public and semipublic buildings, or other uses enumerated in respect of U–3 to U–6, inclusive. The uses of the next 130 feet include all of these, but exclude industries, theaters, banks, shops, and the various other uses set forth in respect of U–4 to U–6, inclusive....

The ordinance is assailed on the grounds that it is in derogation of section 1 of the Fourteenth Amendment to the federal Constitution in that it deprives appellee of liberty and property without due process of law and denies it the equal protection of the law, and that it offends against certain provisions of the Constitution of the state of Ohio. The prayer of the bill is for an injunction restraining the enforcement of the ordinance and all attempts to impose or maintain as to appellee's property any of the restrictions, limitations or conditions. The court below held the ordinance to be unconstitutional and void, and enjoined its enforcement.

Before proceeding to a consideration of the case, it is necessary to determine the scope of the inquiry. The bill alleges that the tract of land in question is vacant and has been held for years for the purpose of selling and developing it for industrial uses, for which it is especially adapted, being immediately in the path of progressive industrial development; that for such uses it has a market value of about $10,000 per acre, but if the use be limited to residential purposes the market value is not in excess of $2,500 per acre; that the first 200 feet of the parcel back from Euclid Avenue, if unrestricted in respect of use, has a value of $150 per front foot, but if limited to residential uses, and ordinary mercantile business be excluded therefrom, its value is not in excess of $50 per front foot.

It is specifically averred that the ordinance attempts to restrict and control the lawful uses of appellee's land, so as to confiscate and destroy a great part of its value; that it is being enforced in accordance with its terms; that prospective buyers of land for industrial, commercial, and residential uses in the metropolitan district of Cleveland are deterred from buying any part of this land because of the existence of the ordinance and the necessity thereby entailed of conducting burdensome and expensive litigation in order to vindicate the right to use the land for lawful and legitimate purposes; that the ordinance constitutes a cloud upon the land, reduces and destroys its value, and has the effect of diverting the normal industrial, commercial, and residential development thereof to other and less favorable locations.

The record goes no farther than to show ... that the normal and reasonably to be expected use and development of that part of appellee's land adjoining Euclid avenue is for general trade and commercial purposes, particularly retail stores and like establishments, and that the normal and reasonably to be expected use and development of the residue of the land is for industrial and trade purposes. Whatever injury is inflicted by the mere existence and threatened enforcement of the ordinance is due to restrictions in respect of these and similar uses, to which perhaps should be added—if not included in the foregoing—restrictions in respect of apartment houses....

A motion was made in the court below to dismiss the bill on the ground that, because complainant (appellee) had made no effort to obtain a building permit or apply to the zoning board of appeals for relief, as it might have done under the terms of the ordinance, the suit was premature. The motion was properly overruled, the effect of the allegations of the bill is that the ordinance of its own force operates greatly to reduce the value of appellee's lands and destroy their marketability for industrial, commercial and residential uses, and the attack is directed, not against any specific provision or provisions, but against the ordinance as an entirety. Assuming the premises, the existence and maintenance of the ordinance in effect constitutes a present invasion of appellee's property rights and a threat to continue it. Under these circumstances, the equitable jurisdiction is clear.

It is not necessary to set forth the provisions of the Ohio Constitution which are thought to be infringed. The question is the same under both Constitutions, namely, as stated by appellee: Is the ordinance invalid, in that it violates the constitutional protection "to the right of property in the appellee by attempted regulations under the guise of the police power, which are unreasonable and confiscatory"?

Building zone laws are of modern origin. They began in this country about 25 years ago. Until recent years, urban life was comparatively simple; but, with the great increase and concentration of population, problems have developed, and constantly are developing, which require, and will continue to require, additional restrictions in respect of the use and occupation of private lands in urban communities. Regulations, the wisdom, necessity, and validity of which, as applied to existing conditions, are so apparent that they are now uniformly sustained, a century ago, or even half a century ago, probably would have been rejected as arbitrary and oppressive. Such regulations are sustained, under the complex conditions of our day, for reasons analogous to those which justify traffic regulations, which, before the advent of automobiles and rapid transit street railways, would have been condemned as fatally arbitrary and unreasonable. And in this there is no inconsistency, for, while the meaning of constitutional guaranties never varies, the scope of their application must expand or contract to meet the new and different conditions which are constantly coming within the field of their operation. In a changing world it is impossible that it should be otherwise. But although a degree of elasticity is thus imparted, not to the *meaning*, but to the *application* of constitutional principles, statutes and ordinances, which, after giving due weight to the new conditions, are found clearly not to conform to the Constitution, of course, must fall.

The ordinance now under review, and all similar laws and regulations, must find their justification in some aspect of the police power, asserted for the public welfare. The line which in this field separates the legitimate from the illegitimate assumption of power is not capable of precise delimitation. It varies with circumstances and conditions. A regulatory zoning ordinance, which would be clearly valid as applied to the great cities, might be clearly invalid as applied to rural communities. In solving doubts, the maxim *sic utere tuo ut alienum non laedas*, which lies at the foundation of so much of the common law of nuisances, ordinarily will furnish a fairly helpful clue. And the law of nuisances, likewise, may be consulted, not for the purpose of controlling, but for the helpful aid of its analogies in the process of ascertaining the scope of, the power. Thus the question whether the power exists to forbid the erection of a building of a particular kind or for a particular use, like the question whether a particular thing is a nuisance, is to be determined, not by an abstract consideration of the building or of the thing considered apart, but by considering it in connection with the circumstances and the locality. A nuisance may be merely a right thing in the wrong place, like a pig in the parlor instead of the barnyard. If the validity of the legislative classification for zoning purposes be fairly debatable, the legislative judgment must be allowed to control.

There is no serious difference of opinion in respect of the validity of laws and regulations fixing the height of buildings within reasonable limits, the character of materials and methods of construction, and the adjoining area which must be left open, in order to minimize the danger of fire or collapse, the evils of overcrowding and the like, and excluding from residential sections offensive trades, industries and structures likely to create nuisances.

Here, however, the exclusion is in general terms of all industrial establishments, and it may thereby happen that not only offensive or dangerous industries will be excluded, but those which are neither offensive nor dangerous will share the same fate. But this is no more than happens in respect of many practice-forbidding laws which this court has upheld, although drawn in general terms so as to include individual cases that may turn out to be innocuous in themselves. The inclusion of a reasonable margin, to insure effective enforcement, will not put upon a law, otherwise valid, the stamp of invalidity. Such laws may also find their justification in the fact that, in some fields, the bad fades into the good by such insensible degrees that the two are not capable of being readily distinguished and separated in terms of legislation. In the light of these considerations, we are not prepared to say that the end in view was not sufficient to justify the general rule of the ordinance, although some industries of an innocent character might fall within the proscribed class. It cannot be said that the ordinance in this respect "passes the bounds of reason and assumes the character of a merely arbitrary fiat." *Purity Extract Co. v. Lynch*, 226 U.S. 192, 204. Moreover, the restrictive provisions of the ordinance in this particular may be sustained upon the principles applicable to the broader exclusion from residential districts of all business and trade structures, presently to be discussed.

It is said that the village of Euclid is a mere suburb of the city of Cleveland; that the industrial development of that city has now reached and in some degree extended into the village, and in the obvious course of things will soon absorb the entire area for industrial enterprises; that the effect of the ordinance is to divert this natural development elsewhere, with the consequent loss of increased values to the owners of the lands within the village borders. But the village, though physically a suburb of Cleveland, is politically a separate municipality, with powers of its own and authority to govern itself as it sees fit, within the limits of the organic law of its creation and the state and federal Constitutions. Its governing authorities, presumably representing a majority of its inhabitants and voicing their will, have determined, not that industrial development shall cease at its boundaries, but that the course of such development shall proceed within definitely fixed lines. If it be a proper exercise of the police power to relegate industrial establishments to localities separated from residential sections, it is not easy to find a sufficient reason for denying the power because the effect of its exercise is to divert an industrial flow from the course which it would follow, to the injury of the residential public, if left alone, to another course where such injury will be obviated. . . .

We find no difficulty in sustaining restrictions of the kind thus far reviewed. The serious question in the case arises over the provisions of the ordinance excluding from residential districts apartment houses, business houses, retail stores and shops, and other like establishments. This question involves the validity of what is really the crux of the more recent zoning legislation, namely, the creation and maintenance of residential districts, from which business and trade of every sort, including hotels and apartment houses, are excluded. Upon that question this court has not thus far spoken. The decisions of the state courts are numerous and conflicting; but those which broadly sustain the power greatly outnumber those which deny it altogether or narrowly limit it, and it is very apparent that there is a constantly increasing tendency in the direction of the broader view. . . .

The decisions [adopting the broader view] agree that the exclusion of buildings devoted to business, trade, etc., from residential districts, bears a rational relation to the health and safety of the community. Some of the grounds for this conclusion are promotion of the health and security from injury of children and others by separating dwelling houses from territory devoted to trade and industry; suppression and prevention of disorder; facilitating the extinguishment of fires, and the enforcement of street traffic regulations and other general welfare ordinances; aiding the health and safety of the community, by excluding from residential areas the confusion and danger of fire, contagion, and disorder, which in greater or less degree attach to the location of stores, shops, and factories. Another ground is that the construction and repair of streets may be rendered easier and less expensive, by confining the greater part of the heavy traffic to the streets where business is carried on. . . .

The matter of zoning has received much attention at the hands of commissions and experts, and the results of their investigations have been set forth in comprehensive reports. These reports which bear every evidence of painstaking consideration, concur in the view that the segregation of residential, business and industrial buildings will make it easier to provide fire apparatus suitable for the character and intensity of the development in each section; that it will increase the safety and security of home life, greatly tend to prevent street accidents, especially to children, by reducing the traffic and resulting confusion in residential sections, decrease noise and other conditions which produce or intensify nervous disorders, preserve a more favorable environment in which to rear children, etc. With particular reference to apartment houses, it is pointed out that the development of detached house sections is greatly retarded by the coming of apartment houses, which has sometimes resulted in destroying the entire section for private house purposes; that in such sections very often the apartment house is a mere parasite, constructed in order to take advantage of the open spaces and attractive surroundings created by the residential character of the district. Moreover, the coming of one apartment house is followed by others, interfering by their height and bulk with the free circulation of air and monopolizing the rays of the sun which otherwise would fall upon the smaller homes, and bringing, as their necessary accompaniments, the disturbing noises incident to increased traffic and business, and the occupation, by means of moving and parked automobiles, of larger portions of the streets, thus detracting from their safety and depriving children of the privilege of quiet and open spaces for play, enjoyed by those in more favored localities—until, finally, the residential character of the neighborhood and its desirability as a place of detached residences are utterly destroyed. Under these circumstances, apartment houses, which in a different environment would be not only entirely unobjectionable but highly desirable, come very near to being nuisances.

If these reasons, thus summarized, do not demonstrate the wisdom or sound policy in all respects of those restrictions which we have indicated as pertinent to the inquiry, at least, the reasons are sufficiently cogent to preclude us from saying, as it must be said before the ordinance can be declared unconstitutional, that such provisions are clearly arbitrary and unreasonable, having no substantial relation to the public health, safety, morals, or general welfare.

It is true that when, if ever, the provisions set forth in the ordinance in tedious and minute detail, come to be concretely applied to particular premises, including those of the appellee, or to particular conditions, or to be considered in connection with specific complaints, some of them, or even many of them, may be found to be clearly arbitrary and unreasonable. But where the equitable remedy of injunction is sought, as it is here, not upon the ground of a present infringement or denial of a specific right, or of a particular injury in process of actual execution, but upon the broad ground that the mere existence and threatened enforcement of the ordinance, by materially and adversely affecting values and curtailing the opportunities of the market, constitute a present and irreparable injury, the court will not scrutinize its provisions, sentence by sentence, to ascertain by a process of piecemeal dissection whether there may be, here and there, provisions of a minor character, or relating to matters of administration, or not shown to contribute to the injury complained of, which, if attacked separately, might not withstand the test of constitutionality. In respect of such provisions, of which specific complaint is not made, it cannot be said that the landowner has suffered or is threatened with an injury which entitles him to challenge their constitutionality. . . .

The relief sought here is . . . an injunction against the enforcement of any of the restrictions, limitations, or conditions of the ordinance. And the gravamen of the complaint is that a portion of the land of the appellee cannot be sold for certain enumerated uses because of the general and broad restraints of the ordinance. What would be the effect of a restraint imposed by one or more of the innumerable provisions of the ordinance, considered apart, upon the value or marketability of the lands, is neither disclosed by the bill nor by the evidence, and we are afforded no basis, apart from mere speculation, upon which to rest a conclusion that it or they would have any appreciable effect upon those matters. Under these circumstances, therefore, it is enough for us to determine, as we do, that the ordinance in its general scope and dominant features, so far as its provisions are here involved, is a valid exercise of authority, leaving other provisions to be dealt with as cases arise directly involving them.

And this is in accordance with the traditional policy of this court. In the realm of constitutional law, especially, this court has perceived the embarrassment which is likely to result from an attempt to formulate rules or decide questions beyond the necessities of the immediate issue. It has preferred to follow the method of a gradual approach to the general by a systematically guarded application and extension of constitutional principles to particular cases as they arise, rather than by out of hand attempts to establish general rules to which future cases must be fitted. This process applies with peculiar force to the solution of questions arising under the due process clause of the Constitution as applied to the exercise of the flexible powers of police, with which we are here concerned.

Decree reversed.

[Justices Van Devanter, McReynolds, and Butler dissented.]

Notes

1. *Cumulative Zoning v. Noncumulative or Exclusive Zoning.* Thanks to this case, cumulative zoning frequently is called *Euclidean* zoning (only coincidentally suggesting the geometric shapes of regulatory zoning reminiscent of Euclidean geometry). A less common zoning scheme is *noncumulative* or *exclusive* zoning. Under this scheme, the uses allowed in each district are exclusive; for example, the ordinance would forbid industrial uses in a residential district and residential uses in an industrial district. Is there any reason to view a cumulative zoning scheme more or less favorably than an exclusive zoning scheme? Why might a municipality choose to implement a cumulative scheme rather than an exclusive scheme (or vice-versa)?

2. *Judicial Deference: Zoning Enactment vs. Application.* The plaintiff in *Euclid* challenged the validity of the zoning scheme as a whole, arguing that the *mere existence* of the "unreasonable and confiscatory" zoning scheme imposed an unconstitutional injury to persons owning land covered by the scheme. The Court held the ordinance to be "a valid exercise of authority," but left unanswered the question of whether any particular aspect of such legislation might be unconstitutional as applied to an affected parcel of land.

The Court addressed this question two years later in *Nectow v. City of Cambridge*, 277 U.S. 183, 48 S.Ct. 447, 72 L.Ed. 842 (1928). Nectow owned slightly more than three acres of land that fell within two different zones. The vast majority of his land fell within an unrestricted zone, while about two-thirds of an acre—bordered to the south by industrial uses (a Ford assembly plant and a soap factory) and to the north and west by residences (located across Henry Street to the north and Brookline Street to the west)— fell within a residential zone. Nectow challenged the constitutionality of the zoning ordinance as it applied to the smaller portion placed in the residential zone.

The *Nectow* Court reiterated the *Euclid* standard of review, noting that a zoning ordinance will be upheld unless the ordinance " 'has no foundation in reason and is a mere arbitrary or irrational exercise of power having no substantial relation to the public health, the public morals, the public safety or the public welfare in its proper sense.' " *Nectow,* 277 U.S. at 187–88 (quoting *Euclid,* 272 U.S. at 395). A court-appointed master had found that placing Nectow's land in a residential district "would not promote the health, safety, convenience and general welfare of the inhabitants of that part of the defendant City." *Id.* at 187. The Court concluded that

> [t]his finding . . . supported by other findings of fact, is determinative of the case. That the invasion of the property . . . was serious and highly injurious is clearly established; and, since a necessary basis for the support of that invasion is wanting, the action of the zoning authorities comes within the ban of the Fourteenth Amendment and cannot be sustained. [*Id.* at 188.]

Because the restricted land was "of little value for the limited uses permitted by the ordinance," the Court held that application of the ordinance to Nectow's land failed to satisfy the "substantial relation" test. *Id.*

To what extent should courts generally defer to a municipality's application of its legislative zoning decision? When do *Euclid* and *Nectow* suggest a challenged zoning ordinance will be upheld or overturned?

2. *The Zoning Process: Searching for Flexibility and Fairness*

Following the Court's validation of zoning in *Euclid,* zoning regulation swept through the country. By the early 1930s, more than half the states had adopted the Standard Zoning Enabling Act (SZEA) or something similar,[3] and hundreds of communities had adopted zoning ordinances. Presently, the vast majority of cities with a population greater than 10,000 have enacted zoning ordinances, as have many counties, townships and villages. Every large metropolitan area (other than Houston, Texas) guides land use and growth through the use of planning and zoning.

Within zoned communities, one or more landowners may wish to use their land in a manner prohibited by the existing zoning. Likewise, a community (or some segment of the community) may wish to make the existing zoning more restrictive and thereby prevent one or more parcels of land from being used in a manner that existing zoning would otherwise permit. As the SZEA provisions suggest, changes in authorized or prohibited uses can occur in a variety of ways:

- First, the community may *amend the zoning ordinance.* If the local ordinance does not permit a desired use within a particular zone under any circumstances, a landowner may urge the community's legislative body (*e.g.,* the city or town council) to amend the zoning ordinance to "upzone" her parcel (*i.e.,* to move the parcel "up" the inverted pyramid into a less restrictive classification that permits the desired use). Similarly, if the community wishes to preclude a presently allowed use, it must amend the ordinance

---

3. Absent an enabling statute such as the SZEA, communities that are not "char- ter" or "home rule" municipalities would lack the authority to engage in zoning.

to "downzone" the parcel (*i.e.*, to move the parcel "down" the inverted pyramid into a more restrictive classification that precludes the undesired use).

- Second, the community may issue a *"special use"* or *"conditional use"* permit. These permits are allowed only if the ordinance expressly authorizes zoning officials to grant specific permission for the desired use within that zone. Such authorization usually is built into a zoning ordinance when a municipality anticipates a special or related use within a zone (*e.g.*, a school within a residential zone), but does not want to allow an unlimited right to make such a use given the potential for negative externalities if the use is not managed properly.

- Third, the community may grant a particular landowner an administrative *variance* from the strict application of the zoning classification to her specific parcel. Officials may allow a variance when a zoning ordinance significantly impairs a landowner's use of her land and the variance will not impair the comprehensive plan's general design for that zone.

Reading the language of the SZEA, can you identify the statutory language that authorizes these three types of changes?

STANDARD STATE ZONING ENABLING ACT

(Recommended by U.S. Dept. of Commerce, 1926)

§ 1. Grant of Power. For the purpose of promoting health, safety, morals, or the general welfare of the community, the legislative body of cities and incorporated villages is hereby empowered to regulate and restrict the height, number of stories, and size of buildings and other structures, the percentage of lot that may be occupied, the size of yards, courts, and other open spaces, the density of population, and the location and use of buildings, structures, and land for trade, industry, residence or other purposes.

§ 2. Districts. For any or all of said purposes the local legislative body may divide the municipality into districts of such number, shape, and area as may be deemed best suited to carry out the purposes of this act; and within such districts it may regulate and restrict the erection, construction, reconstruction, alteration, repair, or use of buildings, structures, or land. All such regulations shall be uniform for each class or kind of buildings throughout each district, but the regulations in one district may differ from those in other districts.

§ 3. Purposes in View. Such regulations shall be made in accordance with a comprehensive plan and designed to lessen congestion in the streets, to secure safety from fire, panic, and other dangers; to promote health and the general welfare; to provide adequate light and air; to prevent the overcrowding of land; to avoid undue concentration of population; to facilitate the adequate provision of transportation, water, sewerage, schools, parks, and other public requirements. Such regulations shall be made with reasonable consideration, among other things, to the character of the district and its peculiar suitability for particular uses, and with a view to conserving the value of buildings and encouraging the most appropriate use of land throughout such municipality.

§ 4. **Method of Procedure.** The legislative body of such municipality shall provide for the manner in which such regulations and restrictions and the boundaries of such districts shall be determined, established, and enforced, and from time to time amended, supplemented, or changed. However, no such regulation, restriction, or boundary shall become effective until after a public hearing in relation thereto, at which parties in interest and citizens shall have an opportunity to be heard. At least 15 days' notice of the time and place of such hearing shall be published in an official paper, or a paper of general circulation, in such municipality.

§ 5. **Changes.** Such regulations, restrictions, and boundaries may from time to time be amended, supplemented, changed, modified, or repealed. In case, however, of a protest against such change, signed by the owners of more than 20 per cent or more either of the area of the lots included in such proposed change, or of those immediately adjacent in the rear thereof extending ___ feet therefrom, or of those directly opposite thereto extending ___ feet from the street frontage or such opposite lots, such amendment shall not become effective except by the favorable vote of three-fourths of all members of the legislative body of such municipality. The provisions of the previous section relative to public hearings and official notice shall apply equally to all changes or amendments.

§ 6. **Zoning Commission.** In order to avail itself of the powers conferred by this act, such legislative body shall appoint a commission, to be known as the zoning commission, to recommend the boundaries of the various original districts and appropriate regulations to be enforced therein. Such commission shall make a preliminary report and hold public hearings thereon before submitting its final report, and such legislative body shall not hold its public hearings or take action, until it has received the final report of such commission. Where a city plan commission already exists, it may be appointed as the zoning commission.

§ 7. **Board of Adjustment.** Such local legislative body may provide for the appointment of a board of adjustment, and in the regulations and restrictions adopted pursuant to the authority of this act may provide that the said board of adjustment may, in appropriate cases and subject to appropriate conditions and safeguards, make special exceptions to the terms of the ordinance in harmony with its general purpose and intent and in accordance with general or specific rules therein contained.

The board of adjustment shall consist of five members, each to be appointed for a term of three years and removable for cause by the appointing authority upon written charges and after public hearing. . . .

The board shall adopt rules in accordance with the provisions of any ordinance adopted pursuant to this act. Meetings of the board shall be held at the call of the chairman and at such other times as the board may determine. Such chairman, or in his absence the acting chairman, may administer oaths and compel the attendance of witnesses. All meetings of the board shall be open to the public. The board shall keep minutes of its proceedings, showing the vote of each member upon each question, or, if absent or failing to vote, indicating such fact, and shall keep records of its examinations and other official actions, all of which shall be immediately filed in the office of the board and shall be a public record.

Appeals to the board of adjustment may be taken by any person aggrieved or by any officer, department, board, or bureau of the municipality affected by any decision of the administrative officer. Such appeal shall be taken within a reasonable time, as provided by the rules of the board, by filing with the officer from whom the appeal is taken and with the board of adjustment a notice of appeal specifying the grounds thereof. The officer from whom the appeal is taken shall forthwith transmit to the board all the papers constituting the record upon which the action appealed from was taken.

An appeal stays all proceedings in furtherance of the action appealed from, unless the officer from whom the appeal is taken certifies to the board of adjustment after the notice of appeal shall have been filed with him that by reason of facts stated in the certificate a stay would, in his opinion, cause imminent peril to life or property. In such case proceedings shall not be stayed otherwise than by a restraining order which may be granted by the board of adjustment or by a court of record on application on notice to the officer from whom the appeal is taken and on due course shown.

The board of adjustment shall fix a reasonable time for the hearing of the appeal, give public notice thereof, as well as due notice to the parties in interest, and decide the same within a reasonable time. Upon the hearing any party may appear in person or by agent or by attorney.

The board of adjustment shall have the following powers:

    1.   To hear and decide appeals where it is alleged there is error in any order, requirement, decision, or determination made by an administrative official in the enforcement of this act or of any ordinance adopted pursuant thereto.

    2.   To hear and decide special exceptions to the terms of the ordinance upon which such board is required to pass under such ordinance.

    3.   To authorize upon appeal in specific cases such variance from the terms of the ordinance as will not be contrary to the public interest, where, owing to special conditions, a literal enforcement of the provisions of the ordinance will result in unnecessary hardship,

and so that the spirit of the ordinance shall be observed and substantial justice done.

In exercising the above-mentioned powers such board may, in conformity with the provisions of this act, reverse or affirm, wholly or partly, or may modify the order, requirement, decision, or determination appealed from and may make such order, requirement, decision, or determination as ought to be made, and to that end shall have all the powers of the officer from whom the appeal is taken.

The concurring vote of four members of the board shall be necessary to reverse any order, requirement, decision, or determination of any such administrative official, or to decide in favor of the applicant on any matter upon which it is required to pass under any such ordinance, or to effect any variation in such ordinance.

Any person or persons, jointly or severally, aggrieved by any decision of the board of adjustment, or any taxpayer, or any officer, department, board, or bureau of the municipality, may present to a court of record a petition, duly verified, setting forth that such decision is illegal, in whole or in part, specifying the grounds of the illegality. Such petition shall be presented to the court within 30 days after the filing of the decision in the office of the board. . . .

§ 8. **Enforcement and Remedies.** The local legislative body may provide by ordinance for the enforcement of this act and of any ordinance or regulation made thereunder. A violation of this act or of such ordinance or regulation is hereby declared to be a misdemeanor, and such local legislative body may provide for the punishment thereof by fine or imprisonment or both. It is also empowered to provide civil penalties for such violation.

In case any building or structure is erected, constructed, reconstructed, altered, repaired, converted, or maintained, or any building, structure, or land is used in violation of this act or of any ordinance or other regulation made under authority conferred hereby, the proper local authorities of the municipality, in addition to other remedies, may institute any appropriate action or proceedings to prevent such unlawful erection, construction, reconstruction, alteration, repair, conversion, maintenance, or use, to restrain, correct, or abate such violation, to prevent the occupancy of said building, structure, or land, or to prevent any illegal act, conduct, business, or use in or about such premises.

---

a. *Amendments and Conditional Uses.* Assume that Key wants to operate a restaurant and bakery out of a large home she inherited near the center of a sizable residential zone in Smithville. Smithville's zoning ordinance does not allow retail bakeries or other commercial uses within a residential zone. Key has heard some of the neighbors complain, however, that there are no restaurants or bakeries within two miles of the neighborhood. In fact, because Key's restaurant would be relatively small (and thus result in little traffic and noise), several of her neighbors are enthusiastic about her plans.

As suggested above, Key could ask the town council to amend the zoning ordinance. In this situation, however, the potential "upzoning" of Key's land presents uncertainties. First, zoning classifications often have an inherently inflexible, "all or nothing" quality that can make rezoning of individual parcels problematic. If Smithville upzones Key's land to "commercial," she could operate not only a bakery, but also any other use permissible in a commercial zone—a risk that might dissuade Smithville's Town Council from upzoning Key's parcel. Second, the mere fact that a few of Key's neighbors do not object does not mean that reclassification of Key's land would be consistent with Smithville's comprehensive plan. Even if Key succeeded in persuading the Town Council to upzone the land, a dissenting neighbor might subsequently sue, claiming that the rezoning decision was invalid "spot zoning"—*i.e.*, singling out a parcel of land for treatment that differs from the treatment of surrounding lands.

Alternatively, the zoning ordinance might authorize other uses—known as *conditional* or *special* uses, or sometimes as *"special exceptions"*—but only if the landowner obtains a "special use" or "conditional use" permit. To obtain such a permit, the landowner satisfies specific conditions set forth in the ordinance. In a traditional residential zone, for example, Key ordinarily could not operate a restaurant and bakery without an amendment of the zoning ordinance. But if Smithville's ordinance allows for conditional commercial uses in residential districts "if not inconsistent with a residential environment," Key may be able to obtain a conditional use permit administratively—if she can persuade the zoning board that her proposed use is compatible with the surrounding neighborhood—and thereby avoid the greater cost and risk of amending the ordinance.

Building flexibility into a zoning regime risks inept or corrupt use of that flexibility—potentially creating the very sort of harm that zoning is supposed to avoid. Sometimes, courts have struggled to evaluate challenges to rezoning and conditional zoning decisions. Should there be limits upon a municipality's ability to incorporate flexibility into its zoning ordinance? Should Smithville be able to rezone Key's parcel in exchange for a promise by Key to use the land only for a restaurant and bakery, and no other commercial use? Consider the following materials.

CHRISMON v. GUILFORD COUNTY

Supreme Court of North Carolina.
322 N.C. 611, 370 S.E.2d 579 (1988).

MEYER, JUSTICE. This was an action by plaintiffs for a declaratory judgment with regard to an amendment to the Guilford County, North Carolina, zoning ordinance. Specifically, plaintiffs sought a judgment declaring that the amendment to the ordinance adopted 20 December 1982 rezoning defendant Bruce Clapp's 8.57 acres of land was unlawful and therefore void. The principal issue presented on this appeal is whether the trial court committed reversible error in affirming the validity of the rezoning in question. The Court of Appeals reversed, holding, first, that the rezoning in question constituted illegal "spot zoning" and, second, that it also constituted illegal "contract zoning." We hold that the Court of Appeals erred in both of these conclusions, and accordingly, we reverse.

The facts underlying the case are undisputed. Defendant Bruce Clapp ... had been operating a business on a 3.18–acre tract of property adjacent to his residence in Rock Creek Township, Guilford County, since 1948. Mr. Clapp's business consisted, first, of buying, drying, storing, and selling grain and, second, of selling and distributing lime, fertilizer, pesticides, and other agricultural chemicals. The distinction between these two principal elements of Mr. Clapp's business is important to the disposition of this case.

In 1964, Guilford County adopted a comprehensive zoning ordinance. The ordinance zoned Mr. Clapp's 3.18–acre tract, as well as an extensive area surrounding his tract, as "A–1 Agricultural" (hereinafter "A–1"). Under this particular zoning classification, one element of the business—namely, the grain drying and storing operation—constituted a permitted use. Significantly, however, the sale and distribution of the lime, fertilizer, pesticides, and other agricultural chemicals were not uses permitted by the A–1 classification. However, because this latter activity pre-existed the ordinance, Mr. Clapp was allowed to continue to sell agricultural chemicals on the 3.18–acre tract adjacent to his own home. Under the ordinance, though such sales constituted a nonconforming use, the sales could be carried on, so long as they were not expanded.

In 1969, plaintiffs William and Evelyn Chrismon bought a tract of land from Mr. Clapp and built a home there. Plaintiffs' lot is located at the south side of the intersection of North Carolina Highway 61 and Gun Shop Road. Highway 61 runs north and south, while Gun Shop Road, a small, unpaved road, begins at Highway 61 and runs east. Mr. Clapp's residence is located on the north side of the intersection, directly across Gun Shop Road from plaintiffs' residence. Adjacent to plaintiffs' lot is an additional 5.06–acre tract, also owned by Mr. Clapp. Prior to 1980, that tract had been used by its owner for the growing of tobacco.

Beginning in 1980, however, Mr. Clapp moved some portion of his business operation from the 3.18–acre tract north of Gun Shop Road to the 5.06–acre tract south of Gun Shop Road, directly adjacent to plaintiffs' lot. Subsequently, Mr. Clapp constructed some new buildings on this larger tract, erected several grain bins, and generally enlarged his operation. Concerned by the increased noise, dust, and traffic caused by Mr. Clapp's expansion, plaintiffs filed a complaint with the Guilford County Inspections Department. The Inspections Department subsequently notified Mr. Clapp, by letter dated 22 July 1982, that the expansion of the agricultural chemical operation to the larger tract adjacent to plaintiffs' lot constituted an impermissible expansion of a nonconforming use. The same letter informed Mr. Clapp further that, though his activity was impermissible under the ordinance, should he so desire, he could request a rezoning of the property.

Shortly thereafter, Mr. Clapp applied to have both of the tracts in question, the 3.18–acre tract north of Gun Shop Road and the 5.06–acre tract south of Gun Shop Road, rezoned from A–1 to "Conditional Use Industrial District" (hereinafter CU–M–2). He also applied for a conditional use permit, specifying in the application that he would use the property as it was then being used and listing those improvements he would like to make in the next five years. Under the CU–M–2 classification, Clapp's agricultural chemical operation would become a permitted use upon the issuance of the conditional use permit. The Guilford County Planning Board met on 8 September 1982 and voted to approve the recommendation of the Planning Division that the property be rezoned consistent with Mr. Clapp's request.

On 20 December 1982, pursuant to appropriate notice, the Guilford County Board of Commissioners held a public hearing concerning Mr. Clapp's rezoning application. Members of the Board heard statements from Mr. Clapp, from plaintiffs, and, also, from plaintiffs' attorney. Several additional persons had previously spoken in favor of Mr. Clapp's rezoning request at earlier Board meetings, stating that Mr. Clapp's business provided a service to the farmers in the immediate vicinity. The Board had also been presented with a petition signed by eighty-eight persons favoring the rezoning. Having considered the matter, the Board members voted to rezone the tracts in question from A–1 to CU–M–2, and as a part of the same resolution, they also voted to approve the conditional use permit application.

. . .[P]laintiffs brought this action seeking to have both the zoning amendment and the conditional use permit declared invalid. After a trial without a jury, the trial court found, among other things, that the sale and distribution of the agricultural chemicals were uses compatible with the agricultural needs of the surrounding area. The trial court concluded further that the rezoning was neither "spot zoning" nor "contract zoning" and also that the County had not acted arbitrarily in making its decision. The trial court made neither findings of fact nor conclusions of law with regard to the issuance of the conditional use permit. . . . [Editors' Note: The court of appeals reversed the decision of the trial court on both grounds.]

. . .[W]e hold today that the practice of conditional use zoning is an approved practice in North Carolina, so long as the action of the local zoning authority in accomplishing the zoning is reasonable, neither arbitrary nor unduly discriminatory, and in the public interest. . . .

The practice of conditional use zoning . . . is one of several vehicles by which greater zoning flexibility can be and has been acquired by zoning authorities. Conditional use zoning anticipates that when the rezoning of certain property within the general zoning framework described above would constitute an unacceptably drastic change, such a rezoning could still be accomplished through the addition of certain conditions or use limitations. Specifically, conditional use zoning occurs when a governmental body, without committing its own authority, secures a given property owner's agreement to limit the use of his property to a particular use or to subject his tract to certain restrictions as a precondition to any rezoning.

It is indeed generally agreed among commentators that, because it permits a given local authority greater flexibility in balancing conflicting demands, the practice of conditional use zoning is exceedingly valuable. 1 A. Rathkopf & D. Rathkopf, The Law of Zoning and Planning § 27.05 (4th ed. 1987). One of the early leading [zoning] scholars ... addressed the importance of this increased flexibility ... as follows:

> Conditional zoning is an outgrowth of the need for compromise between the interests of the developer seeking appropriate zoning changes for his tract, and the neighboring landowner whose property interests would suffer if the most intensive use permitted by the new classification were instituted. In an attempt to reconcile these conflicting pressures, the municipality will authorize the proposed change but minimize its adverse effects by imposing conditions. [Shapiro, *The Case For Conditional Zoning*, 41 Temp.L.Q. 267, 280 (1968).] ...

[T]he action here is consistent with the observations of Shapiro.... Before the now-disputed zoning occurred, the tracts of land in question, and all of the surrounding land for some miles, were classified under the comprehensive zoning plan as A–1.... While the rezoning of the two tracts to M–2 Industrial would clearly allow the desired agricultural chemical operation, it would also clearly allow for activities substantially inconsistent with the surrounding A–1 areas.[4] Herein lies the usefulness of conditional use zoning. By rezoning these tracts CU–M–2, the desired activity becomes a conforming use, but by virtue of the attendant conditions, uses undesirable under these circumstances can be limited or avoided altogether.

Notwithstanding the manifest benefits of conditional use zoning, there has ... been some divergence of opinion amongst courts and commentators alike as to the legal status of the practice. In fact, the initial judicial response to conditional use zoning was to condemn the practice as invalid per se. *See, e.g., Hartnett v. Austin*, 93 So.2d 86 (Fla.1956); *V.F. Zahodiakin Eng'r Corp. v. Zoning Board of Adjustment*, 86 A.2d 127 (N.J. 1952). Those courts falling into this category have objected to conditional use zoning on the several grounds that it constitutes illegal spot zoning; that it is not, on the specific facts, authorized by the state's zoning enabling legislation; and that it results in an improper and illegal abandonment of the local government's police powers.

---

4. For example, permitted uses in a district zoned under the M–2 Industrial classification would include, among other things, manufacturing facilities of virtually any kind, fuel oil dealerships, waste recycling facilities, and public utility storage depots.

...[Today many] jurisdictions, which comprise a growing trend, have concluded, among other things, that zoning legislation provides ample authority for the practice; that the use under the practice of carefully tailored restraints advanced, rather than injured, the interests of adjacent landowners; and that the practice is an appropriate means of harmonizing private interests in land and thus of benefitting the public interest....

Consistent with the above, this Court holds today that conditional use zoning, when carried out properly, is an approved practice in North Carolina. Like the jurisdictions we expressly join today, we are persuaded that the practice, when properly implemented, will add a valuable and desirable flexibility to the planning efforts of local authorities throughout our state. In our view, the "all or nothing" approach of traditional zoning techniques is insufficient in today's world of rapid industrial expansion and pressing urban and rural social and economic problems.

Having so stated, we hasten to add that, just as this type of zoning can provide much-needed and valuable flexibility to the planning efforts of local zoning authorities, it could also be as easily abused. We recognize that critics of the practice are to a limited extent justified in their concern that the unrestricted use of conditional use zoning could lead to private or public abuse of governmental power. We have said, however, that, in order to be legal and proper, conditional use zoning, like any type of zoning, must be reasonable, neither arbitrary nor unduly discriminatory, and in the public interest. It goes without saying that it also cannot constitute illegal spot zoning or illegal contract zoning as those two concepts are developed in the pages which follow. The benefits of the flexibility of conditional use zoning can be fairly achieved only when these limiting standards are consistently and carefully applied....

We turn now to the question of spot zoning. As we noted above, in its opinion below, the Court of Appeals held that the rezoning ... constituted an illegal form of "spot zoning," ... [citing] three principal reasons for its conclusion: (1) the rezoning was not called for by any change of conditions on the land; (2) the rezoning was not called for by the character of the district and the particular characteristics of the area being rezoned; and (3) the rezoning was not called for by the classification and use of nearby land.

While this Court agrees with some portions of the analysis employed by the Court of Appeals, we must disagree with that court's final conclusion. In our firmly held view, the rezoning accomplished in this case, while admittedly constituting a form of spot zoning, constituted a legal, and not an illegal form of spot zoning. Notwithstanding the Court of Appeals' conclusion to the contrary, we find that, on the facts of this case, the county did show a reasonable basis for the rezoning at issue....

We note as an initial matter that there is substantial disagreement amongst jurisdictions across the nation as to both the proper definition of and the legal significance of the term "spot zoning." Jurisdictions have essentially divided into two distinct camps. One group, the majority of jurisdictions, regards the term "spot zoning" as a legal term of art referring to a practice which is *per se* invalid. See 2 A. Rathkopf & D. Rathkopf, The Law of Zoning and Planning § 28.01 (4th ed. 1987); 1 R. Anderson, American Law of Zoning § 5.12 (3d ed. 1986)....

> Spot zoning amendments are those which by their terms single out a particular lot or parcel of land, usually small in relative size, and place it in an area the land use pattern of which is inconsistent with the small lot or parcel so placed, thus projecting an inharmonious land use pattern. Such amendments are usually triggered by efforts to secure special benefits for particular property owners, without proper regard for the rights of adjacent landowners. These are the real spot zoning situations. Under no circumstances could the tag of validity be attached thereto. [2 E. Yokley, Zoning Law and Practice § 13–3 at 207 (4th ed. 1978).]

A somewhat smaller group of jurisdictions, including our own, has taken a different approach. In these jurisdictions, it has been stated that "spot zoning" is a descriptive term merely, rather than a legal term of art, and that spot zoning practices may be valid or invalid depending upon the facts of the specific case. See 2 E. Yokley, Zoning Law and Practice § 13–5 (4th ed. 1978); 2 A. Rathkopf & D. Rathkopf, The Law of Zoning and Planning § 28.01 n.1 (4th ed. 1987)....

We are firmly amongst this latter group of jurisdictions which has held that spot zoning is not invalid per se. For example, in this Court's opinion in *Blades v. City of Raleigh*, 187 S.E.2d 35 (N.C. 1972), we defined "spot zoning" as follows:

> A zoning ordinance, or amendment, which singles out and reclassifies a relatively small tract owned by a single person and surrounded by a much larger area uniformly zoned, so as to impose upon the small tract greater restrictions than those imposed upon the larger area, or so as to relieve the small tract from restrictions to which the rest of the area is subjected, is called "spot zoning." [*Id.* at 45.]

However, having so defined the practice, we hastened to add that the practice is not invalid per se but, rather, that it is beyond the authority of the municipality or county and therefore void only "in the absence of a clear showing of a reasonable basis" therefor. *Id.* . . .

...In the view of this Court, the Board did in fact clearly show a reasonable basis for its rezoning of Mr. Clapp's two tracts from A–1 to CU–M–2. We are particularly persuaded, first, by the degree of public benefit created by the zoning action here and, second, by the similarity of the proposed use of the tracts under the new conditional use zone to the uses in the surrounding A–1 areas.

At the outset, we note that a judicial determination as to the existence or nonexistence of a sufficient reasonable basis in the context of spot zoning is, and must be, the "product of a complex of factors." 1 R. Anderson, American Law of Zoning § 5.13 at 364 (3d ed. 1986). The possible "factors" are numerous and flexible, and they exist to provide guidelines for a judicial balancing of interests. Among the factors relevant to this judicial balancing are the size of the tract in question; the compatibility of the disputed zoning action with an existing comprehensive zoning plan; the benefits and detriments resulting from the zoning action for the owner of the newly zoned property, his neighbors, and the surrounding community; and the relationship between the uses envisioned under the new zoning and the uses currently present in adjacent tracts. . . .

Turning our attention to the case before us, we find the latter two of the above-mentioned factors to argue forcefully for the proposition that the rezoning activity here was supported by a reasonable basis. First, the relative benefits and detriments accruing to Mr. Clapp, Mr. Chrismon, and the surrounding area as a result of the rezoning are instructive. It has been stated that the true vice of illegal spot zoning is in its inevitable effect of granting a discriminatory benefit to one landowner and a corresponding detriment to the neighbors or the community without adequate public advantage or justification. Accordingly, while spot zoning which creates a great benefit for the owner of the rezoned property with only an accompanying detriment and no accompanying benefit to the community or to the public interest may well be illegal, spot zoning which provides a service needed in the community in addition to benefitting the landowner may be proper.

Courts from other jurisdictions have held, for example, that the mere fact that an area is rezoned at the request of a single owner and is of greater benefit to him than to others does not make out a case of illegal spot zoning if there is a public need for it. *See, e.g., Jaffe v. City of Davenport*, 179 N.W.2d 554 (Iowa 1970); *Sweaney v. City of Dover*, 234 A.2d 521 (N.H. 1967). . . .

Turning to the facts of the case at bar, it is manifest that Mr. Clapp . . . has reaped a benefit by the Board's action. Specifically, by virtue of the Board's decision to rezone the tracts from A–1 to CU–M–2, Mr. Clapp will be able to carry on the otherwise illegal storage and sale of agricultural chemicals on both of his two tracts along Gun Shop Road in rural Guilford County. It is also beyond question that the plaintiffs in this case, the Chrismons, have simultaneously sustained a detriment. They, of course, would prefer that Mr. Clapp carry on his agricultural chemical operation somewhere other than next door to their home. Notwithstanding this, and consistent with the authority excerpted above, it is important, in our view, to consider this in the added context of both the benefits of the rezoning for the surrounding community and for the public interest.

As the Court of Appeals quite correctly conceded in its opinion below, "[t]he evidence clearly shows that Mr. Clapp's operation is beneficial to area farmers." *Chrismon v. Guilford County*, 354 S.E.2d 309, 313–14. The record reveals that members of the farming community surrounding the disputed land spoke in favor of the rezoning action during a meeting of the Guilford County Board of Commissioners prior to the ultimate meeting of 20 December 1982. Moreover, the record also reveals that, at one of the Board's meetings concerning the proposed rezoning, the Board was presented with a petition signed by some eighty-eight area residents favoring the action. While this Court understands that it was the Chrismons alone who lived next door to the operation, we do note that it was the Chrismons, and no one else, who spoke up against the rezoning.

In addition to this record evidence of substantial community support for Mr. Clapp's proposed use, there is additional and more objective evidence that the operation constitutes a use valuable to the surrounding community. The area in the vicinity of Mr. Clapp's operation is zoned for some miles as exclusively A–1 and is used by many for farming activities. Quite independent of the indications from members of the community that they have a subjective need for Mr. Clapp's services, it cannot be gainsaid that services of this type—namely, the storage and sale of pesticides, lime, and fertilizer—are valuable in a farming community such as that here. It has been held elsewhere that community-wide need for commercial or industrial facilities usually takes precedence over the objections of several adjacent property owners. *See Citizens Ass'n of Georgetown, Inc. v. D.C. Zoning Comm'n*, 402 A.2d 36 (D.C.App.1979). We believe that to be the case here.

A second factor that we find important in the determination of a reasonable basis for the spot zoning here is the similarity between the proposed use of the tracts under the new conditional use zone and the uses already present in surrounding areas. . . .

The compatibility of the uses envisioned in the rezoned tract with the uses already present in surrounding areas is considered an important factor in determining the validity of a spot zoning action. . . . One court has described the evil to be avoided as "an attempt to wrench a single small lot from its environment and give it a new rating which disturbs the tenor of the neighborhood." *Magnin v. Zoning Commission*, 138 A.2d 522, 523 (Conn. 1958). . . .

While significant disturbances such as the rezoning of a parcel in an old and well-established residential district to a commercial or industrial district would clearly be objectionable, this is clearly not such a case. We note first that, in actuality, the rezoning of the tracts in question from A–1 to CU–M–2, with all of the attendant restrictions and conditions, really represents very little change. The A–1 classification . . . allows all of Mr. Clapp's current operation except for the storage and sale of agricultural chemicals. The most noticeable activity, and the activity we suspect the plaintiffs would most like to be rid of—namely, the storage and sale of grain—is a conforming use under the A–1 classification and can legally continue irrespective of any zoning change. In addition, the conditions accompanying the disputed rezoning in the form of the conditional use permit essentially restrict Mr. Clapp to the very activities in which he is currently engaging—the storage and sale of agricultural chemicals—and nothing more.

Second, this is simply not a situation ... in which a radically different land use, by virtue of a zoning action, appears in the midst of a uniform and drastically distinct area. No parcel has been "wrenched" out of the Guilford County landscape and rezoned in a manner that "disturbs the tenor of the neighborhood." ... [T]he area surrounding the tracts in question is uniformly zoned as A–1 agricultural.... Conforming uses under the A–1 district include such disparate uses as single family dwellings, sawmills, fish or fowl hatcheries, farms, hospitals, and grain mills like the one Mr. Clapp was in fact operating here. In our view, the use of the newly rezoned tracts, pursuant to a CU–M–2 assignment, to store and sell agricultural chemicals is simply not the sort of drastic change from possible surrounding uses which constitutes illegal spot zoning....

We turn finally to the question of contract zoning.... [T]he Court of Appeals also held that the rezoning in question constituted illegal "contract zoning" and was therefore invalid and void for that alternative reason. Relying for support primarily on this Court's decision in *Allred v. City of Raleigh*, 178 S.E.2d 432, the Court of Appeals stated, in relevant part, as follows:

> [T]he county's action here also constitutes "contract zoning." Rezoning lacks a permissible basis where it is done "on consideration of assurances that a particular tract or parcel will be developed in accordance with restricted approval plans." *Allred*, 178 S.E.2d at 441.

> ...In effect, the rezoning was done on the assurance that Mr. Clapp would submit an application for a conditional use permit specifying that he would use the property only in that manner. The rezoning here was accomplished as a direct consequence of the conditions agreed to by the applicant rather than as a valid exercise of the county's legislative discretion. [*Chrismon v. Guilford County*, 354 S.E.2d 309, 314 (citations omitted).]

We must disagree with the Court of Appeals. In the view of this Court, the Court of Appeals, in its approach to the question of whether the rezoning at issue in this case constituted illegal contract zoning, improperly considered as equals two very different concepts—namely, valid conditional use zoning and illegal contract zoning. By virtue of this treatment of the two quite distinguishable concepts, the Court of Appeals has, for all intents and purposes, outlawed conditional use zoning in North Carolina by equating this beneficial land planning tool with a practice universally considered illegal. In fact, for the reasons we will develop below, the two concepts are not to be considered synonymous. Moreover, we hold that the rezoning at issue in this case—namely, the rezoning of Mr. Clapp's two tracts of land from A–1 to CU–M–2—was, in truth, valid conditional use zoning and not illegal contract zoning.

Illegal contract zoning properly connotes a transaction wherein both the landowner who is seeking a certain zoning action and the zoning authority itself undertake reciprocal obligations in the context of a bilateral contract. One commentator provides as illustration the following example:

> A Council enters into an agreement with the landowner and then enacts a zoning amendment. *The agreement, however, includes not merely the promise of the owner to subject his property to deed restrictions; the Council also binds itself to enact the amendment and not to alter the zoning change for a specified period of time.* Most courts will conclude that by agreeing to curtail its legislative power, the Council acted ultra vires. Such contract zoning is illegal and the rezoning is therefore a nullity. [Shapiro, *The Case for Conditional Zoning*, 41 Temp. L.Q. 267, 269 (1968) (emphasis added).]

As the excerpted illustration suggests, contract zoning of this type is objectionable primarily because it represents an abandonment on the part of the zoning authority of its duty to exercise independent judgment in making zoning decisions.

. . . [V]alid conditional use zoning, on the other hand, is an entirely different matter. Conditional use zoning . . . is an outgrowth of the need for a compromise between the interests of the developer who is seeking appropriate rezoning for his tract and the community on the one hand and the interests of the neighboring landowners who will suffer if the most intensive use permitted by the new classification is instituted. One commentator has described its mechanics as follows:

> An orthodox conditional zoning situation occurs when a zoning authority, *without committing its own power,* secures a property owner's agreement to subject his tract to certain restrictions as a prerequisite to rezoning. These restrictions may require that the rezoned property be limited to just one of the uses permitted in the new classification; or particular physical improvements and maintenance requirements may be imposed. [Shapiro, *The Case For Conditional Zoning*, 41 Temp. L.Q. 267, 270–71 (1968).]

In our view, therefore, [there are two] principal differences between valid conditional use zoning and illegal contract zoning. . . . First, valid conditional use zoning features merely a unilateral promise from the landowner to the local zoning authority as to the landowner's intended use of the land in question, while illegal contract zoning anticipates a bilateral contract in which the landowner and the zoning authority make reciprocal promises. Second, in the context of conditional use zoning, the local zoning authority maintains its independent decision-making authority, while in the contract zoning scenario, it abandons that authority by binding itself contractually with the landowner seeking a zoning amendment. . . .

[H]aving carefully reviewed the record in the case, we find no evidence that the local zoning authority . . . entered into anything approaching a bilateral contract with . . . Mr. Clapp. The facts of the case reveal that, pursuant to a filed complaint from the Chrismons, the Guilford County Inspections Department, by a letter dated 22 July 1982, notified Mr. Clapp that his expansion of the agricultural chemical operation to the tract adjacent to plaintiffs' lot constituted an impermissible expansion of a nonconforming use. More important for purposes of this issue, the letter informed Mr. Clapp of his various options in the following manner: "Mr. Clapp, there are several courses of action available to you in an effort to resolve your Zoning Ordinance violations: . . . 2. You may request rezoning of that portion of your land involved in the violations. This is not a guaranteed option."

Shortly after receiving this letter, Mr. Clapp applied to have both of his tracts of land—the 3.18–acre tract north of Gun Shop Road and the 5.06–acre tract south of Gun Shop Road—rezoned from A–1 to CU–M–2. He also filed written application for a conditional use permit, specifying in the application that he would continue to use the property as it was then being used and, in addition, listing those changes he would like to make in the succeeding five years. While these applications were ultimately approved by the Guilford County Board of Commissioners after a substantial period of deliberation which we highlight below, we are quite satisfied that the only promises made in this case were unilateral— specifically, those from Mr. Clapp to the Board in the form of the substance of his conditional use permit application. As the letter excerpted above makes clear, no promises whatever were made by the Board in exchange, and this rezoning does not therefore fall into the category of illegal contract zoning.

Second, and perhaps more important, the Board did not, by virtue of its actions in this case, abandon its position as an independent decision-maker. . . . On the contrary, we find that the Board made its decision in this matter only after a lengthy deliberation completely consistent with both the procedure called for by the relevant zoning ordinance and the rules prohibiting illegal contract zoning. . . .

Pursuant to proper notice, the Guilford County Board of Commissioners held a public meeting on 20 December 1982 regarding both applications and heard numerous statements from all of the concerned parties. During at least one previous meeting, members of the community had spoken in favor of Mr. Clapp's rezoning request, numerous ideas had been introduced concerning use of the property, and the Board was presented with a petition signed by eighty-eight persons favoring the rezoning request. While the Court of Appeals' opinion seems to suggest that the ultimate result of the 20 December 1982 meeting was a foregone conclusion, the record simply does not reveal as much. Instead, the record reveals that the Board made its final decision only after what appears to have been a thorough consideration of the merits of Mr. Clapp's applications for rezoning and for a conditional use permit, as well as of the various alternatives to granting those applications.[5] . . .

5. The official minutes of the 20 December 1982 Board of Commissioners meeting reveal discussion of "attempts [that] had been made to resolve differences between

Accordingly, the decision of Court of Appeals is hereby reversed. The case is remanded to that court for further remand to the Superior Court, Guilford County, for reinstatement of the original judgment denying plaintiffs' action for a declaratory judgment and affirming the zoning action of the Guilford County Board of Commissioners. . . .

Notes

1. *"Nonconforming" Uses.* When a municipality enacts or substantially amends a zoning ordinance, some existing land uses may not comply with the new or amended ordinance. The law generally characterizes these land uses as *nonconforming uses.* Prior to the zoning ordinance in Guilford County, Clapp had the right to use his land selling agricultural chemicals, and in fact had made an investment based upon this use. Although the zoning ordinance reflects a municipal decision to prohibit such uses within A–1 zones, the ordinance could be seen as destroying the value of Clapp's investment in the previously permitted use and thus effecting a "taking" of Clapp's private property. To address this concern, most zoning ordinances "grandfather" such pre-existing uses and allow owners to continue the pre-existing uses as "nonconforming uses."

Because nonconforming uses are, by definition, inconsistent with the municipality's long-term plan for the area, the municipality's eventual goal is to eliminate nonconforming uses. Accordingly, municipalities have developed a number of different approaches to facilitate the termination of nonconforming uses without effecting an unconstitutional taking. Later in this chapter, we examine the success or failure of these approaches.

As a practical matter, the *Chrismon* decision allows Clapp to expand his nonconforming use to an additional parcel of land. Think back to *Brown v. Voss* (page 595), in which the servient landowner successfully challenged the dominant landowner's attempt to use an access easement to benefit additional land. Is the expansion of use in *Chrismon* analogous to the one in *Brown*? Why or why not?

2. *Judicial Review of Zoning Amendments.* What constitutes a good reason for singling out a parcel and treating it for zoning purposes in a fashion that differs significantly from the surrounding land? Carefully review the factors listed in *Chrismon* (page 885), which courts typically use in evaluating a municipality's rezoning decision. Can you explain how and why each listed factor is relevant to deciding the validity of a zoning amendment? Are some perhaps more important than others? What other factors might a court sensibly consider?

(a) *Spot Zoning*? Some jurisdictions use the term "spot zoning" as a legal term of art, carrying the implicit legal conclusion that a particular rezoning is illegal. In these states, a court would first evaluate the amendment to determine whether there was any reasonable basis for the amend-

---

the owner and his neighbors." These attempts to resolve the problem short of rezoning the property apparently included the removal of one grain dryer from the property, the planting of trees along the property line, the placement of canvas covers over the grain bins, and discussions with the Environmental Protection Agency concerning other ways of reducing dust and noise.

ment consistent with the comprehensive zoning plan. If so, the court would conclude that the amendment was not "spot zoning." If not, the court would characterize the amendment as "spot zoning" and invalidate it. How does *Chrismon's* analysis of the validity of spot zoning differ from this view?

(b) *Accordance with a Comprehensive Plan.* What does it mean to say that a particular rezoning decision must be "consistent with" or "in accordance with" a comprehensive plan? We have already seen that the universally required comprehensive plan may be a distinct document, or may be inferred from the zoning classifications designated by the municipality. Should the zoning officials treat the comprehensive plan as a controlling instrument, or as an advisory tool? *Compare Barrie v. Kitsap County*, 93 Wash.2d 843, 613 P.2d 1148 (1980) (plan is advisory) *with Machado v. Musgrove*, 519 So.2d 629 (Fla. Dist. Ct. App. 1987) (plan is controlling). Which view do you think is preferable? Why?

(c) *The "Change or Mistake Rule."* Some states permit rezoning only where either the original zoning is found to have been a "mistake," or the change is justified by "changed circumstances" subsequent to the original zoning. *See, e.g., Citizens for Mount Vernon v. City of Mount Vernon*, 133 Wash.2d 861, 947 P.2d 1208 (1997); *Board of Supervisors of Fairfax County v. Snell Constr. Corp.*, 214 Va. 655, 202 S.E.2d 889 (1974). Is this a sensible prerequisite to rezoning? Consider the following excerpt from an opinion dissenting from application of this "change-or-mistake rule."

Let us examine the syllogisms upon which this "change-or-mistake" rule rests. As I see them they are:

Major premise: The comprehensive zoning plan was a good plan when enacted; the plan is good today, if physical conditions have not changed.

Minor premise: Physical conditions have not changed.

Conclusion: The plan is good today.

The "mistake" part of the "change-or-mistake" rule is founded on another such syllogism, equally grim, which goes like this:

Major premise: Today's plan is a good plan, but differs from the original plan; if physical conditions have not changed, the original plan must have been bad.

Minor premise: Physical conditions have not changed.

Conclusion: The original plan must have been bad. . . .

The "change-or-mistake" rule derived from the syllogisms above set forth is rendered erroneous by the simple truth: "Ideas change."

In my opinion, the correct rule in considering the validity of rezoning ordinances is whether or not the ordinance is unreasonable, arbitrary or capricious. [*MacDonald v. Board of County Comm'rs*, 238 Md. 549, 578–79, 210 A.2d 325, 341–42 (1965) (Barnes, J., dissenting).]

(d) *Review of Rezoning as a "Legislative" or "Judicial" Act.* In reviewing zoning decisions, should courts treat them as legislation and give them the deference typically accorded legislation in our governmental system? Or should courts treat rezoning as a quasi-judicial act subject to more searching judicial review? Effectively, courts taking the latter view have eliminated the normal presumption of validity that attaches to zoning decisions and have placed on the landowner the burden of proving that the amendment conforms to the comprehensive plan and benefits the common welfare. *See, e.g., Fasano v. Board of County Comm'rs of Washington County,* 264 Or. 574, 507 P.2d 23 (1973). Courts in other states have rejected the *Fasano* approach. For example, consider the analysis in *Quinn v. Town of Dodgeville,* 120 Wis.2d 304, 354 N.W.2d 747 (App. 1984):

> The line between legislative and judicial actions may occasionally blur, but the fact is that an ordinance amendment, whether it affects a large or a small parcel, or many property owners or only one, is a decision to change an existing ordinance, a legislative function. It does not adjudicate existing rights where, as here, a property owner proposing a zoning change desires to use the property for a purpose not authorized by the ordinance. Nearby owners cannot claim a property interest in the present zoning of plaintiff's property. . . .

> To declare that an act by a legislative body is judicial to obtain a greater scope of judicial review is, in our view, an unduly pragmatic approach which ignores the division of governmental functions according to their legislative, judicial or executive character. For us to convert a legislative function to a judicial function through a name change would substitute result orientation for functional analysis. [354 N.W.2d at 754.]

3. *Conditional Use Zoning.* Should the fact that a zoning ordinance authorizes conditional use zoning mean that the municipality *must* approve of conditional uses that do not pose a risk of significant harm to adjoining landowners? On this point, zoning ordinances vary. Some ordinances set forth specific criteria that one must satisfy to obtain a conditional use permit; once the applicant satisfies those criteria, the appropriate municipal body (most frequently a board of zoning adjustment) *must* issue the permit. *See, e.g., Keiger v. Winston–Salem Bd. of Adjustment,* 278 N.C. 17, 178 S.E.2d 616 (1971). Other ordinances purport to give the municipality broad discretion. *See, e.g., Gorham v. Town of Cape Elizabeth,* 625 A.2d 898 (Me. 1993) (upholding denial of special use permit to convert single-unit home to multi-unit home, based upon perceived adverse effect on value of adjacent land). Which approach seems preferable? Why?

4. *Conditional Use Zoning vs. "Contract Zoning"?* Although many jurisdictions have found conditional use zoning to be acceptable, most jurisdictions generally frown upon contract zoning. Is the distinction that the *Chrismon* court draws between valid conditional zoning and unlawful contract zoning a meaningful distinction? The *Chrismon* court suggests that contract zoning is troublesome because the municipality is relinquishing some of its legislative authority by entering into a bilateral agreement. Why is this a problem? Does contract zoning present other problems?

Consider these questions in light of the following example. Suppose that Brown owns a parcel of land along one of the busiest streets in a residential zone. Because the adjacent parcel is occupied by a gas station (a valid nonconforming use), Brown cannot find a purchaser for the parcel at a price he is willing to accept. Thus, Brown seeks to have his parcel rezoned commercial for the purpose of building a small "neighborhood" hardware store. The City Council does not object to Brown's proposed use, but (based upon concerns raised by neighbors) does not want Brown to be able to make any other commercial use of the land. The City Council considers two different ways of proceeding with Brown's application:

- It could propose to Brown that if he will impose a covenant on the land stating "This parcel shall be used for no commercial purpose other than a hardware store," it will hold the necessary hearings and pass a rezoning amendment placing his land in a commercial zone.

- It could rezone the parcel to a conditional use commercial classification in which only a limited number of commercial uses would be available, subject to permitting requirements.

Should courts treat these two different approaches to rezoning differently? Based on the *Chrismon* court's critique of contract zoning, what potential problems exist with the first approach to rezoning? Does the second approach really involve a unilateral promise on the part of the applicant (Brown) as opposed to a bilateral agreement? Why should it matter? Should it matter that with conditional use zoning the "conditions" are part of the zoning ordinance, whereas with contract zoning the "conditions" frequently are extrinsic to the zoning ordinance? Why or why not? *See Cederberg v. City of Rockford*, 8 Ill.App.3d 984, 291 N.E.2d 249 (1972) (invalidating contract zoning). Should a court uphold the second approach as valid conditional use zoning? *See Goffinet v. County of Christian*, 65 Ill.2d 40, 2 Ill.Dec. 275, 357 N.E.2d 442 (1976) (allowing conditional zoning).

Finally, suppose that Wells seeks an amendment to rezone 236 acres that she owns in Smithville from agricultural to heavy industrial. The Smithville City Council amends the zoning ordinance to rezone the land "on the condition that it be used solely to construct and operate a synthetic gas production plant. Upon cessation of use as a gasification facility, said land will revert to its previous Agricultural classification." Is this zoning amendment valid? Does conditional zoning with a reverter effectively differ from granting a conditional use permit? Does the reversion clause present any problems? [Who decides when the reversion takes effect? What happens when the reversion takes effect?] *Compare Goffinet, supra* (enforcing zoning ordinance containing reverter clause) *with Scrutton v. County of Sacramento*, 275 Cal.App.2d 412, 79 Cal.Rptr. 872 (1969) (invalidating automatic reversion clause).

5. *Remedies for Invalid Contract Zoning.* In *Cederberg v. City of Rockford, supra* note 4, the court concluded not only that the agreed-upon covenant was void, but that the zoning amendment enacted pursuant to the unlawful contract zoning was also void. By contrast, in *Carlino v. Whitpain Investors*, 499 Pa. 498, 453 A.2d 1385 (1982), the court allowed the rezoning to stand and simply invalidated the covenant. Which remedy is preferable? Which imposes a greater penalty to discourage inappropriate conduct? Which does the most to promote the public welfare?

6. *Procedural Due Process.* The SZEA requires a public hearing prior to the enactment of a zoning ordinance or amendment. In many communities, as in *Chrismon*, there will be two hearings upon zoning amendments— one before the planning and zoning commission and another before the city

council or county commission. The SZEA also states that the municipality must publish notice of the public hearing (such as by a legal notice in the newspaper) at least 15 days prior to the hearing. Though some ordinances follow the SZEA's minimal publication notice, many ordinances now require that the municipality provide notice to the affected landowner(s) and, in some cases, a number of their nearest neighbors.

If the municipality fails to comply with its statutory notice obligations, affected landowners may challenge a zoning amendment based upon its procedural irregularity. In this regard, it is dangerous for a municipality to rely upon publication notice alone, even if its zoning ordinance deems such notice sufficient. The Supreme Court has concluded that the U.S. Constitution requires a state or local government, prior to taking action affecting an interest in property, to provide the owner with notice that is reasonably calculated under the circumstances to apprise him or her of the proposed action. *Mennonite Bd. of Missions v. Adams*, 462 U.S. 791, 103 S.Ct. 2706, 77 L.Ed.2d 180 (1983); *Mullane v. Central Hanover Bank & Trust Co.*, 339 U.S. 306, 70 S.Ct. 652, 94 L.Ed. 865 (1950). If the names and addresses of the affected parties are reasonably ascertainable, this means notice by mail or personal service. *Mennonite Bd. of Missions*, 462 U.S. at 795; *Mullane*, 339 U.S. at 314. Some courts have specifically imposed these requirements in the zoning context. *See, e.g., Harris v. County of Riverside*, 904 F.2d 497 (9th Cir. 1990); *American Oil Corp. v. City of Chicago*, 29 Ill.App.3d 988, 331 N.E.2d 67 (1975).

LAWYERING EXERCISE
(Client Counseling and Dispute Resolution)

SITUATION: Brown owns a parcel of land that is zoned agricultural. He wishes to have the parcel rezoned as residential and to develop it for single family housing and duplexes. At the first hearing, a number of neighbors express opposition to the rezoning. The Planning and Zoning Commission tables the matter and directs the parties to discuss the problem.

TASK: How would you advise Brown to proceed with discussions with the neighbors? Assuming Brown and the neighbors reach an acceptable negotiated resolution, how would you advise Brown regarding options for implementing the agreement? Which option would you recommend?

---

b. *Variances*. When a landowner wants to build in a manner that fails to comply with various height or area restrictions, or to use her land in a manner not permitted within the existing zone—but does not want to go through the amendment process—the landowner may seek a *variance* from the applicable restrictions. There are two types of variances—*use variances* (variances from limitations on use) and *area variances* (variances from dimensional limitations such as setback requirements). The variance request is a site-specific, use-specific request generally decided by an administrative tribunal (such as a board of zoning appeals or board of zoning adjustment). What functions do variances serve that are not already served by amendments and conditional use zoning?

MATTHEW v. SMITH

Supreme Court of Missouri.
707 S.W.2d 411 (1986).

WELLIVER, JUDGE. This is an appeal from a circuit court judgment affirming the Board of Zoning Adjustment's decision to grant Jim and Susan Brandt a variance. The Brandts purchased a residential lot containing two separate houses upon a tract of land zoned for a single-family use. The court of appeals reversed the circuit court judgment, and the case was then certified to this Court by a dissenting judge. We reverse and remand.

The Brandts own a tract of land comprising one and one-half plotted lots. When they purchased the property in March of 1980, there already were two houses on the land, one toward the front of Erie Street and one in the rear. Each of the buildings is occupied by one residential family as tenants of the Brandts. The two houses apparently have been used as separate residences for the past thirty years, with only intermittent vacancies. The property is zoned for Single Family Residences. At the suggestion of a city official, the Brandts applied for a variance which would allow them to rent both houses with a single family in each house. After some delay, including two hearings by the Board of Zoning Adjustment of Kansas City, the Board granted the application. Appellant, Jon Matthew, a neighboring landowner challenged the grant of the variance and sought a petition for certiorari from the Board's action. § 89.110, RSMo 1978. The circuit court affirmed the Board's order; on appeal, the court of appeals held that the Board was without authority to grant the requested variance. A dissenting judge certified the case to this Court....

Under most zoning acts, [Boards of Zoning Adjustment or Appeals] have the authority to grant variances from the strict letter of the zoning ordinance. The variance procedure "fulfil[s] a sort of 'escape hatch' or 'safety valve' function for individual landowners who would suffer special hardship from the literal application of the ... zoning ordinance." *City & Borough of Juneau v. Thibodeau*, 595 P.2d 626, 633 (Alaska 1979). *See also* A. Rathkopf, 3 The Law of Zoning and Planning § 38 (1979); N. Williams, 5 American Planning Law § 129.05 (1985). It is often said that "[t]he variance provides an administrative alternative for individual relief that can avoid the damage that can occur to a zoning ordinance as a result of as applied taking litigation." D. Mandelker, Land Use Law, at 169 (1982). The general rule is that the authority to grant a variance should be exercised sparingly and only under exceptional circumstances.

Both the majority of courts and the commentators recognize two types of variances: an area (nonuse) variance and a use variance. . . . As the name indicates, a use variance is one which permits a use other than one of those prescribed by the zoning ordinance in the particular district; it permits a use which the ordinance prohibits. A nonuse variance authorizes deviations from restrictions which relate to a permitted use, rather than limitations on the use itself, that is, restrictions on the bulk of buildings, or relating to their height, size, and extent of lot coverage, or minimum habitable area therein, or on the placement of buildings and structures on the lot with respect to required yards. Variances made necessary by the physical characteristics of the lot itself are nonuse variances of a kind commonly termed "area variances." Many zoning acts or ordinances expressly distinguish between the two types of variances. When the distinction is not statutory, "the courts have always distinguished use from area variances." D. Mandelker, Land Use Law, at 167 (1982). Some jurisdictions, whether by express statutory directive or by court interpretation, do not permit the grant of a use variance.

Past decisions in this State have placed Missouri within those jurisdictions not permitting a use variance. This line of cases would suggest that the Brandts are not entitled to the variance. They seek a variance to use the property in a manner not permitted under the permissible uses established by the ordinance. The ordinance clearly permits only the use of the property for a single family residence. The applicant is not seeking a variance from the area and yard restrictions which are no doubt violated because of the existence of the second residence. Such an area variance is not necessary because the applicant has a permissible nonconforming structure under the ordinance.

Commentators, however, have questioned the rationale underlying the Missouri cases. These past cases . . . are based upon the premise that the granting of a use variance would be an unconstitutional delegation of power to the Board to amend the ordinance. *See generally* Mandelker, *Delegation of Power and Function In Zoning Administration*, 1963 Wash. U.L.Q. 60, 68–71. This view has long since been repudiated by most jurisdictions, and it is contrary to the express language of § 89.090, RSMo 1978, which grants the Board the "power to vary or modify the application of any of the regulations or provisions of such ordinance relating to the use, construction or alteration of buildings or structures, or the use of land." We, therefore, hold that under the proper circumstances an applicant may obtain a use variance.

Section 89.090, RSMo 1978 delegates to the Board of Adjustment the power to grant a variance when the applicant establishes "practical difficulties or unnecessary hardship in the way of carrying out the strict letter of such ordinance . . . so that the spirit of the ordinance shall be observed, public safety and welfare secured and substantial justice done." . . .

Almost all jurisdictions embellished the general concepts of "unnecessary hardship" or "practical difficulties" by further defining the conditions an applicant must satisfy before obtaining a variance. Quite often, local zoning ordinances "summarize that case law by spelling out the same more specific standards in the ordinance, for the convenience of everybody." N. Williams, *supra*, § 131.02, at 28. The North Kansas City Ordinance, for example, provides in part:

> Section 27. Board of Adjustment....
>
> B. **Standards.** 1. The board of adjustment may vary the provisions of this ordinance as authorized in this section, but only when it shall have made findings based upon evidence presented to it in the following specific cases: (a) That the property in question cannot yield a reasonable return if permitted to be used only under the conditions allowed by the regulations governing the district in which it is located; (b) That the plight of the owner is due to unique circumstances; and (c) That the variance, if granted, will not alter the essential character of the locality....

Unfortunately, any attempt to set forth a unified structure illustrating how all the courts have treated these conditions would, according to Professor Williams, prove unsuccessful. Williams observes that the law of variances is in "great confusion" and that aside from general themes any further attempt at unifying the law indicates "either (a) [one] has not read the case law, or (b) [one] has simply not understood it. Here far more than elsewhere in American planning law, muddle reigns supreme." N. Williams, *supra*, § 129.01, at 12. Yet, four general themes can be distilled from variance law and indicate what an applicant for a variance must prove:

> (1) relief is necessary because of the unique character of the property rather than for personal considerations; and
>
> (2) applying the strict letter of the ordinance would result in unnecessary hardship; and the
>
> (3) imposition of such a hardship is not necessary for the preservation of the plan; and
>
> (4) granting the variance will result in substantial justice to all.

See A. Rathkopf, *supra*, § 37.06; N. Williams, *supra*, § 129.06. Although all the requirements must be satisfied, it is generally held that " '[u]nnecessary hardship' is the principal basis on which a variance is granted." D. Mandelker, Land Use Law, at 167.

Before further examining the contours of unnecessary hardship, jurisdictions such as Missouri that follow the New York model rather than the Standard Act need to address the significance of the statutory dual standard of "unnecessary hardship" or "practical difficulties." Generally, this dual standard has been treated in one of two ways. On the one hand, many courts view the two terms as interchangeable. On the other hand, a number of jurisdictions follow the approach of New York, the jurisdiction where the language originated, and hold that "practical difficulties" is a slightly lesser standard than "unnecessary hardship" and only applies to the granting of an area variance and not a use variance. The rationale for this approach is that an area variance is a relaxation of one or more incidental limitations to a permitted use and does not alter the character of the district as much as a use not permitted by the ordinance.

In light of our decision to permit the granting of a use variance, we are persuaded that the New York rule reflects the sound approach for treating the distinction between area and use variances. To obtain a use variance, an applicant must demonstrate, inter alia, unnecessary hardship; and, to obtain an area variance, an applicant must establish, inter alia, the existence of conditions slightly less rigorous than unnecessary hardship.

While today we enter a field not yet developed by case law in our own jurisdiction, other jurisdictions provide some guidance for determining what is required to establish unnecessary hardship when granting a use variance. . . . *Otto v. Steinhilber*, 282 N.Y. 71, 24 N.E.2d 851, 853 (1939) contains the classic definition of unnecessary hardship:

> Before the Board may exercise its discretion and grant a variance upon the ground of unnecessary hardship, the record must show that (1) the land in question cannot yield a reasonable return if used only for a purpose allowed in that zone; (2) that the plight of the owner is due to unique circumstances and not to the general conditions in the neighborhood which may reflect the unreasonableness of the zoning ordinance itself; and (3) that the use to be authorized by the variance will not alter the essential character of the locality.

Quite often the existence of unnecessary hardship depends upon whether the landowner can establish that without the variance the property cannot yield a reasonable return. "Reasonable return is not maximum return." *Curtis v. Main*, 482 A.2d 1253, 1257 (Me.1984). Rather, the landowner must demonstrate that he or she will be deprived of all beneficial use of the property under any of the permitted uses. . . . Most courts agree that mere conclusory and lay opinion concerning the lack of any reasonable return is not sufficient; there must be actual proof, often in the form of dollars and cents evidence. . . . Such pronouncements and requirements of the vast majority of jurisdictions illustrate that, if the law of variances is to have any viability, only in the exceptional case will a use variance be justified.

The record before this Court is fraught with personality conflicts and charges of bias on the part of one of the Board members. Also, the record is without sufficient evidence to establish unnecessary hardship.[6]

---

6. [Missouri's] Constitution requires that the decision of the Board be reviewed to determine if it is authorized by law and supported by competent and substantial evidence. When the Brandts initially applied for a variance and a hearing was held, there were no minutes of the proceeding and the circuit court had to send the case back to the Board before it could review the Board's order. Nothing in the record indicates why this occurred, but the statute expressly requires that such minutes be transcribed. . . . § 89.080, RSMo 1978. Compliance with this requirement is necessary if there is to be any meaningful review exercised by the circuit court. . . .

The only evidence in the record is the conclusory opinion of Brandt that they would be deprived of a reasonable return if not allowed to rent both houses. No evidence of land values was offered; and, no dollars and cents proof was presented to demonstrate that they would be deprived of all beneficial use of their property. Appellant, in fact, was not permitted to introduce such evidence. The Board, therefore, was without authority to grant a use variance upon this record.

The record, however, indicates that the Brandts may be entitled to a nonconforming use under the ordinance. A nonconforming use differs from a variance. Nonconforming uses are those that are in existence prior to and at the time of adoption of the zoning ordinance and which have been maintained from that time to the present. The North Kansas City Zoning Ordinance provides:

> Any nonconforming building, structure or use which existed lawfully at the time of the adoption of this ordinance and which remains nonconforming, and only such building, structure or use which shall become nonconforming upon the adoption of this ordinance or any subsequent amendment thereto, may be continued in accordance with the regulations which follow. [§ 5.B North Kansas City Zoning Ordinance.]

The ordinance further provides that one loses the right to a nonconforming use if the property is abandoned as a nonconforming use for a period of more than six months. § 5.C(4). The record indicates that a city official, based upon what was apparently scant evidence, suggested to the Brandts that they may have lost their right to a nonconforming use. There is no substantial evidence in this record indicating the length of time the property may have been unoccupied. Nothing in the record indicates whether the Brandts may have been refurbishing the property or looking for tenants during any such time. Nothing suggests that the Brandts intended to abandon their nonconforming use during the period of time the property may have been unoccupied. Both the trial court and counsel for the Board suggest that the Brandts "may very well have a valid nonconforming use of the premises in question." We do not believe that anything in the record indicates that the Brandts have waived their right to or abandoned their claim of a nonconforming use.

The judgment of the circuit court is reversed and the cause is remanded back to the circuit court with directions that the cause be remanded back to the Board of Adjustment with directions that the applicants be permitted to present evidence warranting the grant of a variance and to amend their application to claim a nonconforming use of the premises and for such hearing and decision as may be required consistent with this opinion.

Notes

1. *Use Variance or Area Variance?* Consider the following language from the North Kansas City ordinance, which defines the term "lot" as a

"parcel of land occupied by, or intended for occupancy by, one principal building, unified groups [sic] of buildings for principal use, and having access to a public street. A lot may be one or more platted lots, or tracts as conveyed, or parts thereof." § 3(7). The ordinance also provided that "[e]very dwelling hereafter constructed, reconstructed, moved or altered shall provide a lot area of not less than three thousand eight hundred fifty square feet per family." § 8. In *Matthew*, the land on which the two homes were located contained roughly 1–1/2 times the square footage required for one home.

The opinion in *Matthew* treats the requested variance as a use variance. Do you agree? On what basis might you argue that it instead constitutes an area variance? *See Matthew v. Smith*, 707 S.W.2d 411, 419 (Robertson, J., concurring). Can you explain why it matters?

2. *Use Variances and the "Unnecessary Hardship" Standard.* Why require such a high standard for allowing a use variance? Are the applicable concerns similar to those involving spot zoning? In considering these questions and the ones below, review the statement of criteria for granting a use variance from New York's *Otto* decision (quoted in *Matthew* on page 898) and the four themes identified in *Matthew* as being relevant to the grant of a variance (page 897).

(a) *Hardship?* What evidence must an owner present to demonstrate hardship? Must the owner prove that the land cannot yield a reasonable return absent the requested variance? May the unique circumstances required to satisfy the unnecessary hardship standard relate to the owner of the land, or must they relate solely to the land in question? *See Belgarde v. Kocher*, 215 A.D.2d 1002, 627 N.Y.S.2d 128 (1995) (problem must arise from nature of land, not personal circumstances of owner); *State ex rel. Tucker v. McDonald*, 793 S.W.2d 616 (Mo. Ct. App. 1990) (same).

(b) *Unnecessary?* What does the word "unnecessary" add to the unnecessary hardship standard? If the hardship is necessary to serve the purposes of the zoning ordinance, should the landowner be denied a use variance?

3. *Area Variances and the "Practical Difficulties" Standard.* As *Matthew* notes, many jurisdictions do not distinguish between the "practical difficulties" test and the "unnecessary hardship" test. *See, e.g., Snyder v. Zoning Bd. of Adjustment*, 74 Wis.2d 468, 247 N.W.2d 98 (1976) (two tests should be read together). In other states, however, courts have purported to treat these as distinct standards. For example, *Matthew* states that the practical difficulties test requires the existence of conditions "slightly less rigorous" than unnecessary hardship. What does this mean? *Compare O'Keefe v. Donovan*, 199 A.D.2d 681, 605 N.Y.S.2d 150 (1993) (granting frontage and setback variances for land on which owner wanted to build house for daughter with lupus because the variances would not change character of neighborhood or impact value of neighboring homes) *with Munnelly v. Town of East Hampton*, 173 A.D.2d 472, 570 N.Y.S.2d 93 (1991) (denying lot size variance that would have allowed one lot to be divided into two nonconforming lots; fact that land bought for $150,000 could be sold for only $220,000, rather than for greater profit, does not justify area variance).

4. *New York's Balancing Test for Area Variances.* In response to judicial confusion regarding the practical difficulties test—particularly the

extent to which it required evidence of significant economic hardship—the New York legislature enacted a new standard for area variances. The new standard requires the zoning board to weigh " 'the benefit to the applicant' against 'the detriment to the health, safety and welfare of the neighborhood or community' if the area variance is granted." N.Y. Town Law § 267–b[3][b]. Specifically, the statute requires a zoning board to consider the following:

(1) whether an undesirable change will be produced in the character of the neighborhood or a detriment to nearby properties will be created by the granting of the area variance;

(2) whether the benefit sought by the applicant can be achieved by some other method, feasible for the applicant to pursue, other than an area variance;

(3) whether the requested area variance is substantial;

(4) whether the proposed variance will have an adverse effect or impact on the physical or environmental conditions in the neighborhood or district;

(5) whether the alleged difficulty was self-created, which consideration shall be relevant to the decision ... but shall not necessarily preclude the granting of the area variance.

Is this a more sensible approach? Why or why not? How does this change the "practical difficulties" standard discussed above? *See, e.g., Tarantino v. Zoning Bd. of Appeals*, 228 A.D.2d 511, 644 N.Y.S.2d 296 (1996). Because many states, like Missouri, have modeled their zoning enabling acts on New York's, this change in New York may lead to similar changes in other states.

5. *Landowner and Municipal Mistakes and Variances.* How should mistakes by owners or by municipalities impact a landowner's entitlement to an area variance? Assume Brown spent more than $250,000 building a residence (pursuant to a building permit issued by the town) before discovering that it violated the town setback requirements. At that point, Brown sought an area variance, to which a number of neighbors objected. Should the fact that Brown created the violation himself disqualify him from obtaining a variance? *Compare Bloom v. Zoning Bd. of Appeals*, 233 Conn. 198, 658 A.2d 559 (1995) (insufficient hardship when structures were built pursuant to mistakenly issued building permit) *with Board of Adjustment v. McBride*, 676 S.W.2d 705 (Tex. App. 1984) (variance appropriate when setback violation occurred due to inaccurate site plan approved by city). What if Brown instead spent $250,000 to purchase a completed home, knowing that it was in violation of setback requirements? As a policy matter, should this knowledge preclude Brown from obtaining a variance? *See Spence v. Board of Zoning Appeals*, 255 Va. 116, 496 S.E.2d 61 (1998) (no).

6. *Variance Procedure and Procedural Competence.* The court in *Matthew* chastised the board for failing to maintain minutes of its hearings so as to facilitate judicial review of its decisions. These problems often plague zoning boards of appeal, which tend to consist of citizen volunteers who may not always appreciate the nuances of due process. For example, in *Burke v. Village of Colonie Zoning Bd. of Appeals*, 199 A.D.2d 611, 604 N.Y.S.2d 343 (1993), the board denied a use variance and instead granted an area

variance, which it considered "lesser relief." The court reversed, holding that the board's notice of the hearing focused solely on the request for a use variance and therefore deprived both the applicant and interested neighbors of the opportunity to present evidence tailored to the different standard applicable to area variances. *See generally* Jesse Dukeminier, Jr. & Clyde L. Stapleton, *The Zoning Board of Adjustment: A Case Study in Misrule*, 50 Ky. L.J. 273 (1962).

Some commentators have documented the extent to which zoning appeals boards fail to abide by substantive standards for decisionmaking:

> Eighty-one percent of all appeals were successful in Boston, eighty-five percent in Cambridge, Massachusetts. Sixty-seven percent of all variance requests were approved in Austin, Texas, and seventy-four percent in Milwaukee. If a system can be judged by the frequency of departures from it, zoning fails spectacularly. . . .

> . . . During a study made in Philadelphia, the board granted seventy-seven percent of appeals in which there were no protesters, but only twenty-four percent of those in which a protesting party appeared. In Boston, the figures were eighty-one percent of all appeals as opposed to sixty percent of protested appeals, and in Lexington–Fayette County, Kentucky, eighty-five as opposed to sixty-three percent. The appearance of protesting parties before the appeal board may in some instances perform the helpful function of defining the entire community's attitude toward a proposed project. In many other cases, however, the protesters probably constitute only one interest group, which may or may not represent the best interests of the area affected. It seems likely that such protesters serve more as an unprincipled check upon the equally unprincipled granting of variances and exceptions than as an accurate guide for policy judgments. [Note, *Administrative Discretion in Zoning*, 82 Harv. L. Rev. 668, 673, 675 (1969).]

Consistent with this analysis, one rural Missouri practitioner has observed that in "the real world," the primary "rule" a board of zoning appeals will follow in considering a variance focuses on the extent of neighborly opposition—if there is no opposition, the board generally grants the variance without regard to the legal standard; if the variance is opposed, then the legal standard takes on significance. Do you think that such a "rule" is objectionable? Why or why not?

----

c.   *Nonconforming Uses.* When a municipality enacts or amends a zoning ordinance, existing land uses that do not comply with the new use regulations—*nonconforming uses*—present a problem for municipalities. Zoning ordinances generally "grandfather" such preexisting uses of land, in recognition of the landowner's investment in a lawful pre-existing use. Nonetheless, because nonconforming uses are inconsistent with the municipality's long-term plan for the area, municipalities have developed a number of different approaches to promote the ultimate elimination of nonconforming uses.

IN RE APPEAL OF MISEROCCHI

Supreme Court of Vermont.
170 Vt. 320, 749 A.2d 607 (2000).

SKOGLUND, J. Applicants appeal from decisions of the environmental court that (1) denied on summary judgment their request for a variance, and (2) denied after trial approval for a change in use from agricultural to residential. We conclude that applicants do not need either change-of-use approval or a variance to change the use of their nonconforming structure from one permitted use to another permitted use. Thus, we reverse the decisions of the environmental court to the extent that it held otherwise.

The environmental court made the following findings. In 1988, applicants acquired an eighteen-acre parcel in the Town of Clarendon with a barn that was formerly used to store agricultural equipment. The parcel is in a residential district of the town, in which both agricultural uses and one-family dwellings are permitted uses. The barn is forty feet wide and one hundred feet long, with the longer dimension running along the road. The barn is set back ten to twenty feet from the edge of the pavement. The town zoning regulations require, in a residential district, a minimum forty-foot setback from the edge of the road. Thus, the barn is nonconforming with the setback requirement.

Applicants claimed that the 1988 zoning administrator told them that they did not need a permit to alter the interior of the building for a residence, but that exterior renovations would require a permit. Applicants installed a water supply and sewage disposal system and installed a mobile home at the back of and partially inside the barn. In 1995, a subsequent zoning administrator told them that the residential use was a violation of the zoning regulations, and appellants applied for change-of-use approval. The zoning board of adjustment addressed the request as if it were a request for conditional-use approval. As the environmental court recognized, there is no zoning regulation that requires conditional-use approval to allow a change in use from one permitted use to another permitted use in a noncomplying structure. Nonetheless, the zoning board of adjustment granted a conditional-use permit to allow applicants to renovate part of the barn to use as a dwelling, by adding not more than two bedrooms and a bathroom, provided they did not change the shape of the building. The zoning board of adjustment also limited the use of the barn as a dwelling to ten years. Applicants did not appeal.

Subsequently, in 1996, applicants applied for (1) a change-of-use permit to remove the ten-year limitation on their residential use of the structure, and (2) for a variance to add skylights to the front and an addition to the rear of the building. The zoning board of adjustment denied both the change-of-use permit and the variance. On appeal, the environmental court ruled on summary judgment that applicants did not meet the criteria for a variance, but also ruled that "[i]n general, no variance should be necessary for a residence or an addition or accessory structure beyond the 40–foot setback." Because the applicants had not provided the court with sufficient information as to the specific project proposed, the court ruled that the issue was not suitable for summary judgment.

Following a trial on the request for a change-of-use permit, the court reiterated that applicants need no permit for any of their plans for residential use behind the forty-foot setback because this is a permitted use in the residential zone. Although recognizing that the zoning board of adjustment erred in considering the change-of-use request as a request for conditional-use approval, the court also applied the conditional-use factors in 24 V.S.A. § 4407(2). The court denied the application for permanent residential use of the part of the barn within the forty-foot setback because it would increase the intensity of the use of the noncomplying part of the structure. . . .

We will uphold the environmental court's construction of a zoning regulation unless the construction is clearly erroneous, arbitrary or capricious. Here, we conclude that the court's construction is clearly erroneous. To begin with, the court erred by considering the factors in 24 V.S.A. § 4407(2) in deciding whether to grant change-of-use approval. Section 4407(2) pertains to permitting for conditional uses. This section is not applicable because applicants want to use the barn as a residence. Residential use—one-family dwelling—is a permitted use in the residential district, not a conditional use. *See* Town of Clarendon Zoning Regulations § 430. Thus, applicants do not need a conditional-use permit to use the barn as a residence.

This case therefore involves a nonconforming use, rather than a conditional use. Nonconforming uses are governed by 24 V.S.A. § 4408. Section 4408(a)(1) defines a "nonconforming use" as "a use of land or a structure [that] does not comply with all zoning regulations" but that was in compliance prior to enactment of the regulations. Section 4408(a)(2) defines a "noncomplying structure" to be a structure or part thereof that does not comply with the zoning regulations but was in compliance before the enactment of the regulations. Therefore, the barn in this case is a noncomplying structure because the structure is in the setback area. It is also a nonconforming use, however, because the structure does not comply with all zoning regulations, specifically the setback requirements. Indeed, all noncomplying structures will also be nonconforming uses under the statute.

Section 4408(b) authorizes municipalities to "regulate and prohibit expansion and undue perpetuation of nonconforming uses," which includes noncomplying structures. It specifies four actions that the municipalities may control: (1) changes of nonconforming uses to other nonconforming uses, (2) extension or enlargement of nonconforming uses, (3) resumption of nonconforming uses after abandonment or discontinuance, and (4) movement or enlargement of a structure containing a nonconforming use. The statute authorizes municipalities to regulate these changes in nonconforming uses but does not command any particular action. Thus, we turn to the municipal zoning regulation to determine how the municipality regulates nonconforming uses.

Section 4408 is implemented by Town of Clarendon Zoning Regulations § 280, which provides:

Any non-conforming use of structures or land except those specified below may be continued indefinitely, but:

1. Shall not be moved, enlarged, altered, extended, reconstructed or restored (except as provided below).

2. Shall not be changed to another non-conforming use without approval by the Board of Adjustment.

3. Shall not be re-established or restored without approval by the Board of Adjustment if such use has been discontinued for a period of six months, or has been changed to, or replaced by a conforming use.

Zoning regulations are construed under general rules of statutory construction. Thus, we are bound by the plain and ordinary meaning of the language, unless it is uncertain. Because land use regulation is in derogation of the common law, any ambiguity is resolved in favor of the landowner. . . .

There are two problems with the framework of § 280. First, § 280 fails to provide any criteria for the two exceptions under which the board of adjustment may evaluate whether to approve a change in nonconforming use. Absent any criteria or guidelines, "the applicant for a permit is left uncertain as to what factors are to be considered." *Town of Westford v. Kilburn*, 300 A.2d 523, 526 (1973). Moreover, a decision arrived at without reference to any standards or principles is arbitrary and capricious, *see id.*; such ad hoc decision-making denies the applicant due process of law. The lack of guiding standards in § 280 may explain in part why both the zoning board and the environmental court turned to the guidelines for conditional-use approval to provide some principled basis for their decisions. Section 280 provides no such guidelines as a basis for denying approval, however.

Second, § 280 appears to prohibit all alterations of nonconforming uses, no matter how minor, but allows the board of adjustment to grant approval routinely for major changes, *i.e.*, changes from one nonconforming use to another nonconforming use, and restoring a discontinued, nonconforming use. Indeed, under the plain language of § 280, a nonconforming use cannot be altered at all unless it is changed to another nonconforming use or discontinued and then restored. This construction is simply not rational. *See Stowe Club Highlands*, 668 A.2d at 1277 (rejecting as irrational construction of zoning regulation that reconstruction or replacement of nonconforming structure is allowed while enlargement or substantial alteration is prohibited).

To avoid this irrational result, and the alternative, a standardless approval procedure, we construe § 280 narrowly to address only a change to the nonconforming use. Applicants here do not propose to change their nonconforming use, the setback.

They plan to change only from one permitted use to another permitted use, a change that is not regulated by § 280. Thus, under § 280, applicants may continue the nonconforming use of the land—the setback—indefinitely, provided they do not move, enlarge, alter, extend, reconstruct or restore the nonconforming use—again, the setback. Accordingly, we hold that applicants do not need approval to proceed with their plans because they do not propose any change to the nonconforming use; they propose only to change the use of the barn from agricultural to residential. This construction also resolves any ambiguity in § 280 in favor of the landowner....

We also conclude that the environmental court erred in denying change-of-use approval solely on the grounds that the change in use from agricultural to residential would increase the intensity of the use of the noncomplying part of the structure. Section 280 does not specifically address an increase in intensity of use of a nonconforming use. Decisions addressing an increase in intensity of use ordinarily involve nonconforming business activities. In such cases, most courts have held that a mere increase in the volume or intensity of a nonconforming business activity is not prohibited by a zoning regulation prohibiting an extension or enlargement of a nonconforming use. *See* 1 K. Young, Anderson's American Law of Zoning §§ 6.38, 6.50 (4th ed.1996); *see, e.g., DiBlasi v. Zoning Bd. of Appeals*, 624 A.2d 372, 376 (Conn. 1993) (mere increase in amount of business is not illegal expansion of original nonconforming use).

Although there are few cases addressing an increase in intensity of use of a noncomplying structure, generally a mere increase in the intensity of use of a noncomplying structure is not prohibited. *See, e.g., Seaside Properties v. Zoning Bd. of Appeals*, 542 A.2d 746, 747 (Conn.Ct. App. 1988) (regulations do not prohibit change in use of summer cottage, with nonconforming lot size and setback, to year-round use). We recognize that a goal of zoning is to phase out nonconforming uses, but absent a regulation specifically prohibiting an increase in the intensity of use of a noncomplying structure, we decline to create a rule contrary to the majority of law on this issue.

Finally, we conclude that the ruling of the environmental court—restricting residential use to the part of the barn behind the forty-foot setback—is clearly erroneous. Nothing in 24 V.S.A. § 4408 or zoning regulation § 280 directs such a result. Allowing applicants to use only part of the barn is impractical. Not surprisingly, no case has been presented to us that limits a permitted activity to the complying part of a noncomplying structure.

Much of the difficulty in this case arises from the merger of the concepts of nonconforming activities and noncomplying structures under the single denotation "nonconforming use." In general, zoning law distinguishes between the two concepts. "Use" restrictions limit the activities that may take place within a certain area, while "bulk" restrictions control setbacks and size, shape and placement of buildings on the property. See 7 P. Rohan, Zoning and Land Use Controls § 42.01[4], at 42–9 (1991).

Thus, zoning regulations usually provide different restrictions for nonconforming activities and noncomplying structures. *See Stowe Club Highlands*, 668 A.2d at 1276 (definitions in Stowe zoning ordinance carefully differentiate nonconforming use and nonconforming structure). This distinction is helpful because rules applying to nonconforming activities often cannot be easily applied to noncomplying structures and vice versa.

Zoning regulation § 280 does not distinguish between the two concepts, and therefore, it is difficult to apply in this case because its directives more aptly apply to nonconforming activities than to noncomplying structures. Restrictions that specifically address noncomplying structures are preferable because they provide clearer guidance to landowners, zoning boards and courts. There are three common types of restrictions on alterations to noncomplying structures. First, some limitations may be very restrictive, confining alterations to those related to safety regulations. Second, the most common type of limitation prescribes the maximum amount of money, often as a percentage of the value of the building, that may be spent to alter a noncomplying building. Finally, some regulations limit alterations of noncomplying structures to those that do not increase the nonconformity. Our decision here is consistent with the third and least restrictive of these options.

In sum, the nonconforming use, the setback of the barn, may be continued indefinitely. See Town of Clarendon Zoning Regulations § 280. Only a change in the nonconforming use, in this case the setback, requires approval. None of the changes applicants want to make involve a change in the setback. Thus, they need no change-in-use approval, no conditional-use permit and no variance.

Reversed.

Notes

1. *Political Justifications for Protecting Nonconforming Uses.* Many believe that zoning ordinances grandfather nonconforming uses to protect the community from a "takings" claim brought by a landowner who would have to discontinue a previously allowed use. Once you understand the "regulatory takings" material discussed later in the chapter, however, you will see that restrictions on nonconforming uses rarely would give rise to a compensable "regulatory taking." So when an "unzoned" community is contemplating the enactment of a zoning ordinance, what other reasons might motivate community leaders to grandfather nonconforming uses? What is the community concerned about?

2. *Expansion or Change of Nonconforming Uses.* Suppose that Nice acquires land presently used as a doctor's office (a nonconforming use in a

residential zone) and plans to use the land as a headquarters for distribution of food and services to local indigent and low-income residents. The zoning ordinance does not permit Nice's proposed use within a residential zone. Should Nice be allowed to modify the nonconforming use? Would your answer change if Nice wanted to open a dance club? Resolution of such questions may depend upon whether the zoning ordinance prohibits changes to nonconforming uses or instead merely restricts such changes to other less offensive uses. *See Huff v. Board of Adjustment of Independence*, 695 S.W.2d 166 (Mo. Ct. App. 1985) (no change allowed under local ordinance). If your municipality were implementing a zoning ordinance, would you suggest that the zoning ordinance take a "prohibitive" approach to changes in nonconforming uses? Why or why not?

Litigation also arises regarding whether certain conduct actually constitutes an expansion or modification of a nonconforming use. For example, in *City of Crowley v. Prejean*, 173 So.2d 832 (La. Ct. App. 1965), an owner who leased one trailer home (pursuant to a nonconforming use) wanted to install additional rental trailers on the same parcel. The court held that the zoning ordinance, which provided that "[s]uch use may be extended throughout the building provided no structural alterations are made," allowed for expansion to accommodate the additional trailers. The court compared the case to one involving a beauty parlor operated in someone's home in which the number of customers simply increased over time. Is the court's analogy persuasive? *Cf. Kirkpatrick v. Village Council of Pinehurst*, 138 N.C.App. 79, 530 S.E.2d 338 (2000) (disallowing "expansion" of campground from 50 to 150 sites within same area).

3. *Abandonment of a Nonconforming Use.* Zoning ordinances commonly provide that a nonconforming use terminates if the use is abandoned. For an interesting example of the application of such a provision, see *Blake v. City of Phoenix*, 157 Ariz. 93, 754 P.2d 1368 (Ct. App. 1988) (landowner had gradually changed character and intensity of use from raising plants for wholesale distribution to operating full-scale retail nursery; board denied permit to continue nonconforming use, concluding that change reflected abandonment of original use). Under what circumstances should the court conclude an owner has abandoned a nonconforming use? Suppose that Reuben operates a tavern as a nonconforming use. Reuben loses his liquor license for a period of six months after his third violation for serving alcohol to minors. Unable to operate profitably without liquor sales, Reuben decides to take a six-month vacation and close his bar. Six months later, when Reuben recovers his license and attempts to reopen the bar, the city sues to enjoin his operation on the grounds of abandonment. What result? *Compare Lewis v. City of Atl. Beach*, 467 So.2d 751 (Fla. App. 1985) *with Badger v. Town of Ferrisburgh*, 168 Vt. 37, 712 A.2d 911 (1998) *and Wyatt v. Board of Adjustment–Zoning of the City & County of Denver*, 622 P.2d 85 (Colo. App. 1980).

4. *Destruction of Nonconforming Uses.* Municipalities frequently argue that the destruction of a nonconforming use terminates the owner's right to continue that use. The results in these cases vary depending upon the language of the zoning ordinance and the specific circumstances surrounding the use and its destruction. For example, suppose that Reuben operates a tavern as a nonconforming use. As a result of a kitchen fire, Reuben's tavern

is destroyed. When Reuben attempts to rebuild and reopen the tavern, the city refuses to issue him a certificate of occupancy to operate the tavern, arguing that the fire terminated Reuben's right to continue the nonconforming use. Should this argument succeed? *Compare South Coventry Twp. Bd. of Supervisors v. Zoning Hearing Bd. of South Coventry Twp.*, 732 A.2d 12 (Pa. Comm. 1999) (ordinance allowed rebuilding of nonconforming use only within twelve months of destruction; no right to rebuild after five years) *with Dougherty v. Board of Appeal of Billerica*, 41 Mass.App.Ct. 1, 668 N.E.2d 363 (1996) (building entirely destroyed by fire could not be rebuilt under ordinance prohibiting reconstruction when building is damaged 65% or more).

    5. *Amortization and Registration of Nonconforming Uses.* In a majority of states, municipalities allow an owner to amortize a nonconforming use— *i.e.*, to continue the use for a limited period of time so that the owner can amortize (recover) some or all of the owner's investment in the nonconforming use. After this amortization period expires, the owner may no longer engage in the nonconforming use. Jay M. Zitter, *Validity of Provisions for Amortization of Nonconforming Uses*, 8 A.L.R.5th 391 (1993). Some states, however, do not permit termination of nonconforming uses in this manner. For example, in 1999 the Minnesota legislature—in response to a court decision upholding a two-year amortization schedule for a nonconforming cement plant—amended the state's zoning enabling statute to preclude municipalities, with limited exceptions, from terminating nonconforming uses by amortization. 1999 Minn. Sess. Law Serv. Ch. 96 (S.F. 854) (West) (amending Minn. Stat. §§ 394.21, 462.357).

    In states permitting amortization of nonconforming uses, litigation generally focuses on the reasonableness of the amortization period. Suppose that Easton had acquired a parcel and nonconforming convenience store in Westville three years ago for $240,000. In response to neighbor complaints, Westville's zoning officials want to implement an ordinance to amortize nonconforming uses such as Easton's. Over what period must Westville permit Easton to amortize his convenience store? Should the three years he has owned the store count for amortization purposes? Why or why not? *See, e.g., National Adver. Co. v. County of Monterey*, 1 Cal.3d 875, 83 Cal.Rptr. 577, 464 P.2d 33 (1970) (allowing immediate removal of some, but not all, of defendant's billboards following implementation of billboard ban). If the store building needs $25,000 in roof repairs in order to remain open for business, must Westville allow Easton to extend the amortization period accordingly? *See, e.g., Neighborhood Comm. on Lead Pollution v. Board of Adjustment of Dallas*, 728 S.W.2d 64 (Tex. App. 1987).

    Some states have a registration system, which requires landowners to register a nonconforming use or risk losing the right to continue the nonconforming use. A registration system gives municipalities a snapshot of the nonconforming uses in existence at the time a new ordinance takes effect, eliminating the proof problems that arise if nonconformity is not evaluated until years later. *See, e.g., Lawrence v. Clackamas County*, 164 Ore. App. 462, 992 P.2d 933 (1999) (evaluating whether nonconforming use existed when zoning ordinance enacted in 1964). A registration requirement also may eliminate some nonconforming uses if the landowners fail to comply with the registration requirement.

6. *Estoppel and Vested Rights*. Suppose that a landowner receives some type of governmental approval (such as a building permit) and then invests significant resources in planning in reliance on the approval—only to discover, before completing construction, that the municipality subsequently has enacted or amended its zoning ordinance to preclude the contemplated use. In such circumstances, the landowner's proposed use is not a valid nonconforming use, because the use was not in existence when the ordinance took effect. The landowner may attempt to argue that the municipality should be "estopped" by its prior approval from exercising its zoning authority to bar this planned use. In some jurisdictions, the landowner's estoppel claim may be identified as a claim that she has acquired a "vested right" to proceed with the planned use.

To estop a municipality from applying its zoning ordinance to block the approved use (or to successfully claim a "vested right" to proceed with development), the landowner must demonstrate that she incurred substantial expenses in good faith, reasonable reliance on appropriate government action, and that it would be inequitable and unjust for municipal rezoning to take away the landowner's ability to proceed with development. *See* Grayson P. Hanes & J. Randall Minchew, *On Vested Rights to Land Use and Development*, 46 Wash. & Lee L. Rev. 373 (1989). Each of these factors merits separate attention.

(a) *"Government Action."* A landowner has no vested right in existing zoning. To claim estoppel or vested rights, a landowner must be able to point to some specific governmental action on which she relied. Some jurisdictions hold that a landowner does not have a claim until the municipality issues a building permit, *see, e.g., Avco Cmty. Developers, Inc. v. South Coast Reg'l Comm'n*, 17 Cal.3d 785, 132 Cal.Rptr. 386, 553 P.2d 546 (1976); *but see Santa Margarita Area Residents Together v. San Luis Obispo County Bd. of Supervisors*, 84 Cal.App.4th 221, 100 Cal.Rptr.2d 740 (2000) (noting legislation had superseded *Avco* by authorizing development agreements that can "freeze" zoning prior to issuance of building permit). Other jurisdictions will allow a claim based on the issuance of a special use permit or the approval of a site plan. *See, e.g., Board of Supervisors v. Medical Structures, Inc.*, 213 Va. 355, 192 S.E.2d 799 (1972).

(b) *"Substantial Expenditures."* Courts generally do not consider the mere purchase of land as a substantial expenditure. *See, e.g., County Council v. District Land Corp.*, 274 Md. 691, 337 A.2d 712 (Ct. Spec. App.1975); *but see May Dep't Stores Co. v. County of St. Louis*, 607 S.W.2d 857 (Mo. Ct. App. 1980) (land acquisition costs that include premium because of intended use constitute substantial reliance expenditures). Similarly, expenditures associated with preliminary plans and pre-approval expenditures generally do not justify a vested rights claim. *Belvidere Twp. v. Heinze*, 241 Mich.App. 324, 615 N.W.2d 250 (2000); *but see Town of Largo v. Imperial Homes Corp.*, 309 So.2d 571 (Fla. Dist. Ct. App. 1975) (preliminary expenses considered reliance expenses). Finally, although courts generally treat post-application expenses as reliance expenditures, these expenses still must be "substantial." Some courts consider the absolute amount expended, *e.g., Board of Supervisors v. Medical Structures, Inc., supra*, while others look at the expenses relative to the costs of the overall project, *e.g., City of Rochester v. Barcomb*, 103 N.H. 247, 169 A.2d 281 (1961).

(c) *"Good Faith" Reliance.* Should the landowner's good faith focus solely upon his subjective belief, or an objective assessment of whether a reasonable person would have incurred the expenses in question? For example, suppose that Peters decides to build a shopping center on his land, despite the significant objection of many adjacent residential owners. After Peters obtains a building permit and spends $1,000,000 beginning construction, objections to the proposed center reach such intensity that the city rezones the parcel for residential use only, and the city advises Peters that it will not issue certificates of occupancy. Can Peters claim "good faith" reliance? Would it matter if, at the time Peters began construction, the neighbors had introduced a resolution before the city council seeking to rezone the property for residential use? *Compare Kasparek v. Johnson County Bd. of Health,* 288 N.W.2d 511 (Iowa 1980) (expenditure in good faith, as proposed zoning ordinance not effective until official enactment by local governing body) *with Stowe v. Burke,* 255 N.C. 527, 122 S.E.2d 374 (1961) (no vested right where landowner hurriedly spent $50,000 in anticipation of pending rezoning of parcel). What if Peters failed to request a building permit until a petition for rezoning had been filed? *See, e.g., Boron Oil Co. v. Kimple,* 445 Pa. 327, 284 A.2d 744 (1971) (because proposed zoning ordinance was "pending," borough manager did not act improperly in denying building permit). If you represented a developer, how would you advise your client to minimize the extent to which a rezoning might place the client's investment at risk?

LAWYERING EXERCISE
(Client Counseling)

BACKGROUND: As *Matthew* and *Miserocchi* demonstrate, claims for nonconforming uses, variances and/or conditional uses or special uses can cause confusion not only for landowners, but for city planners, lawyers and even judges. In a compelling example of such confusion, the West Virginia Supreme Court treated a request for a conditional use permit as a request for a variance, only to recognize its mistake four years later in a subsequent appeal. *See Harding v. Board of Zoning Appeals,* 159 W.Va. 73, 219 S.E.2d 324 (1975) ("A special exception, unlike a variance, does not involve the varying of the ordinance, but rather compliance with it."), *overruling Miernyk v. Bd. of Zoning Appeals,* 155 W.Va. 143, 181 S.E.2d 681 (1971). What role can a lawyer play in helping a client avoid these types of confusing situations?

SITUATION 1: Assume you represent the Brandts in the *Matthew* case. The Brandts want to be able live in one house and rent out the other house. Someone from the city has expressed that they need to obtain a variance. The Brandts want you to advise them on the most cost-effective approach to solving their legal problem.

TASK 1: What advice would you offer them about where to start in trying to solve their problem? Can they continue a nonconforming use? Do they need a variance? Can they get a variance? Why?

SITUATION 2: Assume you represent the Miserocchis. After receiving the decision from the Vermont Supreme Court (and your bill for services in representing them), they express some concern about whether they should have to pay your bill given that they should not have had to pursue the permit at all.

TASK 2: How would you respond to the Miserocchis?

3. *Flexibility in Zoning and Modern Zoning Schemes*

Since the 1960s, in both urban and suburban settings, zoning has become increasingly prevalent and sophisticated. In addition to conditional uses, zoning officials have embraced other techniques to provide flexibility to land use planners and landowners alike. This section briefly explores some of these zoning techniques.

a. *Overlay Zones.* You can best understand the concept of an "overlay" zone by thinking of a zoning map constructed with a series of translucent sheets. The first sheet may show residential zones in one color, commercial zones in another color, and industrial zones in a third color. A second, third or fourth sheet may then be laid over the first, identifying additional restrictions (such as height or area limitations, historical areas, green space, wetlands or floodplain) that may apply to varying residential, commercial or industrial classifications. For example, rather than specify within each district how and where historical preservation guidelines may apply, the municipality may instead create an overlay zone map that identifies the relevant historical preservation areas in all districts. Thus, a landowner may own a parcel within a commercial district and also within a floodplain overlay district. This landowner would need to consider both the allowed uses and restrictions applicable to the commercial district as well any restrictions that apply to parcels within a floodplain district.

If an overlay district imposes additional restrictions on some property within a given district, would the overlay district violate the state zoning enabling statute if the statute requires uniform regulations within a district? *Compare Jachimek v. Superior Court*, 169 Ariz. 317, 819 P.2d 487 (1991) (yes) *with A–S–P Assocs. v. City of Raleigh*, 298 N.C. 207, 258 S.E.2d 444 (1979) (no, because all land within overlay zone is treated uniformly). In a jurisdiction such as Arizona, what must a municipality do to implement the desired restrictions?

b. *Bonus Zoning or Incentive Zoning.* If permitted by state statute, bonus zoning or incentive zoning allows landowners to secure the relaxation of certain zoning restrictions in exchange for the development of desired public amenities. For example, a developer may be allowed a greater density of development (*i.e.*, more lots or units, which may translate into more profit) in exchange for providing certain public amenities such as low-income housing, open space, parks, parking, or rapid transit facilities. The municipality accepts the generally undesirable aspects of increased density in exchange for the benefits of new public amenities that the municipality perhaps could not have afforded to provide otherwise.

To avoid challenges that its use constitutes unlawful contract zoning, municipalities may enact the bonus zoning or incentive zoning system as part of the comprehensive zoning ordinance so that there is "transparency"—*i.e.*, so that developers and the general public have access to the information detailing the trade-offs the municipality is willing to make. Are the tradeoffs worth it? Do municipalities have the sophistication and capacity to evaluate these trades adequately? Do conflicts of interest make any deal suspect? *See* Judith Wegner, *Utopian Visions: Cooperation Without Conflicts in Public/Private Ventures*, 31 Santa Clara L. Rev. 313 (1991).

   c. *Planned Unit Developments (PUDs)*. PUDs operate either through a rezoning or a conditional use permit. Unlike a normal rezoning—in which the owner's contemplated use is irrelevant because the rezoning authorizes any allowed use in the district—a rezoning to a PUD focuses entirely on the specific contemplated use. PUDs also often integrate some form of incentive zoning, permitting greater density in some portions of the development in exchange for public amenities such as open space, parks, or greater municipal control over the specific type of development. *See* Jan Z. Krasnowiecki, *Planned Unit Development: A Challenge to Established Theory and Practice of Land Use Control*, 114 U. Pa. L. Rev. 47 (1965).

   If the PUD is implemented through rezoning, then (as discussed previously on pages 891–92), a court generally will view the municipality as engaging in legislative action—and thus will evaluate the rezoning decision deferentially to determine whether it is reasonably in compliance with the comprehensive plan. If the PUD is implemented through a conditional use permit, then it is an administrative decision of a board of zoning appeals or a board of zoning adjustment. Such a decision may be subject to more stringent judicial review, particularly to determine whether the municipal legislature provided meaningful standards and whether the board complied with such standards. *See City of Miami v. Save Brickell Ave.*, 426 So.2d 1100 (Fla. Dist. Ct. App. 1983).

   PUDs are not a panacea, however. PUDs generally are available only in states where the zoning enabling statute explicitly or implicitly authorizes such flexibility. Moreover, the flexibility associated with PUDs is limited. Once the PUD is approved, the landowner has little flexibility as any substantial changes will require some type of municipal approval. *See Makowski v. City of Naperville*, 249 Ill.App.3d 110, 187 Ill.Dec. 530, 617 N.E.2d 1251 (1993) (because relocation of road was not "major change" to PUD, municipality did not need to comply with specific procedures for major changes).

   d. *Development Agreements.* Development agreements have evolved as a way to provide municipalities with the flexibility associated with incentive zoning or PUDs, while providing developers with something akin to vested rights protection. These agreements serve primarily to assure landowners—particularly those investing in a project being developed in phases—that they will not lose their investment as a result of a change in zoning. Several states, such as California and Florida, have legislatively authorized municipalities engaged in planning and zoning to use development agreements. In Nebraska, the Supreme Court approved use of a development agreement even absent express statutory delegation. *Giger v. City of Omaha*, 232 Neb. 676, 442 N.W.2d 182 (1989).

4. *Hot Topics in Zoning—Exclusionary Zoning, Urban Sprawl, Regional Zoning and Smart Growth*

a. *Exclusionary Zoning.* During the early 20th Century, many municipalities had ordinances that compelled racial segregation within certain areas. In *Buchanan v. Warley*, 245 U.S. 60, 38 S.Ct. 16, 62 L.Ed. 149 (1917), the Supreme Court invalidated the Louisville, Kentucky, zoning ordinance under the Due Process Clause because it imposed unreasonable restraints on the alienation of property. Although explicit racial segregation ordinances should have disappeared after *Buchanan*, many communities ignored the decision, and litigation regarding explicit segregation ordinances continued into the late 1940s. *See, e.g., Monk v. City of Birmingham*, 87 F.Supp. 538 (N.D. Ala. 1949), *aff'd*, 185 F.2d 859 (5th Cir. 1950).

More recently, exclusionary zoning disputes have involved zoning ordinances that are facially neutral, but exclude certain types of uses and structures, thereby excluding some population of people, usually low-income people, from a particular zone or area. In some communities, the low-income population is comprised disproportionately of people of color—which means that exclusionary zoning may have a "disparate impact" on a protected class under the Fair Housing Act. A handful of cases have explored the exclusionary zoning concept in various contexts, and the following materials discuss each in turn.

(1) *The* Mount Laurel *Cases—State Constitutional Law.* In the early 1970s, the New Jersey Supreme Court decided Mount Laurel, New Jersey, adopted a zoning ordinance that prohibited attached townhouses, apartments (except on farms for agricultural workers) and mobile homes. The residential zones all provided for single-family, detached residences, and the largest residential zone provided for relatively large lot sizes and minimum floor area requirements. The local NAACP chapter sued to invalidate the ordinance, arguing that the ordinance was intended to exclude low-income persons (and particularly low-income persons of color) from residing within the Mount Laurel community.

In *Southern Burlington County NAACP v. Township of Mount Laurel*, 67 N.J. 151, 336 A.2d 713 (1975) ["*Mount Laurel I*"], the New

Jersey Supreme Court held that each New Jersey municipality had an obligation under the general welfare provision of the New Jersey Constitution to provide its "fair share" of the present and prospective regional need for low- and moderate-income housing. In the process, the court held that because Mount Laurel's zoning ordinance failed to provide sufficient areas in which affordable multi-family housing could be built, it was presumptively contrary to the general welfare.

Perhaps somewhat predictably, this decision did not sit well with Mount Laurel and many other New Jersey communities. As a result, more litigation followed as courts explored the contours of this "fair share" obligation. In 1983, the New Jersey Supreme Court reaffirmed the basic principles of *Mount Laurel I* in *Southern Burlington County NAACP v. Township of Mount Laurel*, 92 N.J. 158, 456 A.2d 390 (1983) ["*Mount Laurel II*"], but altered the way in which landowners, municipalities and courts would assure its implementation. Specifically, the court imposed on municipalities an affirmative obligation to (a) remove excessive restrictions and exactions[7] that made development of low- and moderate-income housing impossible and (b) promote low- and moderate-income housing through subsidies or other incentive programs. In addition, the court provided for "builder's remedies" and the institution of a special panel of judges to hear cases raising exclusionary zoning issues. In response to *Mount Laurel II*, the New Jersey legislature enacted the Fair Housing Act of 1985, which created an administrative agency responsible for assuring that municipal zoning schemes provide for a fair share of affordable housing. The New Jersey Supreme Court upheld the constitutionality of the Act in *Hills Development Co. v. Township of Bernards*, 103 N.J. 1, 510 A.2d 621 (1986).

An extensive literature has developed over the last two decades as people have tried to evaluate the impact of the *Mount Laurel* decisions while reflecting on the causes of and responses to exclusionary zoning. *See* Charles M. Haar, Suburbs Under Siege: Race, Space and Audacious Judges (1996); David L. Kirp, *et al.*, Our Town: Race, Housing and the Soul of Suburbia (1995).

(2) *Exclusionary Zoning—Federal Law.* In *Village of Arlington Heights v. Metropolitan Housing Development Corp.*, 429 U.S. 252, 97 S.Ct. 555, 50 L.Ed.2d 450 (1977), the Village of Arlington Heights had refused the Metropolitan Housing Development Corporation's (MHDC)

---

7. In simple terms, an "exaction" is the term used to describe the "price" that a developer of land must pay to obtain the necessary development approvals from a municipality. For example, as a condition of granting municipal approval for a residential subdivision, the municipality may at-tempt to require the developer to dedicate some portion of the land for a public purpose (such as a park). Later in this chapter (page 969), we explore the extent to which the Constitution places constraints upon a municipality's authority to impose exactions.

request to upzone a parcel to permit multi-family low-income housing. MHDC sued, alleging that the village had violated the Equal Protection Clause and the federal Fair Housing Act. The Supreme Court denied MHDC's equal protection claim, holding that MHDC had not proved "that discriminatory purpose was a motivating factor in the Village's decision." The Court remanded the case, however, for further determination regarding MHDC's statutory claim. On remand, the Seventh Circuit ruled that the village's failure to rezone did have a discriminatory impact based upon race, but remanded the case again—concluding that the failure to rezone would violate the Fair Housing Act only if the village had no other land properly zoned and suitable for federally subsidized low-income housing. *Metropolitan Hous. Dev. Corp. v. Village of Arlington Heights*, 558 F.2d 1283 (7th Cir. 1977). Before the district court could hold its first hearing, however, the parties agreed to a settlement under which the village would annex and zone land for multi-family development and commercial development for several years, with MHDC agreeing to develop 190 units of subsidized rental housing on that land. Over the objections of several neighbors of the parcel to be annexed, including the Village of Mount Prospect, the district court and the Seventh Circuit affirmed the consent decree memorializing the settlement. *Metropolitan Hous. Dev. Corp. v. Village of Arlington Heights*, 469 F.Supp. 836 (N.D. Ill. 1979), *aff'd*, 616 F.2d 1006 (7th Cir. 1980).

In a more recent case, a Texas federal district court concluded "that Sunnyvale's actions in maintaining a one-acre zoning ordinance, in enacting a resolution banning apartments, and in refusing to consider the rezoning application [in question], have a discriminatory effect on African–Americans *and* are motivated by a discriminatory purpose, all in violation" of the Fair Housing Act. *Dews v. Town of Sunnydale*, 109 F.Supp.2d 526, 530 (N.D. Tex. 2000). These types of challenges to zoning ordinances are likely to continue as affordable housing and racial segregation continue to present tensions and challenges in many communities.

Exclusionary zoning issues also have arisen with respect to people with disabilities and group homes. In *City of Edmonds v. Oxford House, Inc.*, 514 U.S. 725, 115 S.Ct. 1776, 131 L.Ed.2d 801 (1995), the city attempted to preclude Oxford House from opening a group home because the home would contain more than five persons unrelated by genetics, blood, or marriage, in violation of the city ordinance. The Court ruled that the ordinance violated the FHA. Although the FHA permits "any reasonable local, State or Federal restrictions regarding the maximum number of occupants permitted to occupy a dwelling," the Court held that the provision exempted only maximum occupancy limits of general application—it did not exempt an ordinance defining "family" as "persons related by genetics, adoption, or marriage [regardless of number], or a group of five or fewer [unrelated] persons.''

LAWYERING EXERCISE
(Client Counseling—An Affordable Housing Developer Client)

SITUATION 1: Assume you represent the Housing Affordability Land Trust ("HALT"). HALT recently acquired seven parcels of land in Munsterville, with the goal of constructing multi-family, low-income housing, which is greatly needed in the community. Four of the parcels are contiguous, and together comprise a tract of approximately six acres presently zoned R–3 (which allows 20 units per acre). HALT has had architectural plans drawn up for three apartment complexes containing a total of 72 units. It has applied for a building permit for these apartment complexes, which it can construct as a matter of right in the R–3 zone under the present zoning regime. The other three parcels are in the R–2 district (two units per acre), and together they comprise approximately four acres located adjacent to an existing nonconforming apartment complex. HALT would like to rezone this four-acre parcel to R–3 so that it could build four 10-unit low-income townhouses. It plans to submit a request to rezone the four-acre parcel as soon as it receives the building permit for the apartment complexes on the six-acre parcel. HALT is aware that some local citizens are concerned about the growth of multi-family housing in Munsterville and have asked the Mayor to consider downzoning most of the R–3 land to R–2 and to reduce the density of the remaining R–3 land to six units per acre.

TASK 1: HALT applied for the building permit over five weeks ago. In its experience, building permits normally are issued within two to three weeks when the building plans comply with the municipal building code and are consistent with existing zoning. HALT is concerned that "something may be going on regarding our building permit" and has asked for your advice. Should HALT simply take an informal approach with continued low-key discussions with the Building Inspector's office, or should it contact the Mayor's office and threaten litigation seeking a writ of mandamus to compel the issuance of the building permit? How would you advise HALT? What other information would you want to gather before advising HALT?

SITUATION 2: Now assume that the Town has issued HALT's building permit for the apartments, and that last week, HALT began grading operations on the six-acre parcel and submitted its request to rezone the four-acre parcel for purposes of developing its low-income townhouses. Upon learning of these events, and in response to requests from concerned citizens, the Mayor placed increased pressure on the Town Attorney to expedite the downzoning amendment for the remaining R–3 acreage. Accordingly, the Town Attorney promptly scheduled a hearing for the Town Council to consider the downzoning request and notified the owners of the affected parcels, including HALT.

TASK 2: You represent HALT, which now has to decide whether to proceed with additional investment in the project. The apartment project had an expected schedule of approximately six months, and HALT likely could complete about one-half of that schedule in the next two months—the period of time that must pass before the Town Council could take action on the downzoning and have it become effective. But HALT has no hope of getting the entire apartment project completed within that time. How would you advise HALT? What other information would you want to obtain before you offer advice to HALT?

b. *Urban Sprawl.* If you reflect on the relationship between zoning structures, the multi-jurisdictional nature of most metropolitan communities, and the American love of the automobile, you should be able to appreciate how these factors have contributed to one of the significant realities of our time—urban sprawl. The 20th Century saw not only the continued migration of people from rural areas to cities, it also saw the migration of people from cities to the suburbs and the "exurbs." As people began driving more, states began building more and larger roads to minimize traffic problems. This made it easier for people to commute into the cities for work (and other activities) from greater distances, which in turn prompted the market transformation of land from agricultural use to residential and commercial use.

Although suburban communities have not always been the catalysts for this evolution, they have frequently responded by competing with other communities to attract residents and businesses that can support the public infrastructure and the public fisc. Zoning represents one way that these communities compete for residents and businesses. Communities often seek to plan and zone their land in a way that will be attractive to prospective business owners and residents, on the theory that the addition of new business and new residents should promote economic prosperity for the community and its citizens. For example, in response to an increased demand in the marketplace for larger residential lots (as there has been over the last several decades), communities have created residential zoning classifications that require larger minimum lot sizes. [Compare the minimum lot sizes described in the Euclid zoning ordinance—in which one zone allowed lots as small as 700 square feet—with modern suburban zoning ordinances that frequently require a minimum lot size of 10,000 square feet in some residential zones (and as much as five or ten acres in other residential zones—200,000 square feet or more).] These much larger minimum lot sizes, by greatly reducing population density, accelerate the problems of urban sprawl (as they require proportionately more land to accommodate new population growth). Moreover, as increased demand for suburban home ownership raises the price of land closest to the cities, some people must move farther from the city to find affordable land, further exacerbating urban sprawl and the associated traffic problems.

This brief introduction is not meant to provide a complete picture of the causes of urban sprawl. A complex array of factors have contributed to urban sprawl, including not only general market forces and zoning, but also government subsidies for highway construction and ownership of single-family homes and more nuanced factors such as property taxes and educational funding formulas, busing for education (which contributed to "white flight" in many cities), and changes in manufacturing industries and the services sector. This overview is designed simply to emphasize that zoning has had a significant role in creating the sprawl.

c. *Regional Zoning and Growth Controls.* To combat both the problems associated with urban sprawl and exclusionary zoning impacts, many states have implemented regional zoning schemes. Under these schemes, local zoning authorities represent just the first level of zoning approval, with a regional board or commission providing another level of zoning approval; at this second level, the decisionmaker can take regional issues into account in deciding whether an area municipality can implement its local zoning decision. In Oregon, Florida and California, the state legislatures have enacted state or regional land use schemes. Some of these regional schemes, such as Oregon's Land Conservation and Development Commission, are designed to address "growth control" and exclusionary zoning issues by focusing on regional impacts of local zoning decisions. For example, growth control limitations applied to the area around Portland, Oregon, have encouraged both "in-fill" development in the areas close to the city and more high-density development than is common in the suburbs and exurbs in other metropolitan areas. But the growth control limitations, by limiting the available supply of land for housing, also have increased the cost of housing and have thus exacerbated the problem of affordable housing. Other schemes are designed to protect specific resources—for example, the South Carolina Coastal Council or the California Coastal Commission, each of which is responsible for approving or rejecting development in sensitive coastal zones.

As more states implement regional zoning structures or state land use plans, landowners now have multiple decisionmakers with whom they must communicate regarding their development ideas. This makes the development process more complicated, time-consuming and expensive—which can further exacerbate the problem of providing affordable housing. When federal environmental concerns get added to the mix—such as concerns about filling of wetlands or destruction of habitat for endangered species—landowners must deal with the federal government, which provides an additional regulatory regime and another layer of decisionmakers representing the federal issues at stake.

d. *Smart Growth.* The most recent mantra among zoning mavens is alternatively described as "sustainable development" or "smart growth." Sustainable development and smart growth advocates believe that communities can combat the problems of urban sprawl through a more rational (and more flexible) approach to zoning. Unlike the classic Euclidean model, smart growth promotes integration of appropriate forms of commercial development interspersed among more densely populated residential communities that are more "walkable." This is sometimes referred to as "New Town" development or "new urbanism"—because it reflects a "new" manifestation of the older town composition: smaller yards (more dense population), occasionally with some multi-family housing throughout the area, and scattered constellations of commercial development within walking distance of a significant population of residents. [Some older urban areas reflect this model. For example, St. Paul, Minnesota, has scattered areas of commercial development every six to ten blocks along the major east-west and north-south streets running through residential areas.]

While developers and communities around the country have begun to implement "smart growth" or "sustainable development" initiatives, there are several issues that need to be resolved if "smart growth" is going to be truly sustainable. First, how will communities that have developed on the Euclidean zoning model be able to adapt to a new paradigm for land use planning? Second, to what extent will homebuyers and renters give up large yards and a corresponding greater sense of privacy in exchange for smaller yards, "walkability" and perhaps a greater sense of community? While "smart growth" presents an intriguing possibility as a way in which zoning can diminish rather than exacerbate sprawl, it remains to be seen how many communities will adopt "smart growth" as a new zoning paradigm, and whether consumers will embrace it as a desirable option in the marketplace.

C. EMINENT DOMAIN, REGULATORY TAKINGS, AND EXACTIONS

1. *Eminent Domain*

What happens when a state decides that it wants to take title to someone's private property to build a road, dam, park, government building, or other public works project? Normally, the state will proceed as any other prospective buyer of land—it will negotiate with the landowner involved, attempt to agree on a price and other terms, and (if the parties reach agreement) purchase the land in a voluntary transaction. But what happens if the landowner refuses to sell? In such cases, the state can exercise its power of *eminent domain* (also known as its *condemnation* authority) and take title to the property in question, even over the owner's objection, as long as the state's action satisfies constitutional requirements—*i.e.*, as long as the state is taking the property for a "public use" and pays "just compensation" to the owner. Thus, as we explained in Chapter 1, the exercise of eminent domain results in an objective determination of the land's value; using the Calabresi/Melamed framework (page 11), it protects a landowner using a liability rule rather than a property rule.

The condemnation process generally begins with the filing of a petition in court and the appointment of a commission (frequently, a number of county residents as specified by statute) to determine the level of compensation due. Once the commission files its report, either party may file an exception that seeks to establish that "just compensation" requires either more or less than the amount established by the commission. Parties who wish to contest the commission's award generally have a right to a jury trial.

Most eminent domain litigation focuses on the determination of the proper amount of "just compensation," but the language of the Fifth Amendment's Takings Clause highlights other issues that sometimes arise when a state attempts to exercise its eminent domain authority. First, is the state taking a *private property* interest so as to trigger the just compensation requirement? This issue should be familiar to you given earlier materials in this book addressing whether a particular person had a "property" interest.[8] Second, is property being taken for a *"public purpose"* or a *"public use"*? The *Kelo v. City of New London* decision presented in Chapter 1 (page 32) provided some understanding of the facets of the "public purpose" or "public use" debate. The following case provides a different perspective.

KELO v. CITY OF NEW LONDON

Supreme Court of the United States.
125 S.Ct. 2655, 162 L.Ed.2d 439 (2005).

[Editors' Note: The opinion appears in Chapter 1 on page 32.]

COUNTY OF WAYNE v. HATHCOCK

Supreme Court of Michigan.
471 Mich. 445, 684 N.W.2d 765 (2004).

YOUNG, J.... [Editors' Note: To obviate concerns about noise caused by an expansion of its airport, Wayne County bought a number of neighboring parcels through voluntary sales. The county subsequently proposed using the acquired land for a large business and technology park with a conference center, hotel accommodations, and a recreation facility. The proposal—known as the "Pinnacle Project"—was projected to create 30,000 jobs and add $350 million in tax revenue for the county while broadening the county's tax base from predominantly industrial to a mixture of industrial, service and technology.

Having acquired over 1,000 acres, the county determined that it needed an additional 46 parcels (comprising nearly 300 acres) that were distributed throughout the project area in a checkerboard fashion. After acquiring 27 of these parcels through voluntary sales, the county determined that further negotiations with the owners of the remaining 19

---

8. In some instances, this issue arises when the state attempts to condemn an interest other than a fee simple interest in land, such as a professional football franchise, *e.g., City of Oakland v. Oakland Raiders,* 32 Cal.3d 60, 183 Cal.Rptr. 673, 646 P.2d 835 (1982); a possibility of reverter, *e.g., Ink v. City of Canton,* 4 Ohio St.2d 51, 212 N.E.2d 574 (1965); a leasehold interest, *Bi-State Dev. Agency v. Nikodem,* 859 S.W.2d 775 (Mo. Ct. App. 1993); an unexercised option to purchase, *e.g., County of San Diego v. Miller,* 13 Cal.3d 684, 119 Cal.Rptr. 491, 532 P.2d 139 (1975); or a promissory servitude, *e.g., Dible v. City of Lafayette,* 713 N.E.2d 269 (Ind. 1999).

parcels would be futile and initiated condemnation actions to obtain the remaining parcels. The affected landowners challenged the constitutionality of the condemnation actions, maintaining that the Pinnacle Project would not serve a public purpose. The trial court held that the Pinnacle Project served a public purpose as defined by *Poletown Neighborhood Council v. Detroit*, 410 Mich. 616, 304 N.W.2d 455 (1981) (a case in which the Michigan Supreme Court upheld the condemnation of private property throughout Detroit's Poletown neighborhood for the purpose of transferring the property to an automobile manufacturer). The court of appeals affirmed, although a concurring opinion argued that the *Poletown* decision was "poorly reasoned, wrongly decided, and ripe for reversal."]

Art. 10, § 2 of Michigan's 1963 Constitution provides that "[p]rivate property shall not be taken for public use without just compensation therefor being first made or secured in a manner prescribed by law." Plaintiffs contend that the proposed condemnations are not "for public use," and therefore are not within constitutional bounds. Accordingly, our analysis must now focus on the "public use" requirement of Art. 10, § 2. . . .

This case does not require that this Court cobble together a single, comprehensive definition of "public use" from our pre–1963 precedent and other relevant sources. The question presented here is a fairly discrete one: are the condemnation of defendants' properties and the subsequent transfer of those properties to private entities pursuant to the Pinnacle Project consistent with the common understanding of "public use" at ratification? For the reasons stated below, we answer that question in the negative.

When our Constitution was ratified in 1963, it was well-established in this Court's eminent domain jurisprudence that the constitutional "public use" requirement was not an absolute bar against the transfer of condemned property to private entities. It was equally clear, however, that the constitutional "public use" requirement worked to prohibit the state from transferring condemned property to private entities for a private use. Thus, this Court's eminent domain jurisprudence—at least that portion concerning the reasons for which the state may condemn private property—has focused largely on the area between these poles.

Justice Ryan's *Poletown* dissent accurately describes the factors that distinguish takings in the former category from those in the latter according to our pre–1963 eminent domain jurisprudence. Accordingly, we conclude that the transfer of condemned property is a "public use" when it possess[es] one of the three characteristics in our pre–1963 case law identified by Justice Ryan.

First, condemnations in which private land was constitutionally transferred by the condemning authority to a private entity involved "public necessity of the extreme sort otherwise impracticable." The "necessity" that Justice Ryan identified in our pre–1963 case law is a specific kind of need:

[T]he exercise of eminent domain for private corporations has been limited to those enterprises generating public benefits whose very existence depends on the use of land that can be assembled only by the coordination central government alone is capable of achieving.

Justice Ryan listed "highways, railroads, canals, and other instrumentalities of commerce" as examples of this brand of necessity....

Second, this Court has found that the transfer of condemned property to a private entity is consistent with the constitution's "public use" requirement when the private entity remains accountable to the public in its use of that property....

Thus, in the common understanding of those sophisticated in the law at the time of ratification, the "public use" requirement would have allowed for the transfer of condemned property to a private entity when the public retained a measure of control over the property.

Finally, condemned land may be transferred to a private entity when the selection of the land to be condemned is itself based on public concern. In Justice Ryan's words, the property must be selected on the basis of "facts of independent public significance," meaning that the underlying purposes for resorting to condemnation, rather than the subsequent use of condemned land, must satisfy the Constitution's public use requirement.

The primary example of a condemnation in this vein is found in *In re Slum Clearance*, a 1951 decision from this Court. In that case, we considered the constitutionality of Detroit's condemnation of blighted housing and its subsequent resale of those properties to private persons. The city's *controlling purpose* in condemning the properties was to remove unfit housing and thereby advance public health and safety; subsequent resale of the land cleared of blight was "incidental" to this goal. We concluded, therefore, that the condemnation was indeed a "public use," despite the fact that the condemned properties would inevitably be put to private use....

The foregoing indicates that the transfer of condemned property to a private entity ... would be appropriate in one of three contexts: (1) where "public necessity of the extreme sort" requires collective action; (2) where the property remains subject to public oversight after transfer to a private entity; and (3) where the property is selected because of "facts of independent public significance," rather than the interests of the private entity to which the property is eventually transferred.

The exercise of eminent domain at issue here—the condemnation of defendants' properties for the Pinnacle Project and the subsequent transfer of those properties to private entities—implicates none of the saving elements noted by our pre–1963 eminent domain jurisprudence.

The Pinnacle Project's business and technology park is certainly not an enterprise "whose very existence depends on the use of land that can be assembled only by the coordination central government alone is capable of achieving." To the contrary, the landscape of our country is flecked with shopping centers, office parks, clusters of hotels, and centers of entertainment and commerce. We do not believe, and plaintiff does not contend, that these constellations required the exercise of eminent domain or any other form of collective public action for their formation.

Second, the Pinnacle Project is not subject to public oversight to ensure that the property continues to be used for the commonweal after being sold to private entities. Rather, plaintiff intends for the private entities purchasing defendants' properties to pursue their own financial welfare with the single-mindedness expected of any profit-making enterprise. The public benefit arising from the Pinnacle Project is an epiphenomenon of the eventual property owners' collective attempts at profit maximization. No formal mechanisms exist to ensure that the businesses that would occupy what are now defendants' properties will continue to contribute to the health of the local economy.

Finally, there is nothing about the act of condemning defendants' properties that serves the public good in this case. The only public benefits cited by plaintiff arise after the lands are acquired by the government and put to private use. Thus, the present case is quite unlike *Slum Clearance* because there are no facts of independent public significance (such as the need to promote health and safety) that might justify the condemnation of defendants' lands.

We can only conclude, therefore, that no one sophisticated in the law at the 1963 Constitution's ratification would have understood "public use" to permit the condemnation of defendants' properties for the construction of a business and technology park owned by private entities. Therefore, the condemnations proposed in this case are unconstitutional under art. 10, § 2.

Indeed, the only support for plaintiff's position in our eminent domain jurisprudence is the majority opinion in *Poletown*. In that opinion per curiam, a majority of this Court concluded that our Constitution permitted the Detroit Economic Development Corporation to condemn private residential properties in order to convey those properties to a private corporation for the construction of an assembly plant. . . .

. . . [T]he majority opinion in *Poletown* is most notable for its radical and unabashed departure from the entirety of this Court's pre–1963 eminent domain jurisprudence. The opinion departs from the "common understanding" of "public use" at the time of ratification in two fundamental ways.

First, the majority concluded that its power to review the proposed condemnations is limited because

> [t]he determination of what constitutes a public purpose is primarily a legislative function, subject to review by the courts when abused, and the determination of the legislative body of that matter should not be reversed except in instances where such determination is palpable and manifestly arbitrary and incorrect.

The majority derived this principle from a *plurality* opinion of this Court and supported the application of the principle with a citation of an opinion of the United States Supreme Court concerning judicial review of congressional acts under the Fifth Amendment of the federal constitution. Neither case, of course, is binding on this Court in construing the takings clause of our state Constitution, and neither is persuasive authority for the use to which they were put by the *Poletown* majority.

It is not surprising, however, that the majority would turn to nonbinding precedent for the proposition that the Court's hands were effectively tied by the Legislature. As Justice Ryan's dissent noted: "In point of fact, this Court has *never* employed the minimal standard of review in an eminent domain case which is adopted by the [*Poletown*] majority.... Notwithstanding explicit legislative findings, this Court has always made an *independent* determination of what constitutes a public use for which the power of eminent domain may be utilized." Our eminent domain jurisprudence since Michigan's entry into the union amply supports Justice Ryan's assertion. Questions of public *purpose* aside, whether the proposed condemnations were consistent with the Constitution's "public use" requirement was a constitutional question squarely within the Court's authority....

Second, the *Poletown* majority concluded, for the first time in the history of our eminent domain jurisprudence, that a generalized economic benefit was sufficient under art. 10, § 2 to justify the transfer of condemned property to a private entity. Before *Poletown*, we had never held that a private entity's pursuit of profit was a "public use" for constitutional takings purposes simply because one entity's profit maximization contributed to the health of the general economy....

Every business, every productive unit in society, does ... contribute in some way to the commonweal. To justify the exercise of eminent domain solely on the basis of the fact that the use of that property by a private entity seeking its own profit might contribute to the economy's health is to render impotent our constitutional limitations on the government's power of eminent domain. *Poletown*'s "economic benefit" rationale would validate practically *any* exercise of the power of eminent domain on behalf of a private entity. After all, if one's ownership of private property is forever subject to the government's determination that another private party would put one's land to better use, then the ownership of real property is perpetually threatened by the expansion plans of any large discount retailer, "megastore," or the like....

Because *Poletown*'s conception of a public use—that of "alleviating unemployment and revitalizing the economic base of the community"— has no support in the Court's eminent domain jurisprudence before the Constitution's ratification, its interpretation of "public use" in art. 10, § 2 cannot reflect the common understanding of that phrase among those sophisticated in the law at ratification. Consequently, the *Poletown* analysis provides no legitimate support for the condemnations proposed in this case and, for the reasons stated above, is overruled....

Notes

1. *Federalism in Constitutional Law*. Is *Hathcock* still good law after the U.S. Supreme Court's decision in *Kelo*? Why or why not?

2. *Is "Public Use" a Meaningful Limit on Government Power?* Interpretation of the Public Use Clause has two components. First, there is a substantive component: what does the term "public use" mean? During the latter part of the 19th Century, courts tended to construe the "public use" requirement in a relatively narrow fashion, requiring that the public actually use or have the right to use the condemned property. During the 20th Century, court decisions evolved a broader construction—that the use be for a public purpose, *i.e.*, of benefit to the public or in the public interest. *See* Lawrence Berger, *The Public Use Requirement in Eminent Domain,* 57 Or. L. Rev. 203, 205–209 (1978). As indicated in *Kelo*, the U.S. Supreme Court has embraced this broader "public purpose" construction, finding it to be coterminous with a sovereign's police powers. *See Hawaii Hous. Auth. v. Midkiff*, 467 U.S. 229, 242, 104 S.Ct. 2321, 81 L.Ed.2d 186 (1984). Compare the U.S. Supreme Court's discussion of "public use" with the Michigan Supreme Court's discussion in *Hathcock*. Which of these two approaches seems to impose greater constraints on the state's exercise of eminent domain for economic development purposes?

The second component of the "public use" analysis is procedural: how much deference should the judiciary give to a legislature's determination that a condemnation serves a public use? Reading *Kelo* and its precursors, *Berman v. Parker* (upholding federal "urban renewal" legislation) and *Hawaii Housing Authority v. Midkiff* (upholding land redistribution plan to counter oligopoly in land ownership), one might easily conclude that judicial deference to legislative judgment is so great that courts have rendered the "public use" requirement almost meaningless. As the Supreme Court stated in *Midkiff*, 467 U.S. 229, 241 (1984): "[W]here the exercise of the eminent domain power is *rationally related to a conceivable public purpose*, the Court has never held a compensated taking to be proscribed by the Public Use Clause." How does this test compare with the standard employed by the Michigan Supreme Court in *Hathcock*? Which view is more appropriate from a federalism or separation of powers perspective?

3. *Who May Exercise the Power of Eminent Domain?* While the power of eminent domain generally resides in the federal or state government, state legislatures have enacted enabling statutes that delegate condemnation authority to cities, counties, and other governmental bodies such as school districts or redevelopment authorities. In addition, many states have chosen to promote economic development by authorizing some regulated entities, such as railroads and utilities, to exercise eminent domain authority. Further, as noted in Chapter 8 (page 570), some states have even delegated eminent domain authority to private individuals where necessary to condemn a private access easement to an otherwise landlocked parcel. Why might such delegations of authority make sense as a matter of public policy?

4. *Calculating "Just Compensation."* Courts have generally understood "just compensation" to require payment of "fair market value." This mea-

sure does not reflect some potentially significant "costs" suffered by the property owner as a result of the taking, including relocation costs, commercial goodwill, or sentimental value. Some statutes specifically provide for recovery of relocation costs or for goodwill associated with having operated at a specific location. *See, e.g.*, Ark. Code Ann. § 22–9–701 (relocation assistance); Cal. Code Civ. Proc. § 1263.510 (goodwill). Should "just compensation" also account for sentimental value? Can you think of a "rough justice" way to account for sentimental value?

Some circumstances create particular difficulties for calculating "just compensation." For example, consider the following:

(a) *Timing Issues.* Suppose that Smithville identifies a site for a new city office building, but cannot persuade the owner of the land to sell it. The City Council then downzones the land (from the broadest commercial zone to a narrower commercial zone permitting fewer uses) and shortly thereafter institutes a condemnation proceeding. How, and at what point, should the court calculate the "fair market value" of the parcel? *See, e.g., City of Baltimore v. Kelso Corp.*, 281 Md. 514, 380 A.2d 216 (Ct. Spec. App. 1977).

(b) *Partial Takings.* What compensation must the owner receive when the state takes only part of her land? For example, suppose that Newtown condemns a 20–foot strip of Smith's land for street widening. Can Smith recover on the basis that the taking has diminished the value (on a per-square foot basis) of the remainder of her land? Can you explain why such a diminishment might occur? What if the taking actually enhanced the value (on a per-square foot basis) of the remainder of her land? Can you explain why such an enhancement might occur? *See, e.g., Los Angeles County v. Continental Dev. Corp.*, 16 Cal.4th 694, 66 Cal.Rptr.2d 630, 941 P.2d 809 (1997); *State v. Templeman*, 39 Wash.App. 218, 693 P.2d 125 (1984). What if Smith's neighbor, Hansen, does not lose any land as a result of Newtown's street widening, but nonetheless experiences a significant diminishment in the value of her land as a result? Can Hansen also receive compensation as a result of the condemnation of Smith's land? Why or why not?

(c) *Potential for Variance or Zoning Amendment.* The City of Columbia attempts to condemn Peters's land for an office building. Peters offers evidence that although the land is presently zoned residential, he could have obtained a variance that would have allowed him to make a limited commercial use that would have increased the value of the parcel by $25,000. Should the court take this evidence into account in valuing the land? *See, e.g., City of Baltimore v. Kelso Corp., supra* (landowner may offer evidence of value based on possibility of rezoning); *Department of Transp. v. VanElslander*, 460 Mich. 127, 594 N.W.2d 841 (1999) (state may offer appraisal evidence showing that landowner's remaining land has greater value due to landowner's ability to obtain a variance).

5. *Legislative Backlash.* The *Kelo* decision has prompted a barrage of legislation proposed to curb what the public perceives as an abuse of the eminent domain power. The legislation varies widely in its scope and emphasis. If you were a legislative aide, how would you analyze the following proposals?

(a) "In no event shall a public purpose be construed to include the exercise of eminent domain solely or primarily for the purpose of economic development."

(b) "A municipality or county may not condemn property for the purposes of private retail, office, commercial, industrial, or residential development; or primarily for enhancement of tax revenue; or for transfer to a person, nongovernmental entity, public-private partnership, corporation, or other business entity; provided, however, the provisions of this subsection shall not apply to the use of eminent domain based upon a finding of blight in an area covered by any redevelopment plan or urban renewal plan."

(c) " 'Public use' means that (1) any entity vested with the power of eminent domain must own, operate, and retain control over the condemned property for the performance of a public function, or (2) the public-at-large must have a fixed, definite, and enforceable right to possess, occupy, and enjoy the condemned property. A mere public purpose or public benefit, including but not limited to the purpose or benefit of economic development, does not constitute the requisite public use for property to be condemned by eminent domain."

(d) "If a public entity desires to exercise the power of eminent domain to acquire property for private ownership or control, including for economic development, the public entity shall, prior to any taking by eminent domain, submit a description of the property to be acquired, along with the public purpose behind said acquisition, to the voters within its jurisdiction for their approval or rejection."

LAWYERING EXERCISE
(Problem–Solving and Counseling)

SITUATION: You represent the County of Wayne following the decision in *Hathcock*. The County of Wayne still wants to pursue the industrial park development project known as the Pinnacle Project.

TASK: In light of the three categories described by the Michigan Supreme Court as representing appropriate uses of eminent domain, identify two strategies the County might pursue to allow it to exercise eminent domain against the successful landowners in *Hathcock* and proceed with the Pinnacle Project.

LAWYERING EXERCISE
(Legal Analysis and Oral Argument)

BACKGROUND: When a case is argued on appeal, the lawyers have a limited amount of time to persuade the judges to rule in their favor. The following excerpt sets forth the basic elements to be addressed and a traditional order of presentation. The actual presentation is likely to vary, depending on the intensity of the questioning from the bench.

1. ***The Opening Statement***: The opening statement introduces you as counsel and describes the nature of the case.... A

proper introduction of the issues should combine essential facts and legal analysis to describe the case in a nutshell and enable the judges to focus on specific issues presented. The introduction should highlight the core theory and give the court enough information to follow the arguments.

2. ***Concise Outline of Legal Arguments***: After introducing yourself and the case, . . . give the court a concise outline of the legal arguments. . . . This summary outline gives the judges a pattern in which to fit later arguments, indicates the order in which matters will be discussed, and enables the court to defer its questions until the appropriate time.

3. ***Statement of Facts***:. . . Even when judges are well-prepared, they will not have memorized the case and may not have decided which facts are important. A good statement of relevant facts can therefore set the stage for them to listen to your arguments. . . . The statement of facts should be framed and delivered in a manner that presents an identifiable point of view. However, if the facts are too obviously slanted or misleading, you will lose credibility with the court.

4. ***The Arguments***:. . . You should present your strongest points early in the argument, using an "inverted pyramid" structure: most important/weighty to least. This both attracts the court's attention and ensures that these points are not omitted if time runs out. As in the brief, state conclusions first and then support them with facts and law. . . .

You should organize your presentation with appropriate attention to both fact and law, and make connections between the two as much as possible. . . . Unless you integrate the factual and legal elements of your argument, no court will ever be able to understand your position or rule in your favor. . . . [Bd. of Student Advisers, Harvard Law School, Introduction to Advocacy: Research, Writing, and Argument (6th ed. 1996).]

SITUATION: The National City Raceway, a privately owned enterprise, wants to expand its parking facilities. Race track owners contacted the adjoining landowner, New Earth Environmental, to discuss purchasing some land, but New Earth refused to discuss the matter. Race track officials then turned to the Southwestern Development Authority, which agreed to use its eminent domain powers to condemn New Earth's land and transfer it to the race track. The SDA made an offer to purchase for $1 million. New Earth rejected the offer, but indicated a willingness to negotiate. The SDA instead filed a condemnation action, and a jury found that $900,000 was just compensation for the property. The SDA immediately quitclaimed the property to the race track. The SDA claims that the new parking facility will benefit the area in two ways:

(1) It will improve public safety. A state transportation agency official testified that the agency was working with the race track to develop a parking plan that would eliminate a safety hazard on sur-

rounding state and interstate highways. Officials had explored the possibility of building a parking garage on the race track's existing land, but the proposal was rejected because it would cost three times more than buying the adjacent land.

(2) It will provide economic benefits, allowing the race track to generate more than $13 million in additional revenue each year, as well as benefits trickling down to other businesses (e.g., hotels, restaurants, gas stations, and other services used by racing fans), and increased taxes paid by all of the businesses.

TASK: Assume that you are in a jurisdiction that has not yet determined which legal standard to apply in interpreting the "public use" clause of the state constitution. Write out the oral argument that you would make for your client (as assigned by your instructor), arguing for one of the standards set forth in *Kelo* and *Hathcock* and how it would apply to the facts set forth above.

2. *Inverse Condemnation and Regulatory Takings*

Suppose that Smith County dams a river for the purpose of generating hydroelectric power—and in the process, creates a reservoir that completely floods Brown's land—but never initiates a condemnation proceeding against Brown's land. Because the dam has caused a physical invasion of Brown's land, the dam is analytically comparable to a taking. As a result, the law permits Brown to initiate a lawsuit—generally called an "inverse condemnation" action—to prove that Smith County has "taken" his land and must pay him just compensation. When the conduct complained of in an inverse condemnation action involves a permanent "physical" invasion—a deprivation of some aspect of the owner's right to exclude the public—the Supreme Court consistently has held that the property owner is entitled to compensation, regardless of how small a diminishment in value may result from the intrusion. *See Loretto v. Teleprompter Manhattan CATV Corp.*, 458 U.S. 419, 102 S.Ct. 3164, 73 L.Ed.2d 868 (1982) (easement for cable wires); *Kaiser Aetna v. United States*, 444 U.S. 164, 100 S.Ct. 383, 62 L.Ed.2d 332 (1979) (public navigation access); *United States v. Cress*, 243 U.S. 316, 37 S.Ct. 380, 61 L.Ed. 746 (1917) (repeated flooding of land caused by water project).

Does the constitutional "takings" equation change if the state does not take legal title to the property or physically invade the land, but instead only regulates the land's use in a way that reduces its value? For example, suppose that the state wants to preserve certain land as open space free from private development. The state could negotiate with the landowners in question to take fee simple title, or to acquire conservation easements, but in either instance the state likely would have to pay the seller's price or "just compensation" (if the state and seller cannot agree on a price). What if the state—which wants to avoid paying any compensation—simply exercises its police power authority by imposing land use regulations so stringent that the owner will be unable to develop a significant portion of the land? Has the state, in effect, taken that portion of the land, thereby entitling the landowner to compensation in an inverse condemnation action (*i.e.*, a regulatory taking)?

As the following cases highlight, claims regarding regulatory takings have presented the Supreme Court with some particularly thorny questions during the last few decades.

PENN CENTRAL TRANSPORTATION CO. v. CITY OF NEW YORK

Supreme Court of the United States.
438 U.S. 104, 98 S.Ct. 2646, 57 L.Ed.2d 631 (1978).

MR. JUSTICE BRENNAN delivered the opinion of the Court. The question presented is whether a city may, as part of a comprehensive program to preserve historic landmarks and historic districts, place restrictions on the development of individual historic landmarks—in addition to those imposed by applicable zoning ordinances—without effecting a "taking" requiring the payment of "just compensation." Specifically, we must decide whether the application of New York City's Landmarks Preservation Law to the parcel of land occupied by Grand Central Terminal has "taken" its owners' property in violation of the Fifth and Fourteenth Amendments.

Over the past 50 years, all 50 States and over 500 municipalities have enacted laws to encourage or require the preservation of buildings and areas with historic or aesthetic importance. These nationwide legislative efforts have been precipitated by two concerns. The first is recognition that, in recent years, large numbers of historic structures, landmarks, and areas have been destroyed without adequate consideration of either the values represented therein or the possibility of preserving the destroyed properties for use in economically productive ways. The second is a widely shared belief that structures with special historic, cultural, or architectural significance enhance the quality of life for all....

New York City, responding to similar concerns and acting pursuant to a New York State Enabling Act,[9] adopted its Landmarks Preservation Law in 1965. *See* N.Y.C. Admin. Code, ch. 8–A, § 205–1.0 et seq. (1976).... The city believed that comprehensive measures to safeguard desirable features of the existing urban fabric would benefit its citizens in a variety of ways: *e.g.*, fostering "civic pride in the beauty and noble accomplishments of the past"; protecting and enhancing "the city's attractions to tourists and visitors"; "support[ing] and stimul[ating] business and industry"; "strengthen[ing] the economy of the city"; and promoting "the use of historic districts, landmarks, interior landmarks and scenic landmarks for the education, pleasure and welfare of the people of the city." § 205–1.0(b).

---

9. *See* N.Y.Gen.Mun.Law § 96–a (McKinney 1977). It declares that it is the public policy of the State of New York to preserve structures and areas with special historical or aesthetic interest or value and authorizes local governments to impose reasonable restrictions to perpetuate such structures and areas.

The New York City law is typical of many urban landmark laws in that its primary method of achieving its goals is not by acquisitions of historic properties,[10] but rather by involving public entities in land-use decisions affecting these properties and providing services, standards, controls, and incentives that will encourage preservation by private owners and users. While the law does place special restrictions on landmark properties as a necessary feature to the attainment of its larger objectives, the major theme of the law is to ensure the owners of any such properties both a "reasonable return" on their investments and maximum latitude to use their parcels for purposes not inconsistent with the preservation goals.

The operation of the law can be briefly summarized.... [The] Landmarks Preservation Commission (Commission) ... first performs the function ... of identifying properties and areas that have "a special character or special historical or aesthetic interest or value as part of the development, heritage or cultural characteristics of the city, state or nation." If the Commission determines, after giving all interested parties an opportunity to be heard, that a building or area satisfies the ordinance's criteria, it will designate a building to be a "landmark," situated on a particular "landmark site," or will designate an area to be a "historic district." After the Commission makes a designation, New York City's Board of Estimate, after considering the relationship of the designated property "to the master plan, the zoning resolution, projected public improvements and any plans for the renewal of the area involved," may modify or disapprove the designation, and the owner may seek judicial review of the final designation decision. Thus far, 31 historic districts and over 400 individual landmarks have been finally designated, and the process is a continuing one.

Final designation as a landmark results in restrictions upon the property owner's options concerning use of the landmark site. First, the law imposes a duty upon the owner to keep the exterior features of the building "in good repair" to assure that the law's objectives not be defeated by the landmark's falling into a state of irremediable disrepair. Second, the Commission must approve in advance any proposal to alter the exterior architectural features of the landmark or to construct any exterior improvement on the landmark site, thus ensuring that decisions concerning construction on the landmark site are made with due consideration of both the public interest in the maintenance of the structure and the landowner's interest in use of the property.

In the event an owner wishes to alter a landmark site, three separate procedures are available through which administrative approval

10. The consensus is that widespread public ownership of historic properties in urban settings is neither feasible nor wise. Public ownership reduces the tax base, burdens the public budget with costs of acquisitions and maintenance, and results in the preservation of public buildings as museums and similar facilities, rather than as economically productive features of the urban scene. *See* Wilson & Winkler, *The Response of State Legislation to Historic Preservation*, 36 Law & Contemp. Prob. 329, 330–331, 339–340 (1971).

may be obtained. First, the owner may apply to the Commission for a "certificate of no effect on protected architectural features": that is, for an order approving the improvement or alteration on the ground that it will not change or affect any architectural feature of the landmark and will be in harmony therewith. Denial of the certificate is subject to judicial review.

Second, the owner may apply to the Commission for a certificate of "appropriateness." Such certificates will be granted if the Commission concludes—focusing upon aesthetic, historical, and architectural values—that the proposed construction on the landmark site would not unduly hinder the protection, enhancement, perpetuation, and use of the landmark. Again, denial of the certificate is subject to judicial review. Moreover, the owner who is denied either a certificate of no exterior effect or a certificate of appropriateness may submit an alternative or modified plan for approval. The final procedure—seeking a certificate of appropriateness on the ground of "insufficient return"—provides special mechanisms, which vary depending on whether or not the landmark enjoys a tax exemption, to ensure that designation does not cause economic hardship.

Although the designation of a landmark and landmark site restricts the owner's control over the parcel, designation also enhances the economic position of the landmark owner in one significant respect. Under New York City's zoning laws, owners of real property who have not developed their property to the full extent permitted by the applicable zoning laws are allowed to transfer development rights to contiguous parcels on the same city block. . . .

This case involves the application of New York City's Landmarks Preservation Law to Grand Central Terminal (Terminal). The Terminal, which is owned by the Penn Central Transportation Co. and its affiliates (Penn Central), is one of New York City's most famous buildings. Opened in 1913, it is regarded not only as providing an ingenious engineering solution to the problems presented by urban railroad stations, but also as a magnificent example of the French beaux-arts style.

The Terminal is located in midtown Manhattan. Its south facade faces 42d Street and that street's intersection with Park Avenue. . . .

On August 2, 1967, following a public hearing, the Commission designated the Terminal a "landmark" and designated the "city tax block" it occupies a "landmark site." The Board of Estimate confirmed this action on September 21, 1967. Although appellant Penn Central had opposed the designation before the Commission, it did not seek judicial review of the final designation decision.

On January 22, 1968, appellant Penn Central, to increase its income, entered into a renewable 50–year lease and sublease agreement with appellant UGP Properties, Inc. (UGP), a wholly owned subsidiary of Union General Properties, Ltd., a United Kingdom corporation. Under the terms of the agreement, UGP was to construct a multistory office building above the Terminal. UGP promised to pay Penn Central $1 million annually during construction and at least $3 million annually thereafter. The rentals would be offset in part by a loss of some $700,000 to $1 million in net rentals presently received from concessionaires displaced by the new building.

Appellants UGP and Penn Central then applied to the Commission for permission to construct an office building atop the Terminal. Two separate plans, both designed by architect Marcel Breuer and both apparently satisfying the terms of the applicable zoning ordinance, were submitted to the Commission for approval. The first, Breuer I, provided for the construction of a 55–story office building, to be cantilevered above the existing facade and to rest on the roof of the Terminal. The second, Breuer II Revised, called for tearing down a portion of the Terminal that included the 42d Street facade, stripping off some of the remaining features of the Terminal's facade, and constructing a 53–story office building. The Commission denied a certificate of no exterior effect on September 20, 1968. Appellants then applied for a certificate of "appropriateness" as to both proposals. After four days of hearings at which over 80 witnesses testified, the Commission denied this application as to both proposals.

The Commission's reasons for rejecting certificates respecting Breuer II Revised are summarized in the following statement: "To protect a Landmark, one does not tear it down. To perpetuate its architectural features, one does not strip them off." [In rejecting] Breuer I . . . the Commission stated:

> [We have] no fixed rule against making additions to designated buildings—it all depends on how they are done. . . . But to balance a 55–story office tower above a flamboyant Beaux–Arts facade seems nothing more than an aesthetic joke. Quite simply, the tower would overwhelm the Terminal by its sheer mass. . . .

Appellants did not seek judicial review of the denial of either certificate. Because the Terminal site enjoyed a tax exemption, remained suitable for its present and future uses, and was not the subject of a contract of sale, there were no further administrative remedies available to appellants as to the Breuer I and Breuer II Revised plans. Further, appellants did not avail themselves of the opportunity to develop and submit other plans for the Commission's consideration and approval. Instead, appellants filed suit in New York Supreme Court, Trial Term, claiming, inter alia, that the application of the Landmarks Preservation Law had "taken" their property without just compensation in violation of the Fifth and Fourteenth Amendments and arbitrarily deprived them of their property without due process of law in violation of the Fourteenth Amendment. Appellants sought a declaratory judgment, injunctive relief barring the city from using the Landmarks Law to impede the construction of any structure that might otherwise lawfully be constructed on the Terminal site, and damages for the "temporary taking" that occurred between August 2, 1967, the designation date, and the date when the restrictions arising from the Landmarks Law would be lifted.

The trial court granted the injunctive and declaratory relief, but severed the question of damages for a "temporary taking."

Appellees appealed, and the New York Supreme Court, Appellate Division, reversed. 377 N.Y.S.2d 20 (1975). The Appellate Division held that the restrictions on the development of the Terminal site were necessary to promote the legitimate public purpose of protecting landmarks and therefore that appellants could sustain their constitutional claims only by proof that the regulation deprived them of all reasonable beneficial use of the property.... The Appellate Division concluded that all appellants had succeeded in showing was that they had been deprived of the property's most profitable use, and that this showing did not establish that appellants had been unconstitutionally deprived of their property.

The New York Court of Appeals affirmed. 366 N.E.2d 1271 (1977)....

The issues presented by appellants are (1) whether the restrictions imposed by New York City's law upon appellants' exploitation of the Terminal site effect a "taking" of appellants' property for a public use within the meaning of the Fifth Amendment, which of course is made applicable to the States through the Fourteenth Amendment, *see Chicago, B. & Q. R. Co. v. Chicago*, 166 U.S. 226, 239 (1897), and, (2), if so, whether the transferable development rights afforded appellants constitute "just compensation" within the meaning of the Fifth Amendment. We need only address the question whether a "taking" has occurred.

Before considering appellants' specific contentions, it will be useful to review the factors that have shaped the jurisprudence of the Fifth Amendment injunction "nor shall private property be taken for public use, without just compensation." The question of what constitutes a "taking" for purposes of the Fifth Amendment has proved to be a problem of considerable difficulty. While this Court has recognized that the "Fifth Amendment's guarantee ... [is] designed to bar Government from forcing some people alone to bear public burdens which, in all fairness and justice, should be borne by the public as a whole," *Armstrong v. United States*, 364 U.S. 40, 49 (1960), this Court, quite simply, has been unable to develop any "set formula" for determining when "justice and fairness" require that economic injuries caused by public action be compensated by the government, rather than remain disproportionately concentrated on a few persons. *See Goldblatt v. Hempstead*, 369 U.S. 590, 594 (1962). Indeed, we have frequently observed that whether a particular restriction will be rendered invalid by the government's failure to pay for any losses proximately caused by it depends largely "upon the particular circumstances [in that] case." *United States v. Central Eureka Mining Co.*, 357 U.S. 155, 168 (1958); *see United States v. Caltex, Inc.*, 344 U.S. 149, 156 (1952).

In engaging in these essentially ad hoc, factual inquiries, the Court's decisions have identified several factors that have particular significance. The economic impact of the regulation on the claimant and, particularly, the extent to which the regulation has interfered with distinct invest-ment-backed expectations are, of course, relevant considerations. *See Goldblatt v. Hempstead, supra*, 369 U.S., at 594. So, too, is the character of the governmental action. A "taking" may more readily be found when the interference with property can be characterized as a physical inva-sion by government, *see, e.g., United States v. Causby*, 328 U.S. 256 (1946), than when interference arises from some public program adjust-ing the benefits and burdens of economic life to promote the common good.

"Government hardly could go on if to some extent values incident to property could not be diminished without paying for every such change in the general law," *Pennsylvania Coal Co. v. Mahon*, 260 U.S. 393, 413 (1922), and this Court has accordingly recognized, in a wide variety of contexts, that government may execute laws or programs that adversely affect recognized economic values. Exercises of the taxing power are one obvious example. A second are the decisions in which this Court has dismissed "taking" challenges on the ground that, while the challenged government action caused economic harm, it did not interfere with interests that were sufficiently bound up with the reasonable expecta-tions of the claimant to constitute "property" for Fifth Amendment purposes.

More importantly for the present case, in instances in which a state tribunal reasonably concluded that "the health, safety, morals, or gener-al welfare" would be promoted by prohibiting particular contemplated uses of land, this Court has upheld land-use regulations that destroyed or adversely affected recognized real property interests. *See Nectow v. Cambridge*, 277 U.S. 183, 188 (1928). Zoning laws are, of course, the classic example, *see Euclid v. Ambler Realty Co.*, 272 U.S. 365 (1926) (prohibition of industrial use); *Gorieb v. Fox*, 274 U.S. 603, 608 (1927) (requirement that portions of parcels be left unbuilt); *Welch v. Swasey*, 214 U.S. 91 (1909) (height restriction), which have been viewed as permissible governmental action even when prohibiting the most benefi-cial use of the property. *See Goldblatt v. Hempstead, supra*, 369 U.S. at 592–593.

Zoning laws generally do not affect existing uses of real property, but "taking" challenges have also been held to be without merit in a wide variety of situations when the challenged governmental actions prohibited a beneficial use to which individual parcels had previously been devoted and thus caused substantial individualized harm. *Miller v. Schoene*, 276 U.S. (1928), is illustrative. In that case, a state entomolo-gist, acting pursuant to a state statute, ordered the claimants to cut down a large number of ornamental red cedar trees because they produced cedar rust fatal to apple trees cultivated nearby. Although the statute provided for recovery of any expense incurred in removing the cedars, and permitted claimants to use the felled trees, it did not provide compensation for the value of the standing trees or for the resulting decrease in market value of the properties as a whole. A unanimous Court held that this latter omission did not render the statute invalid.

The Court held that the State might properly make "a choice between the preservation of one class of property and that of the other" and since the apple industry was important in the State involved, concluded that the State had not exceeded "its constitutional powers by deciding upon the destruction of one class of property [without compensation] in order to save another which, in the judgment of the legislature, is of greater value to the public." *Id*. at 279.

Again, *Hadacheck v. Sebastian*, 239 U.S. 394 (1915), upheld a law prohibiting the claimant from continuing his otherwise lawful business of operating a brickyard in a particular physical community on the ground that the legislature had reasonably concluded that the presence of the brickyard was inconsistent with neighboring uses....

Pennsylvania Coal Co. v. Mahon, 260 U.S. 393 (1922), is the leading case for the proposition that a state statute that substantially furthers important public policies may so frustrate distinct investment-backed expectations as to amount to a "taking." There the claimant had sold the surface rights to particular parcels of property, but expressly reserved the right to remove the coal thereunder. A Pennsylvania statute, enacted after the transactions, forbade any mining of coal that caused the subsidence of any house, unless the house was the property of the owner of the underlying coal and was more than 150 feet from the improved property of another. Because the statute made it commercially impracticable to mine the coal, *id*. at 414, and thus had nearly the same effect as the complete destruction of rights claimant had reserved from the owners of the surface land, *see id*. at 414–415, the Court held that the statute was invalid as effecting a "taking" without just compensation....

Finally, government actions that may be characterized as acquisitions of resources to permit or facilitate uniquely public functions have often been held to constitute "takings." *United States v. Causby*, 328 U.S. 256 (1946), is illustrative. In holding that direct overflights above the claimant's land, that destroyed the present use of the land as a chicken farm, constituted a "taking," *Causby* emphasized that Government had not "merely destroyed property [but was] using a part of it for the flight of its planes." *Id*., 328 U.S. at 262–263, n. 7....

In contending that the New York City law has "taken" their property in violation of the Fifth and Fourteenth Amendments, appellants make a series of arguments, which, while tailored to the facts of this case, essentially urge that any substantial restriction imposed pursuant to a landmark law must be accompanied by just compensation if it is to be constitutional. Before considering these, we emphasize what is not in dispute. Because this Court has recognized, in a number of settings, that States and cities may enact land-use restrictions or controls to enhance the quality of life by preserving the character and desirable aesthetic features of a city, *see Village of Belle Terre v. Boraas*, 416 U.S. 1, 9–10 (1974); *Berman v. Parker*, 348 U.S. 26, 33 (1954); *Welch v. Swasey*, 214 U.S., at 108, appellants do not contest that New York City's objective of preserving structures and areas with special historic, architectural, or cultural significance is an entirely permissible governmental goal. They also do not dispute that the restrictions imposed on its parcel are appropriate means of securing the purposes of the New York City law. Finally, appellants do not challenge any of the specific factual premises of the decision below. They accept for present purposes both that the parcel of land occupied by Grand Central Terminal must, in its present state, be regarded as capable of earning a reasonable return, and that the transferable development rights afforded appellants by virtue of the Terminal's designation as a landmark are valuable, even if not as valuable as the rights to construct above the Terminal. In appellants' view none of these factors derogate from their claim that New York City's law has effected a "taking."

They first observe that the airspace above the Terminal is a valuable property interest, citing *United States v. Causby, supra.* They urge that the Landmarks Law has deprived them of any gainful use of their "air rights" above the Terminal and that, irrespective of the value of the remainder of their parcel, the city has "taken" their right to this superadjacent airspace, thus entitling them to "just compensation" measured by the fair market value of these air rights.

Apart from our own disagreement with appellants' characterization of the effect of the New York City law, the submission that appellants may establish a "taking" simply by showing that they have been denied the ability to exploit a property interest that they heretofore had believed was available for development is quite simply untenable. Were this the rule, this Court would have erred not only in upholding laws restricting the development of air rights, *see Welch v. Swasey, supra,* but also in approving those prohibiting both the subjacent, *see Goldblatt v. Hempstead,* 369 U.S. 590 (1962), and the lateral, *see Gorieb v. Fox,* 274 U.S. 603 (1927), development of particular parcels. "Taking" jurisprudence does not divide a single parcel into discrete segments and attempt to determine whether rights in a particular segment have been entirely abrogated. In deciding whether a particular governmental action has effected a taking, this Court focuses rather both on the character of the action and on the nature and extent of the interference with rights in the parcel as a whole—here, the city tax block designated as the "landmark site."

Secondly, appellants, focusing on the character and impact of the New York City law, argue that it effects a "taking" because its operation has significantly diminished the value of the Terminal site. Appellants concede that the decisions sustaining other land-use regulations, which, like the New York City law, are reasonably related to the promotion of the general welfare, uniformly reject the proposition that diminution in property value, standing alone, can establish a "taking," *see Euclid v. Ambler Realty Co.,* 272 U.S. 365 (1926) (75% diminution in value caused by zoning law); *Hadacheck v. Sebastian,* 239 U.S. 394 (1915) (87-1/2% diminution in value); *cf. Eastlake v. Forest City Enterprises, Inc.,* 426 U.S. at 674 n. 8, and that the "taking" issue in these contexts is resolved by focusing on the uses the regulations permit. Appellants, moreover, also do not dispute that a showing of diminution in property value would not establish a taking if the restriction had been imposed as a result of historic-district legislation, see generally *Maher v. New Orleans*, 516 F.2d 1051 (CA5 1975), but appellants argue that New York City's regulation of individual landmarks is fundamentally different from zoning or from historic-district legislation because the controls imposed by New York City's law apply only to individuals who own selected properties.

Stated baldly, appellants' position appears to be that the only means of ensuring that selected owners are not singled out to endure financial hardship for no reason is to hold that any restriction imposed on individual landmarks pursuant to the New York City scheme is a "taking" requiring the payment of "just compensation." Agreement with this argument would, of course, invalidate not just New York City's law, but all comparable landmark legislation in the Nation. We find no merit in it.

It is true, as appellants emphasize, that both historic-district legislation and zoning laws regulate all properties within given physical communities whereas landmark laws apply only to selected parcels. But, contrary to appellants' suggestions, landmark laws are not like discriminatory, or "reverse spot," zoning: that is, a land-use decision which arbitrarily singles out a particular parcel for different, less favorable treatment than the neighboring ones. *See* 2 A. Rathkopf, The Law of Zoning and Planning 26–4, and n. 6 (4th ed. 1978). In contrast to discriminatory zoning, which is the antithesis of land-use control as part of some comprehensive plan, the New York City law embodies a comprehensive plan to preserve structures of historic or aesthetic interest wherever they might be found in the city, and as noted, over 400 landmarks and 31 historic districts have been designated pursuant to this plan....

Next, appellants observe that New York City's law differs from zoning laws and historic-district ordinances in that the Landmarks Law does not impose identical or similar restrictions on all structures located in particular physical communities. It follows, they argue, that New York City's law is inherently incapable of producing the fair and equitable distribution of benefits and burdens of governmental action which is characteristic of zoning laws and historic-district legislation and which they maintain is a constitutional requirement if "just compensation" is not to be afforded. It is, of course, true that the Landmarks Law has a more severe impact on some landowners than on others, but that in itself does not mean that the law effects a "taking." Legislation designed to promote the general welfare commonly burdens some more than others. The owners of the brickyard in *Hadacheck*, of the cedar trees in *Miller v. Schoene*, and of the gravel and sand mine in *Goldblatt v. Hempstead*, were uniquely burdened by the legislation sustained in those cases.[11] Similarly, zoning laws often affect some property owners more severely than others but have not been held to be invalid on that account. For example, the property owner in *Euclid* who wished to use its property for industrial purposes was affected far more severely by the ordinance than its neighbors who wished to use their land for residences.

In any event, appellants' repeated suggestions that they are solely burdened and unbenefited is factually inaccurate. This contention overlooks the fact that the New York City law applies to vast numbers of structures in the city in addition to the Terminal—all the structures contained in the 31 historic districts and over 400 individual landmarks, many of which are close to the Terminal. Unless we are to reject the judgment of the New York City Council that the preservation of landmarks benefits all New York citizens and all structures, both economically and by improving the quality of life in the city as a whole—which we are unwilling to do—we cannot conclude that the owners of the Terminal have in no sense been benefited by the Landmarks Law. Doubtless appellants believe they are more burdened than benefited by the law, but that must have been true, too, of the property owners in *Miller, Hadacheck, Euclid,* and *Goldblatt....*

Rejection of appellants' broad arguments is not, however, the end of our inquiry, for all we thus far have established is that the New York City law is not rendered invalid by its failure to provide "just compensation" whenever a landmark owner is restricted in the exploitation of property interests, such as air rights, to a greater extent than provided for under applicable zoning laws. We now must consider whether the interference with appellants' property is of such a magnitude that "there must be an exercise of eminent domain and compensation to sustain [it]." *Pennsylvania Coal Co. v. Mahon,* 260 U.S., at 413. That inquiry may be narrowed to the question of the severity of the impact of the law on appellants' parcel, and its resolution in turn requires a careful assessment of the impact of the regulation on the Terminal site.

Unlike the governmental acts in *Goldblatt, Miller, Causby,* ... and *Hadacheck,* the New York City law does not interfere in any way with the present uses of the Terminal. Its designation as a landmark not only permits but contemplates that appellants may continue to use the property precisely as it has been used for the past 65 years: as a railroad terminal containing office space and concessions. So the law does not interfere with what must be regarded as Penn Central's primary expec-

---

11. Appellants attempt to distinguish these cases on the ground that, in each, government was prohibiting a "noxious" use of land and that in the present case, in contrast, appellants' proposed construction above the Terminal would be beneficial. We observe that the uses in issue in *Hadacheck, Miller,* and *Goldblatt* were perfectly lawful in themselves. They involved no "blameworthiness, ... moral wrongdoing or conscious act of dangerous risk-taking which induce[d society] to shift the cost to a pa[rt]icular individual." Sax, *Takings and the Police Power,* 74 Yale L.J. 36, 50 (1964). These cases are better understood as resting not on any supposed "noxious" quality of the prohibited uses but rather on the ground that the restrictions were reasonably related to the implementation of a policy—not unlike historic preservation—expected to produce a widespread public benefit and applicable to all similarly situated property....

tation concerning the use of the parcel. More importantly, on this record, we must regard the New York City law as permitting Penn Central not only to profit from the Terminal but also to obtain a "reasonable return" on its investment.

Appellants, moreover, exaggerate the effect of the law on their ability to make use of the air rights above the Terminal in two respects. First, it simply cannot be maintained, on this record, that appellants have been prohibited from occupying any portion of the airspace above the Terminal. While the Commission's actions in denying applications to construct an office building in excess of 50 stories above the Terminal may indicate that it will refuse to issue a certificate of appropriateness for any comparably sized structure, nothing the Commission has said or done suggests an intention to prohibit any construction above the Terminal. The Commission's report emphasized that whether any construction would be allowed depended upon whether the proposed addition "would harmonize in scale, material and character with [the Terminal]." Since appellants have not sought approval for the construction of a smaller structure, we do not know that appellants will be denied any use of any portion of the airspace above the Terminal.

Second, to the extent appellants have been denied the right to build above the Terminal, it is not literally accurate to say that they have been denied all use of even those pre-existing air rights. Their ability to use these rights has not been abrogated; they are made transferable to at least eight parcels in the vicinity of the Terminal, one or two of which have been found suitable for the construction of new office buildings. Although appellants and others have argued that New York City's transferable development-rights program is far from ideal, the New York courts here supportably found that, at least in the case of the Terminal, the rights afforded are valuable. While these rights may well not have constituted "just compensation" if a "taking" had occurred, the rights nevertheless undoubtedly mitigate whatever financial burdens the law has imposed on appellants and, for that reason, are to be taken into account in considering the impact of regulation.

On this record, we conclude that the application of New York City's Landmarks Law has not effected a "taking" of appellants' property. The restrictions imposed are substantially related to the promotion of the general welfare and not only permit reasonable beneficial use of the landmark site but also afford appellants opportunities further to enhance not only the Terminal site proper but also other properties. . . .

MR. JUSTICE REHNQUIST, with whom THE CHIEF JUSTICE and MR. JUSTICE STEVENS join, dissenting. . . . The question in this case is whether the cost associated with the city of New York's desire to preserve a limited number of "landmarks" within its borders must be borne by all of its taxpayers or whether it can instead be imposed entirely on the owners of the individual properties.

Only in the most superficial sense of the word can this case be said to involve "zoning." Typical zoning restrictions may, it is true, so limit the prospective uses of a piece of property as to diminish the value of that property in the abstract because it may not be used for the forbidden purposes. But any such abstract decrease in value will more than likely be at least partially offset by an increase in value which flows from similar restrictions as to use on neighboring properties. All property owners in a designated area are placed under the same restrictions, not only for the benefit of the municipality as a whole but also for the common benefit of one another. In the words of Mr. Justice Holmes, speaking for the Court in *Pennsylvania Coal Co. v. Mahon*, 260 U.S. 393, 415 (1922), there is "an average reciprocity of advantage."

Where a relatively few individual buildings, all separated from one another, are singled out and treated differently from surrounding buildings, no such reciprocity exists. The cost to the property owner which results from the imposition of restrictions applicable only to his property and not that of his neighbors may be substantial—in this case, several million dollars—with no comparable reciprocal benefits. And the cost associated with landmark legislation is likely to be of a completely different order of magnitude than that which results from the imposition of normal zoning restrictions. Unlike the regime affected by the latter, the landowner is not simply prohibited from using his property for certain purposes, while allowed to use it for all other purposes. Under the historic-landmark preservation scheme adopted by New York, the property owner is under an affirmative duty to preserve his property as a landmark at his own expense. To suggest that because traditional zoning results in some limitation of use of the property zoned, the New York City landmark preservation scheme should likewise be upheld, represents the ultimate in treating as alike things which are different. The rubric of "zoning" has not yet sufficed to avoid the well-established proposition that the Fifth Amendment bars the "Government from forcing some people alone to bear public burdens which, in all fairness and justice, should be borne by the public as a whole." *Armstrong v. United States*, 364 U.S. 40, 49 (1960)....

The Fifth Amendment provides in part: "nor shall private property be taken for public use, without just compensation." In a very literal sense, the actions of appellees violated this constitutional prohibition. Before the city of New York declared Grand Central Terminal to be a landmark, Penn Central could have used its "air rights" over the Terminal to build a multistory office building, at an apparent value of several million dollars per year. Today, the Terminal cannot be modified in any form, including the erection of additional stories, without the permission of the Landmark Preservation Commission, a permission which appellants, despite good-faith attempts, have so far been unable to obtain....

While neighboring landowners are free to use their land and "air rights" in any way consistent with the broad boundaries of New York zoning, Penn Central, absent the permission of appellees, must forever maintain its property in its present state. The property has been thus subjected to a nonconsensual servitude not borne by any neighboring or similar properties.

Appellees have thus destroyed—in a literal sense, "taken"—substantial property rights of Penn Central. . . .

As early as 1887, the Court recognized that the government can prevent a property owner from using his property to injure others without having to compensate the owner for the value of the forbidden use. [*Mugler v. Kansas*, 123 U.S. 623, 668–669.] . . .

Thus, there is no "taking" where a city prohibits the operation of a brickyard within a residential area, *see Hadacheck v. Sebastian*, 239 U.S. 394 (1915), or forbids excavation for sand and gravel below the water line, *see Goldblatt v. Hempstead*, 369 U.S. 590 (1962). Nor is it relevant, where the government is merely prohibiting a noxious use of property, that the government would seem to be singling out a particular property owner.

The nuisance exception to the taking guarantee is not coterminous with the police power itself. The question is whether the forbidden use is dangerous to the safety, health, or welfare of others. . . .

Appellees are not prohibiting a nuisance. The record is clear that the proposed addition to the Grand Central Terminal would be in full compliance with zoning, height limitations, and other health and safety requirements. Instead, appellees are seeking to preserve what they believe to be an outstanding example of beaux-arts architecture. Penn Central is prevented from further developing its property basically because too good a job was done in designing and building it. The city of New York, because of its unadorned admiration for the design, has decided that the owners of the building must preserve it unchanged for the benefit of sightseeing New Yorkers and tourists. . . .

Even where the government prohibits a noninjurious use, the Court has ruled that a taking does not take place if the prohibition applies over a broad cross section of land and thereby "secure[s] an average reciprocity of advantage." *Pennsylvania Coal Co. v. Mahon*, 260 U.S., at 415, 43 S.Ct., at 160. It is for this reason that zoning does not constitute a "taking." While zoning at times reduces individual property values, the burden is shared relatively evenly and it is reasonable to conclude that on the whole an individual who is harmed by one aspect of the zoning will be benefited by another.

Here, however, a multimillion dollar loss has been imposed on appellants; it is uniquely felt and is not offset by any benefits flowing from the preservation of some 400 other "landmarks" in New York City. Appellees have imposed a substantial cost on less than one one-tenth of one percent of the buildings in New York City for the general benefit of all its people. It is exactly this imposition of general costs on a few individuals at which the "taking" protection is directed. The Fifth Amendment "prevents the public from loading upon one individual more than his just share of the burdens of government, and says that when he surrenders to the public something more and different from that which is exacted from other members of the public, a full and just equivalent shall be returned to him." *Monongahela Navigation Co. v. United States*, 148 U.S. 312 (1893). . . .

As Mr. Justice Holmes pointed out in *Pennsylvania Coal Co. v. Mahon*, "the question at bottom" in an eminent domain case "is upon whom the loss of the changes desired should fall." 260 U.S., at 416. The benefits that appellees believe will flow from preservation of the Grand Central Terminal will accrue to all the citizens of New York City. There is no reason to believe that appellants will enjoy a substantially greater share of these benefits. If the cost of preserving Grand Central Terminal were spread evenly across the entire population of the city of New York, the burden per person would be in cents per year—a minor cost appellees would surely concede for the benefit accrued. Instead, however, appellees would impose the entire cost of several million dollars per year on Penn Central. But it is precisely this sort of discrimination that the Fifth Amendment prohibits.

Appellees in response would argue that a taking only occurs where a property owner is denied all reasonable value of his property.[12] The Court has frequently held that, even where a destruction of property rights would not otherwise constitute a taking, the inability of the owner to make a reasonable return on his property requires compensation under the Fifth Amendment. But the converse is not true. A taking does not become a noncompensable exercise of police power simply because the government in its grace allows the owner to make some "reasonable" use of his property. "[I]t is the character of the invasion, not the amount of damage resulting from it, so long as the damage is substantial, that determines the question whether it is a taking." *United States v. Cress*, 243 U.S. 316, 328 (1917); *United States v. Causby*, 328 U.S., at 266. *See also Goldblatt v. Hempstead*, 369 U.S., at 594.

Over 50 years ago, Mr. Justice Holmes, speaking for the Court, warned that the courts were "in danger of forgetting that a strong public desire to improve the public condition is not enough to warrant achieving the desire by a shorter cut than the constitutional way of paying for the change." *Pennsylvania Coal Co. v. Mahon*, 260 U.S., at 416, 43 S.Ct., at 160. The Court's opinion in this case demonstrates that the danger thus foreseen has not abated. The city of New York is in a precarious

---

12. Difficult conceptual and legal problems are posed by a rule that a taking only occurs where the property owner is denied all reasonable return on his property. Not only must the Court define "reasonable return" for a variety of types of property (farmlands, residential properties, commercial and industrial areas), but the Court must define the particular property unit that should be examined. For example, in this case, if appellees are viewed as having restricted Penn Central's use of its "air rights," all return has been denied. *See*

Pennsylvania Coal Co. v. Mahon, 260 U.S. 393 (1922). The Court does little to resolve these questions in its opinion. Thus, at one point, the Court implies that the question is whether the restrictions have "an unduly harsh impact upon the owner's use of the property;" at another point, the question is phrased as whether Penn Central can obtain "a 'reasonable return' on its investment;" and, at yet another point, the question becomes whether the landmark is "economically viable."

financial state, and some may believe that the costs of landmark preservation will be more easily borne by corporations such as Penn Central than the overburdened individual taxpayers of New York. But these concerns do not allow us to ignore past precedents construing the Eminent Domain Clause to the end that the desire to improve the public condition is, indeed, achieved by a shorter cut than the constitutional way of paying for the change.

Notes

1. *Balancing Public and Private Interests—Is Uncompensated Regulation an Appropriate Means to a Legitimate Public End?* The rhetoric of the opinions in *Penn Central* reflects the tension between enabling the government to act in the public interest to address externalities through land use regulation and ensuring that government does not excessively burden individual landowners by such measures. Note that this represents a separate means/end question than the one discussed following *Kelo* (page 43). There, Professor Merrill argued that even when the government is pursuing a legitimate public purpose, there is a "means" question concerning whether the government should be making market purchases rather than exercising the power of eminent domain. Here, the comparison is changed slightly: should the government pursue public purposes by exercising the power of eminent domain (so that the public at large bears the cost) or by exercising its authority to regulate land (so that the cost falls on a smaller number of individuals)?

The majority in *Penn Central* works from a premise that sounds something like an efficiency argument—"[g]overnment hardly could go on if to some extent values incident to property could not be diminished without paying for every such change in the general law" (quoting *Pennsylvania Coal Co. v. Mahon*, 260 U.S. 393, 413, 43 S.Ct. 158, 67 L.Ed. 322 (1922)). But why couldn't government "go on"? If the public at large benefits from having Grand Central Terminal preserved, should that benefit come at the expense of Penn Central (via lost land value due to preservation regulations) or from the general public (through the cost of a condemnation award, payable from tax revenues)?

2. *The Significance of* Penn Central's *Three-Factor Test.* The *Penn Central* opinion articulated three factors relevant to a regulatory takings claim: (a) "[t]he economic impact of the regulation on the claimant [the owner whose property is burdened by the regulation]," (b) "the extent to which the regulation has interfered with [that owner's] distinct investment-backed expectations," and (c) "the character of the governmental action."

Shortly after *Penn Central*, the Court muddied the regulatory takings issue by erroneously restating the nature of the takings inquiry as follows: "The application of a general zoning law to particular property effects a taking if the ordinance *does not substantially advance legitimate state interests* or denies an owner economically viable use of his land." *Agins v. Tiburon*, 447 U.S. 255, 260–61, 100 S.Ct. 2138, 65 L.Ed.2d 106 (1980) (emphasis added). This statement created confusion for more than two decades, with some courts referencing *Penn Central*, some referencing *Agins*, and some referencing both. The Supreme Court corrected the error in 2005, stating that the *Agins* formula was derived from substantive due process analysis and "has no proper place in our takings jurisprudence." *Lingle v. Chevron U.S.A., Inc.*, 125 S.Ct. 2074, 2083, 161 L.Ed.2d 876 (2005).

Following *Lingle*, therefore, *Penn Central's* three-factor test provides the only formula for deciding non-categorical takings claims. The following material explores the significance of each of these three factors in more detail.

3. *Understanding* Penn Central's *Three-Factor Test.* How do courts apply the *Penn Central* three-factor test? What does each factor encompass?

(a) *Impairment of Economic Value.* This factor considers the severity of the economic loss suffered by the landowner—*i.e.*, the diminution of property value caused by the regulation. New York's application of the historic preservation ordinance meant that Penn Central lost virtually all economic value attributable to vertical development above Grand Central Station. The Court noted, however, that Penn Central continued to earn a reasonable return on its overall investment in Grand Central Station, even though it was not able to generate additional revenue associated with vertical development above Grand Central Station.

This analysis raises a question regarding the proper "denominator" to use in determining how much the regulation has diminished the property's value. Assume that the air rights had a value of $10 million, and that Grand Central Station as a whole had a value of $100 million (including the $10 million in air rights). Should the Supreme Court evaluate the loss in comparison to the value of the parcel as a whole (a 10% diminishment in value—$10 million/$100 million), or in comparison to the value of only the impacted air rights (a 100% diminishment in value—$10 million/$10 million)? How does *Penn Central* define the "denominator" against which a court should measure the impairment of economic value? How does the dissent view the question differently? Which approach makes more sense as a matter of policy?[13]

(b) *"Investment–Backed Expectations."* This factor seems to reflect the notion that the application of a regulation to a landowner is more likely to be a taking if a citizen has invested resources in reasonable reliance upon the

---

13. This "denominator" issue played a key role in the decision in *Pennsylvania Coal Co. v. Mahon*, discussed at length in *Penn Central*. Although the statute at issue in *Pennsylvania Coal* required the mining company to leave *some* coal in place to support the surface estates, it did not preclude mining completely—leaving open the possibility that the mining company could have earned a "reasonable return" from the coal it could legally mine. Although the majority treated the statute as a taking, finding that the statute "went too far," Justice Brandeis dissented, criticizing the opinion because the majority focused on a segmented denominator—*i.e.*, it looked at the extent to which the coal company expe-

rienced impairment in value solely with regard to the minerals that the statute required the coal company to leave in place. More recently, however, in a 5–4 decision in *Keystone Bituminous Coal Ass'n v. DeBenedictis*, 480 U.S. 470, 107 S.Ct. 1232, 94 L.Ed.2d 472 (1987), the Court implicitly rejected the *Pennsylvania Coal* approach to defining the denominator. The case involved a similar statute regulating coal mining to prevent subsidence. The Court held that the statute did not effect a regulatory taking because the owners of the regulated mineral rights could obtain a reasonable return despite the obligation to leave coal in place to support the surface estates located above the mines.

pre-existing state of the law. Note that when Grand Central Terminal was built, well before the enactment of the historic preservation ordinance, it was constructed with roof supports that would enable construction of a tower above the roof of the station. Does this fact suggest that Penn Central had a reasonable investment-backed expectation that it should be able to build such a tower? Was it foreseeable that the city's desire to protect Grand Central's facade—as manifested in its historic preservation ordinance— would preclude Penn Central from building a tower onto the terminal? Does it matter? How does the Court's analysis in *Penn Central* inform your understanding of this term? We will return to this issue after the *Lucas* opinion (page 965).

(c) *The Character of the Governmental Action.* The *Penn Central* Court notes that "[a] 'taking' may more readily be found when the interference with property can be characterized as a physical invasion by government than when interference arises from some public program adjusting the benefits and burdens of economic life to promote the common good." Here again, the Court does not provide a definitive statement, but more of a sliding scale. Where a particular regulation falls on this scale depends in large part upon the general policies underlying the takings analysis. As the Court recognizes in *Penn Central*, "[g]overnment could hardly go on if to some extent values incident to property could not be diminished without paying for every such change in the general law." Nonetheless, the Court also emphasized that the "Fifth Amendment's guarantee . . . [is] designed to bar Government from forcing some people alone to bear a burden which, in all fairness and justice, should be borne by the public as a whole[.]"

Using this analysis, what types of laws are more likely to be a taking? Which ones are less likely to be a taking? Is it accurate to say that as long as the state acts within its police powers to regulate some type of noxious behavior, it has not "taken" someone's property through regulation? Does the dissent have a valid point with its harm-benefit analysis—*i.e.*, that a taking should be found when a regulation does not prevent a harm, *i.e.*, is not focused on "nuisance prevention," but compels a landowner to confer a benefit on the public?

(d) *How Do the Three Factors Relate to One Another?* The Supreme Court has not been very explicit about how the three-factor test works in practice, other than to say that it is an "ad hoc" formula. The case law applying the three-factor test at best allows one to deduce some crude understandings. First, modest impairments in economic value generally are inadequate to give rise to a taking. The impairment needs to be truly significant if the landowner even wants to have a chance of succeeding with a regulatory takings claim. Second, courts will weigh the economic impact (and particularly investment-backed expectations) in relation to the character of the government action. In *Penn Central*, for example, the Court observed that when a case has involved land use regulations reasonably related to the promotion of the general welfare, the courts "uniformly reject the proposition that diminution in value, standing alone, can establish a 'taking.'" 438 U.S. at 131 (citing 75% diminution in value in *Village of Euclid v. Ambler Realty Co.*, 272 U.S. 365, 47 S.Ct. 114, 71 L.Ed. 303 (1926) and 87.5% diminution in value in *Hadacheck v. Sebastian*, 239 U.S. 394, 36 S.Ct. 143, 60 L.Ed. 348 (1915)). Does the *Penn Central* test suggest a balancing of interests similar to the way that the Restatement (Second) of Torts (page 845) would balance similar concerns with respect to the law of nuisance? Consider the following analogy: "The law of nuisance is to trespass as the law of regulatory takings is to physical takings." In what ways does this analogy make sense? In what ways does this analogy fail?

4. *Transferable Development Rights.* In *Penn Central*, the Court touched upon, but did not decide, the extent to which transferable development rights (TDRs) should be accounted for in the takings equation. Through the use of TDRs, a landowner can capture some of the value associated with unused development potential on her property by transferring the development potential to neighboring parcels. Think of the development potential of a parcel as a box containing a certain volume of cubic feet, depending upon area limitations (such as front and side setbacks) and height limitations. In jurisdictions with TDR programs, when additional regulations (such as the historic preservation ordinance in *Penn Central*) preclude a landowner from using some of the volume in the box, the landowner has the right to transfer the unusable volume to neighboring parcels. Indeed, after the decision in *Penn Central*, Penn Central was able to sell to neighboring landowners several hundred thousand cubic feet of development potential.

Following *Penn Central*, it was unclear how TDRs were to be considered in the takings analysis. The *Penn Central* majority suggested that the value of the TDRs was relevant in deciding whether a taking had occurred (in assessing the economic impact of the regulation). [How did the Court resolve that inquiry?] In dissent, however, Justice Rehnquist (in a portion of the opinion deleted from your textbook) analyzed the appellee's argument that the TDRs constitute "just compensation." Noting that "just compensation" requires "full and perfect equivalent for the property taken[,]" Justice Rehnquist would have remanded the case for a determination of whether the TDRs met that standard. Justice Scalia reiterated this position in *Suitum v. Tahoe Regional Planning Agency*, 520 U.S. 725, 117 S.Ct. 1659, 137 L.Ed.2d 980 (1997). The case dealt largely with whether Suitum's takings claim was premature because she had not received a final determination regarding the extent to which she could pursue the TDRs relating to land that she could not develop under the zoning ordinance. However, Justice Scalia's concurrence (joined by O'Connor and Thomas) emphasized his view that TDRs did not relate to whether a taking had occurred, but instead related solely to whether a governmental entity had provided adequate compensation when a taking had occurred.

5. *Temporary Takings.* Prior to 1987, many courts and commentators had assumed that when a landowner successfully challenged the application of a government regulation as a regulatory taking, the court would issue an injunction precluding the government from enforcing the regulation. If the government still wished to pursue the policies reflected in the regulation, it then had a choice of either taking title to the relevant property interest through the exercise of eminent domain or amending the regulation to eliminate the aspects that resulted in a taking. Under this approach, however, the landowner received no compensation for the period during which the regulation had been in effect—the "temporary takings" period. Only in a few states did the conclusion that a regulatory taking had occurred trigger an obligation to compensate for the period of the temporary taking.

See Gene R. Rankin, *The First Bite at the Apple: State Supreme Court Takings Jurisprudence Antedating* First English, 20 Urb. Law. 417, 429 (1990).

The Court finally addressed this issue squarely in *First English Evangelical Lutheran Church v. County of Los Angeles*, 482 U.S. 304, 107 S.Ct. 2378, 96 L.Ed.2d 250 (1987), holding that a landowner who suffers a regulatory taking has a claim for compensation beginning with the date the regulation first impacted the land:

> Once a court determines that a taking has occurred, the government retains the whole range of functions already available—amendment of the regulation, withdrawal of the invalidated regulation, or exercise of eminent domain. . . . [But] no subsequent action by the government can relieve it of the duty to provide compensation for the period during which the taking was effective. [482 U.S. at 321.]

How does *First English* alter the bargaining positions of developers and the government? If you represented a municipality considering how to enforce its open space ordinance, how would your advice change as a result of the Court's decision in *First English*?

———————

In response to the enactment of increasingly stringent environmental regulation by federal and state legislatures and agencies, and the increasing hurdles to federal suits alleging a regulatory taking, a "property rights" movement began to flourish in the late 1980s and early 1990s. Believing that an increasingly conservative Supreme Court might demonstrate greater willingness to protect private property rights, advocates sought a case that would allow the Court to clarify or reshape the law of regulatory takings. The case that reached the Court—*Lucas v. South Carolina Coastal Council*—was expected to provide the Court with an opportunity to make a bold departure from the Court's previous regulatory takings doctrine. As you read the *Lucas* case and the accompanying notes, reflect on the extent to which the decision really reshapes the law of regulatory takings.

LUCAS v. SOUTH CAROLINA COASTAL COUNCIL

Supreme Court of the United States.
505 U.S. 1003, 112 S.Ct. 2886, 120 L.Ed.2d 798 (1992).

JUSTICE SCALIA delivered the opinion of the Court. In 1986, petitioner David H. Lucas paid $975,000 for two residential lots on the Isle of Palms in Charleston County, South Carolina, on which he intended to build single-family homes. In 1988, however, the South Carolina Legislature enacted the Beachfront Management Act, S.C.Code Ann. § 48–39–250 *et seq.* (Supp.1990), which had the direct effect of barring petitioner from erecting any permanent habitable structures on his two parcels. A state trial court found that this prohibition rendered Lucas's parcels "valueless." This case requires us to decide whether the Act's dramatic effect on the economic value of Lucas's lots accomplished a taking of private property under the Fifth and Fourteenth Amendments requiring the payment of "just compensation."

South Carolina's expressed interest in intensively managing development activities in the so-called "coastal zone" dates from 1977 when, in the aftermath of Congress's passage of the federal Coastal Zone Management Act of 1972, 86 Stat. 1280, as amended, 16 U.S.C. § 1451 *et seq.*, the legislature enacted a Coastal Zone Management Act of its own. *See* S.C.Code Ann. § 48–39–10 *et seq.* (1987). In its original form, the South Carolina Act required owners of coastal zone land that qualified as a "critical area" (defined in the legislation to include beaches and immediately adjacent sand dunes, § 48–39–10(J)) to obtain a permit from the newly created South Carolina Coastal Council (Council) (respondent here) prior to committing the land to a "use other than the use the critical area was devoted to on [September 28, 1977]."

In the late 1970's, Lucas and others began extensive residential development of the Isle of Palms, a barrier island situated eastward of the city of Charleston. Toward the close of the development cycle for one residential subdivision known as "Beachwood East," Lucas in 1986 purchased the two lots at issue in this litigation for his own account. No portion of the lots, which were located approximately 300 feet from the beach, qualified as a "critical area" under the 1977 Act; accordingly, at the time Lucas acquired these parcels, he was not legally obliged to obtain a permit from the Council in advance of any development activity. His intention with respect to the lots was to do what the owners of the immediately adjacent parcels had already done: erect single-family residences. He commissioned architectural drawings for this purpose.

The Beachfront Management Act brought Lucas's plans to an abrupt end. Under that 1988 legislation, the Council was directed to establish a "baseline" connecting the landward-most "point[s] of erosion ... during the past forty years" in the region of the Isle of Palms that includes Lucas's lots. S.C.Code Ann. § 48–39–280(A)(2) (Supp.1988). In action not challenged here, the Council fixed this baseline landward of Lucas's parcels. That was significant, for under the Act construction of occupiable improvements was flatly prohibited seaward of a line drawn 20 feet landward of, and parallel to, the baseline. § 48–39–290(A). The Act provided no exceptions.

Lucas promptly filed suit in the South Carolina Court of Common Pleas, contending that the Beachfront Management Act's construction bar effected a taking of his property without just compensation. Lucas did not take issue with the validity of the Act as a lawful exercise of South Carolina's police power, but contended that the Act's complete extinguishment of his property's value entitled him to compensation regardless of whether the legislature had acted in furtherance of legitimate police power objectives. Following a bench trial, the court agreed. Among its factual determinations was the finding that "at the time Lucas purchased the two lots, both were zoned for single-family residential construction and ... there were no restrictions imposed upon such use of the property by either the State of South Carolina, the County of Charleston, or the Town of the Isle of Palms." The trial court further found that the Beachfront Management Act decreed a permanent ban on construction insofar as Lucas's lots were concerned, and that this prohibition "deprive[d] Lucas of any reasonable economic use of the lots, ... eliminated the unrestricted right of use, and render[ed] them value-less." The court thus concluded that Lucas's properties had been "tak-en" by operation of the Act, and it ordered respondent to pay "just compensation" in the amount of $1,232,387.50.

The Supreme Court of South Carolina reversed. It found dispositive what it described as Lucas's concession "that the Beachfront Manage-ment Act [was] properly and validly designed to preserve ... South Carolina's beaches." 404 S.E.2d 895, 896 (1991). Failing an attack on the validity of the statute as such, the court believed itself bound to accept the "uncontested ... findings" of the South Carolina Legislature that new construction in the coastal zone—such as petitioner intended— threatened this public resource. *Id.* at 898. The court ruled that when a regulation respecting the use of property is designed "to prevent serious public harm," *id.* at 899 (citing, *inter alia*, *Mugler v. Kansas*, 123 U.S. 623 (1887)), no compensation is owing under the Takings Clause regard-less of the regulation's effect on the property's value.

Two justices dissented. They acknowledged that our *Mugler* line of cases recognizes governmental power to prohibit "noxious" uses of property—*i.e.*, uses of property akin to "public nuisances"—without having to pay compensation. But they would not have characterized the Beachfront Management Act's "primary purpose [as] the prevention of a nuisance." 404 S.E.2d, at 906 (Harwell, J., dissenting). To the dissenters, the chief purposes of the legislation, among them the promotion of tourism and the creation of a "habitat for indigenous flora and fauna," could not fairly be compared to nuisance abatement. *Id.* at 906. As a consequence, they would have affirmed the trial court's conclusion that the Act's obliteration of the value of petitioner's lots accomplished a taking. . . .

Prior to Justice Holmes' exposition in *Pennsylvania Coal Co. v. Mahon*, 260 U.S. 393 (1922), it was generally thought that the Takings Clause reached only a "direct appropriation" of property, *Legal Tender Cases*, 12 Wall. 457, 551, 20 L.Ed. 287 (1871), or the functional equiva-lent of a "practical ouster of [the owner's] possession," *Transportation Co. v. Chicago*, 99 U.S. 635, 642 (1879). Justice Holmes recognized in *Mahon*, however, that if the protection against physical appropriations of private property was to be meaningfully enforced, the government's power to redefine the range of interests included in the ownership of property was necessarily constrained by constitutional limits. 260 U.S. at 414–415. If, instead, the uses of private property were subject to unbri-dled, uncompensated qualification under the police power, "the natural tendency of human nature [would be] to extend the qualification more and more until at last private property disappear[ed]." *Id.* at 415. These considerations gave birth in that case to the oft-cited maxim that, "while property may be regulated to a certain extent, if regulation goes too far it will be recognized as a taking." *Ibid.*

Nevertheless, our decision in *Mahon* offered little insight into when, and under what circumstances, a given regulation would be seen as going "too far" for purposes of the Fifth Amendment. In 70–odd years of succeeding "regulatory takings" jurisprudence, we have generally eschewed any "set formula" for determining how far is too far, preferring to "engag[e] in ... essentially ad hoc, factual inquiries." *Penn Central Transportation Co. v. New York City*, 438 U.S. 104, 124 (1978) (quoting *Goldblatt v. Hempstead*, 369 U.S. 590, 594 (1962)). *See* Epstein, *Takings: Descent and Resurrection*, 1987 S.Ct. Rev. 1, 4. We have, however, described at least two discrete categories of regulatory action as compensable without case-specific inquiry into the public interest advanced in support of the restraint. The first encompasses regulations that compel the property owner to suffer a physical "invasion" of his property. In general (at least with regard to permanent invasions), no matter how minute the intrusion, and no matter how weighty the public purpose behind it, we have required compensation. For example, in *Loretto v. Teleprompter Manhattan CATV Corp.*, 458 U.S. 419 (1982), we determined that New York's law requiring landlords to allow television cable companies to emplace cable facilities in their apartment buildings constituted a taking, even though the facilities occupied at most only 1–1/2 cubic feet of the landlords' property. *See also United States v. Causby*, 328 U.S. 256, 265 (1946) (physical invasions of airspace); *cf. Kaiser Aetna v. United States*, 444 U.S. 164 (1979) (imposition of navigational servitude upon private marina).

The second situation in which we have found categorical treatment appropriate is where regulation denies all economically beneficial or productive use of land. As we have said on numerous occasions, the Fifth Amendment is violated when land-use regulation "does not substantially advance legitimate state interests or denies an owner economically viable use of his land." *Agins* [*v. Tiburon*, 447 U.S. 255, 260 (1980)].[14]

---

14. Regrettably, the rhetorical force of our "deprivation of all economically feasible use" rule is greater than its precision, since the rule does not make clear the "property interest" against which the loss of value is to be measured. When, for example, a regulation requires a developer to leave 90% of a rural tract in its natural state, it is unclear whether we would analyze the situation as one in which the owner has been deprived of all economically beneficial use of the burdened portion of the tract, or as one in which the owner has suffered a mere diminution in value of the tract as a whole.... Unsurprisingly, this uncertainty regarding the composition of the denominator in our "deprivation" fraction has produced inconsistent pronouncements by the Court. *Compare Pennsylvania Coal Co. v. Mahon*, 260 U.S. 393, 414 (1922) (law restricting subsurface extraction of coal held to effect a taking), *with Keystone Bituminous Coal Assn. v. DeBenedictis*, 480 U.S. 470, 497–502 (1987) (nearly identical law held not to effect a taking); *see also id.*, at 515–520 (Rehnquist, C.J., dissenting); Rose, *Mahon Reconstructed: Why the Takings Issue is Still a Muddle*, 57 S.Cal.L.Rev. 561, 566–569 (1984). The answer to this difficult question may lie in how the owner's reasonable expectations have been shaped by the State's law of property—*i.e.*, whether and to what degree the State's law has accorded legal recognition and protection to the particular interest in land with respect to which the takings claimant alleges a diminution in (or elimination of) value. In any event, we avoid this difficulty in the present case, since the "interest in land" that Lucas has pleaded (a fee simple interest) is an

We have never set forth the justification for this rule. Perhaps it is simply, as Justice Brennan suggested, that total deprivation of beneficial use is, from the landowner's point of view, the equivalent of a physical appropriation. *See San Diego Gas & Electric Co. v. San Diego*, 450 U.S., at 652 (dissenting opinion). "[F]or what is the land but the profits thereof[?]" 1 E. Coke, Institutes, ch. 1, § 1 (1st Am. ed. 1812). Surely, at least, in the extraordinary circumstance when no productive or economically beneficial use of land is permitted, it is less realistic to indulge our usual assumption that the legislature is simply "adjusting the benefits and burdens of economic life," *Penn Central Transportation Co.*, 438 U.S., at 124, in a manner that secures an "average reciprocity of advantage" to everyone concerned, *Pennsylvania Coal Co. v. Mahon*, 260 U.S., at 415. And the functional basis for permitting the government, by regulation, to affect property values without compensation—that "Government hardly could go on if to some extent values incident to property could not be diminished without paying for every such change in the general law," *id.*, at 413—does not apply to the relatively rare situations where the government has deprived a landowner of all economically beneficial uses.

On the other side of the balance, affirmatively supporting a compensation requirement, is the fact that regulations that leave the owner of land without economically beneficial or productive options for its use—typically, as here, by requiring land to be left substantially in its natural state—carry with them a heightened risk that private property is being pressed into some form of public service under the guise of mitigating serious public harm. As Justice Brennan explained: "From the government's point of view, the benefits flowing to the public from preservation of open space through regulation may be equally great as from creating a wildlife refuge through formal condemnation or increasing electricity production through a dam project that floods private property." *San Diego Gas & Elec. Co., supra*, 450 U.S., at 652 (dissenting opinion). The many statutes on the books, both state and federal, that provide for the use of eminent domain to impose servitudes on private scenic lands preventing developmental uses, or to acquire such lands altogether, suggest the practical equivalence in this setting of negative regulation and appropriation. . . .

We think, in short, that there are good reasons for our frequently expressed belief that when the owner of real property has been called upon to sacrifice all economically beneficial uses in the name of the common good, that is, to leave his property economically idle, he has suffered a taking.[15]

estate with a rich tradition of protection at common law, and since the South Carolina Court of Common Pleas found that the Beachfront Management Act left each of Lucas's beachfront lots without economic value.

15. Justice Stevens criticizes the "deprivation of all economically beneficial use" rule as "wholly arbitrary," in that "[the] landowner whose property is diminished in value 95% recovers nothing," while the landowner who suffers a complete elimination of value "recovers the land's full val-

The trial court found Lucas's two beachfront lots to have been rendered valueless by respondent's enforcement of the coastal-zone construction ban. Under Lucas's theory of the case, which rested upon our "no economically viable use" statements, that finding entitled him to compensation. Lucas believed it unnecessary to take issue with either the purposes behind the Beachfront Management Act, or the means chosen by the South Carolina Legislature to effectuate those purposes. The South Carolina Supreme Court, however, thought otherwise. In its view, the Beachfront Management Act was no ordinary enactment, but involved an exercise of South Carolina's "police powers" to mitigate the harm to the public interest that petitioner's use of his land might occasion. By neglecting to dispute the findings enumerated in the Act or otherwise to challenge the legislature's purposes, petitioner "concede[d] that the beach/dune area of South Carolina's shores is an extremely valuable public resource; that the erection of new construction, inter alia, contributes to the erosion and destruction of this public resource; and that discouraging new construction in close proximity to the beach/ dune area is necessary to prevent a great public harm." 404 S.E.2d at 898. In the court's view, these concessions brought petitioner's challenge within a long line of this Court's cases sustaining against Due Process and Takings Clause challenges the State's use of its "police powers" to enjoin a property owner from activities akin to public nuisances.

It is correct that many of our prior opinions have suggested that "harmful or noxious uses" of property may be proscribed by government regulation without the requirement of compensation. For a number of reasons, however, we think the South Carolina Supreme Court was too quick to conclude that that principle decides the present case. The "harmful or noxious uses" principle was the Court's early attempt to describe in theoretical terms why government may, consistent with the Takings Clause, affect property values by regulation without incurring an obligation to compensate—a reality we nowadays acknowledge explicitly with respect to the full scope of the State's police power. We made this very point in *Penn Central Transportation Co.*, where, in the course of sustaining New York City's landmarks preservation program against a takings challenge, we rejected the petitioner's suggestion that *Mugler* and the cases following it were premised on, and thus limited by, some objective conception of "noxiousness":

ue." This analysis errs in its assumption that the landowner whose deprivation is one step short of complete is not entitled to compensation. Such an owner might not be able to claim the benefit of our categorical formulation, but, as we have acknowledged time and again, "[t]he economic impact of the regulation on the claimant and . . . the extent to which the regulation has interfered with distinct investment-backed expectations" are keenly relevant to takings analysis generally. *Penn Central Transportation Co. v. New York City*, 438 U.S. 104,

124 (1978). It is true that in at least some cases the landowner with 95% loss will get nothing, while the landowner with total loss will recover in full. But that occasional result is no more strange than the gross disparity between the landowner whose premises are taken for a highway (who recovers in full) and the landowner whose property is reduced to 5% of its former value by the highway (who recovers nothing). Takings law is full of these "all-or-nothing" situations.

[T]he uses in issue in *Hadacheck, Miller,* and *Goldblatt* were perfectly lawful in themselves. They involved no "blameworthiness, . . . moral wrongdoing or conscious act of dangerous risk-taking which induce[d society] to shift the cost to a pa[rt]icular individual." Sax, *Takings and the Police Power,* 74 Yale L.J. 36, 50 (1964). These cases are better understood as resting not on any supposed "noxious" quality of the prohibited uses but rather on the ground that the restrictions were reasonably related to the implementation of a policy—not unlike historic preservation—expected to produce a widespread public benefit and applicable to all similarly situated property. [438 U.S., at 133–134, n. 30.]

"Harmful or noxious use" analysis was, in other words, simply the progenitor of our more contemporary statements that "land-use regulation does not effect a taking if it 'substantially advance[s] legitimate state interests'. . . ." *Nollan [v. California Coastal Comm'n],* 483 U.S. at 834 (quoting *Agins v. Tiburon,* 447 U.S. at 260); *see also Penn Central Transportation Co., supra,* 438 U.S. at 127; *Euclid v. Ambler Realty Co.,* 272 U.S. 365, 387–388 (1926).

The transition from our early focus on control of "noxious" uses to our contemporary understanding of the broad realm within which government may regulate without compensation was an easy one, since the distinction between "harm-preventing" and "benefit-conferring" regulation is often in the eye of the beholder. It is quite possible, for example, to describe in either fashion the ecological, economic, and esthetic concerns that inspired the South Carolina Legislature in the present case. One could say that imposing a servitude on Lucas's land is necessary in order to prevent his use of it from "harming" South Carolina's ecological resources; or, instead, in order to achieve the "benefits" of an ecological preserve. Whether one or the other of the competing characterizations will come to one's lips in a particular case depends primarily upon one's evaluation of the worth of competing uses of real estate. A given restraint will be seen as mitigating "harm" to the adjacent parcels or securing a "benefit" for them, depending upon the observer's evaluation of the relative importance of the use that the restraint favors. Whether Lucas's construction of single-family residences on his parcels should be described as bringing "harm" to South Carolina's adjacent ecological resources thus depends principally upon whether the describer believes that the State's use interest in nurturing those resources is so important that any competing adjacent use must yield.[16]

16. In Justice Blackmun's view, even with respect to regulations that deprive an owner of all developmental or economically beneficial land uses, the test for required compensation is whether the legislature has recited a harm-preventing justification for its action. Since such a justification can be formulated in practically every case, this amounts to a test of whether the legislature has a stupid staff. We think the Takings Clause requires courts to do more than insist upon artful harm-preventing characterizations.

When it is understood that "prevention of harmful use" was merely our early formulation of the police power justification necessary to sustain (without compensation) any regulatory diminution in value; and that the distinction between regulation that "prevents harmful use" and that which "confers benefits" is difficult, if not impossible, to discern on an objective, value-free basis; it becomes self-evident that noxious-use logic cannot serve as a touchstone to distinguish regulatory "takings"— which require compensation—from regulatory deprivations that do not require compensation. *A fortiori* the legislature's recitation of a noxious-use justification cannot be the basis for departing from our categorical rule that total regulatory takings must be compensated. If it were, departure would virtually always be allowed. The South Carolina Supreme Court's approach would essentially nullify *Mahon's* affirmation of limits to the noncompensable exercise of the police power. Our cases provide no support for this: None of them that employed the logic of "harmful use" prevention to sustain a regulation involved an allegation that the regulation wholly eliminated the value of the claimant's land. *See Keystone Bituminous Coal Assn.*, 480 U.S., at 513–514 (Rehnquist C.J., dissenting).

Where the State seeks to sustain regulation that deprives land of all economically beneficial use, we think it may resist compensation only if the logically antecedent inquiry into the nature of the owner's estate shows that the proscribed use interests were not part of his title to begin with. This accords, we think, with our "takings" jurisprudence, which has traditionally been guided by the understandings of our citizens regarding the content of, and the State's power over, the "bundle of rights" that they acquire when they obtain title to property. It seems to us that the property owner necessarily expects the uses of his property to be restricted, from time to time, by various measures newly enacted by the State in legitimate exercise of its police powers; "[a]s long recognized, some values are enjoyed under an implied limitation and must yield to the police power." *Pennsylvania Coal Co. v. Mahon*, 260 U.S. at 413. And in the case of personal property, by reason of the State's traditionally high degree of control over commercial dealings, he ought to be aware of the possibility that new regulation might even render his property economically worthless (at least if the property's only economically productive use is sale or manufacture for sale). *See Andrus v. Allard*, 444 U.S. 51, 66–67 (1979) (prohibition on sale of eagle feathers). In the case of land, however, we think the notion pressed by the Council that title is somehow held subject to the "implied limitation" that the State may subsequently eliminate all economically valuable use is inconsistent with the historical compact recorded in the Takings Clause that has become part of our constitutional culture.

Where "permanent physical occupation" of land is concerned, we have refused to allow the government to decree it anew (without compensation), no matter how weighty the asserted "public interests" involved, *Loretto v. Teleprompter Manhattan CATV Corp.*, 458 U.S., at 426—though we assuredly would permit the government to assert a permanent easement that was a pre-existing limitation upon the land-owner's title. We believe similar treatment must be accorded confiscatory regulations, *i.e.*, regulations that prohibit all economically beneficial use of land: Any limitation so severe cannot be newly legislated or decreed (without compensation), but must inhere in the title itself, in the restrictions that background principles of the State's law of property and nuisance already place upon land ownership. A law or decree with such an effect must, in other words, do no more than duplicate the result that could have been achieved in the courts—by adjacent landowners (or other uniquely affected persons) under the State's law of private nuisance, or by the State under its complementary power to abate nuisances that affect the public generally, or otherwise.

On this analysis, the owner of a lake-bed, for example, would not be entitled to compensation when he is denied the requisite permit to engage in a landfilling operation that would have the effect of flooding others' land. Nor the corporate owner of a nuclear generating plant, when it is directed to remove all improvements from its land upon discovery that the plant sits astride an earthquake fault. Such regulatory action may well have the effect of eliminating the land's only economically productive use, but it does not proscribe a productive use that was previously permissible under relevant property and nuisance principles. The use of these properties for what are now expressly prohibited purposes was always unlawful, and (subject to other constitutional limitations) it was open to the State at any point to make the implication of those background principles of nuisance and property law explicit. *See* Michelman, *Property, Utility, and Fairness, Comments on the Ethical Foundations of "Just Compensation" Law*, 80 Harv.L.Rev. 1165, 1239–1241 (1967). In light of our traditional resort to "existing rules or understandings that stem from an independent source such as state law" to define the range of interests that qualify for protection as "property" under the Fifth and Fourteenth Amendments, this recognition that the Takings Clause does not require compensation when an owner is barred from putting land to a use that is proscribed by those "existing rules or understandings" is surely unexceptional. When, however, a regulation that declares "off-limits" all economically productive or beneficial uses of land goes beyond what the relevant background principles would dictate, compensation must be paid to sustain it.

The "total taking" inquiry we require today will ordinarily entail (as the application of state nuisance law ordinarily entails) analysis of, among other things, the degree of harm to public lands and resources, or adjacent private property, posed by the claimant's proposed activities, *see, e.g.*, Restatement (Second) of Torts §§ 826, 827, the social value of the claimant's activities and their suitability to the locality in question, *see, e.g., id.*, §§ 828(a) and (b), 831, and the relative ease with which the alleged harm can be avoided through measures taken by the claimant and the government (or adjacent private landowners) alike, *see, e.g., id.*, §§ 827(e), 828(c), 830. The fact that a particular use has long been engaged in by similarly situated owners ordinarily imports a lack of any common-law prohibition (though changed circumstances or new knowledge may make what was previously permissible no longer so, *see id.,* § 827, Comment g). So also does the fact that other landowners, similarly situated, are permitted to continue the use denied to the claimant.

It seems unlikely that common-law principles would have prevented the erection of any habitable or productive improvements on petitioner's land; they rarely support prohibition of the "essential use" of land, *Curtin v. Benson,* 222 U.S. 78, 86 (1911). The question, however, is one of state law to be dealt with on remand. We emphasize that to win its case South Carolina must do more than proffer the legislature's declaration that the uses Lucas desires are inconsistent with the public interest, or the conclusory assertion that they violate a common-law maxim such as *sic utere tuo ut alienum non laedas.* As we have said, a "State, by ipse dixit, may not transform private property into public property without compensation...." *Webb's Fabulous Pharmacies, Inc. v. Beckwith,* 449 U.S. 155, 164 (1980). Instead, as it would be required to do if it sought to restrain Lucas in a common-law action for public nuisance, South Carolina must identify background principles of nuisance and property law that prohibit the uses he now intends in the circumstances in which the property is presently found. Only on this showing can the State fairly claim that, in proscribing all such beneficial uses, the Beachfront Management Act is taking nothing.[17]

The judgment is reversed, and the case is remanded for proceedings not inconsistent with this opinion. So ordered....

JUSTICE BLACKMUN, dissenting. Today the Court launches a missile to kill a mouse.

The State of South Carolina prohibited petitioner Lucas from building a permanent structure on his property from 1988 to 1990. Relying on an unreviewed (and implausible) state trial court finding that this restriction left Lucas' property valueless, this Court granted review to determine whether compensation must be paid in cases where the State prohibits all economic use of real estate. According to the Court, such an occasion never has arisen in any of our prior cases, and the Court imagines that it will arise "relatively rarely" or only in "extraordinary circumstances." Almost certainly it did not happen in this case.

Nonetheless, the Court presses on to decide the issue, and as it does, it ignores its jurisdictional limits, remakes its traditional rules of review, and creates simultaneously a new categorical rule and an exception (neither of which is rooted in our prior case law, common law, or

---

17. Justice Blackmun decries our reliance on background nuisance principles at least in part because he believes those principles to be as manipulable as we find the "harm prevention"/"benefit conferral" dichotomy. There is no doubt some leeway in a court's interpretation of what existing state law permits—but not remotely as much, we think, as in a legislative crafting of the reasons for its confiscatory regulation. We stress that an affirmative decree eliminating all economically beneficial uses may be defended only if an objectively reasonable application of relevant precedents would exclude those beneficial uses in the circumstances in which the land is presently found.

common sense). I protest not only the Court's decision, but each step taken to reach it. More fundamentally, I question the Court's wisdom in issuing sweeping new rules to decide such a narrow case. . . .

Petitioner Lucas is a contractor, manager, and part owner of the Wild Dune development on the Isle of Palms. He has lived there since 1978. In December 1986, he purchased two of the last four pieces of vacant property in the development.[18] The area is notoriously unstable. In roughly half of the last 40 years, all or part of petitioner's property was part of the beach or flooded twice daily by the ebb and flow of the tide. Between 1957 and 1963, petitioner's property was under water. Between 1963 and 1973 the shoreline was 100 to 150 feet onto petitioner's property. In 1973 the first line of stable vegetation was about halfway through the property. Between 1981 and 1983, the Isle of Palms issued 12 emergency orders for sandbagging to protect property in the Wild Dune development. Determining that local habitable structures were in imminent danger of collapse, the Council issued permits for two rock revetments to protect condominium developments near petitioner's property from erosion; one of the revetments extends more than halfway onto one of his lots. . . .

The Beachfront Management Act includes a finding by the South Carolina General Assembly that the beach/dune system serves the purpose of "protect[ing] life and property by serving as a storm barrier which dissipates wave energy and contributes to shoreline stability in an economical and effective manner." S.C.Code Ann. § 48–39–250(1)(a) (Supp.1990). The General Assembly also found that "development unwisely has been sited too close to the [beach/dune] system. This type of development has jeopardized the stability of the beach/dune system, accelerated erosion, and endangered adjacent property." § 48–39–250(4); *see also* § 48–39–250(6) (discussing the need to "afford the beach/dune system space to accrete and erode").

If the state legislature is correct that the prohibition on building in front of the setback line prevents serious harm, then, under this Court's prior cases, the Act is constitutional. "Long ago it was recognized that all property in this country is held under the implied obligation that the owner's use of it shall not be injurious to the community, and the Takings Clause did not transform that principle to one that requires compensation whenever the State asserts its power to enforce it." *Keystone Bituminous Coal Assn. v. DeBenedictis*, 480 U.S. 470, 491–492 (1987). The Court consistently has upheld regulations imposed to arrest a significant threat to the common welfare, whatever their economic effect on the owner. . . .

---

18. The properties were sold frequently at rapidly escalating prices before Lucas purchased them. Lot 22 was first sold in 1979 for $96,660, sold in 1984 for $187,500, then in 1985 for $260,000, and, finally, to Lucas in 1986 for $475,000. He estimated its worth in 1991 at $650,000. Lot 24 had a similar past. The record does not indicate who purchased the properties prior to Lucas, or why none of the purchasers held on to the lots and built on them.

Even if I agreed with the Court that there were no jurisdictional barriers to deciding this case, I still would not try to decide it. The Court creates its new takings jurisprudence based on the trial court's finding that the property had lost all economic value. This finding is almost certainly erroneous. Petitioner still can enjoy other attributes of ownership, such as the right to exclude others, "one of the most essential sticks in the bundle of rights that are commonly characterized as property." *Kaiser Aetna v. United States*, 444 U.S. 164, 176 (1979). Petitioner can picnic, swim, camp in a tent, or live on the property in a movable trailer. State courts frequently have recognized that land has economic value where the only residual economic uses are recreation or camping. *See, e.g., Turnpike Realty Co. v. Dedham*, 284 N.E.2d 891 (1972), *cert. denied*, 409 U.S. 1108 (1973); *Hall v. Board of Environmental Protection*, 528 A.2d 453 (Me.1987). Petitioner also retains the right to alienate the land, which would have value for neighbors and for those prepared to enjoy proximity to the ocean without a house. . . .

Yet the trial court, apparently believing that "less value" and "valueless" could be used interchangeably, found the property "valueless." The court accepted no evidence from the State on the property's value without a home, and petitioner's appraiser testified that he never had considered what the value would be absent a residence. The appraiser's value was based on the fact that the "highest and best use of these lots . . . [is] luxury single family detached dwellings." The trial court appeared to believe that the property could be considered "valueless" if it was not available for its most profitable use. Absent that erroneous assumption, I find no evidence in the record supporting the trial court's conclusion that the damage to the lots by virtue of the restrictions was "total." I agree with the Court that it has the power to decide a case that turns on an erroneous finding, but I question the wisdom of deciding an issue based on a factual premise that does not exist in this case, and in the judgment of the Court will exist in the future only in "extraordinary circumstance[s]." . . .

The Court's willingness to dispense with precedent in its haste to reach a result is not limited to its initial jurisdictional decision. The Court also alters the long-settled rules of review.

The South Carolina Supreme Court's decision to defer to legislative judgments in the absence of a challenge from petitioner comports with one of this Court's oldest maxims: "[T]he existence of facts supporting the legislative judgment is to be presumed." *United States v. Carolene Products Co.*, 304 U.S. 144, 152 (1938). Indeed, we have said the legislature's judgment is "well-nigh conclusive." *Berman v. Parker*, 348 U.S. 26, 32 (1954).

Accordingly, this Court always has required plaintiffs challenging the constitutionality of an ordinance to provide "some factual foundation of record" that contravenes the legislative findings. *O'Gorman & Young [v. Hartford Fire Ins. Co.*, 282 U.S. 251, 258 (1931)]. In the absence of such proof, "the presumption of constitutionality must prevail." *Id.* at 257. We only recently have reaffirmed that claimants have the burden of showing a state law constitutes a taking. *See Keystone Bituminous Coal*, 480 U.S. at 485.

Rather than invoking these traditional rules, the Court decides the State has the burden to convince the courts that its legislative judgments are correct. Despite Lucas' complete failure to contest the legislature's findings of serious harm to life and property if a permanent structure is built, the Court decides that the legislative findings are not sufficient to justify the use prohibition. Instead, the Court "emphasize[s]" the State must do more than merely proffer its legislative judgments to avoid invalidating its law. In this case, apparently, the State now has the burden of showing the regulation is not a taking. The Court offers no justification for its sudden hostility toward state legislators, and I doubt that it could....

The Court does not reject the South Carolina Supreme Court's decision simply on the basis of its disbelief and distrust of the legislature's findings. It also takes the opportunity to create a new scheme for regulations that eliminate all economic value. From now on, there is a categorical rule finding these regulations to be a taking unless the use they prohibit is a background common-law nuisance or property principle....

This Court repeatedly has recognized the ability of government, in certain circumstances, to regulate property without compensation no matter how adverse the financial effect on the owner may be....

The Court recognizes that "our prior opinions have suggested that 'harmful or noxious uses' of property may be proscribed by government regulation without the requirement of compensation," but seeks to reconcile them with its categorical rule by claiming that the Court never has upheld a regulation when the owner alleged the loss of all economic value. Even if the Court's factual premise were correct, its understanding of the Court's cases is distorted. In none of the cases did the Court suggest that the right of a State to prohibit certain activities without paying compensation turned on the availability of some residual valuable use.[19] Instead, the cases depended on whether the government interest was sufficient to prohibit the activity, given the significant private cost.

These cases rest on the principle that the State has full power to prohibit an owner's use of property if it is harmful to the public. "[S]ince no individual has a right to use his property so as to create a nuisance or otherwise harm others, the State has not 'taken' anything when it

---

19. *Miller v. Schoene*, 276 U.S. 272 (1928), is an example. In the course of demonstrating that apple trees are more valuable than red cedar trees, the Court noted that red cedar has "occasional use and value as lumber." *Id.* at 279. But the Court did not discuss whether the timber owned by the petitioner in that case was commercially salable, and nothing in the opinion suggests that the State's right to require uncompensated felling of the trees depended on any such salvage value. To the contrary, it is clear from its unanimous opinion that the *Schoene* Court would have sustained a law requiring the burning of cedar trees if that had been necessary to protect apple trees in which there was a public interest: The Court spoke of preferment of the public interest over the property interest of the individual, "to the extent even of its destruction." *Id.* at 280.

asserts its power to enjoin the nuisance-like activity." *Keystone Bituminous Coal*, 480 U.S., at 491, n.20. It would make no sense under this theory to suggest that an owner has a constitutionally protected right to harm others, if only he makes the proper showing of economic loss. . . .

Ultimately even the Court cannot embrace the full implications of its per se rule: It eventually agrees that there cannot be a categorical rule for a taking based on economic value that wholly disregards the public need asserted. Instead, the Court decides that it will permit a State to regulate all economic value only if the State prohibits uses that would not be permitted under "background principles of nuisance and property law."[20]

Until today, the Court explicitly had rejected the contention that the government's power to act without paying compensation turns on whether the prohibited activity is a common-law nuisance. The brewery closed in *Mugler* itself was not a common-law nuisance, and the Court specifically stated that it was the role of the legislature to determine what measures would be appropriate for the protection of public health and safety. In upholding the state action in *Miller*, the Court found it unnecessary to "weigh with nicety the question whether the infected cedars constitute a nuisance according to common law; or whether they may be so declared by statute." 276 U.S. at 280. Instead the Court has relied in the past, as the South Carolina court has done here, on legislative judgments of what constitutes a harm.

The Court rejects the notion that the State always can prohibit uses it deems a harm to the public without granting compensation because "the distinction between 'harm-preventing' and 'benefit-conferring' regulation is often in the eye of the beholder." Since the characterization will depend "primarily upon one's evaluation of the worth of competing uses of real estate," the Court decides a legislative judgment of this kind no longer can provide the desired "objective, value-free basis" for upholding a regulation. The Court, however, fails to explain how its proposed common-law alternative escapes the same trap.

The threshold inquiry for imposition of the Court's new rule, "deprivation of all economically valuable use," itself cannot be determined objectively. As the Court admits, whether the owner has been deprived of all economic value of his property will depend on how "property" is defined. The "composition of the denominator in our 'deprivation' fraction," is the dispositive inquiry. Yet there is no "objective" way to define what that denominator should be. "We have long understood that any

---

20. Although it refers to state nuisance and property law, the Court apparently does not mean just any state nuisance and property law. Public nuisance was first a common-law creation, see Newark, *The Boundaries of Nuisance*, 65 L.Q.Rev. 480, 482 (1949) (attributing development of nuisance to 1535), but by the 1800's in both the United States and England, legislatures had the power to define what is a public nuisance, and particular uses often have been selectively targeted. *See* Prosser, *Private Action for Public Nuisance*, 52 Va. L.Rev. 997, 999–1000 (1966); J. Stephen, A General View of the Criminal Law of England 105–107 (2d ed. 1890). The Court's references to "common-law" background principles, however, indicate that legislative determinations do not constitute "state nuisance and property law" for the Court.

land-use regulation can be characterized as the 'total' deprivation of an aptly defined entitlement.... Alternatively, the same regulation can always be characterized as a mere 'partial' withdrawal from full, unencumbered ownership of the landholding affected by the regulation...." Michelman, *Takings*, 1987, 88 Colum.L.Rev. 1600, 1614 (1988)....

Even more perplexing, however, is the Court's reliance on common-law principles of nuisance in its quest for a value-free takings jurisprudence. In determining what is a nuisance at common law, state courts make exactly the decision that the Court finds so troubling when made by the South Carolina General Assembly today: They determine whether the use is harmful. Common-law public and private nuisance law is simply a determination whether a particular use causes harm. *See* Prosser, *Private Action for Public Nuisance*, 52 Va.L.Rev. 997, 997 (1966) ("Nuisance is a French word which means nothing more than harm"). There is nothing magical in the reasoning of judges long dead. They determined a harm in the same way as state judges and legislatures do today. If judges in the 18th and 19th centuries can distinguish a harm from a benefit, why not judges in the 20th century, and if judges can, why not legislators? There simply is no reason to believe that new interpretations of the hoary common-law nuisance doctrine will be particularly "objective" or "value free." Once one abandons the level of generality of *sic utere tuo ut alienum non laedas*, one searches in vain, I think, for anything resembling a principle in the common law of nuisance....

Finally, the Court justifies its new rule that the legislature may not deprive a property owner of the only economically valuable use of his land, even if the legislature finds it to be a harmful use, because such action is not part of the "long recognized" "understandings of our citizens." These "understandings" permit such regulation only if the use is a nuisance under the common law. Any other course is "inconsistent with the historical compact recorded in the Takings Clause." It is not clear from the Court's opinion where our "historical compact" or "citizens' understanding" comes from, but it does not appear to be history....

[Editors' Note: Justice Blackmun disagreed with Justice Scalia's historical analysis in several respects. First, Justice Blackmun noted that "[t]he principle that the State should compensate individuals for property taken for public use was not widely established in America at the time of the Revolution," observing that in the early 19th Century, state governments often took property for roads and other public projects without paying compensation to the owners. Second, he noted that throughout the 19th Century, judges held that "the Constitution protected possession only, and not value." Third, he noted that "state courts historically have been less likely to find that a government action constitutes a taking when the affected land is undeveloped." Finally, he observed that "history does [not] indicate any common-law limit on the State's power to regulate harmful uses even to the point of destroying all economic value," noting that "[n]othing in the discussions in Congress concerning the Takings Clause indicates that the Clause was limited by the common-law nuisance doctrine."]

In short, I find no clear and accepted "historical compact" or "understanding of our citizens" justifying the Court's new takings doctrine. Instead, the Court seems to treat history as a grab bag of principles, to be adopted where they support the Court's theory, and ignored where they do not. If the Court decided that the early common law provides the background principles for interpreting the Takings Clause, then regulation, as opposed to physical confiscation, would not be compensable. If the Court decided that the law of a later period provides the background principles, then regulation might be compensable, but the Court would have to confront the fact that legislatures regularly determined which uses were prohibited, independent of the common law, and independent of whether the uses were lawful when the owner purchased. What makes the Court's analysis unworkable is its attempt to package the law of two incompatible eras and peddle it as historical fact....

Notes

1. *Categorical or "Per Se" Takings.* Justice Scalia's opinion identifies two categories of *per se* takings—physical takings (as exemplified by *Loretto*) and regulatory takings that deny a landowner all economic value associated with her land (as exemplified by *Lucas*). What is the legal significance of identifying a regulation as a *per se* or categorical taking? What is the relationship between these categorical tests and *Penn Central*'s three-factor test? If you were a bringing a lawsuit on behalf of a landowner, which test would you try to argue first? Which test would be your fall-back position?

Thinking more critically, is Justice Scalia's second category of takings really a *per se* test? Is it accurate to say that *Lucas* creates a new category of *per se* takings when a regulation causes 100% diminishment in value, or does the "background principles of state law of property and nuisance" exception effectively mean that the *Lucas* formula cannot function as a *per se* rule? Alternatively, is it possible to argue that *Lucas* establishes *three* categorical rules?

2. *Character of the Governmental Action Revisited.* The *Lucas* opinion revisits the harm/benefit distinction evident in the majority and dissenting opinions in *Penn Central*. Justice Scalia's opinion initially rejects the harm/benefit rationale as a conceptual foundation for regulatory takings law (pages 954–56). Subsequently (page 957), however, Justice Scalia notes that even when a regulation deprives a landowner of all economically feasible use, the state need not provide compensation if the regulation's limitation on use inheres "in the title itself, in the restrictions that background principles of the State's law of property and nuisance already place upon land ownership." Conceptually, does this "exception" reintroduce the very harm/benefit distinction Scalia labored so hard to eliminate? Reflect carefully on the limitations contained in the "State law of property and nuisance" exception to a "total taking." Why do you think Justice Scalia finds this more palatable than the "harm/benefit" distinction discussed earlier in his opinion

and emphasized in Justice Blackmun's dissent? [In answering this question, think about who will decide whether a limitation inheres in the "State's law of property and nuisance."]

3. *Much Ado About Nothing?* As noted in Justice Blackmun's dissent, the factual and procedural record on which *Lucas* came to the Court may suggest that *Lucas* is a decision of little significance. Rarely will there occur a situation in which a regulation deprives a parcel of "all economically feasible use," because even land incapable of development typically has some residual value. So why did Justice Scalia and the dissenting justices spend so much time talking about the "background principles of state property and nuisance law"? What do you think Justice Scalia might have been trying to accomplish more broadly in the realm of regulatory takings jurisprudence by eviscerating the "harm/benefit" distinction and creating the "background principles" concept?

4. *Legislative Efforts to Protect Property Rights.* In addition to challenging government regulations through judicial actions, property rights advocates also have turned to state legislatures and Congress seeking greater protection for private property. These efforts resulted in the enactment of property rights legislation in nearly 20 states by 1995. These statutes generally take one of two forms. Most are *assessment* statutes, which simply compel state agencies to assess whether regulations will result in a regulatory taking under the existing interpretations of the state and federal constitutions. Five states passed *compensation* statutes, which provide that if a state regulation diminishes value by more than a certain percentage, the state must compensate the affected landowners. Jerome M. Organ, *Understanding State and Federal Property Rights Legislation*, 48 Okla. L. Rev. 191, 199–211 (1995). What does a state legislature accomplish by passing an "assessment" statute? If you were a "property rights" advocate, would you be satisfied by your state's enactment of an assessment statute? What different goals would a state legislature address by enacting a "compensation" statute?

Notably, most of these statutes do not apply to any regulations in effect when the statutes were enacted. *See, e.g.*, Fla. Stat. Ann. § 70.001(12); Tex. Govt. Code Ann. § 2007.003 (Vernon). How does such an approach square with Justice Scalia's suggestion in *Lucas* regarding the types of regulations that inhere in title under state property and nuisance law?

5. *Reasonable Investment–Backed Expectations Revisited.* In *Palazzolo v. Rhode Island*, 533 U.S. 606, 121 S.Ct. 2448, 150 L.Ed.2d 592 (2001), the Court addressed one of the questions left unanswered in *Lucas* concerning the parameters of the "background principles of state property and nuisance law" that inform a landowner's investment-backed expectations. Palazzolo owned a parcel of land containing both wetlands and an "upland" portion that was not implicated by wetland regulations. Palazzolo made two proposals to develop the wetlands with a beach house, but the Rhode Island Coastal Resources Management Council rejected both proposals pursuant to a statute, enacted prior to Palazzolo's purchase of the land, that allowed filling of the wetlands only for a "compelling public purpose." Palazzolo argued (under *Lucas*) that the regulation rendered the land valueless. In response, the State argued (a) that the land was not rendered valueless because the upland portion of the parcel was worth at least $200,000 for residential

development, and (b) that the statute predated Palazzolo's purchase, preventing him from claiming that he had legitimate investment-backed expectations in developing the parcel. The Rhode Island Supreme Court agreed with each of these arguments, and Palazzolo appealed to the U.S. Supreme Court.

In the state court's view, the statute predating Palazzolo's acquisition of the property was relevant in two ways—first, as a "background principle" of state law that would completely offset Palazzolo's claim that he had been deprived of all economic value of his property under the *Lucas* rule; and second, to demonstrate that Palazzolo lacked a reasonable investment-backed expectation under the *Penn Central* test. The U.S. Supreme Court rejected the first of these applications, stating that the mere enactment of a statute prior to a landowner's acquisition of title does not necessarily make the statute part of the "background principles of property and nuisance law" for subsequent owners. In reaching this conclusion, the Court noted that a regulation "cannot be a background principle for some owners but not for others." The Court agreed, however, with the Rhode Island Supreme Court's determination that the remaining value of Palazzolo's land defeated his *Lucas* claim. Accordingly, the Court remanded the case for reconsideration of the *Penn Central* three-factor analysis.

Left unresolved, however, was exactly how the statute predating Palazzolo's acquisition should be treated under the *Penn Central* test. In a concurring opinion, Justice O'Connor cautioned against reading too much into the majority decision, stating that:

> Today's holding does not mean that the timing of the regulation's enactment relative to the acquisition of title is immaterial to the *Penn Central* analysis. Indeed, it would be just as much error to expunge this consideration from the takings inquiry as it would be to accord it exclusive significance. Our polestar instead remains the principles set forth in *Penn Central* itself and our other cases that govern partial regulatory takings. Under these cases, interference with investment-backed expectations is one of a number of factors that a court must examine. Further, the regulatory regime in place at the time the claimant acquires the property at issue helps to shape the reasonableness of those expectations. [533 U.S. at 633.]

Justice Scalia, however, argued that the pre-acquisition existence of a regulation "should have no bearing upon the determination of whether the restriction is so substantial as to constitute a taking"—unless the restriction qualifies as one of the "background principles of the State's law of property and nuisance" under *Lucas*. *Id.* at 637. Who has the better of this argument? If you were the judge hearing this case on remand, how would you proceed?

6. *The Denominator Issue Revisited.* The *Lucas* case intensified the debate over the proper denominator to be used in determining the economic impact of a regulation. [Can you explain why?] The issue resurfaced—with a twist—in *Tahoe-Sierra Preservation Council, Inc. v. Tahoe Regional Planning Agency*, 535 U.S. 302, 122 S.Ct. 1465, 152 L.Ed.2d 517 (2002). As a result of two moratoria issued by the planning agency, all development was prohibited for a period of 32 months while the agency attempted to develop a plan for environmentally sound growth on Lake Tahoe. A group of landown-

ers brought a *Lucas* claim, alleging that they had been completely deprived of all economic value of their property for the 32–month period. Before reading on, can you see how the denominator analysis applies in that situation?

A majority of the Supreme Court reiterated the "whole parcel" denominator concept used in *Penn Central*. Even though the moratorium prevented all economic development of the parcel for the entire 32 months, the Court noted that the economic impact had to be compared not against the 32–month time period, but against the entire potential duration of possession and use associated with the fee simple estate. In a dissent, however, Justice Thomas (joined by Justice Scalia) argued that the denominator is the 32–month "temporal slice" of the property's infinite life. In their view, the case fell under the *Lucas* rule because the moratorium constituted a total deprivation of economic value during that time period.

7. *Ripeness—Of Finality and Exhaustion of State Remedies.* Before reaching the merits of the case, the *Lucas* Court determined that the case was ripe for review even though the South Carolina legislature enacted a variance option following the commencement of the case that Lucas conceivably could have pursued.

The Court had addressed the ripeness requirements for pursuing a takings claim in federal court in two cases in the mid–1980s. In *Williamson County Regional Planning Commission v. Hamilton Bank of Johnson City*, 473 U.S. 172, 105 S.Ct. 3108, 87 L.Ed.2d 126 (1985), the Court gave two reasons why the takings claim in that case was not "ripe" for decision. First, the developer had not gotten a "final" determination about what would be allowed by the county because the developer never sought a variance (which might have addressed many of the inconsistencies between the developer's plans and the county ordinances). Second, the developer had not pursued an inverse condemnation action in state court. Because state regulation can amount to a regulatory taking only if the state fails to provide just compensation, the Court reasoned that the developer could not meet this test without first pursuing an action for compensation in state court.

In *MacDonald, Sommer & Frates v. Yolo County*, 477 U.S. 340, 106 S.Ct. 2561, 91 L.Ed.2d 285 (1986), the Court similarly rejected a developer's claim on ripeness grounds because the developer had not shown that the planning commission would have rejected less intense forms of development. In so holding, however, the Court suggested that in some instances, pursuing revised plans might be futile and therefore unnecessary. This futility exception manifested itself in *City of Monterey v. Del Monte Dunes at Monterey, Ltd.*, 526 U.S. 687, 119 S.Ct. 1624, 143 L.Ed.2d 882 (1999), where a developer had refined and resubmitted its proposal several times to meet the city's ever-changing demands. The district court dismissed the claims as unripe, but the Ninth Circuit reversed, holding that "to require additional proposals would implicate the concerns expressed about repetitive and unfair procedures expressed in [*MacDonald*]." 526 U.S. at 698–99 (*citing* 920 F.2d at 1501–06). How did the Court apply these principles in the *Lucas* case?

Collectively, the ripeness cases establish significant procedural obstacles to federal court regulatory takings litigation—effectively forcing most landowners to exhaust all potential avenues for recourse under state and local land use regulation processes. Some questions for you to consider here: Is such an exhaustion requirement prudent where constitutional rights are at stake? How do *Williamson County* and *MacDonald* alter the bargaining positions of landowners and state and local governments? To what extent do *Williamson County* and *MacDonald* increase the "transaction costs" landowners can expect as they try to develop their land? In representing a developer, what could you do to accelerate the process for obtaining a final decision? If you were a rational planner acting on behalf of a county planning commission, how would you respond to a developer who asks: "What will you allow us to do?"

8. *Registration and Amortization of Nonconforming Uses.* Recall our discussion of termination of nonconforming uses through registration and/or amortization (page 907). Given what you have learned about regulatory takings, how would you evaluate whether a registration requirement for a nonconforming use or an amortization provision for a nonconforming use amounts to a regulatory taking? *See, e.g., United States v. Locke,* 471 U.S. 84, 105 S.Ct. 1785, 85 L.Ed.2d 64 (1985) (registration requirement for preservation of mining claims on federal land did not give rise to a taking); *Board of Zoning Appeals v. Leisz,* 702 N.E.2d 1026 (Ind. 1998) (registration requirement for nonconforming use was not a taking and ordinance amortizing nonconforming use was constitutional).

LAWYERING EXERCISE
(Client Counseling and Legal Analysis of Regulatory Takings)

SITUATION: Assume that Flanagan purchased 40 acres of land outside of Moosetown in 1975 for $40,000. Flanagan gradually began developing a subdivision, with roughly 28 one-acre lots being developed and sold by 1995—providing Flanagan a return of over $400,000 on his original $40,000 investment. As of 1995, Flanagan retained ownership of only three one-acre lots.

Garcia similarly purchased 40 acres of land outside of Moosetown in 1980, for a price of $50,000. Although portions of Garcia's land were relatively low-lying, the entire parcel was well-drained at the time of Garcia's purchase. As development ensued on surrounding parcels, however, changes in surface water runoff patterns resulted in the creation of a five-acre swampy area on Garcia's land. In 1995, Garcia hired a developer to create plans showing a handful of development options. Based on the developer's initial estimates, the most economically remunerative development would require between 25 and 30 lots of about one acre each, with a projected value of $750,000.

In 1996, the city of Moosetown annexed Flanagan's and Garcia's parcels (along with numerous others) in response to increasing development. The express objective of this annexation was to minimize urban sprawl by preserving existing open areas. After the annexation, Moosetown zoned about 27 acres of Garcia's land and half of Flanagan's remaining land in a residential zone, with a four-acre minimum lot size. Moosetown also placed Garcia's other 13 acres and the balance of

Flanagan's land—all of which was near a "walking/biking" trail—in an "open space" zone that permitted no structures. Further, the five-acre swampy area on Garcia's land (located within the residential zone) was also subject to an overlay wetlands zone, requiring the land to be maintained in its natural state. The annexation and zoning destroyed Garcia's development plans, limiting him to no more than five lots with a projected value of $125,000. The zoning and minimum lot size also effectively prevents Flanagan from building on his remaining three one-acre lots.

Garcia sought to have the parcel rezoned, but the city denied the rezoning request, as well as Garcia's subsequent request for a variance. Flanagan has not requested a variance.

TASKS: Garcia and Flanagan want to know whether they have a meaningful likelihood of success if they pursue a regulatory takings claim in federal court. How would you advise Garcia and Flanagan? What additional information, if any, would you want to obtain to advise them? *See Loveladies Harbor, Inc. v. United States*, 28 F.3d 1171 (Fed. Cir. 1994); *Allingham v. City of Seattle*, 109 Wash.2d 947, 749 P.2d 160 (1988). Would it be appropriate for you to represent both of them in their claims against the City? Why or why not? [Hint: To answer this question, you may wish to reconsider the conflict of interest materials presented at the end of Chapter 9 (pages 841–43).]

3. *Exactions and Impact Fees*

Many communities have begun to use zoning authority as a means to force private development to absorb a portion of the cost of public infrastructure needed to sustain that development. For example, a city considering a developer's request to subdivide land for residential development may try to "exact a price" for its approval. This "price" may take the form of an "impact fee" to help finance the cost of public infrastructure (such as roads, sewers, and schools) needed to address the "impact" caused by the additional development. Alternatively, this price may take the form of the landowner's agreement to dedicate (transfer title to) a portion of the land to the city for public purposes (such as a park, a school, or greenspace). In deciding whether such "exactions" amount to regulatory takings, the Supreme Court has developed a separate set of tests, reflected in the following two cases.

NOLLAN v. CALIFORNIA COASTAL COMMISSION

Supreme Court of the United States.
483 U.S. 825, 107 S.Ct. 3141, 97 L.Ed.2d 677 (1987).

JUSTICE SCALIA delivered the opinion of the Court.... The Nollans own a beachfront lot in Ventura County, California. A quarter-mile north of their property is Faria County Park, an oceanside public park with a public beach and recreation area. Another public beach area, known locally as "the Cove," lies 1,800 feet south of their lot. A concrete seawall approximately eight feet high separates the beach portion of the

Nollans' property from the rest of the lot. The historic mean high tide line determines the lot's oceanside boundary.

The Nollans originally leased their property with an option to buy. The building on the lot was a small bungalow, totaling 504 square feet, which for a time they rented to summer vacationers. After years of rental use, however, the building had fallen into disrepair, and could no longer be rented out.

The Nollans' option to purchase was conditioned on their promise to demolish the bungalow and replace it. In order to do so, under Cal.Pub. Res. Code Ann. §§ 30106, 30212, and 30600 (West 1986), they were required to obtain a coastal development permit from the California Coastal Commission. On February 25, 1982, they submitted a permit application to the Commission in which they proposed to demolish the existing structure and replace it with a three-bedroom house in keeping with the rest of the neighborhood.

The Nollans were informed that their application had been placed on the administrative calendar, and that the Commission staff had recommended that the permit be granted subject to the condition that they allow the public an easement to pass across a portion of their property bounded by the mean high tide line on one side, and their seawall on the other side. This would make it easier for the public to get to Faria County Park and the Cove. The Nollans protested imposition of the condition, but the Commission overruled their objections and granted the permit subject to their recordation of a deed restriction granting the easement.

On June 3, 1982, the Nollans filed a petition for writ of administrative mandamus asking the Ventura County Superior Court to invalidate the access condition. They argued that the condition could not be imposed absent evidence that their proposed development would have a direct adverse impact on public access to the beach. The court agreed, and remanded the case to the Commission for a full evidentiary hearing on that issue.

On remand, the Commission held a public hearing, after which it made further factual findings and reaffirmed its imposition of the condition. It found that the new house would increase blockage of the view of the ocean, thus contributing to the development of "a 'wall' of residential structures" that would prevent the public "psychologically ... from realizing a stretch of coastline exists nearby that they have every right to visit." The new house would also increase private use of the shorefront. These effects of construction of the house, along with other area development, would cumulatively "burden the public's ability to traverse to and along the shorefront." Therefore the Commission could properly require the Nollans to offset that burden by providing additional lateral access to the public beaches in the form of an easement across their property. The Commission also noted that it had similarly conditioned 43 out of 60 coastal development permits along the same tract of land, and that of the 17 not so conditioned, 14 had been approved when the Commission did not have administrative regulations in place allowing imposition of the condition, and the remaining 3 had not involved shorefront property. . . .

Had California simply required the Nollans to make an easement across their beachfront available to the public on a permanent basis in order to increase public access to the beach, rather than conditioning their permit to rebuild their house on their agreeing to do so, we have no doubt there would have been a taking. To say that the appropriation of a public easement across a landowner's premises does not constitute the taking of a property interest but rather (as Justice Brennan contends) "a mere restriction on its use," is to use words in a manner that deprives them of all their ordinary meaning. Indeed, one of the principal uses of the eminent domain power is to assure that the government be able to require conveyance of just such interests, so long as it pays for them. Perhaps because the point is so obvious, we have never been confronted with a controversy that required us to rule upon it, but our cases' analysis of the effect of other governmental action leads to the same conclusion. We have repeatedly held that, as to property reserved by its owner for private use, "the right to exclude [others is] 'one of the most essential sticks in the bundle of rights that are commonly characterized as property.' " *Loretto v. Teleprompter Manhattan CATV Corp.*, 458 U.S. 419, 433 (1982), quoting *Kaiser Aetna v. United States*, 444 U.S. 164, 176 (1979). In *Loretto* we observed that where governmental action results in "[a] permanent physical occupation" of the property, by the government itself or by others, *see* 458 U.S. at 432–433, n. 9, "our cases uniformly have found a taking to the extent of the occupation, without regard to whether the action achieves an important public benefit or has only minimal economic impact on the owner," *id.* at 434–435. We think a "permanent physical occupation" has occurred, for purposes of that rule, where individuals are given a permanent and continuous right to pass to and fro, so that the real property may continuously be traversed, even though no particular individual is permitted to station himself permanently upon the premises. . . .

Given, then, that requiring uncompensated conveyance of the easement outright would violate the Fourteenth Amendment, the question becomes whether requiring it to be conveyed as a condition for issuing a land-use permit alters the outcome. We have long recognized that land-use regulation does not effect a taking if it "substantially advance[s] legitimate state interests" and does not "den[y] an owner economically viable use of his land," *Agins v. Tiburon*, 447 U.S. 255 (1980). *See also Penn Central Transportation Co. v. New York City*, 438 U.S. 104, (1978) ("[A] use restriction may constitute a 'taking' if not reasonably necessary to the effectuation of a substantial government purpose"). Our cases have not elaborated on the standards for determining what constitutes a "legitimate state interest" or what type of connection between the regulation and the state interest satisfies the requirement that the former "substantially advance" the latter. They have made clear, however, that a broad range of governmental purposes and regulations satisfies these requirements. *See Agins v. Tiburon, supra*, 447 U.S., at 260–262 (scenic zoning); *Penn Central Transportation Co. v. New York City, supra* (landmark preservation); *Euclid v. Ambler Realty Co.*, 272 U.S. 365 (1926) (residential zoning). The Commission argues that among these permissible purposes are protecting the public's ability to see the beach, assisting the public in overcoming the "psychological barrier" to using the beach created by a developed shorefront, and preventing congestion on the public beaches. We assume, without deciding, that this is so—in which case the Commission unquestionably would be able to deny the Nollans their permit outright if their new house (alone, or by reason of the cumulative impact produced in conjunction with other construction) would substantially impede these purposes, unless the denial would interfere so drastically with the Nollans' use of their property as to constitute a taking.

The Commission argues that a permit condition that serves the same legitimate police-power purpose as a refusal to issue the permit should not be found to be a taking if the refusal to issue the permit would not constitute a taking. We agree. Thus, if the Commission attached to the permit some condition that would have protected the public's ability to see the beach notwithstanding construction of the new house—for example, a height limitation, a width restriction, or a ban on fences—so long as the Commission could have exercised its police power (as we have assumed it could) to forbid construction of the house altogether, imposition of the condition would also be constitutional. Moreover (and here we come closer to the facts of the present case), the condition would be constitutional even if it consisted of the requirement that the Nollans provide a viewing spot on their property for passersby with whose sighting of the ocean their new house would interfere. Although such a requirement, constituting a permanent grant of continuous access to the property, would have to be considered a taking if it were not attached to a development permit, the Commission's assumed power to forbid construction of the house in order to protect the public's view of the beach must surely include the power to condition construction upon some concession by the owner, even a concession of property rights, that serves the same end. If a prohibition designed to accomplish that purpose would be a legitimate exercise of the police power rather than a taking, it would be strange to conclude that providing the owner an alternative to that prohibition which accomplishes the same purpose is not.

The evident constitutional propriety disappears, however, if the condition substituted for the prohibition utterly fails to further the end advanced as the justification for the prohibition.... [H]ere, the lack of nexus between the condition and the original purpose of the building restriction converts that purpose to something other than what it was. The purpose then becomes, quite simply, the obtaining of an easement to serve some valid governmental purpose, but without payment of compensation. Whatever may be the outer limits of "legitimate state interests" in the takings and land-use context, this is not one of them. In short, unless the permit condition serves the same governmental purpose as the development ban, the building restriction is not a valid regulation of land use but "an out-and-out plan of extortion." *J.E.D. Associates, Inc. v. Atkinson*, 432 A.2d 12, 14–15 (1981). . . .

The Commission claims that it concedes as much, and that we may sustain the condition at issue here by finding that it is reasonably related to the public need or burden that the Nollans' new house creates or to which it contributes. We can accept, for purposes of discussion, the Commission's proposed test as to how close a "fit" between the condition and the burden is required, because we find that this case does not meet even the most untailored standards. The Commission's principal contention to the contrary essentially turns on a play on the word "access." The Nollans' new house, the Commission found, will interfere with "visual access" to the beach. That in turn (along with other shorefront development) will interfere with the desire of people who drive past the Nollans' house to use the beach, thus creating a "psychological barrier" to "access." The Nollans' new house will also, by a process not altogether clear from the Commission's opinion but presumably potent enough to more than offset the effects of the psychological barrier, increase the use of the public beaches, thus creating the need for more "access." These burdens on "access" would be alleviated by a requirement that the Nollans provide "lateral access" to the beach.

Rewriting the argument to eliminate the play on words makes clear that there is nothing to it. It is quite impossible to understand how a requirement that people already on the public beaches be able to walk across the Nollans' property reduces any obstacles to viewing the beach created by the new house. It is also impossible to understand how it lowers any "psychological barrier" to using the public beaches, or how it helps to remedy any additional congestion on them caused by construction of the Nollans' new house. We therefore find that the Commission's imposition of the permit condition cannot be treated as an exercise of its land-use power for any of these purposes. Our conclusion on this point is consistent with the approach taken by every other court that has considered the question, with the exception of the California state courts. . . .

We are left, then, with the Commission's justification for the access requirement unrelated to land-use regulation: "Finally, the Commission notes that there are several existing provisions of pass and repass lateral access benefits already given by past Faria Beach Tract applicants as a result of prior coastal permit decisions. The access required as a condition of this permit is part of a comprehensive program to provide continuous public access along Faria Beach as the lots undergo development or redevelopment." That is simply an expression of the Commission's belief that the public interest will be served by a continuous strip of publicly accessible beach along the coast. The Commission may well be right that it is a good idea, but that does not establish that the Nollans (and other coastal residents) alone can be compelled to contribute to its realization. Rather, California is free to advance its "comprehensive program," if it wishes, by using its power of eminent domain for this "public purpose," *see* U.S. Const., Amdt. 5; but if it wants an easement across the Nollans' property, it must pay for it.

Reversed.

JUSTICE BRENNAN, with whom JUSTICE MARSHALL joins, dissenting. Appellants in this case sought to construct a new dwelling on their beach lot that would both diminish visual access to the beach and move private development closer to the public tidelands. The Commission reasonably concluded that such "buildout," both individually and cumulatively, threatens public access to the shore. It sought to offset this encroachment by obtaining assurance that the public may walk along the shoreline in order to gain access to the ocean. The Court finds this an illegitimate exercise of the police power, because it maintains that there is no reasonable relationship between the effect of the development and the condition imposed.

The first problem with this conclusion is that the Court imposes a standard of precision for the exercise of a State's police power that has been discredited for the better part of this century. Furthermore, even under the Court's cramped standard, the permit condition imposed in this case directly responds to the specific type of burden on access created by appellants' development. Finally, a review of those factors deemed most significant in takings analysis makes clear that the Commission's action implicates none of the concerns underlying the Takings Clause. The Court has thus struck down the Commission's reasonable effort to respond to intensified development along the California coast, on behalf of landowners who can make no claim that their reasonable expectations have been disrupted. The Court has, in short, given appellants a windfall at the expense of the public. . . .

Notes

1. *Public Benefits and Private Burdens.* Prior to the decision in *Nollan,* California granted the public lateral access across the wet sand portion of the beach (beyond the high-water mark). With this in mind, if a beachgoer wished to go from Faria County Park to the Cove, what could they have done? What additional rights was the Commission seeking to obtain for beachgoers? How significant an impairment would the Nollans have experienced as a result of giving up these additional rights requested by the Commission?

2. *Exactions—Other Options for Preserving Viewing Access for the Public.* The *Nollan* Court concluded that the lack of nexus between the condition (requiring the Nollans to grant lateral access to the beach) and the original purpose of the building restriction (to limit impacts on "visual access") justified characterizing the city's condition as extortionate. In reaching this conclusion, the Court suggested that courts should accord less deference to a municipality's exercise of the police power for uncompensated physical invasions than for compensated ones. What justifies this reduction in deference?

The *Nollan* standard obviously implies that a municipality may impose an exaction without compensation if it can demonstrate an essential nexus between the exaction and the legitimate governmental interest that the municipality seeks to advance. Under what circumstances would an appropriate "nexus" exist to justify an exaction without compensation? Would height and width restrictions on any building have been allowable? What about an easement allowing the public to enter onto the Nollan property to view the ocean? An easement allowing direct access to the beach (rather than lateral access along the beach)? To what extent does the "essential nexus" test meaningfully constrain municipal efforts to impose appropriate conditions in permits for development?

3. *Exactions—Physical Invasions.* Applying the categorical rule regarding physical invasions reflected in *Loretto* and *Kaiser*, the Supreme Court began its analysis in *Nollan* with the following statement:

> Had California simply required the Nollans to make an easement across their beachfront available to the public on a permanent basis in order to increase public access to the beach, rather than conditioning their permit to rebuild their house on their agreeing to do so, we have no doubt there would have been a taking.

Given the categorical rule regarding physical invasions, why is it ever permissible for the government, as a condition to the granting of a permit, to require the landowner to give up their right to compensation for a physical invasion? What is the analytical premise on which the Court bases its conclusion that the Commission, under different circumstances, could have required the Nollans to provide an easement for viewing the ocean without compensating the Nollans? Does the Court's subsequent decision in *Lucas* erode this analytical premise? Why or why not?

4. *Sidewalks and Takings.* Assume you represent Cheever, a landowner seeking to develop a subdivision in Columbia, Missouri. The City of Columbia has established the goal of becoming a "walkable city," with a network of sidewalks on all residential streets if possible. As one of the conditions for approval of a subdivision, Columbia requires that the developer provide a system of sidewalks to permit the public to walk through the subdivision without having to walk in streets. Cheever doesn't want to provide the sidewalks. Cheever contacts you for advice on whether he can use *Nollan* as a basis to prevent Columbia from requiring sidewalks as a condition to his permit request. How would you advise him?

Now assume that you represent Laitos, a Columbia resident who owns a single lot with a modest two-bedroom bungalow. The lot does not have a sidewalk—because Laitos constructed the bungalow before Columbia began its sidewalk initiatives—but one of the neighboring lots has a sidewalk that comes up to the boundary between the two lots. Laitos seeks a building permit to expand the bungalow into a much roomier four-bedroom house. Columbia's building inspector conditions approval of Laitos's building permit upon Laitos's agreement to install a sidewalk and grant public access across the sidewalk. Laitos contacts you for advice on whether he can use *Nollan* as a basis to prevent Columbia from imposing this condition. How would you advise him?

DOLAN v. CITY OF TIGARD

Supreme Court of the United States.

512 U.S. 374, 114 S.Ct. 2309, 129 L.Ed.2d 304 (1994).

CHIEF JUSTICE REHNQUIST delivered the opinion of the Court. Petitioner challenges the decision of the Oregon Supreme Court which held that the city of Tigard could condition the approval of her building permit on the dedication of a portion of her property for flood control and traffic improvements. We granted certiorari to resolve a question left open by our decision in *Nollan v. California Coastal Comm'n* of what is the required degree of connection between the exactions imposed by the city and the projected impacts of the proposed development.

The State of Oregon enacted a comprehensive land use management program in 1973. Ore.Rev.Stat. §§ 197.005–197.860 (1991). The program required all Oregon cities and counties to adopt new comprehensive land use plans that were consistent with the statewide planning goals.... Pursuant to the State's requirements, the city of Tigard ... developed a comprehensive plan and codified it in its Community Development Code (CDC). The CDC requires property owners in the area zoned Central Business District to comply with a 15% open space and landscaping requirement, which limits total site coverage, including all structures and paved parking, to 85% of the parcel. After the completion of a transportation study that identified congestion in the Central Business District as a particular problem, the city adopted a plan for a pedestrian/bicycle pathway intended to encourage alternatives to automobile transportation for short trips. The CDC requires that new development facilitate this plan by dedicating land for pedestrian pathways where provided for in the pedestrian/bicycle pathway plan.[21]

The city also adopted a Master Drainage Plan (Drainage Plan). The Drainage Plan noted that flooding occurred in several areas along Fanno Creek, including areas near petitioner's property. The Drainage Plan also established that the increase in impervious surfaces associated with continued urbanization would exacerbate these flooding problems. To combat these risks, the Drainage Plan suggested a series of improvements to the Fanno Creek Basin, including channel excavation in the area next to petitioner's property. Other recommendations included ensuring that the floodplain remains free of structures and that it be preserved as greenways to minimize flood damage to structures. The Drainage Plan concluded that the cost of these improvements should be shared based on both direct and indirect benefits, with property owners

---

21. CDC § 18.86.040.A.1.b provides: "The development shall facilitate pedestrian/bicycle circulation if the site is located on a street with designated bikepaths or adjacent to a designated greenway/open space/park. Specific items to be addressed [include]: (i) Provision of efficient, convenient and continuous pedestrian and bicycle transit circulation systems, linking developments by requiring dedication and construction of pedestrian and bikepaths identified in the comprehensive plan. If direct connections cannot be made, require that funds in the amount of the construction cost be deposited into an account for the purpose of constructing paths."

along the waterways paying more due to the direct benefit that they would receive. . . .

Petitioner Florence Dolan owns a plumbing and electric supply store located on Main Street in the Central Business District of the city. The store covers approximately 9,700 square feet on the eastern side of a 1.67–acre parcel, which includes a gravel parking lot. Fanno Creek flows through the southwestern corner of the lot and along its western boundary. The year-round flow of the creek renders the area within the creek's 100–year floodplain virtually unusable for commercial development. The city's comprehensive plan includes the Fanno Creek floodplain as part of the city's greenway system.

Petitioner applied to the city for a permit to redevelop the site. Her proposed plans called for nearly doubling the size of the store to 17,600 square feet, and paving a 39–space parking lot. The existing store, located on the opposite side of the parcel, would be razed in sections as construction progressed on the new building. In the second phase of the project, petitioner proposed to build an additional structure on the northeast side of the site for complementary businesses, and to provide more parking. The proposed expansion and intensified use are consistent with the city's zoning scheme in the Central Business District. CDC § 18.66.030.

The City Planning Commission granted petitioner's permit application subject to conditions imposed by the city's CDC. The CDC establishes the following standard for site development review approval: "Where landfill and/or development is allowed within and adjacent to the 100–year floodplain, the city shall require the dedication of sufficient open land area for greenway adjoining and within the floodplain. This area shall include portions at a suitable elevation for the construction of a pedestrian/bicycle pathway within the floodplain in accordance with the adopted pedestrian/bicycle plan."

Thus, the Commission required that petitioner dedicate the portion of her property lying within the 100–year floodplain for improvement of a storm drainage system along Fanno Creek and that she dedicate an additional 15–foot strip of land adjacent to the floodplain as a pedestrian/bicycle pathway. The dedication required by that condition encompasses approximately 7,000 square feet, or roughly 10% of the property. In accordance with city practice, petitioner could rely on the dedicated property to meet the 15% open space and landscaping requirement mandated by the city's zoning scheme. The city would bear the cost of maintaining a landscaped buffer between the dedicated area and the new store. . . .

The Commission made a series of findings concerning the relationship between the dedicated conditions and the projected impacts of petitioner's project. First, the Commission noted that "[i]t is reasonable to assume that customers and employees of the future uses of this site could utilize a pedestrian/bicycle pathway adjacent to this development for their transportation and recreational needs." The Commission noted that the site plan has provided for bicycle parking in a rack in front of the proposed building and "[i]t is reasonable to expect that some of the users of the bicycle parking provided for by the site plan will use the pathway adjacent to Fanno Creek if it is constructed." In addition, the Commission found that creation of a convenient, safe pedestrian/bicycle pathway system as an alternative means of transportation "could offset some of the traffic demand on [nearby] streets and lessen the increase in traffic congestion."

The Commission went on to note that the required floodplain dedication would be reasonably related to petitioner's request to intensify the use of the site given the increase in the impervious surface. The Commission stated that the "anticipated increased storm water flow from the subject property to an already strained creek and drainage basin can only add to the public need to manage the stream channel and floodplain for drainage purposes." Based on this anticipated increased storm water flow, the Commission concluded that "the requirement of dedication of the floodplain area on the site is related to the applicant's plan to intensify development on the site." . . .

Petitioner appealed to the Land Use Board of Appeals (LUBA) on the ground that the city's dedication requirements were not related to the proposed development, and, therefore, those requirements constituted an uncompensated taking of their property under the Fifth Amendment. In evaluating the federal taking claim, LUBA assumed that the city's findings about the impacts of the proposed development were supported by substantial evidence. Given the undisputed fact that the proposed larger building and paved parking area would increase the amount of impervious surfaces and the runoff into Fanno Creek, LUBA concluded that "there is a 'reasonable relationship' between the proposed development and the requirement to dedicate land along Fanno Creek for a greenway." With respect to the pedestrian/bicycle pathway, LUBA noted the Commission's finding that a significantly larger retail sales building and parking lot would attract larger numbers of customers and employees and their vehicles. It again found a "reasonable relationship" between alleviating the impacts of increased traffic from the development and facilitating the provision of a pedestrian/bicycle pathway as an alternative means of transportation.

The Oregon Court of Appeals affirmed, rejecting petitioner's contention that in *Nollan v. California Coastal Comm'n* we had abandoned the "reasonable relationship" test in favor of a stricter "essential nexus" test. The Oregon Supreme Court affirmed. The court also disagreed with petitioner's contention that the *Nollan* Court abandoned the "reasonably related" test. Instead, the court read *Nollan* to mean that an "exaction is reasonably related to an impact if the exaction serves the same purpose that a denial of the permit would serve." 854 P.2d at 443. The court decided that both the pedestrian/bicycle pathway condition and the storm drainage dedication had an essential nexus to the development of the proposed site. Therefore, the court found the conditions to be reasonably related to the impact of the expansion of petitioner's business. . . .

. . .Without question, had the city simply required petitioner to dedicate a strip of land along Fanno Creek for public use, rather than conditioning the grant of her permit to redevelop her property on such a dedication, a taking would have occurred. *Nollan, supra*, 483 U.S. at 831. Such public access would deprive petitioner of the right to exclude others, "one of the most essential sticks in the bundle of rights that are commonly characterized as property." *Kaiser Aetna v. United States*, 444 U.S. 164, 176 (1979).

On the other side of the ledger, the authority of state and local governments to engage in land use planning has been sustained against constitutional challenge as long ago as our decision *in Euclid v. Ambler Realty Co.*, 272 U.S. 365 (1926). "Government hardly could go on if to some extent values incident to property could not be diminished without paying for every such change in the general law." *Pennsylvania Coal Co. v. Mahon*, 260 U.S. 393, 413 (1922). A land use regulation does not effect a taking if it "substantially advance[s] legitimate state interests" and does not "den[y] an owner economically viable use of his land." *Agins v. Tiburon*, 447 U.S. 255, 260 (1980).

The sort of land use regulations discussed in the cases just cited, however, differ in two relevant particulars from the present case. First, they involved essentially legislative determinations classifying entire areas of the city, whereas here the city made an adjudicative decision to condition petitioner's application for a building permit on an individual parcel. Second, the conditions imposed were not simply a limitation on the use petitioner might make of her own parcel, but a requirement that she deed portions of the property to the city. In *Nollan, supra*, we held that governmental authority to exact such a condition was circumscribed by the Fifth and Fourteenth Amendments. Under the well-settled doctrine of "unconstitutional conditions," the government may not require a person to give up a constitutional right—here the right to receive just compensation when property is taken for a public use—in exchange for a discretionary benefit conferred by the government where the property sought has little or no relationship to the benefit. *See Perry v. Sindermann*, 408 U.S. 593 (1972).

Petitioner contends that the city has forced her to choose between the building permit and her right under the Fifth Amendment to just compensation for the public easements. Petitioner does not quarrel with the city's authority to exact some forms of dedication as a condition for the grant of a building permit, but challenges the showing made by the city to justify these exactions. She argues that the city has identified "no special benefits" conferred on her, and has not identified any "special quantifiable burdens" created by her new store that would justify the particular dedications required from her which are not required from the public at large.

In evaluating petitioner's claim, we must first determine whether the "essential nexus" exists between the "legitimate state interest" and the permit condition exacted by the city. *Nollan*, 483 U.S. at 837. If we find that a nexus exists, we must then decide the required degree of connection between the exactions and the projected impact of the proposed development. We were not required to reach this question in *Nollan*, because we concluded that the connection did not meet even the loosest standard. 483 U.S. at 838. Here, however, we must decide this question. . . .

. . . Undoubtedly, the prevention of flooding along Fanno Creek and the reduction of traffic congestion in the Central Business District qualify as the type of legitimate public purposes we have upheld. It seems equally obvious that a nexus exists between preventing flooding along Fanno Creek and limiting development within the creek's 100–year floodplain. Petitioner proposes to double the size of her retail store and to pave her now-gravel parking lot, thereby expanding the impervious surface on the property and increasing the amount of stormwater run-off into Fanno Creek.

The same may be said for the city's attempt to reduce traffic congestion by providing for alternative means of transportation. In theory, a pedestrian/bicycle pathway provides a useful alternative means of transportation for workers and shoppers. . . .

The second part of our analysis requires us to determine whether the degree of the exactions demanded by the city's permit conditions bear the required relationship to the projected impact of petitioner's proposed development. *Nollan, supra*, 483 U.S. at 834, quoting *Penn Central*, 438 U.S. 104, 127 (1978) (" '[A] use restriction may constitute a taking if not reasonably necessary to the effectuation of a substantial government purpose' "). Here the Oregon Supreme Court deferred to the . . . "city's unchallenged factual findings" supporting the dedication conditions and found them to be reasonably related to the impact of the expansion of petitioner's business. 54 P.2d at 443.

The city required that petitioner dedicate "to the city as Greenway all portions of the site that fall within the existing 100–year floodplain [of Fanno Creek] . . . and all property 15 feet above [the floodplain] boundary." In addition, the city demanded that the retail store be designed so as not to intrude into the greenway area. The city relies on the Commission's rather tentative findings that increased stormwater flow from petitioner's property "can only add to the public need to manage the [floodplain] for drainage purposes" to support its conclusion that the "requirement of dedication of the floodplain area on the site is related to the applicant's plan to intensify development on the site."

The city made the following specific findings relevant to the pedestrian/bicycle pathway:

> In addition, the proposed expanded use of this site is anticipated to generate additional vehicular traffic thereby increasing congestion on nearby collector and arterial streets. Creation of a convenient,

safe pedestrian/bicycle pathway system as an alternative means of transportation could offset some of the traffic demand on these nearby streets and lessen the increase in traffic congestion.

The question for us is whether these findings are constitutionally sufficient to justify the conditions imposed by the city on petitioner's building permit. Since state courts have been dealing with this question a good deal longer than we have, we turn to representative decisions made by them.

In some States, very generalized statements as to the necessary connection between the required dedication and the proposed development seem to suffice. *See, e.g., Billings Properties, Inc. v. Yellowstone County*, 394 P.2d 182 (1964); *Jenad, Inc. v. Scarsdale*, 218 N.E.2d 673 (1966). We think this standard is too lax to adequately protect petitioner's right to just compensation if her property is taken for a public purpose.

Other state courts require a very exacting correspondence, described as the "specifi[c] and uniquely attributable" test. The Supreme Court of Illinois first developed this test in *Pioneer Trust & Savings Bank v. Mount Prospect*, 176 N.E.2d 799, 802 (1961). Under this standard, if the local government cannot demonstrate that its exaction is directly proportional to the specifically created need, the exaction becomes "a veiled exercise of the power of eminent domain and a confiscation of private property behind the defense of police regulations." *Id.* We do not think the Federal Constitution requires such exacting scrutiny, given the nature of the interests involved.

A number of state courts have taken an intermediate position, requiring the municipality to show a "reasonable relationship" between the required dedication and the impact of the proposed development. Typical is the Supreme Court of Nebraska's opinion in *Simpson v. North Platte*, 292 N.W.2d 297, 301 (1980), where that court stated:

> The distinction, therefore, which must be made between an appropriate exercise of the police power and an improper exercise of eminent domain is whether the requirement has some reasonable relationship or nexus to the use to which the property is being made or is merely being used as an excuse for taking property simply because at that particular moment the landowner is asking the city for some license or permit.

Thus, the court held that a city may not require a property owner to dedicate private property for some future public use as a condition of obtaining a building permit when such future use is not "occasioned by the construction sought to be permitted." *Id.* at 302. . . .

We think the "reasonable relationship" test adopted by a majority of the state courts is closer to the federal constitutional norm than either of those previously discussed. But we do not adopt it as such, partly because the term "reasonable relationship" seems confusingly similar to the term "rational basis" which describes the minimal level of scrutiny under the Equal Protection Clause of the Fourteenth Amendment. We think a term such as "rough proportionality" best encapsulates what we hold to be the requirement of the Fifth Amendment. No precise mathematical calculation is required, but the city must make some sort of individualized determination that the required dedication is related both in nature and extent to the impact of the proposed development....

...We turn now to analysis of whether the findings relied upon by the city here, first with respect to the floodplain easement, and second with respect to the pedestrian/bicycle path, satisfied these requirements.

It is axiomatic that increasing the amount of impervious surface will increase the quantity and rate of storm-water flow from petitioner's property. Therefore, keeping the floodplain open and free from development would likely confine the pressures on Fanno Creek created by petitioner's development. In fact, because petitioner's property lies within the Central Business District, the Community Development Code already required that petitioner leave 15% of it as open space and the undeveloped floodplain would have nearly satisfied that requirement. But the city demanded more—it not only wanted petitioner not to build in the floodplain, but it also wanted petitioner's property along Fanno Creek for its Greenway system. The city has never said why a public greenway, as opposed to a private one, was required in the interest of flood control.

The difference to petitioner, of course, is the loss of her ability to exclude others. As we have noted, this right to exclude others is "one of the most essential sticks in the bundle of rights that are commonly characterized as property." *Kaiser Aetna*, 444 U.S. at 176. It is difficult to see why recreational visitors trampling along petitioner's floodplain easement are sufficiently related to the city's legitimate interest in reducing flooding problems along Fanno Creek, and the city has not attempted to make any individualized determination to support this part of its request.

The city contends that recreational easement along the Greenway is only ancillary to the city's chief purpose in controlling flood hazards. It further asserts that unlike the residential property at issue in *Nollan*, petitioner's property is commercial in character and therefore, her right to exclude others is compromised....

Admittedly, petitioner wants to build a bigger store to attract members of the public to her property. She also wants, however, to be able to control the time and manner in which they enter. The recreational easement on the Greenway is different in character from the exercise of state-protected rights of free expression and petition that we permitted in [*PruneYard Shopping Center v. Robins*, 447 U.S. 74 (1980)]. In *PruneYard*, we held that a major private shopping center that attracted more than 25,000 daily patrons had to provide access to persons exercising their state constitutional rights to distribute pamphlets and ask passersby to sign their petitions. *Id.* at 85. We based our decision, in part, on the fact that the shopping center "may restrict expressive activity by adopting time, place, and manner regulations that will minimize any interference with its commercial functions." *Id.* at 83. By contrast, the city wants to impose a permanent recreational easement upon petitioner's property that borders Fanno Creek. Petitioner would lose all rights to regulate the time in which the public entered onto the Greenway, regardless of any interference it might pose with her retail store. Her right to exclude would not be regulated, it would be eviscerated.

If petitioner's proposed development had somehow encroached on existing greenway space in the city, it would have been reasonable to require petitioner to provide some alternative greenway space for the public either on her property or elsewhere. But that is not the case here. We conclude that the findings upon which the city relies do not show the required reasonable relationship between the floodplain easement and the petitioner's proposed new building.

With respect to the pedestrian/bicycle pathway, we have no doubt that the city was correct in finding that the larger retail sales facility proposed by petitioner will increase traffic on the streets of the Central Business District. The city estimates that the proposed development would generate roughly 435 additional trips per day. Dedications for streets, sidewalks, and other public ways are generally reasonable exactions to avoid excessive congestion from a proposed property use. But on the record before us, the city has not met its burden of demonstrating that the additional number of vehicle and bicycle trips generated by the petitioner's development reasonably relate to the city's requirement for a dedication of the pedestrian/bicycle pathway easement. The city simply found that the creation of the pathway "could offset some of the traffic demand . . . and lessen the increase in traffic congestion."

As Justice Peterson of the Supreme Court of Oregon explained in his dissenting opinion, however, "[t]he findings of fact that the bicycle pathway system *'could* offset some of the traffic demand' is a far cry from a finding that the bicycle pathway system *will,* or *is likely to,* offset some of the traffic demand." 854 P.2d at 447 (emphasis in original). No precise mathematical calculation is required, but the city must make some effort to quantify its findings in support of the dedication for the pedestrian/bicycle pathway beyond the conclusory statement that it could offset some of the traffic demand generated. . . .

The judgment of the Supreme Court of Oregon is reversed, and the case is remanded for further proceedings consistent with this opinion. . . .

JUSTICE STEVENS, with whom JUSTICE BLACKMUN and JUSTICE GINSBURG join, dissenting. . . . Applying its new [rough proportionality] standard, the Court finds two defects in the city's case. First, while the record would adequately support a requirement that Dolan maintain the portion of the floodplain on her property as undeveloped open space, it does not support the additional requirement that the floodplain be dedicated to the city. Second, while the city adequately established the traffic increase that the proposed development would generate, it failed to quantify the offsetting decrease in automobile traffic that the bike path will produce. Even under the Court's new rule, both defects are, at most, nothing more than harmless error.

In her objections to the floodplain condition, Dolan made no effort to demonstrate that the dedication of that portion of her property would be any more onerous than a simple prohibition against any development on that portion of her property. Given the commercial character of both the existing and the proposed use of the property as a retail store, it seems likely that potential customers "trampling along petitioner's floodplain," are more valuable than a useless parcel of vacant land. Moreover, the duty to pay taxes and the responsibility for potential tort liability may well make ownership of the fee interest in useless land a liability rather than an asset. That may explain why Dolan never conceded that she could be prevented from building on the floodplain. The City Attorney also pointed out that absent a dedication, property owners would be required to "build on their own land" and "with their own money" a storage facility for the water runoff. Dolan apparently "did have that option," but chose not to seek it. If Dolan might have been entitled to a variance confining the city's condition in a manner this Court would accept, her failure to seek that narrower form of relief at any stage of the state administrative and judicial proceedings clearly should preclude that relief in this Court now.

The Court's rejection of the bike path condition amounts to nothing more than a play on words. Everyone agrees that the bike path "could" offset some of the increased traffic flow that the larger store will generate, but the findings do not unequivocally state that it will do so, or tell us just how many cyclists will replace motorists. Predictions on such matters are inherently nothing more than estimates. Certainly the assumption that there will be an offsetting benefit here is entirely reasonable and should suffice whether it amounts to 100 percent, 35 percent, or only 5 percent of the increase in automobile traffic that would otherwise occur. If the Court proposes to have the federal judiciary micro-manage state decisions of this kind, it is indeed extending its welcome mat to a significant new class of litigants. Although there is no reason to believe that state courts have failed to rise to the task, property owners have surely found a new friend today.

The Court has made a serious error by abandoning the traditional presumption of constitutionality and imposing a novel burden of proof on a city implementing an admittedly valid comprehensive land use plan . . . .

In our changing world one thing is certain: uncertainty will characterize predictions about the impact of new urban developments on the risks of floods, earthquakes, traffic congestion, or environmental harms. When there is doubt concerning the magnitude of those impacts, the public interest in averting them must outweigh the private interest of the commercial entrepreneur. If the government can demonstrate that the conditions it has imposed in a land-use permit are rational, impartial and conducive to fulfilling the aims of a valid land-use plan, a strong presumption of validity should attach to those conditions. The burden of demonstrating that those conditions have unreasonably impaired the economic value of the proposed improvement belongs squarely on the shoulders of the party challenging the state action's constitutionality. That allocation of burdens has served us well in the past. The Court has stumbled badly today by reversing it.

I respectfully dissent.

JUSTICE SOUTER, dissenting. This case, like *Nollan*, invites the Court to examine the relationship between conditions imposed by development permits, requiring landowners to dedicate portions of their land for use by the public, and governmental interests in mitigating the adverse effects of such development. *Nollan* declared the need for a nexus between the nature of an exaction of an interest in land (a beach easement) and the nature of governmental interests. The Court treats this case as raising a further question, not about the nature, but about the degree, of connection required between such an exaction and the adverse effects of development. The Court's opinion announces a test to address this question, but as I read the opinion, the Court does not apply that test to these facts, which do not raise the question the Court addresses.

First, as to the floodplain and Greenway, the Court acknowledges that an easement of this land for open space (and presumably including the five feet required for needed creek channel improvements) is reasonably related to flood control, but argues that the "permanent recreational easement" for the public on the Greenway is not so related. If that is so, it is not because of any lack of proportionality between permit condition and adverse effect, but because of a lack of any rational connection at all between exaction of a public recreational area and the governmental interest in providing for the effect of increased water runoff. That is merely an application of *Nollan*'s nexus analysis. As the Court notes, "[i]f petitioner's proposed development had somehow encroached on existing greenway space in the city, it would have been reasonable to require petitioner to provide some alternative greenway space for the public." But that, of course, was not the fact, and the city of Tigard never sought to justify the public access portion of the dedication as related to flood control. It merely argued that whatever recreational uses were made of the bicycle path and the one foot edge on either side, were incidental to the permit condition requiring dedication of the 15–foot easement for an 8–foot-wide bicycle path and for flood control, including open space requirements and relocation of the bank of the river by some five feet. It seems to me such incidental recreational use can stand or fall with the bicycle path, which the city justified by reference to traffic congestion. As to the relationship the Court examines, between the recreational easement and a purpose never put forth as a justification by the city, the Court unsurprisingly finds a recreation area to be unrelated to flood control.

Second, as to the bicycle path, the Court again acknowledges the "theor[etically]" reasonable relationship between "the city's attempt to reduce traffic congestion by providing [a bicycle path] for alternative means of transportation," and the "correct" finding of the city that "the larger retail sales facility proposed by petitioner will increase traffic on the streets of the Central Business District." The Court only faults the city for saying that the bicycle path "could" rather than "would" offset the increased traffic from the store. That again, as far as I can tell, is an application of *Nollan*, for the Court holds that the stated connection ("could offset") between traffic congestion and bicycle paths is too tenuous; only if the bicycle path "would" offset the increased traffic by some amount, could the bicycle path be said to be related to the city's legitimate interest in reducing traffic congestion.

I cannot agree that the application of *Nollan* is a sound one here, since it appears that the Court has placed the burden of producing evidence of relationship on the city, despite the usual rule in cases involving the police power that the government is presumed to have acted constitutionally. Having thus assigned the burden, the Court concludes that the City loses based on one word ("could" instead of "would"), and despite the fact that this record shows the connection the Court looks for. Dolan has put forward no evidence that the burden of granting a dedication for the bicycle path is unrelated in kind to the anticipated increase in traffic congestion, nor, if there exists a requirement that the relationship be related in degree, has Dolan shown that the exaction fails any such test. The city, by contrast, calculated the increased traffic flow that would result from Dolan's proposed development to be 435 trips per day, and its Comprehensive Plan, applied here, relied on studies showing the link between alternative modes of transportation, including bicycle paths, and reduced street traffic congestion. *Nollan*, therefore, is satisfied, and on that assumption the city's conditions should not be held to fail a further rough proportionality test or any other that might be devised to give meaning to the constitutional limits. As Members of this Court have said before, "the common zoning regulations requiring subdividers to ... dedicate certain areas to public streets, are in accord with our constitutional traditions because the proposed property use would otherwise be the cause of excessive congestion." *Pennell v. San Jose*, 485 U.S. 1, 20 (1988) (Scalia, J., concurring in part and dissenting in part). The bicycle path permit condition is fundamentally no different from these.

In any event, on my reading, the Court's conclusions about the city's vulnerability carry the Court no further than *Nollan* has gone already, and I do not view this case as a suitable vehicle for taking the law beyond that point. The right case for the enunciation of takings doctrine seems hard to spot.

Notes

1. *"Essential Nexus" and "Rough Proportionality."* The *Dolan* decision suggests that analysis of exactions is a two-step process. First, a court must determine whether there is an essential nexus between the legitimate governmental interest sought to be protected and the permit condition being imposed. If not, the condition is invalid under *Nollan*. If such a nexus exists, however, then a court must decide whether the degree of the exaction bears a "rough proportionality" to the impact of the proposed development.

Justice Souter's dissent suggests that the Court unnecessarily created the "rough proportionality test," as the Court could have resolved the case under *Nollan*'s "essential nexus" framework. Are you persuaded by Justice Souter's analysis? Why do you think the majority in *Dolan* decided to add the "rough proportionality" prong to the "essential nexus" test rather than simply apply the "essential nexus" test to decide the case? [Hint: Review the discussion in note 2 following *Nollan*.]

Why did the majority in *Dolan* conclude that the city's conditions were not roughly proportional to the burden resulting from the proposed development? How does the dissent evaluate the "rough proportionality" question differently than the majority? As you reflect on that question, consider these two issues:

(a) *Burden of Proof.* The *Dolan* majority concluded that a municipality cannot simply make a "conclusory statement" that a permit condition is needed to address impacts from the proposed development: "No precise mathematical calculation is required, but the city must make some sort of individualized determination that the required dedication is related both in nature and extent to the impact of the proposed development." Does this statement go beyond the inquiry reflected in *Nollan*? If so, how? Is this consistent with the traditional deference that courts have accorded municipalities to define "public purpose" in eminent domain proceedings? Can you offer any reasons that might justify such heightened scrutiny of municipal action?

(b) *Relative Benefits and Burdens.* Did the majority fail to account for some "benefits" that Dolan would have experienced as a result of having the conditions imposed? How should a court account for such benefits in evaluating "rough proportionality"?

2. *Impact Fees.* In some cases, a municipality may not require an exaction from a developer, but may instead impose an "impact fee"—*i.e.*, a fee charged to help the municipality finance the public infrastructure associated with the proposed development. The use of impact fees to finance public infrastructure presents a number of legal issues. Much litigation over impact fees focuses upon whether a municipality has the power under state law to levy impact fees, either by its own initiative or upon popular vote. Some states take a very narrow view of local government power, essentially permitting local governments to exercise only those powers expressly delegated to them by the state legislature and construing any expressly delegated powers narrowly. [You may study this principle, known as "Dillon's Rule," in greater detail in a course on Local Government Law.] In such states, if no

state statute specifically authorizes municipalities to impose impact fees, or permits them only for certain types of infrastructure expenses, impact fees may not be a very viable land use planning tool. Furthermore, developers often have challenged impact fees as being "taxes," and thus subject to state law limitations upon the taxing authority of local government units (such as, for example, total revenue caps or popular approval requirements). *Compare State v. City of Port Orange*, 650 So.2d 1 (Fla. 1994) (invalidating transportation utility charge as a "tax") *with Bloom v. City of Fort Collins*, 784 P.2d 304 (Colo. 1989) (characterizing similar charge as authorized "fee," not unauthorized "tax").

In states that authorize the collection of impact fees, should such fees be subject to the *Nollan/Dolan* analysis? The Ohio Supreme Court recently held that the "dual rational nexus test" from *Nollan/Dolan* applied to an impact fee for funding road improvements. *Home Builders Ass'n of Dayton & the Miami Valley v. City of Beavercreek*, 89 Ohio St.3d 121, 729 N.E.2d 349 (2000). Other courts have concluded that if the municipality calculates fees on a development-by-development basis, then the *Nollan/Dolan* analysis applies. *See, e.g., Ehrlich v. City of Culver City*, 12 Cal.4th 854, 50 Cal. Rptr.2d 242, 911 P.2d 429 (1996) (recreation impact fee of $280,000, calculated on ad hoc basis, lacked rough proportionality to development's impact). If the municipality assesses impact fees based on a legislatively determined formula, however—for example, a fee equivalent to 1% of any development's total value for a fund for the city to purchase and publicly display art—some jurisdictions have held that such fees are not exactions subject to *Nollan/Dolan*, because they are not ad hoc discretionary conditions and/or because they fall within the municipality's general ability to regulate aesthetics. *See, e.g., Home Builders Ass'n v. City of Scottsdale*, 183 Ariz. 243, 902 P.2d 1347 (Ct. App. 1995) (nondiscretionary water resources development fee), *modified on other grounds*, 187 Ariz. 479, 930 P.2d 993 (1997) (*Dolan* analysis subsumed within Arizona's statutory requirement of a reasonable relationship); *Parking Ass'n v. City of Atlanta*, 264 Ga. 764, 450 S.E.2d 200 (1994) (landscaping requirements reflect regulatory condition, not an exaction).

3. *Common Interest Communities Mandated by Local Government.* As discussed in Chapter 8, modern subdivision regulations often effectively shift to developers (and eventually to community associations) the financial costs of community infrastructure and quasi-public facilities such as streets, lighting, parks, water and sewer facilities—and, in some cases, even services such as trash collection and snow removal. As Professor Winokur has argued, local governments have used planning and development regulation as a conscious strategy for relieving strain on the public treasury. *See* James L. Winokur, *Critical Assessment: The Financial Role of Community Associations*, 38 Santa Clara L. Rev. 1135 (1998). Does the law of exactions apply to any or all of the requirements (and incentives) by which local governments assure private provision and maintenance of this infrastructure? On what theories presented in this chapter would you frame a developer's argument against a land use regulatory agency's insistence on provision of such infrastructure?

Index

References are to Pages

†